**Fenner**
**Fluid Power**

DIVISION OF FENNER AMERICA, INC.

SONY.

Radisson
HOTELS INTERNATIONAL®

Steelcase®

LANDS' END®
DIRECT MERCHANTS

McDonald's®

ServiceMASTER.

Rockwell Automation

Allen-Bradley

A·B QUALITY

# Operations Management
*Concepts in Manufacturing and Services*

# Operations Management

## Concepts in Manufacturing and Services

**Robert E. Markland**
*University of South Carolina*

**Shawnee K. Vickery**
*Michigan State University*

**Robert A. Davis**
*Texas A & M University*

**West Publishing Company**

*Minneapolis/Saint Paul   New York   Los Angeles   San Francisco*

## PRODUCTION CREDITS

*Text and Cover Design*   Rokusek Design
*Cover Image*   Joe Cornish, Tony Stone Images
*Copy Editing*   Polly Kummel
*Illustrations*   Miyake Illustration
*Composition*   Carlisle Communications, Ltd.
*Index*   Schroeder Indexing Services

Photo credits and text acknowledgements follow index.

Production, Prepress, Printing and Binding by West Publishing Company.

## WEST'S COMMITMENT TO THE ENVIRONMENT

In 1906, West Publishing Company began recycling materials left over from the production of books. This began a tradition of efficient and responsible use of resources. Today, up to 95 percent of our legal books and 70 percent of our college and school texts are printed on recycled, acid-free stock. West also recycles nearly 22 million pounds of scrap paper annually– the equivalent of 181,717 trees. Since the 1960s, West has devised ways to capture and recycle waste inks, solvents, oils, and vapors created in the printing process. We also recycle plastics of all kinds, wood, glass, corrugated cardboard, and batteries, and have eliminated the use of Styrofoam book packaging. We at West are proud of the longevity and the scope of our commitment to the environment.

British Library Cataloguing-in-Publication Data. A catalogue record for this book is available from the British Library.

Library of Congress Cataloging-in-Publication Data
Markland, Robert E.
    Operations management : concepts in manufacturing and services / Robert E. Markland, Shawnee K. Vickery, Robert A. Davis.
       p.  cm.
    Includes index.
    ISBN 0-314-04398-5 (Hard)
    1. Production management.  I. Vickery, Shawnee.  II. Davis, Robert, 1947-  .  III. Title.
TS155.8.M35  1995
658.5--dc20

94-30524
CIP

 TEXT IS PRINTED ON 10% POST CONSUMER RECYCLED PAPER    PRINTED WITH SOY INK

# BRIEF TABLE OF CONTENTS

Preface  xviii

SECTION ONE        Introduction to Operations Management

INTRODUCTION       A Preview of Operations Management  1

CHAPTER 1          Manufacturing Operations  5

CHAPTER 2          Service Operations  39

SECTION TWO        Operations Strategy

CHAPTER 3          Operations Strategy  73

SECTION THREE      Strategic Decision Categories in Operations Management

CHAPTER 4          Forecasting Demand for Products and Services  109

CHAPTER 5          Product Planning and Process Design  157

CHAPTER 6          Long-range Capacity Planning and Facility Location  193

CHAPTER 7          Managing Quality  283

CHAPTER 8          Technological Developments in Operations
                   Management  291

CHAPTER 9          Organization and Human Resources  323

SECTION FOUR       Operation Planning and Control

CHAPTER 10         Materials and Logistics Management  355

CHAPTER 11         Aggregate Production Planning  381

CHAPTER 12         Independent Demand Inventory Management  427

CHAPTER 13         Dependent Demand Inventory Management  473

CHAPTER 14         Medium- and Short-range Capacity Planning  515

CHAPTER 15         Shop Floor Control  549

CHAPTER 16         Just-In-Time Production  581

CHAPTER 17         Design and Scheduling of Service Systems  605

CHAPTER 18         Project Management  647

CHAPTER 19         Quality Analysis, Measurement and Improvement  683

SECTION FIVE       Operations Strategy Revisited

CHAPTER 20         Building Competitive Advantage  723

SECTION SIX        Tutorials

TUTORIAL 1         Transportation Problem  742

TUTORIAL 2         Decision Analysis  760

TUTORIAL 3         Linear Programming  776

TUTORIAL 4         Simulation  790

TUTORIAL 5         Waiting Line Models  804

Appendix: Tables  818

Index  826

Acknowledgments  842

# TABLE OF CONTENTS

**Preface, xviii**

## SECTION ONE
Introduction to Operations Management

**INTRODUCTION**
► **A Preview of Operations Management, 1**
Strategic Operations Management, 3

**CHAPTER 1**
► **Manufacturing Operations, 5**
Introduction, 6
The Transformation Process, 6
  Productivity and the Transformation Process, 7
  Managing the Transformation Process: The
    Operations Manager, 9
*Operations Management in Practice 1.1: Portrait of
  Operations Manager, 10*
  Ecologically Sound Manufacturing, 11
Types of Manufacturing Operations, 11
*Operations Management in Practice 1.2: Green
  Manufacturing at AT&T, 12*

Project Manufacturing, 12
The Job Shop, 13
Line-Flow Production, 13
*Operations Management in Practice 1.3: Tablet
  Production at Burroughs Wellcome Co., Greenville,
  N.C., 14*
  Batch Production, 15
Company Activities and Strategic Advantage: The
  Value Chain, 15
The History of Operations Management, 18
  Eli Whitney, 18
  Frederick Winslow Taylor, 20
  Henry Ford, 21
  Alfred P. Sloan, Jr., 23
  The Field of Operations
    Management, 23
Recent Trends in Operations Management, 24
  Just-in-Time Production, 24
  Total Quality Management, 25
  Computers and Computer-Related Operations
    Technologies, 26
  Time-based Competition, 27
  Business Process Reengineering, 28
  The Service Factory, 28
*Operations Management in Practice 1.4:
  Reengineering at Ford Motor Co., 29*
Summary, 31
Key Terms, 32
Discussion Questions, 33
Selected References, 33
*Case Study: Time-based Competition at Northern
  Telecom, 35*

**CHAPTER 2**
► **Service Operations, 39**
Introduction, 40
Defining Services, 41
  Comparing Service and Manufacturing
    Operations, 43
  Classifying Service and Manufacturing
    Operations, 43

Characteristics of Service Operations, 45
  High Consumer Contact, 45
  Consumer Participation, 46
  Perishability of Services, 46
  Site Selection Dictated by Consumer's
    Location, 47
  Labor Intensiveness, 47
  Variable, Nonstandard Output, 48
  Intangibility of the Service Output, 48
  Difficulty of Measuring Service Productivity, 49
*Operations Management in Practice 2.1: Service
Companies—Working to Raise Productivity, 50*
  Difficulty of Measuring Service Quality, 51
Strategic Approaches to Service Operations
  Management, 51
  The Service Process Matrix, 51
*Operations Management in Practice 2.2:
ServiceMaster—Stressing Dignity to its Workers, 54*
  The Strategic Service Vision, 55
Service-Sector Trends, 55
  Increased International Competition, 57
  Improving Productivity and Competitiveness in
    Services, 59
*Global Operations Management 2.3: British
Airways—Taking Off in New Directions, 60*
*Operations Management in Practice 2.4: Using
Computers to Improve Service , 62*
  Technology and Automation in Services, 63
  Adequacy of Service Jobs, 63
*Operations Management in Practice 2.5: J.C.
Penney—Riding the Third Wave of Information
Technology, 65*
  Greater Quality Emphasis in Services, 67
Summary, 68
Key Terms, 69
Discussion Questions, 69
Selected References, 69–70
*Case Study: Blockbuster Entertainment, 71*

**CHAPTER 3**
► **Operations Strategy, 73**
Introduction, 74
Business-level Strategic Planning, 75
  Functional Area Involvement in Business-level
    Strategic Planning, 77
  The Generic Business Strategies, 77
*Operations Management in Practice 3.1: Strategic
Positioning at Haskell of Pittsburgh, 80*
Operations Strategic Planning, 81
  Operations as a Competitive Weapon, 83
  Operations Competitive Priorities, 84
  Strategic Operations Choices, 85
*Global Operations Management 3.2: Competitive
Priorities at Meiji Seika Kaisha, Ltd. (Pharmaceutical
Manufacturing at Odawara), 86*
Categories of Strategic Operations Decisions, 88
  Product or Service Planning, 88
  Process Design and Technology Management, 88
  Long-range Capacity Planning and Facility
    Location, 90
  Quality Management, 91
  Manufacturing or Service Organization, 91
  Human Resource Management, 91
  Operations Planning and Control, 92
Vertical Linkages: The Value Chain Revisited, 92
  Vertical Integration and Outsourcing, 93
  Supply Chain Management, 93
  Assembler-Supplier Relationships in Japan, 95
Global Integration of Operations, 97

*Operations Management in Practice 3.3:* Global Manufacturing Integration at Xerox, 99
Summary, 100
Key Terms, 102
Discussion Questions, 102
Selected References, 103
*Case Study:* Operations Strategic Planning at Allen-Bradley, 104

Qualitative Forecasting Methods, 119
  Naïve Extrapolation, 121
  Sales Force Composite, 121
  Jury of Executive Opinion, 121
  The Delphi Method, 121
  Market Research Surveys, 122
*Global Operations Management 4.1:* A National Delphi Study of System Waste in India, 123
Quantitative Forecasting Methods—Time Series
  Analysis Models, 125
  Time Series Smoothing, 125
  Time Series Decomposition, 135
*Operations Management in Practice 4.2:* Forecasting at Rubbermaid Home Products Division , 136
Quantitative Forecasting Methods—Associative
  Models, 136
  Regression Models, 137
  Econometric Models, 143
Measuring Forecasting Error, 144
  Absolute Measures of Forecasting Error, 144
  Relative Measures of Forecasting Error, 146
Monitoring and Controlling Forecasts, 146
Using Computers in Forecasting, 150
Summary, 150
Key Terms, 151
Discussion Questions, 152
Problems, 152
Selected References, 155

## ► SECTION THREE

Strategic Decision Categories in Operations Management

**CHAPTER 4**
**► Forecasting Demand for Products and Services, 109**
Introduction, 110
Characteristics of Demand, 110
  Factors Influencing Demand, 111
  Demand Components, 113
The Forecasting Process, 114
  Establish Objectives for the Forecast, 115
  Determine What to Forecast, 115
  Specify the Time Period for the Forecast, 116
  Gather and Analyze Data, 117
  Select a Forecasting Method, 117
  Make the Forecast, 118
  Present the Forecast Results, 118
  Monitor and Control the Forecast, 118
Approaches to Forecasting–A Preview, 119

**CHAPTER 5**
**► Product Planning and Process Design, 157**
Introduction, 158
Assessing Customers' Needs and Wants, 158
  Technology-Driven New Product Ideas, 159
  New Product Ideas from Market Research, 159
  The Voice of the Customer, 159
*Operations Management in Practice 5.1:* The Birth of the "Pump", 160
Customer Satisfaction, 161
  Selecting Features for Products and Services, 161
  Customer-Driven New Product Ideas, 162
  Quality Function Deployment, 164
  From the House of Quality to Operations
    Requirements, 168
  Applications of QFD to New Product Design, 170
  Improving Designs Through Simplification and
    Value Analysis, 170
Design for Manufacturability, 172
  Concurrent Engineering, 172

Implementing Cross-Functional Teams in
   DFM, 174
Process Design and Layout for Manufacturing and
   Service Systems, 174
   Projects: Processes That Don't Flow, 175
   Intermittent Flow Configurations, 176
   Line-Flow Configurations, 178
   Cellular Manufacturing, 181
   Production Line Approach to Service, 181
Strategic Issues in Process Design, 182
   Product and Process Innovation, 183
   The Product-Process Matrix, 184
*Operations Management in Practice 5.2:*
   *Air-Conditioner Firms Put Chill on Plans, 185*
Designing for the Environment, 185
*Operations Management in Practice 5.3: DuPont*
   *Generates Energy from Garbage, 187*
Summary, 188
Key Terms, 189
Discussion Questions, 189
Selected References, 189
*Case Study: Union-Camp Corporation, 191*

**CHAPTER 6**
► **Long-range Capacity Planning and**
   **Facility Location, 193**
Introduction, 194
An Overview of Capacity Planning, 194
   The Importance of Capacity Planning, 194
   Defining and Measuring *Capacity*, 195
   Measuring System Effectiveness, 196
   Focused Facilities, 197
Capacity Strategies, 197
*Operations Management in Practice 6.1: Allison*
   *Transmission's Focused Factory—Partnering with*
   *Suppliers, 198*
   Capacity Cushions, 199
   Strategic Timing of Capacity Changes, 199
   Sizing Capacity Changes, 201
Making Capacity-Planning Decisions, 202
   Steps in the Capacity-Planning Process, 203
   Using Decision Trees in Capacity Planning, 205
An Overview of Location Decisions, 207
   Why Location Decisions Are Important, 207
   Location Options, 208
   A General Approach to Making Location
      Decisions, 208
Factors Affecting Location Decisions, 209
   Regional, Community, and Site
      Considerations, 210

Dominant Facility Location Factors in
   Manufacturing, 212
Dominant Facility Location Factors in
   Services, 213
*Operations Management in Practice 6.2: A Successful*
   *Group Move by Alfa-Laval, 214*
Making the Single-Facility Location Decision, 215
   Detailed Cost Analysis, 215
*Operations Management in Practice 6.3: The Charlotte*
   *Panthers Choose a Preseason Training Facility, 216*
   Factor Rating Systems, 216
   Center of Gravity Method, 218
   Locational Cost-Volume-Profit Analysis, 220
Making Multiple-Facility Location Decisions, 222
   Plant Charters Approach, 222
   Transportation Method, 223
   Heuristics, 225
   Simulation, 226
   Optimization Methods, 226
Strategic Trends in Location Decisions, 227
   Business Park Proliferation, 228
   Factories: Research and Development
      Linkages, 229
   Globalization of Production, 229
*Global Operations Management 6.4: Maquiladora*
   *Industry—Locating Plants in Mexico, 231*
   The Sun Belt Phenomenon, 232
*Global Operations Management 6.5: Why BMW*
   *Cruised into Spartanburg, 233*
Summary, 233
Key Terms, 234
Discussion Questions, 234
Problems, 235
Selected References, 238
*Case Study: Georgia-Pacific Corp., 239*
*Case Study: Pohang Iron and Steel Co., Ltd., 249*

**CHAPTER 7**
► **Managing Quality, 253**
Introduction, 254
Quality in Historical Perspective, 254
Quality Management as a Strategic Issue, 256
   ISO9000 International Standards, 257
*Operations Management in Practice 7.1: The*
   *Ritz-Carlton Hotel Co., 258*
*Role of Quality in Manufacturing Strategy, 258*
*Operations Management in Practice 7.2: Chrysler*
   *Mounts Campaign to Cut Defects, 260*
   Malcolm Baldrige National Quality Award, 261
Quality Management Leadership, 263

*Operations Management in Practice 7.3:* 1993
  *Baldrige Award Winners, 264*
  W. Edwards Deming, 265
  Joseph M. Juran, 266
  Philip B. Crosby, 267
Definitions of Quality, 268
  Quality as Excellence, 268
  Quality as Conformance to Specifications, 268
  Quality as Fitness for Use, 269
  Quality as Value for the Price, 269
Quality-related Product Characteristics, 270
Quality-related Service Characteristics, 271
Costs of Quality, 272
  Classifying the Costs of Quality, 272
  Interaction of Quality Costs, 273
Total Quality Management, 275
  TQM Requirements, 275
  TQM Implementation Process, 280
  Barriers to Implementing TQM, 282
Business Process Reengineering, 282
*Operations Management in Practice 7.4:*
  *Reengineering Taco Bell, 284*
Summary, 285
Key Terms, 287
Discussion Questions, 287
Selected References, 287
*Case Study: Cadillac Motor Car Co., 288*

**CHAPTER 8**
**▶ Technological Developments in**
  **Operations Management, 291**
Introduction, 292
Role of Technology in Today's Business
  Environment, 293
*Operations Management in Practice 8.1: Jumping*
  *Ahead by Going High Tech, 294*
  Technology and the Environment, 294
*Operations Management in Practice 8.2: Technology in*
  *Sports, 295*
  Technology-Focused Strategic Alliances, 296
*Global Operations Management 8.3: Japan Bids for*
  *Global Leadership in Clean Industry, 297*
Transferring New Technology from Concept to
  Reality, 298
Implementing New Technology, 299
Fixed, Programmable, and Flexible Automation, 300
*Operations Management in Practice 8.4: Today's*
  *Advanced Manufacturing Options, 302*
Computer-Integrated Manufacturing, 302
  Computer-Aided Design, 304

Computer-Aided Manufacturing, 304
*Operations Management in Practice 8.5: U.S.*
  *Manufacturers Wary on Automation, 307*
Technological Improvements for Support, 309
  Artificial Intelligence: Adaptive Technology for the
    '90s, 310
*Global Operations Management 8.6: Tomorrow's*
  *Manufacturing Technologies, 311*
  Virtual Reality, 312
*Operations Management in Practice 8.7: The Marvels*
  *of "Virtual Reality," 314*
  Technological Improvements in
    Communications, 314
Summary, 315
Key Terms, 316
Discussion Questions, 316
Selected References, 317
*Case Study: Pavilion Technologies, 318*

**CHAPTER 9**
**▶ Organization and Human Resources, 323**
Introduction, 324
Strategic Human Resources Planning, 324
Sociotechnical Organizations, 325
  Adaptive Organizational Structures, 327
  Keys to Worker Productivity, 327
*Operations Management in Practice 9.1: Dramatic*
  *Turnaround: X-ray Processing Time Cut*
  *81 Percent, 329*
Human Resources Issues of the 1990s, 330
  Government Regulations, 330
  Work Force Diversity, 330
  Manager as Leader, 331
  Participative Management, 331
  Team Activities, 332
*Operations Management in Practice 9.2: American*
  *Express Office Takes Team Approach to Work, 334*
  Fear in the Workplace, 335
  Training and Development, 338
*Operations Management in Practice 9.3: Reducing the*
  *Bile Factor at Heinz, 339*
  Benefits, Compensation, Recognition, and
    Reward, 342
*Operations Management in Practice 9.4:*
  *Hewlett-Packard Flexes Its Days, 343*
  The Inevitability of Change, 345
Work Measurement, 346
  Time Studies, 346
  Elemental Standard Times, 350
  Predetermined Standard Times, 350

Summary, 351
Key Terms, 353
Discussion Questions, 353
Problems, 353
Selected References, 354

## ► SECTION FOUR

Operation Planning and Control

**CHAPTER 10**
**► Materials and Logistics Management, 355**
Introduction, 356
Business Logistics for Strategic Advantage, 356
Scope of Logistics, 357
　Logistics System Components, 357
　Logistics Component Integration, 358
　Logistical Elements, 360
Logistics Issues, 361
　Purchasing, 361
*Operations Management in Practice 10.1: An Integrated Logistics Success, 362*
　Transportation, 367
*Global Operations Management 10.2: Double Eagle: Last Year's Vision, This Year's Reality, 371*
　Warehousing, 372
　Customer Service, 372
Strategic Trends in Logistics Management, 373
*Global Operations Management 10.3: How Managers Can Succeed Through SPEED, 374*
　Third-Party Logistics Services, 374
　Environmental Sensitivity, 375
　Just-in-Time Logistics, 376

Summary, 377
Key Terms, 378
Discussion Questions, 378
Problems, 378
Selected References, 379

**CHAPTER 11**
**► Aggregate Production Planning, 381**
Introduction, 382
The Concept of Aggregation, 382
　Products, 383
　Labor, 383
　Time, 384
An Overview of Production Planning, 384
　Long-range Planning, 385
　Medium-range Planning, 385
　Short-range Planning, 386
Framework for Aggregate Production Planning, 386
*Operations Management in Practice 11.1: A "Bridging" Approach to Aggregate Planning, 387*
　The Production-Planning Environment, 387
　Strategies for Aggregate Production Planning, 391
Techniques for Aggregate Production Planning, 393
　Trial-and-Error Method, 393
　Mathematical Techniques, 400
　Summary of Aggregate Production-Planning Methods, 406
*Global Operations Management 11.2: Aggregate Planning in U.K. Manufacturing Companies, 409*
Aggregate Planning in Service Companies, 408
*Operations Management in Practice 11.3: Developing a Staffing Plan for a Public Safety Department Merger, 414*
Implementing Aggregate Production Plans—Managerial Issues, 415
Hierarchical Production Planning, 416
*Operations Management in Practice 11.4: Improved Hierarchical Production Planning at Owens-Corning Fiberglass, 419*
Summary, 422
Key Terms, 423
Discussion Questions, 423
Problems, 424
Selected References, 426

**CHAPTER 12**
**► Independent Demand Inventory Management, 427**
Introduction, 428
Independent and Dependent Demand, 429

Basic Inventory Concepts, 429
  Types of Inventories, 429
  How to Measure Inventory, 430
  Reasons for Holding Inventories, 432
*Operations Management in Practice 12.1: Shrink
  Inventory? Lands' End Builds Inventory to Increase
  Sales, 433*
  Inventory Costs, 433
  Classifying Inventory Items, 435
  Inventory Records, 436
*Operations Management in Practice 12.2: Inventory
  Management At Ellett Brothers—The Need for an ABC
  Analysis, 437*
  Objectives of Inventory Control, 438
How Much to Order: Economic Order Quantity
  Models, 438
  Economic Order Quantity: Constant Demand, No
    Shortages, 439
  Economic Order Quantity: Constant Demand,
    Shortages Allowed, 443
  Economic Order Quantity: Uniform
    Replenishment Rate, Constant Demand, No
    Shortages, 447
  Economic Order Quantity: Quantity
    Discounts, 450
  Sensitivity Analysis for the EOQ Model, 452
When to Order: The Continuous Review
  Systems, 453
  Determining the Reorder Point, 454
  Service Levels, Safety Stock, and Shortages, 459
When to Order: The Periodic Review System, 463
Comparing the Continuous Review and Periodic
  Review Systems, 465
*Operations Management in Practice 12.3:
  Multiechelon Inventory Management at IBM, 466*
Summary, 467
Key Terms, 468
Discussion Questions, 468
Problems, 469
Selected References, 471


**CHAPTER 13**
▶ **Dependent Demand Inventory
  Management: Material Requirements
  Planning, 473**
Introduction, 474
  The Development of Material Requirements
    Planning (MRP), 474
*Operations Management in Practice 13.1: MRP at
  Steelcase, 475*

MRP Prerequisites, 475
  The Master Production Schedule, 477
  Bills of Material , 478
  Inventory Records, 480
The MRP Process, 480
  MRP Records, 480
  Timing Conventions, 480
  MRP Record Calculations, 481
An MRP Example, 482
  Low-level Coding, 483
  Gross-to-Net Requirements Explosion, 483
Important Observations, 486
  Loss of Visibility for Low-level Components, 486
  Minimum Length for the Planning
    Horizon, 487
  MRP System Nervousness, 487
  Freezing the Master Production Schedule, 490
  Lumpiness of Demand, 490
Lot Sizing, 492
  Lot-for-Lot, 493
  Fixed Order Quantity, 493
  Period Order Quantity, 494
  Lot Sizing and MRP System Nervousness, 495
  The Importance of Lot Sizing, 495
Use of MRP Systems, 496
Some Practical Considerations in Using MRP, 497
  Uncertainty, 497
  Modular Bills of Material, 498
  Closed Loop MRP, 498
  MRP II—Manufacturing Resource Planning, 499
Implementation of MRP, 499
  Existing Systems and the Informal System, 499
  Information Requirements, 500
  Inventory Control , 500
  Keys to Successful Implementation, 501
  An MRP Implementation Plan, 501
*Operations Management in Practice 13.2: MRP and
  the Real Cost of Inventory Losses at Gendex, 503*
Summary, 504
Key Terms, 505
Discussion Questions, 505
Problems, 506
Selected References, 514


**CHAPTER 14**
▶ **Medium- and Short-Range Capacity
  Planning, 515**
Introduction, 516
  The Need for Capacity Planning, 506
  Strategic Implications of Capacity Planning, 517

Capacity Planning and the Production Planning and Scheduling Framework, 517
    Capacity Planning as a Trial-and-Error Process, 519
*Operations Management in Practice 14.1: Capacity Planning Makes the Shop Floor Manageable at Minnesota Wire & Cable Co., 520*
Capacity Planning Example, 521
Rough-Cut Capacity-Planning Method, 521
    Capacity Planning Using Overall Factors (CPOF), 521
    Capacity Planning Using Capacity Bills (CB), 525
    Capacity Planning Using Resource Profiles (RP), 527
Comparison of Rough-Cut Method Results, 531
Detailed Capacity Planning, 532
    Capacity Requirements Planning (CRP), 532
    Using CRP, 535
Capacity Planning and Service Operations, 536
*Operations Management in Practice 14.2: Capacity Planning in a Make-to-Order Environment at Borsig Valve Co., 537*
*Summary, 538*
*Key Terms, 540*
*Discussion Questions, 540*
*Problems, 540*
*Selected References, 547*

## CHAPTER 15
## ▶ Shop Floor Control, 549
Introduction, 550
    The Task of the Shop-Floor Control Manager, 551
Shop-Floor Control in Continuous and Repetitive Operations, 552
    Continuous Process Shop-Floor Control, 552
    Repetitive Operation Shop-Floor Control, 552
    Mixed-Model Assembly in Repetitive Manufacturing, 553
Shop-Floor Control in Intermittent, Job Shop Operations, 554
    Terminology, 554
    Performance Measures in Job Shop Floor Control, 557
Scheduling Intermittent Job Shop Processes, 560
    Input-Output Control, 560
    Order Review and Release, 561
    Scheduling and Sequencing, 562
    Gantt Chart Construction, 563
    Johnson's Rule for Fixed-Sequence, Two-Machine Problems, 567

Data Collection and Order Disposition, 569
Innovative Control: Theory of Constraints, 569
*Operations Management in Practice 15.1: Streamline Manufacturing: Sun Microsystems, Inc., 570*
*Operations Management in Practice 15.2: Synchronous Manufacturing—Quaker Furniture, 573*
International Issues in Shop-Floor Control, 574
Summary, 576
Key Terms, 577
Discussion Questions, 577
Problems, 578
Selected References, 579
*Case Study: Hoops University, 580*

## CHAPTER 16
## ▶ Just-in-Time Production, 581
Introduction, 582
Just-in-Time Production, 583
    Origins of JIT Philosophy, 583
*Operations Management in Practice 16.1: Back from the Future—Gearing Up for the Productivity Challenge, 584*
JIT Misunderstandings and Myths, 585
Motivation for JIT Implementation, 585
*Operations Management in Practice 16.2: Just-in-Time at Acme Manufacturing, 586*
Total Business Cycle Management, 587
Managing Material Flows, 589
    Set-up Reduction and the EOQ Lot Size, 589
    Inventory Reduction Caution, 591
Just-in-Time System Requirements, 592
    Production Flexibility Along the Supply Chain, 592
    Schedule Stability and Discipline, 593
    Comprehensive Quality Assurance, 593
    Creating Teams of Competent, Empowered Employees, 595
    JIT Systems and Signals, 595
    Logistics Systems to Support JIT Delivery, 597
*Operations Management in Practice 16.3: Some Manufacturers Drop Efforts to Adopt Japanese Techniques, 598*
Implementation of Just-in-Time, 598
Coordinating JIT and Material Requirements Planning, 600
Summary, 601
Key Terms, 602
Discussion Questions, 602
Selected References, 602

**CHAPTER 17**
▶ **Design and Scheduling of Service Systems, 605**
Introduction, 606
The Evolution of the Service System, 607
  Service Strategy, 607
  The Service Package, 609
*Operations Management in Practice 17.1: Pampering the American Motorist, 612*
Strategic Approaches to Service System Design, 613
  Production-Line Approach, 614
*Global Operations Management 17.2: Innovative Retail Service Systems—ATMs in Japan, 617*
  Isolating the Technical Core Approach, 617
  Consumer Participation Approach, 620
Strategies for Managing Service Demand, 621
  Price Incentives, 624
  Promoting Off-peak Demand, 624
  Partitioning Demand, 625
  Inventorying Demand—Reservation Systems, 625
  Inventorying Demand—Queueing Systems, 625
*Operations Management in Practice 17.3: SABRE—The Evolution of an Airline Demand Management System, 626*
  Developing Complementary Services, 626
Strategies for Controlling Service Supply, 626
  Daily Work Shift Scheduling, 628
  Weekly Work Shift Scheduling, 629
  Part-time Staffing, 632
  Cross-training Employees, 633
  Customer Self-service, 633
  Adjusting or Sharing Capacity, 633
Vehicle Routing, 633
  The Clarke-Wright Savings Heuristic, 634
Summary, 638
Key Terms, 639
Discussion Questions, 639
Problems, 639
Selected References, 641
*Case Study: National Technological University, 642*

**CHAPTER 18**
▶ **Project Management, 647**
Introduction, 648
  Work Breakdown Structures (WBS), 650
  Gantt Charts, 651
PERT and CPM, 652
  Construction of a Project Management Network, 653
  Calculating the Completion Time for a Project, 656

*Operations Management in Practice 18.1: Project Management for Product Launch at Oldsmobile, 659*
Managing Project Resources, 660
  Developing Project Budgets, 660
  Monitoring and Controlling Project Costs, 661
  Resource Limitations, 664
  Time/Cost Trade-offs in Project Management, 664
*Operations Management in Practice 18.2: Using Project Management Tools to Facilitate Communication in Building Construction at Michigan State University, 668*
PERT Networks and Uncertain Time Estimates, 669
Guidelines for Managing Projects, 672
*Operations Management in Practice 18.3: Platform Teams in the U.S. Auto Industry, 674*
Summary, 677
Key Terms, 678
Discussion Questions, 678
Problems, 678
Selected References, 682

**CHAPTER 19**
▶ **Quality Analysis, Measurement, and Improvement, 683**
Introduction, 684
Total Quality Management Implementation Process, 684
Process Analysis for Continuous Improvement, 684
*Operations Management in Practice 19.1: Government Division: North Island Navy Depot, 686*
*Operations Management in Practice 19.2: Service Division: New York Telephone, 687*
Process Improvement Model, 687
*Operations Management in Practice 19.3: Manufacturing Division: Boise Cascade's DeRidder Mill, 688*
*Operations Management in Practice 19.4: Small Organization Division: Fitchburg Coated Products, 689*
*Operations Management in Practice 19.5: Not-for Profit Division: Swedish-American Hospital, 690*
Benchmarking, 692
Data Collection, Analysis, and Presentation, 694
Statistical Tools for Process Improvement, 701
  Statistical Sampling and Control, 702
  Sampling and the Central Limit Theorem, 703
  Using Statistics to Test Inferences About Quality Control, 703
  Process Control Charts, 703
  Control Limits Versus Specification Limits, 711
  Acceptance Sampling, 713

Summary, 716
Key Terms, 717
Discussion Questions, 718
Problems, 718
Selected References, 720
*Case Study:* *Process Improvement Activities, 721*

# ► SECTION FIVE

Operations Management Revisited

## CHAPTER 20
## ► Building Competitive Advantage: Allen-Bradley's World Contractor Facility, 723

Introduction, 724
Allen-Bradley's World Contactors, 724
  The World Contactor Facility, 725
Identifying Strategic Threats and Opportunities, 726
The Competitive Challenge, 727
  Defining Competitive Advantage, 728
  The Foundation for Success, 729
Building Competitive Advantage: Toward
  World-Class Manufacturing, 730
  Cost, 731
  Quality, 731
  Flexibility and Lead Times, 732
Technologies and Methods, 732
  Concurrent Engineering and the Team
    Approach, 733
  Computer-Integrated Manufacturing and the
    Productivity Pyramid, 734
  Bar Coding, 736
  Total Quality Management, 736

Just-in-Time Manufacturing, 737
  Human Resources Management, 737
World-Class Manufacturing: Outcomes and
  Benefits, 738
Summary, 739
Discussion Questions, 740
Selected References, 741

# ► SECTION SIX

Tutorials

## TUTORIAL 1
## ► The Transportation Problem, 742

Introduction, 742
Mathematical Structure of the Transportation
  Problem, 742
Solving the Transportation Problem, 743
  Finding an Initial Basic Feasible Solution, 744
  Moving to an Optimal Solution: The
    Stepping-Stone Method, 746
Special Situations, 750
  Alternative Optimal Solutions, 750
  Unacceptable Transportation Routes, 750
  Degeneracy, 750
  The Unbalanced Transportation Problem, 751
  Changes in Transportation Costs, 752
  Profit Maximization Transportation Problems, 754
Summary, 754
Key Terms, 755
Discussion Questions, 755
Problems, 755
Selected References, 759

## TUTORIAL 2
## ► Decision Analysis, 760

Introduction, 760
Dominated Alternatives, 761
Decision Making Under Uncertainty, 761
  Optimistic (Maximax) Criterion, 761
  Pessimistic (Maximin) Criterion, 762
  Coefficient of Optimism (Hurwicz) Criterion, 762
  Equally Likely Criterion, 763
  Minimax Regret Criterion, 763
Decision Making Under Risk, 764
Expected Value Criterion, 765
Decision Trees, 765
Decision Making With Additional Information, 766
  Expected Value of Perfect Information, 766
  Accuracy of Additional Information, 767

Bayes' Theorem, 767
Evaluating and Using Additional Information, 769
Summary, 771
Key Terms, 772
Discussion Questions, 772
Problems, 772
Selected References, 775

**TUTORIAL 3**
▶ **Linear Programming, 776**
Introduction, 776
Formulating a Linear Programming Model, 776
Assumptions Used in Linear Programming, 777
Mathematical Structure of the Linear Programming
  Model, 777
Graphical Solutions to Linear Programming
  Problems, 777
Solving Linear Programming Problems Using the
  Simplex Method, 779
  Technical Steps in the Simplex Method, 779
  Summary of the Steps in the Simplex Method:
    Maximization Problems, 784
Shadow Prices, 784
Other Issues in Linear Programming, 785
  Other Types of Constraints ($\geq$ and =), 785
  Minimization Problems, 785
  Sensitivity Analysis, 785
Summary, 786
Key Terms, 786
Discussion Questions, 786
Problems, 786
Selected References, 789

**TUTORIAL 4**
▶ **Simulation, 790**
Introduction, 790
An Overview of Simulation, 791
  Steps in a Simulation Study, 791
  Simulating Exogenous Inputs, 791
  Simulating the System, 795

Simulation Languages, 800
Summary, 800
Key Terms, 801
Discussion Questions, 801
Problems, 801
Selected References, 803

**TUTORIAL 5**
▶ **Waiting Line Models, 804**
Introduction, 804
Structure of Waiting Line Problems, 805
  The Input Process, 805
  The Waiting Line (Queue), 807
  The Service Facility, 808
Operating Characteristics of Waiting Line
  Models, 810
Notation Used for Waiting Line Models, 810
Data Collection and Model Validation, 811
Decision Variables in the Analysis of Waiting
  Lines, 811
The Single-Channel, Single-Phase Waiting Line
  Model, 811
  Application of the Single-Channel, Single-Phase
    Waiting Line Model, 812
The Multiple-Channel, Single-Phase Waiting Line
  Model, 813
  Application of the Multiple-Channel, Single-Phase
    Waiting Line Model, 813
Other Waiting Line Models, 814
Summary, 814
Key Terms, 815
Discussion Questions, 815
Problems, 815
Selected References, 817

  **Appendix: Tables, 818**
  **Index, 826**
  **Acknowledgments, 842**

This book thoroughly covers the major concepts and issues necessary for an introductory course in operations management. It includes the discussion of topics involving the production of both goods and services, as both are important to the economies of developed and developing countries. The operations function is a primary business function that has a major effect on production, productivity, and quality. In conjunction with marketing and finance, it is critical to a company's success in a competitive environment. The operations function lies at the core of a business, for the operations area is responsible for most of the labor, materials, equipment, information, energy, and capital used to manufacture products and/or provide services. As we approach the twenty-first century, the need to improve quality and productivity has never been more important. To compete internationally requires a basic understanding of the operations function.

The field of operations management prepares managers to face the competitive challenge of effectively managing organizational resources. It is a blend of analytical tools and strategic issues. *Operations management* merges topics from accounting, industrial engineering, behavioral management, management science, and statistics. In today's competitive environment, organizations must approach the operations management function more strategically than many organizations approached this function in the past. In this text, we view the operations function as critical in enabling organizations to gain a competitive edge. The text emphasizes the importance of viewing operations from a strategic perspective throughout, and we present tools and techniques for solving problems in the context of meeting a company's strategic goals. This strategic emphasis also appears in the organization of the text.

Our objective in writing this text is to enable students to become better managers, particularly if they find themselves working in operations management. A sizeable part of the U.S. and international workforce is employed in operations jobs. These jobs are important and challenging, and they can lead to rewarding and successful careers. To achieve this objective, we have established several goals for the students who use this text. First, we want them to gain a thorough understanding of what operations managers do in manufacturing and service firms. Second, we want students to understand the tools and techniques that operations managers use in making operating decisions. Third, we hope that students who use this text will discover the excitement that marks this vibrant, dynamic, and rapidly changing field. Finally, we trust that the text will introduce some of the many challenges facing those who manage the operations function in service or manufacturing organizations.

## MAJOR THEMES IN *OPERATIONS MANAGEMENT*

In developing this textbook, we attempted to focus on the major themes currently shaping the field of operations management. These themes, woven into the fabric of the text, are outlined below:

- *International operations* The book stresses the importance of the globalization of operations management. This theme, introduced in Chapters 1 and 2, is expanded upon throughout the book.
- *Services* The book covers service operations extensively. Chapter 2 introduces service operations management, and Chapter 17 discusses the design and scheduling of service systems. Numerous service operations examples appear throughout the book.
- *Quality* The text emphasizes the importance of quality and continuous improvement. Chapter 7 provides perspective on managing quality, and Chapter 19 discusses quality analysis, measurement, and improvement.
- *Strategy* The book also highlights the strategic nature of operations management. One entire chapter, Chapter 3, discusses operations strategy in depth. This chapter includes a case involving operations strategic planning at Allen-Bradley. Strategic issues are discussed throughout the book. The concluding chapter, which revisits the strategic nature of operations management, reflects on what Allen-Bradley has done to become a world-class manufacturer.

- *Technology* The book discusses extensively the use of computers and other technologies in operations management. An entire chapter, Chapter 8, reviews technological developments in operations management. A number of the end-of-chapter problems require computer solutions.
- *Environmental issues* Environmental issues are becoming increasingly important to the field of operations management. Discussed throughout the text, these issues also are featured in two case studies, Union-Camp Corporation (Chapter 5) and Georgia-Pacific Corporation (Chapter 6).

# TEACHING AND LEARNING AIDS

The textbook contains numerous features designed to increase its value as a teaching and learning tool. Among the teaching aids we have included are the following:

- *Preview Section* The book begins with a preview section that provides a broad overview of the entire text. In this preview section, we explain the organization of the book in terms of strategic operations decision categories.
- *Flexible Organization* We have attempted to organize the textbook in a manner that offers flexibility in the order of topics and in the depth of coverage. The contents of the book allow for considerable flexibility in course design. After covering Chapters 1, 2, and 3, instructors can rearrange the remaining chapters to reflect their teaching preferences. Moreover, they can supplement the book's quantitative material by assigning material from any of the five tutorials grouped at the end of the text.
- *Chapter Outlines* Each chapter opens with an outline that provides a quick overview of the topics covered in the chapter.
- *Learning Objectives* Each chapter begins by listing a set of learning objectives designed to guide students as they study the chapter. These learning objectives are reviewed and summarized at the chapter's end.
- *Operations Management in Practice Boxes* Each chapter contains several Operations Management in Practice boxes, indicated by the symbol ▮, that provides examples of managerial practices in actual companies. Both manufacturing-oriented and service-oriented boxes are included.

- *Global Operations Management Boxes* Most chapters contain Global Operations Management boxes, indicated by the symbol ▮, that provide examples of international operations management practices.
- *Key Terms* Key terms are boldfaced and defined where they first appear in the text. They then appear in an end-of-chapter terms list for easy review.
- *Solved Demonstration Problems* Throughout the text, when a new technique is presented, we immediately apply it to a problem and work out a solution for the student.
- *End-of-Chapter Questions and Problems* The text includes numerous end-of-chapter exercises and problems. These relevant questions and problems are both qualitative and quantitative in scope.
- *Cases* The text includes ten end-of-chapter cases that relate to chapter content and include discussion questions. Illustrative videos supplement several of these cases.
- *Quantitative Tutorials* The text contains five separate quantitative tutorials: Transportation Problem, Decision Analysis, Linear Programming, Simulation, and Waiting Line Models. These tutorials appear at the end of the text, allowing instructors to use them flexibly with the several chapters to which they apply. Problems relating to the quantitative techniques described in the tutorials appear at the ends of various chapters; these problems relate techniques to specific problem situations.
- *Full-Color Art* Full-color art and photography throughout the text will stimulate and enhance the student's learning experience. Full-color photographs introduce each chapter and complement the text material. Color also strengthens the pedagogy of the text by adding visual contrast and clarity to various diagrams.

# ANCILLARY MATERIALS

To assist course instructors and students, a number of ancillary materials are available to supplement this text. They include:

## For the Instructor

- *Instructor's Manual with Solutions,* prepared by Allison McKinney Wilkins (University of Utah), includes chapter and lecture outlines with suggestions for classroom presentation, and a guide to the overhead transparencies package. The solutions were done by the text authors using the Dennis & Dennis software (see below). The manual also includes a detailed guide to the video package by Ranga Ramasesh (Texas Christian University).

- *Test Bank,* by Drew Rosen (University of North Carolina–Wilmington) and L. Wayne Shell (Nicholls State University), features 1400 test items, including true/false, multiple-choice, extended-problem, and essay questions and short-answer problems.
- *ASTOUND presentation software,* with material by Allison McKinney Wilkins (University of Utah), features visually exciting graphics and demonstrations of text material. These are available as transparencies or as electronic files for multi-media presentations.
- *Video package including seven in-text video cases.* More than twenty additional videos profile large companies (including Motorola, Xerox, Hewlett-Packard, Harley-Davidson, UPS, and Great Dane Trailer) and focus on small business applications (Kiefer Paper Company—TQM, Pavilion Technologies—Artificial Intelligence, Lucas Western Flight Structures—JIT, Hudson Tool and Die—Continuous Improvement) and service organizations (Price/Costco, Minnesota Twins, and First Bank). An extensive video guide by Ranga Ramasesh (Texas Christian University), included in the instructor's manual, provides the length of each video, a brief description, and lecture integration suggestions tied directly to the text.
- *250 Transparencies* feature key figures from the text as well as unique teaching graphics that illustrate key concepts.

## For the Student:

- *Decision Support Systems for Production/Operations Management software for the IBM PC,* by Terry L.

Dennis, Laurie B. Dennis, and Dan Joseph (all of the Rochester Institute of Technology), invites students to solve production and operations management problems on-line.
- *Study Guide,* by Rosen and Shell, includes chapter outlines, review materials, key terms, definitions, and multiple-choice, extended-problem, and application questions.
- *INSIGHTS: Readings in Operations Management* is available for those professors who wish to supplement the text material with articles from the current business press. This softcover book contains twenty selections that discuss contemporary issues in operations management.

## ACKNOWLEDGMENTS

This textbook has resulted from the efforts of a great number of people. The entire publishing team at West Educational Publishing has been unflagging in their support and encouragement. In particular, Rick Leyh, our executive editor, has been a constant source of advice, wise counsel, and often-needed prodding. His editorial judgment and commitment to quality are admirable. His able assistant, Alex von Rosenberg, helped us immensely with the many details that are part of producing a finished textbook. Polly Kummel, copy editor, turned our rough copy into a polished product, and Tom Modl, production editor, transformed our manuscript into an actual textbook by keeping us on schedule. Special thanks go to John B. Jensen, University of Southern Maine, for his help in proofing, error-checking, and obtaining solutions to problems, and to Bret J. Wagner, University of Delaware, for his invaluable assistance and developmental work on Chapters 1, 13, 14, and 18 and Tutorials 2 and 4.

Finally, we greatly appreciate the many comments and suggestions made by our colleagues who reviewed the materials for this textbook. They include:

# A Preview of Operations Management

The term *operations management* encompasses the body of knowledge concerning management of the day-to-day operations of any type of company. Whether the company is primarily a producer of physical goods or a provider of intangible services, the operations function lies at the core of the business. The operations function is usually responsible for most of the labor, materials, equipment, information, energy, and capital used to manufacture products and/or provide services.

One example of a manufacturing operation is Executive Furniture, Inc., (EFI) located in Huntingburg, Indiana. EFI's manufacturing unit produces wood and laminated case goods (desks, cabinets, bookcases, conference tables) for business purposes. Another example is Burroughs Wellcome Co., which is headquartered in Research Triangle Park, North Carolina. Burroughs Wellcome Co. manufactures chemicals and pharmaceuticals (Sudafed, Actifed) in its production facility in Greenville, North Carolina. Still another example is General Motors' Quad 4 Engine Plant in Lansing, Michigan. This plant manufactures the well-known Quad 4 engine and supplies engines to many of General Motors' assembly facilities. The Quad 4 engine is used in such vehicles as the Achieva and the Cutlass 442. All these companies are classified as manufacturing operations, because they produce physical goods (office furniture, chemicals, pharmaceuticals, and engines).

*General Motor's Quad 4 Engine Plant in Lansing, Michigan manufactures the popular Quad 4 Engine.*

In contrast to a manufacturing operation, a service operation primarily provides services to its customers. Sometimes the business provides the services in conjunction with a physical product that is minimally processed or prepared (such as food served in a restaurant). Delta Airlines in Atlanta is a service operation; the service it provides is transportation. Other types of services involve the transfer of knowledge and/or the provision of counsel and advice to customers. Michigan State University in East Lansing provides one group of its customers (students) with an education in the form of baccalaureate, master's, and doctoral degrees. H&R Block, the national tax-preparation chain, services its customers by preparing their tax returns.

Although we are making a distinction between manufacturing operations and service operations, we should note that manufacturing operations often provide services to their customers in conjunction with physical products. For example, Executive Furniture services its customers by delivering, unloading, and placing furniture. Burroughs Wellcome Co. provides detailed product information to the physicians prescribing its pharmaceuticals by means of its in-house staff of doctors, scientists, and pharmacists.

Manufacturing and service operations have many similarities, but they also have significant differences. In light of these important differences and the growing importance of the service economy this textbook devotes two chapters to service-focused companies. Chapter 2, Service Operations, points out the key differences between a manufacturing environment and a service environment. Chapter 17, Design and Scheduling of Service Systems, highlights the important issue of scheduling in a service-focused environment. The text also incorporates both manufacturing and service-related issues in each chapter where appropriate.

The long-term survival of most companies is based largely on management's ability to effectively and efficiently manage organizational resources. The discipline of operations management prepares managers to better accept this competitive challenge. Of primary concern today is the need for a more strategic view of operations than that taken by many organizations in the past. The importance of viewing operations from a strategic perspective is emphasized throughout this text.

## Strategic Operations Management

If the United States is to reestablish its industrial supremacy, operations—and specifically manufacturing—must be viewed as a competitive weapon. Fortunately companies have begun to comprehend the strategic importance of operations and become seriously involved with a variety of activities aimed at developing and enhancing their operations capabilities.[1] Managers are learning how to accurately measure performance in such areas as quality, cost, flexibility, service, and speed. Plans are being developed in light of clearly defined competitive priorities. Strategically important decision categories in operations have been identified, and managers have begun to understand how decision making in these areas affects a company's ability to compete on a global basis. We thoroughly examine the relationship of these categories to competitive advantage in Chapter 3, Operations Strategy.

[1]Arnoldo C. Hax, "Preface: Manufacturing Strategy Papers," *Interfaces* 15 (November–December 1985): 1.

| Strategic Operations Decision Category | Associated Textbook Chapter(s) |
|---|---|
| Product or Service Planning | Chapter 4: Forecasting Demand for Products and Services<br>Chapter 5: Product Planning and Process Design |
| Process design and technology management | Chapter 5: Product Planning and Process Design<br>Chapter 8: Technological Developments in Operations Management |
| Long-range capacity planning and facility location | Chapter 6: Long-range Capacity Planning and Facility Location |
| Quality management | Chapter 7: Managing Quality |
| Manufacturing or service organization | Chapter 9: Organization and Human Resources |
| Human resources management | Chapter 9: Organization and Human Resources |
| Operations planning and control | Chapter 10: Materials and Logistics Management<br>Chapter 11: Aggregate Production Planning<br>Chapter 12: Independent Demand Inventory Management<br>Chapter 13: Dependent Demand Inventory Management (MRP)<br>Chapter 14: Medium-and Short-range Capacity Planning<br>Chapter 15: Shop Floor Control<br>Chapter 16: Just-in-Time Production<br>Chapter 17: Design and Scheduling of Service Systems<br>Chapter 18: Project Management<br>Chapter 19: Quality Analysis, Measurement, and Improvement |

TABLE 1
Organization of the Textbook

This textbook is organized according to the *strategic operations decision categories*: product or service planning, process design and technology management, long-range capacity planning and facility location, quality management, manufacturing or service organization, human resource management, and operations planning and control. Table 1 lists the strategic decision categories and their corresponding textbook chapters. Note that Chapters 1, 2, 3, and 20 do not appear in this table. Chapters 1 and 2 introduce manufacturing operations and service operations, respectively, whereas Chapter 3 examines *operations strategy*. Finally, Chapter 20 provides an in-depth case study of Allen-Bradley's World Contactor Facility to show how operations can provide competitive advantage.

The orientation of this textbook is strategic. Viewing operations from a strategic standpoint is essential for understanding how operations contributes to the creation of value and ultimately to competitive advantage. Only by seeing the total picture can one understand the contribution of each part. Topics such as production planning, quality management, and process technology are more meaningful when viewed in a strategic context—the interrelationships among them become evident. The primary objectives of this textbook are to show students the strategic importance of operations and to enable them to build a solid knowledge base for managing operations in the twenty-first century.

# Manufacturing Operations

*The greatest threat to America's long-term well-being is our collective indifference to the future of manufacturing.*

DON DAVIS, president, Allen-Bradley Co., Rockwell International

## CHAPTER 1

**Introduction**

**The Transformation Process**
OPERATIONS MANAGEMENT IN PRACTICE 1.1: Portrait of an Operations Manager
OPERATIONS MANAGEMENT IN PRACTICE 1.2: Green Manufacturing at AT&T

**Types of Manufacturing Operations**
OPERATIONS MANAGEMENT IN PRACTICE 1.3: Tablet Production at Burroughs Wellcome Co., Greenville, N.C.

**Company Activities and Strategic Advantage: The Value Chain**

**The History of Operations Management**

**Recent Trends in Operations Management**
OPERATIONS MANAGEMENT IN PRACTICE 1.4: Reengineering at Ford Motor Co.

**Case Study: Time-based Competition at Northern Telecom**

## Introduction

The success of companies in the global marketplace depends on their ability to provide quality products and services at competitive prices. U.S. industry's continuing struggle to compete effectively in the international marketplace has increasingly focused on operations as the principal path to industrial resurgence. Increasingly, companies have begun to recognize that their futures depend on the effectiveness and efficiency of their manufacturing operations and that operations management is crucial to the long-run competitiveness of a company.

As we noted in the Preview to Operations Management, the major focus of Chapter 1 is manufacturing operations, as opposed to service operations (which are examined in Chapter 2). Thus, in this chapter we are concerned with the concepts, systems, and methods that relate to the effective management of a manufacturing operation. A **manufacturing operation** produces physical goods. The goods may be materials, components, and/or products that are used as inputs to other manufacturing systems (such as chemicals, lumber, oil, refrigeration coils, electric motors, camera lens, and engines), or they may be goods intended for final consumption (such as pharmaceuticals, furniture, gasoline, refrigerators, hair dryers, cameras, and automobiles). Although we focus on manufacturing operations in this chapter, we also examine some concepts and approaches that are applicable to service operations, hence there are references to *service operations* throughout.

## The Transformation Process

A manufacturing operation or service operation is a system that transforms a set of inputs into an output or set of outputs. The objective is to produce outputs with value to the customer that is greater than the cost of producing them. Inputs to the transformation process include human resources (managers and workers); capital investment in facilities and processes, technology, materials, land, and energy; and external and internal information. External information comes from the outside environment (government agencies, customers). The process itself generates internal information as part of a feedback/control loop (cost data, performance data).

Outputs of manufacturing operations are primarily physical goods but may include such auxiliary services as rapid delivery, product installation, and repairs. Outputs of service operations are primarily intangible but often include physical

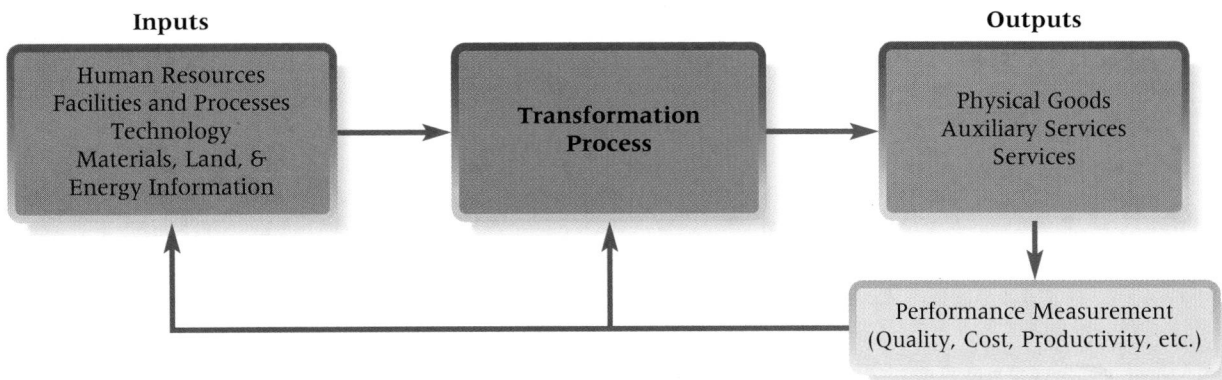

goods that are prepared but not produced by the system, such as legal documents, tax returns, and restaurant food. Figure 1.1 illustrates the transformation process.

## Productivity and the Transformation Process

**Productivity** is the total value of the outputs (goods and/or services) produced by the transformation process and divided by the total cost of the inputs (labor, materials, equipment). The basic productivity equation is

$$\text{Productivity} = [\text{Total Outputs}] \, / \, [\text{Total Inputs}]$$

Productivity can be increased in three ways:

- By using the same amounts of inputs to produce more output
- By using smaller amounts of inputs to produce the same amount of output
- By using smaller amounts of inputs to produce more output

For example, by streamlining operations a company can increase its output using smaller amounts of inputs. The nation's railroads cut back from nearly 27,000 locomotives and 440,000 workers in 1982 to 18,000 locomotives and 260,000 workers in 1992 and hauled almost 50 percent more freight. Or, by using better process technology, a company can generate more output using the same levels of inputs. At the huge U.S. Steel works in Gary, Indiana, a rebuilt strip mill rolls 6,000 tons of hot steel in an eight-hour shift; before modernization and a change in work practices, it produced only 4,000 tons in the same time period.[1]

Productivity studies often focus on the productivity of the manufacturing sector. A recent study of cross-national productivity levels concluded that in most manufacturing industries, U.S. workers are still more productive than workers in Japan or Germany. The study showed U.S. workers to be more productive than German workers in all industries investigated and more productive than the Japanese in all but the machinery and equipment sector. In manufacturing generally, German and Japanese workers were found to produce at a rate 82 percent of that of U.S. workers'.[2]

[1]Marc Levinson and Rich Thomas, "The Roaring '90s?," *Newsweek*, February 22, 1993, pp. 28—29.
[2]Bart van Ark and Dirk Pilat, "Cross Country Productivity Levels: Differences and Causes" (paper presented at the Brookings Papers on Economic Activity—Microeconomics [BPEA—MICRO] meeting, Brookings Institution, Washington, D.C., June 1993).

FIGURE 1.2
Manufacturing
Productivity—Average
Annual Change, 1987–1991

Source: Christopher Heye, "Five Years
After: A Preliminary Assessment of
U.S. Industrial Performance Since
*Made in America*," working paper No.
93-009WP, Industrial Performance
Center, Massachusetts Institute of
Technology Boston, September 1993,
pp. 10–11.

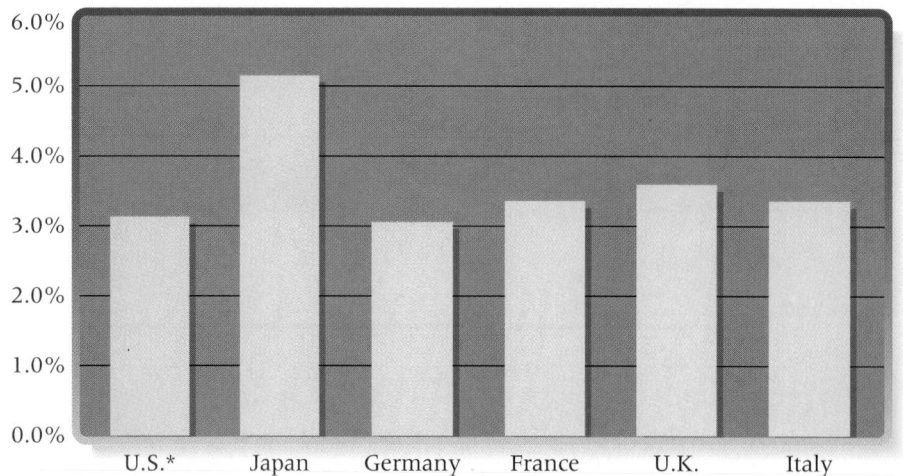

* For purposes of comparison U.S. figures are adjusted to exclude the national accounts price indexes
revision.

A more common measure of cross-national trends in manufacturing productivity is the growth rate of productivity (the percentage of change in productivity
from one period to the next). This measure is related to the long-term prosperity
and wealth of nations. Figure 1.2 depicts average annual changes in manufacturing productivity for the United States, Japan, Germany, France, the United
Kingdom, and Italy for the period 1987—1991. The data suggest that since the
late 1980s U.S. manufacturing productivity has been growing roughly at the
same rate as that of the European countries' although still more slowly than in
Japan. However, more recent data point to continued increases in the productivity of U.S. manufacturing.[3]

In 1989 the Massachusetts Institute of Technology (MIT) Commission on
Industrial Productivity analyzed the competitiveness of U.S. companies in eight
industries. The commission observed that the United States had surrendered to
overseas competitors most, if not all, production of certain product groups
(televisions) and a large percentage of entire industries (consumer electronics
and machine tools) and that American industry showed worrisome signs of
weakness. Much of the evidence gathered by the MIT commission pointed to the
manufacturing sector as the area in which the American advantage in cost and
quality had been most severely eroded.[4]

Much of the blame for declining productivity growth and other problems
related to competitiveness, such as inadequate quality, insufficient capital spending, and sluggish technological innovation, was attributed to "human behavior—
especially American managers' attitudes, capabilities, and strategies—particularly
in the areas of manufacturing and technological development."[5] According to
Richard K. Lester, executive director of the MIT Council on Industrial Productiv-

[3]Christopher Heye, "Five Years After: A Preliminary Assessment of U.S. Industrial Performance Since
*Made In America*," working paper No. 93–009WP, Industrial Performance Center, Massachusetts
Institute of Technology, Boston, September 1993, pp. 10—11.
[4]Michael L. Dertouzos, Richard K. Lester, and Robert M. Solow, *Made in America: Regaining the
Productive Edge* (New York: HarperPerennial, 1990): 1—22, 31.
[5]Robert H. Hayes, Steven C. Wheelwright, and Kim B. Clark, *Dynamic Manufacturing* (New York: Free
Press, 1988), p. 11.

ity, by 1993 many U.S. managers had begun to take productivity, cost, and quality issues more seriously, and they had made some progress in those areas.[6]

## Managing the Transformation Process: The Operations Manager

**Operations managers** play a critical role within their organizations—they ultimately are responsible for the success of their manufacturing or service units. The operations manager works closely with top management in setting the strategic direction of the company and in defining the competitive priorities of the manufacturing or service operation.

In working to achieve strategic goals, an operations manager is engaged in a wide variety of activities. These activities encompass the well-known management functions of planning, organizing, staffing, directing, and controlling.

Two essential attributes of an effective operations manager are a solid technical knowledge base and people skills. An operations manager must fully understand the company's products or services, the process and process technologies used to manufacture the products or provide the services, and the operating systems, methods, and techniques that govern the transformation process. Many chapters in this textbook are designed to provide students with a solid foundation upon which to build their technical competence as operations managers.

Operations managers also must be able to work with people effectively. They must be able to make decisions and communicate them to other managers and to the work force and to motivate both managers and the work force to implement those decisions. An operations manager must be approachable and accessible to other managers and the work force and genuinely open to their participation and ideas. An operations manager must recognize that it is people, both managers and workers, who ultimately determine the success or failure of an organization. Chapter 9, Organization and Human Resources, considers in greater detail issues related to dealing with people. Operations Management in Practice 1.1 describes the career path and challenges facing one successful operations executive.

Operations managers play a vital role within their companies and within society as a whole. As noted earlier, managers of manufacturing and service operations hold the key to increased productivity for their companies and hence contribute to a higher standard of living for themselves and their employees.

Another area in which an operations manager can have substantial societal influence is ethics. The issue of ethics relative to business conduct will become increasingly important as competitive pressures intensify in the twenty-first century. Major corporations throughout the United States are proactively addressing the challenge in a variety of ways. These include (1) developing codes of ethics and statements of values; (2) increasingly open discussion among executives and managers concerning ethical issues and how to deal with them; and (3) effectively implementing ethical policies to ensure compliance.[7]

A related area in which operations managers can affect their companies in positive ways while also having a positive effect on current and future generations is **ecologically sound manufacturing**, or **green manufacturing**. As these terms imply, the operations manager runs the manufacturing process in an environmentally responsible way.

[6]Interview with author, October 12, 1993.
[7]*Corporate Ethics: A Prime Business Asset* (New York: Business Roundtable, February 1988).

## OPERATIONS MANAGEMENT IN PRACTICE 1.1

# Portrait of an Operations Manager

*Dr. Gabriel R. Cipau*

Burroughs Wellcome Co. in Research Triangle Park, North Carolina, is the U.S. affiliate of Wellcome, an international pharmaceutical company dedicated to the discovery and marketing of products that promote human health and quality of life. Wellcome pioneered the development of effective antiviral therapy and holds an enviable commercial position in this area, with products such as Retrovir for the treatment of human immunodeficiency virus (HIV) infection. Until recently Dr. Gabriel R. Cipau was the senior vice president of production and engineering at Burroughs Wellcome (USA). He was responsible for chemical manufacturing and pharmaceutical formulation at the Greenville, North Carolina, production unit, one of Wellcome's major manufacturing sites worldwide. He recently was promoted to president of Nippon Wellcome, Osaka, Japan, a joint venture of Wellcome and Sumato Chemical of Japan.

Here is a summary of some of the milestones of Cipau's career with Burroughs Wellcome (USA). In 1970, Cipau joined Burroughs Wellcome as a project engineer after completing a doctoral degree in chemical engineering and physics from the Polytechnical Institute of Timisora. He obtained a masters degree in chemistry from East Carolina University, Greenville, North Carolina in 1973 and was appointed department head of the new Scientific Computing Department in research, development, and medical (RD&M) in 1975. In 1979, he was appointed vice president of production and engineering and unit manager. In the 1980s he obtained an M.B.A. from Duke University, was elected to the company's board of directors, and was appointed executive manager for Retrovir (zidovudine). In 1989 he was appointed senior vice president of production and engineering.

Over the years Cipau has faced several major challenges. One has been the continuous evolution of technology in the pharmaceutical and chemical industries. The rapid growth of knowledge of pharmaceutical and chemical products since the mid-1970s has led to more stringent standards. As a result, the technology for developing products has shifted dramatically. In 1970 Burroughs Wellcome formulated most of its pharmaceutical products as ointments, tablets, or ampules. Today, the company also produces vials, film-coated tablets, capsules, and a myriad of other product presentations. Also, the technologies used in 1970 were extremely conventional; most manufacturing operations were manual. Today, manufacturing is almost entirely automated using such technologies as film coating and septic filling. Advanced computer controls in chemical manufacturing have practically eliminated all labor. As Cipau states, "The evolution of technology has been a major challenge—to try to keep up with what is happening and not fall behind."

Another major challenge has been people. When it introduced new technologies, management had to retrain people and develop their skills so they could work effectively in the computerized, high-tech environment. Most people who worked for the company in 1970 are still with it today, but the technologies they used then and now are entirely different. The training of employees and the human resources issues related to training have been challenging.

## Ecologically Sound Manufacturing[8]

Although the boundaries of environmental responsibility are not yet clearly defined, it encompasses three operations-related issues: which products a company should bring to market and, specifically, the product and packaging materials that should be used to do so; the degree to which companies should engage in open disclosure of pollution and health information; and how companies can reduce waste at the source, thereby preventing pollution.

From an operations perspective the last question is the most challenging, because the best way to prevent pollution is by designing processes that do not generate harmful emissions. In the long-run this may also prove more cost effective than catching emissions at the end of a smokestack.

Several well-known U.S. companies have reaped substantial savings from aggressive environmental programs. 3M's Pollution Prevention Pays program, organized in 1975, was one of the first sustained waste-reduction efforts by a leading American company. 3M's program, which uses cross-disciplinary teams of employees for problem solving, has saved the company $500 million, with an equally dramatic decrease in emissions. Dow Chemical's Waste Reduction Always Pays program, which began in 1986, has resulted in more than seven hundred projects that save the company millions of dollars a year. Westinghouse's Achievements in Clean Technology project, formalized in 1989, has had similar successes. In one Westinghouse metal-finishing plant in Puerto Rico, the company cut dragout—the contamination accidentally carried as chemicals flow from one tank to another—by 75 percent simply by shaking the tank to remove solids before releasing the chemical to the next tank. Operations Management in Practice 1.2 describes the commitment of AT&T to green manufacturing.

## Types of Manufacturing Operations

One way to classify manufacturing operations is by the amount of processing the product requires after the company receives an order from a customer. At one end of the processing spectrum is the **make-to-order (MTO)** company. This company does not begin processing the material for and components of the product until it has received an order from a customer. In some cases the company may not even procure the material and components until after it receives the order. The latter case is especially common when the company competes on the basis of product customization and serves its customer base by providing unique and/or highly specialized items. The MTO company also bases its production planning on firm customer orders.

At the opposite end of the spectrum is the **make-to-stock (MTS)** company, which manufactures products and places them in inventory before it receives customers' orders. Either the customer purchases the product directly from inventory at a retail outlet or the company ships the product "off the shelf" from finished goods inventory at the factory or at a distribution center. Make-to-stock companies rely heavily on demand forecasting in planning the production of their products with respect to product mix and volume. Chapter 4 deals extensively with the subject of demand forecasting.

Another variation is the assemble-to-order company. The **assemble-to-order company (ATO)** manufactures standardized, option modules according

[8]Adapted from Art Kleiner, "What Does It Mean to Be Green?" *Harvard Business Review* 69 (July—August 1991): 39, 44, 46.

# Green Manufacturing at AT&T

In August 1989 AT&T publicly proclaimed it would eliminate all chlorofluorocarbon (CFC) emissions from its manufacturing processes by 1994. CFCs are chemicals that are widely believed to be eating the earth's protective ozone layer high in the stratosphere. The CFCs used in cleaning compounds, mostly by electronics companies, make up about 17 percent of all CFC usage worldwide (390 billion pounds annually), and AT&T is the fifth biggest emitter of CFCs, after General Motors Corp., United Technologies, IBM, and General Electric Co.

For years AT&T has set an industry standard with its corporate environmental policies, particularly regarding CFCs, hazardous waste, and worker safety. The company is best known for its early and aggressive decision to apply research dollars to CFC alternatives. Like IBM, Digital Equipment Corp. (DEC), Northern Telecom, and Hewlett-Packard, AT&T is exploring alternative solvents and aqueous detergent cleaners. AT&T has set up a multidisciplinary team to explore a variety of alternatives to CFCs: aqueous cleaning, solvents, terpenes, low-solids fluxes, and altered manufacturing processes. While AT&T's Singapore plant is its first facility to be CFC free in the production of circuit boards (by using low-solids flux technology), its other facilities have a long way to go.

Changing capital-intensive processes is difficult, and AT&T is approaching redesign selectively. The chief focus is on designing new products and processes that generate fewer pollutants.

to forecasts it has made and then assembles a specific combination or package of modules after receiving the customer's order. The classic example is the automobile manufacturer. After receiving orders from a host of dealers, the manufacturer specifies the exact build schedule for the automobiles; the schedule is based on the options ordered by customers—automatic or manual transmission, air conditioning, standard versus digital control panel, leather, cloth, or vinyl seating, and so on. The many components for assembling the automobiles would have been ordered or started into production before receiving the dealers' orders based upon demand forecasts. Thus, the major processing remaining when the orders come in is assembly. This approach shortens the time between placement of the customer's order and the customer's receipt of the product—this interval is called the *order cycle time*—as compared with the make-to-order approach.

Another way to classify production operations is according to the amount of flexibility that characterizes the system. Here, **flexibility** is the ability of the operation to efficiently produce highly customized and unique products.

## Project Manufacturing

The most flexible type of manufacturing operation is a project. **Project manufacturing** is usually associated with big, costly, and highly customized items such as aircraft carriers, nuclear submarines, space shuttles, bridges, commercial buildings, and homes. The manufacturer sends all materials for constructing the product to the manufacturing site as they are needed.

These projects usually take more time to complete than other types of manufacturing. For example, the construction of a home can take two to three months, whereas the construction of a submarine can take more than a year. In many instances the same personnel or teams of workers work on a project for significant portions of the construction time.

## The Job Shop

The next most flexible type of production operation is the job shop. The **job shop** is characterized by a process-focused grouping of resources. Production equipment, machinery, or workstations are grouped and arranged according to the function or process that they perform. A separate area is set aside for each process that comprises the set of processes or manufacturing steps needed for manufacturing a given product or set of products. Products move either singly or in small batches from one processing area to another as they are made.

The term *job shop* is appropriate, because the process-oriented organization of resources facilitates the manufacture of many different jobs, or products. The pattern of flow for job shop production is usually jumbled or random, because the routes through the shop of various jobs, or products, can vary greatly. Another term frequently applied to job shop production is *intermittent production,* because the equipment and processing centers within the job shop are usually not in continuous use. Although a job shop can produce products to order or for stock, it is particularly well suited for the manufacture of a wide range of customized products and hence is most often associated with make-to-order companies.

## Line-Flow Production

At the opposite end of the flexibility continuum is line-flow production. **Line-flow production** is characterized by a product-focused grouping of resources. Equipment, machinery, and workstations are set up in a serial pattern or sequence that is dictated by the steps required for manufacturing the product. The manufacturer dedicates equipment and labor to various product lines so that different products do not have to compete for resources; the flow of materials and product is relatively continuous. This production system is specifically designed for high-volume production.

Because the processing pattern is fixed and production resources are dedicated, manufacturers often use line-flow production for standard, make-to-stock products or for assembling option modules and components in an assemble-to-order environment. Examples of line-flow production systems include production lines or assembly lines for making engines, household appliances, washing machines, and automobiles.

Some line-flow production systems do not produce discrete units of product but manufacture products in bulk, the raw materials of which are blended or processed in voluminous quantities. Because this type of production is characterized by a continuous flow of large quantities of bulk product, the term **continuous flow production** is used to distinguish it from the manufacture of discrete units by an assembly line or production line.

Continuous flow production often involves chemical or physical reactions. Industries that produce products in this manner are called *process industries.* Examples of process industries include petroleum refining, chemical production, food processing, and paper production.

# Tablet Production at Burroughs Wellcome Co., Greenville, N.C.

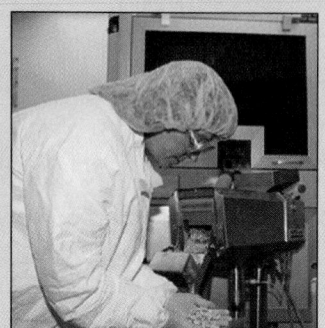

*Tablet compression at Burroughs Wellcome Co. Photo courtesy of Burroughs Wellcome Co.*

Eleven of Burroughs Wellcome's tablet products are differentiated from others in its tablet line based on a unique aspect of their manufacture: Two identical manufacturing rooms and associated equipment are dedicated solely to the processing of these products for a certain stage of their manufacture. Employees refer to the dedicated rooms as the "R5" processing rooms, and the products are known companywide as the "R5" products. Thus, the eleven products share critical manufacturing resources with other tablet products, but they have exclusive use of the R5 rooms. (The company defines *critical resources* as manufacturing rooms, equipment, labor, and totes [huge metal tubs for mixing raw material ingredients].)

Batch production for the R5 products consists of five sequential manufacturing stages for nine products and seven sequential manufacturing stages for two products, followed by shipping. The stages are defined according to the departments that perform the operations that comprise the manufacturing process. The stages of batch production are depicted in Figure 1.3.

Production starts with the drug stock department, which weighs the dry raw ingredients according to the drug formula released by the chief pharmacist. After the weighing, each dry ingredient is sifted into a *tote*. The department then measures the liquid ingredients and mixes them according to specifications.

Next, the granulation department blends the dry ingredients. Granulation begins when the dry and liquid ingredients (including active ingredients) are combined in a special mixer. The granulated mixture proceeds immediately to an aeromatic dryer, which dries the granules of product formed by the mixing operation. After drying, the granules are chopped into the required particle size. The mixing of the dry and liquid ingredients, the aeromatic drying, and the chopping operation form the subset of stage 2 operations that are performed using the dedicated equipment in the R5 rooms. The granulation phase concludes with a final blending of the granulated mixture in a tote blender.

In the third stage of the process, the granulated mixture is gravity fed into a compressing machine. Different types of compressing machines are required, depending on the product being processed. The compressing machine molds tiny portions of the granulated mixture into the desired tablet size and shape. During this stage quality assurance technicians periodically sample the tablets as they are ejected from the compressing machine. The finished tablets are stored in small plastic buckets.

The fourth stage of manufacture is quality assurance. Technicians perform a battery of tests on the finished bulk product before the tablets are released for further processing and/or packaging.

For two of the R5 products, the next stage is sugarcoating. One product also requires printing. Afterward, both products undergo a second set of quality assurance tests before the tablets are released for packaging.

The packaging department handles the last manufacturing stage, bottling and labeling the tablets and packing them in cartons for shipment. Technicians perform final quality assurance tests before shipment. Because there is little lead time for the final quality assurance check, it is considered part of the packaging stage. Each of the eleven products spawns a set of finished items—-the same tablets are packaged in components of different shapes and sizes (a blister pack of forty-eight tablets, a bottle of one hundred tablets).

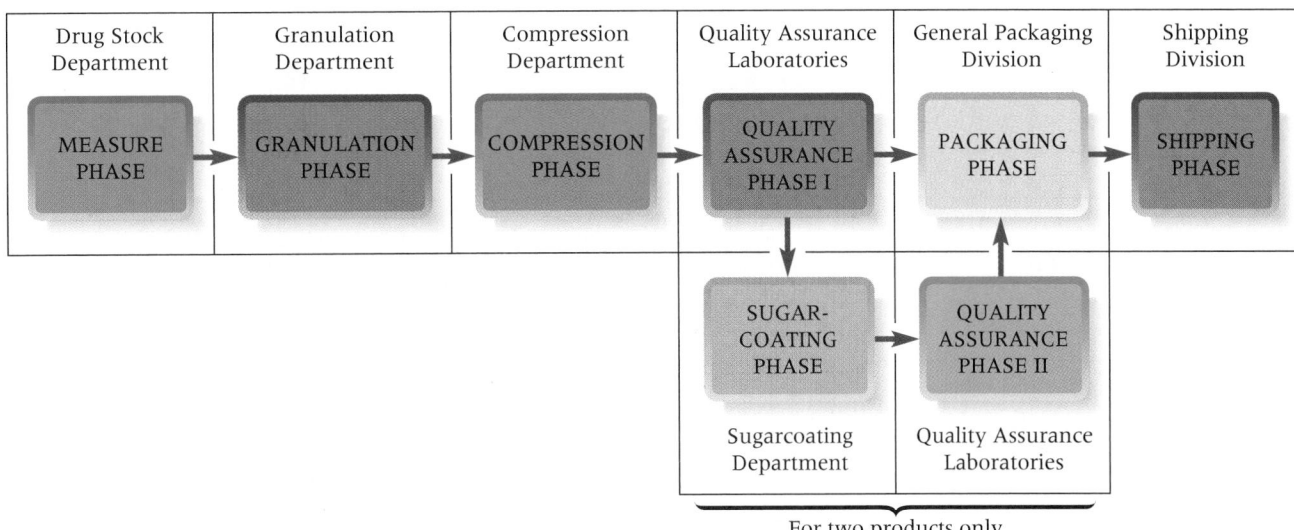

FIGURE 1.3
Stages of Batch Production at
Burroughs Wellcome Co.

## Batch Production

The job shop and line-flow production are at opposite ends of the flexibility continuum. Line-flow production systems are largely inflexible, because they are designed to efficiently produce large quantities of fairly standard products. In contrast, job shops are extremely flexible—they are capable of efficiently producing a wide variety of products, even one-of-a-kind products. Many production systems exhibit features of both systems—that is, they are *hybrids.*

Many hybrids are **batch production** systems. Burroughs Wellcome Co. in Greenville, North Carolina, uses a batch production system to produce drugs in tablet form. Tablet production is a serial process; the stages of production are similar for all products. However, production of the tablets occurs in discrete batches, or lots. Operations Management in Practice 1.3 describes the production system for eleven of Burroughs Wellcome's tablet products.

## Company Activities and Strategic Advantage: The Value Chain[9]

Every company is a collection of activities that design, produce, market, deliver, and support its products (or services). Each activity can contribute to a company's cost position relative to its competitors and/or enable the company to differentiate its products (or services) from those of competitors. One approach to examining a company's activities and their relationship to competitive advantage is the value chain. The value chain is a conceptual model that can help a company recognize strategically important activities, examine the behavior of its costs, and identify existing and potential ways to differentiate its products (or services).

In competitive terms *value* is defined as the amount buyers are willing to pay for a product (or service). Total revenue—price multiplied by the number of units

[9]Adapted from Michael Porter, "The Value Chain and Competitive Advantage," chap. 2 in *Competitive Advantage* (New York: Free Press, 1985), pp. 33—61.

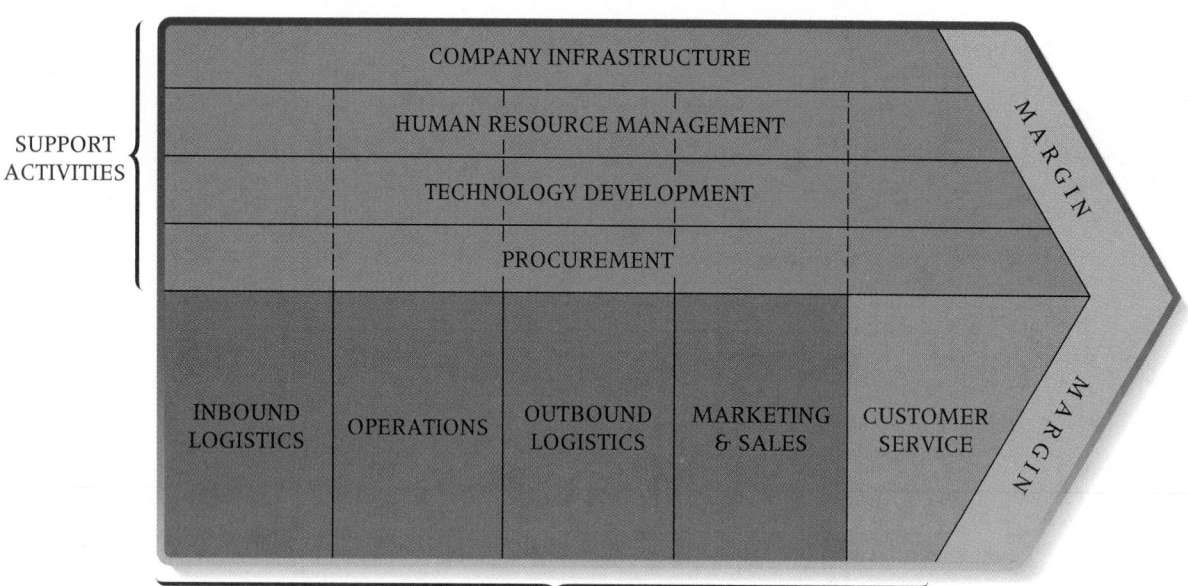

FIGURE 1.4
The Value Chain

Source: Adapted from Michael Porter, *Competitive Advantage* (New York: Free Press, 1985), p. 370.

sold—is the measure of value. For a company to be profitable, the value of its product (or service) must exceed its cost. Providing better value for buyers than competitors is the ultimate goal of a company's business strategy. Chapter 3 covers business strategy and competitive advantage in greater detail.

The **value chain** schematically depicts the total value generated by a company; it is comprised of value activities and margin. Value activities, such as assembly, packaging, product testing, and so on, are physically and technologically distinct activities. They are the building blocks a company uses to provide a product (or service) valuable to its customers. Margin is the difference between total value and the collective cost of performing value activities.

Value activities fall into two broad groups, primary activities and support activities. Primary activities are concerned with the physical creation of the product (or service) and its sale and transfer to the buyer, including postsale customer service. Support activities undergird primary activities and each other by providing purchased inputs, technology, human resources, and other companywide functions. The conceptual framework in Figure 1.4 is an illustration of the value chain and its primary and support activities. The dotted lines in the figure represent the association of procurement, technology development, and human resource management with individual primary activities as well as with the entire value chain. Note that the company's infrastructure is not associated with particular primary activities but supports the value chain as a whole.

As shown in Figure 1.4, primary activities fall into five categories and support activities into four categories. Table 1.1 lists and defines each subcategory for a manufacturer.

Primary and/or support activities can be crucial to a company's competitive advantage. For example, operations is important in the furniture industry, where the ability to rapidly adjust production volume can significantly affect a company's profitability and market share. In the automobile industry, where purchased materials and components represent a sizable portion of the sales dollar, procure-

| **Primary Activities** | **Support Activities** |
|---|---|
| *Inbound Logistics.* Activities associated with receiving, storing, and disseminating inputs to the product, such as handling materials, warehousing, controlling inventory, and scheduling vehicles | *Procurement.* Activities associated with procuring inputs, such as raw materials, supplies, and other consumable items, as well as such assets as machinery, equipment, and buildings |
| *Operations.* Activities associated with transforming inputs into the final product, such as machining, assembling, packaging, testing, maintaining equipment, and operating the facility | *Technology development.* A range of activities involving different scientific disciplines that are directed toward improving the product, the process, and the company's information systems |
| *Outbound logistics.* Activities associated with collecting, storing, and physically distributing the product to customers, such as handling and warehousing finished goods, operating delivery vehicles, and processing orders | *Human resource management.* Activities involved in recruiting, hiring, training, developing, and compensating all personnel |
| *Marketing and sales.* Activities associated with providing a means by which customers can purchase the product and inducing them to do so, such as advertising, promotion, selling, quoting, selecting markets and channels and maintaining relationships with them, and pricing | *Firm infrastructure.* Activities that include general management, planning, finance, accounting, legal, government affairs, and quality management |
| *Customer Service.* Activities associated with providing service to enhance or maintain the value of the product, such as installing, repairing, training, supplying parts, and adjusting the product | |

Source: Adapted from Michael Porter, *Competitive Advantage*. New York: Free Press, 1985, pp. 39–49.

TABLE 1.1
Primary and Support Value Activities

ment is a major priority. In the steel industry, a company's process technology makes the single greatest contribution to success.

Although value activities are the building blocks of competitive advantage, the value chain is not a collection of independent activities. Value activities are interrelated by *linkages* within the chain. A linkage is the relationship between the way one value activity is performed and the cost or performance of another. Linkages often reflect trade-offs among activities. For example, a more costly product design may reduce service costs later on. Linkages may also reflect the need to coordinate value activities. For example, on-time delivery requires the close coordination of operations, outbound logistics, and service activities (installation). Thus, competitive advantage derives from linkages among value activities in addition to the activities themselves. In recent years the intensity of global competition has forced U.S. companies to recognize the importance of linkages.

Figure 1.5 shows a typical organizational structure for a manufacturer superimposed on the value chain. Note two aspects of the diagram. First, production has broad responsibility for many value chain activities. In other words, manufacturing has significant responsibility for many activities that are critical to the success or failure of a company.

Second, Figure 1.5 shows that functional areas such as production, marketing, and purchasing interface to create value for the customer. Better integration of functional areas can improve competitive positioning. For example, a competitively priced, quality product often requires the close integration of research and development (R&D), marketing, production, and purchasing to ensure its design

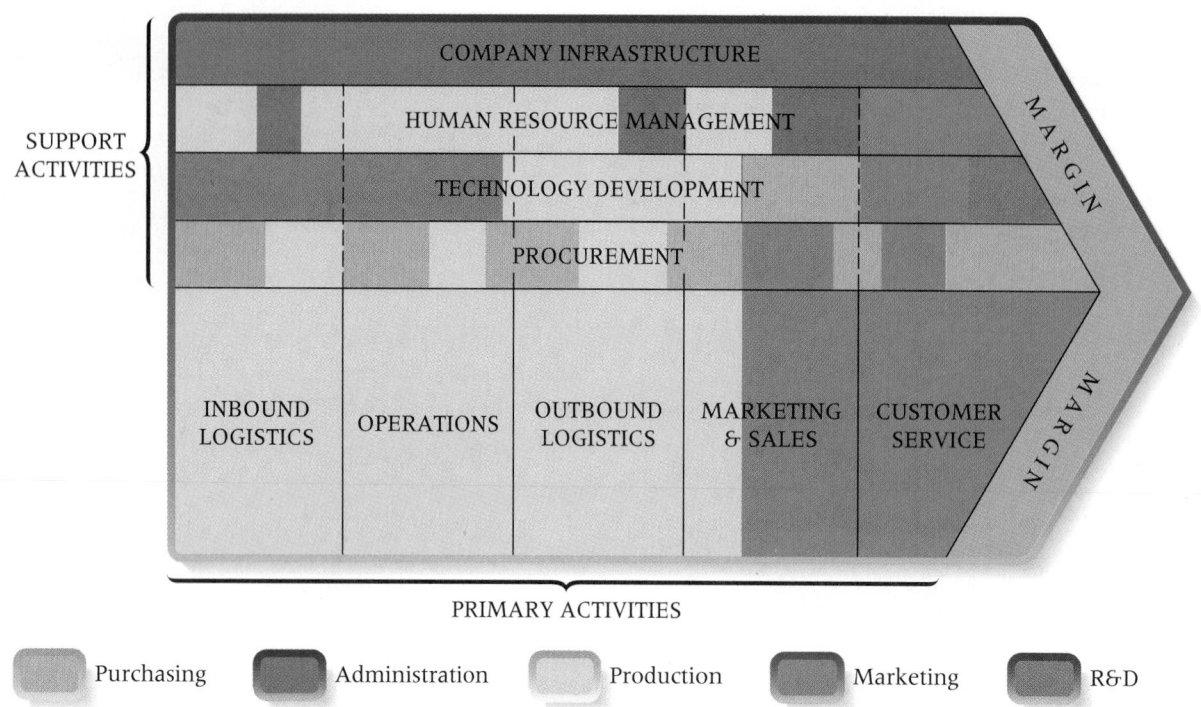

SUPPORT ACTIVITIES

COMPANY INFRASTRUCTURE

HUMAN RESOURCE MANAGEMENT

TECHNOLOGY DEVELOPMENT

PROCUREMENT

MARGIN

MARGIN

INBOUND LOGISTICS

OPERATIONS

OUTBOUND LOGISTICS

MARKETING & SALES

CUSTOMER SERVICE

PRIMARY ACTIVITIES

Purchasing    Administration    Production    Marketing    R&D

FIGURE 1.5
The Value Chain and Typical
Organizational Structure

Source: Adapted from Michael Porter,
*Competitive Advantage.* New York: Free
Press, 1985, p. 60.

meets customers' needs yet is easy to manufacture. One popular method for achieving such integration is the use of cross-functional teams. A **cross-functional team** consists of individuals from different functional areas within a business organization who assemble to accomplish a strategically important goal. However, a company may have to redesign its entire organizational structure to more closely conform to and support its unique value chain.

## The History of Operations Management

The task of managing operations has existed for most of human history. The construction of the Great Wall of China, the pyramids of Egypt and the cathedrals of Europe all required effective management of labor and materials. While the task of managing operations has existed for centuries, the recognition of operations management as a field to be developed and studied is recent. In the United States the development of manufacturing and the consideration of management issues related to manufacturing began with Eli Whitney and the invention of the cotton gin in the late 1700s. The discussion that follows describes some of the "giants" in the field of operations and some key events that contributed to the growth of operations, first as an industrial function and then as an academic discipline.

## Eli Whitney[10]

Eli Whitney had completed his education at Yale University and was about to begin a career as a tutor in South Carolina when he invented the cotton gin.

[10]Adapted from Jeanette Mirsky, *The World of Eli Whitney* (New York: Macmillan, 1952).

Roller gins were available, but they could process only black seed cotton, which could be grown successfully only in the coastal areas of South Carolina and Georgia. Large regions of the South could easily grow green seed cotton, which has high-quality fibers. However, separating the cotton fibers from the green seeds was difficult and time consuming.

Whitney had come to South Carolina at the request of Phineas Miller, to tutor the children of a neighboring planter, a Major Dupont. The tutoring position did not work out, but while he was staying with Miller, Whitney developed the idea for the cotton gin:

> [I] involuntarily happened to be thinking on the subject and struck out a plan of a Machine in my mind, which I communicated to Miller. . . . He was pleased with the Plan and said that if I would pursue it and try and experiment to see if it would answer, he would be at the whole expense, I should lose nothing but my time, and if I succeeded we should share the profits.[11]

Within ten days Whitney had built a prototype, and on June 1, 1793, he built a hand-operated model that could clean ten times the cotton that a manual laborer could clean in the same amount of time and do it more effectively.

Miller and Whitney applied for a patent in June 1793; it was granted on March 14, 1794. They decided the best plan was to set up their own cotton ginneries. Five pounds of raw cotton produced $1\frac{2}{3}$ pounds of clean cotton. The partners would give one pound to the grower and keep two-thirds of a pound as payment. This should have been a lucrative business, but Miller and Whitney experienced many problems.

First, building machinery was difficult because the United States had few skilled workers. Quality raw materials were also scarce. Furthermore, whereas producing cotton gins in large quantities was difficult, it was not difficult to copy them. The high price charged by Whitney, coupled with the ease with which a moderately skilled craftsman could make a gin, led many to infringe on the Whitney patent. A further setback was a fire in the partners' New Haven, Connecticut, factory in 1795. The loss of production capacity increased the pressure cotton growers felt to infringe on the Whitney patent.

Whitney and Miller never profited from the cotton gin as much as they should have. Legal setbacks, patent infringement, and credit difficulties made the business a tough one. Yet, their invention transformed the United States. The U.S. cotton business grew dramatically after the gin was invented. In 1791 U.S. cotton production was fewer than 190,000 pounds, and essentially none was exported. By 1812 England was importing 63 million pounds, half of which was grown and ginned in the United States. By 1825, the year Eli Whitney died, U.S. exports to England alone totaled 171 million pounds, three-fourths of all cotton imported by the British.

While Whitney and Miller pursued the cotton gin business and battled to protect the patent for years, Whitney pursued a second, and perhaps more important, business. On June 14, 1788, Whitney signed a contract to provide the federal government with 10,000 stands of arms (muskets with bayonets and ramrods). He was to deliver the first 4,000 arms on September 30, 1799, and the final 6,000 on September 30, 1800, at a price of $13.40 each. Manufacturing 10,000 muskets in the United States was almost unthinkable, especially considering that Whitney had never manufactured a weapon and had no production facility.

---

[11] Mirsky, *The World of Eli Whitney*, p. 66.

With no skilled base of craftsmen, such as existed in England and France, Whitney understood that the only way to build a large quantity of arms in the United States was to develop a musket based on interchangeable parts and to develop production machinery and processes that put the capability of precision work in the machines and not in the hands of the worker.

Whitney's original plans were wildly optimistic. He made his first delivery, 500 arms, on September 26, 1801 — 3,500 muskets short and two years late. The final shipment was not made until January 23, 1809. Whitney produced the arms within the original contract price (excluding improvements to which both parties agreed), but he required advance payments much larger than originally planned, and the schedule performance was perhaps the worst in U.S. military procurement history. Were it not for the threat of war with France, the desperate need for domestic arms manufacture, Whitney's personal reputation, and the wisdom of Secretary of the Treasury Oliver Wolcott—who continued and modified the contract several times—Whitney's pioneering work would not have succeeded.

The concept of interchangeable parts was fundamental to the furthering of the Industrial Revolution in the mid-1800s. It required the development of tools and techniques that any worker could use. The United States at the time was suffering from a severe worker shortage, and the methods of Eli Whitney allowed less-skilled workers to produce a higher-quality product more efficiently. As for the Whitney Arms Co., it lasted for ninety years under the direction of Whitney's son and grandson, until it was sold to the Winchester Arms Co.

## Frederick Winslow Taylor

The Industrial Revolution brought many technical developments. However, it was not until the early 1900s, when Frederick Winslow Taylor started the scientific management movement, that the management of manufacturing operations gained significant attention. Taylor detailed his philosophy in a paper, "Shop Management," that he presented to the American Society of Mechanical Engineers (ASME) in 1903. He followed up in 1911 with a book, *The Principles of Scientific Management*. Taylor wrote that "the principle object of management should be to secure the maximum prosperity for the employer, coupled with the maximum prosperity for each employee." According to Taylor's **scientific management** approach, management had four responsibilities, or duties:

- To develop a science for each element of a man's work
- To scientifically select and then train, teach, and develop each worker, instead of requiring workers to choose their own work and train themselves as best they could, which had been the practice
- To heartily cooperate with the workers to ensure all work was performed in accordance with the principles of scientific management
- To ensure an almost equal division of work and responsibility between management and workers, with managers taking over all work for which they were better suited than the workers to perform. (Past practice had been to throw almost all work and the greater part of the responsibility to the workers.)[12]

[12]Frederick W. Taylor, *Scientific Management* (New York: W. W. Norton, 1967), pp. 36—37.

Taylor's pioneering work is largely unappreciated today. According to Robert Chapman Wood,

> When people today think of Taylor (if they think of him at all), they tend to think of dehumanizing time-motion studies, as made famous in Charlie Chaplin's *Modern Times* and in *Cheaper by the Dozen* by Frank Gilbreth Jr. and Ernestine Gilbreth Carey. This does an enormous disservice to Taylor. . . . What Taylor principally urged was what came to be known as the systems approach to manufacturing: the idea that every part of a factory or a whole organization should be scientifically analyzed and redesigned to achieve the most efficient output. Managers should look at every aspect of a manufacturing operation as a piece of an integrated system, and should think through the consequences for the entire system of fiddling with any of its parts.[13]

## Henry Ford[14]

Mass production is closely identified with Henry Ford and the Model T. Ford's Model T revolutionized America by providing the masses with economical transportation. Ford had been building cars for some time before he manufactured the first Model T on October 1, 1908. By 1924 he had made 10 million Model Ts, and by 1926 he had made 13 million. At a time when cars were considered a luxury for the rich, Ford recognized an inexpensive, durable car could tap a huge market.

Henry Ford developed or refined many production concepts with the Model T. He integrated his company vertically; that is, he not only manufactured the Model T but also owned the coal mines, ore boats, steel mills, and glass plants that provided or produced its raw materials. While he did not invent the assembly line, he applied it to automobile manufacturing with astonishing gains in productivity. He more than doubled wages in 1914, to $5 per hour, a radical move at the time.

Ford was an innovator, a man ahead of his time. Many of the ideas he espoused in 1925 are still valid today. For example, he wrote of his views on quality and waste, which are crucial issues in the 1990s:

> We will use material more carefully if we think of it as labour. For instance, we will not so lightly waste material simply because we can reclaim it—for salvage involves labour. The ideal is to have nothing to salvage. . . .
>
> Time waste differs from material waste in that there can be no salvage. The easiest of all wastes, and the hardest to correct, is the waste of time, because wasted time does not litter the floor like wasted material.[15]

In 1924 Henry Ford owned 55 percent of the U.S. automobile market, but that figure slipped to 45 percent the next year. The design of the Model T was becoming obsolete. The Model T was open bodied, and the market was moving to closed-body models. In response Ford made a number of changes to the Model T in 1925:

> Last year, we made certain changes to the end of turning out somewhat better cars. The engine we did not touch—that is, the heart of the car.

[13]Robert Chapman Wood, "A Lesson Learned and a Lesson Forgotten," *Forbes*, February 6, 1989, pp. 71—72.
[14]Adapted from Henry Ford, *Today and Tomorrow* (Garden City, N.Y.: Doubleday, Page, 1926).
[15]Ford, *Today and Tomorrow*, pp. 91, 110.

*An early Model T assembly line
at Ford Motor Co.*

In all, eighty-one changes, major and minor, were involved. None of these changes was made lightly. The new designs were thoroughly tried out all over the country in actual service for many months.

After we had decided to make the changes, the next step was to plan how it could be done.

We set a date to begin changing over. The planning department had to calculate on just the amount of material which would keep production going at full speed until that date and then permit production to stop without having any material [left] over. It had to make the same calculations for our thirty-two associated plants and for the forty-two branches.

In the meantime, hundreds of drawings had to be made by the engineers for the building of the new dies and tools. We arranged to make this change without a wholesale shutdown. We "staggered" the process, changing one department at a time, so that by the time the last change was made production had caught up to the last department involved.[16]

These changes were not enough to stop the slide in market share. Model T sales dropped from 2 million units in 1925 to 1.55 million in 1926, a drop of 22.5 percent. Ford realized he had to replace the Model T. The change to a new design, the Model A, was not accomplished as smoothly as the design changes of 1925. The Ford production facilities were geared for making one product in high volume in an extremely efficient manner. To change to the Model A, Ford completely shut down his River Rouge production facility in May 1927 and kept it closed for almost a year. According to Alfred P. Sloan, Jr.,

[16]Ford, *Today and Tomorrow,* pp. 87—88.

Mr. Ford regained sales leadership again in 1929, 1930 and 1935, but, speaking in terms of generalities, he had lost the lead to General Motors. Mr. Ford, who had had so many brilliant insights in earlier years, seemed never to understand how completely the market had changed from the one in which he made his name and to which he was accustomed.[17]

# Alfred P. Sloan, Jr.[18]

Alfred P. Sloan, Jr., the chief executive of General Motors from 1923 to 1946, did understand how the market was changing and used his insights to turn General Motors from a conglomeration of small car companies into the world's biggest automobile manufacturer. He realized that he could not beat Ford at the low end of the market, so he developed a strategy of marketing cars in different price ranges, starting at a price above that of the Model T but offering more features. In 1921 General Motors had ten cars in seven lines, many of which competed with each other. Sloan developed a product policy that reduced the number of car lines to six (Chevrolet, Oakland, two Buicks, Oldsmobile, and Cadillac) but that covered a range of prices.

Sloan was responsible for several developments in the auto industry—installment selling (through General Motors Acceptance Corp. [GMAC]), accepting used cars as trade-ins, using automotive stylists, and changing models annually. He practiced management by exception—for most of the 1920s he left the Buick and Cadillac divisions alone; he wrote that "it is far better that the rest of General Motors be scrapped than any chances taken with Buick's earning power."[19]

Sloan was a modern manager, educated at the Massachusetts Institute of Technology (home today of the Sloan School of Management) as an electrical engineer. He was adept at understanding the car market and developing strategies that took advantage of the direction in which the market was moving. The structure of General Motors under his direction, semiautonomous automotive divisions under central corporate control, was a result of his view of the ideal management of a big industrial corporation—centralized planning with decentralized control. The model was widely applied by many different businesses in the years that followed and enjoys widespread use today.

# The Field of Operations Management

Industrial management was the precursor to modern operations management. As one of the first management disciplines to be studied at many U.S. colleges and universities, it was available as early as the 1930s. However, intense interest and emphasis on management science, or operations research, largely overshadowed the study of production operations after World War II. **Management science** is the application of quantitative models and methods to business problems.

Management science methods were widely applied in manufacturing, perhaps more so than in any other business area. Much of twentieth-century operations literature focuses on the application of mathematical models and techniques (linear programming, simulation, inventory models) to operations problems. It was not until the 1970s that operations management began to attract substantial recognition as an area of study distinct from management science.

[17]Alfred P. Sloan, Jr., *My Years with General Motors* (Garden City, N.Y: Doubleday, 1963), pp. 162—163.
[18]Adapted from Sloan, *My Years with General Motors*, pp. 58–70; 149–168.
[19]Sloan, *My Years with General Motors*, p. 61.

The recognition of operations management as a field in its own right was spurred by the development of **material requirements planning (MRP)**. This methodology, which began as a better method of ordering parts and materials than some of the standard inventory models of the time, quickly evolved into something more. MRP provided a way to keep order due dates valid even after the orders had been released to the shop floor or to outside vendors. It could detect when the due date of an order (when the order is scheduled to arrive in house or be completed in house) was out of synch with its need date (when the arrival or completion of the order is required by the manufacturer). This was a monumental breakthrough. For the first time manufacturers had a way to keep order priorities valid in a constantly changing environment.[20]

Although conceptually simple, MRP requires the manipulation of massive amounts of data, which forced most companies that wanted to use it to turn to computers. That led increasing numbers of companies to use computers for planning and control of their operations.

During the late 1970s and early 1980s, techniques for planning capacity requirements were linked with MRP. Tools were developed to support production planning and master production scheduling. Also incorporated were systems to aid in executing the plan—shop floor control systems for the "in-house factory" and vendor scheduling for "outside factories." The expanded system became known as *closed loop MRP*, because it provided planners with feedback from the shop floor and the company's suppliers so that they could alter plans as the necessity to do so arose. Eventually, closed loop MRP expanded to include the ability to translate the operating plan (expressed in manufacturing terms such as product units) into financial terms ( dollars) and the ability to simulate plans to assess their effects on units and dollars. The new system, **manufacturing resource planning (MRP II),** provided a comprehensive approach to the effective planning of resources for a manufacturing organization.[21]

# Recent Trends in Operations Management

During the 1980s several events provoked interest in and study of operations management. These events included the successful use of just-in-time production by the Japanese and their equally effective use of total quality management. At the same time computer use was growing rapidly—for planning and control and for computer-related production technologies (computer-aided design, computer aided-manufacturing, flexible manufacturing systems). More recent are the introduction of time-based competition and increased emphasis on business processes (as embodied by business process reengineering). Finally, there has been increased emphasis on the service factory. Such trends have prompted U.S. managers to fully recognize the strategic importance of operations and to better understand its effect on a company's competitiveness.

## Just-in-Time Production

**Just-in-time production** is a system of manufacturing that seeks increased responsiveness to customer demand by eliminating waste and increasing produc-

---

[20]Thomas F. Wallace, *MRP II: Making It Happen—The Implementers' Guide to Success with Manufacturing Resource Planning* (Essex Junction, Vt.: Oliver Wright Limited Publications, 1985), p. 5.
[21]Wallace, *MRP II*, pp. 5–7.

tivity. In a just-in-time manufacturing system producing one unit more than what is needed is considered wasteful. The goal is to produce exactly what is needed to satisfy current demand—no more, no less. The system pulls materials and products as required to meet production requirements or demand. The root of all evil is inventory, because it hides problems, such as poor quality, on the shop floor. The dramatic reductions in inventory levels, phenomenally high levels of quality, and short manufacturing lead times of just-in-time systems in Japan quickly gained the attention of American managers.

Satisfying only what current demand required often meant the manufacture of small lot sizes, even a lot size of one. The Japanese made the production of small lots economically feasible by dramatically reducing machine setup times. Setups that once took hours now took minutes, even seconds. This allowed for the economical production of small lots and freed up the capacity of the machine, thus greatly increasing productivity.[22]

Just-in-time systems require the coordination of production schedules and defect-free output at each processing stage, because the system has so little slack (inventory). In other words, managers, workers, and suppliers also must be totally committed and completely involved. The objective is to be as responsive as possible to customers' demands and needs by continually reducing manufacturing lead time through incremental improvements to the system. Chapter 16 provides a comprehensive discussion of just-in-time production.

## Total Quality Management

Quality has always been an important aspect of production. After World War II industrial product quality stagnated in the United States. American companies had almost no foreign competition, because most of Europe and Japan had been devastated. The lack of external competition lasted until the 1970s; in the interval U.S. companies devoted little effort to improving product quality.

Americans traditionally viewed quality as a given and believed that the only way to improve quality was by inspecting more stringently, which would mean higher rates of rejection and therefore higher costs. Quality pioneers such as W. Edwards Deming did not find an audience in the United States receptive to their messages about quality and how to achieve it. After World War II Deming went to Japan, at the request of General Douglas MacArthur's staff. In Japan he found a receptive audience.

In the 1980s U.S. companies quickly adopted Japanese perspectives on quality because they were forced to: The Japanese had made significant gains in key U.S. markets by providing high-quality, low-cost products. Some basic principles characterize the Japanese view of quality, which is known as **total quality management (TQM).** First, quality is built in, not inspected in. Second, improving quality saves money. If quality is viewed as the result of increased inspection, quality costs money. But if quality improves because a company improves the design of the product and its production process, the company reduces waste and scrap, saves money in production, and increases customer satisfaction.

A third principle of quality is **continuous improvement** (*kaizen* in Japanese). This approach pursues incremental improvements in products and pro-

---

[22]Shigeo Shingo, *A Revolution in Manufacturing: The SMED System* (Stamford, Conn.: Productivity Press, 1985).

FIGURE 1.6
American and Japanese
Vehicle Production,
1979–1994

Source: *Automotive News*, December
20, 1993.

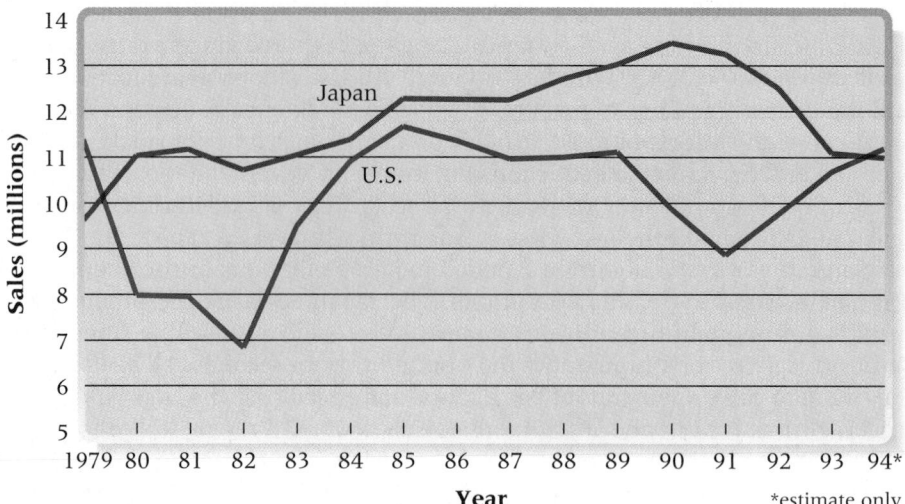

cesses on an on-going basis. For example, if the company's current level of
product defects is 0.01 per million, it sets a new goal of 0.001 defects per million.
The related concept of *zero defects* states that no level of defects is acceptable,
which means that quality must be continually improved.

The importance of product quality is evident in the experience of the U.S. auto
industry in the late 1970s and early 1980s, when U.S. auto manufacturers saw
their market share drop rapidly while the Japanese share of the U.S. car market
was increasing dramatically—primarily as a result of higher product quality. Fortunately, U.S. auto makers have begun to reverse the trend. See Figure 1.6 for a
comparison of recent automobile sales for the United States and Japan.

## Computers and Computer-Related Operations Technologies

The computer has revolutionized society. In manufacturing the effect of the
computer is evidenced in a number of operations-related technologies such as
computer-aided design (CAD) and computer-aided manufacturing (CAM). Chapter 8, Technological Developments in Operations Management, discusses these
technologies in detail.

Many planning and control systems, such as MRP, cannot be used without
the computer. Furthermore, many if not all of the latest product- and process-
related technologies are computer based.

Whereas the development of computers has increased the ability of managers and workers to handle and manipulate data, it has also increased the demand
for people capable of using and understanding computer-based production
technologies. Workers who previously operated a simple milling machine now
find that the job requires them to effectively operate a computer-controlled
machining center, which requires new and different skills.

Although a flexible manufacturing system can change the production of
parts on a real-time basis, it must be driven by a decision-making mechanism,
perhaps a decision support system. However, the operations manager remains
responsible for the system and its results. So while computers have increased the
ability of managers to manage operations effectively, they also require managers
to know how to use computers.

# Time-based Competition

Products and services no longer compete solely on price and quality. Time (delivery speed or time to market) is also a factor. **Time-based competition (TBC)** extends just-in-time principles to every facet of the product delivery cycle, from research and development to manufacturing and procurement and on through to marketing and distribution.[23] Time-based competition has two driving forces: the application of just-in-time throughout the product delivery cycle and the belief that effectiveness is contingent upon closeness to the customer ("closeness to the customer" refers to the company's degree of knowledge of the customer and its ability to use that knowledge to respond to customers' needs).[24]

Companies engaged in time competition include Atlas Door, Motorola, and Toyota. Atlas Door beats competitors on lead time by more than ten weeks. Motorola boasts that it can ship its pagers within two hours of receiving an order. And Toyota, considered the originator of just-in-time production and time-based competition, can deliver a car in Japan eight days after receiving the order.[25]

Examples of time-based competition abound in the service sector as well. Federal Express guarantees overnight delivery ("Absolutely, positively overnight!"). Federal Express was the brainchild of Frederick W. Smith, who developed the concept of an overnight delivery service as a project for a graduate school class in business administration. Although he got a C on the project, Smith's idea forever changed the nature of the competition in the package delivery industry.[26]

Technology often facilitates time-based competition. For example, electronic data interchange (EDI) now processes orders automatically and alerts the production function to a customer's order the moment it comes in. The result is a reduction in order lead time and therefore an improvement in customer service. Technologies such as CAD-CAM allow companies to greatly reduce new product development and introduction times. For example, Atlas Door uses CAD to achieve rapid order entry and design.

New methodologies have also fostered time-based competition. One important methodology is concurrent engineering for developing and introducing new products. Developing and introducing new products once was characterized by various functional areas working in sequence on a project. As one department completed its task (design engineering), it would pass the product on to the next department (manufacturing) with minimal integration of functional area expertise.

With **concurrent engineering**, representatives of all areas of the company—marketing, sales, service, purchasing, engineering, research and development, and manufacturing—form product teams. Team members often work in one facility, and their constant interaction not only speeds the development of products but improves the product's quality and reduces its cost. A well-coordinated product development team can determine whether a product design that is optimal from an engineering standpoint is optimal from other viewpoints, such as ease of manufacture. This evaluation is essential, because design deci-

[23]Patricia E. Moody, *Strategic Manufacturing: Dynamic New Directions for the 1990's* (Homewood, Ill.: Dow-Jones Irwin, 1990), p. 191.
[24]Joseph D. Blackburn, *Time-Based Competition: The Next Battleground in American Manufacturing* (Homewood, Ill.: Business One-Irwin, 1991), p. 69.
[25]Blackburn, *Time-Based Competition*, p. 66, 70, 84.
[26]Blackburn, *Time-Based Competition*, pp. 231—232.

sions have a major effect on the product's manufacturability and therefore on its ultimate cost of production. Early in the design phase a cross-functional team can evaluate trade-offs relating to design and manufacturability to select the course of action that will maximize the company's long-run profitability.

The case study at the end of this chapter examines how one company bases its competitive edge on time. The case study describes how Northern Telecom used time-based competition to change its operations and infrastructure so it could deliver its products faster than ever before. The case also discusses how Northern Telecom uses technologies such as CAD-CAM and EDI and methods such as concurrent engineering.

## Business Process Reengineering[27]

**Business process reengineering** is the fundamental rethinking and radical redesign of business processes to dramatically improve cost, quality, service, and speed. Reengineering a company means throwing out all existing structures, procedures, and systems and inventing completely new ways to organize and accomplish work. It seeks quantum leaps in performance by starting over.

Total quality management and reengineering have several characteristics in common (both recognize the importance of business processes, both emphasize the needs of the customer), but one difference is significant. Quality programs work within the framework of a company's existing processes and seek to enhance or modify them by means of continuous (incremental) improvement. Reengineering seeks performance breakthroughs by discarding existing processes and starting over with entirely new ones. Many manufacturers (Ford Motor Co.) and service operations (Taco Bell) have responded to competitive pressures by successfully applying business process reengineering. Operations Management in Practice 1.4 describes Ford's experience.

## The Service Factory[28]

The trend of the future is the **service factory**, which competes not only on the basis of its products but also on the basis of its services. Such services include informational support for customers, dependable and speedy delivery, product installation, after-sales service, and trouble-shooting.

Manufacturing companies that prosper in the twenty-first century will anticipate and respond to a broad range of customer needs by combining valuable services with superior products. The manufacturing unit will become the center of the company's activities to attract and retain customers—activities that are now too often located in separate and distant areas of the organization. Operations managers and workers alike will have direct and continuing contact with customers to better service their needs.

The manufacturing operations of some leading edge American companies (Allen-Bradley, Hewlett-Packard, and Tektronic) already reflect the increasing strategic importance of product-related services in the global economy. Their manufacturing facilities are well on their way to becoming full-fledged service

---

[27]Adapted from Michael Hammer and James Champy, "Reengingeering—-The Path to Change," chap. 2 in *Reengineering the Corporation: A Manifesto for Business Revolution* (New York: HarperBusiness, 1993), pp. 31—49.

[28]Adapted from Richard B. Chase and David A. Garvin, "The Service Factory," *Harvard Business Review* 67 (July—August 1989): 61—69.

## OPERATIONS MANAGEMENT IN PRACTICE 1.4

# Re-engineering at Ford Motor Co.

In the early 1980s Ford was looking for ways to cut overhead and administrative costs. One department it focused on was accounts payable, which paid the bills submitted by Ford's suppliers. At the time the department had more than five hundred employees. Management suspected that using computers to automate some functions would cut the number of accounts payable employees by 20 percent.

Ford was enthusiastic about its plan to downsize accounts payable, until it visited Mazda, a Japanese company in which Ford had recently acquired a 25 percent interest. Visiting Ford executives found only five people in Mazda's accounts payable department.

The Ford executives realized that Ford's accounts payable unit was roughly five times bigger than it should be. They also realized that to achieve such a profound reduction in work force, Ford would have to rethink the entire process in which accounts payable played a critical role: procurement.

Under Ford's procurement system, purchasing agents would write an order and send a copy to accounts payable. When material control received the goods, it would send a copy of the receiving documentation to accounts payable. Meanwhile, the vendor would send accounts payable an invoice for the goods. Accounts payable would then have to match the purchase order with the receiving document and the invoice. If all three matched, accounts payable would write a check. The documents usually matched, but clerks in accounts payable would spend most of their time rectifying the mismatches by investigating the problem, holding up payment in the interim, and generating still more paperwork.

One way to improve the operation might have been to help the accounts payable clerk investigate more efficiently, but Ford chose to prevent mismatches in the first place. Ford designed a radically different procurement process that uses invoiceless processing. When Ford buyers issue purchase orders to vendors, they simultaneously enter the information in an on-line database. As before, vendors send goods to the receiving dock. When the goods arrive, the receiving clerk checks the database to determine whether they correspond with an outstanding purchase order. Only two possibilities exist: They match or they do not. If the goods do not correspond with an outstanding purchase order in the database, the clerk sends the goods back. If they match, the clerk accepts the goods and pushes a button on the computer terminal's keyboard to signal the database that the goods have arrived. The computer automatically issues and sends a check to the vendor at the appropriate time.

Today only 125 people work in accounts payable at Ford.

---

factories with respect to the range of value activities they perform and the level of interaction between manufacturing personnel and customers.

Allen-Bradley's World Contactor facility, which manufactures contactors and relays (on-off switches) for the global marketplace, serves as a showroom for the company's products. The factory is a working demonstration of the systems, processes, and products that Allen-Bradley manufactures. The many customers who tour this facility quickly become aware of the company's world-class

*Allen-Bradley's World Contactor facility serves as a showroom for systems, processes, and products that Allen-Bradley produces.*

manufacturing capabilities and the superior quality and reliability of Allen-Bradley's products.

The quality department of Hewlett-Packard's Fort Collins Systems Division, which manufactures computers and technical workstations, has been significantly involved in generating valuable information for customers. Initially, quality managers developed customer surveys and collected data on competitors' products for in-house use. Later, they formed a partnership with Hewlett-Packard's marketing department so the company could better exploit the factory's expertise in quality. Over time, the division generated new kinds of information about quality and presented it in user-friendly formats. For example, customers received reports that were easy to understand and videotapes that documented product tests and field performance.

Tektronic, an electronic equipment manufacturer, has pioneered direct communication between customers and employees on the shop floor by inserting a postcard in the shipping carton of every oscilloscope it sells. The postcard contains the names of the workers who built the oscilloscope and the toll-free number of a telephone on the shop floor. Six people who work in the repair area of the factory (and have received telephone training) answer customers' calls. Several customers call every day to ask how to use the product, complain about its performance, and ask for information about other Tektronic products. Workers and managers meet daily to review customers' concerns. If necessary, workers follow these meetings up with additional conversations with customers to ensure satisfaction.

A company's business strategy should drive the development and implementation of a service factory. It should emphasize those services that provide the most value to customers. Factories become service factories when managers and workers thoroughly understand customers' needs and are willing to work openly with various departments and at all levels to delight customers with their products.

---

## ► Summary

This chapter explored basic concepts in operations management and emphasized their application to manufacturing. It introduced the transformation process and the concept of productivity. The chapter also discussed the responsibilities and role of the operations manager, different types of production systems, and using the value chain model to strategically examine a company's activities. A brief history of operations management focused on those individuals who have made significant contributions to U.S. industry. Finally, the chapter explored recent trends in operations management that highlight the strategic importance of operations. Because the keystone of this book is strategic operations, subsequent chapters emphasize the strategic effects of the various concepts, methods, and techniques described in the remainder of this textbook.

### Learning Objective 1: Describe the basic difference between manufacturing and service operations.

The major difference between manufacturing and service operations is that manufacturing operations produce physical goods and service operations provide services. However, a manufacturing operation may provide auxiliary services to its customers, such as technical information and support, product installation, and repair, and a service system may provide its customers with minimally processed physical goods as part of its services package (such as a martini for an airline passenger traveling first class).

### Learning Objective 2: Define *productivity* and give some examples of how operations managers contribute to productivity.

Productivity is the total value of a company's outputs divided by the total cost of its inputs. To increase productivity, a company can generate more output by using the same amounts of inputs, generate the same output by using smaller amounts of inputs, or generate more output by using smaller amounts of inputs. Because operations managers are responsible for the transformation process, they are directly responsible for its productivity. Operations managers can increase productivity by using better or more advanced process technologies or by improving the systems and methods that drive the production (or service) operation.

### Learning Objective 3: Identify different types of manufacturing operations.

The most flexible production operation is project manufacturing. Project manufacturing is used for manufacturing big and costly items such as space shuttles. Typically, materials required for construction are transported to a designated manufacturing site as needed. The next most flexible type of production is the job shop. Job shops group resources according to the process they perform. Products move singly or in small batches from one processing area to another according to their processing requirements. The route a product takes through the job shop may vary substantially from one product to another. The least flexible type of production is line-flow production, which is characterized by resources grouped by product. Because this system uses fixed processing patterns and production resources are often dedicated, it is typical for manufacture of large quantities of standard products or for assembly of large numbers of option modules. Manufacturing processes that exhibit features of both the job shop and line-flow production are hybrids. Batch production, a common hybrid, is characterized by the manufacture of products in discrete batches or lots.

### Learning Objective 4: Discuss the value chain and its relationship to competitive advantage.

The value chain is a conceptual model that helps a company identify strategically important activities, better understand and evaluate its cost structure, and recognize how its products and/or services are or could be distinct from competitors' offerings. The value chain is comprised of value activities, which are the building blocks of competitive advantage. Competitive advantage derives from individual value activities and the ways in which these activities are related, coordinated, or linked.

**Learning Objective 5: Identify key people in the history of operations management and summarize their achievements.** Some key individuals in the history of operations management and their achievements are as follows:

1. Eli Whitney and the invention and production of the cotton gin; also, Whitney's founding of the arms industry in the United States (late 1700s). Producing large quantities of arms required the use of interchangeable parts, which was key to furthering the Industrial Revolution.
2. Frederick Winslow Taylor and his scientific management philosophy (early 1900s). The main thrust of Taylor's work was a systems approach to manufacturing—the idea that every part of a manufacturing organization should be analyzed scientifically and redesigned to achieve the most efficient production.
3. Henry Ford and mass production. In the early 1900s Ford revolutionized America by providing economical transportation to the masses with his Model T. Ford was also a pioneer in the use of vertical integration to achieve competitive advantage.
4. Alfred P. Sloan, Jr., turned General Motors from a conglomeration of small car companies into the world's biggest automobile manufacturer (1920s). Sloan made numerous contributions to the automobile industry (the annual model change) and pioneered the use of centralized planning with decentralized control. He was also adept at identifying market trends and developing strategies that took advantage of them.

**Learning Objective 6: Describe recent trends in operations management.** Recent trends in operations management include just-in-time manufacturing and total quality management. The Japanese used just-in-time production, their innovation, and total quality management, a U.S. transplant, to gain substantial market share in selected U.S. industries in the 1970s and early 1980s. Just-in-time production focuses on responsiveness to customers by eliminating waste and increasing productivity. It embodies the key

concept that a manufacturing organization should produce only that which is necessary to satisfy immediate demand and that producing more is wasteful. Total quality management focuses on product and process quality and espouses the twin ideas that quality is built in, not inspected in, and that it is always cheaper to do it right the first time. A central thread of this philosophy is the concept of continuous improvement, which is directed at serving the customer better.

Another important trend is time-based competition; it represents an extension of the just-in-time philosophy to the entire product delivery cycle. Using this approach, companies concentrate on reducing the time for bringing products to market, reducing the time for delivering products, and in general, increasing the speed with which strategically important activities are performed to respond more effectively to customers' needs.

Still another significant trend is the radical redesign of business processes known as business process reengineering. Reengineering seeks performance breakthroughs by discarding existing processes and starting over with entirely new ones.

Finally, the service factory will become increasingly important as manufacturing enters the twenty-first century. The service factory competes not only on the basis of its products but also on the basis of its services. Such services include informational support for customers, dependable and speedy delivery, product installation, after-sales service, and troubleshooting.

**Learning Objective 7: Discuss the importance of viewing operations from a strategic perspective.** Operations must be viewed from a strategic perspective to understand how manufacturing or service operations contribute to the creation of value for customers and ultimately to a company's ability to compete globally. The strategic framework also shows managers how various concepts, technologies, and methods can be used to create a sustainable competitive advantage. Once managers understand the strategic importance of operations, they pay more attention to developing operations capabilities.

## ► Key Terms

| | | |
|---|---|---|
| assemble-to-order (ATO) | concurrent engineering | cross-functional team |
| batch production | continuous flow production | ecologically sound manufacturing |
| business process reengineering | continuous improvement | flexibility |

green manufacturing

job shop

just-in-time production

line-flow production

make-to-order (MTO)

make-to-stock (MTS)

management science

manufacturing operation

manufacturing resource planning (MRP II)

material requirements planning (MRP)

operations manager

productivity

project manufacturing

scientific management

service factory

time-based competition (TBC)

total quality management (TQM)

value chain

# ▶ Discussion Questions

1. Describe the basic differences between manufacturing operations and service operations. Provide several examples of each type of operation (see Preview of Operations Management).

2. Discuss how the value chain model can be used to improve the competitive positioning of a company.

3. Identify the inputs and outputs for three of the following kinds of companies:
   a. Mortgage loan company
   b. Textbook publisher
   c. Motel
   d. Toy manufacturer
   e. Textile mill

4. Define the term *productivity* and discuss ways manufacturers can improve productivity.

5. Describe the different categories of manufacturing operations that are based on the amount of processing that occurs before the customer places an order. Provide an example of each type of operation.

6. Describe the major difference between the job shop and line-flow production. Which type of manufacturing process characterized the production of Henry Ford's Model T?

7. What was the greatest contribution that Eli Whitney made to the Industrial Revolution?

8. Discuss a recent trend in operations. Provide an example of a company with which you are familiar that has been significantly influenced by this trend.

9. What are some qualities and abilities a successful operations manager must have? In what activities is an operations manager involved on a daily basis?

10. What are the basic strategic decision categories in operations management? (See Preview of Operations Management.)

# ▶ Selected References

Berkman, Barbara N. "AT&T's Big Push to Stay Ahead of Environmental Woes." *Electronic Business* 15 (September 18, 1989): 33—36.

Blackburn, Joseph D. *Time-Based Competition: The Next Battleground in American Manufacturing*. Homewood, Illinois: Business One-Irwin, 1991.

Business Roundtable. *Corporate Ethics: A Prime Business Asset*. New York: Business Roundtable, February 1988.

Chase, Richard B. and David A. Garvin. "The Service Factory." *Harvard Business Review* 67 (July—August 1989): 61—69.

Dertouzos, Michael L., Richard K. Lester, and Robert M. Solow. *Made in America: Regaining the Productive Edge*, New York: HarperPerennial, 1990.

Ford, Henry. *Today and Tomorrow*. Garden City, N.Y.: Doubleday, Page, 1926.

Hammer, Michael. "Reengineering Work: Don't Automate, Obliterate," *Harvard Business Review* 68 (July—August 1990): 104—112.

Hammer, Michael, and James Champy. *Reengineering the Corporation: A Manifesto for Business Revolution*, New York: HarperBusiness, 1993.

Hayes, Robert H., Steven C. Wheelwright, and Kim B. Clark. *Dynamic Manufacturing*. New York: Free Press, 1988.

Heye, Christopher. "Five Years After: A Preliminary Assessment of U.S. Industrial Performance Since *Made in America*." Working paper No. 93–009WP, Industrial Performance Center of the Massachusetts Institute of Technology, Boston, September 1993.

Kleiner, Art. "What Does It Mean to Be Green?" *Harvard Business Review* 69 (July—August 1991): 38—47.

Merrills, Roy. "How Northern Telecom Competes on Time." *Harvard Business Review* 67 (July—August 1989): 108—114.

Mirsky, Jeanette. *The World of Eli Whitney*. New York: Macmillan, 1952.

Moody, Patricia E. *Strategic Manufacturing: Dynamic New Directions for the 1990s*. Homewood, Ill.: Dow-Jones Irwin, 1990.

Orlicky, Joseph. *Materials Requirements Planning*. New York: McGraw-Hill, 1975.

Porter, Michael. *Competitive Advantage*. New York: Free Press, 1985.

Shingo, Shigeo. *A Revolution in Manufacturing: The SMED System*. Stamford, Conn.: Productivity Press, 1985.

Sloan, Alfred P., Jr. *My Years with General Motors*. Garden City, N.Y.: Doubleday, 1963.

Starr, Martin K. (ed.). *Global Competitiveness: Getting the U.S. Back on Track*. New York: W.W. Norton, 1988.

Taylor, Frederick W. *Scientific Management*. New York: W.W. Norton, 1967.

Wood, Robert Chapman. "A Lesson Learned and a Lesson Forgotten." *Forbes*, February 6, 1989, pp. 70—78.

# Northern Telecom

Northern Telecom traces its roots back more than a century—to eight years after Alexander Graham Bell invented the telephone. In its long life the company has experienced many periods of strong growth, but the period of growth that started in the late 1970s was perhaps its most challenging. At that time Northern Telecom introduced the first fully digital switch. The digital switch was vastly superior to its electromechanical counterparts. Independent telephone companies quickly boosted Northern Telecom's 1978 sales to 130 percent of the previous year's. In 1981 AT&T approved the switches for its affiliates, which boosted demand even higher. By 1984, when AT&T was broken up under government order, sales of digital switches had soared to $2.5 billion, an increase of more than 1,200 percent in an eight-year period.

Northern Telecom's response was to hire 1,500 more people and double its production each year for the next three years. However, management did not want to just add new capacity to meet demand, because doing so would drive up costs as quickly as profits. So management also focused on moving more product through its existing marketing, engineering, and manufacturing departments and more rapidly.

By 1985 a number of Northern Telecom's competitors had introduced their own fully digital switches. Northern Telecom no longer had a unique product. Sales began to slow. Added competitive pressure came from attempts by the biggest players in telecommunications to increase their market share and from deregulation. Customers were demanding higher quality, more sophisticated products, and lower prices.

To satisfy the customer demand for new products Northern Telecom released products to the market faster. This created an additional problem, because the company had traditionally reduced production costs by making changes after the new product was on the market. With the proliferation of new products Northern Telecom was making thousands of engineering changes—on average, someone issued a change order every two hours. Most changes added little value to the product or added it too late, and their cost accounted for more than 20 percent of Northern Telecom's manufacturing overhead.

Although Northern Telecom was coping well with the pressures, management was not convinced it was positioned for long-term success. The company had implemented just-in-time systems at some plants and was considering the adoption of other popular management approaches (computer-integrated manufacturing, automation); management concluded that these methods would only fine tune existing processes, providing a short-term advantage at best.

After careful consideration management decided that the best response to global competition, rapid technological change, and ever-shorter product life cycles, was to completely rethink Northern Telecom's manufacturing processes. In early 1985 the company formed a twelve-person operations council, composed of senior operations managers from the divisions across the United States and from headquarters. The divisions had similar product technologies but manufactured different products and had different competitive priorities. The council's mandate was to develop a cohesive manufacturing strategy for the 1990s.

After a year of meetings and consultations at the division level, the operations council defined three strategic objectives for the next five years for remaining competitive: increasing customer satisfaction by at least 20 percent, as measured by the annual customer survey; reducing manufacturing overhead as a percentage of sales by 50 percent; and cutting inventory days by 50 percent. The basic strategic thrust was to double throughput speed without increasing overhead or inventory levels and simultaneously increasing customer satisfaction.

In addition to defining a corporationwide strategic initiative, the operations council identified the actions necessary for accomplishing it.:

1. Shortening the time between a customer's specification of a new product and its installation to less than twelve months for product enhancements and less than nine months for application features

2. Attaining an initial product cost no greater than 110 percent of its ultimate cost (instead of depending on the company's normal procedure of continual cost reductions during the product's manufacture)
3. Cutting manufacturing cycle time from months to two weeks or less and in one case to less than eight hours
4. Ensuring that product documentation was ready at the time the product was released by subjecting documentation to the same process controls, metrics, and objectives that applied to products
5. Measuring quality against customers' expectations.

Senior managers quickly realized that the operations council had done far more than develop a new manufacturing strategy. It had defined a new way of doing business that focused on the entire product delivery process and affected every segment of the organization. But what intrigued senior managers the most was the element common to all strategic objectives—time. Northern Telecom clearly needed to do things *faster* to satisfy its customers. The key requirements are highly trained people, an efficient process, and organizational systems supportive of time and quality.

Senior managers separated different segments of the new strategy into core programs and allowed each division to decide how to implement the programs. Six core programs were defined: new product introduction and change, procurement practices, manufacturing process improvement, operations planning and scheduling, product delivery costs, and installation field service. Each division was to eventually make time-based improvements in all core areas but would select one core program initially and champion it throughout the Northern Telecom organization. However, three programs were identified as top priorities: manufacturing process improvement, new product introduction and change, and procurement.

By 1989 Northern Telecom had made substantial progress in implementing its priority programs and had begun to implement the others. In the three years that had passed, the manufacturing process improvement progressed the most, achieving 50 percent of the company's five-year objectives. One product's production lead time dropped from 9 to 2.4 weeks.

A key element of the manufacturing process improvement was total quality control (TQC). Supervisors and line operators received training in quality control and the power to shut down a line in the event of a quality problem. When this happened, all work stopped until the problem was resolved. Production suffered early in the program, but progress quickly brought production ahead of previous records for time, efficiency, and quality. With TQC came a reduction in manufacturing lot sizes and inventories. Instead of pushing a week's worth of material to the line, workers pull material from inventory as they need it.

As the pull system began to work, Northern Telecom worked with its suppliers to improve quality and on-time delivery to further reduce inventory levels. Also, customers were invited to the firm's design laboratories and manufacturing facilities to ensure that products would meet their expectations and needs.

Northern Telecom also made substantial progress in introducing and changing products. By focusing on time Northern Telecom reduced its new product introduction interval by 20 percent in some cases and by more than 50 percent in others, depending upon the division and product.

The division that championed the new product introduction and change began by using cross-functional product teams composed of members from various departments (design, manufacturing, and marketing). In the past each department had done its job in isolation from other departments and in a linear sequence. R&D developed designs and built prototypes and then "threw them over the wall" to manufacturing. Now product teams assembled at the inception of a product and continued to meet until it was launched. Because team members shared ideas about what was commercially important, technically feasible, and how to manufacture the product while it was still on the drawing board, they solved problems earlier and less expensively.

The pioneering product team found that computer-aided design (CAD) and electronic transfer of designs (EDI) enabled team members to work together and eliminated confusion about which design was current or which functional group was suggesting a change. The smoothness of the new process and dramatic decrease in the time required for design changes forced an immediate change in Northern Telecom's entire design philosophy. Almost every division now uses cross-functional teams at the beginning of the new product process.

Procurement practices also improved. Northern Telecom now works closely with its suppliers to ensure that their materials meet its quality and delivery standards. Initially, one Northern Telecom division developed a system for examining vendors' performance and certifying vendors. Eventually, the supplier certification program went companywide. As a result, Northern Telecom's supply base decreased from 9,300 vendors in 1984 to 2,500 in 1988.

Northern Telecom's infrastructure (training programs, compensation schemes, internal financial reporting methods) reflected its historical, cost-based strategy. The infrastructure also changed to conform with and support the new time-based strategy. Management recognized that the core programs would not succeed without the support of the firm's organizational infrastructure.

The company used several approaches to reconfigure its infrastructure to support time-based competition. First, groups of middle managers participated in week-long sessions at Northern Telecom's corporate training and development center to learn the basics of time-based competition. Later, the center developed a special two-day course for first-level managers and professionals. Eventually, all of Northern Telecom's eight thousand middle managers, supervisors, and professionals will have the opportunity to attend such sessions.

Another important element of Northern Telecom's infrastructure was information technology. Because time-based competition requires instant access to information wherever it is needed, the company put new emphasis on such technologies such as CAD and CAM. The contribution of CAD to decreasing product development cycle times was noted earlier.

Northern Telecom also reviewed its financial and accounting systems and realized that company managers did not have the numbers they needed to operate effectively in a time-based environment. To remedy this Northern Telecom's accountants introduced a profit-and-loss statement for internal use in early 1987. The new profit-and-loss statement replaced absorption accounting with an expense-based system that more accurately captured the real cost drivers of the company's operations. In the past administrative costs (human resources, accounting, and business systems) had been absorbed into overhead and allocated according to labor, material cost, or machine hours. Under the new activity-based cost system, these costs appeared as line items on the profit-and-loss statement. Highlighting these expenses eliminated the incentive to bury them in inventory. More important, the new system made it easier to identify the real sources of costs and motivated managers to address problems immediately. Northern Telecom also examined its capital justification process. It traditionally had used financial payback as the sole criterion for capital investment. The revised system allowed managers to justify projects on the basis of quality improvements and time savings.

Last, Northern Telecom adjusted its incentive structure to encourage workers to be flexible and knowledgeable so they could react more rapidly to customers' needs. For example, a "pay-for-skill" program implemented at one plant gave workers raises for each new task they mastered. People who once performed one narrowly defined task now performed many different tasks. Job categories at this plant have been reduced from twenty-five to five.

Northern Telecom's time-based strategy has been immensely successful. The company has realized substantial benefits with respect to reducing product cycle time, inventory, and operations overhead and increasing customer satisfaction over a five-year period. Northern Telecom's managers believe that improving product delivery is a continuous process. The company reassesses its overall strategy and performance on a five-year cycle, making adjustments as necessary. After all, there is no time to stand still in a time-based environment.

Adapted from Roy Merrills, "How Northern Telecom Competes on Time," *Harvard Business Review* 67 (July–August 1989): 108–114.

## ▶ Case Discussion Questions

1. Describe how Northern Telecom implemented its time-based manufacturing strategy. Why do you think Northern Telecom had each division select one core program that it would tackle first and then champion throughout the organization?
2. How was Northern Telecom's infrastructure reconfigured to support its time-based manufacturing strategy?
3. Describe the advantages of activity-based costing.

## CHAPTER 2

# Service
# Operations

*This is truly the Age of Service. The transition from an economy based on manufacturing to one based on service is one of the most important trends in American life, and certainly in the business world.*

J. W. MARRIOTT, JR.

**Introduction**

**Defining** *Services*

**Characteristics of Service Operations**
*OPERATIONS MANAGEMENT IN PRACTICE 2.1: Service Companies— Working to Raise Productivity*

**Strategic Approaches to Service Operations Management**
*OPERATIONS MANAGEMENT IN PRACTICE 2.2: ServiceMaster—Stressing Dignity to its Workers*

**Service-Sector Trends**
*GLOBAL OPERATIONS MANAGEMENT 2.3: British Airways—Taking Off in New Directions*
*OPERATIONS MANAGEMENT IN PRACTICE 2.4: Using Computers to Improve Service*
*OPERATIONS MANAGEMENT IN PRACTICE 2.5: J.C. Penney—Riding the Third Wave of Information Technology*

*After completing this chapter you should be able to*

1.  Define service activities
2.  Classify service operations
3.  Describe the unique characteristics of service operations

4.  Discuss strategic approaches to service operations management
5.  Summarize major service-sector trends

# Introduction

The U.S. employment trend is unmistakably clear. About 70 percent of U.S. jobs now originate in the **service sector**, which includes all economic activity other than agriculture, mining, construction, and manufacturing (see Table 2.1). From 1970 to 1990 about 9 percent of the work force shifted from the goods-producing sector to the service sector, and by the year 2000 the service sector is expected to provide four of five jobs.

The trend for the gross national product is similar. Today, the service sector of the U.S. economy accounts for about 72 percent of the gross national product.

T A B L E   2 . 1
Jobs Trends in the U.S. Economy, 1970–1990

| | Percentage of Work Force | | | Change 1970–1990 |
|---|---|---|---|---|
| | *1970* | *1980* | *1990* | |
| **Goods-producing Sector** | | | | |
| Agriculture, Forestry, and Fishing | 4.40 | 3.39 | 2.70 | −1.70 |
| Manufacturing | 26.37 | 22.10 | 17.97 | −8.40 |
| Mining | 0.66 | 0.99 | 0.62 | −0.04 |
| Construction | 6.12 | 6.26 | 6.53 | +0.41 |
| **Subtotal** | 37.55 | 32.74 | 27.82 | −9.73 |
| **Service Sector** | | | | |
| Transportation/Communication | 6.76 | 6.57 | 6.90 | +0.14 |
| Wholesale/Retail Trade | 19.08 | 20.33 | 20.58 | +1.50 |
| Finance Services | 5.01 | 6.04 | 6.80 | +1.79 |
| Business Service | 1.78 | 2.38 | 4.52 | +2.74 |
| Personal Services | 5.43 | 3.87 | 3.96 | −1.47 |
| Entertainment/Recreation | 0.91 | 1.05 | 1.27 | +0.36 |
| Professional Services | 16.40 | 19.99 | 21.49 | +5.09 |
| Public Administration | 5.69 | 5.38 | 4.76 | −0.93 |
| **Subtotal** | 61.06 | 65.61 | 70.28 | +9.22 |
| **Total** | 98.61 | 98.35 | 98.10 | |

NOTE: Totals do not equal 100.0% because of rounding in various categories.

Source: U.S. Department of Commerce, Bureau of the Census, *Statistical Abstract of the United States 1992* (Washington, D.C.: U.S. Government Printing Office, 1992), p. 396.

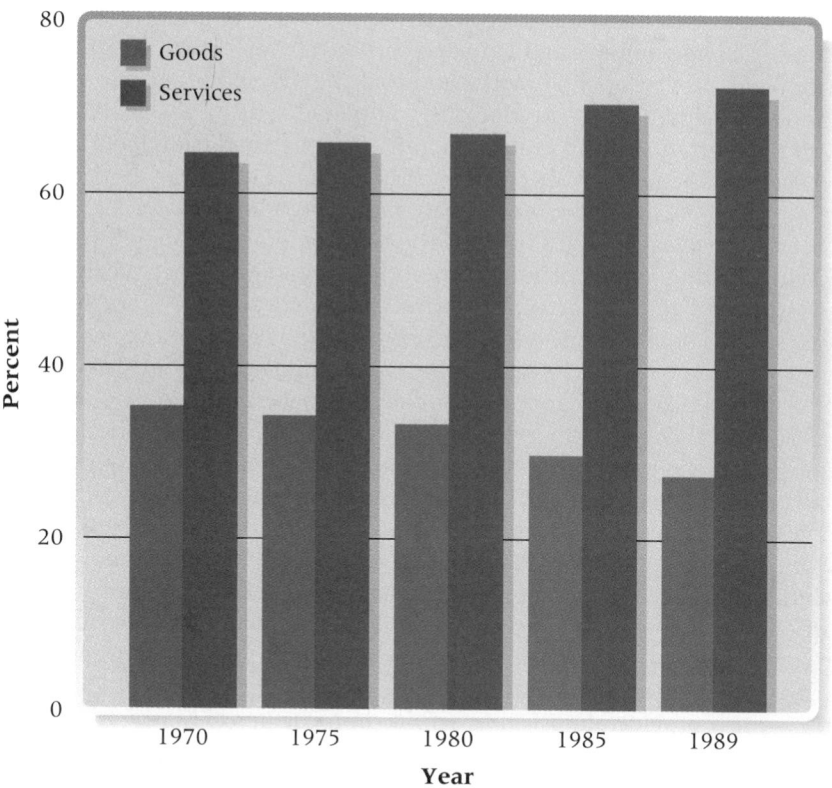

**FIGURE 2.1**
U.S. Gross National Product

Source: U.S. Department of Commerce, U.S. Bureau of the Census, *Statistical Abstract of the United States 1992* (Washington, D.C.: U.S. Government Printing Office, 1992), p. 429.

Figure 2.1 presents manufacturing and service contributions to the gross national product for selected years.

What has caused these trends? Perhaps one major factor is the increasing effectiveness of the goods-producing sector. The nineteenth century saw a major shift from agriculture to manufacturing, because the enormous increase in agricultural productivity allowed people (men, anyway) the freedom to pursue other occupations. Manufacturing productivity has increased rapidly in this century, displacing workers to the service industries. People now have to contend with the service-based nature of the economy—the way in which services are conceived, evaluated, and managed. This presents operations managers with both tremendous opportunities and tremendous challenges.

This chapter introduces the operations function in service systems. We define and characterize service operations and discuss how they are different from manufacturing operations, which were discussed in Chapter 1. We also provide an overview of major service-sector trends. (Chapter 17 offers a detailed discussion of the design and scheduling of service systems.)

## Defining *Services*

To what does the term *services* refer? In an economically advanced country such as the United States many organizations take raw materials, process them into intermediate materials, and transform the intermediate materials into finished end products, called **goods**. But many organizations provide something of value by facilitating the production of goods or offering services. **Services** are economic activities that produce a place, time, form, or psychological utility for the

*A service worker at a ski resort provides a customer with ski equipment.*

consumer. A discount store, such as Kmart or Wal-Mart, provides a place for purchasing a large number and variety of products. A car wash, or a Jiffy-Lube oil change shop, provides people with time that they would otherwise spend doing automobile maintenance. The monthly statement sent by the bank or a broker provides important information in a form that is understandable and useful. When people attend a sporting event, a rock concert, or a movie, they receive a psychological benefit. These services are basically intangible.

Service businesses typically assist their customers by transporting, blending, packaging, storing, or performing some other operation. Some service organizations, such as banks or accounting firms, provide mainly intangible services; others, such as an automobile leasing service, provide customers with a tangible product. Still other service organizations (automotive tune-up shops) both sell and install parts. A particular operation does not necessarily provide only services or only physical goods. When we go to a restaurant, we do so primarily for the intangible services it provides—preparing and serving food—although the food is actually a tangible product. The purchase of a tangible good almost always involves the receipt of some sort of service that makes life easier. Goods and services are not completely distinct but instead are the two end points of a continuum. Figure 2.2 compares different types of service operations. At left in Figure 2.2 are self-service grocery stores, which provide little service and have little contact with customers. In the middle are restaurants and auto maintenance shops, where service becomes much more important. At right in Figure 2.2 are motels, which provide almost pure service in a customized fashion.

Five major types of services have developed in response to the stages and economic conditions through which various societies have passed. They are

*Unskilled personal services.* Housekeeping services and street vending—**unskilled personal services**—are the initial service activities of developing societies.

FIGURE 2.2
A Comparison of Different
Types of Service Operations

Source: Earl W. Sasser, R. Paul Olsen, and D. Daryl Wyckoff, *Management of Service Operations: Text, Cases, and Readings* (Boston: Allyn & Bacon, 1978), p. 11.

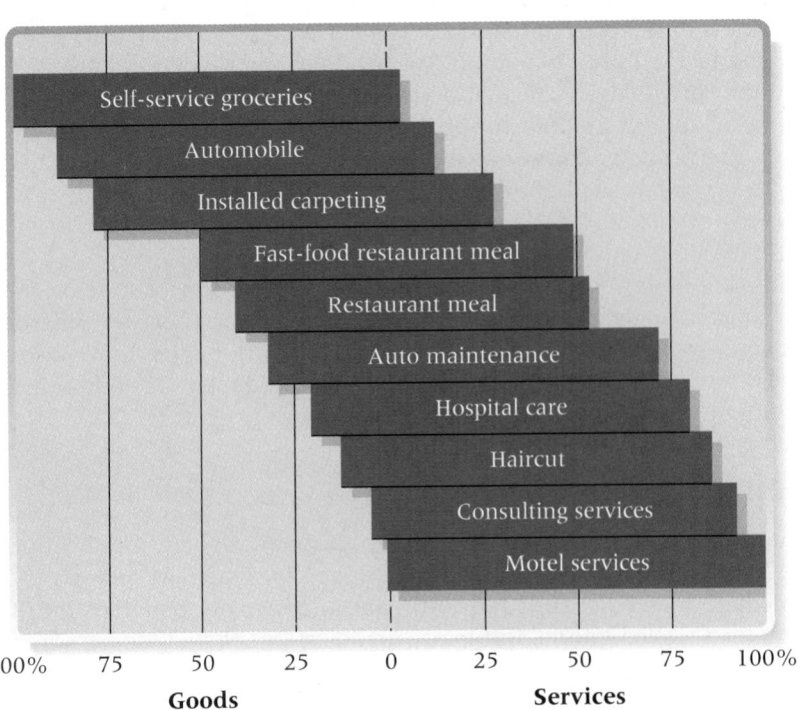

*Skilled personal services.* As productivity improves in agricultural societies and production rises above the subsistence level, industrialization and trade develop. The **skilled personal services** of artisans, shopkeepers, wholesale and retail merchants, repair and maintenance people, and financial clerks become prominent in the economy. Likewise, a need arises for complex government and government services to support the industrialization and its accompanying urbanization.

*Industrial services.* As industry becomes competitive, it needs support services—the work of lawyers, accountants, bankers, and insurance firms, real estate brokers, and commodities traders, known collectively as **industrial services.**

*Mass consumer services.* As industrialization increases the general wealth of the population, people have more discretionary income, which in turn creates consumer demand for such discretionary services **(mass consumer services)** as airlines, hotels, auto rental companies, and entertainment. The health and wellness industries get a major boost from increased consumer discretionary income.

*High-technology business services.* Technological innovations such as microprocessors, lasers, satellites, and biomedical engineering create new services and aid in the automation of existing services. Information services, consulting, and satellite communications are prominent examples of **high-technology business services.**[1]

## Comparing Service and Manufacturing Operations

Making operating decisions for services and manufacturing is similar in many ways. Any organization can be placed on a continuum between pure manufacturing and pure service. Pure manufacturing occurs in organizations that produce a tangible good and have little direct contact with the customer, such as in mining, farming, and heavy manufacturing. Pure service occurs in organizations that provide an intangible service and have substantial direct contact with the customer, such as in medical services, legal services, and consulting. Of course, many organizations both produce tangible goods and offer intangible services. They fall somewhere in the middle of the continuum. For example, AT&T Corp. manufactures telephones and provides telemarketing services to its customers; IBM manufactures a wide range of computers and provides an array of computer-related services.

The key characteristic of the service organization is the interaction of customer and organization. The interaction may be highly personal, between the customer and a "server" in the service company. Or the interactions may be apersonal, between customers and the service organization's equipment.

## Classifying Service and Manufacturing Operations

A production system involves a set of components, the function of which is to convert a set of materials into some desired product. Like their manufacturing counterparts, service organizations try to make this conversion, or transformation, process as effective as possible. Table 2.2 provides several examples of the conversion processes found in typical service systems.

[1]Ronald K. Shelp, John C. Stephenson, Nancy S. Truitt, and Bernard Wasow, *Service Industries and Economic Development* (New York: Praeger, 1985), pp. 3–5.

| Service System | Primary Inputs | System Components | Conversion Process | Desired Output | Managers |
|---|---|---|---|---|---|
| **College or University** | High school graduates | Books, buildings, personnel | Knowledge transmission, skills development (informational) | Educated People | Administrators, professors |
| **Hospital** | Patients | Doctors, nurses, supplies, equipment | Health care (physiological) | Healthy people | Chief of staff, head nurse |
| **Restaurant** | Customers | Food, cooks, equipment, servers | Food preparation, food serving, (physical preparation and exchange) | Satisfied customers | Head chef, restaurant managers |
| **Video Store** | Customers | Videotapes, sales clerks | Promotion of products, filling of orders (exchange) | Satisfied customers | Store manager |
| **Police Department** | Crime victims | Police officers, dispatchers, radios, automobiles, equipment | Detection of crimes, arrests of criminals (public service) | Acceptable crime rate, peaceful community | Police chief, assistant chiefs, sergeants |

T A B L E   2 . 2
Conversion Processes—
Typical Service Systems

Service operations generally do not produce tangible products, but they still can be classified much as manufacturing operations are, that is, according to the degree of standardization of their service, as shown in Table 2.3.

**Project**  Most of us have dealt with individuals who provide professional services, such as lawyers, doctors, and architects. Such professionals typically work for a number of individuals—clients, patients, or builders. They must perform several interrelated, complicated tasks, usually in some specific sequence. A lawyer usually has an initial consultation with a client to discuss general legal problems. Often more detailed discussions and perhaps some legal research follow. From this the lawyer recommends a course of action, which may involve a trial and is often long term in nature. The lawyer's work for the client, referred to in operations management terms as a **project,** ends when the legal problem is resolved.

**Job Shop**  When we need something done in a specific way, we generally seek a **job shop** operation. Someone who needs new clothes can go to a custom tailor and specify size, color, style, and type of material. This type of job shop offers each customer a great deal of flexibility, but its flow of customers may not be steady.

| Type | Description | Manufacturing Examples | Services Examples |
|---|---|---|---|
| Project | Long duration, unit volume, custom product | Construction project, shipbuilding | Consulting, software development |
| Job shop | Short duration, low volume, custom product | Hand-tailored clothing, sign making | Gourmet restaurant, automotive repair shop |
| Line flow | Short duration, high volume, standard product | Appliance plant, automobiles | Fast-food restaurant, oil change/lubrication shop |
| Continuous flow | Continuous processing, homogeneous manner | Cereal plant, oil refinery | Ambulance service, police and fire service, ATMs |

TABLE 2.3
Types of Operations

**Line Flow** A **line flow** operation delivers standard services in an assembly-line fashion. Typically, customers of an automated car wash drive into line in front of the car wash, position their cars over a device that moves the cars forward, and select and pay for the type of car wash service they desire (wash only, wash and dry, or wash, dry, and wax). The sequence of operations then follows some prescribed order, depending on how that car wash is organized. It uses special equipment and few workers, who also are specialized. Little flexibility is possible and bottlenecks often occur.

**Continuous Flow** A **continuous flow** operation delivers a homogeneous service using a continuous process. Emergency medical teams and police and fire protection are examples of continuous flow services. They operate on a continuous, twenty-four-hour basis. They provide an intangible service by making people feel secure and protected. When necessary they also provide other services, such as saving lives, arresting criminals, and extinguishing fires. Automatic teller machines (ATMs) are another example of a continuous flow service.

## Characteristics of Service Operations

Service operations have a number of characteristics that stand in contrast to those of manufacturing operations. The service operations manager must understand these characteristics, because they define the competitive environment of service operations.

### High Consumer Contact

In most manufacturing environments consumers have no contact with the production system. For example, have you ever been involved with the manufacturer of an automobile or a refrigerator you have purchased? Probably not; instead, you have purchased these items through a retailer. Contrast this to a typical service operation, which has a high degree of customer contact. As a college or university student you are an excellent example of a customer who is a participant in the service process. You attend lectures, study, take exams, receive grades, and finally receive your degree.

Some researchers have suggested that services break down into five categories of customer contact, because the type of contact can vary so greatly:

1. Entire operations that require constant physical contact— barbers and cosmetologists are examples.

*Higher education institutions, like the University of South Carolina, provide educational services to a broad constituency.*

2. Services that require constant communication with the customer, who may be remote—an emergency medical or police dispatcher is an example.
3. Services that require sporadic personal contact with the customer—medical and legal services are examples.
4. Entire services that require sporadic telephone (remote) communication with the customer—financial services (stock brokers) and management consulting firms are examples.
5. Services that entail customer contact, either in person or by telephone, only before and at the beginning and end of the service—tailors, dry cleaners, and car rental agencies are examples.[2]

## Consumer Participation in the Service Process

Because the consumer is so often involved, the service process requires its managers to pay more attention to location and atmosphere than other businesses require. We usually associate the service we receive with the physical surroundings of the facility. For example, compare your feelings about a typical fast-food outlet and a fashionable restaurant.

Another important aspect of the service process is the extent to which consumers are actively involved. As educators we believe that students learn best through their own efforts and involvement. Likewise, doctors making diagnoses rely heavily on information patients provide. You probably have noticed that your college cafeteria or local fast-food restaurant has eliminated serving and clean-up personnel. As a result, you have become an important part of the service process and probably expect faster service and less expensive meals as compensation.

## Perishability of Services

The typical demand pattern for service is immensely time dependent, exhibiting cyclic behavior with much variation between the peaks and valleys. Americans customarily eat lunch between noon and 1 P.M., which means that restaurants experience considerable demand during this one-hour period. Demand for automotive repair services is much higher at the beginning of the work week; their customers typically arrive early in the morning. Transportation services experience much higher demand during holiday periods and during the summer months.

A service is a perishable commodity. It usually cannot be stored. A doctor or a dentist tries to see patients throughout the period designated as office hours. An empty seat on an airplane or in movie theater or a vacant room in a hotel is a lost opportunity. The perishable nature of service capacity is even more of a problem when the service experiences rush hours and slack times.

Manufacturers, on the other hand, can inventory durable goods in anticipation of future demand. The operations manager for a manufacturer can use inventories to buffer demand fluctuation and can produce at a constant and efficient level. In contrast, the operations manager for a service cannot inventory those services. This does not mean that service inventories do not exist. A hospital must maintain a supply of medications and an availability of rooms and

[2]Robert G. Murdick, Barry Render, and Roberta S. Russell, *Service Operations Management* (Boston, Mass.: Allyn & Bacon, 1990), p. 29.

beds, for example. The big difference is that these inventories are part of the service process, not its result. They are used and transformed during the provision of the service.

Operations managers for service companies can deal with the perishability aspect in several ways. First, they can smooth demand by requiring reservations or appointments or by providing discounts for certain time periods. Second, they can adjust service capacity by using part-time workers during peak hours or by scheduling workers according to demand. Third, they can simply force customers to wait—to stand in line at the bank until a teller becomes available. Chapter 6, on aggregate planning, and Chapter 17, on scheduling for service systems, discuss these issues further.

## Site Selection Dictated by Consumer's Location

Because many service organizations have direct contact with their customers, they must locate relatively nearby. Either the consumer goes directly to the service facility, as is the case for a restaurant, movie theater, or video rental store, or the service comes to the consumer, as is the case for ambulance or fire service and home repairs.

Some exceptions are obvious. Banking by mail and the proliferation of catalog and television shopping services are prime examples of services linked to customers by technology. The Internal Revenue Service is another example of a service organization that has a widely dispersed set of locations. In higher education the National Technological University (NTU), with administrative headquarters in Ft. Collins, Colorado, uses advanced educational and telecommunications technology to hold classes for graduate engineers and technical professionals and managers throughout the United States at their workplaces (see the NTU case study at the end of Chapter 17).

Because of the time and cost of travel many small service centers often are located close to prospective customers. This contrasts somewhat with manufacturing, which commonly has much bigger facilities that serve regional, national, or international markets.

## Labor Intensiveness

In most service companies labor is the major competitive resource, because the employees interact directly with the customers. This creates opportunities as well as problems. One opportunity is the reward that service employees gain because they typically have a more personal and humanized work experience than their counterparts in manufacturing. Another major opportunity is providing the customer with an excellent experience. One study profiled ten service workers and their jobs and concluded that "since service personnel at the bottom of the totem pole are often the major points of contact between customers and the organization, the performance and demeanor of these individuals can have a powerful effect on the quality of service delivered."[3] The ten service workers also indicated a high level of enthusiasm for their jobs and work experiences, primarily as a result of positive feedback from customers.

[3]Christopher H. Lovelock et al., "Ten Service Workers and Their Jobs," in *Managing Services: Marketing, Operations and Human Resources*, ed. Christopher H. Lovelock (Englewood Cliffs, N.J.: Prentice-Hall, 1988), p. 329.

One problem for service companies is keeping the work force educated in using the latest information or technology. Educating and training the people who supply services is so important that many service companies have organized their own schools. Among these are Holiday Inn University, Marriott's Learning Center, McDonald's Hamburger University, and the Control Data learning centers. These institutions teach technical skills, such as accounting systems or cash management techniques, and interpersonal skills, such as how to analyze a transaction or deal with conflict.[4]

Another problem that services face is employee morale. An unhappy service employee who is sole contact for consumers can do grievous harm to the company. Many services try to deal with this problem by infusing their employees with corporate values and focusing their attention on being a positive factor in the success of the business. Studies have shown that developing a positive relationship between first-line service personnel and customers is possible only when first-line service personnel and their supervisors have a positive relationship.[5]

Both manufacturing and services may vary from capital intensive (mostly equipment based) to labor intensive (mostly labor based), as illustrated in Figure 2.3. In manufacturing, chemical producers are highly automated, but a jewelry maker relies on personal skills to make a ring or bracelet. In services a car wash provides highly automated service, whereas lawyers provide highly specialized, personalized service.

## Variable, Nonstandard Output

Some service companies are labor intensive and produce a variable, nonstandard product. A barber shop, a health club, and a tax service all provide services tailored to the needs of the individual customer. The service varies because the customer's needs vary. The labor-intensive nature of service operations makes it difficult to standardize what employees do. In Chapter 17 we discuss ways in which service companies try to achieve uniformity in service delivery.

## Intangibility of the Service Output

Manufacturing companies generally produce tangible, durable products; service companies generally produce intangible, perishable products. This distinction is not perfect and has several ramifications. First, patents and licensing agreements protect the tangible goods produced by manufacturers. Copyrights and trademarks offer some protection to service companies, but the intangible nature of a service makes solid legal protection difficult. Some service companies, however, succeed in protecting the uniqueness of their delivery systems by using franchising to quickly capture and secure the market to establish a brand name.

Second, intangibility can pose a problem for the consumer. Often, the consumer's major reason for selecting a particular service firm is its reputation, because the consumer really has no way to test the service. Governments and professional associations regulate many services, but "buyer beware" is a particularly important warning for consumers of services. Problems and service failures will occur, and good service organizations deal with them effectively.

[4]Richard Normann, *Service Management: Strategy and Leadership in Service Businesses* (Chichester, England: Wiley, 1984), pp. 44–50.
[5]Benjamin Schneider, *The Service Organization: Climate Is Crucial* (New York: AMACOM, 1980).

**Manufacturing Firms**

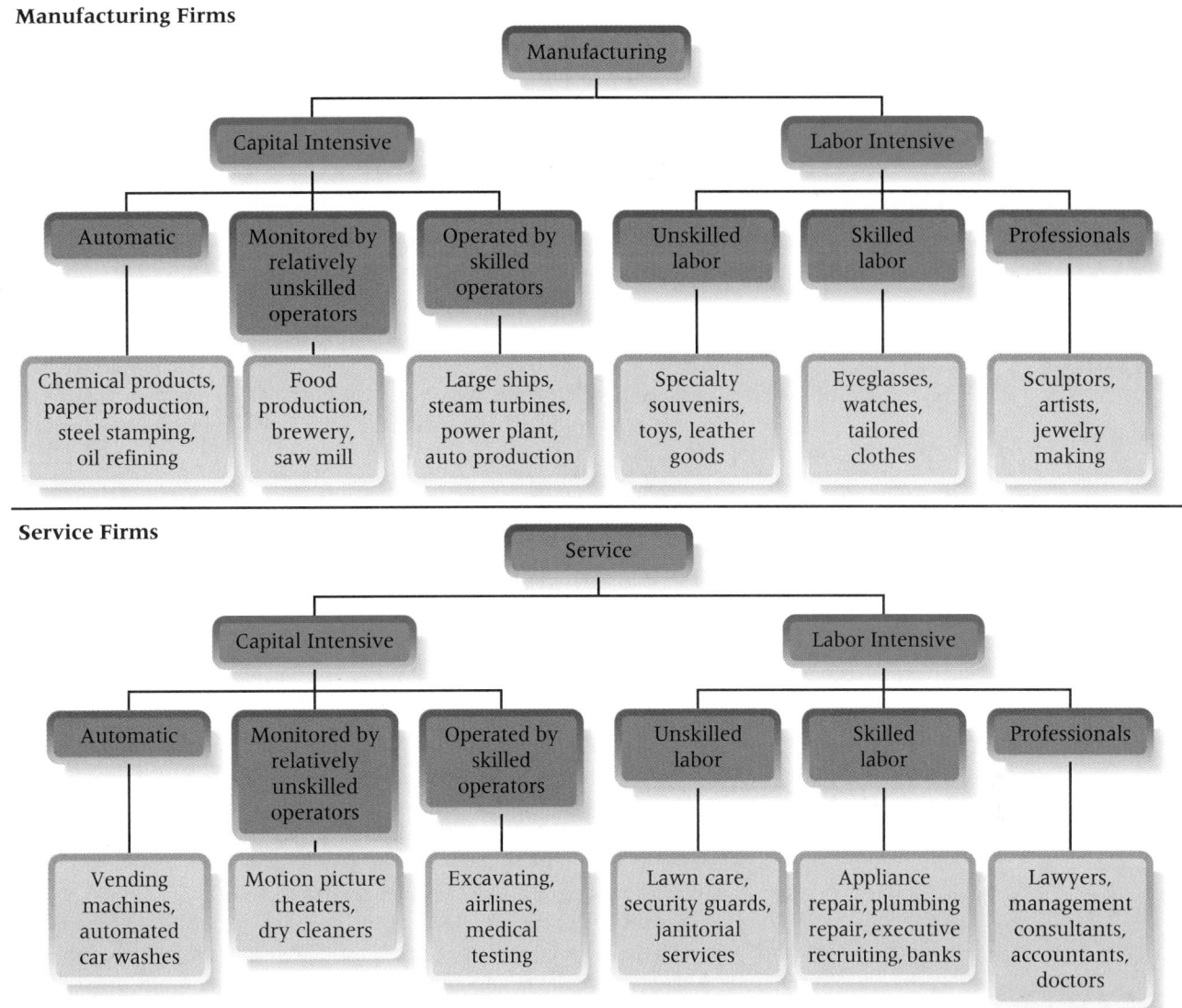

**Service Firms**

F I G U R E   2 . 3
Classifying Firms by Capital
Intensity and Labor Intensity

Source: Dan R. E. Thomas, "Strategy
Is Different in Service Businesses,"
*Harvard Business Review* 56, No. 4.
(July–August 1978): 161.

## Difficulty of Measuring Service Productivity

Trying to measure the productivity of a service organization can be a difficult and frustrating task. Simply counting the number of customers served is often not sufficient, because it does not measure the quality of the service. More important, service companies typically operate with a widely varying customer base, whereas many traditional methods of measuring productivity are based on standard units.

One approach to measuring service productivity is to use indexes that measure some aspect of productivity and then evaluate the change in those indexes over time. For example, retail stores and grocery stores often measure productivity by sales per square foot or sales per employee. Entertainment

# Service Companies— Working to Raise Productivity

Sleep Inn, a franchise hotel chain run by Manor Care, Inc., is a good example of a service company that is working to improve its productivity. A typical 100-bed Sleep Inn employs only 12 full-time workers, 13 percent fewer than the average no-frills hotel. Manor Care is using the assembly-line concept to design the Sleep Inns. David Elmore, vice president of the chain observes, "As we engineered the Sleep Inn product, we attempted to drive down the labor content." To keep the housekeeping staff small, night stands in Sleep Inn rooms are bolted to the wall so housekeepers need not to take time to vacuum around the legs. The closet has no door for housekeepers to open and shut. The shower stall is round, eliminating corners that collect dirt. As a result, cleaning a Sleep Inn room, which is only 70 percent as big as the industry standard, takes only twenty minutes, ten minutes less than the industry average.

The Sleep Inn's computer-based security system helps its owners track the housekeepers' time to the minute. To enter a room housekeepers must insert a card that tells the front office computer where they are. The same computer system eliminates the need for the front desk to handle keys, because guests use their own credit cards to unlock doors. The same security system can bar a guest's access to the room after check-out time and automatically start and stop a room's heating and air-conditioning system. In another labor-saving move the night desk clerk does the Sleep Inn's daily laundry in a high-tech washer and dryer installed behind the desk.

Service companies are using many other approaches to improving productivity. Some install new machines. McDonald's is testing a grill that cooks hamburgers on both sides at once, thereby eliminating the hamburger flipper.

Training is another approach. ARA Services of Philadelphia, a food service, now trains cafeteria employees in the best way to hold a green pepper while cleaning it.

Reducing employee turnover is still another approach. "When you're training 100,000 kids a year, if you cut turnover down a bit, you save money," says Richard Millard, who directs restaurant employee relations for PepsiCo's Pizza Hut chain. After conducting employee focus groups to figure out how to please its teenage work force, Pizza Hut abandoned its brown polyester uniform in favor of khaki pants and striped, short-sleeved shirts. It also is improving kitchen air conditioning, testing a tuition-aid plan, and teaching managers "to manage with a softer style," Millard says.

The rush to improve productivity in services is also based on today's tight labor market and tomorrow's expected labor shortages. "If you look at the demographics in the years ahead, there just aren't going to be enough service people, says John Riley, Manor Care's top personnel executive.

services frequently gauge productivity by the percentage of seats filled in a theater or sports arena. A company might measure a software engineer's productivity by the number of projects finished on time and within budget. But how do you measure the productivity of a psychologist, a physician, a police officer, or a college professor?

Any measure of service productivity should take into account the quality of the service. If a bank has numerous processing errors or if a hospital has many dissatisfied patients, productivity as measured solely by quantity of work will be overstated. Low quality requires repeating the service, which lowers productivity.

Operations Management in Practice 2.1 provides examples of several service companies that are taking innovative steps to increase productivity.

## Difficulty of Measuring Service Quality

Because services usually involve intangible products, measuring their quality is often difficult and frustrating. For example, consider a typical visit to a fast-food restaurant. In this service encounter you may equate quality with the food you are served, the speed with which you are served, or the manners and efficiency of your food server. Quality of service can be measured in many ways.

The perception of its user determines the quality of a service. A typical service has several attributes. Users have an expectation of what they will receive and a perception of the degree to which their expectation was met. The ratio of expectation to perception determines the quality of the service. Researchers conducted extensive, in-depth interviews with service company executives to identify the most important attributes of service quality. They isolated five variables for improving service quality:

- Tangibles—the appearance of physical facilities, equipment, personnel, and communication materials
- Reliability—the ability to perform the promised service dependably and accurately
- Responsiveness—a willingness to help customers and to provide prompt service
- Assurance—knowledge and courtesy of employees and their ability to convey trust and confidence
- Empathy—the provision of caring, individualized attention to customers[6]

The researchers defined *service quality* as the gap between expectations of service and the perception of the service experience. Their research points out the complexity and difficulty of measuring service quality.

# Strategic Approaches to Service Operations Management

The service sector of the U.S. economy has produced many new jobs as new types of services have evolved. This has created a need for strategic approaches to managing service operations; in the material that follows we explore two broad, strategic approaches.

## The Service Process Matrix

Roger Schmenner contends that two elements can be used to classify service businesses and allow for the systematic investigation of the changes and challenges for management. The first is the labor intensity of the service business.

[6]Leonard L. Berry, Valarie A. Zeithaml, and A. Parasuraman, "Five Imperatives for Improving Service Quality," *Sloan Management Review* 31 (Summer 1990): 29–38.

*Delta Air Lines is an example of a "service factory" in which there is a low degree of labor intensity and a low degree of consumer interaction and customization.*

Labor intensity is the ratio of the cost of labor to the value of the plant and equipment. An example of a highly labor-intensive business is a law office, which has negligible amounts of plant and equipment but incurs a large amount of worker time, effort, and cost. An example of a service that is not labor intensive is an airline, which requires a major investment in expensive equipment and relatively less worker time, effort, and cost.

The second major element of a service business combines the degree to which the consumer interacts with service providers and the degree to which the company customizes its service for the consumer. A service with a high level of interaction is one in which the consumer can actively intervene in the service process to request additional service or to ask that some aspect be deleted. A service with a high level of customization will strive to satisfy the full range of the consumer's need. A fine restaurant exemplifies a service business that encourages a high degree of customization and interaction. Here the customer orders and dines at a leisurely pace, and a waiter is constantly available to satisfy requests. At the other extreme is a fast-food restaurant such as McDonald's, where the customer has limited interaction and not much customization.[7]

Schmenner developed a **service process matrix**, a method for categorizing a wide range of service businesses as "high" or "low" in terms of degree of labor intensity and degree of interaction and customization. Service businesses that have relatively low labor intensity and a low degree of customer interaction and customization are called *service factories*. An airline or a hotel is a good example of a service factory. Those services with a middling degree of interaction with and customization for the customer are called *service shops*, which are much like the job shops in manufacturing. A hospital is an example of a service shop.

Service businesses that have a high degree of labor intensity and a low degree of customer interaction and customization are referred to as *mass services*. A retail store is an example of a mass service. Services with high degrees of

[7]Roger W. Schmenner, "How Can Service Businesses Survive and Prosper?" *Sloan Management Review* 27 (Spring 1986): 21–22.

interaction that also offer the customer customization are called *professional services*. An accounting firm is an example of a professional service.

The challenges faced by service managers are related to the position of a service business within the service process matrix, which includes twenty challenges in all. Strategically, service businesses need to determine which quadrant of the service process matrix they are in (see Figure 2.4) and pay close attention to all the managerial challenges that apply.

The service process matrix also is useful for investigating the strategic changes in service operations over time, which is important because service industries change so rapidly.

In Figure 2.4 note that various service businesses have moved in increments toward the diagonal that runs from the professional service to the service

F I G U R E   2 . 4
Strategic Operation Changes Within the Service Process Matrix

Source: Roger Schmenner, "How Can Service Businesses Survive and Prosper?" *Sloan Management Review* 27, No. 3 (Spring 1986): 29.

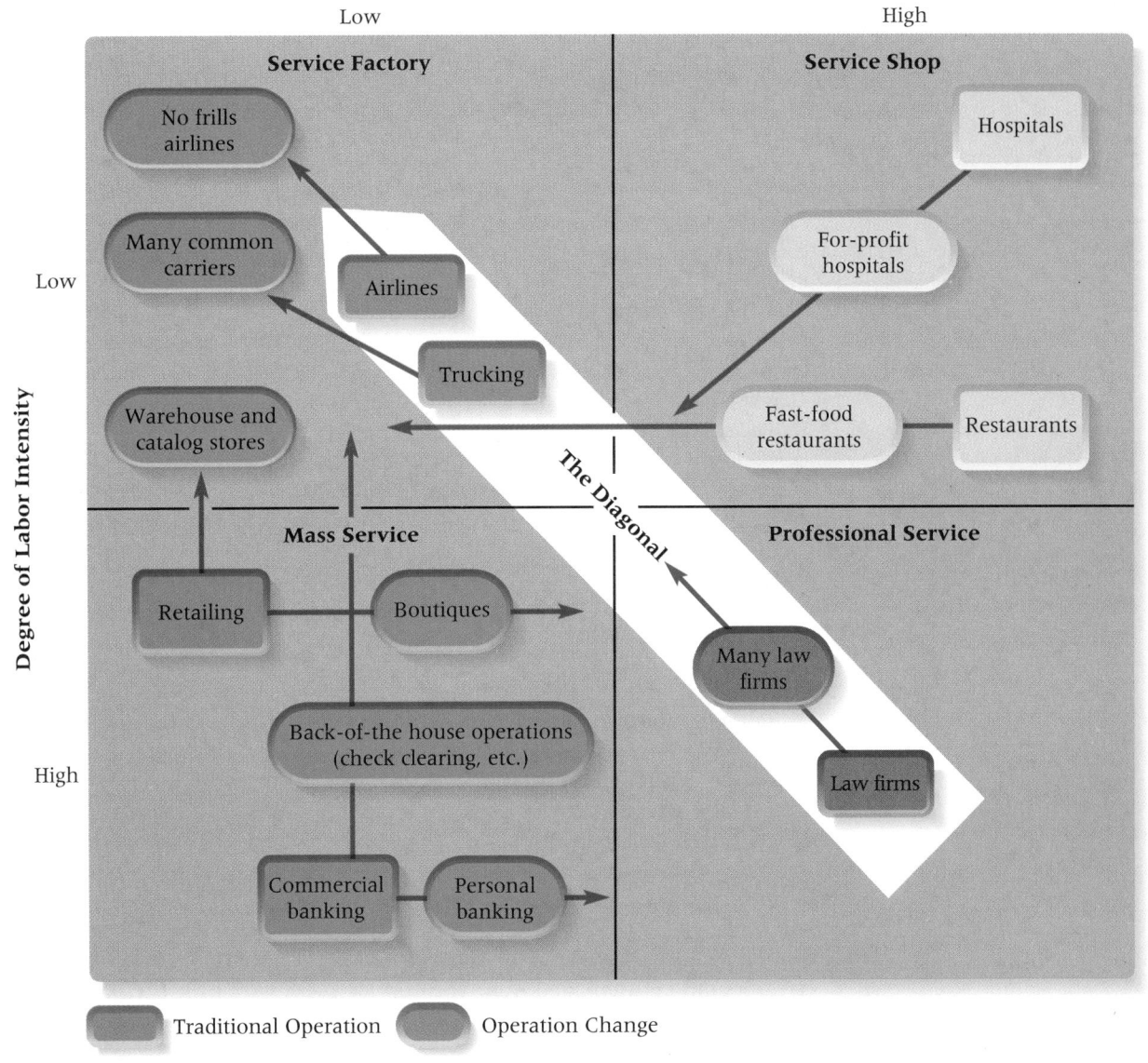

**Degree of Interaction and Customization**

# Service-Master—Stressing Dignity to Its Workers

ServiceMaster Industries, which provides housekeeping and other services to hospitals, schools, and corporations, was founded on the basis of religious principles. Its first corporate objective is "to honor God in all we do." A wooden model that sits on officers' desks shows a symbol for God supporting and balancing flocks that represent profit, achievement, and personal growth.

In 1989 ServiceMaster, headquartered in Downers Grove, Illinois, had sales of $1.6 billion, profits of $68 million, and almost 19,000 employees. As part of its service package ServiceMaster provides advice on what repairs are needed, preventive maintenance that should be done, and inspections that are required.

ServiceMaster is renowned for stressing the dignity of the work performed by janitors, groundskeepers, launderers, and others of its employees. It does so out of a belief, as William Pollard, chairman and chief executive officer, states, that "every individual is created in the image of God and has worth."

This philosophy apparently is working. The company grew sixfold in the 1980s by combining contracts to supervise support personnel at hospitals, schools, and factories in the United States and abroad with a growing line of care and maintenance services. Its profit margins on $1.6 billion in operating revenues also have risen, and the stock is favored by Wall Street analysts.

ServiceMaster attempts to minimize the stratification of the work force that is a common morale problem in U.S. companies. It requires its managers to spend time doing the jobs of the people they supervise. Its training techniques stress empathizing with workers. It expects managers to weigh the development of employees in making every operating decision. ServiceMaster also tries to improve morale by emphasizing the value of manual labor. For example, a hospital cleaning worker is asked to think about mopping a floor in terms of contributing to patients' well being rather than as performing a boring chore.

The corporate philosophy seems to be working. ServiceMaster apparently has been able to define and encourage a corporate ethic without specifying a moral code to support it. As Pollard says, success "comes down to basic principles: Most people want to do a good job. If they're given the right tools, recognized for and praised for performance, they're going to respond."

factory. For example, commercial banks have used automation to make check clearing and credit card operations less labor intensive. At the same time they have attempted to provide greater customization for their personal banking services by offering their customers a wide array of banking services.

Second, some service businesses already located on the diagonal have attempted to move up the slope from professional service to service factory. For example, law firms have begun to use paralegals and other lower-cost labor to provide services that require less labor intensity and customization.

Overall, greater control of labor costs and greater efficiency are the driving forces behind the move toward, and up, the diagonal in the service process matrix. Many service operations managers find the service process matrix useful for understanding the strategic nature of competitive and managerial challenges they face.

## The Strategic Service Vision

Another strategic approach to service operations management is based on integrating marketing and operations in one function. Researchers have proposed a strategic service vision involving four basic elements: target market segments, service concept, operating strategy, and service delivery. Three integrative elements—positioning, value-cost leveraging, and service systems integration—weld the four strategic elements.

Finding **target market segments** requires the service manager to identify the common characteristics of important market segments, the important needs of these market segments, and the strengths of various competitors. Specifying a **service concept** involves establishing expectations for service in the minds of customers and employees. The service organization's careful **positioning** of itself (finding a niche) in the competitive environment of a selected market links the target market and the service concept.

Next, the service operations manager develops an **operating strategy**, which addresses the roles of operations, finance, marketing, quality, and productivity, and the cost of service. Managers then use the **value-cost leveraging** process, which requires decisions on standardization versus customization, how to manage supply and demand, and how to control quality, to link the service concept and its operating strategy. The goal of the exercise thus far is a service that the customer perceives to be of greater value than the actual cost of supplying the service. The operations manager uses the final strategic element, the **service delivery system**, to establish the specific roles of people, technology, equipment, layout, and procedures. **Service systems integration** links the proposed service delivery system to the overall operating strategy.

The best service companies apply their strategic service vision to their employees and to their customers. ServiceMaster, based in Downers Grove, Illinois, manages support services for hospitals, schools, and industrial companies. It has turned its strategic service vision inward, toward its employees, by providing educational and motivational programs to help its workers "be something." Operations Management in Practice 2.2 describes how ServiceMaster strives to help its employees recognize the dignity of their work. Another example is Shouldice Hospital near Toronto, which specializes in the repair of hernias using only a local anesthetic. This allows the doctor and the patient to talk during the operation. The hospital has achieved a remarkably low readmission rate by emphasizing the doctor-patient contact.[8]

# Service-Sector Trends

Many sociologists and economists have studied economic growth and have classified the countries of the world as three types of societies:

*Preindustrial society.* Much of the world's population, particularly those people in less developed countries, lives in a preindustrial society. They are engaged in agriculture, mining, fishing, and forestry, using human and animal labor and basic tools. Their life is one of subsistence and is

---

[8]James L. Heskett, W. Earl Sasser, Jr., Christopher W. L. Hart, *Service Breakthroughs: Changing the Rules of the Game* (New York: Free Press, 1990), pp. 18–30, 51, 201.

dependent on the weather. Their productivity is low and little technology is available in a **preindustrial society**.

*Industrial society.* In the **industrial society** manufacturing is the predominant activity. Factories use technology to make efficient the production of goods, which is coordinated by bureaucratic and hierarchical organizations. The overall objective of making goods efficiently is more important than the role of the individual.

*Postindustrial society.* The goal of the **postindustrial society** is a high standard of living, its quality of life, as measured by such services as health, education, and recreation. The individual is important, and information becomes the key resource. The services found in the postindustrial society, such as information processing, transportation, and utilities, develop rapidly to support industrial development. Also, banking, real estate, and insurance services proliferate, as do wholesale and retail trade, as people consume goods.[9]

The United States exhibits the characteristics of a postindustrial society in which service operations are of major importance. Let's examine some trends in the service sector of our economy.

[9]Daniel Bell, *The Coming of Post-Industrial Society: A Venture in Social Forecasting* (New York: Basic Books, 1973).

FIGURE 2.5
U.S. Balance of
Trade—Services

Source: Allen Sinai, "The Service Economy at a Glance—Better Days Ahead," *The Service Economy* (April 1993): Table 3, p. 16.

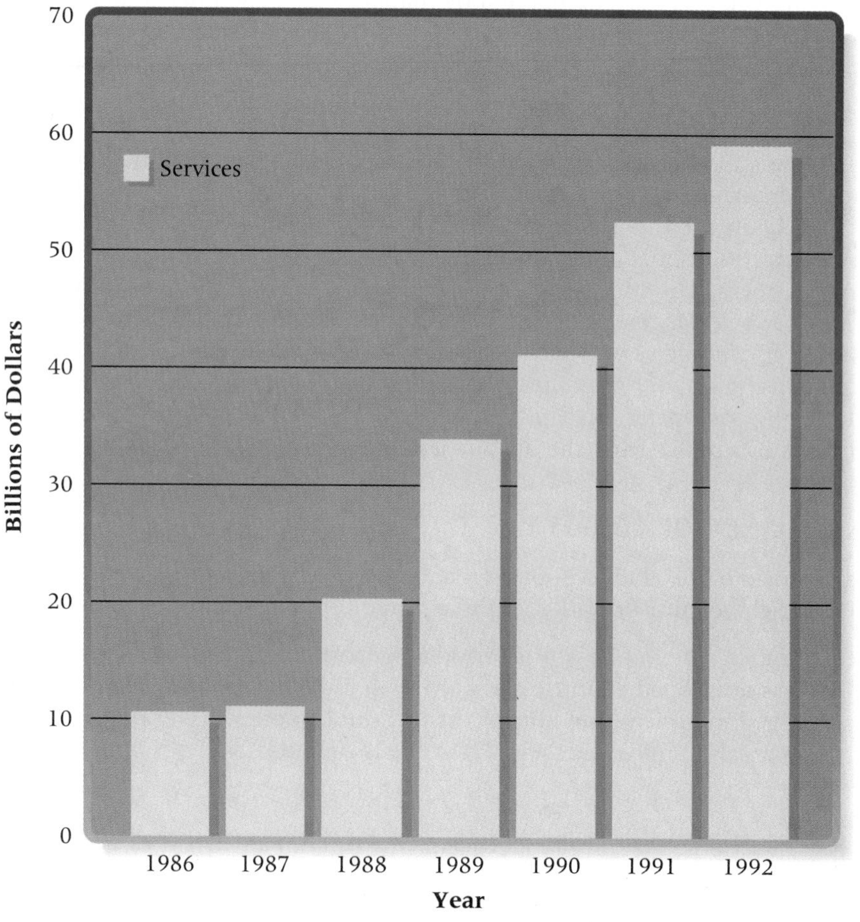

## Increased International Competition in Services

As service workers in the United States make bank loans, serve fast foods, make financial transactions using computer terminals, and provide health care and recreational services, they typically have not worried much about foreign competition. Some services are now becoming vulnerable to increased foreign competition, primarily because of technological advances.

Obtaining an international perspective on services is difficult. Economists use a variety of measures, including revenues, receipts, expenditures, and investment income. For calculating balance of payments economists traditionally have defined *international service transactions* as a mixture of cross-border trade in the service industries (true business services), military expenditures, travel and transportation receipts, and net income from foreign investment. Figure 2.5 summarizes the balance of trade by U.S. service companies for 1986 to 1992. The figures show a steady growth in the U.S. balance of trade in services.

Figure 2.6 shows the position of the American private business services with respect the four major foreign trading partners of the United States. Of particular interest is the U.S. services trade surplus with Japan, given the sizable overall trade deficit with that country.

A more critical appraisal of the international services sector reveals that the United States is having problems maintaining its superiority. International competitors have made inroads in several of the individual sectors that make up the

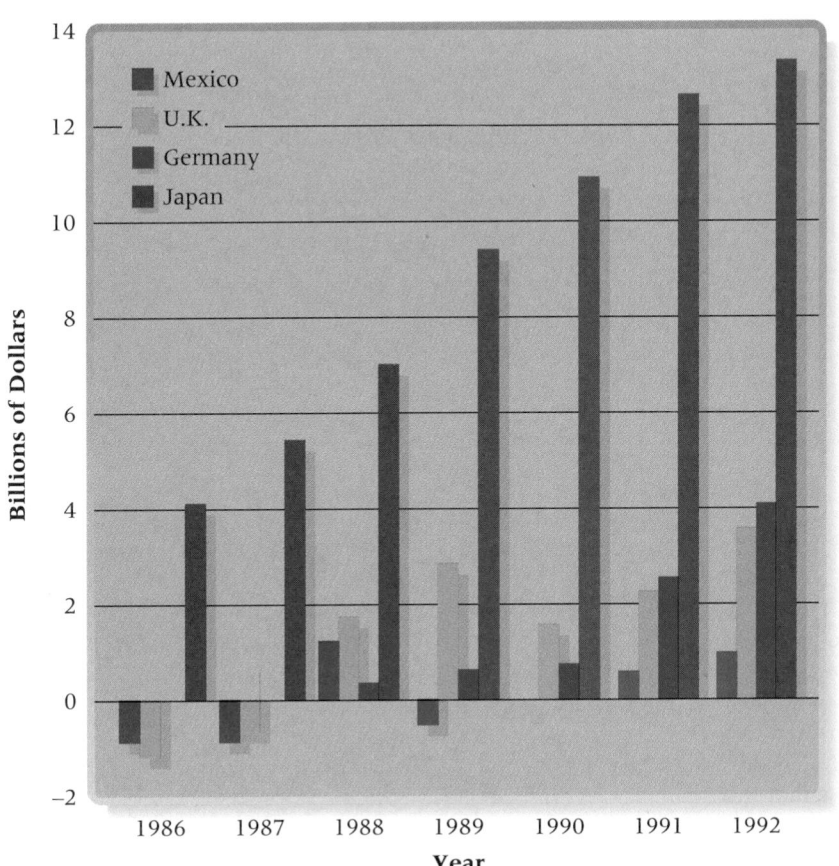

FIGURE 2.6
U.S. Bilateral Services Trade—Selected Countries

Source: Allen Sinai and Zoharo Sofianou, *The Service Economy* "U.S. Trade Data—An Update," (July 1993): Table 2, p. 16.

| Target | Purchaser | Amount in millions |
|---|---|---|
| **Entertainment** | | |
| MCA | Matsushita Electric (Japan) | $ 7,907 |
| Columbia Pictures | Sony Corp. (Japan) | 4,714 |
| MGM/UA Communications | Pathe Communications (U.S. parent, Italian controlled) | 1,670 |
| **Technicolor Holdings** | Carlton Communications (Great Britain) | 780 |
| MTM Entertainment | Television South (Great Britain) | 320 |
| RKO Theaters | Cineplex Odeon (Canada) | 169 |
| **Hotels** | | |
| Intercontinental (Grand Met) | Salson Group (Japan) | 2,270 |
| Motel 6 | Accor (France) | 2,262 |
| Holiday Inn | Bass PLC (Great Britain) | 2,225 |
| Hilton International (UAL) | Ladbroke Group (Great Britain) | 1,070 |
| Ramada Inc. | New World Development (Hong Kong) | 540 |
| **Advertising** | | |
| Ogilvy Group | WPP Group (Great Britain) | 798 |
| J. Walter Thompson | WPP Group (Great Britain) | 541 |
| Ted Bates Worldwide | Saatchi & Saatchi (Great Britain) | 450 |
| **Miscellaneous Business Services** | | |
| Manpower Inc. | Blue Arrow PLC (Great Britain) | 1,345 |
| Rent-A-Center Inc. | Thorn EMI (Great Britain) | 570 |
| Honeywell Information Systems | NEC Corp & Compagnie des Machines Bull (France) | 527 |
| UAL Apollo Reservation System (50% share) | Covia Partnership (Great Britain) | 500 |
| Network Security Corp. | Inspectorate International (Switzerland) | 390 |
| **Retail Trade** | | |
| Federated and Allied Department Stores | Campeau Corp. (Canada) | 11,264 |
| Saks Fifth Avenue (B.A.T.) | Investcorp Bank (Bahrain) | 1,500 |
| Brooks Brothers (Campeau) | Marks & Spencer (Great Britain) | 750 |
| Zale Corp. | People's Jewelers (Canada) | 607 |
| Kay Jewelers | Ratners Group (Great Britain) | 450 |

TABLE 2.4
Notable Foreign Acquisitions of U.S. Service Companies, 1986–1991

total services area. Table 2.4 summarizes recent foreign acquisitions of U.S. service companies.

Foreign competitors have captured major sectors of the U.S. manufacturing base. Now the service industries are facing the same kind of competition. Technological developments afford great opportunities, but they also allow for much greater competition. For example, more than one hundred data entry operations for U.S.-based companies are off shore, and most are foreign owned. Advances in computers and telecommunications have made it much easier for securities houses, banks, accounting, and advertising firms to expand their global operations, and foreign firms have been aggressive in all these service areas.

| Target | Purchaser | Amount in millions |
|---|---|---|
| **Transportation and Communications** | | |
| McCaw Cellular (22% Interest) | British Telecom (Great Britain) | 1,500 |
| Soo Line | Canadian Pacific (Canada) | 390 |
| Sitmar Cruises | Peninsular & Oriental Steam (Great Britain) | 210 |
| Delta Air Lines (5% Interest) | Swiss Air (Switzerland) | 193 |
| Delta Air Lines (5% Interest) | Singapore Airlines (Singapore) | 181 |
| Majestic Shipping (Loews) | Hellesport Shipping (Great Britain) | 154 |
| **Insurance** | | |
| Farmers Group | B.A.T. Industries (Great Britain) | 5,158 |
| Fireman's Fund Insurance | Alliance AG (Germany) | 3,100 |
| Equitable Life Assurance Society (share) | Groupe Axa S.A. (France) | 1,000 |
| Home Insurance (Ambase) | TVH Acquisition (Sweden) | 970 |
| Maryland Casualty Co. | Zurich Insurance (Switzerland) | 740 |
| Reliance Group | Winterthur Swiss Insurance (Switzerland) | 630 |
| **Banking** | | |
| First Maryland Bancorp | Allied Irish Banks (Ireland) | 1,101 |
| First Jersey National | National Westminster Bank (Great Britain) | 820 |
| Citizens Financial Group | Royal Bank of Scotland (Scotland) | 790 |
| First NH Banks | Bank of Ireland (Ireland) | 776 |
| Marine Midland | Hong Kong & Shanghai Banking (Hong Kong) | 758 |
| **Securities and Other Financial Services** | | |
| CIT Group (Manufacturers Hanover) | Dai-Ichi Kangyo (Japan) | 1,280 |
| First Boston | Credit Suisse-First Boston (Switzerland) | 1,100 |
| Shearson Lehman Bros. (American Express, share) | Nippon Life (Japan) | 538 |
| Goldman Sachs (share) | Sumitomo Bank (Japan) | 500 |
| Aubrey Lanston | Industrial Bank of Japan (Japan) | 234 |

Source: Stephen S. Roach, "Services Under Siege—The Restructuring Imperative," *Harvard Business Review 69,* (September–October 1991): 89.

TABLE 2.4
Continued

Deregulation of the airline industry has encouraged foreign competition, and foreign airlines often have the added benefit of government sponsorship.

Many bright spots still remain in the U.S. service sector. The United States is clearly the leader in software development and telecommunications. Its health-care technology and higher education systems are preeminent. It also has an excellent distribution system, and its entertainment industry is the envy of the world. Global Operations Management 2.3 provides insights to British Airways' new approaches to international competition.

# Improving Productivity and Competitiveness in Services

As Table 2.1 showed, the transformation of the U.S. work force has been stunning. Between 1980 and 1990 the service sector created nearly 20 million new jobs, more than enough to compensate for the losses in manufacturing.

**GLOBAL OPERATIONS MANAGEMENT 2.3**

## British Airways— Taking Off in New Directions

With Sir Colin Marshall as its chairman British Airways is taking off in new directions. Marshall's business philosophy stresses consistency—in achieving high standards, maintaining them, and then seeking "the odd way of tweaking them a little bit higher."

British Airways is the world's first airline to adopt the policy of "branding" its individual classes of services. The British Airways brands start with *Concorde* for its fleet of seven supersonic commercial aircraft, which primarily serves London–New York and London-Washington. The goal of the *First Class* brand is providing the best subsonic airline catering service. *Club World,* the business-class brand, aims to deliver international business travelers to their destinations relaxed and ready to do business. *World Traveller* tries to keep passengers happy by using catering, various amenities, and other special perks. *Super Shuttler* links London and four other British cities. *Skyflyers* provides services and amenities for children, while they are traveling with parents or alone. British Airways is a world leader in branding its subcategories of service to give each class of service a perception of added value.

British Airways is teaming up with USAir to bring their customers a "world" of service. The first area in which the two airlines plan to work together is code sharing. Common codes for USAir and British Airways flights are expected to give customers more travel opportunities and alternatives. Other benefits include coordinated schedules, shorter intervals between connecting flights, and smoother baggage transfers.

On March 21, 1990, British Airways announced the "World's Biggest Offer" (WBO), its campaign to bring back customers after the Gulf War, which caused fuel prices, and therefore airline ticket prices, to rise substantially. The campaign involved giving away fifty thousand seats—every seat on its international flights in and out of England on April 23, 1991. Some 5.3 million people applied for the seats, and the World's Biggest Offer was a huge success in boosting air travel for British Airways.

British Airways is one of the most profitable airlines in the world. Marshall cites British Airways' team service philosophy as the key to its success, noting, "I think it comes down to the whole employee group working as a team, much more than they have in the past, and the enthusiasm they generate."

Services employ many people, but they do not use them very productively. Figure 2.7 shows that productivity in the nonmanufacturing sector (a good indicator of productivity in the service sector) came to a halt in the mid-1970s and made only small gains through 1989.

The reasons for slower growth in service productivity include

- The fluctuating business cycle: Service-sector business cycles have historically been mild relative to those experienced by the goods-producing sector. Downturns in the U.S. economy have displaced workers from the goods-producing sector to the service sector, resulting in an overall lowering of service productivity. Recent labor reductions in service industries are likely to yield higher productivity in the next business cycle.

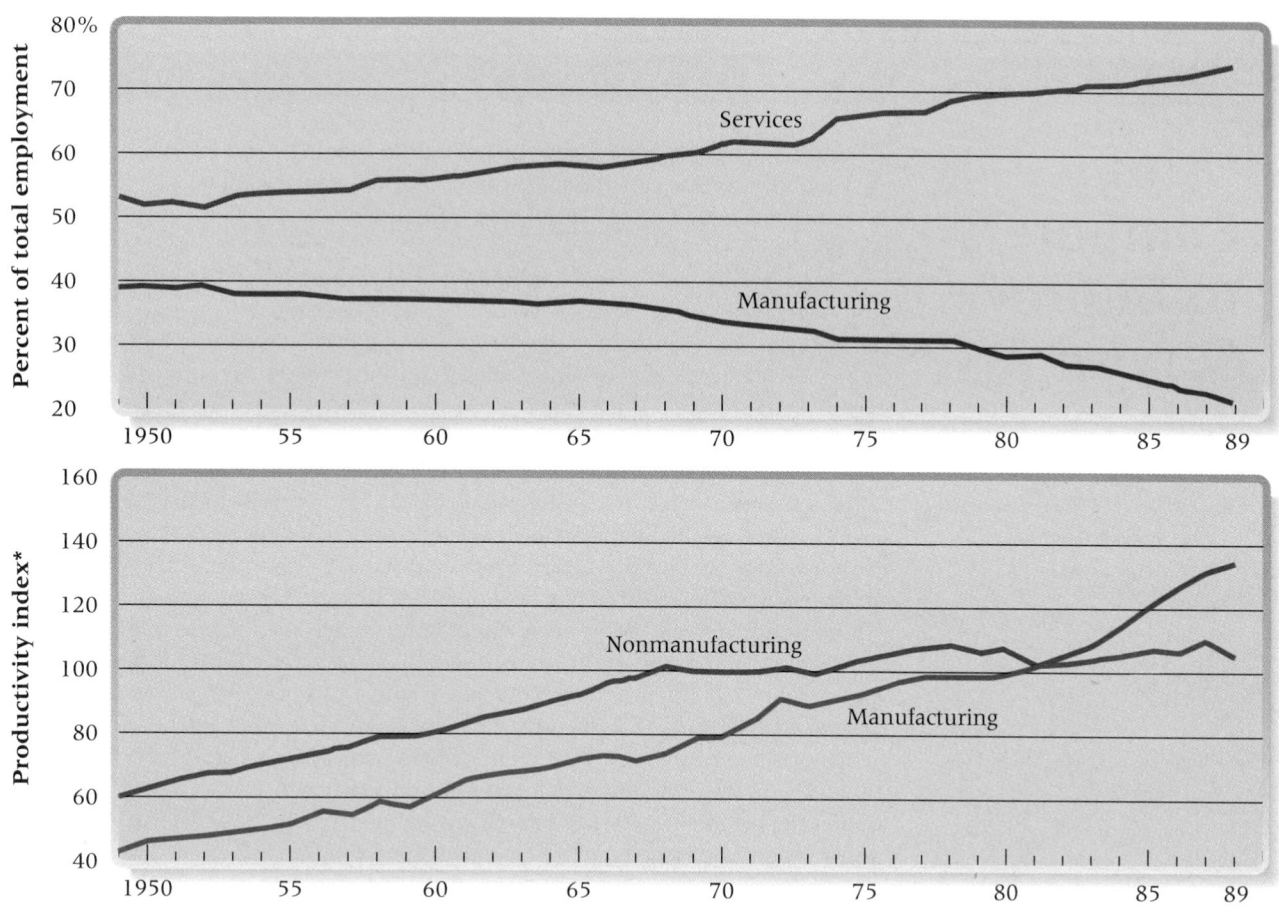

*Measures productivity relative to its base performance in 1982

Source: U.S. Bureau of Labor Statistics

■ The changing mix of service industries: The changes in the mix of services offered tend to slow the growth of overall service productivity. As more services with low productivity, such as fast food and prepared food, laundry services, and child care, grow in importance, overall service productivity tends to decrease.

■ The inadequacy of education and training: Because labor is an inherent part of the service sector, inadequate education and training of service workers are significant factors that decrease overall service industry productivity. Many institutions do not provide the education that service workers need in order to use an increasing variety of high-tech equipment.

■ The problems of the financial services industry: The financial services industry experienced major problems at the end of the 1980s. Troubles at thrifts, in real estate, and in banks led to a drop in their productivity and that of related service activities.[10]

Associated with these reasons for slower growth is the overall measurement problem. Significant problems in measuring service productivity include whether

FIGURE 2.7
Comparison of Employment and Productivity

Source: Stephen S. Roach, "Services Under Siege—The Restructuring Imperative," *Harvard Business Review* 69, (September–October 1991): 83.

[10]Allen Sinai and Zaharo Sofianou, "The Service Economy—Productivity Growth Issues," *The Service Economy* 6 (January 1992): 11–16.

# OPERATIONS MANAGEMENT IN PRACTICE 2.4

# Using Computers to Improve Service

Service aided by a computer is becoming the norm. Recent improvements in computer technology allow for speedy response to telephone inquiries and enable customers to obtain answers to questions at any hour of the day or night.

Some service companies are beginning to use "expert systems" to help answer customers' technical questions. Because turnover in customer service operations can be high, and because training employees properly can take a long time, service companies are developing expert systems that store information to build a base of expertise that remains when employees leave. Answer Computer, Inc., in Sunnyvale, California, is one example of a firm that uses computer technology to provide such an expert system. Otis Elevator Co., a subsidiary of United Technologies Corp., is using an expert system and laptop computers to speed repairs. Otis installs devices that work like airplane flight recorders to record the performance of its elevators. When elevators break down, repair technicians use their portable computers to call up a list of potential problems from the expert system.

Companies also are using image processing, which involves electronic document scanning and storage, to reduce the time a customer spends on the phone with a company. Philip Lakernick, chief executive of Maria Parham Hospital in Henderson, North Carolina, says that a new image-processing system developed by GeneSysData Technologies, Inc., of Hunt Valley, Maryland, has cut from thirty minutes to one minute the time it takes to find a patient's chart.

Another technological breakthrough is computer systems that enable telephone switches and standard computers to speak the same language. For example, a credit card customer calling with a question can punch in an account number while on hold. The telephone switch relays the number to the computer, which retrieves the customer's records. The computer then relays the records back to the phone switch and transmits them to the customer services employee's computer screen. Lee Figuiolo, a vice president at Progressive Casualty Insurance Co. in Cleveland, Ohio, says that IBM's CallPath system links telephones and computers at his company and makes it easier to reroute phone calls. Similarly, Thomas Powell & Associates, a software firm in Boca Raton, Florida, that specializes in voice systems, has announced a system that lets golfers reserve tee-off times by dialing a computer and following a set of voice prompts.

"Services is becoming the determining factor for maintaining competitiveness in more and more businesses," suggests William Davidow, a venture capitalist and coauthor of *Total Customer Service: The Ultimate Weapon*. Certainly, computer technology is a key element in improving services.

existing statistics adequately measure service production, whether the price indexes satisfactorily adjust for quality, and whether the hours counted are comparable over time.

However, more recent economic information is more encouraging. According to data from the Bureau of Labor Statistics, eating and drinking places, for example, scored a 3.5 percent gain in 1991 after years of declining productivity.

Commercial banks posted a 6.2 percent productivity jump in 1990. Electricity utilities surged 2.7 percent in 1991—double the rate from 1973 to 1990—while telecommunications rang up a 5.6 percent increase, and rail transportation thundered ahead at 8.3 percent. Even more recent numbers come from Morgan Stanley Bank, which has analyzed Bureau of Labor Statistics data to create an aggregate productivity rate for the nonfarm, nonmanufacturing sector as a whole. The bank's data suggest that the service productivity growth rate hit a healthy 3.2 percent in late 1992.[11] Operations Management in Practice 2.4 details how several companies are using computers to improve service.

## Technology and Automation in Services

Many of us think of the service sector in terms of fast-food restaurants or video rental stores. This tends to distort the true complexity and technical sophistication of service businesses. In reality the service sector is a major market for high technology. Along with the automation of factories, as represented by robotics and computerized manufacturing control systems, has come a simultaneous automation of the service sector. Since 1980 the service sector has put nearly all its capital improvement money into information technology. One author estimates that 80 to 85 percent of all investment in information technology occurs in the service industries.[12] The use of technology and automation in service industries is proliferating. Table 2.5 presents several such examples.

Technology can be useful at four different points in the service process:

- Processing the customer. Personal services such as medical, cosmetics, and entertainment typically "process the customer." They use technology to surpass competitors or process customers more efficiently, which the medical industry has done with magnetic resonance imaging.
- Processing the customer's materials. Photo processing, dry cleaning, and car washing are examples of processing the customer's materials.
- Processing information. Data and information processing can improve many services, such as financial planning information that mutual fund owners can access, and news reports by newspapers and television news shows. Technological advances in this area are quite rapid.
- Creating new services. Technology can create completely new services by developing new products or processes, such as cellular telephones and fax machines.[13]

Operations Management in Practice 2.5 illustrates J.C. Penney's use of technology in retail services.

## Adequacy of Service Jobs

Are service jobs good jobs? Are today's service jobs as good as yesterday's manufacturing jobs? We have discussed the dramatic shift from manufacturing

---

[11]Myron Magnet, "Good News for the Service Economy," *Fortune*, May 3, 1993, p. 47.
[12]Patrick T. Harker, "Services and American Competitiveness," *The Service Economy* 6 (January 1992): 4.
[13]Murdick, Render, and Russell, *Service Operations Management*, pp. 285–290.

TABLE 2.5
Examples of Automation in
Service Industries

| Service Industry | Automation Examples |
|---|---|
| Education | Personal computers |
| | Electronic calculators |
| | Language translation computers |
| | Speak and spell computer systems |
| Health care | CAT scanners |
| | Fetal monitoring systems |
| | Medical information systems |
| | Dentists' chair systems |
| Financial services | Electronic funds transfer |
| | Automatic teller machines |
| | Encoded check processors |
| | Automated trust portfolio analysis |
| Restaurants/Food services | Vending machines |
| | Automatic french fryer |
| | Rotating service cafeteria |
| | Optical scanners |
| Hotel/Motel services | Electronic reservation systems |
| | Elevators/escalators |
| | Electronic key/lock systems |
| | Automatic sprinkler systems |
| Leisure/Recreation services | Television games |
| | Disney World/Epcot Center |
| | Video disc machines |
| Transportation | Air traffic control systems |
| | Automatic toll booths |
| | Rapid transit systems |
| | Autopilots |
| Utilities/Government services | Optical mail scanners |
| | Airborne warning/control systems |
| | One-person garbage trucks |
| | Mail sorting machines |
| Communications | Phone answering machines |
| | Word processors |
| | Electronic mail systems |
| | Copying machines |
| Wholesale/Retail trade | Automatic car wash |
| | Automated distribution warehouse |
| | Automated security systems |
| | Telemarketing systems |

Source: David A. Collier, *Service Management: The Automation of Services* (Reston, Va.: Reston, 1985), pp. 22–23.

jobs to service jobs in the U.S. economy. As a result, many economists, business leaders, labor leaders, and politicians contend that we are becoming a nation of hamburger flippers, sales clerks, and tune-up specialists. They suggest that we may be heading for long-run trouble, including declining incomes, less economic development, and lower living standards. They note that service jobs do not generate as much economic growth as manufacturing jobs, because they pay less and are less productive. But as Figure 2.8 shows, service jobs in the private sector began to pay almost as much as manufacturing jobs in 1990.

**OPERATIONS MANAGEMENT IN PRACTICE 2.5**

# J.C. Penney— Riding the Third Wave of Information Technology

J.C. Penney has earned a reputation as a pioneer in the use of technology in retail services. Dale Evans, vice president and director of Penney's information systems department in 1990, spent his career developing systems for the company. He started as a programmer in 1964, long before information technology was considered the key to retail services that it has become.

Evans views retail service technology at J.C. Penney as consisting of two major waves, each lasting about fifteen years. The first wave, 1960–1974, involved automating specific functions, such as accounting, accounts payable, and the credit system. Also, the company made some attempt to use technology to track sales and inventories. As early as 1966 Penney was experimenting with ground-breaking ideas, such as installing cash registers that track inventory.

The second wave, 1975–1989, was marked by the installation of transaction-processing systems, on-line credit authorizations, and **electronic data interchange** (integrated systems that use telephones or another technology to link computers at two organizations so they can exchange data). The major goal of service retailers during this period was to capture data.

The third wave of information technology began in 1990. According to Evans, it is characterized by the replacement of outmoded technologies. For example, Penney spent more than $200 million to replace its outdated cash registers with **bar code scanning** at all stores. A bar code is a pattern of wide and narrow black bands and alternating white spaces that a computer reads with the aid of an optical scanner or wand. The Penney system uses an NCR 7052 register that accepts most scanning equipment. At each checkout area, sales personnel use a pen, a laser gun, or a vertical scanner, depending on the type of merchandise in the department, to record sales. Each NCR 7052 also has a built-in magnetic stripe reader that checks the customer's credit and signals approval to the register, which prints a single sales slip that the customer signs.

Penney also plans to increase its electronic data interchange network from five hundred suppliers to more than five thousand. It also is developing computer-aided design workstations for designing merchandise, especially private label apparel. **Computer-aided design (CAD)** is used to create new parts or products or alter existing ones. It uses powerful desktop computers and graphics software to manipulate geometric shapes. Evans observes that "one CAD station we're now testing can process 30 million instructions per second. It can create pictures of merchandise that doesn't exist, move things around and provide details down to the thread count level."

In summary, Evans says, "Technology is advancing so rapidly that each time we change, it's a tremendous improvement. I would never want to go back."

In this context the former dean of the Sloan Business School at the Massachusetts Institute of Technology, Lester Thurow, contends that the United States cannot look to its service sector for salvation, because no country has yet succeeded in exporting services and the domestic service sector is not going to grow all that much.[14] Other economists argue that a service-driven economy

[14]Charles C. Mann, "The Man with All the Answers," *Atlantic Monthly*, January 1990, p. 56.

FIGURE 2.8
Comparison of Service Wages
and Manufacturing Wages

Source: U.S. Department of
Commerce, U.S. Bureau of the
Census, *Statistical Abstract of the United
States 1992* (Washington, D.C.: U.S.
Government Printing Office, 1992),
p. 410.

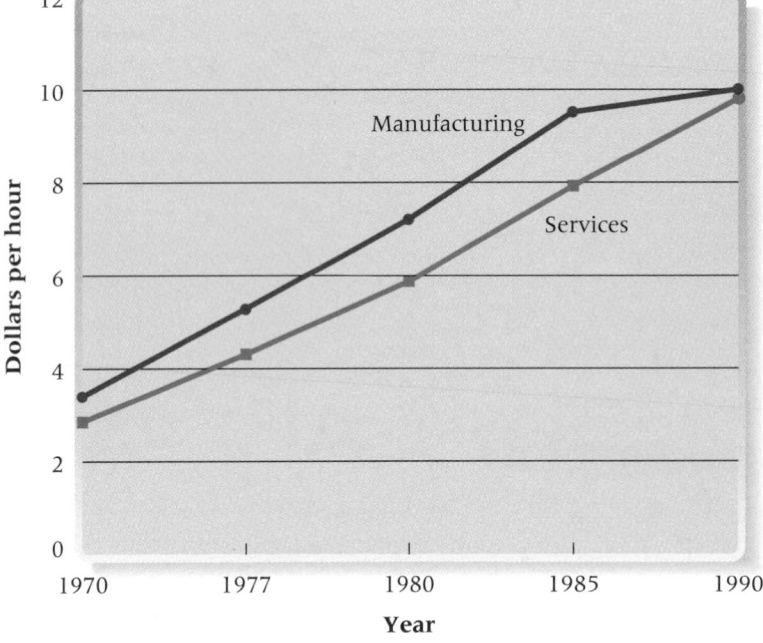

*At L. L. Bean a customer service
representative provides assistance
over the phone.*

must depend on sales to basic industries to survive. Big service support networks—including utilities, distributors, and financial, accounting, and consulting firms—will surely be hurt if manufacturing continues to decline. Equally troublesome is that services are expected to face aggressive foreign competition, both in export markets and at home.[15]

[15]Joan Berger, "The False Paradise of a Service Economy," *Business Week*, March 3, 1986, p. 78.

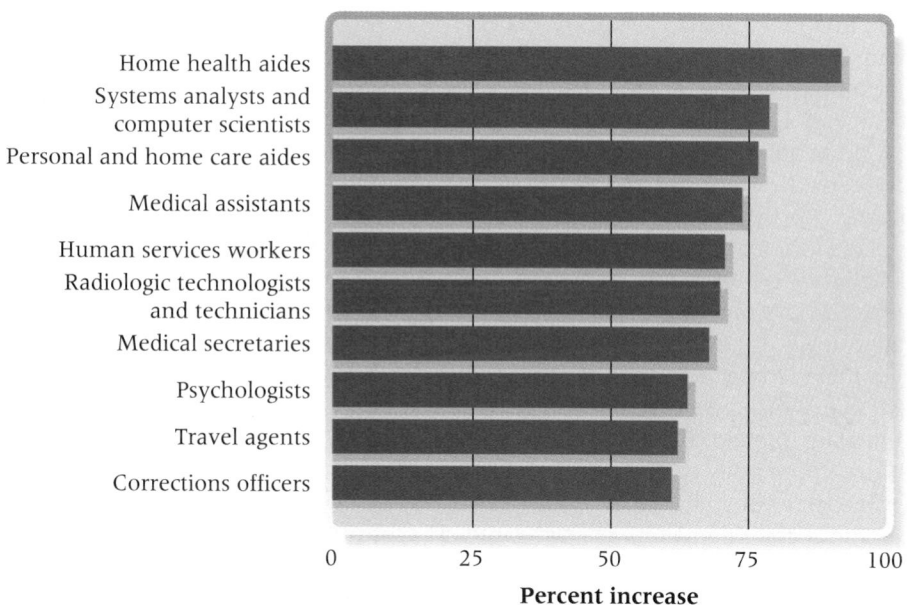

FIGURE 2.9
Job Growth in Ten
Fastest-growing Occupations,
1990–2005

Source: U.S. Department of
Commerce, U.S. Bureau of the
Census, *Statistical Abstract of the United
States 1992* (Washington, D.C.: U.S.
Government Printing Office, 1992),
p. 380.

Others argue that whereas the shift to services is indeed changing the type of work done by many Americans, the fear of deindustrialization is greatly exaggerated. One report suggests reason for optimism, because of the boom in capital spending in the service sector. It shows more than 90 percent of the new jobs created since 1969 have been in the service sector.[16] Moreover, the fastest-growing job categories within the service sector are those that are better paying—professional and technical, including accountants, lawyers, engineers, doctors, and scientists. Figure 2.9 presents a prediction of job growth from 1990 to 2005, for the ten fastest-growing occupations. Virtually all the jobs are in the service sector and are in the higher-paying categories of the service sector.

## Greater Quality Emphasis in Services

Product quality has come to the forefront in American industry. Consumers have become smarter shoppers, seeking greater value and lower prices, and service providers are becoming aware that product quality is the key to competitiveness in international markets.

Much of the published work on quality focuses on manufactured goods, but managers are paying more attention to emphasizing quality in services. One reason is the general perception that service quality is not good. Thomas Peters, a management consultant and coauthor of *In Search of Excellence*, states this perception when he says, "In general, service in America stinks."[17]

Improving quality is becoming a major objective in service companies throughout the United States. Among the major success stories is Federal Express. "We knew from day one that the focus in this company would be on providing a high-quality service," says W. Jack Roberts, former vice president for

[16]U.S. Department of Commerce, Bureau of the Census, *Statistical Abstract of the United States 1992* (Washington, D.C.: U.S. Government Printing Office, 1992), p. 380.
[17]Quoted in Stephen Koepp, "Pul-eeze! Will Somebody Help Me?" *Time*, February 2, 1987, p. 49.

audit and chief quality officer at Federal Express.[18] The U.S. Commerce Department recognized the quality efforts of Federal Express when it awarded it its Malcolm Baldridge National Quality Award in 1990. Federal Express handles an average of 1.5 million packages every night with few problems.

There are many other examples of services that emphasize quality. L.L. Bean, the Freeport, Maine, mail-order house, is well known for leading its industry in quality. As Bean president Leon Gorman acknowledged, "It's just a day-in, day-out, on-going, never-ending, unremitting, persevering, compassionate type of activity."[19] Nordstrom, Inc., headquartered in Seattle, operates big department stores throughout the country and has built an enviable reputation for providing a high level of customer service. Hotelier J. Willard Marriott, Sr., started asking customers what they thought of Marriott's service and for sixty years personally read every response card and suggestion his company received.[20] Delta Airlines, American Express, Florida Power & Light, and Citicorp are other examples of service companies that have developed good reputations for the quality of the service they provide.

The recognition that survival—much less growth—in the service sector is a function of quality led to the increasing emphasis on quality. Service companies have witnessed what has happened to manufacturers that allowed the quality of their products to deteriorate. They also recognize that providing high-quality service to keep a customer is much less expensive than acquiring a new one. Service quality has a major effect on the ability to attract and retain both customers and employees, and it contributes directly to superior productivity.

[18]Peter Bradley, "Making Quality Fly," *Purchasing* 110 (January 17, 1991): 100.
[19]Bro Uttal, "Companies That Serve You Best," *Fortune*, December 7, 1987, p. 98.
[20]Barry Farber, and Joyce Wycoff, "Customer Service: Evolution and Revolution," *Sales & Marketing Management* 143 (May 1991): 44.

## ► Summary

The service sector has assumed an increasing importance in the U.S. economy and in world trade. Service companies typically have several unique characteristics that operations managers must understand in order to manage their operations effectively.

**Learning Objective 1: Define service activities.** Services are economic activities that produce a place, time, form, or psychological service for the consumer. Service companies typically help their customers by transporting, blending, packaging, storing, or performing some other operation. Many service companies provide intangible services, but others provide both tangible goods and intangible services.

**Learning Objective 2: Classify service operations.** Service operations generally do not produce tangible products, but they still can be classified much as manufacturing operations are, according to the degree to which their project or service is standardized. Project services include consulting and software development. Job shop services include gourmet restaurants and automotive repair shops. Line flow services include fast-food restaurants. Continuous flow services include police and fire departments.

**Learning Objective 3: Describe the unique characteristics of service operations.** Service operations have a number of characteristics that are different from those found in manufacturing operations: high consumer contact, active consumer participation in the service, perishability of services, consumer preferences that dictate the location of service facilities, labor intensiveness, intangibility, variable and non-standard products, difficulty in measuring services, and difficulty in measuring quality.

**Learning Objective 4: Discuss strategic approaches to service operations management.** Strategic approaches to service operations management include the service process matrix and the strategic service vision. The service process matrix is based on understanding the interaction between the degree of labor intensity and the degree consumer interaction and customization in the service process. The strategic service approach focuses on identifying target market segments, specifying a service concept, developing an operating strategy, and linking the concept for the service and its operating strategy by a considering value and cost.

**Learning Objective 5: Summarize major service-sector trends.** The service sector is seeing several important trends. Among them are increased international competition in services, emphasis on improving productivity and competitiveness, more reliance on technology and automation, a concern about the adequacy of service jobs, and a greater emphasis on quality.

## ► Key Terms

bar code scanning
computer-aided design (CAD)
continuous flow
electronic data interchange
goods
high-technology business services
industrial services
industrial society
line flow

mass consumer services
operating strategy
positioning
postindustrial society
preindustrial society
project
service concept
service delivery system

service process matrix
service sector
service systems integration
services
skilled personal services
target market segments
unskilled personal services
value-cost leveraging

## ► Discussion Questions

1. What are the major ways in which services operations differ from manufacturing operations?
2. What are the implications for the United States' becoming a services-based economy?
3. Why are quality and productivity often more difficult to measure in service operations than in manufacturing operations?
4. In what ways might the management style of a service operations manager differ from that of a manufacturing operations manager?
5. For some service industries with which you are familiar, describe some ways they are trying to improve productivity.
6. For a particular services business with which you are familiar, identify and discuss the major characteristics of service operations.

7. Explain how to use the service process matrix to analyze the strategic changes in services operations over time.
8. Are services jobs good jobs? Explain why you think they are or are not.
9. Describe the role of computers and information technology in improving service operations.
10. Discuss some international ramifications of service operations.
11. For a particular service business with which you are familiar, describe its conversion process and identify the major elements of the process.
12. Compare the consumer's perception of quality in service and in manufactured goods.

## ► Selected References

Albrecht, Karl. *At America's Service: How Corporations Can Revolutionize the Way They Treat Their Customers.* Homewood, Ill.: Dow Jones-Irwin, 1988.

Albrecht, Karl, and Ron Zemke. *Service America! Doing Business in the New Economy.* Homewood, Ill.: Dow Jones-Irwin, 1985.

Bowen, David E., Richard B. Chase, Thomas G. Cummings, and Associates. *Service Management Effectiveness: Balancing Strategy, Organization, Human Resources, Operations, and Marketing.* San Francisco: Jossey-Bass, 1990.

Collier, David A. *Service Management: The Automation of Services.* Reston, Va.: Reston, 1985.

———. *Service Management: Operating Decisions.* Englewood Cliffs, N.J.: Prentice-Hall, 1987.

Czepiel, John A., Michael R. Solomon, and Carol Suprenant. *The Service Encounter.* Lexington, Mass.: Heath, 1985.

Fitzsimmons, James A., and Mona J. Fitzsimmons. *Service Management for Competitive Advantage.* New York: McGraw-Hill, 1994.

Fitzsimmons, James A., and Robert S. Sullivan. *Service Operations Management.* New York: McGraw-Hill, 1982.

Heskett, James L., *Managing in the Service Economy.* Boston: Harvard Business School Press, 1986.

Heskett, James L., W. Earl Sasser, Jr., and Christopher W. L. Hart. *Service Breakthroughs: Changing the Rules of the Game.* New York: Free Press, 1990.

Lovelock, Christopher H. *Services Marketing: Text, Cases, and Readings.* Englewood Cliffs, N.J.: Prentice-Hall, 1984.

———. *Managing Services: Marketing, Operations, and Human Resources.* Englewood Cliffs, N.J.: Prentice-Hall, 1988.

Murdick, Robert G., Barry Render, and Roberta S. Russell. *Service Operations Management.* Boston: Allyn & Bacon, 1990.

Normann, Richard, *Service Management: Strategy and Leadership In Service Businesses.* Chichester, England: Wiley, 1984.

Sasser, W. Earl, R. Paul Olsen, and D. Daryl Wyckoff. *Management of Service Organizations: Text, Cases, and Readings.* Boston: Allyn & Bacon, 1978.

Shelp, Ronald K., John C. Stephenson, Nancy S. Truitt, and Bernard Wasow. *Service Industries and Economic Development.* New York: Praeger, 1985.

Voss, Christopher, Colin Armistead, Bob Johnston, and Barbara Morris. *Operations Management in Service Industries and the Public Sector.* Chichester, England: Wiley, 1985.

Zeithaml, Valarie A., A. Parasuraman, and Leonard L. Berry. *Delivering Service Quality.* New York: Free Press, 1990.

# Blockbuster Entertainment

As the world moves into the twenty-first century, Blockbuster Entertainment Corp., headed by chairman and chief executive officer H. Wayne Huizenga, will be there waiting with an amazing array of theme parks, video and music centers, virtual reality advertising centers, and neighborhood entertainment plazas. The growth and size of the services empire of Blockbuster Entertainment is a truly amazing American success story.

It all started with a trash route. The Huizenga family moved to Fort Lauderdale in 1953 when Wayne was a freshman in high school. After graduation and an army stint, he returned to Fort Lauderdale and bought a truck and a list of commercial waste customers that generated profits of about $500 a month.

Hard work and diligence led to the founding of Waste Management, Inc., in 1971. Huizenga then made a series of mergers and acquisitions that transformed his company into the world's biggest waste collector and disposer. He resigned from Waste Management, Inc., in 1984 to pursue other business interests.

He was attracted to the home video market, a small service industry characterized by numerous mom-and-pop retailers. Huizenga invested in Blockbuster, a Dallas chain founded by David Cook that had a modest eighteen stores. In 1987 an investor group led by Huizenga took over full management of the company and moved its headquarters to Fort Lauderdale. As of December 1993 Blockbuster had almost four thousand video stores around the world. Plans call for adding two thousand stores in the near future.

What has caused this phenomenal growth? According to Huizenga, "Steve Berrard [Blockbuster's president] and I have a saying. We're no smarter than the competition, so if we expect to accomplish twice as much, we have to work twice as hard." Huizenga says that Cook had an excellent concept for the company, one that was better than anyone else's in the industry. This led Huizenga to believe that Blockbuster could be the industry leader. He applied the same techniques he used with Waste Management, Inc.: a series of rapid mergers and acquisitions. Huizenga recalls, "We were very aggressive on the operational side—finding real estate and building the stores—but we were very conservative when it came to the balance sheet side." - For four years in a row Blockbuster Video averaged a new store opening every seventeen hours.

Blockbuster has been incredibly profitable. Huizenga's personal wealth has been estimated at $500 million. Blockbuster expects to generate a free cash flow of more than $2 billion through 1998. Huizenga recognizes that Blockbuster must diversify into other businesses.

Although his company's success has been spectacular, Huizenga sees the Blockbuster of tomorrow as a vast, global entertainment service company unlike anything that now exists. Topping its list of challenges are the Blockbuster Entertainment Centers and Blockbuster Park in south Florida.

The Blockbuster Entertainment Centers (under design in late 1993 with prototypes under construction) will generally be 20,000 to 50,000 square feet. According to Huizenga, "With the new technologies we can do a lot of things that weren't profitable before. You don't have to go up fourteen stories for a simulated roller coaster ride. With a virtual reality helmet you can go anywhere without leaving your seat."

Blockbuster Park is a one-of-a-kind entertainment complex, with professional sports as anchors. Located between Miami and Fort Lauderdale, its designers envision it as a phase-in project over several years. The first phase, to be completed by 1996, is the hockey arena and home for Huizenga's Florida Panthers. Construction on the 50,000-seat, retractable-roof ballpark for Huizenga's Florida Marlins will follow, with work on the park between the two sports venues progressing simultaneously. Huizenga plans to build a theme park, emphasizing high-tech attractions, on the northwest corner of the property. A separate water theme park is also planned. Eventually, the village will also have a championship-caliber golf course, a sports museum, movie, television, and recording studios, hotels, restaurants, shops, a movie theater with twenty to thirty screens, and virtual reality arcades.

Huizenga is known as a warm, unpretentious, and upbeat chief executive who is generous with his time and money. He and his wife were honored as Broward County's "Outstanding Philanthropists for 1990" for the extensive charitable work done by the Huizenga Family Foundation. When describing his amazing rise to the top of the entertainment services industry, Huizenga has a classically simple explanation: "Anyone can do what I'm doing. You just have to figure out how to keep the customer happy."

Source: Bernie Ward, "Wayne's Midas Touch," *Sky Magazine*, December 1993, pp. 56–65.

## ► Discussion Questions

1. What are the major reasons for Blockbuster Entertainment Corp.'s great success?
2. What is your appraisal of Blockbuster Entertainment's prospect for the future?
3. How might technological advances affect the home video market?

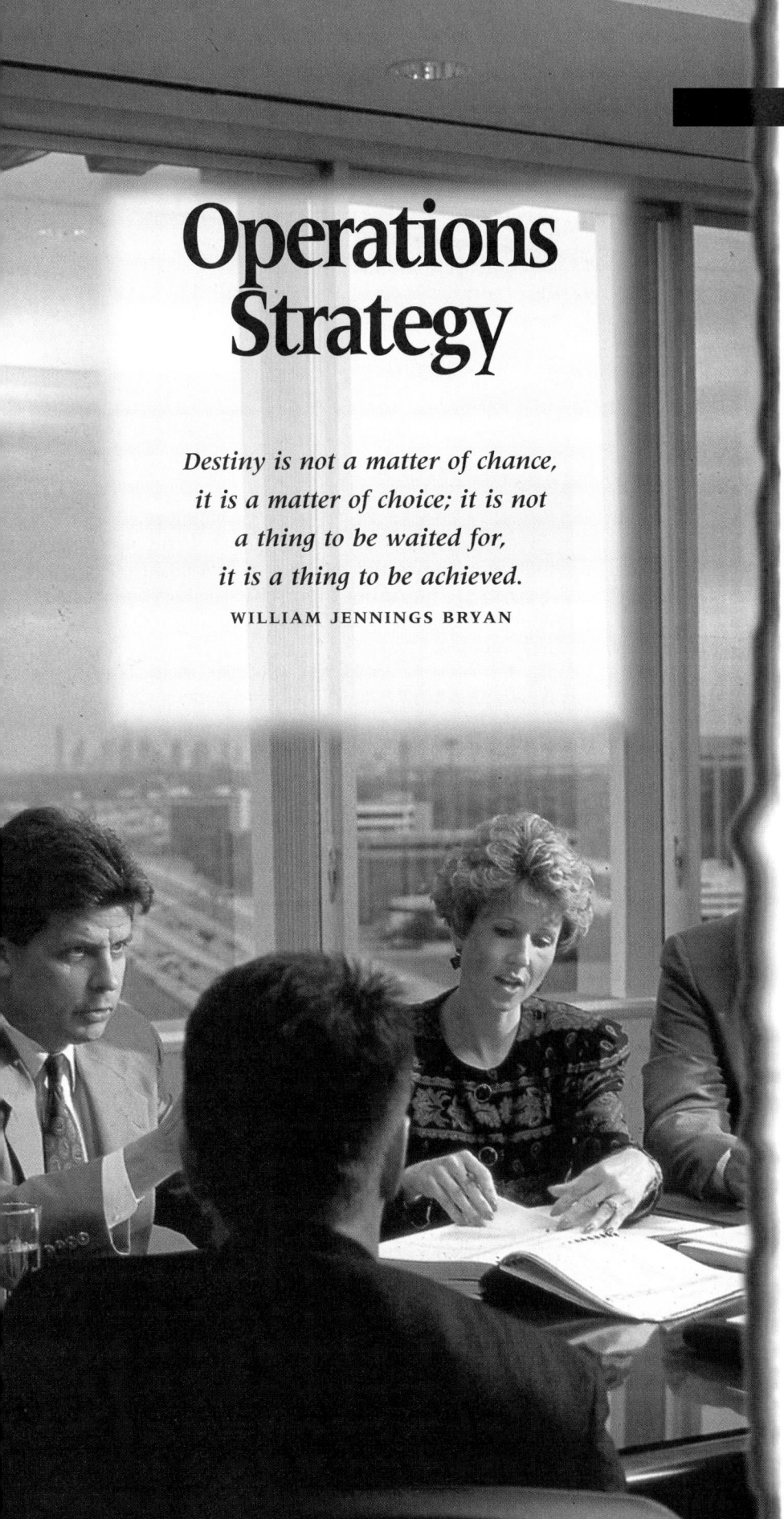

## CHAPTER 3

# Operations Strategy

*Destiny is not a matter of chance,
it is a matter of choice; it is not
a thing to be waited for,
it is a thing to be achieved.*

WILLIAM JENNINGS BRYAN

**Introduction**

**Business-level Strategic Planning**
*OPERATIONS MANAGEMENT IN
    PRACTICE 3.1: Strategic Positioning at
    Haskell of Pittsburgh*

**Operations Strategic Planning**
*GLOBAL OPERATIONS MANAGEMENT
    3.2: Competitive Priorities at Meiji Seika
    Kaisha Ltd. (Odawara)*

**Categories of Strategic Operations
Decisions**

**Vertical Linkages: The Value Chain
Revisited**

**Global Integration of Operations**
*GLOBAL OPERATIONS MANAGEMENT
    3.3: Global Integration of Operations at
    Xerox*

**Case Study: Operations Strategic
Planning at Allen-Bradley**

# Introduction

The purpose of strategic planning is to ensure the long-run profitability of a business organization. Implicit in strategic planning is recognition of the basic structure of business organizations. Companies that operate several businesses have three levels, known as the **strategic planning hierarchy:** the corporate, business, and functional, or product, levels. For single-business companies, the corporate and business levels are combined.

Although the strategic planning process is similar at each level, its focus is different. **Corporate-level strategic planning** is concerned with developing an overall plan to effectively guide the corporation as a whole. It defines the corporate mission, identifies the company's strategic business units (SBU, a single business or collection of related businesses that can be planned and operated as an independent organization), analyzes the corporation's portfolio of businesses to determine the best allocation of resources for each business, and identifies new business opportunities. Corporate-level strategic planning provides the framework within which individual business units do their own strategic planning.[1]

**Business-level strategic planning** is concerned with strategic choices that enable the SBU, or company, to successfully compete with businesses in the same field. Planning at this level means specifying the company's strategic objectives (high-quality products, low costs, short time to market) and the methods for attaining them (advanced process technologies to achieve high-quality at low cost; concurrent engineering for rapid development and introduction of new products). **Functional or product-level strategic planning** is closely linked to business-level strategic planning because the functional or product organizations within the company implement its strategic objectives and determine which tactics or methods to use to achieve those objectives. Participation by functional or product-level managers also provides valuable information for formulating business strategy.[2]

Just as corporate-level strategic planning provides a framework for business-level strategic planning, so business-level strategic planning guides strategic planning at the functional or product level. Figure 3.1 shows this hierarchy of relationships.

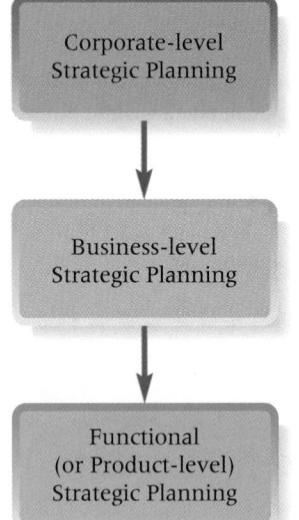

FIGURE 3.1
The Strategic Planning Hierarchy

[1]Philip Kotler, *Marketing Management: Analysis, Planning, Implementation, and Control*, 6th ed. (Englewood Cliffs, N.J.: Prentice-Hall, 1988), pp. 36–49.
[2]Garry D. Smith, Danny R. Arnold, and Bobby G. Bizzell, *Business Strategy and Policy*, 2d ed. (Boston: Houghton Mifflin, 1988), pp. 15–16.

Operations strategic planning is easiest to understand within the context of business-level strategic planning. With this in mind, we discuss business-level strategic planning and examine the relationship between it and operations strategic planning. Our discussion focuses on process (how to plan) as well as content (what to plan for).

# Business-level Strategic Planning[3]

The goal of business-level strategic planning is to effectively relate a business unit or company to its external environment. Thus, the first step in business-level strategic planning is to analyze the company's external environment. A company's external environment has two parts: the industry environment in which it competes and its macroenvironment, the broader economic, social, demographic, political, legal, technological, and global setting of the industry. Although a company has little direct control over its macroenvironment, trends in this area can substantially affect the magnitude of opportunities or threats facing the company. In contrast to a company's macroenvironment, its industry environment consists of elements that directly affect the company, such as competitors, customers, and suppliers. The structure of the industry can strongly influence its competitive rules and the strategies available to a company.

An important task of business managers is to identify opportunities and threats facing the company within its industry. They can do this by analyzing the competitive forces at work in the company's industry environment. Michael Porter of the Harvard Business School has developed a framework to help managers do this. The model views the state of competition in an industry as dependent on five forces:

- The threat of new companies entering the industry
- The threat of substitute products and/or services
- The bargaining power of buyers
- The bargaining power of suppliers
- The rivalry among competitors.

Combined, these forces determine the intensity of competition and profitability within an industry.

Within this framework a weak competitive force may be an opportunity, because it allows a company to earn greater profits; a strong competitive force can be a threat, because it affects profits negatively. Business managers must recognize opportunities and threats and respond with appropriate strategic choices.

An equally important task is assessing the company's internal capabilities. The company must evaluate its strengths and weaknesses and how these factors affect its ability to compete in the marketplace. For example, a strength in a certain area does not automatically translate into a competitive advantage for the company. First, the area may not be important with respect to the company's external environment. Second, even if it is important, competitors may be equally strong in that area. What is important, then, is that the company's strength is relatively greater than its competitors' in a strategically important factor. Such a strength is called a **distinctive competence.** Thus, while two

---

[3]Adapted from Michael E. Porter, "Competitive Strategy: The Core Concepts, " chap. 1 in *Competitive Advantage* (New York: Free Press, 1985), pp. 1–30; and Kotler, "Laying the Groundwork Through Strategic Planning," chap. 2 in *Marketing Management*, pp. 33–64.

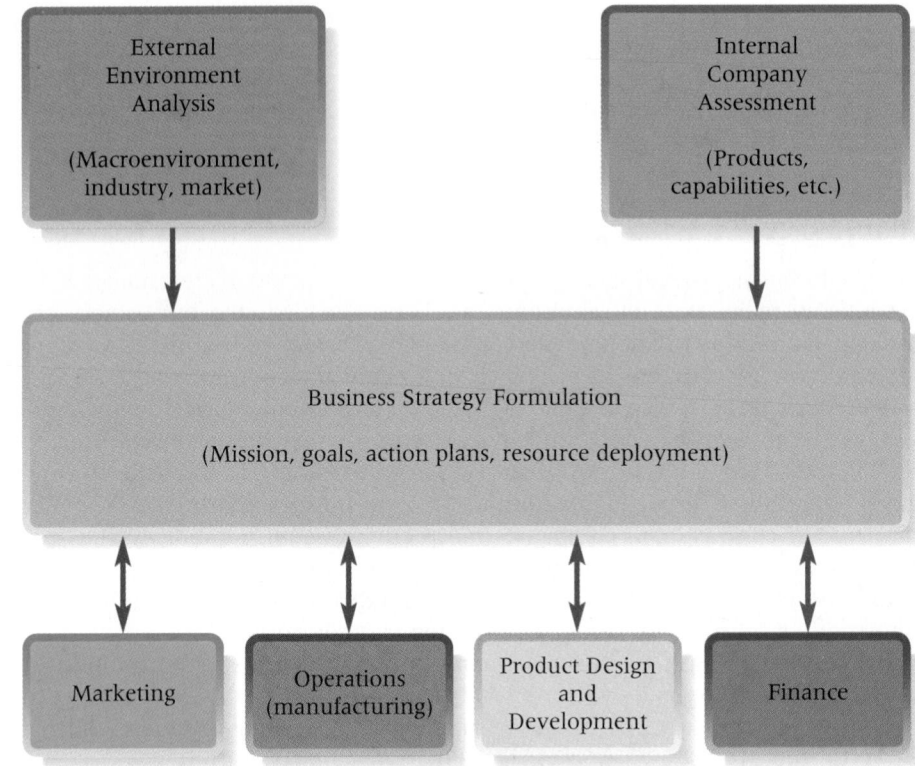

competitors may enjoy low manufacturing costs, the one with the lower costs
has the competitive advantage, assuming that low cost is strategically important
within the industry.

The company does not have to address all its weaknesses (some may be
strategically unimportant) or tout all its strengths (again, some may be strategically unimportant). The larger issue is whether the company should limit itself to
those opportunities it already has the strengths to exploit and seek to become
even stronger in these areas, and/or consider other opportunities, for which it
will have to develop new and different strengths.

Business-level strategic planning begins with an assessment of a company's
external environment and its internal capabilities for competing in that environment. This is graphically depicted in a process model of business-level strategic
planning in Figure 3.2. As part of the business-level strategic planning process a
company develops a broad statement of its values and the role it intends to
assume with respect to its customers, suppliers, competitors, and employees. This
*business mission statement* serves as a general guide for strategic planning. For
example, the mission statement of Kellogg, the famous American food manufacturer, is "Kellogg is a global company committed to building long-term growth in
volume and profit and to enhancing its worldwide leadership position by
providing nutritious food products of superior value."[4]

A company formulates its business strategy so that it is in accord with its basic
mission. The company defines specific objectives and how to achieve them.
Implementation might include companywide action plans, programs, and poli-

[4]Kellogg Company, *Kellogg Company Philosophy* (Battle Creek, Mich.: Kellogg Co., 1992), p. 1.

cies. For example, if one of the company's strategic goals is product quality, top management might implement a companywide total quality management (TQM) program. As noted earlier, the functional or product areas within the company would carry out such plans, programs, and policies (see Figure 3.2).

Business-level strategic planning is also concerned with allocating resources to support the company's strategic goals. Resource deployment is an essential component of business-level strategic planning, because it provides the financial wherewithal for carrying out the action plans, programs, and policies. Thus, resource deployment determines the budgets within which functional areas such as manufacturing must operate.

## Functional Area Involvement in Business-level Strategic Planning

The functional areas of the company are actively involved in implementing its strategic directives. Functional areas are responsible for carrying out the broad programs, policies, and/or action plans that have been formulated to achieve the company's strategic goals. They also are responsible for defining their own strategies and action plans to support these goals and improve functional unit capabilities.

While the marketing and finance departments have played major roles historically in formulating a company's business strategy, this has not been the case for manufacturing. During the 1950s and 1960s the typical company's major emphasis was on growth in sales and market share; executives from marketing and finance—not manufacturing—often dominated top management. Although manufacturing managers typically were responsible for 75 percent of the company's investment, 80 percent of its personnel, and 85 percent or more of its expenditures for materials and equipment, top management often failed to recognize the strategic importance of manufacturing issues.[5]

Since the late 1970s, however, strategic planning experts have recognized participation and involvement of all functional areas as critical to the success of business-level strategic planning. Most experts agree that the strategic planning process should facilitate participation and contribution by all major functional areas within the company (see double-headed arrows in Figure 3.2). Wickham Skinner of the Harvard Business School and other experts in operations management have long touted the importance of **operations strategic planning,** or manufacturing strategic planning, and its integration with strategic planning at the business level. Fortunately, more and more companies are realizing the critical contribution that operations strategic planning can make to the overall competitiveness of a company. Because many capabilities with the greatest competitive value reside in a company's manufacturing organization, business strategy must become much more explicit about, and reliant on, manufacturing considerations.[6]

## The Generic Business Strategies

The essence of business-level strategic planning is to take offensive or defensive actions to create a defendable or advantageous position within an industry in

[5]Wickham Skinner, *Manufacturing in the Corporate Strategy* (New York: Wiley, 1978), p. 4.
[6]Robert H. Hayes and Gary P. Pisano, "Beyond World-Class: The New Manufacturing Strategy," *Harvard Business Review* 72 (January–February 1994): 86.

order to successfully cope with the five competitive forces and thereby realize a superior return on investment for the company. Obviously, a company might pursue many different strategies. However, at the broadest level two basic types of strategies, called *generic strategies*, enable a company to outperform its industry competitors: cost leadership and differentiation.[7]

The first strategy is achieving **cost leadership** within the industry. Important components of this strategy include aggressively constructing efficient-scale facilities; emphasizing operating efficiency; vigorously controlling and reducing costs and overhead, particularly in such areas as research and development (R&D), service, sales force, and advertising; and avoiding marginal customer accounts. Under this strategy company managers devote a great deal of attention to reducing costs, although they do not ignore quality, service, and other areas.

The second generic strategy, **differentiation,** is for the company to differentiate its product or service by creating a product or service that is recognized industrywide as unique and able to command a premium price because of the uniqueness of its attribute(s). Such products include the Ferrari Testarosa, Rolex watches, and Dom Perignon champagne. Company managers devote much attention to product differentiation, although they do not ignore cost reduction. The approach the company might choose for differentiating its products from those of competitors may include one or more of the following: quality, brand image, superior performance, innovative technology, reliability, many features or options, superb customer service, superior accessibility to product, and rapid delivery.

Research has shown that the generic strategies of differentiation and cost are not mutually exclusive—a company can pursue them simultaneously. The consensus is that generic strategies are actually dimensions along which a company can score high or low. For example, a recent study of the furniture industry found that 28 percent of the companies studied classified themselves as pursuing strategies that emphasized only differentiation; 51 percent classified themselves as placing primary emphasis on differentiation and secondary emphasis on cost; 14 percent identified their strategies as placing primary emphasis on cost and secondary emphasis on differentiation, and 3 percent stated they pursued a strategy of cost leadership.[8]

Whether a company pursues a strategy of differentiation, cost, or some combination thereof, it must determine the specific combination of elements, objectives, or priorities that define its strategy, or *strategic positioning*, within its industry or industry segment. Within the framework of the generic strategies a strategic element, objective, or priority is a competitive ability that the company is seeking to acquire, sustain, or improve upon to allow it to differentiate itself relative to its competitors' and/or to lower its costs relative to its competitors'. Table 3.1 lists competitive abilities a company might select in defining its strategic position and gives the average of each item's strategic importance (on a scale of 1 to 7, where 1 = least importance and 7 = most importance) for the sixty-five companies participating in the furniture study cited earlier. Operations Manage-

---

[7]Porter, *Competitive Advantage,* pp. 15–16. Porter also defines a third generic strategy, called *focus,* which means finding a niche within an industry. However, the basic types of competitive advantage are low cost and differentiation, regardless of whether a company's scope of competitive activity is narrow or broad.

[8]Shawnee K. Vickery, Cornelia Droge, and Robert E. Markland, "Production Competence and Business Strategy: Do They Affect Business Performance?" *Decision Sciences* 24 (March–April 1993): 435–456.

| Strategic Element | Average Strategic Importance (1 to 7 scale) |
|---|---|
| Company reputation | 6.6 |
| Quality (conformance to specs) | 6.4 |
| Delivery dependability | 6.3 |
| Postsale customer service | 6.1 |
| Responsiveness to target markets | 6.0 |
| Low production cost | 6.0 |
| Personal sales proficiency | 5.9 |
| Delivery speed | 5.9 |
| New product development | 5.8 |
| Design quality/innovation | 5.8 |
| Presale customer service | 5.6 |
| Product durability | 5.5 |
| Production lead time | 5.5 |
| Target market identification and selection | 5.5 |
| Widespread distribution coverage | 5.5 |
| Product reliability | 5.5 |
| Product improvement | 5.3 |
| Brand image | 5.3 |
| New product introduction | 5.3 |
| Broad product line | 5.2 |
| Product development cycle time | 5.1 |
| Volume flexibility | 5.1 |
| Competitive pricing | 4.9 |
| Selective distribution | 4.9 |
| Process flexibility | 4.8 |
| Advertising/promotion | 4.7 |
| Low cost distribution | 4.6 |
| Product flexibility | 4.0 |
| Product technological innovation | 3.5 |
| Low price | 2.8 |
| Original product development | 2.6 |

*Adapted from Shawnee K. Vickery, Cornelia Droge, and Robert E. Markland, "Production Competence and Business Strategy: Do They Affect Business Performance?" *Decision Sciences* 24, (March–April 1993): 435–456.

ment in Practice 3.1 describes the strategic positioning of one company in the furniture industry.

The ultimate purpose of strategic positioning is to focus an organization's resources, capabilities, and energies on building a sustainable advantage over its competitors in one or more areas. Such an advantage may derive, for example, from lower cost, from higher product performance, from more innovative products, or from superior service. This does not mean that a company's competitors will not occasionally match or better its competitive position for a short period of time by acquiring new technology, establishing production in a low-cost location, or moving rapidly to exploit a narrow window of market opportunity. But if the goal is to develop a sustainable competitive advantage, a company's efforts must be directed at developing specific organizational competencies and relationships that are difficult for competitors to match.

# Strategic Positioning at Haskell of Pittsburgh

Haskell of Pittsburgh is an autonomous manufacturer (privately held company) of steel office furniture that employs 450 people and has annual sales of approximately $38 million. Historically, Haskell of Pittsburgh targeted its products for purchasers in the middle price range, who were basically insensitive to furniture design.

However, in recent years a sensitivity to design entered the high-price end of the market, and the steel office furniture industry developed a strong sense that successful manufacturers are in either the high-price end of the market, which is design sensitive, or in the budget end of the market, which is design insensitive. That meant that companies targeting the mid-price range felt a lot of pressure to move up or down. Many of Haskell of Pittsburgh's competitors in the mid-price market moved up to compete with such industry leaders as Steelcase and Herman Miller. Others moved down, distributing their products through wholesalers and competing against such low-cost giants as HON Industries.

But during this period Haskell of Pittsburgh detected a new trend: Customers in the mid-price range were becoming design sensitive. Haskell of Pittsburgh made the bold decision to stay in the mid-price range but offer furniture that would appeal to design-sensitive consumers.

The strategy significantly influenced the way Haskell of Pittsburgh produces and distributes its products. The company changed from being a high-volume producer of standard furniture to a low-volume producer of a broad and highly customized product line. Because the distribution channel for the latter is entirely different from the former, the company's distribution channel also changed drastically. Haskell of Pittsburgh now sells its furniture through design-oriented retailers that work closely with independent interior designers, architects, and specifiers.

The gamble has paid off handsomely for Haskell of Pittsburgh, which now is one of the few manufacturers of design-sensitive, mid-priced steel office furniture. Many of the company's former competitors that had scrambled to move up or down have declared bankruptcy. Nevertheless, Haskell of Pittsburgh recognizes that it will have to become increasingly cost conscious to remain competitive within its niche; it intends to eventually become the low-cost producer of design-sensitive steel office furniture for the mid-price range.

In pursuing its strategy Haskell of Pittsburgh emphasizes product flexibility, process flexibility, delivery reliability, product durability, target market identification and selection, responsiveness to target markets, selective distribution coverage, the selling proficiency of its independent sales force, and the company's reputation.

Many companies around the world have become household names because of their success in doing this: Hewlett-Packard has become synonymous with innovation and Toyota with reliable automobiles. Which business functions a company decides to emphasize depends on the competitive advantage it is trying to attain. For example, Caterpillar's enduring reputation for dependability is based both on product design and on the logistics system that services its independent dealers.[9]

## Operations Strategic Planning

**Operations strategy** is a collective pattern of choices that determines the structure, resources, and infrastructure of the operations system and is directed toward supporting business-level strategies. As noted earlier, a company's business strategy provides the context in which it develops and formulates its

[9]Robert H. Hayes, Steven C. Wheelwright, and Kim Clark, *Dynamic Manufacturing* (New York: Free Press, 1988), p. 20.

*The Hallmark Desk (left) is representative of Haskell of Pittsburgh's older product lines. The System One Workplaces Table Group (right) demonstrates the aesthetic appeal and flexibility of Haskell of Pittsburgh's newer, more design-sensitive furniture. This product can be easily reconfigured for spur-of-the-moment team meetings.*

*Caterpillar products are known for their dependability.*

operations strategy. More specific, the company's business strategy conveys to operations the strategic objectives that constitute the basis upon which the company is competing. The strategic objectives for which operations is responsible, in whole or in part, are called *operations competitive priorities* (quality of design, delivery speed, low production cost) and provide the starting point for making strategic choices in operations. As described in Preview to Operations Management, there are seven major categories in which strategic choices are made:

Product or service planning
Process design and technology management
Long-range capacity planning and facility location
Quality management
Manufacturing or service organization
Human resource management
Operations planning and control

Strategic decision making in these seven categories should entail consideration of the competitive priorities for operations and their relative importance. Figure 3.3, a graphic representation of a process model of operations (manufacturing) strategic planning, in relation to business-level strategic planning, illustrates this. The strategic choices made by operations govern the scope of its activities and how operations will deploy its resources. Operations strategic planning also provides valuable information for business-level strategic planning (note the arrows in Figure 3.3).

Once the company has established its operations competitive priorities, it must set specific, measurable goals in relation to current performance for each of them. Usually this is done on an annual basis. Examples of measurable goals for a given set of competitive priorities are

Quality of conformance: Reduce the percentage of defective products from 0.01 to 0.001.
Delivery speed: Reduce order lead time from six weeks to two weeks.
Delivery Reliability: Increase the percentage of orders delivered on time from 95 percent to 100 percent.
Process Flexibility: Reduce set-up time from one hour to fifteen minutes on critical production lines.

After strategic choices have been made, the next stage is implementation. Implementation commonly involves projects and programs designed to ensure that strategic decisions are carried out. Projects and programs are tactical, so a company must evaluate their effectiveness regularly to determine whether they should be changed. Another important aspect of implementation is drawing up and adopting specific and appropriate budgets for operations projects and programs and adhering to them carefully.

The final stage in operations strategic planning is measuring and assessing operations performance. The operations unit must measure its performance on each competitive priority (reliability of delivery measured by the percentage of orders shipped on time) and communicate the results to management. This stage identifies operations' strengths and weaknesses, especially in relationship to the company's business strategy. Feedback on the performance of the operations unit provides important information for correcting tactics and planning business strategies. For example, if operations has great strength in an important area

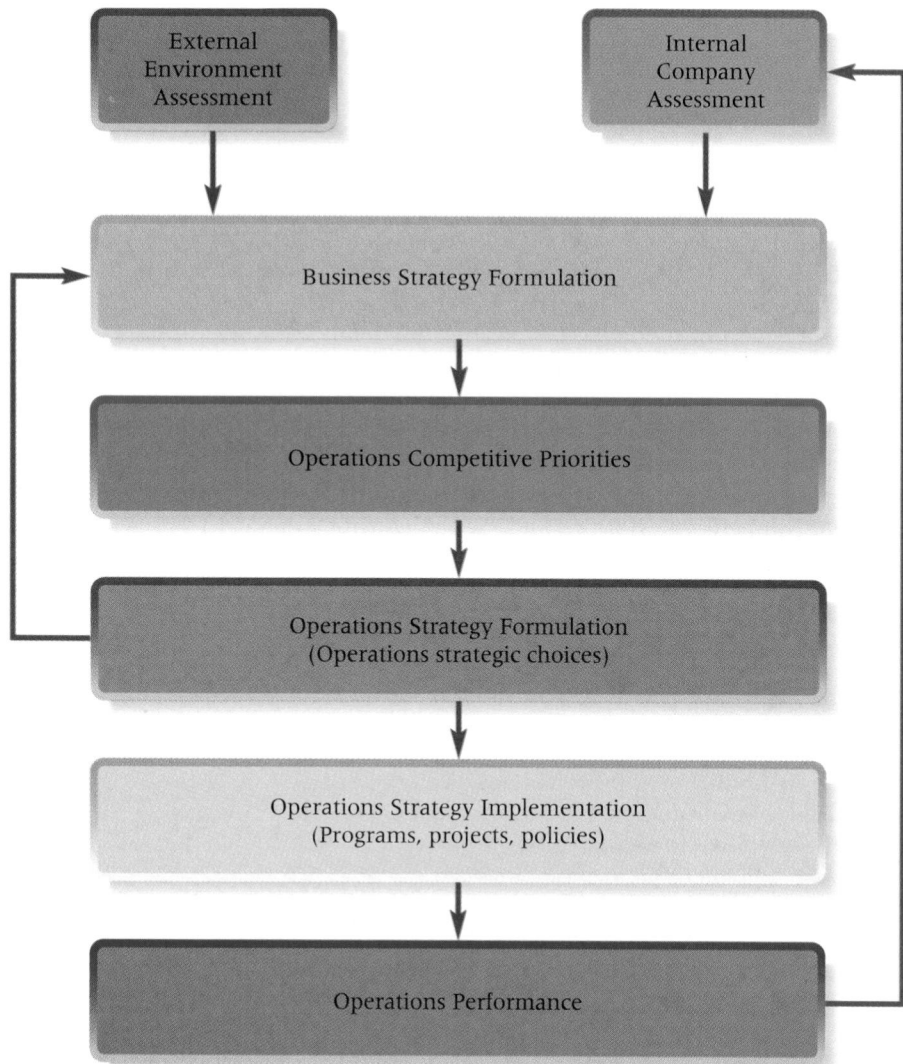

FIGURE 3.3
A Process Model of
Operations (Manufacturing)
Strategic Planning

*Adapted from Shawnee K. Vickery,
"A Theory of Production Competence
Revisited," *Decision Sciences* 22,
(May–June 1991): 635–643.

relative to major competitors (distinctive competence), that strength may influence how the company will compete in the future.

## Operations as a Competitive Weapon

The process model of operations strategic planning shows how important operations is in supporting and implementing a company's business strategy. It also shows the criticality of the information that operations provides to business-level strategic planning. However, if operations is to become a competitive weapon, it must become visible and proactive in defining the competitive advantage that the company will pursue. Top management must consult with operations to get its perspective on (1) the major issues facing the business, (2) the strategies that other functional areas or departments are proposing and (3) the options open to operations. Also, operations must clearly communicate to top management the constraints under which it operates and the capabilities it can exploit. Furthermore, operations must seek collaborative relationships with other departments. In summary, operations must share equally with other functions in defining the company's business strategy as well as in implementing it.

## Operations Competitive Priorities

As discussed earlier, the company's business strategy conveys to operations the strategic objectives that form the basis upon which the company is competing. The strategic objectives for which operations is primarily responsible are termed **operations competitive priorities.** The competitive priorities for operations include low manufacturing cost, product flexibility, volume flexibility, design quality, product reliability, quality of conformance, customer service, new product introduction, delivery dependability, and delivery speed. Table 3.2 offers an expanded list of operations competitive priorities and their definitions.

The **Manufacturing Futures Survey,** an ongoing research study by collaborating universities and researchers, has reported a wealth of information about the competitive priorities and manufacturing strategies of its respondents, which include Japanese manufacturers, American manufacturers, and European manufacturers of machinery and electronic, consumer, industrial, and basic

T A B L E  3 . 2
Competitive Priorities for Operations

**Product flexibility (customization):** The ability to handle difficult, nonstandard orders, to meet special customer specifications, and to produce products characterized by numerous features, options, sizes, and/or colors

**Volume flexibility:** The ability to rapidly adjust capacity in order to accelerate or decelerate production in response to changes in customer demand

**Process flexibility (product mix flexibility):** The ability to produce small quantities of product cost efficiently so that product mix changes are easy to accommodate

**Low production cost:** The ability to minimize the total cost of production (inclusive of labor, materials, and operating costs) through efficient operations, process technology, and/or scale economies

**New product introduction:** The ability to rapidly introduce large numbers of product improvements/variations or totally new products

**Delivery speed:** The ability to reduce the time between order taking and customer delivery to as close to zero as possible

**Delivery dependability:** The ability to exactly meet quoted or anticipated delivery dates and quantities

**Production lead time:** The ability to reduce the time it takes to manufacture products

**Product reliability:** The ability to lengthen the time to product failure or malfunction

**Product durability:** The ability to maximize the life of the product

**Quality (conformance to specifications):** The ability to manufacture a product with operating characteristics that meet established performance standards

**Design quality (design innovation):** The ability to provide a product with capabilities, features, styling, and/or operating characteristics (performance) that are either superior to those of competing products or unavailable in competing products

**Postsale customer service:** The ability to service the customer after the sale of the product to ensure continuing customer satisfaction

T A B L E   3 . 3
Rankings of Competitive
Priorities from
Manufacturing Futures
Survey (1992)

| Competitive Ability | Rank | | |
|---|---|---|---|
| | U.S. | Europe | Japan |
| Conformance quality | 1 | 1 | 4 |
| Reliability/Durability | 2 | 2 | 1 |
| On-time delivery | 3 | 3 | 6 |
| Performance quality | 4 | 7 | 2 |
| Low price | 5 | 5 | 7 |
| Product support | 6 | 8 | 15 |
| Fast delivery | 7 | 4 | 5 |
| New product introduction | 8 | 6 | 11 |
| Broad product line | 9 | 12 | 8 |
| After-sales service | 10 | 10 | 10 |
| Customization | 11 | 9 | 3 |
| Rapid design change | 12 | 11 | 9 |
| Product mix flexibility | 13 | 13 | 13 |
| Broad distribution | 14 | 15 | 14 |
| Volume flexibility | 15 | 14 | 12 |

Courtesy of Jeffrey G. Miller and Jay S. Kim, Boston University.

goods.[10] Table 3.3 lists the top competitive priorities by rank for U.S., European, and Japanese manufacturers for 1992. Note that conformance quality, reliability/durability, and on-time delivery were the top three priorities of U.S. and European companies, whereas Japanese companies ranked reliability/ durability first, performance quality second, and customization (product flexibility) third.

In general Japanese companies consider quality, dependability (delivery), cost, and flexibility as priorities to be addressed *sequentially* over time rather than conflicting strategic goals. The Japanese believe that a company must achieve a minimum level of quality before it can offer dependability and minimum levels of quality and dependability before it can be cost efficient.[11] Because most Japanese manufacturers have achieved outstanding levels of quality, dependability, and cost efficiency, they are now concentrating on flexibility or speed of response. Operations Management in Practice 3.2 describes the competitive priorities of Meiji Seika Kaisha, Ltd., a Japanese pharmaceutical manufacturer.

## Strategic Operations Choices

Once a company establishes competitive priorities for operations, the operations unit must configure itself in a way that achieves, and continually enhances, the competitive advantage the company is seeking. This requires a series of coordinated decisions, or **operations strategic choices.** These decisions can be structural or infrastructural in nature. Structural decisions focus on facilities and

[10]Arnoud De Meyer, Jinichiro Nakane, Jeffrey G. Miller, and Kasra Ferdows, "Flexibility: The Next Competitive Battle—The Manufacturing Futures Survey," *Strategic Management Journal* 10 (March–April 1989): 135–144.

[11]J. Nakane, *Manufacturing Futures Survey in Japan: A Comparative Survey, 1983–1986* (Tokyo: System Science Institute, Waseda University, May 1986).

# Competitive Priorities at Meiji Seika Kaisha, Ltd. (Pharmaceutical Manufacturing at Odawara)

Meiji Seika Kaisha, Ltd., began as a manufacturer of biscuits and caramels in 1916 and soon became Japan's foremost maker of chocolates and other sweets. Over the years the company diversified into a wider range of food production, including canned foods. In 1946 Meiji Seika used its expertise in fermentation to diversify further, into the manufacture of antibiotics. Today, the company is Japan's leading manufacturer of antibiotics (Augmentin, Meicelin) and enjoys international acclaim for the high quality of its products.

Developing new products is extremely important to Meiji Seika. Building on its pioneering fermentation technology, the company is applying it to materials synthesis and to genetic engineering to develop a wide range of new products. The substantial costs associated with Meiji Seika's extensive research and development mean that its products must recover those expenditures and it is always under pressure to reduce costs. Although 80 percent of Meiji Seika's sales come from antibiotics, intense global competition has made them less profitable. Also, pharmaceutical prices are regulated by the Japanese government, which has mandated a 10 percent price reduction every year from 1980 to 1990.

Because its market is so competitive, Meiji Seika has invested heavily in research and development, production, and marketing, and has strengthened its organization to improve operations. By 1990 the company had also expanded its global operations by exporting its products to sixty countries and by selling its technology through joint ventures overseas. Meiji Seika's annual pharmaceutical sales were about 60 billion Yen ($400 million) in 1990.

One of the company's major pharmaceutical manufacturing facilities is located in Odawara. The major products manufactured at the Odawara plant are antibiotics, digestive enzymes, anti-inflammatory drugs and analgesics, and disinfectants. This plant's top competitive priorities are the ability to develop new products, quality, cost, sales, and delivery. Quality and cost are key priorities because of the difficulty of new product development and the government's control of prices.

Quality management is the basis for operations at the Odawara plant. Product safety and reliability are most important. The plant uses product testing (sampling), storage of samples, periodic inspection and tuning of equipment and scales, proper validation of the production process, maintenance of product records by production lot, quality checks at each production stage, and the collection and analysis of customer claims to maintain quality and continuously improve what it is doing. Most of Meiji Seika's production lines are automated, but the current level of automation does not eliminate defective products. The company's long-range planning includes greater automation to eliminate the manufacture of defective products and allow it to maintain consistent quality and high (and consistent) levels of production.

Meiji Seika has several strategies for reducing cost. The company anticipates that additional automation and the use of part-time workers will cut its full-time work force by 20 percent by 1995. It expects to reduce its costs for materials by using imported materials instead of domestic and to reduce energy costs by operating in shifts to increase efficiency and by decreasing its air conditioning in a certain manufacturing room when it is not in use.

equipment and typically require highly visible capital investments. These decisions include

- How much total capacity to provide, how that capacity should be broken up into specific facilities, and where the facilities should be located
- What production or service processes, equipment, and technologies to provide within those facilities

In contrast, infrastructure refers to the people, policies, and systems that determine how the facilities and equipment are managed:

- Product or service planning—forecasting demand for products or services, new product (or service) development processes
- Human resource policies and practices—staffing and training policies and systems that measure and reward performance
- Quality—policies and systems that promote quality
- Operations systems—operations planning and control systems
- Organization design or organizational structure[12]

All these decisions fall into seven **strategic operations decision categories,** which are set forth in Figure 3.4 and structure the organization of this book. In the section that follows we describe each category and how it relates to achieving operations competitive priorities.

But before we examine the categories, we must note that operations plays a significant, but not major, role in an *eighth* strategic decision category. Decision

[12]Peter T. Ward, G. Keong Leong, and David L. Snyder, "Manufacturing Strategy: An Overview of Currect Process and Content Models," in *Manufacturing Strategy: The Research Agenda for the Next Decade, Proceedings of the Joint Industry University Conference on Manufacturing Strategy,* ed. J. E. Ettlie, M. C. Burnstein, and A. Fiegenbaum (Ann Arbor, Mich.: January, 1990), pp. 189–199.

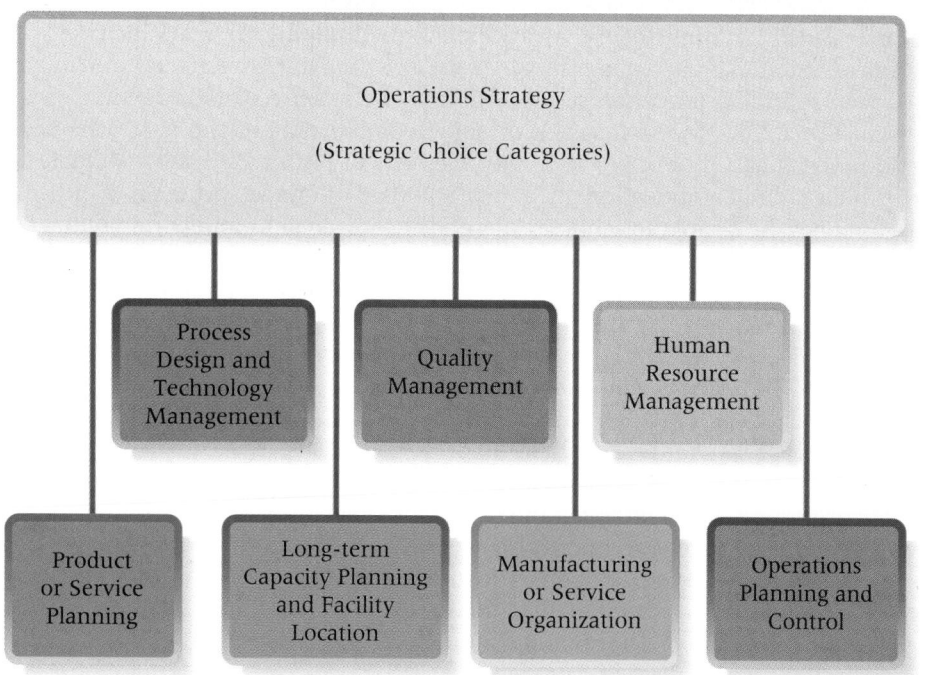

FIGURE 3.4
Strategic Operations Decision Categories

making in this category determines which materials, systems, and services a company should produce or provide internally, which it should buy from outside sources, and the kind of relationships the company should establish with its suppliers and members of its distribution channel. Although operations managers play key roles and are actively involved in these strategic choices, decision making in this category transcends the boundaries of the operations unit. In view of this, we will examine this category later, in the section titled Vertical Linkages: The Value Chain Revisited.

# Categories of Strategic Operations Decisions
## Product or Service Planning

Most companies must continuously plan their products or services in order to respond to and anticipate customers' needs, wants and desires. The importance of product or service planning is heightened by such factors as intense national and global competition, expiration of patents, and rapid technological innovation within an industry.

Developing new products for existing markets, developing original products that create entirely new markets, improving existing products, devising innova- tive product technologies, developing and introducing new products rapidly, and offering a broad product line are some of the ways a company can strategically position itself with respect to its products or services. In certain industries a company's competitive edge from one or more of these factors may determine its long-term survival as well as its short-term success. In the furniture industry study we cited earlier, several of these items were given high strategic importance ratings (see Table 3.1).

## Process Design and Technology Management

*Process design* pertains to the arrangement or grouping of manufacturing (or service) resources (machinery, labor). As we discussed in Chapter 1, a fundamental decision regarding process design is whether the resources of production will be product-focused, process-focused, or some combination of the two. Chapter 1 also noted that a product-focused arrangement of resources is most suitable for the high-volume production of a few standard products, whereas a process- focused design is most suitable for manufacturing small to moderate volumes of a wide range of custom products.

The choice of design for a process is closely related to production volumes and the degree to which a company's products are standardized. A model, called the **product process matrix,** depicts the relationship of these variables and appears in Figure 3.5. Note that the diagonal of the matrix represents suitable matches between type of production operation, relative to production volume, and degree of standardization. The experts who devised the model argue that production systems that fall off the diagonal shown in Figure 3.5 have flow patterns and product volume/standardization characteristics that do not match, which can hinder company performance.

*Process technology* pertains to the actual method used to transform raw materials, purchased components, and/or informational inputs into finished goods and services, whether manual, automatic, or mental. In most cases a range

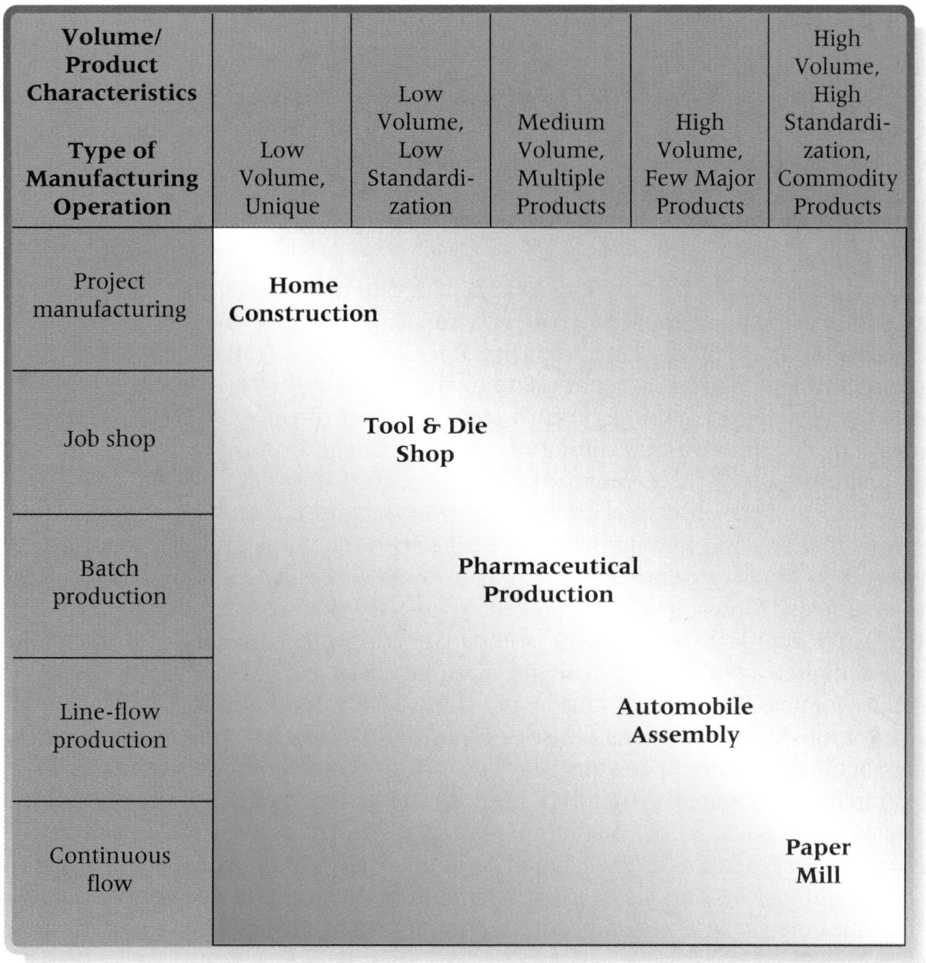

FIGURE 3.5
The Product Process Matrix

| Volume/ Product Characteristics / Type of Manufacturing Operation | Low Volume, Unique | Low Volume, Low Standardi- zation | Medium Volume, Multiple Products | High Volume, Few Major Products | High Volume, High Standardi- zation, Commodity Products |
|---|---|---|---|---|---|
| Project manufacturing | **Home Construction** | | | | |
| Job shop | | **Tool & Die Shop** | | | |
| Batch production | | | **Pharmaceutical Production** | | |
| Line-flow production | | | | **Automobile Assembly** | |
| Continuous flow | | | | | **Paper Mill** |

of technologies is available for defining a specific process; each has advantages and disadvantages. In selecting the appropriate technology an operations manager must weigh the advantages and disadvantages of each in light of the company's competitive priorities.

New operations technologies available to companies include fixed and programmable automation, industrial robots, flexible manufacturing systems (FMS), computer-integrated manufacturing (CIM), electronic data interchange (EDI), and bar coding. We introduce and discuss these technologies in Chapter 8.

New operations technologies often enable a company to improve its competitive stance with respect to quality, service, flexibility, and/or cost. Consider programmable automation, an automatic process that can be reprogrammed to handle different components or products. Programmable automation provides a company with the ability to change its product mix rapidly so that it can manufacture small quantities of many different products at costs much lower than would otherwise be possible. Thus, programmable automation facilitates product and process flexibility, low production cost, competitive pricing, and a broad product line.

# Long-range Capacity Planning and Facility Location[13]

Long-range planning for capacity involves the size and timing of changes in capacity in relation to changing demands; facility location is concerned with where operations capacity will be located. Both involve making structural choices that have long-term consequences with respect to a company's ability to compete. The discussions that follow introduce these topics from a strategic perspective; Chapter 6 treats long-range capacity planning and facility location in detail.

*Capacity decisions* and *capacity strategies* are different animals. Authorization of a request to expand capacity triggers a capacity decision; the formulating of a capacity strategy places each capacity decision in the context of a long-term sequence of such decisions that relate to the company's overall strategic plan. In the simplest terms manufacturing's strategic view of capacity is its philosophy regarding the amount and timing of capacity changes in response to changes in demand in light of the company's strategic goals.

One example of a capacity strategy is maintaining a *capacity cushion,* which means building and maintaining extra capacity so that it is available as soon as it is needed. Another capacity strategy is to build a *negative cushion,* which means the company is more likely to run out of capacity than to have unused capacity. The latter approach provides the company with a high capacity utilization rate and a higher average return on its manufacturing investment than would be otherwise possible. Such a policy may lead to a slow deterioration in a company's market position, but it can also support cost-oriented strategic goals (low production cost, low price, competitive pricing). Ford Motor Co. is an excellent example of a company that has used the negative cushion successfully. Still another approach is to attempt to match, as nearly as possible, a company's production capacity to its anticipated demand. Many companies use this strategy.

Location decisions also can provide substantial support for the company's strategic objectives. Several important criteria for selecting a business location are

Access to markets or distribution centers
Access to suppliers and resources
Community amenities and government regulations
Competitive considerations
Environmental considerations
Interaction with the rest of the corporation
Availability and cost and/or skill of labor
Attractiveness of the site
Taxes and financing
Transportation
Utilities and services

For example, LUI, a make-to-order manufacturer of laminated office furniture, located one of its two production facilities on the West Coast for the sole purpose of increasing its access to markets. LUI managers felt that having a West Coast presence was critical to developing and penetrating local markets.

The third major consideration in developing an integrated capacity and facilities strategy is the degree of specialization characterizing a manufacturing

[13]Robert H. Hayes and Steven C. Wheelwright, *Restoring Our Competitive Edge: Competing Through Manufacturing* (New York: Wiley, 1984), 46–117.

or service facility. A closely related concept is **factory focus,** the notion that a factory—or any organization—will perform better with a narrow, clearly defined set of tasks or priorities than with a broad, somewhat ambiguous set of tasks.[14] Whatever its competitive priorities, a manufacturing or service unit is better able to succeed with few objectives than with many, perhaps inconsistent, objectives.

Researchers have observed at least six ways to focus a plant: by market, by product, by volume, by process, by product and market, and by geography. Determining which of these (or which combination) is most appropriate for a given organization is central to developing an integrated strategy for capacity and facilities.

## Quality Management

As the 1992 rankings for performance quality, reliability/durability, and conformance quality of European, North American, and Japanese companies indicate, quality is a fundamental competitive priority worldwide. Conformance quality and reliability/durability were the top two priorities for European and North American companies, whereas reliability/durability and performance quality were the top two priorities for Japanese companies (see Table 3.3).

Quality management encompasses the strategies, programs, methods, and organizational culture that a company uses to achieve its quality objectives. For example, Japanese companies have used companywide total quality management programs for many years to reach the levels of quality for which they are renowned worldwide. The entire culture of a Japanese organization is directed at fostering quality with a view to continuous improvement, called *kaizen* in Japanese. Chapters 7 and 19 examine the related topics of quality management and quality analysis, measurement, and improvement.

## Manufacturing or Service Organization

The way in which a manufacturing or service unit is organized has important strategic implications. European companies that participated in the Manufacturing Futures Survey included reorganization of manufacturing in their top ten action plans. Increasingly, companies are recognizing the critical effects of organizational structure on their ability to compete and are moving to create the structure they need. Organizational structure can positively affect priorities related to quality, cost, service, and flexibility. Chapter 9 covers manufacturing or service organization in greater detail.

## Human Resource Management

Another area of critical strategic importance is human resource management. World-class competitors place great emphasis on training and motivating their work forces. Japanese, North American, and European manufacturers consider education their most important motivational tool, although European manufacturers also emphasize financial incentives. Human resource issues that appeared in the top ten action plans in the Manufacturing Futures Survey were direct

---

[14]Wickham Skinner, "The Focused Factory," *Harvard Business Review* 52 (May–June 1974): 113–121, and *Manufacturing in the Corporate Strategy,* pp. 69–80.

labor motivation, supervisor training, worker safety, and horizontal job enlargement (giving workers a broader range of tasks). A motivated and highly trained work force can be a major asset for achieving all of a company's strategic objectives. A key attribute of world-class competitors is innovative human resource management that encourages excellence, teamwork, and fast attainment of new skills and rewards employees for their direct contributions.[15] Chapter 9 provides a comprehensive review of human resource management.

## Operations Planning and Control

A major portion of this textbook is devoted to operations planning and control systems (see Chapters 10 to 19). These systems are important components of a company's manufacturing infrastructure. Although they are tactical in nature, they have critical strategic implications. For example, the Japanese have used just-in-time production systems to achieve phenomenal success with respect to responding to customers, reducing manufacturing costs (by dramatically reducing manufacturing lead times and inventory levels), increasing delivery speed, and improving delivery dependability. U.S. companies have successfully used hybrid MRP/JIT systems to achieve these same goals. Also, shop-floor control systems have been instrumental in enabling companies to reduce manufacturing lead times and costs and to provide their customers with better delivery service.

## Vertical Linkages: The Value Chain Revisited[16]

Chapter 1 introduced the value chain. The value chain consists of value activities that are interrelated by linkages between the way one value activity is performed and cost or performance of another value activity. For example, how a company procures its raw materials has a direct bearing on the cost of its finished products and the efficiency of its production line. Note too that such relationships exist not only *within* a company's value chain but also *between* a company's value chain and the value chains of its suppliers and the members of its distribution channel (wholesalers, distributors, retailers, transportation carriers, warehouses). The latter are called *vertical linkages*. The performance of a supplier or channel member affects the cost and/or performance of a company's activities and vice versa.

Consider, for example, a company's suppliers. They provide products or services that the company uses in its value chain. The suppliers' value chains interact with the company's value chain in multiple ways (the company's procurement department interacts with the suppliers' order-entry system). Such linkages provide opportunities for the company to enhance its competitive positioning and for its suppliers to benefit as well. A company might accomplish this by influencing the configuration of its suppliers' value chains to jointly optimize the performance of certain activities and/or by improving the coordination between its value chain and its suppliers' chains. The key point is that the company's relationship with its suppliers can be one in which *both* gain; one need not gain at the expense of the other. Xerox, for example, provides its suppliers with computer access to its manufacturing schedule. This enables its suppliers to

---

[15]Craig Giffi, Aleda V. Roth, Gregory M. Seal, *Competing in World-Class Manufacturing: America's 21st Century Challenge* (Homewood, Ill.: Business One–Irwin, 1990), p. 204.
[16]Adapted from Porter, *Competitive Advantage*, chap. 2.

ship parts precisely when Xerox needs them and provides Xerox's suppliers with the information they need to effectively plan production.

Note that distribution channel members' relationships with companies are similar to suppliers' relationships with companies. Channel members have value chains through which a company's product passes. Channel members perform activities such as sales, advertising, and retail display that may substitute for or complement the company's activities in these areas. A company's value chain and its channel members' chains have many points of contact: selling, order entry, shipping, and so on. Coordinating and jointly optimizing the activities of the company and its channel members can improve the competitive positioning of both.

## Vertical Integration and Outsourcing

Vertical linkages, like linkages within a company's value chain, are frequently overlooked. Even if these relationships are recognized, independent suppliers or channel members or a history of adversarial relationships can impede the coordination and/or collaborative optimization of performance necessary to generate mutual benefits. Sometimes, coordinating and optimizing vertical linkages with coalition partners or subsidiaries is easier than with independent companies; thus, some companies may vertically integrate (either backward, by increasing its control of suppliers, or forward, by increasing control of its distribution channel members) to improve coordination or optimize performance. Wal-Mart, for example, uses its own fleet of trucks to achieve its strategic objective of rapidly replenishing inventory.[17]

Nevertheless, new management approaches and new information technologies (electronic data interchange) are making it easier for companies to coordinate their activities with the activities of their independent suppliers and channel members and to collaboratively optimize performance. The result is that outsourcing is becoming more common in many industries. For example, Ford Motor Co. typically outsources everything but its core technologies (transmissions, engines, vehicle assembly).

Whether the effect of vertical integration (or outsourcing) on a company's ability to compete is positive or negative depends on the individual company, the activity involved, and the industry setting. What is more important, however, is the way in which vertical linkages are *managed*, regardless of whether the relationship is with an outside supplier or in-house division. This important topic is addressed next.

## Supply Chain Management[18]

The **supply chain** is the connected series of value activities that is concerned with the planning, coordinating, and controlling of materials, parts, and finished products from suppliers to the final customer. Figure 3.6 illustrates the supply chain. It has two distinct flows: materials and information. The supply chain spans the value chains of the manufacturing or service company, its suppliers,

---

[17]George Stalk, Philip Evans, and Lawrence E. Shulman, "Competing on Capabilities: The New Rules of Corporate Strategy," *Harvard Business Review* 70 (March–April 1992): 58.

[18]Adapted from Graham Stevens, "Integrating the Supply Chain," *International Journal of Physical Distribution and Materials Management* 19 (No. 8, 1989): 3–8; and John B. Houlihan, "International Supply Chain Management," *International Journal of Physical Distribution and Materials Management* 15 (No. 1, 1985): 22–38.

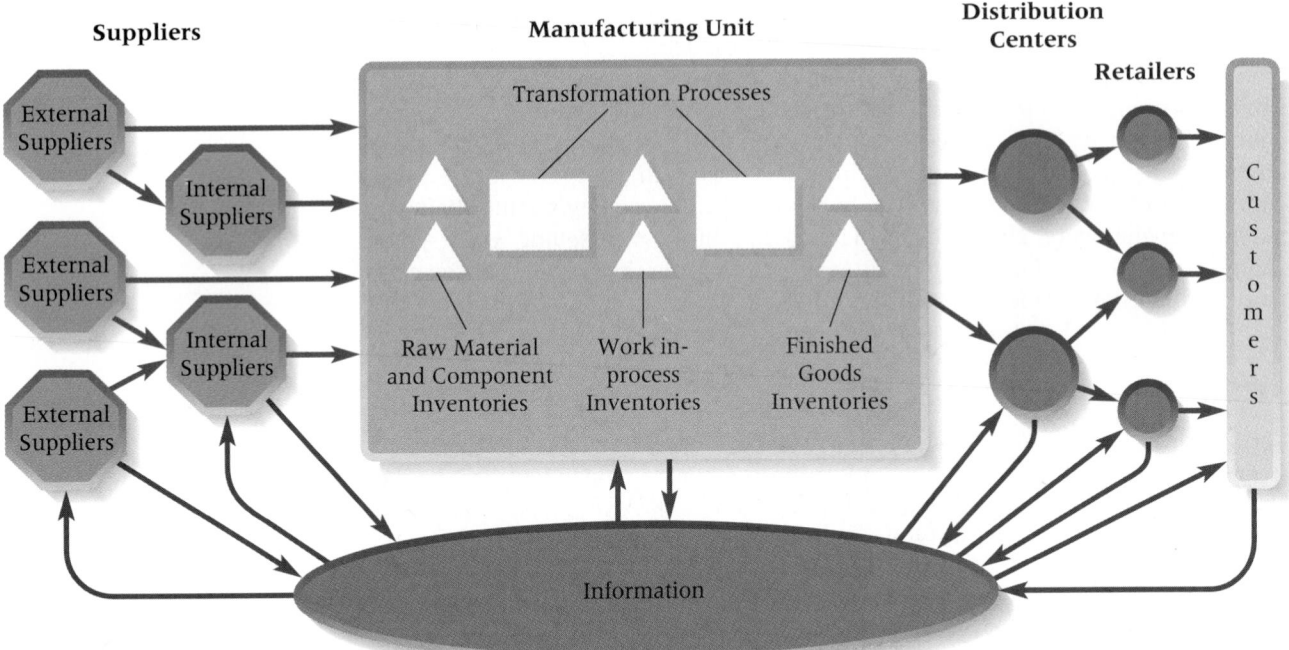

FIGURE 3.6
The Supply Chain

and its distribution channel members, beginning with the supply of raw materials and ending with the customer's purchase of the final product.

**Supply chain management** has four basic characteristics:

- It treats the supply chain as a single entity, not a series of autonomous functions or segments.
- It calls for and depends upon strategic decision making. "Supply" is the shared objective of every function or segment in the chain because of how supply affects total costs and market share.
- It views inventories as last resorts for resolving imbalances between various segments of the supply chain. The exemplary performance of Japanese companies underscores the opportunities that exist for reducing the high inventories that characterize the supply chains of many European and U.S. companies.
- It embraces the integration of systems throughout the chain, which goes beyond the superficial contact that is traditional.

The objective of supply chain management is to synchronize the requirements of the final customer with the flow of materials and information along the supply chain in order to reach a balance between high customer service and cost. Customer service is the yield of the entire system and results from the combined efforts of all functions or segments of the supply chain, both internal (marketing, procurement, operations) and external (suppliers, distribution channel members).

To achieve a balance between cost and service a company's managers must think in terms of a single, integrated chain rather than its individual segments. For example, managers too often laud the importance of one or more functional areas within the company to the detriment of the company as a whole. Thus, supply chain management requires a dramatic shift from the traditional emphasis on protecting turf to an integrative mind set. Managers must become increasingly "process" oriented, in contrast to "function" oriented. They must recognize that business processes, not functions, create value for the customer and that such processes typically transcend functional unit boundaries and even company boundaries. Cross-functional teams and organizations with fewer levels of management are becoming increasingly prevalent as companies attempt to integrate their various functional departments as well as their outside suppliers and channel members.

Effective management of the supply chain is *customer driven.* This means the company must penetrate its customers' businesses to understand their products, cultures, markets, and organizations to ensure it is attuned to its customers' needs and requirements. The customer must be fully integrated into the company's supply chain to ensure its competitive advantage.

Suppliers as well as customers should be fully integrated into the supply chain. This requires a fundamental change in the way business is conducted— from an adversarial relationship to one of mutual support and cooperation. The cooperation starts at the early stages of product development and involves management at all levels. It also includes the dependable and timely supply of high-quality products delivered directly to the production line; sharing product, process, and cost information; exchanging technology and collaborating on design as necessary; and a long-term agreement that spells out a framework for analyzing costs, establishing prices, and sharing profits.

The way in which a company manages its suppliers is one critical aspect of supply chain management. Whether the suppliers are in-house or independent makes surprisingly little difference. Assembler-supplier relationships in Japan provide much information about effective supply chain management.

## Assembler-Supplier Relationships in Japan[19]

In Japan assembler-supplier relationships are an integral part of the just-in-time– total quality management (JIT/TQM) production system. For JIT/TQM production suppliers deliver components directly to the assembly line, either hourly or several times a day, with no inspection of incoming parts. Also, the Japanese assemblers' use of production smoothing, a technique for keeping the total production volume (not mix) as constant as possible, allows them to maximize the productivity of their own workers (who are viewed as fixed costs) and to ensure a steady volume of business for their suppliers.

In examining assembler-supplier relationships in Japan, we focus on the Japanese automobile industry and begin with product development. At the start of product development the Japanese assembler selects all necessary suppliers. The leading Japanese auto makers use fewer than 300 suppliers for each car (compared with 1,000 to 2,500 for Western manufacturers). The suppliers are easy to identify, because they typically are supplying the same parts for the assembler's other models and are long-term members of the assembler's supplier group. Most important is that these suppliers are not selected on the basis of bids but rather on the basis of past relationships and performance.

---

[19]Adapted from James P. Womack, Daniel T. Jones, and Daniel Roos, "Coordinating the Supply Chain," chap. 6 in *The Machine That Changed the World* (New York: HarperPerennial, 1991), pp. 138–168.

Japanese car makers use many fewer suppliers than their Western counterparts, because they assign a whole component, such as seats, a steering assembly, or an electrical system, to what they call a *first-tier supplier*. **First-tier suppliers** are responsible for working as an integral part of the assembler's product development team in developing a new product. The auto maker gives its first-tier suppliers performance specifications. For example, if a supplier is assigned a brake system, the auto maker specifies that the brakes must stop a 2,200-pound car traveling 60 miles per hour within 200 feet and do this ten times in succession without failing; the brakes should fit into a space at the end of each axle that measures 6″ x 8″ x 10″; and the supplier must deliver the brakes to the assembly plant for $40 per set. Note that the assembler does not specify what the brakes are to be made of or how they are to work—these are engineering decisions for which the supplier is responsible.

A first-tier supplier has a team of second-tier suppliers. **Second-tier suppliers** get the job of fabricating individual parts. The second-tier suppliers are usually manufacturing specialists—companies with strong backgrounds in process engineering and plant operations. The second-tier suppliers may assign responsibilities to other companies, which would then constitute a third or even fourth tier in the Japanese supply pyramid.

The nature of supply arrangements in Japan means that the assembler might know relatively little about certain parts or systems. However, even when the assembler is only casually acquainted with the supplier's technology and totally dependent on a single component supplier, the car maker is careful to learn as much as possible about the supplier's production costs and quality. Furthermore, the Japanese car maker does not delegate to the outside supplier the design of certain parts that are considered vital to the success of the car, either because a part requires proprietary technology or because consumers believe that a good auto maker makes that part in house. Key examples of parts usually reserved for the assembler's in-house divisions are engines, transmissions, major body panels, and computerized repair and diagnostic systems.

An open flow of sensitive information characterizes the supply system in Japan. It is made possible by a rational framework for determining costs, prices, and profits that encourages the two parties to work together for mutual benefit rather than view one another with mutual distrust. The framework is a basic contract that not only expresses the assembler's and supplier's long-term commitment to work together but also establishes ground rules for determining prices, establishing quality assurance, ensuring prompt ordering and delivery, guarding proprietary rights, and supplying materials. The contract provides the basis for a cooperative relationship that is fundamentally different from the relatively adversarial relationships between supplier and assembler in the West.

The contract that establishes prices and provides for joint analysis of costs provides the foundation for a cooperative relationship. First, the Japanese auto maker establishes a target price for the vehicle and then works backward with its suppliers to determine how the vehicle can be made for that price while allowing it and its suppliers a reasonable profit. The result of this process is a *cost target*.

To meet the cost target the assembler and supplier break down the costs of each stage of production, identifying each factor that could lower the cost of each part. Then the first-tier (whole component) supplier begins to bargain with the car maker, not on price but on how to reach the target and make a reasonable profit.

Once the part is in production, the Japanese use a method called *value analysis* to achieve further cost reductions. **Value analysis** is a method for comprehensively analyzing the costs of each manufacturing step to identify the steps that have a critical effect on cost and figure out how to make them less expensive. Typically, such cost savings come from continuous improvement, the introduction of new tooling, or redesigning the part.

Obviously, Western manufacturers also try to analyze costs, but the JIT/TQM manufacturing systems of Japan make it much easier to do this accurately. Because set-up times are minimal and production runs are short and frequent, cost estimators do not have to wait days or weeks to calculate average cost performance over several production runs. Accurate and representative cost data are collected quickly—the machine operators themselves can collect them.

For the Japanese supply system to function properly the supplier must share a substantial amount of its proprietary information about costs and manufacturing methods with the auto maker. Both parties review each detail of the supplier's production process, searching for ways to reduce costs and improve quality. In return the car maker recognizes the supplier's need to make a reasonable profit. The contractual agreements on profit sharing provide the supplier with the incentive to improve performance, because they guarantee that the supplier keeps all the profits derived from its cost-saving innovations and continuous improvement activities.

Under a formal agreement to share profits from joint activities and assign to suppliers profits that accrue from the supplier's initiatives, the car maker relinquishes the right to monopolize the benefits of the supplier's ideas. On the other hand, the Japanese car maker gains the increased willingness of its suppliers to innovate, make cost improvements, and work collaboratively. Note that the contractual agreement, which espouses a long-term commitment and specifies a rational framework for determining prices, profit sharing, quality assurance, and so on, is the foundation for the Japanese supply system. American managers would have to fundamentally change their thinking and attitudes, but they could easily adapt such an agreement,because it is not culture specific.

Because Japanese assemblers such as Toyota are so successful at delegating to suppliers much of the responsibility for engineering and fabricating parts, they do much less in house than their Western counterparts such as General Motors. Toyota itself accounts for only 27 percent of the total cost of the materials, tools, and finished parts for making a car. It produces 4 million vehicles per year with only 37,000 employees. General Motors provides 70 percent of the value in the 8 million vehicles it makes and needs 850,000 employees worldwide to do it. One factor is that Toyota is more efficient in everything it does. But much of the differences derives from Toyota and other Japanese car makers doing many fewer things.

# Global Integration of Operations[20]

In the 1980s companies faced the challenge of competing internationally. Those that ignored international markets frequently found international companies competing in their own backyard with better products at a lower cost. One big advantage of competing internationally is learning about global competitors *before* they start taking market share. But competing globally will not be enough in the twenty-first century. The successful multinational companies will be globally

---

[20]Adapted from Michael E. McGrath and Richard W. Hoole, "Manufacturing's New Economies of Scale," *Harvard Business Review* 70 (May–June 1992): 94–102.

*Xerox is a pioneer in the global integration of manufacturing operations.*

integrated. **Global integration of operations** means a company manages all of its operations worldwide as a single entity or system in order to maximize competitive advantage in both its domestic and international markets. Recent political developments such as the European Community and the North American Free Trade Agreement (NAFTA) only increase the pressure to integrate globally. To achieve global integration of operations companies should focus on five basics: *product development, purchasing, production, demand management,* and *order fulfillment.*

International design teams can greatly improve the product development process. Instead of designing a product for one market and then reengineering it for other markets, design teams can develop a core product that allows for simple variations and derivatives to meet the needs of different markets. In some cases overdesigning a product in order to meet the stringent regulatory requirements of only one market may be more efficient. A single overdesigned product often can bring scale economies that bring costs below those for redesigning a product for a special market. International design teams are better at staying abreast of technological developments and changing trends. Communication can be a problem for international design teams, but technological developments such as e-mail and teleconferencing can reduce the difficulties.

Globally integrated purchasing operations can lead to significant cost savings. One approach is to develop global commodity management teams that can identify important raw materials and components and develop international sources. Some low volume, low cost products should be purchased locally, especially if transportation costs are high. But for many products consolidating the company's requirements increases the company's leverage with suppliers, which means it can obtain better prices and more favorable delivery schedules. Global product development strategies that seek to standardize components in new products can further the integration of global purchasing.

## GLOBAL OPERATIONS MANAGEMENT 3.3

# Global Integration of Operations at Xerox

To respond to international competition in the 1980s Xerox developed a strategy for globally integrating its manufacturing. It used several projects to implement the strategy, resulting in improved product quality and significant cost savings.

One of Xerox's first global integration efforts came in 1982. It formed a central purchasing group of commodity managers to identify and develop suppliers that could deliver high-quality, low-cost components on a global basis. The commodity managers reduced Xerox's global supply base from five thousand suppliers to just over four hundred, saving more than $100 million annually.

In 1983 Xerox introduced its Leadership Through Quality program to provide a common language of quality and a standard set of management practices for its worldwide operations. The company followed this in 1985 with a product-delivery process to standardize product development procedures. Now multinational, cross-disciplinary teams are responsible for developing new products for all major markets. The integrated team approach has eliminated the task of reengineering products for different markets and has cut as much as a year from product development times.

In 1988 Xerox created a multinational task force that identified specific facility requirements to facilitate global integration. As a result, Xerox requires all of its plants to adopt international standards for processes that are common to all operations (data bases for materials management); they can be modified only to meet local needs (such as government reporting requirements). The implementation of global standards allows Xerox managers to accurately compare product cost and inventory data at its various plants.

In 1989 Xerox managers realized that they could achieve significant inventory reductions by more closely linking customer orders and production. Xerox formed the multinational Central Logistics and Asset Management (CLAM) organization to integrate the supply chain across geographic boundaries. The result of CLAM's efforts was a reduction in worldwide inventory levels of $500 million. In 1991 a CLAM team, in conjunction with several operating groups, created a western hemisphere distribution center for spare parts to consolidate the safety stocks previously held in the United States, Canada, and Latin America, bringing savings of several million dollars annually.

As a leader in global integration Xerox has had to develop its strategy largely by trial and error. Its approach was to focus on projects that addressed specific problems. Global integration of purchasing operations was the first project, because it was likely to yield the best and fastest results. The project approach is advantageous because it allows a company to set concrete objectives, minimize disruption to existing operations, and clearly evaluate the success of its efforts.

The multinational company also can improve global integration in its production operations. They can be managed as part of an integrated production system instead of as isolated operations. Locating component operations in low-cost countries such as Malaysia and putting assembly operations closer to the market may make sense, even if the manufacturing costs are higher. Integrating manufacturing operations means that they should be balanced both vertically (throughout the supply chain) and horizontally (between plants that produce the same products). The challenge is to try to manage far-flung operations as if they are a single manufacturing facility.

Many companies take a top-down approach to demand management. Senior managers at the company's headquarters develop an annual forecast at the beginning of each fiscal year that is given to manufacturing operations for production planning purposes. The approach has two problems: The forecasts tend to be inaccurate, because they do not consider local information, and the forecasts become political, because financial analysts use them to evaluate the company. As a result, top-down forecasts are both inaccurate and difficult to modify. The globally integrated approach to demand management is to develop a global forecasting system that collects data from the local level, integrates it on the global level, and then distributes the consolidated information to the local operations. Forecasts are a critical input to production planning, inventory management, supplier negotiations, and sales quotas. To achieve global integration, demand management systems must be accurate and flexible so that local managers can use forecasts effectively.

Global integration also improves order filling. Digital Equipment Corporation (DEC) has streamlined its order-fulfillment process by developing a new system that requires that an order be entered only once. DEC sells computer systems that are produced at many facilities around the world. Previously, DEC's order-filling system was not integrated, resulting in a wasteful negotiation process between plants and distribution centers. The integrated order-filling process reduces the number of transactions, streamlines the distribution process, improves delivery time, and increases the accuracy of orders.

A useful exercise for global integration is for a company to publicly declare a global mission, develop a profile of its capabilities and then identify options, pick a plan of action, and target specific results. The company's management must publicly state the goal of global integration, telling employees, customers, and suppliers what its global ambitions are and what they mean for the company. This must be followed by an evaluation of the company's capabilities—the strengths it can use to its advantage and the weaknesses that must be corrected. Management must use the global mission statement and an analysis of the company's capabilities to develop candidate programs and activities for meeting the company's vision of global integration. The company should then choose which programs and activities to pursue and specify the results anticipated. A comparison of actual results and expected results identifies successes to build on and failures to eliminate. Xerox (presented in Global Operations Management 3.3) provides a good example of how a company can globally integrate operations by developing specific projects.

# ▶ Summary

This chapter introduced strategic planning concepts for planning at the business and functional or product levels. It presented operations strategy in the context of business-level strategic planning so that the relationship between the two levels of planning is clear. It emphasized the importance of the participation of all top functional managers (including operations managers) in business-level strategic planning and the critical role that operations plays in enabling a company to compete successfully. We examined briefly the seven categories of strategic operations decisions (see Figure 3.4 and Table 1 in "A Preview to Operations Management") and explored their relationship to competitive advantage. The chapter revisited the value chain model, presented in Chapter 1, to introduce the topics of vertical integration, outsourcing, and supply chain management. Finally, the chapter discussed the necessity of globally integrating operations.

### Learning Objective 1: Discuss the generic business strategies relative to the five competitive forces.

The state of competition in an industry depends on five competitive forces: the threat of new entrants, the threat of substitution, the bargaining power of buyers, the bargaining power of suppliers, and the rivalry among current competitors. The strongest force or forces are the most important with respect to formulating strategy.

Business-level strategic planning means developing strategies and related actions to deal effectively with the five forces and thereby realize a superior return on investment for the company. Many different strategies might accomplish this, but two internally consistent strategies enable a company to outperform its industry competitors: overall cost leadership and differentiation.

The first strategy is for the company to achieve cost leadership within its industry by introducing a set of functional policies directed to this end (constructing efficient-scale facilities, vigorously pursuing cost reductions from experience, emphasizing operating efficiency, and tightly controlling costs and overhead). The second generic strategy is for the company to differentiate its product or service by creating one that is recognized industrywide as unique and that can command a premium price because of its uniqueness. A company can use many methods (innovative product technology, superb customer service, rapid delivery) to differentiate its product or service.

### Learning Objective 2: Describe operations strategic planning and understand its relationship to business-level strategic planning.

Business-level strategic planning specifies the strategic objectives for the company and how to accomplish them. Operations strategic planning is closely related, because operations is responsible for implementing company goals as they relate to manufacturing or service provision. The strategic goals for which operations holds primary responsibility or shares major responsibility with other functional units are called *operations com-*

*petitive priorities* (low cost, rapid delivery, volume flexibility). The business-level strategic planning process communicates the strategic posture of the company to operations so that it knows which operations competitive priorities are most important and can work to achieve them. These competitive priorities guide decision making with respect to the seven categories of strategic choices (product or service planning, long-range capacity planning and facility location, and so on). Also, participation by operations managers provides valuable information for guiding business-level strategy.

### Learning Objective 3: Define three competitive priorities related to flexibility in operations.

- Product flexibility (customization): the ability to handle difficult, nonstandard orders, to meet special customer specifications, and to produce products that have many features, options, sizes and/or colors
- Volume flexibility: the ability to rapidly adjust production capacity in response to changes in customer demand
- Process flexibility: the ability to produce small quantities of product cost efficiently in order to easily accommodate product mix changes

### Learning Objective 4: Identify the seven operations strategic choices or decision categories.

- Product or service planning—planning to satisfy customers' needs and wants and anticipate their desires
- Process design and technology management—arranging or grouping the resources of production or service (equipment, labor), selecting the technologies used for manufacturing products or providing services, and the related management issues
- Long-range capacity planning and facility location—sizing and timing of capacity changes relative to demand and deciding where to locate the capacity
- Quality management—having a fundamental approach to conducting business that encompasses planning, monitoring, controlling, and improving quality at all levels of an organization
- Manufacturing or service organization—designing the manufacturing or service organization to support the performance outcomes the company desires.

- Human resource management—managing the most important resource of an organization: people and their hiring, promotion, training, motivation, and reward
- Operations planning and control—using the tactical and operational procedures, methods, and systems that govern routine planning, monitoring, and controlling of production, quality, inventories, information, materials movements, and so forth

## Learning Objective 5: Describe supply chain management.

Supply chain management is concerned with planning, coordinating, and controlling materials, parts, and finished products from suppliers to the final customer. Supply chain management has four basic characteristics: It views the supply chain as a single entity; it is based on the assumptions that strategy drives decision making and supply is the common goal of every segment of the chain; it treats inventories as last resorts for resolving imbalances in various segments of the supply chain; and it is integrated across functional units and company boundaries.

## Learning Objective 6: Discuss the five basics of globally integrated operations.

The five basics of global integration of operations are product develop-ment, purchasing, production, demand management, and order fulfillment. Global integration of product development means designing a core product for all markets that can be varied easily to satisfy specific markets or overdesigning a single product for all markets. The goal is to meet the regulatory require-ment of the most demanding market but allow for scale economies in manufacturing.

Global integration of purchasing generally means using global commodity teams to identify and develop international sources for important raw materials and components for a company's worldwide manufactur-ing operations and consolidating purchasing in order to obtain better prices and service.

The global integration of production operations means that various manufacturing operations throughout the world are managed as a single manufacturing system and the company makes strategic decisions such as plant location in view of the total system.

The globally integrated approach to managing de-mand means developing a global forecasting system that collects data from the local level, integrates them on the global level, and distributes the consolidated information to the local operations. Finally, global integration of order fulfillment means a centralized order entry system for all plants and distribution centers worldwide.

## ► Key Terms

| | | |
|---|---|---|
| business-level strategic planning | global integration of operations | second-tier supplier |
| corporate-level strategic planning | Manufacturing Futures Survey | strategic operations decision |
| cost leadership | operations competitive priorities | categories |
| differentiation | operations strategic choices | strategic planning hierarchy |
| distinctive competence | operations strategic planning | supply chain |
| factory focus | operations strategy | supply chain management |
| first-tier supplier | product-level strategic planning | value analysis |
| functional strategic planning | product process matrix | |

## ► Discussion Questions

1. Select a Fortune 500 company and describe its strategic positioning.
2. Why should all functional areas within the company, including operations, participate in business-level strategic planning?
3. Select an industry group and determine which operations competitive priorities are most important for that industry and why.
4. Identify some of the reasons a company may elect to vertically integrate in order to better control its distribution channels.
5. Provide an overview of the major principles and characteristics of assembler-supplier relationships in Japan.
6. Identify and discuss some current examples of manufacturing companies with globally integrated operations. What benefits have they realized?
7. Why is measuring performance with respect to a company's strategic goals or priorities important? Discuss some measures that might be used to evaluate a company's performance with respect to product or service quality.

8. Discuss the long-term contractual arrangement that Japanese companies have with their suppliers, and explain why it forms the basis of assembler-supplier relationships in Japan.

9. Compare and contrast the strategic positioning of Wal-Mart versus Kmart based on information in recent business journals or periodicals.

10. Why are operations-related considerations becoming more important in formulating business strategy? Describe some current examples of companies that have gained competitive advantage primarily from manufacturing.

## ► Selected References

De Meyer, Arnoud, Jinichiro Nakane, Jeffrey G. Miller, and Kasra Ferdows. "Flexibility: The Next Competitive Battle—The Manufacturing Futures Survey." *Strategic Management Journal* 10 (March–April 1989): 135–144.

Giffi, Craig, Aleda V. Roth, and Gregory M. Seal. *Competing in World-Class Manufacturing: America's 21st Century Challenge*. Homewood, Ill.: Business One–Irwin, 1990.

Hammer, Michael, and James Champy. *Reengineering the Corporation: A Manifesto for Business Revolution*. New York: HarperBusiness, 1993.

Hayes, Robert H., and Gary P. Pisano. "Beyond World-Class: The New Manufacturing Strategy." *Harvard Business Review* 72 (January–February 1994): 77–86.

Hayes, Robert H., and Steven C. Wheelwright. *Restoring Our Competitive Edge: Competing Through Manufacturing*. New York: Wiley, 1984.

Hayes, Robert H., Steven C. Wheelwright, and Kim Clark. *Dynamic Manufacturing*. New York: Free Press, 1988.

Houlihan, John B. "International Supply Chain Management." *International Journal of Physical Distribution and Materials Management* 15, No. 1 (1985): 22–38.

Kotler, Philip. *Marketing Management: Analysis, Planning, Implementation, and Control*, 6th ed. Englewood Cliffs, N.J.: Prentice-Hall, 1988.

McGrath, Michael E., and Richard W. Hoole. "Manufacturing's New Economies of Scale." *Harvard Business Review* 70 (May–June 1992): 94–102.

Nakane, J. *Manufacturing Futures Survey in Japan: A Comparative Survey 1983–1986*. Tokyo: System Science Institute, Waseda University, May 1986.

Porter, Michael E. *Competitive Advantage*. New York: Free Press, 1985.

Schmenner, Roger W. *Making Business Location Decisions*. Englewood Cliffs, N.J.: Prentice-Hall, 1982.

Skinner, Wickham. "The Focused Factory." *Harvard Business Review* 52 (May–June 1974): 113–121.

———. *Manufacturing in the Corporate Strategy*. New York: Wiley, 1978.

Smith, Garry D., Danny R. Arnold, and Bobby G. Bizzell. *Business Strategy and Policy*, 2d ed. Boston: Houghton Mifflin, 1988.

Stalk, George, Philip Evans, and Lawrence E. Shulman. "Competing on Capabilities: The New Rules of Corporate Strategy." *Harvard Business Review* 70 (March–April 1992): 57–69.

Stevens, Graham. "Integrating the Supply Chain." *International Journal of Physical Distribution and Materials Management* 19 (No. 8, 1989):3–8.

Vickery, Shawnee K. "A Theory of Production Competence Revisited."*Decision Sciences* 22 (May–June 1991): 635–643.

Vickery, Shawnee K., Cornelia Droge, and Robert E. Markland. "Production Competence and Business Strategy: Do They Affect Business Performance?" *Decision Sciences* 24 (March–April 1993): 435–455.

Womack, James P., Daniel T. Jones, and Daniel Roos. *The Machine That Changed the World*. New York: HarperPerennial, 1991.

# Allen-Bradley

## CASE STUDY: OPERATIONS STRATEGIC PLANNING

Allen-Bradley Co., Inc., a Rockwell International company, is a leading international manufacturer of industrial automation products and control and information systems. Allen-Bradley products are designed to help companies become more competitive by linking control and information through the manufacturing or processing operations. Allen-Bradley employs 12,000 people worldwide and had sales of $1.7 billion in 1993. Its worldwide headquarters is in Milwaukee, Wisconsin.

Allen-Bradley offers a broad spectrum of solid-state and electromechanical control devices, along with data communication systems and data acquisition networks. The products include control logic, operator interface, sensors, motion control, quality management, and information-processing and communications products. Allen-Bradley provides worldwide customer support services for its products, including technical training, system start-up services, preventive maintenance, on-call services, applications engineering, software support, project management, and parts repair and replacement.

Three major product-oriented groups and one division comprise Allen-Bradley's business organization: the Power Products Group (motor contactors and starters, relays), the Automation Group (computer numerical controls, programmable controllers), the Applied Systems Group (motor control centers), and the Motion Control Division (encoders).

Allen-Bradley's manufacturing mission is to support the strategic objectives of the company, in particular its globalization objectives, by assuring that manufacturing facilities worldwide provide the company with a competitive advantage through optimized cost, quality, asset utilization, and customer service. Manufacturing strategic planning at Allen-Bradley has three levels: *global, group* or *division,* and *manufacturing site.*

At the global level, Allen-Bradley's Global Manufacturing Committee (GMC) is responsible for strategic planning activities. As Figure 1 shows, GMC has seventeen subcommittees that have their own missions or charters. For example, the Global Manufacturing Strategic Planning Subcommittee charter consists of three major charges: to assure content consistency between division/group manufacturing strategic plans and the global manufacturing strategy; to assure that each manufacturing location has a manufacturing strategic plan approved by the general manager at that site; and to review and recommend approval of capital spending plans related to manufacturing investments. The chairman of the Global Manufacturing Committee is the senior vice president of operations. The executive committee of the GMC is composed of senior business and manufacturing executives.

The Global Manufacturing Committee meets an average of twice a year. The various subcommittees meet as required to accomplish their charters. Charters are reviewed and altered if necessary at the biannual meetings. The GMC reviews site strategies and revises them as necessary to respond to business demands.

At the group level strategic planning activities are carried out by planning teams. For example, one group's planning team, consists of seventeen managers and directors with responsibilities in manufacturing, industrialization, materials, facilities, information systems, and quality assurance. Figure 2 shows the group level strategic planning process. Within a group a manufacturing strategy is established for each major product family or business segment, thus allowing the manufacturing strategy to be tailored to the needs of the particular business segment. Manufacturing strategies are on a par with marketing or product development strategies, for example, and all strategies support the major objectives of the business. The company reviews its manufacturing strategies annually.

Manufacturing strategies (group level) are reviewed and evaluated in terms of seven "key success factors," which are depicted in Figure 3. Allen-Bradley has developed quantitative measures for its seven key factors. For example, it uses the following metrics to assess delivery compliance:

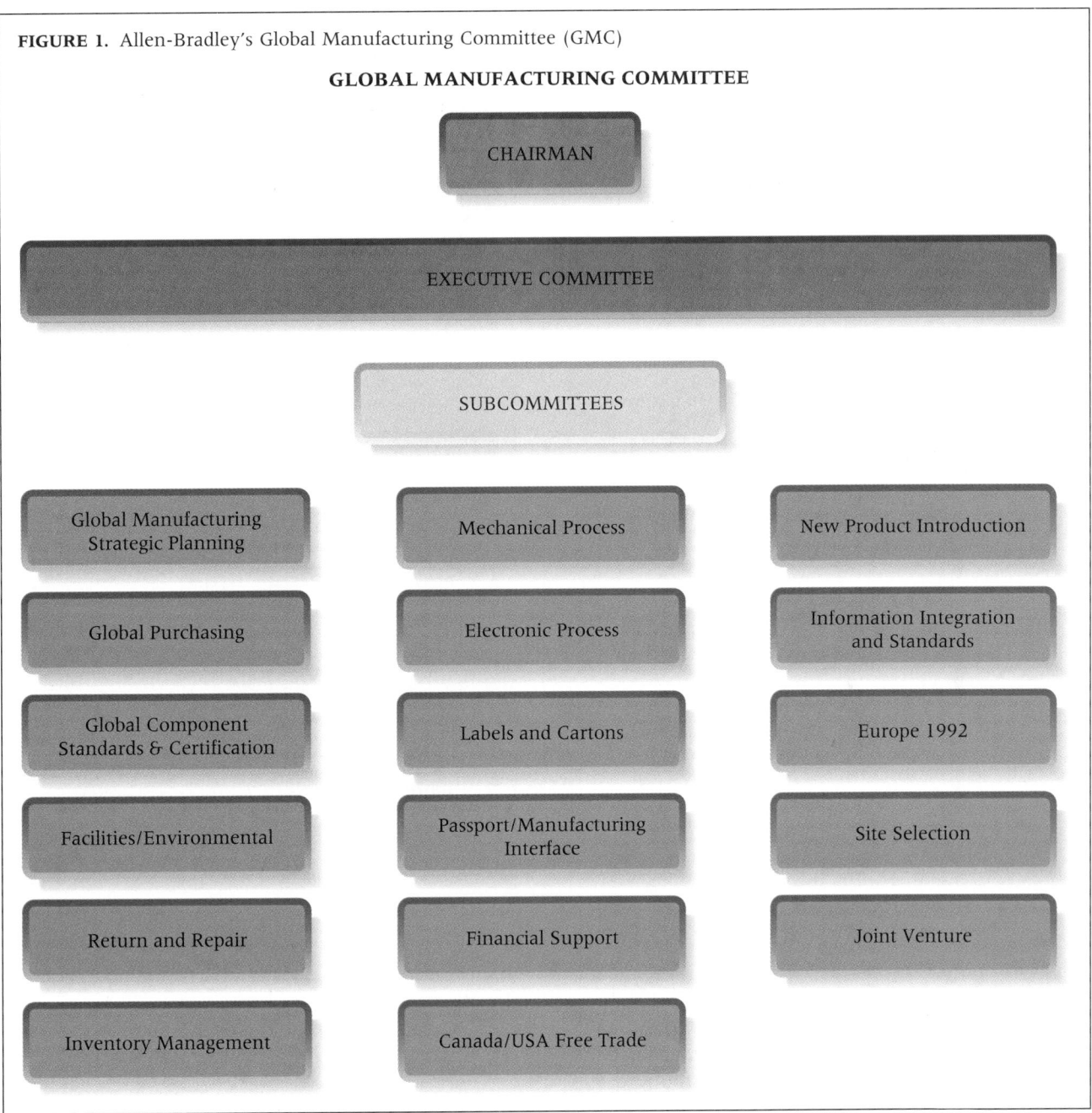

**FIGURE 1.** Allen-Bradley's Global Manufacturing Committee (GMC)

**GLOBAL MANUFACTURING COMMITTEE**

CHAIRMAN

EXECUTIVE COMMITTEE

SUBCOMMITTEES

| | | |
|---|---|---|
| Global Manufacturing Strategic Planning | Mechanical Process | New Product Introduction |
| Global Purchasing | Electronic Process | Information Integration and Standards |
| Global Component Standards & Certification | Labels and Cartons | Europe 1992 |
| Facilities/Environmental | Passport/Manufacturing Interface | Site Selection |
| Return and Repair | Financial Support | Joint Venture |
| Inventory Management | Canada/USA Free Trade | |

1. Sales dollars past due
2. Sales dollars more than two weeks past due
3. Number of order items past due
4. Compliance with date promised (measures variance around date promised)

5. Delivery to order complete (percentage of orders [sales dollars] completed on time)

Allen-Bradley uses management by objectives (MBO) to implement its manufacturing strategies.

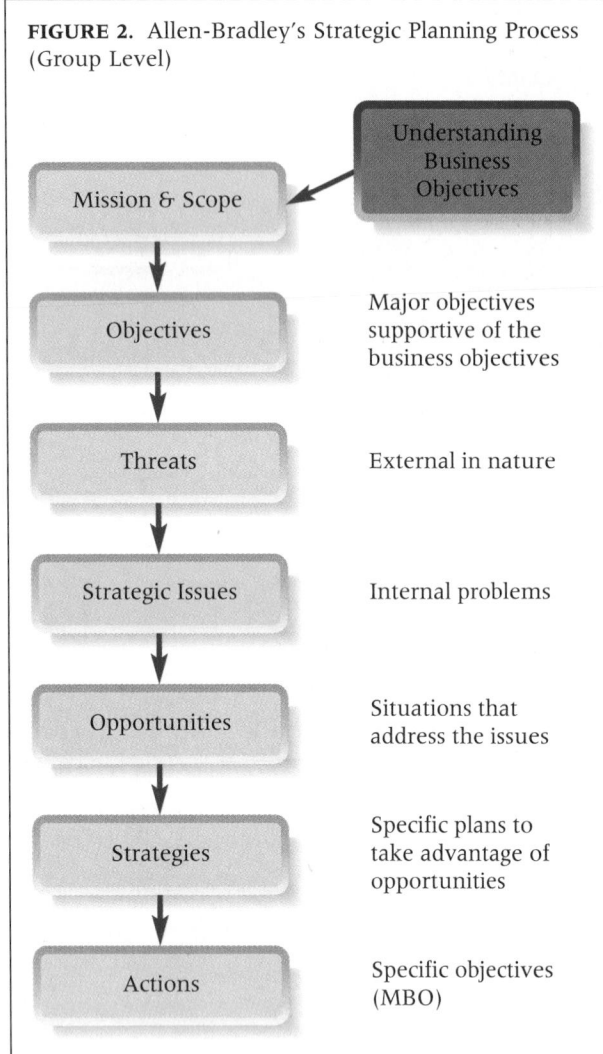

**FIGURE 2.** Allen-Bradley's Strategic Planning Process (Group Level)

Understanding Business Objectives

Mission & Scope

Objectives — Major objectives supportive of the business objectives

Threats — External in nature

Strategic Issues — Internal problems

Opportunities — Situations that address the issues

Strategies — Specific plans to take advantage of opportunities

Actions — Specific objectives (MBO)

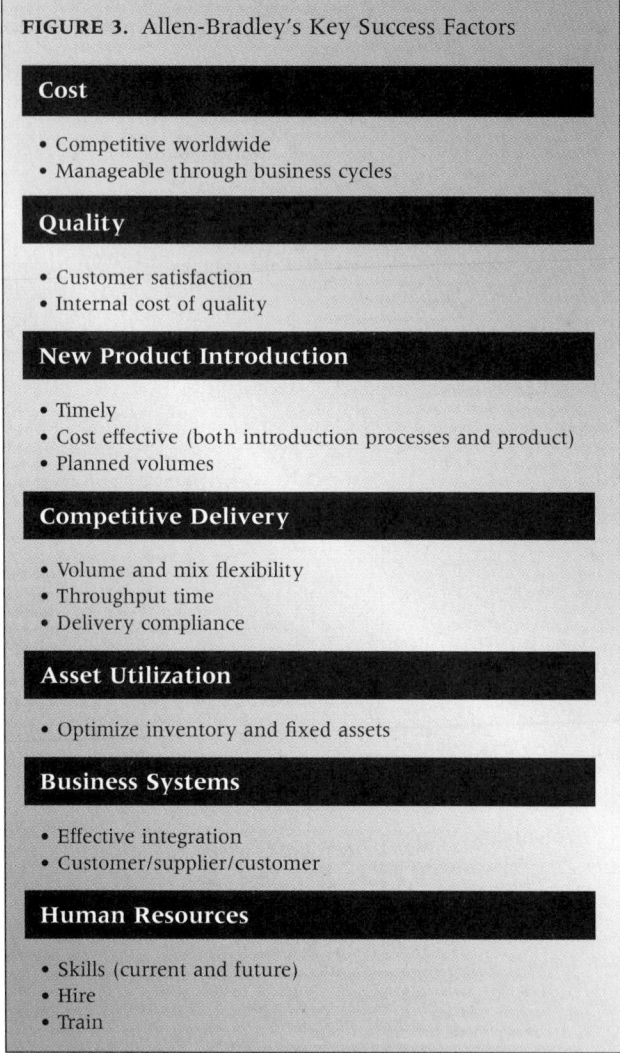

**FIGURE 3.** Allen-Bradley's Key Success Factors

**Cost**
- Competitive worldwide
- Manageable through business cycles

**Quality**
- Customer satisfaction
- Internal cost of quality

**New Product Introduction**
- Timely
- Cost effective (both introduction processes and product)
- Planned volumes

**Competitive Delivery**
- Volume and mix flexibility
- Throughput time
- Delivery compliance

**Asset Utilization**
- Optimize inventory and fixed assets

**Business Systems**
- Effective integration
- Customer/supplier/customer

**Human Resources**
- Skills (current and future)
- Hire
- Train

Figure 4 provides several examples of the action plans, desired responses, and assignments of responsibility that guide and facilitate the implementation process. Many of the strategies, approaches, and methods that appear in Figure 4 are introduced and examined in this textbook.

Strategies lead to actions at Allen-Bradley, and many company programs trace their roots to operations strategic planning. Typical strategic initiatives include total quality management systems (TQMS)/ total quality for customer satisfaction (TQCS); the industrialization process; an electronic manufacturing strategy; stockless production; computer-integrated

manufacturing, strategic manufacturing planning, and the World Contactor facility. Chapter 20 provides an in-depth study of one of Allen-Bradley's highly successful strategic initiatives, its World Contactor facility.

## ► Case Discussion Questions

1. Discuss Allen-Bradley's key success factors.
2. Why are quantitative measures of performance important?
3. Describe how Allen-Bradley implements manufacturing strategies.

**FIGURE 4.** Some Examples of Strategies and Action Plans from Allen-Bradley's Operations Strategic Plan 1991–1995

**Strategy**

**1.0 Effect continuous improvement through a prevention-based system**

| Action Plan | Action | Response or Need | Person(s) Responsible |
|---|---|---|---|
| 1.01 | Maintain/obtain quality certification status (TQMS, ISO 9000, etc.) | Develop/revise policies and procedures | All |
| | | Perform audits | All |
| 1.02 | Expand use of statistical methods | Continue training at all levels | (AF) |
| | | Assure process capability per ICG Policy 46-28 and fabrication TQC certification– | |
| | | 1–All new products | JD/JH/MFS |
| | | 2–Stockless production products/direct delivery parts | RAB/TR/DT RA/GE |
| | | 3–Others as appropriate | RAB/TR/DT RA/GE |
| | | Use statistical methods and problem-solving techniques to improve yields | RAB/TR/DT RA/GE |

**3.0 Industrialize new, existing, and strategic partners' products in parallel with product development and consistent with global business stategies**

| Action Plan | Action | Response or Need | Person(s) Responsible |
|---|---|---|---|
| 3.01 | Continue to analyze competitors' products | Review high contribution margin products | RA/RAB/TR |
| | | Review specific technologies as required | RA/RAB/TR |
| 3.02 | Manage and reduce product introduction durations | Use project management tools | DF/JD/JH/MFS |
| | | Monitor project milestones | DF/JD/JH/MFS |
| | | Measure aggregate product introduction duration and reduce it | DF/DC |
| 3.03 | Expand operations involvement in early stages of product development | Implement effective cross-function business teams | JD/JH/MFS |
| | | Plan for industrialization of strategic partner products | JD/JH/MFS |

**4.0 Configure operations to become a world-class manufacturer of products for global markets**

| Action Plan | Action | Response or Need | Person(s) Responsible |
|---|---|---|---|
| 4.01 | Analyze competitors | Work with development, marketing, and sales to provide a feedback network. Identify A-B personnel with knowledge of or who have contacts with competitors | LY |
| | | Review per key success factors | All |
| 4.02 | Reduce costs | | |
| | 4.02.1 Apply new methods, procedures, and techniques that minimize resources used | Stockless II | GE/DC |
| | | Direct delivery of fabricated and purchased parts | JK |
| | | MSOP | TC/JK |
| | | Set-up reduction | GE |
| | | Manufacturing cells | All |
| | | SPC | (AF) |

## CHAPTER 4

# Forecasting Demand for Products and Services

*I have but one lamp by which my feet are guided, and that is the lamp of experience. I know of no way of judging the future but by the past. . . .*

PATRICK HENRY

Introduction

Characteristics of Demand

The Forecasting Process

Approaches to Forecasting—
  A Preview

Qualitative Forecasting Methods
*GLOBAL OPERATIONS MANAGEMENT
  4.1: A National Delphi Study of System
  Waste in India*

Quantitative Forecasting
  Methods—Time Series Analysis
  Models
*OPERATIONS MANAGEMENT IN
  PRACTICE 4.2: Forecasting at
  Rubbermaid Home Products Division*

Quantitative Forecasting
  Methods—Associative Models

Measuring Forecasting Error

Monitoring and Controlling
  Forecasts

Using Computers in Forecasting

## Introduction

Forecasting is a critical element in virtually every significant management decision. Accurate forecasting enables the manager to select the right combination of human and material resources to produce the physical goods or services provided by the company. Forecasts serve as the basis for long-run corporate planning. The marketing function forecasts sales in order to assign sales personnel to territories and to plan the introduction of new products. Finance and accounting use forecasts to determine budgets and for cost control, whereas operations uses forecasting in many ways—for capacity planning, facility layout, scheduling, and inventory control. Finally, personnel uses forecasts to make hiring decisions and develop compensation and benefits packages.

A **forecast** is a statement or inference about the future that usually involves using information from the past to make predictions. Perfect forecasting is generally not possible; even a carefully and rigorously prepared forecast can be wrong. But this does not mean that we should not continually strive to improve forecasting models and methodologies. The forecast provides the foundation for coordinating various activities throughout the company. When the various parts of a company base their plans and efforts on a common forecast, their efforts become mutually supportive and beneficial. What is really important in the forecasting process is involving all functional areas of the company in the continual review of forecasts. The goal is continual improvement in accuracy and finding ways to avoid inaccurate forecasts.

This chapter considers various aspects of forecasting. Its primary emphasis is on demand forecasting because demand forecasting is important to the operations function. Still, product or service demand is but one factor that requires forecasting. We focus on forecasting using a demand **time series,** which is a time-ordered sequence of observations made at some regular interval over time (hourly, weekly, monthly, quarterly, yearly). Typical demand time series use sales from previous time periods. This chapter discusses the steps necessary to prepare a forecast, basic forecasting techniques, measures of forecasting error, and how to monitor and evaluate forecasts.

## Characteristics of Demand

Demand forecasting has a major effect on planning and decision making throughout all areas of a company, especially the operations function. Before we address the details of the forecasting process and review specific methods for making forecasts, we will look at some factors that influence demand and define the major components of demand for goods or services.

| Internal Factors | External Factors |
|---|---|
| Sales budgets | Business cycle |
| Advertising | Competition |
| Price incentives | Consumerism |
| Product/Service design | World events |
| Rebate policies | Government actions |
| Backlogs | Product life cycle |

TABLE 4.1
Factors Influencing Demand
for Goods or Services

## Factors Influencing Demand

Numerous factors influence the demand experienced by a particular company, factors both internal, which it generally can control and external, over which the typical company can exercise little influence. Table 4.1 lists some factors that can influence the demand for a company's goods or services.

**Internal Factors** Internal decisions that influence demand often are part of the overall demand management strategy used by the company. Pricing, advertising, sales promotions, and rebates are among the marketing devices companies use to influence demand for their products or services, as are product design, packaging, and overall product quality. The company's service reputation is another important factor.

Companies may use price incentives to promote demand in off-peak times. Telephone companies offer lower evening and weekend rates, and ski resorts offer lower rates for times other than holiday weeks.

Companies use backlogs to smooth out peaks and valleys in demand. Professionals, such as doctors, dentists, and lawyers, usually require an appointment, which allows them to match capacity and demand. Many producers promise a delivery date for an order that balances their work load and capacity.

**External Factors** The most important external factor influencing demand is the general state of the economy. It cannot be controlled by any one company; different companies and different industries find the business cycle constantly affects demand for their products and services.

Table 4.2 presents some common business cycle demand indicators with their corresponding sources of information. **Leading indicators** are those time series with turning points that typically precede the peaks and troughs of the general business cycle. **Coincident indicators** are those time series with turning points that closely match the turning points of the business cycle. **Lagging indicators** are those time series with turning points that typically follow the peaks and troughs of the general business cycle. Indicator series such as those shown in Table 4.2 can be valuable to companies interested in figuring out where they are with respect to the economy. For example, a major U.S. manufacturer of wood products closely monitors housing starts as a predictor of the overall demand for its products.

The demand for any product, or service, passes through stages during its **product life cycle,** the period of time encompassing a product's introduction, growth, maturity, decline, and phase out. Figure 4.1 shows the five demand stages in the product life cycle. Demand conditions are different at each stage in a product's life cycle. As Figure 4.1 shows, stage 2 (growth) is characterized by rapid growth in demand. This will, however, undoubtedly stimulate competition, which will then slow demand in stage 3 (maturity).

Another important factor is *consumerism,* a term that encompasses consumer tastes, consumer attitudes about products or services in relation to the environment, and the image a product or service projects. We have witnessed dramatic changes in consumer tastes and perceptions, particularly those related to auto-

**TABLE 4.2**
Examples of Demand
Indicators and Their Sources

| Leading Indicators | Sources of Information |
|---|---|
| Average work week, manufacturing | *Employment and Earnings,* Bureau of Labor Statistics, U.S. Department of Labor |
| Net business formation | *Business Conditions Digest* (Series 12), U.S. Department of Commerce |
| New building permits, private housing units | *Business Conditions Digest* (Series 29), U.S. Department of Commerce |
| Stock Price Index, S&P 500 | *Business Conditions Digest* (Series 19), U.S. Department of Commerce |

| Coincident Indicators | Sources of Information |
|---|---|
| Unemployment rate | *Employment and Earnings,* Bureau of Labor Statistics, U.S. Department of Labor |
| Gross national product | *Survey of Current Business,* U.S. Department of Commerce. |
| Industrial production | *Federal Reserve Bulletin,* Board of Governors, Federal Reserve System |

| Lagging Indicators | Sources of Information |
|---|---|
| Investment expenditures, plant and equipment | *Survey of Current Business,* U.S. Department of Commerce |
| Business inventories | *Business Conditions Digest* (Series 70), U.S. Department of Commerce |
| Commercial and industrial loans outstanding | *Business Conditions Digest* (Series 72), U.S. Department of Commerce |

**FIGURE 4.1**
Demand Stages in Product
Life Cycle

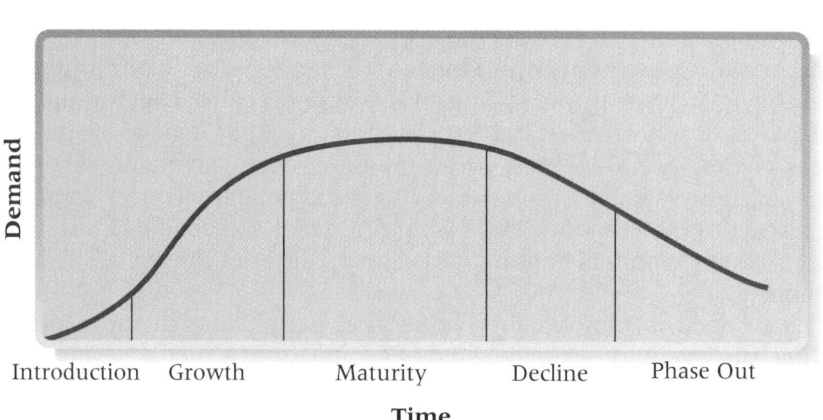

mobiles and electronics. Demand for foreign automobiles and electronic products has soared primarily because of consumers' perceptions of superior quality.

Competition in the form of pricing, advertising, and promotions has a significant effect on sales. World events are also important—we need only consider petroleum products as one primary example. Governmental actions, such as the approval of a particular drug for release to the consumer marketplace, are another important external factor.

## Demand Components

The demand for a product or a service breaks down into five major components:

Average
Trend
Cyclical
Seasonal
and Random (irregular) or Random error

Figure 4.2 illustrates a demand time series over a five-year period, showing the components of average, trend, seasonal, and random error.

**Average** simply reflects the central tendency of the time series. **Trend** describes the general upward or downward movement of demand over time. The

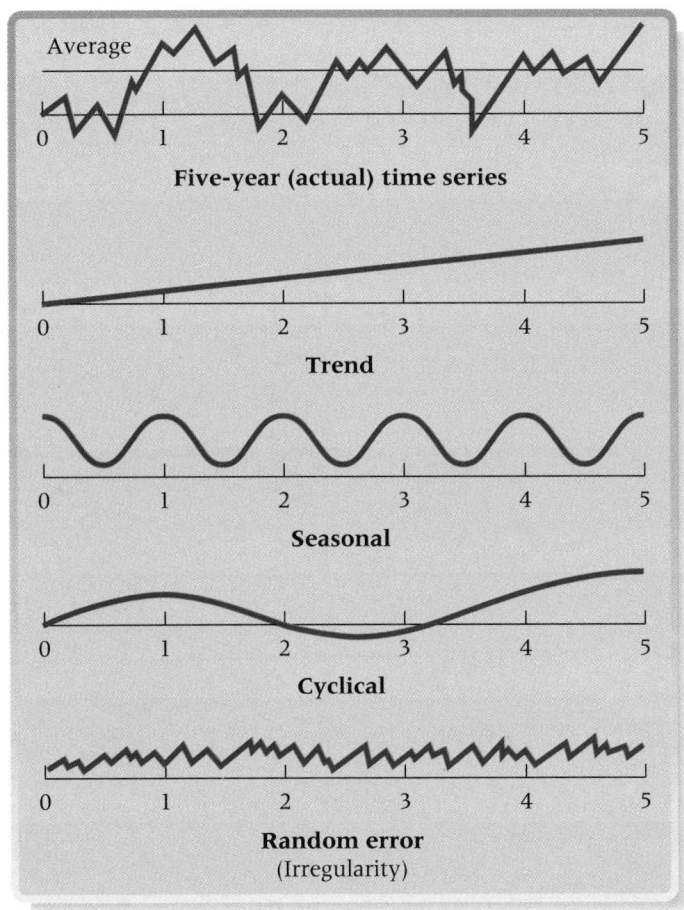

F I G U R E   4 . 2
Demand Time Series and Its Components

trend may be linear or nonlinear. **Cyclical** refers to the recurrent upward and downward wavelike conditions that occur over time because of general economic or political conditions. These cycles usually last longer than one year. **Seasonal** is a short-term (a year or less), regular fluctuation caused by such seasonal influences as weather, month of the year, or timing of holidays. **Random error** is a series of short, erratic movements that follows no discernible pattern and cannot be forecast. These fluctuations are those that cannot be explained by the average, trend, cycle, or seasonal. The random component represents the discrepancy between the combined effects of the average, trend, cycle, and seasonal components and the actual demand. It is unpredictable; forecasts for random components are never 100% accurate.

## The Forecasting Process

The forecasting process enables the manager to base decisions on the future values of some variable or the future occurrence of some event. The complete forecasting process has eight steps, as shown in Figure 4.3. Proper forecasting requires communication and cooperation between managers who use the fore-

FIGURE 4.3
Steps in the Forecasting Process

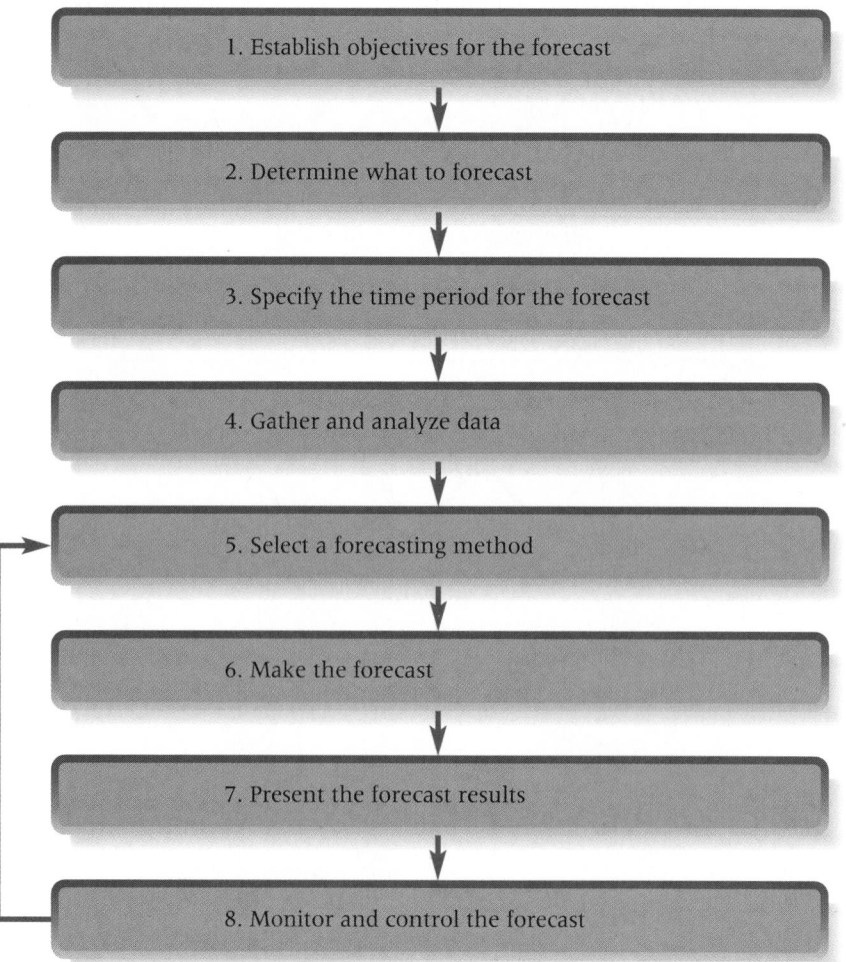

1. Establish objectives for the forecast

2. Determine what to forecast

3. Specify the time period for the forecast

4. Gather and analyze data

5. Select a forecasting method

6. Make the forecast

7. Present the forecast results

8. Monitor and control the forecast

casts and the technicians who actually prepare them. Communication and cooperation are critical to the ultimate success of forecasting.

## Establish Objectives for the Forecast

Managers must state the objectives for the forecast clearly at the beginning. The statement of forecasting objectives includes an appraisal of the purpose of the forecast—how it will be used. For example, the operations manager may need a forecast of the yearly demand for a new product that a special piece of equipment can produce.

In this situation, a subjective forecast may be sufficient to allow the manager to make a good decision about acquiring new equipment. In another situation, the operations manager may need to schedule the work force for a particular time period. The forecast of demand for the period, translated into production requirements, requires a fairly high degree of accuracy.

Trade-offs between cost and accuracy are also a vital consideration in establishing forecasting objectives. Inaccurate forecasting can result in missed sales, carrying too much inventory, or not having enough workers to provide service to customers. Forecasting accuracy tends to improve with the more rigorous, mathematically sophisticated forecasting methods, which also tend to be more costly. The costs associated with choosing a particular forecasting method are of three types:

- Development costs associated with the particular forecasting method, typically the cost of writing or purchasing a computer software forecasting package
- Data storage costs for the forecasting software, usually computer data storage costs
- Costs associated with repeated use of the forecasting software, usually computer running time costs

Figure 4.4 plots the relative cost of making forecasts versus the relative accuracy of the forecasts, using a representative set of forecasting techniques of varying sophistication, which is discussed in detail later in this chapter. In the hypothetical situation represented by Figure 4.4, the optimal cost region produces a reasonable balance between cost and accuracy. In general, the forecasting method chosen should be in this optimal region, although other considerations may influence the choice of a forecasting method.

## Determine What to Forecast

Once overall forecasting objectives are clear, we must decide exactly what to forecast. Let's say that we want to make a sales forecast for a certain product. We need to decide whether we want the sales forecast to be in total dollars of sales revenues or in total units. Determining what to forecast may not be as easy as it seems, and it does require good communication between the forecast preparer and the forecast user.

FIGURE 4.4
Cost Versus Accuracy—
Alternative Forecasting
Methods

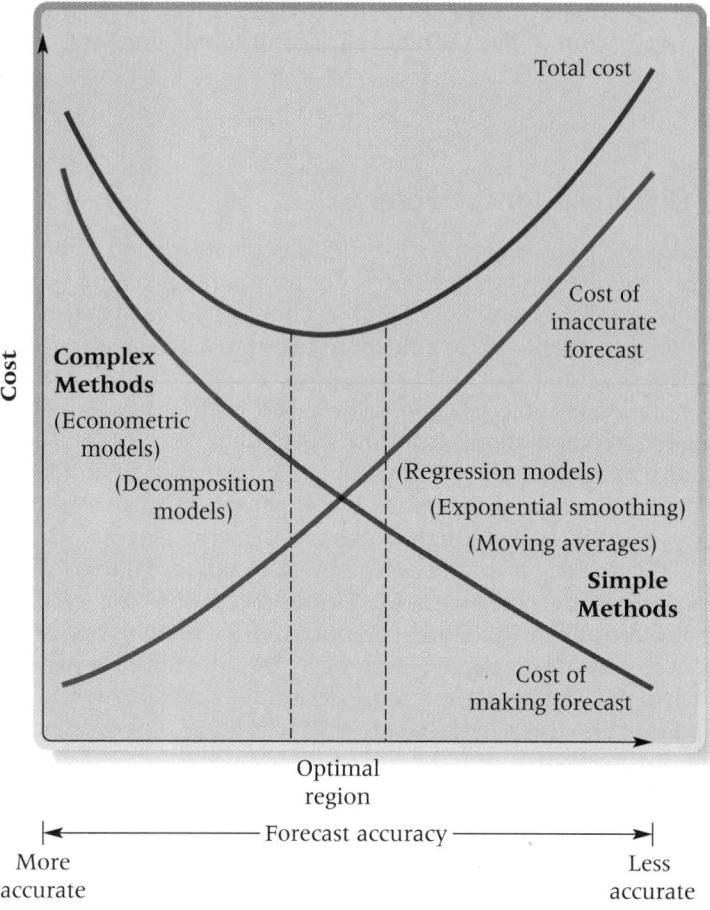

## Specify the Time Period for the Forecast

Specifying the time period for the forecast is important, because forecasting accuracy generally decreases as the length of the forecasting horizon increases. Let's consider the production scheduling and planning process that typically takes place at several levels in a corporation. Forecasting for the master production schedule usually is done for the short term, say, weekly or from one to three months. Forecasting for production planning usually is done for the medium term, ranging from quarterly forecasts to forecasts for as much as two years in the

TABLE 4.3
Time Spans—Forecasting
Applications

| Time Horizon | Forecasting Application | Forecasting Quantity | Forecasting Methods |
|---|---|---|---|
| Short term (0–3 months) | Inventory management, master production scheduling, work force scheduling | Individual product | Moving average, Exponential smoothing (Quantitative) |
| Medium term (3 months–2 years) | Production planning, purchasing, distribution | Product families | Regression, Time series analysis (quantitative) |
| Long term (2 years +) | Capacity planning, facility location | Total sales | Delphi method, market research (qualitative) |

future. Forecasting for capacity planning usually is for the long term, typically two years or more into the future. So the time span involved in a particular forecasting application may be an important consideration in choosing an appropriate forecasting method.

Table 4.3 shows how forecasting applications can be classified according to their time spans; the methods are discussed in detail later in the chapter.

## Gather and Analyze Data

Data for forecasting may come from internal or external sources. Internal data would seem to always be readily available. Unfortunately, this is often not the case because the data may not be available in the appropriate form—total sales rather than sales by product line or in sales dollars rather than sales units. So gathering internal data for forecasting requires communication and cooperation.

External data are available from a wide variety of sources. Federal, state, and local government agencies provide information, usually at low cost. Trade associations, professional groups, and some corporations and nonprofit institutions are also sources of external data.

## Select a Forecasting Method

The forecaster has many methods to select from when attempting to make a particular forecast. Two general approaches to forecasting are qualitative and quantitative. **Qualitative forecasting methods** are primarily subjective or judgmental in nature. **Quantitative forecasting methods** either try to extend historical data into the future or to develop associative models that use causal variables.

*Production forecasts for various plants around the world are presented to a group of plant managers.*

Several general items should be considered in selecting a forecasting method:

1. Type and amount of data available
2. Underlying pattern of the data
3. Forecast time horizon
4. Technical ability of the person making the forecast
5. Use of the forecast
6. Attitude of the user in regard to specific forecasting methods

Selecting a forecasting method is so important that we address it in detail in the next section, in which we will explain several forecasting methods and provide guidelines for their use.

## Make the Forecast

Actually making the forecast may be the easiest part of the entire process, because you will most likely use computer software to actually make the calculations. Many forecasting software packages are available for computers of all sizes. Software packages such as General Electric's *Time Series Forecasting System* and IBM's *Consumer Goods System* (*COGS*) and *Inventory Management Program and Control Technique* (*IMPACT*) are available for use on mainframe computers. Since the introduction of personal computers, virtually hundreds of forecasting software packages have been developed. Many software packages for PCs are attractively priced and provide a wide range of forecasting techniques.

Selection of a forecasting software package should be based on the following factors:

Number and type of forecasting methods provided
Cost of buying or leasing the package
Ease of use in terms of data input and program maintenance
Presentation features of the package

## Present the Forecast Results

The next step in the forecasting process is presenting the results. Forecasts often go to management in both oral and written form. Because forecasts typically involve extensive tables and sets of numbers, the results should be presented in the most interesting manner possible. Extensive use of graphs and diagrams, particularly in oral presentations, is highly desirable; color graphics are particularly effective.

## Monitor and Control the Forecast

A measurement of the forecast accuracy should accompany every forecast. **Forecast error,** the deviation of the forecast from what actually occurred, should be measured and evaluated. The objective here is to find out why the errors occurred and to determine whether the magnitude of the errors affected decisions that were based on the forecast. Monitoring and evaluating the forecast error may lead to changing certain aspects of the forecasting process or even to using a different forecasting method, shown in Figure 4.3 as a feedback loop.

Most software packages provide extensive monitoring and control procedures for errors. A later section of the chapter describes specific procedures for monitoring and controlling forecasts.

## Approaches to Forecasting—A Preview

As we observed earlier, there are two broad approaches to forecasting. The first approach involves qualitative, or subjective, predictions based on intuition and judgment or uses market surveys.

**Judgment methods** require the manager to use experience, intuition, personal values, guesses, and the opinions of others to arrive at a forecast. **Counting methods** are exactly what the term suggests—surveying and counting the number of people who will buy (or say they will buy) a product or the number of people who will attend some event. A **census,** or survey of the entire population, is another method. Or, we can take a **sample** by surveying a portion of the population and then making an estimate about the whole population. Obviously, counting methods are subject to error, because some people may not answer truthfully or may change their minds after making their response.

The second approach uses objective historical data and mathematical and statistical techniques to determine a summary value that is used as the forecast of the future. The two major types of quantitative forecasting methods are time series analysis and associative, or causal, methods.

**Time series analysis methods** are quantitative models that base forecasts on the assumption that the past is a good predictor of the future. For example, time series methods are typically used when considering several years of demand data for the product and the underlying relationships and trends in this data appear to be measurable and relatively stable. An obvious weakness is that new factors can throw off the prediction.

**Associative,** or **causal, methods,** such as regression models, are mathematical and incorporate variables or factors that might influence demand. For example, forecasters typically use associative models when they have several years of demand for the product being considered, have determined a relationship between the product demand and other socioeconomic factors, and have corresponding time series for the other socioeconomic factors.

Table 4.4 provides a brief summary of some forecasting methods that fall within these four categories.

## Qualitative Forecasting Methods

Qualitative forecasting methods are perhaps the simplest and fastest ways to make forecasts. They allow us to include "soft" information such as personal opinions, guesses, and the opinions of others. They are used when there is not enough time to gather and analyze quantitative data. Or they may be useful when political and economic conditions are changing rapidly and information may be unavailable. Among the more commonly used qualitative forecasting methods are naïve extrapolation, sales force composite, jury of executive opinion, the Delphi technique, and market research surveys.

## Judgment Methods

**Naïve extrapolation:** the application of a simple assumption about the economic outcome of the next time period, or a simple, if subjective, extension of the results of current events

**Sales force composite:** a compilation of estimates by salespeople (or dealers) of expected sales in their territories, adjusted for presumed biases and expected changes

**Jury of executive opinion:** the consensus of a group of "experts," often from a variety of functional areas within a company

**Delphi technique:** a successive series of estimates independently developed by a group of "experts," each of whom, at each step in the process, uses a summary of the group's previous results to make new estimates

## Counting Methods

**Market testing:** representative buyers' responses to new offerings, tested and extrapolated to estimate the products' future prospects

**Consumer market survey:** attitudinal and purchase intentions data gathered from representative buyers

**Industrial market survey:** data similar to consumer surveys but fewer more knowledgeable subjects sampled, resulting in more informed evaluations

## Time Series Methods

**Moving averages:** recent values of the forecast variables averaged to predict future outcomes

**Exponential smoothing:** an estimate for the coming period based on a constantly weighted combination of the forecast estimate for the previous period and the most recent outcome

**Time series extrapolation:** a prediction of outcomes derived from the future extension of a least squares function fitted to a data series that uses time as an independent variable

**Time series decomposition:** a prediction of expected outcomes from trend, seasonal, cyclical, and random components, which are isolated from a data series

**Box-Jenkins:** a complex, computer-based iterative procedure that produces an autoregressive, integrated moving average model, adjusts for seasonal and trend factors, estimates appropriate weighting parameters, tests the model, and repeats the cycle as appropriate

## Causal Methods

**Correlation methods:** predictions of values based on historic patterns of covariation between variables

**Regression models:** estimates produced from a predictive equation derived by minimizing the residual variance of one or more predictor (independent) variables

**Econometric models:** outcomes forecast from an integrated system of simultaneous equations that represent relationships among elements of the national economy derived from combining history and economic theory

Source: David M. Georgoff and Robert G. Murdick, "Manager's Guide to Forecasting," *Harvard Business Review* 64, No. 1 (January–February 1986): 110–120.

TABLE 4.4
Summary of Common Forecasting Methods

## Naïve Extrapolation

The simplest of all forecasting methods is to assume that the next period will be identical to the current period. Doing this to make forecasts is **naïve extrapolation.**[1] Naïve extrapolation has the advantage of requiring a minimum amount of information. For example, you are responsible for spare parts inventory at a plant, and you recall that the plant used ten of a certain spare part last month. So, expecting the same for next month, you forecast your needs accordingly. The obvious disadvantage of naïve extrapolation is that it tends to not be accurate.

## Sales Force Composite

Using the collective opinions of a company's sales force is often an excellent way to make a subjective forecast. The sales force is usually a good source of information, because it has direct contact with a company's customers.

To make a **sales force composite** forecast, the forecaster asks members of the sales force to estimate sales for each of their products within their respective territories. The estimates are often subjective, based on the salesperson's "feel" for the situation. They may include estimates of the pessimistic, optimistic, and most likely levels of sales. The sales manager then aggregates these estimates by product line and/or geographic area. The firm's total sales forecast is a combination of the product line and/or geographical forecasts.

One major drawback to this approach is that it is inherently biased. Salespeople may not be able to distinguish between what their customers say and actually do. Also, the sales manager may use the estimates to set sales quotas for products and/or sales territories, which may cause salespeople to underestimate sales so that they can exceed them. The sales manager can offset the underestimation bias but must be careful not to introduce other biases into the forecast.

## Jury of Executive Opinion

Highly paid executives are expected to be knowledgeable of their areas of responsibility. Bringing them together and soliciting their opinions is another way to develop a forecast. To obtain a breadth of opinions, selecting these people from several functional areas of the company (finance, marketing, and production) often is helpful. This **jury of executive opinion** approach again has the advantage of speed. It usually does not require the collection and analysis of data—subjective opinions are used most often. The forecaster can solicit these opinions through interviews or by holding a group meeting of the "jury" of executives. An advantage of the latter approach is that it can stimulate group discussion and greater insights. One disadvantage is that an executive with a strong personality can dominate the group and bias the results.

## The Delphi Method

The **Delphi method** is a process for obtaining a consensus forecast from a group of experts while maintaining their anonymity. It was originally developed by the

[1]Many other authors classify naïve extrapolation as a quantitative method (a moving average of one period). We prefer to classify extrapolation as a qualitative method, to be consistent with the summary shown in Table 4.4.

Rand Corp. in 1948 to evaluate what an atomic bomb attack would do to the United States. Since that time it has been applied to a number of uncertainty scenarios and for making subjective forecasts and is one of the most widely used qualitative forecasting methods.[2]

Application of the Delphi method begins with selecting a panel of experts willing to answer questions about a particular forecasting problem. Usually, panel members are kept separate, asked not to confer, and are not identified to each other. The objective of the Delphi method is to obtain a reliable consensus while eliminating undesirable group interaction. The coordinator of the Delphi group begins by asking each member to make a written estimate of the forecast. The coordinator then collects, edits, and summarizes the initial estimates. Members of the Delphi group receive the summary, and they are asked to make a second, more refined estimate. The entire process is repeated until the coordinator feels that the panel has reached a consensus or narrowed the range for the forecast. The individual answers help to ensure the anonymity that reduces the effect of a particularly aggressive or socially dominant individual. Presenting the summaries in terms of quartile responses avoids the danger of conformity to a majority opinion, which is common in committee decision making. The Delphi method may not produce a single forecast; the final forecast may be expressed instead as a statistical range.

A major advantage of the Delphi method is that it eliminates much of the personal conflict or dominance by one individual that is so often a part of group decision making. Another advantage is that the Delphi group can provide a broad range of judgments. It also can be faster and less expensive than other group decision-making methods.

A major disadvantage of the Delphi method is that studies have failed to prove that Delphi forecasts achieve a high degree of accuracy. Another disadvantage is anonymity frees panel members of accountability and responsibility.

Global Operations Management 4.1 describes the use of the Delphi method in analyzing waste management in India.

## Market Research Surveys

A final type of qualitative forecasting method is the market research survey. As Table 4.4 shows, market surveys can be done either of mass consumers or of industrial consumers and are categorized as counting methods. They involve a systematic approach to creating and testing hypotheses about the market.

The first step in conducting a **market research survey** usually involves constructing a questionnaire that solicits personal, economic, demographic, or marketing information. Second is the selection of a representative sample of consumer households or industrial customers. Usually, sampling is random. Third, the questionnaire is administered through telephone polling, mailings, or personal interviews. The final step is analyzing the data and testing various hypotheses.

Market research surveys are widely used for a variety of forecasting problems, ranging from the short term (new product sales) to the long term (buying

[2]Spyros Makridakis, Steven C. Wheelwright, and Victor E. McGee, *Forecasting: Methods and Applications* (New York: Wiley, 1983), p. 652.

**GLOBAL OPERATIONS MANAGEMENT 4.1**

# A National Delphi Study of System Waste in India

The increased pace and volume of manufacturing, agriculture, distribution, and services have been responsible for the ever-increasing consumption of natural and manufactured resources. The primary emphasis has been on resource management, although waste management also is important. To learn about the amount of waste produced by various sectors of the Indian economy in order to forecast the future, researchers conducted a national Delphi study in 1990.

The researchers classified all organized activity in India in eight sectors:

Agriculture

Energy

Industry

Commerce

Transport and communications

Education and research

Social services

General services

The researchers used a two-stage Delphi procedure. The 280 panelists for the first stage included eminent social scientists, economists, and researchers; some had previous experience in conducting and participating in Delphi experiments. Analysis of the initial results indicated that the following issues should be studied further:

1. Relative rankings of sectors with respect to wastefulness
2. Relative ranking of waste of various resources
3. Relative ranking of some main reasons for waste
4. Self-rating of respondents
5. Relative ranking of functional areas of waste management

The second stage of the Delphi study focused on these issues and involved 125 participants. This table provides information about the most wasteful sectors:

| Sector | 1990 Conditions as Estimated by Respondents (%) | Conditions for 2010 as Projected by Respondents (%) |
|---|---|---|
| Agriculture | 24 | 10 |
| Energy | 29 | 26 |
| Industry | 4 | 5 |
| Commerce | 0 | 0 |
| Transport and Communications | 1 | 0 |
| Education and research | 22 | 17 |
| Social services | 8 | 19 |
| General services | 12 | 23 |

Seventy-five percent of the respondents were of the opinion that the energy, agriculture, and education and research were the most wasteful in 1990. The respondents predicted that energy, general services, and social services would be the most wasteful in 2010.

continued

This table provides information about the experts' opinions of which resources are and will be wasted most:

| Resource | 1990 Conditions as Estimated by Respondents (%) | Conditions for 2010 as Projected by Respondents (%) |
|---|---|---|
| Labor | 78.4 | 82.3 |
| Materials | 10.8 | 6.9 |
| Energy | 4.9 | 2.0 |
| Capital | 2.0 | 2.9 |
| Land and buildings | 0.0 | 0.0 |
| Technology and information | 1.0 | 1.0 |
| Utilities and services | 2.9 | 4.9 |

The respondents reached near consensus—78.4% and 82.3%, respectively, felt that labor was the resource most wasted in 1990 and would be in 2010.

Overall, the national study presented a pessimistic view of the socioeconomic importance of waste management in India. It indicated a low level of awareness of waste management, despite its prominence in media reports. The study also suggested that there would be little improvement by the year 2010.

*At a shopping mall a consumer is interviewed during a market research survey.*

intentions five years in the future). They require a great deal of skill to handle correctly and can involve great expense. They can provide a lot of useful forecasting information, but lengthy questionnaires often have a poor response rate and provide extensive findings that are hard to analyze.

# Quantitative Forecasting Methods— Time Series Analysis Models

Quantitative forecasting methods are applicable when three general conditions are present:

- There is a reliable set of information about the past, a time-ordered sequence of observations taken at regular intervals over a period of time (hourly, weekly, monthly, quarterly, yearly)
- The time series information can be expressed in quantitative terms
- It is reasonable to assume that the pattern exhibited by the information from the past will continue into the future.

Time series analysis models try to predict future occurrences based on data from the past. The forecaster is not concerned with changes in internal or external factors that may affect the forecast. For example, we might simply collect demand information for four months, calculate the average monthly demand, and use this as our forecast for the next month.

Time series analysis models can be further divided into time series smoothing and time series decomposition.

## Time Series Smoothing

Historical time series data typically contain a certain amount of random variation, or "noise," which tends to obscure the underlying pattern of the data. This randomness may arise from many sources, and it cannot be reliably predicted. So, it is often useful to smooth out the data by averaging several observations; this makes the underlying pattern of the data more apparent.

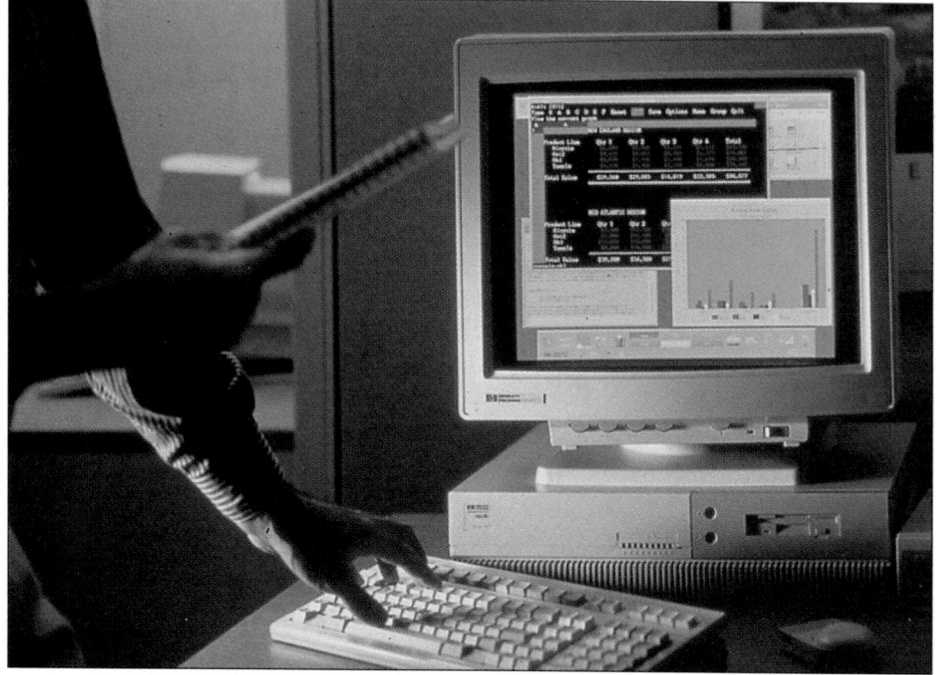

*Personal computers facilitate using a wide array of forecasting techniques, and enable operations personnel to make forecasts quickly and cheaply.*

**Simple Average** The **simple average** is an average of past demand in which all periods have equal weight. The simple average is computed as

$$\text{Simple Average (SA)} = \frac{\text{Sum of demands for all past periods}}{\text{Number of demand periods}}$$

$$= \frac{D_t + D_{t-1} + \ldots + D_{t-(N-1)}}{N} \qquad (4\text{-}1)$$

where

$$D_t = \text{Demand in the current period}$$
$$D_{t-1} = \text{Demand in the past period}$$
$$D_{t-(N-1)} = \text{Demand in the last period for which data was available}$$
$$N = \text{Total number of time periods}$$

To illustrate the computation of a simple average, consider the following example:

---

**EXAMPLE 4.1**

Susan Gardner owns and operates a video rental store. The demand for one of her best videos for the current month and the previous five months follows this pattern:

$$D \text{ current month, } t = 150 \text{ rentals}$$
$$D \text{ past month, } t-1 = 100 \text{ rentals}$$
$$D \text{ two months ago, } t-2 = 130 \text{ rentals}$$
$$D \text{ three months ago, } t-3 = 110 \text{ rentals}$$
$$D \text{ four months ago, } t-4 = 170 \text{ rentals}$$
$$D \text{ five months ago, } t-5 = 180 \text{ rentals}$$

$$\text{Simple Average} = \frac{D_t + D_{t-1} + D_{t-2} + D_{t-3} + D_{t-4} + D_{t-5}}{N}$$

$$= \frac{150 + 100 + 130 + 110 + 170 + 180}{6} = 840/6$$

$$= 140 \text{ rentals} \qquad (4\text{-}2)$$

---

A forecast for the next month would be $F_{t+1} = \text{SA} = 140$ rentals. While the demand in any one period may be above or below the average, the average demand tends to represent the true underlying demand pattern. As the number of periods used to calculate the average increases, the averaging process tends to reflect the central tendency of the demand process, and the effect of extreme random deviations is less.

One major aspect of the simple average method is that the demand in all past periods enters equally into the calculation. However, if the true demand pattern actually changes over time, the simple average may not truly reflect the most recent past, and hence the future, because all past demand periods are weighted equally. Using a simple moving average somewhat overcomes the disadvantage.

**Simple Moving Average** A **simple moving average** is an average computed for a specified number of recent time periods. A new demand data point becomes available for each period and is included in the average, and the oldest demand observation is excluded. Again, a specific number of observations is used in the

| Month | Time Period | Observed Demand | Three-Month Moving Average | Five-Month Moving Average |
|---|---|---|---|---|
| January | 1 | 150 | – | – |
| February | 2 | 100 | – | – |
| March | 3 | 130 | – | – |
| April | 4 | 110 | 126.67 | – |
| May | 5 | 170 | 113.33 | – |
| June | 6 | 180 | 136.67 | 132.00 |
| July | 7 | 190 | 153.33 | 138.00 |
| August | 8 | 210 | 180.00 | 156.00 |
| September | 9 | 180 | 193.33 | 172.00 |
| October | 10 | 200 | 193.33 | 186.00 |
| November | 11 | 190 | 196.67 | 192.00 |
| December | 12 | 220 | 190.00 | 194.00 |

TABLE 4.5
Moving Average—Video Rental Demand Data

averaging process. Once the forecaster has selected the number of past periods to be used in the calculation, it is a constant, and the forecaster gives demands within this time frame equal weight. The average "moves," in the sense that after each demand period elapses, the forecaster adds demand for the newest period and deletes the demand for the oldest period before making the next calculation.

The simple $N$-period moving average is computed as

$$\text{Simple Moving Average (MA)} = \frac{\text{Sum of demands for the last } N \text{ periods}}{\text{Number of periods used in the moving average } (N)}$$

$$= \frac{D_t + D_{t-1} + \ldots + D_{t-(N-1)}}{N} \tag{4-3}$$

where

$D_t$ = Demand in the current period
$D_{t-1}$ = Demand in the past period
$D_{t-(N-1)}$ = Demand in the last period for which the moving average is computed
$N$ = Number of periods used in the moving average

To illustrate the computation of a simple moving average, consider the following example:

**EXAMPLE 4.2**

Gardner has collected a year's worth of data concerning the rental demand for her best video. She would like to determine three-month and five-month moving averages for her year's worth of data. Table 4.5 presents the observed demand and summarizes her computations.

The three-month moving average for April computes as follows:

$$\text{Three-Month Moving Average (April)} = \frac{D_{Mar} + D_{Feb} + D_{Jan}}{3}$$

$$= \frac{130 + 100 + 150}{3} = \frac{380}{3} = 126.67 \tag{4-4}$$

The five-month moving average for June computes as follows:

$$\text{Five-Month Moving Average (June)} = \frac{D_{May} + D_{Apr} + D_{Mar} + D_{Feb} + D_{Jan}}{5}$$

$$= \frac{170 + 110 + 130 + 100 + 150}{5} = 132.00$$

(4-5)

Figure 4.5 displays the three-month and five-month moving averages, along with the actual observed demand. A three-month moving average forecast for the next period would be $F_{t+1} = MA_3 = 190 \text{ units}$; a five-month moving average forecast for the next period would be $F_{t+1} = MA_5 = 194$ *units*.

The advantage of the moving average method is that it helps to smooth out abrupt fluctuations in the demand pattern and can provide a more stable estimate for demand. The number of time periods included in the moving average somewhat controls the stability of response to a change in the demand pattern. **Stability** is the property of not fluctuating erratically so that the forecast follows the basic demand pattern. Observe that the five-month moving average is more stable than the three-month moving average. On the other hand, the **responsiveness** of the forecast—the ability to adjust to changes in the demand pattern—is greater if the average uses fewer periods. Observe that the three-month moving average is more responsive than the five-month moving average. Stability and responsiveness conflict. If the demand pattern appears to have relatively small random fluctuations, use a responsive forecasting method. If the

FIGURE 4.5
Comparison of Three-Month
and Five-Month Moving
Averages

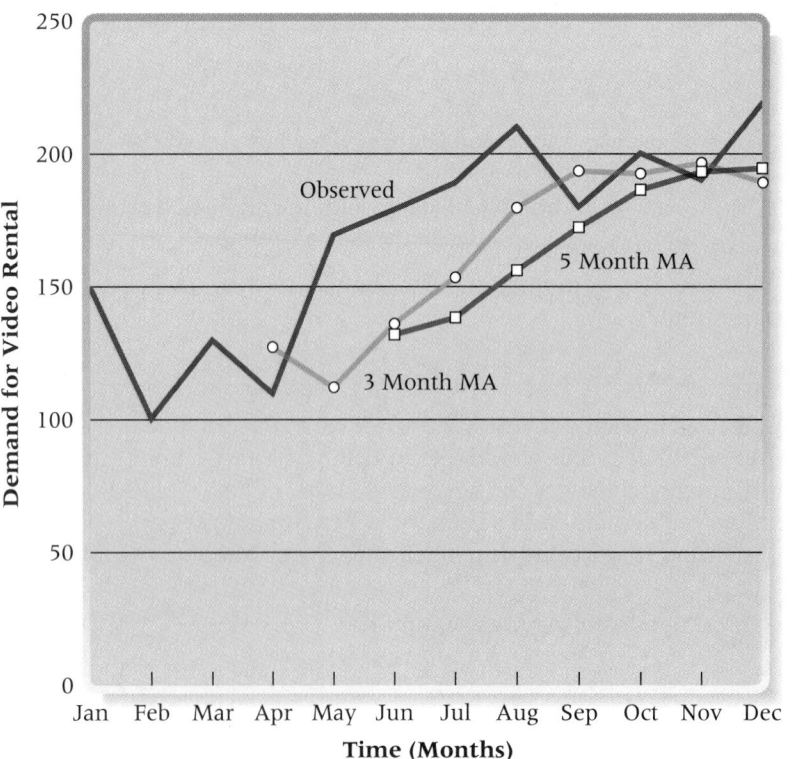

demand pattern appears to have relatively large random fluctuations, use a stable forecasting method.

**Weighted Moving Average**   A **weighted moving average** is a moving average in which the forecaster assigns more weight to certain time periods. A forecaster usually varies weights so that recent demand data influence the forecast more than older demand data. This method provides a more rapid response to recent changes in the demand pattern.

The $N$-period weighted moving average is computed as

Weighted Moving Average (WMA) $= W_t D_t + W_{t-1} D_{t-1} + \ldots + W_{t-(N-1)} D_{t-(N-1)}$

$$(4\text{-}6)$$

where

$$0 \leq W_t \leq 1.0 - \text{weight for period } t$$
$$0 \leq W_{t-1} \leq 1.0 - \text{weight for period } t-1$$
$$\cdot \qquad \cdot$$
$$\cdot \qquad \cdot$$
$$\cdot \qquad \cdot$$
$$0 \leq W_{t-(N-1)} \leq 1.0 - \text{weight for period } t-(N-1)$$
$$W_t + W_{t-1} + \ldots + W_{t-(N-1)} = 1.0$$

The following example illustrates the weighted moving average process:

---

**EXAMPLE 4.3**

Lexington County Medical Center wants to forecast its patient demand for next week. It has experienced patient demand in the last three weeks of $D_t = 750$; $D_{t-1} = 725$; and $D_{t-2} = 690$, respectively. It wishes to weight these demands as $W_t = 0.60$; $W_{t-1} = 0.30$; and $W_{t-2} = 0.10$, respectively. The three-period weighted moving average is computed as

$$\text{Three-Period Weighted Moving Average (WMA)} =$$
$$W_t D_t + W_{t-1} D_{t-1} + W_{t-2} D_{t-2} = (0.60)(750) + (0.30)(725) + (0.10)(690)$$
$$= 450 + 217.5 + 69 = 736.5 \qquad (4\text{-}7)$$

The forecast for next week's patient demand would be $F_{t+1} = WMA = 736.5$

---

The advantage of the weighted moving average forecasting process is that it allows the forecaster to use judgment in weighting more heavily the demand experience of recent months. The disadvantage is that the choice of the weights is still a subjective process in which errors can occur.

**Single Exponential Smoothing**   Exponential smoothing is a special type of weighted moving average. Moving averages have two general limitations. First, the data required to compute moving averages can be extensive if many periods are used in the moving average and if the number of items requiring a forecast is also great. Fortunately, rapidly increasing computer storage capability has made this a relatively minor problem. Second, the simple moving average forecasting process gives equal weight to each of the past $N$ demands and no weight to demand in periods prior to $t-(N-1)$. In general, that true demand pattern is more likely to be reflected by the demand from more recent time periods. So, recent demand values should be given relatively more weight in the forecasting process than older demand observations. Exponential smoothing addresses both problems inherent in the use of a moving average.

Exponential smoothing is so named because of the special way it weights each of the past demands. The pattern of weights is exponential—demand for the most recent time period is weighted most heavily, and then the weights placed on successively older time periods decay exponentially. To illustrate, we now explain the computational aspects of single exponential smoothing. The equation used in **single exponential smoothing,** also called **simple exponential smoothing,** to produce a forecast uses only three pieces of data: the actual demand for the most recent time period, the forecast made for the most recent time period, and the exponential smoothing constant. The general form of the single exponential smoothing equation is

$$F_{t+1} = \alpha D_t + (1 - \alpha) F_t \qquad (4\text{-}8)$$

where

$$F_{t+1} = \text{Forecast of next period's demand}$$
$$D_t = \text{Actual demand in most recent period}$$
$$F_t = \text{Demand forecast in most recent period}$$
$$\alpha = \text{Exponential smoothing constant, } 0.0 \leq \alpha \leq 1.0$$

The implications of exponential smoothing are easier to examine if we expand the general form of the single exponential smoothing equation just presented. We first expand equation 4-8 by replacing $F_t$ with its components as follows:

$$F_{t+1} = \alpha D_t + (1 - \alpha) [\alpha D_{t-1} + (1 - \alpha) F_{t-1}] = \alpha D_t + \alpha(1 - \alpha) D_{t-1} + (1 - \alpha)^2 F_{t-1} \qquad (4\text{-}9)$$

We continue expanding by replacing $F_{t-1}$ with its components, $F_{t-2}$ with its components, and so on, resulting in this equation:

$$F_{t+1} = \alpha D_t + \alpha(1 - \alpha) D_{t-1} + \alpha(1 - \alpha)^2 D_{t-2} + \alpha(1 - \alpha)^3 D_{t-3} + \ldots + \alpha(1 - \alpha)^{N-1} D_{t-(N-1)} \qquad (4\text{-}10)$$

In equation 4-10 the weights applied to each of the past demand values decrease exponentially, hence the term *exponential smoothing*. The smoothing

TABLE 4.6
Nadir Electronics—Video
Disk Player Demand Data

| Time Period | Observed Demand (000 Units) |
|---|---|
| 1 | 110 |
| 2 | 120 |
| 3 | 150 |
| 4 | 180 |
| 5 | 120 |
| 6 | 100 |
| 7 | 90 |
| 8 | 140 |
| 9 | 170 |
| 10 | 190 |
| 11 | 200 |
| 12 | 220 |

constant, $\alpha$, is a decimal between 0 and 1 and is chosen in a manner that makes the values forecast fit the past data accurately. The choice of $\alpha = 0.0$ would result in a forecast that would not be adjusted in any way, regardless of the demand that occurred. This would be a constant forecast, and it would also be totally unresponsive to changes in the actual demand pattern. Conversely, the choice of $\alpha = 1.0$ would result in a forecast that would always equal the last actual demand value. This forecast would be the naïve extrapolation forecast discussed earlier. It would be a very responsive forecast, but it would also be very unstable with respect to any fluctuations in the actual demand pattern.

**EXAMPLE 4.4**

The following example illustrates the application of single exponential smoothing: Nadir Electronics manufactures video disk players and is interested in applying exponential smoothing to twelve months of demand data it has collected. Table 4.6 shows video disk player demand data for Nadir Electronics for one year (twelve time periods).

The initial problem with actually applying exponential smoothing is that in the first period for which a forecast is to be made, $F_{t+1}$, we have no forecast for the previous period, $F_t$. This problem can be resolved by averaging the demands for several early periods to get an initial forecast, or the forecaster can simply use the first observed value as the first forecast. Using the latter approach with the Nadir Electronics data shown in Table 4.6, we set $F_1 = 110$, the actual demand value for the first period (because no forecast is available for the first period). Using the single exponential smoothing equation, with $\alpha = 0.1$

$$F_{t+1} = \alpha D_t + (1 - \alpha) F_t \quad \text{(general formula)} \tag{4-11}$$
$$F_{t=2} = \alpha D_{t=1} + (1 - \alpha) F_{t=1} \quad \text{(forecast—period 2)}$$
$$= (0.1)\,110 + (1 - 0.1)\,110 = 11 + 99 = 110 \tag{4-12}$$
$$F_{t=3} = \alpha D_{t=2} + (1 - \alpha) F_{t=2} \quad \text{(forecast—period 3)}$$
$$= (0.1)\,120 + (1 - 0.1)\,110 = 12 + 99 = 111 \tag{4-13}$$
$$F_{t=4} = \alpha D_{t=3} + (1 + \alpha) F_{t=3} \quad \text{(forecast—period 4)}$$
$$= (0.1)\,150 + (1 - 0.1)\,111 = 15 + 99.9 = 114.9 \tag{4-14}$$

and so forth.

The effect that the choice of the value of $\alpha$ has on the single exponential smoothing process is shown in Figure 4.6. A value of $\alpha = 0.9$ produces little smoothing in the forecast but instead reacts quickly to changes in the demand pattern. Conversely, a value of $\alpha = 0.1$ gives considerable smoothing but is relatively unresponsive to changes in the demand pattern. Overall, a value of $\alpha = 0.9$ produces the most accurate forecast.

Table 4.7 presents a summary of the single exponential smoothing computations for $\alpha$ values of 0.1, 0.5, and 0.9. It includes forecasts made for period 13 (one month beyond the end of the observed demand).

Single exponential smoothing has as its advantages its operating simplicity and its minimal requirements for data. Its main disadvantage is that the forecaster must choose a value of $\alpha$. This choice is usually made through a trial-and-error process in which the forecaster chooses a value for $\alpha$ that minimizes some measure of the forecast error. As the data in Figure 4.7 show, the

FIGURE 4.6
Actual and Single
Exponentially Smoothed
Forecasts—Nadir Electronics

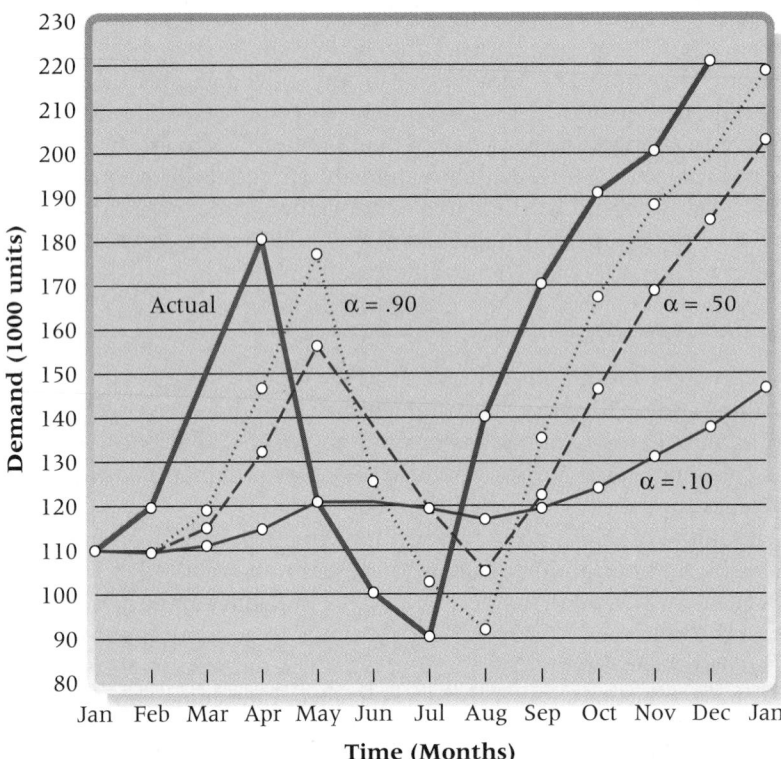

TABLE 4.7
Single Exponentially
Smoothed Forecasts—
Nadir Electronics

| | Time | Observed Demand | α = 0.1 | | α = 0.5 | | α = 0.9 | |
|---|---|---|---|---|---|---|---|---|
| Month | Period | (000 Units) | Forecast | Error | Forecast | Error | Forecast | Error |
| Jan. | 1 | 110 | 110.00 | 0.000 | 110.00 | 0.000 | 110.00 | 0.000 |
| Feb. | 2 | 120 | 110.00 | 10.000 | 110.00 | 10.000 | 110.00 | 10.000 |
| Mar. | 3 | 150 | 111.00 | 39.000 | 115.00 | 35.000 | 119.00 | 31.000 |
| Apr. | 4 | 180 | 114.90 | 65.100 | 132.50 | 47.500 | 146.90 | 33.100 |
| May | 5 | 120 | 121.41 | −1.410 | 156.25 | −36.250 | 176.69 | −56.690 |
| June | 6 | 100 | 121.27 | −21.269 | 138.13 | −38.125 | 125.67 | −25.669 |
| July | 7 | 90 | 119.14 | −29.142 | 119.06 | −29.063 | 102.57 | −12.567 |
| Aug. | 8 | 140 | 116.23 | 23.772 | 104.53 | 35.469 | 91.26 | 48.743 |
| Sept. | 9 | 170 | 118.61 | 51.395 | 122.27 | 47.734 | 135.13 | 34.874 |
| Oct. | 10 | 190 | 123.74 | 66.255 | 146.13 | 43.867 | 166.51 | 23.487 |
| Nov. | 11 | 200 | 130.37 | 69.630 | 168.07 | 31.934 | 187.65 | 12.349 |
| Dec. | 12 | 220 | 137.33 | 82.667 | 184.03 | 35.967 | 198.77 | 21.235 |
| Jan. | 13 | | 145.60 | | 202.02 | | 217.88 | |

"best" value of α, on the basis of most closely following the actual data, is 0.9. Why this value of α produces the best fit for the forecast is revealed in Figure 4.6, which indicates that the actual demand pattern over time has a great deal of variability. Using a higher value of α makes the single exponentially smoothed forecast responsive to the fluctuating demands.

Choosing an appropriate value for α has perplexed forecasters since the inception of simple exponential smoothing. The forecaster confronts two problems in making this choice. First, we may need a fairly long time series to

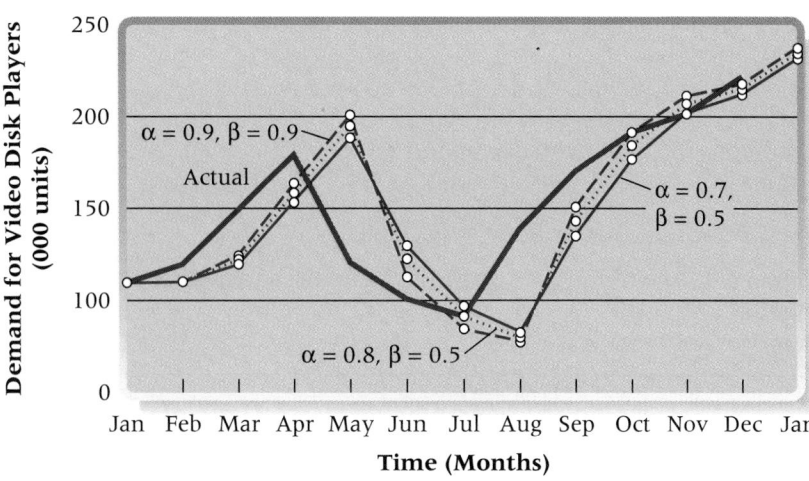

determine the best $\alpha$. Some software packages for PCs can search for the best value of $\alpha$ for a particular time series. What these programs do is set $\alpha = 0.00$, increment $\alpha$ in steps of, say, 0.05 or 0.1 to $\alpha = 1.0$, and determine the "best" forecast based on minimizing some error measure. The value of $\alpha$ that produces the best performance is then used for future forecasts. The more time periods available for the time series, the better the determination of the best $\alpha$ will be. Second, even if we can select a good $\alpha$ using the procedure outlined here, the underlying demand pattern may change in the next period. So, we really need some automatic way to track and change the values of $\alpha$.

Two methods have been proposed for controlling the values of alpha. The first method requires the forecaster to measure the amount of error between the forecast and actual demand.[3] If this error is large, $\alpha$ is set high ($\alpha = 0.8$), and if the error is small, $\alpha$ is set low ($\alpha = 0.2$). Values of $\alpha$ are specified on the basis of this error; they are not computed.

The second method uses a tracking signal to determine whether the forecast is tracking actual changes in demand.[4] The tracking signal is defined by the exponentially smoothed absolute forecast error. The value of $\alpha$ is then set equal to this tracking signal and varies from period to period in the range of $0.0 \leq \alpha \leq 1.0$.

### Double Exponential Smoothing
Single exponential smoothing, like any moving average technique, fails to respond to trends. A variation for incorporating a trend in an exponentially smoothed forecast is called *double exponential smoothing*. The basic idea behind **double exponential smoothing** is to compute a single exponential smoothing forecast and then adjust it for a positive or negative lag in trend.

Several double exponential smoothing models are available. The one discussed here uses two smoothing constants. The first smoothing constant, $\alpha$, is used to smooth the randomness of the overall time series. The second smoothing constant, $\beta$, is used to smooth the trend of the time series.

The exponentially smoothed forecast of next period's demand is found by using the single exponential smoothing equation:

$$F_{t+1} = \alpha D_t + (1 - \alpha)F_t \qquad (4\text{-}15)$$

[3]D. Clay Whybark, "A Comparison of Adaptive Forecasting Techniques," *Logistics and Transportation Review* 8, No. 3 (1972): 13–26.
[4]D. W. Trigg and D. H. Leach, "Exponential Smoothing with an Adaptive Response Rate," *Operational Research Quarterly* 18, No. 1 (March 1967): 53–59.

Next, the exponentially smoothed trend factor $(T_{t+1})$ is calculated by using the formula

$$T_{t+1} = \beta(F_{t+1} - F_t) + (1 - \beta)T_t \tag{4-16}$$

The trend-adjusted exponentially smoothed forecast is then calculated by using the formula

$$\text{Adjusted } F_{t+1} = F_{t+1} + [(1 - \beta)/\beta]T_{t+1} \tag{4-17}$$

In equation 4-17 the term $[(1 - \beta)/\beta]$ is a factor used to further adjust for the lag in the trend.

---

**EXAMPLE 4.5**

The use of double exponential smoothing can also be illustrated by using the Nadir Electronics video disk player data. To perform double exponential smoothing we need an initial estimate for the smoothed demand forecast and the smoothed trend. The initial estimate for the smoothed demand forecast can be set equal to the average demand for several early time periods or simply set equal to the first observed actual demand value. The initial value of the smoothed trend can be estimated from a plot of the time series or set equal to zero.

Using the simple approach, we set $F_1 = 110$, the actual demand value for the first period, and $T_1 = 0$. Using the single exponential smoothing equation, with $\alpha = 0.7$,

$$F_{t=1} = \alpha D_t + (1 - \alpha)F_t \quad \text{(general formula)} \tag{4-18}$$
$$F_{t=2} = \alpha D_{t=1} + (1 - \alpha)F_{t=1}$$
$$= (.7)110 + (1 - 0.7)110 = 77 + 33 = 110 \tag{4-19}$$
$$F_{t=3} = \alpha D_{t=2} + (1 - \alpha)F_{t=2}$$
$$= (0.7)120 + (1 - 0.7)110 = 84 + 33 = 117 \tag{4-20}$$
$$F_{t=4} = \alpha D_{t=3} + (1 - \alpha)F_{t=3}$$
$$= (0.7)150 + (1 - 0.7)117 = 105 + 35.1 = 140.1 \tag{4-21}$$

and so forth.

Next, using the exponentially smoothed trend factor equation, with $\beta = 0.5$,

$$T_{t+1} = \beta(F_{t+1} - F_t) + (1 - \beta)T_t \quad \text{(general formula)} \tag{4-22}$$
$$T_{t=2} = \beta(F_{t=2} - F_{t=1}) + (1 - \beta)T_{t=1}$$
$$= (0.5)(110 - 110) + (1 - 0.5)0 = 0 \tag{4-23}$$
$$T_{t=3} = \beta(F_{t=3} - F_{t=2}) + (1 - \beta)T_{t=2}$$
$$= (0.5)(117 - 110) + (1 - 0.5)0 = 3.5 + 0 = 3.5 \tag{4-24}$$
$$T_{t=4} = \beta(F_{t=4} - F_{t=3}) + (1 - \beta)T_{t=3}$$
$$= (0.5)(140.10 - 117) + (1 - 0.5)(3.5) = 11.55 + 1.75 = 13.3 \tag{4-25}$$

and so forth.

Finally, the trend adjusted exponentially smoothed forecast is calculated as

$$\text{Adjusted } F_{t+1} = F_{t+1} + [(1 - \beta)/\beta]T_{t+1} \quad \text{(general formula)} \tag{4-26}$$
$$\text{Adjusted } F_{t=2} = F_{t=2} + [(1 - \beta)/\beta]T_{t=2}$$
$$= 110 + [(1 - 0.5)/0.5]0 = 110 + (1)(0) = 110 \tag{4-27}$$
$$\text{Adjusted } F_{t=3} = F_{t=3} + [(1 - 0.5)/0.5]T_{t=3}$$
$$= 117 + (1)3.5 = 120.5 \tag{4-28}$$

$$\text{Adjusted } F_{t=4} = F_{t=4} + [(1 - 0.5)/0.5]T_{t=4}$$
$$= 140.10 + (1)13.3 = 153.40 \tag{4-29}$$

and so forth.

Table 4.8 presents a summary of the double exponential smoothing computations for paired values of $\alpha = 0.7$, $\beta = 0.5$; $\alpha = 0.8$, $\beta = 0.5$; and $\alpha = 0.9$, $\beta = 0.5$. Note that it includes forecasts made for period 13 (one month beyond the end of the observed demand).

The effect of the choices for different values of $\alpha$ and $\beta$ in the double exponential smoothing process can be seen in Figure 4.7. It shows that the most accurate forecast was obtained by using $\alpha = 0.9$, $\beta = 0.5$ (the forecasts made using these values of $\alpha$ and $\beta$ most accurately followed the demand observed).

**Other Exponential Smoothing Models**   Many other (higher order) exponential smoothing models are available. One such model, the Winters' triple exponential smoothing model, can be used to forecast demand when both trend and seasonal patterns are present.[5] Such models are more difficult to use, because they require the forecaster to estimate additional forecasting parameters. They are beyond the level of this introductory textbook; the more interested reader should consult some of the specialized forecasting references provided at the end of this chapter.

Operations Management in Practice 4.2 illustrates the use of exponential smoothing forecasting models at Rubbermaid Home Products Division.

## Time Series Decomposition

It is assumed that the time series being forecast consists of an underlying pattern plus some random error, as follows:

$$\text{Time series value} = \text{underlying pattern} + \text{random error} \tag{4-30}$$

[5]Peter R. Winters, "Forecasting Sales by Exponentially Weighted Moving Averages," *Management Science* 6, No. 3 (April 1960): 334–342.

**TABLE 4.8**
Double Exponentially Smoothed Forecasts— Nadir Electronics

| Month | Period | Observed Demand (000 Units) | $\alpha = 0.7$, $\beta = 0.5$ Forecast | Error | $\alpha = 0.8$, $\beta = 0.5$ Forecast | Error | $\alpha = 0.9$, $\beta = 0.5$ Forecast | Error |
|---|---|---|---|---|---|---|---|---|
| Jan. | 1 | 110 | 110.00 | 0.00 | 110.00 | 0.00 | 110.00 | 0.00 |
| Feb. | 2 | 120 | 110.00 | 10.00 | 110.00 | 10.00 | 110.00 | 10.00 |
| Mar. | 3 | 150 | 120.50 | 29.50 | 122.00 | 28.00 | 123.50 | 26.50 |
| Apr. | 4 | 180 | 153.40 | 26.60 | 158.40 | 21.60 | 163.10 | 16.90 |
| May | 5 | 120 | 188.64 | −68.64 | 194.68 | −74.68 | 199.68 | −79.68 |
| June | 6 | 100 | 127.91 | −27.91 | 120.44 | −20.44 | 111.66 | −11.66 |
| July | 7 | 90 | 95.03 | −5.03 | 88.84 | 1.16 | 84.01 | 5.99 |
| Aug. | 8 | 140 | 81.34 | 58.66 | 78.14 | 61.86 | 76.32 | 63.68 |
| Sept. | 9 | 170 | 134.82 | 35.18 | 141.82 | 28.18 | 149.59 | 20.41 |
| Oct. | 10 | 190 | 176.15 | 13.85 | 183.46 | 6.54 | 189.44 | 0.56 |
| Nov. | 11 | 200 | 201.20 | −1.20 | 206.24 | −6.24 | 209.68 | −9.68 |
| Dec. | 12 | 220 | 211.54 | 8.46 | 214.02 | 5.98 | 215.34 | 4.66 |
| Jan. | 13 | | 230.05 | | 233.19 | | 235.72 | |

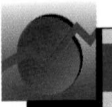

# Forecasting at Rubbermaid Home Products Division

Top managers as well as personnel from all functional areas participate in forecasting at Rubbermaid Home Products Division (HPD) in Wooster, Ohio. Responsibility for participating is widely distributed, both horizontally and vertically. The forecasts use several statistical forecasting techniques, and monitoring for errors is constant. The company uses the forecasts in both short-term and long-term business plans.

HPD divides its six hundred products into ten product lines, which are further subdivided into product groups. Forecasts are initially made for units and then translated into total dollars for items, groups, and product lines. HPD also uses the forecasts to determine color and raw materials requirements at three manufacturing locations.

Each product line is assigned to a group product manager who reports directly to the vice president of marketing and who also supervises one or more product managers. The marketing department also employs a manager of marketing information who supervises a forecast analyst and reports to the manager of inventory planning and forecasting. Forecasting is accorded prime importance in overall planning at HPD.

The annual forecast, which is made about midway through each year, drives the planning process. This forecast relies heavily on the opinions and knowledge of the group product managers and the product managers.

Forecasts for thirty, sixty, and ninety days are made each month, during the "forecast week." The forecasters use exponential smoothing methods and other, more sophisticated, time series analysis models. Several levels of management at HPD review these forecasts and often alter or revise them. Ultimately, the revised forecasts lead to a detailed set of manufacturing plans. Management reviews the forecasts and manufacturing plans each week. The secret to successful forecasting at HPD is the involvement of all levels of management on a continuous basis.

The underlying pattern is then decomposed into components. The four components most often used in time series decomposition are those discussed earlier, namely, the trend, cycle, seasonal, and random error.

Time series decomposition methods are among the oldest approaches to forecasting; economists have used them since the early 1900s. The decomposition method used most often today is known as *Census II* and was developed by the Bureau of the Census of the U.S. Department of Commerce.

A detailed discussion of time series decomposition and its use in forecasting will not be presented here. The references for this chapter include detailed discussions of time series forecasting using decomposition.

## Quantitative Forecasting Methods—Associative Models

A variable that is determined by some other factor, or factors, is referred to as a **dependent variable.** In regression analysis the variable being predicted is the dependent variable. An **independent variable** is one whose values are determined outside of the system being modeled. An independent variable is used in a causal relationship to predict values of a dependent variable. Associative forecasting methods assume that the dependent variable to be forecast has a relationship with one or more independent variables. For example, the forecaster may want to predict demand for a product (dependent variable) as a function of these independent variables

1. Advertising expenditure for the product
2. Price of the product
3. Consumer discretionary income

When using an associative forecasting model, the forecaster attempts to determine the underlying relationship between the dependent variable and the independent variable(s) and then uses this relationship to forecast future values of the dependent variable. In a sense, the use of an associative model allows the forecaster to interject subjectivity in the forecasting process by choosing the independent variables to be considered.

## Regression Models

**Regression models** are used to study the relationship between the dependent variable and one or more independent variables. The forecaster chooses a **regression equation** to measure this relationship and then uses it to forecast future values of the dependent variable. We begin our discussion with **simple linear regression,** which measures the relationship between a single dependent variable and a single independent variable.

**Simple Linear Regression** Company officers at Fairfield Manufacturing have observed that their product demand increases in relation to their advertising expenditures. Joan Wilhoit, vice president of marketing for the company, would like to know if she can use advertising expenditures to predict product demand. She has collected the data shown in Table 4.9.

**EXAMPLE 4.6**

As a first step in the linear regression process we need to verify that the plausibility of a linear relationship between the dependent and independent variables. One effective way to do this involves a **scatter diagram,** which plots the dependent variable along the $X$ axis and the independent variable along the $Y$ axis. Figure 4.8 shows the scatter diagram for the Fairfield Manufacturing data. This scatter diagram shows that a linear relationship between the variables does exist.

TABLE 4.9
Units Demanded and Advertising Expenditures—Fairfield Manufacturing

| Units Demanded (in 000) | Advertising Expenditures ($ 000) |
|---|---|
| 90 | 5 |
| 140 | 10 |
| 260 | 20 |
| 340 | 30 |
| 460 | 40 |

FIGURE 4.8
Scatter Diagram for
Forecasting of Number of
Units Demanded As A
Function of Level of
Advertising Expenditures

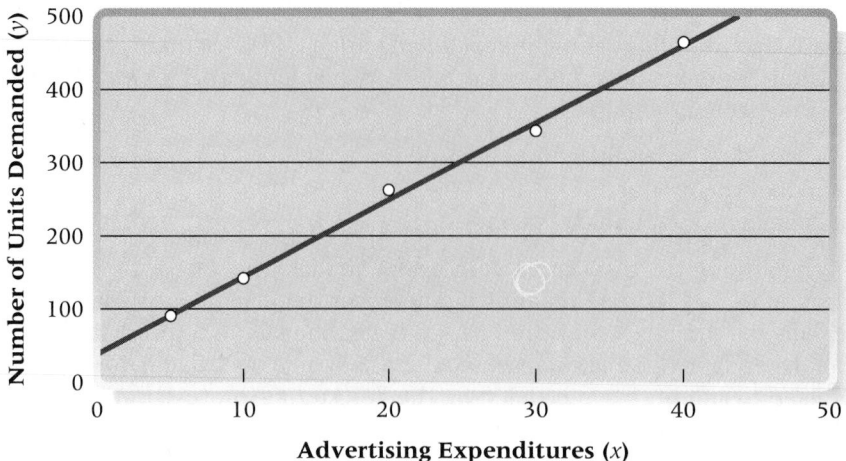

Having verified that a linear relationship does exist, we will now perform a regression analysis. This involves computing the coefficients of the simple linear regression model. The simple linear regression model is given by

$$Y_i = a + bX_i + \epsilon_i \qquad \text{for } i = 1, 2, \ldots, n \tag{4-31}$$

where

$Y_i$ = Dependent variable (units demanded)
$a$ = **Regression constant,** *or* **intercept**
$b$ = **Slope** of the regression equation
$X_i$ = Independent variable (advertising expenditures)
$\epsilon_i$ = Estimated error for observation $i$; a random variable

The intercept and slope values are computed by using the method of least squares. The rationale for the method of **least squares** is that the square of the distance between the actual observation and the fitted regression line should be minimized by the appropriate choice of $a$ and $b$. To illustrate, consider Figure 4.9,

FIGURE 4.9
Simple Linear
Regression—Least Squares
Method

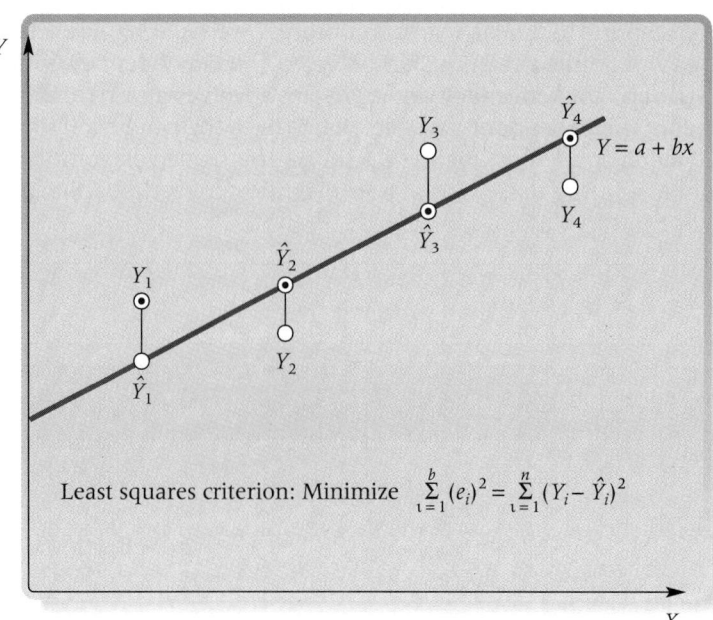

in which the observed (actual) values are labeled as $Y_1$, $Y_2$, $Y_3$, and $Y_4$; the points estimated by the fitted regression line are labeled as $\hat{Y}_1$, $\hat{Y}_2$, $\hat{Y}_3$, and $\hat{Y}_4$; and the deviations from the fitted regression line are labeled as $e_1$, $e_2$, $e_3$, and $e_4$. Each deviation can be computed as $e_i = Y_i - \hat{Y}_i$, and any value on the fitted regression line can be computed as $Y_i = a + bX_i$. The least squares criterion is used to determine the values of $a$ and $b$ so that the sum of the squared deviations between the actual and forecasted values is as small as possible. This implies that we should

$$\text{Minimize} \sum_{i=1}^{n}(e_i)^2 = \sum_{i=1}^{n}(Y_i - \hat{Y}_i)^2 = \sum_{i=1}^{n}[Y_i - (a + bX_i)]^2 \tag{4-32}$$

By differentiating this expression with respect to $a$ and $b$, and setting the corresponding derivatives equal to zero,[6] we obtain

$$b = \frac{\sum_{i=1}^{n} X_i Y_i - \sum_{i=1}^{n} X_i \sum_{i=1}^{n} Y_i}{n \sum_{i=1}^{n} X_i^2 - (\sum_{i=1}^{n} X_i)^2} = \frac{\sum_{i=1}^{n}(X_i - \bar{X})(Y_i - \bar{Y})}{\sum_{i=1}^{n}(X_i - \bar{X})^2} \tag{4-33}$$

$$a = \frac{\sum_{i=1}^{n} Y_i}{n} - b\frac{\sum_{i=1}^{n} X_i}{n} = \hat{Y} - b\bar{X} \tag{4-34}$$

where

$n$ = number of observations (data points) used to fit the regression line.

**EXAMPLE 4.7**

To illustrate the procedure involved in computing $a$ and $b$, Table 4.10 uses the data shown in Figure 4.8. The relevant computations and the resulting parameters for the regression line are obtained by using equations 4-33 and 4-34.

$$\bar{Y} = \frac{1290}{5} = 258 \qquad \bar{X} = \frac{105}{5} = 21 \tag{4-35}$$

$$b = \frac{n \sum_{i=1}^{n} X_i Y_i - \sum_{i=1}^{n} X_i \sum_{i=1}^{n} Y_i}{n \sum_{i=1}^{n} X_i^2 - (\sum_{i=1}^{n} X_i)^2} = \frac{5(35,650) - (105)(1,290)}{5(3,025) - (105)^2} \tag{4-36}$$

$$= \frac{178,250 - 135,450}{15,125 - 11,025} = \frac{42,800}{4,100} = 10.439$$

$$a = \bar{Y} - b\bar{X} = 258 - 10.439(21) = 258 - 219.22 = 38.78 \tag{4-37}$$

$$\text{Thus,} \qquad \hat{Y} = a + bX = 38.78 + 10.439X \tag{4-38}$$

We use this regression equation to forecast the number of units demanded, given a certain advertising expenditure. For example, assume that our next period's advertising expenditures will be $35,000. Using the regression equation we just computed, our demand forecast is

*Demand Forecast:* $\hat{Y} = 38.78 + 10.439X$

$$= 38.78 + 10.439(35)$$
$$= 38.78 + 365.37 = 404.15 \ (404,150 \text{ units}) \tag{4-39}$$

[6]For simplicity we will omit the detailed steps involved in this differentiation process and focus only on its results.

| Data Point $i$ | Units Demanded $Y_i$ | Advertising Expenditures $X_i$ | $Y_i^2$ | $X_i^2$ | $X_i Y_i$ |
|---|---|---|---|---|---|
| 1 | 90 | 5 | 8,100 | 25 | 450 |
| 2 | 140 | 10 | 19,600 | 100 | 1,400 |
| 3 | 260 | 20 | 67,600 | 400 | 5,200 |
| 4 | 340 | 30 | 115,600 | 900 | 10,200 |
| 5 | 460 | 40 | 211,600 | 1,600 | 18,400 |
| Total | 1,290 | 105 | 422,500 | 3,025 | 35,650 |

**TABLE 4.10**
Simple Linear Regression
Computations

We typically also want to measure the accuracy of the fitted regression model. One commonly used measure of the accuracy of the fitted regression model is the **standard error of the estimate,**[7] defined as

$$\text{Standard Error of the Estimate (SEE)} = \sqrt{\frac{\sum_{i=1}^{n}(Y_i - \hat{Y}_i)^2}{n-2}} \qquad (4\text{-}40)$$

The standard error of the estimate is similar to the standard deviation, except that it is based on the mean square vertical deviations of the actual observations from the fitted regression line rather than the deviations from the mean. Computation of the standard error of the estimate allows the forecaster to compare regression models and to make statements about confidence intervals for the predicted values of $Y_i$. If we assume that demand is distributed normally around the fitted regression line, as shown in Figure 4.10, a 68% confidence interval is obtained by moving ±1 standard errors of the estimate from the predicted values. Similarly, a 95% confidence interval is obtained by moving ±2 standard errors of the estimate from the predicted values.

**EXAMPLE 4.8**

For example, if the fitted regression model is

$$\hat{Y}_i = 100 + 10X_i \qquad (4\text{-}41)$$

the predicted value of $Y_i$ for $X_i = 2$ is

$$\hat{Y}_i = 100 + 10(2) = 120 \qquad (4\text{-}42)$$

If the corresponding value of $SEE = 5$, the forecaster can state the following

| 68% Confidence Interval | Prob $(\hat{Y}_i - 1\ SEE \leq$ true value of $Y_i \leq \hat{Y}_i + 1\ SEE) =$ | (4-43) |
|---|---|---|
| | Prob $(120 - 5 \leq$ true value of $Y_i \leq 120 + 5) = 0.68$ | |
| | Prob $(115 \leq$ true value of $Y_i \leq 125) = 0.68$ | |

| 95% Confidence Interval | Prob $(\hat{Y}_i - 2\ SEE \leq$ true value of $Y_i \leq \hat{Y}_i + 2\ SEE) =$ | |
|---|---|---|
| | Prob $(120 - 2[5] \leq$ true value of $Y_i \leq 120 + 2[5]) = 0.95$ | |
| | Prob $(110 \leq$ true value of $Y_i \leq 130) = 0.95$ | (4-44) |

Naturally, the smaller the value of the standard error of the estimate is, the more accurate the model is.

---

[7]For simple linear regression in general, the denominator in this expression is $n - k$, where $k$ is the number of regression constants.

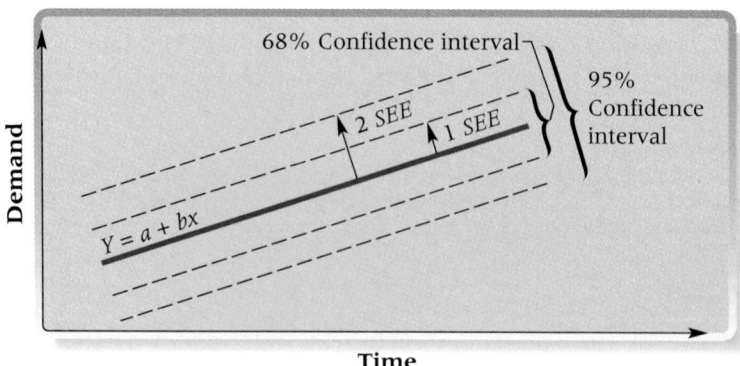

FIGURE 4.10
Confidence Intervals—Fitted
Regression Line

A second commonly used measure of the accuracy of the fitted regression model is the correlation coefficient, $r$. The **correlation coefficient** is a relative measure of the association between the independent and dependent variables. It can vary from 0 (indicating no correlation) to ±1 (indicating perfect correlation). When the correlation coefficient is greater than 0, the two variables are said to correlate positively, and when it is less than 0, they are said to correlate negatively. A **positive correlation** coefficient means that the independent and dependent variables increase or decrease in the same manner. A **negative correlation** coefficient means that the independent variable increases while the dependent variable decreases or vice versa. Figure 4.11

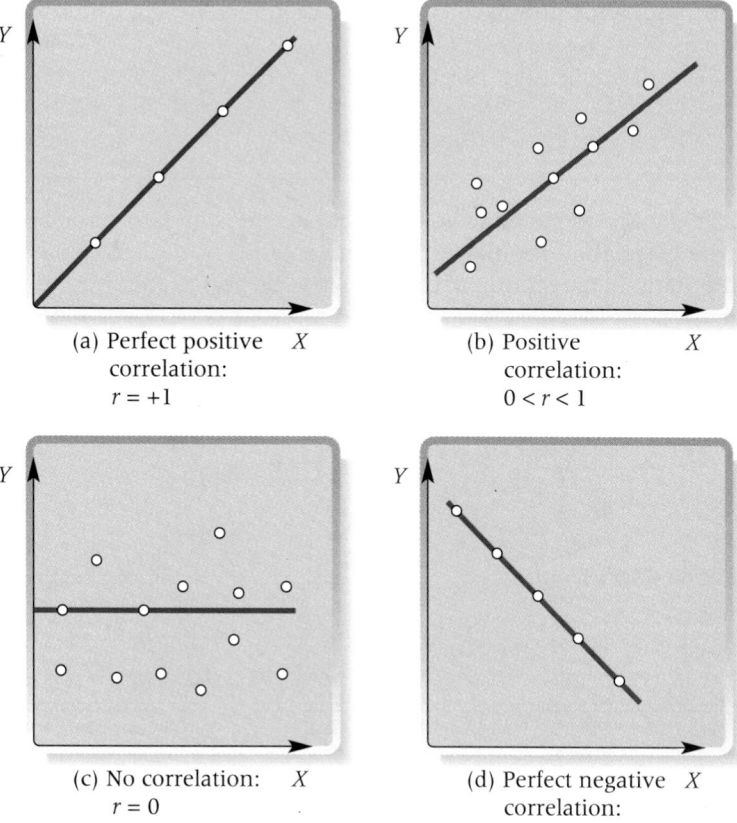

(a) Perfect positive correlation: $r = +1$

(b) Positive correlation: $0 < r < 1$

(c) No correlation: $r = 0$

(d) Perfect negative correlation: $r = -1$

FIGURE 4.11
Examples of Various Values
of the Correlation Coefficient

shows four plots that illustrate various values of the correlation coefficient. The sign of the correlation coefficient is always the same as the sign of the regression coefficient, $b$, in a simple regression model. The correlation coefficient is computed as

$$\text{Correlation Coefficient } (r) = \frac{n \sum_{i=1}^{n} X_i Y_i - \sum_{i=1}^{n} X_i \sum_{i=1}^{n} Y_i}{\sqrt{[n \sum_{i=1}^{n} X_i^2 - (\sum_{i=1}^{n} X_i)^2][n (\sum_{i=1}^{n} Y_i^2 - (\sum_{i=1}^{n} Y_i)^2]}} \qquad (4\text{-}45)$$

The square of the correlation coefficient, referred to as the *coefficient of determination*, is also a useful measure of regression model accuracy. The **coefficient of determination** is the ratio of the variation in the data explained by the fitted regression line to the total variation in the data. The coefficient of determination is computed as

$$\text{Coefficient of Determination } (r^2) = \frac{\text{Sum of explained variation in the data}}{\text{Sum of total variation in the data}}$$

$$= \frac{\sum_{i=1}^{n} (\hat{Y}_i - \overline{Y})^2}{\sum_{i=1}^{n} (Y_i - \overline{Y})^2} \qquad (4\text{-}46)$$

It indicates the percentage of the total variation that is explained by the regression line and measures how well the observations fit the regression line.

---

**EXAMPLE 4.9**

Let's use the data from example 4.6 to calculate the standard error of the estimate, the correlation coefficient, and the coefficient of determination. These computations are summarized in Table 4.11 and as follows:

$$\text{Standard Error of the Estimate (SEE)} = \sqrt{\frac{\sum_{i=1}^{n} (Y_i - \hat{Y}_i)^2}{n - 2}}$$

$$= \sqrt{\frac{324.92}{5 - 2}} = \sqrt{\frac{324.92}{3}} = \sqrt{108.31} = 10.4 \qquad (4\text{-}47)$$

$$\text{Correlation Coefficient } (r) = \frac{n \sum_{i=1}^{n} X_i Y_i - \sum_{i=1}^{n} X_i \sum_{i=1}^{n} Y_i}{\sqrt{[n \sum_{i=1}^{n} X_i^2 - (\sum_{i=1}^{n} X_i)^2][n \sum_{i=1}^{n} Y_i^2 - (\sum_{i=1}^{n} Y_i)^2]}}$$

$$= \frac{5(35,650) - (105)(1,290)}{\sqrt{[5(3,025) - 11,025][5(422,500) - 1,664,100]}} = \frac{178,250 - 135,450}{\sqrt{(4,100)(448,400)}}$$

$$= \frac{42,800}{42,877} = 0.998 \qquad (4\text{-}48)$$

$$\text{Coefficient of Determination } (r^2) = \frac{\sum_{i=1}^{n} (\hat{Y}_i - \overline{Y})^2}{\sum_{i=1}^{n} (Y_i - \overline{Y})^2} = \frac{89,357}{89,680} = 0.996 \quad (4\text{-}49)$$

**Multiple Linear Regression** A forecasting method in which one dependent variable is predicted as a function of two or more independent variables is **multiple linear regression**. The general form of the multiple linear regression equation is

$$\hat{Y} = a + b_1X_1 + b_2X_2 + \ldots + b_kX_k + \epsilon \quad (4\text{-}50)$$

For example, to project sales a forecaster would analyze several factors, such as prices, advertising expenditures, competition, and time, to test for their influence on sales. One important underlying assumption of multiple regression analysis is that the independent variables do not correlate with each other. This means that the changes in the dependent variable $Y$ caused by changes in one independent variable, $X_1$, and changes in a second independent variable, $X_2$, are not related.

Because multiple regression analysis typically involves several independent variables, it is much more complex than simple linear regression analysis. Computing the regression equation coefficients becomes more difficult. Fortunately, the widespread availability of specialized computer programs now makes it possible to quickly and efficiently perform multiple regression analyses. Other problems arise in such analyses, namely, that they can require a large amount of data.

A detailed discussion of multiple linear regression is beyond the scope of this textbook. Several references at the end of the chapter provide good discussion of this topic.

## Econometric Models

Another type of causal approach to forecasting involves econometric models. An **econometric model** is a set of simultaneous linear equations involving several interdependent variables. Econometric models typically use systems of multiple

T A B L E  4 . 1 1
Computation of Standard Error of the Estimate, Correlation Coefficient, and Coefficient of Determination

| | $Y_i$ | $X_i$ | $\hat{Y}_i$ | $(Y_i - \hat{Y}_i)$ | $(Y_i - \hat{Y}_i)^2$ | $(Y_i - \overline{Y})$ | $(Y_i - \overline{Y})^2$ | $(\hat{Y}_i - \overline{Y})$ | $(\hat{Y}_i - \overline{Y})^2$ |
|---|---|---|---|---|---|---|---|---|---|
| | 90 | 5 | 90.98 | −1.98 | 3.92 | −168 | 28,224 | −167.02 | 27,896 |
| | 140 | 10 | 143.17 | −3.17 | 10.05 | −118 | 13,924 | −114.83 | 13,186 |
| | 260 | 20 | 247.56 | 12.44 | 154.75 | 2 | 4 | −10.44 | 109 |
| | 340 | 30 | 351.95 | −11.95 | 142.80 | 82 | 6,724 | 93.95 | 8,827 |
| | 460 | 40 | 456.34 | 3.66 | 13.40 | 202 | 40,804 | 198.34 | 39,339 |
| Total | 1,290 | 105 | | | 324.92 | | 89,680 | | 89,357 |

regression equations to predict sales for a single firm, sales for an entire industry, demand for a particular product or commodity, or economic factors for a geographic region. Each regression equation in an econometric model involves the effect of particular external, or exogenous, variable(s) on the dependent variable that is being forecast. The objective in econometric modeling is to simultaneously solve all the regression equations and obtain the parameters of the model.

A detailed discussion of econometric models is beyond the scope of this book. The reader interested in learning more about econometric models should consult the references provided at the end of this chapter.

## Measuring Forecasting Error

As part of the forecasting process, and in order to evaluate alternative forecasting methods, forecasting effectiveness must be measured. This usually means using some measure of forecast error.

**Forecast error** is the numerical difference between the actual demand and the forecasted demand for a specific time period, $i$:

$$\text{Forecast Error}_i = \text{Actual Demand}_i - \text{Forecasted Demand}_i \qquad (4\text{-}51)$$

Obviously, the forecaster would like the forecasting errors to be as small as possible and would choose a forecasting method that accomplishes this objective.

There are numerous ways to measure forecasting error. We divide several of the more commonly used measures of forecasting error into two categories: absolute measures and relative measures.

### Absolute Measures of Forecasting Error

Absolute measures of forecasting error are so named because the error measurements used are made in an absolute manner without any consideration of the underlying level of demand. Three commonly used absolute measures of forecasting error are

$$\text{Mean Square Error (MSE)} = \frac{\sum_{i=1}^{N}(\text{Actual Demand}_i - \text{Forecasted Demand}_i)^2}{N} \qquad (4\text{-}52)$$

$$\text{Standard Deviation (SD or }\sigma) = \sqrt{\frac{\sum_{i=1}^{N}(\text{Actual Demand}_i - \text{Forecasted Demand}_i)^2}{N}} \qquad (4\text{-}53)$$

$$\text{Mean Absolute Deviation (MAD)} = \frac{\text{Sum of absolute deviations for all periods}}{\text{Total number of periods evaluated}} = \frac{\sum_{i=1}^{N}|\text{Actual Demand}_i - \text{Forecasted Demand}_i|}{N} \qquad (4\text{-}54)$$

In practice either the standard deviation or the mean absolute deviation is most commonly used. Some practitioners may prefer MAD, because it is easier to use. MAD is the average of several absolute deviations that are measured without regard to their sign. It measures the extent, but not the direction, of the forecasting error. Assuming that the forecasting errors distribute normally, the following relationship exists between the standard deviation and the mean absolute deviation:

$$\text{Standard Deviation} \sim 1.25 \, (\text{MAD}) \qquad (4\text{-}55)$$
$$\text{or MAD} \sim 0.80 \, \text{Standard Deviation} \qquad (4\text{-}56)$$

To illustrate the computations involved in using the three absolute measures of forecasting error, consider example 4.10:

---

**EXAMPLE 4.10**

An electronics company that manufactures a personal computer for the "home user" market estimated its monthly demand for the first four months of the year to be 1,000 units per month. Later, the actual demands were observed to be 900, 1,200, 800, and 1,300, respectively.

Table 4.12 summarizes the data used to calculate the various measures of forecasting error.

Use the information shown in Table 4.12 to compute the three absolute measures of forecasting error as follows:

$$\text{MSE} = \frac{(-100)^2 + (200)^2 + (-200)^2 + (300)^2}{4} = \frac{180,000}{4}$$
$$= 45,000 \text{ units} \qquad (4\text{-}57)$$

$$\sigma = \sqrt{\frac{(-100)^2 + (200)^2 + (-200)^2 + (300)^2}{4}} = \sqrt{45,000} = 212.1 \text{ units} \qquad (4\text{-}58)$$

$$\text{MAD} = \frac{|900 - 1,000| + |1,200 - 1000| + |800 - 1,000| + |1,300 - 1000|}{4}$$
$$= \frac{800}{4} = 200 \text{ units} \qquad (4\text{-}59)$$

---

**TABLE 4.12**
Data Used for Calculating Various Measures of Forecasting Error

| Period (Month) | Actual Demand | Forecasted Demand | Forecast Error | Absolute Forecast Error | [Forecast Error]$^2$ |
|---|---|---|---|---|---|
| 1 | 900 | 1,000 | −100 | 100 | 10,000 |
| 2 | 1,200 | 1,000 | 200 | 200 | 40,000 |
| 3 | 800 | 1,000 | −200 | 200 | 40,000 |
| 4 | 1,300 | 1,000 | 300 | 300 | 90,000 |
| Total | 4,200 | 4,000 | 200 | 800 | 180,000 |

## Relative Measures of Forecasting Error

Relative measures of forecasting error take into account the relative magnitude of the forecasting errors with respect to the underlying demand level. Three commonly used relative measures of forecasting error are

Coefficient of Variation (CVAR)

$$= \frac{\text{Standard Deviation of Forecasting Error}}{\text{Mean of the Actual Demand}}$$

$$= \frac{\sqrt{\dfrac{\sum\limits_{i=1}^{N} (\text{Actual Demand}_i - \text{Forecasted Demand}_i)^2}{N}}}{\dfrac{\sum\limits_{i=1}^{N} \text{Actual Demand}_i}{N}} \tag{4-60}$$

Mean Percentage Error (MPE)

$$= \sum_{i=1}^{n} \frac{\text{Actual Demand}_i - \text{Forecasted Demand}_i}{\text{Actual Demand}_i} [100/N] \tag{4-61}$$

Mean Absolute Percentage Error (MAPE)

$$= \sum_{i=1}^{N} \left| \frac{\text{Actual Demand}_i - \text{Forecasted Demand}_i}{\text{Actual Demand}_i} \right| [100/N] \tag{4-62}$$

All the relative measures of forecasting error are defined with respect to the actual level of demand that is occurring. The coefficient of variation scales the standard deviation of the forecasting error to the average demand level. The mean percentage error averages the percentage errors over all the time periods and is a relative measure of the bias present in the forecast. The mean absolute percentage error averages the absolute percentage errors over all the time periods.

---

**EXAMPLE 4.11**

Again, using the information given in Table 4.12, the three relative measures of forecasting error are computed as follows:

$$\text{CVAR} = \frac{212.1}{4,200/4} = \frac{212.1}{1,050} = 0.2020 \ (20.20\%) \tag{4-63}$$

$$\begin{aligned} \text{MPE} &= [(-100/900) + (200/1200) + (-200/800) + \\ &\quad (300/1300)](100/4) \\ &= [(-0.1111) + (0.1667) + (-0.2500) + (0.2308)](100/4) = 0.91\% \end{aligned} \tag{4-64}$$

$$\begin{aligned} \text{MAPE} &= [\,|-100/900| + |200/1200| + |-200/800| \\ &\quad + |\,300/1300\,|\,](100/4) \\ &= [(0.1111) + (0.1667) + (0.2500) + (0.2308)](100/4) \\ &= 18.92\% \end{aligned} \tag{4-65}$$

---

# Monitoring and Controlling Forecasts

To control the forecasting process forecasts should be monitored. One simple way to do this is to visually compare actual data and the forecasts. A second method involves using a tracking signal, and a third method uses control charts.

T A B L E  4 . 1 3
Areas Within Control Limits

| Number of MADs | Corresponding Number of Standard Deviations | Area Within Control Limits |
|:---:|:---:|:---:|
| ±1 | ±0.798 | 57.048% |
| ±2 | ±1.596 | 88.946% |
| ±3 | ±2.394 | 98.334% |
| ±4 | ±3.192 | 99.856% |

The tracking signal measures whether a forecasting method is biased over time. The **tracking signal** is the ratio of the cumulative forecast error to the corresponding value of MAD:

$$\text{Tracking Signal} = \frac{\sum_{i=1}^{N}(\text{Actual Demand}_i - \text{Forecasted Demand}_i)}{\text{MAD}} \tag{4-66}$$

The tracking signal is recalculated each time the actual demand data for a period become available and the forecast is revised. If the forecasting method is performing well, the tracking signal should remain small (close to zero), because positive and negative deviations will balance each other. If actual demand varies significantly from forecast demand in several periods, the numerator of equation 4–66 will also increase, and the tracking signal will deviate significantly from zero.

The resulting values of the tracking signal are often compared with predetermined control limits. A **control limit** is the generally acceptable level for something (in this case the tracking signal). The control limits are defined, or described, in statistical terms. Table 4.13 shows the area within the control limits for a range of 0 to 4 MADs (or their corresponding number of standard deviations). Control limits are typically specified on the basis of experience and judgment. For example, if we are forecasting high value items, we may want to set lower control limits. Doing so will cause more forecasts to be outside the control limits, which requires effort in order to investigate the underlying causes.

**EXAMPLE 4.12**

Table 4.14 presents the computations for the tracking signal for Example 4.5 involving video disk player demand forecasts made using double exponential smoothing, with $\alpha = 0.8$, $\beta = 0.5$ (see Table 4.8).

The tracking signal for this example is plotted in Figure 4.12. Observe that the tracking signal began positive, went higher, then went lower, and finally went positive again. Overall, it was positive for eight out of the eleven months forecast, an indication of an underforecasting bias in the forecasting process. Control limits of ± 3 MAD are specified in Figure 4.12. Only one value of the tracking signal (for month 4) reached these control limits. Given that all 11 of the tracking signal values were within the control limits, we would conclude that the forecast is performing adequately at present.

| Month | Time Period | Actual Demand $A_i$ | Forecasted Demand $F_i$ | Error or Deviation $(A_i - F_i)$ | \|Deviation\| $\|A_i - F_i\|$ | Sum of Deviations | Sum of \|Deviations\| | MAD | Tracking Signal |
|-------|-------------|---------------------|-------------------------|----------------------------------|-------------------------------|-------------------|------------------------|------|-----------------|
| Jan.  | 1  | 110.00 | 110.00 | 0.00    | 0.00  | 0.00   | 0.00   | 0.00  | 0.00  |
| Feb.  | 2  | 120.00 | 110.00 | 10.00   | 10.00 | 10.00  | 10.00  | 10.00 | 1.00  |
| Mar.  | 3  | 150.00 | 122.00 | 28.00   | 28.00 | 38.00  | 38.00  | 19.00 | 2.00  |
| Apr.  | 4  | 180.00 | 158.40 | 21.60   | 21.60 | 59.60  | 59.60  | 19.86 | 3.00  |
| May   | 5  | 120.00 | 194.68 | −74.68  | 74.68 | −15.08 | 134.28 | 33.57 | −0.45 |
| June  | 6  | 100.00 | 120.44 | −20.44  | 20.44 | −35.52 | 154.72 | 30.94 | −1.14 |
| July  | 7  | 90.00  | 88.84  | 1.16    | 1.16  | −34.36 | 155.88 | 25.98 | −1.32 |
| Aug.  | 8  | 140.00 | 78.14  | 61.86   | 61.86 | 27.50  | 217.74 | 31.11 | 0.88  |
| Sept. | 9  | 170.00 | 141.82 | 28.18   | 28.18 | 55.68  | 245.92 | 30.74 | 1.81  |
| Oct.  | 10 | 190.00 | 183.46 | 6.54    | 6.54  | 62.22  | 252.46 | 28.05 | 2.22  |
| Nov.  | 11 | 200.00 | 206.24 | −6.24   | 6.24  | 55.98  | 258.70 | 25.87 | 2.16  |
| Dec.  | 12 | 220.00 | 214.02 | 5.98    | 5.98  | 61.96  | 264.68 | 24.06 | 2.57  |

Note:  $MAD_2 = 10.00/1 = 10.00$         Tracking Signal$_2$ = 10.00/10.00 = 1.00
$\phantom{Note:}$  $MAD_3 = 38.00/2 = 19.00$         Tracking Signal$_3$ = 38.00/19.00 = 2.00
$\phantom{Note:}$  $MAD_4 = 59.60/3 = 19.86$         Tracking Signal$_4$ = 59.60/19.86 = 3.00

$\phantom{Note:}$  $MAD_{12} = 264.68/11 = 24.06$         Tracking Signal$_{12}$ = 61.96/24.06 = 2.57

TABLE 4.14
Tracking Signal Computations—Double Exponential Smoothing, $\alpha = 0.8$, $\beta = 0.5$

FIGURE 4.12
Tracking Signals—Double Exponential Smoothing Forecasts, $\alpha = 0.8$, $\beta = 0.5$

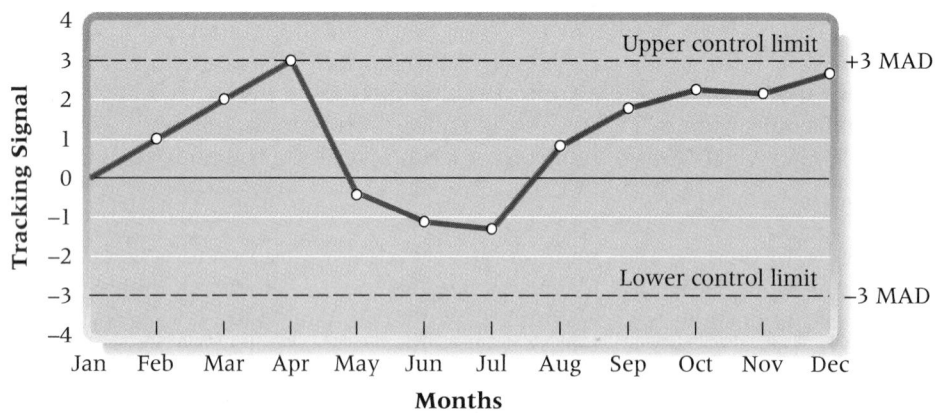

Instead of computing MAD as we did in Table 4.14, we can make a single exponentially smoothed forecast of MAD using

$$MAD_i = \alpha \,|\text{Actual Demand}_i - \text{Forecasted Demand}_i| + (1 - \alpha)\,MAD_{i-1} \quad (4\text{-}67)$$

This approach has certain advantages, because less historical data have to be retained for each period's forecast of MAD and more recent forecasting performance can be weighted more heavily.

A third method for monitoring and controlling forecasts is through the use of a control chart. The **control chart** method requires the setting of upper and lower limits for individual forecast errors (instead of cumulative forecast error, as is done for the tracking signal). It is based on two assumptions:

1. The forecast errors distribute randomly around a mean of zero
2. The distribution of the forecast errors is normal

Earlier, we discussed the standard deviation of the forecasting errors as one of the absolute measures of forecasting error (see equation 4-55). For a normal distribution, about 95% of the individual forecasting errors can be expected to fall within limits of $0 \pm 2\sigma$, and about 99% of the individual forecasting errors can be expected to fall within limits of $0 \pm 3\sigma$. Individual forecast errors that fall outside these limits can then be taken as indications that corrective action is needed.

---

**EXAMPLE 4.13**

For the data presented in Table 4.14 the standard deviation of the forecasting errors can be computed as

$$\sigma = \sqrt{\frac{\sum_{i=1}^{N} (\text{Actual Demand}_i - \text{Forecasted Demand}_i)^2}{N}}$$

$$= \sqrt{\frac{(120.0 - 110)^2 + (150.0 - 122.0)^2 + \ldots + (220.0 - 206.24)^2}{11}}$$

$$= \sqrt{\frac{12{,}084.82}{11}} = 33.15 \text{ units} \tag{4-68}$$

Figure 4.13 is a control chart for the forecasting errors (for this same set of data). The control limits were set at $\pm 3$ MAD $= \pm 2.394\sigma = \pm (2.394)(33.15 \text{ units}) = \pm 79.36$ units, for comparison with Figure 4.12. All 11 individual forecasting errors are within these control limits. The control chart suggests that this forecasting process is just as good as the tracking signal method.

---

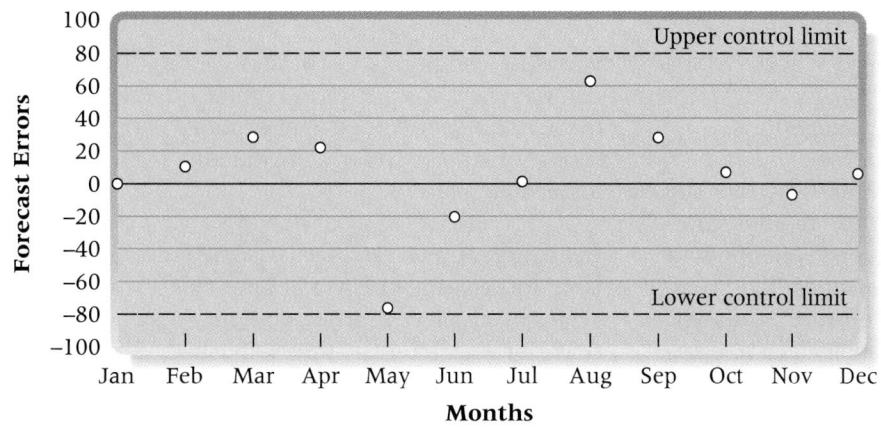

**FIGURE 4.13**
Control Chart—Double Exponential Smoothing Forecasts, $\alpha = 0.8$, $\beta = 0.5$

In general, the control chart approach is superior to the tracking signal approach. The major weakness of the tracking signal method is that it uses cumulative errors. This can mask big positive and negative individual errors that can offset each other. The control chart method compares every single error individually with the control limits.

## Using Computers in Forecasting

In forecasting practice today the computer is an extremely important tool. In this chapter we have explained the underlying computations for several forecasting methods. The computations become time consuming and tedious as the amount of data increases, so the assistance provided by computers is highly desirable. For certain forecasting models, such as multiple regression and econometric models, the computations are so complicated that the computer affords the only practical way to proceed.

Many sophisticated computer-based forecasting programs are available. Among the most widely used packages are *BMDP* (*Biomedical Computer Programs*), *SAS* (*Statistical Analysis System*), and *SPSS* (*Statistical Package for the Social Sciences*). One or more of these packages is usually available, in either mainframe or personal computer versions, or both, at most colleges and universities.

PC-based software packages for specialized forecasting, such as exponential smoothing and regression analysis, are also widely available. A discussion of such packages is beyond the scope of this book, and new entrants in this area appear frequently.

A number of computer software packages that teach these techniques are available for use with textbooks such as this. The packages generally cover a wide range of management science and statistical techniques, including forecasting. The software package accompanying this textbook is *Decision Support Systems for Production/Operations Management* by Terry L. Dennis, Laurie B. Dennis, and Dan Joseph (St. Paul, Minn.: West Educational Publishing, 1994). This software package can be used to solve many of the problems at the end of this chapter and other chapters in the book.

## ► Summary

Forecasting is basic to the planning effort of the operations manager. Good forecasts are critical for both short-term and long-term planning efforts.

**Learning Objective 1: Identify and describe the major components of a time series.** A time series has five major components. The average component reflects the mean value of the time series. The trend component describes the general upward or downward movement of the time series. The cyclical component portrays the recurrent upward and downward wavelike conditions in the time series. The seasonal component is a short-term regular fluctuation caused by seasonal influences. The random component is a series of short erratic movements that follow no discernible pattern.

**Learning Objective 2: Discuss the steps involved in the forecasting process.** The forecasting process typically involves a series of eight steps. First, objectives for the forecast are established. Second, what will be forecast is defined. Third, the time period for the forecast is specified. Fourth, data is gathered and analyzed. Fifth, the forecasting method is selected. Sixth, the actual forecast is produced. Seventh, the forecast results are presented. Eighth, the forecast is monitored and evaluated.

## Learning Objective 3: Explain qualitative approaches to forecasting.
Qualitative forecasting methods are primarily subjective or judgmental. They allow for the inclusion of personal opinions, guesses, and the opinions of others in producing a forecast. Among the more commonly used qualitative forecasting methods are naïve extrapolation, sales force composition, jury of executive opinion, the Delphi method, and market research surveys.

## Learning Objective 4: Explain quantitative approaches to forecasting.
Quantitative forecasting methods try either to extend historical data into the future or to develop associative models that use causal variables to make a forecast. They use a time-ordered sequence of quantitative observations about the forecasts. Among the more commonly used quantitative forecasting methods are simple averages, simple moving averages, weighted moving averages, exponential smoothing, time series decomposition, linear regression, and econometric models.

## Learning Objective 5: Distinguish between absolute and relative measures of forecasting errors.
The effectiveness of a forecast is measured by the forecasting error, defined as the difference between the actual, or observed, demand and the demand forecast. There are many ways to measure forecasting errors. Absolute measures of forecasting error do not consider the underlying level of demand, while relative measures of forecasting error do. Common absolute measures of forecasting error are (1) mean square error, (2) standard deviation, and (3) mean absolute deviation. Common relative measures of forecasting error are (1) coefficient of variation, (2) mean percentage error, and (3) mean absolute percentage error.

## Learning Objective 6: Describe ways to monitor and control forecasts.
Monitoring and controlling forecasts involves observing actual data and forecasts and changing the forecasting process when necessary. One simple way to do this is to visually compare actual data and forecasts. The tracking signal method measures whether a forecasting method is biased over time and compares the cumulative forecasting error with the corresponding value of the mean absolute deviation. The control chart method requires the setting of upper and lower limits for individual forecast errors instead of the cumulative forecast error.

## ► Key Terms

| | | |
|---|---|---|
| associative (causal) methods | judgment methods | sales force composite |
| average | jury of executive opinion | sample |
| census | lagging indicators | scatter diagram |
| coefficient of determination | leading indicators | seasonal |
| coincident indicators | least squares | simple average |
| control chart | market research survey | simple exponential smoothing |
| control limits | multiple linear regression | simple linear regression |
| correlation coefficient | naive extrapolation | simple moving average |
| counting methods | negative correlation | single exponential smoothing |
| cycle | positive correlation | slope |
| Delphi method | product life cycle | standard error of the estimate |
| dependent variable | qualitative forecasting methods | stability |
| double exponential smoothing | quantitative forecasting methods | time series |
| econometric model | random error | time series analysis methods |
| forecast error | regression constant | tracking signal |
| forecast | regression equation | trend |
| independent variables | regression model | weighted moving average |
| intercept | responsiveness | |

## ► Discussion Questions

1. Why is the forecasting time horizon important in choosing a forecasting method?
2. What are the major factors that should be considered in choosing a forecasting method?
3. Explain what is meant by the cost/accuracy trade-off in selecting a forecasting model.
4. Name and describe the major components into which time series data decompose.
5. Why is exponential smoothing a better forecasting method than a simple moving average?
6. What factors determine the smoothing constant that is used in exponential smoothing?
7. What is the difference between an absolute and a relative measure of forecasting error?
8. What is the relationship between MAD and the standard error of the forecast? What do they measure? How are they used?

9. What are some of the main benefits and weaknesses of the Delphi technique?
10. Why are quantitative forecasting techniques generally superior to qualitative forecasting techniques? What are some limitations of quantitative forecasting techniques?
11. Describe the major ways to control forecasts.
12. What are the advantages of establishing control limits for forecasts?
13. You have many items in your product line and must prepare weekly forecasts for each item. What forecasting method would you recommend? Why?
14. What are the advantages and disadvantages of making forecasts using exponential smoothing?
15. What are the advantages and disadvantages of making forecasts using regression methods?

## ► Problems

1. The Strictly Running store experienced the following running shoe demand during the past year:

| Month | Demand for Running Shoes |
|---|---|
| January | 1,150 |
| February | 1,180 |
| March | 1,200 |
| April | 1,000 |
| May | 1,050 |
| June | 1,100 |
| July | 1,250 |
| August | 1,200 |
| September | 1,280 |
| October | 1,300 |
| November | 1,350 |
| December | 1,300 |

Strictly Running would like to use this data to make forecasts for months 6–12 using the following models:
a. Moving average—3 periods
b. Moving average—5 periods
c. Single exponential smoothing—$\alpha = 0.1$
d. Single exponential smoothing—$\alpha = 0.5$
e. Single exponential smoothing—$\alpha = 0.9$
Use the actual data for months 3, 4, and 5 for initializing model a, the actual data for months 1, 2, 3, 4, and 5 for initializing model b, and the average of the data for months 1, 2, 3, 4, and 5 for initializing models c, d, and e.

2. For each forecasting model in problem 1 compute the following measures of forecasting accuracy:
a. Mean square error
b. Standard deviation

c. Mean absolute deviation
d. Coefficient of variation
e. Mean percentage error
f. Mean average percentage error
What conclusions can you draw by comparing these measures of forecasting accuracy for the various forecasting models?

3. The Nostate Auto Insurance Co. had the following claims experience during the past two years:

| Month | Year 1 | Year 2 |
|---|---|---|
| January | 500 | 1,300 |
| February | 550 | 1,700 |
| March | 480 | 1,500 |
| April | 510 | 1,800 |
| May | 490 | 2,100 |
| June | 530 | 2,500 |
| July | 600 | 2,700 |
| August | 650 | 2,600 |
| September | 720 | 2,900 |
| October | 750 | 3,200 |
| November | 890 | 3,500 |
| December | 1,050 | 4,000 |

Nostate would like to use this data to make forecasts for months 8–24 using the following models:
a. Moving average—7 months
b. Exponential smoothing—$\alpha = 0.2$
c. Exponential smoothing—$\alpha = 0.5$
d. Exponential smoothing—$\alpha = 0.9$
Use the actual data for initializing months 1–7 for initializing model a and the average of the data for months 1–7 for initializing models b, c, and d.

**4.** For each forecasting model in problem 3 compute the following measures of forecasting accuracy:
   **a.** Mean square error
   **b.** Standard deviation
   **c.** Mean absolute deviation
   **c.** Coefficient of variation
   **e.** Mean percentage error
   **f.** Mean average percentage error
   What conclusions can you draw by comparing these measures of forecasting accuracy for the various forecasting models?

**5.** The Outspokin Bicycle Shop's monthly bicycle demand is as follows:

| Month | Demand for Bicycles |
|---|---|
| January | 650 |
| February | 700 |
| March | 810 |
| April | 800 |
| May | 900 |
| June | 980 |

   **a.** Use a three-month simple average to compute the forecast for April, May, and June.
   **b.** Use a three-month simple moving average to compute the forecast for April, May, and June.
   **c.** Use a three-month weighted moving average (weights of 0.2, 0.3, and 0.5) to compute the forecast for April, May, and June.
   **d.** Which of the three forecasting methods would you recommend for this company? Why?

**6.** An electric motor manufacturer has experienced quarterly demand for its biggest motor as follows:

| Quarter | Electric Motor Demand |
|---|---|
| 1 | 50 |
| 2 | 52 |
| 3 | 48 |
| 4 | 50 |
| 5 | 49 |
| 6 | 46 |
| 7 | 48 |
| 8 | 44 |

   **a.** Calculate a weighted moving average forecast for quarter 9, using a three-quarter moving average model and weighting the most recent period three times as heavily as each of the previous two periods.
   **b.** Do the forecasting results you obtained and a visual examination of the data indicate a better weighting scheme? Why?

**7.** First Union Bank of Charlotte, North Carolina, wishes to make a forecast of its future check-processing requirements. It has collected the following set of data:

| Month | Actual Number of Checks Processed (1990) | Actual Number of Checks Processed (1991) |
|---|---|---|
| January | 52,000 | 72,000 |
| February | 55,000 | 78,000 |
| March | 58,000 | 84,000 |
| April | 62,000 | 80,000 |
| May | 60,000 | 88,000 |
| June | 57,000 | 96,000 |
| July | 63,000 | 110,000 |
| August | 65,000 | 105,000 |
| September | 62,000 | 115,000 |
| October | 70,000 | 130,000 |
| November | 75,000 | 135,000 |
| December | 77,000 | 140,000 |

   **a.** Use this data to make single exponentially smoothed forecasts with $\alpha$ values of 0.1, 0.3, 0.5, 0.7, and 0.9. Use the actual number of checks processed in January 1990 (52,000) as the initial forecast.
   **b.** Use this data to make moving average forecasts with $N$ values of 3, 5, and 7 months.
   **c.** Assuming that the pattern will extend into the future, what values of $\alpha$ and $N$ should management select in order to minimize the forecasting errors? (Note: Use MAD as the measure of forecasting error.)
   **d.** Use this data to make double exponentially smoothed forecasts using $\alpha = 0.3$, $\beta = 0.9$. Again, use the actual number of checks processed in January 1990 (52,000) as the initial forecast.

**8.** Sales of the Elite leather travel bag have grown steadily during the past ten years. Robert Marcum, president of Marcum Leather, predicted in 1981 that sales of the Premier leather travel bag would be 500,000 units in 1982. Use the following information and exponential smoothing with $\alpha = 0.90$ to develop forecasts for 1983 through 1992.

| Year | Sales |
|---|---|
| 1982 | 545,000 |
| 1983 | 540,000 |
| 1984 | 550,000 |
| 1985 | 575,000 |
| 1986 | 600,000 |
| 1987 | 590,000 |
| 1988 | 620,000 |
| 1989 | 660,000 |
| 1990 | 710,000 |
| 1991 | 725,000 |
| 1992 | ? |

**9.** For problem 8, compute the following measures of forecasting accuracy:
   **a.** Mean square error
   **b.** Mean absolute deviation

10. Analyze the forecasting errors for the time series in problem 8 by using a smoothing constant of $\alpha = 0.6$. Which smoothing constant produces the most accurate forecast, $\alpha = 0.9$ or $\alpha = 0.6$?

11. Plot the sales data from problem 8. What does this plot show? Develop forecasts for 1983 through 1992, using this same data and double exponential smoothing with $\alpha = 0.6$, $\beta = 0.9$, and $\alpha = 0.8$, $\beta = 0.9$. Plot these forecasts. What do they show?

12. For problem 11 compute the following measures of forecasting accuracy:
    a. Mean square error
    b. Mean absolute deviation
    Which set of smoothing constants produces the most accurate forecast?

13. The number of patients treated at the Lexington Medical Center during the last twelve weeks is as follows:

| Week | Number of Patients Treated |
|------|----------------------------|
| 1 | 390 |
| 2 | 380 |
| 3 | 360 |
| 4 | 380 |
| 5 | 420 |
| 6 | 360 |
| 7 | 420 |
| 8 | 450 |
| 9 | 400 |
| 10 | 460 |
| 11 | 440 |
| 12 | 420 |

The center's medical director, Jane Bryson, had originally forecast that 375 patients would be treated in week 1. Use the information presented in the table and exponential smoothing with $\alpha = 0.5$ to develop forecasts for weeks 2 through 12.

14. For problem 13 compute the following measures of forecasting accuracy:
    a. Mean square error
    b. Mean absolute deviation

15. Analyze the forecasting errors for the time series in problem 13 by using a smoothing constant of $\alpha = 0.75$. Which smoothing constant produces the most accurate forecast, $\alpha = 0.5$ or $\alpha = 0.75$?

16. Plot the patient treatment demand in problem 13. What does this plot show? Develop forecasts for weeks 2 through 12, using this same data and double exponential smoothing with $\alpha = 0.5$, $\beta = 0.5$, and $\alpha = 0.9$, $\beta = 0.5$. Plot these forecasts. What do they show?

17. For problem 16 compute the following measures of forecasting accuracy:
    a. Mean square error
    b. Mean absolute deviation
    Which set of smoothing constants produces the most accurate forecast?

18. Determine the linear regression equation for the following data:

| Month | 1 | 2 | 3 | 4 | 5 | 6 |
|-------|----|----|----|----|----|----|
| Demand | 13 | 36 | 36 | 37 | 38 | 43 |
| Month | 7 | 8 | 9 | 10 | 11 | 12 |
| Demand | 45 | 50 | 55 | 60 | 60 | 69 |

Use the computed linear regression equation to calculate the next month's forecasts.

19. Consider the following set of cost and production data for the Phillips Boat Anchor Co.:

| Total Cost (per $1,000) | Units Produced (in 1,000s) |
|-------------------------|----------------------------|
| 35 | 5 |
| 13 | 2 |
| 40 | 6 |
| 52 | 7 |
| 65 | 10 |
| 60 | 9 |

   a. Determine the linear regression equation for this set of data.
   b. Compute the standard error of the estimate (SEE).
   c. Compute the correlation coefficient, $r$.
   d. Compute the coefficient of determination, $r^2$.

20. This table provides data on test scores of various people and their subsequent data entry productivity.

| Person | Test Score | Data Entry Productivity |
|--------|-----------|--------------------------|
| A | 50 | 450 |
| B | 70 | 610 |
| C | 60 | 500 |
| D | 40 | 400 |
| E | 30 | 280 |
| F | 40 | 1,000 |
| G | 30 | 280 |
| H | 65 | 570 |
| I | 80 | 740 |
| J | 55 | 500 |
| K | 70 | 610 |
| L | 75 | 680 |
| M | 60 | 550 |
| N | 40 | 350 |

a.  Plot these data on a graph with the test score as the $X$ axis and the data entry productivity as the $Y$ axis.
b.  Determine the linear regression equation for this set of data.
c.  What data entry productivity would you expect for a person who had a test score of 85?
d.  Compute SEE.
e.  Compute $r$.
f.  Compute $r^2$.
g.  Compute a 95% confidence interval for the forecast you made for the person who had a test score of 85.

21.  The manufacturer of a new type of stereo headset for joggers is trying to determine how television advertising expenditures affect its sales. Sales revenue and advertising expenditure data indicate the following:

| Time Period | Sales (in thousands) | Stereo Headset Advertising Expenditures (in thousands) |
|---|---|---|
| 1 | $100 | $ 20 |
| 2 | 110 | 30 |
| 3 | 130 | 35 |
| 4 | 180 | 40 |
| 5 | 220 | 60 |
| 6 | 290 | 70 |
| 7 | 350 | 90 |
| 8 | 410 | 100 |
| 9 | 460 | 100 |
| 10 | 500 | 100 |
| 11 | 520 | 100 |
| 12 | 540 | 110 |
| 13 | 600 | 150 |
| 14 | 650 | 150 |
| 15 | 700 | 170 |

a.  Plot these data on a graph with the stereo headset sales as the $Y$ axis and the advertising expenditures as the $X$ axis.

b.  Determine the linear regression equation for this set of data.
c.  What level of stereo headset sales would you expect for an advertising expenditure of $200,000?
d.  Compute SEE.
e.  Compute $r$.
f.  Compute $r^2$.
g.  Compute a 95% confidence interval for the forecast you made for an advertising expenditure of $200,000.

22.  For problem 1c
a.  Determine the tracking signal.
b.  Plot the tracking signal and decide whether the forecasting procedure is acceptable, using $= \pm 3$ MAD as the control limit.
c.  Plot the control chart for the individual errors of this forecasting process, using $= \pm 3$ MAD as the control limit. What can you say about the forecasting process?

23.  For problem 8
a.  Determine the tracking signal.
b.  Plot the tracking signal and decide whether the forecasting procedure is acceptable, using $= \pm 3$ MAD as the control limits.
c.  Plot the control chart for the individual errors of this forecasting process, using $= \pm 3$ MAD as the control limits. What can you say about the forecasting process?

24.  For problem 13
a.  Determine the tracking signal.
b.  Plot the tracking signal and decide whether the forecasting procedure is acceptable, using $= \pm 3$ MAD as the control limits.
c.  Plot the control chart for the individual errors of this forecasting process, using $= \pm 3$ MAD as the control limits. What can you say about the forecasting process?

# ► Selected References

Abraham, J., and J. Ledoter. *Statistical Methods for Forecasting.* New York: Wiley, 1983.

Bowerman, B. L., and R. T. O'Connell. *Time Series Forecasting.* Boston: Duxbury, 1986.

Box, G.E.P., and G. Jenkins. *Time Series Analysis: Forecasting and Control.* San Francisco: Holden-Day, 1976.

Brown, Robert G. *Statistical Forecasting for Inventory Control.* New York: McGraw-Hill, 1959.

Cryer, J. *Time Series Forecasting.* Boston: Duxbury, 1986.

Hanke, John E., and Arthur G. Reitsch. *Business Forecasting.* Boston: Allyn & Bacon, 1981.

Makridakis, Spyros, and Steven C. Wheelwright, ed. *The Handbook of Forecasting: A Manager's Guide.* New York: Wiley, 1982.

Makridakis, Spyros, Steven C. Wheelwright, and Victor E. McGee. *Forecasting: Methods and Applications.* New York: Wiley, 1983.

Nelson, Charles R. *Applied Time Series Analysis for Managerial Forecasting.* San Francisco: Holden-Day, 1973.

Neter, John, William Wasserman, and Michael H. Kutner. *Applied Linear Regression Models.* Homewood, Ill.: Richard D. Irwin, 1989.

Pankratz, Alan. *Forecasting with Univariate Box-Jenkins Models.* New York: Wiley, 1983.

Pindyck, Robert S., and Daniel L. Ruhenfeld. *Econometric Models and Economic Forecasts.* New York: McGraw-Hill, 1981.

Wilson, J. Holton, and Barry Keating. *Business Forecasting.* Homewood, Ill.: Richard D. Irwin, 1990.

## CHAPTER 5

# Product Planning and Process Design

*The world is full of willing people,
some willing to work, the rest
willing to let them.*

ROBERT FROST (1878–1963)
AMERICAN POET

**Introduction**

**Assessing Customers' Needs and Wants**
*OPERATIONS MANAGEMENT IN PRACTICE 5.1: The Birth of the ''Pump''*

**Customer Satisfaction**

**Design for Manufacturability**

**Process Design and Layout for Manufacturing and Service Systems**

**Strategic Issues in Process Design**
*OPERATIONS MANAGEMENT IN PRACTICE 5.2: Air-Conditioner Firms Put Chill on Plans*
*OPERATIONS MANAGEMENT IN PRACTICE 5.3: DuPont Generates Energy from Garbage*

# Introduction

Product planning and process design are strategic decisions for manufacturing and service operations. Although these topics usually have been treated separately, the modern business environment requires that companies accomplish product planning and process design at the same time. To properly convey how planning and design overlap, several sections of this chapter discuss them in tandem.

We should note here the contributions of the Japanese in helping American companies understand the need for and procedures used in designing effective products and processes. Most notable is the work of Japanese engineer Genichi Taguchi. He experimented with ways to achieve optimal design and pointed out that designers should be held accountable for losses that result from poor design. He also believed that designers should be held responsible for losses incurred by society when products become unusable or cause societal problems, and he developed the concept of the *loss function*, a method of measuring societal losses that stem from poor design.

His view of designing for "loss minimization" is important, but others see customer satisfaction as the primary objective of manufacturers and service providers, the approach we take in this chapter. We assume that customers want to deal with socially responsible companies that provide environmentally responsible products.

Companies that produce products and services with superior designs and features plan in order to satisfy and, they hope, delight their customers. Their customers become their best advertising. Speaking with loyal customers of Macintosh computers, Lexus automobiles, Maytag appliances, Federal Express overnight shipping services, or visitors to Disney World quickly provides a lesson in what "satisfied customer" means. Behind the success of each of these superior products and services is a process carefully designed to ensure timely, defect-free operations with features the customers want.

## Assessing Customers' Needs and Wants

Keeping customers is the best single strategy that a company can use against its competition. While manufacturers strive for "zero defects," service companies must strive for "zero defections."[1] This is not a new idea, and leading companies are beginning to translate its profound importance into action. Traditional views of product design and production processes focus on the "tension" between new product ideas driven by technology and those gleaned from market research. No longer is either approach sufficient for a company to enjoy long-term success.

## Technology-Driven New Product Ideas

Consider the situation that Thermalux, a manufacturer of aerogels, faced in 1991. Aerogels are substances that look like glass, feel like Styrofoam, and are extremely light weight. They are great insulators and fairly harmless environmentally. A Stanford University researcher developed the technology in the 1930s, but it was ignored for years. As the *Wall Street Journal* reported, the aerogel was a "solution looking for a problem."[2]

Thermalux raised $2 million in seed money from public and private sources for development, but in its zeal to develop a technologically sophisticated product, it did not develop a market for it. One potential application was found to be as improved insulation for refrigerators. Refrigerators now use insulating material that contains environmentally dangerous fluorocarbons. Because Thermalux never manufactured the product in large quantities, it had difficulty quoting a price for the large amount that a refrigerator manufacturer would need.

## New Product Ideas from Market Research

If developing technology and then looking for its application is not the best path, why not rely on market research? Let's consider the effectiveness of market research for identifying potential demand for microwave ovens. Although they can be found in most homes today, in the 1960s microwave ovens were an unfamiliar technology. The devices began appearing with vending machines, which allowed the selling of reheatable foods. Had market researchers interviewed cooks in their homes, they would have had to explain the technology, describe how cooking in this fashion was the same as or different from conventional cooking, and justify the price. Such a survey likely would not have yielded any indication of the potentially explosive growth in demand for microwave ovens.

## The Voice of the Customer

If the technology-driven model and the market research-driven model are each incomplete approaches to product and service design, what should companies do to ensure that they develop products that anticipate customers' needs and wants? The answer is to hear what customers are saying and form close relationships with them. This will ensure the company's ability to anticipate customers' needs and to respond. Operations Management in Practice 5.1

---

[1]Frederick F. Reichheld and W.E. Sasser, Jr., "Zero Defections: Quality Comes to Services," *Harvard Business Review* 68, (September–October, 1990): 105.

[2]John R. Emshwiller, "Thermalux Seeks Customers for a New Technology," *Wall Street Journal*, February 15, 1991, p. B2.

# The Birth of the "Pump"

Reebok had a terrific idea: a basketball sneaker with inflatable air cushions for better ankle support. But the idea had a problem: how to inflate the air bags? Some at Reebok suggested an ugly box that clumsily attached to the heel of the sneaker. Seeking something better, the company hired John Zoccai, 43, a Boston designer with clear plastic glasses and a taste for red paisley ties. From visiting playgrounds around Boston and talking to young hoopsters, he and his team kept refining the features of the new shoe. For example, he helped Reebok design a pump that tucked neatly into the shoe's tongue. Aspiring Michael Jordans simply pushed an orange button that, fittingly, looked like a basketball.

When Reebok introduced the Pump, as it's now called, at an Atlanta trade fair in February 1989, archrival Nike showed up with a similar inflating shoe that had a major difference. The Nike required playground stars to carry a separate hand pump. Preferring Reebok's design, retail buyers flocked to the Pump. Nike eventually dropped its shoe. To date, Reebok's revenues from the Pump are approaching $200 million.

illustrates how listening to customers can benefit product design and profitability.

Business success depends on continuing to advance products and services that anticipate demand. One new product is not sufficient. Two years after IBM introduced the personal computer (PC) in late 1981, "clones" became available and now represent the bulk of the PC market. Competitors copy new production processes quickly, and lower labor costs will not ensure success. For several years U.S. companies complained about Japan's low wage rates, claiming they gave the Japanese an unfair competitive advantage. Now the Japanese are concerned about wage rates in Korea, Malaysia, and India. Nor can government regulation guarantee success. The Japanese computer market is protected, yet IBM enjoys a healthy share of that market. When the United States asked Japanese auto makers to observe voluntary quotas in the U.S. market, the quotas merely provided them with an incentive to design cars for the mid-size market, which has a higher profit margin and was a market in which the Japanese had not previously been big players. Finally, neither size nor market share will guarantee success. In the 1960s General Motors controlled more than 50 percent of the U.S. car market. Since then its market share has dropped steadily, to less than 40 percent.[3]

Alone, one new product, new process, lower labor costs, government regulation, or size cannot create a sustainable competitive advantage. Organizations create sustainable advantage by recognizing that they are in business not simply to provide products or services but because their customers want them to survive, grow, and prosper. If customers do not receive excellent service and alternatives are available, they will take their business elsewhere. The sooner managers in all types of industries recognize this, the better.

[3]Miland M. Lele, *The Customer Is Key* (New York: Wiley, 1987), pp. 1–2.

# Customer Satisfaction

**Customer satisfaction** means meeting or exceeding customers' requirements for a product or service. Assessment of the degree of satisfaction is usually made on at least three measures:

- Whether the product or service includes the features that are most important to the customer
- Whether the company can respond to customers' demands in a timely manner, a criterion that is especially important for custom products and services
- Whether the product or service is free of defects and performs as expected

In this customer-oriented approach a **defect** is any deviation from the customer's expectations for the product or service.

# Selecting Features for Products and Services

When a product or service is in the design phase, "listening to the voice of the market" is not just a catchy phrase. It's an imperative. The design team must evaluate the target market, its wants and needs, and the company's capability to design products to satisfy that market. Product and service development generally follows an inverted pyramid that begins with many ideas and results in a relatively small number of products and services that reach the market. Companies that listen to their customers are more likely to introduce successful products that require less fine tuning to the tastes and preferences of the market than the products of companies that do not listen to their customers. The process that proceeds from an idea to a final product includes the following steps:

- Generating ideas
- Selecting features
- Producing a preliminary design
- Developing a prototype
- Test marketing the prototype
- Mass marketing the final product

The idea phase for some products can produce literally hundreds of thousands of possibilities. Consider the number of writers who have ideas for popular novels and the number of rock bands that are writing songs. In each case the authors or song writers begin with a creative idea, then determine which market-driven features to include. What are readers of best sellers looking for? What do buyers of hit songs want? How do those market-oriented considerations provide opportunities that writers or musicians can match to their creative vision? Traditional market research is unlikely to provide the answer. Rather, the book or song writer needs to observe the world within which readers or listeners live, then interpret a view of the world that will evoke their experiences. While some authors or bands can do this and maintain commercial success for many years, new talent constantly moves in and out of the marketplace. While writing popular novels or music might at first seem to be an unusual example, it actually parallels the process used by big corporations and small businesses to develop new ideas for products and services.

*A view of an early McDonald's restaurant. Some things have changed but the golden arches remain.*

The first McDonald's restaurant was in San Bernardino, California. By definition the customers in San Bernardino were the test market, just as the local region in which an emerging rock band plays is the test market for music that may one day be recorded and distributed nationwide. Over time, market requirements have changed and McDonald's has effectively responded by fine-tuning its layout, menu, and service delivery system. The configuration and features of McDonald's restaurants have changed to include indoor seating, playgrounds, breakfast, meals for children, salads, burritos, pizza, ice cream, chicken, fish, and many others. McDonald's has also demonstrated its commitment to protecting the environment by replacing most of its styrofoam packaging with paper.

Environmental concerns also encouraged European car makers to develop an entire class of tiny automobiles. Designers of these cars listened to what their customers were saying: They wanted greater fuel efficiency and more mobility in the narrow, crowded European streets.

## Customer-driven New Product Ideas

If market research questionnaires are not sufficient for providing new ideas for products and services, how do successful companies listen to their customers? Several Japanese companies observe the customer instead of asking questions. Toyota USA employs a small team of anthropologists to study the cultural setting within which Americans choose to live. Using the California market as a leading indicator of lifestyle trends, the anthropologists observe people in their homes, because that is where customers most obviously express their preferences for living conditions. They note the volume at which residents set their TVs; whether they listen to the radio while watching television; how they arrange food and dishes in their cabinets; how individuals interact with one another; the types, brightness, colors, patterns, and degrees of lighting people prefer; and the spareness or clutter of their homes.

What does this have to do with designing an automobile that will be released in five years? Toyota wants to anticipate the interior environment and exterior appearance that are most likely to delight its customers. It seeks a certain touch and feel that the customer will find familiar and exciting. Asking questions of the customer at the earliest stages of design is unlikely to yield useful information for a car that will not be released for several years.

Hitachi also uses indirect analysis to identify new characteristics for household appliances that will appeal to its Japanese customers. Hitachi's product designers observed that more Japanese women were joining the work force, which meant that they would have to do laundry early in the morning or late in the evening (Japanese men are highly traditional). Hitachi subsequently designed a quiet washing machine for a marketplace that never had considered noise to be an important factor. Hitachi gained significant market share with its quieter machine before competitors could redesign their products. Hitachi also recognized that demand for dryers would increase because working women would not hang laundry to air dry and that making room in the home for a dryer would be difficult because Japanese homes are small. Hitachi developed a single appliance for washing and drying clothes.

Designers at Matsushita, manufacturer of electronic devices sold under the Panasonic label in the United States, were unhappy with some features of their automatic bread-making machine and refined them by observing the best bread maker in Tokyo. They modified the mechanisms for mixing ingredients, kneading dough, and the temperature settings; the new product produced bread that met customers' requirements more closely than did the prototype—and delighted them because they could use it to make high-quality fresh bread at home.

Such design techniques are becoming common at top organizations. Aware that changing demographics present a growing market of older consumers, Procter & Gamble redesigned boxes of Tide for easier opening. General Motors plans to slightly enlarge the knobs on Oldsmobiles, make visual displays easier to read, and simplify operating instructions. Seventeen percent of Americans are disabled; the advocacy group Opening Door lobbies hotel chains to redesign their hotels to accommodate disabled travelers. Recognizing the size and potential of that market, Embassy Suites designed and opened a fully accessible resort facility near Disney World in Orlando, Florida. Embassy Suites requires its employees to attend a three-day etiquette course on how to provide service to disabled people and has equipped its rooms with talking clocks for the blind, roll-in showers, low sinks, and accessible beds.

Design disasters also have encouraged companies to listen to their customers. Most people found the early videocassette recorders (VCRs) almost impossible to program, and customer surveys revealed that most owners seldom used VCRs except to watch rented movies. It was a classic case of features and functions dictated by design engineers who were excited by the sophistication of the product but had little regard for the frustration experienced by users. Newer VCR models are much easier to use, but most people are not willing to discard a difficult but still working unit. VCR Plus+ observed this phenomenon and produced a remote control device that bypasses owners' systems to program their

VCRs. To tell their VCRs to record a program, users simply enter the code number published next to each program in the weekly television viewer guide book.

## Quality Function Deployment

A formal technique for translating the voice of the customer into the language of design and manufacturing engineers is **quality function deployment (QFD)**. Developed in Mitsubishi's Kobe, Japan, shipyards in the 1970s, QFD helps development teams rank the features of products and services according to customers' preferences, needs, and wants. The benefits of QFD include

Fewer changes after product or service is introduced
Shorter product/service development time
Lower costs
Increased productivity
Greater customer satisfaction
Bigger market share
Improved communication within the organization
Better data for refining the design of future products/services.[4]

The complete QFD technique involves constructing a series of sequentially developed matrices. One dimension of each matrix lists the characteristics or attributes—or *what* needs to be included in the design—and the other dimension addresses *how* this will be accomplished. The first matrix, often called the **House of Quality,** is the most popular feature of this technique.[5] Companies often never go beyond the House of Quality to use the complete QFD technique. Figure 5.1 illustrates the general steps for developing the House of Quality.

Most applications of QFD to date are in the manufacturing area, but the technique is just as applicable to the service sector. Suppose you are the owner of a fast-food restaurant in a college town. You are concerned that your operation is not providing the level of customer satisfaction you need to sustain your business in the face of continued competition. You recently learned of the QFD technique in your operations management class and think that you should use its six steps. Let's see how you might proceed. As we discuss the application of the six steps, refer to Figure 5.2, the House of Quality for this example.

**Step 1: Consider the Voice of the Customer.**  In this step you determine what you should be doing in your business. You can obtain some of this information by simply asking the customer and get other important information by watching your customers. Japanese companies often design a prototype of a new product and make it available at some public location such as a shopping mall. Mall patrons are encouraged to handle the product and make comments about their perceptions. Company representatives are on hand to write the comments down so they can be reviewed later.

For our example, suppose you solicit customers' suggestions and develop a list of customers' needs and wants, often referred to as *customer attributes*. What you might learn from talking to customers (see Customer Attributes in Figure 5.2) is that they want fast food service, food that tastes good, food served warm,

[4]Gregg Stocker, "Quality Function Deployment: Listening to the Voice of the Customer," *American Production and Inventory Control Society—The Performance Advantage* 1, (September 1991): 44–48.
[5]John Hauser and Don Clausing, "The House of Quality," *Harvard Business Review* 66, (May–June 1988): 63–73.

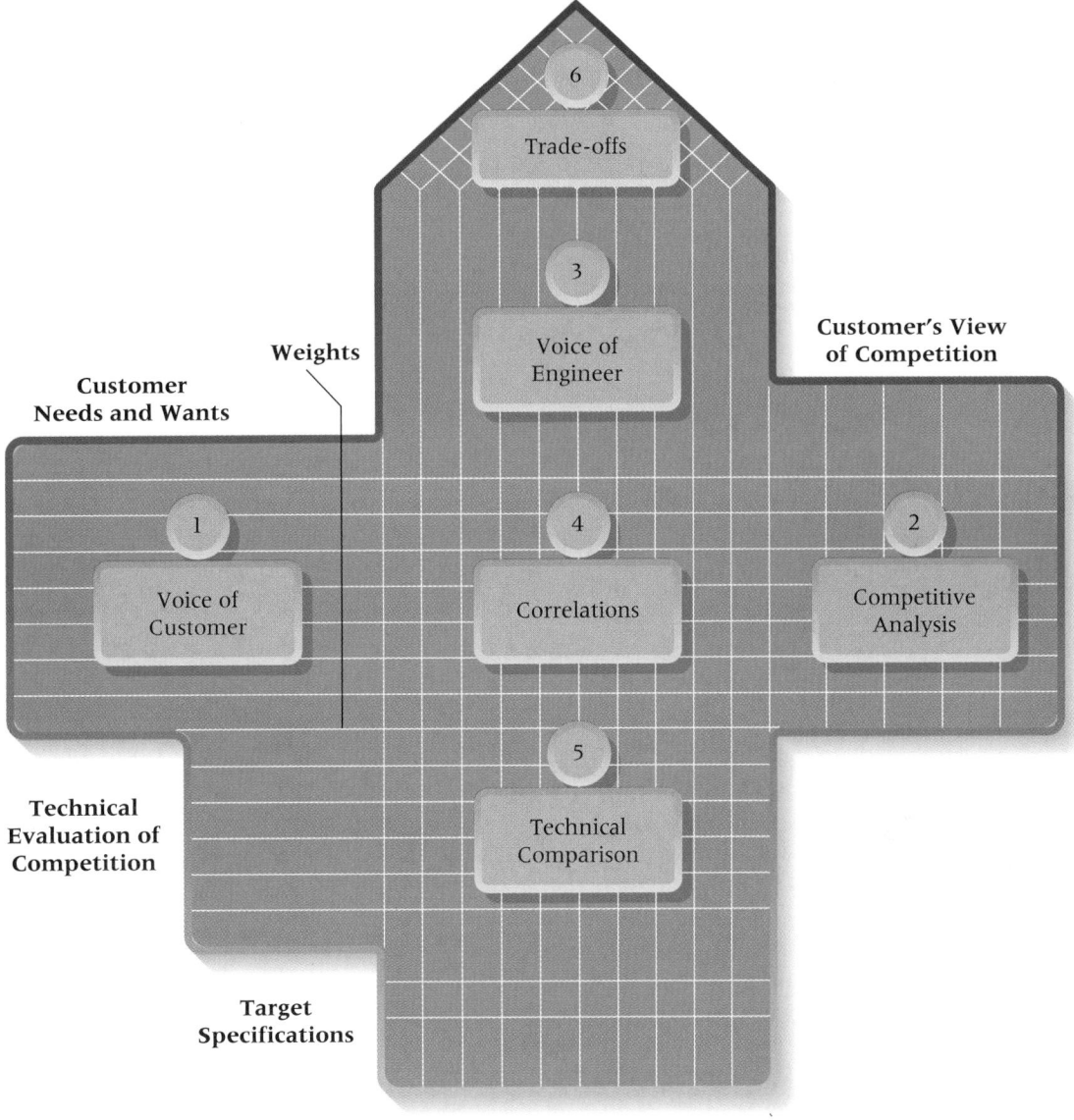

6

Trade-offs

3

Voice of
Engineer

**Weights**

**Customer
Needs and Wants**

**Customer's View
of Competition**

1

Voice of
Customer

4

Correlations

2

Competitive
Analysis

5

Technical
Comparison

**Technical
Evaluation of
Competition**

**Target
Specifications**

FIGURE  5.1
Steps in the House of
Quality

a variety of food selections, and low prices. Next, you need to go back to your customers and ask them to assign a weight to each attribute to reflect its relative importance. This will allow you to focus on those that are most important to your customers.

Note that the weights in Figure 5.2 are expressed as percentages and total 100 percent. This method is preferable to simply ranking the attributes from first to last, because the percentages provide insight about how strongly customers feel about the relative importance of each attribute.

**Step 2: Perform Competitive Analysis.** Next, you must determine how well your restaurant is satisfying your customer attributes as compared with your competitors. You must conduct your competitive analysis through the eyes of the customer. (Business owners sometimes hire consultants to do this.) Suppose you

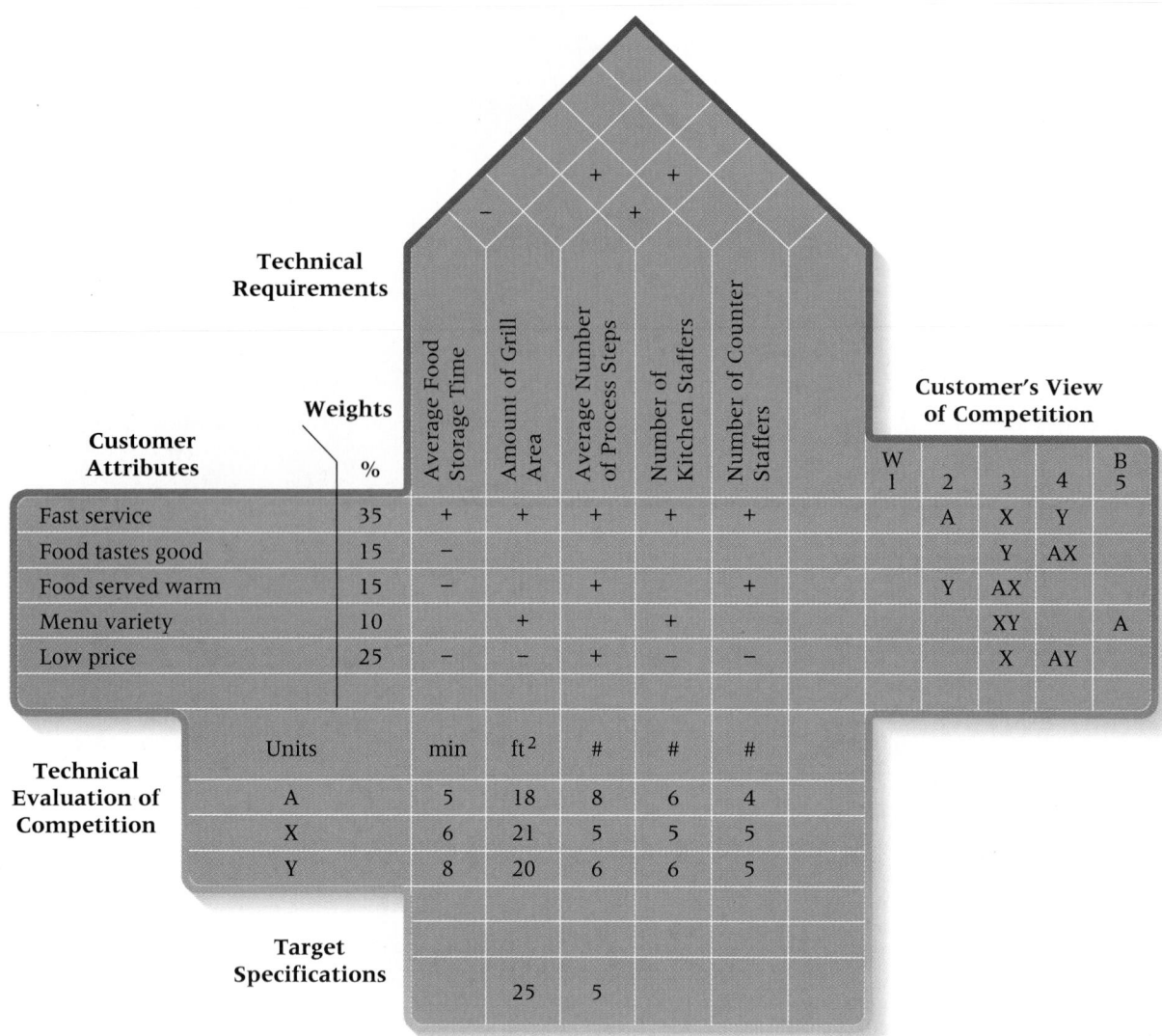

FIGURE 5.2
Using the House of Quality

have two key competitors. Label your company *A* and the competition *X* and *Y*, which are the labels we used in Figure 5.2. Note that you should ask customers to rank your company and the competition on a five-point scale; 5 represents the *best* performance and 1 represents the *worst* performance.

Figure 5.2 yields the information that your restaurant is behind the competition in the attribute for "fast service," ahead of the competition for "menu variety" attribute, and about the same for the other attributes. Of primary importance here is that our customers weighted the "menu variety" attribute as less important than any other attribute and the "fast service" attribute as most important of all. By completing just the first two steps of the House of Quality, you have learned a lot about your business.

**Step 3: Consider the Voice of the Engineer.** What are the technical steps of your operation that affect customer attributes? How might you change these technical elements to better serve your customers? These technical elements are referred to as *technical requirements* and must be stated in terms that are measurable. For example, you can serve your customers faster by preparing food in advance and keeping it warm until they order it. So one measurable technical requirement that you could use to capture this factor might be the average amount of time that prepared food sits until you serve it. Other measurable technical requirements that affect customer attributes include the amount of grill area, the average number of steps in the process of serving a customer, the average number of kitchen staffers, and the number of counter staffers.

**Step 4: Look for Correlations.** What are the relationships between the customers' desired attributes and the technical requirements? These correlations are shown as a plus or minus sign in the body of the House of Quality. For example, preparing more food in advance may speed customer service (+), but it may also negatively affect the taste (-) and temperature (-) of the food. It also may mean that you will throw out more food because it did not sell, which would negatively affect prices (-). Sometimes symbols other than + or - are used to denote these correlations. Alternative symbols would allow identification of strong versus weak, positive and negative correlations. Understanding how changing the measurements of the technical requirements will affect the customer attributes is an important element of the process.

This step can be difficult to complete, because it requires a thorough understanding of the technical requirements and consideration of many issues. Remember that QFD is not a technique for finding an optimal solution to a problem; it is useful for soliciting information from customers and using it in the most effective way to improve their satisfaction.

**Step 5: Perform Technical Comparison with Competitors.** Now you need to compare the measures of your technical requirements and those of the competition. This step is very similar to step 2, where customers were asked to assess how well your restaurant satisfied their key attributes as compared with how well your competitors did that. Here, the engineering staff is looking at your measures of the technical requirements and comparing them with the competitions'. How much food do your competitors prepare in advance and hold? How big are their grills? Recognize the difficulty of determining accurate measures of competitors' technical elements. Figure 5.2 shows where to enter this information on the matrix, under Technical Evaluation of Competition. Note that the matrix specifies the unit of measure for each requirement.

**Step 6: Evaluate Design Trade-offs.** The roof of the House of Quality provides information related to trade-offs in the technical requirements. Improving one technical requirement often has a negative effect on another requirement. You need to assess the trade-offs and enter your conclusions at the top of the house, again using pluses and minuses. Figure 5.2 shows the correlations the engineers found for your restaurant.

For example, if you wish to speed up customer service, you need to have food available more quickly. You can either hold more food prepared with existing grill space or you can increase grill area and hold no more food. There is probably no need to do both. Therefore, this relationship is shown at the top of the House of Quality as a minus sign between the first two technical requirements. Similarly, if grill area is increased, you may need more kitchen staffers. This positive relationship is indicated by a plus sign between the second and fourth technical requirements. It is important to understand the effect of changing the value of one technical requirement on the other requirements of the process. Often in improving a process, what seems to be the best course of action is not, because of the negative effects on other elements of the process.

## From the House of Quality to Operations Requirements

Your House of Quality is complete. You have a better understanding of your customers' needs and expectations and some measure of how well they think you are performing. You have also identified the technical requirements that work together to provide some level of customer satisfaction, and you can see the relationship between your technical requirements and your customers' needs and expectations. You are now in a better position to identify how you can change the technical requirements to provide the biggest improvement in customer satisfaction at the lowest cost, in terms of both time and dollars. You can use the information collected and presented in the matrix and your knowledge and good judgment to determine new specifications for those technical elements that should be changed. The new Target Specifications in the House of Quality in Figure 5.2 represent what you want to do: expand your grill area and cut the number of steps in the food preparation process.

As we noted earlier, the QFD process goes through four phases of development.[6] The House of Quality is the first and arguably most important phase. It is often unnecessary to continue beyond the first phase as in our restaurant example. Implementing the new target specifications may be simple enough to accomplish without further detailed analysis. But target specifications for many manufacturing applications will require much more analysis to determine new specifications for component parts or even processes used to produce the components. We will briefly discuss the other phases here. The outputs of the House of Quality provide inputs to the next phase, which is illustrated in Figure 5.3.

In general applications the second phase of QFD matches the parts and components of the product or service to the target specifications from the House of Quality. The goal is to determine whether the engineering measurements associated with the components can meet the requirements specified in phase 1, or whether components must be redesigned or substituted. Once again, the important, new, and challenging requirements from the Components Matrix become inputs for the third matrix.

The Process Characteristics Matrix compares the new parts and components with the measurements of performance for the manufacturing system. The purpose is to determine whether the manufacturing or service delivery system can produce and deliver parts and components that meet the new requirements. The outcome of the third matrix determines which new manufacturing or service processes must be developed in order to meet the requirements of the Components Matrix.

Finally, the Process Characteristics Matrix determines the important, new, or challenging specifications for the manufacturing or service system. These requirements must then be compared with the process capabilities of our current operations in the Process Control Matrix. This fourth and final phase of QFD compares the statistical process capabilities of current technologies and systems with the capabilities that would be needed in order to meet the manufacturing needs.

[6]Stocker, "Quality Function Development," pp. 44–48.

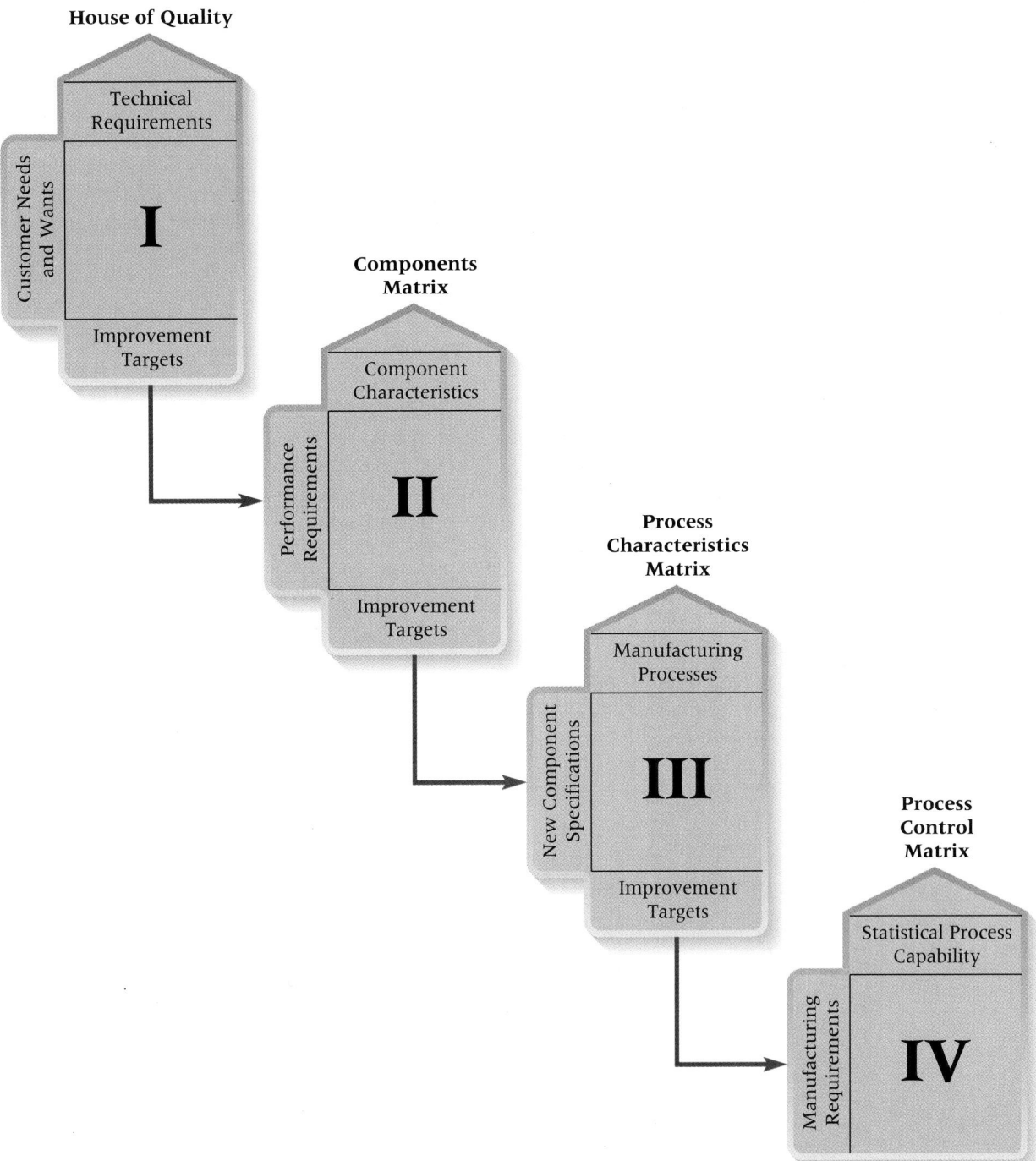

FIGURE 5.3
Four Phases of Quality
Function Deployment (QFD)

## Application of QFD to New Product Design

The German small appliance manufacturer Braun introduced a coffeemaker in 1972 that received design awards for its sleek, modern appearance and its ability to brew good coffee. Unfortunately, the product proved unprofitable and Braun removed it from the market. Braun replaced it in 1984 with a well-designed unit that was more traditional in appearance. What went wrong? The initial design required two heating elements rather than one and used expensive materials and assembly methods. The price at which Braun had to offer the earlier model was too high in comparison to competing models from other manufacturers and the relative range of features that these products included. The Braun design was intended to delight the customer, and it did but at an unacceptable price-to-value ratio.

Although the initial results of the 1992 opening of Euro Disney near Paris were less than anticipated, the amusement park still is a good example of service design using QFD principles. Disney designers determined which features of the theme parks in Florida and California were most appealing to Europeans and which features of the United States were at the top of Europeans' list of interests. Thus in addition to familiar Disney themes and characters, the attractions and hotels use themes from New York City and "the West." Thus, hotels and restaurants have metropolitan, "Old West," and "New West" environments. "Bonjour, pardner!"

IBM used QFD to develop its January 1992 release of a PS/2 computer designed for use in schools. The PS/2-25 is directed at the elementary and secondary school market and includes a configuration of graphics capability, memory, and color, along with two popular networking modes. IBM developed the unique configuration by comparing customers' needs and wants to technical capabilities. The design phase included two thousand interviews and countless observations of the school environment by IBM design engineers; it also recognized that schools wanted a single standard design to simplify training and maintenance.

## Improving Designs Through Simplification and Value Analysis

Lexmark discovered the pleasure of simplicity by simplifying product designs before manufacturing its products. By forming a cross-functional team of designers and engineers Lexmark hoped to reduce the number of parts in its laser printer. The team used a computer-aided design and computer-aided manufacturing tool (CAD/CAM) to test alternative designs for manufacturability. Its goal was to combine and reduce the number of parts and to substitute snap fasteners for nuts and bolts without changing the appearance or function of the printer. Lexmark's product has fewer parts than a similar machine designed by rival Hewlett-Packard and many fewer screws and bolts than it once had. The company had planned to use robotic assembly but found the machine was easy and economical to assemble by hand. CAD-CAM is discussed further in Chapter 8.

A product designer uses **value analysis** to assess the characteristics of the product, the customers who will buy it and how they will use it, and the objective of the company in launching it. Having this information allows the product designer to make better trade-offs in costs versus features that could be included in the product. Value analysis considers the function of the product and each of its components. The result is a concise and clear definition of the role of each part. This can serve as a springboard for considering alternative parts and configurations that provide better function, are easier to implement, and better satisfy the needs of the customer. Black & Decker Corp. often combines value analysis with a conscious attempt to improve the product according to market-driven criteria. When Black & Decker designers were doing a value analysis of a finishing sander, they determined that the first three parts to fail were the switch, the flexible post, and the pad on the sander. They were able to improve these components by sealing the switch and changing the materials used to make the flexible post and the pad. The final design had only 22 percent of the parts in the original, because it combined or eliminated some functions and others were redesigned. The redesign also cut assembly time and component costs.

Simplifying the design of new and existing products is one of the principal weapons a company can use to improve its products. Competitors will take over many of a company's profitable products and services if the company does not constantly listen to its customers and improve performance accordingly. The design phase presents the richest opportunity to satisfy customers and reduce costs.

Figure 5.4 illustrates the relationship between the percentage of cost attributed to design, material, labor, and overhead and the influence of those costs on manufacturing costs. Design represents only 5 percent of the cost of most manufactured goods, but characteristics of that design affect 70 percent of the manufacturing-related costs. Superior designs can thus reduce costs in 70 percent of manufacturing activities, whereas labor can reduce costs in only 5 percent of manufacturing activities. One IBM manufacturing division measured the cost of correcting defects at various stages of design, testing, and delivery to the customer. It determined that finding and correcting defects at the manufacturing and testing stage cost thirteen times more than correcting the cause of the defect at the design stage. Correcting defects that are found at the customer's installation are one hundred times more costly than at the design stage. Clearly, companies that want to reduce the cost of defects will focus on design activities.

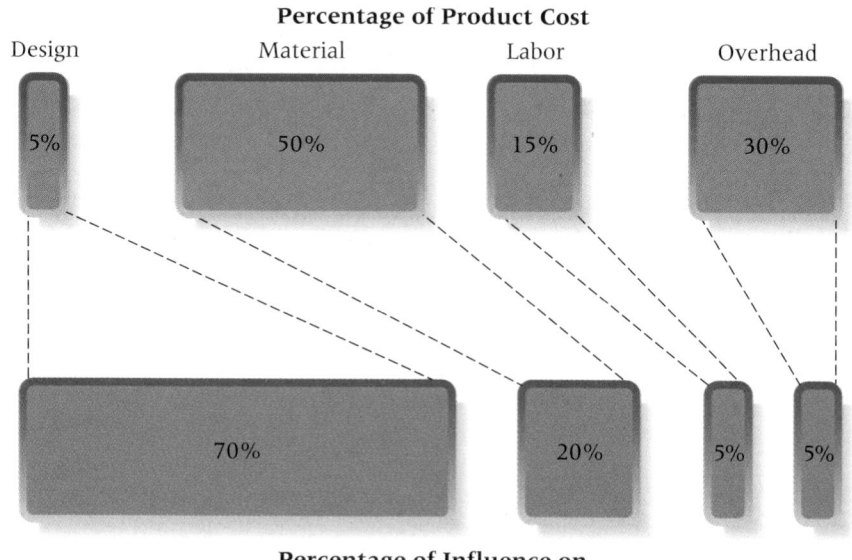

**Percentage of Product Cost**

| Design | Material | Labor | Overhead |
| --- | --- | --- | --- |
| 5% | 50% | 15% | 30% |

70%    20%    5%    5%

**Percentage of Influence on
Manufacturing Cost**

FIGURE 5.4
Cost Breakdown for New Product

# Design for Manufacturability

Thus far the importance of designing products and services to include the features that satisfy customers has been central to our discussion of design. If a defect is some failure to meet the customer's needs and wants, good design methods will help ensure the right features and value to meet customers' expectations. However, the issue of timeliness as a dimension of customer satisfaction also affects product and service design. Once a company has determined its customers' needs and wants, how can it bring new products and services to the marketplace more quickly? Automobile industry analysts have described shorter development cycles (**cycle time** is defined as the time between the release of one model until the release of the next) as auto makers' next battlefield. During its business slump in the 1970s Xerox was surprised that a Japanese competitor was able to bring new designs to market in half the time Xerox required and at half the development cost. Because labor is a big part of development cost, the time-cost relationship for Xerox's competition is not surprising. After sweeping reorganization and considerable new investment, by 1988 Xerox had cut its development time to approximately two years, and it continued to make significant improvements into the 1990s. Similar stories can be told about Honeywell's "Tiger Team" and the industrial controls division of Allen-Bradley Corp. Each of these companies learned to reduce development time by using the principle of concurrent engineering.

## Concurrent Engineering

**Concurrent engineering** involves overlapping activities in product and process development that were previously performed sequentially, in tandem. Companies traditionally designed new products and services and stated the complete specifications. The design then went to the manufacturing team, often with little additional communication, for development of the process for manufacturing the product or delivering the service. If the product specifications meant that manufacturing was difficult or expensive, the company assumed those specifications were necessary to meet the needs of the customer. The first improvement in this model came when companies began conducting a formal design review with both groups, design and manufacturing, present at the same meeting. This permitted quick and perceptive manufacturing engineers to question some of the more difficult design features and seek simplification.

In the most advanced companies design and manufacturing engineers now serve on **cross-functional teams** that may also include representatives from marketing, cost accounting, and other areas. This approach provides an atmosphere conducive not only to the exchange of information but also to true problem solving—a cooperative rather than competitive environment that is referred to as **design for manufacturability (DFM)**. These companies measure and reward their teams according to their ability to bring market-driven product designs to customers quickly and at a price that is possible only when they avoid unnecessary costs.

Figures 5.5 and 5.6 illustrate the greater effectiveness of concurrent engineering practices over sequential development in reducing development cycle time. When the development activities are sequential, as illustrated in Figure 5.5, the prototypes typically have problems with functionality or excessive cost that are subsequently "solved" by last-minute engineering changes. When the product

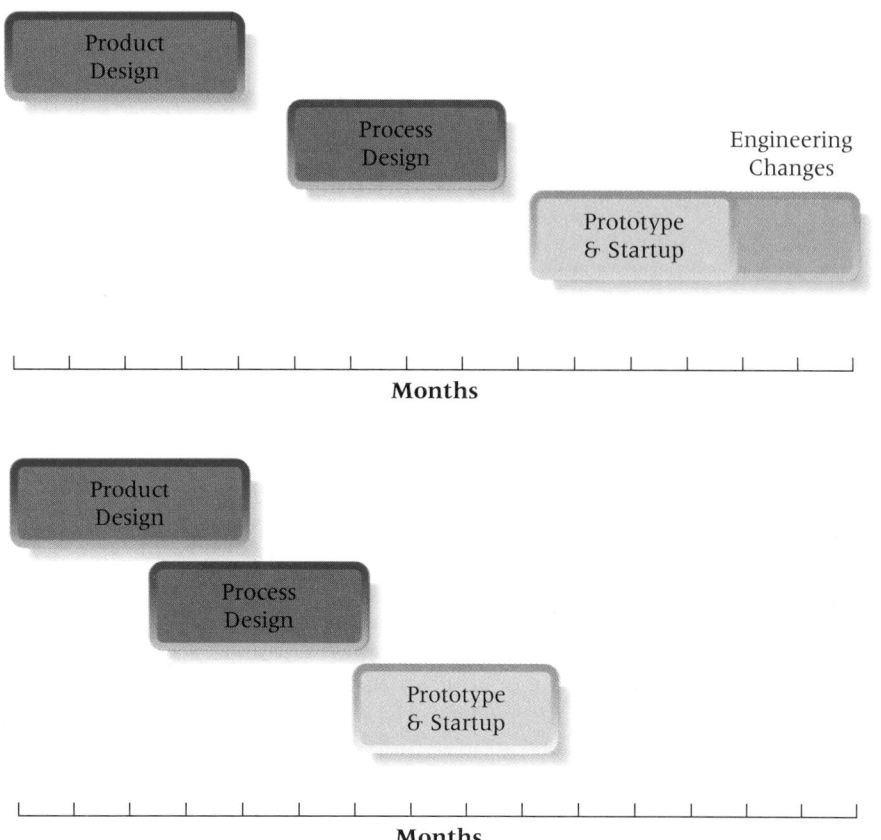

FIGURE 5.5
Sequential Development
Activities

FIGURE 5.6
Overlapping Development
Activities

and process design activities overlap, cycle time improves and engineering changes to correct mismatches between design requirements and process capabilities are rare (see Figure 5.6). Consider what happened at Chrysler Corp. in the early 1960s. The designers ordered a big fin for the middle of the trunk on a particular model of the Plymouth. It was a magnificent fin, but no stamping machine in manufacturing could press it. Factory workers had to weld each fin by hand onto the trunk hood, leading to high cost and some conformity problems. Chrysler scrapped the idea at the last minute. Manufacturing was not even represented on Chrysler design teams until 1981, which meant that Chrysler usually increased its program budgets for new vehicle designs by 25 to 40 percent just to account for the cost of last-minute engineering changes.

American and European auto makers once took more than sixty months to develop new models (compared with the Japanese cycle of just over forty months), but Western auto makers improved their organizations, resulting in more competitive development cycles. The very best companies are extending the concepts of concurrent engineering and design for manufacturability to include customer involvement at each stage of development. IBM's Rochester, Minnesota, division—winner of the U.S. Department of Commerce's Malcolm Baldrige National Quality Award—has collapsed its development timetable by combining concurrent engineering practices, cross-functional development teams, and consistently involving customers throughout the process.

Ford has extended design for manufacturability to include suppliers, because a significant portion of the components of Ford products are outsourced. So that its DFM methods will succeed, Ford has given long-term contracts to suppliers that have the capability to produce excellent parts. Such **strategic alliances** between buyers and sellers have been critical to the development of superior designs.

## Implementing Cross-Functional Teams in DFM

If the methods required to reduce design cycle time and achieve product and service designs that meet customers' needs are so obvious, why has it taken so long for organizations to respond? Young, aggressive members of organizations often find the effects of organizational inertia difficult to understand. Many factors in organizations, including status, hinder DFM success. Companies often pay designers more than they pay manufacturing engineers, and the designers may have more education and more discretion and autonomy in their positions. Furthermore, the project team will be more successful if its work is measured and rewarded as teamwork.

Another indicator of whether a DFM team can succeed is whether the two groups report to a common superior. The senior manager will have the incentive to promote cooperation and use common measures of success for each group. If the design group reports up through several levels to the vice president for engineering, and manufacturing engineers report through a similar number of levels to the vice president for manufacturing or materials management, the teams are less likely to function effectively. Another success indicator is how often individuals move from design to manufacturing and vice versa in the same organization. The more lateral moves there are, the more likely it is that cross-functional teams can succeed. Finally, top management must provide the teams with leadership and budget flexibility.

Project factors also influence the cooperation between design and manufacturing during the project. To be successful the project team must have clear goals, constant membership with low turnover, and regular meetings; and the company must make clear that participation on the team is a significant factor in the promotion and reward of individual members. Solving design and manufacturing problems requires that members be capable of viewing problems from the perspective of both functions and that they be willing to share information. Computer-based data on manufacturability and process guidelines will improve the success and speed of the project.

Finally, recent research studies indicate that the factors with the greatest effect on DFM success are supplier and customer involvement. How do you know whether DFM has succeeded? Measure the dollars committed for tooling and facilities before the design phase is complete. Track the number of engineering changes after specifications were released, compare that number with numbers from sequential development, and note whether the engineering changes came at the beginning or end of the development cycle. Start-up time, from first unit produced to acceptable production levels, should also be faster than for sequential development.

## Process Design and Layout for Manufacturing and Service Systems

Mapping or diagramming the flow of material, information, and people through a system produces a model of the production process. The range of process flow configurations in manufacturing and service systems can be grouped into categories according to common features in their flow patterns and some general principles regarding how they function. These general categories are imperfect for describing any particular operation precisely, but they are useful for comparing the opportunities and challenges presented by some common configurations. Let's use some familiar examples to build a conceptual model of some typical process types and elaborate upon them.

## Projects: Processes That Don't Flow

In the simplest case imagine a product or service for which virtually no flow is visible. Material, workers, and information come to the site and depart from it, but the product does not really move, or flow. One example is the construction of a concrete bridge on an interstate highway. If we mounted a camera near the site and recorded a frame of film every hour, we could trace over several weeks or months the arrival and departure of resources, but the bridge stays in place. This configuration is frequently called a **project**. The challenge to the manager of a project-type process configuration is to ordinate the sequence and timing of activities so that work can proceed efficiently. In a service context a project configuration might be the installation of a new computer and an associated network connecting each person who works in a business.

One feature of projects is that the product or service delivered has unique aspects. The site requirements make the interstate highway bridge unique, although the materials and processes needed to build it may be similar to what many other bridges require. The computer system has some unique features, and some features that do not really distinguish it from other computer networks. This is also true of handcrafted goods. Whether they are made to order or made in anticipation of a sale, handcrafted goods made by one individual rarely flow

*This bridge under construction represents a project type layout where material, equipment, and labor is brought to the job site.*

from workstation to workstation. A made-to-measure suit or dress, a piece of jewelry, and work of art are examples of projects on a somewhat smaller scale. Costs for production of unique products usually are higher than for other production processes. Traditionally, producers of these items are referred to as **jobbers**.

## Intermittent Flow Configurations

Most manufacturing and service operations need to process a variety of products or services simultaneously and efficiently. A process configuration used when flexibility is needed and the number of units to be produced is small is called a **job shop**. Material flows through the facility as it is processed by the various workstations. The workstations are laid out according to the type of process performed. This type of layout is often called a **process-oriented layout**. As Figure 5.7 shows, all the people and equipment involved in the packing operation are located in the same general area. The same would be true for the painting, sanding, cutting, and other functional areas of the job shop in Figure 5.7. Customer orders would be routed through the facility to the various processes as they are needed. At any time a job shop would normally contain several orders for a different number of units of a variety of products or services.

A glance across the floor of the typical job shop reveals some idle workstations and others with stacks of work to be processed. That is the nature of the job shop. Many different orders compete for the general purpose equipment in the workstations. The manager must decide the order in which the jobs are to be processed. This is not a simple task, because each job has different characteristics such as processing time required, type of item involved, customer name, date promised the customer, and many others. An order may spend a considerable amount of time awaiting its turn for processing at workstations before it is completed. The move-and-wait nature of a job shop has given rise to the term **intermittent production**.

The most significant advantage of the job shop is its flexibility for processing a wide variety of products or services in low volume. The most significant disadvantage is the cost per unit. Cost in a job shop tends to be high for several reasons. First, the cost of handling materials is relatively high because unfinished materials must be transported from station to station for processing. The increased material movement translates into longer times till completion. Other costs often are high because the facilities are not working at full capacity. Because one characteristic of the job shop is flexibility, all orders do not require all the processes available. When those processes are not needed, they sit idle.

One simple example of a job shop is a kitchen. The refrigerator, freezer, dishwasher, oven, stove top, microwave, cutting board, and knife are general purpose equipment. Given a variety of raw materials (food) a cook can prepare a virtually endless variety of dishes. Certain groups of food command dominant patterns of flow in the kitchen, but almost any sequence of operations might occur at the various workstations. The benefits of having this variety are partially offset by low and inefficient utilization of resources and high costs. Compare, for example, the percentage of time that the oven in a home and an oven in a cookie factory are in use. The average utilization of equipment in job shops usually is low. Consider the layout of your local hospital. Because hospitals must be able to respond to (process) a wide range of patients' needs, they are most often arranged in job shop fashion. All the people, equipment, and material required to

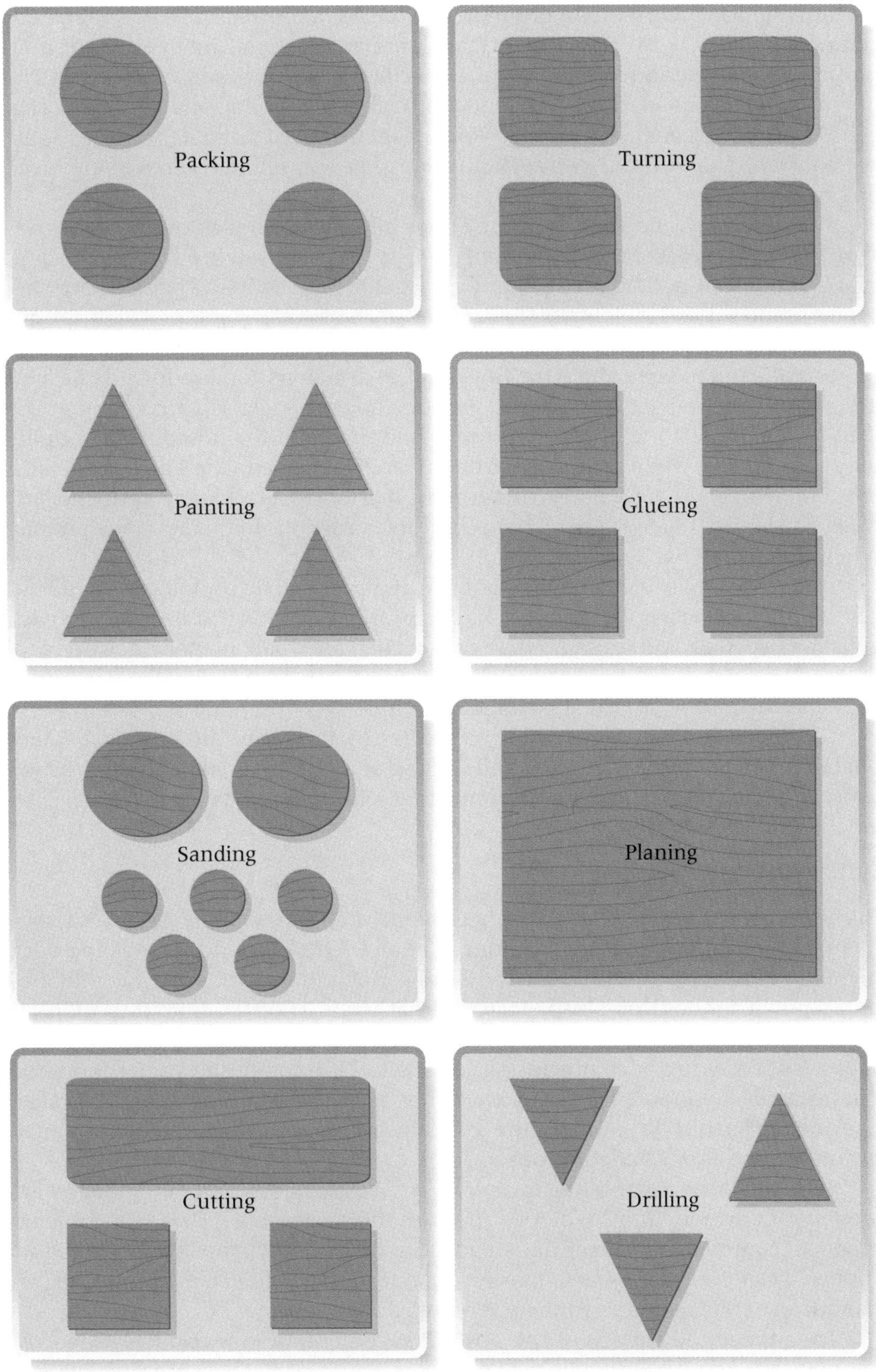


FIGURE 5.7
Process-Oriented Layout for Job Shops

perform similar processes are grouped together. The hospital has an emergency room, laboratory, x-ray room, pharmacy, cardiac care unit, intensive care unit, and other units designed to perform a specific set of functions (processes). The admitting department routes patients through the hospital much as the chef routes meals through a kitchen. Some patients need only lab work. Some patients need lab work, x-ray, then admission for further care. Some need emergency care.

Woodworking and metal-cutting shops also are examples of job shop configurations. An industrial woodworking facility has departments that have groups of machines that perform similar functions. One area contains planers, another sanders, and a third table saws, for example. The manager routes wood for different projects or orders from department to department according to the steps required for manufacturing. Drawings and instructions for producing the part accompany the wood. The task of the job shop manager is to coordinate the routing and scheduling of orders through the shop and to attempt to determine alternative routes when certain departments are overloaded. The skill level of most job shop workers is high. Each worker must master the machinery in the department and be able to read and follow technical instructions for building the product when it reaches that department.

If the job shop is busy, predicting when an order will be completed is difficult. This is one reason why restaurant kitchens are fairly underutilized. Only with considerable skill and coordination can a chef and staff prepare a variety of entrees to be delivered simultaneously to a large party. That is possible only when they have plenty of available cooking capacity.

Chapter 15, Shop Floor Control, addresses many of the complex issues related to the efficient scheduling and routing of a variety of jobs through the job shop as well as the sequencing of competing jobs on a particular machine.

## Line-Flow Configurations

Both the project and job shop configurations are inappropriate in an environment of low variety and high volume. The need for efficiency in dealing with higher volumes of output has given rise to a different type of process configuration, known as the **flow shop**. Material that tends to flow, sometimes uninterrupted from beginning to end of the overall process, is characteristic of flow shops. The order in which processing steps must be accomplished determines the arrangement of processes along the flow path; this arrangement is called **product-oriented layout.** Figure 5.8 illustrates a general product-oriented layout for line-flow configurations.

Some products, such as microwave ovens, refrigerators, and automobiles, are produced in discrete units, whereas others (nondiscrete units), such as petroleum products, concrete, and chemicals, are not. For discrete units the degree of product variety dictates either a batch process or an assembly line. Items produced in nondiscrete units require a configuration of continuous flow.

The primary advantage of the flow-shop configuration is relatively low cost per unit. The cost of setting up the facilities is considerable, because the line uses special purpose equipment and it often is necessary to have several pieces of that equipment. However, the higher volume produced by the line-flow configuration reduces the per unit cost. The primary disadvantage of this approach is the lack of flexibility to adapt to changes in markets or customers' wishes.

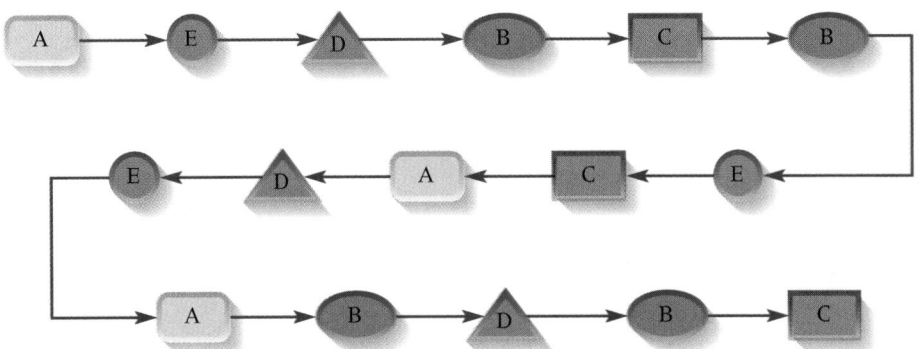

FIGURE 5.8
Product-Oriented Layout for
Flow Shops

Product flows through processes A–E in a sequence dictated by the assembly requirements of the product.

**Batch Processes.** Some discrete unit operations have characteristics that allow production of the products or services in batches or lots. The batch process can be considered a hybrid of the job shop and flow shop configurations. **Batch processes** offer less flexibility than the job shop but more efficiency, gained primarily from less product variety, higher volume, and more dominant material flows. Traditional steel manufacturing is a batch process. Fed by batches of several tons, the blast furnace heats cauldrons of molten ore and metals, then pours the steel into molds to produce ingots. After the batch of ingots cools, the ingots are reheated and rolled into sheets or slabs or pulled into bars or coils. The process permits manufacture of a variety of steel products, but that is an advantage only when a customer demands this variety. If a steel producer is making sequential batches with nearly identical metallurgical properties, it would be more efficient to use "continuous casting" processes to avoid the ingot stage of production and move directly from molten metal to bars, rods, and slabs. That is precisely the technique that has been used by Nucor Corp. in developing its highly efficient minimills. The former steel giants are now most competitive in specialty steel markets that take advantage of their batch processes.

Another example of a batch process is the production of Baskin-Robbins ice cream. Common equipment mixes different flavors of ice cream in batches, then pours them into three-gallon containers for delivery to stores. The only way to maintain the variety of flavors while producing ice cream at regional facilities is to use batch processes. Note that batch processes usually produce discrete units of the product. The manager schedules the products to be produced and assures that important quality characteristics are consistent from batch to batch.

**Assembly Lines.** When product or service variety is very low and volume is high, some material flow patterns dominate. By designing a manufacturing system around these dominant flows, products can be efficiently produced. Products typically move from operation to operation in small lots with little work-in-process inventory buildup. This type of operation is often referred to as an *assembly line* or **repetitive process.**

One immediately observable feature of an **assembly line** is the discrete units of production. Whether it is an aircraft assembly line moving airframes that fill buildings measured in football-field lengths, chickens being cut into parts for packaging, or the assembly of semiconductors, each unit of production moves

*Robotic welders complete their tasks at this Ford assembly plant.*

from workstation to workstation as value is added to the product. The task of the manager is to train and motivate workers, help identify and correct process problems, balance the line, and provide help with maintenance.

A key to customer satisfaction is timeliness, so one way to improve assembly lines is to cut the time it takes to switch from producing one item to another. Vans's shoes are made in the United States, unlike most athletic shoes, which are made in China, South Korea, and Malaysia. Made of canvas, suede, or velvet with rubber soles, Vans' sneakers are known for their unusual styles and colors. Most sports shoe manufacturers require six months to fill custom orders, but Vans' will put any shoes it makes in any size in a store within nineteen days. This permits dealers to adjust their orders to hot styles and colors, eliminating the need for end-of-season discounts that erode profit margins. Vans' also has a unique management style. Teams of workers in a mini-line operation get a daily quota of shoe orders. When they finish the order, they go home—paid for eight hours' work, although they often work less. The teams manage themselves, cutting administrative costs. Vans' employs only three managers to supervise 1,700 factory workers.

**Continuous Flow Processes.** Some manufacturing processes, such as a petro-chemical refinery, use a continuous flow of material, called the **continuous flow process**. Crude oil enters the system at one end and is heated, cooled, chemically catalyzed, and separated by molecular weight. This process yields many chemical by-products as well as the primary products, which include jet fuel, kerosene, gasoline, wax, and lubricants. The flow never stops as the product moves from vessel to pipe to container. An observer never sees a discrete unit of the product, and workers seldom touch it. What workers and managers do is to monitor and adjust the flow of materials to ensure that the process is stable and uninter-rupted. The start-up and shut-down cycles in these systems are complex and difficult to regulate. Redundancy is designed into these systems, and production continues twenty-four hours a day, seven days a week.

The plant shuts down only for annual maintenance and expansion projects. The manager's key tasks are to plan capacity, maintain operations, and keep the work force motivated and trained. Other systems that use continuous process technologies include nuclear power plants, sugar refineries, and paper mills. These systems are efficient, because they constantly add value to the product while it is in production. The system has no unnecessary waiting time between operations, and the flow is synchronized and perfectly balanced.

## Cellular Manufacturing

Recent years have seen relatively few innovations in process design and facility layout. Most companies improve their facilities incrementally when they don't have to add big machinery. Once heavy equipment is in place, it is almost never moved. Thus the design phase of facility layout, done properly, yields significant savings.

Early attempts to analyze facility layout involved complex mathematical programs. These models used departmental weighting schemes to ensure that departments were located near one another when that was appropriate. They seldom generated solutions much better than those developed by people familiar with the process. Now many companies use **animated computer simulation techniques** to evaluate alternative layouts. Designers use these techniques to develop mathematical models of facilities for processing people and material. Repeated "what if" experiments with these models test whether one layout is superior to another under some specified performance measure.

Perhaps the most significant innovation in process design in the second half of this century was **cellular manufacturing**, a concept that groups the various products produced in a job shop according to common features, including size, processing steps, and materials. The **parts families** produced by this grouping are assigned to manufacturing cells, such as those illustrated in Figure 5.9. The cells contain the machines necessary to complete most of the processing steps for that family of parts.

Sometimes an expensive machine (such as the planing device in Figure 5.9) cannot be assigned to a single department, or technological considerations (such as the special environmental factors related to painting) do not support breaking departments into cells.

Service operations also have used cellular manufacturing methods to reorganize and reduce their cycle times. Many companies have created a cluster of employees with the mix of skills and authority to speed travel arrangements and compensation, process health insurance claims, or receive training in new skills.

## Production Line Approach to Service

The various configurations illustrate the trade-off between variety and efficiency in manufacturing operations. Many successful service companies have correctly determined that custom services are not always what the customer seeks. The success of McDonald's standard menu selections is evidence that hot, quick, and inexpensive are more important attributes to many customers than food that is cooked to order and brought to the table. McDonald's has used batch line processes for what was assumed to be a job shop operation. To succeed,

FIGURE 5.9
Manufacturing Cells

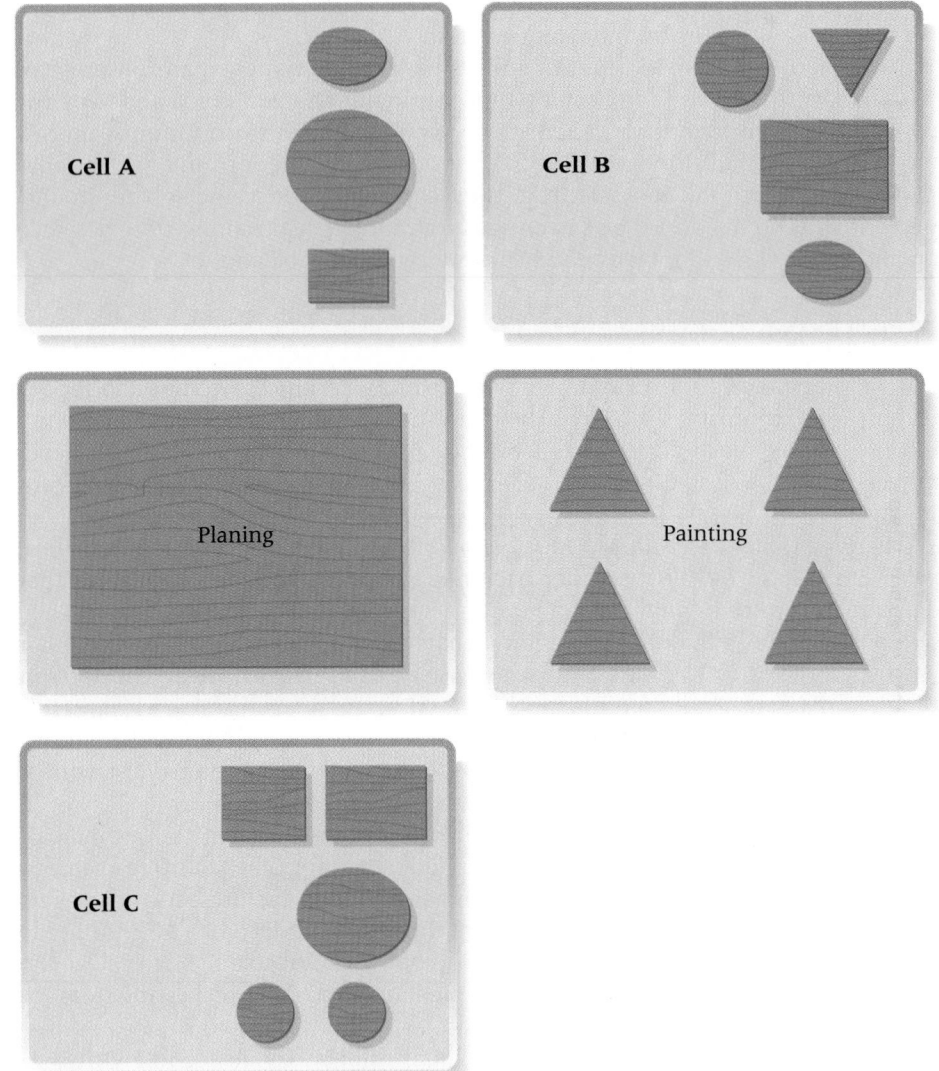

McDonald's had to cut the variety of products it offered and standardize its methods of preparation. One result is consistency. During long trips with cranky kids many parents are delighted that McNuggetts taste exactly as they do at home.

Travel agencies, insurance companies, and even legal practices that specialize in a narrow line of services, provided efficiently and inexpensively, have used service standardization.

## Strategic Issues in Process Design

Before we discuss how to select a process for a manufacturing or service operation that results in a competitive advantage, we need to review some principles of the product life cycle. As Figure 5.10 illustrates, the **product life cycle** is an indicator for the change in volume of demand for products during the introductory, growth, maturity, and decline periods. When the product is new,

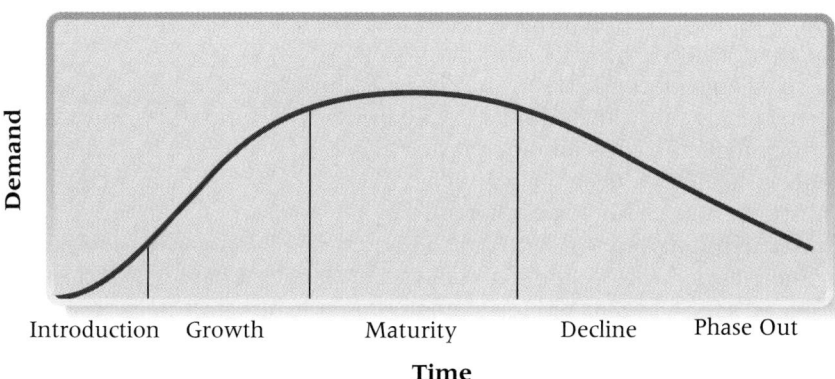

FIGURE 5.10
Product Life Cycle

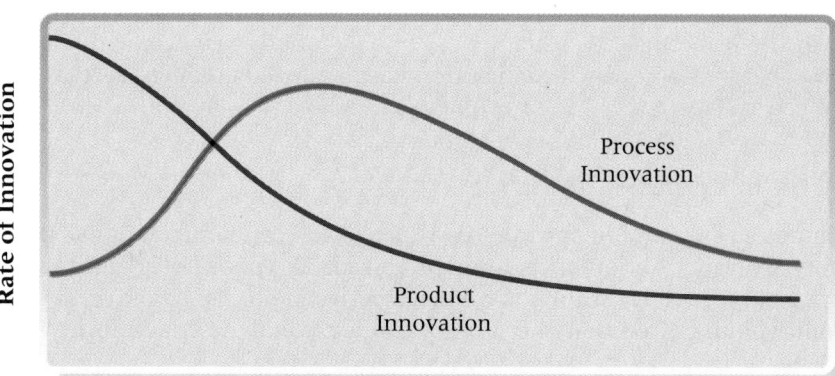

FIGURE 5.11
Interaction of Product and
Process Innovation

production costs are high, volumes are low, and the growth of sales is slow. The maximum rate of demand at maturity and the length of time the product sustains that demand are important elements in selecting technologies for manufacturing.

## Product and Process Innovation

A product's position in its life cycle is closely related to the predictable rate of change in both its design and the design of the technology used to produce or deliver it. Figure 5.11 shows how product and process innovation interact[7] The time axis is identical to the time axis on the product life cycle in Figure 5.10.

When a product is new, the market scrutinizes the features of the prototype or first-run products. That's why many companies first introduce their products in test markets. In Figure 5.11 the rate of product innovation is high. The process innovation is low, because less expensive, general technology is producing small batches or production runs. As the product gains market acceptance and moves into the growth phase, the rate of product innovation slows and the design becomes stable. The higher volume of demand becomes sufficient to justify investing in special purpose machines and adopting batch or line methods of production. Process innovation is high during this phase. Finally, when the market is saturated, the product moves into its maturity phase. In this phase

[7]William J. Abernathy and James M. Utterbark, "Patterns of Industrial Innovation," *Technology Review* 80, (June–July 1978): 40–42.

demand rates are level and product innovation unlikely. Therefore, the predicted level of change in the product and the process is low.

The challenge of the 1990s is the compression of product life cycles. To meet customers' needs and wants companies are bringing new products and variations of existing products to market much faster than ever before. This means that the time once available for developing efficient technology no longer exists. Companies must invest in technologies that are flexible and responsive. These **flexible manufacturing systems (FMS)** are designed to operate with flow-line efficiency and job shop variety and to handle small batches. Chapter 8, Technological Developments in Operations Management, presents these technologies in greater detail.

Many factors affect the speed with which companies develop new products or processes. For example, extraordinary incentives are often required to initiate innovation. Competition also affects the speed of innovation. Although competition in the marketplace is usually healthy, Operations Management in Practice 5.2 describes a case in which competition has hampered product-process innovation.

## The Product Process Matrix

As Figure 5.11 implies, companies can match process configurations with the volume and variety of products to be produced. The **product process matrix** illustrated in Figure 5.12 shows the linkage between process pattern and product mix and volume. Note that the process configurations described earlier in this

FIGURE 5.12
Product Process Matrix

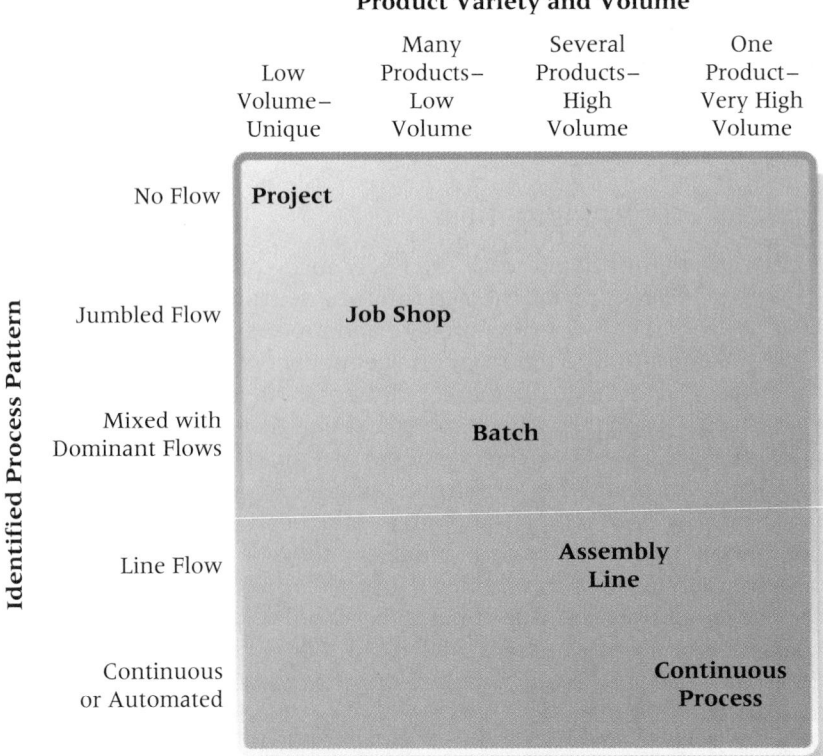

## Air-Conditioner Firms Put Chill on Plans

The U.S. and more than 80 other countries reached a landmark pact last year to halt the production of ozone-eating chlorofluorocarbons, or CFCs, after 1995. But the global campaign to phase out the use of the chemical compounds is stalled in the sub-basements of corporations and businesses around the world. The chief holdup is a multibillion dollar marketing brawl dubbed the "Chiller Wars."

This internecine contest is being waged among the producers of the next generation of industrial air conditioners, called chillers, that are free of CFCs. Two of the largest companies, Carrier Corporation and Trane Company, are competing for the largest slice of that emerging market. They are attacking each other's choice of ozone-friendly alternatives as either dangerous to human health or the environment.

It is the sparring between chiller makers that is most often blamed by regulators and building-industry officials for the confusion and inaction among CFC users. For instance, Carrier attacks Trane by citing laboratory studies two years ago that showed that Trane's favored coolant, HCFC-123, caused benign tumors in rats. Carrier also notes that workers handling the coolant are allowed only relatively low exposure levels. Further says Carrier, HCFC-123 still contains a small amount of chlorine, the element in CFCs that actually damages the ozone layer.

Trane, whose machines account for more than half the chillers in the country, counters that the safety concerns about HCFC-123 are overblown. What's more, Carrier's coolant of choice, the hydrofluorocarbon HFC-134a, causes too much global warming, Trane asserts. Trane machines, which operate at relatively low pressures, can't use HFC-134a, which is designed to work at high pressures.

The chemical companies that make CFCs and alternatives aren't directly taking sides in the Chiller Wars. But DuPont, which makes the broadest range of CFC alternatives, including HCFC-123 and HFC-134a, says it is happy to have customers choose any item on the menu. The Chiller Wars don't show signs of ending soon, even though Trane says it is time for the industry to work together to phase out CFCs.

---

chapter are listed on a diagonal in the body of the matrix. The matrix specifies the most efficient configuration given mix and volume considerations and the flow pattern of products through the process. Deviation into one of the blank corners of the matrix results in excessive unit costs, either from failing to invest in technology in the upper half of the matrix or from investing in technology too specific for the application and poorly used in the lower half of the matrix. As you might predict, production of fledgling products should be handled by job shops or subcontracted until sales volumes permit investment.

## Designing for the Environment

In the 1970s and 1980s the Green party emerged in what was then West Germany with a central platform of environmental protection and improvement; several Greens were elected to the West German parliament, the Bundestag. Although few, party members successfully sponsored environmental protection legislation. Meanwhile, advocacy groups such as the French-based international organization Greenpeace and national groups such as the Sierra Club in the United States became increasingly active. The public initially saw them as fringe groups with radical ideas that were fundamentally opposed to business and industrial development. In recent years, however, business and industry have come to understand the limited ability of the environment to absorb and process chemical and biological wastes and the benefits of being known to consumers as environment-conscious organizations. Also contributing to their heightened environmental sensitivity has been the expense of sending wastes to landfills full of material that will not decompose in our lifetimes. As a result, some companies now contend that "it's good business to be green."

The product and process decisions by environment-conscious companies are one indication of how society can affect operations. Consider the job shop operation started by Julie Lewis of Lake Oswego, Oregon. Her company, NQI, Inc., produces a walking shoe made entirely of recycled materials that she says meet all the criteria for a good walking shoe. The shoe, called the Deja-Shoe, has a sole made of used tires, eyelets made from discarded metals, and uppers made from plastic that is a by-product of the production of disposable diapers. The design includes components from recycled coffee filters and brown paper bags.

Parents love the convenience and health benefits of disposable diapers, but a 1990 survey of new mothers found that 23 percent were using cloth diapers, up 3 percent from 1987 and the first rise in ten years. The increase can be traced largely to environmental concerns. Cotton diaper manufacturers are responding by improving their product designs. Some new cotton diapers include built-in vinyl liners and Velcro tabs, which address customers' needs for safety and convenience.

Office furniture maker Herman Miller of Zeeland, Michigan, a company that has embraced participatory management for forty years, has banned the use of tropical woods such as rose wood and Honduran mahogany from its premier lines. When employee Bill Foley realized that the company's use of tropical hardwoods was contributing to the depletion of rain forests, he and a coworker drafted a policy of only using wood from carefully managed forests. Herman Miller also uses technology that has saved the company $900,000 annually through selling or trading recyclable materials and $1.4 million annually by reducing its packaging. When Joe Azzarello, a Herman Miller engineer, calculated that recycling was impractical for the 800,000 styrofoam cups that employees used annually, the company replaced them with 5,000 ceramic mugs bearing the Buckminster Fuller quotation, "On Spaceship Earth there are no passengers . . . only crew."

Estimates of waste per dollar of goods sold found that American companies were five times more wasteful than Japanese companies and twice as wasteful as German companies in 1990. Still, U.S. companies are improving—Carrier Corp. invested $500,000 to eliminate toxic lubricants, resulting in annual inventory savings of $1.2 million, and AT&T cut $3 million from its annual costs by removing an ozone-depleting compound from its circuit-board manufacturing process. Recent legislation in Germany mandates that companies focus on the recyclability of finished goods. As of 1994, anyone who sells electronic equipment in Germany is required to recycle the customer's old equipment. The German Ministry of the Environment determined that the country had been generating 800,000 metric tons of electronic waste annually.

Recycling old automobiles has become big business in the United States. Ninety-five percent of this country's automobiles are believed to end up in some form of reclamation facility. Recyclers salvage approximately 75 percent of each

**OPERATIONS MANAGEMENT IN PRACTICE 5.3**

# DuPont Generates Energy from Garbage

In November 1993 an unusual public/private partnership was formed to address the never ending supply of trash being generated and related environmental problems. Included in the partnership are three counties in rural North Carolina, the Fayetteville Works of DuPont, and Houston based VEDCO Energy Corporation.

The 330,000 residents of Hoke, Bladen, and Cumberland counties generate nearly 230,000 tons of solid waste per year. Under the plans of this venture, landfills in Hoke and Bladen counties will be closed before they even reach capacity. Where will the trash go? Most will be converted to energy for DuPont to use in its manufacturing process. The new source of energy will replace the more than 3 million gallons of oil DuPont currently burns each year. Through this venture, the existing landfill in adjoining Cumberland county will be able to accept all refuse collected from the three county area and not utilized in the energy conversion process. The project is expected to extend the useful life of the Cumberland landfill by 100 years.

Statistics indicate that currently in the US, only 15 percent of solid waste is recycled, while 20 percent is burned and 85 percent is deposited in landfills. Under the proposed project, 25 percent will be recycled, 65 percent will be burned, and 10 percent will go to landfills. The project, expected to be operational by mid-1995, involves the construction of two separate facilities: a mixed waste processing facility located at the Cumberland county landfill, and an energy generating facility located on the grounds of the DuPont Fayetteville Works facility. Trash from the three county area and beyond will be delivered to the mixed waste processing facility and separated into essentially three main streams of material: recyclables, non-recoverables sent to the landfill, and material suitable for fuel sent to the energy generating facility. There will be two processing lines each able to process 60 tons of waste per hour. About 60 percent of the material will be non-recyclable combustible and will be transported by truck to the energy generating facility about 20 miles away.

For each ton of material burned in the energy conversion process, the equivalent of two barrels of oil or half a ton of coal will be saved. Energy not needed by DuPont will be sold to Carolina Power & Light company for other use. Even the ash left over from the burning process will be recovered and sold to a local asphalt company for use in its production process. When operational, the facility will be one of the most modern waste recovery facilities in the world, providing clean and inexpensive energy as well as recycling valuable materials. Landfill demand will be reduced by 160,000 tons per year and 45,000 tons of material will be recycled each year.

vehicle's weight, mostly iron and steel.[8] While some waste is usually inevitable in a manufactured product, reducing the level of waste through effective product design will lower facility operating costs.

Operations Management in Practice 5.3 describes an innovative public/private joint venture designed to address environmental concerns.

[8]William J. Hampton, "Meeting the Automotive Environmental Challenge," *Business Week*, November 1, 1993, p. 93.

# ► Summary

The ability of American companies to effectively compete in the future relies greatly on their ability to design products and services that consistently meet or exceed customers' expectations. Because global competition is increasing, companies are searching for ways to differentiate their products or services to maintain their advantage. This chapter discussed issues related to product and service design, customer satisfaction, and efficient delivery systems.

## Learning Objective 1: Describe differences in technology-driven, market-research driven, and customer-driven new product ideas.

Technology-driven new product ideas result from advances in technology, often accidental and without immediate commercial application. Market research-driven new product ideas result from information solicited from the marketplace. Market research often identifies consumer demand for products that previously had been demanded only for commercial use. Making them suitable for the general public sometimes requires only minor changes in product design. Customer-driven new product ideas result from active communication with customers. By continually listening to your customers, you will be better able to respond to their changing needs and expectations.

## Learning Objective 2: List the steps associated with the House of Quality.

**Step 1:** Listen to your customers. Find out what their needs and expectations are.

**Step 2:** Determine how well your customers think you are meeting their needs and expectations and how well the competition is doing that.

**Step 3:** Have the engineering staff determine the technical requirements for satisfying customer attributes.

**Step 4:** Determine the relationship between the technical requirements and customer attributes. Look for positive and negative correlations.

**Step 5:** Compare measurements of the technical requirements with similar measures of your competitors' requirements.

**Step 6:** Determine the relationships among the technical requirements. Again, look for positive and negative correlations. Ensure that the design or redesign of product or service addresses those features that have the most effect on key customer attributes.

## Learning Objective 3: Explain the advantages of concurrent engineering.

Concurrent engineering overlaps design activities to shorten the overall time required to get a new product or redesigned product to market. The time saved may be the difference between financial disaster and recovering research and development costs and making a profit. Concurrent engineering is usually undertaken by a cross-functional team of personnel from engineering, manufacturing, marketing, cost accounting, and any other areas with a vested interest in the product or service.

## Learning Objective 4: Outline characteristics of projects, job shops, batch processes, assembly lines, and continuous flow processes.

Low volume, unique demand, and absence of product flow characterize projects. Job shops use general purpose machinery, which provides a large degree of flexibility. The ability to produce small batches of highly variable products makes this configuration appropriate for many applications. Production of products in batches or lots characterizes the batch process, a technique that offers more flexibility in the number of different products that can be produced. Assembly lines use repetitive activities to produce discrete, visible units of product and can produce limited varieties of product because of its relative inflexibility. A continuous flow of material characterizes continuous flow processes; an observer never sees a discrete unit of the product, and workers seldom touch it.

## Learning Objective 5: Explain why continuous flow configurations are more efficient than a job shop.

Job shops offer the ability to produce small batches of highly variable products, but that flexibility has a cost. The functional layout of a job shop means that products are routed through the facility in sequences pegged to the processing requirements of the product, resulting in often excessive material-handling costs. Each workstation needs sequencing rules for identifying which job to process next, because work often piles up at each station. Some jobs are there for a first processing, some for a second processing, and so on. Each job may be owed to a customer on a different date; because of the complexity of the work environment, that date is often difficult to meet. Products processed in continuous process configurations do not stop and are not handled. No inventory builds between steps, and no one has to decide which job to process next.

**Learning Objective 6: Construct a product process matrix, and explain why operating off its diagonal is inefficient.** Figure 5.12 shows the configurations most appropriate for different product-process characteristics. Deviating from the diagonal of the matrix results in using a configuration not suited to that product or process. For example, using a project configuration is inefficient when several products must be produced in high volume. That environment is more suited to a line configuration.

## ▶ Key Terms

animated computer simulation techniques
assembly line
batch process
cellular manufacturing
concurrent engineering
continuous flow process
cross-functional team
customer satisfaction
cycle time

defect
design for manufacturability (DFM)
flexible manufacturing system (FMS)
flow shop
House of Quality
intermittent production
job shop
jobber
parts families
process-oriented layout

product life cycle
product process matrix
product-oriented layout
project
prototype
quality function deployment (QFD)
repetitive process
strategic alliance
value analysis

## ▶ Discussion Questions

1. What is customer satisfaction? Identify a company you think is exceptionally good at satisfying customers. What does that company do to make you think that?
2. Describe the typical path of activity that products follow, from idea generation to marketwide availability.
3. Responding to changing customers' needs is critical for successful companies. Provide an example of a company that you feel responds to changes in customers' needs. Provide an example of a company that has a history of not responding to changes in customers' needs.
4. What is quality function deployment? What are its benefits?
5. Explain the use of the House of Quality in product and service design.
6. What is value analysis? Why is it used?
7. What are the benefits of concurrent engineering?

8. What are the benefits of cross-functional teams? Why have organizations been slow to develop cross-functional teams? What can companies do to help ensure the success of cross-functional teams?
9. Compare and contrast continuous processes, assembly lines, batch processes, and flow shops. Which of these line-flow configuration(s) would you use to manufacture each of the following: gasoline? automobiles? steel?.
10. How can the stage of the product life cycle influence process design? What would be the most appropriate process configuration for manufacturing a product in a limited test market?
11. What are some of the changes manufacturers are making because of their increased awareness of the importance of the environment?
12. What is cellular manufacturing? When is it appropriate to use cellular manufacturing?

## ▶ Selected References

Barabba, Vincent P., and Gerald Zaltman, *Hearing the Voice of the Market*. Boston: Harvard Business School Press, 1991.

Buchholz, R. A. "Corporate Responsibility and the Good Society: From Economics to Ecology." *Business Horizons* 34, (July 1991): 19–31.

Camp, Robert C. *Benchmarking: The Search for Industry Best Practices That Lead to Superior Performance.* Milwaukee: ASQC Quality Press, 1989.

Clark, Kim, and Takahiro Fujimoto. *Product Development Performance.* Boston: Harvard Business School Press, 1991.

Hauser, John R., and Don Clausing. "The House of Quality." *Harvard Business Review* 66, (May–June 1988): 63–73.

Lele, Miland. *The Customer Is Key.* New York: Wiley, 1987.

Post, J. E. "Managing as If the Earth Mattered." *Business Horizons* 34, (July 1991): 32–38.

Whiteley, Richard C. *The Customer-Driven Company.* Reading, Mass.: Addison-Wesley, 1991.

# Union Camp

Union Camp Corp., headquartered in Wayne, New Jersey, is a leading manufacturer of paper, packaging, chemicals, and building products. The company ranks among the top two hundred U.S. industrial companies in sales and employs about twenty thousand people worldwide. Domestic operations extend from Florida to Maine and west to California. Union Camp also has operations in twenty-four other countries.

The paper manufacturing segment consists of four pulp and paper mills. Two produce fine white paper for business forms, printing, direct mail, and other communications uses. The other two mills produce unbleached kraft paper and linerboard, primarily packaging materials.

Union Camp's network of forty-six packaging plants converts more than half of its unbleached kraft production into boxes and bags for consumer and industrial products. Four packaging plants produce plastic bags and films. Two others produce folding cartons.

The company's other domestic manufacturing plants include nine building products operations, four chemical plants, and three flavors and fragrances facilities. Other domestic activities involve residential and commercial land development. Overseas the company has corrugated container plants, chemical plants, and flavor and fragrance facilities.

The company's Corporate Technology Center at Princeton is its central research and development facility. Its chemical development laboratories are located at its Savannah, Georgia, manufacturing complex and Jacksonville, Florida, chemical plant. Flavor and fragrance development laboratories are in Montvale, New Jersey, the United Kingdom, and Singapore. A woodlands research facility is in Rincon, Georgia.

Southeastern woodlands provide the raw material base for most of Union Camp's products. Union Camp's woodlands, which furnish 50 percent of the company's raw materials for its pulp mills and sawmills, total about 1.7 million acres in six states.

Compared with other major producers in the industry, Union Camp has relatively few pulp and paper mills, but they are all large-scale facilities. Two are the biggest of their kind in the world. This concentration of high production capabilities at a few,

highly efficient sites is a major factor in Union Camp's performance as one of the lowest-cost producers in the industry.

The company continually invests to upgrade and modernize its facilities to produce high-quality products as efficiently as possible. For the five-year period of 1988 to 1992 alone, it spent about $2.5 billion on such programs.

## Eastover

Union Camp's Eastover, South Carolina, mill specializes in fine paper production and can produce more than 1,750 tons per day of fine paper and 300 tons per day of bleached pulp. Business communications, advertising, direct marketing, publishing, and commercial printing use these products.

The Eastover mill opened in 1984 at an initial cost of $500 million and underwent a $750 million expansion, completed in 1991. The facility was designed as the industry's "mill of the future," using the latest technology in the paper-making process, taking the needs of its workers into account, and providing facilities with state-of-the-art equipment.

## Environmental Compatibility

Union Camp is a large and complex company that uses significant amounts of water and energy in its manufacturing processes. Its environmental programs are crucial in maintaining a balance of resource conservation, clean air and water, and the important social and economic benefits it provides. Throughout its corporate history the company has attempted to be responsible in its stewardship of the environment.

Its carefully managed forests provide important benefits to air, water, and wildlife. The company plants more than three trees for every one it cuts. And scientists, conservationists, and recreation enthusiasts benefit immensely from access to the company's lands.

Nearly one hundred full-time environmental experts help ensure that all Union Camp plants operate in full compliance with environmental regulations. And the company backs up that commitment with its vast technological resources and capital, which allow it to use the most effective environmental control equipment. In 1990 alone the company spent more than $46 million on environmental improvements.

Most of the company's products—paper and packaging—are recyclable. The company has a long history of recycling waste paper at its mills and recently made capital improvements that have significantly increased the amount of waste that those mills can recycle. A high-level task force is examining ways for Union Camp to expand its participation in the recycling business.

Fine papers, particularly the uncoated business grades, were a growth segment for decades for Union Camp, but in the late 1970s the company faced a problem. Union Camp could not expand its fine paper mill at Franklin, Virginia, and needed a new mill.

In selecting a new mill location the company examined sites in fourteen states. The company selected Eastover, South Carolina, and purchased the site in 1981 because of its desirable combination of transportation, water, labor, governmental, and environmental factors.

As all large projects do, Eastover began as an idea. Union Camp set out to build the safest, most efficient, and environmentally compatible facility of its kind in the world. Throughout construction and operation of the Eastover mill Union Camp scrupulously guarded the water, air, earth, and heritage of the community from abuse and carelessness.

## The Water

At Eastover, Union Camp draws its water from the Wateree River. To minimize the amount taken from the river, the water is used over and over again—as many as twenty-two times before it is released. Controls within the mill and an extensive treatment system ensure that the water's color, temperature, dissolved oxygen, solids content, and oxygen demand more than meet environmental standards. Its intake system is designed not to disturb fish, fish eggs, navigation, or the natural beauty of the river.

It uses oxygen bleaching to whiten its paper, a process that uses less water than other methods and minimizes the contaminants that are by-products of other pulp-bleaching systems. Union Camp has been in the forefront of oxygen bleaching in the United States. It installed its first oxygen line at its Franklin, Virginia, mill in 1981 and, including the Eastover expansion, it has three of only a handful in this country.

## The Air

At Eastover, Union Camp installed a system that significantly reduces sulfur emissions and therefore the "rotten eggs" odor so often associated with paper mills. A system that operates at 99.9 percent efficiency collects odorous gases from many points in the manufacturing process and incinerates them to prevent their escape into the atmosphere. Once these gases are burned, they are odorless and colorless.

Union Camp is installing a new, leading-edge technology that strips many of the odor-producing compounds and forms by-product chemicals that are recycled in the pulp-making process. This system is new to North America and is being pioneered by Union Camp at Eastover.

## The Earth

Of the 4,400 acres owned by Union Camp at Eastover, 1,000 are still being farmed—strong evidence of the compatibility of the mill with its agricultural surroundings. Its management practices prevent the loss of topsoil and the runoff of agricultural chemicals to the surrounding waterways. Such conservation farming techniques have led to awards from the Soil Conservation Society of America and the Richland County Soil and Water Conservation District. Clemson University uses the Eastover site to demonstrate best agricultural practices to its students.

## The Heritage

Union Camp has completely rehabilitated the historic Kensington mansion, located on the site, to preserve it for future generations. The year-long project was completed in 1984. Roughly two thousand visitors annually tour the mansion, guided by employees who volunteer. It's a reflection of Union Camp's philosophy of putting every asset to its highest and best use—with care.

## ▶ Discussion Questions

1. In constructing and operating its Eastover, South Carolina, paper mill what environmental factors did Union Camp consider?
2. How did environmental concerns affect process design at Eastover?
3. What kinds of environmental problems might Union Camp face in the future?

# Long-range Capacity Planning and Facility Location

*Today corporate decisions about production and location are driven by the dictates of global competition, not by national allegiance.*

ROBERT B. REICH

**Introduction**

**An Overview of Capacity Planning**
*OPERATIONS MANAGEMENT IN PRACTICE 6.1: Allison Transmission's Focused Factory—Partnering with Suppliers*

**Capacity Strategies**

**Making Capacity Planning Decisions**

**An Overview of Location Decisions**

**Factors Affecting Location Decisions**
*OPERATIONS MANAGEMENT IN PRACTICE 6.2: A Successful Group Move by Alfa-Laval*
*OPERATIONS MANAGEMENT IN PRACTICE 6.3: The Charlotte Panthers Choose a Preseason Training Facility*

**Making the Single-Facility Location Decision**

**Making Multiple-Facility Location Decisions**

**Strategic Trends in Location Decisions**
*GLOBAL OPERATIONS MANAGEMENT 6.4: Maquiladora Industry—Locating Plants in Mexico*
*GLOBAL OPERATIONS MANAGEMENT 6.5: Why BMW Cruised into Spartanburg*

**Case Study: Georgia-Pacific Corp. A Case Study in Capacity Planning and Facility Location**

**Case Study: Pohang Iron and Steel Co., Ltd. Increasing Capacity in the Korean Steelmaking Industry**

**LEARNING OBJECTIVES**

*After completing this chapter you should be able to*

1. Discuss the importance of capacity planning
2. Define *capacity* and explain how it is measured
3. Describe the major steps in the capacity planning process

4. Define the linkages between capacity planning and facility location
5. Explain why location decisions are important
6. Discuss the major factors affecting location decisions

# Introduction

The focus of this chapter is on two intertwined strategies, or long-term decisions. The first addresses the questions of how much a plant should produce, how big a warehouse should be, and what level of service a service company should provide. The second considers the questions of where the plant(s), warehouse(s), or service facility(ies) should be located.

Questions involving "how much" are categorized as capacity planning. Capacity decisions are made at two levels. Long-term capacity decisions concern investments in new facilities and equipment and typically involve a two- to five-year time period. They are the subject of this chapter. Short-term capacity decisions concern work force size, overtime, subcontracting, and inventories. We will discuss short-term capacity plans in Chapter 11.

Questions involving "where" are categorized as facility location. Facility location decisions have many strategic implications: They affect operating costs, particularly the costs associated with obtaining raw materials and distributing finished products, and they influence price and the competitive ability of the company.

Capacity and location decisions are circular. When a company decides to make a new product, offer a new service, make more of an existing product, or provide more of an existing service, it needs to plan for capacity. The demand for products or services is a function of location, so the location decision is tied to the capacity decision. There is a growing tendency for producers to locate close to both their suppliers and their customers, because they get faster delivery of raw materials and components and can deliver their products faster. Service companies typically try to locate near their customers to gain a competitive edge with respect to time and place.

# An Overview of Capacity Planning

We begin this chapter by exploring various aspects of making capacity planning decisions, starting with an overview of capacity planning and followed by a review of capacity strategies. We then examine specific techniques for making capacity planning decisions.

## The Importance of Capacity Planning

Capacity planning is extremely important to all sizes and types of companies and is among the first decisions that a company has to make. If a company has too much capacity, its inventory levels may rise or it may underuse its work force and equipment. If a company has too little capacity, it can lose customers to competitors or be forced to use subcontracting.

Capacity decisions are also important because building capacity usually requires significant capital, and a company can incur significant losses when its capacity needs are reduced. For example, if we decide that we need a new plant to increase our capacity, we will spend many millions of dollars on the new plant and its equipment. If the need for additional capacity does not materialize, the result will be losses as a result of overcapacity. Similarly, adding people for a second shift can be costly if they cannot be used effectively. Quality and productivity improvements can increase capacity, but achieving such improvements also requires additional expenditures.

## Defining and Measuring Capacity

In simple terms *capacity* is the productive capability of a facility, usually measured as a quantity of output per unit of time, the rate of output that can be achieved from a manufacturing or service process. For example, an automotive service center can perform so many brake jobs per day, or an electronic calculator manufacturer can produce so many calculators per month.

For companies with diverse products lines, measuring capacity may be more difficult. General Motors and Ford produce both automobiles and trucks. Anheuser-Busch produces many brands of beers, in bottles, cans, and kegs. When the units are reasonably similar, a company can use a common unit of measurement. General Motors and Ford measure capacity as the output of vehicles, and Anheuser-Busch and Coors measure capacity as the output of barrels of beer. When product mix is diverse, input measures sometimes define capacity. For example, a simple measure of a hospital's capacity is its number of beds. A hospital in Manning, South Carolina, with fifty beds is small, whereas a hospital in Columbia, South Carolina, with five hundred beds is large. Similarly, a theater may measure its capacity by number of seats, or a restaurant may measure its capacity in tables. Airlines measure their capacity in available seat miles (ASMs) over some time period; one ASM means one seat is available for one passenger for one mile. So, many situations call for measuring capacity by inputs rather than outputs.

There are a variety of measures and definitions of capacity. Most common, **capacity** refers to the maximum productive capability of a facility or the maximum rate of output from a process. There are several ways of viewing "maximum" capacity. Operations managers often talk about **design capacity**, which is the target output rate, or maximum capacity, for which the production facility was designed. For example, a manufacturing plant may have been designed to produce a maximum of five thousand air conditioners per year. The company may not have achieved this goal, or it may have exceeded it.

Another common term is **effective capacity**, which refers to the maximum rate of output achievable, given the quality standards, scheduling constraints, machine maintenance, work force capabilities, and product mix of the company. This capacity is a reduction of the design capacity that reflects typical operating conditions. The effective capacity cannot exceed the design capacity, and it will normally be less than the design capacity. For example, the effective capacity of the air-conditioner manufacturing plant might be 4,500 air conditioners per year under typical operating conditions.

The **actual capacity**, or **actual output rate**, reflects the rate of output that the plant actually achieves. It is normally less than effective capacity because machines break down, workers are absent, materials are defective, and materials or assemblies run short. When evaluating the actual operation of a production system, planners commonly reduce the effective capacity by 15 percent or more.

Another characteristic of capacity is it frequently has a variety of restrictions. For example, the number of mechanics, the number of parts personnel, the number of service bays, and even the number of people writing up the service orders may limit an auto service center's capacity. Any of these factors can become a bottleneck that limits the auto service center's actual capacity to less than its design capacity or its effective capacity. A **bottleneck** is any operation that limits output in the production or service sequence.

We should make one last note, about using the word *maximum* in various measures of capacity. Overtime or subcontracting can increase capacity, but a company cannot sustain this type of maximum capacity for long periods of time. For example, most employees do not want to work excessive overtime at a maximum capacity level for very long.

Given the measures of capacity we have discussed, we can observe that the capacity of a facility can be defined in many ways. This means that we must use the terms for describing capacity carefully.

## Measuring System Effectiveness

Companies also find the various methods of measuring capacity useful in evaluating the effectiveness of the production system. They use two measures of production system effectiveness:

$$\textbf{Capacity utilization} = \frac{\text{Actual capacity (output)}}{\text{Design capacity}} \quad (6\text{-}1)$$

$$\textbf{Capacity efficiency} = \frac{\text{Actual capacity (output)}}{\text{Effective capacity}} \quad (6\text{-}2)$$

Both measures are expressed as percentages and require measuring the numerator and denominator in similar units and time periods (machines hours/day, patients/day, dollars of output/month).

Utilization measures how much a facility is being used and can also be calculated as the ratio of the hours of capacity used to the hours of capacity available. Efficiency is a short- and medium-range measure of how well the company is using its production system.

Operations managers typically focus first on efficiency and try to adjust the work force with part-time workers or by using overtime and subcontracting. These procedures usually cause higher costs. Then the operations manager has to consider capacity utilization: Companies with rates of utilization that are either too high or too low contract or expand their design capacity by adjusting existing facilities or building new facilities.

Consider the following example, which is an illustration of these two measures.

**EXAMPLE 6.1**    Willets VCR Repair Co. has collected the following information on its operations:

Design capacity = 24 VCR repairs/day
Effective capacity = 18 VCR repairs/day
Actual capacity (output) = 12 VCR repairs/day

$$\text{Capacity utilization} = \frac{\text{Actual capacity}}{\text{Design capacity}}$$

$$= \frac{12 \text{ VCR repairs/day}}{24 \text{ VCR repairs/day}} = 50\% \qquad (6\text{-}3)$$

$$\text{Capacity efficiency} = \frac{\text{Actual capacity}}{\text{Effective capacity}}$$

$$= \frac{12 \text{ VCR repairs/day}}{18 \text{ VCR repairs/day}} = 67\% \qquad (6\text{-}4)$$

In this case, capacity efficiency (67 percent) looks pretty good. But capacity utilization is only 50 percent. This indicates that the company needs to improve its actual capacity (output).

## Focused Facilities

The concept of the *focused factory* states that a production facility is most efficient when it concentrates on a fairly limited set of production objectives. This enables the operations manager to concentrate resources and motivate the work force toward a single goal.[1]

Adoption of this concept causes some companies to stop building huge production facilities. Instead of attempting to satisfy all demand with one huge plant, a company builds several smaller plants, one for each market. Or the company might split one plant for producing all the components and assembling the final product into two plants, one producing the components and one assembling the final product. This decision means that each of the smaller plants can focus on its own process technology.

Other companies create plants within plants (PWPs). PWPs have separate management organizations, work forces, equipment, processes, and production control methods. This brings the concept of the focused factory to the operating level.

Whirlpool Corp.'s manufacturing facility in Columbia, South Carolina, is a good example of a focused factory. Whirlpool is the world's biggest appliance company, with sales of more than $6 billion worldwide in 1990. It manufactures and markets a full line of major home appliances and appliance-related products under nine brand names in forty-five countries (its U.S. brands are Whirlpool, Kitchen Aid, Kenmore, and Roper). The Columbia plant is a 251,800-square-foot facility that manufactures component parts for automatic washing machines, clothes dryers, dishwashers, and garbage disposals. It uses three PWPs. The first is an injection-molding plant that produces approximately 320 different plastic parts. The second is a machining plant that produces basket drive tubes, spin pinions, and agitator shafts for washing machines. The third produces pumps for automatic washing machines. The overall focus is on manufacturing a wide range of component parts and then shipping them on to three assembly plants in Ohio.

Operations Management in Practice 6.1 describes the focused factory approach used by Allison Transmission.

## Capacity Strategies

A specific capacity strategy should precede the capacity decision, which, if approved, results in authorization of a capital request to expand capacity. A

[1]Wickham Skinner, "The Focused Factory," *Harvard Business Review* 52 (May–June 1974): 113–121.

# Allison Transmission's Focused Factory—Partnering with Suppliers

Allison Transmission, a division of General Motors that makes transmissions for medium- and heavy-duty trucks, took an unusual approach to designing a manufacturing plant for its new World Transmission. "A lot of companies have manufacturing organizations, production control organizations, and so forth," says Charlie Clevenger, manager of materials management for the World Transmission. "Here it's different. The receiving function (for material) is really an extension of our supplier management organization. The shipping function is becoming an extension of the assembly organization."

This factory within a factory occupies about 300,000 square feet within 4 million square feet of the sprawling Allison Transmission complex in Allisonville, Indiana. Within this focused factory Allison's managers have taken "partnering" with suppliers to a new level. Allison's supplier management organization is responsible for having transmission parts delivered to specific spots on the factory floor in an area called *focused stores*. Manufacturing is responsible for pulling materials from these stores and building transmissions.

Steve Sprecher, an industrial engineer, describes how Allison designed its focused factory. "If you look at each area, you can see that it can support itself," he says. "Each area will be equipped with its own dock, storage points, dedicated manufacturing service areas, dedicated buffer area of finished parts before assembly, et cetera." The general layout of the factory is a series of concentric circles. Goods received enter the factory on the outer circle. The material flows inward toward manufacturing departments, through the focused stores area. No walls separate manufacturing and subassembly areas. Allison also maintains a nearly antiseptic atmosphere with white machines and immaculate floors. The machining areas are laid out in small triangles or U shapes. This requires less handling of parts than the traditional layout of a row of machines. Often a part can be given to the next operator or put in a basket and moved a short distance for more machining. Each machine and department is set up to run at the plant rate, not at the machine's capacity.

Allison Transmission's new focused factory, based on partnering with its suppliers, is working. Its new plant is highly efficient, with about 30 percent of the incoming parts exempt from inspection. This will increase to 100 percent with only occasional sampling.

capacity strategy provides a longer-term perspective for viewing individual, shorter-term capacity decisions.

A company typically bases its capacity strategy on a series of assumptions and predictions about technological innovations, long-term marketing, and the behavior of competitors, including

1. The predicted growth and variability of primary demand
2. The costs of building and operating plants of different sizes
3. The rate and direction of technological innovation
4. The likely behavior of competitors

**5.** The anticipated effects of international competitors, markets, and sources of supply[2]

A capacity strategy is a key element of a firm's overall manufacturing strategy. It should embody the corporate philosophies discussed in Chapter 3.

Before we look at the process of making capacity decisions, let's examine three aspects of capacity strategy: capacity cushions, timing of capacity changes, and sizing of capacity changes.

## Capacity Cushions

Companies generally strive for high utilization rates, but capacity utilization rates that get close to 100 percent flirt with danger. In practice many companies operate at an capacity utilization of 80 to 85 percent. Capacity utilization rates above 85 percent can result in declining quality and productivity or the loss of orders.

Many companies use a **capacity cushion**, defined as the amount by which the average utilization rate falls below 100 percent. Specifically,

$$\text{Capacity Cushion} = 100 - \text{Capacity Utilization Rate} \qquad (6\text{-}5)$$

**EXAMPLE 6.2**

Assume that we have a plant for which the actual monthly output is 1 million units, whereas the design capacity is 1.1 million units per month. For this plant

$$\text{Capacity Utilization} = \frac{1,000,000 \text{ units}}{1,100,000 \text{ units}} = 91\% \qquad (6\text{-}6)$$

$$\text{Capacity cushion} = 100 - 91\% = 9\% \qquad (6\text{-}7)$$

In 1988–1989 manufacturers had an average capacity cushion of about 15 percent. In 1990 their capacity cushion rose to 17 percent, and in 1991 it rose to slightly more than 20 percent. The capacity cushion varies by industry and by companies within an industry. Capital-intensive industries typically have smaller capacity cushions, of 10 percent or less. Utilities are capital intensive, but they maintain capacity cushions in excess of 15 percent in order to prevent any breaks in service to their customers.

The idea of a capacity cushion can be useful in developing a long-term capacity strategy. By focusing on the capacity cushion the capacity strategy that evolves requires adding or subtracting capacity in chunks, or discrete increments, such as ten units per change.

## Strategic Timing of Capacity Changes

Assuming that demand will grow steadily and that it will add capacity in chunks, a company can use three capacity-timing strategies, as shown in Figure 6.1.

**Strategy 1: Anticipate and Lead Demand**  This is an expansionist strategy, involving big but infrequent increases in capacity. Using it, the company tries to

[2]Robert H. Hayes and Steven C. Wheelwright, *Restoring Our Competitive Edge: Competing Through Manufacturing* (New York: Wiley, 1984), p. 46.

**Strategy 1: Anticipate and lead demand.**

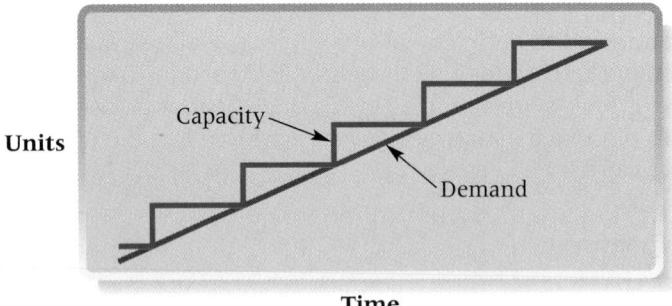

**Strategy 2: Closely follow demand.**

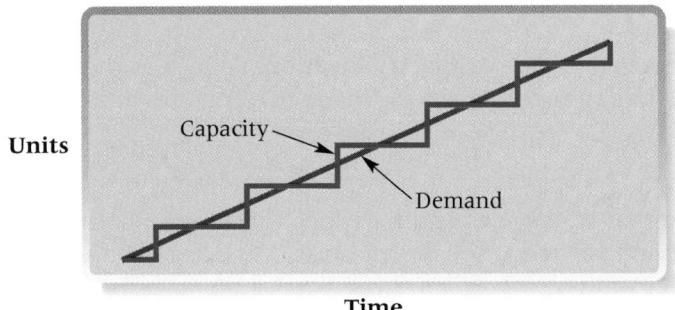

**Strategy 3: Lag demand.**

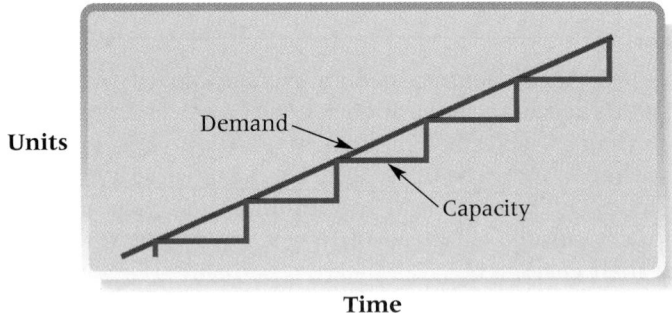

build and maintain a positive capacity cushion so that the likelihood of running short is less than the likelihood of having excess capacity. This strategy is aggressive: The company uses capacity as a weapon to preempt expansion by competitors or to signal major marketing efforts. The company may be able to lure customers away from competitors who are capacity constrained. Or this strategy can enable a company to guard its market share from competitors in a growing market.

**Strategy 2: Closely Follow Demand** This strategy implies a matching of production capacity to the demand forecast and is simply one of trying to have about the right amount of capacity over time. For example, the company would time the construction of a new plant to correspond exactly to its need for additional capacity.

**Strategy 3: Lag Demand** This is a very conservative, "wait-and-see" strategy. Using it, the company tries to build a negative capacity cushion so that the likelihood of running short is greater than the likelihood of having excess capacity. This strategy assures the company of higher use of its capacity and tends to produce a higher return on investment. This has been a typical strategy of U.S. management, criticized because it can lead to erosion of market share over the long run, although it does minimize the risk of underusing existing capacity.

Companies often use several variations of the three strategies.

## Sizing Capacity Changes

Over a period of time a company has an ideal, or optimal, level of operation in terms of its average unit cost of output. The level of capacity at which the average unit cost is at a minimum is called the **best operating level**, illustrated in Figure 6.2. At low levels of output a few units must absorb the fixed cost of the facilities and equipment, which produces a high average unit cost of output. As output increases, average unit cost decreases, until the company achieves some minimum average unit cost. Beyond that point the average unit cost again increases because other factors such as worker fatigue, absenteeism, equipment breakdowns, reduced communication, and scheduling problems overcome the gains from the absorption of the fixed costs.

Historically, many companies have used the concept of **economies of scale** in making capacity decisions. The basic idea is both simple and compelling: As a facility's size (or *scale*) becomes bigger and its production volume increases, the average unit cost for its output drops. This happens because each additional unit of output absorbs part of the fixed operating costs. The reduction in average unit cost continues until the facility becomes so big that complexities, lack of communication, poor coordination of material flows, and staffing problems arise. At some size **diseconomies of scale** occur—the plant becomes too big to operate efficiently. Figure 6.3 shows economies and diseconomies of scale. Overall, the 100-seat restaurant is preferable from the perspective of economy of

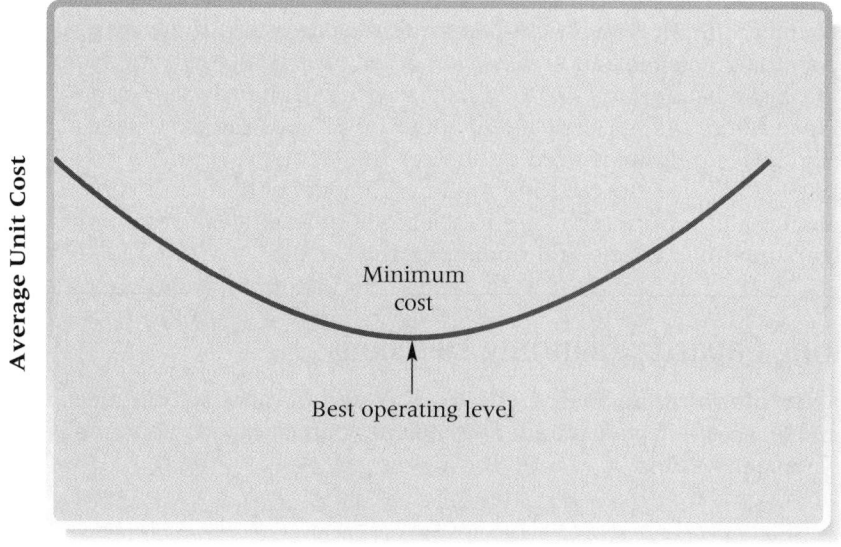

FIGURE 6.2
Best Operating Level

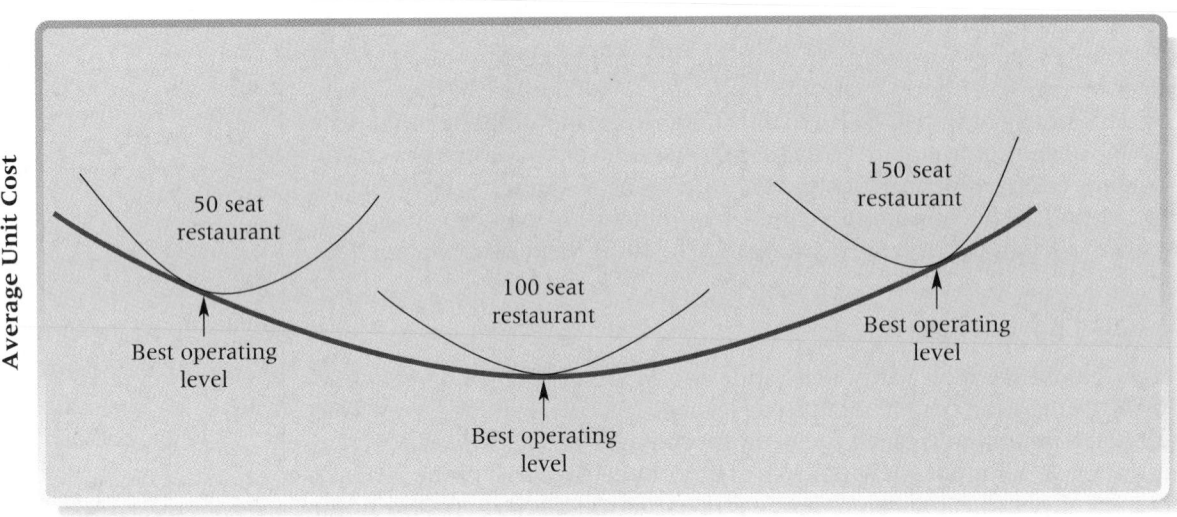

FIGURE 6.3
Economies and Diseconomies
of Scale

scale, because the average unit cost at its best operating level is less than that of
either the 50-seat restaurant or the 150-seat restaurant. The smaller and bigger
restaurants have higher unit costs and exhibit diseconomies of scale.

Figure 6.3 also shows that each size of restaurant has economies and
diseconomies of scale. As the output approaches the restaurant's best operating
level, each of the three different sizes of restaurants realizes economies of scale.
Diseconomies of scale occur above the best operating level.

---

**EXAMPLE 6.3**

Determining the best size and operating level is not easy. But many companies use this approach. Burger King (BK) reported evaluating three sizes of
restaurants:

- BK-500, yearly sales of $500,000–$700,000
- BK-700, yearly sales of $700,000–$900,000
- BK-900, yearly sales in excess of $900,000

For example, the BK-500 is designed for trading areas (customer bases) of
5,000 to 10,000 people and breaks even at just over $500,000. An average
BK-500 easily handles sales of $675,000 a year with hourly sales capacity
of $550 per hour. As sales reach $700,000 the BK-500 can no longer maintain standards for desired speed of service. Similar analyses for the BK-700
and BK-900 allowed Burger King restaurant operators to more clearly
match sales and service capacities to select the most efficient restaurant
configuration for each site and trading area.[3]

---

# Making Capacity Planning Decisions

**Capacity planning** involves specifying the level of capacity that meets market
demand in a cost-effective manner. Companies initiate capacity planning projects
for five major reasons:

[3]William Swart and Luca Donno, "Simulation Modeling Improves Operations Planning and Productivity of Fast Food Restaurants," *Interfaces* 11 (December 1981): 35–46.

■ Increasing demand—Companies simply want to expand in their marketplace; this is the most common reason that companies initiate capacity planning.

■ Dropping demand—Companies use capacity planning to review their capacity, a process that may lead to the closing or sale of a plant.

■ Changing technology—A major technological change may encourage, or even force, a company to plan for a transition that requires replacing or upgrading its plant's equipment.

■ Changing environment—A company's external environment, such as government legislation (the pollution control legislation of the 1970s), or major changes in competition may trigger capacity planning in order to meet the challenges.

■ Spotting opportunities—A company that sees a way to significantly improve its competitive position initiates capacity planning to take advantage of the opening.

## Steps in the Capacity Planning Process

Effective capacity planning requires the execution of a series of steps.

**Step 1: Audit and Evaluate Existing Capacity and Facilities** The major objective of this step is to define and measure the capacity of individual facilities and the company as a whole. This step must be comprehensive, taking into account the cost structure and performance characteristics of the technologies used in these facilities.

**Step 2: Forecast Capacity or Facilities Requirements** Companies sometimes take this step in parallel with the first step. It involves forecasting future requirements by technology, product or market, and geographic area and considers external (competitive) as well as internal factors. A critical decision is choosing the time period that is appropriate for the capacity planning process.

Capacity changes are generally long term (more than one year). But a company must relate its long-term capacity plans to its other plans that are of shorter duration. Figure 6.4 suggests one such "linking" approach in which capacity planning is broken into four different time frames:

Long-range planning (more than one year)
Annual planning (one year)
Short-term scheduling (up to three months)
Dispatching (less than one month)

Figure 6.4 emphasizes that each segment of capacity planning is naturally linked to those segments that have longer and shorter durations. Also, the level of managers involved is different for each time period. For example, whereas top management is likely to be involved directly with long-range capacity planning, plant and shop-floor managers typically schedule and dispatch job orders.

**Step 3: Define Alternatives for Meeting Requirements** Considering a variety of alternatives for meeting requirements is important and means considering options other than the obvious one of simply expanding existing production capabilities. This step requires a great deal of creativity and ingenuity.

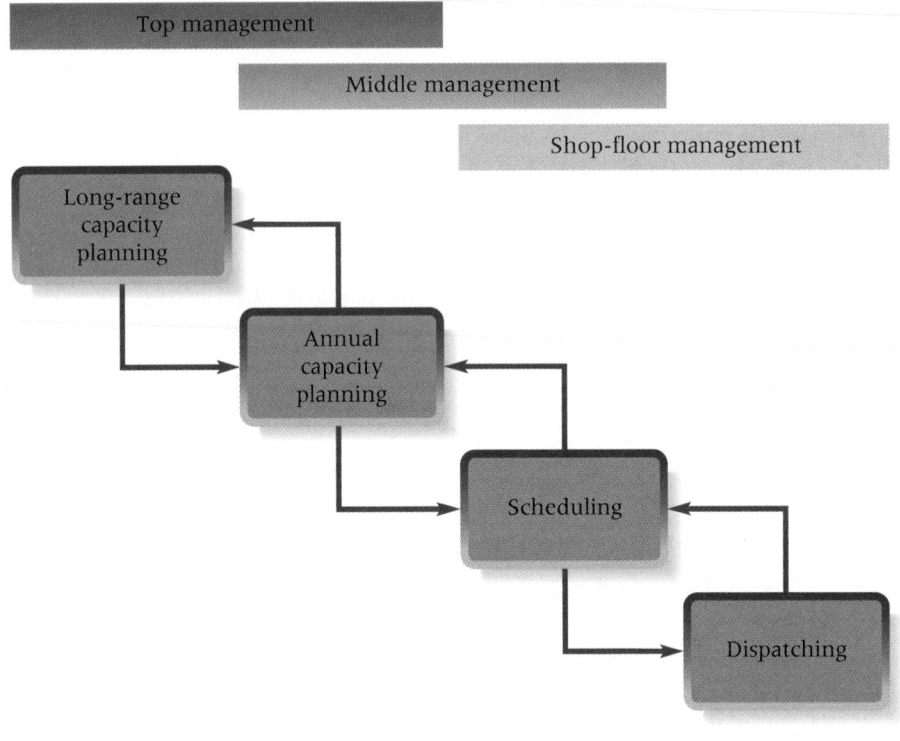

**Step 4: Perform Financial Analyses of Each Alternative** Once it has defined the capacity planning alternatives, the company must evaluate them using financial techniques that include payback, accounting rate of return, discounted cash flow, and internal rate of return.

**Step 5: Assess Key Qualitative Issues for Each Alternative** This important step entails reviewing the qualitative factors that are relevant to each alternative. Qualitative factors are those that either cannot be quantified or those for which the company cannot obtain quantitative information. For example, a company will often need to assess how a certain capacity change alternative fits with its competitive environment and business strategy.

**Step 6: Select One Alternative to Pursue** In this step the company selects a specific alternative to pursue. Pursuing the alternative means subjecting it to the entire approval process, including the capital budgeting procedure. This step may require the company to use certain quantitative techniques (we will discuss one such technique, decision tree analysis, shortly). This step also involves the selling of the alternative to corporate management.

**Step 7: Implement the Alternative Chosen** This step involves two important issues. First, the company needs to define the performance measures it will use to monitor the project's implementation. Second, it must identify and provide those resources that will have the greatest effect on the overall success of the project.

**Step 8: Audit and Review Actual Results**    Most companies do not audit results in any systematic way, but reviewing the results of major capacity changes against both project milestones and costs is important, because the company needs to know how well the capacity planning has been done and because the information will be useful in future capacity planning efforts. This review should also contain an appraisal of whether the completed project is supporting the company's strategic objectives.[4]

## Using Decision Trees in Capacity Planning

A **decision tree** is a graphic model of a set of alternatives and their consequences; it provides a clear picture of capacity decisions and their outcomes over time. Managers who use it can see exactly what is happening at each stage of the decision-making process, because it shows the logical progression of each decision. Professional journals report interesting applications of decision trees to capacity planning for air quality control equipment and postal automation equipment.[5] (Tutorial 2, Decision Analysis, at the end of the book, provides an expanded discussion of decision trees.)

Let's consider a simplified example that illustrates the use of a decision tree in capacity planning.

---

**EXAMPLE 6.4**

The Crabapple Microcomputer Co. is considering the expansion of its manufacturing capacity by purchasing a "through-hole" soldering machine. Its major alternatives are to do nothing (not purchase any machine), purchase a small machine, purchase a medium-size machine, or purchase a big machine. This through-hole soldering machine would allow Crabapple to produce a new type of circuit board; the market for the new circuit board is not known. If the company buys a big machine and finds a favorable market exists, it could realize a profit of $150,000. But purchasing a big machine would result in a $75,000 loss if the market proves unfavorable. If Crabapple buys a medium-size machine, it would see a profit of $90,000 in a favorable market but a loss of $20,000 in an unfavorable market. If it buys a small machine, it would realize a $50,000 profit in a favorable market but a $5,000 loss in an unfavorable market. Not purchasing any machine will result in no profit or loss.

The management of Crabapple Microcomputer Co. has recently conducted a market survey and has concluded that there is a 0.4 probability of a favorable market for the new type of circuit board and a 0.6 probability of an unfavorable market for the new type of circuit board.

---

[4]Hayes and Wheelwright, *Restoring Our Competitive Edge,* pp. 118–155.
[5]Thomas J. Madden, Michael S. Hyrnick, and James A. Hodde, "Decision Analysis Used to Evaluate Air Quality Control Equipment at Ohio Edison Company," *Interfaces* 13 (February 1983): 66–75; and Jacob W. Ulvila, "Postal Automation (Zip + 4) Technology: A Decision Analysis," *Interfaces* 17 (March–April 1987): 1–12.

Figure 6.5 presents a completed and solved decision tree for Crabapple Microcomputer Co.

In Figure 6.5 node A is a decision node from which the company may select one of four alternatives. Nodes 1, 2, and 3 are state-of-nature nodes from which one of multiple states of nature will occur. The payoffs, expressed in dollars, are at the far right of each of the tree's branches. The probabilities appear in parentheses next to each state of nature. The expected monetary value (EMV) for each state-of-nature node is then calculated and placed by its node, using the following equation:

$$EMV\ (A_i) = \sum_{j=1}^{n} (P_j)\ (O_{ij}) \qquad (6\text{-}8)$$

where

$EMV\ (A_i)$ = the expected monetary value for alternative i
$P_j$ = the probability of the occurrence state of nature j
$O_{ij}$ = the monetary outcome resulting from alternative $A_i$ and state of nature j

As Figure 6.5 shows, the highest expected monetary value, $28,000, occurs for node 2, purchase of a medium-size machine. This approach to making a capacity decision indicates that Crabapple Microcomputer Co. should purchase the medium-size machine.

FIGURE 6.5
Decision Tree—Crabapple
Microcomputer Co.

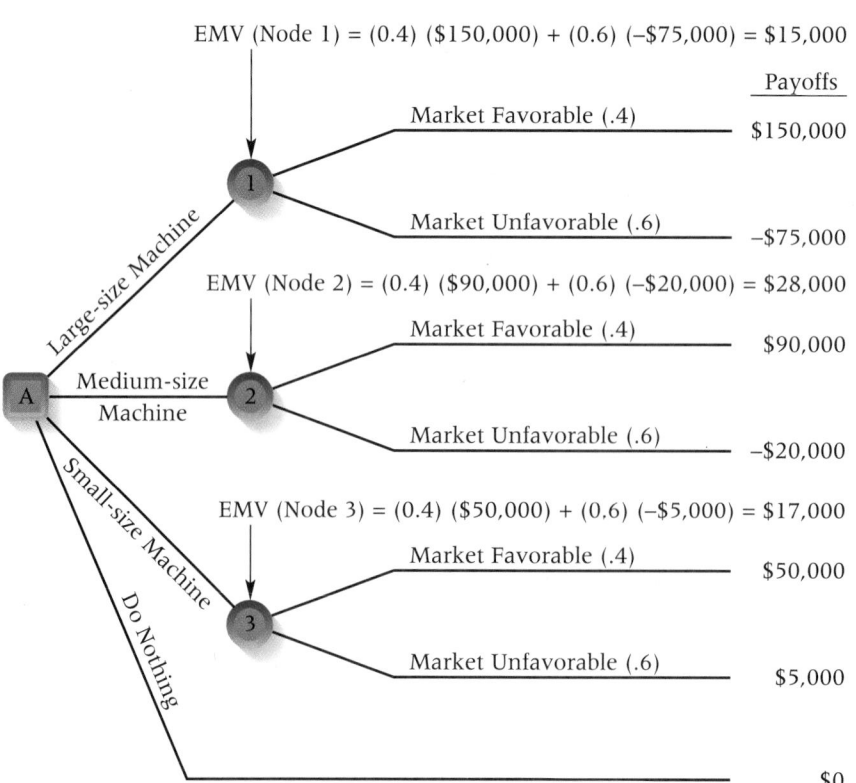

EMV (Node 1) = (0.4) ($150,000) + (0.6) (–$75,000) = $15,000

Payoffs

Market Favorable (.4) — $150,000

Market Unfavorable (.6) — –$75,000

EMV (Node 2) = (0.4) ($90,000) + (0.6) (–$20,000) = $28,000

Market Favorable (.4) — $90,000

Market Unfavorable (.6) — –$20,000

EMV (Node 3) = (0.4) ($50,000) + (0.6) (–$5,000) = $17,000

Market Favorable (.4) — $50,000

Market Unfavorable (.6) — $5,000

Large-size Machine
Medium-size Machine
Small-size Machine
Do Nothing

$0

# An Overview of Location Decisions

Making a location decision is a key element in the strategic planning process for organizations of all types and sizes. It is linked to the capacity decision aspect of strategic planning that we discussed in the first part of this chapter. The smallest mom-and-pop grocery store has to have a good location, just as does the Japanese car manufacturer locating a plant in the United States for the first time. Location problems are on-going for existing companies; they are among the first problems that new companies consider. The remainder of this chapter explores various facets of making location decisions: an overview of the process, a review of the factors that affect location decisions, techniques for deciding whether to build a single facility or several in a variety of locations, the decisions themselves, and trends.

## Why Location Decisions Are Important

Companies make location decisions relatively infrequently, usually in response to a major capacity problem. If demand has grown, a plant may have become too small to satisfy that demand. Constructing a new plant at another location becomes an attractive alternative. The service sector can use new locations to expand markets or as part of an overall marketing strategy. Some companies, in both the manufacturing and service sectors, have to relocate because of changing labor conditions and major shifts in customer demand. Certain types of companies make location, or relocation decisions, based on the availability of raw materials for their manufacturing process.

Location decisions have a profound influence on a company's operations and profitability. A location decision, once made, cannot be changed easily. Closing a plant or warehouse that has been located in the wrong place is a costly

*The Saturn automobile production facility, located in Springhill, Tennessee, is composed of a large number of manufacturing and service facilities and is designed to allow for capacity expansion.*

proposition. Location decisions have a long-term effect on both revenues and operating costs: A location in a high labor cost area, or one where transportation costs are excessive, can be a difficult problem that can require many years to solve.

## Location Options

Managers have several broad options available for making location decisions (assuming that they need to provide additional capacity). The first, and perhaps simplest, option is to do nothing, using internal capacity adjustment techniques instead. Among these techniques are additional shifts, paying overtime, and using subcontracting. This option is essentially medium-term capacity planning, or aggregate planning and is discussed in detail in Chapter 11.

A second option is to expand the existing facility, which is viable only if expansion is possible at the existing location. Its cost can make it attractive.

A third option is to maintain the existing facility or facilities and add an additional facility or facilities elsewhere. This option is more costly than the previous two options and will also create a system of plants, or service facilities. This means that the manager will have to take into account the operation of the total system. For example, if the opening of a new plant in another location causes an existing plant to be underused, the company will have accomplished little.

A fourth option is to close an existing facility and move to another location, the most costly option. A company needs to make a careful and thorough analysis of its capacity problems before selecting this option.

## A General Approach to Making Location Decisions

Figure 6.6 presents a general approach to making location decisions. The general approach consists of the following steps:

1. Perform a company-oriented needs assessment, reviewing the following factors:
   (a) Size of company—outputs, revenues, profits, people
   (b) Company objectives
   (c) Market niche
   (d) Number/sizes of plants/warehouses
2. Determine strategies for making location decisions, analyzing the following:
   (a) Dominant location factors
   (b) Products/markets emphasis
   (c) Company competencies
   (d) Risk orientation
3. Search for a feasible region using both objective and subjective criteria. This search may be aided by either quantitative or nonquantitative techniques and is broad based.
4. Develop location alternatives, which may be either specific communities, or specific sites in a community.
5. Evaluate and compare the location alternatives, using either quantitative or nonquantitative techniques.
6. Select a specific site.

The first two steps typically involve higher-level managers and decision makers. They would be done as a part of overall corporate planning, in the development

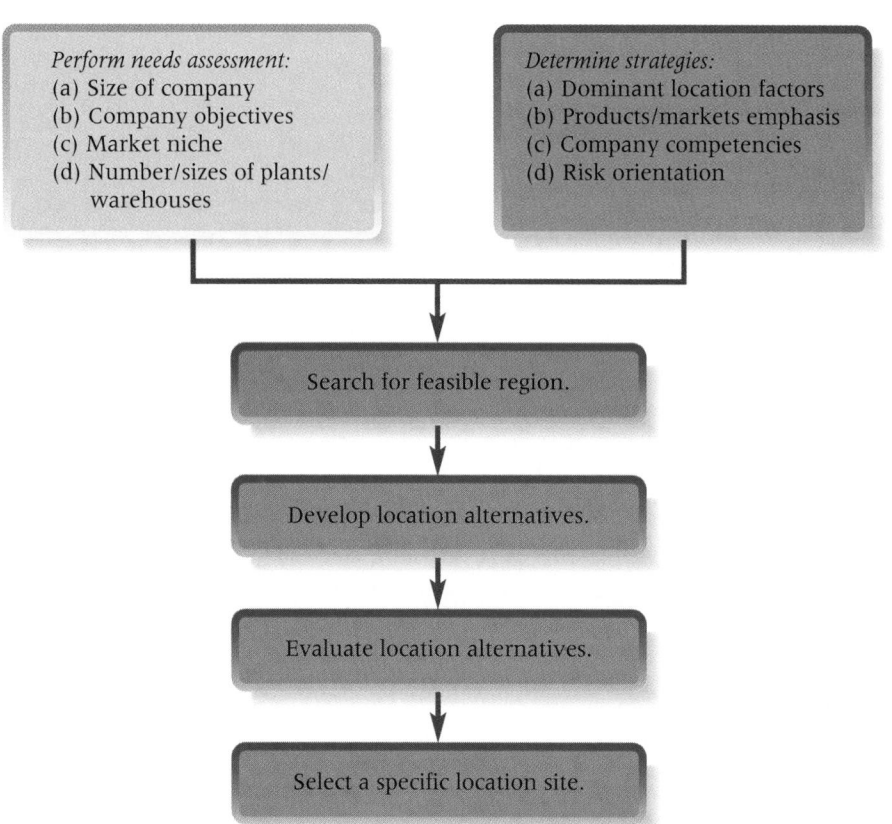

FIGURE 6.6
General Approach to Making
Location Decisions

of a business plan. The operations manager, assisted by other functional areas of the company, would perform the final four steps. The remainder of this chapter elaborates on these steps.

## Factors Affecting Location Decisions

**Facility location** involves determining a geographic location for a company's operation. A manufacturer can subdivide the facility location problem into plant or factory location and warehouse location. Many factors, such as raw material and supply costs, distribution costs, and regional costs, influence both problems. For a service firm, the principal facility location problem is selecting a site close to its customers.

In practice operations managers often use comprehensive checklists that consider a multitude of factors to analyze facility location problems. Table 6.1 presents a typical checklist of factors considered in location decisions. Because so many factors can affect facility location, the manager needs to first consider those factors that will have a major effect on the company's competitive position. For example, transportation costs are a major portion of the delivered cost of food products and will be of particular significance to that type of company. The manager can downplay or even ignore secondary factors in many instances. In the discussion that follows we will focus on those factors that dominate facility location decisions. The Georgia-Pacific case study at the end of this chapter illustrates the use of a primary set of facility location factors in making an actual facility location decision.

TABLE 6.1
Checklist of Factors for
Location Decisions

1. Labor availability
2. Labor costs
3. Unionization
4. Transportation availability (highways, waterways, railroads, airports)
5. Electric power and fuel supply
6. Water supply and sewage system
7. Climate and weather
8. Wage scales
9. Taxes
10. Market proximity
11. Population and population trends
12. Suppliers and supporting services
13. Pollution/environmental considerations
14. Land availability and costs
15. Construction costs
16. Zoning restrictions
17. Higher education facilities
18. Medical and hospital facilities
19. Schools, churches, and recreational facilities
20. Police and fire protection
21. Region-state-community attitudes
22. General living standards
23. Communication systems
24. Financial systems
25. Preference of management

Operations managers have to be concerned with four generic types of problems associated with facilities design:

- The **location problem** addresses where to locate new facilities, assuming that company knows and uses as a given the flow of goods between its new facilities and its customers' locations.
- The **allocation problem** considers how to allocate the movement of items to the existing routes that link the facilities, assuming that the company has decided the number and locations of all facilities.
- The **location-allocation problem** requires the manager to determine the number of facilities, their locations, and the amount of interaction with existing facilities and customers' locations.
- The **facility layout problem** encompasses several types of problems, including the arrangement of production shops and storerooms in a plant, machine tools and equipment in a job shop, or merchandise in a service facility or warehouse.

This chapter discusses the first three types of problems listed; Chapter 5 considered the problem of facilities layout.

## Regional, Community, and Site Considerations

Managers make location decisions by selecting, in turn, a region, a community within the region, and a site within the community. Thus the search process starts broadly and then narrows and becomes more focused. A common term for the evaluation of alternative regions and communities is *macroanalysis*, whereas the term *microanalysis* describes the evaluation of specific sites in the community. But the three factors quite often are linked. For example, companies often consider community and site factors together, because they are so tightly intertwined.

**Regional Considerations** Regional considerations vary according to the size and scope of the company. For a multinational company the region may be an entire continent or several countries. For a big U.S. company it may be the Southeast or the West. For a smaller U.S. company the region may be a particular state. Many factors, including market proximity, raw materials' proximity, transportation accessibility, labor supply, public services, and climate, influence the choice of a region.

**Community Considerations** Having selected a region, we next look for a specific community within that region. The choice of a community in which to locate may be the major decision for certain types of service organizations, such as hospitals and educational institutions. Factors that influence community location decisions are labor supply, wage levels, tax structures, living standards, educational and recreational opportunities, and community attitudes. Quite often communities actively campaign to attract new businesses as sources of employment for their residents and as sources of tax revenue. The availability of utilities and transportation are also important in community location decisions.

**Site Considerations** After choosing the community, the company must select an exact site within the community. Managers should compare available sites to a checklist, such as that shown in Table 6.2.

Among the factors listed in Table 6.2, the primary considerations are often those involving land, transportation, and zoning. The selection of the final site is subject to the following constraints:

- The site must be accessible to a certain number of employees with certain labor skills and backgrounds.
- The site must be located within a defined geographical area.

TABLE 6.2
Site Selection Checklists

1. Transportation access (highways, railways, airports)
2. Availability of services (water, electric, gas, sewer system)
3. Zoning
4. Land availability
5. Land cost
6. Fire and police protection
7. Soil characteristics (bearing and drainage)
8. Construction costs
9. Availability of land for expansion and parking
10. Availability of building or improvements on site
11. Air and water pollution restrictions
12. Neighborhood characteristics
13. Taxes
14. Availability of communication facilities
15. Access to educational, recreational, and cultural facilities
16. Neighborhood characteristics of the site
17. Access to financial facilities

- The site must have access to certain modes of transportation.
- The site must be capable of supporting a structure of a certain size and weight.

## Dominant Facility Location Factors in Manufacturing

Research has determined that five groups of factors dominate location decisions for new manufacturing plants. These dominating factors, along with the percentage of respondents who found each essential in selecting a new location, are as follows:

**Favorable Labor Climate (76 Percent)** More than three-quarters of the respondents reported that a favorable labor climate was a dominant factor in making facility location decisions. A favorable labor climate in turn is a function of the cost and availability of labor in an area, prevailing wage rates, labor productivity, work attitudes, and union strength. The U.S. textile industry has made a major shift, from northeastern to southern states because of lower labor costs and weak unions in southern states. Other labor-intensive industries that have emphasized labor climate in making facility location decisions are furniture manufacturing and consumer electronics makers.

**Proximity to Markets (55 Percent)** Half of the respondents said that locating near their markets was extremely important. This is particularly true for products that are bulky or heavy or involve high transportation rates for outbound finished goods. Food makers, paper manufacturers, and metals makers all try to locate close to their markets.

**Quality of Life (35 Percent)** Respondents in general judged quality of life to be of less importance, but executives from highly technical industries rated it at the

*Located in the heart of downtown Dallas, the Baylor Medical Center uses the Japanese inspired JIT philosophy in working with its supplier, Owens & Minor.*

top of their list of important factors. The latter find quality schools, good recreational facilities, and attractive physical surroundings to be very important, because they are important to the highly educated and mobile work force that comprises the high-tech industries.

**Proximity to Suppliers and Resources (31 Percent)** The survey respondents generally rated proximity to suppliers and resources to be much less important than proximity to markets. An obvious exception was industries that process bulky or heavy raw materials, because inbound transportation costs are a dominant consideration for such industries. A good example is food processing; facilities are typically located near farms.

**Proximity to the Parent Company's Facilities (25 Percent)** The final factor that the survey respondents considered important was proximity to the parent company's other facilities. They cited this factor because of the many supply and communication linkages in companies that have multiple facilities.[6]

A host of additional factors may be important in a specific decision, among them, climate; utility costs; local and state taxes; proximity to rail lines, major highways, or airports; financing incentives offered by state or local governments; land and construction costs; and relocation costs.

Operations Management in Practice 6.2 illustrates how Alfa-Laval Thermal Co. successfully relocated from one region of the country to another.

## Dominant Facility Location Factors in Services

Being close to customers is the primary consideration for service industries. Few people are willing to travel great distances to obtain services, so the proximity of the service facility to its customers dominates all other factors. Revenues reflect a well-chosen location for a service facility. Service managers can estimate potential revenue by considering traffic flows and volumes, general retail activity, residential density, and income levels.

Nine dominant factors relate to location and site selection for service companies:

*Customers.* Service facilities should be close to customers. A service that emphasizes the convenience of its location is referred to as *customer based.*

*Cost.* A location where operating costs are the lowest becomes the dominant consideration for certain types of service companies. Wholesalers and specialty shops typically make location decisions based on cost.

*Competitors.* Some service businesses base their location decisions on being close to competitors. Being close to competitors attracts customers, and the service can observe, evaluate, and copy its competitors. For example, we often see groups of car dealerships or fast-food restaurants located close together.

*Support systems.* Service companies often make their location decisions based on the proximity of support systems. For example, doctors' offices, pharmacies, hotels, and motels typically locate near big medical centers.

*Geographic/environmental factors.* Geographical or environmental factors become the major determining factor for certain types of service businesses. Geographic or environmental factors drive location decisions for

[6]Roger W. Schmenner, *Making Business Location Decisions* (Englewood Cliffs, N.J.: Prentice-Hall, 1982), pp. 22–42.

# A Success-ful Group Move by Alfa-Laval

Typically, when a company relocates from one region of the country to another, only 50 percent of the employees who are asked to move will actually do so, even when the company offers a comprehensive incentive program. When Swedish-owned Alfa-Laval Thermal Co., a manufacturer of heat transfer equipment, decided to relocate from several states to Richmond, Virginia, in the summer of 1990, its president, Kirk Spitzer, was determined to obtain a positive response from at least 60 percent of its employees.

Alfa-Laval faced a complicated relocation. Its manufacturing and service facility was located in Poughkeepsie, New York, its corporate administration was in Fort Lee, New Jersey, and a small satellite office in Houston, Texas, conducted its sales and marketing efforts. Alfa-Laval used two human resources and real estate consulting companies—respectively, Moran, Stahl and Boyer, based in New York, and LaSalle Partners, headquartered in Chicago—to investigate potential sites. They considered sixty-five cities and targeted seven for more in-depth studies.

Spitzer felt that location would be an important issue in retaining employees. So the consultants stressed employee-related concerns such as quality of life, economic base, affordable housing, demographics, and schools. Also, as Spitzer observed, "From a corporate standpoint, because we bring in product from Sweden, we needed to be near a major seaport and within a one-day truck route from that port to our headquarters. It was also important to be able to service our business clients and then ensure our people didn't have to break ties with the East Coast."

In late 1988 the Alfa-Laval decided to build its $20 million Heat Transfer Center in Richmond, Virginia. This decision handed Spitzer his major task—obtaining the support of his employees. His effort was actually two pronged: determining which employees should be asked to relocate and determining what incentives would entice the most valued employees to relocate. In July 1989 the company announced the details of its relocation policy, including:

Retaining a finance company in Richmond to provide mortgage rate discounts

Reimbursing all expenses involved in the purchase of a new home, including points, title costs, and legal fees

Providing a resettlement allowance of as much as two months' salary (based on annual salary) with a maximum payment of $7,000

Providing the services of Richmond Relocation Co. for all needs, including helping spouses to find new employment

Reimbursing expenses related to home sales, including broker or real estate fees. Also, if an employee's home did not sell quickly, Alfa-Laval guaranteed the residence would be purchased by a third party at the appraised value.

Spitzer realized that the company also needed a well-rounded communications program. In July 1989 the company created an in-house relocation newsletter to communicate news of the impending move to employees. Although the information in the newsletter was not earth shattering, it did help dispel rumors and fill in information gaps. Just before the February 1, 1990, deadline for relocation decisions, the company had a package of gifts delivered to each employee's home. Inside were twelve presents with cheerful tags that told of the attractions of the Richmond area and the opportunities for employees there. The cost of each gift package was $200.

A remarkable 73 percent of Alfa-Laval's employees moved to Richmond.

recreational services. For example, a ski resort has to be located in a mountainous area that is blanketed by snow for several months each year.

*Business climate.* The business climate of a particular state or city may be conducive to certain types of service businesses. For example, Boston has many institutions of higher education. Hartford, Connecticut, and Des Moines, Iowa, serve as headquarters for many insurance companies.

*Communications.* High-speed communication is a major location factor for several types of service businesses. This factor leads large banks and financial institutions such as brokerage houses and mutual fund companies to locate in big, highly developed cities that have excellent communications facilities.

*Transportation.* A good transportation network may be the deciding location factor for certain service businesses. For example, mail-order companies locate where transportation networks are good.

*Personal desires of the chief operating officer.* A more subjective location factor can be the personal desire of the CEO. For example, Wal-Mart is headquartered in Arkansas because its CEO, Sam Walton, was a native and wanted the company located there.[7]

Operations Management in Practice 6.3 reviews how the Charlotte Panthers, a new National Football League franchise, chose Wofford College as their preseason training site.

# Making the Single-Facility Location Decision

Single-facility problems are normally location problems, because the uniqueness of the single facility (it is the only facility, so it has to provide all its customers with products or services) automatically resolves the allocation aspect. The techniques we will describe are useful for locating manufacturing facilities (plant or warehouses) or service facilities. In practice managers may use certain techniques more frequently for manufacturing facility location decisions and other techniques more frequently for service facility location decisions. We will present examples of both.

## Detailed Cost Analysis

The most direct way to make a facility location decision is to perform a detailed cost analysis of each alternative site. Such an analysis can consider a wide range of costs and address present value calculations.

**EXAMPLE 6.5**

Table 6.3 shows a detailed cost analysis; it compares the current location of a plant in Columbia, South Carolina, with alternative community sites, in Charlotte and Raleigh. As the table shows, the Columbia location is less attractive than either of the alternatives. Overall, the Raleigh location would produce annual cost savings of almost 30 percent over the Columbia location.

---

[7]Robert G. Murdick, Barry Render, and Roberta S. Russell, *Service Operations Management* (Boston: Allyn & Bacon, 1990), pp. 141–142.

# The Charlotte Panthers Choose a Preseason Training Facility

Richardson Sports, the Charlotte, North Carolina, sports marketing company, was recently awarded a National Football League expansion franchise. It used the College of Business Administration at the University of South Carolina (USC) to help it determine the optimal location for its new team's preseason training facility.

In the summer of 1993 a field consulting team from the USC business school studied twenty-six locations at colleges and universities in North and South Carolina and examined eight in detail. The study team based its recommendation on several location criteria, after ranking the eight locations according to

- Playing field conditions
- Gymnasium availability
- Locker room facilities
- Training room facilities
- Weight room facilities
- Classroom availability
- Distance from Charlotte
- Local lodging accommodations

The team considered no Division 1A football schools, such as South Carolina, Clemson, Duke, Wake Forest, North Carolina, or North Carolina State, because of the size of their own football programs and potential conflicts in the use of facilities. Team members also conducted personal interviews and analyzed the economic impact of locating a training facility at each site.

In late spring 1994 Richardson Sports announced that it would hold preseason training at Wofford College in Spartanburg, South Carolina. According to Professor Robert Markland, faculty director of the study team, "The site that Richardson Sports eventually chose, Wofford College, was one of the top recommendations of the MBA study team."

## Factor Rating Systems

**Factor rating systems** are among the techniques most used widely for making location decisions. They allow operations managers to incorporate their personal opinions as well as quantitative information in the location decision process. The factor rating combines diverse factors in an easy-to-understand format that produces a composite value for each alternative.

The factor rating procedure follows a series of logical steps:

1. Determine a list of relevant factors for the location decision factors from a list such as that shown in Table 6.1.
2. Assign a weight to each factor that indicates its importance relative to all the other factors. Typically, these factors will add up to 1, 10, or 100.
3. Specify a common scale for all factors. Typically, this scale will be 1, 10, or 100.
4. For each alternative location determine the score for each factor, using the scale specified.

| Operating Expenses | Columbia, S. C. (Current Location) | Charlotte, N. C. (Alt. 1) | Raleigh, N. C. (Alt. 2) |
|---|---|---|---|
| **Transportation** | | | |
| Inbound | $ 302,942 | $ 212,209 | $ 307,467 |
| Outbound | 480,605 | 361,268 | 393,402 |
| **Labor** | | | |
| Hourly, direct and indirect costs | 2,520,943 | 2,339,790 | 2,146,087 |
| Fringe benefits | 304,189 | 187,571 | 126,070 |
| **Plant overhead** | | | |
| Rent or carrying costs | 271,436 | 290,000 | 280,000 |
| Real estate taxes | 43,345 | 39,000 | 34,000 |
| **Personal property and other** | | | |
| Locally assessed taxes | 16,899 | — | — |
| Fuel for heating | 19,260 | 11,000 | 9,500 |
| **Utilities** | | | |
| Power | 56,580 | 61,304 | 41,712 |
| Gas | 18,460 | 19,812 | 13,767 |
| Water | 12,474 | 8,200 | 4,500 |
| Treatment of sewage | 6,376 | — | 2,300 |
| **State factors** | | | |
| State taxes | 67,811 | 73,400 | 44,920 |
| Workers' compensation insurance | 30,499 | 24,000 | 14,000 |
| **Total** | $4,151,819 | $3,727,554 | $3,417,725 |
| **Savings through construction of new plant** | | | |
| New plant layout | | $ (310,000) | $ (310,000) |
| **Reduced materials handling** | (38,000) | (38,000) | |
| **Elimination of current local interplant movements** | | (70,000) | (70,000) |
| **Reduced public warehousing** | (30,000) | (30,000) | |
| **Reduced supervisory personnel** | | (27,000) | (27,000) |
| **Savings through new construction** | | $ (475,000) | $ (475,000) |
| **Annual operating costs** | $4,151,819 | $3,252,554 | $2,942,725 |
| **Potential annual savings over present location** | | $ 899,265 | $1,209,094 |
| **Percentage of savings** | | 21.7% | 29.1% |

TABLE 6.3
Detailed Cost Analysis Example

| Factor | Factor Weight (0–100) | Factor Scores (0–100) | | Weighted Factor Scores | |
|---|---|---|---|---|---|
| | | *Alt. 1* | *Alt. 2* | *Alt. 1* | *Alt. 2* |
| Residential density | 40 | 80 | 60 | 3,200 | 2,400 |
| Highway accessibility | 30 | 50 | 90 | 1,500 | 2,700 |
| Land and construction costs | 20 | 70 | 60 | 1,400 | 1,200 |
| Property taxes | 10 | 50 | 40 | 500 | 400 |
| | 100 | | | 6,600 | 6,700 |

TABLE 6.4
Factor Rating
Procedure—New Life Health
Clubs, Inc.

5. Multiply the score for each factor by its factor weight, and add the results for each location alternative.
6. Select the alternative with the highest composite score.

The service company example that follows is an illustration of the factor rating procedure.

**EXAMPLE 6.6**

New Life Health Clubs, Inc., is trying to evaluate two alternative sites for a new fitness center in Charleston, South Carolina. Table 6.4 provides the relevant factors, factor weights, factor scores, and the associated computations required to produce composite scores for each of the alternatives. Based on the composite weighted factor scores, alternative 2 is preferable.

## Center of Gravity Method

The **center of gravity method** is a technique that is useful for locating a single facility, usually a distribution warehouse. The method considers existing facilities, the distances between them, the location of markets, and the volume of goods to be shipped. It assumes that the transportation cost is directly proportional to both the distance and the volume shipped. Managers often use additional simplifying assumptions: that inbound and outbound transportation costs are equal and that it does not cost more to ship less than full loads. The overall objective of the method is to determine a location that minimizes the weighted distance between the distribution warehouse and its market, where the distance is weighted by the volumes shipped.

**EXAMPLE 6.7**

Consider Southeastern Steel Co., which is attempting to locate a distribution warehouse for its steel products somewhere in the state of South Carolina. It has an old and outdated distribution warehouse in Columbia, South Carolina, that ships to four major centers of market demand in addition to supplying the Columbia area. Information on the average monthly demand volumes for the five (total) demand centers appears in Table 6.5.

In using the center of gravity method, we begin by placing the existing locations on a grid of coordinates. The starting point for and the scale of the grid are arbitrary. Its purpose is to establish relative distances between locations. One possibility is to use longitude and latitude, another is to simply put standard graph paper over an ordinary road map. Figure 6.7

| Location | Monthly Demand (thousand tons) |
|---|---|
| Charleston | 250 |
| Columbia | 150 |
| North Augusta | 300 |
| Rock Hill | 300 |
| Greenville | 250 |

TABLE 6.5
Average Monthly Demand—Southeastern Steel Co. Locations in South Carolina

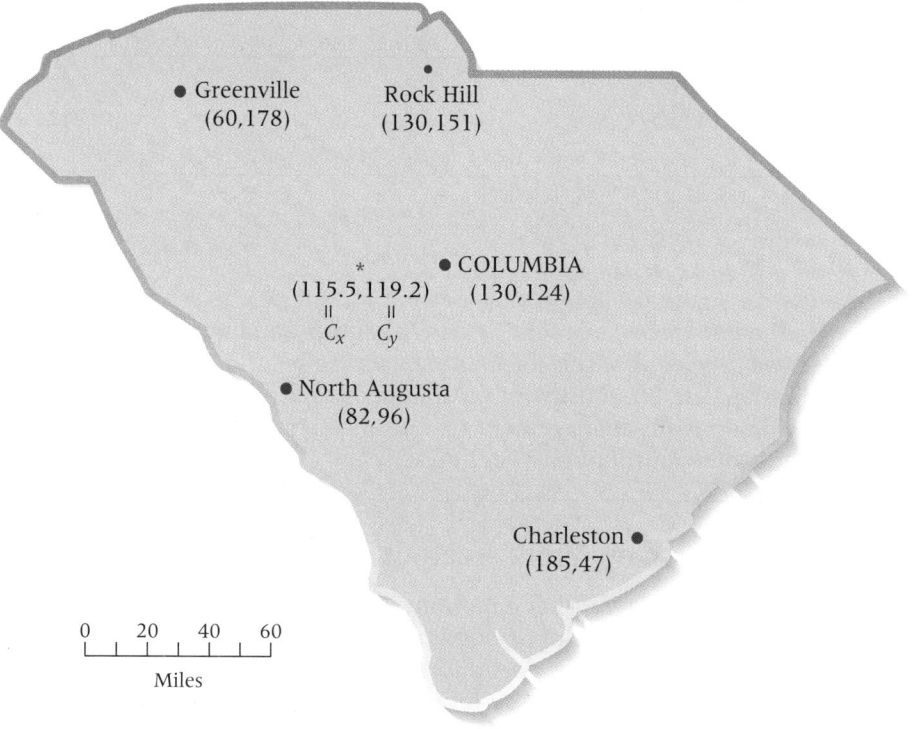

FIGURE 6.7
Coordinate Locations for Southeastern Steel Co. Facilities in South Carolina

presents the coordinate locations of the five Southeastern Steel Co. locations in South Carolina.

To determine the center of gravity, calculate the $x$ and $y$ coordinates that produce the minimum weighted transportation costs; use the following formulas:

$$C_x = \frac{\sum\limits_{i=1}^{N} d_{ix} V_i}{\sum\limits_{i=1}^{N} V_i} \qquad (6\text{-}9)$$

$$C_y = \frac{\sum\limits_{i=1}^{N} d_{iy} V_i}{\sum\limits_{i=1}^{N} V_i} \qquad (6\text{-}10)$$

where

$$C_x = x \text{ coordinate of the center of gravity}$$
$$C_y = y \text{ coordinate of the center of gravity}$$
$$d_{ix} = x \text{ coordinate of the ith location}$$
$$d_{iy} = y \text{ coordinate of the ith location}$$
$$V_i = \text{volume moved to or from the ith location}$$
$$N = \text{number of locations}$$

Use the coordinate information shown in Figure 6.7 and the average monthly demand (volume) information shown in Table 6.5 to calculate the coordinates of the center of gravity:

$$C_x = \frac{(185 \times 250) + (130 \times 150) + (82 \times 300) + (130 \times 300) + (60 \times 250)}{250 + 150 + 300 + 300 + 250}$$

$$\frac{144{,}350}{1250} = 115.5 \tag{6-11}$$

$$C_y = \frac{(47 \times 250) + (124 \times 150) + (96 \times 300) + (151 \times 300) + (178 \times 250)}{250 + 150 + 300 + 300 + 250}$$

$$\frac{148{,}950}{1250} = 119.2 \tag{6-12}$$

The asterisk on Figure 6.7 shows this location ($C_x = 115.5$, $C_y = 119.2$). By placing the grid over a map of the state of South Carolina, shown in Figure 6.7, we can see that this location happens to be at one of the interchanges on Interstate 20, southwest of Columbia, South Carolina. This would provide company management with a starting point for searching for a site for its new distribution warehouse.

## Locational Cost-Volume-Profit Analysis

Demand volume is one of the important variables that affects a location's desirability. As a result, **locational cost-volume analysis** or **locational cost-volume-profit analysis** can be useful tools in selecting a location. Certain costs associated with having a facility in a location will be fixed, and other costs will vary with the location's business volume. The overall cost structure of different locations will be different. Sales volumes will also vary by location.

A manager can do these analyses by using a spreadsheet or a graphic representation. For brevity we will illustrate only the locational cost-volume analysis. This procedure is based on the following assumptions for each location:

1.  Fixed costs are constant throughout the range of probable volume.
2.  Variable costs are linear throughout the range of probable volume.
3.  Only one product, or product family, is produced.
4.  The required volume can be accurately forecast for some specified time period.

The example that follows illustrates locational cost-volume analysis.

**EXAMPLE 6.8**

Hickory Furniture Co. is considering four plant locations in North Carolina. The fixed and variable costs for the four locations appear in Table 6.6. Figure 6.8 shows these fixed and variable costs as plotted for the expected output level of 12,000 units per year. The graph shows the ranges for which the various alternatives will yield the lowest costs. We can see that High Point and Lenoir are equal at a total annual output of 1,000 units. To verify this, substitute 1,000 units in the total annual cost equations for these two plants:

*High Point          Lenoir*

$$\$1,000,000 + 400(1,000 \text{ units}) = \$1,100,000 + \$300(1,000 \text{ units})$$
$$\$1,400,000 = \$1,400,000 \qquad (6\text{-}13)$$

Similarly, we can see that Lenoir and Hickory are equal at a total annual output of 9,500 units. To verify this, substitute 9,500 units in the total annual cost equations for these two plants:

*Lenoir          Hickory*

$$\$1,100,000 + \$300(9,500 \text{ units}) = \$3,000,000 + \$100(9,500 \text{ units})$$
$$\$3,950,000 = \$3,950,000 \qquad (6\text{-}14)$$

Overall, we observe that the High Point location will be preferable only at a low total annual output level (1,000 units or fewer). Thus the Lenoir location is preferable for the total annual output range of 1,000 units to 9,500 units. Above 9,500 units, the total annual output of Hickory is preferable. The Thomasville location is never preferable.

| Location | Fixed Cost per Year | Variable Cost per Thousand Units |
|---|---|---|
| Hickory, N. C. | $3,000,000 | $100 |
| Lenoir, N. C. | 1,100,000 | 300 |
| High Point, N. C. | 1,000,000 | 400 |
| Thomasville, N. C. | 2,000,000 | 400 |

T A B L E   6 . 6
Fixed and Variable Costs—Potential Plant Locations

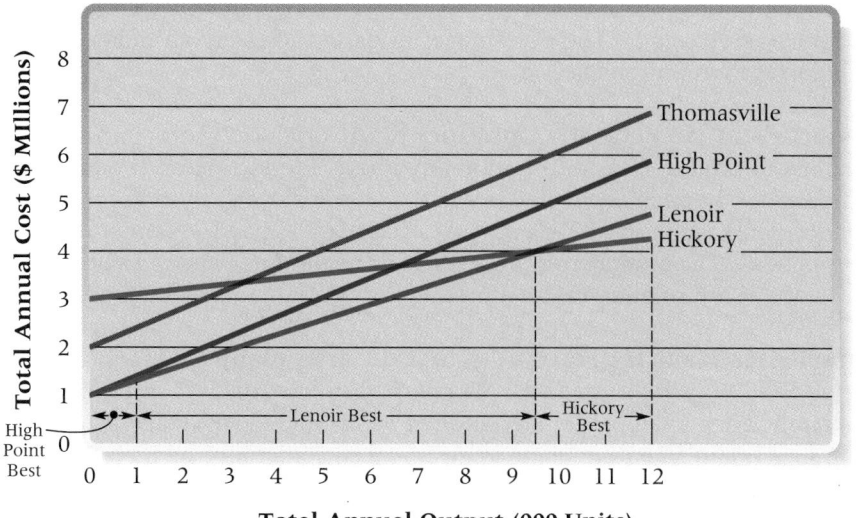

F I G U R E   6 . 8
Plots of Fixed and Variable Costs—Hickory Furniture Co.

Locational cost-volume-profit analysis is done in the same manner except that the profits associated with various output levels are plotted for the alternative locations. The lowest-cost location may not be the same as the maximum-profit location, unless the prices and volumes are the same for all locations.

## Making Multiple-Facility Location Decisions

Multiple facility-location decisions are much more complicated than the single-facility location decision. First, the possibility of multiple locations means that such problems are necessarily much larger. Second, multiple-facility problems can result in both location and location-allocation models. The number of facilities, their locations, and the amount of interaction with existing and new facilities and customer locations all become decision problems for multiple-facility location-allocation models. The essential questions to be answered are

1. How many facilities should there be?
2. Where should the facilities be located?
3. What should the capacity of each facility be?
4. Which facility should service which customer?
5. What products/services should each facility provide?

The models that answer these questions are even bigger and more complicated.

A vast amount of research has looked at multiple-facility location decisions, leading to the development of many techniques and models. The material that follows describes some of the more important techniques and provide examples by way of addressing location problems, allocation problems, and combined location-allocation problems. All the problems fall within the general framework of multiple-facility location decisions.

### Plant Charters Approach

One strategic approach to the multiple-facility location problem is the **plant charters** approach used by manufacturing companies that have several plants. A study of 410 major U.S. manufacturers showed that they used four distinct multiplant strategies that govern the "charters" under which these plants operate and orient them to the focused factory concept discussed earlier. There are four types of plants; the percentages in parentheses are an indication of the frequencies found in practice.

**Product Plant (58 Percent)**  A **product plant** produces a certain product line, or family of products, for distribution anywhere. Product plants produce canned or frozen foods; their locations are typically constrained by natural resources. Product plants tend to be independent, with separate management and engineering functions. The product responsibilities of the product plant are numerous and changeable—the rule is continual product innovation and product mix changes.

**Market-Area Plant (31 Percent)**  A **market-area plant** produces most, if not all, of the company's products; distribution is confined to the surrounding geographic area. Examples of market-area plants include beverages, staple foods, some steel, many paper products, glass and glass containers, metal containers, oil refining, some chemicals, and some furniture. The dominant location factor for this type of plant is proximity to market: It often produces heavy or bulky items that incur high outbound transportation costs. Market-area plants tend to be smaller, unionized, and more dependent than product plants.

**Process Plant (9 Percent)**  A **process plant** produces a certain segment of the full production process. A process plant often produces components, or subassemblies, that are fed to one or more final assembly plants. Examples of process plants are the component plants for motor vehicles, computers, and machine tools. Other examples are found in vertically integrated industries, such as aluminum and forest products, segments of which may be linked to natural resources or energy. Process plants tend to be highly capital intensive and are the most dependent on the parent corporation. Process plants are controlled as cost centers.

**General Purpose Plant (3 Percent)**  The **general purpose plant** is oriented toward flexibility—it can be assigned any of a number of responsibilities: products, market areas, process segments, or a combination for varying lengths of time. U.S. Department of Defense suppliers (aerospace and shipbuilding) and consumer package goods companies that market products with short life cycles use general purpose plants. This type of plant is likely to be a profit center. Also, it is most likely to be influenced by customer orders, with products made to customers' specifications and production triggered by customers' orders that it receives directly.[8]

The plant charters approach is a strategic way to look at multiple-facility location decisions. It is not really a location technique, but it does provide a useful framework for the multiple-facility location decision process.

## Transportation Method

Transportation costs often are the most important factor in multiple-facility location decisions. Transportation costs can be those associated with the movement of raw materials to plants or those associated with the movement of the finished goods to the customers.

For a multiple-facility network, which is composed of several existing plants and several existing customers' locations, determining the overall transportation cost may be difficult. This allocation problem has a number of variables that require evaluation. If we want to determine the consequences of adding a facility to an existing multiple-facility network, we have an even more difficult problem.

The **transportation method** of linear programming has proved to be useful in solving both types of problems. It is a special algorithm that can be used to determine the least expensive way to transport raw materials or products from several supply points to several demand destinations. It can be used to determine the best allocations for an existing multiple-facility network or to analyze new multiple-facility configurations. (Tutorial 1 at the end of the book provides more detail on the transportation method.)

---

The Dartnell Co., headquartered in St. Louis, manufactures plastic body parts for automobiles. It has manufacturing facilities in San Diego, St. Louis, and Orlando and maintains distribution warehouses in Salt Lake City and Detroit. Because of the influx of automobile manufacturing to the Southeast, it is contemplating opening a new distribution warehouse in

**EXAMPLE 6.9**

---

[8]Roger W. Schmenner, "Multiplant Manufacturing Strategies Among the Fortune 500," *Journal of Operations Management* 2 (February 1982): 77–86.

that region. The president and chief executive officer of the company, Linda Dartnell, has made a factor rating study of cities in the Southeast. She has concluded that either Atlanta or Knoxville would be good locations.

Dartnell remembers studying the transportation method in her operations management course at Washington University. She has directed her vice president for manufacturing operations, Bob Abernethy, to make such a study of the potential new warehouse locations. Abernethy has collected the information, shown in Table 6.7, relevant to this problem. He made separate transportation method analyses of each alternative.

Table 6.8 presents the optimal transportation method solution to the problem of locating the new warehouse in Atlanta. Note that the three plants have 5,000 units of excess capacity (monthly), so the optimal solution includes a dummy location requiring 5,000 units. The monthly shipping cost for a new distribution warehouse located in Atlanta is $365,000.

Table 6.9 presents the optimal transportation method solution to the problem of locating the new warehouse in Knoxville. Note that the 5,000 units of excess capacity (monthly) is again assigned to a dummy location. The monthly shipping cost for a new distribution warehouse located in Knoxville is $375,000.

Clearly, Atlanta is the preferable location for the new distribution warehouse.

TABLE 6.7
Dartnell Co.—Plant Capacities: Warehouse Demands and Shipping Costs

**Plant Capacities (Units)**

| | |
|---|---|
| *San Diego* | 10,000 |
| *St. Louis* | 25,000 |
| *Orlando* | 15,000 |

**Warehouse Demands (Units)**

| | |
|---|---|
| *Salt Lake City (existing)* | 15,000 |
| *Detroit (existing)* | 20,000 |
| *Atlanta(new)* | 10,000 |
| *Knoxville (new)* | 10,000 |

**Shipping Cost (Dollars per Unit)**

| FROM | Salt Lake City | Detroit | Atlanta | Knoxville |
|---|---|---|---|---|
| San Diego | 8 | 12 | 10 | 9 |
| St. Louis | 11 | 7 | 8 | 9 |
| Orlando | 14 | 13 | 9 | 10 |

| Demand<br>Supply | Salt Lake City | Detroit | Atlanta | Dummy | Total Supply |
|---|---|---|---|---|---|
| San Diego | 8.0<br>(10,000) | 12.0 | 10.0 | 0 | 10,000 |
| St. Louis | 11.0<br>(5,000) | 7.0<br>(20,000) | 8.0<br>(0) | 0 | 25,000 |
| Orlando | 14.0 | 13.0 | 9.0<br>(10,000) | 0<br>(5,000) | 15,000 |
| Total Demand | 15,000 | 20,000 | 10,000 | 5,000 | 50,000 |
| Minimum Monthly Shipping Cost = $365,000 | | | | | |

TABLE 6.8
Optimal Solution—Dartnell Co.'s New Warehouse in Atlanta

| Demand<br>Supply | Salt Lake City | Detroit | Knoxville | Dummy | Total Supply |
|---|---|---|---|---|---|
| San Diego | 8.0<br>(10,000) | 12.0 | 9.0 | 0 | 10,000 |
| St. Louis | 11.0<br>(5,000) | 7.0<br>(20,000) | 9.0<br>(0) | 0 | 25,000 |
| Orlando | 14.0 | 13.0 | 10.0<br>(10,000) | 0<br>(5,000) | 15,000 |
| Total Demand | 15,000 | 20,000 | 10,000 | 5,000 | 50,000 |
| Minimum Monthly Shipping Cost = $375,000 | | | | | |

TABLE 6.9
Optimal Solution—Dartnell Co.'s New Warehouse in Knoxville

# Heuristics

**Heuristics** are general guidelines, or "rules of thumb," for obtaining feasible, but not necessarily optimal, solutions to problems. Researchers have developed various heuristics and applied them to many multiple-facility location problems.

One of the first heuristics solved a two-stage (plant → warehouse → customer) location-allocation problem, which had multiple products and capacity-constrained plants and warehouses.[9] The computerized heuristic program had two parts:

■ The main program, which located one warehouse at a time until the total system cost showed an increase

[9]Alfred A. Kuehn and Michael J. Hamburger, "A Heuristic Program for Locating Warehouses," *Management Science* 9 (July 1963): 643–666.

■ The bump-and-shift routine, which tried to change the solution obtained by the main program by dropping existing warehouses or by shifting their current location

For a set of twelve sample problems this early heuristic provided solutions close to the optimum in most cases.

## Simulation

**Simulation** is the process of developing a descriptive model of a particular problem and then conducting experiments that use the model to determine performance measures for the problem. It provides descriptive information that can be used to evaluate various alternatives. For multiple-facility location (or location-allocation) problems it provides information that allows the analyst to look at different locations on a case-by-case basis. One major advantage of simulation is that it permits the consideration of a virtually unlimited number of products, plants, warehouses, and customers. (Tutorial 4 at the end of the book provides more detail on simulation.)

Managers have used simulation extensively to analyze a wide variety of multiple-facility location (or location-allocation) problems. Two experts analyzed distribution systems as large as 12 plants, 25 commodities, 100 warehouse locations, and 5,000 customers.[10] Other researchers developed the *Distribution System Simulator*, which was later marketed by IBM.[11]

Ralston Purina Co. used a large-scale simulation model as an aid in making warehouse location decisions.[12] The simulation model included all, or a portion of, ten midwestern states. It consolidated customer demand within this geographical area into twenty-nine demand analysis areas. Five field warehouses and four plants (with accompanying warehouses) served the geographical areas. The company simulated random demand at each demand center, by product type, for a three-month period and found that demand was satisfied by using the closest warehouse that had inventory available. Ralston Purina ultimately simulated thirty-two field warehouse locational patterns and collected information about inventory levels, transportation costs, warehouse operating costs, and penalty costs. Table 6.10 presents the distribution cost summary for simulation experiments involving alternative warehouse locations. These simulation experiments showed that the least costly alternative would be to consolidate the five existing field warehouses into three, at a savings of $132,000 per year.

## Optimization Methods

**Optimization methods** encompass a wide range of techniques designed to produce a set of "best" locations, or location-allocation decisions. We have already discussed one such optimization technique, the transportation method. In general, optimization methods attempt to provide models of problems with some or all of the following characteristics:

[10]Harvey N. Shycon and Richard B. Maffei, "Remarks on the Kuehn-Hamburger Paper," *Management Science* 9 (July 1963): 667–668.

[11]H. M. Connors et al., "The Distribution System Simulator," *Management Science* 18 (April 1972): B-425–B-453.

[12]Robert E. Markland, "Analyzing Geographically Discrete Warehousing Networks by Computer Simulation," *Decision Sciences* 4 (April 1973): 216–236.

| Type of Cost | Warehouse Configuration | | | | | |
|---|---|---|---|---|---|---|
| | *Five Field Warehouses* | *Four** Field Warehouses* | *Three** Field Warehouses* | *Two** Field Warehouses* | *One** Field Warehouse* | *Zero Field Warehouses* |
| **Transportation Costs*** | | | | | | |
| Mfg. Facility→Customer | $514 | $530 | $525 | $567 | $574 | $ 665 |
| Mfg. Facility→Field Warehouse | 36 | 30 | 20 | 17 | 10 | 0 |
| Field Warehouse→Customer | 60 | 51 | 42 | 20 | 28 | 0 |
| Subtotal | 610 | 611 | 587 | 604 | 612 | 665 |
| **Warehousing Costs** | | | | | | |
| Field Warehouses | 30 | 25 | 16 | 13 | 6 | 0 |
| Mfg. Facility Warehouses | 303 | 304 | 310 | 313 | 316 | 320 |
| Subtotal | 333 | 329 | 326 | 326 | 322 | 320 |
| **Penalty Costs** | | | | | | |
| Order Shifting Costs | 12 | 8 | 9 | 7 | 5 | 22 |
| Back Ordering Costs | 4 | 2 | 4 | 4 | 3 | 4 |
| Subtotal | 16 | 10 | 13 | 11 | 8 | 26 |
| **Total Distribution Costs** | $959 | $950 | $926 | $941 | $942 | $1011 |

*Transportation costs associated with interplant and interwarehouse shipments are not shown for the sake of brevity. They were of small magnitude and did not vary significantly between the various simulation runs.
**Minimum cost combination for the particular warehouse configuration.

TABLE 6.10
Distribution Cost Summary—Three-Month Period: Alternative Warehouse Configurations ($000)

1. Multiple products
2. Two stages of distribution (plants → warehouses → customers)
3. Productive capacity limits for plants
4. Size limits for warehouses
5. Each customer served by a single warehouse
6. Various constraints on the distribution system configuration
7. Minimum service levels

Among the more well-known optimization methods are mixed integer programming, specialized branch-and-bound procedures, and the Benders decomposition approach. Hunt-Wesson Foods, Inc., has used the Benders decomposition approach successfully for very large problems.[13] The *Harvard Business Review* reported that the analysis led Hunt-Wesson to change its distribution network, which saved more than $1 million.

## Strategic Trends in Location Decisions

A tremendous number of new plants, warehouses, office buildings, stores, and service buildings are built every year in the United States and much remodeling and expansion of existing facilities takes place. In total, industrial renovation and construction is a major driving force in our economy. Looking at location

[13]Arthur M. Geoffrion, "Better Distribution Planning with Computer Models," *Harvard Business Review* 54 (July–August 1976): 92–99.

decisions and how they are made is interesting, and it is possible to identify at least four major trends: business park proliferation, factory/research and development linkages, globalization of production, and the Sun belt phenomenon.

## Business Park Proliferation

Types of business parks include

1.  Science parks—primarily oriented toward research and development activities
2.  Office parks—primarily oriented toward administrative activities
3.  Industrial parks—typically contain manufacturing or production facilities
4.  Mixed-use parks—combine administrative and manufacturing activities
5.  Fly-in parks—combine one or more of the activities of the other parks with an airport facility

The 1990 geo-sites survey done by *Site Selection* magazine reports that overbuilt markets and weakening demand are translating into attractive business park leasing deals, and corporate real estate executives can choose from an increasingly broad array of business park options. Perhaps never before has the time been better to hunt for quality business park space.

Florida leads all states in the number of business parks. Other top states in total number of parks include California (527), Ohio (451), Texas (410), Illinois (391), and Georgia (355). In 1990 the world had almost 10,000 business parks, more than 7,600 of which were in the United States. Figure 6.9 is a map that shows the locations of business parks in North America.

Another major trend this study observed is the increasing emphasis park developers are placing on the quality of park space. Corporations now prefer to locate facilities in those business parks that are not only functional but also esthetically pleasing and capable of providing recreational amenities.

**FIGURE 6.9**
North American Business
Parks, 1990

Source: Tim Venable, "Attractive
Business Park Deals for Corporate
Tenants on Rise,"*Site Selection* 35
(December 1990): 1308.

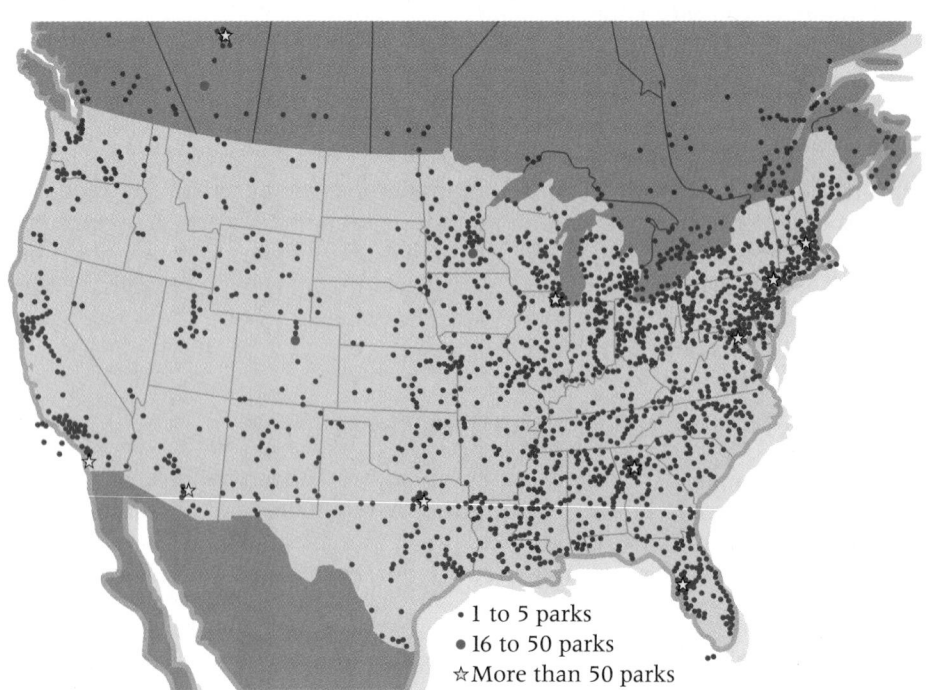

- • 1 to 5 parks
- ● 16 to 50 parks
- ☆ More than 50 parks

T A B L E   6 . 1 1
R&D Facility Location
Factors

| Top-Rated Factors in Recent R&D Facility Locations | |
| --- | --- |
| 1. High concentration of engineers and scientists in work force | 1.49 |
| 2. Proximity to universities | 1.55 |
| 3. Proximity to corporate operations/manufacturing | 1.63 |
| 4. Proximity to corporate headquarters | 1.81 |
| 5. Availability of industry-specific training | 1.86 |
| 6. Proximity to R&D centers | 1.98 |
| 7. Quality of life comparable to a resort area | 2.26 |
| 8. Science or technology park site | 2.38 |
| 9. State science advisory commission or authority to promote high-tech concerns | 2.52 |
| 10. State seed money available | 2.66 |

Source: Jack Lyne, "Many U.S. Firms Poised to Relocate R&D Facilities Closer to the Factory Floor," *Site Selection* 35, No. 6 (June 1990): 631.
Note: Average scores listed. Highest possible rating equals 1.0. Lowest possible rating equals 3.0.

In today's competitive business park market, amenities are playing a significant role in attracting corporate tenants. The *Site Selection* survey showed that meeting and conference rooms are the most common business park amenity, followed by sandwich shops, full-service restaurants, jogging trails, hotels, day-care centers, and printing centers.[14]

## Factories: Research and Development Linkages

Although U.S. research facilities are considered to be the best in the world, American companies have not done well in transforming technical findings into high-quality manufacturing processes and products.

Many U.S. companies are planning to relocate their research and development facilities closer to the factory floor. The 1990 geo-technology survey made by *Site Selection* magazine shows that almost 60 percent of corporate real estate executives have adopted this approach. Many consider this successful research and development strategy to be a key element in Japan's global technological preeminence.

Judging from survey results, many U.S.-based corporations may soon move their R&D facilities. Forty-eight percent of survey respondents said they planned to move R&D closer to operations within the next three years, while 32 percent said the move would come within the next five years.[15]

The top-rated factors in recent R&D facility locations appear in Table 6.11.

## Globalization of Production

American companies have had foreign operations for many years, and the multinational identity of American companies is not a new phenomenon. Robert B. Reich, U.S. secretary of labor, says that "what is new is that American-owned multinationals are beginning to employ large numbers of foreigners relative to their American work forces, are beginning to rely on foreign facilities to do most

[14]Tim Venable, "Attractive Business Park Deals for Corporate Tenants on the Rise," *Site Selection* 35 (December 1990): 1306–1318.
[15]Jack Lyne, "Many U.S. Firms Poised to Relocate R&D Facilities Closer to the Factory Floor," *Site Selection* 35 (June 1990): 630–632.

of their technologically complex activities, and are beginning to export from their foreign facilities—including bringing products back to the United States."[16]

Examples of this new phenomenon abound. Forty percent of IBM's worldwide work force are citizens of countries other than the United States, and the percentage is increasing. After cutting its American work force by 10 percent and buying N.V. Philips's appliance business, Whirlpool employs 43,500 people around the world in forty-five countries, most of them non-American. Texas Instruments, which does most of its research, development, design, and manufacturing in east Asia, employs more than 5,000 people in Japan alone. Taiwan includes AT&T, RCA, and Texas Instruments among its biggest exporters. More than 100,000 Singaporians work for more than 200 U.S. corporations, and American corporations employ 11 percent of the industrial work force of Northern Ireland.

Perhaps an even more dramatic development is the arrival of foreign corporations in the United States. In 1977 about 3.5 percent of the value added to and employment of Americans in manufacturing originated in foreign-owned companies. By 1987 the number had grown to almost 8 percent. In 1991 foreign-owned companies employed 30 million Americans, roughly 10 percent of our manufacturing workers. These non-U.S. companies are vigorously exporting from the United States. Sony exports audiotapes and videotapes from its Dothan, Alabama, factory. Sharp exports 100,000 microwave ovens a year from its factory in Memphis, Tennessee. Toshiba America is sending projection televisions from its Wayne, New Jersey, plant to Japan. Honda annually exports 50,000 cars to Japan from its Ohio production base, actually making more cars in the United States than in Japan.

Reich also observes that corporate decisions about production and location today are driven by global competition, not national allegiance. Cross-border ownership is booming: Americans are buying into global companies based in Europe and east Asia, and Europeans and Asians are buying into companies based in the United States. When two or more locations are about the same, the company will base its decision on where the global manager can secure the most profitable deal.

The global manager's role is to put everything together, worldwide. For example, Mazda's latest sports car, the MX-5 Miata, was designed in California, financed in Tokyo and New York, prototyped in Worsting, England, and assembled in Michigan and Mexico using advanced electronic components invented in New Jersey and fabricated in Japan. Boeing's next airliner will be designed in Washington State and Japan and assembled in Seattle, with tail cones from Canada, special tail sections from China and Italy, and engines from Great Britain. Saatchi and Saatchi's recent television advertising campaign for Miller Lite beer was conceived in Britain, shot on location in Canada, dubbed in Britain and the United States, and edited in New York.[17]

The activities that add the most value to the global company's products—advanced R&D, sophisticated engineering and design, and complex fabrication and assembly—are not necessarily found in the country in which most of its shareholders and executives live. Ford's state-of-the-art engine factory is in Chihuaha, Mexico, where skilled Mexican engineers produce more than one thousand engines per day with quality equal to the best in the world. In 1990 Hewlett-Packard's German researchers were making significant studies in fiber-optic technologies, its Australian researchers in computer-aided engineering software, and its Singapore researchers in laser printers.

*A supervisor observes a worker assembling telephones at a* maquiladora *plant in northern Mexico.*

[16]Robert B. Reich, "Who Is Us?" *Harvard Business Review* 68 (January–February 1990): 54.
[17]Robert B. Reich, "Who Is Them?" *Harvard Business Review* 69 (March–April 1991): 79.

## GLOBAL OPERATIONS MANAGEMENT 6.4

### *Maquiladora* Industry— **Locating Plants In Mexico**

The term *maquiladora* (inbound) refers to an assembly plant operating in Mexican territory under special customs treatment and liberal foreign investment regulations. Maquiladoras import into Mexico (temporarily duty-free) machinery, equipment, parts, raw materials, and other components used in the assembly or manufacture of semifinished or finished products. The products are then exported back to their originating country or on to a third country.

The growth of the maquiladora program has been spectacular. In 1966 Mexico had 12 maquiladora plants, employing 3,000 workers. By 1980 this had grown to 620 maquiladora plants, with 123,879 workers. By late 1990, 1,977 maquiladora plants were operating, employing 468,773 workers. The industry each year produces more than $12.4 billion in products and more than $3 billion of value-added income for Mexico.

Maquiladora plants were originally very labor intensive and stressed simple manual assembly operations and low-level technology. Recently, technology transfer has brought sophisticated and innovative processes into the maquiladora plant.

U.S. manufacturers have found a great attraction in Mexico's proximity to the U.S. market. The maquiladora industry has historically been closely identified with the Mexico–U.S. border. But maquiladora plants can be found throughout the country today.

Maquiladora manufacturing is expected to remain attractive for small and medium-size companies, especially those opening new markets or coming to Mexico for the first time, but the recent passage of the North American Free Trade Agreement (NAFTA) may change dramatically how foreign-owned businesses operate in Mexico. Some economists suggest that certain NAFTA provisions (such as the environmental regulations) may even make it more difficult to establish maquiladora plants.

---

Since the late 1800s companies have moved their manufacturing locations to take advantage of cheap labor. Managers must now think in terms of a world market for labor, because human capital increasingly flows across national borders. During the 1990s the world's work force is becoming even more mobile, and employers are moving across borders to find the skills they need. Important labor force trends include

- Women entering the labor force in great numbers, especially in the developing countries, where relatively few women have been employed to date
- The rising average age of the world's work force, especially in the developed countries.
- An increasingly well-educated worldwide work force; the developing countries will produce a growing share of the world's high school and college graduates[18]

Global Operations Management 6.4 describes the growth of the *maquiladora* program in Mexico.

[18]William B. Johnston, "Global Work Force 2000: The New World Labor Market," *Harvard Business Review* 69 (March–April 1991): 116–122.

## The Sun Belt Phenomenon

During the 1970s and 1980s, the centers of economic, population, and per capita income growth in the United States shifted from the North to the South and West (to the so-called Sun belt states). The states included in the Sun belt are not precisely defined but usually include the thirteen states of Alabama, Arkansas, Florida, Georgia, Kentucky, Louisiana, Mississippi, New Mexico, North Carolina, Oklahoma, South Carolina, Tennessee, and Texas. Other states often mentioned as part of the Sun belt are Arizona and California, whereas Kentucky is often excluded. Figure 6.10 is a map showing the Sun belt states; the numbers in parentheses indicate the estimated changes in manufacturing employment in various regions to 2010. Growth in the Sun belt has been characterized by the flight of both people and industry from the Frost belt. Industry has moved because of low wages, favorable business climates, low taxes, inexpensive land, energy availability, less unionism and active recruitment of industry by state and local governments. People have moved because of mild climates, sports and recreational facilities, relaxed outdoor living, and the chance to escape from big city congestion and pollution.

The Sun belt is already the most populous region in the United States, and it is expected to grow by 30 percent by 2010. Employment growth rates in all Sun belt states are expected to be greater than for the United States as a whole. The major impetus for overall growth is likely to be manufacturing employment, projected to grow by 55 percent in the Sun belt by 2010.

Global Operations Management 6.5 reviews the issues that influenced BMW's decision to build a plant in South Carolina.

FIGURE 6.10
The Sunbelt States—
Comparative Manufacturing
Employment Changes, to
2010

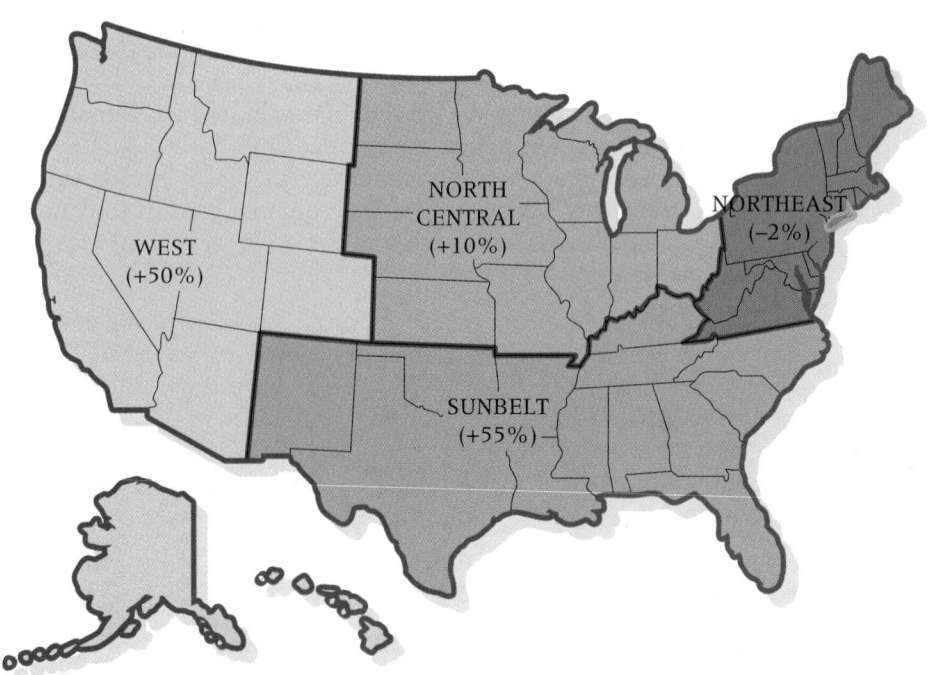

# Why BMW Cruised into Spartanburg

BMW's decision to build a new plant in South Carolina was a resounding vote of confidence in the importance of a qualified work force, the principal criterion set by the company in 1989 when it decided that it needed a new facility outside Germany. It looked at 250 locations worldwide, narrowed the list to 10, and picked one—Spartanburg, South Carolina.

Among the broader issues influencing the negotiations (in addition to the need for a qualified work force) were financing, tax incentives, and infrastructure. But one of the main factors clearly was the state's intense preemployment worker training program. This program supports a work force that already has basic skills. South Carolina has committed to providing all the hand tools, manuals, and classroom facilities, as well as hiring qualified instructors, that businesses in the state need. The state modified its high-quality training program, tailoring it specifically for BMW by extending the state education commitment to three years from the more usual one year. The South Carolina education package for BMW workers includes training in technical skills, leadership–team building, new management techniques, and youth apprenticeship programs. BMW and South Carolina develop all programs for BMW jointly.

Another positive factor from BMW's perspective was South Carolina's business-oriented state government. Also, labor relations are harmonious throughout the state and region. Finally, the state had committed to a $40 million runway extension and modernization of the Greenville-Spartanburg Airport, adjacent to the site of the new auto facility.

The state expects the BMW facility to inject more than $6 billion into the region through 2002, a return of 150 times South Carolina's investment in work force education.

## ► Summary

Capacity planning and location decisions are two major strategic areas of concern for operations managers. They are closely linked and are often inseparable. Globalization of production is having a strong influence on them.

**Learning Objective 1: Discuss the importance of capacity planning.** Capacity decisions are important, because building capacity usually requires significant capital and companies incur significant losses when capacity is reduced. Also, when a company has too much capacity, its inventory levels may rise, or it may underuse its work force and equipment. When a company has too little capacity, it can lose customers to competitors or be forced to use costly subcontracting.

**Learning Objective 2: Define *capacity* and explain how it is measured.** Capacity is usually measured as a quantity of output per unit of time, the rate that a manufacturing or service process can achieve. Operations managers may also refer to *design capacity*, which is the target output rate, or maximum capacity for which the production facility was designed. Another common term is *effective capacity*, which is the maximum rate of output achievable, given quality standards, scheduling constraints, machine maintenance, work force capabilities, and product mix. The actual capacity, or actual output rate, is the rate of output that the operation actually achieves. It is normally less than effective capacity because of machine breakdowns, worker absenteeism, defective materials, and shortages of materials or assemblies.

**Learning Objective 3: Describe the major steps in the capacity planning process.** Effective capacity planning requires the execution of a series of steps:

1. Audit and evaluate the existing facilities and capacity.
2. Forecast facilities and capacity requirements.
3. Define capacity alternatives.
4. Perform financial analyses of the capacity alternatives.
5. Assess key qualitative issues for the capacity alternatives.
6. Select a specific alternative to pursue.
7. Implement the alternative chosen.
8. Audit and review the actual results.

**Learning Objective 4: Define the linkages between capacity planning and facility location.** A company must plan for capacity planning when it decides to make a new product, offer a new service, make more of an existing product, or provide more of an existing service. Because the demand for products or services is a function of location, facility location decisions are necessarily linked to capacity decisions. Both manufacturers and service companies tend to locate near their customers, and manufacturers also try to locate close to their suppliers.

**Learning Objective 5: Explain why location decisions are important.** Location decisions are made relatively infrequently, usually in response to a major capacity problem. Once a location decision is made, it is difficult to change it. Location decisions have a long-term effect on both revenues and operating costs.

**Learning Objective 6: Discuss the major factors affecting location decisions.** Many factors are part of typical location decisions. Among the major factors are labor availability and cost, transportation availability, market proximity, land and/or property availability and cost, utilities availability and costs, region-state-community attitudes, and management's preferences.

## ► Key Terms

actual capacity
actual output rate
allocation problem
best operating level
bottleneck
capacity
capacity cushion
capacity efficiency
capacity planning
capacity utilization
center of gravity method

decision tree
design capacity
diseconomies of scale
economies of scale
effective capacity
facility layout problem
facility location
factor rating systems
general purpose plant
heuristics
location problem

location-allocation problem
locational cost-volume analysis
locational cost-volume-profit analysis
market-area plant
optimization methods
plant charters
process plant
product plant
simulation
transportation method

## ► Discussion Questions

1. Discuss the linkage between capacity planning and facility location.
2. What is the difference between design capacity and effective capacity?
3. Define *capacity* and explain why it is important to the operations manager.
4. What are some major capacity considerations for a business school? How do they differ from those for a typical factory?
5. What are the major steps in the capacity planning process?
6. What are the major capacity strategies that operations managers can use?
7. Describe the major factors in plant location.
8. Explain why location decisions are important.
9. What are the major options for making location decisions?
10. What are the major steps in the facility location process?
11. Why are Sun belt locations attractive for manufacturing facilities?

**12.** Why are foreign locations attractive for U.S. manufacturers? Why are U.S. locations attractive for foreign manufacturers?

**13.** Compare and contrast the decisions that a company must make in locating manufacturing and service facilities.

**14.** Describe the plant charters approach. Under what conditions would each of the four types of production plants be used?

**15.** Develop a list of reasons that a manufacturing company should choose your home town as a location for a new plant.

# ► Problems

**1.** Susan Bromley, operations manager at Enviro-Tech, Inc., has collected data concerning three new plant locations. The fixed and variable costs for these three locations are as follows:

| Location | Fixed Cost per Year | Variable Cost per Unit |
|---|---|---|
| 1 | $ 500,000 | $1,000 |
| 2 | 1,700,000 | 200 |
| 3 | 1,100,000 | 500 |

**a.** Plot the total cost curves for the three potential locations on a graph. Using this graph, identify the range in volume over which each location would be best.

**b.** Calculate the break-even quantity for locations 1 and 2, 1 and 3, and 2 and 3.

**2.** A company is considering three locations for a new distribution warehouse: Durham, North Carolina, Charlottesville, Virginia, and Knoxville, Tennessee. Using the following information, determine the range in volume over which each location would be preferable:

| Location | Fixed Cost per Year | Variable Cost per Unit |
|---|---|---|
| Durham, N.C. | $1,200,000 | $50 |
| Charlottesville, Va. | 1,600,000 | 40 |
| Knoxville, Tenn. | 2,000,000 | 30 |

**a.** Plot the total cost curves for the three potential locations on a graph. Using this graph, identify the range in volume over which each location would be best.

**b.** Calculate the break-even quantity between Durham and Charlottesville, Durham and Knoxville, and Charlottesville and Knoxville.

**3.** Evaluate the decision tree shown in the following diagram:

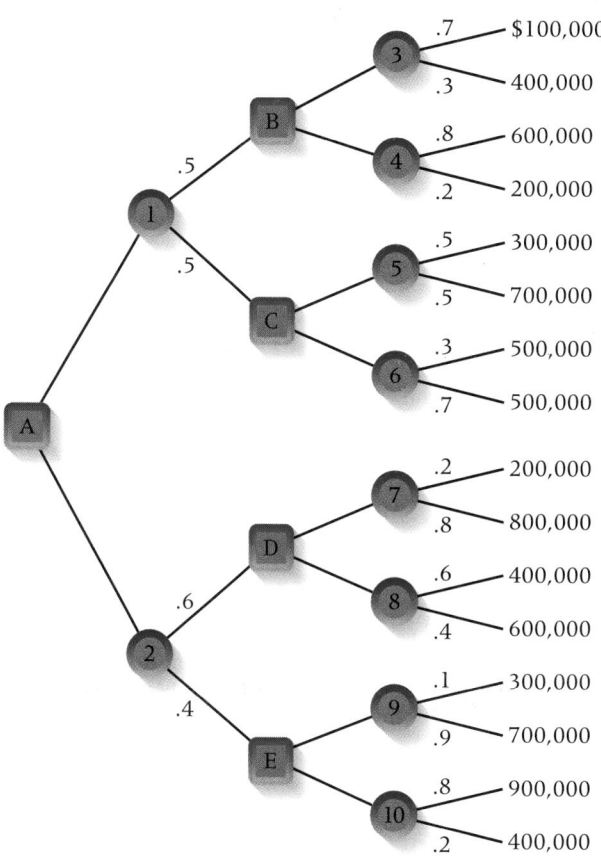

4. Evaluate the decision tree shown in the following diagram:

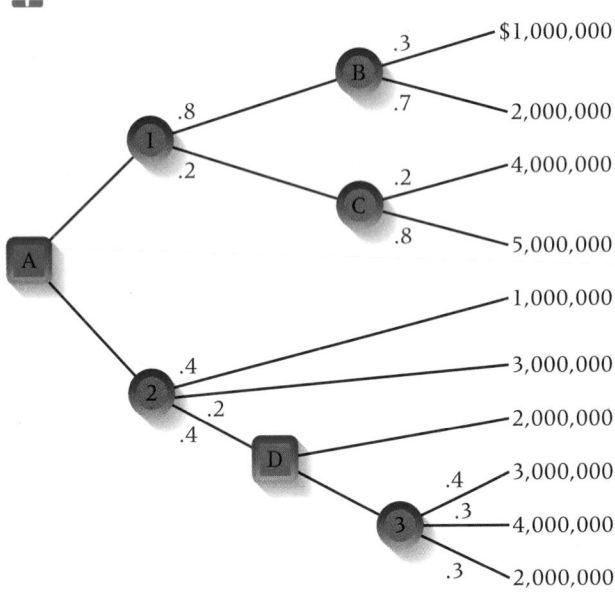

| Decision Variables | New Site | Probability |
|---|---|---|
| Yearly lease cost | | |
| Construction cost | $5,000,000 | |
| Yearly Gross Revenues: | | |
| High ticket sales | 1,000,000 | (0.4) |
| Medium ticket sales | 500,000 | (0.3) |
| Low ticket sales | 500,000 | (0.3) |
| Yearly operating cost | 200,000 | |

6. Jefferson Dewright, a production manager, is trying to decide whether to manufacture a new part in house or subcontract for its manufacture. Subcontracting would cost $15 per unit. Internally, he can use either of two production lines to make the part. On production line 1, the set-up cost would be $10,000 and the variable cost would be $5 per unit. On production line 2, the set-up cost would be $8,000 and the variable cost $8 per unit. Yearly demand for the product is projected as follows:

| Yearly Demand (units) | Probability |
|---|---|
| 20,000 | 0.4 |
| 30,000 | 0.2 |
| 40,000 | 0.4 |

Use this information to develop a decision tree that will help Dewright make his production decision.

5. The owners of the Triple A Columbia Bombers baseball team are facing two options for a baseball park. First, they can sign a lease on the baseball park owned by the city of Columbia. The city will renovate the ball park and provide an initial four-year lease. If the city is satisfied at the end of four years, it will extend the lease for six years. If the city refuses to renew the lease, the Columbia Bombers would have to play their games at the University of South Carolina, which would increase their lease cost by 30 percent, or build a new facility. The owners estimate the likelihood that the city will renew the lease at 70 percent. The second option is for the owners to build a new facility now.

Given this information and that provided in the table that follows, develop a decision tree to help the owners of the Columbia Bombers decide what to do. (Use a ten-year planning horizon, ignoring cost of capital and compounding of interest.)

| Decision Variables | Existing Site | Probability |
|---|---|---|
| Yearly lease cost | $400,000 | |
| Construction cost | | |
| Yearly Gross Revenues: | | |
| High ticket sales | 800,000 | (0.5) |
| Medium ticket sales | 500,000 | (0.3) |
| Low ticket sales | 300,000 | (0.2) |
| Yearly operating cost | 300,000 | |

7. Nu-Process Corp. manufactures molded plastic automobile trim at three locations, plants, A, B, and C. Recently, it secured a large contract from a Japanese auto maker. It has decided to concentrate all its production in one big, new facility, Plant D.

The grid shows the locations of and production volumes at its existing plants.

Use the center of gravity method and the information provided here to determine the best location for plant D.

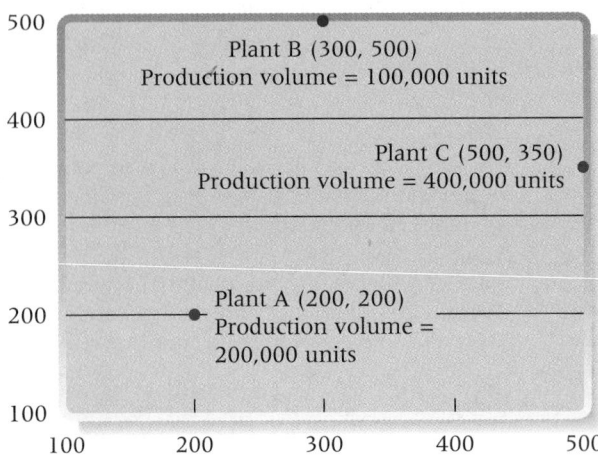

8. Using the information given in problem 7, assume that management decides to shift half its production at plant C to plant A. Would this change the location you proposed for plant D? If so, where should it now be located?

9. Ace Delivery Service is considering relocating its main collection facility from its current location in downtown Charlotte, North Carolina. The building is an old warehouse that is too small and needs a lot of repair work. Also, a significant portion of its delivery business has shifted to business parks in the suburbs.

   Janice Dobson, the manager of Ace Delivery Services, has collected information about its current pickup and delivery points:

| Pickup/Delivery Point | Round Trips per Day | XY Coordinates (miles) |
|---|---|---|
| 1 | 8 | (2,10) |
| 2 | 6 | (3,12) |
| 3 | 12 | (4,9) |
| 4 | 9 | (6,2) |
| 5 | 7 | (12,4) |
| 6 | 4 | (15,3) |

   Use the center of gravity method and the information provided to determine the best location for a new collection facility.

10. Reconsider problem 9 by assuming that delivery points 1 and 2 are closed and that their volumes (round trips per day) are shifted to point 4. Would this change the location of the new collection point? If so, where should it now be located?

11. Aretha Grimes has collected the following information about where to locate a new service facility:

|  |  | | Factor Score | |
|---|---|---|---|---|
| Location Factor | Factor Weight | Location A | Location B | Location C |
| Construction costs | 20 | 7 | 8 | 6 |
| Transportation | 25 | 5 | 9 | 8 |
| Property taxes | 15 | 7 | 6 | 7 |
| Residential density | 10 | 3 | 5 | 5 |
| Land costs | 30 | 7 | 8 | 8 |

Scoring Key: 1 = Poor to 10 = Excellent

   Compute the weighted factor scores for locations A, B, and C. Which location should her company choose?

12. Bob Wing is the operations manager at Century Pool Chemicals Co. He has to decide whether to relocate a major plant and has compiled the following set of information:

|  |  | | Factor Score | |
|---|---|---|---|---|
| Location Factor | Factor Weight | St. Louis | Dallas | Atlanta |
| Construction costs | 20 | 60 | 70 | 50 |
| Transportation | 10 | 90 | 90 | 90 |
| Market proximity | 20 | 60 | 70 | 70 |
| Land costs | 20 | 70 | 50 | 60 |
| Property taxes | 10 | 80 | 60 | 80 |
| Community services | 10 | 80 | 70 | 50 |
| Unionization | 10 | 30 | 70 | 70 |

Scoring Key: 0 = Poor to 100 = Excellent

   Compute the weighted factor scores for St. Louis, Dallas, and Atlanta. Which location should he choose?

TABLE 6.12
Transportation Table for Problem 13.

| Storage Facilities / Refineries | $S_1$ | $S_2$ | $S_3$ | $S_4$ | Refinery Availabilities |
|---|---|---|---|---|---|
| $R_1$ | 80 / 10 | 70 / 6 | 50 | 60 | 16 |
| $R_2$ | 60 | 90 / 4 | 40 / 12 | 80 / 4 | 20 |
| $R_3$ | 50 | 50 | 95 | 90 / 14 | 14 |
| Storage Requirements | 10 | 10 | 12 | 18 | 50 |

TABLE 6.13
Transportation Table for
Problem 14

| Amusement Park Arcade Distribution Center | $APA_1$ | $APA_2$ | $APA_3$ | $APA_4$ | Distribution Center Availabilities |
|---|---|---|---|---|---|
| $DC_1$ | 11.0 | 8.00 (15) | 11.5 | 10.0 (5) | 20 |
| $DC_2$ | 12.5 (30) | 11.0 | 13.5 (5) | 12.0 (10) | 45 |
| $DC_3$ | 11.0 | 9.50 | 11.5 | 11.0 (10) | 10 |
| Requirements | 30 | 15 | 5 | 25 | 75 |

**13.** The Slippery Oil Co. operates three refineries that produce gasoline, which it then ships to four big storage facilities. The monthly quantities (1,000 barrels) for each storage facility, as well as the associated costs, are shown in Table 6.12. This transportation table also provides information about the company's current distribution plan. Does the distribution plan minimize the distribution cost of the Slippery Oil Co.? If not, find a plan that does minimize the distribution cost.

**14.** Video Techtronics manufactures and distributes video games. It has three distribution centers that supply four major video game arcades. The yearly quantities supplied by each distribution center and the yearly requirements for each video arcade are shown in Table 6.13. The transportation table also provides information about the company's distribution plan. Does the distribution plan minimize the cost to Video Techtronics? If not, find a plan that does minimize the distribution cost.

## ▶ Selected References

Buffa, Elwood S. *Meeting the Competitive Challenge: Manufacturing Strategy for U.S. Companies.* Homewood, Ill.: Irwin, 1984.

Francis, R. L., and J. A. White. *Facilities Layout and Location: An Analytical Approach.* Englewood Cliffs, N.J.: Prentice-Hall, 1987.

Freidenfelds, John. *Capacity Expansion: Analysis of Simple Models with Applications.* New York: Elsevier North-Holland, 1981.

Hayes, Robert H., and Steven C. Wheelwright. *Restoring Our Competitive Edge: Competing Through Manufacturing.* New York, Wiley, 1984.

Hill, Terry. *Manufacturing Strategy.* Homewood, Ill.: Irwin, 1989.

Morris, William T. *The Capacity Decision System.* Homewood, Ill.: Irwin, 1967.

Reed, Rudell. *Plant Location, Layout, and Maintenance.* Homewood, Ill.: Irwin, 1967.

Schmenner, Roger W. *Making Business Location Decisions.* Englewood Cliffs, N.J.: Prentice-Hall, 1982.

Skinner, Wickham. *Manufacturing in the Corporate Strategy.* New York: Wiley, 1978.

Stafford, H. A. *Principles of Industrial Facility Location.* Atlanta: Conway, 1980.

Tompkins, James A., and John A. White. *Facilities Planning.* New York: Wiley, 1984.

Tong, Hsin-Min. *Plant Location Decisions of Foreign Manufacturing Investors.* Ann Arbor: University of Michigan Research Press, 1979.

# Georgia-Pacific Corp.

## A CASE STUDY IN CAPACITY PLANNING AND FACILITY LOCATION

## Introduction

Georgia-Pacific Corp., headquartered in Atlanta, Georgia, is one of the world's biggest forest products companies. Founded in 1927 as a hardwood lumber wholesaler in Augusta, Georgia, Georgia-Pacific has grown rapidly through expansions and acquisitions to become a leading integrated manufacturer and distributor of pulp, paper, and building products.

It had net sales of $12.665 billion and net income of $365 million in 1990. It employs roughly sixty thousand people and owns and manages millions of acres of timberland in North America. Georgia-Pacific is committed to improving the quality of air and water, to using solid waste for products and energy to conserve natural resources, and to managing and renewing forests in ways that protect the environmental quality of our timberland resources and meet the demands of the marketplace.

This case study focuses on capacity planning and facility location at Georgia-Pacific, a company that has undergone phenomenal growth and that has operations inextricably linked to the environmental quality of our woodlands. This case illustrates the importance of growth and its linkage to the environment.

## Company History

In 1927 Owen Cheatham, a twenty-four-year-old salesman, borrowed $6,000, added $6,000 of his own money, and bought a lumber yard in Augusta, Georgia. He called the new company the Georgia Hardwood Lumber Co. and began to wholesale hardwood lumber. The company soon began manufacturing operations, and by 1938 it was operating five sawmills throughout the South.

During World War II Cheatham was the biggest supplier of lumber to the U.S. armed forces. In 1947 his company made its first West Coast acquisition, a plywood plant at Bellingham, Washington, and in 1948 changed its name to Georgia-Pacific Plywood and Lumber Co. The ensuing years saw additional acquisitions and name changes until the company

adopted "Georgia-Pacific Corp.," as it is known today, in 1956.

Diversification and continuing acquisition followed. The company entered the pulp and paper business in 1957, opened its first resin adhesive plant in 1959, and added paper converting facilities and its first corrugated container plant in 1961. It entered the tissue business in 1963, acquired a gypsum company in 1965, began construction of a big chemical complex in 1968, acquired an oil and gas company in 1975, entered roofing manufacturing in 1976, and began waferboard production in 1980. During the 1980s it expanded several company operations while selling or writing off other underperforming company assets. In 1982 Georgia-Pacific moved its headquarters from Portland, Oregon, to a new fifty-story skyscraper in Atlanta. In 1990 it completed its merger with Great Northern Nekoosa Corp., adding 55 paper and paperboard converting plants, 83 paper distribution centers, 1 plywood plant, and 2 sawmills.

Georgia-Pacific's history is one of constant growth—by acquiring various companies and by investing in new technologies and manufacturing processes. Growth is a major factor in both capacity expansion and facility location decisions at Georgia-Pacific.

## Georgia-Pacific and the Environment

Trees are one of the most important resources available in the United States. Trees are used in more than five thousand products and improve the quality of our air and water. They also give us shade and beauty and afford a habitat for wildlife. The fabric of our industrial growth has been woven from the forest. Sawmills were among our first manufacturing enterprises, and early settlers viewed our vast forests as inexhaustible. But as America grew, the need for good forest management became apparent.

When Cheatham founded Georgia-Pacific, it did not own any timberlands; it began to acquire them in the 1950s in order to provide its plants and mills with a continuous supply of raw materials. Today, it owns and manages millions of acres of timberland in North America. From loblolly pine and oak in the South to Douglas fir, redwood, and ponderosa pine in the Northwest, from cherry and poplar in the Appalachians to spruce and aspen in the Northeast, Georgia-Pacific owns and manages a wide variety of softwood and hardwood species.

The geographic diversity of Georgia-Pacific's timberlands requires forest management practices best suited to the species, climates, soils, and end uses of the timber. Georgia-Pacific practices forest management, including making harvesting decisions, with the understanding that the company will plant new trees or allow them to regenerate naturally and that it will consistently upgrade the economic value and environmental quality of the land.

Georgia-Pacific manages most of its forests for sawtimber. The logs usually go to sawmills or plywood plants, and the company's pulp and paper mills use the residual chips from the wood products facilities. Georgia-Pacific uses as much of each tree as possible:

The bark and other waste provide biomass fuel for boilers, and sawmill shavings, plywood trim, and sawdust become particleboard. Plywood core, the part of the log remaining after veneer has been peeled off, is sawed into two-by-fours or chipped for use at pulp mills.

Nationwide, Georgia-Pacific plants more than fifty million trees annually. It operates seed orchards, seedling nurseries, and greenhouses in most of its forest regions; natural regeneration predominates in its hardwood forests. But planting the trees is only the beginning. Georgia-Pacific foresters develop forest management plans that provide for growth and protection of the young trees, which they monitor for insects and diseases. Fire prevention is another important consideration.

Georgia-Pacific uses a variety of forest management practices. In some areas this means selective harvesting, whereas in other areas it means clear-cutting or harvesting seed trees to accelerate reforestation. Georgia-Pacific uses clear-cutting to ensure the health of new stands of such softwood species as

**Legend**

- Pulp and paper mills
- Paper converting plants
- Paper distribution
- Building products plants
- Building products distribution
- Chemical plants and research centers

**FIGURE 1.** Georgia-Pacific Operations

loblolly pine and Douglas fir because of their intolerance to shade. Georgia-Pacific also uses carefully controlled burning under the right meteorological conditions to reduce litter buildup, reduce the risk of wildfire, and improve wildlife habitats.

A top priority for Georgia-Pacific is protecting the health and safety of its employees, the communities in which it operates, and its consumers. Its 265 manufacturing facilities annually produce almost 9 million tons of pulp, paper, and paperboard, nearly 12 billion square feet of panel products, and about 2.6 billion board-feet of lumber. Consequently, it must remove large quantities of pollutants from gases discharged to the atmosphere and from effluents entering waterways. Each Georgia-Pacific plant has modern waste water treatment and emission control facilities.

Georgia-Pacific is committed to constant efforts to use manufacturing waste and by-products efficiently, as well as to recycle postconsumer waste. The company manufactures paper and building materials by recycling wastepaper and manufacturing residuals. It uses wood waste and other renewable sources to generate about 60 percent of its energy needs, and it annually recycles more than one million tons of paper and packaging to produce sanitary tissue, fax and computer papers, and containerboard. All of the paperboard that Georgia-Pacific uses to sheathe its gypsum wallboard is recycled, and it uses recycled paper fiber in its asphalt roofing. These efforts make Georgia-Pacific a recycling leader in the U.S. pulp and paper industry, which is reusing more than 33 percent of the country's wastepaper, with a goal of 40 percent by 1995. As much as half of the fiber used by some Georgia-Pacific plants is recycled.

Georgia-Pacific and the forest products industry are genuinely concerned about the quality of our air and water. As a result, the pulp and paper industry alone has spent more than $8 billion on pollution control since 1970; the industry spent $1 billion in 1988 alone. By reducing pollutants such as sulfur dioxide, dioxins, and particulate matter, air and water quality have improved significantly. To this end, Georgia-Pacific pioneered the installation of the wet electrostatic precipitators to control air emissions from flake dryers used in oriented strand board plants.

Environmental considerations have a major influence on Georgia-Pacific's decisions to locate a new facility or expand the capacity of an existing one.

## Operations at Georgia-Pacific Corp.

Georgia-Pacific's 1990 merger with Great Northern Nekoosa Corp. made it one of the nation's leading forest products companies. Figure 1 shows its facilities. It successfully integrated the Georgia-Pacific and Great Northern Nekoosa operations and reorganized its pulp and paper business. In addition, the company's building products business produced operating profits of $423 million despite difficult industry and economic conditions and higher interest costs.

Table 1 presents a comparison of key financial figures for 1989 and 1990.

## Pulp and Paper

The company produces containerboard and packaging, fax and computer papers, market pulp, tissue, groundwood papers, and envelopes at 108 facilities in the United States and one in Canada. Georgia-Pacific's annual paper and paperboard capacity of 7.1 million tons represents about 8 percent of the total annual capacity in the United States. The company also produces 1.8 million tons of market pulp each year for shipment worldwide and

**TABLE 1.** Key Financial Information (1989–1990) (Dollar amounts, except per share; shares are in millions)

| | 1990 | 1989 | Change |
|---|---|---|---|
| Net sales | $12,665 | $10,171 | 25% |
| Net Income | 365 | 661 | (45) |
| Earnings per share | 4.28 | 7.42 | (42) |
| Cash provided by operations* | 1,223 | 1,358 | (10) |
| Cash dividends paid | 139 | 130 | 7 |
| Total assets at year end | 12,060 | 7,056 | 71 |
| Return on equity | 13.4% | 25.1% | |
| Total debt to capital | 63.6% | 40.1% | |
| Cash dividends paid per share of common stock | $1.60 | 1.45 | 10% |
| Shares of common stock outstanding at year end | 86.7 | 86.7 | – |
| Shareholders of record at year end | 48,000 | 49,000 | (2) |
| Employees at year end | 63,000 | 44,000 | 43 |

*Excluding $850 million proceeds from the sale of accounts receivable in 1990

is one of the country's biggest paper distributors, with 82 outlets in 32 states.

Pulp and paper product sales for 1990 by major product lines were as follows:

| Sales Category | Percentage of Sales | Sales $ Million |
|---|---|---|
| Containerboard and packaging | 36% | $2,440 |
| Fax and computer papers | 20% | 1,360 |
| Market pulp | 12% | 779 |
| Tissue | 11% | 719 |
| Groundwood papers | 5% | 305 |
| Paper distribution and envelopes | 15% | 1,027 |
| Other | 1% | 72 |
| | | $6,702 |

## Building Products

Georgia-Pacific is one of the nation's leading manufacturers and distributors of building products. The company produces plywood, oriented strand board and other wood panels, lumber, gypsum products, roofing, chemicals, and other products at 153 facilities located throughout the United States. Georgia-Pacific sells most of its building products through its distribution division, which operates 143 distribution centers in 45 states. In addition, the distribution centers purchase a variety of items from other manufacturers to supplement the company's production and offer a broader line of building products.

Building products sales for 1990 by major product line were as follows:

| Sales Category | Percentage of Sales | Sales $ Million |
|---|---|---|
| Wood panels | 39% | $2,296 |
| Lumber | 33% | 1,966 |
| Gypsum products | 5% | 270 |
| Chemicals | 4% | 247 |
| Roofing | 3% | 192 |
| Other | 16% | 952 |
| | | $5,923 |

## Timber and Timberlands

Georgia-Pacific owns millions of acres of timberland, most of it near the company's manufacturing facilities. Georgia-Pacific's fee timberlands (leased timberlands) and other timber controlled by another party supply a substantial portion of the company's wood fiber requirements. Figure 2 shows the locations and sizes of Georgia-Pacific's North American timberlands.

Georgia-Pacific uses the latest advances in technology to make its production operations more efficient. Computers at its paper mills help it trim multi-ton paper rolls into smaller rolls for less waste. Lasers and computers in its sawmills determine how to cut logs for maximum yield, and thin saws produce more lumber and less sawdust. Laser sensors, computerized controls, and other technological advances installed in its plywood plants allow it to peel the most veneer possible from each log. The company continually invests in new, advanced equipment or in improving existing equipment to make sure that customers receive high-quality products. It also invests both time and money in training employees to apply proven quality control techniques.

## Production Operations: Pine Sawmill, Palatka, Florida

Georgia-Pacific's pine sawmill at Palatka, Florida, is a typical production facility in the forest products industry. Figure 3 is a flow diagram of the production operations there.

Tree-length logs come into the mill by truck, are weighed and off-loaded with mobile log-handling equipment, and stored in the log yard. The mobile log-handling equipment reclaims logs from storage and loads them into the log cut-up system. Here, the logs are cut to multiples of nominal lumber lengths (8 through 20 feet) and conveyed to a "debarker," which removes the bark from the logs; bark is collected and conveyed to a truck loading system for sale as a mulch or as fuel for waste-wood-fired boilers.

Debarked logs are cut to the nominal log lengths; the tops, and other portions of the log that are unacceptable for lumber making, go into a chipper. Meanwhile, the cut logs move to the sawmill, where they are sawed into rough lumber, and the waste is turned into chips.

All the chips pass over a screen that removes pieces that are too fine or too big, the *fines* and the *overs*, respectively. The overs go back through the chipper, then are loaded on trucks that head for sales centers or pulp and paper mills. (From the pine sawmill in Palatka they go to a nearby Georgia-Pacific mill.) The fine chips are combined with the sawdust from the sawmill and from the log cut-up system and are stored for use as a fuel for the kiln.

Meanwhile, the roughly sized green lumber moves to a stacker, where it is stacked in "bunks"

**FIGURE 2.** Georgia-Pacific Timberlands

Legend
• 50,000 acres of Timber
(fee acres, not to scale)

North American Fee Acreage as of January 31, 1992

| State, Country | Fee Acres | State, Country | Fee Acres |
|---|---|---|---|
| Alabama | 82,186 | Oklahoma | 123,645 |
| Arkansas | 778,610 | Oregon | 313,271 |
| California | 321,358 | Pennsylvania | 23,394 |
| Florida | 484,880 | South Carolina | 301,983 |
| Georgia | 923,157 | Tennessee | 69 |
| Kentucky | 13,680 | Texas | 24,599 |
| Louisiana | 124,938 | Viginia | 102,704 |
| Maine | 2,589,305 | Washington | 50,632 |
| Minnesota | 39 | West Virginia | 308,187 |
| Mississippi | 813,040 | Wisconsin | 260,602 |
| North Carolina | 189,377 | Canada | 372,510 |
| | | Total | 8,203,166 |

approximately twelve feet high. One-inch sticks separate the layers to allow air to circulate through the lumber during the drying process. The lumber goes next to the kilns, which dry it further. The lumber cools and stabilizes before moving on to the planing mill, which removes the rough surface, cuts out any defects, and trims the lumber to its required length. The planed and trimmed lumber is stacked into standard package sizes, ready for sale to the customer.

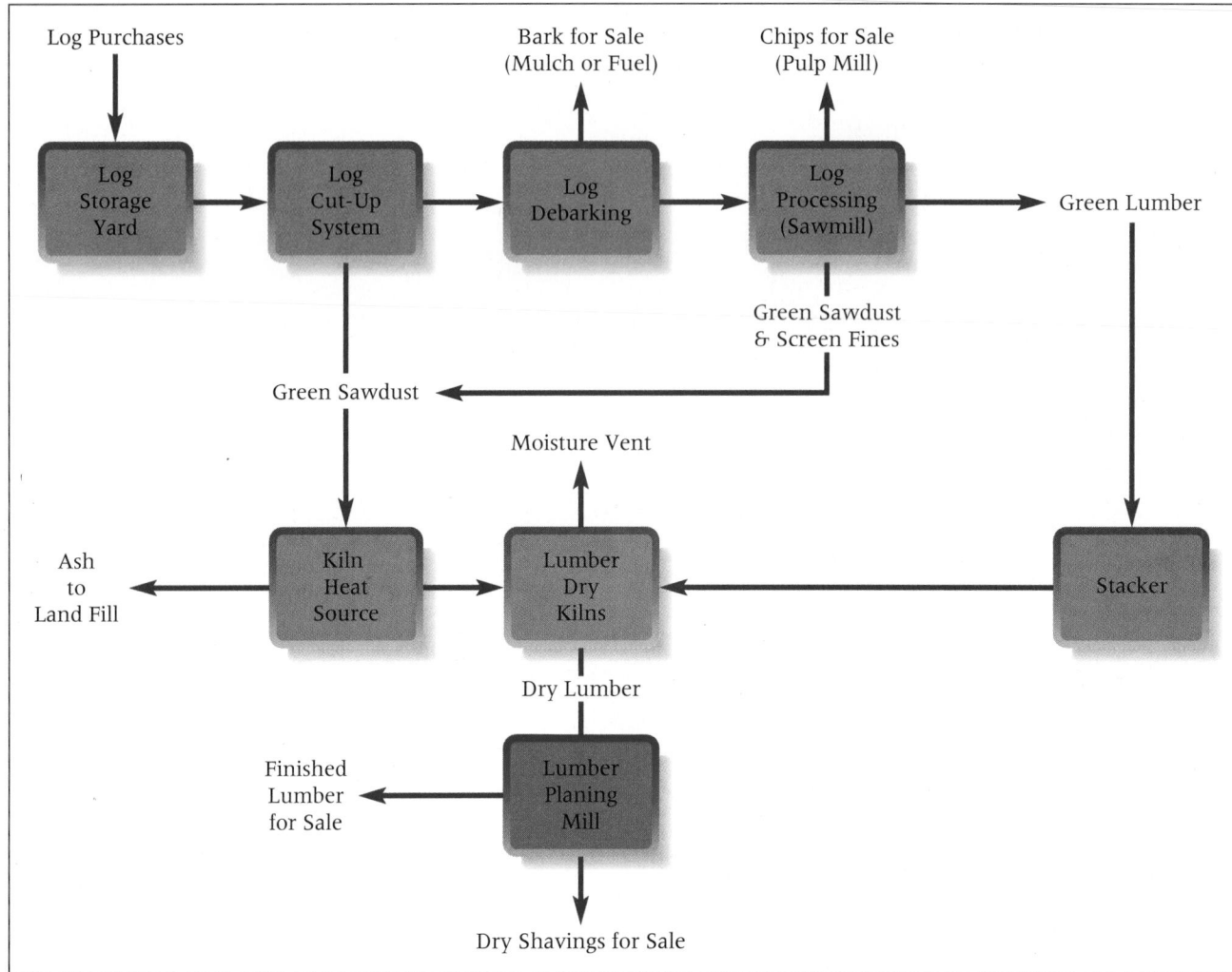

**FIGURE 3.** Flow Diagram—Pine Sawmill, Palatka, Fl.

The system collects the shavings from the planing mill and conveys them to a truck-loading system for sale as a raw material in the manufacture of particleboard and as bedding for chickens and horses.

## Capacity Planning at Palatka

The Palatka pine sawmill is an excellent example of the capacity-planning process at Georgia-Pacific. Georgia-Pacific bases changes in capacity and the timing of the changes primarily on

- Market conditions: As markets grow, Georgia-Pacific increases its production capacity to meet the demands.

- Technology: Changes in technology mean that the company can increase its production capacity with only minor equipment changes.
- Equipment: Georgia-Pacific uses improvements in existing equipment, or installs new equipment, to achieve significant increases in production capacity.

By buying the Palatka pine sawmill from Wadsworth Lumber Co. in 1987, Georgia-Pacific increased its lumber production capacity in a strategic market area. At the time of sale, the capacity of the mill (built in 1970) was seriously restricted, and Wadsworth had been taking its lumber to another location for kiln drying and dressing. Georgia-Pacific expanded the operation and greatly improved its efficiency, adding drying kilns, a planer mill for finishing the lumber on site, and warehouses for storing the finished lumber.

The specific major factors Georgia-Pacific considered in deciding whether to buy and expand the Palatka sawmill in 1987 were

1. Market conditions—This location gave Georgia-Pacific a distinct advantage over its major competitors by positioning it closer to major Florida markets. Because of the rapid population growth in Florida and the boom in home construction, market conditions for a plant were excellent.
2. Raw materials—The company owned forests in the area, which also had other stands of privately owned timber.
3. Environment—The company judged this site, as opposed to alternates, to be environmentally clean, based on a rigorous environmental assessment. Florida has stringent environmental rules that make it more difficult to build a new plant than to purchase a clean existing plant.
4. Economics—The company's analysis of its return on the investment necessary to make changes and build new facilities showed that buying and expanding the sawmill would be economically viable.
5. Labor—Georgia-Pacific's nearby facility meant that the sawmill could draw on a nucleus of trained personnel.
6. Equipment—The existing sawmill had much of the basic equipment Georgia-Pacific required for the operation; it was on a railroad spur and close to a good road system and electricity facilities.

Overall, the mill offered excellent potential for capacity expansion.

Georgia-expanded the sawmill in 1988, and it has contributed greatly to the company's success since that time.

# Production Operations: Oriented Strand Board Plant, Skippers, Virginia

Georgia-Pacific's oriented strand board (OSB) plant at Skippers, Virginia, is another good example of a typical production facility in the forest products industry. Figure 4 is a flow diagram that shows the production operations at Skippers.

As at Palatka, tree-length logs are weighed, off-loaded, and stored. The OSB process begins with loading the stored logs into the log-slasher system, which cuts them to nominal lengths, and moves them to the debarker. The facility reclaims the bark and sends it through a bark hog, which reduces bark and trimmed log ends to acceptable size. The material is stored for use as fuel.

The debarked, eight-foot logs are cut into three short blocks, which disc flakers reduce to "strand" form. Each strand is 1 inch by 4 inches by 0.025 inches thick; they are stored in 5,000-cubic-foot bins that meter them into the flake dryers. Gases from the plant's heating equipment pneumatically convey the strands through the dryers to decrease their moisture content.

Screens separate the excess fine material from the acceptably sized strands. The fines are either sold as "furnish" (raw material) to particleboard plants or stored for fuel. The acceptable strands are stored in bins and ultimately sent to blenders that coat the strands with wax and thermosetting resin. These resinated strands move to the forming machine, where they are placed on a moving belt to form a three-ply "matt" that is 8 feet wide by 24 feet long. A hot press holds the matts under heat and pressure for about five minutes.

The rough edges of the pressed OSBs are trimmed, and the boards are cut to commercial sizes (generally 4 feet by 8 feet but as large as 8 feet by 24 feet). The board may then be sanded or its edges given a tongue-and-groove treatment, depending on the use to which the finished board will be put.

The boards, which are used in construction, are graded, stacked, and strapped, the edges of the board sealed to retard water absorption, and then stored in the warehouse for shipment to the customer.

# Facility Location: The Skippers Oriented Strand Board Plant

The OSB plant at Skippers is an excellent example of the process Georgia-Pacific uses to locate a new facility. In the mid-1980s the company became interested in building additional manufacturing facilities for oriented strand board, a new product and one that required a lot of machinery to manufacture. At that time the company had OSB plants in Maine and North Carolina.

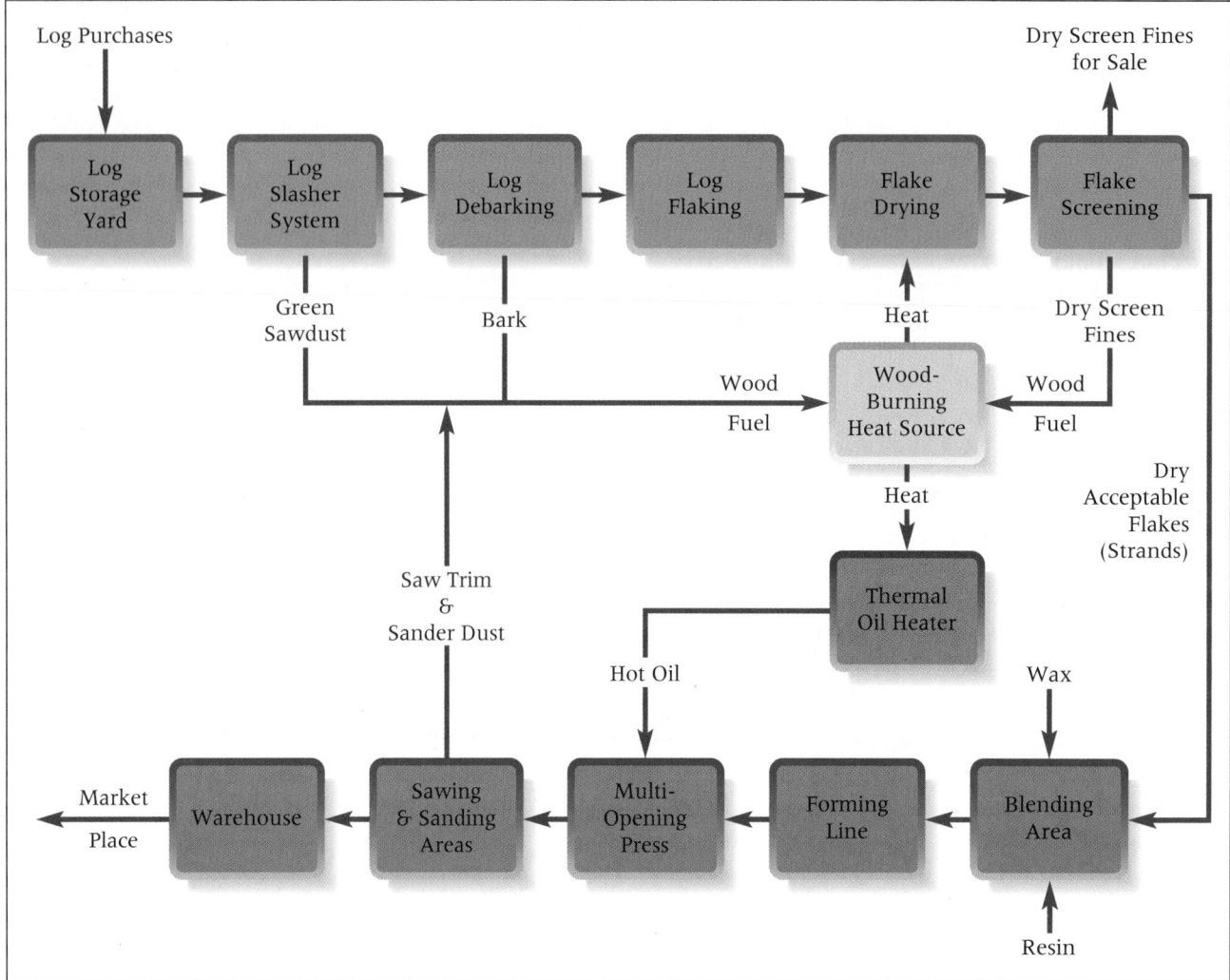

**FIGURE 4.** Flow Diagram—OSB Plant, Skippers, Va.

Georgia-Pacific bases its decision on where to locate new facilities on several major factors:

1. Market conditions—Georgia-Pacific requires a current or anticipated market for the material to be produced and the by-products to be generated. A survey of market conditions indicated demand for the product would be strong and determined that Skippers is within twenty-four hours of two-thirds of the population of the United States.

2. Raw materials—The company requires an adequate supply of reasonably priced raw materials for its plants. Both company-owned and privately owned but competitively priced timber must be available locally. The production of oriented strand board also requires resin plant capacity. The Skippers was near an excellent timber base and resin plant, and plants nearby could use the residuals.

3. Labor—Georgia-Pacific needs a trainable local labor force. The company planned to use team management—all employees are salaried—in the plant. Virginia helped the company find team-oriented employees by screening and evaluating all candidates. The state also reimbursed the company for the cost of training new employees.

4. Government—Georgia-Pacific tries to locate in areas where state and local governments

welcome industry. The company looks at such factors as enforcement attitudes and policies of environmental agencies, taxes (sales, property, workers' compensation, etc.), and the attitudes of the local citizenry toward industry. Georgia-Pacific considered Virginia's laws and enforcement policies to be fair with respect to air, water, and solid waste pollution control. Local government officials and citizens were quite favorably disposed to the proposed new plant at Skippers, primarily because the company was already a factor in the area.

5. Utilities—Georgia-Pacific's operations need a reliable source of electricity at a competitive cost. Similarly, it needs an adequate source of water, either from municipal systems or from wells drilled on site. Availability of natural gas and/or municipal sewage disposal systems can also be important. All the necessary utilities were available at the Skippers site.

Georgia-Pacific uses these factors to establish a preliminary list of plant sites. It emphasizes market conditions and its raw materials surveys. Georgia-Pacific's land management and procurement people work with local and state industrial development groups and representatives from local utilities to compile the list. The company's engineering department reviews the list and makes a final recommendation by focusing on

- Land cost
- Site development cost
- Availability of electrical power, water, and sewers
- Adequacy of highway and rail systems
- Environmental concerns

The return-on-investment analysis of the project as a whole includes information gleaned from the site selection process.

The OSB plant at Skippers, which began operations in 1985, has become the company's northernmost southern plant. It afforded the company a great competitive advantage in the OSB market, because it became the plant closest to the predominant OSB markets and has contributed greatly to the company's success since.

## ▶ Conclusion

Increases in production capacity and the acquisition or building of new production facilities are a way of life at Georgia-Pacific, because it emphasizes growth.

Overall, the company operates in a team fashion by soliciting suggestions and obtaining information from a number of sources and people. It then evaluates potential capacity increases or potential new plant sites by using a checklist of major factors. Decisions in these areas are always made with the goal of contributing to the company's growth, and market demand is an overriding consideration. Environmental considerations are also important, because the company is totally dependent on natural resources, most notably timber, for its existence. Labor, equipment, and technology also are important factors in any decision.

The company does make detailed cost analyses and return-on-investment calculations for its capacity-planning and facility location decisions. As a rule, it does not use optimization, decision tree, or simulation methods. Rather, it stresses the importance of analyzing key decision factors. In relation to the material presented in Chapter 6, we observe that Georgia-Pacific's approach to making decisions in these areas is objective yet qualitative rather than quantitative. The experience and judgment of its management personnel are keys to its successfully increasing capacity and locating new production facilities.

## ▶ Acknowledgements

The preparation of this case was greatly assisted by a number of Georgia-Pacific personnel, including Davis K. Mortensen, executive vice president for building products; W. L. Duke, group vice president for wood products manufacturing; L. G. Chambers, group manager for manufactured board; A. T. Johnson, manager of engineering for the building products manufacturing division; G. W. McVicker, Jr., manager of land and timber for the northeastern region; B. C. Zoffmann, director of corporate communications, W. D. Rose, vice president for millwork and specialties; and C. T. Ellis, general sales manager for molding operations in the millwork and specialities division.

The authors sincerely appreciate the assistance and cooperation of all these individuals. We drew material for the case study from the following sources:

Georgia-Pacific Corp. *Georgia-Pacific Annual Report, 1990.* Atlanta: Georgia-Pacific Corp., 1990.

———. *A Natural Partnership: Georgia-Pacific and the Environment.* Atlanta: Georgia-Pacific Corp., 1990.

———. *Georgia-Pacific 1990 Facts and Statistics.* Atlanta: Georgia-Pacific Corp., December 31, 1990.

———. *Georgia-Pacific Corporation, Operating and Statistical Information, 1990–1991,* Atlanta: Georgia-Pacific Corp., 1991.

Ross, John R. *MAVERICK—The Story of Georgia-Pacific.* Atlanta: Georgia-Pacific Corp., 1980.

## ► Discussion Questions

1. Discuss the production process at Georgia-Pacific's Palatka, Florida, pine sawmill, relating it to the types of manufacturing operations described in Chapter 1.

2. Discuss the production process at Georgia-Pacific's Skippers, Virginia, oriented strand board plant, relating it to the types of manufacturing operations described in Chapter 1.

3. Which capacity-timing strategy does Georgia-Pacific use? What factors influence its capacity-timing strategy?

4. What were the major factors Georgia-Pacific used to make its capacity expansion decision? What other factors might the company have considered?

5. What technique did Georgia-Pacific use in making its facility location decision? What other facility location factors might the company have considered?

6. How do environmental considerations affect capacity-planning and facility location decisions at Georgia-Pacific?

# Pohang Iron and Steel Co., Ltd.

In December 1990 the Kwangyang Steel Works of the Pohang Iron and Steel Co., Ltd., (POSCO) completed the third phase of an expansion project that pushed capacity at Kwangyang to 8.1 million tons annually. The total capacity of POSCO is 17.55 million tons annually, which ranks it third in the world after Nippon Steel of Japan and Usinor-Sacilor of France. At the same time Korea has become the sixth-biggest steel producer in the world, with a total capacity of 25.7 million tons annually.

How has the Korean steel industry, embodied by POSCO, become one of the world's most competitive producers of iron and steel products in just over twenty years? This case provides an overview, from the viewpoint of manufacturing strategy, of this giant in world steelmaking.

By the late 1960s the Korean government had decided to make the construction of an integrated steelworks a major priority in its economic development. At that time Korea could produce only 23 percent of the steel it needed. The result was POSCO, founded in 1968; its first phase, with a capacity of 1.03 million metric tons per year, was completed in 1973 at Pohang, Korea.

A private-sector initiative followed the effort begun by the Korean government. The private initiative took the form of entrepreneurship, and one of its major functions was dealing with the government. The company's founder, and incumbent chairman of its board of directors, Tae-Joon Park, assumed this entrepreneurial role in a dynamic manner, focusing first on government relations and the financing of POSCO's first integrated steelworks and subsequently on strategic markets. For example, in recent years his leadership has stressed the diversification and internationalization of POSCO.

Tae-Joon Park is a legendary figure in Korea. He had no previous experience, but he managed to build the first blast furnace in a developing country. He obtained massive amounts of technical assistance from Japanese steel industry leaders after a proposed international consortium—the Korea International Steel Association—did not work out. He was a major force in all construction activities, developed the company's management structure and operating policies, and created a strong work ethic among its employees. In summary, he is the much admired father of the Korean steel industry.

After POSCO was founded in 1968 the first phase of steelworks was started in 1970 at Pohang, Korea, and completed in 1973 with an initial capacity of 1.03 million metric tons annually. The second phase of the steelworks was completed at Pohang in 1976, bringing the total capacity to 2.6 million metric tons annually; the third phase was completed in 1978, bringing the total capacity to 5.5 million metric tons annually; and the fourth phase was completed in 1983, bringing the total capacity to 9.1 million metric tons annually. The fourth and final phase at Kwangyang was to be completed by late September 1992. At that point POSCO's total steelmaking capacity became 20.8 million metric tons annually. It employed 22,000 people in 1989 and had total sales of $6,408 million. Most important, POSCO produces 80 percent of all steel produced in Korea, and Korea has to import only 18 percent of its steel.

POSCO's initial objective was to position itself as a catalyst for Korean industrialization by manufacturing and supplying a growing volume of low-cost steel to Korean industries. Its basic strategy was to produce at low cost, so that it could sell low-priced products at home. As a consequence Korean steel users have been able to produce at a low price, increase their market share, and expand. POSCO has made an especially important contribution to the rising level of Korean exports. A comparison of costs and prices among international companies shows that POSCO has achieved its strategic goal of being a low-cost producer. More recently it has begun producing specialty steels, emphasizing a wider product range.

POSCO has established itself as a world-class steel and iron producer. The major factors contributing to its international competitiveness are

1. *Reductions in construction costs.* POSCO has been able to keep its construction costs to a minimum without jeopardizing the quality of construction or production, partly because its labor costs are inexpensive but, more important, because Korean construction periods usually are short. POSCO took only 33 months to build its first blast furnace, whereas the first in Italy took 50 months, France 74 months, and India 101 months. POSCO also has secured low-cost investment capital from foreign sources, most notable the Japanese Export-Import Bank. Another important source of capital was the $500 million reparation fund paid by Japan in compensation for that country's earlier colonization of Korea. The average cost of construction, between the Pohang and Kwangyang steelworks, was about $422 per ton of crude steel, compared with steelworks in other countries that cost $600 to $800 per ton of crude steel.

2. *Use of latest technologies.* POSCO has used the latest technologies in both the construction of its steelworks and in its manufacturing processes. A major theme in Korea's economic development has been industrialization through learning and the absorption of technology. Widespread use of apprenticeships, domestically and abroad, in order to increase technical knowledge contributed to Korea's industrial development. Many Korean workers gained practical experience in construction in the Middle East, for example.

3. *Economical plant location and layout.* POSCO was able to economically purchase large tracts of coastal land at Pohang and Kwangyang for the sites of the steelworks. At both sites the Korean government provided the necessary domestic infrastructure to facilitate rapid access to domestic markets. The coastal locations of the steelworks allow easy transfer of raw materials and finished products from and to ships, providing savings on transportation costs. The layouts of the steelworks are designed to move materials through the manufacturing stages with minimal handling.

4. *Economic and stable sources of raw materials.* Korea is almost totally lacking in the raw materials needed to produce steel, but POSCO has been able to secure economic and stable sources of raw materials. It imports most coking coal from three countries, Australia, Canada, and the United States. POSCO is now joint owner of the Mt. Thorley coal mine in Australia and the Greenhills coal mine in Canada. India, Brazil, and Peru supply its iron ore.

5. *Effective human resources management.* During its start-up years one of POSCO's advantages was an abundance of inexpensive labor with military training and discipline. Its labor cost is rising, but it remains low in comparison with other industrialized nations'. For example, in 1988 its labor costs were 45 percent of those experienced by Japan.

POSCO attempts to provide for all the welfare needs of its 22,000 employees. It has built excellent manufacturing facilities, and employee wages are kept higher than the national average for manufacturing. It has also created a complete social welfare system, offering quality housing at reduced rates and free schooling for employees' children at its own well-regarded schools. It also provides extensive shopping, cultural, educational, and recreational facilities.

POSCO personnel undergo extensive training, which uses Japanese training and apprenticeship programs, to overcome the lack of skilled steelmaking expertise in Korea. POSCO founded its own technical high school, where the core curriculum trains students to move into jobs at the company. It also founded a training institute, which runs many management, technical, and language courses. A few employees are selected to go overseas for long study periods financed by the company.

At the managerial level it has adopted a policy that stresses flexibility in responding to changes in its markets. From its beginning POSCO has used management techniques for strategic planning, budgeting, and control, and management by objectives. POSCO made concentrated efforts to computerize its production and business systems and was the first corporation in Korea to introduce local area network and value-added network systems. It also uses television links among Pohang, Kwangyang, and Seoul for its thrice-weekly directors' meetings.

POSCO has made a major commitment to create a comfortable and safe working environment for its workers. Its environmental objectives are embodied in the slogan "A Steel Mill in a Green Park," and it has installed the most advanced pollution control equipment at its steelworks. It invests more than 10 percent of its capital in pollution control equipment, more than three times the industrywide average.

One of POSCO's major strategies for the future is diversification, because it believes that demand for steel in Korea will peak around the turn of the century. It is actively seeking new products and services, most notable in the information/communications and chemical industries. A major problem faced by POSCO in its diversification efforts is the presence of the *chaebol* conglomerates in all major Korean industries, which make entry in an attractive industry difficult. Chaebols are the Korean equivalent of large conglomerates composed of several companies involved in several industries.

To further its long-term diversification strategy, it founded two science and technology institutions in 1987: Research Institute of Science and Technology (RIST), a research institute, and Pohang Institute of Science and Technology (POSTECH), a small university. RIST has four major divisions, more than twenty research departments, and more than four hundred full-time researchers. Its research fields range from economics and management strategy to biomedical engineering, mechatronics, and new materials. POSTECH is a research-oriented institution with a small and select number of students. It maintains a low student-professor ratio, which allows professors to devote more time to basic research. POSCO has formed a three-part system that integrates industry, research, and a university and is designed to encourage interchange in the form of shared personnel, information, and research material.

Another major strategy being pursued by POSCO is increasing the share in its total sales mix of products that add a lot of value during manufacturing. POSCO is behind its major Japanese competitors in developing higher value-added products, and it is attempting to mobilize its research and development resources in RIST to develop new products and to radically improve iron and steelmaking technologies.

The success of the Pohang Iron and Steel Co., Ltd., has indeed been remarkable and has made a major contribution to the emergence of Korea as a economic force in Asia and throughout the world. Future prospects for POSCO remain good, but it does face major problems. One is the pooling of resources in research and development in the United States and Japan by multicompany research consortia; POSCO is a lone, integrated company with limited resources and research capabilities. The relative scarcity of high-quality scrap iron in Korea may retard the application of new technologies such as thin slab and strip casting. Japan is also planning for massive modernization of its steelmaking facilities in the late 1990s and has taken major steps to reduce costs and put more resources into research and development. Finally, a leadership vacuum may occur when Tae-Joon Park retires, although POSCO has prepared for that by creating the post of vice chairman, occupied by an experienced and able executive.

## ▶ Acknowledgements

The authors would like to acknowledge the valuable assistance provided by Dr. Sung-Il Juhn, vice president and executive director of the Management and Economic Research Center at the Research Institute of Science and Technology, Pohang, Korea, in the preparation of this case study. Other sources included

Juhn, Sung-Il. "Challenge of a Latecomer: The Case of the Korean Steel Industry with Specific Reference to POSCO," in *Changing Patterns of International Rivalry: Some Lessons from the Steel Industry*, ed. Etsuo Abe and Yoshitaka Suzuki (Tokyo: University of Tokyo Press), 1991.

Pohang Iron and Steel Co., Ltd., and Research Institute of Science and Technology. Internal company technical reports.

"POSCO's Production Capacity Ranks 3rd in the World," *Korea Herald*, December 5, 1990, special supplement.

## ▶ Discussion Questions

1. What are the major factors that have contributed to POSCO's success in international competition?
2. What are POSCO's major strategies for maintaining its competitive edge in the future?
3. What problems might POSCO face in the future?

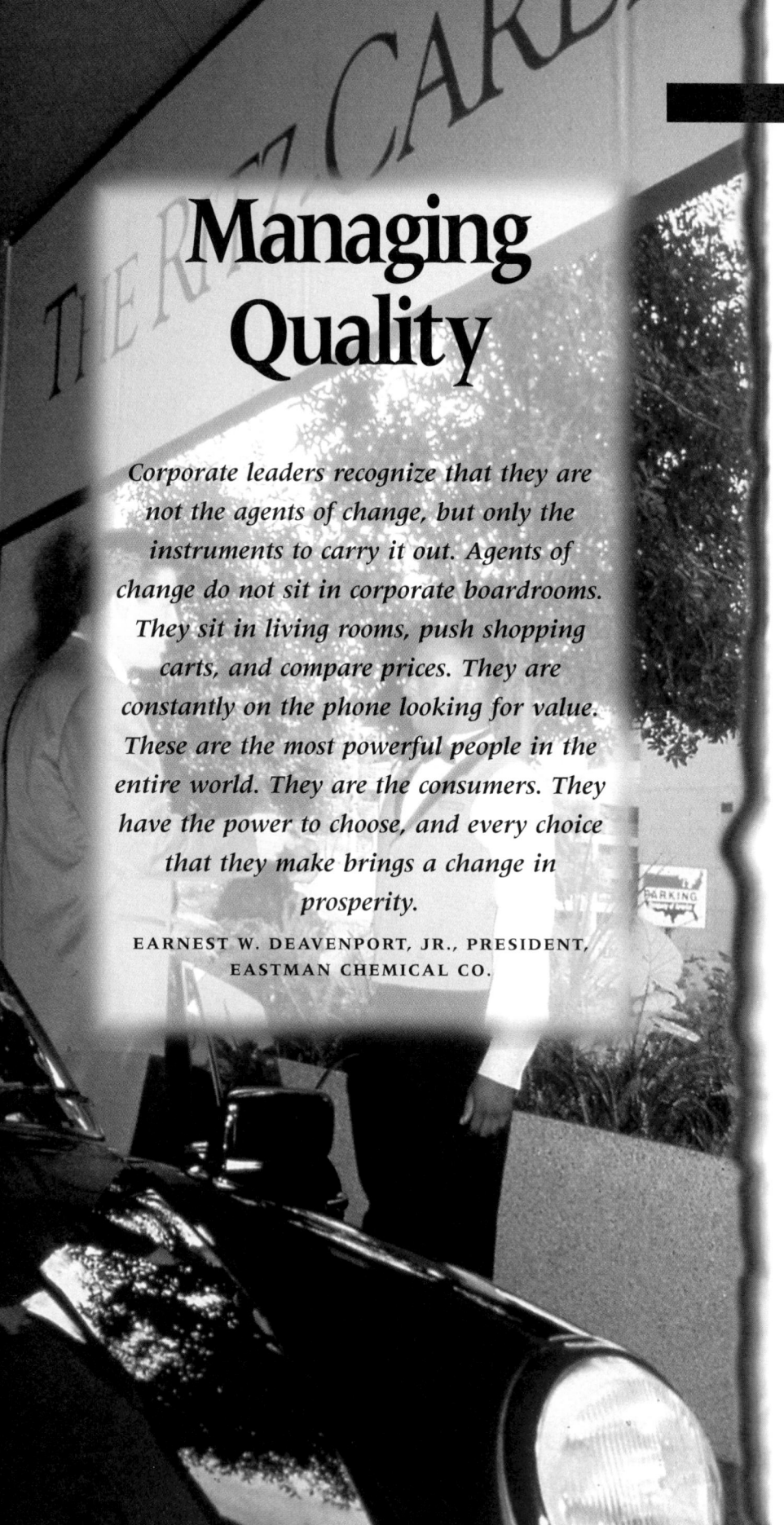

# Managing Quality

*Corporate leaders recognize that they are not the agents of change, but only the instruments to carry it out. Agents of change do not sit in corporate boardrooms. They sit in living rooms, push shopping carts, and compare prices. They are constantly on the phone looking for value. These are the most powerful people in the entire world. They are the consumers. They have the power to choose, and every choice that they make brings a change in prosperity.*

EARNEST W. DEAVENPORT, JR., PRESIDENT, EASTMAN CHEMICAL CO.

## CHAPTER 7

Introduction

Quality in Historical Perspective

Quality Management as a Strategic Issue
*OPERATIONS MANAGEMENT IN PRACTICE 7.1: The Ritz-Carlton Hotel Co.*
*OPERATIONS MANAGEMENT IN PRACTICE 7.2: Chrysler Mounts Campaign to Cut Defects*
*OPERATIONS MANAGEMENT IN PRACTICE 7.3: 1993 Baldrige Award Winners*

Quality Management Leadership

Definitions of Quality

Quality-related Product Characteristics

Quality-related Service Characteristics

Costs of Quality

Total Quality Management

Business Process Reengineering
*OPERATIONS MANAGEMENT IN PRACTICE 7.4: Reengineering Taco Bell*

Case Study: Cadillac Motor Car Co.

1. Summarize historical developments in quality management
2. Describe Deming's chain reaction of quality events
3. Describe the various definitions of *quality*
4. Define three terms used to describe product quality characteristics
5. Define five terms used to describe service quality characteristics

6. Describe the four types of quality costs
7. Define *total quality management*, and list organizational requirements for its successful implementation
8. Describe the difference between continuous process improvement and business process reengineering

## Introduction

The concept of quality in manufacturing and service delivery systems is the subject of a revolution in American industry. Intense competition from Japan and Western Europe in all markets, from automobiles to computer chips, forced American businesses to take a closer look at their business practices. They found that the solution to the international quality challenge was more than a revolution in engineering and operations. It would require rethinking of strategies developed throughout the organization, from marketing and human resources to the financial areas, and a different management style to carry out the new strategies.

The focus of this chapter is on managing the strategic quality activities of the company to enhance competitive position. The concepts discussed in this chapter are not new but are different from those that many organizations are practicing. In fact, most statistical concepts that are an integral part of any comprehensive quality process have been known for well over fifty years. Clearly, this knowledge alone has not been sufficient to reach competitive goals in regard to the quality of products and services.

## Quality in Historical Perspective

Development of the concept and practice of quality in manufacturing and service organizations continues to evolve. In his book *Managing Quality*, David Garvin explains the history of the American quality movement as a sequential changing of focus over time.[1] He calls these significant phases in quality practice the *eras of inspection, statistical quality control, quality assurance,* and most recent, *strategic quality management.*

The initial drive for quality practices in manufactured goods arose from the desire to produce parts that were interchangeable. Rifle and armament manufacturers, the Singer Sewing Machine Co., and McCormick Harvester Co. wanted to be able to replace broken parts on their equipment from a stock of spares. They

[1]David Garvin, *Managing Quality: The Strategic and Competitive Edge* (New York: Free Press, 1988), pp. 3–38.

did it by using "master parts" to which all manufactured parts were compared. The master parts were manufactured to extremely close tolerances, so if a newly produced part precisely matched the master part, it was deemed to be a quality part. The comparison consisted of visual **inspection**, or matching, and later included developing and using gauges to take more precise measurements.

In 1931 W. A. Shewhart of Bell Laboratories began to develop techniques for predicting the quality of manufactured goods by using the relatively new science of statistics. This **statistical quality control** developed in several directions simultaneously. In each case Bell Labs researchers used results obtained from the inspection of a sample of items to infer characteristics of the entire population of items. Shewhart's work was oriented toward process control through inspection and resulted in the development of the first process control charts.

Shewhart's colleagues, Harold Dodge and Harry Romig, used sampling principles to determine the acceptability of a lot of raw material or finished goods. They successfully developed models of the average outgoing quality limit (AOQL) so that they could use samples to make generalizations about the entire manufacturing process. Bell Labs was interested in developing statistical quality control techniques because of its parent company's monopoly on developing the nation's telephone system; the company needed to closely monitor the quality of parts used in its manufacturing process to ensure a steady supply of reliable and interchangeable components for a huge market. The process they developed is called *acceptance sampling.*

During World War II manufacturers of war-related materiel used the information developed by Bell Labs in their production facilities. The MIL-STD (military standard) tables were developed to facilitate use of acceptance sampling. Acceptance sampling was relatively easy and quick to implement, but the decision to use it probably played a significant role in constraining future quality practices in the United States after the war. Most organizations began to focus on the quality of incoming material and the quality of outgoing products, for which acceptance sampling techniques were most useful. Procedures for monitoring the quality of work in process never were widely used. Chapter 19 offers a more thorough description of statistical techniques for the control of quality.

By 1951 Joseph Juran was finding that improving quality could drastically reduce the cost of quality. This idea, plus Armand Feigenbaum's assertion in 1956—that quality is the responsibility of all workers and managers—were the cornerstones of the **quality assurance** approach to quality. In the early 1960s Philip Crosby was an employee at the Martin Co. when it manufactured the first defect-free Pershing missile for the U.S. Army. To do it, Martin Co. enlisted the assistance of every employee to set up, test, and assemble the missile in a way that minimized the risk of a nonconformity. Martin's management realized in retrospect that the change in its philosophy of work force management and participation was the greatest contributor to the zero-defects missile. This early experience of Crosby's undoubtedly contributed to the development of his concept that "quality is free."

Today quality is understood to be a strategic issue that affects everyone and every process within any organization. The remainder of this chapter discusses quality management as a strategic issue and how quality improvement may be "institutionalized" in order to have positive effects on organizational culture. Table 7.1 summarizes the four quality eras.

| Identifying Characteristics | Era of the Quality Movement | | | |
| --- | --- | --- | --- | --- |
| | Inspection | Statistical Quality Control | Quality Assurance | Strategic Quality Management |
| 1. Primary concern | Detection | Control | Coordination | Strategic impact |
| 2. View of quality | A problem to be solved | A problem to be solved | A problem to be solved but one that is attacked proactively | A competitive opportunity |
| 3. Emphasis | Product uniformity | Product uniformity with reduced inspection | The entire production chain, from design to market, and the contribution of all functional groups, especially designers, to preventing quality failures | The market and consumer needs |
| 4. Methods | Gauging and measuring | Statistical tools and techniques | Programs and systems | Strategic planning, goal setting, and mobilizing the organization |
| 5. Role of quality professionals | Inspection, sorting, counting, and grading | Troubleshooting and the application of statistical methods | Quality measurement, quality planning, and program design | Goal setting, education and training, consulting with other departments, and program design |
| 6. Assignment of responsibility for quality | The inspection department | The manufacturing and engineering departments | All departments, although top management is involved only peripherally | Everyone in the organization, with top management exercising strong leadership |
| 7. Orientation and approach | "Inspects in" quality | "Controls in" quality | "Builds in" quality | "Manages in" quality |

Source: David A. Garvin, *Managing Quality* (New York: Free Press, 1988), p. 37.

TABLE 7.1
The Four Major Quality Eras

## Quality Management as a Strategic Issue

Recognizing the competitive advantage that **strategic quality management** can give them, leading U.S. companies are increasingly using the quality of products and services to increase their share of the international market. In each case companies needed to shift their orientation from conforming to design specifications of the product or service to the customer's needs and expectations. In practice these companies seek to exceed their customers' expectations. Motorola, Inc. seeks to delight the customer rather than just meet the customer's requirements.

An organization recognized for its superior quality, the Ritz-Carlton Hotel Co., is a good illustration of the strategic nature of quality management. The hotel chain is known worldwide as a refuge for travelers who expect the best in customer service. In 1992 Ritz-Carlton received the coveted Malcolm Baldrige National Quality Award. Operations Management in Practice 7.1 tells the story of the Ritz.

The quality concept is transforming industry by challenging the survivability of companies around the globe. Quality is the critical issue for the emerging companies of the developing nations that are seeking to become the next wave of suppliers to the wealthy consumers of North America, Western Europe, and Japan. Eastern European companies frequently seek assistance in quality management and technology as they face the challenge of free markets. Also, quality is becoming more difficult to deal with, because new international markets are opening and more companies are competing for a share of those markets. Companies seeking to compete in international markets need some mechanism for demonstrating their commitment to quality.

## ISO9000 International Standards

The International Organization of Standards recently created international standards in conjunction with other organizations, such as the American National Standards Institute (ANSI). The standards are known as the **ISO9000** series, which broadly defines the components of quality in different industries.[2] The broadest element of the ISO9000 series and the most difficult to attain is ISO9001, which provides quality standards for organizations that design, produce, service, and install products. ISO9002 is the same as ISO9001 except that it omits the design and service of products. ISO9003 contains no standards for production and is more suited to a warehousing operation. The final standard, ISO9004, provides information about how to interpret the other standards and is not itself a standard to be met.

A company seeks certification in the particular standards that most pertain to its business. The motivation for certification varies from company to company, but it often is the result of economic self-defense. If you and many other companies sell a product internationally and all your competitors obtain ISO9000 certification, you may be at a disadvantage in international markets. There is much confusion about what ISO9000 certification says about a company. Certification does not necessarily mean that a company produces a quality product. Certification is based on a company's ability to establish procedure by precisely documenting its processes and then showing that it is continuing to follow prescribed procedures. ISO9000 certification guarantees consistency, not quality, and it is not customer focused. It does, however, represent a significant step toward identifying standards recognizable worldwide, which should make it easier for companies to compete in the international marketplace.

[2]Martin Ramsay, "ISO9000: The Myths and Misconceptions," *American Production and Inventory Control Society—The Performance Advantage* (June 1992): 55–58.

## OPERATIONS MANAGEMENT IN PRACTICE 7.1

# The Ritz-Carlton Hotel Co.

The Ritz-Carlton Hotel Company was a 1992 winner of the Malcolm Baldrige National Quality Award. Targeting primarily industry executives, meeting and corporate travel planners, and affluent travelers, the Atlanta-based company manages 31 luxury hotels that pursue the distinction of being the very best in each market. It does so on the strength of a comprehensive service quality program that is integrated into marketing and business objectives. Hallmarks of the program include participatory executive leadership, thorough information gathering, coordinated planning and execution, and a trained work force that is empowered "to move heaven and earth" to satisfy customers. Of these, committed employees rank as the most essential element.

Key product and service requirements of the travel consumer have been translated into Ritz-Carlton "Gold Standards," which include a credo, motto, three steps of service, and 20 "Ritz-Carlton Basics." Each employee is expected to understand and adhere to these standards, which describe processes for solving problems guests may have as well as detailed grooming, housekeeping, and safety and efficiency standards. The corporate motto is "ladies and gentlemen serving ladies and gentlemen." Workers are required to act at first notice to do whatever it takes to provide "instant pacification" in response to a customer complaint. No matter what their normal duties are, other employees must assist if aid is requested by a fellow worker who is responding to a guest's complaint or wish.

Among the data gathered and tracked over time are guest room preventive maintenance cycles per year, percentage of check-ins with no waiting, time spent to achieve industry-best clean room appearance, and time to service an occupied guest room. From automated building and safety systems to computerized reservation systems, Ritz-Carlton uses advanced technology to full advantage. For example, each employee is trained to note guest likes and dislikes. These data are entered in a computerized guest history profile that provides information on the preferences of 240,000 repeat Ritz-Carlton guests, resulting in more personalized service.

The aim of these and other customer-focused measures is not simply to meet the expectations of guests but to provide them with a "memorable visit." According to surveys conducted for Ritz-Carlton by an independent research firm, 92 to 97 percent of the company's guests leave with that impression. Evidence of the effectiveness of the company's efforts also includes the 121 quality-related awards received in 1991 and industry-best rankings by all three major hotel-rating organizations.

## Role of Quality in Manufacturing Strategy

In *Manufacturing Strategy* Terry Hill suggests a useful model for thinking about the role of quality within manufacturing strategy: evaluating a product or service from the perspective of the prospective buyer.[3] A buyer demands that certain characteristics be present in an acceptable combination in order to consider an

[3]Terry Hill, *Manufacturing Strategy* (Homewood, Ill.: Richard D. Irwin, 1989), pp. 44–45.

item in the running. The model terms these features and their respective values **qualifiers**, because the presence of these attributes puts the product on a short list of potentially acceptable alternatives. Buyers usually apply a single criterion to their list of qualified candidates in order to make a selection. The model calls this criterion the **order winner**, because it determines which company actually makes the sale. If a company wins orders because of its low prices, its products had to be of acceptable quality and reliability and their delivery timely in order to make the short list. For example, you may be trying to decide which automobile to buy after graduation. The price you can pay may be a qualifier, as might a list of features that you consider essential. It might also be true that you cannot wait several months for delivery and will choose from cars that are on dealers' lots within thirty miles of your home. Reliability may well be the order winner here.

The challenge to competing companies comes when the order-winning criteria shift. For example, U.S.-based auto makers have been striving to improve conformance to design specifications, reliability, and fuel efficiency to meet the challenge of Japanese and Western European competitors. At the same time Japanese producers have moved the quality criteria from reliable but boxy sedans with a limited range of features to new designs with features designed to delight and "mystify" the buyer. By redefining quality in the eyes of the customer, the Japanese are relegating conformance measures of quality to the category of qualifier, and meeting the new definition of quality will be necessary to win orders. Operations Management in Practice 7.2 describes one American automobile manufacturer's quest to compete internationally.

Companies noted for their services have found that quality or "perceived quality" has always been a significant determinant of an individual's willingness to select one service provider over another. The phrase "perceived quality" reflects the difficulty in assessing quality in a service environment. After a stay in the hospital, how do you assess the quality of care you received? Former patients' comments might include, "I feel better now than I did before," or "They were very nice to me." Both statements may be true, but they do not completely address the question of the quality of the care that the patients received. They are only perceptions. Patients may have received the best medical treatment possible, but bad-tasting hospital food or an unfriendly orderly can significantly affect their perception of the quality of their care. This is a major issue for health care providers interested in improving their competitiveness by improving their quality.

What is it about a department store that makes customers keep coming back? What is it about a department store that makes people swear they'll never be back? These are questions that all service providers need to be asking. Is it the value of the product or the courtesy and competence of the sales associate? Stanley Marcus, founder of Neiman Marcus and a legend in retailing, believes that "retail merchandising is actually very simple: It consists of two factors, customers and goods. If you take good care in the buying of the product, it doesn't come back. If you take good care of your customers, they do come back." He has also said that "the dollar bills I receive at competing banks are exactly alike, what's different are the tellers." Marcus's statements emphasize the important contribution that employees make in affecting customers' perception of the quality of services. Given the ever-increasing competition in all fields, businesses must pay more attention to employee training, not only to the technical skills necessary to provide a quality product but to the interpersonal skills necessary to provide that quality product in a quality way.

# Chrysler Mounts Campaign to Cut Defects

As Chrysler racks up a string of profitable quarters and new product launches, one fact has almost been lost: The Number 3 auto maker has the worst quality record of Detroit's Big Three, as determined by J.D. Power & Associates' annual initial quality survey.

To win buyers away from Honda and Toyota, Chrysler has introduced the Neon which is aimed squarely at the Honda Civic. To be successful, Chrysler made an all-out effort to make certain that the Neon launch was as flawless as possible. The company forced suppliers to explain precisely how they would ensure delivery of flawless parts. Even so, Chrysler discovered that a leaky seal in 1,100 of first 10,000 Neons built could lead to brake loss. Chrysler and AlliedSignal Inc.'s automotive division, supplier of the brakes, fixed the cars, including some 60 already in customer's hands.

J.D. Power tracks initial defects on cars—flaws ranging from a loose knob to an engine that will not start. The firm, which depends on auto makers for its revenues, will not release the names of car companies that perform worse than the industry average (1.07 defects per car in its 1992 survey). But the numbers are widely available within the industry, and they show that on average Chrysler vehicles have 1.35 defects per car. Dodge, Chrysler's volume brand, has 1.48 defects per car, twice Toyota's 0.74 defect rate.

Big Three cars and trucks as a group have more defects than the best of the Japanese—Toyota Motor Corp. and Honda Motor Co. That is one reason why, even as Japanese cars became more expensive recently as the yen rose in value, consumers still bought plenty of Japanese cars. Together, Chrysler, Ford Motor Co. and General Motors Corp. gained only 1.5 points of market share, despite a $2,000–$3,000 price advantage. But Chrysler is trying with considerable urgency to ensure that its newest products perform better than some of its recent launches, including the Chrysler Concorde and the Jeep Grand Cherokee.

Both the Concorde and Cherokee were designed for a low defect rate. They are relatively simple to build, and Chrysler says that a teamwork approach to the new vehicles meant that workers and suppliers helped engineers anticipate problems. But after the Concorde launch in 1992, Chrysler announced two separate recalls. One was to fix a defective washer that could affect steering. Then there was an engine part that could cause piston wear. Chrysler also announced two Grand Cherokee recalls affecting 65% of the vehicles it had built so far. The Jeeps had problems with the rear tailgate latch mechanism and with front suspensions.

Even though J.D. Power rates the Cherokee below the Ford Explorer and the Toyota 4-Runner, Chrysler argues that its new vehicles are extraordinarily popular with those who buy them. They claim that the survey does not adequately reflect this strong customer enthusiasm.

Chrysler is far from satisfied with its quality ratings. In addition to its new demands on suppliers, it is building prototypes earlier. With the Neon, for example, it built a precise version of the car a year before launch and flew some 1,500 workers from Illinois to a prototype assembly plant in Michigan. Workers there cooperated with engineers to perfect the vehicles and the assembly process

*continued*

with the goal of making both as simple as possible. The company also has begun to test drive every single vehicle that rolls off the production line.

At Chrysler's Belvidere, Ill., plant, where the Neon is produced, the goal is to put the Neon on J.D. Power's top-10 list of the most defect-free cars. In the early stages of development, employees drove 50 early Neons 16 hours a day in an attempt to uncover defects before the customer did, and Chrysler demanded that suppliers institute rigorous quality control checks. Even with all these precautions, several problems did occur. Early production runs were slowed because internal audits indicated defect rates were well above Chrysler goals. Even with the difficulties in reducing the number of defects as quickly as it would like, Chrysler believes that it will continue showing substantial improvements in future Power surveys.

## Malcolm Baldrige National Quality Award

President Ronald Reagan established the **Malcolm Baldrige National Quality Award** in 1987 to emphasize the government's interest in encouraging and improving quality awareness in this country. The National Bureau of Standards and the American Society for Quality Control (ASQC) administer the awards jointly and give them annually to as many as two manufacturing companies, two service companies, and two small businesses. The organizations evaluate each nominated company according to a set of criteria, awarding up to one thousand points for a grade. Representatives visit the top point-winners to further investigate the quality of their processes and improvements they have made. Table 7.2 provides the actual criteria and point values for the 1995 award; the list of winners through 1994 appears in Table 7.3. Operations Management in Practice 7.3 high-

*The Malcolm Baldrige National Quality Award is presented to E. W. Deavenport, Jr., chairman and CEO of Eastman Chemical Company, by President Clinton in a ceremony in Washington.*

T A B L E   7 . 2
Malcolm Baldrige National
Quality Award

**1995 Criteria Point Values (1,000 points maximum)**

**Leadership (90 points)**
*Senior Executive Leadership (45)*
*Leadership System and Organization (25)*
*Public Responsibility and Corporate Citizenship (20)*

**Information & Analysis (75 points)**
*Management of Information and Data (20)*
*Competitive Comparisons and Benchmarking (15)*
*Analysis and Use of Company-Level Data (40)*

**Strategic Planning (55 points)**
*Strategy Development (35)*
*Strategy Deployment (20)*

**Human Resource Development and Management (140 points)**
*Human Resource Planning and Evaluation (20)*
*High Performance Work Systems (45)*
*Employee Education, Training, and Development (50)*
*Employee Well-Being and Satisfaction (25)*

**Process Management (140 points)**
*Design and Introduction of Products and Services (40)*
*Process Management: Product and Service Production and Delivery (40)*
*Process Management: Support Services (30)*
*Management of Supplier Performance (30)*

**Business Results (250 points)**
*Product and Service Quality Results (75)*
*Company Operational and Financial Results (130)*
*Supplier Performance Results (45)*

**Customer Focus and Satisfaction (250 points)**
*Customer and Market Knowledge (30)*
*Customer Relationship Management (30)*
*Customer Satisfaction Determination (30)*
*Customer Satisfaction Results (100)*
*Customer Satisfaction Comparison (60)*

| | |
|---|---|
| **1994** | AT&T Consumer Communications Services Unit—Basking Ridge, NJ (Service) |
| | GTE Directories Corp.—Dallas (Service) |
| | Wainwright Industries, Inc.—St. Peters, Mo. (Small business) |
| **1993** | Eastman Chemical Co.—Kingsport, Tenn. (Manufacturing) |
| | Ames Rubber Corp.—Hamburg, N.J. (Small business) |
| **1992** | AT&T Network Systems Group: Transmission Systems Business Unit—Morristown, N.J. (Manufacturing) |
| | Texas Instruments Inc.: Defense Systems & Electronics Group—Dallas (Manufacturing) |
| | Granite Rock Co.—Watsonville, Calif. (Small business) |
| | AT&T Universal Card Services—Jacksonville, Fl. (Service) |
| | Ritz-Carlton Hotel Co.—Atlanta (Service) |
| **1991** | Zytec Corp.—Eden Prairie, Minn. (Manufacturing) |
| | Solectron Corp.—Milpitas, Calif. (Manufacturing) |
| | Marlow Industries—Dallas (Small business) |
| **1990** | Cadillac Motor Car Co.—Detroit (Manufacturing) |
| | IBM Rochester—Rochester, Minn. (Manufacturing) |
| | Federal Express—Memphis (Service) |
| | Wallace Co.—Houston (Small business) |
| **1989** | Xerox Corp.: Business Products & Systems—Fairport, N.Y. (Manufacturing) |
| | Milliken and Co.—Spartanburg, S.C. (Manufacturing) |
| **1988** | Motorola, Inc.—Schaumburg, Ill. (Manufacturing) |
| | Westinghouse Electric Corp.: Commercial Nuclear Fuel Division— Pittsburgh (Manufacturing) |
| | Globe Metallurgical, Inc.—Beverly, Ohio (Small business) |

TABLE 7.3
Malcolm Baldrige National
Quality Award Winners

lights the 1993 winners of the Baldrige award, Ames Rubber Corp. and Eastman Chemical Co.

Hundreds of organizations have successfully used the Baldrige award criteria as a tool for self-assessment. Although many companies have no intention of applying for the award, the criteria provide guidance for management in their improvement efforts. The award has provided a mechanism by which companies may assess their individual performance, compare their organizations with others', and provide recognition for those who have excelled.

Mail-order giant L.L. Bean credits a losing 1988 bid for the award as the beginning of its quality efforts. The assessment process showed L.L. Bean that its customer satisfaction was unsurpassed, but how it won on that point was not always productive. The company was founded on making things right but not necessarily doing it right the first time. Today L.L. Bean is more efficient than ever, mostly as a result of losing and learning from the Baldrige award.

# Quality Management Leadership

Several individuals have made significant contributions to the quality movement in this country and abroad. The list of significant contributors grows each day, but space limits dictate that we discuss only some of the most notable individuals.

# 1993 Baldrige Award Winners

In December of 1993, two companies were recognized by President Clinton for their commitment and success with their quality improvement efforts. President Clinton delighted the crowd by departing from the normal procedure of leaving the stage after the winning companies are introduced and a few remarks are made. This year he and Commerce Secretary Ronald Brown walked among the members of the audience and congratulated the company employees who were in attendance. Congratulation of the employees was definitely in order.

Employees of Ames Rubber have increased their productivity by 48 percent in three years, and their improvement ideas have saved the company more than $3 million. Eastman employees have reduced the time to bring a new product to market by 50 percent since 1990, and their shipping reliability has been consistently near 100 percent over the last four years. Both companies agree that there are three major elements in their total quality processes—Leadership, Teamwork, and Training and education.

Founded in 1949, Ames Rubber manufacturers rubber rollers used to feed paper and transfer fuse toner to paper in office machines, such as copiers, printers, and typewriters. The company has 445 employees who work at four New Jersey sites. Ames Rubber credits one of its customers, Xerox, for providing direction for its quality journey. Ames developed its Excellence Through Total Quality process which involves all employees in achieving a common goal: the full satisfaction of internal and external customers' needs.

To set the climate for change, a steering committee developed a guiding strategy that has two main components. The first is a nine-step quality improvement process for identifying and satisfying customers' requirements. The second is a six-step process for solving problems. It then had to convince the employees that management was behind the process committed to the long term success of the company.

Involvement groups, which meet monthly, were started in all work units to share information and identify problems. Additionally, every employee participates in at least one quality-improvement or problem-solving team. An executive quality improvement team monitors teams activities and provides teams with guidance and resources when necessary.

Since 1988, every employee has received 24 hours of basic training in quality principles, techniques, and tools, but this is soon to be increased to 40 hours. In addition to training, each employee is assigned a coach to ensure that he or she is familiar with the job and with total quality procedures.

Eastman manufactures and markets more than 400 chemicals, fibers, and plastics that are used in many consumer products, such as beverage bottles, bread, window cleaners, aspirin, and computer diskettes. Headquartered in Kingsport, TN, Eastman has 17,750 employees working at manufacturing plants throughout North America and the United Kingdom. Its Quality Management Process is based on focusing on the customer; establishing a mission, vision, and performance indicators; improving processes; and implementing the continuous improvement cycle of plan, do, check, and act.

continued

Eastman's leadership understands that a culture needs to be established that encourages and reinforces people. The technical system of quality will not work unless people believe that they are the key owners of the enterprise and that what they do makes a difference. Managers are constantly trying to identify and eliminate impediments to the "Eastman Way." Through their efforts, the old time card system was eliminated by putting everyone on salary; most reserved parking spaces have been eliminated; the benefits package was equalized for all employees; and the performance appraisal system was revamped.

Like Ames Rubber, Eastman also uses teamwork effectively. It uses the concept of interlocking teams, beginning with a team made up of the president and his vice presidents. Each vice president then forms a team of his or her reports. This continues throughout the organization until nearly all employees are involved. Other teams are formed to improve processes, tackle projects, and build relationships with suppliers and customers.

In addition to job-related training, employees receive quality training in statistics, team building, and problem solving.

## W. Edwards Deming

Probably no individual is more recognized as a quality leader than **W. Edwards Deming**, who died in 1993 at age 93. He devoted his entire life to pursuing quality and improving productivity. Deming began his career by applying statistical principles to quality improvement. In 1950, with American managers uninterested or unwilling to exert the effort to systematically improve manufacturing, Deming went to Japan where he began teaching the principles of statistical quality control to senior managers of Japanese companies. Deming received much of the credit for creating the "Japanese industrial miracle." He is so revered in Japan that the highest honor a company can receive for quality improvement is called the *Deming Prize*. He did not receive similar acclaim in this country until 1980, when NBC aired a news special entitled, "If Japan Can, Why Can't We?"

*We will long remember the contributions of W. Edwards Deming to improving quality standards throughout the world.*

That television show highlighted Deming and the successes he had achieved in Japan. Deming immediately began receiving the recognition and respect from American industry that he deserved. His statistical techniques have served as the underpinnings of a total management system based on a top-to-bottom transformation in regard to quality.

Deming had little time for industry executives he believed were not totally dedicated to improving quality. Executives had to convince him of their sincerity before he would agree to provide them with consultation or training. Deming believed that management can control over 90 percent of all business problems. Also, he believed that companies can improve their productivity, innovation, participation, and profits by making a sincere and focused effort to improve quality. He maintained that the keys are teamwork, training the work force, and the committed leadership of top management. Deming's fourteen points describe his management philosophy; they appear in Table 7.4.

Deming described the effect of quality improvement activities on an organization as a "chain reaction" of desirable events. As Figure 7.1 shows, the rewards for improving quality often are decreases in costs associated with poor quality.

T A B L E   7 . 4
Deming's Fourteen Points for
Quality

1. Create constancy of purpose for the improvement of product and service.
2. Adopt the new philosophy.
3. Cease dependence on mass inspection.
4. End the practice of awarding business based on the price tag alone.
5. Improve constantly and forever the system of production and service.
6. Institute job training and retraining.
7. Institute leadership.
8. Drive out fear.
9. Break down all barriers between staff areas.
10. Eliminate slogans, exhortations, and targets for the work force.
11. Eliminate numerical quotas.
12. Remove barriers to pride of workmanship.
13. Institute a vigorous program of education and retraining.
14. Take action to accomplish the transformation.

Source: Mary Walton, *The Deming Management Method* (New York: Putnam, 1986), pp. 55–88.

F I G U R E   7 . 1
Chain Reaction for Quality
Improvement

Source: Mary Walton, *The Deming
Management Method* (New York:
Putnam, 1986), p.25.

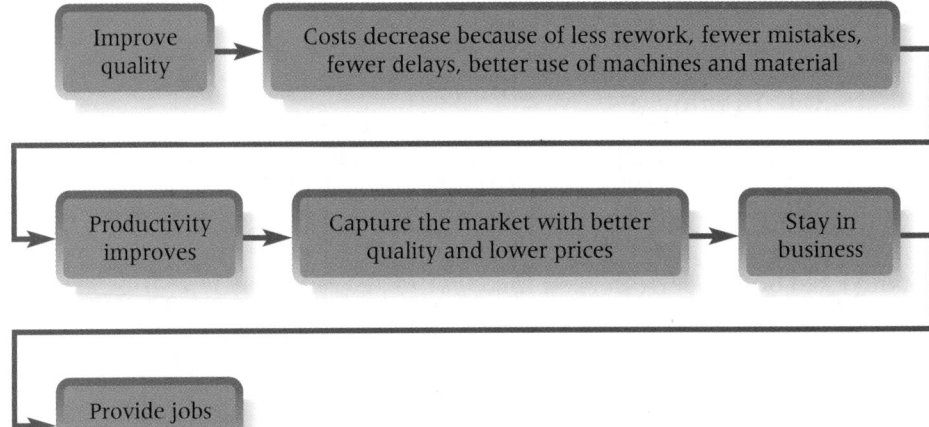

Less scrap and rework, fewer mistakes and delays, and better use of facilities mean lower costs and higher productivity. Better quality and lower-cost products and services are the weapons for capturing a greater share of the market. And capturing a bigger market share will allow the company to continue to grow and prosper in its industry.

## Joseph M. Juran

**Joseph M. Juran** was born in 1904 and worked with Deming in his early years at Western Electric Co. Juran's views parallel many of Deming's. He describes today's quality transformation within businesses as a shift from "little Q" to "big Q."[4] Businesses that practice little Q traditionally focus their quality efforts on the physical product or service provided to their ultimate customers. The movement today is toward big Q, which extends the application of quality

[4]J. M. Juran and F. M. Gryna, *Quality Planning and Analysis*, 3d ed. (New York: McGraw-Hill, 1993), p. 6.

| Quality Planning | Quality Control | Quality Improvement |
|---|---|---|
| Establish quality goals. | Choose control subjects. | Prove the need. |
| Identify customers. | Choose units of measure. | Identify projects. |
| Learn customer's needs. | Set goals. | Organize project teams. |
| Develop product features. | Create a sensor. | Diagnose the causes. |
| Develop process features. | Measure actual performance. | Provide remedies and prove that |
| Establish process controls and | Interpret the difference. | the remedies are effective. |
| transfer them to operations. | Take action on the difference. | Deal with resistance to change. |
| | | Control to hold the gains. |

Source: J. M. Juran and F. M. Gryna, *Quality Planning and Analysis,* 3d ed. (New York: McGraw-Hill, 1993), p. 9.

TABLE 7.5
Universal Processes for
Managing Quality

concepts to all functional activities by recognizing that each associated process has both internal and external customers.

Like Deming, Juran refined many of his quality theories while working with the Japanese. Whereas Deming was focusing on statistical process control, Juran was espousing the concept of total quality control. It is thought that Deming's work with the Japanese had the most immediate and profound effect on Japanese quality, whereas Juran's activities provided the framework for integrating quality concepts throughout the organization.[5] This integration has meant that many Japanese companies continue to realize improvements in quality.

Juran bases his philosophy of quality on three managerial processes: quality planning, quality control, and quality improvement. Table 7.5 shows the activities that each of these managerial processes requires.

## Philip B. Crosby

**Philip Crosby,** probably best known for his 1979 book *Quality Is Free*, was born in 1926 in Wheeling, West Virginia. In that book he explained his views that "doing things right the first time adds nothing to the cost of a product or service, but doing things wrong is what costs money."[6] Crosby became the leader of a crusade that promoted zero defects as the quality standard that all organizations should adopt.

Crosby believes that in order for an organization to change from traditional quality management to an innovative and enduring quality management process, it must understand his "Four Absolutes of Quality Management," which are designed to answer four important questions:[7]

1. *What is quality?* The definition of *quality* is conformance to requirements, not goodness.
2. *What system do we need to institute so that we offer a quality product or service?* The system of quality is prevention, not detection.
3. *Which performance standard should we use to measure the quality of our performance?* The performance standard is zero defects, not "that's close enough."

[5]Otis Port, "W. Edwards Deming and J. M. Juran: Dueling Pioneers,"*Business Week Bonus Issue on the Quality Imperative*, October 25, 1991, p. 17.
[6]Philip B. Crosby, *Quality is Free* (New York: McGraw Hill, 1979), inside front cover.
[7]Philip B. Crosby, *Quality Without Tears: The Art of Hassle-Free Management* (New York: McGraw Hill, 1984), pp. 58–86.

4. *Which system is appropriate for measuring the quality of what we do?* The measurement of quality is the price of nonconformance.

Crosby has been an outspoken critic of the Baldrige award, saying that companies tend to focus more on winning the prize rather than on making long-term, sustainable improvements in quality. He says that many companies use the award guidelines as a checklist of things to do, expecting to have a total quality organization when they finish. Much to a company's dismay, it may end up in worse shape than it had been previously.

Crosby and others may question the award's objectives, administration, or measurement criteria, but the award nevertheless has succeeded in raising the level of quality awareness nationwide. Many believe that the long-term benefits of such awareness will outweigh the short-term concerns about the design or administration of the award.

# Definitions of Quality

The definition of *quality* continues to evolve for goods and services. The lack of a clear definition makes it difficult for organizations to measure, control, and manage quality. So let's discuss several alternative definitions and examples that illustrate how each definition applies to today's business world and its implications.

## Quality as Excellence

Defining quality as the characteristic of attained excellence in a product or service is an elusive yet appropriate definition in some cases. Many products or services convey to the user some sense of personal pleasure or esteem. This certainly represents a challenge to the operations manager, because the precise attainment of that characteristic and its perception by the customer are difficult to ensure. Nevertheless, the perception of a product's excellence can be a significant competitive approach.

The concert piano market is a good illustration of this definition of quality. Major companies in this market include American Steinway and Sons, Yamaha, and Boesendorfer, among others. Every piano has some unique characteristics, despite significant efforts by the manufacturers to use the most carefully selected materials, designs, and workmanship. The temperature and humidity of the room used to manufacture a piano and the site of the concert affect tone and resonance. How, then, does a manufacturer assure the buyer that its instruments are more excellent than the others? Part of the answer is the loyalty of "signature" pianists of significant reputation. For example, Steinway carefully guards its lists of artists who perform on Steinway pianos exclusively, including Maurizio Pollini, Van Cliburn, and Elton John. Boesendorfer lays claim to Frank Sinatra and Stevie Wonder. Because a company has no way to ensure or prove that each of its pianos produces exactly the same sound as the piano used by a Grammy Award winner, its advertising relies heavily on endorsements.

## Quality as Conformance to Specifications

Another approach to defining quality is to measure the extent to which the product or service conforms to design specifications. Does a fast-food restaurant serve its food hot, in correct portions, and in proper packaging? Do the components of a mountain bike work efficiently together ? Each question refers to a measure of conformance. Consider how this definition is different from the excellence criterion. If excellence is the criterion, a Bic does not challenge a Mont Blanc fountain pen, and a Timex does not challenge a Rolex watch. But if each product meets its respective design specifications, we can say that each has achieved its quality objectives. This definition does assume that the design of the product includes specifications for every important aspect of the product or service.

As noted earlier, Crosby's definition of quality is "conformance to require-ments," which is quite different from "conformance to specifications." Basing design specifications on the needs and expectations of the customers eliminates that difference. Today product and service designers are working with customers more closely than ever to help ensure that specifications yield products and services that meet customers' needs and expectations.

## Quality as Fitness for Use

A significant step beyond the conformance definition is to add to it the customer's intended use of the product or service, a definition first articulated by Juran. Known as the *fitness concept,* it requires that the design of the product be appropriate for the conditions and purpose of the user. This definition of quality has a strong component of product liability and consumer education, because the company must correctly assess the knowledge, skill, and intentions of the customer. From a competitive standpoint fitness for intended use is a more accurate way to measure quality. Many companies produce products of good design and exceptional conformance, only to go out of business because they failed to meet the demands of the marketplace. Sony's eventual capitulation to the industry standard for videotape recorder and playback technology was not the result of poor design or manufacture of Sony's Betamax; its product did not consider the market requirement for compatibility of videotape formats from a wide number of producers.

## Quality as Value for the Price

Perhaps the most comprehensive definition of the concept of quality was proposed by Armand Feigenbaum, author of the classic volume *Total Quality Control.*[8] Feigenbaum combines economic and consumer criteria with the con-cepts of fitness, conformance, and excellence. His definition recognizes that our desire for conformance to a requirement is price sensitive. For example, suppose that you place a high value on the percentage of cotton in a shirt or blouse. You would prefer content of 100 percent cotton, assuming that the design, color, and size specifications are acceptable. If an appropriate 100 percent cotton garment sells for $50, and an otherwise identical one containing 80 percent cotton sells for $30, you are forced to weigh the importance of cotton content versus selling price. This definition is user specific, and the array of products and prices that we see each day is an indication of the variety of values that individual consumers place on products and services. Many consumers may not act so rationally when assessing product quality, but manufacturers and service providers no doubt

[8]Armand V. Feigenbaum, *Total Quality Control*, 3d ed. (New York: McGraw-Hill, 1983).

regularly assess the relative value of their products against those of their direct competitors'. This is especially true when the product or service is difficult to differentiate, such as airline service between the same two cities.

## Quality-related Product Characteristics

Closely related to the definitions of quality are the concepts of reliability, durability, and serviceability. None of these product characteristics is a substitute for the defined quality concepts just described, but each may be an important criterion for determining the conformance, fitness, or value of a product or service.

When design engineers describe **product reliability**, they measure it as a statistically random variable representing the mean time between failures (MTBF) for some function of the component or for the entire item. All machines malfunction, and the rate of failure for a particular technology may be well known. Household refrigerators are famous for the years of continuous service they provide. Some photocopying machines require frequent servicing. Yet the underlying statistical distributions for these two machines may well be the same, with different means.

The reliability of a technology can certainly affect the experience of the customer. Imagine that the door to an automatic teller machine has just closed, releasing no money but giving you a receipt that indicates your account has been debited by $30. You have your card, a receipt, and, you hope, the ability to convince the bank that the ATM shortchanged you. Although these machines have a triple redundant sensor system to detect the movement of cash from the machine to the customer, such mistakes occur once in approximately 12,000 withdrawals, according to officials at Chemical Bank in New York.

**Durability** is a concept that applies to products that are generally considered impossible to repair. Incandescent light bulbs are generally treated as replaceable items that are expected to function for some number of hours of normal use. This mean time to failure (MTTF) is similar to the MTBF measure but assumes a single failure at a time determined from some underlying statistical distribution. Some manufacturing technologies permit tight specifications for the design of products, and purchasers can make a warranty claim for early failure. Automobile headlights are an example of this predictable technology. Assuming you use two headlights made by the same manufacturer for the same number of hours under identical conditions, you can expect that they will fail within days of each other. For this reason many consumers replace both when one burns out.

**Serviceability** refers to how easily a repair can return a failed product or machine to functional condition. The principle may apply to the ease of removal of stains from a necktie, the speed at which a television repairer can remove and replace a defective or failed component, or the ease with which a customer can locate, purchase, and replace automobile windshield wipers with an identical pair.

While calculations of reliability, durability, and serviceability are beyond the scope of the discussion in this chapter, these three concepts obviously have a crucial effect on the appropriateness of the design of products. These issues have been of paramount importance in the U.S. automobile manufacturing industry as car makers strive to regain the market share they have lost to foreign producers.

# Quality-related Service Characteristics

We should highlight the similar characteristics that customers use to select their service providers. Because making an accurate assessment of service quality is much more difficult than an assessment of product quality, characteristics of service quality are important issues for managers to address. In their book *Marketing Services* Leonard L. Berry and A. Parasuraman describe five general dimensions of service quality as

- **Reliability:** What is your ability to perform the promised service dependably and accurately?
- **Tangibles:** What is the appearance of your physical facilities, equipment, personnel, and communication materials?
- **Responsiveness:** How willing are you to help customers and provide prompt service?
- **Assurance:** Are the personnel who come in direct contact with the customer knowledgeable and courteous and able to convey trust and confidence?
- **Empathy:** Do you provide care and individual attention to customers?[9]

These dimensions of service quality are useful in helping operations managers design and implement successful service quality initiatives. Successful businesses understand the importance of providing exceptional customer service and continue to assess and improve service delivery systems.

One example of an entrepreneur who truly provides exceptional customer service is Carl Sewell, owner of several automobile dealerships. His book, *Customers for Life*, should be required reading for anyone interested in improving service quality. Sewell expanded his business from about $10 million in sales in 1968 to about $250 million in 1990, with profits showing similar increases. He describes in his book the Ten Commandments of Customer Service:

1. BRING 'EM BACK ALIVE: Ask customers what they want and give it to them again and again.
2. SYSTEMS, NOT SMILES: Saying please and thank you doesn't insure you'll do the job right the first time, every time. Only systems guarantee you that.
3. UNDER-PROMISE, OVER-DELIVER: Customers expect you to keep your word. Exceed it.
4. WHEN THE CUSTOMER ASKS, THE ANSWER IS ALWAYS YES: *Period!*
5. FIRE YOUR INSPECTORS AND CUSTOMER RELATIONS DEPARTMENT: Every employee who deals with clients must have the authority to handle complaints.
6. NO COMPLAINTS? SOMETHING'S WRONG: Encourage your customers to tell you what you're doing wrong.
7. MEASURE EVERYTHING: Baseball teams do it. Football teams do it. Basketball teams do it. You should too.
8. SALARIES ARE UNFAIR: Pay people like partners.
9. YOUR MOTHER WAS RIGHT: Show people respect. Be polite. It works.
10. JAPANESE THEM: Learn how the best really do it; make their systems your own. Then improve them.

[9]Leonard L. Berry and A. Parasuraman, *Marketing Services* (New York: Free Press, 1991), p. 16.

However, Sewell cautions that *"these ten rules aren't worth a damn . . .* unless you make a profit. You have to make money to stay in business and provide good service."[10]

# Costs of Quality

Whereas manufacturing and design engineers typically are responsible for some of the more technological issues in quality assurance for products, operations managers often conduct the analysis of quality-related costs, an important task. Strategic opportunities or threats frequently motivate the launch of aggressive quality management initiatives. Analyzing the costs of quality can provide the financial justification for implementing them. It is not unusual for American manufacturers to have quality-related costs in the range of 20 percent of the cost of goods sold. Carefully planning quality improvement activities not only improves quality but lowers quality-related costs.

## Classifying the Costs of Quality

The American Society for Quality Control (ASQC) has developed a typology of quality-related costs that is based on the work of several quality masters. Operations managers have found the classification system useful for collecting data that are consistent and for identifying the opportunities for controlling quality costs that will have the greatest effects on efficiency. The typology has four categories: internal failure costs, external failure costs, appraisal costs, and prevention costs.

An extremely important truism is that the further along in a process an item is, the more a defect costs. For example, in the design phase of a new product or service, the cost of correcting a defect may be minimal. If that defect goes undetected and the company releases the product or service to the public, it will incur a much greater cost to resolve the problems that result. So what are the implications for quality managers? Control quality all the way back to the source. Create an assessment process that will identify defects as far back in the life cycle of a product or service as possible. In the long run, costs of prevention and assessment will be considerably less than the costs of internal and external failures.

**Internal and External Failure Costs** Where the failure is detected is what distinguishes internal failure costs from external failure costs. **Internal failure costs** are the costs of scrap, rework, reinspection, and low production yields for nonconforming items that are detected before they leave the ownership of the company. Internal failure costs can also include lost production capacity when defective items require more processing time and the cost of downgrading some products to "second quality" for sale at a reduced price. Also, internal failure costs include the cost of performing an analysis to determine the cause of the failure. The manufacturer or service deliverer bears the cost of internal failure; the customer is not involved.

Conversely, **external failure costs** include warranty claims, repairs, and service costs that result when the failure is detected in the marketplace or in the presence of the consumer. In addition to the replacement and service costs

---

[10]Carl Sewell and Paul B. Brown, *Customers for Life* (New York: Pocket Books, 1990), pp. xix–xx.

external failure costs should include such intangibles as lost goodwill and reputation, although these are difficult to quantify. Recalls of automobiles, food, and over-the-counter drugs are examples of costly external failures with the potential to damage reputation.

**Appraisal and Prevention Costs**  **Appraisal costs** include the costs of inspecting material upon arrival, during manufacture, in laboratory tests, and by outside inspectors. Companies must pay for the maintenance, routine calibration, and perhaps certification by government agencies or industry associations of their testing equipment. Each of these costs is attributed to the appraisal of product quality.

When a company invests in the design and development of new quality equipment, evaluates the design of a new product or service, or invests in training or improvement projects, it is incurring **prevention costs.** Other sources of costs related to prevention include the data gathering, analysis, and reporting associated with much of the company's quality measurement and control activities.

## Interaction of Quality Costs

Imagine how the costs associated with quality might change as the number of nonconforming units of products or services increases or decreases. Figure 7.2 illustrates the cost increases in both categories, internal and external failure, as the number of defects increases. Obviously, the best way to minimize failure costs is to prevent defects during processing rather than find them later. The number of nonconforming units will not affect appraisal costs, almost by definition. The

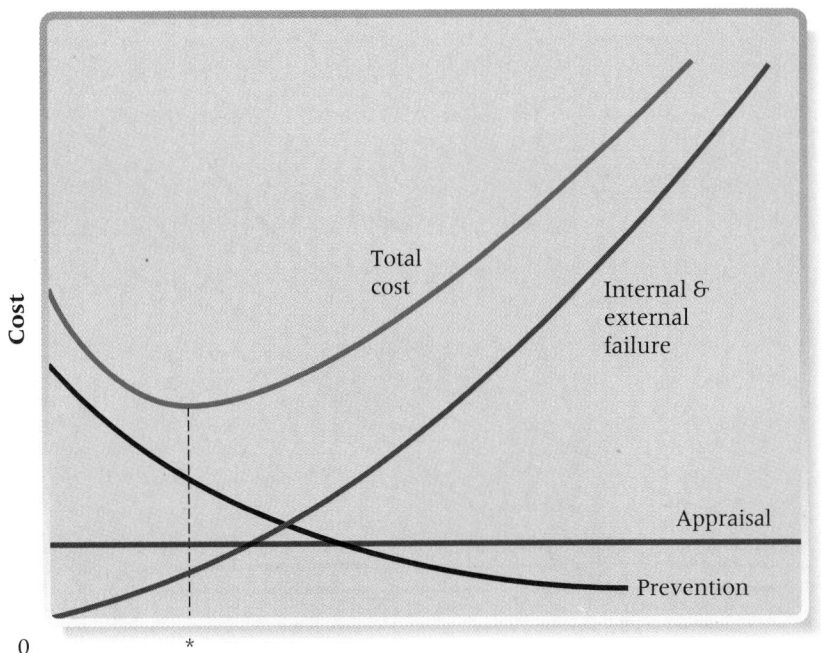

**FIGURE 7.2**
Interaction of Failure, Appraisal, and Prevention Costs

*Optimum proportion of nonconforming products

costs of appraisal, whether from testing, calibration, or inspection, will be constant no matter what the defect rate may be. The behavior of prevention costs as a function of nonconformities is the subject of considerable disagreement. Traditionally, quality professionals, led by Juran, have assumed that the costs associated with prevention increase as the defect rate decreases. The logic of their argument is that some sources of defects are more difficult to uncover than others.

Obvious sources of quality problems are comparatively easy to identify and correct. However, prevention has a threshold at which the marginal cost of finding and correcting the remaining sources of errors increases. Figure 7.2 also illustrates how the marginal cost of prevention increases as the number of nonconforming units decreases. If a manager seeks to minimize the sum of all four quality costs, the minimum total cost probably will be associated with some rate of nonconformities greater than zero.

Leading the opposition to this view is Crosby, who contends that prevention costs do not increase marginally. He claims that no problems are diabolically difficult and that systematic approaches to the prevention of defects do not increase in cost. Crosby and other professionals hold fast to the idea that operations workers are endowed with the ingenuity and creativity to solve problems. Some sources of error do have obvious solutions, but solving others requires more effort rather than more expense. Consider an eight-year-old child who is learning to multiply. After mastering the multiples of six, does the child need to allocate marginally more effort to learn the multiples of seven? We can make the case that the process of learning number facts becomes progressively easier and that this learning process enables the child to engage in even more advanced arithmetic concepts. Figure 7.3 illustrates the view that prevention costs do not increase. Note that the sum of the quality costs becomes minimal at zero defects.

FIGURE 7.3
Crosby's Concept of
Prevention Costs
(No Increase)

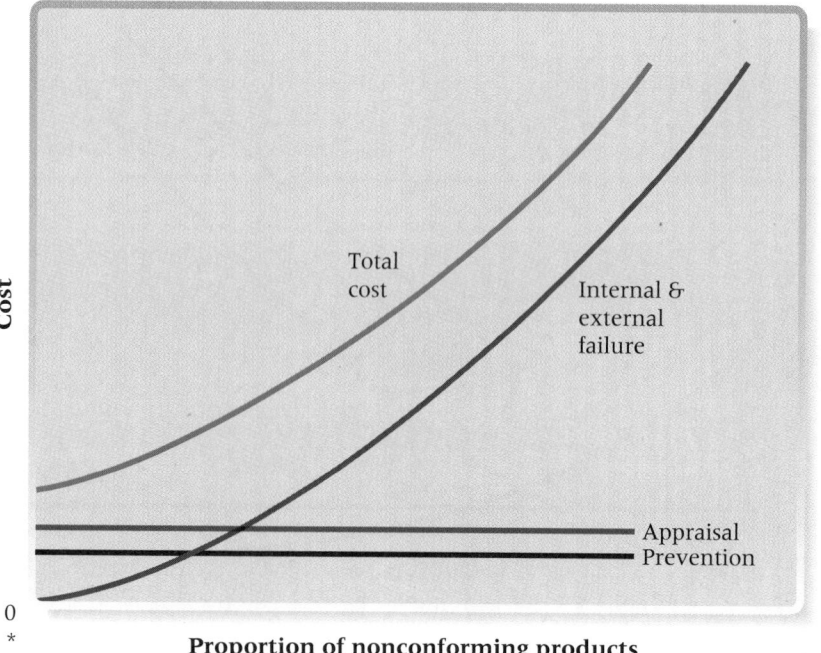

**Proportion of nonconforming products**

*Optimum proportion of nonconforming products

# Total Quality Management

The challenge today is to take the information discussed thus far in this chapter and formulate an organizationwide approach to quality improvement. Many such efforts are underway and go by many names. Terms such as *total quality control (TQC), continuous quality improvement (CQI), continuous process improvement (CPI),* and *total quality management (TQM)* are just a few. We will use the term *total quality management* because it is probably the term most used today. There are no essential differences in TQC, CQI, CPI, and TQM. Actually, there is little difference between what we will describe as TQM and the quality views espoused by Deming and others since the 1950s.

**Total quality management (TQM)** is an organizationwide approach to total customer satisfaction and a continuous process of improvement. During the 1980s the TQM movement spread from manufacturing to all segments of society. In 1988 President Reagan created the Federal Quality Institute (FQI) in Washington, D.C., charging it with the responsibility to promote and facilitate the implementation of TQM concepts at government agencies.[11] The challenge for the institute is enormous: In 1992 federal civilian workers numbered approximately 2.9 million; the FQI's full staff was thirty-five individuals. The institute provides training and consulting services for those agencies interested in learning more about TQM.

Manufacturing organizations, health care institutions, service organizations, educational institutions, and military agencies, including the navy, air force, and army, have reported successful implementation of TQM. It is difficult to imagine an organization that could not benefit from the concepts and practice of TQM.

Misunderstandings about what TQM is and is not are considerable.

TQM *is not*

- Another management fad
- A panacea for all organizational ills
- A quick fix

TQM *is*

- A philosophy and a set of guiding principles and tools for improving quality
- A way to manage an organization based on "total customer" satisfaction and a continuous process of improvement
- The way we would do things if we had not thought of a *worse* way

## TQM Requirements

One recent survey showed that as many as two-thirds of American managers think TQM has failed in their companies.[12] Obviously, there is more to implementing TQM than simply saying the words. Experience has revealed several requirements, listed in Table 7.6, that companies must meet in successfully implementing TQM. Let's look at each requirement to better understand why some implementations are less than successful and why many companies are reluctant to even consider TQM.

**Strategic Quality Planning**   For the tenets of TQM to permeate the culture of an organization, the company must recognize quality as a strategic issue and treat it

[11]Larry Reynolds, "The Feds Join the Quality Movement," *Management Review*(April 1992): 39–40.
[12]Rahul Jacob, "TQM: More Than a Dying Fad?" *Fortune*, October 18, 1993, p. 66.

TABLE 7.6
Total Quality Requirements

- Strategic quality planning
- Clear focus on "customers' " satisfaction
- Effective collection and analysis of information
- Effective use of teamwork and training
- Effective design of products and services
- Effective leadership

as such. This means that quality planning must become part of overall business planning for the entire organization. Strategic quality planning must include a clear vision of what the organization wants to achieve with respect to customer satisfaction and continuous improvement. Communication of this clear vision of quality must permeate the organization to achieve constancy of purpose. All units of an organization must understand the importance of quality and make plans and decisions that contribute to the quality vision.

As part of the strategic planning process many organizations formulate both vision and mission statements. Whereas the vision statement describes some future state of excellence, the mission statement describes why the organization exists. The vision should be inspiring and futuristic. Robert Woodruff, president of Coca-Cola from 1923 to 1955, said, "We will see that every man in uniform gets a bottle of Coca-Cola for five cents wherever he is and whatever it costs." After World War II ended, he said that in his lifetime he wanted everyone in the world to have tasted Coca-Cola. This was quite a vision. At a ceremony marking the opening of Disney World a man introducing Lillian Disney, widow of Walt, said that he wished that Walt Disney could have seen the Orlando park. Lillian Disney stood up, said simply, "He did," and sat down. Visions can be powerful.[13]

The strategic planning process also yields a guide for an organization's quality improvement efforts. For example, an organization should partly base its selection of projects to tackle on each project's contribution to the vision and mission of the company. Without these strategic documents a company can lose direction. It would be like trying to determine the best route to a destination without first knowing the destination.

**Clear Focus on Customer Satisfaction** One of the most significant differences between traditional quality activities and TQM is the redefinition of *customer*. Traditional quality activities focused on the ultimate customer in the market for the product or service offered. The primary weakness of this view of quality is that employees tend to assume that someone else is responsible for quality in their organization. Asked "Who is responsible for quality around here?" a machine operator on a manufacturing floor during the 1970s and early 1980s might well have responded, "Quality control." The same question asked of employees in accounting, marketing, human resources, or even some engineering functions would have resulted in the same answer—if they even had any idea at all.

One requirement of TQM noted earlier is a focus on processes. The focus on processes leads to the immediate recognition that the processes of each job have a customer. Recognizing the existence of these internal customers helps workers understand that they are responsible for the quality of the work they do and are

[13]John C. Maxwell, *Developing the Leader Within You* (Nashville: Thomas Nelson, Inc. 1993). p. 143.

responsible to their customers for that quality. One of the most valuable exercises for employees is being asked by their managers to identify various processes for which they are responsible, who the customers for those processes are, and what the needs and expectations of the customers are. That exercise would be equally valuable for managers.

**Continuous Improvement of Key Processes**  A **process** is an established series of steps or operations that together work toward a desired result or product. We all perform processes daily without ever thinking of them as processes. For example, in order to prepare a research paper you first decide upon a topic, do the research, develop an outline, write, edit, revise the paper, and finally submit the paper to the professor for grading. Could you improve the process you use to complete research projects? What about the process of preparing to go out on Friday night? Getting up in the morning and getting ready to go to class? These are all processes suitable for improvement efforts.

Many successful companies have embraced the concept of continuous process improvement. Rather than setting goals that, once achieved, provide no further incentive for improvement, these companies invest in training, technology, and management policies that promote the improvement of quality and services in every facet of the business. Continuous process improvement is an integral part of the TQM philosophy.

Whereas many U.S. managers treat problems as inevitable and unimprovable, Japanese managers have been effective at challenging the status quo and designing processes that are nearly idiot proof. A Japanese production engineer, Shigeo Shingo, worked with Toyota managers to develop of series of principles that would be useful for identifying the source of quality problems. Called *poka-yoke*, these quality techniques are oriented toward the design of nearly foolproof production systems. For example, if a component attaches to a frame with five fasteners, the system should present the operator with five fasteners at a time. This reduces to almost zero the chance of using fewer than the required number. The term used in Japan to denote continuous process improvement is *kaizen*.

The success of improvement activities depends heavily on the particular projects chosen for improvement. According to Peter Scholtes, author of *Team Handbook*, organizations often make several errors in selecting projects for improvement:[14]

1.  Selecting a process that no one is really interested in—The desire of individual team members to improve a process often drives the improvement effort.
2.  Selecting a desired solution instead of a process—Management might tell a team to "identify ways to reduce inventory replenishment lead time," which is a potential solution to an inventory problem. A more fruitful approach would be to ask the team to investigate the process used to replenish inventory and make recommendations for improving customer service. Reducing lead time may turn out to be the desired solution, but that decision should be based on factual data analysis.
3.  Selecting a process that is in transition—Studying a process that is soon to change is a waste of time. Close coordination ensures that two or more teams are not studying the same process from different angles.

[14]Peter R. Scholtes, *The Team Handbook* (Madison, Wisc.: Joiner and Associates, 1988), p. 3–2.

4. Selecting a system to study, not a process—Be careful that teams do not become too ambitious. Rather than study a system that has several processes, the team should focus on a specific process. Initial projects should be small and have a high probability of success.

**Effective Collection and Analysis of Information** Information is critical for the success of a total quality organization. From strategic planning to day-to-day process improvement activities, the effective collection and analysis of information allows managers to base their decisions on fact more than on intuition. In addition to traditional financial information, useful data include

- Market information about customers' needs and expectations, as well as their perceptions about the company and its products and services
- Information on purchased parts, materials, and general vendor performance
- Information on any gaps between how processes are performing and what customers expect
- Information on the availability of quality measurements for products and services
- Field performance information on mean times between product failures and other warranty and complaint information from customers

Some of this information may be readily available in a organization, some may need to be collected.

**Effective Use of Teamwork and Training** Process improvement relies heavily on the use of teams of individuals as problem solvers. Early team activities for process improvement were in the form of **quality circles.** The Japanese developed the concept; in 1962 the Japan Telephone & Telegraph Corp. registered the first quality circle,[15] and Japanese quality expert Kaoru Ishikawa continues to develop the concept. Effective use of quality circles contributed greatly to Japan's transition to a well-respected and often feared worldwide competitor.

Many companies in this country experimented with quality circles, but only a few succeeded. The team concept is still alive in the United States, but its focus has changed, to problem solving and a focus on specific processes. Chapter 9, Organization and Human Resources, provides a more detailed discussion of team activities.

Regardless whether teams are called *quality circles, problem-solving teams, customer satisfaction teams, process improvement teams*, or whatever, involving workers in process improvement activities is important. Also, team members must have a vested interest in the process they are working to improve. It is not uncommon to find machine operators, engineers, managers, and support staffers working together on the same process improvement team.

For a traditional organization to change to a total quality organization requires the critical evaluation of every element of the organization and change where appropriate. Many employees and managers resist change and are overwhelmed by the amount of change going on around them. Training these employees and managers facilitates their transition to the new and improved organization and is essential.

An early step in implementing TQM is training. The upper levels of the organization usually receive the initial training, an overview of what it takes to

[15]Garvin, *Managing Quality*, p. 188.

become a total quality organization and the benefits the company can expect. Once those individuals have been trained, the ideal situation is for them to train the next level in the organization and so on. Training should cascade throughout the organization down to the lowest levels. The content of the training programs often is different, but the message is always clear: Change is good, change is essential, and change is here to stay.

**Effective Design of Products and Services** As Chapter 5 noted, it is impossible to overstate the importance of developing products and services that meet customers' needs.

The life cycle of most products and services begins with an idea. In some industries market research generates the idea in response to customers' expressed needs for new items and services. In other industries research and development scientists and engineers recognize an opportunity to develop a new product. Translating these ideas into prototype products and services is exciting; it is also the most significant opportunity to influence the ultimate quality of the product or service. Choices of material, equipment, configuration, and features of the product will critically affect the ability of the company to conform to specifications and meet the demands of the marketplace. At this stage the potential for quality improvement is unlimited. The emphasis is on choosing the best values of important factors in the design of the product or service. Remember that the cost of a defect found during the design phase is minimal, whereas the same defect, found only after the product is in the customer's hands, can be tremendously expensive.

A good illustration of importance of specifying the right factors and Genichi Taguchi's experimental design methods involves a Japanese manufacturer of ceramic tile.[16] The manufacturer was having a problem with lack of uniformity in the size of the tiles after they were fired in a kiln in the final stage of processing. The company determined correctly that the temperature inside the kiln was not uniform, a variation that was responsible for the size inconsistency. The manufacturer determined that there were two approaches to correcting the problem. The first and more costly option involved redesigning the process by purchasing a new kiln with more uniform temperature distribution or one with more sophisticated controls. The second was to redesign the product. Kiln managers investigated the tile formulation and experimented with different proportions of materials that comprised the tiles. One ingredient was lime. Increasing the amount of lime from 1 percent to 5 percent of the tile's total content reduced its sensitivity to kiln temperature variations. Subsequent checks of other important features, such as the strength of the tile and the effect of the revised formulation on material costs, showed that increasing the lime content would not cause problems.

In this case the experimenters were lucky. Limestone was the least expensive material used in the tiles, and agalmatolite was the most expensive. Experimentation revealed that using more limestone and less agalmatolite would increase both productivity and quality and decrease costs. Taguchi's ideas on experimental design contribute greatly to companies' ability to effectively design new products and improve existing ones.

**Effective Leadership** The last major requirement for total quality is effective leadership. Without effective leadership a company can attain none of the other

---

[16]Lance A. Ealey, *Quality by Design: Taguchi Methods and U.S. Industry* (Dearborn, Mich.: ASI Press, 1988), pp. 124–127.

requirements. Whether total quality organizations need "managers" or "leaders" is a matter of some debate today. Traditionally, we think of managers' roles as planning, directing, controlling, organizing, and coordinating. The leadership activities that supplement those roles include empowering, coaching, and caring. Leaders in total quality organizations must help create and communicate a clear quality vision and at every opportunity demonstrate their personal commitment to it.

Personal commitment must be more than signing supportive memos that go out to employees. Management must demonstrate its support by attending improvement team meetings, attending and participating in training programs, serving on improvement teams, and participating in reward and recognition ceremonies. Workers are sensitive to the "strategy du jour" and will watch to see whether they should invest their time and energy in another passing management fad. Total quality management is not just another management fad. It is a process of continuous improvement and a never-ending quest for superior customer satisfaction. Traditional managers often find the idea of an empowered work force threatening. They perceive it as a loss of their power. These managers need to understand that their job is simply changing and that their leadership is more important now than ever before. A work force that has the power to make many of the routine decisions will give managers more time to do their jobs more effectively.

## TQM Implementation Process

The actual implementation process adopted by an organization may differ significantly from that used by other organizations. Because each organization has its own culture and TQM often represents a change in that culture, each company must tailor its approach to adopting TQM to suit its individual characteristics. Failure of a company to recognize and draw on its uniqueness will often result in failure. Figure 7.4 illustrates the steps in one general approach to total quality implementation:

1.  Identify critical business issues. Critical business issues often threaten the long-term success or survival of a company. Clear identification of these issues serves as the driving force behind TQM implementation.
2.  Secure the commitment of top management. Top management must help create and communicate a clear vision of quality, and it must be willing to provide the support, both financial and personal, to make the total quality process work. Management must not only talk the talk but walk the walk.
3.  Provide initial training. As noted earlier, the initial training should be general and directed at key members of management. Many organizations seek to achieve a critical mass of trained managers from different areas to ease implementation.
4.  Identify customers' requirements. If a company is to achieve total customer satisfaction, employees must know what it will take to achieve that goal. Market studies, surveys, focus groups, and other approaches are proven and effective sources of information.
5.  Identify key processes. Once a company understands the needs and expectations of its customers, it must identify the processes that have the most significant effects on the satisfaction of those needs and expectations. These will become the processes that the company first considers for improvement.

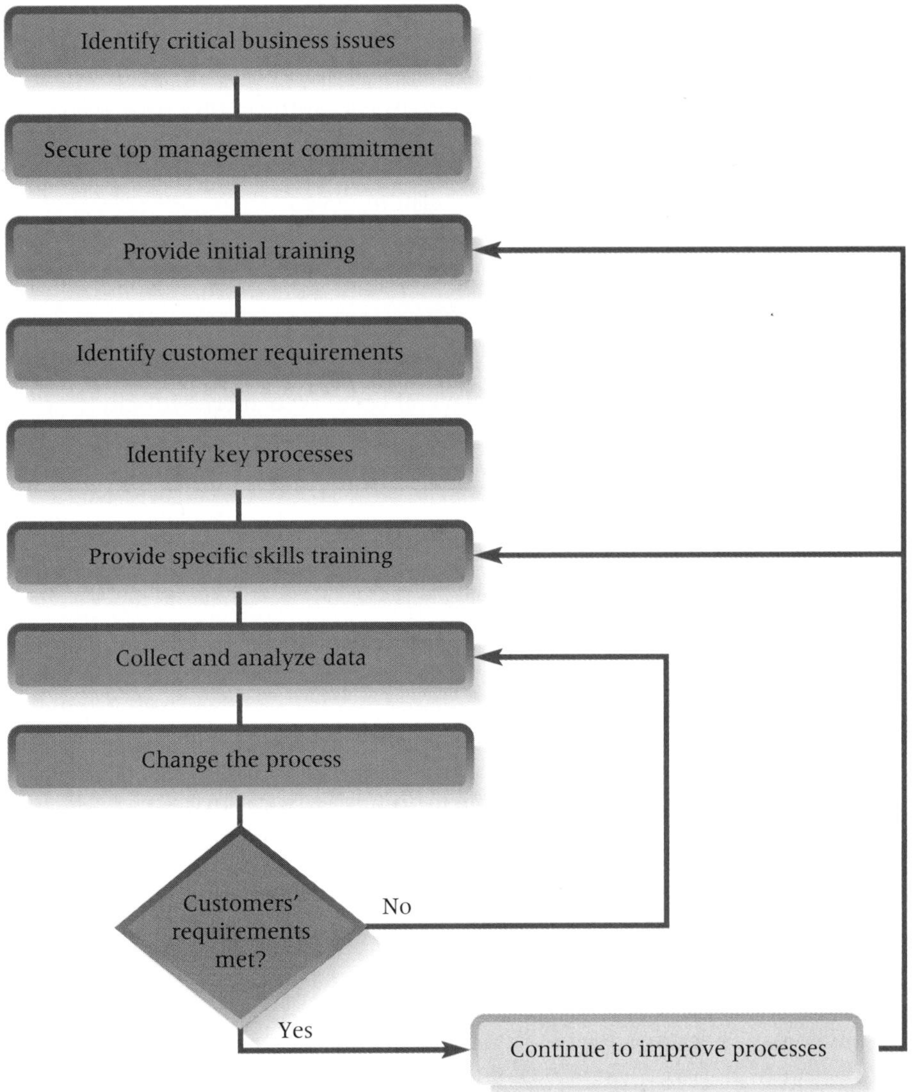

FIGURE 7.4
Implementing Total Quality
Management

6. **Provide specific skills training.** As teams form to improve selected processes, their members will need additional training so that the teams have skills to accomplish their improvement activities.

7. **Collect and analyze data.** Using the tools of total quality, teams will collect data to help them figure out how to improve the process they are reviewing. The basis of the improvement process is first understanding customers' needs and expectations, then measuring to what degree the company already is satisfying those needs and expectations, and finally recommending improvements in the process to increase customers' satisfaction.

8. **Change the process.** After analyzing the effects of various process improvements, the company has to implement the improvements it has selected and measure the actual effect of the changes. If improvements are not achieving desired levels of customer satisfaction, the company will have to collect and analyze more data and institute additional improvements.

9.  Commit to continuous improvement of key processes. This final step in the implementation process is probably the most important. Committing to continuous process improvement implies a never-ending drive toward perfection. The company should maintain communications with customers and continually measure its performance. Improvement teams should form as necessary to stay abreast of customers' changing needs and expectations in an attempt to not only satisfy but also to delight them.

Chapter 19 explores the techniques for analyzing and improving processes.

## Barriers to Implementing TQM

TQM is not a panacea, nor is it easily or quickly implemented in the typical organization. Experience has revealed several barriers to successful implementation:

- Assuming that implementing total quality will quickly and completely cure all the organization's ills
- Top management's failing to provide a demonstration of its commitment to the total quality effort
- Middle management's failing to recognize its new leadership roles and its feeling threatened by a perceived loss of power to employees
- Becoming so obsessive about internal quality activities that critical performance issues, such as financial performance and external customers' needs, are overlooked
- Creating hundreds of improvement teams and failing to provide resources, direction, training, and encouragement to help ensure success
- Adopting an off-the-shelf quality program without modifying it to match the company's unique characteristics
- Failing to link quality goals to financial returns and compensation

Failure of an organization to realize the full potential of total quality often is attributable to one of these barriers. Do organizations find it worthwhile to go through the dramatic and often painful transition to a total quality organization? Those who have been successful say, "Absolutely!" Will textbooks five years from now continue to discuss the merits of total quality management? It is impossible to be certain, but TQM probably won't be covered as a separate chapter, as it is in this book. For companies to compete in ever-changing international markets, total quality must be an integral part of their culture. It will not be something new they attempt to implement successfully but simply the way they do business.

## Business Process Reengineering[17]

**Business process reengineering** is the fundamental rethinking and radical redesign of business processes to achieve dramatic improvements in strategically important measures of performance, such as cost, quality, service, and speed. Reengineering a company means throwing out all existing structures, procedures, and systems and inventing completely new models of organizing and

---

[17]Adapted from Michael Hammer and James Champy, *Reengineering the Corporation: A Manifesto for Business Revolution* (New York: HarperBusiness, 1993), pp. 31–49.

accomplishing work. Reengineering ignores the old rules for how business is organized and conducted and focuses on what *should* be. It seeks quantum leaps in performance by starting over.

Quality programs usually work within the framework of a company's existing processes to enhance or modify them by means of continuous (incremental) improvement. Reengineering seeks performance breakthroughs, not by enhancing or modifying existing processes but often by discarding them and starting over with entirely new ones. Processes must be kept simple to meet the demands for quality, service, flexibility, low cost, and speed in today's global marketplace. The need for simplicity has enormous consequences for how processes should be designed and organizations structured. Operations Management in Practice 7.4 presents one example of this, Taco Bell's effective use of business process reengineering to achieve competitive advantage.

Reengineering is about innovation. It seeks to exploit new technologies to achieve new and different goals. Unfortunately, a common mistake made by companies is to view technology in the context of existing processes. Managers attempt to determine how they can use new technologies to improve or streamline existing operations instead of examining how they can use these technologies to do new and different things. One of the most challenging aspects of reengineering is to identify the new and unfamiliar capabilities of technology instead of focusing on those that are well known.

Finally, managers must recognize that people's needs are greatly influenced by their understanding of what is possible. Breakthrough technology makes possible activities that people have not yet imagined. The ability of technology to break the limiting rules of the past and open up new vistas of possibility is what makes technology critical to reengineering and ultimately to competitive advantage. Chapter 8 provides a more thorough discussion of the role of technology in today's business environment.

# Reengineering Taco Bell

Taco Bell, a subsidiary of PepsiCo, was sick and getting sicker when John E. Martin was named CEO in 1983. Taco Bell had enjoyed a fair degree of success as a regional Mexican-American restaurant chain. In 1982, it had less than 1,500 restaurants and did approximately $500 million in total sales, but its competitors were far ahead. Cumulative real growth from 1978 to 1982 was a negative sixteen percent compared to the total industry's positive six percent. Everyone knew that things had to drastically change if there was to be a long-term future for Taco Bell. The question was how could the organization implement such radical change quickly enough to make a difference. The answer was business process reengineering.

Martin comments that throughout the entire process, the greatest insight gained was that it had to listen to the customer. Taco Bell was a typical command and control organization with operational handbooks to cover every possible situation. It was driven by the process of processing while it tried for bigger, better, and more complicated in nearly everything it did. According to Martin, "If something was simple, we made it complex. If it was hard, we figured out a way to make it impossible." While those activities ensured that everyone always had things to keep them busy, the company lost sight of what mattered to the customers. As Martin says, "Did the customers care that our assistant managers could assemble and disassemble the twelve parts of a deep fryer with a blindfold on? Did they care that somebody in our industry probably wrote a handbook on it, including recommendations for the type of blindfold to use? Did they care, in the final analysis, that we managed to turn the relatively simple business of fast food into rocket science, all under the presumption that it was good for them?"

The company began by creating a new vision for the future. It would no longer be enough to be the leader in the Mexican category of the fast-food industry. Taco Bell would become a competitive force with which all restaurant organizations in all categories would have to address. How was Taco Bell to transform itself from a regional Mexican-American restaurant chain to a national force in the industry? Martin expected that the company's greatest barriers would be the tradition-bound ideas in which many of its employees believed.

Taco Bell's reengineering process began by asking its customers what was important to them. The company was surprised to learn that its customers did not want bigger, better, or fancier things as was first believed. All they wanted was good food, served fast and hot, in a clean environment at an affordable price. The industry always knew of the price sensitivity of customers and focused on reducing the cost of goods sold to ensure price leadership. But the cost of goods sold, primarily food and paper, are the only things that the customers get for their dollar. Maybe the cuts should come in some other form rather than cost of goods sold. It was decided to reduce every expense, except cost of goods sold. Marketing expenses were also reduced under the assumption that a better deal for its customers would sell itself. During the reengineering process, one simple rule was followed, enhance those things that bring value to the customer and change or eliminate those that do not.

continued

Over the years, its reengineering efforts have been responsible for many changes in the organization. For example, a complete reorganization of the human resources was undertaken. Entire levels of management were eliminated and new, more innovative positions were created. The position of "district manager" which traditionally oversaw the operations of five or six restaurants was eliminated. Restaurant managers were given the responsibility for running their own $1 million to $2 million operations without the "help" of upper management. To better reflect the nature of their new jobs, they were renamed restaurant general managers. Some managers were not able to adapt to the new, customer focused management style and left the company.

The restaurant building itself was reengineered. Before 1983, it was common for a Taco Bell restaurant to be 70 percent kitchen and 30 percent customer area. After eight years of reengineering, new restaurants averaged 30 percent kitchen space and 70 percent customer area. This change in restaurant layout was accomplished without decreasing productivity. In fact after the change, top restaurants could be expected to have a peak capacity of about $1,500 per hour compared to about $400 per hour before the change. This improvement in productivity was accomplished even with lower average prices than before.

CEO Martin said, "What we have achieved through reengineering is a synergy of all our processes. As our value-based marketing strategy drives sales and transactions, our efforts at reengineering make those sales more profitable, and at the same time, increase the customer satisfaction ratings we track on a continual basis." Under Martin's guidance, Taco Bell has also reevaluated its target audience. Within the confines of its brick and mortar facilities, its target audience is those who eat at fast-food restaurants (approximately $78 billion). Outside the confines of its walls, the target audience is all people who eat (about $600 billion in the U.S. alone).

Based on this logic, the company is rethinking its market and looking to expand into areas where people congregate. Successful locations have included airports, university campuses, office buildings, and stadiums. In the future, it may be vending machines, supermarkets, schools, retail outlets, or street corners. Taco Bell has averaged earnings increases of 31 percent since 1989, when the rest of the industry is struggling to increase profits at all. It has grown from a regional Mexican-American fast-food company in 1982 to a $3 billion national company because it listened to its customers and was not afraid to change.

## ► Summary

The quality movement is one of the most significant strategic activities taking place in American business today. Companies are completely changing the way they are working with their customers, suppliers, and employees. Many companies are improving productivity and quality and regaining market share from abroad. The road to a total quality organization is difficult to travel, with many potholes that skillful managers must negotiate.

**Learning Objective 1: Summarize historical developments in quality management.** Quality in this country has gone through four phases of development. In the inspection phase of development companies determined quality by comparing their manufactured parts to some master part. If the manufactured part matched the master completely, it was determined to be a quality part. Statistical quality control, developed during the 1930s, made it easier to determine the quality of a batch of parts without actually checking each one. This was the beginning of what is now referred to as *statistical process control* and *acceptance sampling*. The quality assurance phase built on the concepts of statistical quality and promoted the idea that quality is everyone's responsibility. New techniques helped managers measure the cost of quality. Today U.S. industry and services are in the strategic quality management phase. Companies have recognized quality as a strategic weapon and are treating it as such.

## Learning Objective 2: Describe Deming's chain reaction of quality events.

According to Deming, a decrease in costs follows improvement in quality. The improvement in quality and decrease in quality costs improve workers' productivity. Cost savings can be passed on to the customer in the form of lower prices for higher quality, which means a better value for the customer and results in better market share and an expanding customer base. The company stays in business and continues to provide more and more jobs.

## Learning Objective 3: Describe the various definitions of *quality*.

The first definition of quality is excellence. Some products provide customers with a sense of personal pleasure or esteem. Excellence is difficult to measure, but customers know it when they see it. The second definition is conformance to specifications. This definition simply states that so long as a product or service conforms to the design specifications for that product or service, it is a quality product or service. Therefore, a $5 wristwatch that conforms to the design specifications for that watch is a quality watch. The third definition of quality is fitness for use and includes some idea of the customer's intended use for the product. Under this definition, although a product conforms to specifications, it is not a quality product if it does not meet the needs of the customer. The most comprehensive definition of quality is value for the price. This definition combines the other definitions and includes the concept of price sensitivity. Customers determine the quality of a product or service by the perceived value for the money paid.

## Learning Objective 4: Define three terms used to describe product quality characteristics.

*Reliability* of a product is its ability to perform as expected. *Durability* of a nonrepairable product is its ability to last for its expected life span. *Serviceability* of a product refers to the ease of repairing a failed product or machine and returning it to service.

## Learning Objective 5: Define five terms used to describe service quality characteristics.

*Service reliability* refers to the ability to perform a promised service dependably and accurately. *Tangibles* refer to what the customer sees upon entering the facility. *Responsiveness* refers to willingness to help customers and provide prompt service. *Assurance* refers to the customer's perception of the service provider's trustworthiness and the confidence the customer has in that provider. *Empathy* refers to the customer's desire for individual care and attention.

## Learning Objective 6: Describe the four types of quality costs.

Internal failure costs are those incurred when a defect is found before the product reaches the customer. The most common internal failure costs are scrap and rework costs. External failure costs are those incurred when the customer detects the defect. Warranty claims and repair costs are external failure costs. Appraisal costs are those incurred for inspection to identify defects, and prevention costs are those incurred for activities designed to prevent defects.

## Learning Objective 7: Define *total quality management*, and list organizational requirements for its successful implementation.

Total quality management is an organizationwide approach to total customer satisfaction and continuous process improvement. Successful implementation of TQM requires strategic quality planning, a clear focus on internal and external customer satisfaction, continuous improvement of all processes, effective collection and analysis of information, effective use of teamwork and training, effective design of products and services, and effective leadership.

## Learning Objective 8: Describe the difference between continuous process improvement and business process reengineering.

Companies accomplish traditional quality activities within the framework of their existing processes and seek to enhance or modify them by means of continuous improvement. Reengineering seeks performance breakthroughs, not by enhancing or modifying existing processes but by discarding them and starting over with entirely new ones.

## ▶ Key Terms

| | | |
|---|---|---|
| appraisal costs | ISO9000 | quality assurance |
| assurance | Juran, Joseph M. | quality circle |
| business process reengineering | *kaizen* | reliability |
| Crosby, Philip B. | Malcolm Baldrige National Quality Award | responsiveness |
| Deming, W. Edwards | order winner | serviceability |
| durability | *poka-yoke* | statistical quality control |
| empathy | prevention costs | strategic quality management |
| external failure costs | process | tangibles |
| inspection | product reliability | total quality management (TQM) |
| internal failure costs | qualifiers | |

## ▶ Discussion Questions

1. Identify and discuss the eras in the quality movement.
2. Discuss how the qualifiers and order winners may differ for a cash-poor student and an executive of a successful company.
3. What is the Malcolm Baldrige National Quality Award? What are the seven major evaluation areas?
4. Discuss the roles that Deming, Juran, and Crosby have played in the quality movement.
5. How would *you* define quality? How does your definition compare with some current definitions of quality?
6. Compare and contrast product reliability, durability, and serviceability.
7. Use your favorite restaurant to discuss how the restaurant rates in terms of the five general dimensions of service quality.
8. What are the four categories of quality costs? Provide examples in each category.
9. What is total quality management? Suppose you are the owner of a company that has a unique product; as of now you have no competition. Is there any reason for you to implement TQM? Why?
10. Suppose you have been working as a manager of a company for ten years and the boss instructs you to write a memo discussing what needs to be done in order to successfully implement TQM. What would you say?
11. Discuss how effective design of products and services influences the ultimate quality of the product or service.
12. Describe the TQM implementation process.
13. Describe the difference between the continuous process improvement element of total quality management and the concept of business process reengineering. How might you know whether process reengineering is needed?

# Cadillac Motor Car Co.

In 1985 General Motor's Cadillac division ranked low in quality polls. Its image and its sales were suffering. Something had to be done to maintain Cadillac as a viable competitor in the increasingly competitive luxury car market.

Two years later General Motors reorganized Cadillac Motor Car Co. as a single business unit. As General Motor's only integrated automobile division, Cadillac was responsible for the engineering, manufacture, assembly, sales, and marketing of luxury automobiles. The reorganization was a better support for the strategy of simultaneous engineering, which Cadillac had been using since 1985. Simultaneous engineering involves functional areas that interact to conceive, approve, develop, and implement product programs, and Cadillac had been using it as a key strategy for product development and improvement plans. It allowed the company to incorporate its customers' needs and production concerns into the design process.

Simultaneous engineering required increased teamwork and employee involvement, so Cadillac created vehicle teams, management teams, and product development and improvement teams, which were responsible for the quality, cost, timing, and technology of Cadillac's vehicles, systems, and components. More than seven hundred employees, including suppliers and dealers, were responsible for defining, engineering, marketing, and continuously improving Cadillacs.

To succeed with simultaneous engineering Cadillac had to develop partnerships with its suppliers. Cadillac suppliers served on a variety of teams associated with simultaneous engineering; as key suppliers took on additional responsibilities, Cadillac reduced its supplier base to allow for closer, more focused relationships. Cadillac also played a key role in Targets for Excellence, a General Motors development program for suppliers that it designed to bring the continuous improvement culture to suppliers.

Cadillac also established the United Auto Workers–General Motors Quality Network, joint union-management quality councils at the corporate, group, division, and plant levels of the organization.

The Cadillac councils oversee all quality improvement efforts and support the implementation of the business plan. Cooperation of management and union has become part of the company's culture; they share the goal of producing a product that will satisfy the customer.

These initiatives depended on the involvement and teamwork of employees. Cadillac provided employees with the training, environment, and reward structure they needed in order to become an integral part of the quality effort. Cadillac made cross-functional People Strategy Teams responsible for research, design, recommendation, implementation, and evaluation of Cadillac's personnel processes.

As Cadillac worked to improve quality in terms of processes and product, it stressed the importance of focusing on the customer. Cadillac Motor Car Co.'s mission statement stresses that "Cadillac will continuously improve the quality of its products and services to meet or exceed customer expectations and succeed as a profitable business." If a showroom customer criticized a Cadillac before 1986, the comment went from the dealer to the customer service department and then worked its way through six other departments. It was months before the complaint reached anyone who could act on it. This changed as Cadillac became more customer focused. The company expected dealers to call in both negative and positive feedback, which went to the appropriate quality service team. In addition, all new Cadillac owners received questionnaires that invited suggestions for improvement, and Cadillac employees called some customers to get more information. Both line workers and executives of the division participated in the data gathering. The extensive market research allowed Cadillac to better understand customers' needs and wants and what customers consider important. This was important information for the simultaneous engineering process. Cadillac used quality function deployment to translate customers' needs and wants into engineering terms and product specifications.

Cadillac Motor Car Co.'s cultural change was rewarded when it earned the 1990 Malcolm Baldrige

National Quality Award, the most prestigious quality award in America. Cadillac was the first American automobile company to receive the award.

Companies that apply for the Baldrige award are scrutinized in seven areas: leadership, information and analysis, planning, use of human resources, quality assurance of products and services, quality results, and customer satisfaction. Here's how Cadillac performed in each area:

- Leadership. The executive staff is responsible for establishing and communicating the visions, values, and methods of the company. The executive staff also leads the organization through the annual business planning cycle, the process by which Cadillac continuously improves the quality of its people, processes, products, and services. The executive staff empowers employees to develop individual objectives to support the overall organizational objectives.

- Information and analysis. Cadillac conducts extensive market research to assess customers' requirements and satisfaction levels; it also collects data on employee satisfaction, safety and environmental impact of products and processes, dealer sales and service, quality of suppliers' parts and processes, key indicators of internal operations and processes, and competitive benchmarks. It uses a variety of techniques to analyze the information, including simulations, trend charts, and regression analyses.

- Strategic quality planning. Cadillac's business plan is its quality plan. It helps ensure that Cadillac is the "standard of the world" for customer satisfaction and for quality and requires the annual review of the mission statement and strategic objectives, guides internal processes, and provides structure to the development of short-term and long-term goals. Virtually every employee is involved in the planning process in some way. Suppliers and dealers also participate.

- Use of human resources. Cadillac believes that people and people systems represent its most significant competitive advantage. It developed training and reward structures to ensure that employees have necessary skills and incentives to achieve goals in the business plan, and quality teams work to improve personnel processes. Cadillac workers have power; the company sees them as both capable and essential to quality

improvements. Teamwork is a critical component of the quality effort, which means that Cadillac has seen training levels exceed forty hours per employee per year, lower rates of injury and illness, and a decline in employee turnover.

- Quality assurance of products and services. Simultaneous engineering, which brings a product to market, is handled by teams that follow Cadillac's Product Program Management Process (PPMP) for coordinating all aspects of a specific car program. The process has four phases: technology and concept development, product/process development prototype validation, process validation product confirmation, and production and continuous improvement. In the first phase the team converts concepts into a plan that includes a marketing strategy, vehicle content and performance criteria, manufacturing objectives, and other details. The second phase is for formalizing part characteristics and process requirements; the team completes the manufacturing and assembly design and demonstrates vehicle prototypes. Phase 3 includes building pilot vehicles with actual production tools. The last phase is production and continuous improvement.

- Quality results. The increased focus on quality and customer satisfaction has yielded many benefits. Since 1986 the performance of Cadillac's combined product line in the number of things that will go wrong at 50,000 test miles has improved by 67 percent, to levels at or exceeding world-class performance. One Cadillac plant improved its tool transition by 65 percent in just two years. Simultaneous engineering has brought a 56 percent reduction since 1985 in the number of engineering changes issued in a model year. Target build—the percentage of cars built in their scheduled week—has improved 67 percent since 1987. These are just of a few of the many positive outcomes of the quality efforts.

- Customer satisfaction. Cadillac incorporates the needs of the customers in the product design process. Extensive market research keeps the company current in regard to the often changing needs of customers. It also asks customers to suggest improvements. Dealers receive a wide array of customer service programs as well as incentives and activities designed to make them more customer focused. The Cadillac Consumer Relations System, established in 1987, handles calls twenty-four hours a day, seven days a week from Cadillac drivers and potential customers. Customers are obviously satisfied: In 1989 the J.D. Power Customer Satisfaction Index ranked Cadillac the highest domestic marque and fifth overall in the world.

## ► References

Art Durity. "Critics Charge Baldrige Ads Lack Quality." *Personnel* 68 (February 1991): 1–2.

John Phillips, III. "Cadillac in the Nineties." *Car and Driver*, February 1990, p. 25.

Rosetta Riley. "Getting Faster Feedback from Your Customers." *Working Woman*, November 1991, pp. 55–58.

Cadillac. Promotional literature, including *The Quality Story* and *Application Summary*.

## ► Discussion Questions

1. Which of the Baldrige award criteria are most important to the success of a quality effort? Least important? Why?
2. Why is simultaneous engineering so important for Cadillac? How can a service organization use simultaneous engineering?
3. Cadillac recognizes the importance of both internal and external customers. Which customer group is most important? Why?
4. Some criticize Cadillac's advertisements that tout its winning the Baldrige award. Do you think it is appropriate to use this award in advertising? Why? On what grounds might the criticisms be based?

## ► Selected References

Brocka, Bruce, and M. Suzanne Brocka. *Quality Management: Implementing the Best Ideas of the Masters.* Homewood, Ill. : Richard D. Irwin, 1992.

Crosby, Phillip B. *Quality Is Free.* New York: McGraw-Hill, 1979.

Feigenbaum, Armand V., *Total Quality Control,* 3d ed. New York: McGraw-Hill, 1983.

Garvin, David A. *Managing Quality: The Strategic and Competitive Edge.* New York: Free Press, 1988.

Hammer, Michael, and James Champy. *Reengineering the Corporation: A Manifesto for Business Revolution.* New York: Free Press, 1993.

Hauser, John R., and Don Clausing. "The House of Quality." *Harvard Business Review* (May–June 1988): 63–73.

Juran, J. M., and F. M. Gryna. *Quality Planning and Analysis,* 3d ed. New York: McGraw-Hill, 1993.

Sewell, Carl, and Paul B. Brown. *Customers for Life.* New York: Simon & Schuster, 1990.

Walton, Mary. *The Deming Management Method.* New York: Putnam, 1986.

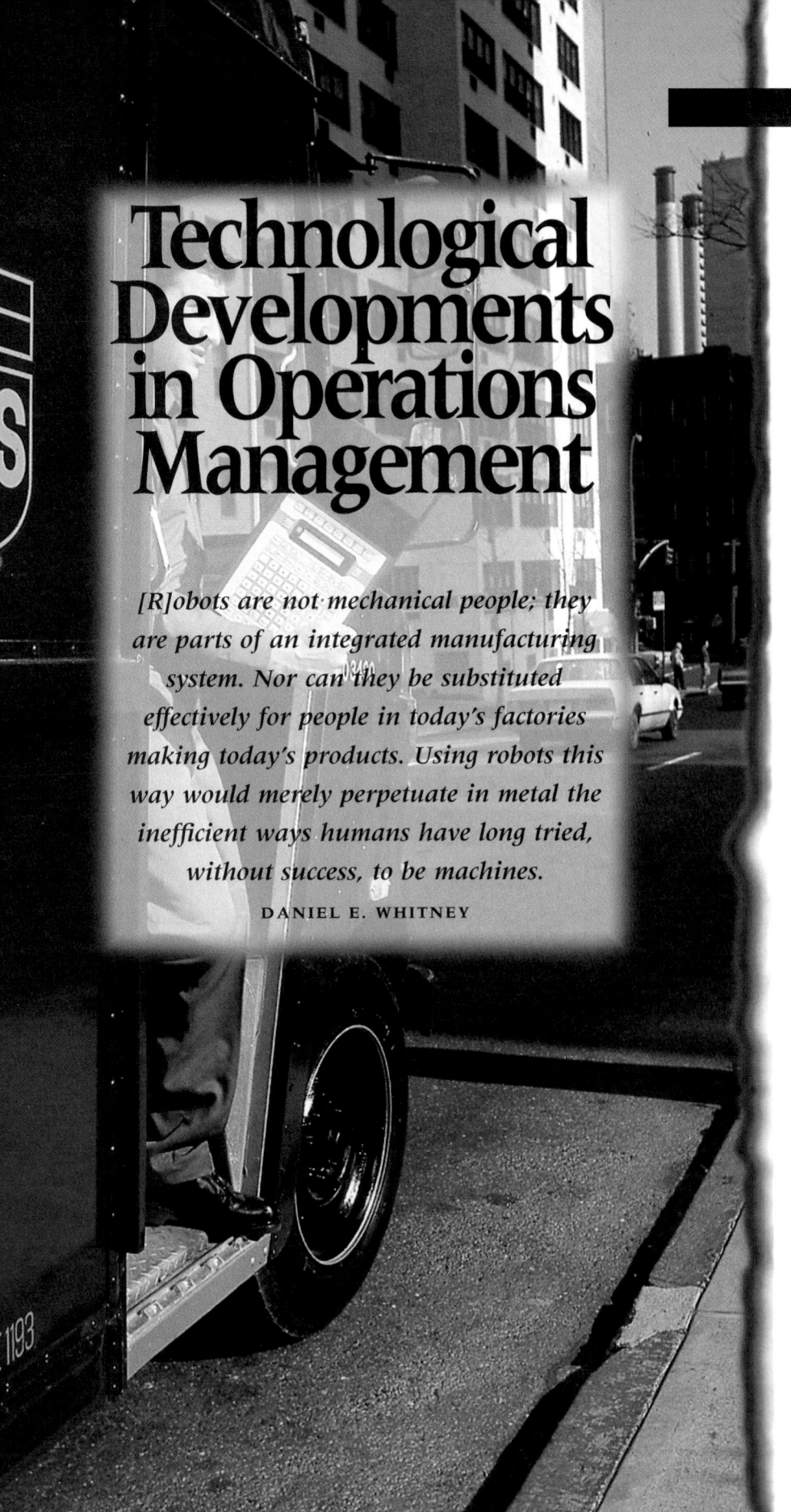

# Technological Developments in Operations Management

*[R]obots are not mechanical people; they are parts of an integrated manufacturing system. Nor can they be substituted effectively for people in today's factories making today's products. Using robots this way would merely perpetuate in metal the inefficient ways humans have long tried, without success, to be machines.*

DANIEL E. WHITNEY

**Introduction**

**Role of Technology in Today's Business Environment**
*OPERATIONS MANAGEMENT IN PRACTICE 8.1: Jumping Ahead by Going High Tech*
*OPERATIONS MANAGEMENT IN PRACTICE 8.2: Technology in Sports*
*GLOBAL OPERATIONS MANAGEMENT 8.3: Japan Bids for Global Leadership in Clean Industry*

**Transferring New Technology from Concept to Reality**

**Implementing New Technology**

**Fixed, Programmable, and Flexible Automation**
*OPERATIONS MANAGEMENT IN PRACTICE 8.4: Today's Advanced Manufacturing Options*

**Computer-Integrated Manufacturing**
*OPERATIONS MANAGEMENT IN PRACTICE 8.5: U.S. Manufacturers Wary on Automation*

**Technological Improvements for Support**
*GLOBAL OPERATIONS MANAGEMENT 8.6: Tomorrow's Manufacturing Technologies*
*OPERATIONS MANAGEMENT IN PRACTICE 8.7: The Marvels of "Virtual Reality"*

**Case Study: Pavilion Technologies**

*After completing this chapter you should be able to*

1. Describe the role of technology in today's business environment
2. Define *technology transfer*, and explain why it is such an important issue
3. Identify the five fallacies commonly associated with implementing new technology
4. Describe the differences in fixed, programmed, and flexible automation
5. Summarize the role of computers in applying technology in manufacturing and service operations
6. Describe the importance of flexibility in today's organizations
7. Identify some key technological developments in manufacturing and service operations, and discuss the advantages they create

## Introduction

Have you ever stopped to think what advances in technology have done for you? Just think about all the things that would not have been available five to ten years ago. Compact disks, electronic pagers, facsimile machines, cellular telephones, camcorders, and laser video disks certainly top the list. Who would have thought that the fancy new personal computer you purchased five years ago would be obsolete today? The world continues to change, and much of that change is attributable to technology.

Technology is one of the most significant issues facing both manufacturing and service companies today. As companies strive for increased productivity by reducing costs, improving quality, and improving customer responsiveness, many have turned to advances in technology as the way to get the most out of their operations. Some companies have been extremely successful at creating strategic advantage through technological advancements, whereas others have looked to technology as a panacea and have been disappointed in their results.

Many technological advancements are computer based. The continuous improvements in computer technology create additional opportunities for applying that technology in new areas of industry, to the benefit of both manufacturing and service businesses. In Chapter 5 we discussed the role of technology in product and process design decisions. In this chapter we will look more specifically at recent technological developments that have helped improve day-to-day operational capabilities. Some technological advancements discussed here are relatively new; others go back to the 1960s. Although some of these technologies may seem dated, they are old only in chronology. In some cases it has taken us decades to understand how to best use these technologies and see evidence of their acceptance in industry. Therefore, they too will be treated as recent advances in technology.

We will also address the importance of exercising care in implementing new technology, because new technology implemented poorly may make operational performance worse, not better. We will introduce you to several companies, both in manufacturing and services, that have been very successful in the implementation and use of technological advances. Chapter 9 investigates the influence of advanced technology on organizational structure and employees.

# Role of Technology in Today's Business Environment

Just exactly what is **technology**? *Webster's II New Riverside Dictionary* defines *technology* as "the application of scientific knowledge, especially in industry or business."[1] Some level of technology is associated with every completed task. A task that involves no new technology is a low-technology task. A task that involves the integration of several new key technologies is considered a high-technology task. For example, in your local grocery store's not too distant past the checkout person manually entered all sales transactions in the cash register. Data entry errors were commonplace. From that level of technology we have progressed to the point that supermarkets use electronic scanners to enter data with much greater accuracy than before. This technology has gone beyond data entry and is being used to maintain inventory records to ensure timely replenishment of stock items. Today technology allows many customers to pay for their groceries with a bank charge card or debit card, and some stores are experimenting with automated checkouts. This is an example of applying newer technology to improve the level of customer service and efficiency.

In general, manufacturing and service operations use technology in order to improve the performance of the organization through

1. Improved product and service quality
2. Lower cost
3. Increased responsiveness to markets
4. Increased responsiveness to customers
5. More flexibility
6. Improved safety
7. Smaller work-in-process inventories
8. Increased long-term profitability

Decision makers must be prepared to evaluate various levels of the technology that is available to support a given set of activities and choose the most appropriate level of technology for their operation. A higher level of technology is not always preferable to a lower level. The key is that changes in technology must be strategic decisions. Investing in expensive new technology just to achieve some short-term objective is not worthwhile. The effects of advanced technology permeate the entire organization and can have profound and long-lasting implications for the competitive abilities of the company. Operations Management in Practice 8.1 recounts how Pitney Bowes, a manufacturer of postage machines, copiers, facsimile machines, and dictating machines, has used technology successfully to increase its competitive advantage.

Both manufacturing and service operations benefit from advances in technology. Companies such as Wal-Mart, Kmart, Federal Express, United Parcel Service, and many others have been using technology for competitive advantage. Chapter 2 introduced you to J.C. Penney's use of technology in service operations (see Operations Management in Practice 2.5).

Technological advances have even played a significant role in the sports world. Rules committees of the International Olympic Committee work to keep track of the application of technological advances that might affect the competi-

[1] *Webster's II New Riverside Dictionary* (Boston: Houghton Mifflin, 1984).

## OPERATIONS MANAGEMENT IN PRACTICE 8.1

# Jumping Ahead by Going High Tech

Making postage meters hardly seems a business to write home about, but the folks at Pitney Bowes in Stamford, Connecticut can barely contain their enthusiasm for their latest product. Introduced in July, 1992, the Paragon mail processor is the paragon of postage meters. It's also a milestone in the march of Pitney Bowes from old-line manufacturer to high-tech growth company.

Feed the Paragon a stack of mail and it seals each letter by spraying a thin jet of water on the glued edge of the envelope flap. Then it weighs the letter in milliseconds, prints the appropriate postage on the corner, and shoots it out the other end of the machine at rates up to 240 pieces per minute. The Paragon employs three kinds of microprocessors; its development generated 75 new patents. Industry analysts predict the machine will bring in at least $100 million in revenues over the next year, which would lead to sales and earnings records.

That's a remarkable achievement for one product, but to CEO George Harvey, the Paragon is even more: it's proof that the company has transformed itself from a stodgy office equipment supplier into a technologically sophisticated manufacturer with its sights set on growth.

No rival offers anything comparable to the Paragon, so Pitney Bowes has a chance to regain market share lost to European companies. The $20,000 system is being promoted as a labor saving device. It is estimated that the Paragon can save the average mail room up to three worker-hours of tedious sorting daily. The vice president of operations and technology says, "You don't have any delays for separating the piles and adjusting the machine. The mail goes through so fast, you need a person on roller skates to take it all away."

*Major cities throughout the world are subject to environmental pollution.*

tiveness of individuals and teams: Today's sports equipment is so good that these committees are asking whether the equipment, not the athletes, is driving world records. They want to be sure that the Olympics is a contest of athletes, not sporting equipment. Operations Management in Practice 8.2 describes how a variety of sports are using technology.

## Technology and the Environment

In a 1991 Gallup Poll, 83 percent of the respondents felt that business and industry were not concerned enough with environmental problems. Other results from that study showed that of the respondents,

78 percent considered themselves to be "environmentalists"
71 percent favored protecting the environment, even at the risk of curbing economic growth
62 percent thought that not enough progress had been made in twenty years, but 80 percent thought that at least some progress had been made
86 percent reported voluntarily recycling newspapers, glass, or aluminum
79 percent reported at least some optimism that our environmental problems would be well under control by 2011

# Technology in Sports

Many of the most dramatic improvements in sports equipment came on the heels of World War II. Diving springboards, for example, were transformed by way of the aircraft industry when Norman Buck introduced a design in 1948 that used 300 interlocking pieces of war-surplus square aluminum tubing. The "Buckboard" soon gave way to designs that used even stronger and lighter aluminum alloys. By the 1960s the enhanced springiness of diving boards made possible dives at the 1-meter height that had previously been performed only at 3 meters.

Today's boards are springier still and provide 15 percent more lift than those of the 1960s. They also feature superior non-skid surfaces, and the light weight and resiliency of the board tip minimize injuries, especially to the head. In fact, the last two feet of the springboard now weigh less than 10 pounds.

Pole vaulting also got a boost from improved materials. In 1960 Herb Jencks, manufacturer of fiberglass fishing poles, had just built a new deep-sea fishing rod 10 feet long and more than an inch in diameter. Jencks's son, a junior-high-school vaulter, borrowed one of his father's poles for a practice vault and, much to his surprise and delight, surpassed his personal best by half a foot. Until then, pole vaulters used bamboo poles and landed in sawdust pits, and the world record was 15 feet. Today the world record is just over 20 feet, thanks to carbon composite poles that are custom built to the vaulter's weight, take-off speed, and hold technique. Foam rubber pits that cushion falls more effectively also allow vaulters to be ever more fearless in their quest for height.

Technology has played a significant role in other sports as well. High technology javelins had to be de-engineered. Aerodynamic models were so advanced that they were being thrown off the field of competition into the stands. Fencing foils, epees, masks and jackets have all been redesigned for safety by using advanced technology. The sports of archery, bicycling, kayaking and discus throwing represent other examples where advanced technology has been applied.

The optimism reflected in this survey is based in part on improvements in technology. Because they are using new technologies to develop intelligent manufacturing systems, new metals, polymers, ceramic and composite materials—and new processes to use these new technologies—manufacturers can use their resources more efficiently and reduce waste.

The motivation for industry to become more environmentally sensitive is partly economic. According to one estimate, the global market for environmental goods and services may be as big as $370 billion a year.[2]

What will be the source of the technological advancements that businesses and services need? Many will result from redirecting defense-related efforts to environmental research. Others will come from joint partnerships of private industry and federal agencies and partnerships of multiple industry groups. One example of such collaboration is a group made up of representatives from the

[2]Robert Engleman, "Technology Paves Way for Greener Future," *Safety & Health* 147 (April 1993): 31–33.

automobile industry, the electric power industry, and the U.S. Department of Energy. The group's mission is to develop batteries for a new generation of electric cars, because public support and use of electric cars is likely to improve the environment greatly; the primary barrier to that end is battery design. Without new battery technology, pollution and energy consumption will continue to increase as the population and the number of automobiles worldwide continue to increase.

Developing more effective recycling procedures and more environmentally sensitive products—and moving away from products, such as styrofoam, that are not biodegradable—are just a few ways businesses and individuals are contributing to a greener environment. Manufacturing companies that conduct business in foreign countries are continually faced with different environmental standards. Motorola's answer to the different standards is to establish one set of high standards for the corporation to use throughout the world. The word *compliance* is not a word that is well received in discussions of environmental standards at Motorola, which prefers to be on the leading edge, continuing to improve and serving as a model for other corporations. Global Operations Management 8.3 describes the activities of some Japanese companies in their quest for global leadership in clean industries.

## Technology-Focused Strategic Alliances

Technology has served as the catalyst for many joint ventures between many companies both in the United States and abroad, especially in high-technology businesses. Companies have organized these **strategic alliances** in an attempt to improve the competitiveness of each member company. They form strategic alliances to gain access to expertise they need and to gain entry to new markets. These partnerships have become an integral part of many organizations' strategic efforts. For example, IBM has joined more than four hundred strategic alliances with various companies in the United States and abroad.[3] Not all strategic alliances have been beneficial. The key reason for failure of an alliance often is that one or more members join the group expecting to satisfy some short-term concern. Other reasons for failure include the personalities of individual parties and cultural differences. The most successful alliances are generally those joined by companies that have a long-term vision and an understanding of and appreciation for each other's culture.

In the mid-1980s the U.S. Department of Defense and U.S. industry formed an alliance called Sematech to support development of technology to assist the ailing semiconductor industry. Half of the funding for Sematech comes from the federal government and half from the twelve member companies. In 1992 Congress told Sematech to spend 10 percent of its 1993 budget on environmental research in order to continue receiving funding.[4] That requirement was consistent with Washington's increasing tendency to make scientific research more practical. Legislators were concerned that the $76 billion annual investment in research and development was not leading to improvements in the nation's well being. The Energy Department plans to spend more than $200 million to transfer

[3]Stratford Sherman, "Are Strategic Alliances Working?" *Fortune*, September 21, 1992, p. 77.
[4]John Markoff, "Environment Is a Mission at Sematech," *New York Times*, October 5, 1992, p. D1.

## GLOBAL OPERATIONS MANAGEMENT 8.3

# Japan Bids for Global Leadership in Clean Industry

The Earth Summit in Rio de Janeiro was an event long on pieties and short on commitment, but where the U.S. and Europe wavered, Japan stood out. After years as an environmental pariah, Japan now hopes to enter what its prime minister Kiichi Mayazawa calls "an era of global citizenry." Japan has realized how new industrial opportunity will be driven by environmental change. Japan already leads the world in environmental friendliness. The amount of sulfur dioxide discharged by Japanese power plants is about four percent of the average discharge from the U.S., and nitrogen oxide discharge is about 11%. One United Nations study shows that global emission of carbon dioxide would fall 36% if other countries adopted Japanese style eco-efficiency.

Japan's push to develop new environmental technology is headed by the Research Institute of Innovative Technology for Earth (RITE), and international participation is encouraged—a rarity for a Japanese institution. Recent projects include Toyota's program to develop genetically engineered trees that utilize more carbon dioxide, the prime pollutant from automobile exhaust. Japan's electrical power industry is devising means of using chlorella to remove carbon dioxide from power plant exhausts. It plans to bubble the exhaust through large beds of the algae, which thrives on carbon. Coral reefs are also being genetically engineered to consume more carbon dioxide as they grow. Most of this new technology will take 20 years to develop. In the shorter term, Japan sees transferring its existing energy efficient technology to developing countries as the best way to deal with global warming. World Bank figures show that developing countries will produce 44% of total carbon emissions in 2050, up from 20% now.

This use of technology raises an important ethical consideration, however. Can the juggernaut of technical progress clean up its own mess? Do we have to face a world on which tropical rain forests and coral reefs, along with wetlands and other wild areas, become relentlessly engineered to the demands of planetary management? Is this really the RITE way to solve our environmental problems?

---

weapons technology from the national labs to industry.[5] The government is already running several programs, and several others are under consideration, as Table 8.1 shows.

Many strategic alliances involve a U.S. company and one or more foreign companies. Each strategic alliance usually is concerned about the technology that might be involved and how that technology should be transferred among alliance members. In the case of foreign alliance members technology transfer becomes a more serious issue, because much of the technology is computer technology, which means that U.S. national security interests are a consideration.

[5]John Carey, "Hey, You in the Ivory Tower. Come on Down," *Business Week*, October 12, 1992, pp. 32–33.

**TABLE 8.1**
Federal Technology Programs

**Uncle Sam's Science Experiments**
*Existing Efforts*

Advanced Technology Program: $50 million in 1992 to support research and
development in everything from ceramics and robotics to superconductivity
High Performance Computing Initiative: $655 million in 1992 to develop faster
computers and the information super highway
Manufacturing Technology Centers: $15 million to support seven centers to
bring manufacturing technology to small factories

*On the Drawing Board*

Civilian Technology Agency: A counterpart to the National Science Foundation
that would focus on applied research
Civilian Technology Development Corp.: A new agency to fund companies
commercializing new technologies
Advanced Manufacturing Initiative: Increased federal funding for research and
development in machine tools and high-technology manufacturing

Source: Mark Lewyn, "Hey You in the Ivory Tower. Come on Down," *Business Week,* October 12,
1992, p. 32.

# Transferring New Technology from Concept to Reality

As defined earlier, technology involves the application of scientific knowledge.
This scientific knowledge results from individuals and organizations that are
committed to improving the technical base of industry. Many universities
sponsor technological research in engineering, computer science, information
processing, physical sciences, and other areas, and many private companies are
seeking their own technological breakthroughs.

Whatever the source of the technological advances, companies must be
careful about attempting to apply the new technology in the business environment. **Technology transfer** is the process by which technology, often newly
developed, is applied in the workplace or shared by members of a strategic
alliance. Many companies spend millions of dollars annually to support university research. Their hope is that the academy will develop new technologies that
will give industry an additional competitive advantage. Transferring this technology from the research lab to the factory floor is often a difficult task.

The transfer of technology among members of a strategic alliance has proved
extremely beneficial in many cases. In 1990 the Minnesota Mining & Manufacturing (3M) Co. made public the results of efforts by 3M and twenty-five other
companies that joined with it in the venture. Each company brought to the
project a particular technical competence and shared it with the entire group.
The resulting product, called Digital Matchprint, is a $300,000 machine that
generates accurate color proofs of a page so that it can be inspected before
printing begins. 3M estimates that it would have taken fifteen years to develop
the new product alone; the alliance developed it in five years.[6]

[6]Jagannath Dubashi, "Best-Practice Companies: 3M," *Financial World* 160 (September 17, 1991): 40.

# Implementing New Technology

Some companies have treated technology as their savior, but many U.S. companies have been relatively slow to adopt new technology. Reluctance is often the result of several barriers to effective implementation of new technology. One such barrier is the difficulty in justifying new technology. Traditional financial accounting practices are not designed to recognize many advantages of new technology. For example, measuring the financial effect of increased responsiveness, flexibility, and quality on the bottom line of the company is difficult. Certainly, the benefits cannot be determined with the same level of precision that the accounting procedures yield for labor and overhead costs. Along those same lines many managers continue to see technology primarily as a way to reduce labor costs. So their approach to financial justification focuses myopically on the labor-savings component of the decision.

Another barrier is that management often fails to understand the capabilities of the new technology. Business researchers Robert Hayes and Ramchandran Jaikumar describe implementing new technology as replacing an old car with a helicopter. They say that "if you fail to understand and prepare for the revolutionary capabilities of these systems, they will become as much an inconvenience as a benefit—and a lot more expensive."[7] After all, the availability of a helicopter opens up an entirely new set of opportunities for the company. Failure to recognize and use these additional opportunities will make the investment marginal at best.

Another key barrier to the implementation of new technology is concern about how it affects the people in the organization. Many think technological change has a detrimental effect on the social element of the organization. Northern Telecom commissioned a study to assess the actual effect of technological change. The study identified five fallacies related to the belief that advanced technology is bad for people:

**Fallacy 1:**   *The main effect of technological change on people is loss of jobs.* In reality technological change may be the only way to preserve jobs in the long term.

**Fallacy 2:**   *The people hit hardest by technological change are hourly workers.* In fact, technological change affects the entire organization. Hourly workers are usually better prepared for change than the professional and engineering employees.

**Fallacy 3:**   *Experts should handle job design and other technical issues.* Yes, the company will need experts, but they must be prepared to work with a diverse group of individuals within the company in order to realize the full potential of the technology.

**Fallacy 4:**   *New, automated systems will reduce the need for interpersonal communication on the factory floor and in the office.* Some people think of the factory of the future as a "lights out" factory that needs no people. But the reality is that automation requires increased communication between workers and management and a greater degree of teamwork and participative management.

---

[7]Robert H. Hayes and Ramchandran Jaikumar, "Manufacturing's Crisis: New Technologies, Obsolete Organizations," *Harvard Business Review* 66 (September–October 1988): 77–78.

| Currently Skillful at Using | | Plan to Use in Future | |
|---|---|---|---|
| *Technology* | *Percentage of Respondents* | *Technology* | *Percentage of Respondents* |
| Computer–aided design (CAD) | 50.4 | Computer–aided manufacturing (CAM) | 50.9 |
| Material requirements planning (MRP) | 26.5 | Just in Time (JIT) | 43.6 |
| Computer–aided manufacturing (CAM) | 26.0 | Computer–aided design (CAD) | 39.5 |
| Manufacturing resource planning (MRP II) | 21.0 | Manufacturing cells | 32.2 |
| Manufacturing cells | 18.2 | Manufacturing resource planning (MRP II) | 29.6 |
| Just in Time (JIT) | 16.4 | Statistical process control (SPC) | 28.6 |
| Statistical process control (SPC) | 16.0 | Material requirements planning (MRP) | 21.3 |
| Robotics | 7.5 | Computer–integrated manufacturing (CIM) | 20.3 |
| Computer–integrated manufacturing (CIM) | 4.9 | Robotics | 14.0 |
| Flexible manufacturing systems (FMS) | 3.9 | Flexible manufacturing systems (FMS) | 9.1 |
| Optimized production technology (OPT) | 1.6 | Optimized production technology (OPT) | 1.6 |
| Automated storage and retrieval systems (AS/RS) | 1.0 | Automated storage and retrieval systems (AS/RS) | 0.5 |

Source: William H. Miller, "CAD Comes into Its Own," *Industry Week* (May 18, 1992): 62.

TABLE 8.2
Results of Advanced
Technology Study

**Fallacy 5:** *Technological change is bad for people.* Technological change can have an adverse effect on any organization through job loss, increased stress, sabotage, and other factors, and cases of each have been reported. But at the same time technological change can create a work environment that supports increased training, greater participation in decision making, improved relationships between workers and management, and a general improvement in the quality of working life in the organization; other cases support these outcomes.[8]

Many companies have implemented advanced manufacturing technologies with varied success. A 1992 study conducted by the National Association of Manufacturers of 385 manufacturing plants from a cross-section of industry asked participants to indicate which advanced technologies they would consider themselves "skillful" in applying. They were also asked to list which technologies they planned to implement. The survey showed that industry had accepted several advanced technologies well but was less receptive to other technologies. Table 8.2 shows the results of the study.

Because much advanced technology involves automation in one form or another, the next section discusses different types of automation used in industry today.

## Fixed, Programmable, and Flexible Automation

**Automation** is defined as the substitution of machine work for human physical and mental work.[9] When many people think of automation they think of robots, but they are but one form of automated equipment.

[8]Andrew Young, Daniel Levi, and Charles Slem, "Dispelling Some Myths About People and Technological Change," *Industrial Engineering* 19 (November 1987): 52–69.
[9]Thomas F. Wallace and John R. Dougherty, *American Production and Inventory Control Society Dictionary*, 6th ed. (Falls Church, Va.: American Production and Inventory Control Society, 1987), p. 2.

Manufacturing and service organizations today are using three basic types of automation: fixed, programmed, and flexible.[10] **Fixed automation** is used primarily in high-volume assembly situations in which the sequence of processing steps is fixed. Fixed automation requires high-volume production in order to spread its great cost over a large number of units and make investment in it economically feasible. The major drawback of fixed automation is its relative inflexibility; adapting the production system to different product designs is extremely difficult.

Manufacturers use **programmable automation** to overcome some of the problems that result from the inflexibility of fixed automation. This type of automation allows the production of different product designs so long as the differences are not dramatic. The production environment usually involves a low or medium volume of units produced in batches. After each batch of a product is produced, the production system is reprogrammed to accommodate the next batch of a different product. One major drawback is that the production system is usually out of service during reprogramming, which means the manufacturer loses valuable productive capacity.

**Flexible automation** is an improvement upon programmable automation. It refers to automated production facilities that can be adapted to a wider variety of product designs; changeovers require minimal down time. Therefore, flexible automation can produce various combinations and schedules of products and does not require batch production. Flexible automation is the way of the future. Improved computer technology will give the shop floor even more flexibility, improving the productivity of the operation. But history has not been kind to the move toward more automation. Operations Management in Practice 8.4 recounts how flexibility was a concern even in the 1920s with Henry Ford's automobile manufacturing operation.

In the 1980s many companies expected to solve all their problems by purchasing automated equipment. Unfortunately, in many cases these major expenditures of capital were not appropriate. For example, after becoming chairman of General Motors in 1981, Roger Smith decided that technology would be the key to improving operations throughout the company. During the 1980s GM invested approximately $80 billion on modernizing its operations worldwide. Soon after, it realized that its enormous spending may have been a mistake. Some production lines halted for hours because of software problems, robots dismembered and painted each other, robots damaged automobiles, and automatically guided vehicles refused to move. The *Economist* estimated that GM may have wasted about 20 percent of what it spent on new technology.[11]

GM learned an expensive lesson about automation and advanced technology. Technology is no panacea. Technology cannot be a substitute for good management, organizational communication, worker training and motivation, product and process design, and relationships with customers and suppliers. Implementing advanced technology requires sharing information across functional lines in an organization. Marketing, sales, purchasing, engineering, human resources, and manufacturing all have to work together in a coordinated effort. Without such cooperation and coordination companies will time and again have experiences such as GM's.

[10]Mikell P. Groover, *Automation, Production Systems, and Computer Integrated Manufacturing* (Englewood Cliffs, N.J.: Prentice-Hall, 1987), pp. 2–3.
[11]"Management Brief: When GM's Robots Ran Amok," *Economist*, August 10, 1991, pp. 64–65.

# Today's Advanced Manufacturing Options

Automobile production in the U.S. was down a million cars in 1927—not because it was a bad year economically, but because Henry Ford's plants took five months, from May 26 to November 1, to switch production from the Model T to Model A.

In 1927, many of Henry's customers and dealers were content to wait, but in today's marketplace such a long changeover could spell corporate suicide. Auto buyers and many other retail and industrial customers as well put a premium on timely delivery. (Incidentally, it took Ford Motor Co. until 1929 to rebound to its 1926 sales level.)

Back then, Ford confronted problems that sound familiar even today—an aging product line beginning to draw yawns in a rough-and-tumble marketplace, and plenty of eager competitors with new and exciting design features. Unfortunately, auto production technology had not progressed much beyond rigidly dedicated factories that rolled out a continuing parade of look alike cars. So Henry had little choice but to shut down and struggle with the changeover.

Today, auto makers and other manufacturers have an alternative—flexible automation. Among the virtues of this emerging technology: its ability to allow rapid conversion of production facilities from one product to another. Had today's spectrum of automation concepts been available in 1927, Henry Ford wouldn't have had to tell his customers to wait.

The next section looks at specific types of technology advancements in use today. Discussing all technological advancements is impossible, so we will focus on a sample of those receiving the most attention.

## Computer-Integrated Manufacturing

The development of **computer-integrated manufacturing (CIM)** goes back to the 1960s, but CIM is a recent concept in terms of its application in American industry. What CIM really means still is a matter of considerable debate. Some people confuse CIM with process automation, although nothing in the concept of CIM suggests the need for automation. Some tend to emphasize the *C* in CIM and refer to it as a computer system used to integrate manufacturing operations. Others focus on the *I* in CIM and consider it a formal structure for integrating all business functions within the organization. Of course, computers are the easiest way to accomplish this integration.

For purposes of this text we will define *CIM* as 'a formal process by which integration of organizational functions may be achieved.' This seems to be the definition most widely accepted today. Another term, which reflect this more recent view of CIM, is **enterprise integration**. Some view CIM as an option, to be adopted or not, whereas others view CIM as an absolute necessity for long-term survival of manufacturing operations.

Regardless of how one defines or views CIM, the role of computer technology in achieving integration cannot be discounted. While management must do the integrating, the computer is the tool that allows successful management of the system. Kenneth Van Winkle, the manager of manufacturing systems at Kimball International, Inc., a furniture manufacturer, leads a staff of ten full-time employees responsible for CIM implementation in Kimball's twenty manufacturing plants. He says that "computer technology is only 20 percent of CIM. The other 80 percent is the business process and people."[12] As H. Lee Hales, a partner in the accounting firm of Coopers & Lybrand, says, "CIM is a way of doing business—not just a specific system or computer applications."[13]

One way to look at CIM is as the umbrella under which all integration comes together. From product-process design through order entry, accounting, and various production activities throughout the distribution network, CIM orchestrates continuity of direction for each function. According to those individuals most experienced with implementing CIM in industry, four simple managerial factors are important for its successful introduction:[14]

- Scoping the CIM program (how much to spend and where?). Issues to be addressed in establishing scope include budget, organization, technical complexity, and logistics.
- Setting goals and objectives (what specific, measurable results are we seeking?). Goals need to be precise and measurable and focused on improving critical processes, products, and facilities. Because the customer may be internal, it is important to state objectives in a customer-centered way.
- Choosing the right time frame for planning (short or long term?). Do not be influenced here by the traditional five-year planning cycle. Once implemented, CIM becomes the framework for the future. The planning horizon should be at least as long as the expected life of current products and technologies. Alcoa uses a twenty-year planning horizon.
- Applying sound methodologies (what is the step-by-step process for getting results with CIM?). Methodologies are like road maps and navigational aids: They tell us where we are, where we are going, and how to get there. Without a formal road map, companies may never get beyond forming a CIM steering committee.

If we were to add a fifth factor the list, it would relate to the human element of the company. Many implementations of new technology, including CIM, have failed because responsible parties failed to prepare the work force to accept, support, and be able to use the new technology.

As noted earlier, CIM links the business functions with the engineering functions of the company. Business functions usually include order entry, accounting, billing, and payroll. Other technologies, such as computer-aided design (CAD) and computer-aided manufacturing (CAM), usually address engineering functions. When used together, CAD-CAM technologies effectively link and coordinate the design function and the manufacturing function. The linkage, illustrated in Table 8.3, means that companies are better able to respond to changes in the marketplace with new products or new designs of existing products. The functions listed in Table 8.3 are not exhaustive; they merely introduce issues involved in enterprise integration through CIM.

---

[12]John H. Sheridan, "The CIM Evolution: Bringing People Back into the Equation," *Industry Week* 241 (April 20, 1992): 30.
[13]H. Lee Hales, "Getting Results with CIM," *American Production and Inventory Control Society—The Performance Advantage* 1 (September 1991): 36.
[14]Hales, "Getting Results with CIM," pp. 31–36.

TABLE 8.3
Scope of Computer-
Integrated Manufacturing

| Computer Integrated Manufacturing | | |
|---|---|---|
| *Engineering Functions* | | *Business Functions* |
| Computer-aided design (CAD) | Computer-aided Manufacturing (CAM) | Order entry<br>Accounting<br>Customer billing<br>Payroll |
| Geometric modeling<br>Product design<br>Automated drafting | Numerically controlled machines<br>Flexible manufacturing systems<br>Automated storage and retrieval<br>Automatic identification of parts | |

The remainder of this chapter is a more detailed explanation of the key functions listed in Table 8.3, giving examples and describing several new technology advancements that support the overall effectiveness of a company. Most are used by manufacturing operations, but some are just as useful in service businesses.

## Computer-Aided Design

**Computer-aided design (CAD)** is defined as the use of computers in interactive engineering drawing and storage of designs. Programs complete the layout, geometric transformations, projections, rotations, magnifications, and interval (cross-section) views of a part and its relationship with other parts.[15] Chapter 5's discussion of product design issues is an example of the use of CAD. More and more companies are using CAD, because the computer technology is improving and the software is becoming more sophisticated. One of the most important uses of CAD today is to quickly create good product designs that are easy to manufacture. Designing for manufacturability should be a primary objective of all design engineers. CAD encourages experimentation, yields better quality products, and helps products get introduced more quickly. As companies introduce new products with shorter life cycles than ever before, the newly introduced product must be easy to manufacture, at low cost and with high quality. Quality products begin with quality product designs.

## Computer-Aided Manufacturing

**Computer-aided manufacturing (CAM)** relates to an organization's planning and control functions for manufacturing and is defined as the use of computers to program, direct, and control production equipment in the fabrication of manufactured items.[16] Process planning, cost estimating, and inventory planning all fall under the manufacturing-planning function. All activities concerned with the control of physical operations, including quality control, material movement and

[15]Wallace and Dougherty, *APICS Dictionary*, p. 6.
[16]Wallace and Dougherty, *APICS Dictionary*, p. 6.

*Computer technology enables designers to be more effective.*

control, and shop floor control, are part of the manufacturing control function of CAM. Typically, CAM applications include coordinating many other technologies used in the manufacture of products. Such technologies include, but are not limited to, numerically controlled machines, robotics, flexible manufacturing systems, automated storage and retrieval systems, and automatic identification systems.

**Numerically Controlled Machines** Technology for **numerically controlled (NC) machine** systems was developed in the 1940s and 1950s, making it the most mature of all the CAM technologies. The most basic NC machines use prerecorded, coded instructions as a means of control. These instructions are coded on punched-paper tapes, which electromechanical tape readers connected to the machines decode. The instructions tell the machine what path to take during the machining process. As computer technology advanced, a new generation of numerically controlled machines, called *computer numerically controlled (CNC) machines*, was developed. The CNC machines attached to a dedicated minicomputer that stored the NC-coded instructions. The most advanced numerically controlled machines are the direct numerically controlled (DNC) machines. DNC is a network of individual machining stations tied to a mainframe computer that instructs the network. Programming NC machines once was a tedious, labor-intensive process; programmers today use special programming languages that make programming quicker and more accurate than ever before.[17] NC machines were the introductory step on the way to the new world of robotics.

**Robotics** The movies and television formed many Americans' perception of robots: images from "The Jetsons" and *RoboCop*, and the characters R2D2 in *Star Wars* and Robot Johnny 5 in *Short Circuit*. In the movies robots have seemed to

[17]James H. Greene, *Production and Inventory Control Handbook*, 2d ed. (New York: McGraw Hill, 1987), p. 10.40.

assume individual personalities; in reality robots are not simply mechanical people. They are an integral part of an integrated, automated manufacturing system. Robots provide consistency, precision, and quality that humans cannot and do so without acting human. They don't need days off, vacations, pay raises, promotions, or motivation, as humans do. They also do not mind working in hazardous locations.

Even with these seemingly obvious benefits the word *robot* has not been a favorite of American manufacturing in recent years. Some companies have had a positive experience, but the implementation of robotic applications has often been an expensive disappointment, for the same reasons that companies have implemented other new technology to their sorrow. The basements of many manufacturing facilities are littered with robotic equipment that was removed from service because it failed to live up to expectations.

**Robotics** is defined as replacing functions previously done by humans with robots that can either be operated by people or run by computer. Difficult, dangerous, or monotonous tasks are likely candidates for robots to perform.[18] While American companies were having limited success with robotics, Japanese manufacturers were developing flexible manufacturing systems of which robots were an integral part. In 1988 Japan employed two-thirds of all robots in use worldwide. In 1989 Japan installed about $2.5 billion-worth of new ones; U.S. companies installed only about $400 million-worth that year.[19]

Flexibility is a key issue in the formulation of strategic plans in Japanese companies and a growing concern in U.S. companies. What is flexibility? Sometimes **flexibility** means quickly changing something that is being done or changing completely to adjust to new product designs. At other times flexibility is the ability to produce in small quantities in order to produce a product mix that may better approximate actual demand and reduce work-in-process inventories. Regardless of the definition of *flexibility*, traditional fixed automation manufacturing facilities, while efficient, are often inflexible.[20] Similarly, extremely flexible operations are often inefficient. An argument can be made for the relative merits of both efficiency and flexibility. Actually, both are desirable, which leads to quite a quandary: How do you get both efficiency and flexibility?

The ease with which they can be programmed and reprogrammed has made the later generations of robots more flexible than ever before. Operations Management in Practice 8.5 describes how General Electric Co. is using robots in a dishwasher plant. The Japanese and several U.S. manufacturers believe that they can achieve both efficiency and flexibility by using flexible manufacturing systems.

### Flexible Manufacturing Systems A **flexible manufacturing system (FMS)**

consists of a group of processing stations (primarily CNC machine tools), physically interconnected by an automated material-handling and storage system and controlled by computer.[21] As its name implies, an FMS cell can process a variety of different product types at the same time at the various workstations. Because FMS requires essentially no set-up time, small lot sizes are economically

[18]Wallace and Dougherty, *APICS Dictionary*, p. 26.
[19]Andrew Tanzer and Ruth Simon, "Why Japan Loves Robots and We Don't," *Forbes*, April 16, 1990, p. 150.
[20]Daniel E. Whitney, "Real Robots Do Need Jigs," *Harvard Business Review* 64 (May–June 1986): 111–112.
[21]Groover, *Automation, Production Systems*, p. 463.

**OPERATIONS MANAGEMENT IN PRACTICE 8.5**

# U.S. Manu-facturers Wary on Auto-mation

In Building No. 3 of General Electric Co.'s sprawling appliance works [in Louisville, Kentucky], technology breeds dishwashers like rabbits.

The automated assembly line is a blur of robots, machine tools and a conveyor system that snakes its way through the building, toting high-tech plastic washer tubs that carry a 10-year warranty.

GE is proud of this $40 million facility. It paid for itself in three years and has helped the firm gain 10 points in the market share for dishwashers. The irony is that technology experts do not consider this automated assembly line to be the wave of the future in American manufacturing. It is referred to as an island of automation. The problem, say experts, is that the GE facility is only capable of making dishwashers. It is simply not flexible enough.

To technology experts, the coming thing in manufacturing is the all-purpose factory, one that is linked together by computer and can produce several products on the same assembly line without costly or elaborate retooling. Flexible and efficient, it could make computers or toaster ovens of different sizes and shapes or of different parts. The ultimate flexible factory could be programmed to roll out many different types of products made on the same day to customer order, eliminating expensive inventory.

That day is not here yet, but scientists have made dramatic strides in flexible manufacturing. Some factories are capable of making a "family" of products or parts on the same line. It's an exciting concept and one that could prove the salvation of U.S. industry as the implementation becomes better developed. It promises the ability to produce according to need while cutting industry costs at the same time.

feasible. In general, each FMS is dedicated to processing a family or group of parts. The material-handling system used will vary, given the particular characteristics of the environment, and the FMS often uses robots to precisely transfer parts from processing station to processing station. Bigger facilities are increasingly using **automated guided vehicles (AGV)** to move parts to and from the FMS cells. The remainder of the material-handling function involves moving material into and out of the warehouse storage area. A completely integrated FMS could use an **automated storage and retrieval system (AS/RS)** to complete the automation of the material-handling function.

**Automatic Identification of Parts** The introduction of technology that provides **automatic identification of parts** has dramatically improved material handling into, through, and out of all types of operations. Several different forms of automatic identification are in use. **Bar coding** is the most used and recognized form of automatic identification and has proved effective in most cases. Bar coding allows computer technology to quickly and accurately collect and effectively manage data. The bar code system involves three elements, the bar code symbol, the symbol reader, and the printing process. The efficiency of the system is related to how well the three elements work together. Table 8.4 summarizes the benefits of bar code technology.

TABLE 8.4
Benefits of Bar Code
Technology

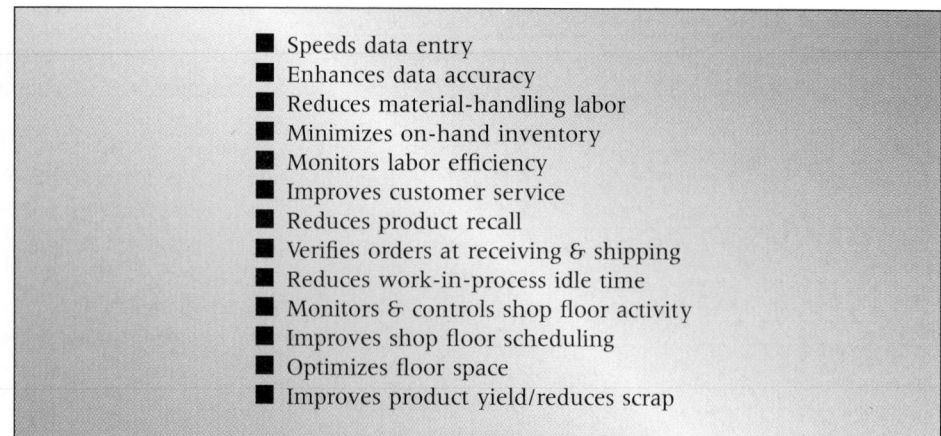

- Speeds data entry
- Enhances data accuracy
- Reduces material-handling labor
- Minimizes on-hand inventory
- Monitors labor efficiency
- Improves customer service
- Reduces product recall
- Verifies orders at receiving & shipping
- Reduces work-in-process idle time
- Monitors & controls shop floor activity
- Improves shop floor scheduling
- Optimizes floor space
- Improves product yield/reduces scrap

Source: Joe LaFeir, "Everything You've Needed to Know About Bar Coding . . . But Just Haven't Asked," *American Production and Inventory Control Society—The Performance Advantage* (May 1992), p. 26.

The service sector has been using bar code technology since the mid-1970s. Grocery stores and other retail establishments recognized the importance of bar coding in improving data entry performance and customer service. Many discount retailers are expanding the use of bar coding to give customers access to scanners throughout the store. Customers are then able to check prices of items that may not be marked clearly. The airline industry has recently made greater use of bar coding in response to customers' complaints about late departures and lost luggage. Northwest Airlines recently announced that it had implemented a systemwide bar code tracking system for luggage.

Bar codes appear on almost every purchase, from soft drinks to automobiles. The code itself is made up of vertical parallel lines of varying widths and can store as many as twenty to thirty characters per inch of coded information. That is more than enough space to store the **universal product code (UPC)** for the item, which tells the computer to respond with the correct price for the item. Research and development in bar coding technology has led to the recent development of a new bar code. The new two-dimensional code contains a stack of as many as 90 one-dimensional bar codes, each just three-hundredths of an inch high. High-speed laser scanners read the new bar codes just as quickly as an ordinary scanner reads a conventional code. Figure 8.1 describes the new two-dimensional bar code technology.

Some situations have environmental conditions, such as temperature, dirt, clutter, or hazardous contamination, that make bar coding ineffective. In those cases radio frequency identification is often more useful. **Radio frequency (RF) identification** systems have three primary components, the tag or transponder, the antenna or scanner, and the reader. The scanning speed and the distance between the reader and the tag determine the size of the RF tag.[22] The tag size for identification of a stationary pallet-load of material would be much smaller than a tag used to identify a moving freight car.

Applying the RF technology is not new. In 1980 a California citizens group sued the Bay Area Rapid Transit (BART) system, claiming that disabled individuals did not have equal access to the system, especially elevators at the stations.

[22]"Radio Frequency for Automatic Identification," *American Machinist & Automated Manufacturing* 131 (March 1987): 96–97.

**This Square Says a Mouthful**
Here's how a whole speech can fit onto a postage stamp or two.

**How It Works**

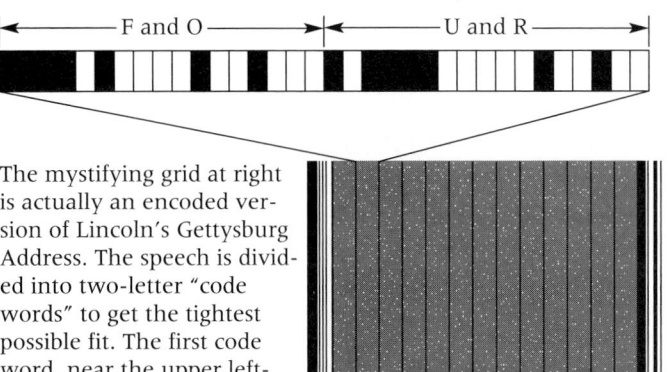

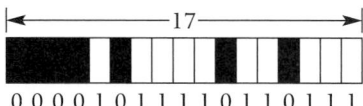

The mystifying grid at right is actually an encoded version of Lincoln's Gettysburg Address. The speech is divided into two-letter "code words" to get the tightest possible fit. The first code word, near the upper left-hand corner, represents the letters F and O, while the second stands for U and R. Together they spell out the first syllable of the famous opening, "Fourscore and seven years ago . . . "

As the scanner's laser beam zigzags downward, it reads the pattern as binary code. The black bars, which absorb the laser light, register as zeroes, while the white spaces, which reflect it, register as ones. Each code word contains 17 bits of information, enough to represent two numbers or letters (here, F and O).

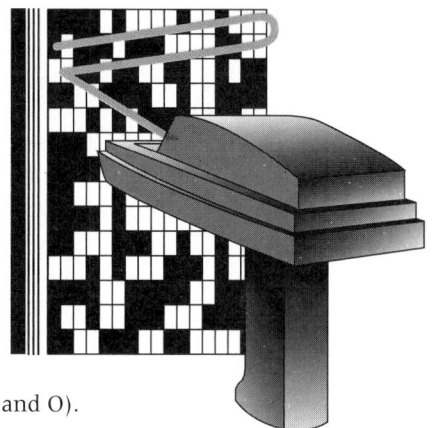

FIGURE 8.1
New Technology in Bar Codes

Source: Mark Alpert, "Building a Better Bar Code," *Fortune*, June 15, 1992, p. 101.

BART's response was to install an RF identification system. Under the new system disabled people apply for and receive a personal identification tag at no charge. The ID tag, about the size of a credit card, activates station elevators. To operate the system a disabled person holds a valid ID tag close to the reader, which is mounted near the elevator. The tag may also be mounted on a wheelchair, allowing the disabled person to ride past the reader to activate the elevator. The group dropped its suit after BART installed the RF system.[23]

Many other technological advances of recent years are having a significant effect on both manufacturing and service companies. These are the technologies that fall more into the category of "support" technologies, which means that they can be useful anywhere in an organization.

# Technological Improvements for Support

Many companies have begun to search for opportunities to extend and improve traditional computer-controlled automation applications. The traditional practice is to use sensors that send information to the computer throughout the manufacturing process. Programs in residence in the computer take the information from the sensors, analyze the data, and structure the best response. The current limitation is that the computer can respond only to those situations that are known to occur or those that are predictable. If a new situation arises, the system is usually not prepared to handle it. This means that the success of the automation depends upon the insight and foresight of those who designed it.

[23]William P. Hakanson, "Automatic Identification for the Disabled," *Mass Transit* 18 (May–June 1991): 45–47.

The lack of adaptability of this technology bothers many researchers. Some researchers have worked for years to develop procedures that allow computers to respond to situations not previously known to them.

## Artificial Intelligence: Adaptive Technology for the '90s[24]

**Artificial intelligence (AI)** is an emerging technology that is based on the computer's expert use of information, usually provided by sensors. The plan is to make the computer act more human in its ability to reason and respond. Artificial intelligence is not new as a field of study, but practical commercial applications are just beginning to surface after more than twenty years of research by computer scientists and engineers. AI is expected to assume an even more important role in computer-controlled automated factories of the future, especially given the increasing availability of high-powered computers and high-capacity data-storage devices.

Basically, AI is a general field of study to which researchers have taken several different approaches. The most developed of these approaches is the expert system. **Expert systems** are knowledge-based systems in which expert human knowledge has been converted to rules for the computer to use. The computer uses the rules to evaluate different situations, always trying to perform as the experts would have performed if they were evaluating the situation. Several examples of expert systems are in use today; Global Operations Management 8.6 describes the use of an expert system to help find fabrication cracks in heavy construction.

Fixed rules such as those used in expert systems cannot solve all problems. For example, using fixed rules to make an accurate model of a chemical process would be quite difficult, because chemical relationships don't follow rules. For example, a group of engineers in the nylon industry could never agree on the specific rules that an expert system would follow. These issues have driven researchers to work on alternative AI approaches, to make systems more adaptable in dynamic environments. This is the next frontier in AI/computer technology.

One exciting AI approach that represents a giant step toward adaptability is **neural networks**, which are based on biological or mathematical models designed to imitate the way the brain works. The plan is to design neural networks that will be capable of learning from past experiences.

Think of the human body as a complex chemical/mechanical plant. In the human body no mathematical equations ensure the balance of bodily operations, yet the body performs a multitude of complex chemical reactions and does so with a high degree of accuracy and dependability for many decades. It performs this complex chemo-mechanical control under constantly changing external and internal conditions, such as body growth, changes in diet, fluctuating weather conditions, and so on. Part of the way that the body is able to achieve control over this complex, high-dimensional, nonlinear system is through a network of millions of neurons that sense the internal state of the body, process the sensory information, and send out signals to the muscles and glands to achieve the response desired.

In a very real and pragmatic way this biological neural network builds an internal model of the function of the body from neural sensory information and

---

[24] Adapted from Pavilion Technologies, *Pavilion Technologies: Company Backgrounder* (Austin, Tex: Pavilion Technologies, 1993), pp. 8–9.

## Tomorrow's Manufacturing Technologies

Manufacturers troubled by fabrication cracking in heavy constructions can get help from a diagnostic system called Weldcrack Expert. This microcomputer software package from TWI (Cambridge, England) uses stored knowledge from leading welding engineers and metallurgists to guide the user through a series of questions about a crack's appearance and location. From the answers, the system diagnoses the probable cause.

TWI reports the expert welding program works well in applications involving many different types of cracks and tears. It can display photographs and schematics of weld microsections and provide operators with more than 30 digitally scanned, metallurgical photographs of classic responses, and results from each session can be stored on disk or printed. This allows the building of a library of case studies for future reference when tackling similar problems.

learns how to control the body based on that model. Recent advances in the mathematics and understanding of the mechanisms of learning, coupled with the power of modern and inexpensive computers, allow the building of artificial neural networks that make and control models of adaptive sensory information in a manner analogous to the function of biological neural networks. In essence, neural network software provides a similar structure that is useful in operating and controlling a manufacturing plant. The Pavilion Technologies case at the end of this chapter describes several applications of this technology in industry.

Neural networks represent a set of powerful mathematical techniques for modeling optimization and control that "learn" processes directly from historical data. Neural nets are nonlinear regression algorithms that can model high-dimensional systems and have a uniform user interface; they work well for both batch and continuous processes, and they can be used in static or dynamic modeling. When coupled with analytical and predictive techniques, neural networks have proved their value in converting historical operating data into real process knowledge.

**Fuzzy logic** is another adaptive technology that is being used effectively in many equipment and plant control applications. The user-friendly linguistic interface of this technology, combined with its numerical underpinning, makes fuzzy logic a natural complement to other adaptive techniques. Fuzzy logic is particularly suited for developing more realistic constraints used for system optimization.

Constraints, such as high and low limits and rate-of-change limitations, are an important and necessary part of optimizing a system. Hard constraints are usually specified in terms of safety limits, such as "The pressure on line 3 should never exceed 1,000 psi." However, near this emergency condition is a gray area, or fuzzy boundary, within which concern increases as the pressure approaches the 1,000 psi mark. Having the system at 999 psi is not desirable, and it probably should not be above 975 psi, depending on how well the pressure can be controlled.

This type of "fuzzy" constraint is easily expressed as a fuzzy rule and can be tied in as a "fuzzy constraint envelope" around the neural network. By contrasting fuzzy rules with the traditional rules of rule-based expert systems, we can see that fuzzy rules are softer and more intuitive in their specification. For example, suppose that a plant operator has an intuition about how to run the plant and his instincts are that "if the temperature on line 5 is too high, I should turn down control valve 3 a little bit." But what are "too high" and "a little bit"?

To incorporate such rules in an expert system a knowledge engineer would usually ask the plant engineer to be more specific. He might define *too high* as 120 degrees and *a little bit* as 10 degrees to the left. These rules would become part of a rule-based expert system. However, the plant engineer usually does not control the plant by firing exactly that rule at exactly that point by exactly that amount. Instead, if the temperature rises to 100 degrees, the engineer may start compensating by turning the control valve to the left by 5 to 6 degrees and increase this adjustment if the system's temperature continues to rise. This gradation is exactly what happens in a fuzzy control system, and it does not have to be encoded as a separate rule. A single fuzzy rule already incorporates this interpolative concept and automatically adjusts reactions accordingly.

Thanks to these new technologies, the computer, not the engineer, does most of the learning about the process. This predictive/adaptive control approach is likely to increase in importance as the power and cost effectiveness of computers, sensors, and storage media continue to increase.

Also underway is a move toward developing **neurocomputers**, which will have the neural networks implemented in the hardware. Implications for such neurocomputers are interesting, especially in complex applications involving robotics and vision. These applications are not as far in the future as we might think. A. J. Vitale, a consultant with the Automation & Productivity Institute, predicts that neurocomputers based on multiprocessor designs will be available as off-the-shelf items by 1995.[25]

Table 8.5 lists some applications of various forms of artificial intelligence technology at work today.

## Virtual Reality

Another exciting technological development receiving attention today is the field of virtual reality. Virtual reality is promising to revolutionize the way people interact with their computers. Many advanced graphics packages allow you to manipulate images on the computer screen; **virtual reality** will allow the operator to participate in the computer's program execution. Operations Management in Practice 8.7 provides a preview of virtual reality. Also, the Blockbuster Entertainment case at the end of Chapter 2 discussed the use of virtual reality as an element of a service organization's overall strategy.

Those involved in the development of this new technology envision countless applications. For example, the designer's ability to hold an item electronically, before the part is ever manufactured, would replace traditional CAD technology. That means that the designer could identify design problems before spending valuable time on building a prototype for evaluation. Virtual reality will mean completing designs faster and with higher quality and greater manufacturability than ever before.

[25]"Future View: Tomorrow's Manufacturing Technologies," *Manufacturing Engineering* 108 (January 1992): 80.

| Industry | Application |
|---|---|
| **Finance** | Shearson Lehman uses neural networks to predict the performance of stocks and bonds. |
| **Human Services** | Merced County in California has an expert system that decides whether applicants should receive welfare benefits. |
| **Telecommunications** | NYNEX has an expert system that helps unskilled workers diagnose customers' phone problems. |
| **Energy** | Arco and Texaco use neural networks to help pinpoint oil and gas deposits deep below the earth's surface. |
| **Government** | The Internal Revenue Service is testing software designed to read tax returns and spot fraud. |
| **Marketing** | Spiegel uses neural networks to determine who on a vast mailing list are the most likely buyers of its products. |
| **Transportation** | American Airlines has an expert system that schedules the routine maintenance of its airplanes. |

Source: Evan I. Schwartz and James B. Treece, "Smart Programs Go to Work," *Business Week,* March 2, 1992, p. 97.

T A B L E   8 . 5
Let Your Software Do the Thinking

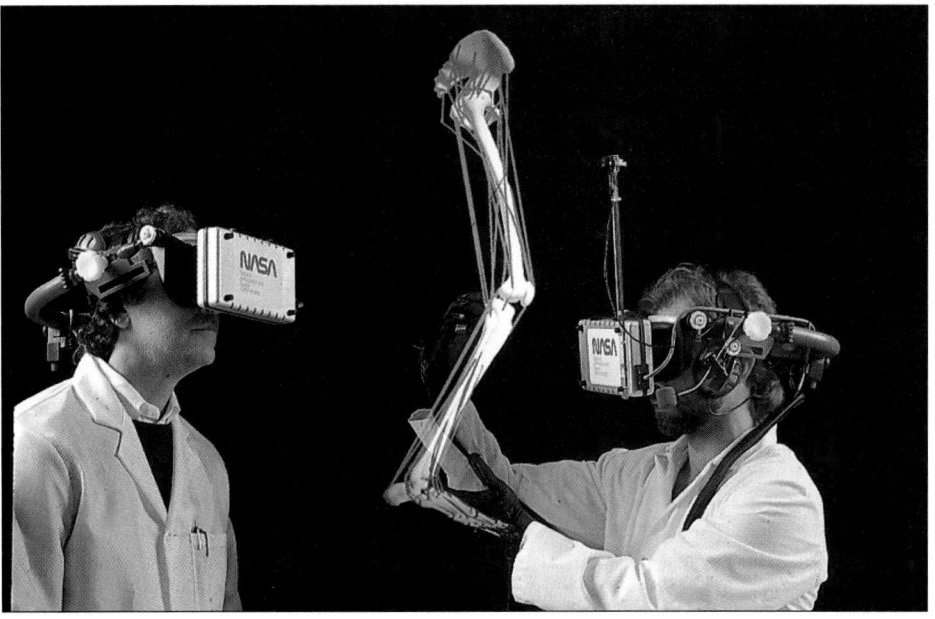

*Virtual reality technology provides researchers with opportunities never before available.*

Consider the entertainment and educational possibilities. What would this course be like if classes could go on field trips without ever leaving the classroom? You would be totally immersed in a three-dimensional image of the destination. Arcade games that use basic virtual reality technology already are available.

OPERATIONS MANAGEMENT IN PRACTICE 8.7

# The Marvels of "Virtual Reality"

Inside a darkened computer lab in Seattle, a Boeing engineering executive dons a bulky headset equipped with blacked-out goggles and pulls on a Lycra glove bristling with wires. Then he points his forefinger at an airplane that looks almost real as it seems to sit on a runway in front of him. In response to his gesture the scene shifts, and he finds himself in front of the airplane. He lifts his finger to walk around it and stops to open a maintenance hatch, revealing a life support system and a pressure gauge. His next command puts him inside the cockpit. He touches a button on the instrument panel to start the engine, then pulls back the throttle.

The plane, a hypothetical tilting-rotor aircraft that Boeing calls VS-X, rumbles down the runway and takes off while he sits back and admires the green-and-brown landscape below through a porthole. After the plane lands, he walks back to the cargo bay and reconfigures the seats inside the plane. Actually, only he is real. The airplane is made entirely of equations residing in computer memory, yet he says flying it feels "pretty convincing." Boeing takes virtual reality serious enough to have had more than 100 of its engineers and executives fly inside the virtual airplane. The company has organized a corporate-wide steering committee to explore potential applications.

## Technological Improvements in Communications

Many other recent technological advancements have led to significant improvements companywide. For example, **electronic data interchange (EDI)** has greatly improved relationships between vendors and customers. As companies move more toward flexibility and responsiveness as goals, they have recognized the need to treat their customers and vendors as partners in their business. That improved relationship is facilitated by sharing information. EDI links key vendors by computer network to a company for sharing up-to-date information. Vendors and companies can rapidly transmit information about purchase orders, invoices, shipping notices, schedule changes, demand shifts, or other problems for appropriate response.

**Electronic mail** has become the preferred method for communicating within many companies. Our society has become characterized by answering machines, call waiting, voice mail, and facsimile machines. Gone are the days of the busy signal, and organizational productivity is improving as a result. **Electronic pagers** have become a necessity for employees throughout many organizations, and some households now use pagers as a form of communication among family members. **Cellular telephones** have expanded our ability to communicate and enhanced the productivity of business people—people use cellular telephones while walking through the airport, driving the car, and visiting a construction site. They have proved so popular in the business world that many people now use them for personal business as well.

Computer technology has also redefined the concept of a formal presentation. Simply using overheads, slides, or video is not enough. Today's professional presentation calls for all of these techniques. Technology is allowing truly multimedia presentations. **Multimedia** technology allows a presenter to combine multiple presentation modes such as text, graphics, photographic still images, animation, sound, and video in a single information-processing environment. One example of a multimedia application was a presentation that the Atlanta Olympic Committee developed: It allowed members of the International Olympic Committee, meeting in Puerto Rico, to "tour" the Atlanta area. The presentation used a combination of video pictures of existing Atlanta facilities and animated examples of proposed facilities. The Atlanta Olympic Committee believes that the presentation was instrumental in winning Atlanta its selection as the host city of the 1996 Summer Olympic Games.[26]

[26]Lisa Ottinger and David Paradice, "Approaches to Research in Multimedia Processing," *1991 Proceedings of the Decision Sciences Institute Annual National Conference*, November 1991.

# ► Summary

Technology is continuing to play a critical role in transforming American businesses into global competitors. Companies must use extreme care in selecting and implementing the most appropriate level of technology for a particular business environment. As computer technology continues to evolve, practical applications are becoming possible that no one ever dreamed of.

**Learning Objective 1: Describe the role of technology in today's business environment.** Technology is useful for improving the performance of the organization. Specifically, it can lead to improved product and service quality, lower costs, increased responsiveness to customers and markets, increased flexibility, improved safety, smaller work-in-process inventories, and greater long-term productivity. Technology also serves as a catalyst for strategic alliances in which two or more companies meet in a joint venture for the good of all parties.

**Learning Objective 2: Define** *technology transfer,* **and explain why it is such an important issue.** Technology transfer is the process by which technology is applied in the workplace or shared between members of a strategic alliance. Private companies and the federal government spend millions of dollars annually on basic research. If new technology proves impossible to transfer from the laboratory to the manufacturing facility, the money may have been wasted.

**Learning Objective 3: Identify the five fallacies commonly associated with implementing new technology.**

1. People lose their jobs.
2. Hourly workers will be the most severely affected.
3. Experts should handle job design and other technical issues.
4. New, automated systems will reduce the need for interpersonal communication on the factory floor and in the office.
5. Technological change is bad for people.

**Learning Objective 4: Describe the differences in fixed, programmed, and flexible automation.** High-volume situations in which the sequence of processing steps is fixed call for fixed automation, but it is inflexible. Programmed automation addresses the inflexibility of fixed automation by allowing the production of batches of different product designs so long as the differences are not dramatic. Flexible automation is the most versatile of the three, because its minimal changeover times allow the production of small batches of a wide variety of products. Flexible automation is the way of the future.

**Learning Objective 5: Summarize the role of computers in applying technology to manufacturing and service operations.** Advances in computer technology have allowed manufacturing technology to progress as far as it has, but we must continue to explore the new frontiers of computer technology. To continue being competitive in this global economy companies must continue moving toward enterprise integration, and computer technology is necessary for their success.

## Learning Objective 6: Describe the importance of flexibility in today's organizations.
Because competition from abroad is growing, companies must learn to respond more rapidly to customers' wishes as well as to changes in the market. They will need to be able to design new products or redesign old products quickly and efficiently. Only then will companies have the chance to capitalize on opportunities while they are available. And the window of opportunity is often quite small. Manufacturing processes must be flexible enough to accommodate new product designs with minimal disruption or time lost.

## Learning Objective 7: Identify some key technical developments in manufacturing and service operations, and discuss the advantages they create.
One example of a key technological development in manufacturing operations is CIM. CIM means that it is possible to improve efficiency by integrating engineering and business functions. Within the CIM framework CAD and CAM technologies facilitate new product design, development, and manufacture. In service operations key technological developments include bar code and optical scanner technology, which improve inventory control and customer service. Also, in both manufacturing and service operations the use of electronic data interchange has dramatically improved communication within the supplier-customer network.

## ► Key Terms

artificial intelligence (AI)
automated guided vehicle (AGV)
automated storage and retrieval system (AS/RS)
automatic identification of parts
automation
bar coding
cellular telephones
computer-aided design (CAD)
computer-aided manufacturing (CAM)
computer-integrated manufacturing (CIM)

electronic data interchange (EDI)
electronic mail
electronic pager
enterprise integration
expert system
fixed automation
flexibility
flexible automation
flexible manufacturing system (FMS)
fuzzy logic
multimedia
neural network

neurocomputer
numerically controlled machine (NC)
programmable automation
radio frequency (RF) identification
robotics
strategic alliance
technology
technology transfer
universal product code (UPC)
virtual reality

## ► Discussion Questions

1. What is technology, and how might increased technology improve organizational performance?
2. Why might strategic alliances be a better method for obtaining higher technology than in-house research and development?
3. The text states that "the most successful alliances are those joined by companies that have a long-term vision." Why is this important?
4. What would be the advantages and disadvantages of having a strategic alliance with a foreign company?
5. What does *technology transfer* mean?
6. Why have U.S. companies often been slow to implement new technology?
7. What are the five common misconceptions regarding advanced technology?
8. What are the three basic types of automation, and how would you distinguish among them? What are the advantages and disadvantages of each?
9. What managerial factors are important in determining the success of CIM?
10. What advantages might a manufacturing facility expect after implementing a complete CIM system?
11. What are CAD and CAM? Why are they often used together?
12. What would be the advantages of using a flexible manufacturing system?
13. What is virtual reality, and how might business use it?
14. What is electronic data interchange? In what ways do you think this technology would improve a business?

► **Selected References**

Greene, James H. *Production & Inventory Control Handbook.* New York: McGraw-Hill, 1987.

Groover, Mikell P. *Automation, Production Systems, and Computer-Integrated Manufacturing.* Englewood Cliffs, N.J.: Prentice-Hall, 1987.

Harmon, Roy L., and Leroy D. Peterson. *Reinventing the Factory.* New York: Free Press, 1990.

Hayes, Robert H., and Steven C. Wheelwright. *Restoring Our Competitive Edge: Competing Through Manufacturing.* New York: Wiley, 1984.

Hunt, V. Daniel. *Computer-Integrated Manufacturing Handbook.* New York: Chapman and Hall, 1989.

Lenz, John E. *Flexible Manufacturing: Benefits for the Low-Inventory Factory.* New York: Marcel Dekker, 1989.

Skinner, Wickham. *Manufacturing: The Formidable Competitive Weapon.* New York: Wiley, 1985.

# Pavilion Technologies

## Introduction

Pavilion Technologies, a spinoff company of the Microelectronics and Computer Technology Corp. (MCC), has developed a revolutionary new class of process control software.

Pavilion, which is based in Austin, Texas, is marketing the software to manufacturing engineers for modeling, optimization, and control of production processes. Initial targets are unit operations in the chemical, petrochemical, and refining industries, where early installations of this software have already produced significant savings for such companies as Eastman Chemical Co. (a winner of the 1993 Malcolm Baldrige National Quality Award). Pharmaceuticals, semiconductor fabrication, power generation, pulp and paper, metals, glass, ceramics, food processing, and other capital-intensive manufacturing and materials processing industries are also potential customers for Pavilion's software.

The advent of low-cost, reliable sensor technology for data collection and dramatic improvements in computer price and performance have transformed the average manufacturing facility into a data-rich environment, with millions of bytes of production information recorded daily. Pavilion has developed unique software that enables manufacturing engineers to use the data to deliver more efficient, higher-quality production with little or no capital investment. It is Pavilion's philosophy that just creating knowledge from historical data is not enough. One must also be able to generate action for improvement. Users already see Pavilion's new technology as a major competitive advantage: Payback is rapid, often measured in weeks; bottom-line results are significant, regularly exceeding six figures annually; and the software is reliable and already operating in many production applications. Pavilion's software, *Process Insights*, allows users of UNIX systems and Digital Equipment VAX/VMS and Alpha workstations to model, optimize, and control manufacturing processes that once were impossible to analyze. The software is based on adaptive technology developed by MCC, early versions of which have been available since 1989. *Process Insights* also is unique in its ability to enable manufacturing engineers to model, optimize, and perform real-time control on their production processes, based solely on the automated analysis of historical data.

Application of this software represents a significant shift in the operations methodology of manufacturing industries that will result in

- Many billions of dollars in operational savings by the coming decade
- Significant reduction in pollutants and waste
- Conservation of energy as well as minimization of associated taxes

For example, the U.S. refining, petrochemical, and chemical industries generate more than $150 billion in revenue per year and spend more than 50 to 60 percent of that amount in production operations. The chemical industry also accounts for 3 to 5 percent of all U.S. energy consumption each year. With new U.S. federal energy taxes expected to add approximately $10 billion in annual costs for the industry, a 2 percent improvement in overall production and energy efficiency would result in billions in savings for these industries. Pavilion Technologies' customers that have already optimized their chemical processes have improved their operations by more than 30 percent.

Similarly, as companies work to comply with the increasingly more stringent requirements of environmental regulations, they are using Pavilion's software to minimize their compliance costs by modeling and controlling burners on incinerators and boilers to manage the complex balance of permissible emissions of nitrous oxide, carbon monoxide, and other effluents.

## Technology Overview

Industrial process control has undergone several major shifts since the beginning of the Industrial Revolution. New methods of controlling the industrial process emerged with the arrival of the equipment necessary for the implementing of the control strategy and at a time of significant advances in the underlying mathematics. The equipment allowed companies to use a new control methodology, and the mathematics described the best way to use the equipment.

Given the historical trend of new equipment and mathematics giving rise to major shifts in control methodologies, what does the future hold? The trend for equipment is clear: faster and less expensive computers, greater capacity, less expensive memory, and low-cost, high-accuracy "smart" sensors. This means that the amount of process data that manufacturers can gather and store is going to increase exponentially. Indeed, many manufacturing facilities are already overwhelmed with data, storing tens or even hundreds of gigabytes of historical process data annually. Yet these same facilities are starved for useful knowledge about their production processes.

Most manufacturers have found existing tools—such as steady-state linear models of a limited number of process variables—inadequate for accurately modeling and optimizing many complex real world processes. In practice many continuous and batch processes exhibit characteristics that make the results of existing modeling and control techniques difficult to apply:

- Plant nonlinearity or uncertainty
- High-dimensional multivariate inputs and control variables with complicated or detrimental interactions
- Inherent and variable time delays
- Inadequate and uncertain measurements
- Plant safety and environmental constraints
- Unknown or uncontrollable changes in such external variables as feed stock, outside temperature, barometric pressure, humidity, and so on
- Multiple constraints on both the process input settings and output target variables
- Optimization criteria and operating constraints expressed imprecisely

The conventional approach to dealing with the high dimensionality of plant dynamics is to split the plant into small unit operations and then optimize each one. However, when the plant as a whole is studied, managers often find that what is best for the individual unit operation may not be what is best for the entire plant. Because older technology has been unable to cope with the problem, manufacturers often miss the larger plantwide opportunities. To date, methods for handling the high dimensionality of optimizing overall plant operations have been very expensive, time consuming, and only feasible for steady-state analysis while offering no practical method for addressing dynamic situations. Fortunately, new technologies are available that can deliver a solution. Artificial neural networks, fuzzy logic, and chaotic systems theory represent a class of powerful mathematical techniques for modeling, controlling, and optimizing that "learns" processes directly from historical data. Furthermore, these data-based neural network models can handle nonlinear and dynamic plant conditions as well as steady-state situations.

In order to make neural network technologies useful, they must be incorporated in efficient algorithms that existing computer equipment can solve. An early algorithm involving neural networks took 4.5 weeks to solve a small problem that involved 12 variables and 1,200 rows of data. During that time a Cray supercomputer was devoted to solving only this problem. It was not uncommon to find real-world problems involving 100 variables and 100,000 rows of data, which would take thousands of years to solve on the Cray, so it seemed unlikely that computer hardware would ever get fast enough to solve real-world problems efficiently. They needed more efficient algorithms to facilitate solutions to large-scale problems. In the late 1980s an algorithm was developed and patented that was 50 million times faster than the original algorithm. That algorithm is an integral part of Pavilion's adaptive software products.

## Pavilion Software Products

*Process Insights*, the company's first standard software product, allows users to model, optimize, and control manufacturing processes that once were extremely difficult to analyze. *Process Insights* leads the user through a simple four-step process of formatting, preprocessing, modeling, and analyzing process data. (The company video accompanying this case illustrates these steps.) The software is designed for use by plant engineers on industrial-strength problems. Its spreadsheets, data transformation tools, and graphics are capable of manipulating data sets of hundreds of megabytes. Its model builder, analyzer, and optimizer generate accurate results without requiring the user to understand the underlying adaptive technologies.

*Process Insights* uses a unique combination of neural network and chaotic systems algorithms to learn the complex interactions of process variables from historical production data. The product also uses concepts from fuzzy logic and fuzzy control theory to allow flexible, real-world definition of process operating constraints. After the historical data for the process have been read in to the program and prepared for modeling, *Process Insights* automatically builds a predictive model that faithfully reflects the underlying dynamics of the process.

When the predictive model is ready for use, the user can validate the model by using a new set of historical data taken from the production unit to test its accuracy. Once validated, this model can be used to predict future performance based on current operating data. *Insights* also allows the user to perform sensitivity analysis to determine the effects of each manipulated (input) variable on each controlled (output) variable. The user can manipulate the sensitivity data to find key relationships among the various factors that affect output product, sometimes leading to improvements in overall control strategy. Next, the software assists the user in achieving target output results by establishing optimum settings for the modi-

fiable process variables. The user then can use that data to run what-if simulations to predict the effects of using those settings in unit operations.

Users who want to perform real-time control can turn to a companion product, the *Process Insights RunTime Software Controller*. The *Controller* software uses model files produced by *Insights* and real-time data from the process control system to make recommendations, either to an operator or directly to the control system, to achieve desired results. Figure 1 illustrates how various Pavilion software products interface with an application environment.

## Pavilion Software Application

Pavilion designs software for specific applications to be used in conjunction with its *Process Insights* and *RunTime Software Controller*. One product recently developed specifically for the chemical industry is designed to aid in monitoring smokestack emissions to ensure compliance with Environmental Protection

**FIGURE 1.** Software Products Interface

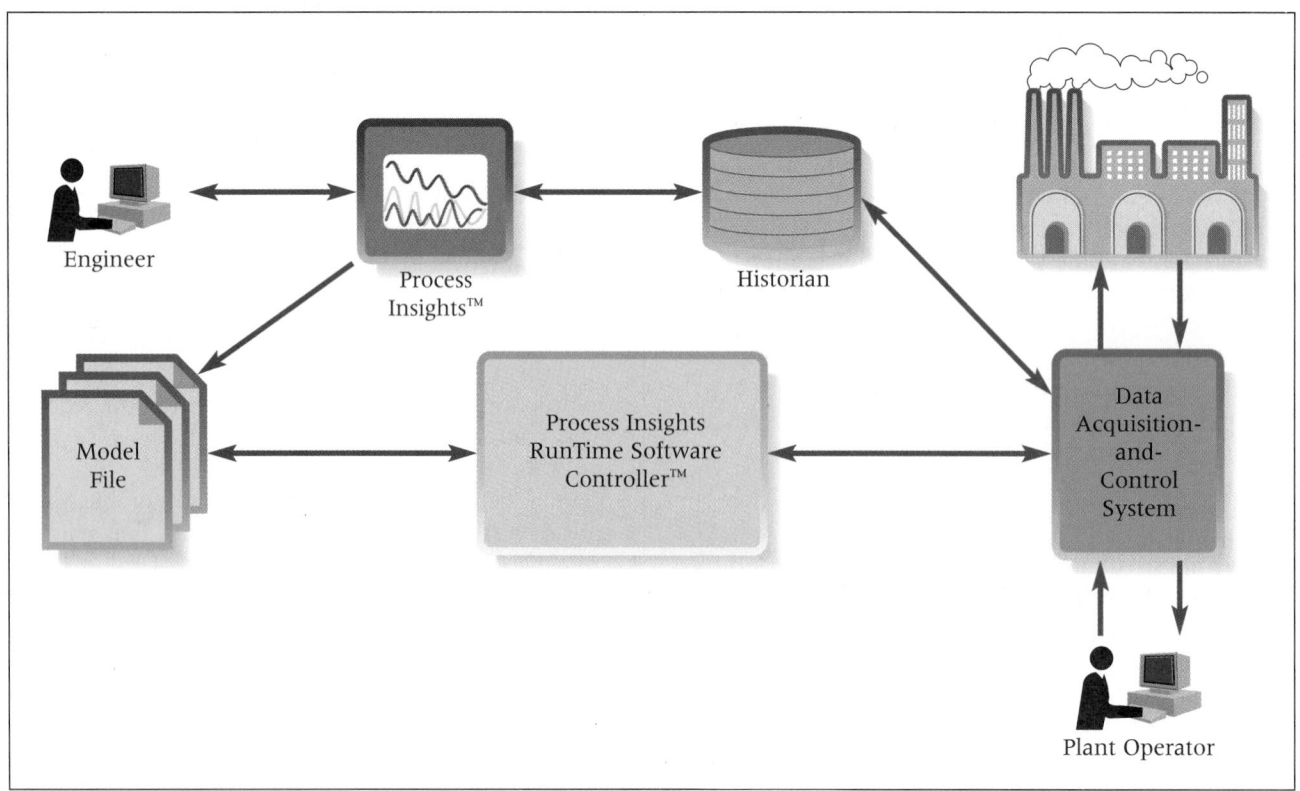

Agency (EPA) standards. Both *Business Week* and *Industry Week* have reported on the success of this application, which is called *Software CEM*.

The EPA has approved the software *CEM* for use, but individual states also must approve it. States can impose environmental standards more restrictive than the federal regulations. To date, Texas, Arkansas, Louisiana, and California have approved use of the software *CEM*.

The 1990 Federal Clean Air Act Amendments require manufacturers to install continuous emissions monitoring systems (CEMS) to monitor such emissions as sulfur dioxide, nitrogen oxides, carbon monoxide, carbon dioxide, and other dangerous elements. The initial cost of a hardware CEMS, with its housing and associated equipment, ranges from approximately $150,000 to $350,000. A CEMS typically relies on delicate instruments that require frequent recalibration and incur significant maintenance costs. A study by the National Petroleum Council reported that the cost of complying with federal and state environmental requirements for U.S. refineries could run as high as $37 billion between 1991 and the year 2000, about $6 billion more than the value of these facilities in 1994.[1]

Pavilion's alternative to hardware CEMS is its *Software CEMS* package, which provides highly accurate emissions measurements. Typically, the accuracy is achieved at one-third the cost of installing the typical hardware CEMS. *Software CEM* is also much less expensive to maintain and operate than the hardware CEMS. In addition, Pavilion's *Software CEM* goes beyond the simple measuring of emissions of the CEMS hardware—the software provides information about the causes of emissions. It can calculate optimal equipment settings for reducing emissions while maintaining product yield and quality, thereby increasing profits.

*Software CEM* is a model-based computer software system that accurately predicts plant emissions from the plant's process sensor readings. The model used by *Software CEM* is created by using Pavilion's *Process Insights* process modeling and optimization software. The software CEM is a versatile system that faithfully predicts emissions even in the extreme operating ranges of unit operations and can be used for a wide variety of different unit operations, including steam boilers, gas turbines, furnaces, reciprocating engines, and so on.

At least one client has found a unique application for *Process Insights*—completing a direct mail promotion for one of its products. Each item was so big that it would have cost approximately $3 to mail. The company expected to send the promotion to approximately 1 million potential customers in order to generate the desired number of responses. After feeding the problem in to the Pavilion software, the company decided to do two mailings. First, it mailed 100,000 units, and 1.5 percent of the recipients responded in the desired way. At that rate, 1 million mailings would generate 15,000 responses. The company used the modeling capability of *Process Insights* to analyze the 1,500 responses to determine the characteristics of those who responded to the promotion. As a result, the company mailed 19,000 more units only to those potential customers who shared the desired characteristics. Fifteen thousand of the 19,000 responded, which meant the company got responses from the same number expected from mailing all 1 million units but at a fraction of the cost.

Industry has developed many other applications for this generic modeling tool. Companies have been using the software for geologic applications, waste water treatment, multivariate statistical process control, pharmaceutical applications, utilities, and many others. The potential applications for an intelligent, adaptive modeling tool for process control seem to be endless.

## ► Acknowledgements

Material for this case was provided by R. Bruce Ferguson, vice president of marketing for Pavilion Technologies, Inc., Austin, Texas, 1994.

## ► Case Discussion Questions

1. Discuss Pavilion's philosophy about the relationship of data, knowledge, and action.
2. Would Pavilion's modeling software be useful for product demand forecasting? Why or why not?
3. Why has Pavilion initially targeted the chemical, petrochemical, and refining industries for its products?
4. What is it about continuous process industries that makes this technology most appealing?

[1]Tim Stevens, "Software Cuts Clean Air Costs," *Industry Week*, January 17, 1994, p. 45.

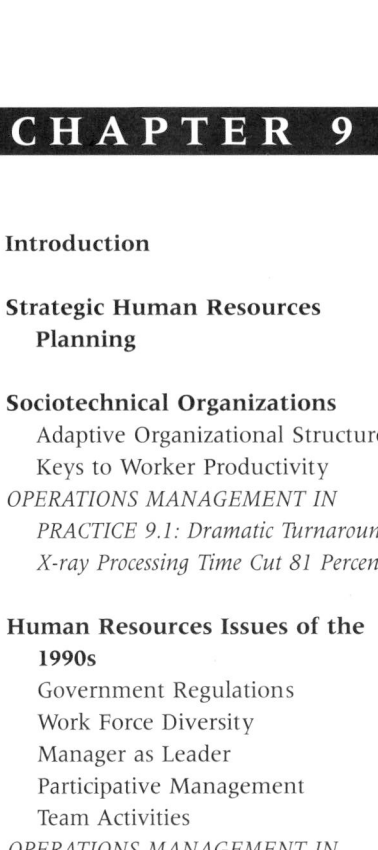

# Organization and Human Resources

*You get gains in productivity only because people work smarter and not harder. That is total profit, and it multiplies several times.*

W. EDWARDS DEMING

## CHAPTER 9

Introduction

**Strategic Human Resources Planning**

**Sociotechnical Organizations**
Adaptive Organizational Structures
Keys to Worker Productivity
*OPERATIONS MANAGEMENT IN PRACTICE 9.1: Dramatic Turnaround: X-ray Processing Time Cut 81 Percent*

**Human Resources Issues of the 1990s**
Government Regulations
Work Force Diversity
Manager as Leader
Participative Management
Team Activities
*OPERATIONS MANAGEMENT IN PRACTICE 9.2: American Express Office Takes Team Approach to Work*
Fear in the Workplace
*OPERATIONS MANAGEMENT IN PRACTICE 9.3: Reducing the Bile Factor at Heinz*
Training and Development
Benefits, Compensation, Recognition, and Reward
*OPERATIONS MANAGEMENT IN PRACTICE 9.4: Hewlett-Packard Flexes Its Days*
The Inevitability of Change

**Work Measurement**
Time Studies
Elemental Standard Times
Predetermined Standard Times

# Introduction

The last two chapters have emphasized dramatic changes taking place in organizations today. The quality movement (Chapter 7) and advances in technology (Chapter 8) have had significant effects on all organizations, most especially on the human resources function. In this chapter we will further explore how the human resources function is changing in order to support a rapidly changing operations environment.

Because the introduction and use of technology in organizations today is rapid, we often refer to them as *sociotechnical organizations* rather than simply *social organizations* or *technical organizations*. Employers and employees today are faced with issues and problems that were not even concerns five years ago. This chapter explores many issues of utmost concern, because they are affecting the short- and long-term operations of the typical company.

# Strategic Human Resources Planning

According to one estimate, U.S. companies have experienced a failure rate of 50 to 75 percent when implementing advanced technology. The primary suspect in this failure has been the explicit neglect of the human factor. With expensive technological investments becoming commonplace companies must consider their people, both in deciding whether to purchase and in how to implement new technology.

Human resources managers can play a significant role in linking human resources management practices with the strategic goals of the company. Through their efforts in planning, staffing, evaluating, compensating, and training and development, they are in a position to significantly affect the culture of the organization. An effective organization requires a human resources function that is proactive rather than reactive. Unfortunately, many human resources organizations spend much of their time responding to personnel problems rather than working to reduce their occurrence, often because top management does not offer support for proactive programs. As competitive pressures mount at the typical company, management demands increased productivity with higher quality levels at lower costs. Unless the employees are properly prepared, they are often unable to meet those demands.

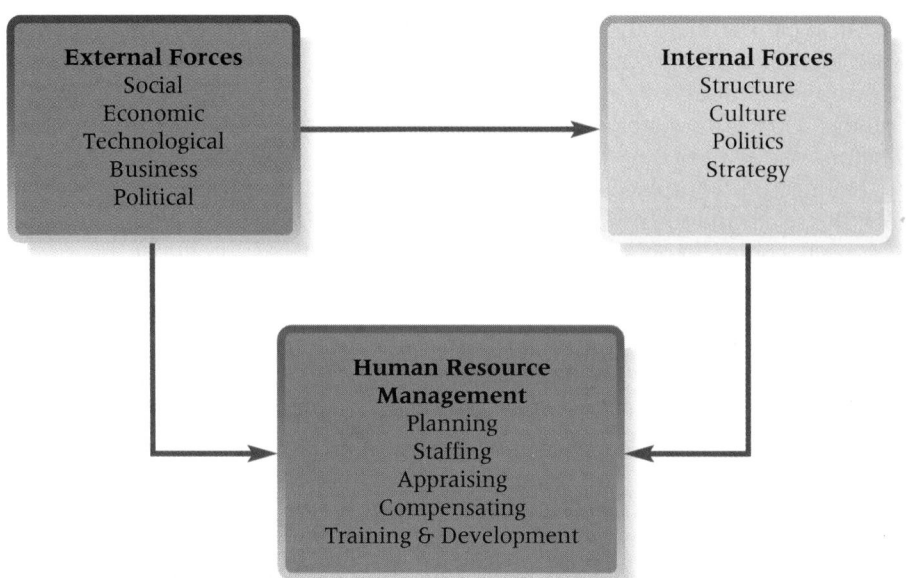

FIGURE 9.1
Model of Strategic Human
Resource Management

Source: Cynthia D. Fisher, Lyle F.
Schoenfeldt, and James B. Shaw,
*Human Resource Management* (Boston:
Houghton Mifflin, 1990): 688.

Ideally, workers in high-performance organizations would themselves continually look for ways to improve productivity, because they perceive it to be in their best interest. To help create such an environment human resources management must be prepared to deal with both the external and the internal pressures that lead to changing requirements. Just as we have discussed the strategic implications of other operations elements, so we consider in this chapter the strategic implications of the human resources element. Figure 9.1 is a model of **strategic human resources management**. As the model shows, various external factors—social, economic, technical, business, and political—influence the internal elements of structure, culture, politics, and strategy. And both affect the development of strategic human resources management.

The first step in using the human resources function strategically is understanding the various elements of an organization and how they interact. The increased use of technology in companies today, coupled with the difficulty of implementing that technology, has forced managers to rethink traditional decision-making processes. They must pay more attention to the effects of technology on the work force when they are making decisions about the work environment. To help managers and decision makers understand increasingly complex organizations, researchers have explored the relationship between the social and technical elements of an organization.

## Sociotechnical Organizations

The term *sociotechnical organization* is thought to have first been used by Eric L. Trist and his associates at the Tavistock Institute in England in the 1950s.[1] Through their research in the coal mines in the United Kingdom they found that simply looking at the human side of the organization would not provide solutions to productivity and morale problems. They decided to also study the

[1]Ron Zemke, "Sociotechnical Systems: Bringing People and Technology Together," *Training* 24 (February 1987): 47–57.

technical environment in which the miners worked, including their equipment, work methods, and procedures. They were surprised to learn that the technical environment influenced personal attitudes and group dynamics, and their findings led to the development of a new school of thought in organizational design.

Seeing the workplace as a **sociotechnical system (STS)** means studying both the social and technical areas of an organization, as well as their interaction, in order to comprehend and effectively address operational problems. Historically, the focus of organizations has been on controlling employee behavior, not on encouraging independent thought or flexibility. Today companies are recognizing the need to change their attitudes about the work force and the value of a well-motivated, trained, and involved work force. As earlier chapters have noted, companies that invest in technology to overcome problems but that fail to consider and involve the work force have been greatly disappointed in the results. Thus, companies must make a conscious effort to blend both the social and technical aspects of any organization in order to reap the benefits of technological change. It is in the social area that most companies have the greatest difficulty, because treating a work force with dignity and concern is a foreign concept to many traditional command-and-control managers.

In his book *Designing Effective Organizations* William Pasmore highlights several recommendations for companies that are considering a move toward a sociotechnical system:

> [T]he social system should receive as much attention during sociotechnical systems design as the technology and the environment.
>
> When it is possible to select members of a social system, as in a new organization . . . , the resulting culture will be stronger if members are relatively homogeneous in their backgrounds and attitudes toward work.
>
> When selecting members of a social system is not possible, the design of the organization should take into account . . . the things that people wish to change . . . maintain . . . and create . . . in the organization.
>
> Adult learning occurs primarily through experience; adaptability is a learned behavior. The more people are involved in experiences which allow them to influence the design of the organization, the more adaptable they and the organization will become.
>
> Activities that offer opportunities to satisfy unfulfilled needs will produce more motivation than activities devoid of such opportunities. . . .
>
> High performance requires commitment; building commitment requires treating people like adults and engaging them fully in shaping their future.[2]

The STS concept did not receive much attention in U.S. companies until the 1960s, and even then few companies were willing to consider its possibilities. Companies such as Sherwin-Williams, Proctor & Gamble, General Foods, and Hewlett-Packard were pioneers in the United States in implementing some of the ideas of STS, especially the use of multifunctional teams. Other companies, including General Motors, Ford, IBM, Motorola, Xerox, General Electric, and many others, followed the movement during the 1970s and 1980s.

Many companies have never heard of Eric Trist, the Tavistock Institute, or STS, but they nonetheless are undergoing significant changes in the way they think of and use their people. Pressures from domestic and foreign competition,

[2]William A. Pasmore, *Designing Effective Organizations: The Sociotechnical Systems Perspective* (New York: Wiley, 1988), p. 49.

labor unions, and the workers themselves have awakened U.S. management to the need for change. As Chapter 7 noted, the total quality management movement has taken hold in many companies as a way to enhance productivity and quality. We cannot overstate the importance of the role of the human element in improving quality and productivity. It is primarily the social element of an organization that will determine the payback from quality improvement efforts. But what of the organizational structure itself? Can the traditional top-down, bureaucratic, hierarchical structure accommodate the emerging need for flexibility, participation, and teamwork, or must the organizational structure change dramatically?

## Adaptive Organizational Structures

Whereas some companies operate in relatively stable industries such as forest products or petroleum products, others operate in dynamic, rapidly changing industries such as electronics, automobiles, communications, and computers. A hierarchical organizational structure may be appropriate for stable industries. But a traditional structure creates barriers that impede communication and cross-functional cooperation in companies in dynamic industries. Companies in these dynamic industries are sensing the most urgent need for flexibility, speed, and adaptability. Dynamic organizations need the ability to quickly and efficiently get new products or major changes in products to market, respond to changes in customers' desires, respond to changes in the marketplace, and deal with frequent problems. These are the organizations that should benefit the most from restructuring that moves toward more adaptive organizational structures.

**Adaptive organizations** are characterized by significant employee involvement—teams, projects, and alliances—designed to unleash employees' creativity.[3] Although the concept of adaptive organizational structure is relatively foreign to most U.S. companies, Apple Computer, Levi Strauss, Xerox, and some others have begun to test its concepts. Some companies are often freeing workers to select the projects and teams with which they would like to work. When a team completes a project, it usually disbands and employees move on to a new team and a new project. The concept of adaptive organizations is similar to the structure used in the construction industry—experts with all the skills a project needs form a team to complete a project. Upon completion a new team forms to tackle the next project.

While this team project orientation sounds useful, it is not without its problems: How are the team assignments to be made and by whom? How long should members be expected to participate on a particular team? How should the employees be evaluated, given that they do not continue to work in one particular environment? Who should be in charge of the individual teams? Answers to these fundamental questions are unique to each organization.

## Keys to Worker Productivity

At the root of organizations' need to be more competitive is their need for improved productivity. Productivity is generally measured as output per unit of input. Companies have always looked for ways to get more for less but have usually adopted a short-term view of their universe in doing so. Many companies

---

[3]Brian Dumaine, "The Bureaucracy Busters," *Fortune*, June 17, 1991, p. 36.

chose automation, only to be disappointed by the results. Decisions made to improve productivity in the short term often adversely affect long-term productivity.

Improvements in technology have improved long-term productivity in some cases, but in others less expensive approaches have led to similar gains because they focus on the worker. Companies need to identify the right mix of technological advancements and worker skill for their particular situation. In STS terminology companies need to find the right social-technical balance. A lower level of technology and a better trained and motivated work force may yield better results than a higher level of technology with less emphasis on the work force. Recognizing this, companies are attempting to unlock the vast stores of knowledge and potential within their workers. For decades companies considered workers a physical resource, because they were paid for what they did, not what they knew. Most successful companies have recognized their workers as an intellectual resource and are exploring their potential. Because of the historical tension between management and labor, some employees prefer to use the term *exploit* rather than *explore* when discussing their new working environment. Operations Management in Practice 9.1 illustrates one company's exploration of its workers' potential to increase their productivity.

Throughout the 1970s and much of the 1980s *productivity* was a dirty word to U.S. workers, because it meant demands that they work faster and harder than usual. Unfortunately, to many managers the call by their superiors for improved productivity meant exactly the same thing. In many companies workers became tired of reports that said that U.S. workers lagged behind Japanese and other international competitors in improving productivity. Workers were being blamed for the poor showing of American products in international markets. And the workers knew better. They knew they were working as hard as they could, and the call to work even harder would have only negative effects on the quality of the product they were producing or the service they were providing.

Fortunately, some companies have listened to their employees and recognized that they often know best. Who is in a better position to recognize potential problems and recommend practical solutions than the people who have worked in that area for years? Companies such as Xerox, IBM, Motorola, Ford, Hewlett Packard, Texas Instruments, Westinghouse, Federal Express, J.C. Penney, Wal-Mart, and many others have learned to unlock employees' potential for the good of the company. They have learned to modify the work environment in ways that encourage improved quality and productivity. A 1992 study by the McKinsey Global Institute of productivity in different countries showed that the United States holds a significant lead over Japan and Europe in output per worker. Specifically, in 1990 a full-time American worker produced $49,000 of goods and services per year. In equivalent dollars' worth of purchasing power a German worker produced $44,000, a Japanese worker produced $38,200, and a British worker $37,100. The study also showed that general merchandise retailing in the United States is more than twice as efficient as that in Japan.[4]

Although U.S. companies choose different approaches to enhancing their individual productivity, their efforts include some or all of the following:

Redefining the role of managers and supervisors as one of leading and
    facilitating

[4]Sylvia Nasar, "U.S. Rate of Output Called Best; Study Affirms Lead over Foreign Rivals," *New York Times*, October 13, 1992, p. C1 (national edition).

# OPERATIONS MANAGEMENT IN PRACTICE 9.1

## Dramatic Turnaround: X-ray Processing Time Cut 81 Percent

A team of employees and managers redesigned the X-ray testing process at Sentara Norfolk General Hospital [in Norfolk, Virginia], cutting it from an average 72.5 hours to 13.8. While patients weren't taking days to go through X-ray, tests were. In 1991, an average 72.5 hours elapsed between the ordering of an X-ray, CAT scan or other radiological test and delivery of a written report to the doctor who ordered it. Approximately 300–500 radiological tests are ordered each day at Norfolk General.

Using a quality improvement program designed by Sentara Health System, a team of nine employees and managers redesigned the X-ray process. The team uncorked hidden bottlenecks, eliminated wasted motion and needless steps and upgraded technology. For the first time, all players in the process were aware of how their performance affected others. This resulted in a reduction from 72.5 hours to 13.8 hours, an impressive 81 percent improvement.

Team members admit that they were defensive when they came to the first meeting in March 1991. After checking everyone's egos at the door, the team's facilitator stressed that personal performance wasn't the issue. Fixing the entire process was. The team's success in making changes depended on getting turf-conscious colleagues from several camps to buy into solutions. The team's diversity and inclusion of managers was key. People who could affect change were part of the process.

The team redesigned the process to cut 14 of the 40 steps to get the reported improvement. The team also persuaded management to invest in newer technology which when installed, is expected to result in a turnaround time of 11 hours. Team members are still not satisfied since they have established a new goal of eight hours and are continuing to improve the process.

Instilling a participative environment in which workers have some say in the design and operation of their work environment

Initiating the use of single- and multidiscipline teams to identify problems and recommend solutions, and often empowering them to actually implement the proposed solution. Some teams share in any monetary savings that result from the improvement

Reducing fear in the workplace that results from uncertainty by enhancing communications throughout the organization, both horizontally and vertically

Investing in training and development for all workers in the organization, from top to bottom

Addressing workers' needs by developing effective benefits, compensation, recognition, and reward programs

Recognizing that organizational change in an organization has a dramatic effect on all employees and that the willingness of a company to welcome change and use it to its advantage will enhance workers' ability to grow and prosper.

This list should be familiar: Our discussion of total quality management in Chapter 7 listed most of the entries as requirements for implementing TQM.

Clearly, an organization must undergo a cultural change from top to bottom. Those companies that succeed at implementing and managing such a cultural change are more likely to survive the 1990s.

## Human Resources Issues of the 1990s

Many critical issues are confronting human resources (HR) practitioners in the 1990s, and they must prepare an effective response to each. In this chapter we discuss many critical issues to highlight the influence of HR decisions on the operations of a company.

### Government Regulations

One of the most significant issues facing HR professionals is the increasing amount of **government regulation.** One such example is the **Americans with Disabilities Act (ADA)**, enacted by Congress in 1990. This act requires that disabled people be granted the same opportunities for employment, advancement, training, compensation, and access as people who do not have disabilities. Another regulation relates to the aging work force. The **Age Discrimination in Employment Act (ADEA)**, as amended in 1986, protects workers aged forty and older from age discrimination. Employers may not in any way limit, segregate, or classify older employees so as to deprive them of opportunities because of their age. As the work force continues to age and retire, the stability of pension plans will be threatened. Their retirement will also place on organizations the additional burden of replacing experienced older workers with young, inexperienced ones.

*Many employers are realizing benefits from hiring physically challenged workers.*

### Work Force Diversity

In addition to an aging work force, other demographic changes are posing challenges. By the year 2000, African Americans, Hispanic Americans, and Asian Americans will make up 53 percent of new work force entrants and 34 percent of all workers, according to estimates.[5] Additionally, the number of women, immigrants, and older adults continues to increase. Whether the source of **work force diversity** is ethnicity, gender, or nationality, it is creating an entirely new set of challenges for managers.

Many recent new programs started by human resources offices are aimed at breaking down barriers between employees that are based on differences in culture, ethnicity, or gender. Recent research by the American Management Association shows that managing diversity is not only the ethical thing to do but can actually be a source of competitive advantage for an organization.[6] Heterogeneous work groups develop more innovative solutions to business problems than homogeneous ones.

Disabled workers, the aging work force, and the increasing diversity of the work force in gender and ethnicity increase the importance of organizations' training and development programs. Many companies are developing internal and external training programs to effectively deal with these increased training

[5]Regina Eisman, "True Colors," *Incentive Journal* 167 (August 1993): 24.
[6]American Management Association, "Managing Diversity for Competitive Advantage," *Management Review* 22 (April 1993): 6.

requirements. Many companies, such as Motorola, Target, and Federal Express, have become noted worldwide for their success.

## Manager as Leader

Another critical issue is the redefining of managers' roles in organizations. This is a difficult change for many _____ _____ible one for some. For example, retired military _____ _____ _____porate managers, because the _____ _____ _____trol management environm _____ _____ _____g great difficulty in char _____ _____ d style. That workers ma _____ _____ is difficult for some trad _____ _____ ,y, quality improvements, _____ _____ ly, management must be w _____ _____ nt.

An effective manager _____ _____ ch, cheerleader, facilitator, negotia _____ _____ is quite a tall order for the tradition.

## Participative Management

With an effective, involved, motivated, a _____ _____ , the company must stress the importance of _____ ir environment. Companies must encourage _____ s relating to their work environment. This i. _____ al organizations, which are characterized by the _____ e- ment. So far as the workers are concerned, one r _____ nt encouraging participation will not erase years o _____ . It took decades for labor-management relations t _____ ave in many companies, and change will not occu _____ sed here is a cultural change, a dramatic shift from the _____.

According to Stanley Herman, **participative management** has ___ ___ basic premises:[7]

- Several heads are better than one.
- Employees are likely to carry out a consensus decision with more enthusiasm than one that is imposed on them.
- Participating in decision making is effective on-the-job training that helps develop subordinates.

Herman says that while each of these premises has merits, participative management can be counterproductive and even reduce workers' effectiveness and job satisfaction in some situations. To avoid these negative effects organizations should take the following precautions:

1. Do not introduce participative management when radical changes are needed quickly.
2. It is seldom economical to try to build a participative team out of people who interact only occasionally.
3. Participation is only conversation unless it produces action.

[7]Stanley M. Herman, "Participative Management Is a Double-Edged Sword," *Training* 26 (January 1989): 55.

4. Effective employee participation need not always include final decision making.

5. Don't ask for participation in making a decision that has already been made. Ask instead how to make it work.

Although these ideas are intuitively appealing, they are new to many managers.

## Team Activities

In trying to create a participative work environment, many companies have turned to teamwork to implement changes. A large-scale movement toward more teamwork has been one of the most important human resources developments in the last decade. Figure 9.2 describes the history and evolution of team activities at U.S. companies, which set the typical pattern for development of team activities. The first team to form usually focuses on a specific problem. These **problem-solving teams**, sometimes referred to as **quality circles**, have been effective in supporting employees' participation and involvement. Once employees accept the use of problem-solving teams and teams succeed and are celebrated, many companies move to the next level of sophistication by forming

FIGURE 9.2
The Evolution of Worker Participation in the United States

Source: John Hoerr, "The Payoff from Teamwork," *Business Week*, July 10, 1989, p. 57.

|  | Problem-Solving Teams | Special Purpose Teams | Self-Managing Teams |
|---|---|---|---|
| **Structure and Function** | Consist of 5 to 12 volunteers, hourly and salaried, drawn from different areas of a department. Meet one to two hours a week to discuss ways of improving quality, efficiency, and work environment. Do not have power to implement ideas. | Duties may include designing and introducing work reforms or new technology, meeting with suppliers and customers, linking separate functions. In union shops, labor and management collaborate on operational decisions at all levels. | Usually 5 to 15 employees who produce an entire product instead of subunits. Members learn all tasks and rotate from job to job. Teams take over managerial duties, including work and vacation scheduling, ordering materials, etc. |
| **Results** | Can reduce costs and improve product quality. But do not organize work more efficiently or force managers to adopt a participatory style. Tend to fade away after a few years. | Involve workers and union representatives in decisions at ever-higher levels, creating atmosphere for quality and productivity improvements. Create a foundation for self-managing work teams. | Can increase productivity 30% or more and substantially raise quality. Fundamentally change how work is organized, giving employees control over their jobs. Create flatter organization by eliminating supervisors. |
| **When Introduced** | Small-scale efforts in 1920s and 1930s. Widespread adoption in late 1970s based on Japanese quality circles. | Early-to-middle 1980s, growing out of problem-solving approach. Still spreading, especially in union sectors. | Used by a few companies in 1960s and 1970s. Began rapid spread in mid to late 1980s, and appear to be wave of future. |

*Teams are formed to study and recommend improvements in key processes.*

**special purpose teams**. These teams usually have more authority and focus on the more sophisticated problems or projects. The highest level of team activity is the **self-managing work team**; their use is not widespread, but many companies see them as their goal. A 1987 survey of 476 large companies by the U.S. General Accounting Office found that 70 percent had formed problem-solving teams. The study also revealed that within those companies less than half of the work force was involved.[8] Operations Management in Practice 9.2 describes efforts by American Express to improve operations through team activities.

Several companies recently have emerged as leaders in the use of team activities. For example, Motorola promotes its Participative Management Program, which is the foundation for its team activities. Motorola uses it to recognize and reward team activities that result in improvements in quality, cycle time, or other operational problems. The program provides awards for group as well as individual efforts. The company is also sponsoring an annual Total Customer Satisfaction (TCS) team competition. TCS teams are cross-functional teams that have members whose jobs range from engineer to machine operator. Teams throughout Motorola submit a report of their successes to a corporate committee, which selects finalists. The teams that emerge as finalists go to corporate headquarters in Schaumburg, Illinois, for the last round of competition, and winners receive wide recognition and suitable reward.

At Westinghouse the main mechanism for continuous improvement is the employee team. It has undertaken several initiatives to encourage team spirit, involvement, and the feeling of ownership by all employees. Milliken and Co. also uses teamwork for continuous improvement. During 1988 Milliken's employees formed more than two thousand teams to address specific challenges involving customers, suppliers, and internal operations.[9] At any given time approximately 75 percent of all Xerox employees are involved in some type of

---

[8]John Hoerr, "The Payoff from Teamwork," *Business Week*, July 10, 1989, p. 58.
[9]"Pushing to Improve Quality," *Research-Technology Management* 33 (May–June 1990): 19–22.

# American Express Office Takes Team Approach to Work

American Express in Plantation, Florida, has thrown away the rule book and put employees in charge of the company. The revolution is part of a planned upheaval throughout a conservative, 150 year old corporation that traditionally revered hierarchy and sent orders flowing from the top down. Now employees feel like they own the place.

"We make decisions on our own," says Scott Ernst, a member of a team that handles card holder inquiries about rental-car companies. "We tell management what we want done." The efforts to change the corporate structure of the Plantation operation have cost time, hard work and more than $2.5 million for initial employee training.

Was it worth all the trouble? The result has been the creation of a more productive work environment and a more enthusiastic workforce that tries harder to please customers and is less likely to leave the company. In short, it has helped them step ahead of the competition.

The 3,500 Plantation employees are organized as work teams of 10 to 12 people. They all get about 60 hours of training in team skills: how to communicate, trust, resolve conflict. Before, the supervisor checked whether subordinates came to work on time. Now that person is a team leader who serves as coach and mentor. The employees used to follow prescribed formulas for getting things done. Now, they must exercise their judgment and help overburdened colleagues, too.

For example, letters written by Ernst and his colleagues used to go to the quality assurance department which checked to see that each one contained a list of specific details. It didn't matter if a detail was a relevant response to the customer's inquiry—if it was missing, quality assurance would reprimand the employees. Now employees decide what to write in their letters.

Other teams are problem solvers. One team figured out how to make the company suggestion box come alive. It has organized 200 volunteers to evaluate all ideas handed in and come up with ways to carry out the feasible ones. Other teams figure out how to make the company a better place to work. They take the results of annual employee satisfaction surveys and formulate and implement ways to change the things with which employees are dissatisfied.

American Express rewards teamwork. A new bonus program calculates payoffs according to how well the whole work team, not the individual employee, handles customer satisfaction.

team project. As of 1990 Cadillac Motor Car Co. reported that it had approximately seventy teams involving about 750 employees.

Clearly, many effective organizations have decided that teamwork is one way to unlock the potential of the work force. Although many companies have come forward to pronounce their successes with team activities, some individuals and organizations consider the increasing use of teamwork undesirable. For example, many union leaders consider the use of team activities a clandestine effort by management to undermine the effectiveness of organized labor. Unions recently suggested to the National Labor Relations Board (NLRB) that teams may violate the National Labor Relations Act of 1935, which prevents companies from creating "paper" unions to undercut legitimate ones, a practice common in the 1930s.[10]

Unions are arguing that the law does not allow management to both create and manage teams unless workers agree. They say that management should be allowed to suggest that employees set up teams but not to require that they do so. Unions are not generally worried about problem-solving teams, because these teams focus on their own work areas. But they draw the line at creating teams that may affect work areas governed by union contract. The test case involved an electrical parts maker called Electromation, Inc. After a year of heavy financial losses management decided in 1988 to skip wage increases for the company's two hundred employees. The employees resisted the move, so management set up what it called "action committees," made up of both hourly workers and managers. The focus of the committees was such problems as absenteeism and pay structures for skilled workers. At about the same time the Teamsters were attempting to organize Electromation's workers. The Teamsters filed an objection to the company's committees with the NLRB. In 1990 the board ruled that the company had violated the National Labor Relations Act by interfering with the effort to unionize.

Despite the board's ruling, it is unlikely that team activities will be outlawed, but the NLRB is likely to provide more rigid guidelines for their formation and management. In general, the rulings indicate that management must exercise care in creating teams and in selecting projects for the teams to address. Specifically, any teams created and led by management that address such issues as rates of pay, conditions of employment, or any other topics that might be covered under a collective bargaining agreement with organized labor may cause problems. Management must be more diligent in its dealings with organized labor to promote the benefits to both sides of increased employee involvement. Only then can labor and management negotiate new contracts that will be beneficial to employers and employees and provide a flexible and participative work force.

## Fear in the Workplace

With all the changes taking place in American industry today the work force is often in constant fear. Employees have fears about pay, job advancement, job security, health, safety, ethics, performance appraisal, ambiguous managerial behavior, and more. That fear is affecting their job performance and their willingness to participate in productivity-enhancing activities. Because many managers tend to persecute the messenger of bad news, many employees are reluctant to bring problems to their attention. W. Edwards Deming pointed out the need to address this fear in order to create and sustain a quality-oriented organizational culture. Managers must be willing to acknowledge the presence of fear, identify its causes, and develop long-term strategies to alleviate the fear.

The most common measure of the degree of fear in an organization is the willingness of its employees to speak up in meetings and express their displeasure about an issue. In an organization in which fear is present, employees deal with that fear by keeping quiet. The employees in turn lose self-confidence, become more dissatisfied with their jobs, and never develop to their full potential. In their book *Driving Fear Out of the Workplace* Kathleen Ryan and Daniel Oestreich point out that "fear is an interactive process involving communication between

---

[10]Aaron Bernstein, "Putting a Damper on That Old Team Spirit," *Business Week*, May 4, 1992, p. 60.

FIGURE 9.3
The Cycle of Mistrust

Source: Adapted from Kathleen D. Ryan and Daniel K. Oestreich, *Driving Fear Out of the Workplace* (San Francisco: Jossey-Bass, 1991): 89.

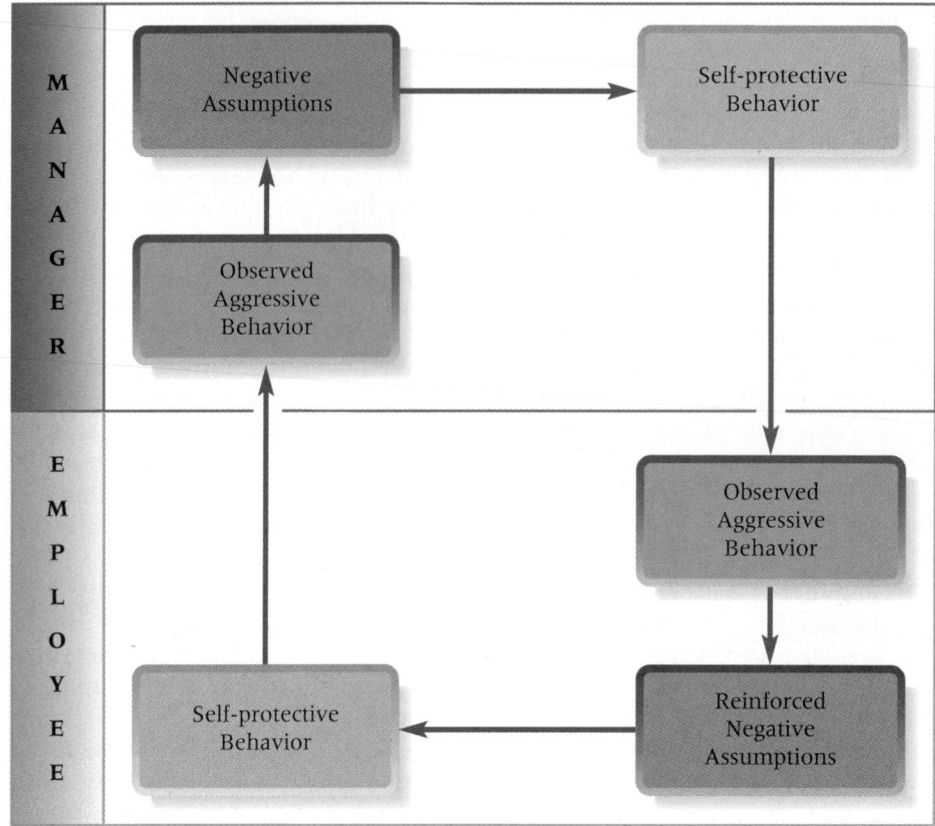

at least two people."[11] In their interviews of 260 employees of 22 companies in the United States, 70 percent said that they had hesitated to speak up at one time or another because they feared some type of repercussion. The authors suggest that companies experience **cycles of mistrust** because negative assumptions and self-protective behavior on the part of managers and employees serve to ensure a self-fulfilling negative relationship. Figure 9.3 illustrates the cycle of mistrust.

From the figure we see that the cycle can begin anywhere, but once started it will continue until broken by some change in the culture of the organization. For example, let's begin with the first block that represents a manager's negative assumptions about an employee's ability, interest, performance, or some other measure. The result is that the manager may behave in self-protective ways. The employee often senses the manager's self-protective posture and interprets it as aggressive. Because the employee perceives the manager as aggressive, the employee does not trust the manager, which often reinforces other negative assumptions the employee has made about the manager. So the employee begins to behave in self-protective ways. The manager interprets this behavior as aggressive and a sign of mistrust, reinforcing the manager's negative assumptions about the employee. If ignored, the cycle of mistrust will continue its harmful effects throughout the organization.

[11]Kathleen D. Ryan and Daniel K. Oestreich, *Driving Fear Out of the Workplace* (San Francisco: Jossey-Bass, 1991), p. 4.

The key to breaking the cycle of mistrust is to change the assumptions from negative to positive. Managers need to think positively about employees until they are proved wrong. They need to assume that their employees possess all the positive characteristics of a good employee. Employees will take note of the positive attitude, so their assumptions are more likely to be more positive. This is not always easy to do. Ryan and Oestreich offer seven strategies for a manager interested in creating an environment full of enthusiasm and trust:

1. *Acknowledge the presence of fear.* Be constantly aware of factors that contribute to fear in the workplace. Don't be afraid to discuss this issue with the employees individually or in groups.

2. *Pay attention to interpersonal conduct.* Employees form many of their assumptions about management through their limited personal contact. Managers need to pay particular attention to how they present themselves to employees. Being overly critical, using abusive language, becoming angry, yelling, insulting, placing blame, and even ignoring are behaviors that contribute to the cycle of fear in the workplace.

3. *Value criticism—reward the messenger.* The traditional approach is to prosecute the messenger if the message is not a good one. This attitude contributes to the level of fear in the workplace, because employees are not willing to share concerns or even suggestions with management for fear of reprisals. Management must create an environment in which criticisms and suggestions are appreciated.

4. *Reduce ambiguous behavior.* Employees perform better in an environment in which information is shared. Secretive meetings, limited direct communication, and unethical conduct of managers contribute to uncertainty, which leads to more fear. Managers must be willing to share as much accurate information as possible so employees will feel more involved. Managers must also quickly respond to employees' questions.

5. *Discuss the undiscussables.* Every group has a set of issues that is not usually discussed. Managers must identify these issues and begin to routinely share information about them. The issues usually include management practices, coworker performance, compensation, job security, and others unique to a particular group.

6. *Collaborate on decisions.* Most employees want to be involved in decisions that relate to them or their work environment. Managers should encourage participation and collaboration in the decision-making process, which should lead to less uncertainty in the environment and reduce fear.

7. *Challenge worst-case thinking.* In a fearful environment people tend to think and expect the worst. These negative thoughts and negative expectations often lead to expected results. Managers must challenge this negativism and worst-case thinking.[12]

By following these commonsense strategies management can greatly reduce fear and uncertainty in the workplace. The result should be a more motivated, involved, and productive work force.

One of the greatest issues causing fear throughout U.S. companies today is the move toward **corporate downsizing**, or *rightsizing*, as it is becoming known. As companies struggle to become internationally competitive, many are finding

---

[12]Ryan and Oestreich, *Driving Fear Out of the Workplace*, pp. 103–232.

that they need to scale back domestic operations. The downsizing is affecting all employees, from the executive suite to the shop or sales floor. Many executives and managers are standing in unemployment lines today, a scene seldom imagined by rational businesspeople. A study conducted by the American Management Association in 1992 asked personnel managers of 836 companies about their companies' worker reduction efforts from July 1991 to June 1992 and about plans for 1993.[13] The survey found that 46.1 percent of the surveyed companies had reduced their work forces in the past year and 25 percent planned to reduce their work forces in 1993. Especially hard hit was middle management, which accounts for only about 8 percent of all jobs, but 22 percent of the losses. Companies have eliminated nearly 2 million middle management positions since 1980, according to estimates.

Many companies have been through the downsizing and have not realized the returns they expected. The message is clear for many companies: Simply reducing head count is not the way to achieve sustainable gains in efficiency. Yes, costs will decrease in the short term, but the effect of the downsizing on the remaining work force can cause costs to increase in the long term. After downsizing, management must get to work immediately. The remaining work force will be in some degree of shock and disarray, partly grieving for their lost comrades and wondering why they were spared. Operations Management in Practice 9.3 tells the story of downsizing effort at Heinz. It is an example of the relationship between total quality management, discussed in Chapter 7, and efforts to improve productivity and efficiency.

Many companies have become so overstaffed and overmanaged that some downsizing is necessary. Common sense dictates that the downsizing should result from careful analysis of the operations of the company, looking for waste, duplication of effort, unnecessary steps, and so on. In the methodical elimination of waste costs will decrease, some jobs will change, and some jobs will be lost. But at least the reductions will be part of a master plan, and the work force will not be cut simply to reduce costs. In some cases employees are so empowered and involved that they actually recommend that their own positions be eliminated because they are wasteful. Only in a special work environment will workers have so little fear that they would make such a recommendation. Of course, these companies do not lay off the workers; they eliminate the work the employees were doing, which yields cost and time savings for the companies. The displaced workers get new positions.

## Training and Development

Another major human resources issue for the 1990s is employee **training and development**. With all the changes taking place in organizations today, including international competitiveness, renewed emphasis on quality, continual improvements in technology, and corporate restructuring and downsizing, increasingly diverse training has become a necessity. At one time companies treated training as something they would do when a specific need arose, but today successful companies view training as an investment in their future. Companies that have recognized the importance of continual education of their work forces are spending millions of dollars annually. One of the most recognized

[13]Charles Boisseau, "Employment Carnage May Continue, Survey Says," *Houston Chronicle*, October 23, 1992, p. 1D.

## OPERATIONS MANAGEMENT IN PRACTICE 9.3

# Reducing the Bile Factor at Heinz

Anthony J.F. O'Reilly, chief executive of Heinz since 1979, realizes that a company, much like a plastic bottle of ketchup, can be squeezed only so much. Even at Heinz, one of industry's most successful cost cutters, downsizing has its limits.

In the 1980s, it closed factories, laid off workers, and revved up production lines with enviable results. Gross profit margins swelled from 33% to 39% of sales, and Heinz posted average earnings increases of 15% per year in a decade when the processed food industry was bedeviled by sluggish growth, merciless competition, and bitter takeover battles.

O'Reilly now realizes that his sharp pencil, while financially successful, alienated workers, interfered with the quality of the products, and left the company still wasting millions of dollars a year on unnecessary work. His solution: stop squeezing and start changing. Concentrate on quality, not cost.

Under the company's total quality management effort, teams of workers are reexamining virtually everything Heinz does—from the way it packages French fries to the way it conducts market research. O'Reilly figures that TQM can save the company $250 million over the next three years, mostly by eliminating waste and rework.

Working in teams creates a sense of interdependence. Jobs are now substantially more sophisticated, interesting, and exciting. Instead of staring mindlessly at a moving belt of peas, carrots, or bottles, workers are now able for example to work the computerized photo-imaging machinery that controls the labeling line.

The advent of TQM has greatly elevated the dignity of the worker at Heinz. In the past there was very little consultation with employees. That led to a natural sense of human irritation and a sense that no one cared that the employee was most knowledgeable about how a process really operated.

leaders in corporate training and education is Motorola, through the introduction of its Motorola University.

Originally called the Motorola Training and Education Center, Motorola University provides one of the most comprehensive and effective corporate training programs in the world. In 1991 Motorola instituted a requirement that each employee receive forty hours of training each year. People in technical positions may receive two or three times that amount. In the average year Motorola offers its employees about 1 million hours of training at a cost of nearly $120 million.[14] Training includes everything from basic reading, writing, and math skills to computer programming, designing for manufacturability, statistical process control, cycle management, foreign languages, cross-cultural training, successful negotiation, and how to handle difficult people. Training is not only for Motorolans; suppliers and customers also participate. Motorola estimates that every dollar it spends on training returns about $30 in productivity gains within a three-year period. William Wiggenhorn, former president of Motorola University, says, "When you buy a piece of equipment, you set aside a percentage for

[14]William Wiggenhorn, "Motorola U: When Training Becomes an Education," *Harvard Business Review* 68 (July–August 1990): 72.

*The power of teamwork was experienced throughout the design, development, and production of the state-of-the-art Boeing 777.*

maintenance. Shouldn't you do the same for people?"[15] Table 9.1 lists and describes other corporate leaders in training and education.

Milliken and Co. also is committed to training its "associates," for whom it too has a forty-hour per year training requirement. In 1988 alone, the company spent $1,300 to train each of approximately 15,000 associates in statistical process control and other skills.[16] Milliken also encourages employees to take other courses and pays the first $50 plus 75 percent of the remaining costs of books, tuition, and fees.

One particular dilemma in industry relates to the ever-increasing need for educated, entry-level employees. Where companies ten years ago may have required only a seventh grade education, those companies today may be requiring a high school diploma. The dilemma lies in what to do about employees who have been with the company for ten to fifteen years. Companies have ended up with workers who have diverse educational backgrounds and are performing the same functions in the organization. How can older employees be brought up to speed so they can compete with the younger ones? Some older employees are illiterate and/or do not speak English, which was acceptable when they were hired. Wiggenhorn tells the story of a supplier for a Motorola plant that was changing its packaging design. Plant management found out quickly that many workers were working by the color of the package, not by what was printed on it, because they could not read. He also tells of a foreign-born employee who did not know the difference between the present tense and the past. The worker was never sure whether people were talking about what *was* happening or what *had* happened. These stories highlight the need for basic skills evaluation and training, especially when companies must be flexible and adaptive to remain competitive. Many companies, including those mentioned earlier, as well as Adolph Coors, GTE, and Exxon, are actively involved in literacy programs for their organizations.

[15]Ronald Henkoff, "Companies That Train Best," *Fortune*, March 22, 1993, p. 22.
[16]"Pushing to Improve Quality," *Research-Technology Management* 33 (May–June 1990): 19–22.

| Company | Training | | Comments |
| --- | --- | --- | --- |
| Employees Worldwide | Percent of Payroll Spent in 1992 | Avg. Hours per Employee per Year | |
| Motorola 107,000 | 3.6% | 36 | The gold standard of corporate training. The company says every $1 spent on education returns $30 in productivity gains. |
| Target 100,000 | N.A. | N.A. | Rapidly expanding retail chain has used Disney-type training to empower frontline employees and improve customer service. |
| Federal Express 93,000 | 4.5% | 27 | Workers take computer-based job competency tests every six to 12 months. Low scores lead to remedial action. |
| General Electric Aircraft Engines 33,000 | N.A. | N.A. | Training budget has shrunk, but new focus on teamwork has helped the division boost productivity in a slumping industry. |
| Andersen Consulting 26,700 | 6.8% | 109 | Replaced 40-hour Business Practices class with interactive video, saving $4 million per year, mostly on travel and lodging. |
| Corning 14,000 (domestic) | 3.0% | 92 | Ordinary employees, nonprofessional educators, do most training. Pay of factory workers rises as they learn new skills. |
| Solectron 3,500 | 3.0% | 95 | Training helped this fast-growing Silicon Valley company win a Baldrige Award in 1991. The 1993 goal: 110 hours per worker. |
| Dudek Manufacturing 35 | 5.0% | 25 | Had to teach basic literacy and math before introducing quality management. Hefty investment has paid off in profits. |

Source: Ronald Henkoff, "Companies That Train Best," *Fortune*, March 22, 1993, p. 64.

TABLE 9.1
Industry Leaders in Training and Education

Another training issue for the 1990s is the need for **cross-cultural training** for employees. As companies become more international, they transfer employees from place to place in order to best use their resources. It's expensive to transfer employees and their families to foreign assignments, and employees and their families need training to prepare for life in a foreign land. They need to learn not only the language but also the customs and culture of the country. Industry is rife with horror stories about terminations of foreign assignments because employees were ignorant of cultural differences. General Motors spends nearly $500,000 each year on cross-cultural training and boasts of a premature return rate of less than 1 percent.[17]

Although we have discussed many examples of training and development, not every company is involved. These examples represent pockets of excellence. According to the American Society for Training and Development, training expenditures for U.S. companies average only 1.4 percent of payroll, and only 10 percent of the nation's workers receive formal training.[18]

[17]Joann S. Lublin, "Companies Use Cross-Cultural Training to Help Their Employees Adjust Abroad," *Wall Street Journal*, August 4, 1992, p. 1B.
[18]Linda Thornburg, "Training in a Changing World," *HR Magazine* 37 (August 1992): 44.

## Benefits, Compensation, Recognition, and Reward

A major question still remains unanswered: If we create comprehensive training programs and give employees the opportunity to become more involved through team activities, will workers line up to take advantage of these opportunities? In many cases the answer is no. The employees must clearly recognize that it is in their best interest to do so. It is up to management to create an environment in which employees ask to be trained and ask to become members of teams. Much of the solution to this problem is based on our earlier discussion of fear in the workplace. Management must clearly communicate the necessity for such training and recognize that many employees may simply be afraid of going back to school for fear of failing. Management must determine what types of incentives will work for their organizations and use those incentives to promote desired behavior.

The term *incentive* in this discussion refers to a family of programs used by management to promote a healthy, productive, creative, and inspired work force. **Incentive** programs can be monetary and/or nonmonetary in nature and range from those relating to employment itself to those that relate more specifically to job performance. Table 9.2 lists general forms of incentives.

This characterization of incentive programs includes benefits and compensation in employment-related programs, whereas job performance-related programs include compensation, recognition, and reward programs. Compensation is listed in both categories, because compensation may or may not be tied to job performance in a particular organization. Let's look at these four forms of incentives in more detail to better understand what is available and what companies are using.

**Benefits** Company **benefits** include such programs as medical, dental, life, and disability insurance coverage, savings and retirement plans, flextime, job sharing, child and elder care assistance, vacations and sick leave, as well as leaves of absence for various family emergencies. The total spending by industry for benefits in 1990 was divided as follows: 3 percent for disability and life insurance, 13 percent for pensions, profit sharing, and other retirement plans, 23 percent for legally required benefits such as Social Security and workers' compensation, 24 percent for medical benefits, and 37 percent for vacation, sick leave, child care, and other paid, time-off benefits.[19] Operations Management in Practice 9.4 describes how Hewlett-Packard thinks of its responsibilities to the work force.

In March 1992 RJR Nabisco announced an innovative program of tuition loan guarantees and company-matched savings plans, so all employees could afford to send their children to college.[20] Some companies are compensating

[19]Jeremy Main, "The Battle over Benefits," *Fortune*, December 16, 1991, p. 92.
[20]Lani Luciano, "The Good News About Employee Benefits," *Money*, June 1992, p. 94.

TABLE 9.2
Incentive Programs

| Employment-Related | Job Performance-Related |
| --- | --- |
| Benefits | Compensation |
| Compensation | Recognition |
| | Reward |

# Hewlett-Packard Flexes Its Days

Katherine Tanelian, with the elaborate title of "world-wide personnel communications manager" at Hewlett-Packard, described how her company, noted for its humane personnel policies, defines a family-friendly company: "This isn't just one problem—day care—it's seventeen. We offer a flexible time-off program which combines traditional sick leave and vacation time. Now, employees receive fifteen flexible days off to use at their discretion in addition to eleven paid holidays. We treat people like adults. We don't ask for doctors' notes. We realized that we had a lot of honest working parents who would call in and say, 'I have to take a vacation day because my son is ill,' while others would simply say, 'I need sick leave.' It's now accepted in the company culture that people will call in and say they need a flex-day—flexible working hours for that day—because their child is ill."

As part of its benefits package, Hewlett-Packard also makes it relatively easy for a new parent to take a leave of several months. Combining all the available increments of paid and unpaid time, a new mother can usually take up to three months off. Plus using the company's job guarantee stipulation, a mother could take an additional four months—though she may not be returning to the same job.

Hewlett-Packard has also introduced a new part-time policy. A new mother may, after having a child, decide that she doesn't want to come back full-time. At that point, she and her supervisors determine if her existing job can be done part-time or if another part-time job is available. So far, less than 5 percent of Hewlett-Packard's employees are part-time workers, but interest in part-time is reported to be increasing.

"Sometimes time is not the problem, finances are. So instead of an on-site center, we offer pretax accounts for dependent care (for the old or young). You can estimate how much you spend for child care or parent care and set it aside for an account that is not taxed. That helps offset the burden."

"Another reason we don't offer on-site day care is equity. We offer the same basic package to all employees, so building a child-care center would not benefit the people who do not have kids. Cost-wise we could afford to do it, but it doesn't feel very equitable."

employees' spouses for lost wages and providing job search assistance to spouses involved in a move. At Motorola an employee with ten years of service cannot be released without the concurrence of the chairman of the board. Motorola also provides for professional counseling for financial, alcohol, drug dependency, or other problems. According to *Money* magazine's 1992 listing of companies with the best employee benefits, the top five slots are held by Levi Strauss, IBM, Proctor & Gamble, Eastman Kodak, and Hewlett-Packard.[21]

When the economy is tight and companies are forced to cut costs wherever they can, the benefit packages of many companies tend to shrink. For example, the spiraling cost of health care has meant that many companies are asking employees to assume more of the cost of their coverage. This one issue has been

[21]Luciano, "Good News," pp. 92–93.

the cause of more than half of all employee strikes in recent years. Benefit packages were once thought to be untouchable, but employers today are beginning to manage their entire benefit packages just as they would manage any of their other costs. Continued attempts to cut back insurance and pension benefits have contributed to the distress and fear that many employees feel.

**Compensation** Compensation, or pay, is a controversial issue in industry today. As companies strive to become world class, they are finding they need to have world-class compensation plans. Achieving world-class status essentially means the organization is flexible and able to effectively change as the market changes around them. This requires a well-trained, well-motivated, and highly creative work force. The compensation plan of an organization often encourages—or discourages—employee behavior that the company sees as desirable.

An effective compensation plan is one that recognizes the increased responsibilities management has placed on the workers for quality, training, maintenance, troubleshooting, team activities, workplace organization, and others and rewards workers for accepting and excelling in those new responsibilities. Traditional compensation plans simply reward a worker for the specific task performed. For example, whether a particular job was machine operator, maintenance technician, sales clerk, office manager, receptionist, or quality inspector, it probably would have a precise, written job description and a specified starting salary with a set of incremental increases based primarily on time served. Employees whose performance far exceeds the norm may or may not be eligible for a merit increase. When compensation plans do not include a merit component, where is the motivation for workers to want more training, to want to become more involved, or to want to participate in problem-solving/quality-improvement team activities? If these are desirable behaviors, the compensation plan must be innovative enough to measure and reward them.

Today organizations are moving toward compensation plans that focus on performance *and* knowledge. Some plans use both fixed and variable components. In one such system promoted by Steve Gross, a noted compensation consultant, "individuals are evaluated for base pay on such variables as ability to communicate, customer focus, dealing with change, interpersonal skills, ability to work on a team, and professional and technical knowledge."[22] The same system evaluates managers on employee development, group productivity, and leadership skills. Both workers and managers are compensated for what the organization actually accomplishes, often through profit-sharing or gain-sharing plans. This compensation model is particularly well suited to organizations adopting the customer focus concept of total quality management.

**Pay-for-performance** plans emphasize long-term improvements. Companies are even beginning to tie executive bonuses to long-term financial or market improvements. Almost all personnel managers at big companies think employees' pay should reflect their performance, but only about half of the compensation plans actually do.

In summary, financial incentives may focus on the individual, team, or the entire organization. Individual financial incentives are based on achieving some predetermined standard of performance. Team financial incentives relate to the team's successful accomplishment of some team objective, such as a problem to

---

[22]Linda Thornburg, "Pay for Performance: What You Should Know," *HR Magazine* 37 (June 1992): 59.

be solved or a project to be completed. Organizationwide financial incentives usually take the form of profit-sharing or gain-sharing plans that reward members of the organization when it reaches some overall financial or market objective. Most critical in many companies today are the team rewards. Teamwork is so new in many organizations that compensation systems do not adequately recognize, assess, and reward team activities. Team rewards need not be solely financial. Many companies have developed innovative approaches to team recognition and rewards that do not involve traditional pay systems. Effective managers recognize that some types of rewards influence employees' long-term behavior and other types may help only in the short term. Identifying and applying the appropriate types of rewards significantly affect whether employees buy new concepts and procedures.

**Recognition and Rewards** When Westinghouse launched its major quality initiative, it took five hundred employees from all levels of the organization to Japan to observe Japanese operations.[23] John Wallace, chief executive officer of Wallace Manufacturing, sends congratulatory letters to associates' homes as a form of recognition for a job well done. One manufacturing facility in Fort Worth gave top-performing employees and teams coupons that essentially were raffle tickets. The better the performance of individuals or teams, the more coupons they received. At the end of the month management would sponsor a wiener roast on the grounds and hold a drawing for several portable color TV sets. Employees knew that excellent performance would not guarantee them a TV, but it certainly improved their chances. These are examples of **recognition and reward** systems in action. In addition to money, picnics, and TV sets, rewards may include special parking, plaques, employee/team of the month designation, special event tickets, and gift certificates.

Management often has trouble deciding what forms of recognition and reward to adopt. Usually, the problem is that management does not consider the wishes and desires of the work force. For example, most managers find it difficult to appreciate the value a machine operator places on pats on the back by management or tokens such as coffee mugs, key rings, and t-shirts. Unfortunately, managers tend to use their own value systems when deciding what their employees would respond to. Why not ask the workers? Employee-centered companies are surveying employees annually to help management and the human resources department develop programs to better respond to the wishes of the work force.

## The Inevitability of Change

If anything is true of all business in the 1990s, it's that change is inevitable. As operations managers and human resources professionals work together to develop a well-motivated and inspired work force for the future, they must not lose sight of this truism. Successful organizations of the future must be flexible, efficient, and able to respond to changes in technology, market conditions, and the economy. Shorter product life cycles and a greater focus on customer satisfaction will drive the need for continual change. Change must become the rule of the organization rather than the exception.

[23]Thomas M. Rohan, "Baldrige Award's Winners Tell How," *Industry Week* 238 (January 16, 1989): 23.

# Work Measurement

In discussing human resources issues in the 1990s, we mentioned terms such as *measurement, improvement,* and *predetermined standards.* Absent from that discussion was any reference to how to establish standards, for without standards it is impossible to accurateiy measure productivity improvements. Activities that cannot be measured cannot be effectively managed or rewarded.

The idea of measuring work is not new. During the late nineteenth century, Frederick W. Taylor, noted as the father of scientific management, committed much of his life to studying work methods and measurement. Much of what we know today is the result of his work. **Work measurement** refers to the task of determining what rate of output a manager may expect from a qualified employee working at a normal pace, using a given technique, raw materials, equipment, and workplace layout to complete a particular task. That amount of time, after adjusting for expected delays, becomes the **standard time** against which managers measure employee or process improvements. Calculating standard time requires precise specification of the environmental conditions present when the standards are established. If any environmental conditions change, the company must reevaluate its standard time for accuracy. Standard times are necessary inputs for incentive pay systems, machine and employee scheduling, cost estimation, budgeting, and capacity planning.

Consider for a moment the capacity-planning application. If a qualified worker can accurately process a product in ten minutes, the capacity of that process would be six units per hour, excluding any time for unexpected delays. If management determines that six units per hour will not satisfy customer demand for the product, it must adjust the process to increase capacity. One way to do that is to divide the process that now takes ten minutes into two segments of five minutes each. Adding an individual to complete the second part of the process should nearly double the capacity of the process. But what of the cost of the additional worker? These are the types of decisions that have to be made continually throughout the organization.

How do companies establish these important standard times? They are using several approaches, including time studies, elemental standard times, and predetermined standard times.

## Time Studies

Sometimes called *stopwatch studies,* **time studies** make estimates of standard times from repeated measurements of a qualified individual accomplishing the same task. It is the most commonly used of all the approaches. Steps for making a time study are as follows:

1. Select the task to be analyzed and identify the worker who will perform it.
2. Discuss with the worker the reason for the analysis and try to dispel any fears the worker may have about the analysis. Ask the employee to accomplish the task normally.
3. Divide the task into necessary elements.
4. Determine the appropriate number of cycles for measuring a particular level of confidence.
5. Time the task and note any suspected deviations from normal practice by the worker.
6. Analyze the collected information and determine the standard time.

The first two steps of the process are extremely important. According to historical evidence, many workers will feel threatened by the analysis and may find subtle ways to increase the duration of the task. That way, the worker feels that a higher time standard will make it easier to meet expectations of the job. For example, if the task can easily be accomplished in twenty minutes, but the standard is set at twenty-five minutes, the worker should be able to comfortably meet expectations. The person doing the analysis must be familiar with the task in order to address these issues.

In step 3 of the process the task is divided into smaller elemental parts, which are timed. There are several reasons for accomplishing this step:

1.  Each element of the task may not be accomplished in every cycle.
2.  Machine-paced and worker-paced elements should be divided as a reference for future improvement efforts.
3.  Some elements may take much longer to accomplish than other elements, which again helps in focusing improvement efforts.
4.  Times for each element may be stored for use later. Other tasks may involve the same or similar elements, so establishing standard times for a new task may be quicker and easier by using the **elemental standard times**, as the times for the different parts are called.

Step 4 of the time study process, determining the number of cycles to study, is important for accuracy considerations. Would you consider making a time standard for everyone in the entire organization to use by analyzing *one* cycle for a selected worker? Probably not. More than likely the analyst will take repeated readings and determine some mean value of observed times as a basis for the standard. As we noted earlier, these standard times become the basis against which companies measure improvements and productivity and determine incentive pay and daily work output. You can be certain that labor unions carefully scrutinize the establishment of standard times by which their membership will have to perform. After all, the desires of the two parties often conflict. Usually, management would prefer standards that allow high rates of output, and unions prefer standards that allow a lower rate of output and more comfortable standards.

The number of cycles to be timed depends primarily upon three factors. First, how do the observed times vary? For example, if readings for ten cycles of the task show little difference, an accurate reading may be achieved with fewer cycles. But if the ten cycles show a lot of variation, timing more cycles will provide a better estimate. The second factor to be considered in determining the number of cycles to time is the degree of accuracy desired. Some tasks are more critical than others, making the desire for accuracy high. For other applications of standard times, the desired accuracy may not be so high. The analyst must understand for what purpose the standard times will be used in order to assess the degree of accuracy needed.

The degree of accuracy is often stated as some percentage of the actual value. For example, we might say that the desired accuracy of the standard is within 5 percent of actual. Finally, the third factor to consider is the degree of confidence that the true, long-run average time will be within a prescribed number of standard deviations of the set time standard. This measure, often called a *Z-score*, is usually determined from a statistical table of standard normal deviates (see Appendix) that relates confidence to standard deviations. For example, a desired confidence of 95 percent means that the true long-run average time to complete the task will be within $Z = 1.96$ standard deviations of the set time standard.

The general procedure would be first to take ten to fifteen cycle measurements. Next, calculate the mean and standard deviation of the observed times. Then determine the degree of accuracy and the level of confidence desired, and substitute the values into the following formula:

$$n = \left[\frac{Zs}{A\overline{X}}\right]^2 \qquad\qquad (9\text{-}1)$$

where

$n$ = total number of cycles to be observed (including those already taken) to achieve the desired level of accuracy

$Z$ = number of standard deviations needed for desired level of confidence

$s$ = standard deviation of values already observed

$A$ = desired accuracy expressed as a decimal value

$\overline{X}$ = mean of values already observed

---

**EXAMPLE 9.1**

Suppose you have taken ten measurements for a task that yields the minutes for the times that follow. You want your estimate to be within 10 percent of the true value, and you want 95 percent confidence in your estimate. How many samples in all should you take?

| Measurement Number | Observed Time |
|---|---|
| 1 | 7.5 |
| 2 | 11.8 |
| 3 | 8.9 |
| 4 | 10.0 |
| 5 | 15.2 |
| 6 | 9.5 |
| 7 | 12.0 |
| 8 | 14.8 |
| 9 | 12.5 |
| 10 | 14.0 |

$\overline{X} = 11.62$      $s = 2.60$      $Z = 1.96$      $A = 0.10$

Substituting into equation 9.1

$$n = \left[\frac{(1.96)\,(2.60)}{(.10)\,(11.62)}\right]^2$$

$$n = 19.23 \text{ rounded to } 20$$

You must round the value for $n$ up to the nearest whole number to achieve the level of accuracy you are seeking. Therefore, you need to collect at least ten more measurements.

---

Note that in Example 9.1 the analyst needed to calculate the standard deviation of the observed values. Several mathematical expressions are available for calculating the sample standard deviation, including the two that follow:

$$s = \sqrt{\frac{\sum(X_i - \overline{X})^2}{n-1}} \qquad\qquad s = \sqrt{\frac{\sum X_i^2 - (\sum X_i)^2/n}{n-1}} \qquad (9\text{-}2)$$

Assuming that in Example 9.1 you went out and collected ten or more additional measurements, you then would calculate the average observed time as follows:

$$\text{Observed Time} = \frac{\sum X_i}{n} \tag{9-3}$$

where

$$\sum X_i = \text{the sum of the observed times}$$
$$n = \text{number of measurements}$$

Will this new calculation for $\overline{X}$ be the time standard to use? Not yet.

To compensate for subjective factors the analyst must adjust this new estimate of mean task duration. The first adjustment recognizes the performance level of the worker being observed, if the analyst perceives that the worker is not performing up to normal levels or if the analyst believes that the worker is performing at a higher level than that expected of the average worker. After adjusting for performance, the observed time becomes the normal time.

$$\text{Normal time} = \text{Observed time} \times \text{Performance rating} \tag{9-4}$$

The analyst uses the performance rating in this relationship to adjust the performance of the worker to what the analyst believes is normal. A base of 1 is used for a worker proceeding at a normal pace. Any value greater than 1 indicates that the worker is working faster than normal, and a value less than 1 indicates the worker is working more slowly than normal. For example, a performance rating of 0.85 would indicate that the worker is working about 15 percent below normal; the analyst would decrease the observed time by 15 percent. Similarly, a performance rating of 1.15 would indicate that the worker is working about 15 percent faster than normal; the analyst would increase the observed time by 15 percent. If the task has been divided into smaller elements, the analyst may apply a performance rating to each element's average time.

So far, we have a calculation for **normal time**, which is the amount of time a qualified worker should take to complete the task if no delays or disruptions occur. It would be ridiculous to expect a worker to perform at the pace indicated by the normal time, because disruptions are unavoidable. Therefore, the second type of adjustment the analyst makes is an allowance for unavoidable delays. The allowance accounts for such interruptions as rest breaks, machine adjustments, engineering changes, and scheduling, material, or inspection delays. The allowance factor is stated as a percentage of the normal time and is expressed in decimal form. For example, if the analyst is using an allowance of 10 percent of normal time, the allowance factor is 0.10. Given the allowance factor, the analyst can calculate the standard time as follows:

$$\text{Standard Time} = \text{Normal Time} \times (1 + \text{Allowance Factor}) \tag{9-5}$$

We cannot conclude our discussion of time studies as a method of measuring work without noting the problems associated with this technique. For example, an analyst can use the technique only for repetitive tasks, because the standard time depends greatly on the conditions under which the measurements were made. Nonrepetitive tasks will differ each time. Also, this technique is not appropriate unless the work situation has a great deal of structure. For example, the technique is inappropriate for measuring tasks that require creativity or innovation. Last, the technique is somewhat subjective. Organized labor complains the most about the performance rating used to convert observed times to normal times. Because these are subjective estimates, they often are a source of contention in labor-management relations.

## Elemental Standard Times

As we noted earlier, dividing the task into its elemental parts and evaluating each element often is helpful. Once the analyst has assembled a data base of normal times for the individual elements, it becomes easier to establish standard times for new tasks that may share some elements of tasks the analyst already has studied. The analyst only needs to identify the elements of the new task, look up the normal times for the elements, and apply any allowances that may be appropriate for the new application. If elements of the task are new, the analyst may do a detailed time study for the new elements and add them to the data base for future reference.

This approach has several advantages. First, the analyst has to conduct fewer costly and time-consuming time studies. Second, the company can price its new products more accurately, because it has determined standard times for most elements of the new task before it produced the product. Third, the company can evaluate the effects on processing time of any changes in work methods or product design without actually making the changes.

## Predetermined Standard Times

The last approach to establishing standard times is similar to the elemental standard time approach. Under the **predetermined standard time** approach the analyst divides each task into detailed micromotions. Frank and Lillian Gilbreth continued the work of Taylor and were instrumental in developing the idea of dividing tasks into micromotions. Frank Gilbreth chose to call the micromotions **therbligs**, from *Gilbreth* spelled backward. He identified several therbligs: search, select, grasp, reach, move, hold, release, position, preposition, inspect, assemble, disassemble, and use.[24] Today published tables of time estimates of these micromotions are available.

One of the most recognized predetermined standard time systems is methods-time measurement (MTM). Developed in the 1940s, the MTM system provides predetermined time values for eight basic hand and finger motions plus body, leg, and foot motions, and eye travel-focus time. The eight basic motions include reach, move, turn, apply pressure, grasp, position, release, and disengage.[25] To use the MTM tables a skilled analyst would first break the task into its most basic micromotions. After considering the characteristics of each motion— for example, how far to reach or move or how much pressure to apply—the analyst would go to the table and add up the predetermined standard times for the micromotions to determine the normal time for the task. The analyst determines the standard time by adding to the normal time any allowances for the particular environment. We must recognize that the table of values came from many repetitions of many different individuals, in many different work

[24]Richard W. Humphreys, *Work Measurement: A Review and Analysis* (Morgantown: Institute of Labor Studies, West Virginia University, 1974), p. 123.
[25]Humphreys, *Work Measurement*, p. 129.

environments, making a particular micromotion. It may be prudent to conduct a time study occasionally to verify the accuracy of this approach for a particular environment.

These three approaches help develop standard times for many repetitive tasks in an organization. The company can use them as a basis for evaluating incentive pay systems or improvement activities. As we noted earlier, measurement is important if the company is to effectively manage and reward an employee's activity. Several notes of caution are in order. Workers generally dislike standards that are created by management and imposed upon them without their participation; gaining employees' acceptance of the standards is difficult. In this new era of empowered workers and participative management styles management must take care to involve the workers whenever possible. A second note of caution involves the changes in technology, product and process design, continuous process improvements, and process reengineering that are becoming commonplace in many organizations. A data base of standard times may become obsolete quickly. The company must take care that the measures are correct for the current work environment and that the existence of the standards does not discourage efforts to improve processes.

## ► Summary

As organizations today attempt to differentiate themselves from the competition, they are looking for any competitive advantage they can find. Successful organizations of the future must be able to respond to a rapidly changing business environment, and to do so they must rely heavily upon the human resources of the company. The organizational culture must change to support a more participative and empowered work force, a vast departure from the traditional command-and-control organization.

**Learning Objective 1: Discuss the use of human resources management as a strategic tool.** An organization will gain the flexibility and responsiveness it needs for the future through a well-trained, motivated, and empowered work force. The company cannot ignore its employees or underestimate the effects of a poorly trained, poorly motivated work force. Technology alone will not make an organization world class. It can help, but companies must change their organizational culture and structure to accommodate the new technology. Through the human resources functions of planning, staffing, evaluating, compensating, and training and development, human resources professionals are in a position to contribute significantly to the strategic goals of the organization.

**Learning Objective 2: Describe the characteristics of an adaptive organizational structure.** An adaptive organization is characterized by significant employee involvement through teams, projects, and alliances; the goal is to unleash employees' productivity and creativity. Such an organizational structure is in contrast to the traditional hierarchical organizations in which the leader sits atop a pyramid and commands from that lofty perch. Adaptive organizations are flexible and dynamic and thrive on change. Employees are well trained, motivated, and willing to do whatever is necessary for the organization to succeed. The sense of ownership and empowerment encourages workers to do their best and to continue to look for ways to improve the organization.

**Learning Objective 3: Describe the changing role of managers as leaders in today's business environment.** The changing role of managers as leaders is one of the major human resources issues of the 1990s. As organizations become more adaptive, management style has to change from commanding to coaching. This change is very difficult for many managers who are accustomed to giving orders and having them carried out. The workplace of the future is one in which employees participate in decisions that affect them and their job environment. The manager's role as leader is to create an environment whereby empowered employees can be as productive as possible.

### Learning Objective 4: Define the term *participative management*, and describe how organizations need to change to benefit from its use.

Participative management is a management style that welcomes the participation of workers in decisions that affect their environment. It is based on three premises:

- Several heads are better than one.
- A consensus decision is likely to be carried out more enthusiastically than one that is mandated.
- Participation in decision making is effective on-the-job training that helps develop subordinates.

Employees will recognize feigned attempts to implement participative management, and they will fail. The movement must be sincere and preceded by increased communication between management and workers to explain the purpose of the movement and what the workers may expect. The company must establish measurement and incentive programs to recognize and reward those who accept the challenge of the new environment.

### Learning Objective 5: Discuss the activities essential for using teams successfully to bring about continuous improvement.

The chapter discussed three types of teams. The most common form of team activity is the problem-solving team. After problem-solving teams are successful, and the company recognizes and celebrates their successes, the next step usually is the formation of special purpose teams. These teams are usually cross-functional and focus on more global problems. The most sophisticated form of team activity is the self-managing work team, which has nearly total control of its work environment, occasionally including hiring, firing, and disciplining. Management becomes involved with these teams only on special occasions. Companies must precede the formation of team activities with the development of an organizational culture that recognizes and rewards team activities. They must use individual incentive programs in combination with group incentive programs to encourage continued participation in team activities. In addition to providing motivation, companies must train team members in problem-solving skills and underline the importance of continuous improvement.

### Learning Objective 6: Describe the "cycle of mistrust" that contributes to fear in the workplace.

Fear in the workplace blocks many attempts to implement any form of organizational change. This fear is the result of many years of mistrust and calloused actions by management against the workers. The cycle of mistrust is a simple model that is used to illustrate how the fear can continue to grow unless the company breaks the cycle. The cycle of mistrust results from a series of negative assumptions by management about workers that leads management to exhibit self-protective behavior that stems from the negative assumptions. Workers often perceive this self-protective behavior as aggressive behavior, which reinforces negative assumptions the workers have about management. The workers respond with self-protective behavior, because management has reinforced their negative assumptions. Management often perceives workers' self-protective behavior as aggressive behavior, which reinforces the negative assumptions the managers hold about the workers. The cycle continues until it is broken.

### Learning Objective 7: Describe differences in various approaches to establishing standard times for work, and calculate sample size and standard times, using the time study approach to work measurement.

Various approaches to establishing standard times differ primarily in the level of detail they consider. The approach used most often is the time study, also known as the stopwatch study. In this approach the focus is on the task itself. The measurements begin after a qualified worker is chosen and prepared. Usually, the analyst divides the task into smaller elements and analyzes each element. The analyst determines the number of cycles to measure by considering the degree of accuracy and confidence the estimate should have. After taking measurements throughout the required number of cycles, the analyst calculates the average observed time, which the analyst then adjusts according to the analyst's subjective estimate of the performance rating of the worker. The result is referred to as the *normal time*, and the analyst applies to the normal time an allowance that accounts for unavoidable delays in the work environment.

The second approach to establishing standard times focuses on the task elements and is called the *elemental standard times approach*. This approach uses standard times for individual elements that the analyst compiled in a data base of previous time studies. The advantage here is that time-consuming and costly time studies are not always necessary for establishing a time standard for a new task. Each task is made up of individual elements, and different tasks often have common elements. Thus, the analyst often can establish the time standard for a new task without having to conduct a time study. The sum of the elemental times is the task's normal time. The analyst then adjusts the normal time to allow for unexpected delays.

The third approach focuses on the micromotions that comprise all elements of a task. Tables of normal times for various micromotions are available for determining task standard times. The analyst simply divides the task into a series of detailed micromotions, refers to the table of normal times for each motion, and adds up the normal times. The analyst then adds the appropriate allowance for unexpected delays, resulting in the standard time.

## ► Key Terms

adaptive organization
Age Discrimination in Employment Act (ADEA)
Americans with Disabilities Act (ADA)
benefits
compensation
corporate downsizing
cross-cultural training
cycles of mistrust
elemental standard times

government regulation
incentive
normal time
participative management
pay for performance
predetermined standard time
problem-solving team
quality circle
recognition and reward
self-managing work team

sociotechnical system (STS)
special purpose team
standard time
strategic human resources management
therblig
time studies
training and development
work measurement
work force diversity

## ► Discussion Questions

1. Why is the human resources function treated as a strategic element?
2. You are the vice president of human resources management at a small electronics company. What are the external forces that may influence the human resources management function?
3. You have been hired as a consultant by a company that wants to better understand its sociotechnical system. Write a brief report defining a sociotechnical system and tracing its development. Also, provide recommendations for the company to follow to ensure success.
4. What are the premises behind participative management?
5. What should organizations do to prevent the potentially negative effects of participative management?
6. Describe the effects that government regulation and work force diversity are having on the typical organization.

7. Compare and contrast these teams: problem-solving teams, special purpose teams, and self-managing teams.
8. Discuss the cycle of mistrust advanced by Ryan and Oestreich.
9. What role should training and development play for companies that want to increase their competitiveness?
10. You work for a company and are in charge of the complete employee incentive program. Discuss the various incentives. What role do these incentives play in motivating employees? What is the best mix of incentives?
11. You are hired by a fast-food chain to conduct a time study. How would you go about determining a time standard for making a hamburger?
12. Briefly discuss the three approaches that can be used to develop standard times.

## ► Problems

1. Given the following observed times of twenty cycles for a task, determine whether you need additional samples to achieve 95 percent confidence that the actual time will be within 10 percent of the observed average.

| Measurement Number | Observed Time | Measurement Number | Observed Time |
|---|---|---|---|
| 1 | 7.5 | 11 | 12.5 |
| 2 | 11.8 | 12 | 11.6 |
| 3 | 8.9 | 13 | 7.8 |
| 4 | 10.0 | 14 | 14.6 |
| 5 | 15.2 | 15 | 9.6 |
| 6 | 9.5 | 16 | 11.8 |
| 7 | 12.0 | 17 | 12.7 |
| 8 | 14.8 | 18 | 13.6 |
| 9 | 12.5 | 19 | 12.8 |
| 10 | 14.0 | 20 | 7.9 |

   a. What is the average observed time for the data?
   b. What is the observed standard deviation for the data?
   c. According to your calculations, what should be the minimum sample size to satisfy accuracy specifications?

2. Suppose that the worker you are observing to collect the data in problem 1 is the company's best worker. You have determined that she can do the task about 20 percent faster than the average worker. You have also estimated that delays in the system waste about 5 percent of the productive time. Using this information, determine the normal time and standard time for this task.

3. Suppose that an analyst has determined that the average observed time for an individual is 10.75 minutes but feels that the worker was holding back. Based on the analyst's judgment, the worker is proceeding 15 percent too slowly.
   a. By how much should the analyst adjust the observed time, given the performance rating?
   b. What normal time would the analyst report?

4. The analyst in problem 3 has determined that the task should be given certain allowances because of the characteristics of the job environment. For example, a personal allowance for breaks and such should be 5 percent, an allowance for regular delays because of equipment problems should be 3 percent, and an allowance for delays resulting from quality problems, including the resolution of the problems by the engineering staff, should be another 2 percent.
   a. What is the total allowance factor?
   b. What would be the standard time reported by the analyst for this particular task?

# ► Selected References

Davis, Donald D. *Managing Technological Innovation*. San Francisco: Jossey-Bass, 1986.

Fisher, Cynthia D., Lyle F. Schoenfeldt, and James B. Shaw. *Human Resource Management*. Boston: Houghton Mifflin, 1990.

Humphreys, Richard W. *Work Measurement: A Review and Analysis*. Morgantown: Institute for Labor Studies, West Virginia University, 1974.

Miller, Eric J., and Albert K. Rice. *Systems of Organization: The Control of Task and Sentient Boundaries*. New York: Tavistock, 1967.

Niebel, Benjamin W. *Motion and Time Study*, 8th ed. Homewood, Ill.: Richard D. Irwin, 1988.

Pasmore, William A. *Designing Effective Organizations*. New York: Wiley, 1988.

Ryan, Kathleen D., and Daniel K. Oestreich. *Driving Fear Out of the Workplace*. San Francisco: Jossey-Bass, 1991.

Skinner, Wickham. *Manufacturing: The Formidable Competitive Weapon*. New York: Wiley, 1985.

## CHAPTER 10

# Materials and Logistics Management

*The time to act is now! The first firm in an industry to implement a real time, interactive logistics information system will have a competitive advantage, the last firm to do so doesn't need to spend the money.*

D. M. LAMBERT AND T. C. HARRINGTON

**Introduction**

**Business Logistics for Strategic Advantage**

**Scope of Logistics**
 Logistics System Components
 Logistics Component Integration
 Logistical Elements
*OPERATIONS MANAGEMENT IN PRACTICE 10.1: An Integrated Logistics Success*

**Logistics Issues**
 Purchasing
 Transportation
*GLOBAL OPERATIONS MANAGEMENT 10.2: Double Eagle: Last Year's Vision, This Year's Reality*
 Warehousing
 Customer Service
*GLOBAL OPERATIONS MANAGEMENT 10.3: How Managers Can Succeed Through SPEED*

**Strategic Trends in Logistics Management**
 Third-Party Logistics Services
 Environmental Sensitivity
 Just-in-Time Logistics

## Introduction

In this age of international markets and competition, a company's competitiveness rests on its ability to provide goods and services when and where they are needed. Before the days of efficient transportation and storage systems customers consumed goods close to their point of origin. If not, the movement of goods was limited to what individuals could carry and store. Limitations in movement and storage systems generally constrained people to consume the narrow range of goods produced locally.[1]

Today efficient and effective transportation and storage systems allow production of products all over the world for global consumption. Transportation and storage are integral elements of what is known as *business logistics*. Some believe that business logistics represents the last major frontier for improved profitability in American industry.

This chapter defines the major components of a business logistics system and identifies the logistics activities that link the company to its suppliers and customers. A primary theme of the chapter is the integrative and multifunctional nature of business logistics, and we describe in some detail the elements of purchasing, transportation, warehousing and storage, and customer service.

## Business Logistics for Strategic Advantage

Industry uses many different labels for the activities we refer to as business logistics: physical distribution, materials management, distribution engineering, logistics management, industrial logistics, marketing logistics, distribution logistics, and transportation management. The **Council of Logistics Management,** a professional organization dedicated to the study and improvement of logistics management, defines **business logistics** as "the process of planning, implementing, and controlling the efficient, cost-effective flow and storage of goods, services and related information from point of origin to point of consumption for the purpose of conforming to customer requirements."[2]

Figure 10.1 depicts a simplified logistics system and illustrates the comprehensive and integrative nature of the logistics process. Logistics activities include

---

[1]Ronald H. Ballou, *Business Logistics Management*, 3d ed. (Englewood Cliffs, N.J.: Prentice-Hall, 1992), p. 1.
[2]Council of Logistics Management.

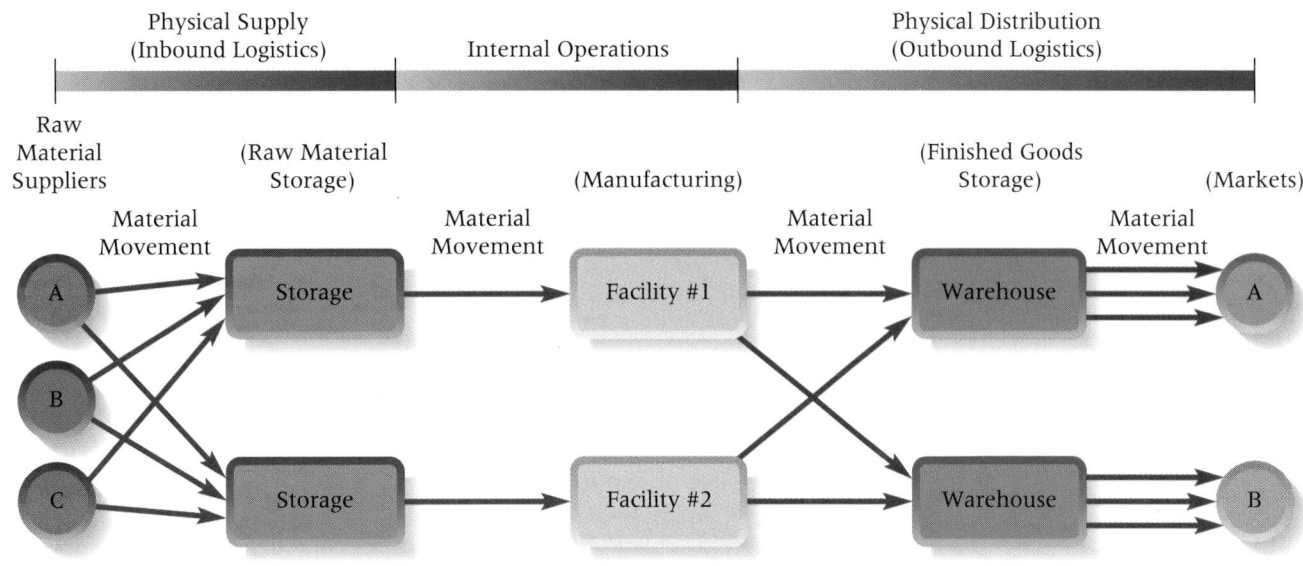

Physical Supply
(Inbound Logistics)

Internal Operations

Physical Distribution
(Outbound Logistics)

Raw
Material
Suppliers

(Raw Material
Storage)

(Manufacturing)

(Finished Goods
Storage)

(Markets)

FIGURE 10.1
Logistics System Components

the management of inventory, transportation, facilities, customer service, and order processing.

In contrast to production, which creates value by changing the form of materials, logistics creates value through changes in time, place, and quantity. Because an item's availability at the right place and time in the right quantities increases its utility, the central task of this service we call *logistics management* is often referred to as ensuring time, place, and quantity utility.[3]

# Scope of Logistics

Business logistics links the sources of raw materials to the locations of the final customers, often by spanning industrywide channels of supply and distribution. These linkages promote both the flow of physical product and logistics-related information, each of which is essential for the efficient and effective integration of the logistics process. In addition, multifunctional value chain linkages with other areas of the company, such as finance, marketing, and production, are an important part of business logistics management.

## Logistics System Components

As Figure 10.1 indicates, the logistics system has three major components, physical supply, internal operations, and physical distribution, each with its own focus and set of responsibilities.

**Physical Supply**  The component sometimes called *inbound logistics, procurement,* or *materials management,* **physical supply** is responsible for the interface between the company's operating processes and its suppliers. We can group the

[3]Roy D. Shapiro and James L. Heskett, *Logistics Strategy: Cases and Concepts* (St. Paul, Minn.: West, 1985), p. 6.

specific responsibilities of the physical supply component into the elements of purchasing, vendor management, inbound transportation, and raw material inventory storage. Key issues addressed within this component include

- How much and when material should be ordered
- From whom the material should be ordered
- Which criteria are appropriate for evaluating suppliers
- By what transportation mode and particular transport service the material should be transported
- Where incoming material should be stored to make the most effective use of resources

**Internal Operations**    Managing the flow of material during the material conversion process is the responsibility of **internal operations;** it plans, schedules, and supports manufacturing operations. Internal operations generally cover the time from when material is drawn from raw material storage until finished goods are placed in storage. Topics such as production planning and control, inventory management, aggregate planning, capacity planning, and just-in-time production systems are all related to this logistical component. This chapter focuses primarily on inbound and outbound logistics, whereas topics relating to the internal operations of the company are covered elsewhere in the text.

**Physical Distribution**    Also known as *outbound logistics,* **physical distribution** provides the interfaces for the company's production or service processes and its customers. The responsibilities of this component include the management of outbound material flows. For many companies this includes demand forecasts, finished goods warehouses and inventories, product packaging, transportation, information transfers, warranty operations, and most important, customer service. Whereas the physical supply component is concerned with *establishing* certain expectations for suppliers, the physical distribution component is concerned with *meeting* the expectations of the company's customers. Key issues include

- The level of customer service that customers expect in terms of product availability, delivery lead time, technical support, and so on
- Whether the network of distribution facilities provides the prescribed level of customer service at minimum cost
- Which items should be stocked in each distribution facility, and how much of each item should be stocked
- Which transportation modes and particular transportation services should be used to replenish distribution facilities and to supply customers

## Logistics Component Integration

As the definition of *logistics* implies, its scope is broad. Given the volume of movement, material storage, scheduling, order processing, and communication taking place in hundreds of thousands of supplier-customer exchanges, the complexities of managing the logistics function become apparent.

Another complicating factor is the frequent lack of a single control point within the company that is responsible for integrating logistics activities. Marketing frequently has primary responsibility for the physical distribution activities, whereas production manages the activities that directly affect manufacturing and its primary objective, producing at the lowest unit cost. Purchasing, which sets policies for the flow of inbound material, has its own functional area or may be part of production. Companies may delegate to a traffic department responsibility for inbound, internal, and outbound transportation, or they may split those responsibilities among the production, marketing, and purchasing functions.

A major shortcoming of such traditional organizational structures is the lack of a single organizational unit that is charged with managing the total logistics process. The various functions may do an excellent job of managing the activities under their direct control, but the efficiency and effectiveness of the organization as a whole suffer unless the entire logistics process is integrated. A simple example is the use of a single truck to make deliveries to a distant customer and on the return trip to pick up supplies from a vendor located near the customer. Unless the interorganizational coordination is tight, companies usually send two trucks to perform these transportation services, wasting corporate resources.

Managing the total logistics pipeline has benefits that exceed managing the sum of the parts. Recognizing this, many companies are directing greater resources toward logistics management and have assigned clear responsibility for logistics integration. Some major companies, such as Quaker Oats, Dow Chemical, Xerox, and Ashland Chemical, have established functional areas for logistics and logistics executives at the vice presidential level. Other companies set up logistics departments that report to the vice presidents of operations or marketing. Such organizational changes are helping to eliminate the myopic functional focus that has been characteristic of U.S. industry in the past.

Figure 10.2 highlights some interfaces among production, marketing, and logistics and several primary activities of each function. Note that some activities,

FIGURE 10.2
Interface of Production, Marketing, and Logistics

Source: Ronald H. Ballou, *Business Logistics Management*, 3d ed. (Englewood Cliffs, N.J.: Prentice-Hall, 1992), p. 24.

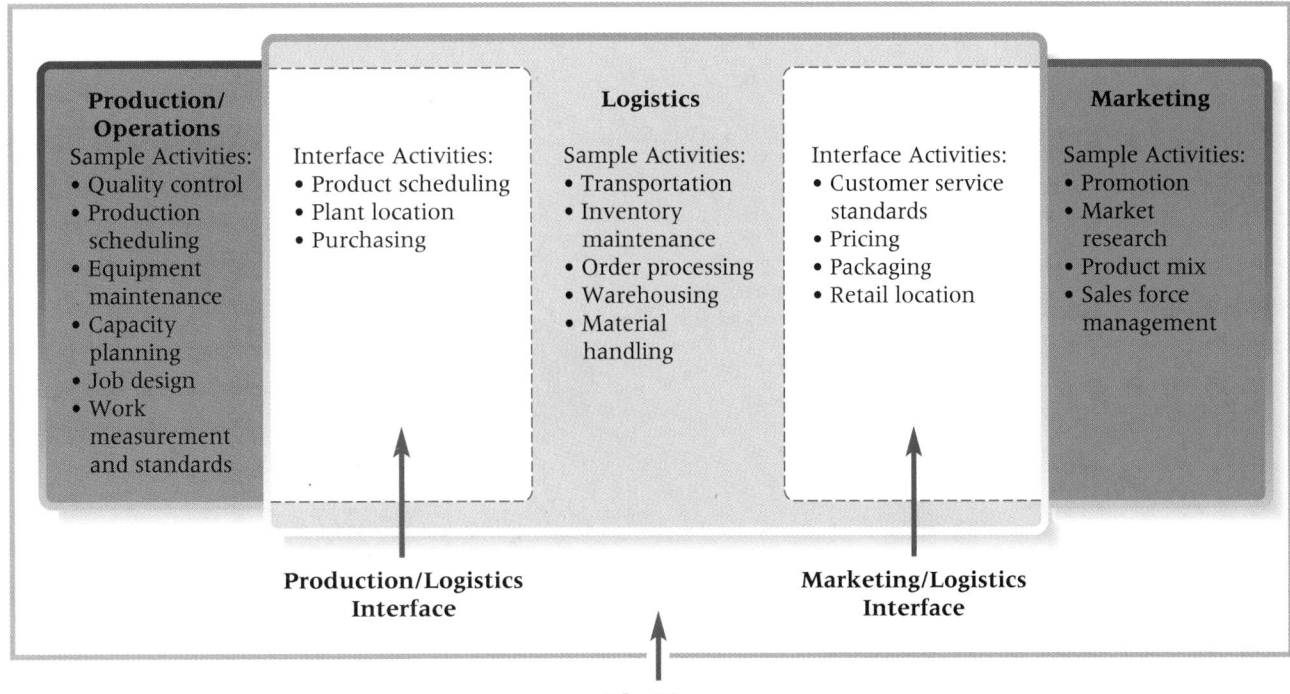

such as packaging, require that logistics interface with a single other function; others, such as transportation, require a broader functional interface.

## Logistical Elements

Many elements must be effectively managed within a company's total logistics system. The precise list of elements may differ from company to company. A company's list of logistical elements might include transportation, facilities, procurement and purchasing, packaging, warehousing and storage, inventory planning and control, demand forecasting, customer service, order processing, and salvage and scrap disposal. Figure 10.3 summarizes the key elements of business logistics.

Table 10.1 summarizes a study of one hundred U.S. businesses across a broad range of industries and provides the specific activities the companies included within their logistics areas. It is not surprising that the bulk of logistics activities centers around the moving and storing activities. However, trends toward greater involvement of logistics in production scheduling, purchasing, and customer service are noticeable. Hence, more companies appear to be recognizing the role of logistics in the value chain and in creating customer value.

Earlier, we focused on the multifunctional integration of the logistics elements; however, integrating the elements among themselves also is important. Effective management of a logistics system often requires trade-offs among the various logistics elements. For example, consider the choice of rail or truck for product shipment. If the objective is to minimize transportation costs, rail would be the appropriate choice, because shipping by rail is less expensive than by truck per hundredweight (cwt) shipped. However, the average transit time for rail is

FIGURE 10.3
Elements of Business
Logistics

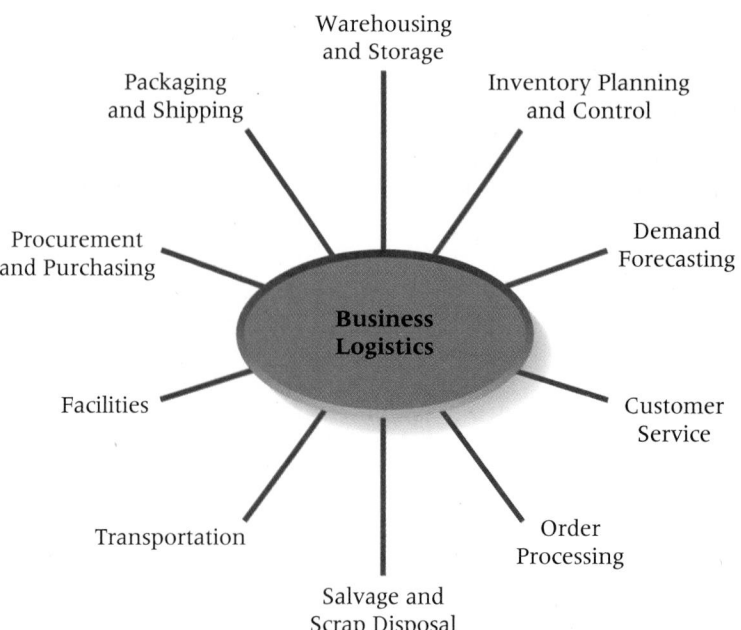

| Activity | Percentage of Firms Indicating Inclusion of the Activity |
|---|---|
| Outbound traffic | 93 |
| Finished goods warehousing | 84 |
| Inbound traffic | 90 |
| Plant warehousing | 73 |
| Finished goods inventory management | 68 |
| Proprietary transportation | 75 |
| Customer service | 64 |
| Order processing | 65 |
| Purchasing | 52 |
| Production planning | 50 |
| Raw material/In-process inventory management | 36 |
| Packaging | 40 |
| Sales forecasting | 41 |

Source: C. John Langley, Jr., and Mary C. Holcomb, "Creating Logistics Customer Value," *Journal of Business Logistics* 13 (1992): 5.

greater and more variable than for truck, which tends to increase systemwide inventories and related costs. In addition, many products shipped by rail require more expensive protective packaging than when shipped by truck, and both the shipping and receiving companies must either be located on a rail siding or transfer the product to and from the rail yard by truck.

This simple example illustrates the potential pitfalls of optimizing a single logistics element (to minimize transportation costs, for example) and neglecting the effect of other elements (delivery time, inventory, packaging, and availability of rail siding). This integrative aspect of logistics management is what makes it complex. However, by better managing this integration the company can improve both the efficiency and effectiveness of serving its customers' needs.

Operations Management in Practice 10.1 examines one company that is striving to develop an integrated logistics system. Note the critical role of the logistics information system in achieving integration.

# Logistics Issues

In this section we discuss in more detail the managerial issues related to purchasing, transportation, warehousing, and customer service. In-depth coverage of several other logistical elements and concepts that are important to the operations manager appear in Chapter 3 (supply chain management), Chapter 4 (forecasting), Chapter 6 (facility location), Chapters 12 and 13 (inventory management) and Chapter 16 (just-in-time production).

## Purchasing

Purchasing is one of the most significant elements of the physical supply component of a logistics system. **Purchasing** is defined as "the acquisition of

## OPERATIONS MANAGEMENT IN PRACTICE 10.1 ◀

# An Integrated Logistics Success

While many firms talk about integrated logistics, SmithKline Beecham Consumer Brands, Pittsburgh, PA, is doing it. SmithKline Beecham is a billion dollar maker of such products as Aqua-Fresh toothpaste, Tums and Contac, with three manufacturing plants and four distribution centers. SmithKline's logistics information system used to be a collection of inefficient home-grown, stand-alone systems.

In 1978, the company acquired Calgon Consumer Products, and its information system finally broke down. Managing the information flows of its various operations became a nightmare. It had a "hodgepodge" of information management systems, not only from the Calgon merger but from the many corporate changes that occurred over the past 10 years.

SmithKline conducted a needs study of all major functional areas affected by the flow of information. From December 1987 to March 1988, input was solicited from finance, purchasing, customer service, information systems, manufacturing, marketing, field sales and logistics as the company sought an accurate picture of how the logistics pipeline and decision making process worked. On the basis of what was learned, a single, centralized information processing system was recommended to handle order entry and warehousing systems to push orders through to shipment.

In April 1988, the committee picked Andersen Consulting's DCS/Logistics customer service and distribution management software. By fall 1990, the DCS/Logistics system was up and running. Today, nearly 150 employees from across the company's manufacturing, planning, distribution and customer service departments simultaneously access the system each day.

Customer service improved drastically because representatives were able to view accurate information at the touch of a finger. Determining customer order status once was virtually impossible; today the information is found in a matter of minutes.

needed goods and services at optimum cost from competent, reliable sources."[4] Several important factors must be considered when purchasing goods and services. For example, how much of a particular item should the company purchase at one time, and when should it order the item? We introduced these quantity- and timing-related issues in Chapter 4, and later chapters will consider specific topics related to inventories. This chapter addresses other critical purchasing questions, including whether the purchase should be made from inside or outside the organization; if the purchase is to be from the outside, from whom the purchase should be made; what ethical issues are involved in purchasing; whether price is the best determinant for selecting suppliers; and how the set of qualified suppliers should be determined.

**Make-or-Buy Decision** The purchasing function is responsible for procuring both goods and services but not necessarily from outside the organization. In

[4]Eberhard E. Scheuing, *Purchasing Management* (Englewood Cliffs, N.J.: Prentice-Hall, 1989), p. 4.

many cases the material or service can be provided in-house. An important issue, known as the **make-or-buy decision,** is deciding whether the company will make some or all of a product or buy it from a supplier.

The make-or-buy decision is often a complex, strategic issue. However, we can reduce the economic considerations to a simple break-even analysis. The question is whether it is cheaper to buy the item or produce it in house. If the item is purchased, the total cost ($TC_{BUY}$) is the unit landed cost ($C$) times demand ($D$):

$$TC_{BUY} = C \times D \tag{10-1}$$

The per unit landed cost includes the purchase price, transportation cost, and any other costs associated with making the purchased item available for use at the company's facility.

If the company makes the item, it incurs the fixed or overhead cost for producing the item *(FC)* plus the per unit variable cost of manufacture *(V)*. If the company does not have the capability or capacity to produce the item, the fixed cost would include the amortized cost of purchasing the required technological expertise and equipment. The total cost of the make decision ($TC_{MAKE}$) is

$$TC_{MAKE} = FC + (V \times D) \tag{10-2}$$

It is more economically attractive for the company to make the item when $TC_{MAKE} < TC_{BUY}$. At the break-even quantity *(B)*, whether the company makes the item or buys it from a vendor does not matter. The break-even quantity is easy to express:

$$TC_{BUY} = TC_{MAKE}$$
$$C \times B = FC + (V \times B)$$
$$(C \times B) - (V \times B) = FC$$
$$B(C - V) = FC$$
$$B = FC/(C - V) \tag{10-3}$$

The break-even analysis oversimplifies the make-or-buy decision. Several other factors, which are not easily quantified, must also be considered. Some of these are

- The desire to develop new strategic process capabilities
- Current capacity utilization and the strategic implications of adding additional capacity
- Availability and lead time for acquiring the necessary technical expertise or equipment for producing the item
- The effect on current vendor relationships
- Assurance of the item's availability and quality
- The nature of the demand (for example, stable demand versus uncertain demand for a new product introduction)

Companies often choose to perform a portion of the work themselves and let vendors provide the rest. This maintains flexibility in the supply source, lessens the risk of not having the part available in the event of a strike at the vendor's plant, and provides a bargaining chip when negotiating the purchase contract.

**Sources of Goods and Services** If the decision is purchase from outside, the purchasing manager must determine the best source to use. Today **sourcing** decisions are becoming increasingly more difficult, because the purchasing manager must evaluate both domestic and international sources. Additionally, as technology continues to change at a rapid pace, buyers must ensure that potential suppliers remain up to date and maintain adequate capacity to meet their service requirements.

The purchasing department is responsible for selecting sources as well as negotiating purchase contracts. It is also responsible for monitoring the performance of the supplier base along important dimensions such as the on-time delivery of the specified quantities, quality, cost, and reliability.

In the last decade many companies have chosen to vertically integrate their operations. **Vertical integration** often brings the sources of supply for key materials and services within the control of the company. For example, General Motors' purchase of Electronic Data Systems ensured that GM would have sophisticated information-processing technology and capabilities. General Motors also controls its supply channels for a majority of its component parts.

In recent years vertical integration has proved to be too expensive or risky for some companies to maintain. The Boeing Co., for example, eliminated many of its component-manufacturing processes and now relies extensively on its suppliers. In doing so the company transformed itself from a manufacturer to an assembler of airplanes. A primary reason for this shift in strategy is to share with suppliers the risk of introducing new aircraft. Japan makes tail sections, Italy makes aircraft skins, and Boeing obtains other components from a variety of sources around the world. The extension of its supplier base has forced Boeing to work more closely with its suppliers; after all, they are partners, sharing the risks and profits associated with the Boeing's product lines.

**International Sourcing**   Today's global economy, with its sophisticated telecommunications and transportation methods, provides more choices than ever before, and more companies rely on **international sourcing.** Several factors make international sourcing much more complex than domestic sourcing. One factor is the difference in cultures. A purchasing agent must be acutely aware of and sensitive to the cultural issues involved in any proposed relationship. Even the need to communicate in another language will often complicate the process. Another factor is the increased uncertainty involved in international dealings, including instability of legal and political systems, instability of foreign transportation methods, or instability of foreign monetary systems. The U.S. government has created federal agencies to assist companies with their foreign trade dealings, but these same agencies often create regulations and levels of bureaucracy that can impede the process.

**Best Value for the Money**   The purpose of purchasing is to buy goods and services at the lowest total cost, not necessarily the lowest price. Many companies have learned the hard way about the overall organizational effects of purchasing the lowest price products and services. If the sole criterion for purchase is price of the material and it does not meet the company's quality standards, the company will ultimately suffer. Material of poor quality can damage equipment, create safety hazards for the workers, cause system down time, and result in significant amounts of rework, warranty repairs, and scrap. The most beneficial item or service to purchase is the one that meets the user's needs and strikes the best balance between cost and quality, sometimes referred to as *value.*

**Value Analysis** **Value analysis** is a disciplined effort to compare the function performed by an item and its cost in an attempt to find a lower-cost alternative. It is usually a team effort by representatives of purchasing, manufacturing, engineering design, transportation, and marketing. Basic questions addressed by the team are

- What the function of the item is
- Whether an alternative product design would lower its manufacture or transportation costs
- Whether the function requires a unique design, or whether a standard design could be used to serve the functional needs of several products
- Whether the items' specifications could be relaxed so that a less costly design still satisfies the functional requirements
- If the company is making the item now, whether it could buy it for less
- Whether the function is necessary for gaining acceptance of the item in the marketplace

Applying value analysis to new products as well as existing ones yields the most value for the money.

**Supplier Evaluation** Companies rate their suppliers on performance dimensions as well as the price and quality of products and services, a process known as **supplier evaluation.** One of the most important is the reliability of the supplier in providing on-time delivery. An unreliable vendor can cause the plant to revise its production schedules or even shut the plant down until the materials come in. Many purchasing departments track vendors' performance in this area and maintain a scorecard. Most managers do not remember when a vendor delivers on time, but they never forget when a critical shipment was late.

In the past companies expected to maintain buffer stocks of procured items just in case a vendor's shipment was late. However, buffer stocks tie up investment capital, require storage space, and cause the company to incur a number of costs related to stocking inventory. A purchasing manager should consider all these factors when evaluating an unreliable but low-cost supplier. With the increased emphasis on just-in-time production and value chain management many companies refuse to do business with an unreliable supplier.

Other evaluation factors include the responsiveness of the vendor to changes in purchase quantities and due dates, the ability of the vendor to provide technical support, and advance notice of price changes. These are just some of the dimensions used to evaluate suppliers' performance.

Traditionally, purchasing managers believed that the greater the number of suppliers for a product, the better. This enabled the buyer to play one supplier against the other to get a deal at the lowest cost possible. The trend today is toward fewer but higher-quality suppliers, reflecting the recognition that suppliers are business partners and that criteria other than price determine a good supplier-customer relationship. By working with a select group of suppliers buyers are better able to communicate their company's product and service requirements and develop lasting relationships that permit the suppliers to better serve those needs.

Many companies have instituted a supplier certification program to help them identify the top-performing suppliers with which they intend to do business and develop long-term relationships. To become certified and maintain

**TABLE 10.2**
Supplier Evaluation Criteria

Quality of product and service
Variability in product and service
Price and terms available
Location of facilities
Condition of facilities (age, size, efficiency, utilization, and sophistication)
Inventory policy
Responsiveness
Reliability
Flexibility
Technical sophistication
Financial standing
Management (capability and attitude)
Workers (skills, training, attitude, and presence of unions)
References (quality, delivery, variability, responsiveness, and problem resolution)

certification a vendor must continuously satisfy a rigorous set of evaluation criteria. The specific criteria vary from company to company; Table 10.2 provides a list of the criteria most often used for evaluating suppliers.

Companies use the criteria to assess a supplier's capability of participating in a supplier-customer partnership that would benefit both parties. As companies continue to reduce their supplier base, many suppliers are becoming more willing to work to become one of the chosen few. The primary advantages to the supplier can include a greater percentage of the customer's total orders; less uncertainty about future orders; shared engineering, manufacturing, and logistics expertise with the partner; and preferential treatment for supplying other needs of the customer as they develop over time. This cooperation and coordination between suppliers and customers can be a win-win situation for both parties.

As we mentioned in Chapter 7, the ISO9000 is one example of a formal supplier certification process instituted in an economic trading area. Similar certification programs exist in the United States and Canada. Some companies view ISO9000-type certification as essential for maintaining good business relations with their most valued customers.

**Ethics in Purchasing** Purchasing agents sometimes confront an offer of free gifts, in the form of tickets to sporting or social events, meals, liquor, trips, and vacations. Salespeople with whom purchasing agents are doing business or are considering doing business usually offer these gifts. Where is the line between normal activity and unethical or even illegal behavior? Many companies have a policy that governs **ethics in purchasing,** preventing buyers from accepting any form of gift from vendors. Some companies simply place restrictions upon the types and values of gifts that their purchasing agents may accept.

Purchasing agents may have a great deal of power because of the volume of business they control. Securing or losing a particular deal can make or destroy a salesperson's career. Such stress, when combined with the fact that purchasing agents may not be paid at a level commensurate with their power, creates an environment that invites abuse.

Another concern is the accuracy of information provided to the purchasing department by the individual or group asking that the department procure a product or service. If the user requests that a particular vendor supply the product or service, the purchasing agent must ensure that valid reasons lie behind the request and that it was not merely a case of personal preference.

# Transportation

The **transportation** element typically accounts for one-half to two-thirds of all logistics costs. Companies frequently assign responsibility for this activity to a traffic department, which determines the transportation requirements for inbound and outbound movements, selects freight carriers for specific shipments, monitors the flow of the company's inbound and outbound shipments and expedites them when necessary, negotiates with carriers to obtain the transportation services required at favorable prices, and evaluates carriers' performance.

**Legal Forms of Carriers** Transportation services take three primary legal forms: private, common, and contract carriers. Private carriers are owned by the shipper and primarily provide in-house transportation services. The primary incentives for using private transportation are improved service and cost savings. Wal-Mart uses a private fleet of trucks to transport products between its distribution centers and stores.

Common carriers serve the general public for a specified range of goods and services and are regulated by appropriate government agencies. Examples of common carriers are UPS, Yellow Freight, and Roadway Express in the trucking industry, Federal Express and American Airlines in the air industry, and Burlington Northern and Union Pacific in the rail industry. Contract carriers provide transportation services that are tailored to the specific needs of a limited set of customers. Union Pacific operates as a common carrier and also contracts to provide specialized transport services for particular customers.

**Transportation Mode Selection** The five primary modes of transportation are rail, truck, air, water, and pipeline.

Rail provides relatively low-cost transport service primarily for the long haul of raw materials (coal, grain, and chemicals) and manufactured products of low value (paper, lumber, and food). This mode accounts for the biggest percentage of tonnage moved within the United States.[5] Progressive railroads have developed such innovative approaches to business as enclosed, trilevel automobile cars, cushioned appliance cars, unit trains, and new pricing techniques.[6] Rail's major competition for hauling manufactured goods comes from the truck mode.

The vast majority of manufactured goods shipped within the United States moves by truck. Advantages of this mode include flexible schedules, door-to-door delivery, relatively rapid and reliable transit times, and the ability and willingness to handle shipment sizes of **less than full truck load (LTL).**

Air shipments represent the most expensive and least used transportation mode. The primary advantage of this mode is speed. Air is best suited for the movement of high-value lightweight items, emergency shipments (spare parts), and perishable goods such as fresh fish, flowers, seasonal fashions, and Shamu the whale. Although air has seen significant increases in the percentage of

[5]Nicholas A. Glaskowsky, Jr., D. R. Hudson, and R. M. Ivie, *Business Logistics* (Orlando, Fla.: Harcourt Brace Jovanovich, 1992), p. 220.
[6]Donald J. Bowersox, D. J. Closs, and O. K. Helferich, *Logistical Management* (New York: Macmillan, 1986), p. 161.

*Intermodal transportation is indicated by the truck trailer being loaded on a train flatcar for further transport.*

tonnage transported, it still represented less than 1 percent of the total tonnage in 1990. With international markets expanding, air cargo is expected to win a bigger share of the high-value, lightweight cargo business.

Water transportation, the oldest of all modes and one of the least expensive, includes ocean, river, and lake transport. The usual cargo is low-value, high-bulk commodities for which a low cost per ton-mile of transportation is more important than speed. Water transport competes primarily with railroads for the inland movement of bulk commodities and raw materials such as iron ore, grains, chemicals, cement, coal, limestone, and petroleum products. It is unchallenged in the transoceanic movement of all but extremely high-value cargo products.[7]

Pipelines provide effective point-to-point shipment of fluids and some non-fluids; most carry petroleum products. Completion of the Trans-Alaska Pipeline in 1977 illustrated to the world the value of pipelines as a mode of transportation. Pipelines operate twenty-four hours a day, seven days a week, unlike most other transportation modes. Their disadvantage is the lack of flexibility in terms of source and destination and the types of material that they can handle.

Each transportation mode requires trade-offs in terms of cost, capability, speed of delivery, and reliability. The ability of the shipment to absorb transportation costs, the urgency of delivery, and shipment size are the primary determinants of which transportation mode is appropriate.

Combinations of some shipment modes are also attractive to shippers. For example, the intermodal option of shipping manufactured goods long distances in truck trailers on rail flat cars (TOFC) provides the low-cost advantage of rail and the door-to-door flexibility of truck.

Containerization plays an important role in facilitating intermodal movements. The goal is to protect the goods and simplify loading and unloading. In TOFC shipments the truck trailer serves as the container. Shipping the container

[7]John F. Magee, W. C. Copacino, and D. B. Rosenfield, *Modern Logistics Management* (New York: Wiley, 1985), p. 124.

on rail flat car (COFC) uses containers specially designed to be stacked on rail cars for long-distance transport. Upon their arrival at the destination a crane lifts and positions the containers on truck trailer chassis for final delivery. This eliminates the need to ship the trailer chassis and promotes more efficient use of rail.

Transocean movements also frequently use containerization and intermodal shipments. Consider a European manufacturer who is supplying a customer in Japan. The European company might pack its manufactured goods in a big container and transport the container by truck to a seaport for loading onto a container ship destined for the East coast of the United States. Upon arrival the crane unloads the container from the ship to a rail car for COFC movement across the continental United States. Upon arrival at a West coast terminal a crane once again loads the container onto a container ship for transoceanic movement. Finally, the container moves by truck from the Japanese seaport to the customer.

The manufacturer in the example exploits the door-to-door delivery capability of truck and the economic efficiency of the water modes. Rail provides a relatively fast and low-cost method for moving the goods across the United States, cutting weeks off the delivery lead time had the shipment moved all the way from Europe to Japan by ship. Containers are especially significant in international shipments. They facilitate movement by protecting the goods during loading, unloading, and while in transit and by promoting efficient handling of the goods. Table 10.3 summarizes the advantages and service features of various transportation modes.

Global Operations Management in Practice 10.2 illustrates the innovative relationship of one supplier, customer, and transporter.

**Freight Consolidation** As a result of economies of shipment volume, carriers usually offer a financial incentive for managers to ship in bigger quantities. In the common carrier trucking industry the freight rate per hundred pounds for shipping less-than-truckload quantities can be almost twice the cost of shipping in truckload (TL) quantities. Transport costs are similar in the rail industry, where

*By double-stacking, more efficient use of transportation facilities can be realized.*

**TABLE 10.3**
Advantages and Service
Features of Transport Modes

| Mode | Advantages/Features |
|---|---|
| **Rail** | Mass movement of goods<br>Large capabilities<br>Extensive geographic coverage<br>Large number of accessorial services<br>Low unit costs<br>Energy efficient<br>Specialized equipment to handle all types of goods |
| **Truck** | Extensive and intensive geographic coverage<br>Point-to-point service<br>Handles all types of goods<br>Flexible<br>Fast<br>Frequent departures |
| **Water** | Mass movement of bulk commodities<br>Lowest cost<br>Large capabilities<br>Preferred mode for long-haul movement of some low-value commodities |
| **Air** | Fastest mode for intermediate to long movements<br>Reduced costs for other logistics components (e.g., inventory)<br>Broad service range<br>Increasing capabilities |
| **Pipeline** | Mass movement of liquid and gas products<br>Large capabilities/capacity<br>Most dependable mode<br>Lowest operating cost and unit cost |

Source: John F. Magee, W. C. Copacino, D. B. Rosenfield, *Modern Logistics Management* (New York: Wiley, 1985): 126.

carload (CL) shipments move at significantly lower rates than do less-than-carload (LCL) shipments.

One way to lower the transportation cost per unit is to consolidate small shipments in one bigger shipment that will move at volume freight rates, a strategy called **freight consolidation,** which is effective for both inbound and outbound shipments.

The automobile industry makes effective use of freight consolidation. For example, General Motors assembles automobiles in several different locations and receives component parts from hundreds of sources. Because of the many locations involved, a shipment from a particular supplier to a particular assembly plant may represent only an LTL shipment. However, the auto industry achieves economies of volume by establishing intermediate consolidation points at which LTL shipments from several suppliers are consolidated and submitted as a single TL shipment.

Similarly, major automobile manufacturers service hundreds of geographic markets, but the number of automobiles going from a particular assembly plant to a particular customer market may be small. Once again, intermediate consoli-

# Double Eagle: Last Year's Vision, This Year's Reality

Costumed jugglers perform at busy intersections, street vendors hawk tomatoes, tortillas and tamales, miniature taxis leap at the smallest advantage in traffic, and towering above them all are some of the handsomest office buildings in North America.

This is not Los Angeles, Toronto or New York; it's Mexico City, the largest metropolis in the world. Its 20 million people live at the heart of an industrial giant, a nation shedding the cocoon of a pastoral myth. Its hotel lobbies bustle with businessmen from five continents, all looking to tap the energy of its work force.

For Union Pacific (UP), that promise of international prosperity is transforming the railroad's traditional orientation as a key link in the East-West transcontinental network. And nothing has stamped the North-South capability on UP's system map more convincingly than the success of Double Eagle Double Stack.

Double Eagle Double Stack is a service that would not have been possible without the combined vision of the Marketing and Sales Automotive and Machinery Group, The Chrysler Corporation, American President Companies (APC), and Ferrocariles Nacionales de Mexico (FNM), the Mexican National Railways.

To be precise, Double Eagle Double Stack is an expedited, run-through train, the AIZ, that bypasses rail yards and stops only for fuel and fresh crews. At 5:15, six mornings a week, the AIZ rolls south from Chicago's Yard Center on an 98 hour, 2,160 mile journey to Mexico City's sprawling Pantaco intermodal terminal. Double Eagle's articulated cars carry more than 30 APC containers loaded with American and Canadian made parts for Chrysler's light truck and auto assembly plants in Mexico City and nearby Toluca. It is business that once belonged to truckers.

One key to Double Eagle's success lies in the special customs arrangements that hasten the train's journey southward. No inspection or delay is necessary at the border because the sealed containers are cleared only after their arrival at the Pantaco terminal. The normal declarations of contents, value and destination have been sent electronically by the shipper, and the computerized documents arrive at customs offices before the Double Eagle even reaches Laredo.

The project has been very successful. For all transportation modes, cross-border traffic generates well over $1 billion annually. Union Pacific's piece of that business now totals $250 million a year. If international tariffs were eliminated, there would be even greater potential for savings.

dation points allow manufacturers to collect finished products from several assembly plants for volume shipment to individual customer markets.

Note that we can look at freight consolidation from two viewpoints. From one, it is a method of reducing freight costs. However, we can also look at it as a method for allowing more frequent and smaller just-in-time shipments from vendors to manufacturing facilities without significantly increasing inbound transportation costs.

Establishing and coordinating the details of a consolidation strategy (number, location, size, layout, and so on of consolidations points) is quite complex. Usually, solving such a problem requires sophisticated mathematical programming, which is beyond the scope of this book.

*Palettes of finished products are loaded onto a truck for transportation to the customer*

# Warehousing

Because of uncertainties in the procurement process and production, companies rely on the accumulation of inventory to help ensure a smooth flow into and through the manufacturing process. Similarly, on the outbound side the uncertainty of demand, volume shipment discounts, and production economics results in the accumulation of finished goods inventory. Regardless of their source, inventories must go into storage, be maintained in usable condition, and forwarded to the next process in the value chain as needed. The **warehousing** logistics element performs these tasks.

Some companies own and operate their own warehouses; others use the services of a public warehouse. In either case, typical warehouse operations

1. Receive and inspect goods. The warehouse receives merchandise from inside or outside the organization, checks the quantity and quality, and then accepts responsibility for the storing material until needed.
2. Identify goods. Warehouse personnel create inventory records that identify the stock keeping units (SKUs) and the quantities of each, often by using bar code technology as discussed in Chapter 8.
3. Sort and dispatch goods to storage. The warehouse sorts the material and places it in the proper storage area for future retrieval.
4. Hold goods. The warehouse holds material in storage under proper care until it is needed.
5. Recall, select, or pick goods. The warehouse retrieves from storage items ordered by internal or external customers and groups them in a manner useful for the next step in the process.
6. Organize the shipment. The warehouse collects the items making up the shipment and checks for order completeness.
7. Dispatch the shipment. The warehouse packages the order, directs it to the correct transportation vehicle, and prepares the necessary shipping and accounting documents.
8. Prepare inventory records. The warehouse forwards information pertaining to the receipt or shipment of the order to the proper location for processing.[8]

# Customer Service

Another important logistics activity is providing **customer service,** which refers to all the activities performed to support the customer during the supplier-customer exchange, including all presale, sale, and postsale activities. Presale activities affect the customer's early perception about a company's ability to provide the product and accompanying service the customer wants. Sale activities affect the customer's level of satisfaction through the company's ability to actually provide the product in a timely and accurate fashion. Postsale activities directly affect the customer's satisfaction through the company's responsiveness to the customer's needs after the sale. Organizations must direct their resources toward identifying customers' needs and expectations during the complete buying experience and ensure that they are met or exceeded.

[8]Magee, Copacino, and Rosenfield, *Modern Logistics Management*, p. 153.

Ronald H. Ballou points out that "from a logistics perspective, customer service is the *result* of all logistic activities."[9] Therefore, organizations must fully understand customers' needs and expectations and design a logistics system that will meet the levels desired. But what is it that customers want? Low price? On-time delivery? Friendly service? The answer is all of the above and more.

In a 1992 study conducted by the professional journal *Traffic Management* and Andersen Consulting's Logistics Strategy Practice, respondents provided the following customer service elements in order of importance:[10]

1. Orders delivered on time
2. Order fill rates
3. Orders delivered complete
4. Order accuracy
5. Handling of customer complaints
6. Order receipt-to-delivery time
7. Courtesy of sales/order takers
8. Carrier performance

According to the survey, on-time delivery is the most important service measure, with 94 percent of respondents saying that they regularly monitor their suppliers' performance on this service element.

Notice that items 1 and 6 are time related. Many companies have designed their logistics systems such that they use time as a competitive advantage. For example, consider that Wal-Mart replenishes its store shelves an average of twice a week rather than the industry average of once every two weeks. A big problem in retail service is correctly guessing what customers will buy and having it in stock when they need it. Speed in resupply can significantly reduce the amount of inventory a retailer must carry to serve this uncertain demand. This reduces costs while providing customers with high levels of product availability. The company uses its private fleet of nearly two thousand trucks, nineteen distribution centers, and a satellite communications system to provide fast and responsive service to its stores. Its logistics system plays a key role in the corporate strategy that has helped Wal-Mart grow into the largest and most profitable discount retailer in the country. Global Operations Management 10.3 provides another example of a company that has effectively used its logistics system to competitive advantage.

## Strategic Trends in Logistics Management

As the world changes around us, organizations must adapt in order to remain competitive. Businesses are constantly looking for ways to provide better products and service to a customer base that is becoming more sophisticated and demanding. Many companies are looking to their logistics system to provide competitive advantage. Perhaps the major trend in logistics management today is the increased awareness of the potential benefits of integrated logistics management. The evidence is the organizational changes that are taking place in major companies to capture these benefits. The increased managerial focus on the strategic benefits of value chain management also serves to heighten the awareness of logistics' potential contribution to creating customer value.

[9]Ballou, *Business Logistics Management*, p. 79.
[10]Staff Report, "Customer Service: The Great Differentiator," *Traffic Management* 31 (November 1992): 41.

# How Managers Can Succeed Through SPEED

Even the world's fastest factory won't offer much competitive advantage if everything it produces gets snagged in the distribution chain, a lesson Benetton, the Italian sportswear company, has knit in its heart. Located in Ponzano, Italy, Benetton makes and distributes 50 million pieces of clothing worldwide each year, mostly sweaters, slacks, and dresses.

Benetton found that the fastest way to run a distribution system is to create an electronic loop linking sales agent, factory, and warehouse. If, say, a saleswoman in one of Benetton's Los Angeles shops finds that she is starting to run out of a best-selling red sweater in early October, she calls one of Benetton's 80 sales agents, who enters the order in his personal computer, which sends it to a mainframe in Italy. Because the red sweater was originally created on a computer-aided design system, the mainframe has all its measurements on hand in digital code, which can be transmitted to a knitting machine. The machine makes the sweaters, which factory workers put in a box with a bar code label containing the address of the Los Angeles store, and the box goes into the warehouse. That's right—one warehouse serves Benetton's 5,000 stores in 60 countries around the world. It cost $30 million, but this distribution center, run by only eight people, moves 230,000 pieces of clothing a day.

Once the red sweaters are sitting snugly in one of 300,000 slots in the warehouse, a computer sends a robot flying. By reading the bar codes, the robot finds the right box and any other boxes being shipped to the Los Angeles store, picks them up, and loads them onto a truck. Including manufacturing time, Benetton can get the order to Los Angeles in four weeks. If the company already has red sweaters in stock, it takes one week. That's quite a performance in the notoriously slow garment industry, where hardly anyone else will even bother with reorders. And if Benetton suddenly realizes that it didn't make any, say, black cardigans and purple blouses this year and they're hot, it can manufacture and ship a "flash collection" of black cardigans and purple blouses in huge quantities in a few weeks.

Three other significant logistical trends are the move toward third-party logistics services, an increasing sensitivity to environmental issues, and the increased use of just-in-time logistics practices.

## Third-Party Logistics Services

Some companies today are farming out, or **outsourcing,** all or part of their logistics functions to third-party organizations. A company might choose to outsource some of its logistics activities for several reasons. First, logistics is fast becoming a high-tech and capital-intensive business, and small companies find it difficult to allocate enough resources to their logistics area to be able to compete effectively. This is particularly true when the company is attempting to supply a geographically dispersed marketplace. Other companies prefer to allocate their scarce resources to other purposes and turn their logistics operations over to specialists. For example, Sun Microsystems outsourced its distribution center operations to Federal Express, giving FedEx's Business Logistics Services group the responsibility for moving Sun computer products from the factory floor to its customers.[11]

According to a 1992 study of Fortune 500 manufacturing companies, companies most commonly turn to **third-party logistics services** for warehousing and consolidating shipments. Almost half of the third-party logistics users said that they are outsourcing these activities. The survey showed that most respondents believe that third parties have exerted a positive influence on their organization and planned to expand their use of third-party services between 1992 and 1995. Fifty-four percent of the respondents cited reduced logistics costs, 48 percent cited higher logistics productivity, and 42 percent cited improved customer service from their outsourcing activities.

## Environmental Sensitivity

Logistics systems create a tremendous amount of waste material to protect goods during shipment and storage. In the very near future it will not be enough for the distribution function to provide the right stuff at the right time at the right place. Distribution will also be responsible for returning cardboard boxes, packing material, strapping bands, shrink wrap, wooden pallets, and another shipping material to the point of origin or arranging for its disposal. No federal law yet requires manufacturers to collect and recycle shipping material, but that may not be true for long. A bill introduced in the Senate in 1992 would have established a national recycling program. Although the bill died on the Senate floor, its sponsors are optimistic about its eventual passage. And nearly three-quarters of the states already have imposed mandatory recycling laws.

The most dramatic example of mandatory recycling today comes from Germany. Under Germany's new recycling law the product manufacturer is responsible for recovering all the packing material used in a shipment.[12] The Avoidance of Refuse Ordinance, as it is called, even gives consumers the legal right to return packing material to retail outlets where they purchased the product. Many U.S. multinational companies operating in Europe have contracted with third-party companies to collect the shipping material for recycling rather than having to haul the material back to the source themselves. Colgate-Palmolive Co., operating in Germany, participates in a "pallet pool" to recycle the pallets used in shipping. It rents pallets from a private company, which picks them up from Colgate-Palmolive customers.

This practice of returning goods to the source, known as **reverse logistics,** is causing managers to rethink their packaging options and logistics systems. Many manufacturers expect that the federal government eventually will mandate recycling and are developing programs now so they will be ready. The logical strategy is to design waste out of the logistics process.

One type of packing material has received special attention. Three states (Massachusetts, Wisconsin, and South Dakota) will soon ban from their landfills the polystyrene peanuts used as filler in packages to protect the product.[13] Technology has come to their aid by developing a packing material, similar to the peanut, which is made from vegetable starch. This material breaks down

[11]Rita Koselka, "Distribution Revolution," *Forbes,* May 25, 1992, p. 58.
[12]James Aaron Cooke, "It's Not Easy Being Green," *Traffic Management* 31 (December 1992): 42.
[13]Staff Report, "HOT Technologies for the '90s: A Tasteful Alternative to Plastic Peanuts," *Traffic Management* 31 (August 1992): 34.

completely when wet so it does not take up landfill space. The starch peanuts cost at least twice as much as polystyrene peanuts but the cost is expected to decrease as more organizations use the product.

## Just-in-Time Logistics

Japanese companies are well known for their use of just-in-time (JIT) concepts for minimizing inventories in their manufacturing and logistics systems. JIT sees inventory as waste and as serving only to cover up operating problems. Examples are safety stocks as protection against a shipment's being late, inventories of items ordered only infrequently and in large quantities, and buffer stocks of inventory that effectively decouple various stages of the manufacturing process.

Instead of pushing materials into the operating system and marketplace, JIT systems attempt to match the flow of material to the demand rate of the customer with only minimal inventory. JIT sees customers as pulling material through the logistics system. If the customer is not buying, obviously the company has no need to move finished goods, produce more of the item, or replenish the components used to produce the item.

The logistics system in Figure 10.1 is a graphic depiction of the JIT concept. The blocks in the figure represent potential storage locations for inventory, and the arrows represent avenues for product flow. The goal of a JIT system is to minimize the size of the blocks and arrows but still meet customers' demands. This can occur only with small production lot sizes and small shipments of each item. The logistics system must work toward daily product movements (or even more frequent movements) that match the daily market requirements and still keep costs down.

JIT requires innovative approaches to logistics management. Wal-Mart responded by linking the information systems of its stores, distribution centers, and suppliers through electronic data interchange (EDI). This provides the complete logistics system with daily updates on customers' demand so that it can use the most accurate demand data to plan replenishment for the entire system. When Wal-Mart needs another truckload of an item, its manufacturer ships it to the Wal-Mart distribution center where Wal-Mart separates it into appropriate quantities for delivery to each store. Wal-Mart consolidates each store's replenishment quantity with products from other manufacturers so that the distribution center sends economical truckload deliveries of hundreds of different items from different manufacturers to the store at one time. In this manner Wal-Mart promotes the use of efficient truckload quantities throughout its logistics system while providing JIT delivery to its stores.

Note that Wal-Mart's suppliers can also pass on their planning information to their suppliers. Hence, they can obtain fresh stocks of raw materials and components just in time to meet their own production needs. The just-in-time philosophy plays such a predominate role in operations and logistics management today that Chapter 16 is devoted to an intensive treatment of the subject.

# ► Summary

A company's competitiveness rests on its ability to provide goods and services when and where they are needed. The logistics system is an important component of the company's value chain, which links the company's operating processes to both its suppliers and customers. The integrative and multifunctional nature of business logistics provides an avenue for more efficiently and effectively satisfying customers' needs.

**Learning Objective 1: Describe the responsibilities of the three major logistics components.** The physical supply component is responsible for inbound material movement that links the suppliers and the operations process. The internal operations component is responsible for managing the in-process material flow within the manufacturing process. The physical distribution component is responsible for outbound material movement that links the customer and the operations process.

**Learning Objective 2: List the various elements of a company's logistics function.** The precise list of elements may differ from company to company, but a general list would include transportation, facilities, procurement and purchasing, packaging, warehousing and storage, inventory planning and control, demand forecasting, customer service, order processing and salvage, and scrap disposal.

**Learning Objective 3: Discuss what integrated logistics management means.** Traditionally, companies assign the various elements of logistics to different functional areas within the company. This can lead to optimization of the individual logistical elements but suboptimization of the logistics system as a whole. The integrated logistics management concept stresses looking at all the parts of the logistics puzzle simultaneously and considering trade-offs between these parts when making decisions.

**Learning Objective 4: Discuss the issues involved in effective supplier selection.** In many cases a company has the option to purchase needed material or services from within the organization. If it decides to use an outside source, the company must decide which source to use. The choice should not rest solely on the issue of price. Other issues—quality, reliability, and on-time delivery—are often even more important than price, and the company may be able to use an international source rather than a domestic source. The purchasing agent must be careful to recognize the uncertainties surrounding international business affairs.

**Learning Objective 5: Discuss the five basic modes of transportation.** The five basic modes of transportation include rail, truck, air, water, and pipeline. Rail shipments usually are low cost, but rail time schedules offer little flexibility. Truck shipments offer highly flexible schedules, door-to-door delivery, and the ability to handle shipments of less than a full load. Air shipments are the most expensive but offer speedy delivery. This mode is especially well suited for lightweight or perishable goods. Water transport is usually the lowest cost per ton-mile but slow and competes primarily with railroads for basic bulk commodities and raw materials such as iron ore, grains, chemicals, cement, coal, limestone, and petroleum products. It is unchallenged in the transoceanic movement of all but high-value or time-critical goods. The pipeline mode of transport provides effective point-to-point shipment of fluids and some nonfluids. Most pipelines today carry petroleum.

**Learning Objective 6: Describe the role of customer service in a company's logistics system.** Customer service refers to the level of satisfaction with the chain of activities performed in the supplier-customer exchange. Product quality, service quality, accuracy of order process, courtesy of salespersons, and on-time delivery are just a few elements that join together to determine the overall level of customer service. Customer service is the result of all logistics activities. Companies must analyze any proposed changes to the logistics system to determine their effect on customer service.

**Learning Objective 7: Discuss the advantages and disadvantages of using third-party logistics services.** By farming out some logistics activities to outside service providers, a company may better focus its resources on other key business activities. Logistics today is a high-tech and quite capital-intensive operation. Rather than make that capital commitment, many companies prefer to let another company that has a comparative advantage handle some elements of the logistics function.

However, using a third-party logistics service involves a certain amount of loss of control, and it does not promote development of internal strategic logistics capabilities.

## ► Key Terms

business logistics
Council of Logistics Management
customer service
ethics in purchasing
freight consolidation
internal operations
international sourcing

less than full truck load (LTL)
make-or-buy decision
outsourcing
physical distribution
physical supply
purchasing
reverse logistics

sourcing
supplier evaluation
third-party logistics services
transportation
value analysis
vertical integration
warehousing

## ► Discussion Questions

1. Discuss the role of logistics in today's business environment. Is the role different than it was ten years ago?
2. What are some of the environmental factors that are increasing the importance to business of effective logistics activities?
3. Describe the activities involved in the interface of production, marketing, and logistics.
4. What are the issues involved in achieving a totally integrated logistics system?
5. There must be advantages to a company's reducing its supplier base, because so many companies are doing it. What might those advantages be?
6. You are a purchasing agent for a big discount retailer and have been contacted by a company that wishes to supply goods to your company. What factors do you think would be important to use in evaluating the new supplier?
7. What factors should a company consider when choosing a method of transportation for a shipment of goods?

8. Imagine that a shipment of components is being delivered to your loading dock from a supplier. Describe what will happen to that shipment from the time it arrives until it is eventually sent to manufacturing for use.
9. How might you decide which measure or measures of customer service should receive the most attention in your operation?
10. Why is the number of third-party logistics providers increasing? What advantages do they offer?
11. Why do companies sometimes use intermodal shipments? What role do containers play in intermodal shipments?
12. List the business logistics elements. What role would each element play in the following organizations:
    a. A soft drink bottler and distributor?
    b. An appliance manufacturer?
    c. A general merchandise retailer?
    d. A fast-food restaurant?
13. What is the purpose of JIT logistics? What special challenges does it present for operations managers?

## ► Problems

1. A manufacturer can either produce a certain part in house or buy it from an outside vendor. The company needs 70,000 of those parts each year. Consider the following cost data that have been collected:

| Source | Fixed Cost | Variable Cost per Unit |
|--------|-----------|----------------------|
| Make | $10,125 | $12.50 |
| Buy | – | 14.75 |

    a. Should the company make or buy the part? Why?
    b. At what quantity would it not matter whether the company made or bought the part?

2. Suppose you make an item that has an annual demand of 35,000 units. The annual overhead costs for the facility, equipment, and administration are $300,000, and the variable costs of the item are $80 per unit.
    a. If a vendor offers to supply the item at a unit cost of $88, what should you do?
    b. Are there any other factors to consider before making your decision? What are they?
3. Mary's Mustang Interiors manufactures and sells a variety of reproduction parts for restoring classic Ford Mustangs. Mary buys weather stripping from a distributor in South Carolina for $210 per set. She

sells approximately 50 sets per year. If Mary can lease a machine for making weather stripping for $2,000 per year and the variable production costs are $100 per unit, should Mary's make or buy the weather stripping?

4. What is the break-even demand quantity for the data in question 3?

5. XYZ Computers buys disk drives at a delivered price of $48. A foreign supplier offers a $40 unit price, but the buyer must pay the freight costs and import duties. If the freight costs are $3.50 per unit and import duty is 15 percent of the item price, from whom should XYZ Computers buy? Are there any other factors that XYZ should consider? What are they?

6. Jorge's Taco Barn uses 1,600 dozen fresh tortillas each month for which Jorge pays $.75 per dozen. Jorge is considering leasing a tortilla press so he can make his own. He figures his labor and material costs will be $.50 per dozen. What is the maximum monthly lease Jorge could pay and still come out ahead?

7. A company currently purchases television cabinets from a nearby supplier for $40 per unit plus a $4 transportation charge for shipping them to the final assembly plant. Another vendor offers to make the cabinets in Mexico for a sales price of $34 each and ship them to the final assembly plant by rail for $6 per unit. About 4 percent of the cabinets coming out of Mexico by rail will have to be scrapped because of damage during transport. If the company uses 500,000 cabinets per year, should the company change vendors or keep its current vendor? Why?

# ► Selected References

Ballou, Ronald H. *Business Logistics Management*, 3d ed. Englewood Cliffs, N.J.: Prentice-Hall, 1992.

Bowersox, Donald J., D. J. Closs, and O. K. Helferich. *Logistical Management*, 3d ed. New York: Macmillan, 1986.

Johnson, James C., and D. F. Wood. *Contemporary Physical Distribution and Logistics*, 3d ed. New York: Macmillan, 1986.

Magee, John F., W. C. Copacino, and D. B. Rosenfield. *Modern Logistics Management*. New York: Wiley, 1985.

Scheuing, Eberhard E. *Purchasing Management*. Englewood Cliffs, N.J.: Prentice-Hall, 1988.

Shapiro, Roy D., and James L. Heskett. *Logistics Strategy: Cases and Concepts*. St. Paul, Minn.: West, 1985.

Stock, James R., and D. M. Lambert. *Strategic Logistics Management*, 2d ed. Homewood, Ill.: Richard D. Irwin, 1987.

## CHAPTER 11

# Aggregate Production Planning

*It is a bad plan that admits of no modification.*

LIVY (TITUS LIVIUS)

**Introduction**

**The Concept of Aggregation**

**An Overview of Production-Planning Activities**
*OPERATIONS MANAGEMENT IN PRACTICE 11.1: A "Bridging" Approach to Aggregate Planning*

**Framework for Aggregate Production Planning**

**Techniques for Aggregate Production Planning**
*GLOBAL OPERATIONS MANAGEMENT 11.2: Aggregate Planning in U.K. Manufacturing Companies*

**Aggregate Planning in Service Companies**
*OPERATIONS MANAGEMENT IN PRACTICE 11.3: Developing a Staffing Plan for a Public Safety Department Merger*

**Implementing Aggregate Production Plans—Managerial Issues**

**Hierarchical Production Planning**
*OPERATIONS MANAGEMENT IN PRACTICE 11.4: Improved Hierarchical Production Planning at Owens-Corning Fiberglas*

*After completing this chapter you should be able to*

1. Position aggregate production planning within the capacity decision hierarchy of the company
2. Discuss the concept of aggregation
3. Describe production-planning activities at various levels and over various time periods
4. Define the major inputs, both external and internal, to the production-planning process
5. Describe the major costs in aggregate production planning

6. Discuss the major strategies used in aggregate production planning
7. Describe the various techniques used for aggregate production planning. In addition, you should be able to apply trial-and-error methods and simple linear programming models to aggregate planning problems.
8. Discuss hierarchical production planning and relate it to aggregate production planning

# Introduction

All businesses operate according to a plan. Aggregate planning is a "macro" approach to planning—*aggregation* refers to the idea of focusing on overall capacity, rather than individual products or services. For example, assume that we are trying to prepare product plans for Black & Decker Co. This company manufactures hundreds of products at numerous plants and has thousands of employees. To prepare a production plan for each product and employee that would satisfy marketing demand or financial guidelines would be virtually impossible. Even if we could prepare such a plan, it would require a tremendous commitment of time and resources. Over time we would have to constantly repeat the same massive planning effort. Because of this, production plans are made in an aggregated fashion according to products, labor, and time.

In this chapter we introduce the concept of aggregate planning, discuss strategies and techniques for aggregate planning, and review the costs associated with aggregate planning. We conclude by suggesting ways to implement the aggregate production plan.

In a hierarchical framework aggregate planning links facilities planning from above with scheduling below. Figure 11.1a shows these linkages. Facilities planning sets limits for aggregate planning, which in turns sets limits for scheduling. These decisions proceed from the top down and work as a feedback loop in which the process is constantly undergoing revision.

Figure 11.1b presents the time frame for such decisions. Scheduling decisions are short range, a few months or less. Aggregate planning decisions are medium range, from a few months to one year or eighteen months. Facilities-planning decisions are long range, from a year to five years or more.

# The Concept of Aggregation

Aggregate planning, or **aggregate production planning**, is medium-term capacity planning that typically encompasses a time period (also referred to as a time *horizon*) of two to eighteen months. It involves determining the best quantity to produce and selecting the lowest-cost method that will provide flexibility in capacity while meeting production requirements. In manufacturing

FIGURE 11.1
Capacity Decisions Hierarchy

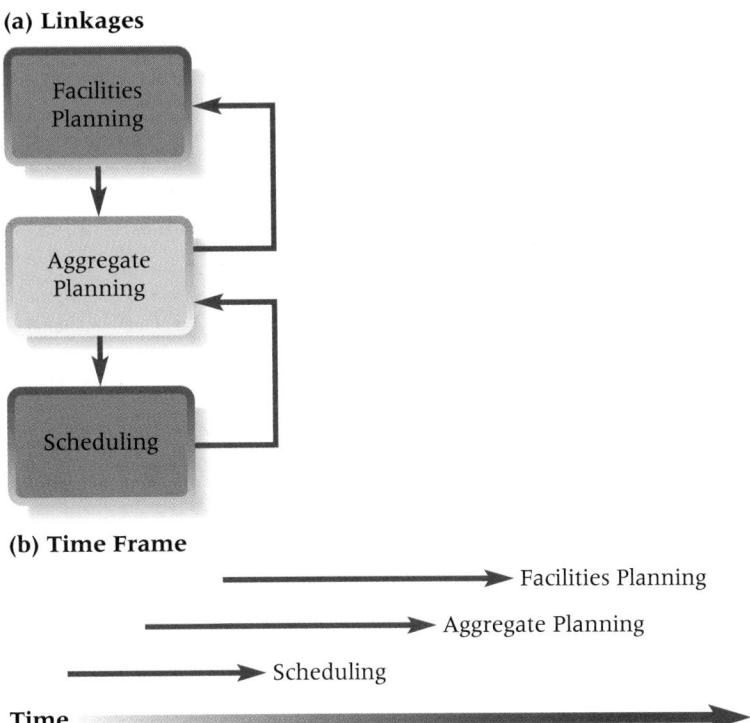

**(a) Linkages**

Facilities Planning

Aggregate Planning

Scheduling

**(b) Time Frame**

Facilities Planning

Aggregate Planning

Scheduling

**Time**

environments aggregate planning means determining the size of the work force, rates of production, and levels of inventory. This process results in what is called a **production plan**. In service situations aggregate planning entails scheduling of staff that considers customers' service needs and perhaps the limits of machine capacity. This process results in what is called a **staffing plan**. Aggregation, or grouping, is done according to products, labor, and time.

## Products

The most common type of aggregation is by product. Usually, a product family is a group of products that are manufactured similarly and have common labor and material requirements. Sometimes, marketing or accounting/financial requirements determine product families. However it is done, the idea is to create a set of broad product families, which facilitates aggregation and avoids details.

## Labor

Another common type of aggregation is by labor—a company can aggregate its work force by product family if, for example, it devotes a specific plant to a given product family. In another situation a company might distribute its entire work force among several plants with each plant producing all product families. In this case the work force could be considered as a single aggregate group.

## Time

A third type of aggregation is by time. In aggregate planning the time period is usually about one year. But aggregate plans require updating during this planning period, and the question is how often a planner should update. Again, the idea is not to update so frequently that it creates disruptions and is distracting. At the same time planners need to update to allow for seasonality or to reflect sudden changes. Companies commonly use monthly or quarterly planning periods.

## An Overview of Production Planning

Production planning links top management and manufacturing. The production plan summarizes the production resources needed to achieve the strategic objectives of the company. It specifies time-phased production rates, work force levels, and inventory requirements while considering customers' requirements and capacity limitations.

A company has to plan its production activities at several levels and for various time periods. Figure 11.2 presents an overview of production-planning activities for various time periods.

FIGURE 11.2
Production-Planning
Activities and Levels

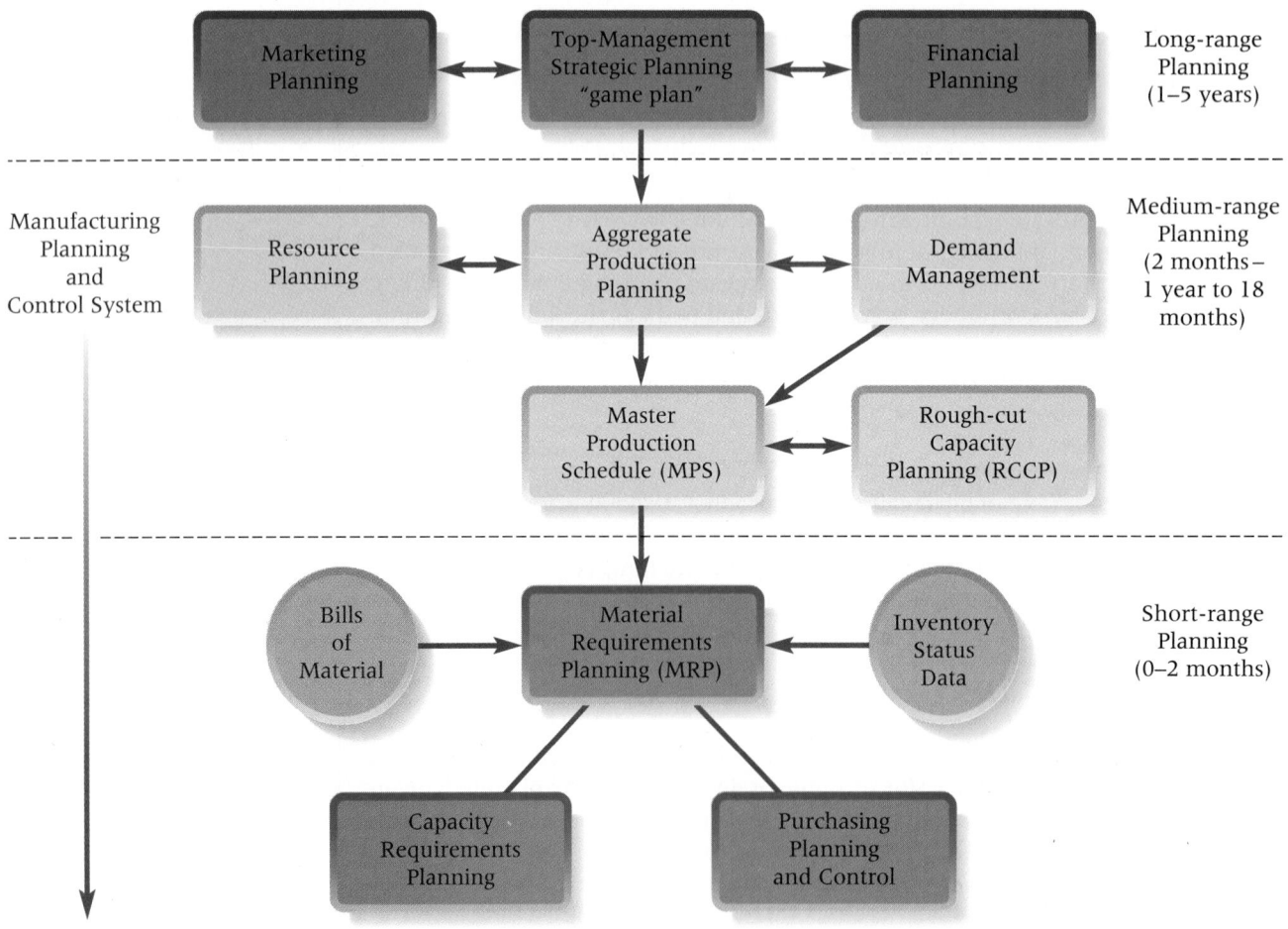

## Long-range Planning

**Long-range planning** is usually done on an annual basis. Long-range plans address a time period that covers one to five or more years hence. It is corporate, or top management, strategic planning and results in a statement of organizational goals and objectives.

Top management must resolve the broad trade-offs in order to bring consistency to the functional plans of marketing, finance, and production. The overall context within which management makes the trade-offs is often called a *game plan*. The game plan reflects both the strategy and the tactics of the company for responding to its economic and political environments.

The strategic plan of the company has elements that link marketing, finance, and production. Marketing planning considers both market penetration and the objectives for the product line, as well as such issues as pricing, quality, and new markets. Financial planning analyzes the financial consequences of the marketing objectives in terms of cash flow, working capital requirements, capital investment needs, and return on investment goals.

## Medium-range Planning

**Medium-range planning** usually addresses a time period of about two months to one year or eighteen months hence. The increments for medium-range planning are months or quarters. Medium-range planning decisions relate to general levels of employment, output, and inventories.

The aggregate production plan states what manufacturing has to do so that the company can meet its overall objectives. It links and provides for dialogue between manufacturing and top management, as well as between marketing and finance. The production plan must be stated in aggregated terms that everyone can understand. Some companies express the aggregate production plan as the dollar value of total monthly, quarterly, or yearly output. Other companies state the production plan in terms of total units for each product line.

The link between aggregate production planning and managing demand is also important. Demand management includes order entry, order promising, physical distribution coordination, and forecasting. Demand management must include every source of demand and weigh the demand against manufacturing capacity. Another important link to aggregate production planning is with resource planning. Resource planning involves the long-range planning of facilities and requires the translation of extended production plans into capacity requirements on an aggregate basis.

Both demand management and resource planning are part of the manufacturing planning-and-control (MPC) system. Aggregate production planning precedes and directs MPC decision making and serves as the basis for creating the more detailed set of MPC decisions. The production plan is in turn linked to the master production schedule, which is a disaggregation of the production plan. It generates the amounts and dates for the manufacture of specific end products. The **master production schedule (MPS)** is usually fixed for some short time period, say, six to eight weeks or longer. A final important aspect of medium-range planning is **rough-cut capacity planning**, so called because it gives only a rough approximation of actual resource requirements. This type of planning is a review of the master production schedule to make sure that it does not violate capacity constraints.

## Short-range Planning

**Short-range planning** looks about two months into the future. The time period for short-range planning is typically a week. Short-range decisions involve scheduling jobs, loading machines, and sequencing the jobs.

In short-range planning the master production schedule feeds directly into **material requirements planning (MRP)**. MRP determines the period-by-period plans for all component parts and raw materials required to make the products included in the MPS. MRP has two other major inputs. The first is the bill of materials that shows, for each part number, which other part numbers the manufacturing system requires as components. The second is the inventory status, which states by part number how many of each item are on hand, how many are allocated to work in process, and how many have already been ordered.

MRP also has a number of important links. Among these are capacity requirements planning and purchasing planning and control. **Capacity requirements planning** provides a detailed schedule of when each work center is to run each operation. **Purchasing planning and control** concerns the acquisition and control of purchased items, as specified by MRP.

These two types of planning are only a small portion of the detail that exists below the MRP level. We will not go further at this point; Chapter 13 discusses MRP in detail. Operations Management in Practice 11.1 describes how Wright Line, Inc., handles aggregate planning.

## Framework for Aggregate Production Planning

Aggregate production planning focuses on setting production rates by broad product groups for an intermediate time period. It uses the company's adjustable capacity—the size of the work force, the number of hours per week they work, the number of shifts used, and the extent of subcontracting. Its objectives are to determine the best quantity to produce during each time period in the intermediate framework and to specify the lowest-cost method of adjusting capacity to meet the production requirements.

Traditionally, aggregate production planning involves work force levels, production rates, and inventory levels. **Work force level** is the number of workers required for production. **Production rate** is the number of units produced per time period. **Inventory level** is the balance of unused units carried forward from the previous period. Two academic researchers, Joseph H. Mellichamp and Robert M. Love, have formally stated the aggregate production-planning problem this way: Given the demand forecast $F_t$ for periods $t = 1, 2, \ldots,$ $T$ in a planning horizon, determine the production level $P_t$, inventory level $I_t$, and work force level $W_t$ that minimize the relevant costs during the planning period.[1] Implicit in this statement is that the aggregate production plan should be optimal (least costly). This is not often possible, but the company should try to develop plans that use resources in the best way and at the lowest cost possible. The aggregate production plan should always be at least feasible in terms of being within the capacity of the company and satisfying the major portion of demand.

---

[1]Joseph M. Mellichamp and Robert M. Love, "Production Switching Heuristics for the Aggregate Planning Problem," *Management Science* 24 (August 1978): 1242.

# A "Bridging" Approach to Aggregate Planning

Wright Line, Inc., of Worcester, Massachusetts, uses aggregate planning as a bridge between its tactical plan and implementing material requirements planning. The company manufactures products for management, filing, handling, and protection of information media. It built its aggregate plan around a standard cost system; the plan encompassed all product families within its factory.

The first part of the aggregate plan consisted of orders, backlogs, and shipments. Orders measure the rate of incoming orders and are forecast by the marketing department. Backlog is the status of unshipped customer orders; the company's Aggregate Planning Committee devises its backlog plan from information provided by marketing, finance, manufacturing, and inventory planning. Shipments are the rate at which finished goods are shipped to customers.

The second part of the aggregate plan consists of inventory-receipted value, alternative receipts, and net receipts. The third part of the aggregate plan consists of the response from manufacturing. Manufacturing develops its own "mini" aggregate plan in response to the value standards specified by the total aggregate plan. The master scheduler takes into consideration changes in levels of work-in-process and parts inventories, lead times, throughput, and scrap to determine what the factory needs in order to produce at the rate envisioned in the total plan. Current capacity is another consideration. Both the second and third parts of the aggregate plan are negotiable. Trade-offs between an aggregate plan that calls for level loads and inventory levels are common.

Wright Line has been able to reduce its finished goods inventory levels by 45 percent while maintaining a service level of 95 percent. It did this by using a system that everyone understood because it used standard cost calculations.

## The Production-Planning Environment

Aggregate production planning takes place in a complex environment that has a number of external and internal factors, as Figure 11.3 shows. The external inputs to the production-planning process are generally outside the production planner's direct control. For example, the production planner cannot control subcontracting capacity, although subcontracting may be included in the aggregate plan.

Companies generally align their internal inputs to the production-planning process and the various functions of the company. The internal inputs may be controllable in varying degrees. For example, plant and equipment capacities are usually fixed in the short run, and union contracts may limit changes in the work force. But inventory may offer great flexibility.

Because the internal inputs to the production-planning process are so diverse and complex, several objectives may conflict. Among the common objectives of production planning are to

1. Minimize costs
2. Maximize profits
3. Minimize inventory levels

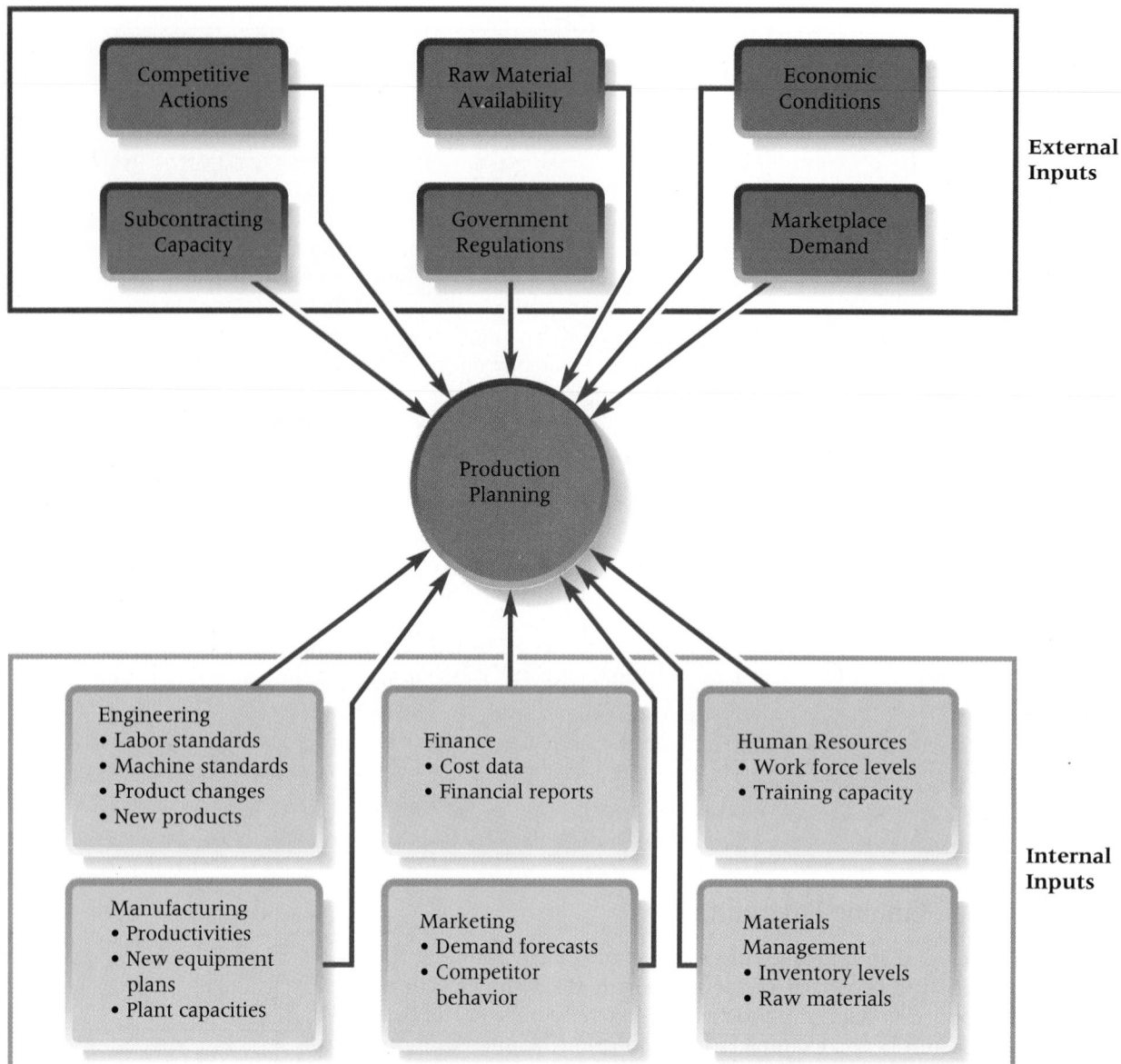

FIGURE 11.3
The Production-Planning
Environment

**4.** Minimize changes in work force levels
**5.** Minimize use of overtime
**6.** Minimize use of subcontracting
**7.** Minimize changes in production rates
**8.** Minimize number of machine set-ups
**9.** Minimize idle time for plant and personnel
**10.** Maximize customer service

The conflicts in these objectives are apparent. Minimizing changes in work force levels and maximizing customer service both conflict with minimizing inventory. Maximizing profits may not be possible without changing work force levels or using overtime. Overall, cost minimization is the overriding objective in production planning.

Within the production-planning environment various options are available. Two broad options are those influencing demand and those influencing supply.[2]

Companies can modify or influence demand for their product, or service, in several ways, including

- Price incentives. Price incentives are useful for reducing peak demand or stimulating off-peak demand.
- Reservations. Requiring customers to reserve capacity in advance can influence demand.
- Backlogs. Companies can modify demand by asking customers to wait for orders.
- Complementary products or services. Companies that have highly seasonal demand use complementary products or services to smooth out their demand.
- Advertising/promotion. Advertising and promotion can stimulate demand or shift it from peak periods to slack periods.

Some of these factors affect the demand level, whereas others affect the pattern of demand. The factors on which to focus will depend on which elements the company is trying to control.

Companies can also modify or influence the supply of the product or service in several ways, including

- Hiring/firing workers. Perhaps the most direct way to modify supply, how companies use hiring and firing, varies a great deal. Company labor policies or union contracts may restrict this option. Also, hiring/firing entails certain costs, both tangible and intangible. Other resources may constrain the hiring of workers.
- Overtime/slack time. This option is a common choice. It is much less severe than hiring/firing and is quicker and easier to implement. But overtime is costly, and union contracts may restrict its use.
- Part-time/temporary labor. This option is particularly attractive because of the flexibility it affords, and because companies can pay part-time or temporary workers less and not provide them with fringe benefits. Service industries make particular use of part-time or temporary workers.
- Subcontracting. This option involves the use of other companies and is often an effective way to increase or decrease supply. Subcontracting can have disadvantages, including higher costs and lack of control of product quality. Also, subcontracting arrangements frequently must be made well in advance of the anticipated need.
- Cooperative arrangements. Many companies have arrangements to share facilities. Examples include electrical or agricultural cooperatives and airlines that share gates, ramps, and baggage-handling equipment.
- Inventories. Companies can use inventories as a buffer between supply and demand during the time period. Inventories are more useful in manufacturing than in service organizations, but they do incur a holding or carrying cost until they are needed.

Aggregate production-planning methods generally are oriented toward minimizing costs. The usual assumption is that demand is given or fixed. Using options for modifying supply makes cost minimization the logical objective.

---

[2]This topic is also discussed extensively in Chapter 17, Design and Scheduling of Service Systems.

Companies should consider the following costs while planning aggregate production:

- Hiring/firing costs. Hiring costs include the recruitment, screening, and training that enable the employee to become fully productive. Firing costs include severance, certain employee benefits, the cost of realigning the remaining work force, and certain intangibles such as the bad feelings of those people who are fired and the loss of morale for those who are not fired.

- Overtime/slack time costs. Overtime costs usually consist of regular wages plus a premium of 50 to 100 percent. Over a long time period other costs related to employees' health and well being result from overtime. Employers incur slack time costs when they use workers at less than their capacity. However, slack time can provide opportunities for performing maintenance or conducting training without further reducing production.

- Part-time/temporary labor costs. Part-time or temporary labor costs usually are less than those associated with full-time employees because of the difference in benefits and because part-time or temporary workers are simply paid less. Union contracts or operational considerations generally limit the number or percentage of the total work force that a company can use part time or temporarily.

- Subcontracting costs. The cost of subcontracting is simply the subcontractor's fee to provide the needed production. Subcontracting can be more or less costly than making the units at the company's own facility.

- Cooperative arrangement costs. The cost of a cooperative arrangement is analogous to a subcontracting cost and again can be more or less than the cost of making the units at the company's own facility. Companies often enter into cooperative arrangements because costs are lower—each organization pays only partial (shared) costs for facilities/equipment that each would otherwise maintain on a full-time basis.

*Aggregate production planning at Black & Decker Co. is greatly complicated by the company's diverse product line.*

■ Inventory carrying costs. Inventory carrying costs include not only storage and the cost of tying up money that could be invested elsewhere but also the costs of insurance, obsolescence, breakage, spoilage, and deterioration. Inventory carrying costs are often expressed as a percentage of the dollar value of inventory and range from 10 to 40 percent per year.

■ Back order or stock out costs. These costs arise when a company cannot fill an order from existing inventories. They are difficult to estimate but are related to loss of customer goodwill (for back orders) or to loss of sales (for stock outs).

Some or all of these costs may be important in evaluating alternative strategies and solutions to a typical aggregate production-planning problem. Later in this chapter we present examples that illustrate how to use a number of these costs.

## Strategies for Aggregate Production Planning

In broad terms aggregate planners look at the demand forecast or expected demand from the perspectives of both quantity and timing. If total demand and total capacity for the planning period do not match, the planner's major objective is either to increase capacity (if the demand forecast exceeds available capacity) or reduce capacity (if the demand forecast is less than available capacity). But even if total demand and total capacity are reasonably balanced, aggregate planners may still have to deal with the timing of uneven demand during the planning period, as illustrated in Figure 11.4. Uneven demand means that aggregate planners still have the problem of balancing demand and capacity throughout the planning period.

Production managers have several ways of balancing demand and capacity for aggregate planning purposes. Two are pure operations strategies and many are

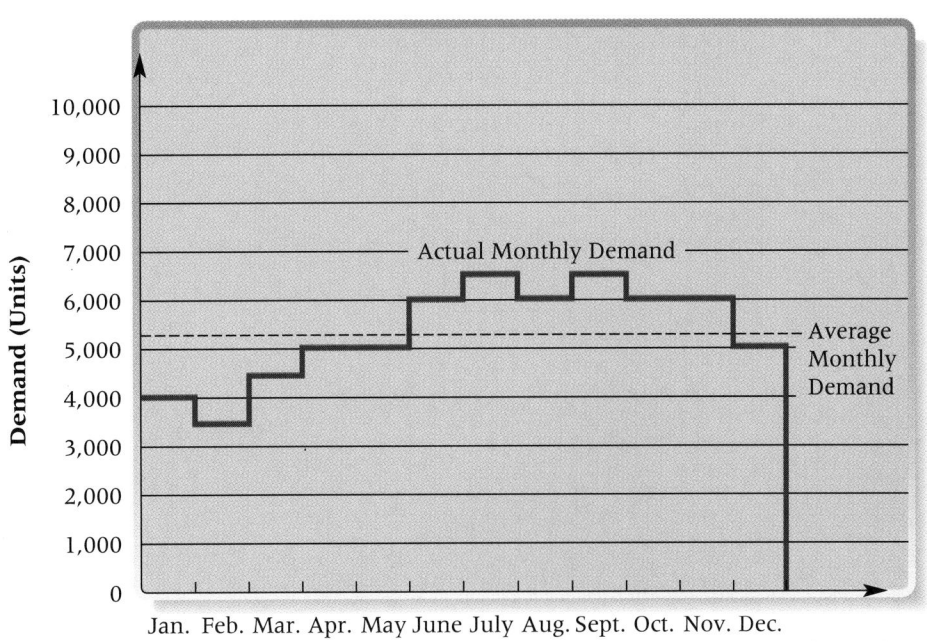

FIGURE 11.4
Uneven Monthly Demand Pattern

combinations of these strategies that planners can use to meet fluctuating demand.

One pure strategy is the **chase strategy**, in which planners adjust production rates or work force levels to match the demand requirements of the planning period. They can implement a chase strategy in several ways: by using overtime and subcontracting or hiring or laying off workers. They do not use inventory to absorb demand fluctuations. The pure chase strategy keeps inventory investment low but demands that planners adjust production rates or work force levels for every period of the plan.

A second pure strategy is the **level strategy**, in which planners maintain a constant production rate or work force level for the duration of the plan. Again, they have several techniques for implementing a level strategy, including increasing inventory levels to satisfy peak demand or allowing backlogs (longer delivery lead times). If the work force is subject to attrition, planners can factor for a constant production rate by using overtime, subcontracting, or even hiring of new workers. The pure level strategy maintains level production rates and a stable work force at the expense of increased inventory investment and perhaps more backlogs and overtime.

**TABLE 11.1**
Production-Planning Information—Forest Hills Tennis Racket Co.

**(a) Demand Information**

| Month | Monthly Demand Forecast— Production Requirements (Units) | Cumulative Production Requirements (Units) | Number of Working Days in Month | Cumulative Number of Working Days | Daily Demand Forecast (Units) |
|---|---|---|---|---|---|
| January | 1,000 | 1,000 | 23 | 23 | 43.5 |
| February | 1,200 | 2,200 | 20 | 43 | 60.0 |
| March | 1,400 | 3,600 | 21 | 64 | 66.7 |
| April | 1,600 | 5,200 | 22 | 86 | 72.7 |
| May | 2,000 | 7,200 | 23 | 109 | 87.0 |
| June | 2,500 | 9,700 | 20 | 129 | 125.0 |
| July | 2,500 | 12,200 | 23 | 152 | 108.7 |
| August | 3,000 | 15,200 | 22 | 174 | 136.4 |
| September | 3,000 | 18,200 | 21 | 195 | 142.9 |
| October | 2,000 | 20,200 | 23 | 218 | 87.0 |
| November | 1,600 | 21,800 | 21 | 239 | 76.2 |
| December | 2,000 | 23,800 | 22 | 261 | 90.9 |

**(b) Cost Information**

| | |
|---|---|
| Materials | $10/unit |
| Inventory holding cost | $1/unit/month |
| Stockout cost | $3/unit/month |
| Subcontracting cost | $24/unit |
| Hiring and training cost | $300/employee |
| Layoff cost | $200/employee |
| Regular time cost | $4/hour |
| Overtime cost | $6/hour |
| Labor hour requirement | 3 hours/unit |

In practice planners have a range of strategies between the pure chase strategy and the pure level strategy. A **mixed strategy** that calls for periodic fluctuations in both inventory levels and work force and production rates is often most appropriate.

# Techniques for Aggregate Production Planning

A number of techniques are available to planners of aggregate production. In broad terms we can categorize them as of two types: trial-and-error methods and mathematical techniques. Despite a considerable body of research devoted to the development and testing of various mathematical models for aggregate production planning, planners more commonly use trial-and-error methods.

## Trial-and-Error Method

The trial-and-error method involves evaluating alternative ways to use production resources to meet production requirements. Production planners evaluate various options until they find one that seems to work well. The method is relatively easy to use and understand. But it requires tedious and time-consuming computations. Recent advances in computer hardware and software make such "what-if" analysis much more efficient. Spreadsheet programs, such as *Lotus 1-2-3* or *EXCEL*, can make trial-and-error calculations very quickly.

EXAMPLE 11.1

The Forest Hills Tennis Racket Co. would like to prepare an aggregate production plan for a one-year period. It has prepared a demand forecast to be used as its production requirements. Table 11.1a shows the demand information and a summary of the working days available each month, and Table 11.1b shows the relevant cost information. To visualize its aggregate planning problem, the company also plots the daily demand forecast for each month in the plan, as shown in Figure 11.5. The company determined the daily demand forecast by dividing the monthly demand forecast by the number of working days in the month. The broken line in Figure 11.5 represents the average daily demand for the entire planning period. To compute average daily demand

$$\text{Average daily demand} = \frac{\text{Total forecasted demand}}{\text{Cumulative working days}}$$
$$= \frac{23,800 \; units}{261 \; days} = 91.2 \; units \; per \; day \qquad (11\text{-}1)$$

Figure 11.5 shows how the daily demand forecast for various months differs from the average daily demand and shows the fundamental nature of the aggregate production-planning problem.

We will analyze four aggregate production plans to determine the one that produces the lowest total cost. For each plan we will assume that the company begins the year with a backlog of one thousand units, does not try to maintain safety stocks, and that its inventory holding cost is based on the inventory level at month's end. Also, we will not try to plan for vacations, sickness, disability, relocation, or death of employees during the year.

FIGURE 11.5
Plot of Daily Demand by
Month—Forest Hills Tennis
Racket Co.

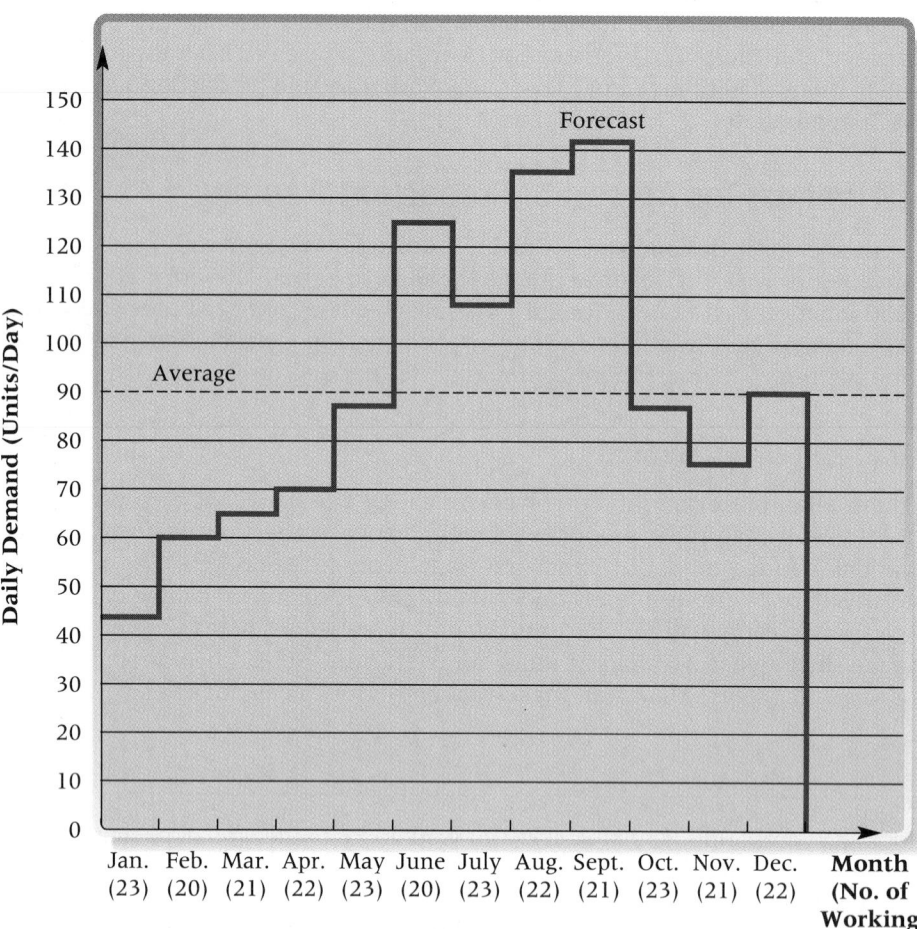

TABLE 11.2
Production Plan 1: Vary
Work Force Levels—Chase
Strategy*

| Month | (1) Monthly Production Requirement | (2) Production Hours Needed (col. 1 × 3) | (3) Number of Working Days in Month | (4) Hours per Month per Employee (col. 3 × 8) | (5) Number of Workers Required (col. 2/col. 4) |
|---|---|---|---|---|---|
| January | 2,000[+] | 6,000 | 23 | 184 | 33 |
| February | 1,200 | 3,600 | 20 | 160 | 23 |
| March | 1,400 | 4,200 | 21 | 168 | 25 |
| April | 1,600 | 4,800 | 22 | 176 | 27 |
| May | 2,000 | 6,000 | 23 | 184 | 33 |
| June | 2,500 | 7,500 | 20 | 160 | 47 |
| July | 2,500 | 7,500 | 23 | 184 | 41 |
| August | 3,000 | 9,000 | 22 | 176 | 51 |
| September | 3,000 | 9,000 | 21 | 168 | 54 |
| October | 2,000 | 6,000 | 23 | 184 | 33 |
| November | 1,600 | 4,800 | 21 | 168 | 29 |
| December | 2,000 | 6,000 | 22 | 176 | 34 |

*Assumes a beginning backlog of 1,000 units and a beginning work force level of 33 employees
[+]Includes the beginning backlog of 1,000 units

*Production Plan 1: Vary work force levels.* Among the pure strategies that the Forest Hills Tennis Racket Co. might use is the chase strategy that we discussed earlier. This strategy assumes that company can hire people with the necessary production skills when it needs them and lay them off with no long-term negative results. Hiring and layoffs keep the labor hours (or employees) exactly equal to the labor hours (or employees) the company needs. Inventory does not accumulate under this strategy. This plan assumes a beginning inventory backlog of one thousand units and a beginning work force level of thirty-three employees. The beginning work force level is exactly what the first month of the plan requires. Table 11.2 summarizes the costs associated with this aggregate production plan.

*Production Plan 2: Use level work force, vary inventories and back orders.* The second pure strategy that the Forest Hills Tennis Racket Co. might use is the level strategy we discussed earlier. This strategy allows inventory to accumulate and fills shortages from a subsequent month's production by using back orders. This plan also uses a beginning backlog of one thousand units. Planners set the (constant) work force level by determining how many workers the company would require if it divided the total yearly production plus the beginning backlog of one thousand units equally for each of the twelve months. This computation is as follows:

$$\text{Level work force} = \frac{\substack{\text{Cumulative yearly} \\ \text{production requirement} \\ \text{+ Beginning backlog (units)}} \times \substack{\text{Labor hour} \\ \text{requirement} \\ \text{(hours/unit)}}}{\substack{\text{Cumulative number of} \\ \text{working days per year (days)}} \times \substack{\text{Labor hours} \\ \text{per day (hours)}}}$$

(11-2)

$$= \frac{24,800 \text{ Units per year} \times 3 \text{ Hours per unit}}{261 \text{ Working days per year} \times 8 \text{ Hours per day}} = \frac{35.6 \text{ Employees}}{\text{(use 36)}}$$

TABLE 11.2
Continued

| Month | (6) Number of Workers Hired | (7) Hiring Cost (col. 6 × $300) | (8) Number of Workers Laid Off | (9) Layoff Cost (col. 8 × $200) | (10) Regular Time Production Cost (col. 2 × $4) |
|---|---|---|---|---|---|
| January | 0 | $ 0 | 0 | $ 0 | $ 24,000 |
| February | 0 | 0 | 10 | 2,000 | 14,400 |
| March | 2 | 600 | 0 | 0 | 16,800 |
| April | 2 | 600 | 0 | 0 | 19,200 |
| May | 6 | 1,800 | 0 | 0 | 24,000 |
| June | 14 | 4,200 | 0 | 0 | 30,000 |
| July | 0 | 0 | 6 | 1,200 | 30,000 |
| August | 10 | 3,000 | 0 | 0 | 36,000 |
| September | 3 | 900 | 0 | 0 | 36,000 |
| October | 0 | 0 | 21 | 4,200 | 24,000 |
| November | 0 | 0 | 4 | 800 | 19,200 |
| December | 5 | 1,500 | 0 | 0 | 24,000 |
| | | $12,600 | | $8,200 | $297,600 |

Total Cost = $318,400

| Month | (1) Monthly Production Requirement | (2) Number of Working Days in Month | (3) Hours per Month per Employee (col. 2 × 8) | (4) Number of Employees# | (5) Production Hours Available (col. 3 × col. 4) | (6) Actual Production (col. 5/3) |
|---|---|---|---|---|---|---|
| January | 1,000 | 23 | 184 | 36 | 6,624 | 2,208 |
| February | 1,200 | 20 | 160 | 36 | 5,760 | 1,920 |
| March | 1,400 | 21 | 168 | 36 | 6,048 | 2,016 |
| April | 1,600 | 22 | 176 | 36 | 6,336 | 2,112 |
| May | 2,000 | 23 | 184 | 36 | 6,624 | 2,208 |
| June | 2,500 | 20 | 160 | 36 | 5,760 | 1,920 |
| July | 2,500 | 23 | 184 | 36 | 6,624 | 2,208 |
| August | 3,000 | 22 | 176 | 36 | 6,336 | 2,112 |
| September | 3,000 | 21 | 168 | 36 | 6,048 | 2,016 |
| October | 2,000 | 23 | 184 | 36 | 6,624 | 2,208 |
| November | 1,600 | 21 | 168 | 36 | 6,048 | 2,016 |
| December | 2,000 | 22 | 176 | 36 | 6,336 | 2,112 |

| Month | (7) Beginning Inventory | (8) Ending Inventory (col. 7 + col. 6−col. 1) | (9) Units Short | (10) Shortage Cost (col. 9 × $3 | (11) Units Excess | (12) Inventory Holding Cost (col. 8 × $1) | (13) Regular Time Production Cost (col. 5 × $4) |
|---|---|---|---|---|---|---|---|
| January | −1,000 | 208 | 0 | $ 0 | 208 | $ 208 | $ 26,496 |
| February | 208 | 928 | 0 | 0 | 928 | 928 | 23,040 |
| March | 928 | 1,544 | 0 | 0 | 1,544 | 1,544 | 24,192 |
| April | 1,544 | 2,056 | 0 | 0 | 2,056 | 2,056 | 25,344 |
| May | 2,056 | 2,264 | 0 | 0 | 2,264 | 2,264 | 26,496 |
| June | 2,264 | 1,684 | 0 | 0 | 1,684 | 1,684 | 23,040 |
| July | 1,684 | 1,392 | 0 | 0 | 1,392 | 1,392 | 26,496 |
| August | 1,392 | 504 | 0 | 0 | 504 | 504 | 25,344 |
| September | 504 | −480 | 480 | 1,440 | 0 | 0 | 24,192 |
| October | −480 | −272 | 272 | 816 | 0 | 0 | 26,496 |
| November | −272 | 144 | 0 | 0 | 144 | 144 | 24,192 |
| December | 144 | 256 | 0 | 0 | 256 | 256 | 25,344 |
| | | | | $2,256 | | $10,980 | $300,672 |
| | | | | | | | Total Cost = $313,908 |

*Assumes a beginning backlog of 1,000 units and a level work force of 36 employees
#(24,800 units × 3 hours per unit)/(261 days × 8 hours per day) = 36 employees

TABLE 11.3
Production Plan 2: Use Level
Work Force, Vary Inventory
and Back Orders—Level
Strategy*

| Month | (1) Monthly Production Requirement | (2) Number of Working Days in Month | (3) Hours per Month per Employee (col. 2 × 8) | (4) Number of Employees | (5) Production Hours Available (col. 3 × col. 4) | (6) Actual Production (col. 5/3) |
|---|---|---|---|---|---|---|
| January | 1,000 | 23 | 184 | 30 | 5,520 | 1,840 |
| February | 1,200 | 20 | 160 | 30 | 4,800 | 1,600 |
| March | 1,400 | 21 | 168 | 30 | 5,040 | 1,680 |
| April | 1,600 | 22 | 176 | 30 | 5,280 | 1,760 |
| May | 2,000 | 23 | 184 | 30 | 5,520 | 1,840 |
| June | 2,500 | 20 | 160 | 30 | 4,800 | 1,600 |
| July | 2,500 | 23 | 184 | 30 | 5,520 | 1,840 |
| August | 3,000 | 22 | 176 | 30 | 5,280 | 1,760 |
| September | 3,000 | 21 | 168 | 30 | 5,040 | 1,680 |
| October | 2,000 | 23 | 184 | 30 | 5,520 | 1,840 |
| November | 1,600 | 21 | 168 | 30 | 5,040 | 1,680 |
| December | 2,000 | 22 | 176 | 30 | 5,280 | 1,760 |

| Month | (7) Beginning Inventory | (8) Ending Inventory (col. 7 + col. 6−col. 1) | (9) Units Short | (10) Subcontracting Cost (col. 9 × $24) | (11) Units Excess | (12) Inventory Holding Cost (col. 8 × $1) | (13) Regular Time Production Cost (col. 5 × $4) |
|---|---|---|---|---|---|---|---|
| January | −1,000 | −160 | 160 | $ 3,840 | 0 | $ 0 | $ 22,080 |
| February | 0 | 400 | 0 | 0 | 400 | 400 | 19,200 |
| March | 400 | 680 | 0 | 0 | 680 | 680 | 20,160 |
| April | 680 | 840 | 0 | 0 | 840 | 840 | 21,120 |
| May | 840 | 680 | 0 | 0 | 680 | 680 | 22,080 |
| June | 680 | −220 | 220 | 5,280 | 0 | 0 | 19,200 |
| July | 0 | −660 | 660 | 15,840 | 0 | 0 | 22,080 |
| August | 0 | −1,240 | 1,240 | 29,760 | 0 | 0 | 21,120 |
| September | 0 | −1,320 | 1,320 | 31,680 | 0 | 0 | 20,160 |
| October | 0 | −160 | 160 | 3,840 | 0 | 0 | 22,080 |
| November | 0 | 80 | 0 | 0 | 80 | 80 | 20,160 |
| December | 80 | −160 | 160 | 3,840 | 0 | 0 | 21,120 |
|  |  |  |  | $94,080 |  | $2,680 | $250,560 |
|  |  |  |  |  |  | Total Cost = | $347,320 |

*Assumes a constant work force level of 30 employees and a beginning backlog of 1,000 units

TABLE 11.4
Production Plan 3: (Lower) Level Work Force, Use Subcontracting—Mixed Strategy*

| Month | (1) Monthly Production Requirement | (2) Production Hours Needed (col. 1 × 3) | (3) Number of Working Days in Month | (4) Hours per Month per Employee (col. 3 × 8) | (5) Number of Workers | (6) Production Hours Available (col. 4 × col. 5) | (7) Actual Production (col. 6/3) | (8) Beginning Inventory | (9) Ending Inventory (col. 8 + col. 7 – col. 1) |
|---|---|---|---|---|---|---|---|---|---|
| January | 1,000 | 3,000 | 23 | 184 | 30 | 5,520 | 1,840 | −1,000 | −160 |
| February | 1,200 | 3,600 | 20 | 160 | 30 | 4,800 | 1,600 | 0 | 400 |
| March | 1,400 | 4,200 | 21 | 168 | 30 | 5,040 | 1,680 | 400 | 680 |
| April | 1,600 | 4,800 | 22 | 176 | 30 | 5,280 | 1,760 | 680 | 840 |
| May | 2,000 | 6,000 | 23 | 184 | 30 | 5,520 | 1,840 | 840 | 680 |
| June | 2,500 | 7,500 | 20 | 160 | 30 | 4,800 | 1,600 | 680 | −220 |
| July | 2,500 | 7,500 | 23 | 184 | 30 | 5,520 | 1,840 | 0 | −660 |
| August | 3,000 | 9,000 | 22 | 176 | 30 | 5,280 | 1,760 | 0 | −1,240 |
| September | 3,000 | 9,000 | 21 | 168 | 30 | 5,040 | 1,680 | 0 | −1,320 |
| October | 2,000 | 6,000 | 23 | 184 | 30 | 5,520 | 1,840 | 0 | −160 |
| November | 1,600 | 4,800 | 21 | 168 | 30 | 5,040 | 1,680 | 0 | 80 |
| December | 2,000 | 6,000 | 22 | 176 | 30 | 5,280 | 1,760 | 80 | −160 |

| (10) Units Short | (11) Overtime Hours Needed (col. 10 × 3) | (12) Overtime Hours Used | (13) Overtime Cost (col. 12 × $6) | (14) Sub-contracting Units Required (col. 11 – col. 12)/3 | (15) Sub-contracting Cost (col. 14 × $24) | (16) Units Excess | (17) Inventory Holding Cost (col. 16 × $1) | (18) Regular Time Production Cost (col. 6 × $4) |
|---|---|---|---|---|---|---|---|---|
| 160 | 480 | 480 | $ 2,880 | 0 | $ 0 | 0 | $ 0 | $ 22,080 |
| 0 | 0 | 0 | 0 | 0 | 0 | 400 | 400 | 19,200 |
| 0 | 0 | 0 | 0 | 0 | 0 | 680 | 680 | 20,160 |
| 0 | 0 | 0 | 0 | 0 | 0 | 840 | 840 | 21,120 |
| 0 | 0 | 0 | 0 | 0 | 0 | 680 | 680 | 22,080 |
| 220 | 660 | 660 | 3,960 | 0 | 0 | 0 | 0 | 19,200 |
| 660 | 1,980 | 1,440 | 8,640 | 180 | 4,320 | 0 | 0 | 22,080 |
| 1,240 | 3,720 | 1,440 | 8,640 | 760 | 18,240 | 0 | 0 | 21,120 |
| 1,320 | 3,960 | 1,440 | 8,640 | 840 | 20,160 | 0 | 0 | 20,160 |
| 160 | 480 | 480 | 2,880 | 0 | 0 | 0 | 0 | 22,080 |
| 0 | 0 | 0 | 0 | 0 | 0 | 80 | 80 | 20,160 |
| 160 | 480 | 480 | 2,880 | 0 | 0 | 0 | 0 | 21,120 |
|  |  |  | $38,520 |  | $42,720 |  | $2,680 | $250,560 |

Total Cost = $334,480

*Assumes a constant work force level of 30 employees, and a beginning backlog of 1,000 units

Maximum overtime possible per month:   16 regular days @ 1 hour/day = 16 hours
4 Saturdays   @ 8 hours/day = 32 hours
48 hours × 30 employees = 1,440 hours

TABLE 11.5
Production Plan 4: (Lower)
Level Work Force, Use
Overtime and Subcontracting
(Mixed Strategy)*

| Cost Category | Plan 1 (Pure Strategy) | Plan 2 (Pure Strategy) | Plan 3 (Mixed Strategy) | Plan 4 (Mixed Strategy) |
|---|---|---|---|---|
| Hiring cost | $ 12,600 | | | |
| Layoff cost | 8,200 | | | |
| Inventory holding cost | | $ 2,256 | $ 2,680 | $ 2,680 |
| Shortage cost | | 10,980 | | |
| Subcontracting cost | | | 94,080 | 42,720 |
| Regular time cost | 297,600 | 300,672 | 250,560 | 250,560 |
| Overtime cost | | | | 38,520 |
| Total cost | $318,400 | $313,908 | $347,320 | $334,480 |

TABLE 11.6
Summary—Costs for Four Aggregate Production Plans

Table 11.3 summarizes the costs associated with this aggregate production plan.

*Production Plan 3: Lower-level work force, use subcontracting.* This is one mixed strategy that the Forest Hills Tennis Racket Co. might use. It assumes that the company will use subcontracting whenever back orders occur and that subcontracting can provide all the units needed to satisfy the back order. This plan assumes that the company needs a constant but lower-level work force of thirty employees. Again, the planners use a beginning inventory backlog of one thousand units and permit inventory to accumulate. Table 11.4 summarizes the costs associated with this aggregate production plan.

*Production Plan 4: Lower-level work force, use overtime and subcontracting.* This is another mixed strategy that the Forest Hills Tennis Racket Co. might use. It assumes the company will use a combination of overtime and subcontracting to exactly meet the demand requirements. It will use overtime first, up to a maximum permissible level, which is computed as

Maximum permissible overtime hours per month = [16 Regular days × 1 Hour per day + 4 Saturdays × 8 Hours per day] × 30 Employees = 1,440 Hours    (11-3)

The company then uses subcontracting as needed to obtain additional units. This plan uses the constant but lower-level work force of thirty employees and the beginning backlog of one thousand units. Inventory can accumulate under this strategy. Table 11.5 summarizes the costs associated with this aggregate production plan.

The final step in the planning process is to summarize and compare the costs associated with the four plans, as in Table 11.6. Table 11.6 shows that the optimal (least costly) aggregate production plan uses the level strategy. Figure 11.6 shows the same four plans graphically, with cumulative production requirements plotted against cumulative production days. Note that aggregate plan 3, which uses subcontracting, and aggregate plan 4, which uses a combination of overtime and subcontracting, result in identical cumulative production.

Obviously, the company could consider many other feasible aggregate production plans. Evaluating each would require completion of tables such as those presented in this example. The company would make a final decision after evaluating a number of such plans. The trial-and-error method does not produce an optimal solution, but recent advances in computer technology and spreadsheet programs allow planners to quickly consider many alternatives. For this reason most aggregate production planning uses this approach.

## Mathematical Techniques

Since the 1950s scholars have proposed a variety of mathematical techniques for aggregate production planning.

**Linear Decision Rule**   One of the earliest mathematical approaches to aggregate production planning was the **linear decision rule**, developed by Charles Holt, Franco Modigliani, and Herbert Simon.[3] The linear decision rule model considers

[3]Charles C. Holt, Franco Modigliani, and Herbert Simon, "A Linear Decision Rule for Production Employment Scheduling," *Management Science* 2 (October 1955): 1–30.

FIGURE 11.6
Graphic Representation—
Four Aggregate Plans

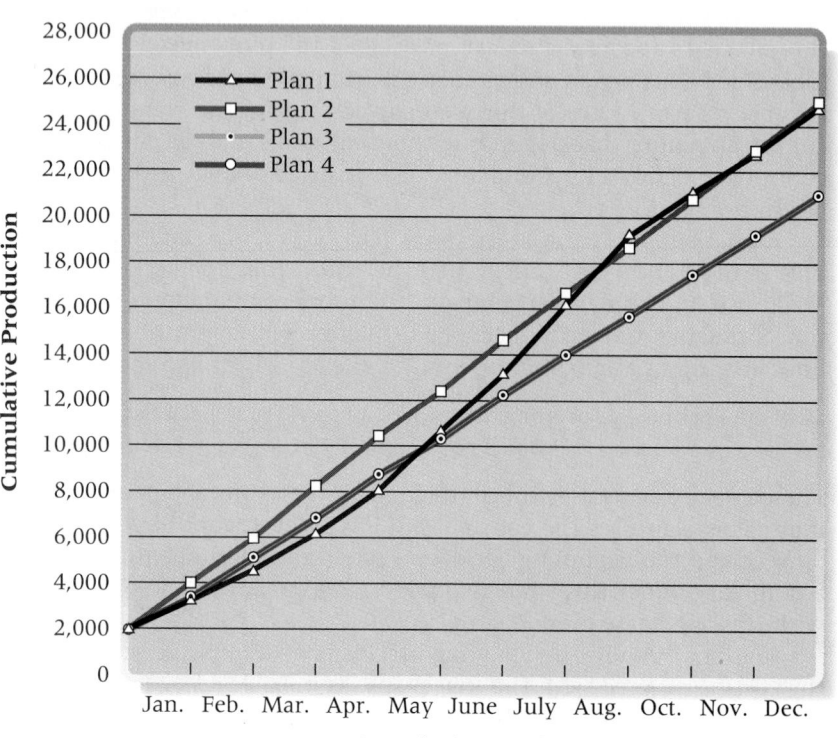

four cost elements: the regular payroll cost, hire/fire cost, overtime/undertime cost, and inventory/backlog cost. The regular payroll cost is expressed as a linear function of the number of workers employed. The other three costs are expressed as quadratic cost functions. The total cost is composed of these four elements and combines the linear and quadratic cost data. Using calculus can minimize the cost function. The result is two decision rules that specify the production output rate and the work force level in each month.

Holt, Modigliani, and Simon tested and implemented the linear decision rule at a paint factory. Although the factory used the rule to some extent, its greatest value perhaps lay in serving as a guideline for evaluating various plans and policies. The rule suffered from certain limitations, including difficulty in specifying and developing cost functions and the impracticality of the solutions it produced.

**Management Coefficient Model** In 1963 Edward H. Bowman proposed a heuristic model that used past management behavior to determine the appropriate coefficients of the production-level and work force decision rules. He suggested that the general production rule, expressed in equation 11-4, could set the production rate for any period.[4]

$$P_t = aW_{t-1} + bI_{t-1} + cF_{t+1} + K \qquad (11\text{-}4)$$

where

$$P_t = \text{The production rate for period t}$$
$$W_{t-1} = \text{The work force in the previous period}$$
$$I_{t-1} = \text{The ending inventory for the previous period}$$
$$F_{t+1} = \text{The forecast of demand for the next period}$$
$$a, b, c, K = \text{Constants}$$

Bowman gathered historical data for $P$, $W$, $I$, and $F$ and used regression analysis to determine values of $a$, $b$, $c$, and $K$. The result was a decision rule based on past managerial behavior that did not explicitly use cost functions. This so-called **management coefficients model** was a major departure from previous practices, which used cost information to make planning decisions.

Bowman compared the performance of the management coefficients model with the linear decision rule and actual practice at four companies. In three out of four cases the management coefficients model produced results superior to those made by the company. In two cases the results were also superior to those derived by the linear decision rule.

**Parametric Production Planning** C. H. Jones proposed another heuristic technique, called **parametric production planning**, in 1967.[5] It allowed the use of more general cost functions, and Jones developed two linear decision rules, for production output and work force size. Parametric production planning uses a grid search procedure to minimize the costs associated with these two linear decision rules. When tested against the linear decision rule method, the parametric production planning approach performed well.

[4]Edward H. Bowman, "Consistency and Optimality in Managerial Decision Making," *Management Science* 4 (January 1963): 100–103.
[5]C. H. Jones, "Parametric Production Planning," *Management Science* 13 (July 1967): 843–866.

**Search Decision Rule**  William H. Taubert developed a method called the **search decision rule** that did not restrict the mathematical form of the cost equations.[6] Taubert used the paint company problem to compare his search decision rule with the linear decision rule. He concluded that the results of the search decision rule were very close to those obtained by using the linear decision rule. In practice several companies have used the search decision rule method.

**Production-Switching Heuristic**  In 1978 Mellichamp and Love developed a **production-switching heuristic** that uses a rule with three levels—-low, medium, and high—of production (and work force).[7] As the name suggests, the procedure switches production from one level to another depending on sales forecasts and inventory. Minimizing some cost function by using a search procedure is the basis for determining the production levels at which switches are made. Using the production-switching heuristic tends to keep period-to-period production changes to a minimum, with significant changes in the work force only when the company reaches the switching points.

**Linear Programming (Simplex Method)**  An early study by Fred Hansmann and Sydney W. Hess used the **simplex method of linear programming** to include hirings and layoffs in aggregate production planning.[8] (Tutorial 3, the linear programming tutorial at the end of this book, discusses the simplex method in greater detail.)

Linear programming models for aggregate production planning attempt to find the optimal production plan for a linear objective function and a set of linear constraints. Example 11.2 illustrates the formulation of a linear programming model for a production-planning problem.

| |
|---|
| **EXAMPLE 11.2** |

You must plan production of a certain product and do not want to use back orders. Each worker can produce 10,000 units per month, working regular hours. You can use overtime production to supplement regular time production, but your company limits overtime to 10 percent of the regular time production in any month. The company also is willing to use subcontracting to supplement regular time production. For formulation purposes let

$D_t$ = (Known) demand in month $t_i$
$W_t$ = Number of employees available at start of month $t$
$H_t$ = Number of employees hired at start of month $t$
$F_t$ = Number of employees fired at start of month $t$
$I_t$ = Inventory level, in units, at end of month $t$
$S_t$ = Subcontracted production, in units, in month $t$
$O_t$ = Overtime production, in units, in month $t$

Your company always operates under the following constraints:

1.  Balance in inventory level:

[6]William H. Taubert, Jr., "A Search Decision Rule for the Aggregate Scheduling Problem," *Management Science* 14 (February 1968): B343–B359.
[7]Mellichamp and Love, "Production-Switching Heuristics," pp. 1242–1251.
[8]Fred Hansmann and Sydney W. Hess, "A Linear Programming Approach to Production and Employment Scheduling," *Management Technology* 1 (January 1960): 46–52.

Ending inventory, previous month + Current month's regular time
production + Current month's subcontracted production + Current
month's overtime production − Current month's demand =
Ending inventory, current month

$$I_{t-1} + 10,000\, W_t + S_t + O_t - D_t = I_t \qquad (11\text{-}5)$$

2. Balance in work force level:

Work force level, previous month + Workers hired, current month −
Workers fired, current month = Work force level, current month

$$W_{t-1} + H_t - F_t = W_t \qquad (11\text{-}6)$$

3. Limits to overtime production:

Overtime production, current month = 10%
(Current month's regular time production)

$$O_t = 0.10\,(10,000\, W_t) \qquad (11\text{-}7)$$

We can specify the objective function, for minimizing cost, as follows: Let

$C_w$ = Regular time wages, per worker, per month
$C_h$ = Cost of hiring one worker
$C_f$ = Cost of firing one worker
$C_i$ = Cost of holding one unit in inventory for one month
$C_s$ = Cost of subcontracting the production of one unit
$C_o$ = Cost of production for one unit using overtime

The objective function is

$$\text{Minimize } Z = \sum_{t=1}^{T} (C_w W_t + C_h H_t + C_f F_t + C_i I_t + C_s S_t + C_o O_t) \qquad (11\text{-}8)$$

*Total cost = Regular time production cost + Hiring cost + Firing cost + Inventory*
*holding cost + Subcontracting cost + Overtime production cost*

Under this formulation each month has six decision variables and three
constraints. If the planning horizon is, say, $T = 12$ months, your problem
formulation would require $12 \times 6 = 72$ decision variables and $12 \times 3 = 36$
constraints. Even for simple problems this approach requires a large number of variables and constraints, and computer software works out the solutions. The major drawbacks of the linear programming approach are that
all the relationships among the variables must be linear and the optimal
values of the decision variables (numbers of workers or production quantities) may be fractional.

**Linear Programming (Transportation Method)** Bowman published an early
aggregate production-planning study that used the **transportation method of
linear programming** to analyze the effects of holding inventory, back ordering,
using overtime, and using subcontracting.[9] (Tutorial 1 at the end of this book
discusses the transportation method in greater detail.) Using the transportation

[9]Edward H. Bowman, "Production Planning by the Transportation Method of Linear Programming,"
*Journal of the Operations Research Society* 4 (February 1956): 100–103.

method assumes that the production planner has a capacity plan that specifies the maximum capacities for regular time, overtime, and subcontractor production for each time period; a (known) demand forecast for each period; and a set of costs, all of which are linearly related to the production quantities.

**EXAMPLE 11.3**

The C.W. Crook Co. is attempting to prepare an aggregate production plan for a three-month period, during which it can use regular time, overtime, or subcontracting. It can also carry inventories and allow back orders. The company has collected the information shown in Table 11.7 as part of its planning process.

Table 11.8 presents the information from Table 11.7 in the form of a transportation tableau. This situation presents three monthly demand forecasts of 800, 1,000, and 1,000 units, and a goal—an ending inventory of 100 units. These amounts appear in the bottom row of the tableau. The beginning inventory is 500 units, and in each month 600, 100, and 150 units are available from regular time, overtime, and subcontracting, respectively. These amounts appear in the far right column of the tableau. The total capacity is 3,050 units, which is 150 units in excess of the total demand requirement of 2,900 units. These 150 units appear as unused capacity in the next to last column. The cost associated with each cell of the tableau appears in the small box in the upper right-hand corner. The inventory holding costs increase in increments of $1 for each period, moving from left to right across the tableau. The costs associated with producing in month 2 to satisfy demand in month 1, and producing in month 3 to satisfy demand in months 1 and 2, increase in increments of $4 (each month) to reflect back-ordering costs.

The circled numbers show the optimal solution for this particular transportation problem. The optimal aggregate production plan uses a combination of regular time production, overtime production, and subcontracting, as Table 11.8 shows. The minimum total cost for this plan is $143,250.

TABLE 11.7
C. W. Crook Co.—Aggregate
Planning Information

| | Month 1 | Month 2 | Month 3 | | |
|---|---|---|---|---|---|
| **Demand Forecast** | 800 | 1,000 | 1,000 | | |
| **Capacities:** | | | | **Costs:** | |
| *Regular Time* | 600 | 600 | 600 | *Regular Time Production* | $ 50/unit |
| *Overtime* | 100 | 100 | 100 | *Overtime Production* | $ 75/unit |
| *Subcontracting* | 150 | 150 | 150 | *Subcontracted Production* | $100/unit |
| | | | | *Inventory Carrying* | $ 1/unit/period |
| **Beginning Inventory** | 500 | | | *Back Order* | $ 4/unit/period |
| **Ending Inventory** | | | 100 | | |

**TABLE 11.8**
Aggregate Production Plan for the C. W. Crook Co. Determined by the Transportation Method

| Supply \ Demand | Month 1 | Month 2 | Month 3 | Ending Inventory | Unused Capacity | Total Capacity (Supply) |
|---|---|---|---|---|---|---|
| **Month** Beginning Inventory | 0 (500) | 1 | 2 | 3 | 0 | 500 |
| **1** Regular Time | 50 (300) | 51 (300) | 52 | 53 | 0 | 600 |
| **1** Overtime | 75 | 76 (100) | 77 | 78 | 0 | 100 |
| **1** Subcontracting | 100 | 101 | 102 | 103 | 0 (150) | 150 |
| **2** Regular Time | 54 | 50 (600) | 51 | 52 | 0 | 600 |
| **2** Overtime | 79 | 75 | 76 (100) | 77 | 0 | 100 |
| **2** Subcontracting | 104 | 100 (150) | 101 | 102 | 0 | 150 |
| **3** Regular Time | 58 | 54 | 50 (600) | 51 | 0 | 600 |
| **3** Overtime | 83 | 79 | 75 (100) | 76 | 0 | 100 |
| **3** Subcontracting | 108 | 104 | 100 (50) | 101 (100) | 0 | 150 |
| **Total Demand** | 800 | 1,000 | 1,000 | 100 | 150 | 3,050 |

Minimum Total Cost = $143,250

**Goal Programming** **Goal programming** is an extension of linear programming that attempts to find a satisfactory level of achievement for multiple objectives, or goals, rather than an optimal outcome for a single objective (which is what linear programming yields). Researchers have reported several applications of goal programming to aggregate production planning.[10]

**Mixed Integer Programming** **Mixed integer programming** is a method for determining optimal aggregate production plans that overcomes some of the limitations imposed by the assumptions used in linear programming. It also allows planners to prepare aggregate production plans for a product family or simply a more detailed plan. Chen Chung and Lee Krajewski developed one such

[10]Richard Deckro and John Hebert, "Goal Programming Approaches to Solving Linear Decision Rule-Based Aggregate Production Planning Models," *IIE Transactions* 16 (December 1984): 308–315; D. A. Goodman, "A Goal Programming Approach to Aggregate Planning of Production and Workforce," *Management Science* 20 (August 1974): 1569–1575; and Sang M. Lee and Laurence J. Moore, "A Practical Approach to Production Scheduling," *Production and Inventory Management* 15 (First quarter 1974): 79–92.

mixed integer programming model for companies that use a make-to-stock competitive strategy for dealing with a seasonal demand for their products.[11] Their study shows that a company's cost structure does affect the appropriate planning period for aggregate planning.

**Simulation Models**    Over the years researchers have developed and used many **simulation models** for aggregate production planning. One early example was the work of Roger Vergin, who used simulation to select the parameters for aggregate production-planning rules.[12] The production planner can use a simulation model to evaluate a variety of cost structures and decision rules. However, simulation models do not always produce optimal solutions, and they may be costly to develop and use. (Tutorial 4, the simulation tutorial at the end of this book, discusses simulation models in greater detail.)

## Summary of Aggregate Production-Planning Methods

In the preceding material we have reviewed a number of aggregate production-planning methods that range from simple charting or graphing procedures to such complicated approaches as mixed integer programming.

[11]Chen Chung and Lee J. Krajewski, "Planning Horizons for Master Production Scheduling," *Journal of Operations Management* 4 (August 1984): 389–406.
[12]Roger C. Vergin, "Production Scheduling Under Seasonal Demand, *Journal of Industrial Engineering* 17 (May 1966): 10–19.

*Candy bars move along the production line at a Cadbury-Schweppes facility in the United Kingdom, where aggregate planning is used to minimize the number of production workers.*

What does a company really do when it faces an array of aggregate production-planning methods? Most companies probably begin by using simple charting or graphing procedures and then move into spreadsheet models. But with the acceptance of computers and modeling approaches in general, companies are making greater use of the mathematical techniques, most commonly linear programming. The answer to the question ultimately is a function of the company's attitude about the value of mathematical modeling in making decisions. Companies that have invested heavily in computer and modeling technology use one or more mathematical techniques to do aggregate planning. Those that have not still use trial-and-error methods and spreadsheet models.

Table 11.9 summarizes the aggregate production-planning methods we have discussed.

TABLE 11.9
Summary—Aggregate Production-Planning Methods

| Technique | Solution Approach | Assumptions | Major Characteristics |
|---|---|---|---|
| 1. Chart/Graphic | Trial and error | None | Produces good but not optimal solution; easy to understand; follows simple logic |
| 2. Linear programming transportation method | Optimizing | Linearity, constant work force | Produces an optimal solution; used when hiring/firing costs are not a consideration |
| 3. Linear programming Simplex method | Optimizing | Linearity | Produces an optimal solution; useful for the general case |
| 4. Linear decision rule | Optimizing | Quadratic cost function | Complex; model is difficult to formulate, and relative cost information may be hard to determine; does produce an optimal decision |
| 5. Management coefficients | Heuristic | Good information is available from managers | Uses multiple regression of previous managerial decisions to make future decision; does not produce an optimal decision |
| 6. Parametric production planning | Heuristic | Linear decision rules | Uses a search procedure to develop decision rules; does not produce an optimal |
| 7. Search decision rule | Heuristic | Any type of cost function | Uses a pattern search procedure to obtain a local minimum of the cost function |
| 8. Goal programming | Optimizing/ Satisficing | Linearity | Allows the consideration of multiple goals in planning; does produce an optimal solution, but this solution may only satisfy goals |
| 9. Production-switching heuristic | Heuristic | Period-to-period production changes should be avoided | Use of three levels for production and work force; does not produce an optimal solution |
| 10. Simulation | Evaluation of many alternatives | None | Very flexible procedure; usually done on a computer to facilitate computations and testing of alternatives; does not produce an optimal solution |
| 11. Mixed integer | Optimizing | Linearity/ nonlinearity | Complex modeling technique; allows for programming consideration of broader problems; does produce an optimal solution |

TABLE 11.10
Annual Profit
Performance—Aggregate
Production-Planning Model

| Aggregate Planning Model | Annual Profit |
|---|---|
| Existing company procedure | $4,420,000 |
| Management coefficients | 4,607,000 |
| Linear decision rule | 4,821,000 |
| Parametric production planning | 4,900,000 |
| Search decision rule | 5,021,000 |

W. B. Lee and B. M. Khumawala did a comparative study of aggregate production-planning techniques.[13] They compared four of the mathematical techniques we have described with the approach to aggregate production planning used by a manufacturing company with an annual sales volume of $11 million. They developed a simulation model of this company's production process and used it to compare the various aggregate planning techniques. Table 11.10 provides the results of their study. As you can see, each of the mathematical techniques performed better than the procedure the company had been using. Overall, the search decision rule method provided the greatest improvement in profit ($601,000, or 14 percent).

Frank L. DuBois and Michael D. Oliff surveyed and reported on the aggregate planning procedures being used by fifty-five U.S. manufacturing companies.[14] They observed that few manufacturers were using the more sophisticated aggregate production-planning models reported in the literature. However, DuBois and Oliff found that more than half (54 percent) of the responding companies were using computer-based aggregate production-planning methods. They concluded that the manufacturers were using relatively simple techniques mostly because they did not have explicit cost data.

Global Operations Management 11.2 discusses a survey of aggregate planning at manufacturers in the United Kingdom.

## Aggregate Planning in Service Companies

Aggregate planning is also important for service companies. Service companies do not produce inventories; they typically make to order rather than make to stock. For service companies aggregate planning results in staffing plans that call for changing the numbers of employees or using subcontracting.

**EXAMPLE 11.4**

C.W. Jones Hauling Services provides a trash-hauling service for Lexington County, South Carolina. The company removes household trash and garbage, as well as grass clippings, small branches, and leaves.

C.W. Jones Hauling has traditionally tried to maintain a stable work force of 400 employees, who pick up 20,000 tons of trash in an average month. Their yearly average is 240,000 tons.

[13]W. B. Lee and B. M. Khumawala, "Simulation Testing of Aggregate Production Planning Models in an Implementation Methodology," *Management Science* 20 (February 1974): 903–911.
[14]Frank L. DuBois and Michael D. Oliff, "Aggregate Production Planning in Practice," *Production and Inventory Management Journal* – (Third quarter 1991): 266–273.

## GLOBAL OPERATIONS MANAGEMENT 11.2

# Aggregate Planning in U.K. Manufacturing Companies

A survey of four hundred manufacturing companies in the United Kingdom indicated that in practice companies often do not perform aggregate planning in the manner prescribed in textbooks. The survey suggested that most aggregate planning approaches lack the scope to accommodate real planning situations and that aggregate planning is influenced by much more than just production considerations.

The vast majority of the respondents said they used empirical data as well as subjective information in aggregate planning. Although most companies said they used quantitative approaches, nearly one-third used more intuitive approaches. More than 70 percent of the companies frequently used computers to develop their aggregate production plans, and about half were using computers and quantitative approaches in their aggregate planning efforts. The survey determined that aggregate planning is the result of influences from many areas of a company. The production function is more concerned than marketing or finance with planning and controlling production and work force levels and with production and labor costs. Both production and finance exert considerable influence in regard to inventory costs.

When faced with increasing demand, the manufacturers responded by (in order of priority)

1. Working overtime
2. Depleting inventories
3. Adding personnel
4. Increasing backlogs

In the face of decreasing demand, the manufacturers responded by (in order of priority)

1. Reducing backlogs
2. Building inventories
3. Reducing work hours
4. Laying off personnel

Most companies said they adhered to their priorities.

The survey concluded that companies still need more realistic aggregate planning systems that truly reflect the interests of managers and reflect various functions and product goals. Such systems would provide a more strategic approach to aggregate planning.

---

Jones Hauling would like to prepare a staffing plan for the coming year. To do so it has prepared a forecast of trash demand, by month, for the next twelve months. Table 11.11a shows the demand information and summarizes the working days available in each month. Table 11.11b shows the relevant cost information. To visualize its staffing plan problem the company has also plotted its monthly demand forecast against its regular time capacity for four hundred employees, as shown in

TABLE 11.11
Staffing Plan
Information—C. W. Jones
Hauling Services

**(a) Demand**

| Month | Trash Demand Forecast (tons) | Number of Working Working Days in Month |
|---|---|---|
| January | 22,000 | 23 |
| February | 18,000 | 20 |
| March | 20,000 | 21 |
| April | 23,000 | 22 |
| May | 24,000 | 23 |
| June | 25,000 | 20 |
| July | 25,000 | 23 |
| August | 24,000 | 22 |
| September | 22,000 | 21 |
| October | 20,000 | 23 |
| November | 19,000 | 21 |
| December | 18,000 | 22 |
| Total | 260,000 | 261 |

**(b) Cost Information**

| | |
|---|---|
| Regular time cost | $6/hour |
| Overtime cost | $ 9/hour |
| Hiring/firing cost | $100/employee |
| Subcontracting cost | $30/ton |

Figure 11.7. The monthly demand forecast is the same as that presented in Table 11.11a. The company can compute its actual monthly capacity by multiplying the number of working days per month by the number of employees and by the average daily capacity of each employee. The average daily capacity per employee is

$$\text{Average daily capacity per employee} = \frac{\text{Total yearly capacity}}{\text{Total yearly working days}} \div 400 \text{ employees}$$

$$= \frac{20,000 \text{ tons per month} \times 12 \text{ months per year}}{261 \text{ Days}}$$

$$\div 400 \text{ employees}$$

$$= 2.30 \text{ tons per day per employee} \qquad (11\text{-}9)$$

For example, the monthly capacity for January is

$$\text{Monthly capacity (January)} = 23 \text{ Working days} \times 400 \text{ Employees} \times$$
$$2.30 \text{ Tons per day per employee}$$
$$= 21,160 \text{ Tons} \qquad (11\text{-}10)$$

The company is evaluating two staffing plans. It would like to minimize the overall cost of its trash-hauling service while maintaining effective and efficient service for its customers. Because of the latter factor, both staffing plans use a chase strategy.

*Staffing Plan 1: Use overtime (only) in any month that has a capacity backlog.* This is a pure chase strategy—Jones Hauling will use overtime only during

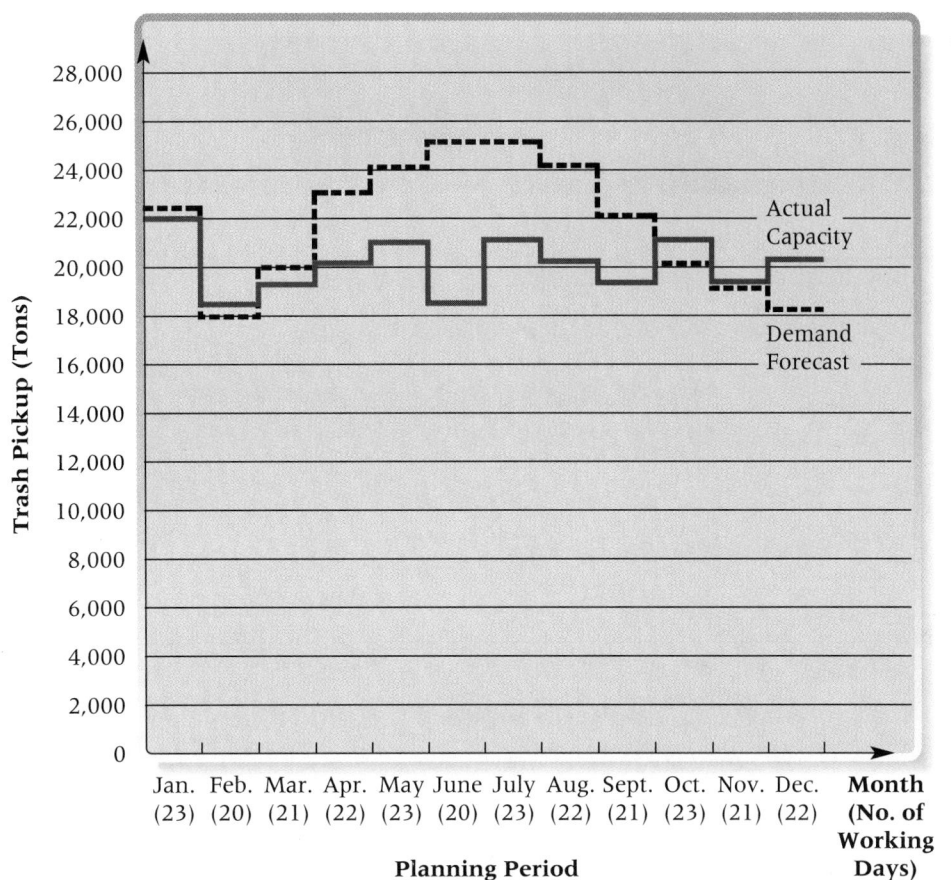

F I G U R E   1 1 . 7
Demand Forecast Versus
Actual Capacity—C. W. Jones
Hauling Services

a month for which the demand forecast exceeds available capacity. Table 11.12 summarizes the costs associated with this staffing plan.

*Staffing Plan 2. Hire an additional forty workers for April through September; use subcontracting for remaining backlogs.* This is another pure chase strategy; it uses both additional workers and subcontracting. Table 11.13 summarizes the costs associated with this staffing plan. For minimizing costs plan 2 is preferable to plan 1. Both plans provide the capacity necessary to meet the demand forecast for each month of the planning period. Both plans also provide for excess capacity in four months. In this service situation excess capacity cannot be inventoried and cannot be avoided. The total cost for plan 2 assumes that any equipment required for the additional forty employees (April through September) will not mean additional costs. If, for example, Jones had to rent or buy more trash-hauling trucks, the plan would have to include that cost.

Operations Management in Practice 11.3 reviews the development of a staffing plan for a public safety department merger in Grosse Pointe Park, Michigan.

| (1) Month | (2) Trash Demand Forecast (tons) | (3) Working Days per Month | (4) Number Employees | (5) Pickup Capacity (col. 3 × col. 4 × 2.30) | (6) Backlog/Excess Capacity (col. 5 − col.2) |
|---|---|---|---|---|---|
| January | 22,000 | 23 | 400 | 21,160 | −840 |
| February | 18,000 | 20 | 400 | 18,400 | 400 |
| March | 20,000 | 21 | 400 | 19,320 | −680 |
| April | 23,000 | 22 | 400 | 20,240 | −2,760 |
| May | 24,000 | 23 | 400 | 21,160 | −2,840 |
| June | 25,000 | 20 | 400 | 18,400 | −6,600 |
| July | 25,000 | 23 | 400 | 21,160 | −3,840 |
| August | 24,000 | 22 | 400 | 20,240 | −3,760 |
| September | 22,000 | 21 | 400 | 19,320 | −2,680 |
| October | 20,000 | 23 | 400 | 21,160 | 1,160 |
| November | 19,000 | 21 | 400 | 19,320 | 320 |
| December | 18,000 | 22 | 400 | 20,240 | 2,240 |
| Totals | 260,000 | 261 | | 240,120 | |

| (1) Month | (7) Backlog in Days (col. 6/919.5) | (8) Regular Time Cost (col. 3 × col. 4 × 8 × $6) | (9) Overtime Cost (400 × col.8 × 8 × $9) | (10) Total Cost (col. 9 + col. 10) |
|---|---|---|---|---|
| January | 1 | $  441,600 | $ 28,800 | $  470,400 |
| February | 0 | 384,000 | 0 | 384,000 |
| March | 1 | 403,200 | 28,800 | 432,000 |
| April | 3 | 422,400 | 86,400 | 508,800 |
| May | 3 | 441,600 | 86,400 | 528,000 |
| June | 7 | 384,000 | 201,600 | 585,600 |
| July | 4 | 441,600 | 115,200 | 556,800 |
| August | 4 | 422,400 | 115,200 | 537,600 |
| September | 3 | 403,200 | 86,400 | 489,600 |
| October | 0 | 441,600 | 0 | 441,600 |
| November | 0 | 403,200 | 0 | 403,200 |
| December | 0 | 422,400 | 0 | 422,400 |
| Totals | | $5,011,200 | $748,800 | $5,760,000 |

TABLE 11.12
Plan 1: Use Overtime (Only)
in Months That Have a
Capacity Backlog

| (1)<br>Month | (2)<br>Trash Demand<br>Forecast<br>(tons) | (3)<br>Working Days<br>per Month | (4)<br>Number<br>Employees | (5)<br>Pickup<br>Capacity<br>(tons<br>(col. 3 × col. 4<br>× 2.30) | (6)<br>Backlog/Excess<br>Capacity<br>(col. 5 − col. 2) |
|---|---|---|---|---|---|
| January | 22,000 | 23 | 400 | 21,160 | −840 |
| February | 18,000 | 20 | 400 | 18,400 | 400 |
| March | 20,000 | 21 | 400 | 19,320 | −680 |
| April | 23,000 | 22 | 400 | 22,264 | −736 |
| May | 24,000 | 23 | 400 | 23,276 | −724 |
| June | 25,000 | 20 | 400 | 20,240 | −4,760 |
| July | 25,000 | 23 | 400 | 23,276 | −1,724 |
| August | 24,000 | 22 | 400 | 22,264 | −1736 |
| September | 22,000 | 21 | 400 | 21,252 | −748 |
| October | 20,000 | 23 | 400 | 21,160 | 1,160 |
| November | 19,000 | 21 | 400 | 19,320 | 320 |
| December | 18,000 | 22 | 400 | 20,240 | 2,240 |
| Totals | 260,000 | 261 | | 252,172 | |

| (1)<br>Month | (7)<br>Regular<br>Time Cost<br>(col. 3 × col.4<br>× 8 × $6) | (8)<br>Subcontracting<br>Cost<br>(col. 6 × $30) | (9)<br>Hire/Layoff<br>Cost<br>(40 × $100) | (10)<br>Total Cost<br>(col. 7 + col. 8<br>+ col. 9 + col.10) |
|---|---|---|---|---|
| January | $  441,600 | $ 25,200 | $ | $  466,800 |
| February | 384,000 | 0 | | 384,000 |
| March | 403,200 | 20,400 | | 423,600 |
| April | 464,640 | 22,080 | 4,000 | 490,720 |
| May | 485,760 | 21,720 | | 507,480 |
| June | 422,400 | 142,800 | | 565,200 |
| July | 485,760 | 51,720 | | 537,480 |
| August | 464,640 | 52,080 | | 516,720 |
| September | 443,520 | 22,440 | | 465,960 |
| October | 441,600 | 0 | 4,000 | 445,600 |
| November | 403,200 | 0 | | 403,200 |
| December | 422,400 | 0 | | 422,400 |
| Totals | $5,262,720 | $358,440 | $8,000 | $5,629,160 |

TABLE 11.13
Plan 2: Hire 40 Additional
Workers April Through
September, Use
Subcontracting for
Remaining Backlogs

# Developing a Staffing Plan for a Public Safety Department Merger

The City of Grosse Pointe Park, Michigan, covers a twenty-two-square mile area northeast of Detroit. In 1986 it had a population of 13,600 people. Its police department consisted of thirty sworn officers, and the fire department, which also provided emergency medical and ambulance service, had nineteen fire fighters and officers. The 1986 budgets were $1.5 million for police and $800,000 for fire, out of a total city budget of $4.8 million.

For several years city officials had discussed the possibility of merging its police department and fire departments. Almost all personnel would be trained as both police officers and fire fighters, and many also would be trained as emergency medical technicians. In January 1985 a city commission reported in favor of a merger by a vote of 11 to 2. By January 1986 the new, innovative police chief had developed a detailed plan for implementing the merger. At this point city officials hired an independent expert to review and evaluate the chief's merger plan.

The premerger fire department of nineteen employees (including the chief), used five employees (three fire fighters, a sergeant, and a lieutenant) to staff the fire station twenty-four hours a day, seven days a week. (The work schedule was twenty-four hours on duty and forty-eight hours off duty.) Most fire personnel were certified as basic emergency medical technicians (EMTs), and the schedule called for a minimum of three EMTs on duty. They were stationed at the city's only fire station, next door to police headquarters.

The police department had thirty officers, and their deployment varied by time of day. On average the department deployed slightly fewer than four patrol cars (in addition to supervisors) and averaged 4.5 officers on the road at any time.

The proposed merger called for reducing the fire department staff of nineteen to nine first-level fire fighters assigned to the fire station. Fire personnel who chose not to assume the additional police role would fill most of these positions, and they would be paid according to the current fire department salary scale. Average fire station staffing would be three fire fighters on station duty at a time (twenty-four hours on duty followed by forty-eight hours off duty). Officers trained in police and fire procedures would cover vacations and sick days.

The merger plan called for using the ten-person reduction in the fire service to fund one additional position in the detective bureau and to assign five more people to patrol-related activities. The five additions would staff one patrol car around the clock.

The merger plan was, in effect, a staffing plan that encompassed both the fire and police departments. The new public safety department would have forty-five employees instead of the forty-nine employed by the two existing departments. The consultant used simulation and waiting line analysis to evaluate response times that would result from the merger plan.

The major findings with regard to fire and emergency medical services were as follows:

■ Fire and emergency medical services were responding to fire and medical emergencies in an average of 2.2 minutes.
■ The merger would mean that the first trained person would arrive at the scene an average of 1.2 minutes faster.

■ Eighty-five percent of the time the first unit at the scene would be a patrol unit.

■ Fire department personnel were averaging thirty-three minutes a day on calls for service, or 2.3 percent of their time.

■ Three (or four) patrol units would be tied up for more than forty-five minutes at the scene of an emergency on an average of once a month.

The major findings with regard to police services were as follows:

■ The police service's average response time was unusually fast, only 1.2 minutes for crimes reported in progress.

■ A merger would reduce police response time by 10 percent.

■ Patrol units were busy with high-priority, uninterruptible calls less than 4 percent of the time.

■ A merger could increase crime prevention activities by 20 percent (by adding patrol personnel).

■ A merger would increase the number of detectives from three to four immediately.

The major findings with regard to cost were as follows:

■ A merger would save an estimated $110,000 per year, excluding increased pay for public safety officers.

■ Each 1 percent increase in salary would reduce the savings by $15,000 (a 7 percent pay raise would consume all projected savings).

The city held a referendum on the proposed merger on June 16, 1986, and voters approved the merger plan. Two years later the city had trained all thirty police officers as fire fighters, and eleven of them also had completed training as emergency medical technicians. Half the fire fighters had cross-trained as police officers; nine others had decided to remain on fire station assignment exclusively. The city had reduced its fire station staffing to three and adjusted its dispatch strategy.

# Implementing Aggregate Production Plans—Managerial Issues

Once a company has finished its aggregate production plan, it has to implement it. Using an aggregate production plan involves breaking it up (disaggregating it) into specific product requirements. In this chapter we have stressed the idea that the best intermediate-term planning works with aggregate units. But when the aggregate production plan goes into effect, the company has to state its production schedules in terms of units of specific products or services.

For example, consider the situation of the Forest Hills Tennis Racket Co. presented in Example 11.1. The aggregate production plan for this company calls for the production of one thousand to three thousand tennis rackets during each month of a twelve-month plan. Of course, the company would be producing several types and models of tennis rackets. Although the rackets would require similar processes for fabrication and assembly, the operations, parts, and materials would vary by type and model. So the company must translate the aggregate amounts of tennis rackets to be produced during the twelve months into specific numbers of tennis rackets by type and model. This must be done so that the company can purchase appropriate materials and parts, schedule production operations, and specify inventory requirements.

Figure 11.2 showed that the result of disaggregating the aggregate production plan is the master production schedule. It serves as the basis for short-range planning and covers only a portion of the time period encompassed by the aggregate production plan. It is also subject to constant updating, as the aggregate production plan is disaggregated and as actual production occurs and inventories and demand fluctuate.

Several managerial issues are involved in aggregate production planning:

1. Each company must tailor its aggregate production planning to its particular situation. A model or technique that works well for one company may not work well for another. This means that companies will continue to have many aggregate production-planning methods from which to choose.
2. Union contracts or a policy that seeks to maintain a level work force may highly constrain aggregate production planning at some companies. In such situations aggregate production planning will provide for a review of such policies or contracts.
3. Companies are likely to have to balance the use of mathematical techniques for aggregate production planning with managerial judgment and experience. Before a company accepts the results from a mathematical model, it should compare the results to past managerial performance.
4. Some companies tend to blur the distinction between production planning and production scheduling. Scheduling changes can mean that decisions affecting work force levels, production requirements, and inventories are made on a week-to-week basis. In this situation management has to perceive that an aggregate planning problem does exist and make the necessary commitment to create a separate aggregate planning function.

# Hierarchical Production Planning

Earlier in this chapter we examined production-planning activities by looking at the time frames for such decisions. Another approach to analyzing aggregate capacity incorporates a philosophy of matching product aggregations to decision-making levels in the organization. **Hierarchical production planning (HPP)** is the term used to describe the process of tailoring the planning structure to the organization. HPP uses a series of mathematical models and follows organizational lines, with managerial participation at each stage. Figure 11.8 presents a framework for HPP.

As Figure 11.8 shows, top-level decisions use aggregate, whereas low-level, or shop-floor, decisions use more detailed data. The planning process first involves specifying which products to produce in which factories. To facilitate this aggregation the planner combines products in logical family groupings and assigns factories according to capital investment costs, manufacturing costs, and transportation costs.

The company then incorporates management's thinking in the plan and makes aggregate production plans for each plant. We discussed specific procedures for aggregate planning earlier in this chapter. The aggregate plan specifies

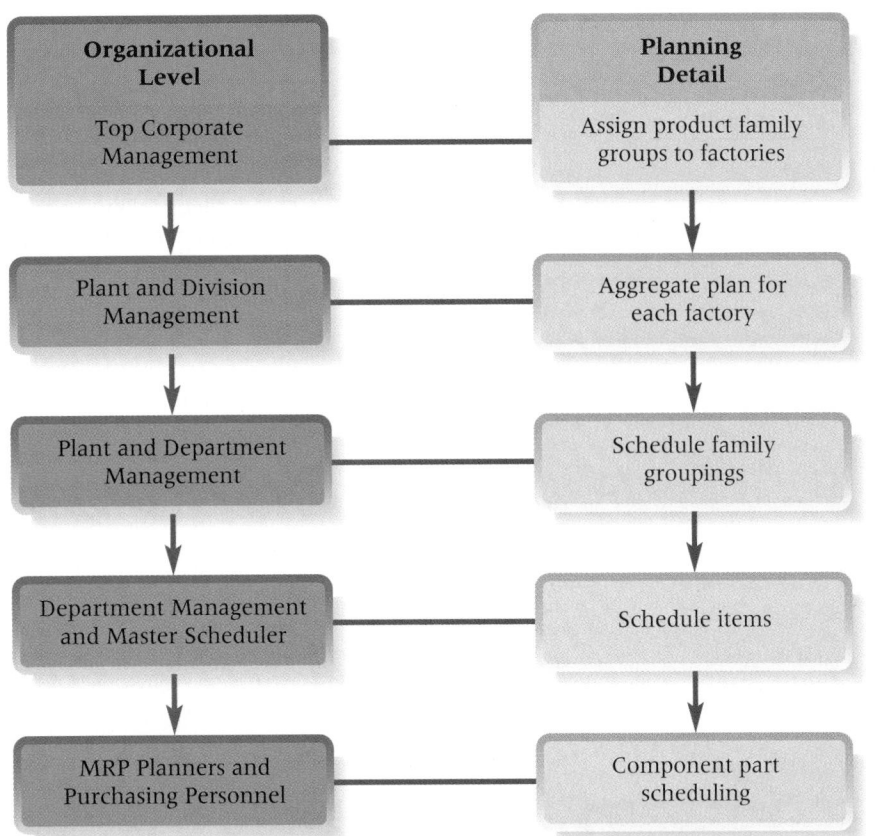

| Organizational Level | | Planning Detail |
|---|---|---|
| **Top Corporate Management** | — | Assign product family groups to factories |
| ↓ | | ↓ |
| Plant and Division Management | — | Aggregate plan for each factory |
| ↓ | | ↓ |
| Plant and Department Management | — | Schedule family groupings |
| ↓ | | ↓ |
| Department Management and Master Scheduler | — | Schedule items |
| ↓ | | ↓ |
| MRP Planners and Purchasing Personnel | — | Component part scheduling |

FIGURE 11.8
A Hierarchical Production-Planning Framework

Source: Thomas E. Vollman, William L. Berry and D. Clay Whybark, *Manufacturing Planning and Control Systems* (Homewood, Ill.: Richard D. Irwin, 1992), p. 631, as adapted from Gabriel D. Bitran, Elizabeth A. Haas, and Arnoldo C. Hax, "Hierarchical Production Planning: A Two-Stage System," *Operations Research* 30, vol.2 (March–April 1982): 232–251.

*Developing a staffing plan for a large service company, such as UPS, is a very complex task.*

FIGURE 11.9
Examples—Hierarchical
Production-Planning Process

Source: Harlan C. Meal, "Putting
Production Decisions Where They
Belong," *Harvard Business Review* 62
(March–April 1984): 101.

FIGURE 11.10
Hierarchical Production-
Planning Characteristics and
Constraints

Source: Harlan C. Meal, "Putting
Production Decisions Where They
Belong," *Harvard Business Review* 62
(March–April 1984): 106.

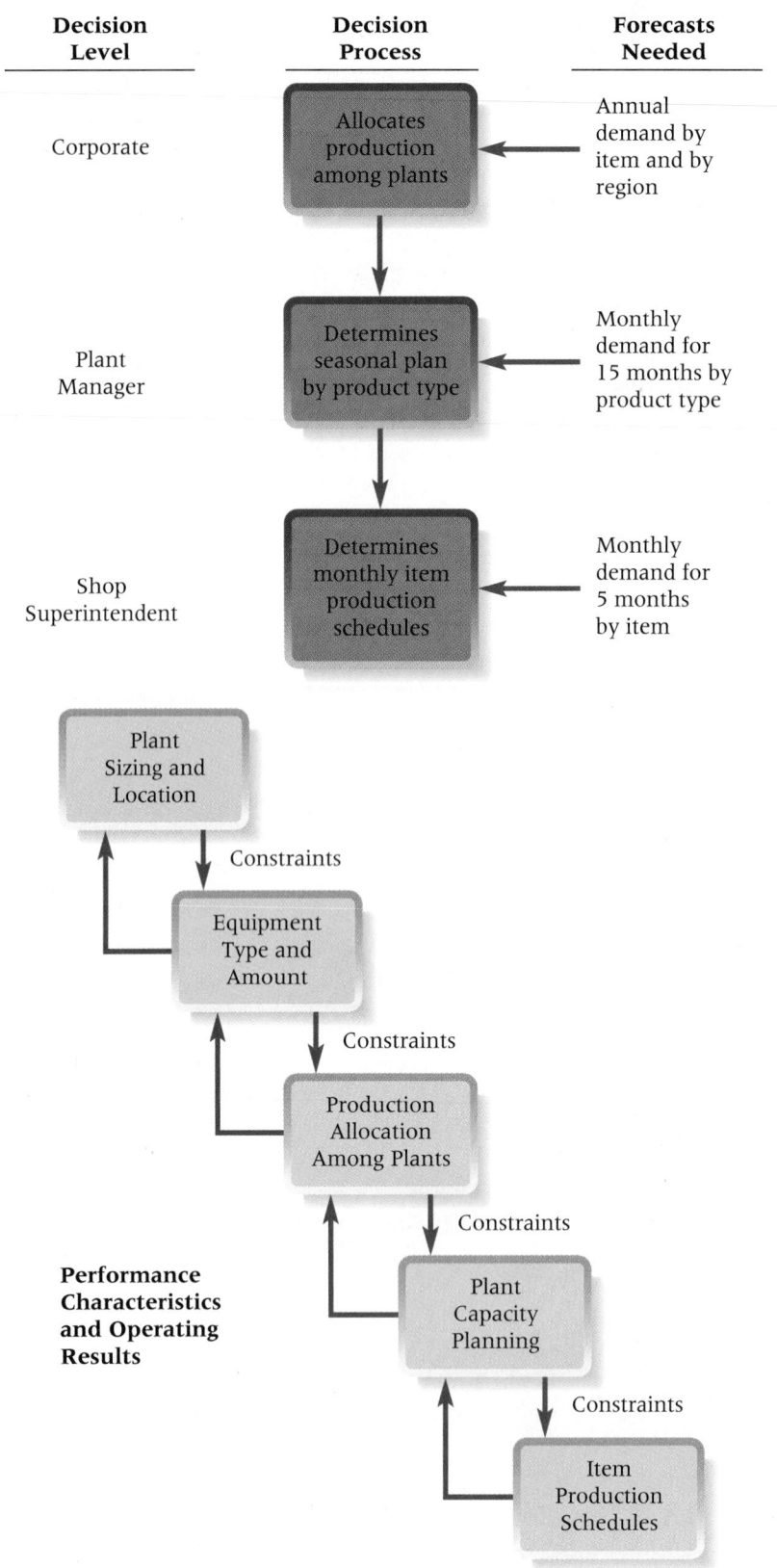

production levels, inventory levels, production schedules, overtime, and so forth for the plant, and the plant is constrained by the specific products and volumes assigned to it. The next step involves scheduling the family groupings within the factory, subject to existing inventories and constraints imposed by the aggregate production plan. Next scheduled are individual items, a process analogous to making a master production schedule (MPS). The MPS is constrained by the previously scheduled family groupings. The final step is scheduling detailed parts and components by using the logic of material requirements planning (MRP).

Figure 11.9 presents three specific examples within an HPP system and shows the decision processes used and the forecasts needed.

Figure 11.10 shows some additional characteristics typically found in HPP systems and the constraints present at successive levels.

The major principle of HPP is that disaggregation should follow organizational lines. A related principle is that only information that is appropriate should be provided at each aggregation level. So we would not provide detailed parts information to the top corporate management group that is assigning product family groups to factories. A final related principle is that the only schedule necessary is for the lead time needed to change decisions. This means that the company can make detailed plans for periods as short as the manufacturing lead times. A major advantage of hierarchical production planning is that each successive level has a simpler structure and less data and can be analyzed by using the simpler models.

Operations Management in Practice 11.4 shows how Owens-Corning Fiberglas handles hierarchical production planning.

# Improved Hier- archical Production Planning at Owens- Corning Fiberglas

In 1982 Owens-Corning Fiberglas (OCF) implemented a hierarchical model at its Anderson, South Carolina, plant to make production scheduling decisions at three distinct levels—aggregate production planning, disaggregate production planning, and job scheduling.

The Anderson plant produces a fiberglass mat used in the marine products industry for constructing boat hulls, as reinforcement in pipeline construction, and in bathtubs and showers. It sells in a variety of widths and lengths, is treated with one of three process binders, and is often trimmed on one or both edges. The entire product line has more than two hundred distinct mat items. Thirty of these represent about 80 percent of total annual demand and are categorized as high-volume standard products. The remaining 20 percent are low-volume specialty products. The production process for fiberglass mat consists of two high-volume, parallel batch production lines that have different capacities. Line 1 produces mats up to seventy-six inches wide; line 2 is limited to materials of sixty-inch width. Line 1 is about three times a fast as line 2. During a typical year overall demand exceeds capacity for about six months.

Since 1982 OCF has seen major advances in manufacturing and information systems and drastic changes in corporate organization and infrastructures. Processing capacities have improved to allow high-volume production of item groups instead of single products. Bigger computers are handling work for single users and networks. Partly in response to a 1986 takeover bid by Wickes Lumber, the company reorganized management and decentralized both the customer service and information management functions.

In response to these developments the company developed a computer-based hierarchical production-planning system. The improved hierarchical production-planning model consists of four modules: aggregate forecasting, aggregate production planning, disaggregate production planning (DPP), and sequencing (heuristic). The system determines

Monthly aggregate demand forecasts for twelve months, individual product forecasts for some thirty high-volume items for three months, and quarterly forecasts for the remaining 170 low-volume products
An aggregate production plan that reflects the pertinent costs for work force, inventory, and overtime
Production lot sizes and line assignments for multiple product groups, inventory for each standard product, and explicit feedback goals regarding actual line use and master schedule feasibility
Specific product sequences for standard and special orders and items in the format of coordinated production groups

Table 11.14 shows a typical aggregate production plan generated by using the production-switching rule. The aggregate production plan specifies the monthly shift settings for the two production lines, the projected monthly aggregate ending inventories, inventory cost, labor cost, hiring/firing costs, and total costs. For example, a shift setting of (4,2) implies that line 1 is operating on four shifts and line 2 is operating on two shifts.

Beginning Inventory          184
Beginning Shift Settings     (3.0)

| Shift Settings | Beginning Inventory | Production | Actual Sales | Ending Inventory | Inventory Cost | Labor Cost | Hiring Cost | Layoff Cost |
|---|---|---|---|---|---|---|---|---|
| (3,0) | 184 | 100 | 132 | 152 | $20,400 | $ 90,000 | $      0 | $    0 |
| (4,0) | 152 | 140 | 124 | 168 | 23,600 | 120,000 | 12,000 | 0 |
| (4,0) | 168 | 140 | 155 | 153 | 20,600 | 120,000 | 0 | 0 |
| (4,1) | 153 | 155 | 187 | 121 | 14,200 | 130,000 | 7,000 | 0 |
| (4,2) | 121 | 170 | 174 | 117 | 13,400 | 140,000 | 7,000 | 0 |
| (4,2) | 117 | 170 | 194 | 93 | 9,300 | 140,000 | 0 | 0 |
| (4,2) | 93 | 170 | 169 | 94 | 9,400 | 140,000 | 0 | 0 |
| (4,1) | 94 | 155 | 132 | 117 | 13,400 | 130,000 | 0 | 3,000 |
| (4,1) | 117 | 155 | 151 | 121 | 14,200 | 130,000 | 0 | 0 |
| (4,1) | 121 | 155 | 167 | 109 | 11,800 | 130,000 | 0 | 0 |
| (4,0) | 109 | 140 | 97 | 152 | 20,400 | 120,000 | 0 | 3,000 |
| (4,0) | 152 | 140 | 140 | 152 | 20,400 | 120,000 | 0 | 0 |

Total inventory costs            $   191,100
Total labor costs                $1,510,000
Total hiring costs               $    26,000
Total layoff costs               $     6,000

Total costs                      $1,733,100

Lower inventory target = 120

Upper inventory target = 150

Minimum monthly aggregate inventory > 90

NOTE: Values for inventory, production, and sales are in 10,000 pounds.

Source: G. Keong Leong, Michael D. Oliff, and Robert E. Markland, "Improved Hierarchical Production Planning," *Journal of Operations Management* 8 (April 1989): 100.

TABLE 11.14
Minimum Cost Aggregate Production Plan Using Actual Sales (with Inventory Restrictions)

# ► Summary

Aggregate production planning establishes work force levels, production requirements, and inventory levels for medium-range plans. It links long-range corporate planning for facilities with short-range operations scheduling. A demand forecast initiates it, and it concludes with disaggregation into the master production schedule.

**Learning Objective 1: Position aggregate production planning within the capacity decision hierarchy of the company.** Aggregate production planning is medium-term capacity planning that typically encompasses a time period of two to eighteen months. Aggregate planning links facilities planning from above with scheduling below.

**Learning Objective 2: Discuss the concept of aggregation.** *Aggregation* refers to the idea of focusing on overall capacity rather than individual products or services. The most common type of aggregation is by product—products that are manufactured similarly and have common labor and material requirements are grouped into families. Another common type of aggregation is by labor, aggregating the work force by product family or specific plants devoted to a product family. A third type of aggregation is by time; the usual aggregate planning time period is about one year.

**Learning Objective 3: Describe production-planning activities at various levels and over various time periods.** Long-range planning, for one to five years hence or more, is done annually. It is top-management strategic planning and results in a statement of organizational goals and objectives. Medium-range planning, for about two to eighteen months hence, is done in monthly or quarterly time increments. Companies make medium-range planning decisions for general levels of employment, output, and inventories. Short-range planning is done for about two months into the future, in weekly time increments. Short-range decisions involve scheduling jobs, loading machines, and sequencing jobs.

**Learning Objective 4: Define the major inputs, both external and internal, to the production-planning process.** The external inputs to the production-planning process are generally outside the direct control of the production planner. They include such factors as economic conditions, raw material availability, government regulations, marketplace demand, competitive actions, and subcontracting capacity. The internal inputs to the production-planning process are generally aligned with the various functions of the company and differ in terms of their controllability. They include information from human resources, materials management, engineering, finance, marketing, and manufacturing.

**Learning Objective 5: Describe the major costs in aggregate production planning.** Aggregate production planning is oriented toward minimizing overall production costs. It considers the following costs: (1) hiring/firing costs, (2) overtime/slack time costs, (3) part time/temporary labor costs, (4) subcontracting costs, (5) cooperative arrangement costs, (6) inventory carrying costs, and (7) back order or stock out costs.

**Learning Objective 6: Discuss the major strategies used in aggregate production planning.** Aggregate planners have the general problem of balancing demand and capacity throughout the planning period. They can use two pure operations strategies, or many combinations of these strategies, to balance demand and capacity. One pure strategy is the chase strategy, in which planners adjust production rates or work force levels to match the demand requirements for the planning period. Overtime and subcontracting, or hirings and layoffs of workers, are the ingredients of a chase strategy. A second pure strategy is the level strategy, which maintains a constant production rate or work force level throughout the planning period. Inventory levels, backlogs, or overtime are the ingredients for a level strategy. In practice companies use a range of mixed strategies between the pure chase strategy and the pure level strategy.

**Learning Objective 7: Describe the various techniques used for aggregate production planning. In addition, you should be able to apply trial-and-error methods and simple linear programming models to aggregate planning problems.** The techniques used for aggregate production planning are of two types: trial-and-error methods and mathematical techniques. Trial-and-error methods involve the evaluation of various options, using spreadsheets, until an acceptable option is found. The many mathematical techniques proposed for aggregate production planning include linear decision rules, management coefficients, parametric production planning, search decision rules, linear programming, goal programming, production-switching heuristics, simulation, and mixed integer programming. In practice most companies probably begin by using simple charting or graphing procedures and move into spreadsheet models. With the widespread acceptance and use of computers companies are making greater use of such mathematical techniques as linear programming. The problems at the end of the chapter offer you an opportunity to apply trial-and-error methods and simple linear programming models to aggregate planning problems.

**Learning Objective 8: Discuss hierarchical production planning and relate it to aggregate production planning.** Hierarchical production planning uses a series of mathematical models, following organizational lines, to tailor the entire planning process to the organization. Hierarchical production planning uses aggregate data for top-level decisions, whereas low-level, or shop floor, decisions use more detailed data. The process begins with assigning product family groups to factories. The next step is specifying aggregate plans for each factory. This is followed by scheduling family groupings with the plants. Next scheduled are individual items by using a process analogous to master production scheduling. The final step is scheduling detailed parts and components by using the logic of material requirements planning.

## ► Key Terms

| | | |
|---|---|---|
| aggregate production planning | master production schedule | rough-cut capacity planning |
| capacity requirements planning | material requirements planning (MRP) | search decision rule |
| chase strategy | medium-range planning | short-range planning |
| goal programming | mixed integer programming | simplex method of linear programming |
| hierarchical production planning | mixed strategy | simulation model |
| inventory level | parametric production planning | staffing plan |
| level strategy | production plan | transportation method of linear programming |
| linear decision rule | production rate | |
| long-range planning | production-switching heuristic | work force level |
| management coefficients model | purchasing planning and control | |

## ► Discussion Questions

1. Why is aggregate production planning necessary?
2. What are the planning levels and associated decisions for operations managers in a typical company?
3. What is the difference between aggregate production planning and production scheduling?
4. What are the major data inputs for the aggregate production-planning process?
5. What are the cost factors that the production-planning process should consider?
6. What are the relationships between the aggregate production plan and other organizational plans?
7. Distinguish between pure and mixed strategies in aggregate production planning.
8. Describe the differences between the chase and level strategies for aggregate production planning.
9. What are the advantages and disadvantages of informal graphic and charting techniques for aggregate production planning?
10. Compare and contrast the production plan for a manufacturing company with a staffing plan in a service company.
11. Briefly describe the following aggregate production-planning techniques, giving an advantage and disadvantage for each:
    a. Transportation method of linear programming
    b. Linear decision rule
    c. Search decision rule
    d. Simulation
12. How does the hierarchical production-planning process relate to actual managerial practices?
13. Discuss the strategic importance of aggregate production planning.
14. Discuss the relationship between aggregate production planning and detailed scheduling.
15. Discuss the importance of forecast accuracy to the overall process of aggregate production planning.

# ► Problems

1. Using the information given in the chapter for the Forest Hills Tennis Racket Co., prepare another production plan that assumes that the work force level is constant at 25 employees, overtime is allowed up to 1,200 hours per month, and subcontracting is used where necessary to prevent backlogs.

2. Using the information given in the chapter for the Forest Hills Tennis Racket Co., prepare another production plan that assumes that the work force level is kept constant at 30 employees, overtime is allowed up to 1,440 hours per month, and inventories and backlogs can vary.

3. Prepare a graph such as that in Figure 11.6 that illustrates the aggregate production plans for problems 1 and 2.

4. Diamond Enterprises produces telephone-answering machines for the personal use market. It needs to develop an aggregate production plan for the six months from January through June. It has compiled the following information:

|  | January | February | March | April | May | June |
|---|---|---|---|---|---|---|
| **Demand Data** |  |  |  |  |  |  |
| *Beginning inventory* | 100 |  |  |  |  |  |
| *Demand Forecast* | 600 | 700 | 800 | 900 | 900 | 800 |

| **Cost Data** |  | **Production data** |  |
|---|---|---|---|
| *Holding Cost* | $ 8/unit/month | *Labor Hours/Unit* | 5 |
| *Shortage Cost* | $20/unit month | *Workdays/Month* | 22 |
| *Hiring Cost/Worker* | $100 | *Beginning Work Force* | 15 |
| *Layoff Cost/Worker* | $200 |  |  |
| *Labor Cost/Hour—Regular Time* | $ 10 |  |  |
| *Labor Cost/Hour—Overtime* | $ 20 |  |  |
| *Subcontracting Cost/Unit* | $ 80 |  |  |

Determine the cost associated with the following production strategies:

a. Exactly meet demand, vary work force levels (assuming a starting work force of 15)

b. Level work force, vary inventories and backlogs

c. Level work force, use subcontracting

d. Exactly meet demand requirements, using overtime and subcontracting (assuming a starting work force of 15 and allowing overtime of 48 hours per month per employee)

5. Prepare a graph that illustrates the aggregate production plans for problem 4.

6. Diamond Enterprises has adopted a company policy that guarantees it will lay off no one. Additionally, it has determined that its overtime policy will allow no more than 9 units per month per worker. It can subcontract for up to 50 units per month at $80 per unit. It has increased its work force to 20 employees. Develop an optimal production plan for this situation, using the transportation method.

7. Great Southwestern Food Co. has made the following demand forecast for cases of its chili in each of the four quarters of next year: 1,000, 700, 1,000, and 1,400. It wishes to begin and end the year with an inventory level of 500 cases of chili. Its production capacity in each quarter is 900 cases on regular time and 250 cases on overtime. The cost to produce a case of chili is $20 on regular time and $30 on overtime. It costs the company $2 per case per quarter to store a case in inventory. It cannot use subcontracting because its chili recipe is proprietary.

Determine an optimal production plan for Great Southwestern Food Co., using the transportation method.

8. Burris Construction Co. uses a six-month "rolling" planning period. It does not use subcontracting but instead maintains an on-call labor force consisting of skilled construction workers. It completes its construction projects using regular time and overtime but limits overtime to 25 percent of regular time

each month. The company plans on the basis of 22 working days of regular time (8 hours per day) each month.

The company's current work force consists of 50 construction workers, who are paid at an hourly rate of $12 per hour. Overtime work is paid at an hourly rate of $18 per hour. If it completes any construction work late, Burris incurs a penalty cost of $5 per hour per month. It may complete work early but that takes a premium of $2 per hour per month.

Construction requirements (in hours) for the next six months are

| January | February | March |
|---------|----------|-------|
| 9,000 | 10,000 | 11,000 |

| April | May | June |
|-------|-----|------|
| 12,000 | 15,000 | 18,000 |

Devise an optimal staffing plan for Burris Construction Co., using the transportation method.

9. Pony Electronics manufactures 19-inch color television sets, 25-inch color television sets, and home entertainment systems. The demand (in units) for these products groups is forecast as follows for the next four quarters:

| | 19" Television | 25" Color Television | Home Entertainment System |
|---|---|---|---|
| Quarter 1 | 10,000 | 2,000 | 12,000 |
| Quarter 2 | 20,000 | 3,000 | 10,000 |
| Quarter 3 | 15,000 | 2,000 | 14,000 |
| Quarter 4 | 25,00 | 5,000 | 20,000 |
| Total | 70,000 | 12,000 | 56,000 |

The hours required to produce one unit of each product and the hourly costs on a regular time or overtime basis are

| | Hours per Unit | Hourly Cost Regular Time | Hourly Cost Overtime |
|---|---|---|---|
| 19" Color Television | 5 | $ 6 | $ 9 |
| 25" Color Television | 8 | 8 | 12 |
| Home Entertainment System | 10 | 10 | 15 |

To store one unit of a product for one quarter costs the following

| 19" Color Television | $6 |
|---|---|
| 25" Color Television | $8 |
| Home Entertainment System | $8 |

The available production hours for each quarter are

| | Regular Hours | Overtime Hours |
|---|---|---|
| Quarter 1 | 180,000 | 80,000 |
| Quarter 2 | 180,000 | 80,000 |
| Quarter 3 | 140,000 | 40,000 |
| Quarter 4 | 120,000 | 30,000 |

The company cannot use subcontracting because of the proprietary nature of the electronic circuitry in its products.

Determine an optimal production plan for Pony Electronics, using the transportation method.

10. Kids Delight manufactures bicycles and wagons. The demand for these products for the four quarters of next year is as follows:

| | Bicycles (units) | Wagons (units) |
|---|---|---|
| Quarter 1 | 10,000 | 5,000 |
| Quarter 2 | 15,000 | 10,000 |
| Quarter 3 | 10,000 | 10,000 |
| Quarter 4 | 20,000 | 15,000 |

To produce each toy requires the following production hours:
Bicycles: 3 hours
Wagons: 2 hours
Kids Delight can produce the toys using regular time or overtime. The available production hours are as follows:

| | Regular Time | Overtime |
|---|---|---|
| Quarter 1 | 50,000 | 15,000 |
| Quarter 2 | 50,000 | 15,000 |
| Quarter 3 | 50,000 | 15,000 |
| Quarter 4 | 50,000 | 15,000 |

Inventory holding costs are as follows:
Bicycles: $3 per quarter
Wagons: $2 per quarter
Production costs are as follows:
Regular time: $6 per hour
Overtime: $9 per hour
Devise an optimal production plan for Kids Delight, using the transportation method.

11. Develop an electronic spreadsheet to perform aggregate production planning by the trial-and-error method. Use the Forest Hills Tennis Racket Co., as described in Example 11.1, as a framework. This problem assumes access to a computer and appropriate software.

12. The production manager at the Delaney Paint Co. is preparing production and inventory plans for next year. She has gathered the following data:

| Quarter | Sales Forecast (units) |
|---|---|
| 1st quarter | 9,900 |
| 2nd quarter | 5,600 |
| 3rd quarter | 9,500 |
| 4th quarter | 15,000 |
| Total | 40,000 |
| Beginning inventory level (quarter 1) | 3,000 units |
| Ending inventory level (quarter 4) | 2,500 |
| Maximum quarterly production: | |
| Eight-hour shift only | 12,000 units/quarter |
| Maximum of two hours' overtime | 3,000 units/quarter |
| Total | 15,000 units/quarter |

NOTE: Delaney forbids the use of overtime unless production need is greater than 1,200 units.

Delaney's labor costs are as follows:

| | |
|---|---|
| Regular time | $3.00 per unit |
| Overtime | $6.00 per unit |

Inventory carrying cost = $0.60 per unit per quarter
Back-ordering cost = $6.00 per unit
Cost of increasing or decreasing the work force = $3.00 per unit change in production. NOTE: This charge is applicable only when production is less than 12,000 units per quarter.

Assume that units are available for sale during the same quarter that they are produced and inventory carrying costs for a quarter are based on the ending inventory for that quarter.

Formulate and solve this problem, using the simplex method.

13. Armstrong Manufacturing Co. is preparing an aggregate production plan for next year. Its production manager, Leon Washington, has compiled the following information:

- Forecast of quarterly demand in hours per quarter: 250,000; 300,000; 400,000; 300,000
- Beginning inventory in hours: 20,000
- Initial employment level: 500 workers
- Hours worked per quarter by each worker: 400 hours of regular time, 100 hours overtime (maximum)
- Inventory holding costs in dollars per hour per quarter: $50
- Cost of regular time in dollars per hour: $5
- Cost of overtime in dollars per hour: $8
- Cost to hire one worker: $1,000
- Cost to fire one worker: $400
- Required ending inventory in hours: 40,000

Formulate and solve this problem, using the simplex method.

## ▶ Selected References

Hax, Arnoldo C., and Dan Candea. *Production and Inventory Management*. Englewood Cliffs, N.J.: Prentice-Hall, 1984.

Hayes, R. H., and S. C. Wheelwright. *Restoring Our Competitive Edge*. New York: Wiley, 1984.

Hill, Terry. *Manufacturing Strategy*. Burr Ridge, Ill.: Richard D. Irwin, 1994.

McLeavy, D. W., and S. L. Narasimhan. *Production Planning and Inventory Control*. Boston: Allyn & Bacon, 1985.

Monden, Yasuhiro. *Toyota Production Systems*. Atlanta: Industrial Engineering and Management Press, 1983.

Plossl, G. W. *Production and Inventory Control: Principles and Techniques*. Englewood Cliffs, N.J.: Prentice-Hall, 1985.

Silver, E. A., and R. Peterson. *Decision Systems for Inventory Management and Production Planning*. New York: Wiley, 1985.

Skinner, C. W. *Manufacturing in the Corporate Strategy*. New York: Wiley, 1978.

Vollman, Thomas E., William L. Berry, and D. Clay Whybark. *Manufacturing Planning and Control Systems*. Homewood, Ill.: Richard D. Irwin, 1988.

## CHAPTER 12

# Independent Demand Inventory Management

*An empty bag cannot stand upright.*

BENJAMIN FRANKLIN

**Introduction**

**Independent and Dependent Demand**

**Basic Inventory Concepts**
*OPERATIONS MANAGEMENT IN PRACTICE 12.1: Shrink Inventory? Lands' End Builds Inventory to Increase Sales*
*OPERATIONS MANAGEMENT IN PRACTICE 12.2: Inventory Management At Ellett Brothers—The Need for an ABC Analysis*

**How Much to Order: Economic Order Quantity Models**

**When to Order: The Continuous Review System**

**When to Order: The Periodic Review System**

**Comparing the Continuous Review and Periodic Review Systems**
*OPERATIONS MANAGEMENT IN PRACTICE 12.3: Multiechelon Inventory Management at IBM*

# Introduction

Virtually all business organizations have problems associated with maintaining inventories. Small retailers, moderate-size wholesalers, and large manufacturing companies all must establish inventory control procedures. So must such service organizations as hospitals and auto repair shops. Good inventory management is important to companies of all sizes and types, for many reasons. First, inventories represent a major commitment of monetary resources. In manufacturing companies materials inventories typically account for more than half of total costs. Second, inventories affect virtually all aspects of a company's daily operations. Third, inventories are a major competitive weapon for many companies. Finally, inventories are the major control problem at many companies.

Inventory management is probably the most discussed and debated topic in manufacturing today. "Zero inventory" became the common phrase and the overriding goal of manufacturers in the mid-1980s. Achieving this goal requires reductions in inventory levels throughout the production process: reducing amounts of raw materials and purchased parts and assemblies by having suppliers deliver them directly; reducing the amount of work in process by using just-in-time production; and reducing the amount of finished goods by shipping to markets as quickly as possible. Evaluation of a manager's performance now tends to be based on **inventory turnover**, defined as the annual cost of sales divided by the average value of inventory. For example, Toyota achieves about thirty-five turnovers per year, compared with about eight for General Motors (as reported in their annual reports). This dramatic difference reflects Toyota's famous just-in-time approach to managing inventory.

Because of the dramatic changes in approaches to inventory management, we faced a dilemma in writing this chapter. Some practitioners and academicians would suggest that the classical models for inventory management, which have been taught and applied for many years, are irrelevant, because fewer companies are using them now. But inventory still plays a major role in every system that produces goods or services—it promotes smooth operations. We finally settled on a balanced approach: We will present only a few of the most important classical inventory management models. Although these inventory management models are perhaps falling into disuse in the manufacturing process, they remain appropriate for many service industries. In particular, effective inventory management is crucial to wholesale and retail merchandisers, which account for more than 40 percent of the U.S. economy.

This chapter explores the concepts and techniques that underlie effective inventory management. In the preceding chapter we addressed aggregate production and inventory planning. This chapter and Chapter 13 concentrate on inventory planning and control for individual items. This chapter also looks at methods for controlling inventories of finished goods, raw materials, purchased parts, and retail items; Chapter 13 describes methods for managing inventories of component parts and subassemblies.

# Independent and Dependent Demand

A key to planning and controlling inventories is whether an item is subject to independent or dependent demand. **Independent demand** items are finished products or parts that are shipped as end items to customers for spare parts or repair. Market conditions influence the demand for such items, and the demand for various end items is unrelated. The requirements for independent demand items (the amount to be produced or the amount to be held as inventory) must be determined separately. The demand for cars is a good example of independent demand, because a car is a complete entity that is not part of another product. Its demand comes from sources outside the car manufacturing company. Forecasting plays a critical role in stocking decisions for independent demand items.

**Dependent demand** items are raw materials, component parts, or subassemblies that are used to produce a finished product. In this situation the demand for raw materials, component parts, or subassemblies depends on the number of finished units to be produced. The requirements for dependent demand items are based simply on the number needed to produce each higher-level item. For example, a car manufacturer who produces 10,000 cars per month will also need 20,000 headlights and 40,000 wheels (not counting spares).

This chapter focuses on the management of independent demand items, such as that for manufactured end items or service industries that sell merchandise at a single location. Chapter 13 focuses on material requirements planning and techniques that are oriented to the dependent demand items found in manufacturing inventories.

# Basic Inventory Concepts

An **inventory** is the stock of an item or a resource used by an organization. Many companies have wide-ranging inventories, consisting of many small items such as paper pads, pencils, and paper clips, and fewer big items such as trucks, machines, and computers. A particular company's inventory is related to the business in which it is engaged. A tennis shop has an inventory of tennis rackets, shoes, and balls. A television manufacturer has parts, subassemblies, and finished TV sets in its inventory. A theater has an inventory of seats, a restaurant has an inventory of tables and chairs, and a public accounting firm has an inventory of accountants.

## Types of Inventories

As Figure 12.1 shows, a materials flow system has inventories in various forms. Inventories for a manufacturing facility consist of three major types, or accounting categories. **Raw materials** are the basic inputs to the manufacturing process. **Work in process** consists of partially finished goods. **Finished goods** are the outputs of the manufacturing process. As Figure 12.1 shows, raw materials

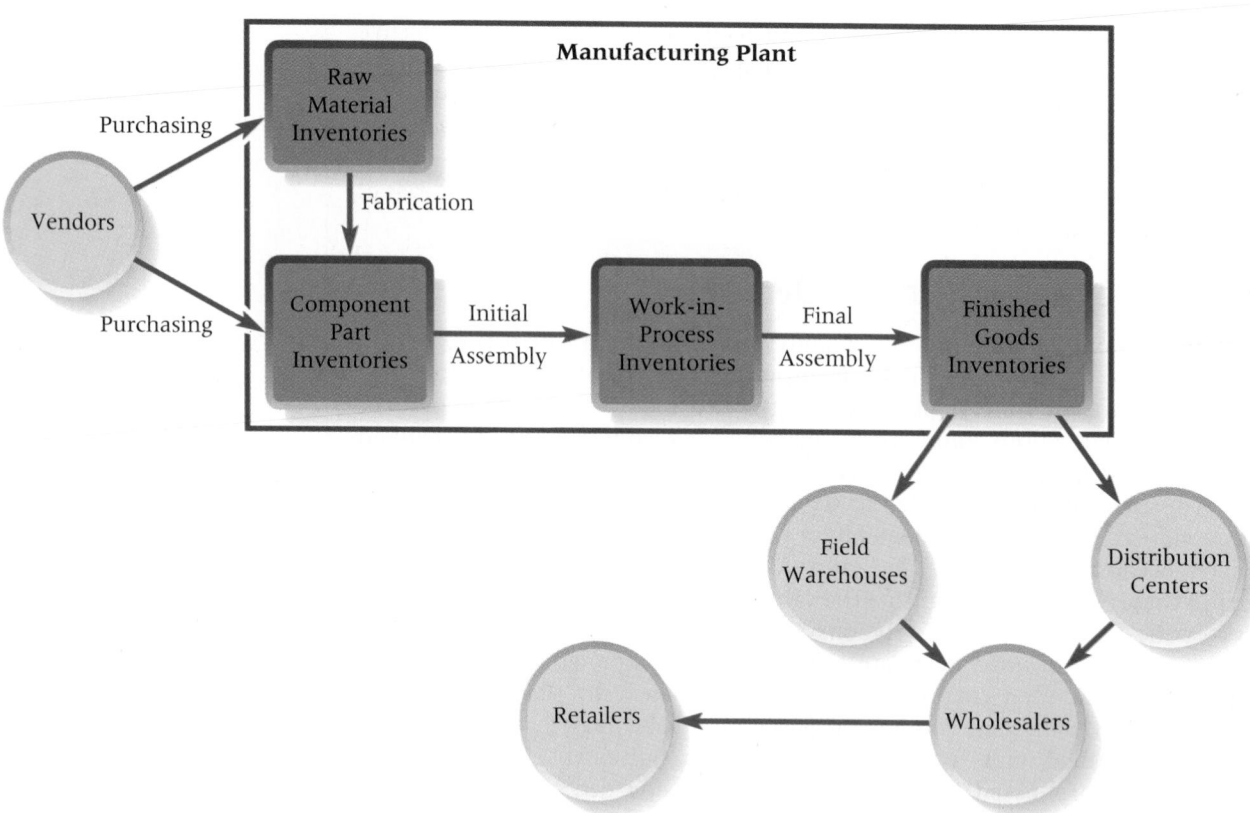

FIGURE 12.1
A Materials Flow System

originate at the supplier and the manufacturing plant keeps them in inventory. The manufacturer then processes these raw materials into component parts, which are also inventories. The manufacturer may purchase other component parts directly from the supplier and then partly assemble those components, which creates a work-in-process inventory. Final assembly turns the work-in-process inventory into finish goods inventory. Manufacturers can hold their finished goods inventories at the plant, distribution centers, a field warehouse, wholesalers, and retailers. Materials flow systems can be more or less complex than that shown in Figure 12.1. Multiplant materials flow systems are much more complex, because inventories have to be controlled at more stocking points.

## How to Measure Inventory

Inventory is a hot topic in manufacturing circles today. Operations managers closely monitor and control inventories to keep them as low as possible while still providing acceptable customer service.

To monitor and control inventories, operations managers need ways to measure inventories. Typically, inventories are measured in three ways: average aggregate inventory value, weeks of supply, and inventory turnover.

Measuring inventories begins with a physical count of units, or a physical measurement of volume or weight. Because the monetary value of various units may vary a great deal, operations managers use the **average aggregate inventory value** to calculate the average total value of all items held in inventory during some time period. We compute the average aggregate inventory value by multiplying the average number of units of each item (the beginning inventory plus ending inventory, divided by two) by its per unit value to obtain the total average value of each item and then add the total average values of all items. The average aggregate inventory value tells the inventory manager just how much of the company's total assets are invested in inventory. Typically, various types of companies will have guidelines for their investment in average aggregate inventory that are based on industry norms.

To calculate the second measure of inventory, **weeks of supply**, divide the average aggregate inventory value by the sales per week at cost. The numerator of this measure includes the value of all inventory items (raw materials, work in process, and finished goods), whereas the denominator includes only the cost of the finished goods sold.

To calculate the third measure of inventory, **inventory turnover (turns)**, divide the annual sales at cost by the average aggregate inventory value maintained during the year. The number of inventory turns achieved by various companies can vary widely.

Illustrations of these measures appear in the examples that follow, which are taken from the 1993 annual reports for Ford Motor Co. and Sears, Roebuck, and Co.

EXAMPLE 12.1

## Manufacturing Company—Ford Motor Co.

Average aggregate inventory value (1992 Ending inventory value + 1993 Ending inventory value)/2 = ($5.451 million + $5.538 million)/2 = $5.495 million    (12-1)

$$\text{Weeks of supply} = \frac{\text{Average aggregate inventory value}}{\text{Annual cost of sales/52 weeks}}$$

$$= \frac{5.495 \text{ million}}{\$85.168 \text{ million/52 weeks}} = 3.35 \text{ weeks} \quad (12\text{-}2)$$

$$\text{Inventory turns} = \frac{\text{Annual cost of sales}}{\text{Average aggregate inventory value}}$$

$$= \frac{\$85.168 \text{ million}}{\$5.495 \text{ million}} = 15.5 \quad (12\text{-}3)$$

EXAMPLE 12.2

## Service Company—Sears, Roebuck, and Co.

Average aggregate inventory value = (1992 Ending inventory value + 1993 Ending inventory value)/2 = ($4.048 million + $3.518 million)/2 = $3.783 million    (12-4)

$$\text{Weeks of supply} = \frac{\text{Average aggregate inventory value}}{\text{Annual cost of Sales/52 weeks}}$$

$$= \frac{3.783 \text{ million}}{47.234 \text{ million/52 weeks}} = 4.17 \text{ Weeks} \quad (12\text{-}5)$$

$$\text{Inventory turns;} = \frac{\text{Annual cost of sales}}{\text{Average aggregate inventory value}}$$

$$= \frac{\$47.234 \text{ million}}{\$3.783 \text{ million}} = 12.5 \quad (12\text{-}6)$$

## Reasons for Holding Inventories

Inventories serve a number of important functions in various companies. Among the major reasons for holding inventories are

1. To meet anticipated customer demand. Companies use **anticipation stock** to satisfy expected demand, and it is particularly important for products that exhibit marked seasonal demand but are produced at uniform rates. Lawn mower manufacturers and children's toy manufacturers build up anticipation stock, which is depleted during peak demand periods.

2. To protect against stock outs. Manufacturers use **safety stock** to protect against uncertainties in either the demand or supply of an item. Delayed deliveries and unexpected increases in demand increase the risk of shortages. Safety stock provides insurance that the company can meet anticipated customer demand without backlogging orders. In Figure 12.1 the plant can invest in safety stocks at several points. Raw materials and component parts can have safety stocks within the manufacturing plant. Finished goods can have safety stocks throughout the materials flow (at the plant, field warehouses, distribution centers, wholesalers, and retailers).

3. To take advantage of economic order cycles. Companies use **cycle stock** to produce (or buy) in quantities larger than their immediate needs. Because of the cost involved in setting up a machine, companies usually find producing in large quantities economical. Similarly, to minimize purchasing costs companies often buy in quantities that exceed their immediate requirements. In both cases, periodic orders, or order cycles, produce more economical overall production costs. The quantity produced is called the **economic lot size**. The quantity ordered is called the *economic order quantity (EOQ)*.

4. To maintain independence of operations. The successive stages in the production and distribution system require a buffer of inventories between them so that they can maintain their independence of operations. For example, the raw materials inventory buffers the manufacturer from problems with a supplier. Similarly, the finished goods inventory buffers factory operations from problems in the distribution system.

5. To allow for smooth and flexible production operations. A production-distribution system needs flexibility and a smooth flow of material. But production cannot be instantaneous so **work-in-process inventory** relieves pressure on the production system. Similarly, manufacturers use **in-transit**, or **pipeline, inventory** to offset distribution delays. Both work-in-process inventories and pipeline inventories are part of a broader classification, called **movement inventories**.

6. To guard against price increases. Manufacturers sometimes use large purchases, or large production runs, to achieve savings when they expect price increases for raw materials or component parts.

In summary, companies hold inventories to buffer against uncertainties in supply (raw materials inventory), the production process (work-in-process inventory), and demand (finished goods inventory).

Operations Management in Practice 12.1 shows the importance of inventories to catalog clothier Lands' End.

# Shrink Inventory? Lands' End Builds Inventory to Increase Sales

In Dodgeville, Wisconsin, the expansion of catalog clothier Lands' End continues. Its November–December 1993 holiday orders were up 26 percent over the same period for 1992, and for the first six months of the company's 1994 fiscal year, the gain was 10 percent.

After some stumbles in the early 1990s Lands' End appears to be approaching its torrid growth of 1987–1990, when sales more than doubled. The company expected to easily exceed $850 million in orders by the end of fiscal 1994.

In pursuing expansion Lands' End consistently builds inventory. It is an example of how the mail-order service business is markedly different from regular retailing, says William T. End, head of the new management team at the thirty-year-old company. (Despite his name, End came from rival L.L. Bean). A complete inventory is vital to cementing customer loyalty, End says. He suggests that "if we don't keep the customers for several years, we don't make money. We need a long-term payback for the expense of coming up with a buyer."

A typical department store shopper may be resigned to missing sizes and colors, but the typical mail-order shopper is not. So Lands' End makes good on back orders by paying the mailing expense.

Lands' End attempts to provide a 90 percent service level. End says he authorized more than $20 million (or nearly 10 percent extra) in inventory for the 1993 Christmas season, but with the heavy consumer rush Lands' End still missed the 90 percent target "by a couple of points."

With U.S. producers accounting for a shrinking share of Lands' End merchandise (about 80 percent) it is "tougher for sure" to secure stocks to maintain desired service levels. But End says it is still doable with the improved inventory control systems available.

## Inventory Costs

In making decisions about inventory levels companies must address a variety of costs.

Each time a company places a purchase order with a supplier or a production order with its own shop, it incurs an **ordering cost**. To buy an item someone has to solicit and evaluate bids, negotiate price terms, decide how much to order, prepare purchase orders, and follow up to make sure that the shipment arrives on time. For example, when we order an item from a supplier, we might incur a $100 cost for placing the order and a cost of $5 for each unit we are ordering. The purchasing cost function for this situation is

Ordering cost
↓

$$\text{Purchasing cost: } c(x) = \$100 + \$5x \text{ for } x > 0 \qquad (12\text{-}7)$$

The fixed portion ($100) of the total purchasing cost is independent of the amount ordered; it is primarily the cost of our clerical and administrative work. Placing a production order for a manufacturing item involves many of the same activities; only the type of paperwork changes.

The **set-up cost** is the cost involved in changing a machine over to produce a different part or item. While someone is adjusting a machine, it is idle and the company incurs the additional costs of the set-up workers. Sometimes the machines are producing trial products, and they will make defective parts until the machine is fine tuned. For example, we have a production process for manufacturing suitcases. The set-up cost for a production run is $1,000, and each suitcase costs $10 to manufacture. The manufacturing cost function for this situation is

$$\text{Set-up cost}$$
$$\downarrow$$

$$\text{Manufacturing cost: } c(x) = \$1,000 + \$10x \text{ for } x > 0 \qquad (12\text{-}8)$$

Many companies treat set-up costs as a fixed quantity and try to make the production lot size as big as possible to spread the set-up cost over as many units as possible. Newer approaches, such as just-in-time manufacturing, mean small lot sizes and working to reduce the set-up cost so that it corresponds to the small lot size. (We discuss this in greater detail in Chapter 16.)

The **holding, carrying,** or **storage cost** is the cost associated with maintaining an inventory until it is used or sold. Holding or storage cost includes the cost of maintaining storage facilities, the cost of insuring the inventory, taxes attributed to storage, costs associated with obsolescence, and costs associated with the capital that is committed to the inventory. The latter is called the *opportunity cost,* an expense incurred by having capital tied up in inventory rather than having it invested elsewhere, and it is frequently the most important component of the inventory holding cost. The opportunity cost is generally equal to the biggest return that the company could obtain from alternative investments. The holding, or storage, cost is usually related to the maximum quantity, average quantity, or excess of supply in relation to demand during a particular time period. For example, in one inventory control modeling effort, a metal-processing company estimated that its annual inventory holding cost was approximately 13 to 15 percent of the original purchase price of the metal commodity. So another common practice is to estimate the annual holding costs as a percentage of the unit cost of the item.

The **stock out,** or **shortage, cost** occurs when the demand for an item exceeds its supply. When a **stock out** or **shortage** occurs, a company faces two possibilities:

■ It can meet the shortage with some type of rush, special handling, or priority shipment.
■ It cannot meet the shortage at all.

The cost associated with a stock out or shortage depends on how the company handles the problem. Consider first the cost incurred when the inventory is on **back order**. In theory demand for the back ordered item is satisfied when the item next becomes available. From a practical standpoint accurately determining the nature and magnitude of the back-ordering cost can be difficult. A small portion of the back-ordering cost, such as the cost of notifying the customer that the item has been back ordered and when delivery can be expected, may be fairly easy to determine. Another portion of the back-ordering cost may involve explicit costs for overtime, special clerical and administrative costs for expediting, and extraordinary transportation charges. Such costs are much more difficult to determine. Finally, a major portion of the back-ordering cost is an implicit cost—it reflects the loss of the customer's goodwill. This is a difficult cost to measure, because it is a penalty cost that accounts for lost future sales. For example, a stereo equipment retailer might have a shortage cost composed primarily of lost goodwill, which it can estimate as 15 percent of the original purchase cost of the stereo system. But when back ordering is not possible or the customer chooses to order from another company, the shortage costs include the costs of notifying the customer, the loss in profit from the sale, and the future loss of goodwill.

The shortage cost may also depend on the size of the shortage and how long the shortage lasts. For example, customers may have written into their purchase contracts specific penalty clauses that are based on shortage amounts and times. In other instances the shortage cost may be a fixed amount regardless of the number of units unavailable or how long the shortage exists.

The **item cost** becomes relevant if a **quantity discount** is available. A company offering quantity discounts drops the price per item when the order is sufficiently large. This becomes an incentive to order greater quantities.

## Classifying Inventory Items

In developing the framework for constructing an inventory model, perhaps the first question is, "What inventory do we want to control?" Because we are focusing on finished goods inventories, one obvious answer would be, "We want to control all our finished goods inventory." Long practical experience and many studies show that for the typical production process or group of items a small number of items in the group will account for the bulk of the total inventory's value. This concept, called **ABC classification**, is one of the most widely known yet least exploited ideas in inventory control. In using an ABC classification we attempt to consider the small number of items that will account for most of the sales dollars and that are the most important to control for effective inventory management.

**EXAMPLE 12.3**

To see how ABC classification works, consider Table 12.1, which provides yearly sales volume data for 10 items. In Table 12.1 we have multiplied the annual sales (in number of units) by the unit cost (the cost for each item) to determine the annual sales dollars associated with each item.

Then we ranked the annual sales dollars. Now consider Table 12.2, which presents the items by rank according to their annual sales dollars. Table 12.2 also shows the cumulative annual dollar sales and the cumulative percentage sales. Assume that we have decided to classify the first 20 percent of the 10 items as the A class, the next 30 percent of the 10 items as the B class, and the remaining 50 percent of the 10 items as the C class.

As Table 12.2 shows, the A items account for approximately 60 percent of the annual sales, the B items account for 25 percent of the annual sales, and the C items account for the remaining 15 percent of the annual sales. Clearly, by concentrating our control efforts on the A items to reduce their inventory by 25 percent, we would have a substantial inventory reduction, even if the C items increased by almost 50 percent.

TABLE 12.1
Yearly Sales Data

| Sales Item | Annual Sales (No. of Units) | Unit Cost | Annual Sales ($) | Rank (Annual Sales, $) |
|---|---|---|---|---|
| F-1 | 40,000 | 0.06 | 2,400 | 7 |
| F-3 | 195,000 | 0.10 | 19,500 | 1 |
| F-7 | 30,000 | 0.09 | 2,700 | 6 |
| H-1 | 100,000 | 0.05 | 5,000 | 3 |
| H-3 | 3,000 | 0.15 | 450 | 10 |
| H-4 | 50,000 | 0.06 | 3,000 | 5 |
| H-6 | 10,000 | 0.07 | 700 | 8 |
| J-1 | 30,000 | 0.12 | 3,600 | 4 |
| J-3 | 150,000 | 0.05 | 7,500 | 2 |
| K-3 | 6,000 | 0.09 | 540 | 9 |

TABLE 12.2
ABC Classification

| Sales Item | Annual Sales ($) | Cumulative Annual Sales ($) | Cumulative Annual Sales (%) | Class |
|---|---|---|---|---|
| F-3 | 19,500 | 19,500 | 43.0 | A |
| J-3 | 7,500 | 27,000 | 59.4 | A |
| H-1 | 5,000 | 32,000 | 70.5 | B |
| J-1 | 3,600 | 35,600 | 78.4 | B |
| H-4 | 3,000 | 38,600 | 85.0 | B |
| F-7 | 2,700 | 41,300 | 90.9 | C |
| F-1 | 2,400 | 43,700 | 96.3 | C |
| H-6 | 700 | 44,400 | 97.8 | C |
| K-3 | 540 | 44,940 | 99.0 | C |
| H-3 | 450 | 45,390 | 100.0 | C |

We should initiate our inventory control procedures where it will do the most good, namely, with those items that are most important from a total dollar-usage standpoint. For example, some companies have concluded that it is much easier to carry a large stock of low-value items and not maintain any sort of control records for these items. They use their savings in time, effort, and expense to closely control the high-value items. We can summarize the rules involved in the proper degree of control as follows:

*A Items:* Very tight control, complete and accurate records; regular review by major decision makers
*B Items:* Less tightly controlled, good records, and regular review
*C Items:* Simplest controls possible, minimal records, large inventories, periodic review, and reordering

Operations Management in Practice 12.2 explains why Ellett Brothers, a large wholesaler, needed ABC classification.

## Inventory Records

Operating an actual inventory system requires the maintenance of accurate inventory records. The company must have information on the level of on-hand

# Inventory Management at Ellett Brothers— The Need for an ABC Analysis

Ellett Brothers Co., located in Chapin, South Carolina, is one of the largest wholesalers of firearms and shooting accessories in the United States. It is a multimillion dollar company that maintains more than 24,000 different products in its inventory. Twice named "Sporting Goods Distributor of the Year" and winner of dozens of awards for sales and service, it consistently ships orders 88 percent complete within six working hours after receiving the order.

Inventory control is of major importance to the company, but despite its efforts several problems remain:

- Lack of focus. The company attempts to control all of its inventory instead of focusing its attention on the most important inventory items. It needs to perform a thorough ABC analysis and develop a more focused program of inventory control. By attempting to control inventories throughout its broad product line, it is failing to concentrate on the small number of inventory items that account for the bulk of its total inventory value.

- High inventories. The company maintains high inventory levels to protect against being unable to fill customers' orders. But inventory turnover is much too low, and it has to sell many items at discounted prices. Simple forecasting of demand for A inventory items would be a first step, followed by the establishment of economic order quantities. Using economic order quantities would also establish better order in its purchasing and inventory control system.

- Stock outs. Despite its high inventory levels, the company experiences many stock outs. Again, it needs to forecast and set realistic reorder points for key items. Because of the lack of forecasting, it tends to purchase too many of certain items. Preliminary EOQ analysis for a sample of important (A) items showed that current order quantities were at least 25 percent bigger than necessary.

- Seasonality. In certain periods of the year (Christmas, fall hunting season) the company sees much seasonality. These one-time inventory decisions are a problem, because the company later has to heavily discount the unsold items. Any inventory control system implemented by this type of wholesaler must consider seasonality.

In summary, Ellett Brothers Co. has been highly successful, primarily as a result of its aggressive marketing efforts and because it offers good service. It has not devoted much attention to inventory control. An ABC analysis of its inventory items, followed by some simple forecasting and the use of economic order quantities, could make it even more profitable.

inventory and the scheduled receipt of items. Some companies check the actual inventory periodically by closing down facilities and physically counting all stocks. Retailers commonly do this. Other companies maintain perpetual inventory records, which record each inventory transaction. Perpetual inventory systems can be manual or computerized.

Accuracy is crucial for effective inventory management. Some companies assign inventory control duties to specific employees, who are then responsible for accuracy. Other companies maintain inventories in locked, secured areas, with limited access. Other companies use **cycle counting**, whereby inventory control personnel physically count a small percentage of the inventory items each day and correct any errors that they find. They check the class A inventory items most frequently. Companies that use computerized inventory systems can check each transaction for logic errors. In short, companies can maintain inventory accuracy in several ways, and doing so pays off both in better service and in overall inventory reduction.

However, we should caution that at the time of final assembly a *C* item is just as important as an *A* item, when the company needs the *C* item to fill a customer's order or to complete assembly of an end item.

## Objectives of Inventory Control

Inventory control has two major objectives. The first objective is to maximize the level of customer service by avoiding understocking. Understocking causes missed deliveries, backlogged orders, lost sales, production bottlenecks, and worse: unhappy customers.

The second objective of inventory control is to promote efficiency in production or purchasing by minimizing the cost of providing an adequate level of customer service. Placing too much emphasis on customer service can lead to overstocking, which means the company has tied up too much of its capital in inventories.

These two objectives often conflict. Achieving high levels of customer service by maintaining certain inventories leads to higher inventory costs and less efficiency in production or purchasing. Inventory control becomes a balancing act. Quite often the operations manager selects a desired level of customer service and attempts to control inventory in a manner that achieves that level of customer service at the lowest cost possible. Also, we have learned that adopting the competitive philosophy of just-in-time manufacturing can increase customer service, production output, and purchasing efficiencies while decreasing inventory costs (see Chapter 16 for more detail).

The operations manager's problem is striking a balance in inventory levels, avoiding both overstocking and understocking. This means that the operations manager must answer two questions:

- When should the company replenish its inventory, or when should the company place an order or manufacture a new lot?
- How much should the company order or produce?

## How Much to Order: Economic Order Quantity Models

Operations managers often answer the fundamental question of how much to order by using an economic order quantity (EOQ) or economic lot size model. We'll discuss four models that specify the optimal order quantity or production lot size in terms of minimizing the annual costs associated with maintaining inventories.

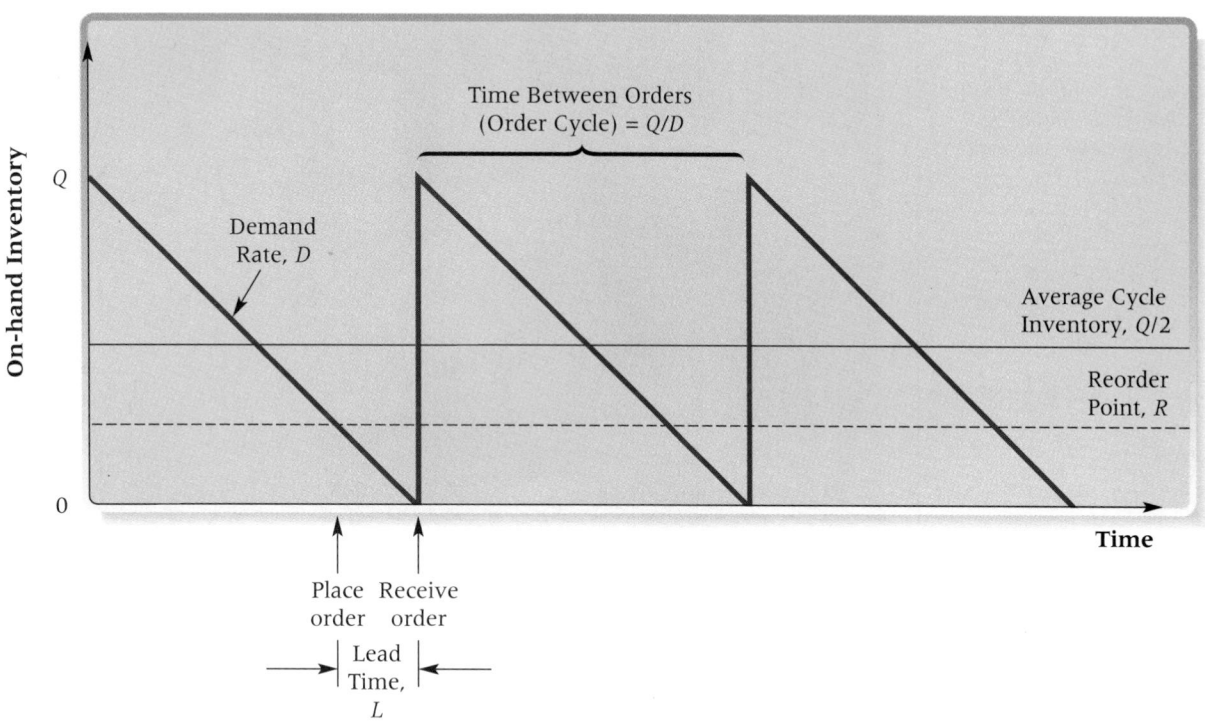

FIGURE 12.2
Economic Order Quantity
Model; Constant Demand,
No Shortages Allowed

## Economic Order Quantity: Constant Demand, No Shortages

The basic **economic order quantity (EOQ)** model is the simplest of the four and is used to determine the quantity that minimizes the annual costs of holding and ordering inventory. It is applicable to a single product or item that is continuously reviewed and is based on these assumptions:

1.  The company knows the demand rate for the item, and it is constant over time.
2.  The company produces the item in lots or purchases it in orders.
3.  Each lot or order arrives in a single delivery.
4.  The company knows the lead time (time from ordering to receipt), and it is constant.
5.  The company's bases its inventory holding cost on average inventory.
6.  Ordering or set-up costs are constant.
7.  The company satisfies all demands for the product (it allows no back orders).
8.  The company cannot obtain quantity discounts.

Figure 12.2 is a graphic depiction of this particular inventory situation. Each inventory cycle begins with the receipt of an order of $Q$ units. The company uses the $Q$ units at a constant rate, $D$, over time. At the **reorder point**, $R$—when the on-hand inventory is barely sufficient to satisfy demand during the **lead time**, $LT$, (the time between placing and receiving an order)—the company places an order of $Q$ units with the vendor. Assuming that both the demand rate and the lead time are constant, the vendor receives the order of $Q$ units exactly when the

*An inventory control specialist makes a physical count of inventory and records the count using a hand-held inventory record keeping device that reads bar codes.*

inventory level reaches zero. This means that there are no shortages. The inventory level varies from $Q$ to zero, so the average inventory level during the inventory cycle is $Q/2$.

For this inventory model the total annual inventory cost is

| Total annual inventory cost | = | Annual inventory item cost | + | Annual inventory ordering cost | + | Annual inventory carrying cost | |
|---|---|---|---|---|---|---|---|
| $TC$ | = | $DC_I$ | + | $\dfrac{D}{Q} C_O$ | + | $\dfrac{Q}{2} C_H$ | (12-9) |

where

$TC$ = Total annual inventory cost
$D$ = Annual demand, in units per year
$C_I$ = Cost of purchasing an item, in dollars
$Q$ = Order quantity, or lot size, in units
$C_O$ = Cost of placing an order, or setup cost for a lot, in dollars
$C_H$ = Annual carrying cost, in dollars per unit per year

Figure 12.3 shows these costs relationships graphically.

The annual inventory ordering cost is a function of the number of orders placed per year, and the ordering cost per order, $C_O$, and is expressed as

$$\text{Annual inventory ordering cost} = \left(\frac{D}{Q}\right) C_O \qquad (12\text{-}10)$$

Because the number of orders made per year, $D/Q$, decreases as the order size, $Q$, increases, the annual inventory ordering cost is inversely related to order size.

The annual inventory carrying cost is a linear function of $Q$:

$$\text{Annual inventory carrying cost} = \left(\frac{Q}{2}\right) C_H \qquad (12\text{-}11)$$

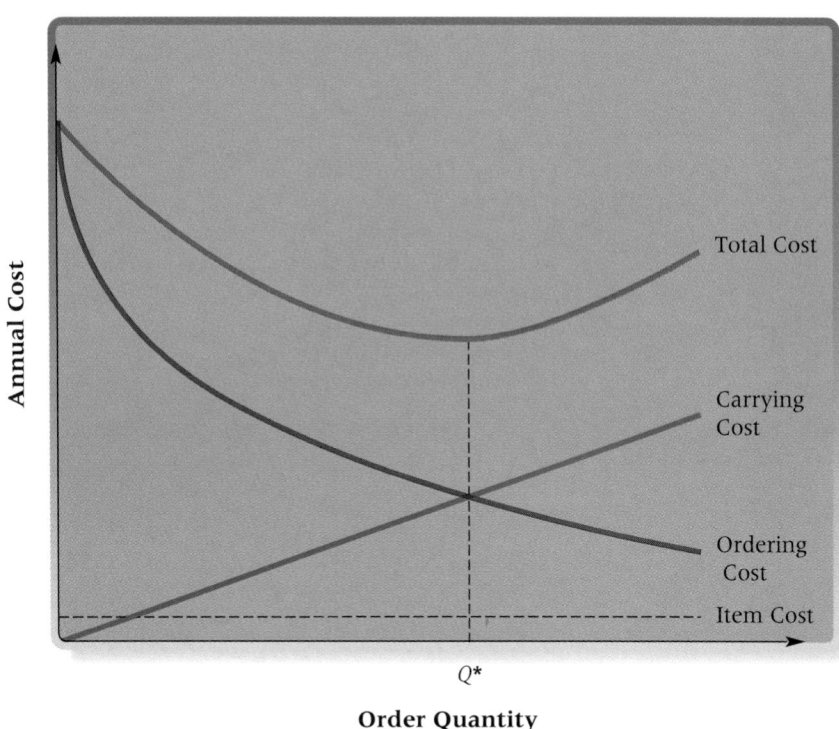

**Order Quantity**

The average inventory is $Q/2$, which is multiplied by the cost of carrying one unit for a year, $C_H$, to arrive at the annual inventory carrying cost.

The cost of the individual items is assumed to be constant, regardless of the size of the order. The inventory item cost, $DC_I$, appears in Figure 12.3 as a broken horizontal line. Observe that it only increases the total inventory cost by the constant amount, $DC_I$, during the entire order quantity range. It does not affect the optimal order quantity, $Q^*$. Therefore, it is not really a relevant cost for the economic order quantity decision, and we can eliminate it from further consideration in the model.

Figure 12.3 shows that the total cost curve is U-shaped and reaches its minimum at the quantity for which carrying and ordering costs are equal. We can use calculus to obtain the expression for the optimal order quantity, $Q^*$, by taking the derivative of total inventory cost with respect to $Q$, setting the derivative to zero, and solving for $Q$. This derivation is as follows:

$$TC = \left(\frac{D}{Q}\right) C_O + \left(\frac{Q}{2}\right) C_H$$

$$\frac{dTC}{dQ} = \left(\frac{-D}{Q^2}\right) C_O + \frac{C_H}{2} = 0$$

$$Q^* = \sqrt{\frac{2D\,C_O}{C_H}} \tag{12-12}$$

Because $\frac{d^2TC}{dQ} > 0$, $Q^*$ is a minimum.

The result of equation 12-12 is the economic order quantity or economic lot size.

FIGURE 12.4
Trade-offs—Inventory Levels
Versus Number of Orders

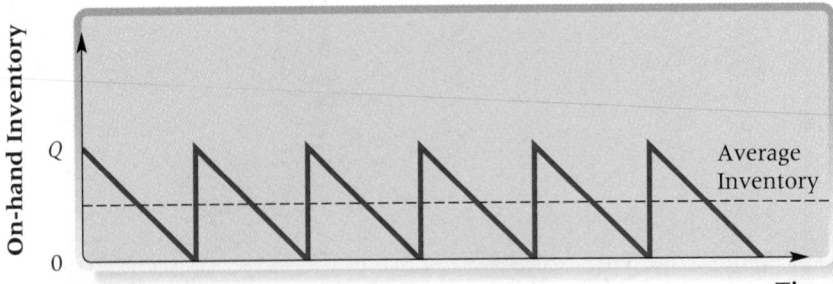

(a) Many orders but low average inventory
- Lower inventory carrying cost
- Higher inventory ordering cost

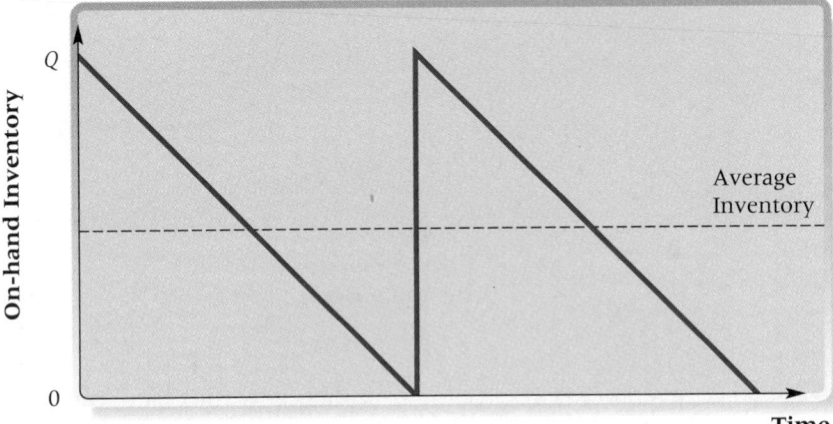

(b) Fewer orders but high average inventory
- Lower inventory ordering costs
- Higher inventory carrying costs

Over a given time period—say, one year—a company can use two policies for making inventory size decisions. First, it can keep the order size small. This will result in a small average inventory, and inventory carrying costs will be low. But this policy will lead to frequent orders, and the annual ordering costs will increase. Second, the company can increase its order size. This will result in less frequent orders, so the annual ordering costs will be low. But this will result in a high average inventory, and the annual inventory carrying costs will increase. Figure 12.4 shows these two contrasting situations.

The number of orders per year is

$$\text{Number of orders per year} = \frac{D}{Q^*} \tag{12-13}$$

The length of the order cycle is

$$\text{Length of order cycle} = \frac{Q^*}{D} \tag{12-14}$$

Finally, the minimum total annual cost is

$$TC = \frac{DC_O}{Q^*} + \frac{Q^* C_H}{2} \tag{12-15}$$

EXAMPLE 12.4

A large retailer of stereo equipment orders one of its disk players from a Japanese company. It has compiled the following data:

Annual demand $(D)$ = 100,000 units
Average monthly demand $(d)$ = 100,000/12 = 8,333 units
Ordering cost $(C_O)$ = $10 per order
Holding cost $(C_H)$ = $2 per unit per year

The optimal EOQ is

$$Q^* = \sqrt{\frac{2DC_O}{C_H}} = \sqrt{\frac{2(100,000)\,(10)}{2}} = 1,000 \text{ units} \qquad (12\text{-}16)$$

The number of orders per year is

$$\text{Number of orders per year} = \frac{D}{Q^*} = \frac{100,000}{1,000} = 100 \qquad (12\text{-}17)$$

The length of the order cycle is

$$\text{Length of order cycle} = \frac{Q^*}{D} = \frac{1,000}{100,000} = 0.01 \text{ year or 3.65 days} \qquad (12\text{-}18)$$

The total annual cost is

$$TC = \frac{DC_O}{Q^*} + \frac{Q^*C_H}{2}$$
$$= \frac{(100,000)\,(10)}{1,000} + \frac{(1,000)\,(2)}{2}$$
$$= 1,000 + 1,000 = \$2,000 \qquad (12\text{-}19)$$

Two other comments are in order here. First, we have developed and illustrated the basic economic order quantity model using an annual time frame. Other time frames, say, quarterly or monthly, can be used for making inventory decisions. The only requirement is that all the terms in the EOQ formula (equation 12-12) must be consistent. For example, if demand is monthly, inventory carrying costs must also be stated in terms of months. Second, inventory carrying costs are sometimes stated as a percentage of the purchase price of the item rather than as a dollar amount per unit. So long as we convert this percentage to a dollar amount, the EOQ formula is applicable.

## Economic Order Quantity: Constant Demand, Shortages Allowed

The inventory problem in Example 12.1 becomes slightly more complicated when a company permits shortages, or back orders, to occur. However, in many situations shortages are economically desirable. Permitting shortages allows the manufacturer or retailer to increase the cycle time, thereby spreading the set-up or ordering cost over a longer time period. Allowing shortages may also be desirable when the unit value of the inventory and therefore the inventory holding cost is high. An example of this situation would be a recreational vehicle dealer who typically will not maintain an inventory of all the expensive

FIGURE 12.5
Economic Order Quantity
Model: Constant Demand,
Shortages Allowed

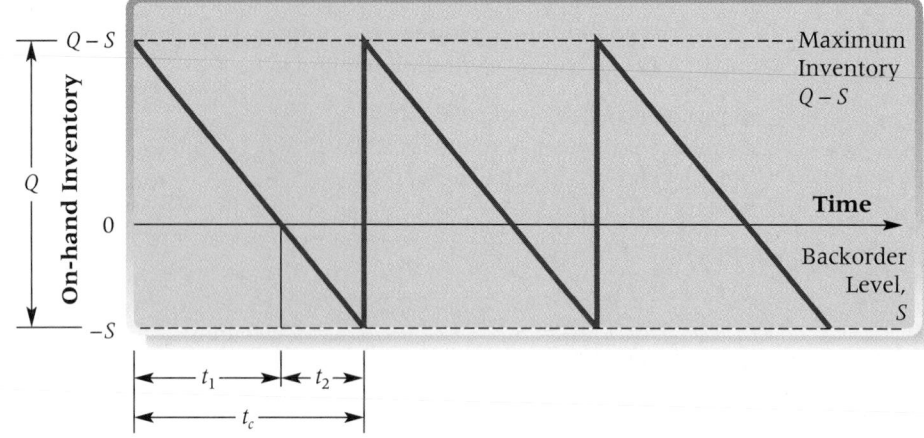

($> \$20,000$) recreational vehicles that are sold. Rather, the dealer will order the particular recreational vehicle that the customer wants at the time of the sale.

In the back order situation customers place an order, no stock is available, and they simply wait until stock becomes available, at which point the order is filled. The company hopes that the waiting period for the back order will be short and its customers will not become impatient or angry.

For the next model we will again use the assumptions of a known and constant demand rate and the instantaneous delivery of goods to inventory. If $S$ represents the amount of the shortage (size of the back order) that has accumulated when the new shipment of size $Q$ arrives, the economic order quantity model with constant demand and permissible shortages has the following major characteristics:

1. When the new shipment of size $Q$ arrives, the company immediately ships the back orders of size $S$ to the customers. The remaining units $(Q - S)$ immediately go into inventory.
2. The inventory level will vary from a minimum of $-S$ units to a maximum of $Q - S$ units.
3. The inventory cycle of $T$ months (days) is divided into two distinct parts: $t_1$ months (days) when inventory is available for filling orders and $t_2$ months (days) when inventory is not available, stock outs occur, and back orders are made.

Figure 12.5 shows this inventory situation graphically. For this inventory model the total annual inventory cost is

| Total annual inventory cost | = | Annual inventory ordering cost | + | Annual inventory carrying cost | + | Annual inventory back-ordering cost |
|---|---|---|---|---|---|---|

$$TC = \left(\frac{D}{Q}\right) C_O + \frac{(Q - S)^2 C_H}{2Q} + \frac{S^2 C_B}{2Q} \qquad (12\text{-}20)$$

where

$TC$ = Total annual inventory cost
$D$ = Annual demand, in units per year
$C_O$ = Cost of placing an order, or set-up cost for a lot, in dollars
$C_H$ = Annual carrying cost, in dollars per unit per year

$Q$ = Order quantity, or lot size, in units
$S$ = Back order quantity in units
$C_B$ = Back-ordering cost, in dollars per unit per year

The annual inventory ordering cost is a function of the number of orders made per year, $(D/Q)$, and the annual inventory ordering cost per order, $C_O$:

$$\text{Annual inventory ordering cost} = \left(\frac{D}{Q}\right)C_O \tag{12-21}$$

The annual inventory holding, or carrying, cost is computed in the following manner. From Figure 12.5 we can see that the positive inventory level ranges from $Q - S$ to 0. This means that the average inventory level is $(Q - S)/2$ for the period of time during which there are no shortages. The time period for which there are no shortages is $t_1$ and is given by $(Q - S)/Q$, and

$$\text{Annual inventory carrying cost} = \frac{(Q - S)^2 C_H}{2Q} \tag{12-22}$$

The annual inventory back-ordering cost is computed similarly. From Figure 12.5 we can see that the shortage, or back order level, ranges from 0 units to $S$ units. This means that the average shortage, or back order level, is $S/2$ while there are shortages or back orders. The time period for which there are shortages is $t_2$ and is represented by $S/Q$. The annual inventory back-ordering cost is

$$\text{Annual inventory back-ordering cost} = \frac{S^2 C_B}{2Q} \tag{12-23}$$

Figure 12.6 shows the pattern for the three individual inventory cost functions and the total inventory cost function for this model. With this model the three cost functions generally do not intersect at a common point. The

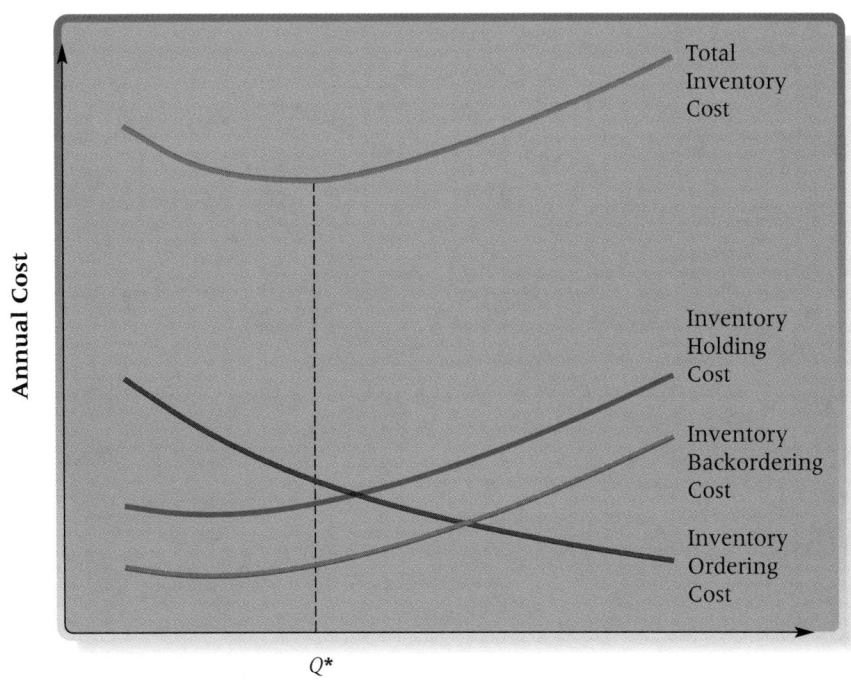

**Order Quantity**

FIGURE 12.6
Inventory Costs—EOQ
Model with Shortages
Allowed

operations manager must use differential calculus to solve for $Q^*$, the optimal economic order quantity, and $S^*$, the optimal maximum shortage level. The optimum values for $Q^*$ and $S^*$ are

$$Q^* = \sqrt{\frac{2DC_O}{C_H}} \sqrt{\frac{C_B + C_H}{C_B}} \qquad (12\text{-}24)$$

$$S^* = Q^* \left( \frac{C_H}{C_B + C_H} \right) \qquad (12\text{-}25)$$

The number of orders per year is

$$\text{Number of orders per year} = \frac{D}{Q^*} \qquad (12\text{-}26)$$

The maximum inventory level is

$$I_{max}{}^* = Q^* - S^* \qquad (12\text{-}27)$$

The average (positive) inventory level is

$$I_{avg}{}^* = \frac{Q^* - S^*}{Q^*} \qquad (12\text{-}28)$$

The length of time during which there are no shortages is

$$t_1{}^* = \frac{Q^* - S^*}{Q^*} \left( \frac{Q^*}{D} \right) = \frac{Q^* - S^*}{D} \qquad (12\text{-}29)$$

The length of time during which there are shortages is

$$t_2{}^* = \left( \frac{S^*}{Q^*} \right) \left( \frac{Q^*}{D} \right) = \frac{S^*}{D} \qquad (12\text{-}30)$$

The length of an inventory cycle is

$$t_c{}^* = t_1{}^* + t_2{}^*$$
$$= \frac{Q^* - S^*}{D} + \frac{S^*}{D} = \frac{Q^*}{D} \qquad (12\text{-}31)$$

Finally, the minimum total annual inventory cost is

$$TC = \left( \frac{D}{Q^*} \right) C_O + \frac{(Q^* - S^*)^2\, C_H}{2Q^*} + \frac{S^{*2}C_B}{2Q^*} \qquad (12\text{-}32)$$

---

**EXAMPLE 12.5**

Maxine's Mobile Home Co. experiences a yearly demand of 500 units for mobile homes; Maxine incurs a cost of $250 every time she places a new order with the factory. She estimates her inventory holding costs at $1,200 per unit per year, and she incurs a shortage cost of $200 per unit per year for each mobile home that a buyer wants but is not on the lot.

The optimal EOQ is

$$Q^* = \sqrt{\frac{2DC_O}{C_H}} \sqrt{\frac{C_B + C_H}{C_B}} = \sqrt{\frac{2(500)\,(250)}{1,200}} \sqrt{\frac{200 + 1,200}{200}}$$

$$= \sqrt{208.33}\ \sqrt{7} = (14.43)\,(2.65) = 38.19 \text{ units (use 38)} \qquad (12\text{-}33)$$

The optimal back order quantity is

$$S^* = Q^* \sqrt{\frac{C_H}{C_B + C_H}} = 38.19 \left( \frac{1,200}{200 + 1,200} \right) = 32.73 \text{ units} \qquad (12\text{-}34)$$

The length of time during which there are no shortages is

$$t_1 = \frac{Q^* - S^*}{D} = \frac{38.19 - 32.73}{500} = \frac{5.46}{500} = 0.011 \text{ year or } 4.00 \text{ days} \quad (12\text{-}35)$$

The length of time during which there are shortages is

$$t_2 = \frac{S^*}{D} = \frac{32.73}{500} = 0.065 \text{ year or } 23.73 \text{ days} \quad (12\text{-}36)$$

The length of an inventory cycle is

$$t_c = t_1{}^* + t_2{}^* = Q^*/D$$
$$= 38.19/500 = 0.076 \text{ years or } 27.73 \text{ days} \quad (12\text{-}37)$$

The maximum inventory level is

$$I_{max}{}^* = Q^* - S^* = 38.19 - 32.73 = 5.46 \text{ units} \quad (12\text{-}38)$$

The number of orders per year is

$$\text{Number of orders per year} = D/Q^*$$
$$= 500/38.19 = 13.09 \text{ orders} \quad (12\text{-}39)$$

The minimum total annual inventory cost is

$$TC = \left(\frac{D}{Q^*}\right) C_O + \frac{(Q^* - S^*)^2 C_H}{2Q^*} + \frac{S^{*2} C_B}{2Q^*}$$
$$TC = \frac{500}{38.19}(250) + \frac{(38.19 - 32.73)^2(1{,}200)}{2(38.19)} + \frac{(32.73)^2 200}{2(38.19)}$$
$$= 3{,}273 + 468 + 2{,}805$$
$$= \$6{,}546 \quad (12\text{-}40)$$

# Economic Order Quantity: Uniform Replenishment Rate, Constant Demand, No Shortages

Let us now consider the situation in which a company supplies units to inventory at a uniform replenishment rate over time, rather than in economic order quantities at specific points in time. This situation occurs when a company is both a producer and user of an item or when it spreads its deliveries over time. In some cases usage and production (or delivery rates) are equal, and inventory will not build up because the company will use all items immediately. More typically, the production or delivery rate, $p$, will exceed the demand, or usage rate, $u$.

Figure 12.7 is a graphic of this inventory situation.

Note that the inventory cycle in Figure 12.7 has two parts. The company both uses and produces items during the first part of the inventory cycle. Inventory builds up at a rate equal to the difference between the production rate and the usage rate. For example, if the production rate is 100 units per month and the usage rate is 25 units per month, inventory will accumulate at the rate of $100 - 25 = 75$ units per month. When production ceases, the second part of the inventory cycle begins: The company will deplete its inventory level at the usage, or demand, rate. Again, this model assumes there are no shortages.

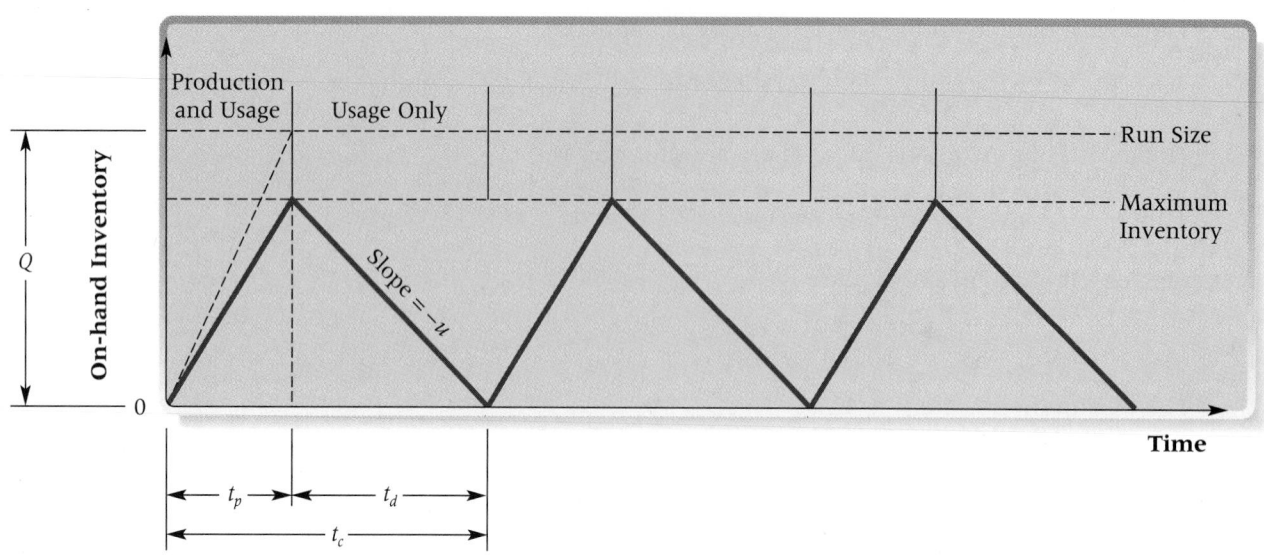

**FIGURE 12.7**
Economic Order Quantity
Model: Uniform
Replenishment Rate,
Constant Demand, No
Shortages

For this inventory model the total annual cost is

$$
\begin{array}{ccccc}
\text{Total} & & \text{Annual} & & \text{Annual} \\
\text{annual} & = & \text{set-up} & + & \text{inventory} \\
\text{inventory} & & \text{cost} & & \text{carrying} \\
\text{cost} & & & & \text{cost}
\end{array}
$$

$$
TC = \left(\frac{D}{Q}\right) C_S + \frac{Q}{2}\left(1 - \frac{u}{p}\right) C_H \tag{12-41}
$$

where

$TC$ = Total annual cost
$D$ = Annual demand, in units per year
$Q$ = Lot size, in units
$C_S$ = Set-up cost for a lot, in dollars
$C_H$ = Annual carrying cost, in dollars per unit per year
$u$ = Usage rate
$p$ = Production rate

The expression for the optimal lot size, $Q^*$, is

$$
Q^* = \sqrt{\frac{2DC_S}{C_H}} \sqrt{\frac{p}{p - u}} \tag{12-42}
$$

The maximum inventory level is

$$
I_{max}^* = Q^*\left(\frac{p - u}{p}\right) = Q^*\left(1 - \frac{u}{p}\right) \tag{12-43}
$$

The average inventory level is

$$
I_{avg}^* = \frac{Q^*}{2}\left(\frac{p - u}{p}\right) = \frac{Q^*}{2}\left(1 - \frac{u}{p}\right) \tag{12-44}
$$

The length of time required to produce a lot is

$$
t_p^* = \frac{Q^*}{p} \tag{12-45}
$$

The length of time required to deplete the maximum on-hand inventory is

$$t_d = \frac{Q^*}{u}\left(1 - \frac{u}{p}\right) \qquad (12\text{-}46)$$

The length of an inventory cycle is

$$\begin{aligned} t_c^* &= t_p^* + t_d^* \\ &= \frac{Q^*}{p} + \frac{Q^*}{u}\left(1 - \frac{u}{p}\right) = \frac{Q^*}{u} \end{aligned} \qquad (12\text{-}47)$$

Finally, the minimum total annual cost is

$$TC = \frac{D}{Q^*}C_S + \frac{Q^*}{2}\left(1 - \frac{u}{p}\right)C_H \qquad (12\text{-}48)$$

---

**EXAMPLE 12.6**

The Great Southern Motor Co. manufactures electric motors. One particular motor has a known and constant demand rate of 2,000 units per year. The fixed cost of the set-up for each production run is $100, and the inventory holding cost is $2 per unit per year. The production rate is 8,000 units per year.

The optimal economic lot size is

$$\begin{aligned} Q^* &= \sqrt{\frac{2DC_S}{C_H}}\sqrt{\frac{p}{p-u}} = \sqrt{\frac{2(2,000)(100)}{2}}\sqrt{\frac{8,000}{8,000 - 2,000}} \\ &= 516 \text{ units} \end{aligned} \qquad (12\text{-}49)$$

The maximum inventory level is

$$I_{max}^* = Q^*\left(1 - \frac{u}{p}\right) = 516\left(1 - \frac{2,000}{8,000}\right) = 387 \text{ units} \qquad (12\text{-}50)$$

The average inventory level is

$$I_{avg}^* = \frac{Q^*}{2}\left(1 - \frac{u}{p}\right) = \frac{516}{2}\left(1 - \frac{2,000}{8,000}\right) = 193.5 \text{ units} \qquad (12\text{-}51)$$

The length of time required to produce a lot is

$$t_p^* = \frac{Q^*}{p} = \frac{516}{8,000} = 0.065 \text{ year or } 23.7 \text{days} \qquad (12\text{-}52)$$

The length of time required to deplete the maximum on-hand inventory is

$$\begin{aligned} t_d^* &= \frac{Q^*}{u}\left(1 - \frac{u}{p}\right) = \frac{516}{2,000}\left(1 - \frac{2,000}{8,000}\right) \\ &= 0.194 \text{ year or } 70.8 \text{ days} \end{aligned} \qquad (12\text{-}53)$$

The length of the inventory cycle is

$$t_c^* = t_p^* + t_d^* = \frac{Q^*}{u} = \frac{516}{2,000} = 0.259 \text{ year or } 94.5 \text{ days} \qquad (12\text{-}54)$$

The total annual cost is

$$\begin{aligned} TC &= \left(\frac{D}{Q^*}\right)C_S + \frac{Q^*}{2}\left(1 - \frac{u}{p}\right)C_H \\ &= \left(\frac{2,000}{516}\right)100 + \frac{516}{2}\left(1 - \frac{2,000}{8,000}\right)2 \\ &= 387 + 387 = \$774 \end{aligned} \qquad (12\text{-}55)$$

## Economic Order Quantity: Quantity Discounts

When we first began to develop the simple economic order quantity model, we observed that the cost of purchasing items is an important factor in certain inventory decisions. However, we assumed that the demand, $D$, and the purchase cost per item, $C_I$, were constant or that the unit cost of an item was independent of the quantity produced. This meant that the quantity ordered did not affect the total inventory cost, so the model did not consider it.

Many service businesses and manufacturing companies provide quantity discounts as an incentive to buy greater quantities of products. Quantity discounts generally mean lower unit costs on items purchased in bigger lots or quantities. When quantity discounts are available, the relevant total annual inventory cost is

| Total annual inventory cost | | Annual inventory ordering cost | | Annual inventory carrying cost | | Annual inventory item cost | |
|---|---|---|---|---|---|---|---|
| $TC$ | $=$ | $\left(\dfrac{D}{Q}\right)C_O$ | $+$ | $\left(\dfrac{Q}{2}\right)C_H$ | $+$ | $DC_I$ | (12-56) |

Figure 12.8 is a graph that shows the relevant annual inventory costs as a function of order quantity when the supplier offers a quantity discount situation. For this figure, if less than $Q_A$ units are ordered the price per unit will be $C_1$; if $Q_A$ up to $Q_B$ units are ordered, the price per unit will be $C_2$; and, if more than $Q_B$ units are ordered, the price per unit will be $C_3$.

For the quantity discount situation, $C_1 > C_2 > C_3$, and there are price breaks associated with the various quantities. This means that the cost per item will be discontinuous. Because the holding cost is a function of the item cost, the cost of holding inventory will also be discontinuous. The ordering cost remains a

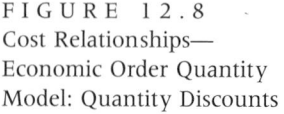

F I G U R E   1 2 . 8
Cost Relationships—
Economic Order Quantity
Model: Quantity Discounts

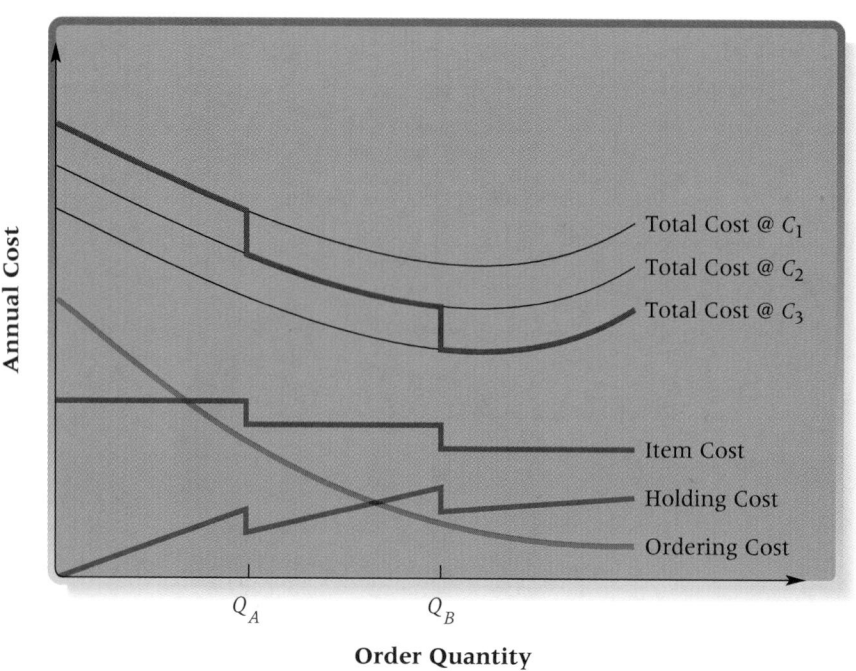

| Discount Category | Order Size | Discount per Order, % | Unit Cost per Item, $C_I$ |
|---|---|---|---|
| A | 0 to 1,499 | 0 | $10.00 |
| B | 1,500 to 2,499 | 2 | 9.80 |
| C | 2,500 + | 5 | 9.50 |

continuous curve, because it has no relationship to the item price. Overall, the total inventory cost curve is discontinuous, shown by connecting portions of the three continuous curves. The continuous curves represent what would happen if the item cost remained constant for all quantities.

In the total annual inventory cost expression, the term $D\,C_I$ is independent of the order quantity $Q$. So we can still use the basic economic order quantity formula that appears in equation 12-12. However, we must now use a three-step process to determine how much we should order so as to minimize the total annual inventory cost in equation 12-56. We can summarize the three-step process as follows:

**Step 1.** Compute $Q^*$ by using the simple EOQ formula in equation 12-12 for the unit cost associated with each discount category.

**Step 2.** For those $Q^*$s that are too small to qualify for the appropriate discount price, adjust the order quantity up to the nearest order quantity that will qualify for the appropriate discount price. NOTE: If a computed $Q^*$ for a given discount price is bigger than the biggest order quantity that qualifies for that particular discount price, we drop that discount price from further consideration, because it cannot lead to the optimal solution.

**Step 3.** For each order quantity determined through steps 1 and 2, compute the total annual inventory cost, using the unit price associated with that order quantity and equation 12-56. The order quantity that yields the minimum total annual inventory cost is the optimal order quantity.

Ace Office Supply Co. is offering discounts on the purchase of boxes of personal computer printer paper. Table 12.3 summarizes the discounts.

Jan Cummings, vice president for materials management for World-wide Overnight Express, is contemplating a large quantity purchase from Ace Office Supply. Her company has more than 1,000 locations throughout the world, and each location needs printer paper. Cummings estimates that her company's annual demand for computer paper is 10,000 boxes, the annual inventory holding costs are 20 percent of the item unit costs, and the ordering costs are $100 per order. Ace will not back order.

We use step 1 of the quantity discount evaluation to compute an optimum economic order quantity for each discount category by using equation 12-12:

$$Q_A^* = \sqrt{\frac{2(10,000)\,(100)}{(0.20)\,(10)}} = 1,000 \text{ boxes} \qquad (12\text{-}57)$$

$$Q_B^* = \sqrt{\frac{2(10,000)(100)}{(0.20)(9.80)}} = 1,010 \text{ boxes} \tag{12-58}$$

$$Q_C^* = \sqrt{\frac{2(10,000)(100)}{(0.20)(9.50)}} = 1,025 \text{ boxes} \tag{12-59}$$

The economic order quantities for the three discount categories are nearly the same—the only difference is the slight change in the inventory holding cost (denominator) in the models. Because $Q_B^*$ and $Q_C^*$ are not sufficiently large to qualify for the appropriate discount, we apply step 2 of the evaluation procedure, and adjust these order quantities up to the nearest order quantity that will permit Cummings to obtain the quantity discount. The revised order quantities become

$$Q_B^* = 1,500 \text{ boxes} \tag{12-60}$$
$$Q_C^* = 2,500 \text{ boxes} \tag{12-61}$$

Next, we apply step 3 of the evaluation process and compute the total annual inventory cost for the order quantities associated with the three discount categories. Table 12.4 summarizes the computations.

Table 12.4 shows that a decision to order 2,500 units at the 5 percent discount rate costs the least. The higher discount rate for an order of this size more than offsets the higher inventory costs that Cummings's company incurs.

## Sensitivity Analysis for the EOQ Model

The various EOQ models we discussed previously assumed that the ordering and holding costs and the demand are all known with certainty. In practice they are, at best, good estimates. Thus, operations managers may find it useful to subject the EOQ formula to sensitivity analysis.

They can write the basic economic order quantity formula as

$$Q^* = \sqrt{\frac{2D\,C_O}{C_H}} \quad \text{or} \quad Q^a = \sqrt{\frac{2D^a\,C_O^a}{C_H^a}} \tag{12-62}$$
$$\text{(Estimated)} \qquad\qquad\qquad \text{(Actual)}$$

where $D$, $C_O$, and $C_H$ are estimated values and the actual values are $D^a$, $C_O^a$, and $C_H^a$. Defining $r$ as the ratio of the actual to estimated EOQ, we have

$$r = \frac{Q^a}{Q^*} = \frac{\sqrt{2D^a C_O^a / C_H^a}}{\sqrt{2D C_O / C_H}} = \sqrt{\left(\frac{D^a}{D}\right)\left(\frac{C_O^a}{C_O}\right)\left(\frac{C_H}{C_H^a}\right)} \tag{12-63}$$

T A B L E  1 2 . 4
Total Annual Inventory
Costs, Quantity Discounts

| Discount Category | Unit Cost per Item, $C_t$ | Economic Order Quantity | Annual Inventory Holding Cost | Annual Ordering Cost | Annual Purchase Cost | Total Annual Cost |
|---|---|---|---|---|---|---|
| A | $10.00 | 1000 | $1,000 | $1,000 | $100,000 | $102,000 |
| B | 9.80 | 1500 | 1,470 | 667 | 98,000 | 100,137 |
| C | 9.50 | 2500 | 2,375 | 400 | 95,000 | 97,775 |

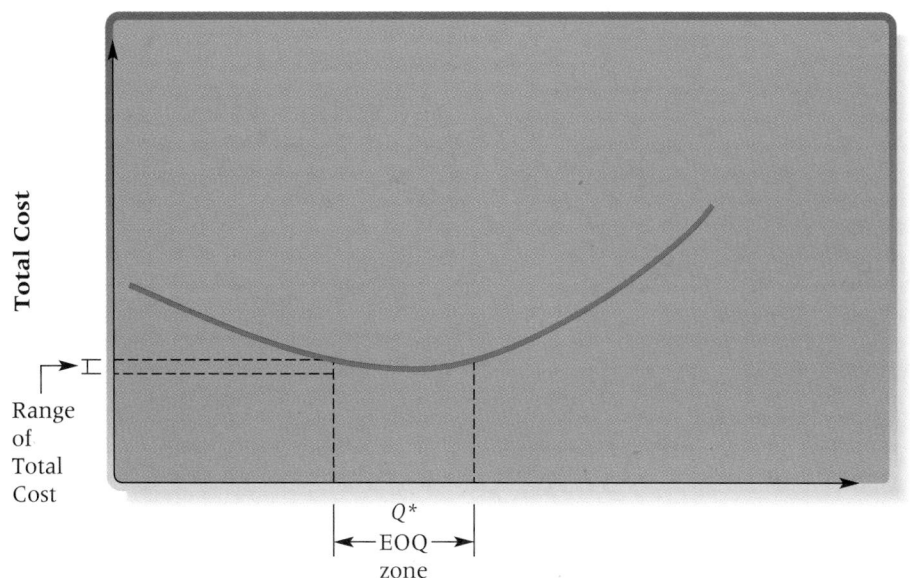

FIGURE 12.9
Total Inventory Cost Versus
EOQ

Total Cost

Range of Total Cost

$Q*$
← EOQ →
zone

---

**EXAMPLE 12.8**

We can see the sensitivity of the EOQ formula if we suppose that the $C_O = 1,000$, $C_H = 100$, and $D = 50,000$. It is discovered that $D^a = 60,000$. Then

$$r = \frac{Q^a}{Q^*} = \sqrt{\left(\frac{D^a}{D}\right)\left(\frac{C_O^a}{C_O}\right)\frac{C_H}{C_H^a}} = \sqrt{\left(\frac{60,000}{50,000}\right)\left(\frac{1,000}{1,000}\right)\left(\frac{100}{100}\right)} \quad (12\text{-}64)$$
$$= 1.095$$

We can see that we underestimated the demand by 16.7 percent (60,000 − 50,000/60,000), whereas we underestimated the economic order quantity by about 8.7 percent, because

$$\frac{Q^*}{Q^a} = \frac{1.0}{1.095} = 0.913 \ (1.000 - 0.913 = 0.087) \quad (12\text{-}65)$$

---

Perhaps the most important issue in sensitivity analysis involves how errors affect the total inventory cost. Figure 12.9 illustrates this property of the total cost. Overall, the total cost is insensitive to small changes, or errors, in cost or demand quantities in the EOQ model. Figure 12.9 shows that the EOQ actually has a "zone" of acceptable values, which produces nearly the same total cost.

# When to Order: The Continuous Review System

We can define inventory control systems in terms of how we decide when to place the order. Using the **continuous review system** to determine when to reorder, we review the remaining quantity of an item each time a withdrawal is made from inventory. In practice operations managers make a physical count of inventory at periodic intervals (daily, weekly, or monthly) to decide how much of each item to order. Many small retailers use this approach, simply checking the quantities on shelves and in the storeroom on a periodic basis. Another very elementary type of continuous review system is the **two-bin system**, which sets aside two containers, or bins, to hold the total inventory of an item. Items are

*Retail inventory at a typical large discount store. Discount store chains order in large amounts in order to receive quantity discounts.*

withdrawn from the first bin until it is empty, at which point it is time to reorder the quantity that will again fill the bin. The second bin contains enough stock to satisfy demand until the order comes in, plus an extra amount to provide a cushion against a stock out. More sophisticated continuous review systems exist for virtually all large retailers. They use computerized cash registers, which are linked to inventory control systems. At sale the clerk enters the item's inventory code, and the computer system automatically reduces the inventory level by one and checks to see whether the reorder point has been reached. If it has, the system initiates a purchase order to replenish the stock.

The continuous review system is also called a **reorder point system (ROP)**, or a **fixed order quantity system**. It works this way: Place an order for $Q$ units whenever a withdrawal brings the inventory to the reorder point, $R$. The continuous review system has only two parameters, $Q$ and $R$, and each new order is of size $Q$. Figure 12.10 shows how a continuous review system operates. Values for $Q$ and $R$ are specified in advance; $Q$ is based on the EOQ, a price-break quantity, or a container size. The downward sloping line in Figure 12.10 represents the on-hand inventory, which is reduced at a fairly steady rate. When the reorder point, $R$, is reached, a new order for $Q$ units is placed. The on-hand inventory continues to drop throughout the lead time, $LT$, until the order arrives and the on-hand inventory increases by $Q$ units. During the lead time the company is vulnerable to stock outs and uses a safety stock to provide protection.

## Determining the Reorder Point

Figure 12.10 shows that the reorder point is a function of the demand rate and the lead time. Four situations involving variations in these factors are possible:

- Constant demand rate, constant lead time
- Variable demand rate, constant lead time
- Constant demand rate, variable lead time
- Variable demand rate, variable lead time

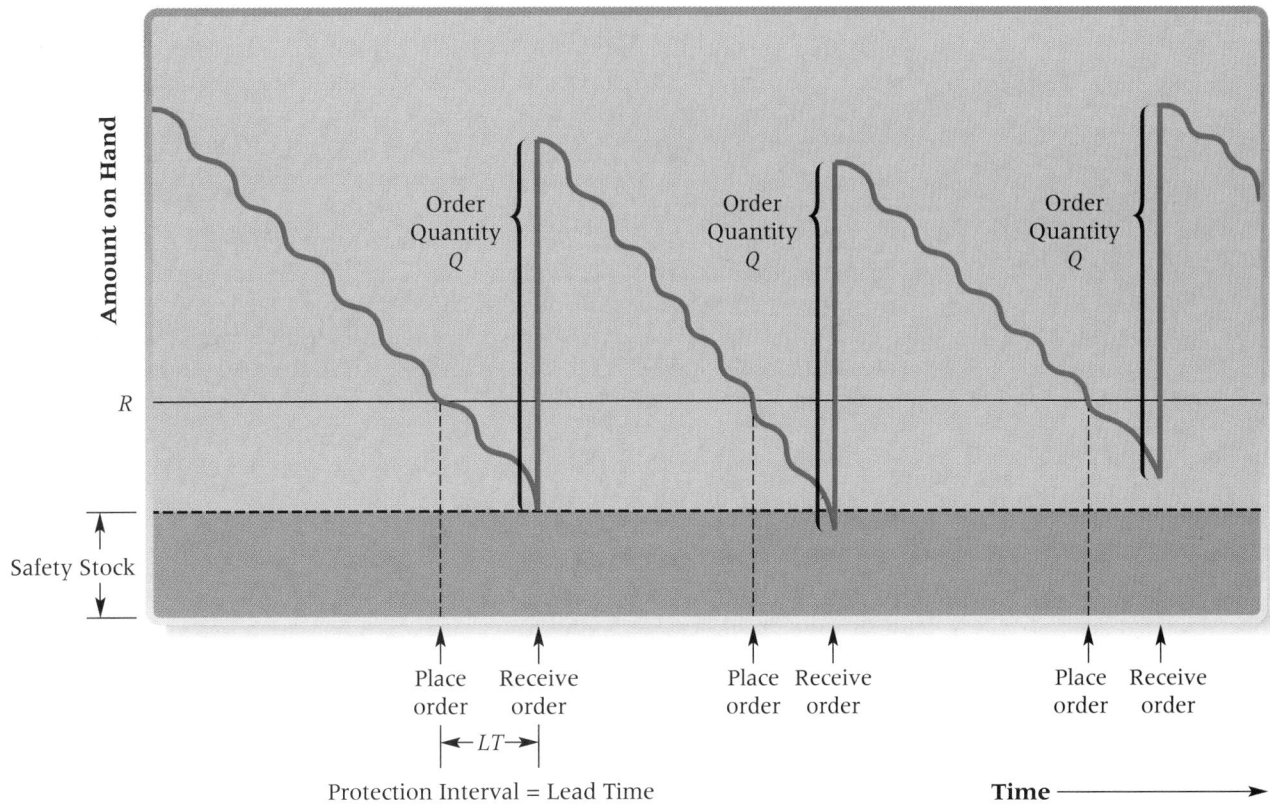

Amount on Hand

Order
Quantity
$Q$

Order
Quantity
$Q$

Order
Quantity
$Q$

$R$

Safety Stock

Place
order

Receive
order

Place
order

Receive
order

Place
order

Receive
order

$\leftarrow LT \rightarrow$

Protection Interval = Lead Time

**Time** ⟶

FIGURE 12.10
Operation of a Continuous
Review Inventory System

Each situation assumes that a normal distribution can adequately describe any variation in either the demand rate or the lead time. Fortunately, this system provides good approximate reorder points even when the actual distributions are not normal.

### Situation 1: Constant Demand Rate and Constant Lead Time
This is the set of conditions assumed for the simple EOQ model. Because both demand and lead time are constant, the company is at no risk of a stock out. For constant demand with constant lead time, the reorder point is

$$R = \text{constant demand during lead time}$$
$$= d \cdot LT \qquad (12\text{-}66)$$

where
$$d = \text{constant demand rate}$$
$$LT = \text{constant lead time}$$

---

Allen Machinery Co. uses four drums of hydraulic fluid for its presses each day. Deliveries of the hydraulic fluid arrive exactly 10 days after Allen Machinery places an order. The reorder point is

**EXAMPLE 12.9**

$$R = d \cdot LT$$
$$= 4 \cdot 10 = 40 \text{ drums} \qquad (12\text{-}67)$$

**Situation 2: Variable Demand Rate, Constant Lead Time** A stock out could occur when the demand rate varies and lead time is constant. To compensate for the variable demand rate the company uses a buffer or safety stock to reduce the risk of a stock out during the lead time.

By carrying a safety stock the company incurs an additional inventory carrying cost. So the operations manager must carefully weigh the cost of carrying safety stock against the insurance it provides.

The company risks a stock out only during the lead time, that is, between the time an order is placed and the time it arrives. Figure 12.11 presents an expanded view of how variable demand might behave during a fixed lead time and how safety stock can reduce the risk of a stock out during that period. As Figure 12.11 shows, a range of demands is possible during the lead time. If demand during the lead time continues at its current rate (solid line), it will just reach the safety stock when the lead time ends and the new order comes in. If demand decreases during the lead time, the inventory will be at point *a*, above the safety stock level. If demand during the lead time increases only slightly, the inventory will be at point *b*, about half-way through the safety stock. If demand during the lead time increases markedly, the inventory will reach points *c* or *d*. At point *c* the safety stock would be depleted. At point *d*, the inventory would be in an out-of-stock or back order condition.

The concept we are describing here is the **cycle-service level**, which is defined as the probability that a stock out will not occur during the lead time of the inventory cycle. A cycle-service level of 90 percent means that there is a 90 percent probability that supply will exceed demand during lead time.

The cycle-service level is

$$\text{Cycle–service level} = 100 \text{ percent} - \text{Stockout risk} \qquad (12\text{-}68)$$

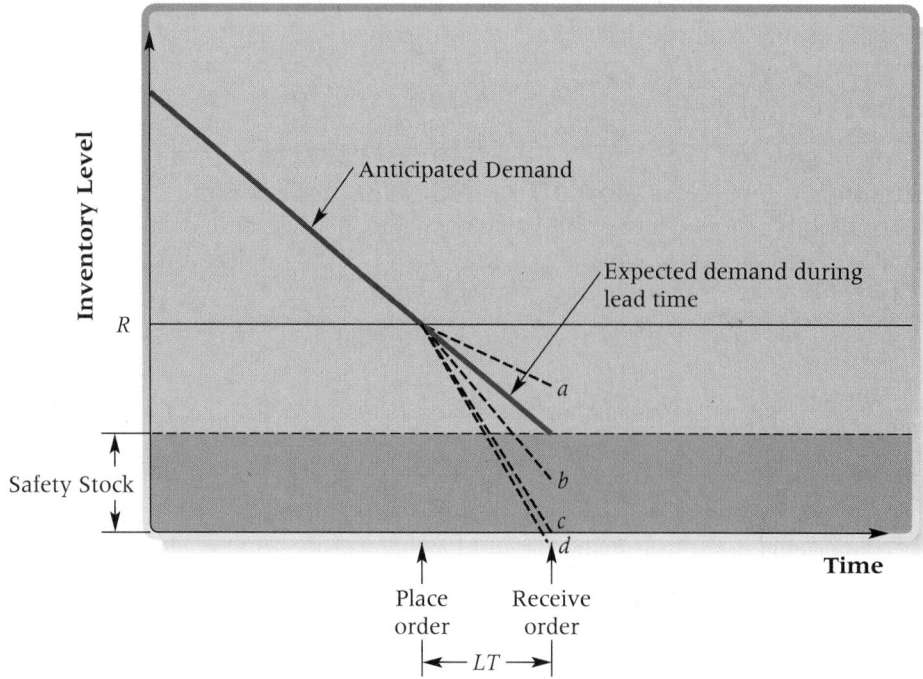

FIGURE 12.11
Lead Time—Safety Stock
Relationships

For variable demand with constant lead time the recorder point is

$$R = \text{Expected demand during lead time} + \text{Safety stock}$$
$$= \bar{d} \cdot LT + Z\sqrt{LT}\,(\sigma_d) \qquad (12\text{-}69)$$

where

$\bar{d}$ = Average demand rate
$LT$ = Constant lead time
$Z$ = Standard normal deviate associated with the cycle-service level
$\sigma_d$ = Standard deviation of the demand rate

**EXAMPLE 12.10**

The average demand that Smash Hits Videos is experiencing for one of its first-run movies is 10 rentals per day. It has examined its rental records for the last 30 days and has found that the daily rental demand for this particular movie is approximately normally distributed and has a standard deviation of 2 rentals per day. Smash Hits Videos does two-day rentals, so its lead time is 2 days. The manager of the company wants to maintain a 95 percent cycle-service level. The reorder point for this movie is

$$R = \bar{d} \cdot LT + Z\sqrt{LT}\,(\sigma_d)$$
$$= 10 \cdot 2 + (1.65)\sqrt{2}\,(2) = 24.65 \text{ rentals (use 25)} \qquad (12\text{-}70)$$

To meet its goal of a 95 percent cycle-service level, Smash Hits Videos should maintain a rental inventory of 25 copies of the video. Figure 12.12 shows this situation graphically.

**Situation 3: Constant Demand Rate, Variable Lead Time** When the demand rate is constant and the variable lead time is normally distributed, the reorder point is

$$R = \text{Expected demand during lead time} + \text{Safety stock}$$
$$= d \cdot \overline{LT} + Z\,d\,\sigma_{LT} \qquad (12\text{-}71)$$

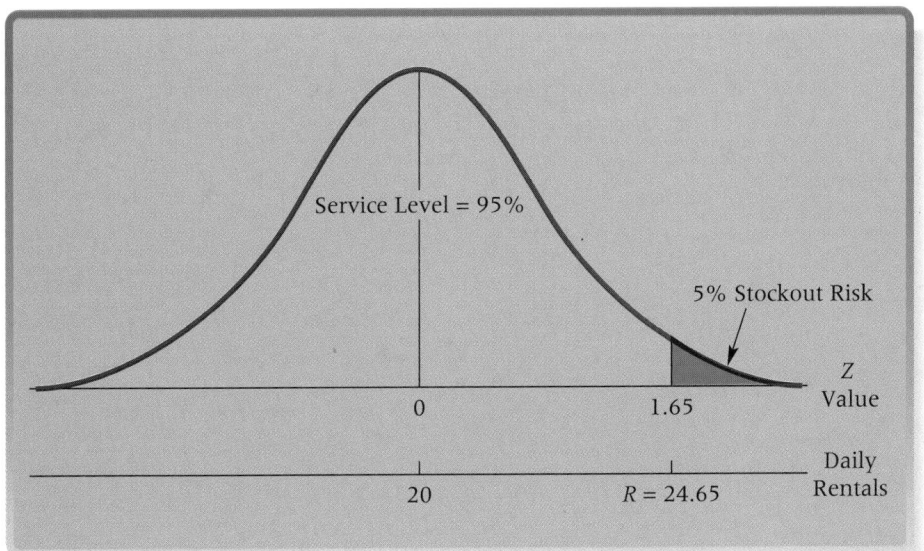

**FIGURE 12.12**
Variable Demand Rate, Constant Lead Time Example

where

$d$ = Constant demand rate
$\overline{LT}$ = Average lead time
$Z$ = Standard normal deviate associated with the cycle-service level
$\sigma_{LT}$ = Standard deviation of the lead time

---

**EXAMPLE 12.11**

The copying machines at Southeastern Technical University regularly use 6 toner cartridges each week. The lead time associated with receiving orders of the toner cartridges is normally distributed with a mean of 0.5 weeks and a standard deviation of 0.25 weeks. A 97 percent cycle-service level is considered desirable. The reorder point for the toner cartridges is

$$R = d \bullet \overline{LT} + Z\,d\,\sigma_{LT}$$
$$= 6(0.5) + 1.88(6)(0.25) = 5.82 \text{ cartridges} \qquad (12\text{-}72)$$

Figure 12.13 depicts this situation.

---

**Situation 4: Variable Demand Rate, Variable Lead Time** Both the demand rate and the lead time are subject to variation in the fourth and final situation. In this case the safety stock generally must be larger in order to compensate for the increased variation. Assuming that the average demand during the lead time and the lead time itself are normally distributed, the total demand during the lead time will also be normally distributed, with an expected value of $\bar{d} \bullet \overline{LT}$. The variance for this expected value is the sum of the variances of the demand and the lead time, and its standard deviation is

Standard deviation of total demand during the lead time:

$$\sigma_{dLT} = \sqrt{\sigma^2_{demand} + \sigma^2_{lead\ time}} \qquad (12\text{-}73)$$

where

$$\sigma_{demand} = \sqrt{\overline{LT}}\,\sigma_d \qquad (12\text{-}74)$$

$$\sigma_{lead\ time} = \bar{d}\,\sigma_{LT} \qquad (12\text{-}75)$$

FIGURE 12.13
Constant Demand Rate,
Variable Lead Time Example

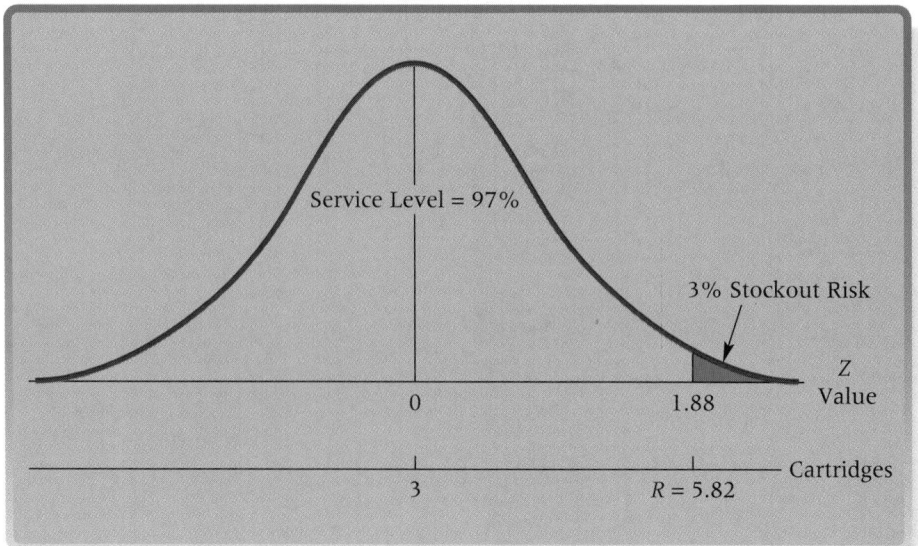

Substituting

$$\sigma_{dLT} = \sqrt{(\sqrt{\overline{LT}}\,\sigma_d)^2 + (\overline{d}\,\sigma_{LT})^2} = \sqrt{\overline{LT}\,\sigma_d^2 + \overline{d}^2\,\sigma_{LT}^2} \qquad (12\text{-}76)$$

When both demand rate and lead time are variable and assumed to be normally distributed, the reorder point is

$$R = \text{Expected demand during lead time} + \text{Safety stock}$$

$$= \overline{d}\,(\overline{LT}) + Z\sqrt{\overline{LT}\,\sigma_d^2 + \overline{d}^2\,\sigma_{LT}^2} \qquad (12\text{-}77)$$

---

**EXAMPLE 12.12**

Sales of 35mm print film at the Photo-Quik Drive Thru are normally distributed, with a mean of 100 rolls per day and a standard deviation of 10 rolls per day. The lead time is also normally distributed, with a mean of 5 days and a standard deviation of 1 day. The Photo-Quik Drive Thru would like to maintain a 90 percent cycle-service level. The reorder point for this example is

$$R = \overline{d}\,(\overline{LT}) + Z\sqrt{\overline{LT}\,\sigma_d^2 + \overline{d}^2\,\sigma_{LT}^2}$$

$$= (100)(5) + 1.28\sqrt{(5)\,(10)^2 + (100)^2\,(1)^2}$$

$$= 500 + 1.28\sqrt{500 + 1,000,000} = 500 + 1.28\sqrt{1,500,000}$$

$$= 500 + 1.28(1225) = 2,068 \text{ rolls} \qquad (12\text{-}78)$$

Figure 12.14 shows this situation graphically.

---

## Service Levels, Safety Stock, and Shortages

Another way to look at service level is as the percentage of units that can be supplied from stock on hand, commonly referred to as the **fill rate**. For example, if the monthly demand for an item is one hundred units, a 95 percent service level, or fill rate, implies that the company can immediately supply ninety-five units from stock and will be short five units. This assumes that numerous small

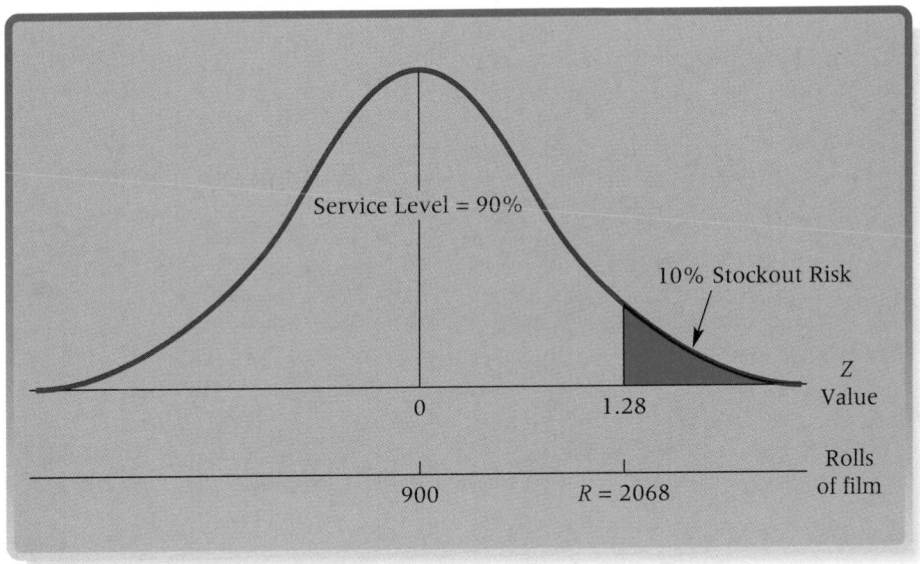

FIGURE 12.14
Variable Demand Rate,
Variable Lead Time Example

## Normal Distribution Service Levels and Unit Normal Loss Function

| z | Lead Time Service Level | E(z) | z | Lead Time Service Level | E(z) | z | Lead Time Service Level | E(z) | z | Lead Time Service Level | E(z) |
|---|---|---|---|---|---|---|---|---|---|---|---|
| -2.40 | 0.0082 | 2.403 | -0.80 | 0.2119 | 0.920 | 0.80 | 0.7881 | 0.120 | 2.40 | 0.9918 | 0.003 |
| -2.36 | 0.0091 | 2.363 | -0.76 | 0.2236 | 0.889 | 0.84 | 0.7995 | 0.112 | 2.44 | 0.9927 | 0.002 |
| -2.32 | 0.0102 | 2.323 | -0.72 | 0.2358 | 0.858 | 0.88 | 0.8106 | 0.104 | 2.48 | 0.9934 | 0.002 |
| -2.28 | 0.0113 | 2.284 | -0.68 | 0.2483 | 0.828 | 0.92 | 0.8212 | 0.097 | 2.52 | 0.9941 | 0.002 |
| -2.24 | 0.0125 | 2.244 | -0.64 | 0.2611 | 0.798 | 0.96 | 0.8315 | 0.089 | 2.56 | 0.9948 | 0.002 |
| -2.20 | 0.0139 | 2.205 | -0.60 | 0.2743 | 0.769 | 1.00 | 0.8413 | 0.083 | 2.60 | 0.9953 | 0.001 |
| -2.16 | 0.0154 | 2.165 | -0.56 | 0.2877 | 0.740 | 1.04 | 0.8508 | 0.077 | 2.64 | 0.9959 | 0.001 |
| -2.12 | 0.0170 | 2.126 | -0.52 | 0.3015 | 0.712 | 1.08 | 0.8599 | 0.071 | 2.68 | 0.9963 | 0.001 |
| -2.08 | 0.0188 | 2.087 | -0.48 | 0.3156 | 0.684 | 1.12 | 0.8686 | 0.066 | 2.72 | 0.9967 | 0.001 |
| -2.04 | 0.0207 | 2.048 | -0.44 | 0.3300 | 0.657 | 1.16 | 0.8770 | 0.061 | 2.76 | 0.9971 | 0.001 |
| -2.00 | 0.0228 | 2.008 | -0.40 | 0.3446 | 0.630 | 1.20 | 0.8849 | 0.056 | 2.80 | 0.9974 | 0.0008 |
| -1.96 | 0.0250 | 1.969 | -0.36 | 0.3594 | 0.597 | 1.24 | 0.8925 | 0.052 | 2.84 | 0.9977 | 0.0007 |
| -1.92 | 0.0274 | 1.930 | -0.32 | 0.3745 | 0.576 | 1.28 | 0.8997 | 0.048 | 2.88 | 0.9980 | 0.0006 |
| -1.88 | 0.0301 | 1.892 | -0.28 | 0.3897 | 0.555 | 1.32 | 0.9066 | 0.044 | 2.92 | 0.9982 | 0.0005 |
| -1.84 | 0.0329 | 1.853 | -0.24 | 0.4052 | 0.530 | 1.36 | 0.9131 | 0.040 | 2.96 | 0.9985 | 0.0004 |
| -1.80 | 0.0359 | 1.814 | -0.20 | 0.4207 | 0.507 | 1.40 | 0.9192 | 0.037 | 3.00 | 0.9987 | 0.0004 |
| -1.76 | 0.0392 | 1.776 | -0.16 | 0.4364 | 0.484 | 1.44 | 0.9251 | 0.034 | 3.04 | 0.9988 | 0.0003 |
| -1.72 | 0.0427 | 1.737 | -0.12 | 0.4522 | 0.462 | 1.48 | 0.9306 | 0.031 | 3.08 | 0.9990 | 0.0003 |
| -1.68 | 0.0465 | 1.699 | -0.08 | 0.4681 | 0.440 | 1.52 | 0.9357 | 0.028 | 3.12 | 0.9991 | 0.0002 |
| -1.64 | 0.0505 | 1.661 | -0.04 | 0.4840 | 0.419 | 1.56 | 0.9406 | 0.026 | 3.16 | 0.9992 | 0.0002 |
| -1.60 | 0.0548 | 1.623 | 0.00 | 0.5000 | 0.399 | 1.60 | 0.9452 | 0.023 | 3.20 | 0.9993 | 0.0002 |
| -1.56 | 0.0594 | 1.586 | 0.04 | 0.5160 | 0.379 | 1.64 | 0.9495 | 0.021 | 3.24 | 0.9994 | 0.0001 |
| -1.52 | 0.0643 | 1.548 | 0.08 | 0.5319 | 0.360 | 1.68 | 0.9535 | 0.019 | 3.28 | 0.9995 | 0.0001 |
| -1.48 | 0.0694 | 1.511 | 0.12 | 0.5478 | 0.342 | 1.72 | 0.9573 | 0.017 | 3.32 | 0.9995 | 0.0001 |
| -1.44 | 0.0749 | 1.474 | 0.16 | 0.5636 | 0.324 | 1.76 | 0.9608 | 0.016 | 3.36 | 0.9996 | 0.0001 |
| -1.40 | 0.0808 | 1.437 | 0.20 | 0.5793 | 0.307 | 1.80 | 0.9641 | 0.014 | 3.40 | 0.9997 | 0.0001 |
| -1.36 | 0.0869 | 1.400 | 0.24 | 0.5948 | 0.290 | 1.84 | 0.9671 | 0.013 | | | |
| -1.32 | 0.0934 | 1.364 | 0.28 | 0.6103 | 0.275 | 1.88 | 0.9699 | 0.012 | | | |
| -1.28 | 0.1003 | 1.328 | 0.32 | 0.6255 | 0.256 | 1.92 | 0.9726 | 0.010 | | | |
| -1.24 | 0.1075 | 1.292 | 0.36 | 0.6406 | 0.237 | 1.96 | 0.9750 | 0.009 | | | |
| -1.20 | 0.1151 | 1.256 | 0.40 | 0.6554 | 0.230 | 2.00 | 0.9772 | 0.008 | | | |
| -1.16 | 0.1230 | 1.221 | 0.44 | 0.6700 | 0.217 | 2.04 | 0.9793 | 0.008 | | | |
| -1.12 | 0.1314 | 1.186 | 0.48 | 0.6844 | 0.204 | 2.08 | 0.9812 | 0.007 | | | |
| -1.08 | 0.1401 | 1.151 | 0.52 | 0.6985 | 0.192 | 2.12 | 0.9830 | 0.006 | | | |
| -1.04 | 0.1492 | 1.117 | 0.56 | 0.7123 | 0.180 | 2.16 | 0.9846 | 0.005 | | | |
| -1.00 | 0.1587 | 1.083 | 0.60 | 0.7257 | 0.169 | 2.20 | 0.9861 | 0.005 | | | |
| -0.96 | 0.1685 | 1.049 | 0.64 | 0.7389 | 0.158 | 2.24 | 0.9875 | 0.004 | | | |
| -0.92 | 0.1788 | 1.017 | 0.68 | 0.7517 | 0.148 | 2.28 | 0.9887 | 0.004 | | | |
| -0.88 | 0.1894 | 0.984 | 0.72 | 0.7642 | 0.138 | 2.32 | 0.9898 | 0.003 | | | |
| -0.84 | 0.2005 | 0.952 | 0.76 | 0.7764 | 0.129 | 2.36 | 0.9909 | 0.003 | | | |

Source: Revised from Robert G. Brown, *Decision Rules for Inventory Management* (New York: Holt, Rinehart and Winston, 1967), pp. 95–103.

TABLE 12.5
Expected Number of Units
Short as a Function of Safety
Stock Standard Deviation

orders, randomly distributed, occur over time. Thus, safety stock is the inventory the company carries to assure that it can provide the level of service it specifies.

In our discussion about computing the reorder point, we did not give any examples involving an expected amount of shortage for a given lead time service level. Quite often, operations managers want to determine the expected number of units by which they will be short.

Operations managers can compute the expected number of units short by using the same statistical concepts. For example, assume that the average weekly demand for an item is ten units with a standard deviation of one unit. If we stock twelve units, the probability that we will be out of stock is the probability that someone will demand thirteen, fourteen, fifteen, or more units. While the idea behind this computation is simple, using it is time consuming and tedious. Fortunately, Robert G. Brown has compiled a table, provided in Table 12.5, that shows how the number of standard deviations of safety stock, the service level, and the expected number of units short correspond. This table is based on the assumption that the distribution of lead time demand can be adequately represented by the normal distribution. Using this assumption, the expected number of units short in each order cycle is

$$E(n) = E(z)\,\sigma_{dLT} \tag{12-79}$$

where   $E(n)$ = Expected number of units short per order cycle
$E(z)$ = Expected number of units short from a normalized table where mean
  = 0 and $\sigma$ = 1 (Table 12.5)
$\sigma_{dLT}$ = Standard deviation of lead time demand

Usually, the operations manager will know the standard deviation of demand, but it will correspond to a time period different than the lead time. For example, demand variation may have been computed from daily demand reports extending over a month, whereas the lead time is only a few days. Fortunately, the following conversion is available for computing the standard deviation of lead time demand:

$$\sigma_{dLT} = \sigma_t \sqrt{\frac{LT}{t}} \tag{12-80}$$

where

$\sigma_t$ = Known standard deviation of demand over some time period $t$
$LT$ = Lead time
$t$ = Time interval corresponding to the standard deviation of demand

For example, assume that we computed the standard deviation of demand to be ten units per day. If our lead time is four days, then

$$\sigma_{dLT} = \sigma_t \sqrt{\frac{LT}{t}} = 10\sqrt{\frac{4}{1}} = 10(2) = 20 \tag{12-81}$$

**EXAMPLE 12.13**

The O'Brien Corp. has determined that its lead time demand is approximately normal, with a mean of 100 units and a standard deviation of 15 units. It seeks to determine the number of units it can expect to be short for a 90 percent lead time service level and the service level that corresponds to an expected shortage of 5 units.

First, for a service level of 0.90, from Table 12.5, $E(z) = 0.048$.

$$E(n) = E(z) \, \sigma_{dLT} = (0.048)(15) = 0.72 \text{ units} \qquad (12\text{-}82)$$

Second, for $E(n) = 5 \text{ units}$

$$
\begin{aligned}
E(n) &= E(z) \, \sigma_{dLT} \\
5 &= E(z)(15) \\
E(z) &= 5/15 = 0.333
\end{aligned}
\qquad (12\text{-}83)
$$

From Table 12.5, this produces a service level of approximately 56 percent (by interpolation).

On a yearly basis the expected number of units short is simply the product of the expected number of units short per cycle and the number of cycles (orders) per year:

$$E(N) = E(n)\left(\frac{D}{Q}\right) \qquad (12\text{-}84)$$

where

$$E(N) = \text{Expected number of units short per year}$$

---

**EXAMPLE 12.14**

Assume that the O'Brien Corp. also experiences yearly demand of 3,000 units and uses an order quantity of size 150. Its expected number of units short per year for a 90 percent lead time service level is

$$E(N) = E(n)\left(\frac{D}{Q}\right) = (0.72)\left(\frac{3,000}{150}\right) = 14.4 \text{ units} \qquad (12\text{-}85)$$

---

It is also useful to talk about the service level in annual terms. On an annual basis

$$
\begin{aligned}
&\text{Expected number of units short per year} \\
&= (1 - \text{Annual service level})(\text{Annual demand}) \\
E(N) &= (1 - SL \text{ annual})\, D
\end{aligned}
\qquad (12\text{-}86)
$$

Also:

$$
\begin{array}{ccc}
\text{Expected number of} & & \text{Expected number of} \quad \text{Number of} \\
\text{units short per year} & = & \text{units short per order} \; \bullet \; \text{orders per} \\
& & \text{order} \qquad\qquad \text{year}
\end{array}
$$

$$E(N) = E(n) \bullet \left(\frac{D}{Q}\right) \qquad (12\text{-}87)$$

Now $E(n) = E(z) \, \sigma_{dLT}$

so, $E(N) = E(z) \, \sigma_{dLT} \bullet \left(\frac{D}{Q}\right) \qquad (12\text{-}88)$

By substitution $(1 - SL$ annual$)\, D = E(z)\,\sigma_{dLT}\left(\dfrac{D}{Q}\right)$  (12-89)

or $(1 - SL$ annual$) = E(z)\,\dfrac{\sigma_{dLT}}{Q}$

---

Let's compute the annual service level for O'Brien Corp. With $E(z) = 0.048$ (Table 12.5) for a 90 percent lead time service level and $Q = 150$, we determine that

$$(1 - SL \text{ annual}) = E(z)\,\frac{\sigma_{dLT}}{Q}$$

$$(1 - SL \text{ annual}) = \frac{(0.048)\,(15)}{150}$$

$$(1 - SL \text{ annual}) = 0.0048$$

$$SL \text{ annual} = 1 - 0.0048 = 0.9952 \qquad (12\text{-}90)$$

**EXAMPLE 12.15**

# When to Order: The Periodic Review System

An operations manager who is using the **periodic review system** checks the inventory position only at fixed time intervals, not continuously. The periodic review system is also called a **fixed time period system** or a **fixed order interval system**. The manager places a new order at the end of each review, and the time between orders is fixed. The manager orders varying quantities at these fixed time intervals, because demand is a random variable that varies between reviews. A good example of the periodic review system is the candy or soft-drink supplier who stocks the candy or soda machines at your college or university. The supplier makes rounds every few days, or once a week, reviews the quantities of candy or soft drinks in the vending machines, and restocks them to a level sufficient until the next review. Figure 12.15 shows the operation of a periodic review system.

The downward sloping line again represents how the periodic review system operates. When the predetermined time since the last review has elapsed, the manager places an order to bring the inventory level up to the desired target

*Work in process and finished goods inventories at a brewery. Breweries have unique inventory control problems because of product spoilage.*

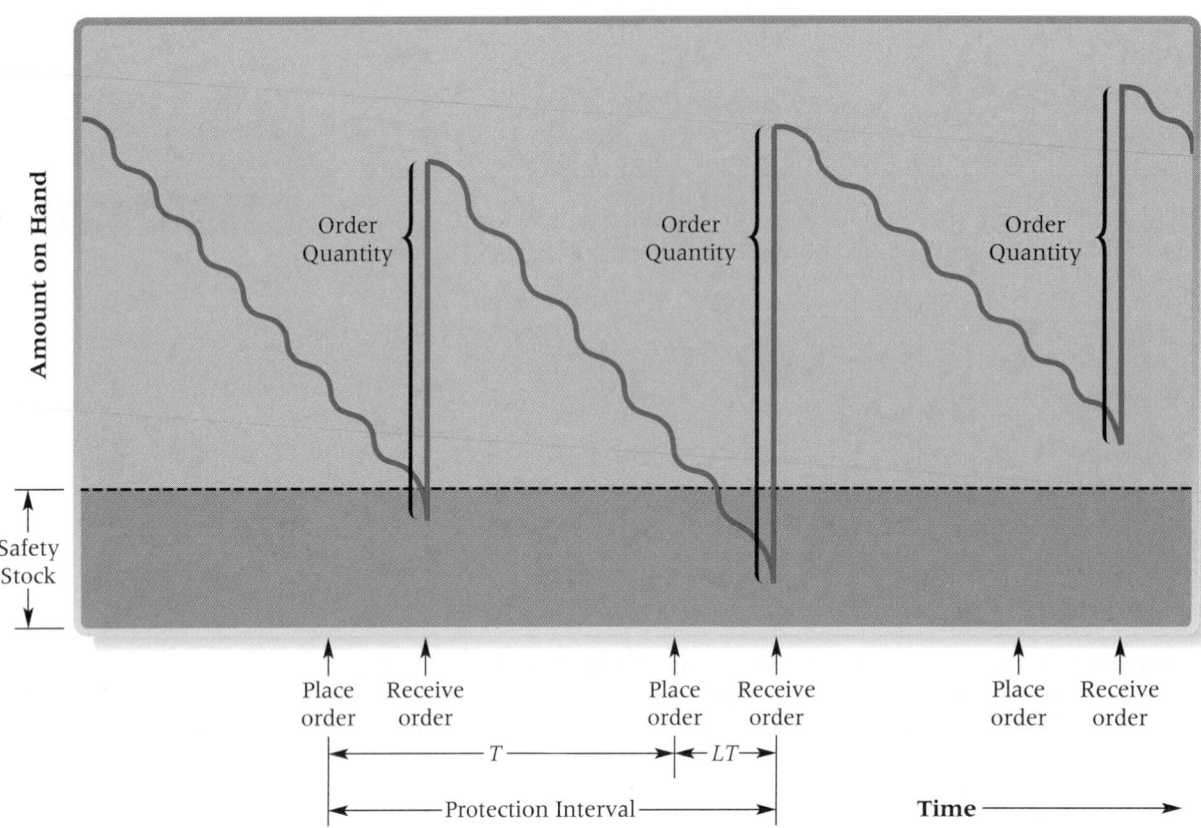

FIGURE 12.15
Operation of a Periodic
Review System

inventory level. As Figure 12.15 shows, the lot sizes vary from cycle to cycle. The order quantity is

$$\text{Order quantity} = \begin{matrix} \text{Expected demand} \\ \text{during the} \\ \text{protection interval} \end{matrix} + \text{Safety stock} - \begin{matrix} \text{Inventory} \\ \text{on hand at} \\ \text{reorder} \\ \text{time} \end{matrix}$$

$$= \bar{d}\,(T + LT) + Z\,\sigma_d\,\sqrt{T + LT} - I \qquad (12\text{-}91)$$

where

$\bar{d}$ = Average demand rate
$LT$ = Lead time
$T$ = Time between reviews
$Z$ = Standard normal deviate associated with the cycle-service level
$\sigma_d$ = Standard deviation of demand over the review and lead time
$I$ = Current inventory level (including items on order)

The demand rate, lead time, and time between reviews can be expressed in any time unit, such as days, weeks, months, or years, so long as it is consistent throughout equation 12-91.

> Hopewell Manufacturing produces a computer monitor. A major component for the monitor is its plastic case (housing). Daily demand for the case is 100 units with a standard deviation of 10 units. The company uses a review period of 30 days, and the lead time is 14 days. It would like to maintain a 95 percent cycle-service level. At the beginning of this review period Hopewell has 50 units in inventory.
>
> The periodic review order quantity is
>
> $$\text{Order quantity} = \bar{d}\,(T + LT) + Z\sigma_d\,\sqrt{T + LT} - I$$
> $$= (100)\,(30 + 14) + (1.65)(10)\,\sqrt{30 + 14} - 50$$
> $$= 4{,}400 + 109 - 50 = 4{,}459 \text{ cases} \qquad (12\text{-}92)$$

**EXAMPLE 12.16**

## Comparing the Continuous Review and Periodic Review Systems

A variety of inventory problems arise in practice. This means that neither the continuous review nor the periodic review system is best in all situations. Table 12.6 compares the two systems.

The first, and major, advantage of the continuous review system is that it requires less safety stock. Its safety stock covers only the lead time, whereas safety stock in the periodic review system covers the lead time and the time between orders. A second advantage is that using fixed lot sizes may make obtaining quantity discounts easier. Physical limitations of the manufacturing process or the service facility may also require a fixed lot size. A third advantage is that this system tends to promote the individualized review of every item, which may be particularly desirable for expensive items. By reviewing inventory items individually the operations manager can reduce total ordering and holding costs.

The periodic review system also has a number of advantages. First and foremost, it is less time consuming and expensive to maintain. Because replenishment occurs at fixed time intervals, it can be part of an employee's duties and can be done on a certain day or part of a day on a regular basis. Fixed replenishment also works well with many transportation systems, where delivery times are fixed on a daily, weekly, or monthly basis. Second, it allows for combining orders to the same supplier, which may promote efficiency, because it eliminates paperwork, reduces ordering cost, and makes checking of orders easier. In some cases combining orders can lead to price breaks. Third, inventory recordkeeping costs are lower, because inventory levels only have to be known when a review is made. For a periodic review system perpetual inventory records are not necessary.

| Continuous Review System Advantages | Periodic Review System Advantages |
|---|---|
| 1. Lower safety stock | 1. Less time consuming and experience to maintain |
| 2. Fixed lot sizes may make it easier to obtain quantity discounts | 2. Allows for combining orders to the same supplier |
| 3. Individual review of items is used, which may be very desirable for expensive items | 3. Inventory recordkeeping cost can be reduced |

TABLE 12.6
Comparison of the Continuous Review and Periodic Review Systems

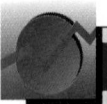

# Multi-echelon Inventory Management at IBM

IBM has implemented Optimizer, a system for flexible and optimal control of spare parts inventory, in its United States service support network. This system is based on recent research in multiechelon inventory theory.

IBM's National Service Division (NSD) is responsible for providing high-quality, postpurchase support to IBM's customers. It has developed an extensive and sophisticated inventory management system to provide customers with prompt and reliable service. Most service calls require parts for replacement, diagnostics, or tools. Rapid deployment of these parts is vital to getting customers' machines fixed and running quickly.

The IBM parts distribution network is a large, complex, multiechelon network, as shown in Figure 12.16. The parts inventory maintained in this network is large, diverse, and valued in billions of dollars. Most inventory is carried at noncentral site locations, and the network processes millions of parts transactions annually. The logistics of the network are managed by a sophisticated information and control system called the Parts Inventory Management System (PIMS).

The major requirement for effective after-sales service support are service level flexibility and inventory efficiency. The basic problem facing IBM's National Service Division was to achieve lower costs while maintaining or improving customer service.

NSD solved the problem by determining a stock control policy for each location and each part that would minimize the expected costs for the whole system and satisfy service constraints for products and specific groupings of parts, called *technology component groups (TCGs)*. The cost function includes (1) replenishment cost-transportation, handling, and order set-up, (2) emergency (expediting) cost, and (3) inventory holding cost. NSD made a comprehensive set of inventory decisions, including:

- The reorder points and stock levels for each part and echelon in the system
- Alternative sources for each part, for both emergency backup and stock
- Policies that determine the priority attached to different classes of demand when shortages arise

When NSD implemented the system on a national basis, it led to a reduction in inventory investment, improved service, enhanced flexibility in responding to changing service requirements, and an improved understanding of the effect of parts operations on customer service. The time-averaged value of inventory recommended by the Optimizer system was 20 to 25 percent below that of the old system. The system also produced a 10 percent improvement in parts availability at the lower echelons while maintaining parts availability at the higher echelons. Overall, NSD achieved an operational efficiency of $20 million a year.

Because each system offers several advantages, operations managers must carefully analyze their inventory situation before selecting the best system for their company.

Operations Management in Practice 12.3 describes multiechelon inventory management at IBM.

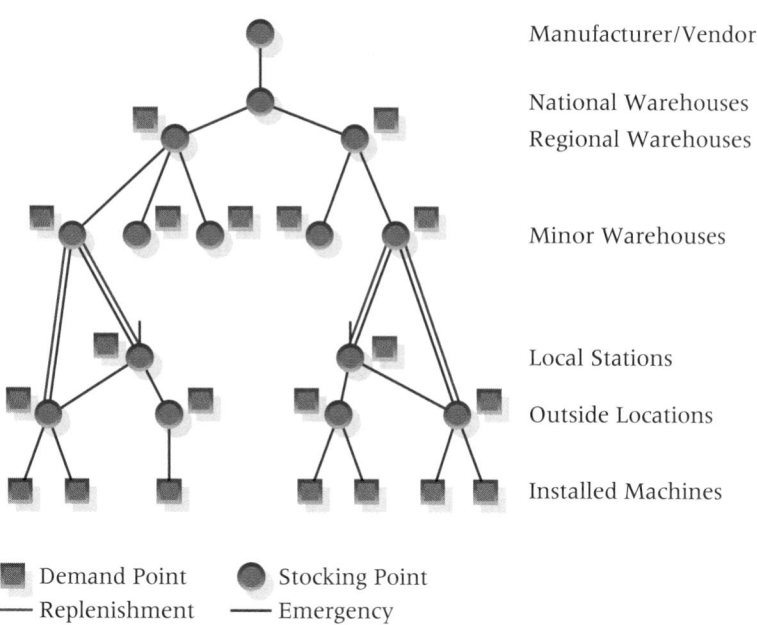

Manufacturer/Vendor

National Warehouses
Regional Warehouses

Minor Warehouses

Local Stations

Outside Locations

Installed Machines

■ Demand Point    ● Stocking Point
— Replenishment    — Emergency

---

## ► Summary

In virtually any organization inventory planning and control is an important issue. Balancing the cost of holding inventory against the cost of providing a reasonable level of customer service is a major managerial objective.

**Learning Objective 1: Discuss the importance of inventory to operations managers.** Regardless of the size of the company, inventories require a major commitment of monetary resources. For example, materials inventories typically account for more than half of all costs at manufacturing companies. Inventories affect virtually all aspects of a company's daily operations, and many companies use them as a competitive weapon. Conversely, they are often a major control problem. Zero inventory has become the overriding goal of manufacturers.

**Learning Objective 2: Characterize independent and dependent demand.** Independent demand items are finished goods or parts that are shipped as end items to customers for spare parts or repair. Market conditions influence the demand for independent items. Dependent demand items are raw materials, component parts, or subassemblies that are used to produce a finished product. The need for dependent demand items is a reflection of the number needed in each higher-level item in which it is used.

**Learning Objective 3: Describe the major types of inventories for manufacturers.** Inventories for a manufacturing facility consist of three major types. Raw materials are the basic inputs to the manufacturing process. Work in process consists of partially finished goods. Finished goods are the outputs of the manufacturing process.

**Learning Objective 4: Discuss the important costs relevant to inventory control.** In making inventory control decisions operations managers must consider several costs. The first is the ordering, or manufacturing cost, which is directly proportional to the amount that is ordered or produced. The second is the holding, carrying, or storage cost, which is the cost associated with maintaining an inventory until it is used or sold. The third is the stock out, or shortage, cost, which occurs when the demand for an item exceeds its supply.

**Learning Objective 5: Describe ways to measure inventory.** Typically, inventories are measured in three ways. First, because the monetary value of various units may vary widely, the average aggregate inventory value is used to add up the total value of all items usually held in inventory during some time period. The second measure of inventory, weeks of supply, is computed by dividing the average aggregate inventory value by the sales per week at cost. The third measure of inventory, inventory turnover (turns), is computed by dividing the annual sales at cost by the average inventory value maintained during the year.

## Learning Objective 6: List the major reasons for holding inventories.
Inventories serve many important functions in various companies. Among the major reasons for holding inventories are to meet anticipated customer demand, to protect against stock outs, to take advantage of economical order cycles, to maintain independence of operations, to allow for smooth and flexible production operations, and to guard against price increases.

## Learning Objective 7: Describe the ABC classification approach and explain its value.
We use the ABC classification approach to attempt to isolate the small number of inventory items that account for most of the sales dollars. By concentrating inventory control efforts in this manner, an operations manager can achieve better overall inventory cost control.

## Learning Objective 8: Contrast continuous review and periodic review inventory systems.
A continuous review inventory system reviews the remaining quantity of an item each time a withdrawal is made from inventory to determine whether it is time to reorder. The continuous review system is also called a *reorder point system* or a *fixed order quantity system*. The periodic review system checks the inventory position only at fixed time intervals rather than continuously. The periodic review system is also called a *fixed time period system* or a *fixed order interval system*. A new order is placed at the end of each review, and the time between orders is fixed. Orders for varying quantities are placed at these fixed time intervals.

## Learning Objective 9: Use various economic order quantity models to determine reorder points, service levels, safety stocks, and expected number of units short.
The problems at the end of the chapter offer you the opportunity to solve various types of inventory models and problems.

## ► Key Terms

| | | |
|---|---|---|
| ABC classification | fixed order quantity system | raw materials |
| anticipation stock | fixed time period system | reorder point |
| average aggregate inventory value | holding cost | reorder point system (ROP) |
| back order | independent demand | safety stock |
| carrying cost | in-transit inventory | set-up cost |
| continuous review system | inventory | shortage |
| cycle counting | inventory turnover (turns) | shortage cost |
| cycle-service level | item cost | stock out |
| cycle stock | lead time | stock out cost |
| dependent demand | movement inventories | storage cost |
| economic lot size | ordering cost | two-bin system |
| economic order quantity (EOQ) | periodic review system | weeks of supply |
| fill rate | pipeline inventory | work in process |
| finished goods | quantity discount | work-in-process inventory |
| fixed order interval system | | |

## ► Discussion Questions

1. What is the opportunity cost of inventory?
2. What are the major functions of inventory?
3. What are the major cost factors in inventory analysis? What is the trade-off among these cost factors? How are they determined in practice?

4. What basic questions must be answered in choosing an inventory control model?
5. Why is the ABC classification procedure useful?
6. What are the major types of inventories?
7. What is the difference between a back order and a lost sale?

8. What are the major assumptions underlying the basic EOQ model?
9. What is meant by a constant demand rate? How realistic is the constant demand rate assumption?
10. Discuss the sensitivity of the EOQ model to changes in the model parameters.
11. What is the effect of a replenishment rate that is less than the demand rate in the uniform replenishment rate model?
12. Discuss the difference in the cost function when quantity discounts are available.
13. What types of costs are associated with back orders? With lost sales?

14. Define and discuss the *cycle-service level*. How is it related to the probability of a stock out?
15. Describe the operation of a continuous review inventory system.
16. Describe the operation of a periodic review inventory system.
17. What type of inventory control system would you advocate for a small manufacturing company? Why?
18. What type of inventory control system would you advocate for a video rental store? Why?

## ▶ Problems

1. Given the following annual demand, annual carrying cost, and ordering cost,

$$D = 7,500 \text{ units per year}$$
$$C_O = \$10,000 \text{ per order}$$
$$C_H = \$.50 \text{ per unit per year}$$

compute
a. The optimal economic order quantity
b. The number of orders per year
c. The length of the order cycle
d. Total annual cost

2. Given the following annual demand, annual carrying cost, and ordering cost,

$$D = 50,000 \text{ units per year}$$
$$C_O = \$500 \text{ per order}$$
$$C_H = \$.25 \text{ per unit per year}$$

compute
a. The optimal economic order quantity
b. The number of orders per year
c. Length of the order cycle
d. Total annual cost

3. The constant annual demand for the beer of the Van Riesling Brewery is 100,000 barrels. The set-up for each production run costs $1,000 and the holding cost is $25 per barrel per month. The brewery tries to avoid shortages. Determine the optimal economic lot size, the number of lots that the brewery should produce per year, the length of the order cycle, and the total annual cost.

4. Given the following annual demand, annual carrying cost, ordering cost, and shortage cost,

$$D = 10,000 \text{ units per year}$$
$$C_O = \$7,500 \text{ per order}$$
$$C_H = \$.50 \text{ per unit per year}$$
$$C_B = \$.10 \text{ per unit}$$

compute
a. The optimal economic order quantity
b. The optimal back order quantity

c. The number of orders per year
d. Length of the order cycle
e. Total annual cost

5. The Outspokin Bicycle Shop experiences a monthly demand for 60 bikes. The shop incurs an order cost of $25 whenever it orders bikes. The inventory holding cost for the bicycle shop is $1 per bicycle per month, and the shortage cost is estimated as $5 per unit. Compute the optimal economic order quantity, the optimal back order quantity, the number of orders per year, the length of the order cycle, and the total annual cost.

6. Runner's World sells 250 pairs of running shoes monthly. It costs the store $15 to place each order with its wholesaler. Each pair of shoes incurs an inventory holding cost of $.75 per month. When sales personnel cannot fit a customer with a pair of shoes, the shop incurs a shortage cost of $2. Determine the optimal economic order quantity, the optimal back order quantity, the number of orders per month, the length of the order cycle, and the total annual cost.

7. Given the following annual demand, annual production rate, annual carrying cost, and set-up cost,

$$D = 15,000 \text{ units per year}$$
$$p = 25,000 \text{ units per year}$$
$$C_H = \$50 \text{ per unit per year}$$
$$C_S = \$500 \text{ per order}$$

compute
a. The optimal economic lot size
b. The maximum inventory level
c. The average inventory level
d. Length of time to produce a lot
e. Length of time to deplete maximum inventory
f. Length of the inventory cycle
g. Total annual cost

8. The Tasty Soup Co. produces chicken noodle soup on a production line that has an annual capacity of

100,000 cans. Its annual demand for chicken noodle soup is 75,000 cans, and the demand rate is constant throughout the year. When it manufactures the chicken noodle soup, cleaning and setting up the production line costs $500. The annual inventory holding cost is estimated to be $.25 per can per year. Determine the optimal economic lot size, the maximum and average inventory levels, the length of the inventory cycle, and the total annual cost.

9. The Nu-Sheen Co. produces car wax on a production line that has a monthly capacity of 10,000 cans. Its annual demand for auto wax is 100,000 cans on a uniform basis. The set-up cost associated with the production of car wax is $250.

   Nu-Sheen estimates the monthly holding cost to be $.50 per can of car wax. What is the appropriate production lot size? Also, compute the maximum and average inventory levels, the length of the inventory cycle, and the total annual cost.

10. The quantity discount schedule for an item is as follows:

| Order Size | Discount | Unit Cost ($) |
|---|---|---|
| 0 to 99 | 0 | 50.00 |
| 100 to 249 | 3% | 48.50 |
| 250 + | 5% | 47.50 |

   If the annual demand for the item is 1,000 units, the ordering cost is $50 per order, and the annual inventory holding cost is 25 percent of the unit cost of the item, find the economic order quantity.

11. The Village Green Hardware Store in White Rock, South Carolina, orders power mowers from a major midwestern manufacturer. The following quantity discount applies to 21-inch, self-propelled, electric start, rotary power mowers:

| Order Size | Discount | Unit Cost ($) |
|---|---|---|
| 0 to 99 | 0 | $90.00 |
| 100 to 199 | 1 | 89.10 |
| 200 to 399 | 2 | 87.30 |
| 400 + | 3 | 85.50 |

   The annual demand for the mowers is 1,000 units, the store's holding cost per year is 10 percent of the unit cost, and its ordering cost is $10 per order. Determine the economic order quantity for this situation.

12. Power Boats, Inc., operates a boat rental concession at Lake Murray, South Carolina. The company uses gasoline at the rate of 5,000 gallons per month. The ordering cost for obtaining the gasoline is $25, and the inventory holding cost is 1 percent of the unit cost. The cost of the gasoline is $1 per gallon for a ordering of less than 5,000 gallons, $.95 per gallon for a purchase of 5,001 to 15,000 gallons, and $.90 per gallon for a purchase of 15,001 gallons or more.

How much gasoline should Power Boats, Inc., order?

13. For problem 1 assume that the demand estimate was incorrect and has an actual value of 10,000 units per year. Compute the percentage error in the previously computed economic order quantity.

14. For problem 2 assume that the values for $D$, $C_O$ and $C_H$ were estimated incorrectly. The correct values are $D = 60,000$ units per year, $C_O = \$400$ per order, and $C_H = \$.20$ per unit per year. Determine the percentage errors in the previously computed economic order quantity and in the total annual cost.

15. For problem 3 assume that the demand estimate was incorrect and has an actual value of 125,000 barrels per year. Compute the percentage error in the total annual cost caused by using the incorrect value for demand.

16. Wagner Industries takes a complete inventory count of all items at the end of each month. It would like to streamline this process without losing overall inventory control. The following is a random sample of 20 of Wagner Industries' storeroom items:

| Item Number | Annual Usage | Unit Value | Item Number | Annual Usage | Unit Value |
|---|---|---|---|---|---|
| 1 | 1,400 | 70.15 | 11 | 2,500 | 10.00 |
| 2 | 1,200 | 30.42 | 12 | 1,200 | 90.50 |
| 3 | 1,000 | 50.65 | 13 | 1,470 | 25.65 |
| 4 | 1,600 | 42.10 | 14 | 1,100 | 72.80 |
| 5 | 2,000 | 80.00 | 15 | 1,650 | 51.90 |
| 6 | 1,800 | 75.11 | 16 | 1,200 | 42.30 |
| 7 | 1,450 | 42.90 | 17 | 1,900 | 35.70 |
| 8 | 1,000 | 32.60 | 18 | 1,120 | 12.00 |
| 9 | 900 | 51.40 | 19 | 1,370 | 85.63 |
| 10 | 1,900 | 32.60 | 20 | 1,410 | 74.90 |

How might Wagner Industries try to reduce its storeroom labor cost? Illustrate by specifying an ABC plan.

17. Jane Austin, the owner and manager of Fashions by Jane, is having a problem trying to control inventory at her store. The following is a sample of some items she stocks, along with the annual usage of each item expressed in annual dollar volume:

| Item | Annual Dollar Usage | Item | Annual Dollar Usage |
|---|---|---|---|
| A | $ 8,000 | N | $30,000 |
| B | 21,000 | O | 56,000 |
| C | 55,000 | P | 7,000 |
| D | 63,000 | Q | 10,000 |
| E | 20,000 | R | 65,000 |
| F | 34,000 | S | 42,000 |
| G | 14,000 | T | 51,000 |
| H | 12,000 | U | 60,000 |
| I | 33,000 | V | 14,000 |
| J | 19,000 | W | 71,000 |

| Item | Annual Dollar Usage | Item | Annual Dollar Usage |
|------|------|------|------|
| K | 80,000 | X | 50,000 |
| L | 72,000 | Y | 4,000 |
| M | 11,000 | Z | 91,000 |

What type of system would you suggest that she use to allocate her time for inventory control? What sort of control should she use for the various items in the list?

18. Twinko's Copy Center uses four cases of copier fluid for its copiers each month. Deliveries of copier fluid arrive exactly one month after Twinko's places an order. What is the reorder point for this situation?

19. Jamal's Auto Supply is experiencing an average daily demand for its best-selling motor oil of 25 cases. By analyzing his sales records for the last six months, Jamal has determined that this demand has a roughly normal distribution with a standard deviation of 5 cases per day. The lead time for restocking cases of oil from his wholesale distributor is 3 days. Jamal wants to maintain a 98 percent service level. What is the reorder point for this situation?

20. An automatic milling machine uses 2,000 feet of half-inch bar stock each day. The lead time for this bar stock is normally distributed with a mean of 5 days and a standard deviation of 2 days. A service level of 98 percent is required for the milling machine's bar stock. What is the reorder point for this situation?

21. Joan's Mail Order House uses customer order forms at the rate of 150 order forms per day with a standard deviation of 10 order forms per day. The demand for order forms is normally distributed. The lead time for resupplying the order forms is also normally distributed with a mean of 6 days and a standard deviation of 2 days. Joan wants to maintain a service level of 98 percent for the order forms. What is the reorder point for this situation?

22. The Wilson Co. has compiled data showing that its lead time demand is approximately normal with a mean of 200 units and a standard deviation of 25 units. It wants to determine
   a. The expected number of units short for a 90 percent lead time service level
   b. The service level corresponding to expected shortages of 20 units

23. The Wilson Co. (see problem 22) experiences annual demand of 2,000 units and uses an order quantity of size 100. For a 90 percent lead time service level, determine its annual service level.

24. The daily demand for a housewares item at Clem's Discount Store is normally distributed with a mean of 15 units and a standard deviation of 3 units. Clem uses a review period of 30 days, and the lead time is 14 days. At the beginning of this review period he has 100 units of the housewares item in inventory. Clem would like to maintain a 98 percent service level. How many units should he order?

25. A dentist orders dental supplies from her supplier every 20 days. The lead time for delivery of the supplies is 5 days. A check of the stock of anesthetics indicates that 250 bottles are on hand. Daily usage of the anesthetic is approximately normally distributed with a mean of 40 bottles and a standard deviation of 5 bottles. The desired service level for anesthetics is 99 percent. How many bottles should the dentist order?

## ▶ Selected References

Brown, Robert G. *Decision Rules for Inventory Management.* New York: Holt, Rinehart and Winston, 1967.
————. *Materials Management Systems.* New York: Wiley, 1977.

Buffa, Elwood S., and Jeffrey G. Miller. *Production—Inventory Systems: Planning and Control.* Homewood, Ill.: Richard D. Irwin, 1979.

Fogarty, Donald W., and Thomas R. Hoffman. *Production and Inventory Management.* Cincinnati: South-Western, 1983.

Greene, J. H. *Production and Inventory Control Handbook.* Falls Church, Va.: American Production and Inventory Control Society, 1984.

Hadley, G., and T. M. Whitin. *Analysis of Inventory Systems.* Englewood Cliffs, N.J.: Prentice-Hall, 1963.

Love, Stephen F. *Inventory Control.* New York: McGraw-Hill, 1979.

Markland, Robert E. *Topics in Management Science.* New York: Wiley, 1989.

Plossl, George W., and W. Evert Welch. *The Role of Top Management in the Control of Inventory.* Reston, Va.: Reston, 1979.

Plossl, George W., and Oliver W. Wight. *Production and Inventory Control.* Englewood Cliffs, N.J.: Prentice-Hall, 1979.

Silver, E. A., and R. Peterson. *Decision Systems for Inventory Management and Production Planning.* New York: Wiley, 1985.

Tersine, Richard J. *Principles of Inventory and Materials Management.* New York: Elsevier North-Holland, 1987.

Vollmann, T. E., W. L. Berry, and D. C. Whybark. *Manufacturing Planning and Control Systems.* Homewood, Ill.: Richard D. Irwin, 1988.

Wight, Oliver W. *Production and Inventory Management in the Computer Age.* Boston: Cahners Books, 1974.

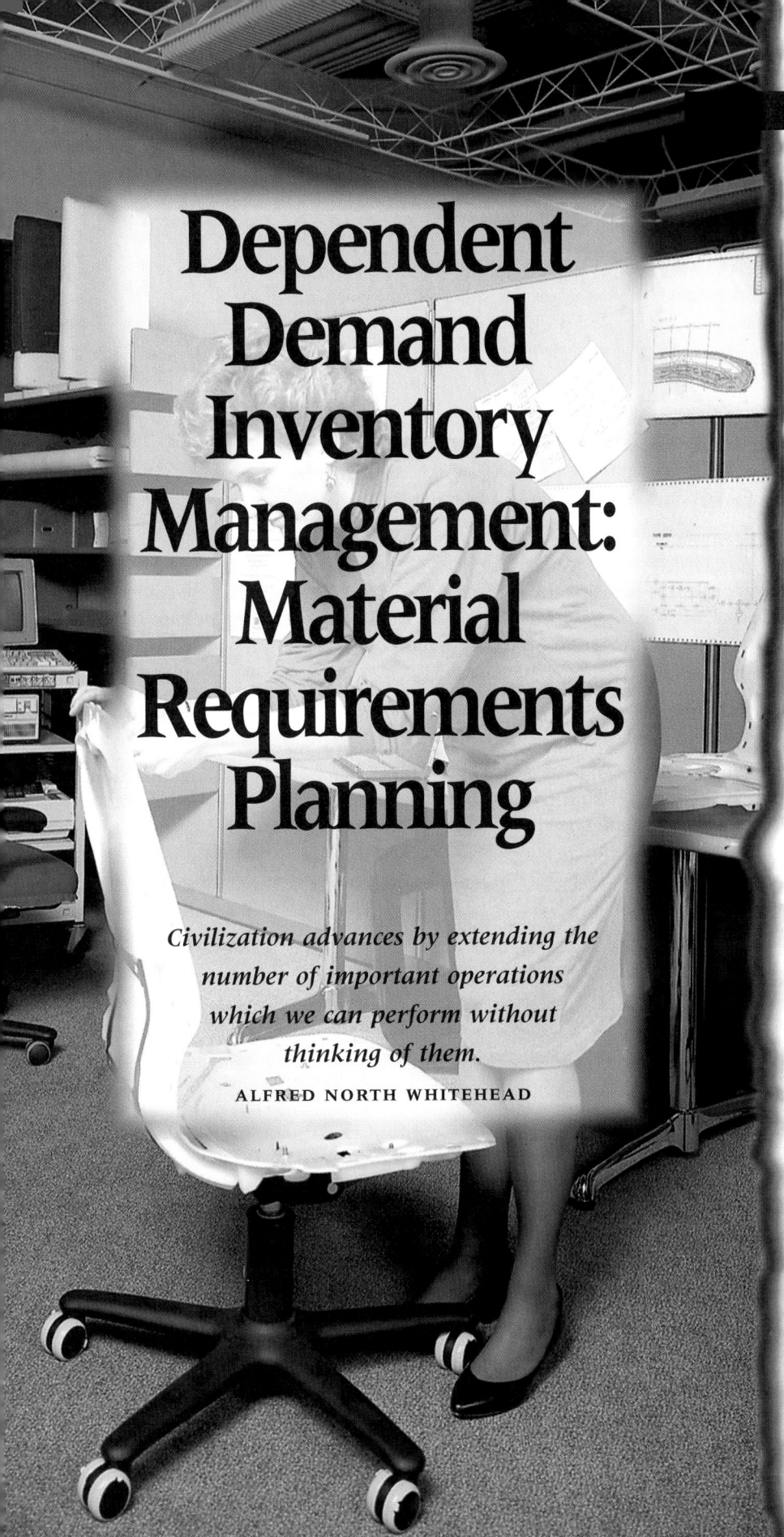

## CHAPTER 13

# Dependent Demand Inventory Management: Material Requirements Planning

*Civilization advances by extending the number of important operations which we can perform without thinking of them.*

ALFRED NORTH WHITEHEAD

**Introduction**
*OPERATIONS MANAGEMENT IN PRACTICE 13.1: MRP at Steelcase*

**MRP Prerequisites**

**The MRP Process**

**An MRP Example**

**Important Observations**

**Lot Sizing**

**Use of MRP Systems**

**Some Practical Considerations in Using MRP**

**Implementation of MRP**
*OPERATIONS MANAGEMENT IN PRACTICE 13.2: MRP and the Real Cost of Inventory Losses at Gendex*

# Introduction

Dependent demand inventory items are raw materials, parts, and assemblies used in the manufacture of a finished product. The term *component* refers to any inventory item that is part of a finished product. Finished products are called *end items*. Because the demand for components depends upon the demand for finished products, we can derive component demand directly from the number of finished products that have been scheduled for production. For example, a car manufacturer who has scheduled the production of 10,000 vehicles (end items) in the coming month will need 10,000 engines, 20,000 headlights, 40,000 wheels, and 10,000 spare tires to execute the production plan.

This chapter on dependent demand inventory management is primarily concerned with **material requirements planning (MRP)**—a production and inventory planning system specifically designed to handle dependent demand inventory items. In the United States it is the system most commonly used for planning material requirements for manufacturing operations. Although the concepts behind MRP are simple, its execution can be complicated. This chapter examines the mechanics of MRP, critical issues associated with MRP implementation, and problems that can arise when using MRP systems.

## The Development of Material Requirements Planning (MRP)

Initially, manufacturers viewed MRP as a better method for ordering components than the independent demand inventory models (see Chapter 12) they had been using during the 1950s and 1960s. However, it has evolved into a comprehensive priority planning system. MRP provides a method that helps keep order due dates valid even after the orders have been released to the shop floor or to outside vendors. MRP systems can detect when the due date of an order (the date the order is scheduled to arrive) is out of alignment with its need date (the date the order is actually required).

During the late 1970s and early 1980s the techniques for helping to plan capacity requirements were tied in with MRP. Tools were developed to support the planning of aggregate production levels and the development of the anticipated build schedule. Systems to aid in executing the plans were incorporated: shop-floor control systems for the "in-house factory" and vendor scheduling for the "outside factories." The expanded MRP system became known as **closed loop MRP**, because it provided feedback from the execution functions to the

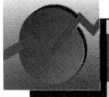

# MRP at Steelcase

Steelcase, one of the largest furniture companies in the world, has long been recognized as a leading user and advocate of MRP. The implementation and use of MRP at Steelcase in the early 1970s were instrumental in the transformation of this company from a small local player to one of the biggest furniture companies in North America. By the late 1970s Steelcase had implemented MRP II as well, which allowed it to integrate its financial, operations, purchasing, and distribution systems. MRP and MRP II allowed Steelcase to successfully handle the tremendous growth the company experienced from the mid-1970s to the late 1980s.

More recently, Steelcase's MRP and MRP II systems have contributed substantially to its success in global markets and continue to serve as important communication vehicles, according to Jim Austhof, production and inventory control manager of Steelcase's chair plant. Austhof says that Steelcase's business strategy is one of time-based competition, particularly with respect to delivery speed. He anticipates that Steelcase eventually will have to revamp its MRP system and integrate it with new systems and approaches to allow Steelcase to continue to increase its delivery speed. Austhof envisions the conversion of Steelcase's current MRP system to a customer-driven MRP hybrid by the year 2010.

planning functions so manufacturers could change plans when necessary. Eventually, practitioners expanded closed loop MRP to provide the ability to translate the operating plan (expressed in manufacturing terms, such as units and gallons) into financial terms (dollars) and the capability to simulate the effects of various plans in terms of both units and dollars. The new system, called **manufacturing resource planning (MRP II)**, was a comprehensive approach for the effective planning of all the resources of a manufacturing organization.[1]

Production and materials planning is critical to the success of a manufacturing company. A company can have the best product designs, the newest manufacturing facilities, the latest equipment, and all the newest production technologies (CAD-CAM, robotics, automated guided vehicles, and so on), but without the ability to plan and schedule production effectively, the company has no ability to compete. MRP has proved to be an effective production and inventory planning system in a wide variety of environments, including Steelcase, as described in Operations Management in Practice 13.1.

## MRP Prerequisites

An MRP system requires three types of information:

- Master production schedule
- Bills of material
- Inventory records

[1]Thomas F. Wallace, *MRP II: Making It Happen* (Essex Junction, Vt.: Oliver Wight Limited Publications, 1985), p. 7.

*The use of MRP and MRP II at Steelcase has helped the company become a world class manufacturer of office furniture.*

A clear understanding of these items is necessary for understanding MRP. The **master production schedule (MPS)** is a detailed production schedule for finished goods or end items that provides the major input to the material requirements planning process. Associated with each finished product or end item is a **bill of material (BOM)**, which describes the dependent demand relationships that exist among the various components (raw materials, parts, subassemblies) comprising the end item. The entire set of bills of material for a company's finished products is called the *bill of material file*. Inventory status data for each product or component (such as amount of inventory on hand, amount on order) are provided by **inventory records**, which also contain planning factors related to lead time, safety stock, and lot sizing.

MRP logic uses the master production schedule, the BOM file, and the inventory records to determine the following for all components:

1.  Planned order quantities
2.  Planned order release dates (to the shop floor or to a vendor)
3.  Planned order due dates

The MRP system calculates the release dates and due dates, taking into consideration the lead times required to produce or procure the components and recognizing the order in which they are assembled into the finished product. If the MRP process is done in conjunction with capacity planning (the subject of Chapter 14), the production facility should have the capacity to complete the component orders on time. The sections that follow provide a detailed discussion of the three prerequisites to MRP.

# The Master Production Schedule

The master production schedule (MPS) is a detailed production schedule for end items. The MPS specifies the quantity of each end item to be produced in each time period of the planning horizon. The *planning horizon* is the length of time for which the company has planned its end-item production. The MPS must cover a span of time at least equal to the maximum cumulative procurement and manufacturing lead time for components for any of the company's finished products.

We can look at the MPS as a contract between marketing and manufacturing. It is not a forecast of demand; rather, it is a schedule that marketing and manufacturing have agreed upon, and it takes into account expected market demand as well as constraints that arise from the production process. Determining whether manufacturing has adequate capacity to execute a proposed MPS is difficult; however, capacity-planning techniques are available to aid in the development of an "executable" or "feasible" MPS (see Chapter 14).

Frequently, the MPS is developed in a hierarchical fashion. First, upper-level management develops an *aggregate production plan*, which specifies production quantities for product families during an extended time horizon. For example, an appliance manufacturer may generate an aggregate production plan encompassing each appliance family (washers, dryers, refrigerators); it specifies the planned levels of production for each family group. From the aggregate production plan comes a master production schedule that specifies the number of each model in a family to produce, given the aggregate family quantities that appear in the production plan. For example, if the product family is refrigerators, the master production schedule specifies how many frost-free model 1187s the factory should produce, how many model 1802 side-by-side refrigerators it should produce, and so forth. The MPS is a more detailed plan than the aggregate production plan and typically has a one-year planning horizon. In contrast, the aggregate production plan is a more general plan and usually has a longer planning horizon than the MPS. Chapter 11 discussed aggregate production-planning methods.

Figure 13.1 presents a framework for production planning and scheduling. Note that the demand forecast is a key input to the production planning process. The aggregate production plan is developed in conjunction with the resource plan (the long-range plan of facilities and resources discussed in Chapter 6) and is based upon forecasts of product demand. The aggregate production plan is the major input to the master production scheduling process. The operations manager can directly evaluate the acceptability of an MPS from a capacity standpoint with rough-cut capacity-planning techniques; a more accurate approach is to use detailed capacity-planning techniques to evaluate the MPS after MRP converts the MPS into detailed component order schedules. If the capacity required by the MPS (and its associated material requirements plan) exceeds the capacity available in the production facility, the company either will have to make additional capacity available (by scheduling overtime or subcontracting) or will have to change the MPS (and material requirements plan) to conform with the available capacity of the production facility. As Figure 13.1 shows, MRP output provides component orders to the shop floor and purchasing.

Figure 13.1 shows a feedback loop that connects purchasing and the shop floor with master production scheduling and material requirements planning.

FIGURE 13.1
Production Planning and
Scheduling Framework

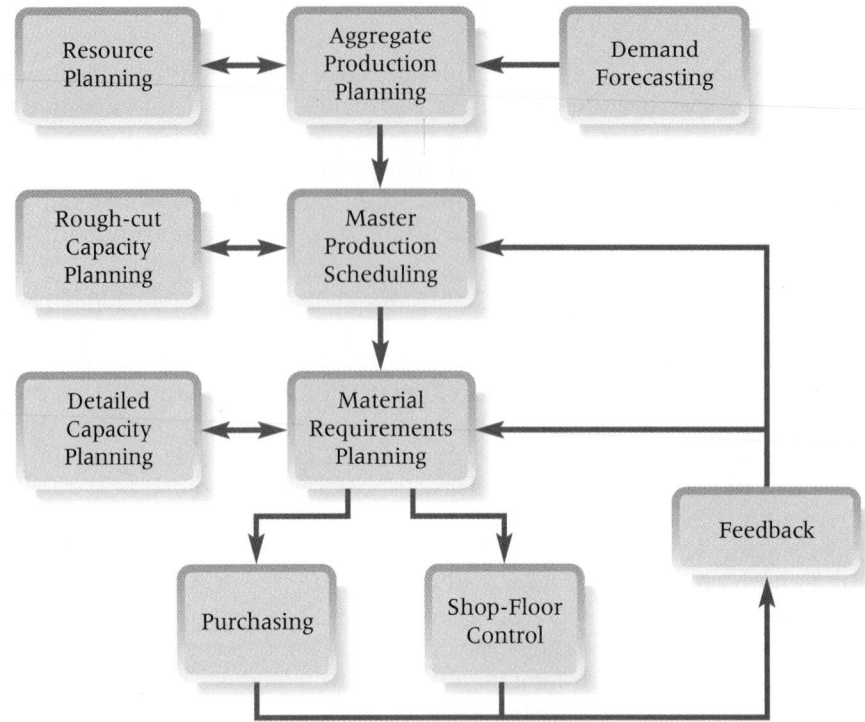

This illustrates a concept called *closed loop MRP* (described later). The operations manager can use feedback on the performance of the shop floor and vendors in executing the material plans to revise current plans and develop better plans and planning factors in the future.

## Bills of Material

A bill of material (BOM) defines the relationship of components to end items. The BOM identifies all components used in the production of an end item, the quantity required, and the order in which the components are assembled. For example, consider the simplified assembly drawing for an office chair, shown in Figure 13.2. The chair is composed of a seat cushion, back cushion, adjuster mechanism, base unit, wheels, and fasteners. To manufacture the chair the wheels, base unit, and adjuster mechanism are assembled into a chair frame, to which the base cushion and back cushion are attached. All eleven fasteners are identical, because the company used concurrent engineering to design the chair, and because common fasteners simplify production and reduce inventory costs. Figure 13.3 shows a BOM for this chair. To simplify the discussion this BOM does not show all purchased raw materials (paint, steel tubing, and so on). This form of the BOM is frequently called a **product structure diagram**.

All items appearing below the end item in a bill of material are referred to as *components*, whether they are raw materials, component parts, or subassemblies. In Figure 13.3 all items, with the exception of the office chair, are components. The term *parent component* describes a component at one level in the BOM that is composed of components from the next lower level in the BOM. The lower-level components are called *child components*. As Figure 13.3 shows, the chair frame is

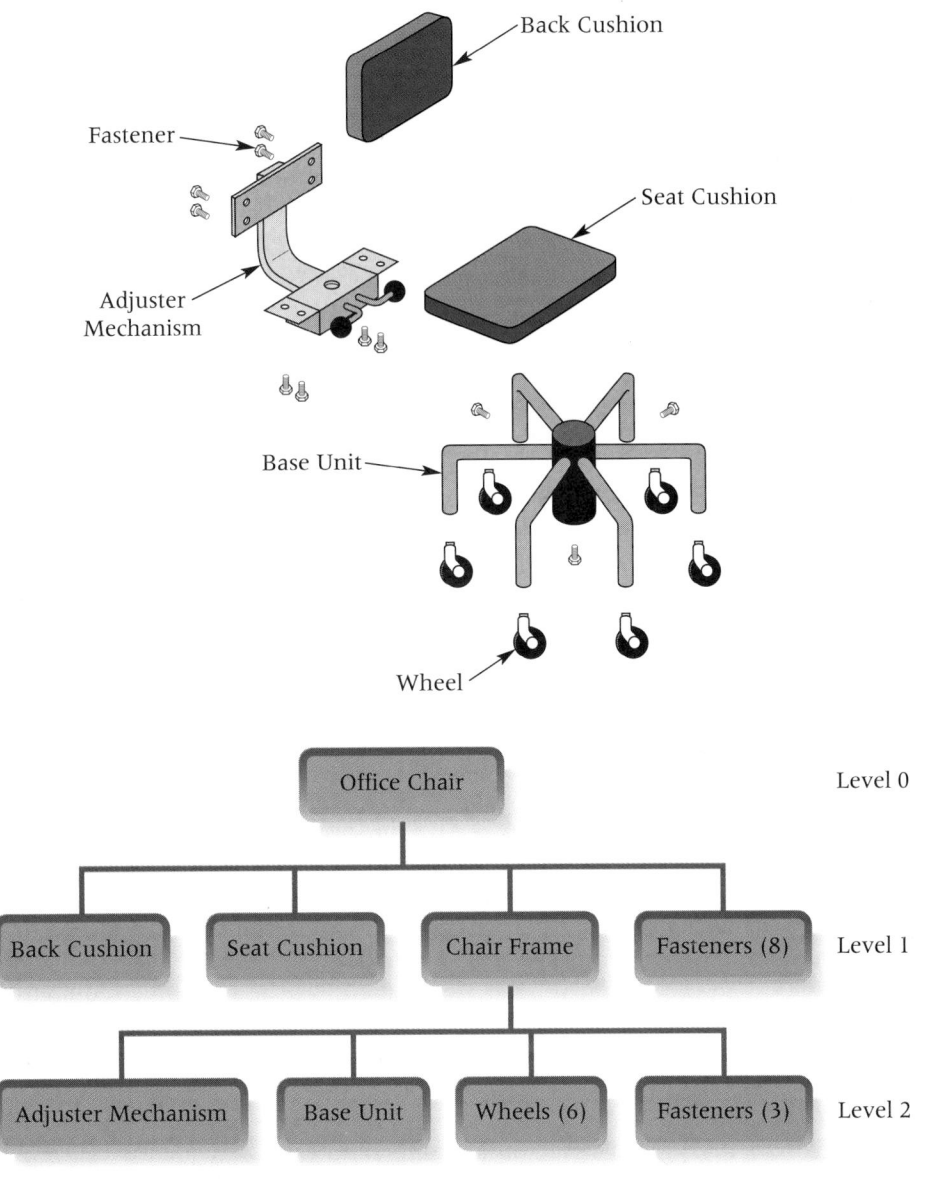

FIGURE 13.2
Assembly Drawing for the
Office Chair Example

Back Cushion

Fastener

Seat Cushion

Adjuster
Mechanism

Base Unit

Wheel

FIGURE 13.3
Bill of Material for the Office
Chair Example

Office Chair — Level 0

Back Cushion    Seat Cushion    Chair Frame    Fasteners (8) — Level 1

Adjuster Mechanism    Base Unit    Wheels (6)    Fasteners (3) — Level 2

a parent to the adjuster mechanism, base unit, wheels, and fasteners. Likewise, the same items are child components in relation to the chair frame.

The levels at which the end item and its components appear in a BOM are numbered in ascending order as we move down through the product structure, starting with level 0 for the end item. As Figure 13.3 shows, the office chair appears at level 0, the back cushion, seat cushion, chair frame, and fasteners appear at level 1, and the adjuster mechanism, base unit, wheels, and fasteners appear at level 2. Note that the fasteners appear at two levels of the BOM in Figure 13.3, levels 1 and 2. Using a component in more than one parent component, is known as *commonality*.

The key to MRP is the *time-phasing* of requirements for components, based upon the structure of the BOM. If the time required to either manufacture or purchase components (lead time) is known, we can determine when orders should be released to the shop floor or outside suppliers to ensure the required components will be available when needed.

## Inventory Records

To determine how many components to order, the operations manager must know the inventory status of each component. Managers use inventory records to maintain inventory status. A company maintains an inventory record for each component; it specifies the item's identification number, the number of components available, the quantity and delivery date(s) for components already ordered, the lot size (purchase order or production quantity) or lot-sizing method used for the item, and the lead time associated with the item. An inventory record may also provide additional information for an item pertaining to factors such as safety stock requirements and scrap allowances. Inventory records are kept up to date by posting inventory transactions that reflect various inventory events (stock receipt, stock disbursement, scrap).

# The MRP Process
## MRP Records

Material requirements planning uses the MPS, BOMs, and inventory records to determine when orders for components should be released to the shop floor or to outside vendors. Figure 13.4 shows a typical **MRP record.** In practice, MRP records are kept as data files in a computer system, which may store information in addition to that shown in Figure 13.4. However, the MRP record format in Figure 13.4 is useful for explaining the MRP process. MRP records can appear in various formats, depending on the computer software being used. Note that the MRP record includes inventory record information.

MRP systems typically use part numbers to track components, although a descriptive name is also entered to help users of MRP system information. The entry *LS* refers to the item's lot size. The entry *LT* is the lead time required to obtain the component. In this example, the lead time is two time periods.

## Timing Conventions

Traditionally, MRP systems divide time into fixed intervals, frequently called *time buckets*. The most commonly used time interval is one week, although the

FIGURE 13.4
A Sample MRP Record

| Part No: G1 | | | | | | | | | | | | |
|---|---|---|---|---|---|---|---|---|---|---|---|---|
| Part Name: Generic Part | | | | | | | | | | | | |
| LS: 50 | LT: 2 | | 1 | 2 | 3 | 4 | 5 | 6 | 7 | 8 | 9 | 10 |
| Gross Requirements | | | 10 | 10 | 15 | 15 | 15 | 20 | 20 | 15 | 10 | 10 |
| Scheduled Receipts | | | | 50 | | | | | | | | |
| Planned Order Receipts | | | | | | | | 50 | | 50 | | |
| Available Balance | | 15 | 5 | 45 | 30 | 15 | 0 | 30 | 10 | 45 | 35 | 25 |
| Planned Order Releases | | | | | | 50 | | 50 | | | | |

appropriate time interval depends on the application. In bucketed MRP systems it is necessary to define the point in the time bucket at which events occur. The most frequently used timing convention is to assume that

1. Orders are placed at the beginning of the time bucket
2. Orders are available at the beginning of a time bucket
3. Demand must be satisfied by the end of a time bucket

The MRP record is constructed so that period 1 is the current period. Under the timing conventions listed earlier an order placed at the beginning of period 4 with a lead time of two periods will arrive in time to be used at the beginning of period 6.

## MRP Record Calculations

The MRP record in Figure 13.4 shows the current inventory status for part number G1 and the planned changes to the inventory status for this part for the next ten time buckets. The first row shows the gross requirements for the component for the next ten periods. **Gross requirements,** or demand for an inventory item, arise from end items or from components that require the item in their construction. The gross requirements for a component must be satisfied from inventory or by purchasing or producing the component. The **scheduled receipts** row shows when purchase or production orders that have already been placed will be available. If the component is manufactured in-house, the entry in the scheduled receipts row shows that a production order has been released to the shop floor for the quantity shown and that the order should be available at the beginning of the period in which the entry is shown. If the component is purchased, the entry shows that a purchase order has been placed and should be received, inspected, and transported to the shop floor in time to be used at the beginning of the period in which the entry occurs. Figure 13.4 shows a scheduled receipt for fifty units in period 2. Because the lead time is two periods, the company ordered this component (production or purchase) at the beginning of the period before the current period. Barring any complications, the company should receive fifty parts at the beginning of period 2.

The last row, **planned order releases**, shows future orders that the company must place to ensure sufficient inventory to meet the gross requirements. An MRP planner implements or executes a planned order when it appears in the current period, not before. When a planned order is executed—that is, released to the shop floor or an outside vendor—it becomes a *scheduled receipt* or *open order.* The MRP system automatically changes planned order releases if the gross requirements for the component change. However, because scheduled receipts are orders that have already been released to the shop floor or outside vendors, changes to gross requirements will not cause the MRP system to change a scheduled receipt. If an MRP planner has canceled or changed a scheduled receipt or open order in some fashion (increased or reduced the quantity) the planner must manually update the MRP system to reflect this change in the scheduled receipt row. The **planned order receipts** row shows when a planned order release should arrive.

The first entry in the *available balance* row shows the inventory level for that component at the beginning of the current period. All other entries in the available balance row show what the inventory level will be at the end of that period if the current plans are executed. Thus, Figure 13.4 shows that fifteen parts were available at the beginning of period 1. Ten of these components are scheduled to be used in period 1, leaving five units to be carried over to period 2. In period 2 the fifty units that the company ordered will be available in addition to the five left over from period 1. Ten of these units will be required in period 2, leaving a balance of forty-five units available at the beginning of period 3. This inventory will be sufficient to satisfy gross requirements for periods 3, 4, and 5. Because no inventory will be carried over to period 6 (the ending inventory for period 5 is zero), the company must plan an order so that the appropriate number of items will be available at the beginning of period 6. Because the lead time for this component is two periods and the lot size is fifty, a planned order release for fifty units is scheduled for period 4, which will result in a planned order receipt of fifty units in period 6. A second planned order for fifty components is scheduled for period 6, which will result in a planned order receipt in period 8. This will provide sufficient inventory to cover periods 8, 9, and 10. Twenty-five units will be left in inventory at the end of period 10.

# An MRP Example

Now we can demonstrate the basic logic of MRP. Suppose that a furniture manufacturer produces two models of an office chair—economy and deluxe. Figure 13.2 shows the chair assembly; the two models are identical, except that the economy model has nylon cloth-covered cushions and a one-way (up/down) adjuster mechanism, whereas the deluxe model has leather-covered cushions and a two-way (up/down and tilt) adjuster mechanism. Table 13.1 shows the *indented bills of material* for the two chairs. The indented BOM is a convenient format for computer output. In addition to item number, item name, and quantity required, Table 13.1 gives the low-level code for each item. The

TABLE 13.1
Indented BOMs for MRP Example

| Item # | Name | Quantity | Low-level Code |
|---|---|---|---|
| 1174 | Economy office chair | – | 0 |
| 2838 | Nylon back cushion | 1 | 1 |
| 2839 | Nylon seat cushion | 1 | 1 |
| 2571 | Fastener—1¼″ | 8 | 2 |
| 3807 | Economy chair frame | 1 | 1 |
| 9805 | 1-way adjuster mechanism | 1 | 2 |
| 8507 | Base unit | 1 | 2 |
| 2571 | Fastener—1¼″ | 3 | 2 |
| 5562 | Wheel | 6 | 2 |
| 1184 | Deluxe office chair | – | 0 |
| 2938 | Leather back cushion | 1 | 1 |
| 2939 | Leather seat cushion | 1 | 1 |
| 2571 | Fastener—1¼″ | 8 | 2 |
| 3817 | Deluxe chair frame | 1 | 1 |
| 9825 | 2-way adjuster mechanism | 1 | 2 |
| 8507 | Base unit | 1 | 2 |
| 2571 | Fastener—1¼″ | 3 | 2 |
| 5562 | Wheel | 6 | 2 |

| Item # | Name | On Hand | Lot Size | Lead Time | Scheduled Receipts | Period |
|---|---|---|---|---|---|---|
| 1174 | Economy office chair | 0 | LFL | 1 | | |
| 1184 | Deluxe office chair | 0 | LFL | 1 | | |
| 2571 | Fastener—1¼" | 600 | 1,000 | 3 | 1,000 | 2 |
| 2838 | Nylon back cushion | 10 | 50 | 2 | 50 | 1 |
| 2839 | Nylon seat cushion | 20 | 50 | 2 | | |
| 2938 | Leather back cushion | 10 | LFL | 1 | 15 | 1 |
| 2939 | Leather seat cushion | 10 | LFL | 1 | 15 | 1 |
| 3807 | Economy chair frame | 50 | 50 | 3 | | |
| 3817 | Deluxe chair frame | 50 | 50 | 3 | 50 | 3 |
| 5562 | Wheel | 700 | 500 | 2 | | |
| 8507 | Base unit | 45 | 50 | 4 | 50 | 1 |
| | | | | | 50 | 3 |
| 9805 | 1-way adjuster mechanism | 25 | 75 | 3 | 75 | 1 |
| 9825 | 2-way adjuster mechanism | 32 | 75 | 3 | | |

**TABLE 13.2**
Inventory Records for Example

low-level code specifies the order in which the MRP records should be processed.

Table 13.2 shows the inventory records for the chairs and the components of the chairs. In this example the company does not hold a finished goods inventory, so its inventory records show no inventory for the economy chair (#1174) or for the deluxe chair (#1184). The lot size for the chairs, leather back cushion, and leather seat cushion, is designated as *LFL*, or *lot-for-lot*. With the lot-for-lot procedure planned orders satisfy the demand for one period only. The term **lot-for-lot** means that for every lot of a parent component, the company purchases or produces one lot of the child component.

## Low-level Coding

Common parts need low-level codes. The low-level code shows the lowest level in *any* BOM at which a component is used. As we noted earlier, the levels at which items appear in a BOM are numbered in ascending order, starting with level 0 for end items (compare Figure 13.3 and Table 13.1). Notice that the fastener, part number 2571, is used to attach the seat cushions to the frame in level 1 and to attach the adjuster mechanism to the base unit in level 2, so the low-level code for the fastener is 2. The low-level code is used to sequence the processing of the MRP records so that the system properly determines the gross requirements for a component. The importance of the low-level coding scheme will become apparent as we explain the example.

## Gross-to-Net Requirements Explosion

Suppose that the company used an aggregate production plan that calls for thirty chairs per period to develop the MPS in Table 13.3. We are now ready to accomplish **gross-to-net requirements explosion**, that is, use MRP records to convert the MPS into component requirements. The first step in the process is to transfer the end-item requirements from the MPS to the gross requirements row in the MRP records for all items with low-level codes of 1. Figure 13.5 illustrates

TABLE 13.3
MPS for MRP Example

| | | | | | Period | | | | | |
|---|---|---|---|---|---|---|---|---|---|---|
| Item # | 1 | 2 | 3 | 4 | 5 | 6 | 7 | 8 | 9 | 10 |
| 1174 | 10 | 10 | 15 | 30 | 30 | 15 | 15 | 15 | 15 | 15 |
| 1184 | 20 | 20 | 15 | 0 | 0 | 15 | 15 | 15 | 15 | 15 |

| Part No: 2838 | | | | | | | | | | | | |
|---|---|---|---|---|---|---|---|---|---|---|---|---|
| Part Name: Nylon Back Cushion | | | | | | | | | | | | |
| LS: 50 | LT: 2 | | 1 | 2 | 3 | 4 | 5 | 6 | 7 | 8 | 9 | 10 |
| Gross Requirements | | | 10 | 10 | 15 | 30 | 30 | 15 | 15 | 15 | 15 | 15 |
| Scheduled Receipts | | | 50 | | | | | | | | | |
| Planned Order Receipts | | | | | | 50 | | | 50 | | | 50 |
| Available Balance | | 10 | 50 | 40 | 25 | 45 | 15 | 0 | 35 | 20 | 5 | 40 |
| Planned Order Releases | | | | 50 | | | 50 | | | 50 | | |

| Part No: 2938 | | | | | | | | | | | | |
|---|---|---|---|---|---|---|---|---|---|---|---|---|
| Part Name: Leather Back Cushion | | | | | | | | | | | | |
| LS: LFL | LT: 1 | | 1 | 2 | 3 | 4 | 5 | 6 | 7 | 8 | 9 | 10 |
| Gross Requirements | | | 20 | 20 | 15 | | | 15 | 15 | 15 | 15 | 15 |
| Scheduled Receipts | | | 15 | | | | | | | | | |
| Planned Order Receipts | | | | 15 | 15 | | | 15 | 15 | 15 | 15 | 15 |
| Available Balance | | 10 | 5 | 0 | 0 | 0 | 0 | 0 | 0 | 0 | 0 | 0 |
| Planned Order Releases | | | 15 | 15 | | | 15 | 15 | 15 | 15 | 15 | |

FIGURE 13.5
MRP Records for Back
Cushions

this for the two types of back cushion, parts 2838 and 2938. We obtain the beginning inventory levels, scheduled receipts, lead times, and lot sizes from the inventory records and include them in the MRP record. Once we have the gross requirements and inventory record information, we can process the low-level code 1 inventory records. The lot size for part 2939 is lot-for-lot (LFL), so the planned orders satisfy demand for one period only. The lot-for-lot procedure results in a zero available balance at the end of each period. Because the beginning balance for part 2939 is not zero, we must assume that something unusual occurred in previous periods, such as a change in the MPS, overproduction of the part, and so on.

Figure 13.6 shows the MRP records for two other low-level code 1 items, the economy and deluxe chair frames (#3807 and #3817) and for a low-level code 2 item, wheels (#5562). The gross requirements for the chair frames come directly

| Part No: 3807 | | | 1 | 2 | 3 | 4 | 5 | 6 | 7 | 8 | 9 | 10 |
|---|---|---|---|---|---|---|---|---|---|---|---|---|
| Part Name: Economy Chair Frame | | | | | | | | | | | | |
| LS: 50 | LT: 3 | | | | | | | | | | | |
| Gross Requirements | | | 10 | 10 | 15 | 30 | 30 | 15 | 15 | 15 | 15 | 15 |
| Scheduled Receipts | | | | | | | | | | | | |
| Planned Order Receipts | | | | | | 50 | | 50 | | | 50 | |
| Available Balance | | 50 | 40 | 30 | 15 | 35 | 5 | 40 | 25 | 10 | 45 | 30 |
| Planned Order Releases | | | 50 | | 50 | | | 50 | | | | |

| Part No: 3817 | | | 1 | 2 | 3 | 4 | 5 | 6 | 7 | 8 | 9 | 10 |
|---|---|---|---|---|---|---|---|---|---|---|---|---|
| Part Name: Deluxe Chair Frame | | | | | | | | | | | | |
| LS: 50 | LT: 3 | | | | | | | | | | | |
| Gross Requirements | | | 20 | 20 | 15 | | | 15 | 15 | 15 | 15 | 15 |
| Scheduled Receipts | | | | | 50 | | | | | | | |
| Planned Order Receipts | | | | | | | | | | | 50 | |
| Available Balance | | 50 | 30 | 10 | 45 | 45 | 45 | 30 | 15 | 0 | 35 | 20 |
| Planned Order Releases | | | | | | | | 50 | | | | |

| Part No: 5562 | | | 1 | 2 | 3 | 4 | 5 | 6 | 7 | 8 | 9 | 10 |
|---|---|---|---|---|---|---|---|---|---|---|---|---|
| Part Name: Wheel | | | | | | | | | | | | |
| LS: 500 | LT: 2 | | | | | | | | | | | |
| Gross Requirements | | | 300 | | 300 | | | 600 | | | | |
| Scheduled Receipts | | | | | | | | | | | | |
| Planned Order Receipts | | | | | | | | 500 | | | | |
| Available Balance | | 700 | 400 | 400 | 100 | 100 | 100 | 0 | 0 | 0 | 0 | 0 |
| Planned Order Releases | | | | | | 500 | | | | | | |

from the MPS. The MRP records show planned orders for fifty economy chair frames in periods 1, 3, and 6 and fifty deluxe chair frames in period 6. Each chair frame requires four different components (adjuster mechanism, base unit, wheels, and fasteners), so the planned orders for chair frames provide the gross requirements for the lower level components that make up the chair frame.

The chairs use the same wheels, so the gross requirements for the wheels are the sum of the planned orders for the two chair frames multiplied by six, the

FIGURE 13.6
MRP Records for Chair Frames and Wheels

| Part No: 2571 | | | 1 | 2 | 3 | 4 | 5 | 6 | 7 | 8 | 9 | 10 |
|---|---|---|---|---|---|---|---|---|---|---|---|---|
| Part Name: Fastener-1¼" | | | | | | | | | | | | |
| LS: 1,000 | LT: 3 | | | | | | | | | | | |
| Gross Requirements | | | 390 | 240 | 390 | 240 | 240 | 540 | 240 | 240 | 240 | 240 |
| Scheduled Receipts | | | | 1,000 | | | | | | | | |
| Planned Order Receipts | | | | | | | | 1,000 | | | 1,000 | |
| Available Balance | | 600 | 210 | 970 | 580 | 340 | 100 | 560 | 320 | 80 | 840 | 600 |
| Planned Order Releases | | | | | 1,000 | | | 1,000 | | | | |

F I G U R E   1 3 . 7
MRP Record for Fasteners

number of wheels per chair. The gross requirements for the wheels result in a planned order for five hundred wheels in period 4.

Figure 13.7 shows the MRP record for the fasteners. The fasteners appear at two levels in the BOM: at level 1, where they are used to attach the cushions to the chair frame, and at level 2, where they are used to attach the adjuster mechanism to the base unit. Thus, the gross requirements for the fastener come from sources at two different BOM levels (see also Figure 13.3). The gross requirements for fasteners in period 1 come from the MPS schedule to produce ten economy chairs and twenty deluxe chairs in period 1 and the planned order for fifty economy chair frames (#3807) in period 1. Note that there is no planned order for deluxe chair frames in period 1. Thus, the gross requirements in period 1 are 8 × (10 + 20 chairs) + 3 × (50 + 0 chair frames) = 390 fasteners.

The use of the low-level code should now be clear. The gross requirements for a component come from the MPS and/or the planned order release schedule(s) for a component's parent component(s). If the MRP record for fasteners was processed before the MRP record for chair frames, the 150 fasteners required to assemble the economy chair frames would not be included in the gross requirements for the fasteners in period 1. Thus the low-level code provides a convenient means to correctly sequence the processing of MRP records. This is an especially important consideration for implementing MRP on a computer.

## Important Observations

Using MRP systems requires an understanding of several issues and a variety of problems. These include the loss of visibility for low-level components, MRP nervousness, minimum length of the planning horizon, freezing the MPS, and "lumpiness" of demand for low-level components.

### Loss of Visibility for Low-level Components

The MPS for the two types of office chairs had a time horizon of ten periods. However, when requirements are time-phased in the gross-to-net explosion process, the time-phasing reduces the planning horizon for the low-level components. Consider the MRP records in Figure 13.6. The chair frames (#3807 and #3817) have a lead time of three periods. This means that to satisfy the MPS requirements for period 10 the latest a production request for chair frames can be released is period 7. Furthermore, consider the wheels (#5562), which as child components to the chair frames receive their gross requirements from the chair frames. The lead time for wheels is two periods. Thus, the latest that a purchase order can be placed to meet requirements for wheels in period 7 (the latest period in which gross requirements can be passed down from the chair frames) is period 5. The result is that whereas the MPS has a planning horizon of ten periods, the planning horizon for wheels is only half that long. This reduction in the planning horizon for low-level components is frequently called a *loss of visibility*.

## Minimum Length for the Planning Horizon

We can now understand with greater clarity why the length of the planning horizon for the master production schedule must be at least equal to the maximum cumulative procurement and production lead time for the components associated with any of a company's finished products. First, consider the wheels, which are characterized by a low-level code of 2. As we can see from Figure 13.3 and Table 13.1, the wheels appear at the very lowest level of the bills of material for the two end items in the sample problem. To determine whether a purchase order must be placed for wheels at the beginning of period 1 (the current period), the gross requirements for wheels must be specified in period 3. To specify gross requirements for wheels in period 3 the operations manager first must determine whether period 3 requires a planned order for chair frames. This requires the specification of gross requirements for chair frames in period 6. Thus, to determine whether to initiate a purchase order for wheels in the current period, the operations manager must be working with an MPS that has a planning horizon of at least six periods.

The MPS planning horizon must be at least as long as the sum of the lead times for any component and all its parent components. This is similar to the idea of a critical path in project management (see Chapter 18). Figure 13.8 shows how to calculate the minimum planning horizon for the economy chair by using an operation setback chart. This chart uses component lead time information with the BOM to show the timing of component production (see Figure 13.3 and Table 13.2). For the chair to be completed in period 8, for example, the cushions, frame and fasteners must be available by the end of period 7. The adjuster mechanism, base unit, wheels, and fasteners must be available at the end of period 4 to begin assembly of the chair frame. The production request for the base unit must be issued at the beginning of period 1 so that it is available in time. Thus, Figure 13.8 shows that the planning horizon (or critical path) must be long enough to order base units for assembly into chair frames and the chair frames must be available in time to assemble the finished chair. The minimum planning horizon for the economy chair is eight periods—the sum of the lead time for the base unit (four periods) plus the lead time to assemble the frame (three periods) plus the assembly time for the chair (one period).

We should note that when the product structure diagram has many levels and the lead times for components are long, the minimum MPS planning horizon can be quite long. This means that product design can have a significant effect on the production-planning process.

## MRP System Nervousness

The time-phasing process used in gross-to-net requirements explosion means that future MPS requirements dictate the material needs in earlier periods. This

FIGURE 13.8
Operation Setback Chart for
Economy Office Chair

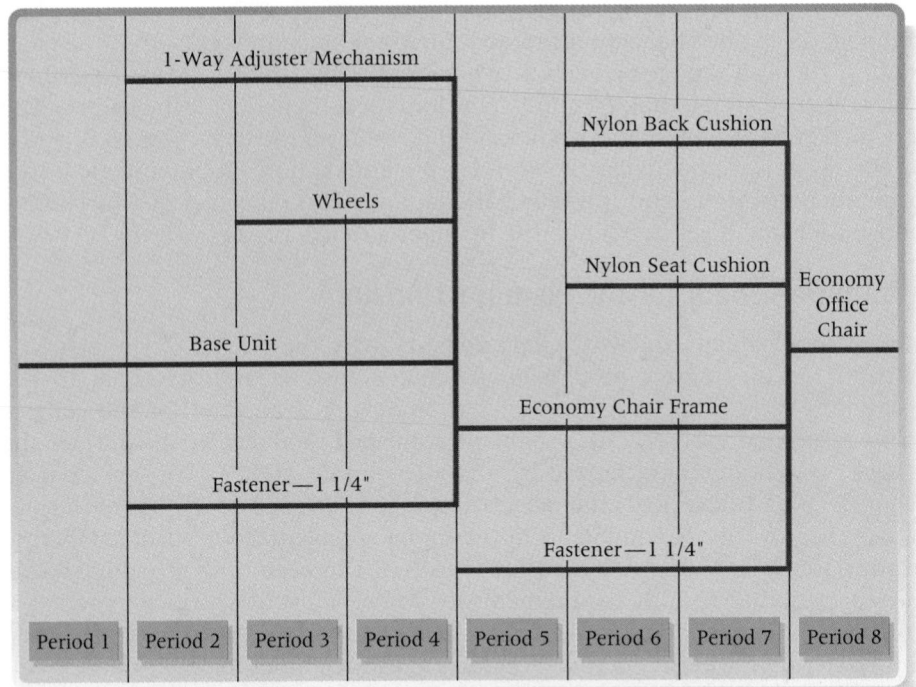

causes a problem known as *MRP system nervousness*. **MRP system nervousness** can be described as a chain reaction: Modifying the MPS in future periods causes changes in material requirements in earlier periods and can result in material shortages in the current period.

Take another look at Table 13.3 and the MRP records for chair frames in Figure 13.6, and suppose that we modify the MPS by adding a requirement for fifteen deluxe chairs in periods 4 and 5. This will cause changes that cascade through the MRP records. Figure 13.9 shows the effect of this MPS change. The change to the MPS changes the gross requirements for the deluxe chair frames, which changes the planned order for fifty chair frames in period 6 to two orders for fifty chair frames, one in period 4 and one in period 7 (see Figure 13.9). This changes the gross requirements for the base units from what they would have been originally. The original gross requirements for fifty base units in periods 1 and 3 and one hundred base units in period 6 as shown in Figure 13.9 changes to gross requirements of fifty units in periods 1, 3, 4, 6, and 7. The gross requirement for fifty units in period 4 causes a negative inventory balance in period 4, because the order to meet this requirement should have been placed before the current period. It should be obvious that changes to the MPS that modify plans in the current period—or worse, create past due orders (orders that should already have been placed to meet planned requirements)—cause serious problems. It should also be obvious that more levels in the BOM or longer lead times will aggravate the effect of changes to the MPS. Furthermore, some lot-sizing methods add to MRP system nervousness.

Three approaches are commonly used to reduce MRP system nervousness. First, the appropriate selection of lot-sizing methods can reduce the problem but will not eliminate it entirely. A second method is to use firm planned orders. **Firm planned orders (FPOs)** involve the manual fixing or freezing of orders by

| Part No: 3817 | | MRP Record for Deluxe Chair Frame with Modified MPS | | | | | | | | | |
|---|---|---|---|---|---|---|---|---|---|---|---|
| Part Name: Deluxe Chair Frame | | | | | | | | | | | |
| LS: 50 | LT: 3 | 1 | 2 | 3 | 4 | 5 | 6 | 7 | 8 | 9 | 10 |
| Gross Requirements | | 20 | 20 | 15 | 15 | 15 | 15 | 15 | 15 | 15 | 15 |
| Scheduled Receipts | | | | 50 | | | | | | | |
| Planned Order Receipts | | | | | | | | 50 | | | 50 |
| Available Balance | 50 | 30 | 10 | 45 | 30 | 15 | 0 | 35 | 20 | 5 | 40 |
| Planned Order Releases | | | | | 50 | | | 50 | | | |

| Part No: 8507 | | Original MRP Record for Base Unit | | | | | | | | | |
|---|---|---|---|---|---|---|---|---|---|---|---|
| Part Name: Base Unit | | | | | | | | | | | |
| LS: 50 | LT: 4 | 1 | 2 | 3 | 4 | 5 | 6 | 7 | 8 | 9 | 10 |
| Gross Requirements | | 50 | | 50 | | | 100 | | | | |
| Scheduled Receipts | | 50 | | 50 | | | | | | | |
| Planned Order Receipts | | | | | | | 100 | | | | |
| Available Balance | 45 | 45 | 45 | 45 | 45 | 45 | 45 | 45 | 45 | 45 | 45 |
| Planned Order Releases | | | 100 | | | | | | | | |

| Part No: 8507 | | Modified MRP Record for Base Unit | | | | | | | | | |
|---|---|---|---|---|---|---|---|---|---|---|---|
| Part Name: Base Unit | | | | | | | | | | | |
| LS: 50 | LT: 4 | 1 | 2 | 3 | 4 | 5 | 6 | 7 | 8 | 9 | 10 |
| Gross Requirements | | 50 | | 50 | 50 | | 50 | 50 | | | |
| Scheduled Receipts | | 50 | | 50 | | | | | | | |
| Planned Order Receipts | | | | | | 50 | 50 | 50 | | | |
| Available Balance | 45 | 45 | 45 | 45 | -5 | 45 | 45 | 45 | 45 | 45 | 45 |
| Planned Order Releases | | 50 | 50 | 50 | | | | | | | |

a production planner so that they are not automatically changed by the MRP system when the MPS is modified.

Implementing and changing FPOs require managerial approval. Because using FPOs tends to limit the chain reactions that result from MPS changes, the third and most effective approach to reducing MRP system nervousness is obvious. If changes to the MPS create problems, changes should be limited. Limiting changes to the MPS is commonly called *freezing the MPS*.

FIGURE 13.9
Effect of MPS Change on MRP Records

## Freezing the Master Production Schedule

Freezing the MPS means that no changes can be made to it for some number of periods into the future. Note that because the cumulative lead time for the chair wheels, chairframes, and final assembly of chairs is six periods (see Figure 13.8 and Table 13.2), freezing the MPS from periods 1 through 6 will avoid any changes to current period plans for the wheels.

Although the MPS can be frozen so that no changes in current period plans for various components are possible, this may not be practical or desirable. For example, if the chief executive officer of a company says that changes must be made to the frozen MPS to accommodate an important customer, changes will have to be made. A change in current period plans is not a problem if the company can accommodate the change—either on the shop floor or by working with the supplier. Although MRP systems operate under the assumption that lead times are constant, in practice they are not. Typically, lead times are set so that they are likely to be met. This means that a big percentage of component orders (purchase orders or production requests) is available earlier than actually needed. Thus, although the planned lead time for a component might be three periods, it might be possible to obtain the components in two periods. Obviously, this would allow a change in the MPS that would normally be considered impossible. Component orders can frequently be expedited—that is, lead times can be reduced by special efforts, such as working overtime, changing job priorities on the shop floor, shipping purchased orders by a faster mode of transportation, purchasing from an alternate supplier, and so on. These efforts usually increase costs, but the benefit gained from making the changes to the MPS may offset the increased costs.

A balanced approach should be taken when changing the MPS. Prohibiting changes may result in production that does not serve the customer, but frequent changes can cause confusion on the shop floor or create difficulties with suppliers. Such difficulties can degrade the integrity of the MRP system—if schedules are changed frequently, no one knows what the true schedule is and employees ignore the schedule.

One way to achieve a better balance between rigid schedules and total chaos is to use time fences. **Time fences** are limits to changes in the MPS for different periods and require approval from different levels in the company. For example, changes to the MPS in periods 1 through 4 might require vice presidential approval, but changes during periods 5 through 8 may require only plant manager approval. After period 8 a formal request from marketing may be all that is necessary. Time fences limit changes to the MPS, yet critical changes can be made with appropriate approval.

## Lumpiness of Demand

Although the MPS for the sample problem has a smooth demand of thirty chairs per period, the demand for components at lower levels in the MPS is not smooth. Note, for example, the lumpiness in the gross requirements for wheels in Figure 13.6. The gross requirements call for three hundred units in periods 1 and 3 and six hundred units in period 6, with zero demand in all other periods. The demand for wheels is "lumpy" because of the lot-sizing procedures used for its parent components (the economy and deluxe chair frames). The demand for chair frames is fairly smooth, but because chair frames are ordered in groups of fifty, the requirements are passed down only at certain periods. Because a chair frame requires six wheels, the lumpiness is amplified. Although the aggregate demand for chairs could be satisfied by providing 180 wheels per period (30 chairs × 6 wheels), the MRP logic creates a lumpiness of demand for wheels. This can be a significant problem because of its implication for in-house or vendor capacity requirements and should be considered when choosing lot-sizing methods.

The operations manager can reduce lumpiness in the gross requirements for wheels by changing the lot size for chair frames from a fixed lot size of fifty to LFL. Figure 13.10 shows the results of this change. Note that the beginning

F I G U R E   1 3 . 1 0
MRP Records for Chair Frames and Wheels Using LFL Lot Sizing

| Part No: 3807 | | | | | | | | | | | |
|---|---|---|---|---|---|---|---|---|---|---|---|
| Part Name:<br>  Economy Chair Frame | | | | | | | | | | | |
| LS: LFL | LT: 3 | 1 | 2 | 3 | 4 | 5 | 6 | 7 | 8 | 9 | 10 |
| Gross Requirements | | 10 | 10 | 15 | 30 | 30 | 15 | 15 | 15 | 15 | 15 |
| Scheduled Receipts | | 10 | 10 | 15 | | | | | | | |
| Planned Order Receipts | | | | | 30 | 30 | 15 | 15 | 15 | 15 | 15 |
| Available Balance | 0 | 0 | 0 | 0 | 0 | 0 | 0 | 0 | 0 | 0 | 0 |
| Planned Order Releases | | 30 | 30 | 15 | 15 | 15 | 15 | 15 | | | |

| Part No: 3817 | | | | | | | | | | | |
|---|---|---|---|---|---|---|---|---|---|---|---|
| Part Name:<br>  Deluxe Chair Frame | | | | | | | | | | | |
| LS: LFL | LT: 3 | 1 | 2 | 3 | 4 | 5 | 6 | 7 | 8 | 9 | 10 |
| Gross Requirements | | 20 | 20 | 15 | | | 15 | 15 | 15 | 15 | 15 |
| Scheduled Receipts | | 20 | 20 | 15 | | | | | | | |
| Planned Order Receipts | | | | | | | 15 | 15 | 15 | 15 | 15 |
| Available Balance | 0 | 0 | 0 | 0 | 0 | 0 | 0 | 0 | 0 | 0 | 0 |
| Planned Order Releases | | | | 15 | 15 | 15 | 15 | 15 | | | |

| Part No: 5562 | | | | | | | | | | | |
|---|---|---|---|---|---|---|---|---|---|---|---|
| Part Name:<br>  Wheel | | | | | | | | | | | |
| LS: 500 | LT: 2 | 1 | 2 | 3 | 4 | 5 | 6 | 7 | 8 | 9 | 10 |
| Gross Requirements | | 180 | 180 | 180 | 180 | 180 | 180 | 180 | | | |
| Scheduled Receipts | | | | | | | | | | | |
| Planned Order Receipts | | | | | 500 | | | 500 | | | |
| Available Balance | 700 | 520 | 340 | 160 | 480 | 300 | 120 | 440 | 440 | 440 | 440 |
| Planned Order Releases | | | 500 | | | 500 | | | | | |

inventory balance has been changed to zero for both types of chair frame, and scheduled receipts have been added to the first three periods of the chair frame records, consistent with the LFL procedure. Under the LFL procedure the gross requirements for the wheels change to a level demand of 180 units per period. Using the LFL procedure for the chair frames passes the level aggregate demand down to the gross requirements for wheels, avoiding the lumpiness problem. However, do not assume that the LFL procedure is always the best. Using LFL for the chair frames smoothed the gross requirements for the wheels, but it increased the number of planned orders for chair frames, which may increase total costs if there are high set-up costs associated with chair frame production.

## Lot Sizing

The key question in lot sizing is whether a planned order should include components that satisfy requirements beyond the period triggering the order. Although lot sizing can have a significant effect on the performance of the MRP system and many lot-sizing methods are available, no optimal method exists. Frequently, obtaining the data required to calculate lot sizes is difficult. Further, many argue that the importance of lot sizing in MRP has been exaggerated.

FIGURE 13.11
Lot-Sizing Example Data

Part No: G1
Name: Generic Component
LT: 0
Ordering Cost: $250
Holding Cost: $1.25 per unit per period
Gross Requirements

| Period | | | | | | | | | |
|---|---|---|---|---|---|---|---|---|---|
| 1 | 2 | 3 | 4 | 5 | 6 | 7 | 8 | 9 | 10 |
| 40 | 30 | 30 | 50 | 60 | 150 | 300 | 140 | 0 | 200 |

FIGURE 13.12a
Lot-for-Lot Example

| Part No: G1 | | | | | | | | | | | |
|---|---|---|---|---|---|---|---|---|---|---|---|
| Part Name: Generic Component | | | | | | | | | | | |
| LS: LFL | LT: 0 | 1 | 2 | 3 | 4 | 5 | 6 | 7 | 8 | 9 | 10 |
| Gross Requirements | | 40 | 30 | 30 | 50 | 60 | 150 | 300 | 140 | 0 | 200 |
| Scheduled Receipts | | | | | | | | | | | |
| Planned Order Receipts | | 40 | 30 | 30 | 50 | 60 | 150 | 300 | 140 | 0 | 200 |
| Available Balance | 0 | 0 | 0 | 0 | 0 | 0 | 0 | 0 | 0 | 0 | 0 |
| Planned Order Releases | | 40 | 30 | 30 | 50 | 60 | 150 | 300 | 140 | 0 | 200 |

| | |
|---|---|
| Ordering Costs: | $2,250.00 |
| Inventory Holding Costs: | 0.00 |
| Total Costs: | $2,250.00 |

We will use the generic component data provided in Figure 13.11 to illustrate three lot-sizing methods. The lead time is assumed to be zero, because it simplifies the discussion.

In these examples we will apply inventory costs only to the available balance quantities; that is, only inventory carried over from one period to the next is assessed for inventory holding charges. For comparison purposes we will apply the fixed order quantity, the period order quantity, and the lot-for-lot procedures to the data in Figure 13.11.

## Lot-for-Lot

The Lot-for-Lot (LFL) procedure produces the MRP record shown in Figure 13.12a. Because LFL places an order in every period there is a gross requirement—the ordering costs are 9 × $250 = $2,250—whereas the inventory holding costs are zero, because only the inventory held over from one period to the next incurs carrying charges.

## Fixed Order Quantity

Frequently, the lot size is a fixed quantity. This may occur when suppliers prefer to sell and ship a certain quantity, so the buyer purchases a **fixed order quantity (FOQ).** A particular part such as fasteners may be packaged in cases;the lot size should be a case (or a multiple number of cases). Bulk raw materials might be ordered in truckloads to obtain shipping discounts. Suppliers may offer quantity discounts that make particular order quantities attractive (see Chapter 12 for a discussion of the quantity discount problem). In the company's own facility producing a fixed quantity may be economical because of a process yield. For example, if a part is stamped out of steel, producing a quantity that uses an entire roll of steel may be more economical than producing a partial roll quantity and then changing to a different product that requires a different type of steel. In process industries, mixing, blending, and other chemical processes are frequently difficult to perform with less than a full batch.

One method of determining a fixed order quantity is the **economic order quantity (EOQ)** equation discussed in Chapter 12. Under a number of assumptions, including a constant rate of demand, we can calculate an economic order quantity, $Q$, for a purchased component as

$$Q = \sqrt{\frac{2DC_o}{C_H}} \qquad (13\text{-}1)$$

where

$D$ = Annual demand, in units per year
$C_o$ = Cost for placing an order, in dollars
$C_H$ = Annual carrying cost, in dollars per unit per year

For a component that is produced in house, the set-up cost $C_S$ replaces the ordering cost $C_o$.

The average demand per period for the generic component is one hundred units (1,000 units/10 periods). Assuming weekly time buckets for fifty weeks per year, the estimate of the annual demand would be five thousand units (100 units/period × 50 periods). Thus, the annual carrying cost per unit per year is $62.50 ($1.25/period × 50 periods). We then can calculate the EOQ as

| Part No: G1 | | | | | | | | | | | | |
|---|---|---|---|---|---|---|---|---|---|---|---|---|
| Part Name: Generic Component | | | | | | | | | | | | |
| LS: EOQ | LT: 0 | | 1 | 2 | 3 | 4 | 5 | 6 | 7 | 8 | 9 | 10 |
| Gross Requirements | | | 40 | 30 | 30 | 50 | 60 | 150 | 300 | 140 | 0 | 200 |
| Scheduled Receipts | | | | | | | | | | | | |
| Planned Order Receipts | | | 200 | | | | 200 | | 260 | 200 | | 200 |
| Available Balance | | 0 | 160 | 130 | 100 | 50 | 190 | 40 | 0 | 60 | 60 | 60 |
| Planned Order Releases | | | 200 | | | | 200 | | 260 | 200 | | 200 |

| Ordering Costs: | $1,250.000 |
|---|---|
| Inventory Holding Costs: | 1,062.50 |
| Total Costs: | $2,312.50 |

**FIGURE 13.12b**
FOQ Lot Sizing Based on the EOQ

$$Q = \sqrt{\frac{(2)(5000)(250)}{62.50}} = 200 \qquad (13\text{-}2)$$

Figure 13.12b shows the MRP record using the EOQ lot size. Note that the planned order for period 7 was 260. Whenever a gross requirement exceeds the EOQ, the operations manager should order the gross requirement quantity. EOQ lot sizing results in five planned orders, so the ordering cost is $1,250. The sum of the on-hand inventory is 850, so the inventory holding cost is $1,062.50.

Because the EOQ method assumes constant demand, it would seem inappropriate for MRP systems. However, if gross requirements for an item are somewhat smooth, the EOQ order quantity might not be too far from the optimum.

## Period Order Quantity

The previous example showed how the EOQ lot size can produce high inventory levels if the level demand assumption is violated. The period order quantity lot-sizing method attempts to reduce this problem. The **period order quantity (POQ)** method converts the economic order quantity to an economic order period. We can calculate the POQ as

$$POQ = \frac{EOQ}{D_p} \qquad (13\text{-}3)$$

where $D_p$ is the average demand per period. Instead of ordering a fixed quantity, the POQ lot size covers the gross requirements for a fixed number of periods. In this example the POQ is two periods (200 units/100 units per period). Figure 13.12c shows the MRP record for the generic component with a POQ of two. The POQ method orders five times, for an ordering cost of $1,250 (the same as for EOQ), but the sum of the available balance is only 370 units, for an inventory carrying cost of $462.50. In this example the POQ method worked much better than the EOQ method, because it reduced the inventory levels in the early periods.

| Part No: G1 | | | | | | | | | | | | |
|---|---|---|---|---|---|---|---|---|---|---|---|---|
| Part Name:<br>  Generic Component | | | | | | | | | | | | |
| LS: POQ | LT: 0 | | 1 | 2 | 3 | 4 | 5 | 6 | 7 | 8 | 9 | 10 |
| Gross Requirements | | | 40 | 30 | 30 | 50 | 60 | 150 | 300 | 140 | 0 | 200 |
| Scheduled Receipts | | | | | | | | | | | | |
| Planned Order Receipts | | | 70 | | 80 | | 210 | | 440 | | | 200 |
| Available Balance | | 0 | 30 | 0 | 50 | 0 | 150 | 0 | 140 | 0 | 0 | 0 |
| Planned Order Releases | | | 70 | | 80 | | 210 | | 440 | | | 200 |

| | |
|---|---|
| Ordering Costs: | $1,250.00 |
| Inventory Holding Costs: | 462.50 |
| Total Costs: | $1,712.50 |

FIGURE 13.12c
POQ Lot Sizing Example

## Lot Sizing and MRP System Nervousness

As we mentioned previously, lot-sizing methods can contribute to MRP system nervousness. One manager has recommended the following lot sizing policy to minimize MRP nervousness for products with several BOM levels: use the fixed order quantity for top levels; use the fixed order quantity or lot-for-lot for intermediate levels; and use the period order quantity for lower levels. This approach should help stabilize requirements at the lower levels of the product structures.[2]

## The Importance of Lot Sizing

Although the academic community has expended much effort in studying lot-sizing methods, industry for many reasons has not exhibited much interest in this research.

First, practitioners are typically wary of complicated procedures. This may be attributable to a lack of understanding, but more likely it stems from a belief that the benefits of a complex lot-sizing mechanism do not outweigh the costs. Second, academic research often is characterized by a variety of unrealistic assumptions and simplifications, such as constant demand.

Like those discussed earlier, most lot sizing procedures ignore the effect of the multilevel demand structure in MRP. Lot-sizing decisions at one level in the BOM affect the lot-sizing decision at lower levels, yet most lot-sizing methods (and all of those described earlier) consider only one level in the BOM at a time.

Another important factor in lot sizing is forecasting errors. A study that compared fourteen lot sizing methods showed that the five lot sizing rules, "which have been found to be the five *best* performers under demand certainty in terms of holding and ordering cost, are also the five *worst* performers in terms of

[2]Daniel C. Steele, "The Nervous MRP System: How To Do Battle," *Production and Inventory Management Journal* 16, No. 4 (4th Quarter 1975), 83–89.

service levels and number of stockout occurrences when forecast errors are present."[3]

The issue of lot sizing is perhaps best summed up by Joe Orlicky, a pioneer in the development of MRP systems: "When it comes to selecting a lot-sizing technique (or techniques) to be incorporated in an MRP system, it is the author's opinion that neither detailed studies nor exhaustive debates are warranted—in practice, one discrete lot-sizing algorithm is about as good as another."[4] However, Orlicky did recommend that the lot-for-lot approach should be used wherever feasible, except in cases of significant set-up costs where other methods (such as POQ) would be more appropriate.

## Use of MRP Systems

Although MRP is a computerized planning system, people make it work. MRP systems use information to make plans based on MRP logic, but it is the **MRP planner** who provides the inputs, modifies schedules, and executes the plan.

One function of the MRP planner is to help develop the MPS. Whereas marketing and manufacturing executives typically develop the MPS, the MRP planner must ensure that the MPS is feasible. This usually involves the capacity planning functions discussed in Chapter 14. As production plans are completed, the MPS rolls forward, meaning that the MRP planner must resolve any discrepancies between the MPS and what was actually produced and must add new MPS requirements to the end of the planning horizon.

The MRP planner is responsible for checking and launching planned orders for the current period (releasing the orders to purchasing or the shop floor). If production requirements change, the MRP planner may delay a due date or expedite production or purchasing, whichever is appropriate. Pegging is a useful technique for the MRP planner to use when scheduled receipts are delayed or the quantity delivered is less than scheduled. **Pegging** relates the gross requirements for a component to the parent component that caused the requirement. In this manner the MRP planner can trace demand up through the product structure file(s) to the MPS. With this information MRP planners can make trade-offs concerning which finished goods orders to delay and then modify the due dates for all components related to the delayed order(s). Pegging also allows the planner to determine which customer order(s) will be delayed in a make-to-order environment, allowing for timely notification of the customer. The MRP planner is also responsible for updating such planning factors as lot size, lead time, and safety stock and correcting any errors in the MRP data.

Many companies have hundreds of finished products made up of tens of thousands of component parts. In these environments MRP systems require large volumes of data and produce large amounts of information. Two techniques are useful for managing the data and output of MRP systems. The first is to divide the finished goods and component parts among several MRP planners so that each planner handles a logical subset of the company's component parts and can become intimately familiar with them. Parts may be organized according to product lines or type of product (wood, sheet metal, electronics, and so on).

Second, rather than printing all MRP records, the computer system can be programmed to print *exception reports*. Exception reports include only those items

---

[3]Urban Wemmerlöv, "The Behavior of Lot-Sizing Procedures in the Presence of Forecast Errors," *Journal of Operations Management* 8 (January 1989): 42.

[4]Joseph Orlicky, *Material Requirements Planning* (New York, McGraw-Hill, 1975), p. 137.

that require the attention of the MRP planner, such as planned order releases in the current time period, scheduled receipts that have not materialized, or projected inventory shortfalls. By separating the important few from the trivial many, exception reports enhance the communication of information from the MRP system to the MRP planner.

# Some Practical Considerations in Using MRP

The application of MRP to a variety of manufacturing environments has led to the development of several techniques to handle specific application problems. This section discusses methods to handle uncertainty in product deliveries or manufacturing yields, means of dealing with product options, closed loop MRP, and manufacturing resource planning, or MRP II.

## Uncertainty

Frequently, there is uncertainty in manufacturing and purchasing processes. Lead times may not be met. Purchased or manufactured parts may not meet quality standards, reducing the quantity received to less than what was planned. Depending on the source of the uncertainty, the MRP planner can use safety stock, safety lead time, or scrap allowances to address such problems.

Safety stock can be used when the quantity of a scheduled receipt is uncertain. **Safety stock** is an inventory balance of a component part that is not used under normal circumstances. Suppose a component is purchased from a vendor who can meet delivery schedules but occasionally has difficulty meeting quality standards. If a scheduled receipt has defective components, the safety stock can make up the loss, and the next purchase order for the components can include parts to return the safety stock to its normal level.

If the quality of a component is usually acceptable but delivery delays are possible, **safety lead time** might be used. Suppose a vendor quotes a planned lead time of four weeks but at times delivers components in five weeks instead of four. In this situation the MRP planner may use a safety lead time of one week by placing orders five weeks before they are needed. Safety lead time is not appropriate for internally produced components, because the planned lead times should be set so that they can be achieved with some confidence. If planned lead times are too long, the production facility will be working on jobs sooner than necessary and in-process inventory levels will be unnecessarily high. Furthermore, if employees notice that production orders frequently are not used until a week or two after the due date, confidence in the MRP system will erode.

If manufacturing processes at times produce bad components, the quantity produced will be less than the quantity ordered. Suppose in the office chair example that the wheels are force-fit into the base unit and that the machine that does this occasionally breaks the wheels or splits the steel tubing of the base unit. If fifty chair frames are required and fifty base units and three hundred wheels are procured, fewer than fifty chair frames may be assembled because of damage to the component parts. If the process that attaches the base unit to the adjuster mechanism occasionally damages parts, the number of chair frames produced may be even lower. If scrap losses are anticipated, a *scrap allowance* may be added to the planned orders. If fifty chair frames are required and scrap is anticipated, the planned order for chair frames may be increased to fifty-two.

Although safety stock, safety lead time, and scrap allowances allow MRP systems to account for uncertainty, these methods also allow the company to ignore these problems rather than look at the source of these errors (poor supplier relations, poorly maintained equipment, poor training). Recent trends in manufacturing, such as JIT production and total quality management (TQM) show that companies gain significant savings when they fix problems rather than accommodate them.

## Modular Bills of Material

Suppose the office chair manufacturer in our sample MRP problem wants to expand the product line by offering the following range of options:

| Component | Options |
|---|---|
| Seat cushions | Leather (tan, brown and black) |
| | Nylon (tan, green, brown and black) |
| Adjuster mechanism | 1–way, 2–way and 3–way |
| Base unit | 5-wheel and 6-wheel |
| Wheels | Bushing, roller bearing, and ball bearing |

The fifteen options create 126 different chair models ($7 \times 3 \times 2 \times 3$). Developing an MPS for 126 different end items would be formidable, and the demand forecasts would lack accuracy. Another approach is to develop an MPS for the fifteen option components, or **option modules,** significantly reducing the forecasting task. To accomplish this the MRP planner must modify the BOM structure so that option modules, rather than the actual end items, appear at the end-item level in the BOM. This type of BOM is known as a **modular bill of material**.

A modular BOM may be easier to develop, but it does not specify how the option modules are to be assembled into finished chairs. A separate document, known as the *final assembly schedule*, is used for this purpose.

## Closed Loop MRP

For an MRP system to be successful the production system must be able to complete component orders on time. Closed loop MRP uses capacity planning and feedback to improve the ability of the production system to complete work as planned. Capacity-planning tools (discussed in Chapter 14) allow the operations manager to adjust the MPS and/or planned order release dates or obtain additional capacity so that shop orders can be completed by their due dates.

MRP planners use a number of planning factors (capacity-planning factors, lead time estimates, safety stocks, safety lead times) and tools (capacity planning, frozen time horizons, firm planned orders) to improve the quality of the materials schedules generated by the MRP system. To determine how well the planning factors and tools are working, MRP planners need feedback from the shop floor and the purchasing department. With effective feedback the MRP planner can revise the planning factors and techniques so that better materials schedules can be developed in the future.

Feedback is also important when suppliers or the shop floor cannot meet order due dates. Timely feedback to MRP planners allows them to develop alternatives or at least to minimize the effect of the problem. For example, production of a batch of a component may not be completed on time, but enough components may be available in on-hand inventory and safety stock to allow the production of a smaller quantity of the parent item to satisfy the MPS until production of the component is completed.

## MRP II—Manufacturing Resource Planning

MRP originally developed as a computer system that was limited to materials planning. As computer technology and MRP systems developed, it became clear that MRP systems maintain extensive information that can be used for other company functions. For example, MRP systems maintain accurate inventory information. Combining this information with cost data allows accounting personnel to have accurate inventory information in meaningful financial terms. Rather than having separate production and accounting systems, a company can expand MRP to meet the requirements for both systems.

MRP II is an expansion of closed loop MRP for managing an entire manufacturing company. MRP II systems provide information that is useful to all functional areas and encourages cross-functional interaction. MRP II supports sales and marketing by providing an order-promising capability. Order promising is a method of tying customers' orders to end items in the MPS. This allows sales personnel to have accurate information on product availability and gives them the ability to give customers accurate delivery dates. MRP II supports financial planning by converting material schedules into capital requirements. A company can use MRP II to simulate the effects of different master production schedules on material usage, labor, and capital requirements. MRP II provides the purchasing department with more than just purchase requisitions. The long-range planned order release schedules can be used to provide purchasing with information for developing long-range buying plans. It is now common for suppliers to directly access a customer's MRP II system to receive up-to-date information on the customer's planned material needs. Information in the MRP II system is used to provide accounting with information on material receipts to determine accounts payable. Shop-floor control information is used to track workers' hours for payroll purposes.

Manufacturing is the central function in a manufacturing company. The information required to successfully plan and schedule production is valuable to the other (supporting) functions in the company. MRP II systems increase a company's efficiency by providing a central source of management information.

# Implementation of MRP

Implementing an MRP system is a monumental effort. The system requires a tremendous amount of information, which must be accurate if the system is to be successful. MRP systems affect all functions within a company—marketing, production, purchasing, accounting, finance, and logistics—to some extent. All personnel who have any interaction with the MRP system require training. Further, they must be committed to making the MRP system work. The problems that occur in implementing MRP are frequently organizational and behavioral rather than technical.

## Existing Systems and the Informal System

If an MRP system is replacing an existing production and inventory control system, the company may see significant resistance to change, even if the existing system has been unsatisfactory. People generally resist change, and they prefer the familiar to the unfamiliar. Also, when a system performs poorly, an informal system develops to deal with problems.

When a production and inventory control system begins to fail, the first sign is usually an increase in order expediting and frequent changes in priorities. Batches of components may be tagged *rush* to help in expediting orders. Frequently, this approach leads to having a rush tag on every basket of parts, which means that no order has priority. If production schedules are unreliable, informal communications between workers and supervisors usually serve to determine which job is more important. Hot lists (lists of critical jobs) serve as the actual production-scheduling tool. Informal systems develop to solve problems, but they can never be effective, because they operate locally with only a small amount of information.

Although an MRP system can provide stable, meaningful materials schedules, employees frequently feel more comfortable with the informal system. When production and inventory planning has been ineffective, a fire-fighting mentality frequently develops—production schedulers and supervisors are constantly moving from one crisis to the next, putting out fires. Fire fighting can be seductive; dealing with problems every day can be exciting, even if it is ineffective. Employees must be convinced that a formal MRP system will provide a better way to plan material requirements and production priorities, and they must be committed to its success.

## Information Requirements

An operating MRP system requires a large amount of timely, accurate data. A detailed discussion of the data requirements or effective organization of the data is beyond the scope of this text. However, a discussion of the types of data required shows the magnitude of the data management task in MRP systems.

Bills of material must be developed for all end items. This task is not simple. Frequent product changes and engineering modifications can make the process of developing a BOM challenging. To maintain the integrity of the BOM, the company must practice effective configuration control, that is, the company must control and coordinate changes to its products to ensure a smooth changeover to new product designs. Failure to control the configuration of products can leave the company with an excess inventory of obsolete parts.

MRP systems require information for each component part. This data can be broken down into two categories, static and dynamic. Static information does not change frequently and typically is stored in a computer file called the **item master file**. Dynamic information is stored in a subordinate item master file. Item master file data include such information as the part number and name, order quantity or lot-sizing method, planned lead time, engineering drawing numbers, production planner code (to identify the production planner responsible for the part), purchasing agent code, and so on. The subordinate item master file would contain inventory status information: available balance, scheduled receipts, purchase order or shop order numbers for scheduled receipts, firm planned orders, location information (storage location for the parts), and so on. The component data are separated into two files so that the subordinate item master file, which must be updated frequently, can be as small as possible to minimize processing time.

## Inventory Control

All MRP data must be accurate to ensure system integrity, but the inventory data are the most difficult to maintain because they change frequently. The MRP inventory data must be compared periodically with the actual physical inventory to maintain accuracy. Two methods of inventory control can be used—*periodic counts* and *cycle counting*. With periodic counts the company's entire inventory is counted at one time and compared with company records. During this period the company limits its transactions to minimize confusion. Periodic counts are frequently performed during standard vacation times when the production facility is idle. Periodic counting involves more than just counting parts. The company must maintain proper housekeeping so that parts are properly located, accessible, and identified. Procedures and forms must be developed, and personnel must be trained. When implementing MRP for the first time, getting inventory under control can be a formidable task.

Cycle counting is useful when the MRP system is in operation and inventory is under control. Cycle counting is a continuous process that does not require production activities to be shut down. In cycle counting a small set of parts is counted during any one period. The inventory count is compared with the MRP system inventory status to determine whether the system is in control. With cycle counting the company's entire inventory eventually is counted. Frequently, cycle counting can be combined with normal material-handling operations.

## Keys to Successful Implementation[5]

A recent study of implementing information technology (MRP is one form of information technology) describes the conditions that relate to successful implementation. Factors that are important to the successful implementation of information technology (IT) are

- Top management support
- Good information technology design
- Appropriate user-designer interaction and understanding

Research on the social changes required by IT implementation shows that success is also related to

- Committing to change and to the implementation effort
- Defining and planning the project extensively
- Using organizational change theories to manage the process

Finally, political research suggests that success depends on recognizing and managing the diverse interests of everyone who will be affected by the new IT. The study particularly emphasized the importance of the human and organizational aspects of IT implementation.

## An MRP Implementation Plan[6]

Our discussion thus far has described important factors in MRP implementation, but it has not provided specific guidance on how to implement an MRP system. Thomas Wallace, an MRP II expert, provides a more prescriptive description of MRP implementation. Figure 13.13 is a graphic representation of Wallace's "proven path." He also views MRP implementation as a task primarily concerned with people, not computer systems. Wallace's plan specifies twelve months for

---

[5]Adapted from Randolph B. Cooper and Robert W. Zmud, "Information Technology Implementation Research: A Technological Diffusion Approach," *Management Science* 36 (February 1990): 123–139.
[6]Adapted from Wallace, *MRP II*.

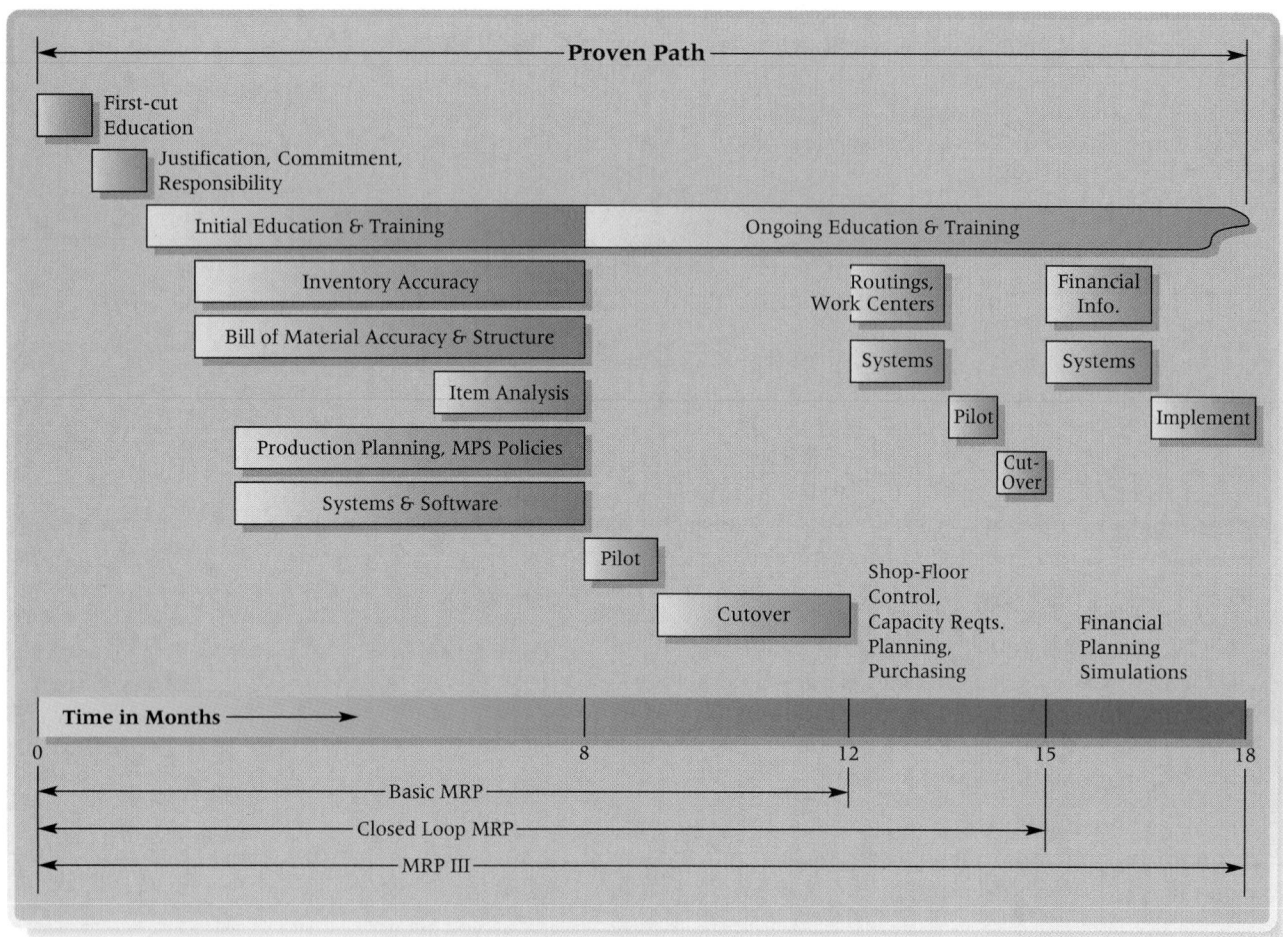

FIGURE 13.13
Wallace's Proven Path for
MRP Implementation

implementing MRP, three months to "close the loop," and three more months to implement MRP II.

His view is that implementing MRP in less time is not practically possible and that allowing more time means that the implementation effort is likely to lose steam.

The process starts with a first-cut education of management in the intricacies of MRP (and MRP II) and developing a consensus that the company should implement MRP. With a proper understanding of MRP management can make more accurate cost and benefit estimates and project benchmarks before making the final decision to go ahead with implementation.

Education is a big part of the implementation process, and it becomes an ongoing activity after implementation. Wallace gives two purposes for education:

■ Transferring facts, which occurs when people learn the whats, whys, and hows
■ Changing behavior, which occurs when people who have lived in the
   world of the informal system become convinced of the need to do their
   jobs differently

Inventory accuracy and BOM accuracy and structure are the most time- (and labor-) consuming steps. Frequently, companies find that developing accurate inventory control systems and gaining control over product configuration pro-

# OPERATIONS MANAGEMENT IN PRACTICE 13.2 ◀

## MRP and the Real Cost of Inventory Losses at Gendex

When Gendex, a Chicago-based supplier of medical and dental equipment, purchased Midwest Medical in 1990, it got more than a manufacturer of dental hand pieces (air-driven, high-speed drill motors): It got MRP II software operating on a Hewlett-Packard HP9000 RISC minicomputer. Gendex's other two divisions, which produced medical and dental x-ray supplies, were not MRP users and were doing much of their production and inventory planning by hand. The medical x-ray division was using the IBM *MAPICS* software but not the MRP module and was spending nearly $1 million to purchase mainframe computer time. Now all three divisions are using the software on the HP9000 minicomputer. The new package allows each division to operate a separate MRP system.

MRP has helped the medical x-ray division make significant improvements in its operations. According to Jim Kettner, Gendex vice president of information services and regulatory affairs, "The medical division's purchased components inventory was out of control. They didn't know what they needed, and they had too much of everything. The MRP system allowed them to get purchased components under control." The MRP system also helped them cut inventory losses by 50 percent in dollar terms. Previously, the inventory system and cost-accounting system were separate, so that no one really appreciated the cost of inventory losses. With the new system inventory losses were no longer expressed in terms of parts but in real dollars, and the company could focus more attention on the part numbers with the highest cost losses.

vide significant cost reductions in and of themselves. Production planning and MPS policies should address four key areas: production planning, master production scheduling, material planning, and engineering changes. The policies should define who is responsible, who is authorized to make changes, what reporting is required, and so forth.

Wallace notes that "software of and by itself cannot make a company a successful MRP II user. However, the lack of a reasonably complete set of software can keep a company from succeeding."[7] Computer software for MRP is widely available for mainframe, minicomputer, and microcomputer systems. Computer Publications, Inc.,[8] sells the *MRP Systems Directory and Buyers Guide*, which provides information on almost two hundred software systems and includes information on how to conduct a detailed evaluation of manufacturing software systems. With the number of systems available a company is unlikely to want to invest in developing its own software system.

There are three ways to actually implement an MRP system: switch over cold turkey, run MRP and the existing system in parallel, or conduct a pilot test and cut over once the pilot test is successfully completed. According to Wallace, the cold turkey approach is too risky: If the old system is discarded and the new system does not work, the company cannot order material and parts and may risk serious financial difficulty. Nor does he recommend the parallel approach. The

*At Gendex, MRP software is run on an HP9000 RISC minicomputer.*

[7]Wallace, *MRP II*, p. 135.
[8]Computer Publications, Inc., 279 Morris Avenue, Providence, Rhode Island 02906.

purpose of a parallel approach is to compare the output of the existing system with the new MRP system. The trouble is, if the company was not using MRP before, the output of the two systems will not be comparable.

With the pilot approach the company implements the MRP system with one product or one small set of products first. The pilot approach minimizes the risk if problems develop. Once the MRP system works with the pilot product(s), the personnel involved with the MRP implementation have seen a demonstration of its usefulness, and expanding the products being handled with MRP will be much easier.

This overview gives some idea of the challenges and important decisions required to implement an MRP system. The critical factor in MRP implementation is getting everyone to support the idea and work toward the goal of making MRP the *only* system used to plan material requirements and order priorities. Operations Management in Practice 13.2 discusses the benefits of using MRP at Gendex, a medical products supplier.

## ► Summary

This chapter provided an introduction to dependent demand inventory management. In a manufacturing environment MRP provides a means of using the dependent demand relationships represented by bills of material to provide timely and accurate material order schedules for production and purchasing.

This chapter illustrated how MRP converts a master production schedule into planned order releases using MRP logic. It presented many important problems in MRP applications, including the loss of visibility for low-level components and MRP nervousness. It also discussed some methods of dealing with these problems, including frozen planning horizons, firm planned orders, and selecting lot-sizing techniques. A number of advanced MRP topics were also discussed, including uncertainty, modular bills of material, closed loop MRP and MRP II. These topics show how MRP has developed to handle the complexities of real manufacturing systems.

Perhaps the most difficult problem with MRP systems is determining an MPS that the company can execute, given the capacity constraints of its production system. Capacity planning is an important MRP topic and is the subject of Chapter 14.

**Learning Objective 1: Describe how MRP logic uses the dependent demand relationships to determine component order release dates and due dates.** MRP uses component lead time data to time-phase component requirements based upon the dependent demand relationships depicted in the BOM file. MRP records are processed according to components' low level codes to specify time-phased component order release dates and due dates.

**Learning Objective 2: Describe how offsetting lead times leads to a loss of visibility for low-level components.** The planned order releases for a component have to allow for the lead time required to manufacture or purchase the component. Thus the component's planned order releases are generated for earlier periods than the periods in which the gross requirements they satisfy appear. The planned order releases appearing in earlier periods create gross requirements in these earlier periods for the component's children. Thus, the planning horizons for low level components are shorter than these for higher level components, leading to a loss of visibility for these items.

**Learning Objective 3: Discuss MRP system nervousness.** The time-phasing process used in MRP means that MPS quantities in future periods affect the planned order release schedules for components in earlier periods including the current period. Because the MPS quantities are based on forecasts, they are subject to change. Changing MPS quantities affects component requirements and can cause material shortages in the current period. Lot-sizing mechanisms can amplify MRP nervousness.

**Learning Objective 4: Discuss the implementation of an MRP system, including data requirements, planning, and the importance of human behavior**

**in implementing MRP.** MRP implementation is a significant effort. MRP requires significant amounts of information. Bills of material must be accurate, and engineering changes must be managed. The company must develop and analyze component information, such as lot sizes, lead times, scrap allowances, safety stock levels, and so on. MRP requires accurate inventory information and the development of inventory controls.

Planning is essential. All employees who are affected by the MRP implementation must be trained and motivated to make the implementation a success. Planning is also necessary to smooth the transition, because the company will have to continue functioning during the transition, and productivity losses because of transition problems cost money.

The human behavior aspect is perhaps the most important. Change is frequently disturbing to people, and they tend to cling to old ways of doing things. Rumors are likely to run rampant during the transition as people worry about the effect of the new system on their jobs. Education and communication are the keys to avoiding such problems.

### Learning Objective 5: Describe some functions of the MRP planner.
The MRP planner is a central figure in a successful MRP system. MRP planners decide whether planned order releases become actual shop orders and requests to purchasing. In many cases they are responsible for determining whether planning factors should be changed or adjusted. They determine the adequacy of an MPS and its feasibility (using the capacity-planning techniques of Chapter 14). The MRP planner usually interacts with shop-floor personnel, helping to determine which orders should be expedited and which should be delayed. MRP planners also replan when the shop floor or a supplier cannot meet a due date.

### Learning Objective 6: Describe situations in which a modular BOM would be appropriate.
Modular BOMs are useful when a number of product options can be combined to produce a large number of end items. In this case planning production of option modules is usually easier and more accurate than planning end items.

### Learning Objective 7: Compare MRP and MRP II.
MRP is a system for determining component order quantities, release dates and due dates based on the MPS, the BOM file and inventory records (on-hand inventory, scheduled receipts, lead times). MRP II is a system in which the entire manufacturing organization shares the manufacturing information provided by the system. MRP II improves the efficiency of the organization and increases the coordination between functions. MRP II provides a coordinated means by which to manage a manufacturing organization.

## ► Key Terms

| | | |
|---|---|---|
| bill of material (BOM) | low-level code | pegging |
| closed loop MRP | manufacturing resource planning (MRP II) | period order quantity (POQ) |
| economic order quantity (EOQ) | master production schedule (MPS) | planned order receipts |
| firm planned order (FPO) | material requirements planning (MRP) | planned order releases |
| fixed order quantity (FOQ) | modular bill of material | product structure diagram |
| gross requirements | MRP planner | safety lead time |
| gross-to-net requirements explosion | MRP record | safety stock |
| inventory records | MRP system nervousness | scheduled receipts |
| item master file | option modules | time fences |
| lot-for-lot (LFL) | | |

## ► Discussion Questions

1. How does the dependent demand inventory relationship simplify the determination of demand for components?
2. Why is the MPS described as a contract between marketing and manufacturing? How does the MPS differ from a forecast of market demand?
3. Why are aggregate production plans, rather than an MPS, used for strategic planning?
4. How does a BOM differ from a component parts list?
5. Why are the BOM levels numbered in ascending order as we move downward in the BOM? What problems could occur if the levels were numbered in *descending* order?
6. Which method of reducing MRP nervousness, freezing the MPS or changing lot-sizing methods, would have the greater effect on marketing?

7. How can product and production process design affect the loss of low-level visibility?
8. Why might EOQ lot sizing produce planned orders that may not be least cost?
9. Why do informal production and inventory control systems develop?
10. Why is configuration control important in MRP systems?
11. Why could cycle counting be used in place of periodic counts if an effective MRP system is in place? What must be done to make cycle counting effective?
12. What functions are typically performed by MRP planners in companies using MRP systems?

13. What types of uncertainty can occur in production and purchasing processes? What methods are available to deal with uncertainty? Are some methods better for some types of uncertainty than others?
14. What problems can occur when using safety stock, safety lead time, or scrap allowances?
15. When is a modular BOM useful? Why is a final assembly schedule required when a modular BOM is used?
16. What advantages would an MRP II system have over a traditional MRP system?

## ▶ Problems

1. The Cool Breeze Co. produces an electric fan (model 42124). The fan is constructed by attaching an electric cord with integral switch (#4122) to an electric motor (#4123) and mounting it in a plastic base unit (#8407) to produce a motorized base (#1208). After testing the motorized base, employees attach fan blades (#1424) and a protective grill (#5509), using five screws (#123) to produce the finished fan.

   Develop a product structure diagram for this problem.
2. Develop an indented bill of material for the fan in problem 1.
3. The Luggit Luggage Co. builds its model 25 briefcase using the following components:

| Part # | Name | Quantity |
|---|---|---|
| 4234 | ABS plastic shell | 2 |
| 1313 | Cloth shell liner | 2 |
| 4275 | Edge trim | 2 |
| 3414 | Hinge | 2 |
| 5917 | Latch | 1 |
| 8471 | Handle | 1 |
| 9243 | Rivets | 88 |

   The cloth liner is attached to the plastic shells, using the edge trim and 30 rivets to produce a finished briefcase half (#3282). Two briefcase halves are attached using 2 hinges and 16 rivets. The latch and handle are then attached using 8 and 4 rivets, respectively.

   Construct a product structure diagram for the briefcase.
4. Develop an indented bill of material for the briefcase in problem 3.

5. Blaster, Inc., builds a high output stereo speaker, Model 888. Construction of the speaker uses the following components:

| Part # | Name | Quantity |
|---|---|---|
| 112 | Side panel | 2 |
| 243 | Top/bottom panel | 2 |
| 324 | Front panel | 1 |
| 485 | Back panel | 1 |
| 521 | Speaker—15″ woofer | 1 |
| 531 | Speaker—4″ midrange | 1 |
| 541 | Speaker—1″ tweeter | 1 |
| 637 | Crossover network | 1 |
| 652 | Connector w/cable | 1 |
| 725 | Fastener—staple | 52 |
| 734 | Fastener—screw | 14 |
| 755 | Grill fasteners | 4 |
| 761 | Adhesive—tube | 3 |
| 847 | Front grill | 1 |

   The speaker is constructed by first building the speaker box (# 1132), which uses 2 side panels, 2 top-bottom panels, a back panel, a connector with cable, 34 staples, and 2 tubes of adhesive. Fourteen screws attach the speakers and crossover network to the front panel to produce the speaker panel assembly (#2143). Eighteen staples and a tube of adhesive join the speaker box and speaker panel assembly, and attaching the grill requires the 4 grill fasteners to produce the finished speaker unit.

   Construct a product structure diagram for the finished speaker.
6. Using the information in problem 5, construct an indented bill of material.

7. Use a lot size of 60 to complete this MRP record:

| Part No: 4122 | | | | | | | | | | | | |
|---|---|---|---|---|---|---|---|---|---|---|---|---|
| Part Name:<br>Cord w/Switch | | | | | | | | | | | | |
| LS: 60 | LT: 3 | 1 | 2 | 3 | 4 | 5 | 6 | 7 | 8 | 9 | 10 |
| Gross Requirements | | 40 | 35 | 5 | 15 | 25 | 20 | 30 | 15 | 10 | 5 |
| Scheduled Receipts | | 60 | | 60 | | | | | | | |
| Planned Order Receipts | | | | | | | | | | | |
| Available Balance | 15 | | | | | | | | | | |
| Planned Order Releases | | | | | | | | | | | |

8. Use LFL lot sizing to complete this MRP record:

| Part No: 4122 | | | | | | | | | | | | |
|---|---|---|---|---|---|---|---|---|---|---|---|---|
| Part Name:<br>Cord w/Switch | | | | | | | | | | | | |
| LS: LFL | LT: 3 | 1 | 2 | 3 | 4 | 5 | 6 | 7 | 8 | 9 | 10 |
| Gross Requirements | | 40 | 35 | 5 | 15 | 25 | 20 | 30 | 15 | 10 | 5 |
| Scheduled Receipts | | 40 | 35 | 20 | | | | | | | |
| Planned Order Receipts | | | | | | | | | | | |
| Available Balance | 15 | | | | | | | | | | |
| Planned Order Releases | | | | | | | | | | | |

9. Given the MPS that follows, fill in the MRP records for problem 1. The finished fan (#42124) is assembled in one period, using LFL lot sizing.

| | | | | | | **Period** | | | | | |
|---|---|---|---|---|---|---|---|---|---|---|---|
| *Item #* | *1* | *2* | *3* | *4* | *5* | *6* | *7* | *8* | *9* | *10* | |
| 42124 | 100 | 120 | 130 | 140 | 150 | 150 | 150 | 150 | 160 | 160 | |

| Part No: 1208 | | | 1 | 2 | 3 | 4 | 5 | 6 | 7 | 8 | 9 | 10 |
|---|---|---|---|---|---|---|---|---|---|---|---|---|
| **Part Name:** Motorized Base | | | | | | | | | | | | |
| LS: 200 | LT: 2 | | | | | | | | | | | |
| Gross Requirements | | | | | | | | | | | | |
| Scheduled Receipts | | | 200 | | | | | | | | | |
| Planned Order Receipts | | | | | | | | | | | | |
| Available Balance | | 50 | | | | | | | | | | |
| Planned Order Releases | | | | | | | | | | | | |

| Part No: 4123 | | | 1 | 2 | 3 | 4 | 5 | 6 | 7 | 8 | 9 | 10 |
|---|---|---|---|---|---|---|---|---|---|---|---|---|
| **Part Name:** Electric Motor | | | | | | | | | | | | |
| LS: 300 | LT: 3 | | | | | | | | | | | |
| Gross Requirements | | | | | | | | | | | | |
| Sceduled Receipts | | | 300 | | | | | | | | | |
| Planned Order Receipts | | | | | | | | | | | | |
| Available Balance | | 100 | | | | | | | | | | |
| Planned Order Releases | | | | | | | | | | | | |

10. Given the MPS that follows, fill in the MRP records for problem 3. The finished briefcase (#25) is assembled in one period, using LFL lot sizing.

| | | | | | **Period** | | | | | |
|---|---|---|---|---|---|---|---|---|---|---|
| Item # | 1 | 2 | 3 | 4 | 5 | 6 | 7 | 8 | 9 | 10 |
| 25 | 40 | 40 | 40 | 40 | 50 | 50 | 50 | 40 | 40 | 40 |

| Part No: 3282 | | | 1 | 2 | 3 | 4 | 5 | 6 | 7 | 8 | 9 | 10 |
|---|---|---|---|---|---|---|---|---|---|---|---|---|
| **Part Name:** Briefcase Half | | | | | | | | | | | | |
| LS: 150 | LT: 1 | | | | | | | | | | | |
| Gross Requirements | | | | | | | | | | | | |
| Scheduled Receipts | | | 150 | | | | | | | | | |
| Planned Order Receipts | | | | | | | | | | | | |
| Available Balance | | 20 | | | | | | | | | | |
| Planned Order Releases | | | | | | | | | | | | |

| Part No: 9243 | | 1 | 2 | 3 | 4 | 5 | 6 | 7 | 8 | 9 | 10 |
|---|---|---|---|---|---|---|---|---|---|---|---|
| Part Name: Rivet | | | | | | | | | | | |
| LS: 5,000 | LT: 2 | | | | | | | | | | |
| Gross Requirements | | | | | | | | | | | |
| Scheduled Receipts | | 5,000 | | | | | | | | | |
| Planned Order Receipts | | | | | | | | | | | |
| Available Balance | 2,000 | | | | | | | | | | |
| Planned Order Releases | | | | | | | | | | | |

11. Given the BOM and MPS that follow, fill in the MRP records for components C and F. Assume LFL lot sizing and a lead time of one period for end items A and D.

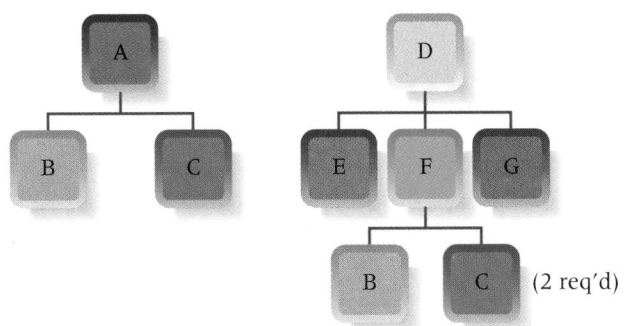

|  |  | | | | | Period | | | | | |
|---|---|---|---|---|---|---|---|---|---|---|---|
| Item # | 1 | 2 | 3 | 4 | 5 | 6 | 7 | 8 | 9 | 10 |
| A | 30 | 20 | 10 | 0 | 0 | 20 | 30 | 20 | 20 | 20 |
| D | 10 | 20 | 20 | 30 | 30 | 30 | 30 | 20 | 20 | 20 |

| Part No: F | | 1 | 2 | 3 | 4 | 5 | 6 | 7 | 8 | 9 | 10 |
|---|---|---|---|---|---|---|---|---|---|---|---|
| LS: 50 | LT: 2 | | | | | | | | | | |
| Gross Requirements | | | | | | | | | | | |
| Scheduled Receipts | | | | | | | | | | | |
| Planned Order Receipts | | | | | | | | | | | |
| Available Balance | 30 | | | | | | | | | | |
| Planned Order Releases | | | | | | | | | | | |

| Part No: C | | | | | | | | | | | | |
|---|---|---|---|---|---|---|---|---|---|---|---|---|
| LS: 150 | LT: 2 | | 1 | 2 | 3 | 4 | 5 | 6 | 7 | 8 | 9 | 10 |
| Gross Requirements | | | | | | | | | | | | |
| Scheduled Receipts | | | 150 | | | | | | | | | |
| Planned Order Receipts | | | | | | | | | | | | |
| Available Balance | | 20 | | | | | | | | | | |
| Planned Order Releases | | | | | | | | | | | | |

12. Given the following information, fill in the MRP record using EOQ lot sizing:

Parts per year: 50
Part #: 4123
Ordering cost: $25
Holding cost: $12.50 per unit per year

| Part No: 4123 | | | | | | | | | | | | |
|---|---|---|---|---|---|---|---|---|---|---|---|---|
| Part Name: Electric Motor | | | | | | | | | | | | |
| LS: EOQ | LT: 2 | | 1 | 2 | 3 | 4 | 5 | 6 | 7 | 8 | 9 | 10 |
| Gross Requirements | | | 10 | 30 | 20 | 50 | 60 | 100 | 80 | 40 | 60 | 50 |
| Scheduled Receipts | | | | | | | | | | | | |
| Planned Order Receipts | | | | | | | | | | | | |
| Available Balance | | 40 | | | | | | | | | | |
| Planned Order Releases | | | | | | | | | | | | |

Calculate the ordering and holding cost, ignoring the initial available balance.

13. Repeat problem 12, using POQ lot sizing.

14. Complete MRP records for components A, B, and C, given the following information:

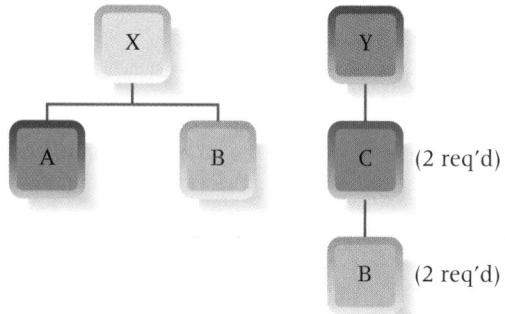

MPS

| | | | | | **Period** | | | | | |
|---|---|---|---|---|---|---|---|---|---|---|
| *Item* | *1* | *2* | *3* | *4* | *5* | *6* | *7* | *8* | *9* | *10* |
| X | 10 | 10 | 20 | 10 | 10 | 20 | 20 | 10 | 15 | 15 |
| Y | 15 | 25 | 20 | 20 | 30 | 20 | 20 | 15 | 25 | 15 |

Inventory Data

| *Item* | *LS* | *LT* | *Initial Inventory* | *Scheduled Receipts* |
|---|---|---|---|---|
| X | LFL | 1 | 0 | – |
| Y | LFL | 1 | 0 | – |
| A | 40 | 2 | 30 | – |
| B | 300 | 2 | 200 | 300 in period 1 |
| C | 100 | 3 | 50 | 100 in period 2 |

| Part Name: A | | 1 | 2 | 3 | 4 | 5 | 6 | 7 | 8 | 9 | 10 |
|---|---|---|---|---|---|---|---|---|---|---|---|
| LS: | LT: | | | | | | | | | | |
| Gross Requirements | | | | | | | | | | | |
| Scheduled Receipts | | | | | | | | | | | |
| Planned Order Receipts | | | | | | | | | | | |
| Available Balance | | | | | | | | | | | |
| Planned Order Releases | | | | | | | | | | | |

| Part Name: B | | 1 | 2 | 3 | 4 | 5 | 6 | 7 | 8 | 9 | 10 |
|---|---|---|---|---|---|---|---|---|---|---|---|
| LS: | LT: | | | | | | | | | | |
| Gross Requirements | | | | | | | | | | | |
| Scheduled Receipts | | | | | | | | | | | |
| Planned Order Receipts | | | | | | | | | | | |
| Available Balance | | | | | | | | | | | |
| Planned Order Releases | | | | | | | | | | | |

| Part Name: C | | 1 | 2 | 3 | 4 | 5 | 6 | 7 | 8 | 9 | 10 |
|---|---|---|---|---|---|---|---|---|---|---|---|
| LS: | LT: | | | | | | | | | | |
| Gross Requirements | | | | | | | | | | | |
| Scheduled Receipts | | | | | | | | | | | |
| Planned Order Receipts | | | | | | | | | | | |
| Available Balance | | | | | | | | | | | |
| Planned Order Releases | | | | | | | | | | | |

15. Complete MRP records for components A, B, and C, given the following information:

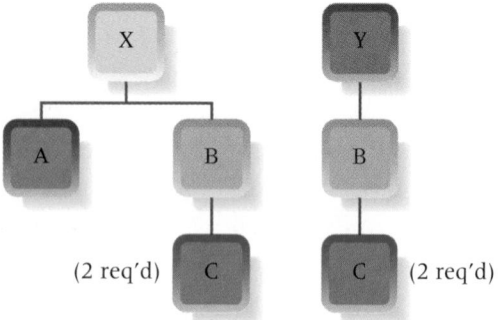

MPS

| | | | | | **Period** | | | | | |
|---|---|---|---|---|---|---|---|---|---|---|
| Item | 1 | 2 | 3 | 4 | 5 | 6 | 7 | 8 | 9 | 10 |
| X | 10 | 10 | 10 | 10 | 10 | 30 | 20 | 15 | 15 | 15 |
| Y | 20 | 20 | 10 | 10 | 10 | 0 | 0 | 15 | 15 | 15 |

Inventory Data

| Item | LS | LT | Initial Inventory | Scheduled Receipts |
|---|---|---|---|---|
| X | LFL | 1 | 0 | – |
| Y | LFL | 1 | 0 | – |
| A | 50 | 2 | 30 | – |
| B | 50 | 2 | 40 | 50 in period 2 |
| C | 150 | 2 | 50 | 150 in period 2 |

| Part Name: A | | 1 | 2 | 3 | 4 | 5 | 6 | 7 | 8 | 9 | 10 |
|---|---|---|---|---|---|---|---|---|---|---|---|
| LS: | LT: | | | | | | | | | | |
| Gross Requirements | | | | | | | | | | | |
| Scheduled Receipts | | | | | | | | | | | |
| Planned Order Receipts | | | | | | | | | | | |
| Available Balance | | | | | | | | | | | |
| Planned Order Releases | | | | | | | | | | | |

| Part Name: B | | 1 | 2 | 3 | 4 | 5 | 6 | 7 | 8 | 9 | 10 |
|---|---|---|---|---|---|---|---|---|---|---|---|
| LS: | LT: | | | | | | | | | | |
| Gross Requirements | | | | | | | | | | | |
| Scheduled Receipts | | | | | | | | | | | |
| Planned Order Receipts | | | | | | | | | | | |
| Available Balance | | | | | | | | | | | |
| Planned Order Releases | | | | | | | | | | | |

| Part Name: C | | 1 | 2 | 3 | 4 | 5 | 6 | 7 | 8 | 9 | 10 |
|---|---|---|---|---|---|---|---|---|---|---|---|
| LS: | LT: | | | | | | | | | | |
| Gross Requirements | | | | | | | | | | | |
| Scheduled Receipts | | | | | | | | | | | |
| Planned Order Receipts | | | | | | | | | | | |
| Available Balance | | | | | | | | | | | |
| Planned Order Releases | | | | | | | | | | | |

16. Calculate the new MRP record, given the following activities in period 1:
   a. The gross requirement in period 1 was changed from 15 to 10 (a customer canceled an order).
   b. The gross requirement in period 11 will be 20 units.
   c. A cycle inventory count revealed that the actual on-hand quantity at the beginning of the week was 30, not 25.
   d. Marketing has asked for a change in the MPS, moving the 25-unit gross requirement for period 5 to period 4.
   e. Based on the canceled order and the revised inventory count, the company released an order for 40 units (rather than 80).

Original MRP Record

| Part No: 4123 | | | | | | | | | | | | |
|---|---|---|---|---|---|---|---|---|---|---|---|---|
| Part Name: Electric Motor | | | | | | | | | | | | |
| LS: 40 | LT: 2 | | 1 | 2 | 3 | 4 | 5 | 6 | 7 | 8 | 9 | 10 |
| Gross Requirements | | | 15 | 20 | 35 | 25 | 25 | 25 | 20 | 30 | 30 | 25 |
| Scheduled Receipts | | | | | | | | | | | | |
| Planned Order Receipts | | | | | | | | | | | | |
| Available Balance | | 25 | 10 | -10 | 35 | 10 | 25 | 0 | 20 | 30 | 0 | 15 |
| Planned Order Releases | | | 80 | | 40 | | 40 | 40 | | 40 | | |

New MRP Record

| Part No: 4123 | | | | | | | | | | | | |
|---|---|---|---|---|---|---|---|---|---|---|---|---|
| Part Name: Electric Motor | | | | | | | | | | | | |
| LS: 40 | LT: 2 | | 2 | 3 | 4 | 5 | 6 | 7 | 8 | 9 | 10 | 11 |
| Gross Requirements | | | | | | | | | | | | |
| Scheduled Receipts | | | | | | | | | | | | |
| Planned Order Receipts | | | | | | | | | | | | |
| Available Balance | | | | | | | | | | | | |
| Planned Order Releases | | | | | | | | | | | | |

# ▶ Selected References

Cooper, Randolph B., and Robert W. Zmud, "Information Technology Implementation Research: A Technological Diffusion Approach," *Management Science* 36 (February 1990): 123–139.

Fogarty, D. W., and T. R. Hoffman. *Production and Inventory Management*. Cincinnati: South-Western Publishing, 1983.

Orlicky, Joseph. *Material Requirements Planning*. New York: McGraw-Hill, 1975.

Steele, Daniel C. "The Nervous MRP System: How to Do Battle," *Production and Inventory Journal* 16, No. 4 (Fourth Quarter, 1975): 83–89.

Vollman, T. E., W. L. Berry, and D. C. Whybark. *Manufacturing Planning and Control Systems*, 3d ed. Homewood, Ill.: Irwin, 1992.

Wallace, Thomas F. *MRP II: Making It Happen*. Essex Junction, Vt: Oliver Wight Limited Publications, 1985.

Wemmerlöv, Urban. "The Behavior of Lot-Sizing Procedures in the Presence of Forecast Errors." *Journal of Operations Management* 8 (January 1989): 37–47.

Wight, O. W. *The Executives Guide to Successful MRP II*, 2d ed. Essex Junction, Vt.: Oliver Wight Limited Publications, 1983.

## CHAPTER 14

# Medium- and Short-range Capacity Planning

*The executive exists to make sensible exceptions to general rules.*

ELTING E. MORISON

Introduction

Capacity Planning and the Production Planning and Scheduling Framework
*OPERATIONS MANAGEMENT IN PRACTICE 14.1: Capacity Planning Makes the Shop Floor Manageable at Minnesota Wire & Cable Co.*

A Capacity Planning Example

Rough-cut Capacity Planning Methods

Detailed Capacity Planning
*OPERATIONS MANAGEMENT IN PRACTICE 14.2: Capacity Planning in a Make-to-Order Environment at Borsig Valve Co.*

Capacity Planning and Service Operations

# Introduction

Chapter 13 showed how to use material requirements planning (MRP) in a dependent demand inventory environment. Using MRP, the MRP planner can determine when to release component shop orders or purchase orders to meet the requirements of the master production schedule (MPS). MRP also allows the MRP planner to determine whether due dates for open orders should be modified. The logic used by MRP assumes that lead times for component parts are constant and sufficient production capacity (labor capacity, machine capacity ) exists to execute the MPS. In practice, lead times are not constant and capacity is not unlimited. Capacity planning provides a way for management to develop a feasible MPS. Without capacity planning MRP is just an order-launching system—it cannot be used to effectively manage the company.

We use capacity-planning techniques to evaluate the feasibility of an MPS, given the (finite) capacity of a company. Shop-floor information on component lead times and processing times provide critical inputs to the capacity-planning process. Capacity-planning techniques estimate the capacity required at each work center in a production facility for each time period of the planning horizon for executing the MPS. The planner then can compare the *capacity required* with the *capacity available* to determine whether the MPS is feasible. As discussed in Chapter 13, capacity planning is a vital component of closed-loop MRP.

## The Need for Capacity Planning

Imagine a manufacturing facility that does not perform some kind of capacity planning. The MRP system will generate shop orders without regard to the capacity constraints of the production facility. Some work centers will invariably become overloaded. Production supervisors will have too many orders to process, and some orders will not be completed on time. Depending on the demand pattern and lot-sizing methods used, different work centers may become congested at different times, resulting in "roving bottlenecks."

The result is reduced confidence in the MRP system. MRP planners will soon find that the shop floor cannot deliver components consistently within the planned lead times. Their response will be to increase planned lead times so that a higher percentage of jobs is completed on time. Although increasing lead times will result in the completion of a higher percentage of orders on time, it will further reduce the visibility of low-level components, and because it will cause shop orders to be placed earlier, more work-in-process (WIP) inventory will be created.

Production supervisors will also respond to the capacity problems. When the work load is high, an informal system will develop among supervisors to determine which jobs are the hot jobs. They will use this informal system, instead of the MRP system, to determine which jobs are really due. Production supervisors will realize that MRP planners are increasing planned lead times and releasing shop orders early. As a result, due dates generated by the MRP system will decrease in importance as the informal system increasingly controls materials planning.

To avoid this scenario managers must check the materials plans generated by an MRP system against available capacity to ensure that they can be completed. If the available capacity is not sufficient for executing the materials plan, managers must take corrective action. They could use overtime or subcontracting to obtain additional capacity and/or modify the MPS.

## Strategic Implications of Capacity Planning

Although the capacity planning techniques we discuss in this chapter are tactical tools (they are used in the day-to-day and week-to-week operation of the company), the company's ability to effectively plan capacity can contribute to its competitive positioning. Capacity planning can do this in two ways: by reducing costs and by improving schedule performance. If a company can manage its capacity better, it can achieve the same level of production with less investment in facilities and labor. Better capacity planning leads to lower levels of WIP inventory, which means reduced costs from lower capital investment and smaller losses from damage and obsolescence. Costs also fall because a facility that manages its capacity well has less need for more expensive production methods such as overtime and subcontracting.

Good capacity management also improves schedule performance. In a make-to-stock environment this means that the company can achieve a higher customer service level with the same investment in finished goods inventory. In the make-to-order environment good capacity planning increases a company's ability to meet due dates, which means it provides better customer service. Although the rest of this chapter is concerned mainly with the mechanics and tactical implications of medium- to short-range capacity planning, we should remember that effective capacity management provides strategic benefits with respect to cost and customer service.

## Capacity Planning and the Production Planning and Scheduling Framework

Figure 14.1 shows the production planning and scheduling framework we introduced in Chapter 13. Note that it shows two overall approaches to capacity planning: rough-cut capacity planning and detailed capacity planning. **Rough-cut capacity planning** methods use simplifying assumptions for approximating capacity requirements based on the MPS. This chapter describes three rough-cut capacity planning techniques:

FIGURE 14.1
Production Planning and
Scheduling Framework

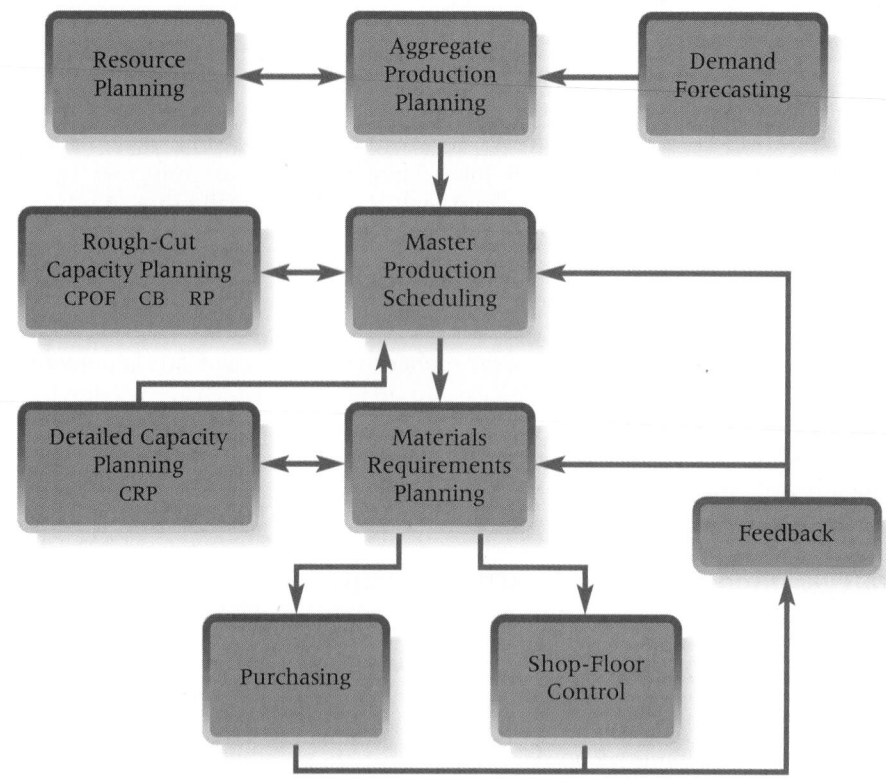

- ■ **Capacity planning using overall factors (CPOF).** Capacity planning using overall factors uses standard capacity factors obtained from production-related accounting records to estimate capacity requirements.
- ■ **Capacity planning using capacity bills (CB).** Capacity planning using capacity bills uses the bill of material (BOM) file and routing and standard time data to more accurately determine capacity requirements.
- ■ **Capacity planning using resource profiles (RP).** Capacity planning using resource profiles considers component lead time information in addition to the BOM and routing and standard time data to provide time-phased capacity estimates.

Figure 14.1 shows rough-cut capacity planning methods are used iteratively to determine a feasible MPS (see double-headed arrows). Managers evaluate an initial MPS by using a rough-cut capacity technique. If the MPS requires more capacity than is available, the company either increases capacity (by using overtime, scheduling a second shift, renting additional equipment, subcontracting, and so on) or by changing the MPS. If it changes the MPS, it then evaluates the revised MPS using the same capacity planning method. This iterative process continues until the capacity required to execute the MPS is roughly equivalent to the capacity available.

The fourth capacity planning technique depicted in Figure 14.1 is **capacity requirements planning (CRP),** a detailed capacity planning method that uses the material plans generated by MRP to estimate the time-phased capacity requirements of a proposed MPS. Because CRP considers the current inventory status and lot sizing of component parts as well as work in process, it is more accurate than any of the rough-cut capacity planning methods. Although CRP is

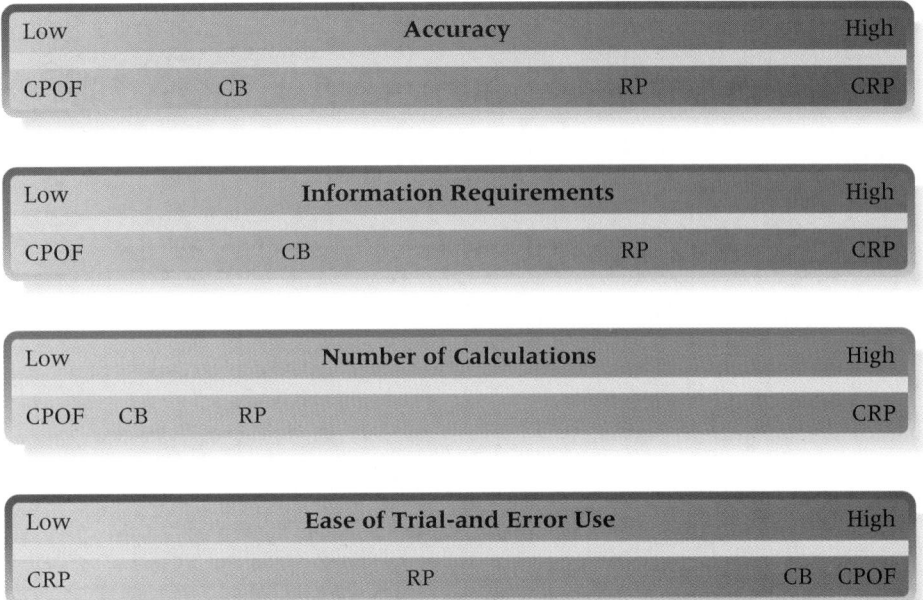

more accurate, it requires more information and a significantly greater number of calculations to estimate capacity requirements.

The four capacity planning techniques we introduce in this chapter have advantages and disadvantages. They differ in accuracy, information requirements, number of calculations, and ease of use in an iterative process. Choosing a capacity planning technique involves a compromise among these factors. Figure 14.2 provides a graphic comparison of the four capacity planning techniques.

## Capacity Planning as a Trial-and-Error Process

It can be difficult to develop an MPS that is feasible with respect to capacity yet meets customer demand. Within an MRP environment this is necessarily a trial-and-error process, because the MRP explosion process does not consider capacity requirements. This process can become especially complicated using CRP. Although CRP is the most accurate capacity planning method, it is often the most difficult to use. First, CRP requires the calculation of all MRP records on each iteration, a process that can take thirty minutes or more, depending on the computer system and software package used and the manufacturing environment (number of products, number of levels in the BOM). Second, lot sizing can magnify the effect of changes. A change that appears to reduce the need for capacity at a work center in a given period may in fact increase it, or it may cause a capacity problem at another work center in a different period.

It may appear that capacity planning in MRP systems is somewhat less than ideal. Unfortunately, this impression is correct. Although many researchers have studied production scheduling in the dependent demand environment in the past thirty years and have developed a number of analytical models to solve this problem, these models typically suffer from a number of limitations. First, they are invariably complicated and difficult to solve. Second, they rely on simplifying assumptions, such as having no component part commonality, restricting lot sizes to integer multiples of the parent component lot size, having only one capacity-

**OPERATIONS MANAGEMENT IN PRACTICE 14.1** ◀

# Capacity Planning Makes the Shop Floor Manageable at Minnesota Wire & Cable Co.

Minnesota Wire & Cable Co. of Saint Paul produces wire products for the medical industry. The company purchases copper wire, extrudes plastic insulation around the wire, cuts it to length and injection-molds connectors on the ends. Until 1990 the company scheduled production with a software package developed in house. The result, according to Jack Rose, computer operations manager, was the "typical chaotic manufacturing environment. Workers didn't know what jobs were coming until they arrived at their work center." In 1990 the company purchased an operations planning and control system that included modules for MPS, MRP, CRP, shop-floor control, and job costing.

The company's new system uses the MPS and MRP modules weekly to generate planned order quantities and due dates. The shop-floor control module combines job routing and standard time data with planned order information to schedule orders backward in the shop. The CRP module is then used to generate work center load reports and also to specify when shop orders will need processing in each work center. The CRP module uses the load profiles to flag capacity problems. Jobs are then rescheduled so that capacity requirements are in line with capacity availability. The result is a smoother production schedule—the capacity required in each work center in each period is fairly constant.

According to Rose, "The MRP system has done a good job in helping us get orders out on time. Capacity planning with the CRP module has allowed us to generate smoother production schedules, and it has given shop-floor personnel the ability to see what orders are coming so they can plan accordingly."

*Capacity planning at Minnesota Wire & Cable Co. provides shop-floor personnel with forward visibility concerning upcoming orders so they can plan accordingly.*

constrained work center, and so on. Finally, because these models are complicated, they are not easily understood by production-scheduling personnel.

Although no optimal approach to scheduling production has been developed, a company must somehow develop schedules for manufacturing products and components. Although MRP in conjunction with capacity planning may not be a perfect system, it is nevertheless a workable system that has proved effective in many production environments. Operations Management in Practice 14.1 discusses the use of capacity planning at Minnesota Wire & Cable Co.

## A Capacity Planning Example

In this chapter we use the MRP example we introduced in Chapter 13 to illustrate all four capacity planning techniques. See Tables 13.1 through 13.3 for the information contained in the indented BOMs, inventory records, and the MPS, respectively. Note that the wheels (part 5562) and the fasteners (part 2571) are not considered in these capacity planning examples because they are purchased components.

Capacity represents any limited resource required in the production of goods or services. Typical resources are labor and machine capacity, but other resources such as tooling and fixtures can also represent capacity that must be managed. In the examples that follow labor is assumed to be the critical resource.

Typically, a manufacturing facility is divided into departments, which are subdivided into work centers. Here we assume that deluxe and economy office chairs are produced in a manufacturing facility that has the departments and work centers shown in Table 14.1. Now we will use the example to illustrate each of the four capacity-planning methods we introduced earlier.

## Rough-cut Capacity Planning Methods
### Capacity Planning Using Overall Factors (CPOF)

CPOF is the simplest rough-cut capacity planning technique. Calculating work center capacity requirements from an MPS requires two pieces of information:

- Total hours of capacity required to produce one unit of an end item (labor time per unit, machine time per unit, and so on)
- Historical work center usage percentages—planning factors

| Department | Work Center | Work Center Number |
|---|---|---|
| Assembly | Chair & frame assembly | 100 |
| | Adjuster assembly | 110 |
| Paint | Metal paint | 200 |
| Upholstery | Fabric cut | 320 |
| | Cushion assembly | 350 |
| Steel fabrication | Cutting | 510 |
| | Bending | 530 |
| | Welding | 560 |
| Quality control | Inspection | 910 |

The first piece of information is standard time data. Frequently, this type of information simply represents average time requirements based on past production-related accounting data. In some cases the company's industrial engineers may have used such methods as time and motion studies to develop this information. Suppose we had the following accounting data for production in the previous month:

| | |
|---|---|
| Economy chair production: | 400 units |
| Deluxe chair production: | 340 units |
| Labor used in economy chair production: | 318 hours |
| Labor used in deluxe chair production: | 292 hours |

For economy chair production the number of labor hours required per chair is

$$\left(\frac{318 \text{ Hours}}{400 \text{ Chairs}}\right) = 0.7950 \text{ Hours per Chair}$$

The same calculation for deluxe office chairs results in 0.8588 hours per chair. We now have the first piece of information we need—standard time data.

To determine the second piece of information, the historical work center usage percentages or planning factors, we need an additional piece of data: the labor charges broken down by work center. Suppose the labor charged in work center 100 last month was 116.5 hours. Note that the total labor used in production is 318 hours + 292 hours = 610 hours. Thus, the historical work center usage percentage for workcenter 100 is

$$\left(\frac{116.5 \text{ Hours in work center } 100}{610 \text{ Total hours}}\right) = 19.10\% \text{ (Usage percentage in work center 100)}$$

Table 14.2 provides the standard time data and planning factors for all the work centers.

For CPOF, estimating the labor capacity required at each work center is a two-step process. First, we calculate the total load on the manufacturing facility

**TABLE 14.2**
Standard Time Data and Planning Factors for CPOF

| Standard Labor Hours for Finished Products | |
|---|---|
| *Item #* | *Standard Labor Hours* |
| 1174 | 0.7950 |
| 1184 | 0.8588 |

| Historical Work Center Percentages | |
|---|---|
| *Work Center* | *Percentage* |
| 100 | 19.10 |
| 110 | 13.30 |
| 200 | 15.94 |
| 320 | 1.40 |
| 350 | 3.92 |
| 510 | 6.32 |
| 530 | 11.64 |
| 560 | 12.74 |
| 910 | 15.64 |
| | 100.00 |

| MPS | Period | | | | | | | | | |
|---|---|---|---|---|---|---|---|---|---|---|
| | 1 | 2 | 3 | 4 | 5 | 6 | 7 | 8 | 9 | 10 |
| #1174 | 10 | 10 | 15 | 30 | 30 | 15 | 15 | 15 | 15 | 15 |
| #1184 | 20 | 20 | 15 | 0 | 0 | 15 | 15 | 15 | 15 | 15 |

Step 1: Total Labor Calculation

| | Period | | | | | | | | | |
|---|---|---|---|---|---|---|---|---|---|---|
| | 1 | 2 | 3 | 4 | 5 | 6 | 7 | 8 | 9 | 10 |
| #1174 | 7.950 | 7.950 | 11.925 | 23.850 | 23.850 | 11.925 | 11.925 | 11.925 | 11.925 | 11.925 |
| #1184 | 17.176 | 17.176 | 12.882 | 0.000 | 0.000 | 12.882 | 12.882 | 12.882 | 12.882 | 12.882 |
| Total | 25.126 | 25.126 | 24.807 | 23.850 | 23.850 | 24.807 | 24.807 | 24.807 | 24.807 | 24.807 |

Step 2: Allocation of Total Labor to Work Centers

| Work Center | Period | | | | | | | | | |
|---|---|---|---|---|---|---|---|---|---|---|
| | 1 | 2 | 3 | 4 | 5 | 6 | 7 | 8 | 9 | 10 |
| 100 | 4.799 | 4.799 | 4.738 | 4.555 | 4.555 | 4.738 | 4.738 | 4.738 | 4.738 | 4.738 |
| 110 | 3.342 | 3.342 | 3.299 | 3.172 | 3.172 | 3.299 | 3.299 | 3.299 | 3.299 | 3.299 |
| 200 | 4.005 | 4.005 | 3.954 | 3.802 | 3.802 | 3.954 | 3.954 | 3.954 | 3.954 | 3.954 |
| 320 | 0.352 | 0.352 | 0.347 | 0.334 | 0.334 | 0.347 | 0.347 | 0.347 | 0.347 | 0.347 |
| 350 | 0.985 | 0.985 | 0.972 | 0.935 | 0.935 | 0.972 | 0.972 | 0.972 | 0.972 | 0.972 |
| 510 | 1.588 | 1.588 | 1.568 | 1.507 | 1.507 | 1.568 | 1.568 | 1.568 | 1.568 | 1.568 |
| 530 | 2.925 | 2.925 | 2.888 | 2.776 | 2.776 | 2.888 | 2.888 | 2.888 | 2.888 | 2.888 |
| 560 | 3.201 | 3.201 | 3.160 | 3.038 | 3.038 | 3.160 | 3.160 | 3.160 | 3.160 | 3.160 |
| 910 | 3.930 | 3.930 | 3.880 | 3.730 | 3.730 | 3.880 | 3.880 | 3.880 | 3.880 | 3.880 |
| Total | 25.126 | 25.126 | 24.807 | 23.850 | 23.850 | 24.807 | 24.807 | 24.807 | 24.807 | 24.807 |

T A B L E   1 4 . 3
Capacity Planning Using
Overall Factors

by using the MPS and the standard labor hour data. We then allocate the total labor requirement to individual work centers by using the historical work center percentages. Table 14.3 shows this two-step calculation for the sample MPS. For example, the total labor requirement in the first period is the sum of the capacity required to produce ten economy office chairs and twenty deluxe office chairs. This calculation is shown in equation 14-1.

$$\begin{pmatrix}\text{Units of}\\ \text{\#1174}\end{pmatrix} \times \begin{pmatrix}\text{Labor hours per}\\ \text{unit of \#1174}\end{pmatrix} + \begin{pmatrix}\text{Units of}\\ \text{\#1184}\end{pmatrix} \times \begin{pmatrix}\text{Labor hours per}\\ \text{unit of \#1184}\end{pmatrix}$$
$$= (10) \times (0.7950) + (20) \times (0.8588)$$
$$= 7.950 + 17.176 = 25.126 \qquad (14\text{-}1)$$

We repeat this calculation for each period in the planning horizon.

Next, we use the historic work center percentages or factors to convert the total labor capacity estimates into work center estimates. For example, for period 1 we calculate the labor requirements for work center 100 as shown in equation 14-2:

$$\begin{pmatrix}\text{Total labor hours}\\ \text{per period}\end{pmatrix} \times \begin{pmatrix}\text{Fraction of total hours}\\ \text{at work center 100}\end{pmatrix}$$
$$= (25.126) \times (0.1910) = 4.799 \qquad (14\text{-}2)$$

The calculations for the CPOF method are simple and require minimal data. Furthermore, the simplicity of the method makes it easy to use in an iterative fashion to achieve a feasible MPS. If the capacity requirement for a work center is too high in a given period, we either adjust the MPS for the period or make additional capacity available in the period. With CPOF it is quite straightforward to determine how to change the MPS to ensure the capacity required in a given period is in alignment with the capacity available.

The benefits of the CPOF method come at the expense of accuracy. The historical work center percentages are accurate only to the extent that the current product mix is identical to the product mix used to generate the planning factors. Also, the CPOF method ignores the time phasing of component requirements, the lot-sizing methods used for component items, and the current status of finished and work-in-process inventories.

Note that the capacity requirements presented in Table 14.3 are rather low—less than five hours per week at any work center. This is because we kept the problem size small to simplify our presentation. Actual furniture manufac-

**TABLE 14.4**
Routing and Standard Time Data

| Item # | Item Name | Lot Size | Operation | Work Center | Work Center Number | Standard Set-up (Labor Hours) | Standard Set-up (Labor hours per unit) | Standard Run Time (Labor hours per unit) | Total Standard Time (Labor hours per unit) |
|--------|-----------|----------|-----------|-------------|--------------------|-------------------------------|----------------------------------------|------------------------------------------|--------------------------------------------|
| 1174 | Economy office chair | LFL(20)* | 1 of 1 | Chair & frame assembly | 100 | 0.12 | 0.006 | 0.084 | 0.090 |
| 1184 | Deluxe office chair | LFL(10)* | 1 of 1 | Chair & frame assembly | 100 | 0.12 | 0.012 | 0.084 | 0.096 |
| 2838 | Nylon back cushion | 50 | 1 of 2 | Fabric cut | 320 | 0.08 | 0.0016 | 0.002 | 0.0036 |
|  |  |  | 2 of 2 | Cushion assembly | 350 | 0.10 | 0.002 | 0.014 | 0.016 |
| 2839 | Nylon seat cushion | 50 | 1 of 2 | Fabric cut | 320 | 0.08 | 0.0016 | 0.002 | 0.0036 |
|  |  |  | 2 of 2 | Cushion assembly | 350 | 0.10 | 0.002 | 0.014 | 0.016 |
| 2938 | Leather back cushion | LFL(10)* | 1 of 2 | Fabric cut | 320 | 0.07 | 0.007 | 0.003 | 0.010 |
|  |  |  | 2 of 2 | Cushion assembly | 350 | 0.02 | 0.002 | 0.014 | 0.016 |
| 2939 | Leather seat cushion | LFL(10)* | 1 of 2 | Fabric cut | 320 | 0.07 | 0.007 | 0.003 | 0.010 |
|  |  |  | 2 of 2 | Cushion assembly | 350 | 0.02 | 0.002 | 0.014 | 0.016 |
| 3807 | Economy chair frame | 50 | 1 of 2 | Chair & frame assembly | 100 | 0.09 | 0.0018 | 0.062 | 0.0638 |
|  |  |  | 2 of 2 | Inspection | 910 | 0.05 | 0.001 | 0.120 | 0.121 |
| 3817 | Deluxe chair frame | 50 | 1 of 2 | Chair & frame assembly | 100 | 0.09 | 0.0018 | 0.062 | 0.0638 |
|  |  |  | 2 of 2 | Inspection | 910 | 0.05 | 0.001 | 0.140 | 0.141 |
| 8507 | Base unit | 50 | 1 of 4 | Cutting | 510 | 0.80 | 0.016 | 0.034 | 0.050 |
|  |  |  | 2 of 4 | Bending | 530 | 0.65 | 0.013 | 0.082 | 0.095 |
|  |  |  | 3 of 4 | Welding | 560 | 0.20 | 0.004 | 0.100 | 0.104 |
|  |  |  | 4 of 4 | Paint | 200 | 0.45 | 0.009 | 0.065 | 0.074 |
| 9805 | 1-way adjuster mechanism | 75 | 1 of 2 | Adj. assembly | 110 | 0.15 | 0.002 | 0.100 | 0.102 |
|  |  |  | 2 of 2 | Paint | 200 | 0.45 | 0.006 | 0.050 | 0.056 |
| 9825 | 2-way adjuster mechanism | 75 | 1 of 2 | Adj. assembly | 110 | 0.15 | 0.002 | 0.120 | 0.122 |
|  |  |  | 2 of 2 | Paint | 200 | 0.45 | 0.006 | 0.055 | 0.061 |

*Because lot sizing is LFL, the average batch size is used for the lot size.

turers may produce thousands of units per week of a wide range of furniture products, which would result in capacity requirements measured in thousands of hours per week.

## Capacity Planning Using Capacity Bills (CB)

Capacity planning using capacity bills (CB) requires more information than CPOF and consequently generates more precise capacity estimates. The CB method uses BOM information (Table 13.1) and routing and standard time data (Table 14.4) in addition to the MPS (Table 13.3). The *routing and standard time data* in Table 14.4 show, for each component part or end item, the lot size used for processing, the work center(s) that must process the part or end item, the order in which the processing must be performed, the standard labor time required to set up the production equipment and the per unit set-up time, the labor time required to process one unit of the part or end-item, and the total labor hours required per unit (per unit set-up plus per unit run time).

The CB approach, like CPOF, cannot determine the number of set-ups required to execute the MPS, because it does not consider the timing of the actual production lots. Thus, this method approximates the capacity required for set-ups. The CB approach calculates a standard set-up time per *unit* by dividing the standard set-up time by the actual lot size (if available) or an estimated lot size (average lot size). As Table 14.4 shows, we computed the standard set-up time per unit for end-item 1174 in work center 100 by dividing the standard set-up time of 0.12 labor hours by the average lot size of twenty units to get an average of 0.006 set-up labor hours per chair. We then added the standard set-up time per unit to the standard run time per unit to obtain the total labor hours per unit. We then used the total labor hours per unit to estimate the capacity required for both set-up and run time. Note that for items that use LFL sizing, we use the average lot size for calculation purposes.

We can rearrange the data in Table 14.4 by work center for each end item by using BOM information (Table 13.1), as shown in Table 14.5. This is a preliminary step in the specification of a **capacity bill** for each end item. Note that Table 14.5 presents the total labor time per unit data in a format that simplifies the calculation of the capacity required at each work center for one unit of an *end item*. We use the data in Table 14.5 to determine the capacity bills for the economy and deluxe office chairs (see Table 14.6). Note that in this example the end items require only one unit of each component. If more than one component is required to manufacture an end item this would be factored into the specification of the capacity bill. For example, if the manufacture of a single end item required three units of a given component, we would multiply the total labor hours per (component) unit (last column, Table 14.4) by three to get the total labor hours per end item in a given work center (columns 3 and 6, Table 14.5).

Table 14.6 shows how to calculate the capacity required for the MPS by using the capacity bills. For example, equation 14-3 shows how to calculate the capacity required at work center 100 in period $i$, where $E_i$ represents the number of economy chairs (#1174) and $D_i$ represents the number of deluxe chairs (#1184) in the MPS for a given period $i$. If $i = 1$, we have the following:

| Economy Office Chair (#1174) | | | Deluxe Office Chair (#1184) | | |
|---|---|---|---|---|---|
| Work Center Number | Item Number | Total Hours per End Item | Work Center Number | Item Number | Total Hours per End Item |
| 100 | 1174 | 0.0900 | 100 | 1184 | 0.0960 |
| | 3807 | 0.0638 | | 3817 | 0.0638 |
| | | 0.1538 | | | 0.1598 |
| 110 | 9805 | 0.1020 | 110 | 9825 | 0.1220 |
| 200 | 8507 | 0.0740 | 200 | 8507 | 0.0740 |
| | 9805 | 0.0560 | | 9825 | 0.0610 |
| | | 0.1300 | | | 0.1350 |
| 320 | 2838 | 0.0036 | 320 | 2938 | 0.0100 |
| | 2839 | 0.0036 | | 2939 | 0.0100 |
| | | 0.0072 | | | 0.0200 |
| 350 | 2838 | 0.0160 | 350 | 2938 | 0.0160 |
| | 2839 | 0.0160 | | 2939 | 0.0160 |
| | | 0.0320 | | | 0.0320 |
| 510 | 8507 | 0.0500 | 510 | 8507 | 0.0500 |
| 530 | 8507 | 0.0950 | 530 | 8507 | 0.0950 |
| 560 | 8507 | 0.1040 | 560 | 8507 | 0.1040 |
| 910 | 3807 | 0.1210 | 910 | 3817 | 0.1410 |
| | | Total Hours: 0.7950 | | | Total Hours: 0.8588 |

TABLE 14.5
Calculation of Capacity Bills

$$\left(\begin{array}{c}\text{Hours at work center 100}\\\text{per unit of \#1174}\end{array}\right) \times (E_i)$$
$$+ \left(\begin{array}{c}\text{Hours at work center 100}\\\text{per unit of \#1184}\end{array}\right) \times (D_i) \qquad (14\text{-}3)$$
$$= (0.1538) \times (10) + (0.1598) \times (20) = 4.734$$

As Figure 14.2 shows, the CB approach is almost as simple as CPOF with respect to the number of calculations and ease of use, but developing and maintaining accurate capacity bills requires significantly greater effort than maintaining the accounting data required for CPOF. However, the advantage of the CB approach is that it has the same accuracy no matter how the product mix changes.

The total capacity requirement calculated by the CB approach is the same as that calculated by the CPOF approach (compare bottom row, Table 14.6, with bottom row, Table 14.3), because the total work required per item is the same under both methods. The difference between the two methods lies in the labor requirements estimated for *each* work center in the various periods of the planning horizon. Compare, for example, the projected load for work center 320 in period 4 using the CB approach (0.216 labor hours, see Table 14.6) with the projected load using the CPOF approach (0.334 labor hours, see Table 14.3).

Both CPOF and CB are ideally suited for spreadsheet execution. Also, because of their ease of use, it is even common for companies that do not use MRP to use these methods to generate feasible schedules.

| Capacity Bill for Part #1174 | | Capacity Bill for Part #1184 | |
|---|---|---|---|
| Work Center | Hours per Item | Work Center | Hours per Item |
| 100 | 0.1538 | 100 | 0.1598 |
| 110 | 0.1020 | 110 | 0.1220 |
| 200 | 0.1300 | 200 | 0.1350 |
| 320 | 0.0072 | 320 | 0.0200 |
| 350 | 0.0320 | 350 | 0.0320 |
| 510 | 0.0500 | 510 | 0.0500 |
| 530 | 0.0950 | 530 | 0.0950 |
| 560 | 0.1040 | 560 | 0.1040 |
| 910 | 0.1210 | 910 | 0.1410 |
| | Total Hours: 0.7950 | | Total Hours: 0.8588 |

| MPS | Period | | | | | | | | | |
|---|---|---|---|---|---|---|---|---|---|---|
| | 1 | 2 | 3 | 4 | 5 | 6 | 7 | 8 | 9 | 10 |
| #1174 | 10 | 10 | 15 | 30 | 30 | 15 | 15 | 15 | 15 | 15 |
| #1184 | 20 | 20 | 15 | 0 | 0 | 15 | 15 | 15 | 15 | 15 |

| Work Center | Period | | | | | | | | | |
|---|---|---|---|---|---|---|---|---|---|---|
| | 1 | 2 | 3 | 4 | 5 | 6 | 7 | 8 | 9 | 10 |
| 100 | 4.734 | 4.734 | 4.704 | 4.614 | 4.614 | 4.704 | 4.704 | 4.704 | 4.704 | 4.704 |
| 110 | 3.460 | 3.460 | 3.360 | 3.060 | 3.060 | 3.360 | 3.360 | 3.360 | 3.360 | 3.360 |
| 200 | 4.000 | 4.000 | 3.975 | 3.900 | 3.900 | 3.975 | 3.975 | 3.975 | 3.975 | 3.975 |
| 320 | 0.472 | 0.472 | 0.408 | 0.216 | 0.216 | 0.408 | 0.408 | 0.408 | 0.408 | 0.408 |
| 350 | 0.960 | 0.960 | 0.960 | 0.960 | 0.960 | 0.960 | 0.960 | 0.960 | 0.960 | 0.960 |
| 510 | 1.500 | 1.500 | 1.500 | 1.500 | 1.500 | 1.500 | 1.500 | 1.500 | 1.500 | 1.500 |
| 530 | 2.850 | 2.850 | 2.850 | 2.850 | 2.850 | 2.850 | 2.850 | 2.850 | 2.850 | 2.850 |
| 560 | 3.120 | 3.120 | 3.120 | 3.120 | 3.120 | 3.120 | 3.120 | 3.120 | 3.120 | 3.120 |
| 910 | 4.030 | 4.030 | 3.930 | 3.630 | 3.630 | 3.930 | 3.930 | 3.930 | 3.930 | 3.930 |
| Total | 25.126 | 25.126 | 24.807 | 23.850 | 23.850 | 24.807 | 24.807 | 24.807 | 24.807 | 24.807 |

TABLE 14.6
Capacity Requirements Using Capacity Bills

Although the CB approach is more accurate than CPOF, it does not incorporate lead time information for time-phasing purposes, actual lot sizes, and the current status of finished goods and WIP inventories. The last rough-cut capacity-planning technique, resource profiles, takes time-phasing into account.

## Capacity Planning Using Resource Profiles (RP)

The resource profiles (RP) method extends the CB approach by considering lead time information. Suppose the lead time data in Table 14.7 were available. This information is more detailed than the lead time information presented in Chapter 13. MRP calculations require lead times for components for determining release dates for an order. RP capacity planning requires lead times for each component *operation* to estimate work center loads. Note that the lead time for a component in a given work center is the sum of the set-up, processing, and queue (waiting) time that the component order experiences. In a production facility that is

| Item # | Item Name | Operation | Work Center | Work Center Number | Operation Lead Time (Periods) |
|---|---|---|---|---|---|
| 1174 | Economy office chair | 1 of 1 | Chair & frame assembly | 100 | 1 |
| 1184 | Deluxe office chair | 1 of 1 | Chair & frame assembly | 100 | 1 |
| 2838 | Nylon back cushion | 1 of 2 | Fabric cut | 320 | 1 |
| | | 2 of 2 | Cushion assembly | 350 | 1 |
| 2839 | Nylon seat cushion | 1 of 2 | Fabric cut | 320 | 1 |
| | | 2 of 2 | Cushion assembly | 350 | 1 |
| 2938 | Leather back cushion | 1 of 2 | Fabric cut | 320 | ½* |
| | | 2 of 2 | Cushion assembly | 350 | ½* |
| 2939 | Leather seat cushion | 1 of 2 | Fabric cut | 320 | ½* |
| | | 2 of 2 | Cushion assembly | 350 | ½* |
| 3807 | Economy chair frame | 1 of 2 | Chair & frame assembly | 100 | 2 |
| | | 2 of 2 | Inspection | 910 | 1 |
| 3817 | Deluxe chair frame | 1 of 2 | Chair & frame assembly | 100 | 2 |
| | | 2 of 2 | Inspection | 910 | 1 |
| 8507 | Base unit | 1 of 4 | Cutting | 510 | 1 |
| | | 2 of 4 | Bending | 530 | 1 |
| | | 3 of 4 | Welding | 560 | 1 |
| | | 4 of 4 | Paint | 200 | 1 |
| 9805 | One-way adjuster mechanism | 1 of 2 | Adjuster assembly | 110 | 2 |
| | | 2 of 2 | Paint | 200 | 1 |
| 9825 | Two-way adjuster mechanism | 1 of 2 | Adjuster assembly | 110 | 2 |
| | | 2 of 2 | Paint | 200 | 1 |

*For the leather cushions the lead time for both operations *combined* is one week; that is, an order for leather cushions completes both operations in a single time period.

TABLE 14.7
Lead Times for Individual Work Centers

operating near capacity (80 percent or higher), the majority of the lead time is usually queue time, not processing time.

We combine these operation lead times with BOM data to produce the **operation setback chart,** shown in Figure 14.3. This chart is a more detailed version of the operation setback chart introduced in Figure 13.8 and clearly shows the importance of time phasing in developing accurate capacity estimates. Recall that under the capacity bills approach we estimate the labor hours for work center 100 in period $i$ for economy chair production, $CE_i^{100}$,

$$CE_i^{100} = \left(\frac{\text{hours at work center 100}}{\text{per unit of \#1174}}\right) \times E_i \qquad (14\text{-}4)$$
$$= 0.1538E_i$$

where $E_i$ is the MPS quantity for economy chairs in period $i$ (see equation 14-3). Under the CB approach we assume the capacity requirement occurs in the *same period* as the MPS quantity. However, Figure 14.3 shows that the MPS quantity for economy chairs in period 8 will require capacity in work center 100 not only in period 8 for *chair* assembly but in periods 5 and 6 as well for *frame* assembly. Under the RP approach, which considers time phasing, we determine the labor requirement in work center 100 (WC100) in period $i$ arising from MPS requirements for economy chairs as:

$$CE_i^{100} = 0.090E_i + (0.0638/2)E_{i+2} + (0.0638/2)E_{i+3} \qquad (14\text{-}5)$$
$$= 0.090E_i + 0.0319E_{i+2} + 0.0319E_{i+3}$$

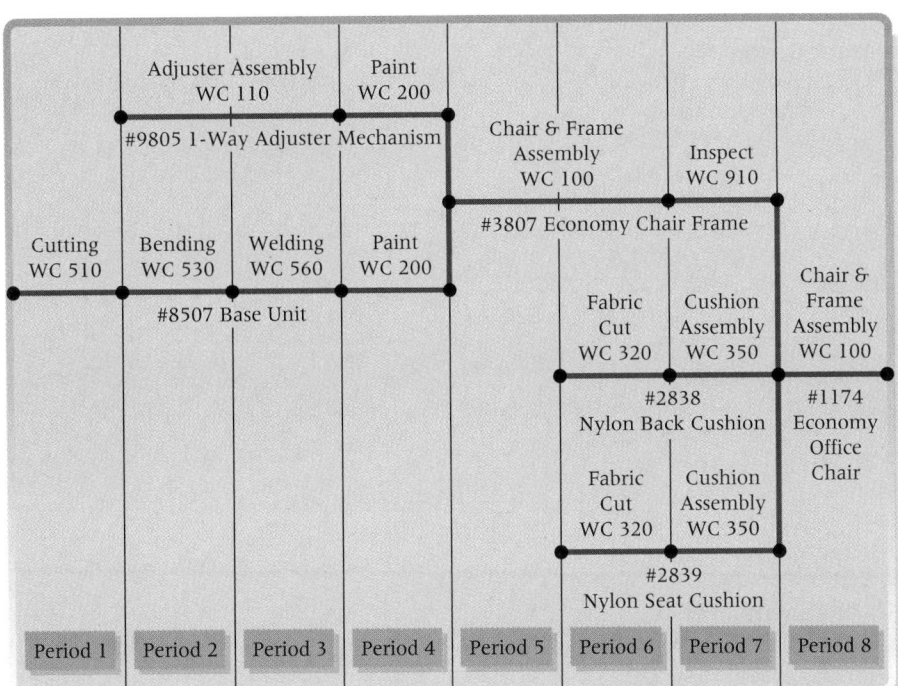

FIGURE 14.3
Operation Setback Chart for
Economy Office Chair

Economy chair production requires 0.090 hours per unit in WC100 for final assembly of the chair and 0.0638 hours per unit in WC100 for assembly of the frame (see Tables 14.4 and 14.5). Final assembly of the economy chair in period $i$ is associated with the MPS quantity in period $i$, whereas the assembly of the frame in period $i$ is associated with MPS quantities occurring two and three periods later, respectively. (see Figure 14.3). Although the lead time for frame assembly is two periods, assembly of the frame is unlikely to occur in both periods of the lead time. (Remember that lead time estimates include set-up, run, and queue times, and they are set conservatively to ensure a high probability of on-time order completion.) Because we are not sure in which period frame assembly will actually occur, we estimate capacity requirements by dividing the processing time equally over the two periods of lead time (0.0638 hours/2). Note that the per unit operation time for the adjuster mechanism assembly in work center 110 must also be divided between two periods because *operation* lead time here is also greater than one period.

With the RP method we can develop an equation for each work center that includes all products. Table 14.8 gives the equations for all work centers in this example for both economy chair and deluxe chair production. With these equations we can easily estimate the capacity requirements for the sample MPS. Table 14.9 shows the results of this process. The obvious difference between these estimates and those of CPOF and CB is the shortened planning horizons for many of the work centers. This is most clearly demonstrated at work center 510, where the capacity requirements for periods 4 through 10 are zero, which are dramatically different from the estimates generated by CPOF and CB. The shortened planning horizons are a result of the loss of low-level visibility we discussed in Chapter 13. The shortened planning horizons of the RP estimates are

TABLE 14.8
Resource Profile Equations
for Example

**Work Center 100**

$$C_i^{100} = 0.090E_i + (0.0638/2)E_{i+2} + (0.0638/2)E_{i+3} + 0.096D_i + (0.0638/2)D_{i+2}$$
$$+ (0.0638/2)D_{i+3}$$
$$= 0.090E_i + 0.0319E_{i+2} + 0.0319E_{i+3} + 0.096D_i + 0.0319D_{i+2}$$
$$+ 0.0319D_{i+3}$$

**Work Center 110**

$$C_i^{110} = (0.102/2)E_{i+5} + (0.102/2)E_{i+6} + (0.122/2)D_{i+5} + (0.122/2)D_{i+6}$$
$$= 0.051E_{i+5} + 0.051E_{i+6} + 0.061D_{i+5} + 0.061D_{i+6}$$

**Work Center 200**

$$C_i^{200} = 0.056E_{i+4} + 0.074E_{i+4} + 0.061D_{i+4} + 0.074D_{i+4}$$
$$= 0.130E_{i+4} + 0.135D_{i+4}$$

**Work Center 320**

$$C_i^{320} = 0.0036E_{i+2} + 0.0036E_{i+2} + 0.010D_{i+1} + 0.010D_{i+1}$$
$$= 0.0072E_{i+2} + 0.020D_{i+1}$$

**Work Center 350**

$$C_i^{350} = 0.016E_{i+1} + 0.016E_{i+1} + 0.016D_{i+1} + 0.016D_{i+1}$$
$$= 0.032E_{i+1} + 0.032D_{i+1}$$

**Work Center 510**

$$C_i^{510} = 0.050E_{i+7} + 0.050D_{i+7}$$

**Work Center 530**

$$C_i^{530} = 0.095E_{i+6} + 0.095D_{i+6}$$

**Work Center 560**

$$C_i^{560} = 0.104E_{i+5} + 0.104D_{i+5}$$

**Work Center 910**

$$C_i^{910} = 0.121E_{i+1} + 0.141D_{i+1}$$

TABLE 14.9
Capacity Requirements Using
Resource Profiles

| MPS | Period | | | | | | | | | |
|---|---|---|---|---|---|---|---|---|---|---|
| | 1 | 2 | 3 | 4 | 5 | 6 | 7 | 8 | 9 | 10 |
| #1174 | 10 | 10 | 15 | 30 | 30 | 15 | 15 | 15 | 15 | 15 |
| #1184 | 20 | 20 | 15 | 0 | 0 | 15 | 15 | 15 | 15 | 15 |

| Work Center | Period | | | | | | | | | |
|---|---|---|---|---|---|---|---|---|---|---|
| | 1 | 2 | 3 | 4 | 5 | 6 | 7 | 8 | 9 | 10 |
| 100 | 4.734 | 4.734 | 4.704 | 4.614 | 4.614 | 4.704 | 4.704 | 3.747 | 2.79 | 2.79 |
| 110 | 3.360 | 3.360 | 3.360 | 3.360 | 1.680 | 0.0 | 0.0 | 0.0 | 0.0 | 0.0 |
| 200 | 3.900 | 3.975 | 3.975 | 3.975 | 3.975 | 3.975 | 0.0 | 0.0 | 0.0 | 0.0 |
| 320 | 0.508 | 0.516 | 0.216 | 0.108 | 0.408 | 0.408 | 0.408 | 0.408 | 0.300 | 0.0 |
| 350 | 0.960 | 0.960 | 0.960 | 0.960 | 0.960 | 0.960 | 0.960 | 0.960 | 0.960 | 0.0 |
| 510 | 1.500 | 1.500 | 1.500 | 0.0 | 0.0 | 0.0 | 0.0 | 0.0 | 0.0 | 0.0 |
| 530 | 2.850 | 2.850 | 2.850 | 2.850 | 0.0 | 0.0 | 0.0 | 0.0 | 0.0 | 0.0 |
| 560 | 3.120 | 3.120 | 3.120 | 3.120 | 3.120 | 0.0 | 0.0 | 0.0 | 0.0 | 0.0 |
| 910 | 4.030 | 3.930 | 3.630 | 3.630 | 3.930 | 3.930 | 3.930 | 3.930 | 3.930 | 0.0 |
| Total | 24.962 | 24.945 | 24.315 | 22.617 | 18.687 | 13.977 | 10.002 | 9.045 | 7.980 | 2.790 |

not the result of a weakness in the method; they stem from the inclusion of time phasing in the capacity estimation process.

## Comparison of Rough-cut Methods Results

Figure 14.4 compares the capacity requirement estimates of the three rough-cut capacity techniques. The total facility work load for the CPOF and CB methods is identical, but the RP method shows a substantial difference because of the time phasing of capacity requirements and the associated loss of visibility. Because the MPS is fairly stable (always thirty chairs per period, with similar total capacity requirements for the economy and deluxe chairs), the three methods give similar results for the first three periods. Comparing the capacity estimates for work center 320 (fabric cut) shows how the methods differ. The CPOF method predicts a fairly stable capacity requirement for the ten periods. The CB approach shows that the change in the MPS to all economy chairs in periods 4 and 5 will reduce the capacity requirements for work center 320. The RP approach shows that the reduced capacity requirements associated with producing only economy chairs in periods 4 and 5 will actually occur in periods 3 and 4 because of time phasing and that time phasing will lead to an extremely low capacity requirement in period 4. The extremely low capacity requirement in work center 320 in period 4 derives from the MPS quantity for economy chairs in period 6 (which is only 15 chairs) and the MPS quantity for deluxe chairs in period 5, which is zero (see equation for work center 320 in Table 14.8).

Although RP is the most accurate rough-cut planning technique, it does not consider the current status of finished goods and WIP inventories and lot sizing. In contrast, capacity requirements planning (CRP), a **detailed capacity planning** method, considers the current status of all finished and WIP inventories in calculating capacity requirement estimates. CRP uses scheduled receipts and planned order receipts from the MRP system to estimate capacity based on actual and anticipated component orders. These scheduled receipts and planned order receipts reflect the actual lot sizes that are being used or will be used in production.

FIGURE 14.4
Comparison of CPOF, CB, and RP

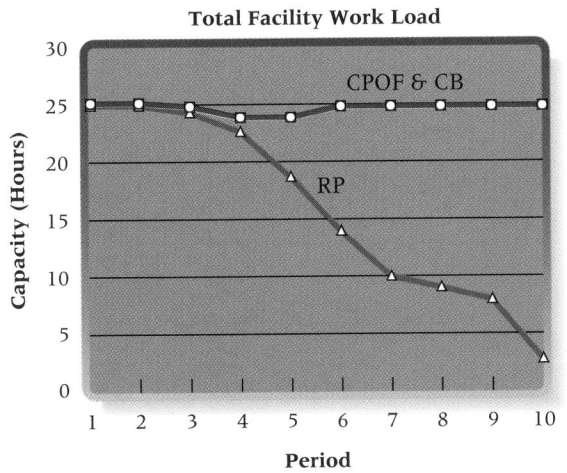

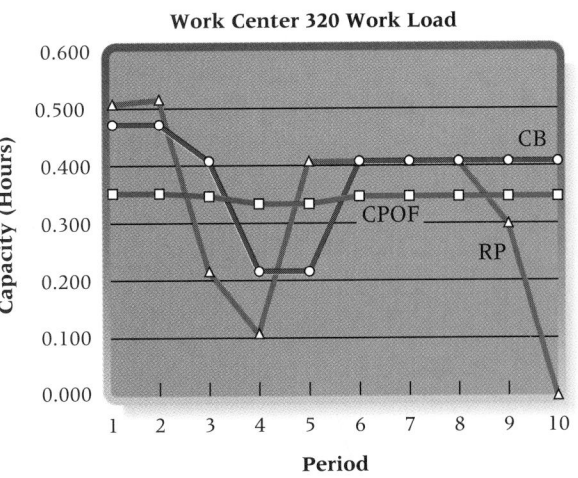

# Detailed Capacity Planning
## Capacity Requirements Planning (CRP)

The CRP method applies routing and standard time data to scheduled receipts and planned order receipts (for component parts) and MPS quantities (for end items) to generate time-phased capacity requirements. CRP requires additional information (the current status of inventory and work in process and the actual lot sizes and release dates from MRP) and significantly more calculations than rough-cut methods but provides capacity estimates that are much more accurate.

Figure 14.5 shows CRP using the operation setback chart. This chart shows that if there is an MPS quantity for chairs (economy or deluxe) in period $i$, work center 100 requires capacity in period $i$. The capacity is required in the same period as the MPS quantity, because the operation lead time for the final assembly of chairs (see Table 14.7) chairs is one period and the MRP timing convention for end items requires that they be completed by the *end* of the

**FIGURE 14.5**
Component Operation Setback Chart

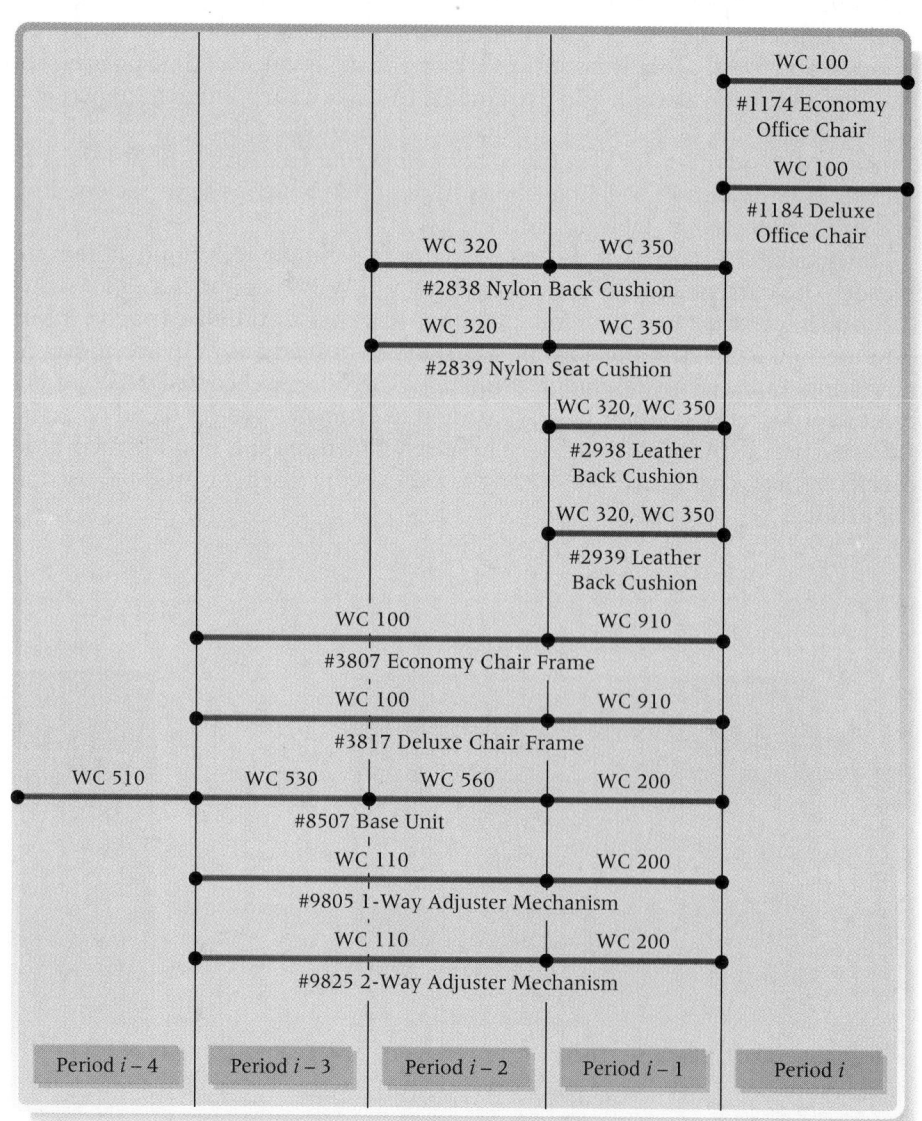

period in which the MPS quantity occurs. In contrast, if there is a planned order receipt for nylon back cushions (#2838) in period *i*, work center 350 requires capacity in period $i - 1$ and work center 320 needs capacity in period $i - 2$. Recall that MRP timing conventions require planned and scheduled receipts to be available at the *beginning* of the time period in which they appear.

We calculate capacity requirements by using the operation setback chart in Figure 14.5, the routing and standard time data in Table 14.4, the operation lead time data from Table 14.7, and MRP system output. The gross-to-net explosion process, described in Chapter 13 produces the component order data, which are shown in Table 14.10 for the sample problem. Table 14.11 shows the CRP calculations for work center 100. Work center 100 requires capacity for the final assembly of economy and deluxe office chairs (#1174 and #1184) and to

TABLE 14.10
MPS and Component
Order Data

| | | | | | Period | | | | | |
|---|---|---|---|---|---|---|---|---|---|---|
| Item # | 1 | 2 | 3 | 4 | 5 | 6 | 7 | 8 | 9 | 10 |
| 1174 | **10** | **10** | **15** | **30** | **30** | **15** | **15** | **15** | **15** | **15** |
| 1184 | **20** | **20** | **15** | **0** | **0** | **15** | **15** | **15** | **15** | **15** |
| 2838 | 50 | | | 50 | | | 50 | | | 50 |
| 2839 | | | 50 | | 50 | | 50 | | | |
| 2938 | 15 | 15 | 15 | | | 15 | 15 | 15 | 15 | 15 |
| 2939 | 15 | 15 | 15 | | | 15 | 15 | 15 | 15 | 15 |
| 3807 | | | | 50 | | 50 | | | 50 | |
| 3817 | | | 50 | | | | | | 50 | |
| 8507 | 50 | | 50 | | | 100 | | | | |
| 9805 | 75 | | | | | 75 | | | | |
| 9825 | | | | | | 75 | | | | |

**KEY**

Scheduled MPS quantity—**Bold**
Scheduled receipt—<u>Underline</u>
Planned receipt—Normal text font

TABLE 14.11
Work Center 100 Capacity
Requirements

| | | | | | | Period | | | | | |
|---|---|---|---|---|---|---|---|---|---|---|---|
| Item # | | 1 | 2 | 3 | 4 | 5 | 6 | 7 | 8 | 9 | 10 |
| 1174 | Set-up | 0.12 | 0.12 | 0.12 | 0.12 | 0.12 | 0.12 | 0.12 | 0.12 | 0.12 | 0.12 |
| | Run | 0.84 | 0.84 | 1.26 | 2.52 | 2.52 | 1.26 | 1.26 | 1.26 | 1.26 | 1.26 |
| 1184 | Set-up | 0.12 | 0.12 | 0.12 | | | 0.12 | 0.12 | 0.12 | 0.12 | 0.12 |
| | Run | 1.68 | 1.68 | 1.26 | | | 1.26 | 1.26 | 1.26 | 1.26 | 1.26 |
| 3807 | Set-up | 0.045 | 0.045 | 0.045 | 0.045 | | 0.045 | 0.045 | | | |
| | Run | 1.55 | 1.55 | 1.55 | 1.55 | | 1.55 | 1.55 | | | |
| 3817 | Set-up | 0.045 | | | | | 0.045 | 0.045 | | | |
| | Run | 1.55 | | | | | 1.55 | 1.55 | | | |
| | Total: | 5.95 | 4.355 | 4.355 | 4.235 | 2.64 | 5.95 | 5.95 | 2.76 | 2.76 | 2.76 |

assemble the economy and deluxe chair frames (#3807 and #3817). Note that because the office chairs are end items with one period lead times for final assembly, work center 100 requires capacity in the same period as the scheduled MPS quantities. Thus, both types of chairs require a set-up in period 1. The set-up time for final assembly of either type of chair is 0.12 hours (see Table 14.4). The run time for economy chairs is the MPS quantity multiplied by the run time per item, or

$$\left(\begin{array}{c}\text{Number}\\\text{of \#1174}\end{array}\right) \times \left(\begin{array}{c}\text{Hours}\\\text{per unit}\end{array}\right)$$
$$(10) \times (0.084) = 0.84 \tag{14-6}$$

Table 14.11 (see item # 1174) shows the set-up time of 0.12 hours and the run time of 0.84 hours for assembly of 10 economy chairs in period 1. The calculation of run time for deluxe chairs is similar. The set-up time and run time for deluxe chairs in period 1 also appear in Table 14.11 (see item #1184).

With respect to chair frame assembly (parts #3807 and #3817), recall that the lead time for this particular assembly operation is two periods (see Table 14.7). As for the RP approach, we divide the set-up and processing times evenly between the two periods of lead time.

Note that for part #3807, Table 14.10 shows a planned order receipt of fifty units in period 4, which means the completed order is due at the beginning of period 4. The operation setback chart in Figure 14.5 shows that a planned receipt for part 3807 in period $i$ requires capacity in work center 100 in periods $i - 2$ and $i - 3$. So the planned receipt of fifty units in period 4 will require capacity at work center 100 in periods 1 and 2. Note that the set-up time for #3807 shown in Table 14.4 is 0.09 hours. To obtain the set-up time required in period 1, we must divide this time by two to allocate the set-up time equally between periods 1 and 2. The result is 0.045 hours, as shown in Table 14.11. We calculate the run time required for the fifty units of #3807 as

$$\left(\begin{array}{c}\text{Number}\\\text{of \#3807}\end{array}\right) \times \left(\begin{array}{c}\text{Hours}\\\text{per part}\end{array}\right)$$
$$(50) \times (0.062) = 3.1 \tag{14-7}$$

As with set-up time, we divide the run time by two to allocate it equally between periods 1 and 2 (3.1/2 = 1.55).

**TABLE 14.12**
Capacity Requirements Using CRP

| Work Center | 1 | 2 | 3 | 4 | 5 | 6 | 7 | 8 | 9 | 10 |
|---|---|---|---|---|---|---|---|---|---|---|
| 100 | 5.95 | 4.355 | 4.355 | 4.235 | 2.64 | 5.95 | 5.95 | 2.76 | 2.76 | 2.76 |
| 110 | | | 8.40 | 8.40 | | | | | | |
| 200 | | 3.7 | | | 15.725 | | | | | |
| 320 | 0.41 | 0.41 | 0.18 | | 0.59 | 0.23 | 0.23 | 0.41 | 0.23 | |
| 350 | 0.46 | 1.26 | 0.80 | 0.80 | 0.46 | 2.06 | 0.46 | 0.46 | 1.26 | |
| 510 | | 4.2 | | | | | | | | |
| 530 | | | 8.85 | | | | | | | |
| 560 | 5.20 | | | 10.20 | | | | | | |
| 910 | | 7.05 | 6.05 | | 6.05 | | | 13.10 | | |
| Total: | 12.02 | 20.975 | 28.635 | 23.635 | 25.465 | 8.24 | 6.64 | 16.73 | 4.25 | 2.76 |

Part 3817 has a scheduled receipt in period 3. This scheduled receipt represents an open shop order. Ideally, information about the current status of this order should be available for the capacity estimation process. In this example we assumed that no information is available about the status of this scheduled receipt, so we treated it as a planned order. Thus, we assume (using Figure 14.5) that the scheduled receipt for fifty units in period 3 has gone through one week of its lead time in work center 100 and will require capacity in period 1 in work center 100 to complete the frame assembly operation. The set-up and assembly run times in work center 100 for part 3817 in period 1 are calculated similarly to part 3807's. This results in an estimated set-up time of 0.045 hours and an estimated run time of 1.55 hours, as depicted in Table 14.11.

Table 14.12 shows the CRP capacity estimates for all work centers for the example. Note that the lumpiness phenomenon (discussed in Chapter 13) is present. Again, this is not a weakness of the method but a more accurate representation of the expected work load on the shop floor. Figure 14.6 illustrates the lumpiness of the capacity requirements. This figure shows capacity requirements will be lumpier than indicated by the rough-cut capacity estimates, both in the total facility and in individual work centers (see work center 320).

## Using CRP

Because the CRP method estimates capacity from planned and scheduled orders for components rather than directly from the MPS, its estimates reflect the lumpiness that results from MRP lot-sizing. With rough-cut capacity planning the only way to correct capacity problems is to add capacity or change the MPS. With CRP we are dealing with actual and planned shop orders, so another method of adjusting capacity is available—the firm planned order (FPO). For example, work center 910 is used to inspect chair frames. The relatively large capacity requirement of 13.10 hours in period 8 (see Table 14.12) is needed to support the planned order receipts of fifty economy frames (#3807) and fifty deluxe frames (#3817) in period 9 (see Table 14.10). The planned order releases for these parts are scheduled in period 6 because the lead time for the chair frames is 3 periods. Releasing one of these orders early would shift some of the capacity require-

FIGURE 14.6
Comparison of CRP and Rough-cut Methods

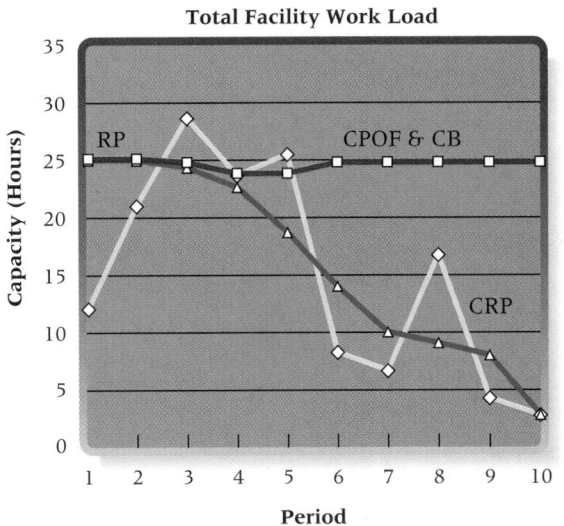
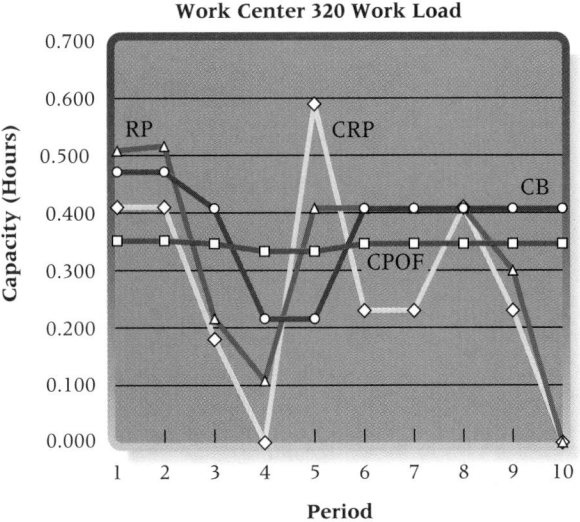

ments at work center 910 to an earlier period, when the capacity requirement is zero. For example, an FPO for fifty units of #3807 could be scheduled in period 5, which would spread the current capacity requirement in period 8 over periods 7 and 8. In this example the FPO smoothes requirements at work center 910. However, smoothing requirements at one work center may increase the lumpiness at another. Unexpected results are more likely to occur if the FPO is used on a component at a higher level in the BOM or if more complicated lot-sizing methods are used.

Using CRP to adjust capacity utilization can be difficult, because the effect of changing the MPS or using FPOs can be difficult to anticipate. To use CRP the MRP planner typically evaluates the capacity requirements of the proposed schedule and attempts to adjust the work load using FPOs or modifications to the MPS. Then the planner must repeat the MRP calculations with the proposed FPOs and MPS changes and reevaluate the capacity needs of the new plan using CRP. Any remaining (or new) capacity problems are corrected using additional FPOs or MPS modifications or perhaps by deleting previous FPOs. Then the planner reruns both MRP and CRP and evaluates the new schedule again. This can be a time-consuming and onerous process. If capacity cannot be adjusted with FPOs or MPS changes, the company must make additional capacity available. Operations Management in Practice 14.2 discusses the use of CRP and FPOs at Borsig Valve Co.

## Capacity Planning and Service Operations

Although this chapter covers capacity planning in relation to manufacturing operations, capacity planning is central to the efficient operation of service operations as well. Service operations have unique features that make the capacity problem different and harder to solve in practice. The service industry literature identifies five unique characteristics:

*Managers of service operations have fewer ways of dealing with capacity problems than managers of manufacturing because services cannot be stored in inventory.*

# Capacity Planning in a Make-to-Order Environment at Borsig Valve Co.

Borsig Valve Co. of Cambridge, Ontario, a subsidiary of Nichols-Radtke, produces ball valves in sizes that range from two inches to 48 inches in diameter for the oil and gas pipeline industry. The company offers many options, including diameter, pressure rating, means of attachment (welded or flanged), above or below ground, type of operator (electric motor or handwheel), and so on. The number of product options suggests a make-to-order approach to production that fortunately is compatible with the oil and gas pipeline business.

Until recently Borsig had been using an in-house, inventory control system to produce shop packets and routings, but the system did not do a good job of managing inventory, evaluating costs, and managing the production shop. According to Bill Neufeld, project leader for implementation of the company's new MRP II system, "Under the old system, the production manager had no way of knowing what was in the shop. He could only release orders to the shop and hope finished product came out the other end." Usually, more than 150 shop orders were on the floor at one time, which is high, considering that the company has only twenty employees. In addition to increasing costs and confusion, the high WIP inventory resulted in lost and damaged parts and lost customer orders when due dates were missed.

The company replaced the old system with an MRP II system that includes a CRP module. The company uses the CRP module to determine the effect of a new order on the shop floor. It also provides a what-if analysis capability for determining whether it can deliver a potential order on time, and what additional resources (overtime, subcontracting, and so on) it will require. The company also uses the CRP module to smooth the production schedule by using firm planned orders to get a level production schedule.

MRP II has dramatically improved the performance of the company's manufacturing operations. The number of open orders on the shop floor now averages twenty-five to thirty. According to Neufeld, who now works at another division of Nichols-Radtke, "I continued to be involved with the implementation for eight months after the system became operational, and in that time not one customer order was late, or at least what I would consider late. With a product that requires from four to six weeks of internal processing, we were consistently completing the orders within one or two days of the scheduled completion date."

■ Customers are participants in the production process.
■ The service provider's performance capability is time perishable. (Service operations cannot store their products in finished goods inventories.)
■ Customers dictate service site location.
■ The service production process is labor intensive.
■ The service product is intangible.[1]

[1]M. Jill Austin, "Planning in Service Organizations," *Advanced Management Journal* 55 (Summer 1990): 7.

Having the customer as part of the production process has a number of implications. Many times the customer must provide input to the service process, and the quality and speed of the customer's input is beyond the control of the provider. Anyone who has experience in the fast-food industry understands that the server can do nothing to speed up the customer's ordering process (or ensure its accuracy). Also, in many cases service speed is seen as evidence of poor service quality. One example is that a patient's dissatisfaction with a doctor's care frequently is the result of the doctor's not having spent enough time with the patient. Because service systems deal with customers, they have little opportunity to handle customers on a basis other than first come, first served (at least in the United States where the culture says first come, first served is fair), even if a different order would provide better service according to some overall measure of customer service.

Because services cannot be stored in inventory, managers of service operations have fewer techniques available for dealing with capacity problems. Capacity can either be physically limited or service limited, and the effective capacity is the lesser of the two.[2] Although demand is generally assumed to be beyond the control of the service provider, some demand management techniques are available, such as price incentives for off-peak usage and the use of reservations and appointments.

For services, medium-range capacity decisions focus on the proper number and type of the work force (full time versus part time, skills, and so on), whereas the short-range capacity decisions are concerned with shift scheduling and job assignment. The medium-range capacity or scheduling problem can be complex. A recent study points out that although part-time employees can reduce the labor hours needed to meet demand, service providers must consider the typically higher turnover rates and reduced efficiency of part-time employees.[3] Various strategic concerns pertain to short-range capacity decisions related to labor scheduling. Some methods for dealing with peak work loads include cross-training of workers, scheduling overlapping shifts so that two shifts are on duty at the same time, and performing only essential tasks during peak periods and using slack periods for supporting tasks. Employee selection and training decisions also obviously affect the labor-scheduling options.

Although capacity planning in the manufacturing and service sectors have similarities, some aspects of the service environment make the capacity-planning problem unique. Capacity planning in the service industries is an area of increasing research and importance.

[2]Sue Perrott Siferd, W. C. Benton, and Larry P. Ritzman, "Strategies for Service Systems," *European Journal of Operational Research* 56 (February 1992): 298.
[3]Vincent A. Mabert, and Michael J. Showalter, "Measuring the Impact of Part-Time Workers in Service Operations," *Journal of Operations Management* 9 (April 1990): 209–229.

## ► Summary

Capacity planning is an important function in closed loop MRP systems and, unfortunately, is also difficult. The goal for any MRP implementation is to achieve a fully functional MRP II system, and capacity planning is key to achieving this goal. The four capacity planning techniques we presented in this chapter provide a spectrum of compromises in accuracy, data requirements, number of calculations, and ease of use.

CPOF is the simplest of the rough-cut techniques, and it requires only basic production-related accounting data. If information is available for estimating the capacity required at each work center for each end item (obtained either from detailed accounting records or industrial engineering studies), the planner can use the CB approach to give more accurate capacity requirement estimates, especially when the product mix changes. If component lead time data are available, the planner can use the RP method, which incorporates time phasing in the capacity estimates.

The rough-cut techniques are simple to use, because they consider only the MPS and ignore actual component lot sizing and timing and current inventory status. Thus, their simplicity of use comes at the expense of accuracy. Maximum accuracy in capacity planning is obtained from CRP. CRP estimates capacity by using MRP output. Although CRP requires more time and effort, it produces much more accurate capacity estimates than the rough-cut methods, and it provides the MRP planner with an additional tool for adjusting capacity requirements—the FPO.

Although much of our discussion in this chapter focused on the technical aspects of capacity planning, the strategic importance of effective capacity management should not be underestimated. A company that manages its capacity well can provide better on-time service and is likely to reduce its expediting costs (overtime and so on). With good capacity planning, management will spend less time in fire-fighting drills, arguing which hot order should be worked on next, and more time improving the company's operations. Capacity planning is an important management tool that provides strategic advantage for both manufacturers and service providers.

### Learning objective 1: Describe how capacity planning relates to material requirements planning (MRP).

Capacity planning is a critical component of a closed loop MRP system. Without capacity planning the MRP system may generate shop orders that cannot be completed on time. Increased use of overtime, late orders, and the development of an informal system are the likely results. Managers are likely to increase planned lead times, increasing WIP inventory and shop-floor congestion. Without capacity planning the integrity of an MRP system can be severely compromised.

### Learning Objective 2: Describe how to use capacity planning techniques to develop a feasible MPS.

Rough-cut capacity planning techniques are used to evaluate the capacity required by a proposed MPS. If the proposed MPS creates a capacity requirement that exceeds the available capacity, the company can increase capacity by adding overtime or subcontracting, or it can change the MPS. The company can reevaluate the revised MPS to determine its capacity requirements and whether to make additional changes.

CRP provides an additional tool for developing a feasible MPS—namely, firm planned orders. Firm planned orders allow managers to shift planned order release dates in time to smooth capacity requirements. With CRP, firm planned orders allow an initially infeasible MPS to be made feasible by adjusting order release dates.

### Learning Objective 3: Compare four capacity planning techniques on the basis of accuracy, information requirements, number of calculations, and ease of use.

The four techniques can be rated in the order they were presented in this chapter: CPOF, CB, RP, and CRP. We presented the techniques in order of increasing accuracy, increasing information requirements, increasing number of calculations, and decreasing ease of use. The rough-cut techniques (CPOF, CB, and RP) are fairly simple and require relatively little information, compared with CRP, but because they do not consider the actual lot sizing used or the current status of inventory, they are less accurate than CRP.

### Learning Objective 4: Understand how to use the various capacity planning methods to estimate capacity requirements, given the required data.

CPOF uses the MPS and production-related accounting data (hours per end item and historic work center percentages) to estimate capacity requirements. CB uses the MPS and data on the individual work center capacity requirements per end item to estimate capacity requirements. The RP method adds time phasing to the CB method to estimate time-phased capacity requirements. CRP uses the actual planned and scheduled order release data from the MRP process with current inventory status and shop-floor data to generate the most accurate capacity estimates.

### Learning Objective 5: Discuss the relationship between the MPS and capacity requirements.

The MPS is the source of capacity requirements. Capacity is needed to fabricate and assemble components into finished goods as specified by the MPS. Thus, changes to the MPS will result in changes to the capacity requirements. The difficulty is that the relationship between MPS requirements and capacity requirements is not direct if lot sizing is used. Changes to the MPS that reduce a capacity problem in one period may increase it in another.

**Learning Objective 6: Discuss how to use firm planned orders to adjust capacity requirements when using CRP.** With CRP, the MRP planner is dealing with the actual planned order releases. If the capacity required in one period exceeds what is available, but excess capacity is available in a previous period, the planner can use a firm planned order to move the order release date from a period of high capacity requirements to a period of lower capacity requirements.

## ▶ Key Terms

capacity bill
capacity planning using capacity bills (CB)
capacity planning using overall
    factors (CPOF)

capacity planning using resource
    profiles (RP)
capacity requirements planning (CRP)

detailed capacity planning
operation setback chart
rough-cut capacity planning

## ▶ Discussion Questions

1. How can effective capacity planning provide strategic advantage?
2. Why should capacity planning techniques be used with MRP systems? What assumptions do MRP systems make with respect to capacity?
3. Why is capacity planning a trial-and-error process?
4. How does an MRP planner use capacity planning techniques to develop a feasible MPS?
5. What options are available for increasing the capacity available?
6. What conditions are necessary for CPOF to make accurate capacity estimates? What conditions facilitate accurate capacity estimates from CB?
7. Is it possible to develop planning factors for CPOF for a new product? Can a capacity bill be developed for a new product?

8. What advantage is gained in using the RP method instead of CPOF or CB?
9. Why are CRP estimates frequently lumpy?
10. How can firm planned orders be used to smooth capacity requirements? What problems can arise from their use?
11. How will the ever-increasing speed and power of computers affect the selection of a capacity-planning method?
12. How does capacity planning for service organizations differ from capacity planning for manufacturing?

## ▶ Problems

1. Given the following data, use CPOF to calculate the capacity required by the proposed MPS:

*Total Processing Time per Unit*

Product X—10 minutes
Product Y—20 minutes

***Standard Allocation***

| | |
|---|---|
| Stamping | 20% |
| Electrical | 20% |
| Assembly | 40% |
| Inspection | 10% |
| Pack & ship | 10% |

***Proposed MPS***

| Product | Period 1 | 2 | 3 | 4 | 5 |
|---|---|---|---|---|---|
| X | 20 | 20 | 10 | 20 | 20 |
| Y | 20 | 30 | 20 | 30 | 10 |

***Capacity Requirements***

| | Period 1 | 2 | 3 | 4 | 5 |
|---|---|---|---|---|---|
| Total | | | | | |
| Stamping | | | | | |
| Electrical | | | | | |
| Assembly | | | | | |
| Inspection | | | | | |
| Pack & Ship | | | | | |

**2.** The Steelplace Co. manufactures two-drawer and three-drawer file cabinets. The following production-related accounting data are available for estimating capacity requirements:

| ***Product*** | ***Standard Hours per Unit*** |
|---|---|
| Two-drawer file | 3.5 |
| Three-drawer file | 4.8 |

| ***Work Center*** | ***Typical Percentage*** |
|---|---|
| Metal stamping | 10 |
| Welding | 45 |
| Painting | 20 |
| Assembly | 25 |

Using the CPOF method, estimate the capacity required to execute the following MPS:

| ***Product*** | ***1*** | ***2*** | ***3*** | ***4*** | ***5*** |
|---|---|---|---|---|---|
| Two-drawer file | 100 | 150 | 150 | 200 | 200 |
| Three-drawer file | 100 | 100 | 200 | 150 | 200 |

**3.** Using the MPS from problem 2, estimate the capacity requirement using the following capacity bills:

| ***Work Center*** | ***Two-Drawer File*** | ***Three-Drawer File*** |
|---|---|---|
| Metal stamping | 0.35 | 0.50 |
| Welding | 1.60 | 1.80 |
| Painting | 0.70 | 1.15 |
| Assembly | 0.85 | 1.35 |
| Total | 3.50 | 4.80 |

**4.** The Pisces Aquarium Co. produces aquariums in three sizes: 10-gallon, 20-gallon, and 30-gallon capacity. The company has divided its production facility into four work centers: glass cutting, assembly, caulking, and packing. The following accounting data are available for these products:

| Product | Standard Hours per Unit |
|---|---|
| 10-gallon tank | 1.8 |
| 20-gallon tank | 2.1 |
| 30-gallon tank | 2.5 |

| Work Center | Typical Percentage |
|---|---|
| Glass cutting | 20 |
| Assembly | 25 |
| Caulking | 40 |
| Packing | 15 |

Using the CPOF method, estimate the capacity required to execute the following MPS:

| Product | 1 | 2 | 3 | 4 | 5 | 6 | 7 | 8 | 9 | 10 |
|---|---|---|---|---|---|---|---|---|---|---|
| 10 gallon | 20 | 15 | 15 | 10 | 0 | 10 | 15 | 20 | 20 | 20 |
| 20 gallon | 10 | 15 | 10 | 15 | 15 | 10 | 10 | 5 | 5 | 10 |
| 30 gallon | 10 | 10 | 10 | 10 | 10 | 15 | 10 | 15 | 15 | 15 |

5. Using the MPS from problem 4, estimate the capacity requirement using the following capacity bills:

| Work Center | 10 gallon | 20 gallon | 30 gallon |
|---|---|---|---|
| Glass cutting | 0.40 | 0.45 | 0.50 |
| Assembly | 0.40 | 0.50 | 0.60 |
| Caulking | 0.70 | 0.80 | 1.00 |
| Packing | 0.30 | 0.35 | 0.40 |
| Total | 1.80 | 2.10 | 2.50 |

6. Refer to problem 3 in Chapter 13. For the parts that are manufactured in house, the following routing and standard time data are available:

| Part # | Lot Size | Operation | Work Center | Standard Set-up (Hours) | Standard Run Time (Hours per Unit) |
|---|---|---|---|---|---|
| 25 | 50 | 1 of 1 | Assembly | 0.20 | 0.40 |
| 4234 | 50 | 1 of 1 | Molding | 1.00 | 0.05 |
| 1313 | 100 | 1 of 2 | Fabric cutting | 0.10 | 0.02 |
|  |  | 2 of 2 | Sewing | 0.04 | 0.08 |
| 4275 | 200 | 1 of 2 | Metal cutting | 0.08 | 0.001 |
|  |  | 2 of 2 | Metal forming | 1.00 | 0.05 |

Use this information to calculate a capacity bill for the model 25 briefcase.

7. The BOM for a product is as follows:

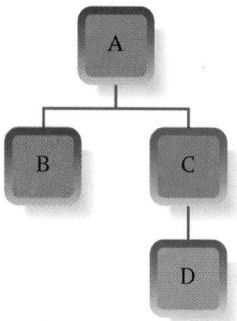

The following information for the components is also available:

| Component | Lot Size | Operation | Work Center | Lead Time (Periods) | Set-up Time | Operation Time (per Unit) |
|---|---|---|---|---|---|---|
| A | LFL* | 1 of 1 | 100 | 1 | 30 | 0.40 |
| B | 100 | 1 of 2 | 300 | 1 | 28 | 0.30 |
|   |   | 2 of 2 | 200 | 1 | 45 | 0.50 |
| C | 100 | 1 of 1 | 200 | 1 | 20 | 0.20 |
| D | 200 | 1 of 2 | 400 | 1 | 35 | 0.06 |
|   |   | 2 of 2 | 300 | 1 | 45 | 0.05 |

*Assume an average lot size of 50 units.

Use the resource profiles method to determine the equations required to estimate capacity.

8. Use the resource profile equations method developed in problem 7 to calculate the capacity required at each work center for periods 1 through 5 to complete the following MPS:

| Product | 1 | 2 | 3 | 4 | 5 |
|---|---|---|---|---|---|
| Two-drawer file | 100 | 150 | 150 | 200 | 200 |

9. Suppose the MRP records that follow were generated for the product in problem 7. Use CRP to calculate the capacity requirements at work center 300.

**Name: Part B**

| LS: 100 | LT: 2 | 1 | 2 | 3 | 4 | 5 | 6 | 7 | 8 | 9 | 10 |
|---|---|---|---|---|---|---|---|---|---|---|---|
| Gross Requirements | | 50 | 50 | 40 | 60 | 20 | 30 | 50 | 60 | 40 | 40 |
| Scheduled Receipts | | 100 | | | | | | | | | |
| Planned Receipts | | | | 100 | | 100 | | | 100 | | 100 |
| Available Balance | 10 | 60 | 10 | 70 | 10 | 90 | 60 | 10 | 50 | 10 | 70 |
| Planned Order Releases | | 100 | | 100 | | | 100 | | 100 | | |

**Name: Part D**

| LS: 200 | LT: 2 | 1 | 2 | 3 | 4 | 5 | 6 | 7 | 8 | 9 | 10 |
|---|---|---|---|---|---|---|---|---|---|---|---|
| Gross Requirements | | 100 | | 100 | | | | 100 | | 100 | |
| Scheduled Receipts | | | | | | | | | | | |
| Planned Receipts | | | | 200 | | | | | | 200 | |
| Available Balance | 150 | 50 | 50 | 150 | 150 | 150 | 150 | 50 | 50 | 150 | 150 |
| Planned Order Releases | | 200 | | | | | | 200 | | | |

Capacity Requirements for Work Center 300

|  | | | | | | *Period* | | | | | |
|---|---|---|---|---|---|---|---|---|---|---|---|
|  | 1 | 2 | 3 | 4 | 5 | 6 | 7 | 8 | 9 | 10 |
| Set-up | | | | | | | | | | |
| Run time | | | | | | | | | | |
| Total | | | | | | | | | | |

**10.** Given the data that follow, calculate the capacity requirements in work centers 100 and 200 by using CRP. Available capacity in work center 200 is 120 hours per period. Is there a capacity problem with the proposed MPS? If so, how would you fix it?

BOM

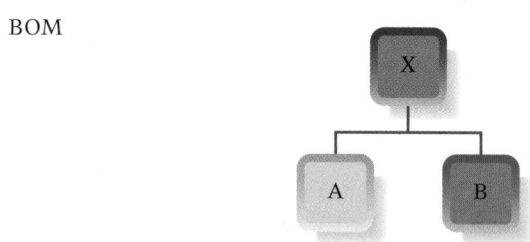

| Component | LS | LT** | Operation | Work Center | Set-up Time (Total) | Processing Time (per Unit) |
|---|---|---|---|---|---|---|
| X | LFL* | 1 | 1 of 1 | 100 | 3 hrs. | 30 min. |
| A | 50 | 1 | 1 of 2 | 200 | 5 hrs. | 1 hr. |
|  |  | 1 | 2 of 2 | 100 | 10 hrs. | 20 min. |
| B | 50 | 1 | 1 of 1 | 200 | 5 hrs | 2 hr. |

*Assume average batch size is 20.
**This is lead time *per operation*.

**MPS**

| | | | | | Period | | | | | |
|---|---|---|---|---|---|---|---|---|---|---|
| Item | 1 | 2 | 3 | 4 | 5 | 6 | 7 | 8 | 9 | 10 |
| X | 15 | 20 | 15 | 15 | 20 | 20 | 20 | 15 | 20 | 20 |

| Part No: | A | | | | | | | | | | |
|---|---|---|---|---|---|---|---|---|---|---|---|
| Part Name: | | | | | | | | | | | |
| LS: 50 | LT: 2 | 1 | 2 | 3 | 4 | 5 | 6 | 7 | 8 | 9 | 10 |
| Gross Requirements | | 15 | 20 | 15 | 15 | 20 | 20 | 20 | 15 | 20 | 20 |
| Scheduled Receipts | | | 50 | | | | | | | | |
| Planned Order Receipts | | | | | | | 50 | | | 50 | |
| Available Balance | 40 | 25 | 55 | 40 | 25 | 5 | 35 | 15 | 0 | 30 | 10 |
| Planned Order Releases | | | | 50 | | 50 | | | | | |

| Part No: | | B | | | | | | | | | | |
|---|---|---|---|---|---|---|---|---|---|---|---|---|
| Part Name: | | | | | | | | | | | | |
| LS: 50 | LT: 1 | | 1 | 2 | 3 | 4 | 5 | 6 | 7 | 8 | 9 | 10 |
| Gross Requirements | | | 15 | 20 | 15 | 15 | 20 | 20 | 20 | 15 | 20 | 20 |
| Scheduled Receipts | | | | 50 | | | | | | | | |
| Planned Order Receipts | | | | | | | 50 | | 50 | | | 50 |
| Available Balance | | 20 | 5 | 35 | 20 | 5 | 35 | 15 | 45 | 30 | 10 | 40 |
| Planned Order Releases | | | | | | 50 | | 50 | | | 50 | |

### Capacity Requirements for Work Center 100

**Period**

| | 1 | 2 | 3 | 4 | 5 | 6 | 7 | 8 | 9 | 10 |
|---|---|---|---|---|---|---|---|---|---|---|
| Set-up | | | | | | | | | | |
| Run time | | | | | | | | | | |
| Total | | | | | | | | | | |

### Capacity Requirements for Work Center 200

**Period**

| | 1 | 2 | 3 | 4 | 5 | 6 | 7 | 8 | 9 | 10 |
|---|---|---|---|---|---|---|---|---|---|---|
| Set-up | | | | | | | | | | |
| Run time | | | | | | | | | | |
| Total | | | | | | | | | | |

11. The Magic-Gadget Co. produces a number of kitchen products, including wall-mounted spice racks. The spice racks are constructed by using components assembled according to the following BOM:

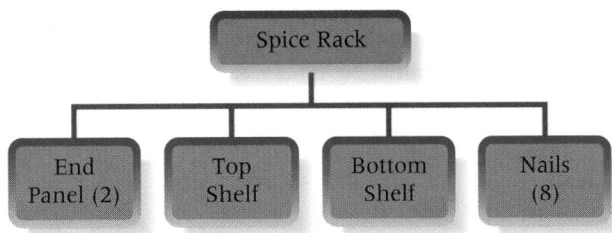

The end panels and shelves are produced in house, and the nails are purchased. Both the end panels and shelves are cut to length from 1″ × 4″ × 12″ #2 yellow pine stock. Holes are drilled in the top shelf to accommodate the spice jars. Both end panels and shelves have their edges shaped on a router, and then they are stained and varnished. The shelves are assembled using eight nails from a pneumatic nailer.

During the past month the accounting department has collected data on the production of spice racks to be used in developing capacity bills.

| Part | Process | Batch Size | Set-up Time | Batch-Processing Time |
|------|---------|-----------|-------------|----------------------|
| End panel | Cutting | 500 | 10 min. | 2 hr. 23 min. |
| | | 500 | 8 min. | 2 hr. 10 min. |
| | Routing | 200 | 27 min. | 2 hr. 15 min. |
| | | 200 | 29 min. | 2 hr. 42 min. |
| | | 200 | 31 min. | 2 hr. 24 min. |
| | Stain & varnish | 200 | 35 min. | 3 hr. 18 min. |
| | | 200 | 40 min. | 3 hr. 6 min. |
| | | 200 | 55 min. | 3 hr. 20 min. |
| Top shelf | Cutting | 500 | 7 min. | 2 hr. 40 min. |
| | Routing | 200 | 25 min. | 2 hr. 6 min. |
| | | 200 | 27 min. | 2 hr. 15 min. |
| | | 200 | 22 min. | 2 hr. 24 min. |
| | Drilling | 200 | 15 min. | 2 hr. 5 min. |
| | | 200 | 16 min. | 1 hr. 56 min. |
| | | 200 | 13 min. | 2 hr. 14 min. |
| | Stain & varnish | 200 | 25 min. | 3 hr. 45 min. |
| | | 200 | 27 min. | 3 hr. 54 min. |
| | | 200 | 22 min. | 3 hr. 43 min. |
| Bottom shelf | Cutting | 500 | 9 min. | 2 hr. 48 min. |
| | | 500 | 12 min. | 2 hr. 55 min. |
| | Routing | 200 | 22 min. | 2 hr. 25 min. |
| | | 200 | 30 min. | 2 hr. 33 min. |
| | | 200 | 26 min. | 2 hr. 17 min. |
| | Stain & varnish | 200 | 22 min. | 3 hr. 28 min. |
| | | 200 | 30 min. | 3 hr. 20 min. |
| | | 200 | 26 min. | 3 hr. 24 min. |
| Spice rack | Assembly | 100 | 5 min. | 1 hr. 20 min. |
| | | 100 | 7 min. | 1 hr. 35 min. |
| | | 100 | 8 min. | 1 hr. 28 min. |

Use this data to construct a capacity bill for the spice rack by using the average processing and set-up time values.

12. The accounting department of Truckin' Tots Toy Co. has been accumulating data for use in capacity-planning that uses overall factors. The company produces three types of plastic toys—an earth mover, a front loader, and dump truck. The company has three departments—molding, assembly, and packaging. The MPS for the last ten periods and the capacity used broken down by end item and work center are provided. Use this data to calculate planning factors for Truckin' Tots' manufacturing operations.

| MPS | Period | | | | | | | | | |
|-----|---|---|---|---|---|---|---|---|---|---|
| | 1 | 2 | 3 | 4 | 5 | 6 | 7 | 8 | 9 | 10 |
| Earth mover | 500 | 700 | 600 | 500 | 500 | 600 | 700 | 600 | 600 | 500 |
| Front loader | 1,200 | 1,300 | 1,200 | 1,000 | 1,300 | 1,200 | 1,100 | 1,200 | 1,400 | 1,500 |
| Dump truck | 2,500 | 2,300 | 2,500 | 3,000 | 2,800 | 2,600 | 2,500 | 2,700 | 2,600 | 2,600 |

*Work Center*
*Breakdown*
*(Hours)*

| | | | | | *Period* | | | | | |
|---|---|---|---|---|---|---|---|---|---|---|
| | 1 | 2 | 3 | 4 | 5 | 6 | 7 | 8 | 9 | 10 |
| Molding | 149.17 | 112.00 | 149.50 | 136.33 | 152.83 | 120.00 | 118.67 | 137.50 | 140.33 | 149.17 |
| Assembly | 224.17 | 204.50 | 214.16 | 217.67 | 233.33 | 233.33 | 212.50 | 217.50 | 222.67 | 245.33 |
| Packing | 85.00 | 63.08 | 84.67 | 78.17 | 87.08 | 78.33 | 66.25 | 75.00 | 74.50 | 83.92 |
| Totals: | 458.33 | 379.58 | 448.33 | 432.17 | 473.25 | 421.67 | 397.42 | 430.00 | 437.50 | 478.42 |

*Product*
*Break Down*
*(Hours)*

| | | | | | *Period* | | | | | |
|---|---|---|---|---|---|---|---|---|---|---|
| | 1 | 2 | 3 | 4 | 5 | 6 | 7 | 8 | 9 | 10 |
| Earth mover | 71.00 | 52.00 | 80.00 | 40.00 | 70.00 | 20.00 | 90.00 | 70.00 | 20.00 | 70.00 |
| Front loader | 175.00 | 147.92 | 150.00 | 134.17 | 182.92 | 145.00 | 122.08 | 155.00 | 185.83 | 203.75 |
| Dump truck | 213.33 | 181.67 | 218.33 | 258.00 | 220.33 | 256.67 | 185.33 | 205.00 | 231.67 | 204.67 |
| Totals: | 458.33 | 379.58 | 448.33 | 432.17 | 473.25 | 421.67 | 397.42 | 430.00 | 437.50 | 478.42 |

## ▶ Selected References

Austin, M. Jill. "Planning in Service Organizations." *Advanced Management Journal* 55 (Summer 1990): 7–12.

Berry, W. L., T. G. Schmitt, and T. E. Vollmann. "Capacity Planning for Manufacturing Control Systems: Information Requirements and Operating Features." *Journal of Operations Management* 3 (November 1982): 13–25.

Fogarty, D. W., and T. R. Hoffman. *Production and Inventory Management.* Cincinnati, Ohio: South-Western Publishing, 1983.

Mabert, Vincent A., and Michael J. Showalter. "Measuring the Impact of Part-Time Workers in Service Operations." *Journal of Operations Management* 9 (April 1990): 209–229.

Siferd, Sue Perrott, W. C. Benton, and Larry P. Ritzman. "Strategies for Service Systems." *European Journal of Operational Research* 56 (February 1992): 291–303.

Vollmann, T. E., W. L. Berry, and D. C. Whybark. *Manufacturing Planning and Control Systems,* 3rd ed. Homewood, Ill.: Irwin, 1992.

## CHAPTER 15

# Shop Floor Control

*A leader is best when people barely know he exists. Not so good when people obey and acclaim him. Worse when they despise him. But of a good leader who talks little, when his work is done and his aim fulfilled, they will say, "We did it ourselves."*

LAO-TZE, CHINESE PHILOSOPHER

Introduction

Shop-Floor Control in Continuous and Repetitive Operations

Shop Floor Control in Intermittent, Job Shop Operations

Scheduling Intermittent Job Shop Processes

Data Collection and Order Disposition
*OPERATIONS MANAGEMENT IN PRACTICE 15.1: Streamline Manufacturing: Sun Microsystems, Inc.*

Innovative Control: Theory of Constraints
*OPERATIONS MANAGEMENT IN PRACTICE 15.2: Synchronous Manufacturing—Quaker Furniture*

International Issues in Shop-Floor Control

Case Study: Hoops University

▶ **L E A R N I N G   O B J E C T I V E S** ◀

*After completing this chapter you should be able to*

1. Discuss the key activities of shop-floor control in continuous, repetitive, and job shop operations
2. Describe the difference between a job's planned lead time and its flow time
3. Describe the negative effects of high levels of work-in-process inventories
4. Describe the measures of shop performance that are best served by SPT (shortest processing time) and EDD (earliest due date) scheduling rules

5. Construct Gantt charts to illustrate sequencing a set of jobs
6. Describe the steps of Johnson's rule, and identify situations to which it is applicable
7. Discuss the key performance measures promoted by the theory of constraints

# Introduction

A manufacturing plant near Jakarta, Indonesia, produces a variety of wire products. The path of material moving through the plant from department to department is complex, and the variety of wire products produced is diverse. When buyers seek information on orders for wire products that are late for delivery, managers can rarely pinpoint the location of that particular order in processing, although the plant's performance is good and the finished items eventually appear in the finished goods warehouse. Wire bales are piled high on every square foot of floor space not occupied with equipment. Investment in this work-in-process inventory is excessive.

This manufacturing problem can be found almost everywhere on earth where there are manufacturing operations. It is symptomatic of the challenge of successfully executing sophisticated manufacturing plans by instituting procedures and methods known as *shop-floor control (SFC)*. The American Production and Inventory Control Society defines shop-floor control as

> A system for utilizing data from the shop floor to maintain and communicate status information on shop orders (manufacturing orders) and on work centers. The major subfunctions of shop floor control are: (1) assigning priority of each shop order, (2) maintaining work-in-process quantity information, (3) conveying shop order status information to the office, (4) providing actual output data for capacity control purposes, (5) providing quantity by location by shop order for work-in-process inventory and accounting purposes, and (6) providing measurement of efficiency, utilization, and productivity of the work force and machines.[1]

This comprehensive definition indicates that the SFC function involves determining a production plan and routing for each order, releasing that order to the production or service facility, tracking its progress and reporting its status when needed, and measuring the performance of the facility based upon the timely, cost-effective completion of those orders.

---

[1]James F. Cox III, J. Blackstone, Jr., and M. Spencer (eds.), *APICS Dictionary*, 7th ed. (Falls Church, Va.: American Production and Inventory Control Society, 1992), p. 46.

## The Task of the Shop-Floor Control Manager

Executing the production plan is frequently the task of first-line supervisors and workers who are directly engaged in the production or service process. Consider the different concerns of managers and workers, given the type of production environment within which they work. At one extreme is the shift supervisor of a petroleum refinery. This is a big, capital intensive operation with a high degree of predictability. The manager probably has a technical degree in an area such as chemical engineering. This would not be her first job after college; this is an interdependent system, and managers must have time to learn how a change in one part of the system effects other parts of the operation. The manager and her work force are primarily concerned with keeping the refinery in continuous operation. Backup and redundant systems mean that performing maintenance during production is possible—the flow of material is rerouted to the backup systems. Any threat of an unanticipated shutdown is critical, whether it be a technical breakdown, labor problem, or shortage of material such as crude oil. Coordinating the logistics of smoothly moving material in and out of the plant is a significant concern. Perhaps once a year the entire facility shuts down for major maintenance activities. Both the workers and manager monitor the flow of material through the system and attempt to detect and solve problems from the data they collect. They can justify virtually any action that is necessary to maintain smooth production, given the high cost of an unplanned shutdown.

The second manager works in repetitive manufacturing in a snack-food manufacturing facility. His level of technical training is not as crucial as the oil refinery manager's is. This facility prepares potato-, corn-, and wheat-flour-based snack foods and confections from raw materials and packages and ships them to intermediate distribution points and institutions in the region. Round-the-clock operations make better use of the equipment, but the manager can start and stop the operation. The operation requires approximately one hour of maintenance and set-up for each start and stop, when the market requirements are for less than twenty-four hours' worth of production. The manager must solve a continuous series of technical problems with technology, coordinating production with repairs and changes in the production plans, and motivating the work force to meet production requirements and solve problems. The flow of material is predictable, but the mix of products produced on the available production lines varies daily. Starting and stopping the process is a regular event, either to accommodate the production plan or because of emergencies. The manager seeks to streamline operations and reduce uncertainty in the system.

The wire plant we described in the introduction to this chapter is the environment of the third manager. The mix of products produced is extensive, and the routing plan of an individual order dictates material movement. Production planning is inexact, and the time required to produce an order is an estimate at best. The precise time required at each work center or department, the time required to move the order from place to place, and the availability of workers and machines at the new work center contribute to this uncertainty. The manager must be skilled at tracking orders and estimating the production load on each work center. The more congested the facility and the wider the variety of new products it produces, the more difficult this task becomes. Workers are frequently skilled employees who can follow complex production instructions, but getting them training on the use of new tools and techniques is a constant challenge that requires coordination from management.

It is easy to see that the execution of production plans in each of these scenarios is a somewhat different task, yet the measures of performance are fairly standard in each case. How well are people and machines utilized? Do they produce the product to specifications? Can they complete the order in time to meet the promised delivery date?

# Shop-Floor Control in Continuous and Repetitive Operations

## Continuous Process Shop-Floor Control

Defining shop-floor control decisions as the decisions shop managers must make would be easy, but our descriptions of the three different facilities indicate that the range of decision making varies widely according to the environment. In process industries such as the refinery the concern is maintaining "linearity" by producing a consistent product at a consistent rate of production. The initial choice of technology and periodic replacement and maintenance of that technology and associated tooling are the most significant determinants in the success of shop-floor control. Routine reporting of the status of the system and accurate prediction of the ability of the system to meet order requirements on time are the key activities of the SFC task.

## Repetitive Operation Shop-Floor Control

Data collection and monitoring are more detailed in the large batch, repetitive operation of the snack-food manufacturer. Scheduled production is subject to change in response to the demands of customers as well as to the need for routine and emergency maintenance. Order control and feedback provide the basis for making these changes in the execution of the schedule. Ideally, the repetitiveness of this process extends through all phases of the operation. Another example is a facility that produces toys. Ideally, the repetitiveness of the toy assembly process should extend to parts fabrication, construction of subassemblies, and ordering materials. Synchronizing each production activity makes the entire system more predictable and easier to manage.

More and more often businesses are using technologies such as electronic data interchange (EDI) to reduce the batch pattern of earlier stages in the production process. If the toy manufacturer purchases hardwood, paint, sanding belts, and metal coils from suppliers on a regular basis, it may attempt to reduce the delivery quantity and increase the frequency of those deliveries. If the manufacturer can transmit the paint colors it used last week electronically, or even by telephone or fax to the paint supplier, the procedure for ordering paint becomes more repetitive. If wood or plastic injection resins are the principal material used in these toys, delivery may be even more frequent—perhaps even daily. This level of synchronization of material delivery, manufacturing, and shipment to the buyer has been effective in improving performance in a variety of manufacturing and service operations.

The Allen-Bradley electrical contactor manufacturing facility is a highly computer-integrated manufacturing facility that was installed in a renovated portion of an existing facility in Milwaukee. The technology is programmable, and the production schedule is matched to customers' orders on a daily basis. As contactors (on-off switches) move through the facility, they are made into several hundred configurations of several basic designs according to customers' requirements. The time that it takes a unit of production, here a lot size of one contactor, to move through the facility is predictable, because Allen-Bradley has invested heavily in technology that permits quick changeover from producing one option to one of the others. The motivation behind the design of this system was to provide quick response to the customer. The Allen-Bradley facility manufactures custom orders the day they arrive and ships them at the end of the one-shift production cycle. This market-driven facility produces a wide variety of contactors each day, and material arrives at the facility daily to replenish the small material stocks. The execution of this customer-oriented, quick-response strategy required the inclusion of an effective SFC system.

## Mixed-Model Assembly in Repetitive Manufacturing

Improving the repetitiveness of manufacturing systems can proceed in two very different ways. One is an attempt to reduce the amount of variability in the product. Reducing the number of options available makes the production schedule and material plan—and their execution—more predictable. This is the strategy that the principal U.S. auto makers adopted during the late 1970s and early 1980s. In an attempt to be more efficient companies such as Chrysler reduced the number of models and options they offered. In this case the strategy was not effective, because it did not meet customers' requirements for variety, although it did streamline operations and reduce costs.

The second approach to improving repetitiveness is to design an SFC system that can respond flexibly to a wide range of designs and options. Cannondale, a bicycle manufacturer based in Connecticut, developed a mixed-model assembly scheme similar to the one frequently described at Toyota. Cannondale produces the full range of bicycle configurations each day, according to demand patterns, at its plant in south-central Pennsylvania. The final assembly of bicycles is a repetitive process that does not require a tremendous degree of flexibility or cross-training for the work force. The components that go with each bicycle frame are collected in a "kit," and assembly of the components by an experienced work force proceeds without hesitation.

Production of the components and wheel sets must be matched to the final assembly schedule for the bicycles. Cannondale does this easily, because wheel set assembly has no complex operations or expensive or lengthy set-ups. But the production of some components requires casting and machining procedures that are not easily synchronized. In these cases the company produces larger lot sizes and sends to inventory the components not needed immediately. Do not, however, assume that fabrication operations and final production schedules are impossible to synchronize. Investment in flexible tooling permits a company to manufacture some fabricated components as they are needed. Components that Cannondale buys from companies such as Shimano are also fabricated using synchronous schedules and regular exchange of production schedule information. Cannondale orders tires, which are delivered in small, mixed lots according to schedule.

Because Cannondale accepts delivery for a wide variety of tire models and sizes in each order, suppliers need not have the capacity to fill a large order for a thousand of one model and size in a single run but can dedicate slower, lower capacity, and less-expensive technology to producing a single size of tire daily to match Cannondale's typical requirements, perhaps changing tread designs if necessary to improve utilization. Cannondale gets the desired mix of tires; the tire producer can invest in less-expensive technology and dedicate it to producing commonly ordered models and sizes while using one tire-forming machine with fast changeover capability to produce the unusual orders.

Earlier stages of production are not always easily synchronized. Some alloys for components are available from a narrow range of suppliers. The manufacturer may have to accept bigger lots until it can ensure a regular supply or the supplier improves its technological capabilities.

# Shop-Floor Control in Intermittent, Job Shop Operations

A wide variety of raw material, manufacturing processes, and specific job data fill the complex manufacturing environment of the job shop. A particular job may never have been manufactured before, and the best materials and methods may not be obvious. Managers and workers alike must be broadly trained to assess the complexities and uncertainty of this production or service system. A hospital emergency room is a good example of a job shop. Each individual who arrives has a medical history unlike any that medical personnel have seen before. The nature of the emergency is impossible to predict and plan in advance, although data on previous accident and emergency rates can assist the hospital with material and staffing plans. The attending physician and a team of physicians, nurses, assistants, and support staff determine the sequence of operations, which they sometimes perform simultaneously. The range of technology and medication available is wider than that found in any other hospital department, where personnel perform a more narrow range of operations. When the emergency room is busy, someone has to assign a relative priority to each patient. The criteria are usually the survivability and seriousness of the injury, using a procedure developed during wartime called *triage*.

The decisions made in the emergency room are undoubtedly more serious than in a typical manufacturing company, but the complexity and uncertainty are almost identical. Managing is stressful, the situation and priorities may change frequently, and the task is data intensive as well. The manufacturing manager must determine the sequence of operations that the job will follow, perhaps taking into consideration the heavy work load that is already on some work centers and avoiding them if possible. Once managers have established a routing, they must estimate the time required at each work center and tally the material required. Finally, they determine the **delivery date,** or due date. In some cases the customer specifies this date, and the manager must determine whether it is possible to produce the order, given the other open orders in the shop and the time required to obtain material if it is not available. In other cases the manager must quote a delivery date, keeping in mind that quick response to the customer is a key competitive criterion in most industries. By quoting a long time to order completion, or **lead time**, and thus a due date far in the future, the shop manager takes the risk that the customer will balk or at the least will seek other suppliers for future orders.

## Terminology

The topic of job shop floor control has been the subject of extensive research from both business and engineering perspectives. Whenever two diverse groups

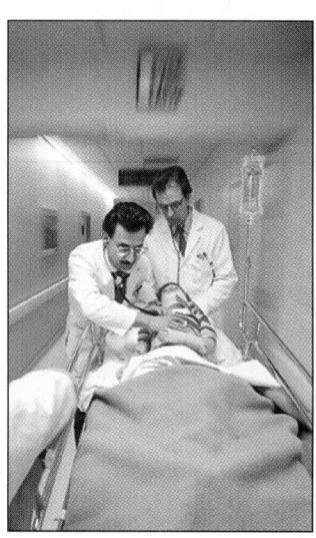

*Hospitals are organized similar to job shops in that people and equipment that perform similar functions are grouped together. Patients are routed through the facility according to their needs. For example, patients may need emergency care, laboratory work, cardiac care, or x-ray.*

study the same issue, they often develop their own language to describe the environment. As high-performance organizations improve efficiency by removing functional boundaries, using a single set of terms becomes even more important. In the remaining sections of the chapter we will carefully define the key terms used in SFC discussions.

For example, people frequently use the terms *job* and *order* interchangeably. A job is a unit of production that follows some sequence of operations. The number of units in the job may be one or several. For example, a job might consist of an order for one prototype machined-metal casting. Another job might require a total of one hundred units of a different casting. The two orders may overlap in material or machines. In fact, they may be for the same customer. However, the definition of a job is typically applied to an order for one or several identical parts. A production lot is the number of units in the order that are produced between process set-ups. The production lot size is usually the same as the order size. The operator sets up the machine to perform an operation, completes repetitive processing operations until the required number have been completed, and then sets the machine up to perform a different operation, usually on a different job. When the order specifies a larger number of units, one hundred, for example, the processing of the hundred units may proceed on one machine, but some of them may be transferred to the next workstation in smaller **transfer lots** in sizes of twenty or fifty. This transfer lot procedure permits part of the job to continue at the next workstation, while some units are still being processed at an earlier stage. This allows the shop to process the order more expeditiously.

The estimated time that is required at an operation is referred to as the **operation processing time**. The total processing time is the sum of the operation processing times for a job. The total time required to complete a job will be *much* longer than the total processing time because of delays from many sources. Some application areas have found that delays are the reason for 90 to 95 percent of the time a job spends in the shop. Sources of order delays include time to accomplish machine set-ups, long queue (wait) times because of the number of units in the production lot, and the time required to move items throughout the series of process stages. Delays are also the result of problems with machinery, personnel, and material. It is easy to see how difficult it is to quote an accurate due date for the customer who is placing an order and wants to know when it will be available. The **planned lead time** is the estimated time that it will take to complete an order, including processing time and delays. The time that the order actually takes to flow through the shop is its **flow time** or **cycle time**.[2]

Suppose an order arrives and specifies fifty units of a component that will require four processing steps. The manager determines that the time for the first processing step is one hour. The second, third, and fourth operations require 4, 2, and 0.5 hours, respectively. The total processing time is the sum of these operation processing times, or 7.5 hours. What is the likelihood that the shop can complete the order in that amount of time? Even assuming that the operation times quoted include time to set up the machine to perform the operation, the

[2]In this chapter we use the terms *cycle time* and *flow time* interchangeably. Using cycle time in this sense is consistent with engineering terminology used in manufacturing environments. Some business texts define cycle time as the time between completions of finished products.

7.5-hour estimate could be close to the true flow time only if every work center were idle, with a trained worker ready to perform the operation as soon as it arrives. This time also assumes that the work centers are located next to one another, arranged as they would be in a repetitive manufacturing process, and that no problems with equipment, material, quality, or design would arise.

The typical job shop can almost never meet these conditions. Thus, the manager estimates the planned lead time for the job, which determines the due date, by using a variety of heuristics, or decision rules. One such rule is to use a standard estimate for the amount of time required to move the order from work center to work center and to include an estimate for the time that the job will wait in the queue of other jobs that require processing there. We can calculate such a planned lead time in several ways.

Suppose a manager is convinced that the total processing time is the best data to use in determining the planned lead time. Using her experience with the flow time required for other jobs in the shop, she estimates that the planned lead time is usually ten times the processing time. That means that the 7.5-hour job would have an estimated completion time of seventy-five hours after it has been released to the shop. Alternatively, the manager may have reason to believe that the number of operations is more useful in estimating the planned lead time. Suppose this particular order has four operations. Historical performance of the shop might indicate that the average operation requires twenty hours from the time of its arrival at the work center to be completed. Using this heuristic, the planned lead time would be eighty hours after release of the order to its first work center.

As we noted earlier, managers use planned lead time to quote delivery dates to the customer or to determine whether it is possible to accept an order when the customer specifies the delivery date. How would this work with each of the heuristic methods we have described? Suppose a six-operation order requires a total of eleven days of processing time. The production schedule is maintained in days, and the shop operates seven days a week. Today is the forty-fifth day of the production year. The customer asks us to quote a delivery date for this order.

## Method 1: Base Planned Lead Time on Total Processing Time

Delay multiplier: $k = 8$

Planned lead time = Delay multiplier × Processing time

$$= 8 \times 11$$
$$= 88 \text{ days}$$

RESULT: Assuming we can release the order to the shop today, its planned delivery date is

$$45 + 88 = \text{day } 133$$

If the customer specifies a delivery date of day 150, we would accept the order knowing that we need not release it to the shop immediately. If the required delivery date is day 120, we would have to assess the situation further. For example, is this a customer whose job warrants special priority? Can we use transfer lots to reduce production time? Can we design a routing that uses machines that are less heavily loaded than the average machine in the shop? Remember, the delay multiplier is based upon past shop performance and may not reflect the current status of the shop.

## Method 2: Base Planned Lead Time on the Number of Operations

Delay multiplier: $k = 9$

Planned lead time = Delay multiplier × Number of operations

$$= 9 \times 6$$
$$= 54 \text{ days}$$

RESULT: Assuming we release the job to the shop immediately, the planned delivery date is

$$45 + 54 = \text{day } 99$$

We apply the same calculations outlined earlier for planned delivery date or to determine the likelihood of meeting a customer's delivery requirements. Note that the expected value of the flow time for the order described depends heavily upon the heuristic we used to estimate lead time and the accuracy of the delay multiplier.

One final term that is used in job shop control is the **completion date**, the actual time that an operation or an order is completed. The actual flow time required to complete a job is the difference between the completion date and the date the order was released to the shop, or

Actual flow time = Completion date − Release date

If we released the order immediately, on day 45, and it was completed and available for delivery on day 110, the actual flow time was sixty-five days.

## Performance Measures in Job Shop Floor Control

The job shop manager's objective is to meet promised due dates, make the best use of people, equipment, and materials, and meet expectations regarding quality, working conditions, and responsiveness to the unanticipated needs of regular customers. It is hoped that the manager applies measures of shop performance that are consistent with these business objectives. Managers use several measures of performance frequently.

The first measure of job shop performance is work-in-process inventory (WIP), which is open orders that have been released but not yet completed. WIP is undesirable and should be reduced for several reasons:

*The automobile racing world understands the need for quick changeover. It is said that races are won in the pits and not on the track. A fast pit stop often makes the difference between winning and losing.*

1. WIP inventory represents a commitment of raw material and processing time that has not yet generated cash flow from the customer. The greater the WIP, the greater the level of this kind of investment.
2. WIP inventory is an indication of long flow times or cycle times. When many orders are open, either the manager has released too many orders or has consistently understated the lead time estimates. Long flow times are not responsive to customers' needs and therefore dull the shop's competitive edge.
3. WIP inventory contributes to shop congestion and confusion. Managers are constantly working to move unfinished goods from place to place; queue discipline is difficult to maintain at work centers. People misplace orders, damage material, and waste time, and the status of open orders is difficult to determine.

Throughput is another important measure of shop performance. **Throughput** is the total volume of output from a process. We can measure how many machined parts are completed per shift or per hour or how many customers a bank drive-through window can process in an hour. All would be measures of throughput for a particular process. In a job shop the throughput is less predictable than in a repetitive or continuous operation. Meeting the customization requirements of buyers has a cost, and the lower efficiency of job shops is just one indication of that cost.

Another traditional measure of performance is **utilization**, or the percentage of time a resource is being used productively. Although high utilization of machinery and people is intuitively appealing and generally advisable, it often encourages managers to make decisions that may be counterproductive in the long term. Releasing more orders to the shop in an attempt to keep everyone busy increases queue time and work-in-process inventory. This is especially true if the busiest operation, known as the **bottleneck operation**, cannot handle the increased load. The increased work load would create more congestion on the shop floor, decrease efficiency, and increase the probability of missing customer due dates.

Reducing lead time is a goal of job shop managers. It captures the benefits of lower WIP, because orders are on the floor for less time, and results in faster and more responsive service for most customers. Being able to complete a customer's order faster and better than the competition may give the shop additional competitive advantage. What strategies can the shop-floor manager use to reduce lead time?

Figure 15.1 represents typical elements of a job's total flow time. A job often waits in queue with other jobs, awaiting its turn for processing. And it waits some more while someone sets up the process for that particular job. After processing, it waits again to be moved. After it moves to the next processing station, the sequence of wait, set up, work, wait, and move begins again. Note that a job's processing time is only a small portion of the total time it spends on the shop floor. As we noted previously, it is not uncommon to find that only 5 to 10 percent of the total flow time is actually value-added time. Activities that do not add value are those that add cost to the product but do not improve it in any way, such as moving, storing, setting up, inspecting, and waiting. When managers attempt to better control flow time, they generally focus on identifying and eliminating, if at all possible, the activities that do not add value. Managers can eliminate these activities in several ways.

**Reduce Set-up Times**   The time required to set up a machine to process an order is one element of lead time. Cutting set-up time not only permits the shop to produce smaller lot sizes more economically but also effectively increases the capacity of the plant by making the machine available for use for longer periods

**FIGURE 15.1**
Elements of Flow Time for a Job

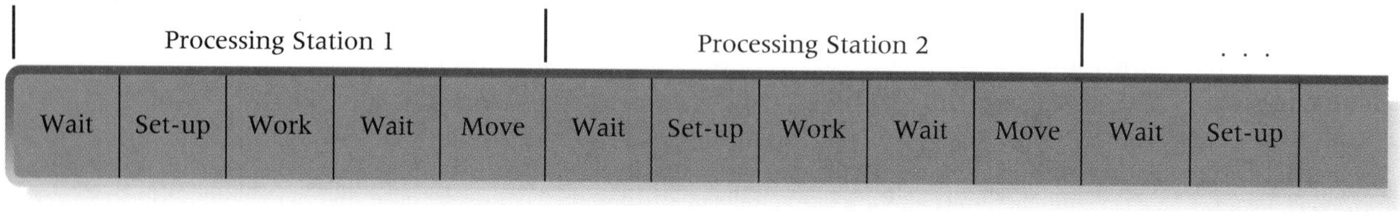

of time, instead of being down for set-ups. In the early 1980s researchers found that the typical Japanese automobile manufacturer required approximately twelve minutes to set up a hood/fender stamping machine. The same set-up for a similar machine in the United States was taking nearly six hours. Consider the implications of this difference. Whereas the Japanese had the luxury of producing in small quantities by setting machines up frequently, the U.S. companies were forced to produce in larger lots to minimize the number of set-ups required. This resulted in a large investment in work-in-process and finished goods inventories and reduced flexibility for the U.S. companies. Most recently, researchers found that U.S. companies have cut set-up time on these types of machines to minutes and sometimes seconds. How have they achieved such dramatic reductions in set-up times? For the most part they changed their philosophy. They finally recognized the problems often associated with long set-ups.

An auto race is a good illustration of the importance of fast and frequent set-ups. An auto race is essentially a race of flow times or cycle times. Each car travels the same distance, but the one that goes the distance in the shortest time wins the race. Breakdowns, accidents, and pit stops interrupt the flow of material (cars) through that system (race track). We can think of the pit stops as similar to a machine set-up in a manufacturing environment.

While the car is in the pit for gas, new tires, cleaned windshield, and so on, it is not being productive. For every instant that the car is in the pit the competition gets farther ahead. So the pit crew is responsible for achieving the shortest pit stop possible. Crew members recognize the importance of a quick set-up and are very good at it. They do not simply ask for volunteers from the crowd to help out. The pit crew is made up of professionals. Pit work is their job, and they practice continually to cut the required time. They do not wait until the car has stopped in the pit area before filling up the gas can or getting four new tires from the trailer. They do these things while the car is still being productive. They recognize that they can accomplish some necessary activities, referred to as *external activities*, while the machine is still running and that they cannot accomplish some activities, the *internal activities*, until the machine has stopped. So the time required to accomplish the list of internal activities determines the amount of time the machine will be out of service, its set-up time. Here is a proven strategy for improving set-up times:

**Step 1:** Everyone must understand the importance of accomplishing a quick set-up.

**Step 2:** Document the list of activities that a complete set-up requires.

**Step 3:** Classify these activities as either internal or external activities.

**Step 4:** Preview the list of internal activities, transfer as many as possible to the external list, and improve the others.

**Step 5:** Identify the tools and equipment required for the set-up and ensure their availability.

**Step 6:** Identify the person or persons who will be responsible for the set-up, train them in the best procedure to follow, and encourage them to practice the procedure frequently, always looking for a better way.

This strategy has proved itself time and time again in industries in which machine set-ups are a critical issue. This is especially true for bottleneck machines, because time lost on a bottleneck machine is lost to the system forever.

**Reduce Queue Times** Jobs wait in queue for their turn on a machine. They wait while the machine is being set up and while someone addresses quality or machine problems. Managers interested in reducing flow times must look carefully at the sources of queue time in an operation. One way to reduce queue time is to make use of **alternative routings** that bypass bottleneck operations that limit production rates. Another way is to delay the introduction of new jobs to the shop to reduce congestion. Many customers change the specifications on special orders during the planned lead time. If work on an order has already started but it is sitting in queues waiting for intermediate processing steps, responding to the customer's modifications may be much more difficult.

**Reduce Material Handling** A well-designed job shop should have departments neighboring one another if they are likely to be in sequence on order-routing sheets. Suppose a large percentage of all jobs coming through a metal-working job shop requires drawing sheet steel from raw material storage, then cutting the steel into pieces of appropriate sizes, and bending the steel pieces to required shapes. It would be logical to consider locating those two processes next to one another and near the raw material storage in order to improve material flow and reduce material handling. Proximity also increases the likelihood of using transfer lots to process an order in two work centers simultaneously.

Reducing set-up times can indirectly improve material handling. With reduced set-up times the shop can produce jobs in smaller lots, which will result in smaller work-in-process inventory. Because the smaller inventory requires less space, the manager can move the processes closer together, thus reducing material handling.

Applying these principles to the example of a hospital emergency room should clarify them. The ER has capacity constraints; noncritical cases should wait outside the ER for available space rather than being shuffled among patients requiring more critical care. The staff uses alternative routings for some patients to avoid overloaded individuals or equipment. Physician's assistants or nurse's aides may replace a preferred care giver when the ER is busy (utilization is high). However, services that involve the patient in the process present special challenges for shop-floor control. How ER personnel prioritize the care of patients may be different than that which some sense of human fairness might predict; they heavily weight the waiting and movement of the patient in determining the quality of the service.

# Scheduling Intermittent Job Shop Processes
## Input-Output Control

We discussed capacity planning on an aggregate level in Chapter 14. At the level of shop-floor control the manager can match input to capacity and output levels fairly easily when the production process is predictable. In complex, less-predictable systems such as job shops the task is more complex. Consider the diagram of a water storage vessel in Figure 15.2. Water flows into the tank through the valve at the top and flows out through a similar valve at the bottom.

When the valves are fixed so that the rate of input and output are identical, the system is stable with virtually any level of water in the tank. The tank water is analogous to the work-in-process load of open orders in the facility. If the

*Careful scheduling and monitoring of work in any organization contributes to timely job completion and satisfied customers.*

FIGURE 15.2
Input-Output Flow
Illustration

process is smooth and continuous, gallons of water in and out are equal, no matter what the WIP level. Therefore, continuous process operations attempt to choose technologies and configurations that keep the WIP level to the lowest value possible. In repetitive systems the level of WIP must be a bit higher to facilitate high levels of utilization at other work centers when one is undergoing repair or maintenance or when a product change initiates a set-up at a work center. In job shops operations occur with less predictability. They require more WIP to maintain high machine utilization, but as we pointed out earlier, there is still a level at which high WIP is dysfunctional. At least one of the "valves" must be flexible to respond to the unpredictability of production. The manager could adjust the output valve by investing in flexible, multipurpose machines that could be deployed to reduce waiting or by investing in excess capacity so that "water" is unlikely to build up in the tank. Both options are costly. Alternatively, the manager could use available capacity by carefully controlling the rate at which new orders enter the input valve. If every customer order is released immediately upon arrival and none is ever turned away, the manager is failing to exercise one of the most important overall controls available. In fact, some practicing managers contend that input-output controls, properly applied, remove the need for detailed shop-floor control procedures.

## Order Review and Release

If the manager has minimized WIP and reduced flow time in a job shop, the sensitive task of reviewing orders and selectively releasing them to the shop requires broad knowledge of the production system, finesse, and a bit of luck. Order release authorizes the beginning of production of an order. It also defines the date that material, tooling, and such instructions as routing sheets and blueprints must be available.

A survey of shop-floor managers shows that they believe that the timely completion of orders according to schedule is closely related to the order release policy. Unfortunately, general understanding of this process is still incomplete. Many researchers have conducted controlled experiments, usually using computer simulation techniques, but they have not conclusively demonstrated the importance of order review and release. More important, because researchers have not determined the critical factors in this procedure, scientific evidence to support the claims of practitioners is lacking. Several explanations for this situation are plausible.

Experiments with simulated manufacturing systems may not capture all elements of a real manufacturing system and thus might ignore some benefits accrued from careful order review and release. Also, some critical factor might be modeled incorrectly in experiments. Several researchers have found that the *pattern* of arrival of orders can have an important effect on the performance of the shop. Others have noted that the *balance* of the load of jobs across work centers is a critical factor that controlled experiments seldom evaluate.

## Scheduling and Sequencing

Input-output control and order review and release procedures often ignore specific information about an order and its routing. However, when more precise information is available regarding open orders that await processing at each work center, the manager can construct sequences of jobs at each work center and establish exact schedules for the start and completion time of each operation. This is a computing-intensive task, but scheduling becomes more and more feasible as the speed of computers increases and the cost of computing continues to drop. Sequencing is the process of prioritizing jobs that are waiting to be processed. The rule used to establish these priorities will have an effect on measures of shop performance. Commonly used sequencing rules, also frequently called *dispatching rules*, include

1. First come, first served. First come, first served (FCFS) is a simple rule by which orders are processed in the sequence in which they arrive. Service applications use it most often, because the sense of fairness is important when dealing with people. Most people standing in line at the bank or grocery store would not accept any sequencing rule but FCFS.
2. Shortest processing time. Shortest processing time (SPT) is the rule that sequences jobs in the queue according to their processing times. Putting the jobs with the shortest processing times first moves those orders through the work center quickly, minimizing the average number of open orders in the shop. This also minimizes the average flow time for jobs in the system. The problem, of course, is that if the shop is never empty, it may never complete some orders with very long processing times. Those cases call for a modified form of SPT that increases a job's priority according to the time it has spent in the shop.
3. Earliest due date. Once again, the earliest due date (EDD) rule can pertain to operation due dates that are set as intermediate production target dates or to the final due date for the complete job. Because each order will eventually become "earliest" as it advances under this rule, difficult orders will not be ignored, as was the case in SPT. Following this rule also leads to the best overall performance when the objective is to minimize the maximum lateness of jobs in the system. A corollary is that EDD does better than other rules at minimizing the variance of lateness. (In fact, these results for EDD and SPT scheduling have been found only in some very restrictive situations in which jobs are being processed by only one machine and all jobs are present at the start of the experiment. However, these relationships have proved to be robust—that is, they are generally true in multimachine processes and in dynamic situations in which jobs are constantly arriving to the shop.)

4. Slack time remaining. *Slack* has a specific definition here: It is the difference between the current point in time and the due date, after subtracting the remaining process time. It reflects the time that is available for moving and waiting. Under the slack time remaining (SLACK) rule jobs with the least slack are processed first. An operations-based version of this rule (SLACK) divides the slack time by the number of operations that remain. The order with the smallest value of that ratio is processed first. This version reflects the importance that is sometimes put on the number of operations rather than on the processing time, as was the case in determining lead time.

5. Critical ratio. The critical ratio (CR) is the difference between the current point in time and the due date, divided by the remaining processing time. This rule attempts to keep all orders as close to schedule as possible, even those that are past their due dates. The order with the smallest ratio is processed first.

The five dispatching rules make up only a sample of the complete set of rules. Other rules include those that focus on the total changeover cost for a sequence of jobs and those that recognize the importance of specific customers.

There are almost as many measures of performance as there are dispatching rules. For our purposes we will focus on four measures that have proved useful:

■ Average flow time. This is a measure of the average amount of time required to complete the total sequence of jobs. As we noted earlier, the SPT rule will yield the lowest average flow time for a set of jobs on a single machine.

■ Average number of jobs in the system. This is a measure of work-in-process inventory generated by a particular sequence. For an organization in which space is limited, minimizing the average number of jobs in the system is important. For most jobs SPT performs particularly well on this measure.

■ Average lateness. This is a measure of the degree of lateness of the average job. This measure does not consider jobs that are early, only those that are late. (In some applications an early job is almost as bad as a late one. In those cases a manager can use a measure of average deviation from target date.)

■ Maximum lateness. This is a measure of the degree of lateness of the latest job.

## Gantt Chart Construction

A common technique used to assess the start and finish times that constitute a schedule is the construction of a Gantt chart, a horizontal bar chart that plots the assignment of critical or scarce resources to jobs during a period of time. The jobs that follow (and the processing time required for each on a single machine) are present at some initial point in time that is equal to zero:

| Job | Processing Time | Due Date |
| --- | --- | --- |
| A | 10 hours | 20 hours |
| B | 5 | 10 |
| C | 12 | 16 |
| D | 4 | 11 |
| E | 20 | 25 |

Assuming that the jobs arrived in alphabetical order, we first will apply the first-come, first-served rule. The Gantt chart describing this sequence of jobs, with start and finish dates for each job, are as follows:

| Job | Start | Finish |
|-----|-------|--------|
| A   | 0     | 10     |
| B   | 10    | 15     |
| C   | 15    | 27     |
| D   | 27    | 31     |
| E   | 31    | 51     |

We can easily use the finish times to calculate the average flow time for the jobs, because they were all released to the shop at time zero. The average flow time is (10 + 15 + 27 + 31 + 51)/5, or 26.8 hours. Using the same data, the SPT rule would yield the sequence D, B, A, C, E, with a average flow time of (4 + 9 + 19 + 31 + 51)/5, or 22.8 hours. This is the Gantt chart for this sequence:

The manager can test other rules and develop a schedule of start and finish times. The sample problem that follows illustrates the five sequencing rules and four performance measures most frequently used for a set of jobs on a single machine.

---

**EXAMPLE 15.1**

**First Come, First Served (FCFS)**

| Job | Processing Time | Due Date |
|-----|-----------------|----------|
| A   | 8 hours         | 12 hours |
| B   | 4               | 5        |
| C   | 7               | 20       |
| D   | 10              | 35       |
| E   | 13              | 47       |
| F   | 5               | 25       |

| Job Sequence | Flow Time | Lateness |
|--------------|-----------|----------|
| A | 0 +  8 =  8 | 0 |
| B | 8 +  4 = 12 | 7 |
| C | 12 +  7 = 19 | 0 |
| D | 19 + 10 = 29 | 0 |
| E | 29 + 13 = 42 | 0 |
| F | 42 +  5 = 47 | 22 |

| Performance Measure | Calculation | Result |
|---------------------|-------------|--------|
| Average flow time | (8 + 12 + 19 + 29 + 42 + 47)/6 | 26.17 hours |
| Average number of jobs in system | [8(6) + 4 (5) + 7 (4) + 10 (3) + 13 (2) + 5 (1)]/47 | 3.34 jobs |
| Average lateness | (0 + 7 + 0 + 0 + 0 + 22)/6 | 4.83 hours |
| Maximum lateness | — | 22 hours |

## Shortest Processing Time (SPT)

| Job | Processing Time | Due Date |
|-----|-----------------|----------|
| A | 8 hours | 12 hours |
| B | 4 | 5 |
| C | 7 | 20 |
| D | 10 | 35 |
| E | 13 | 47 |
| F | 5 | 25 |

| Job Sequence | Flow Time | Lateness |
|--------------|-----------|----------|
| B | 0 + 4 = 4 | 0 |
| F | 4 + 5 = 9 | 0 |
| C | 9 + 7 = 16 | 0 |
| A | 16 + 8 = 24 | 12 |
| D | 24 + 10 = 34 | 0 |
| E | 34 + 13 = 47 | 0 |

| Performance measures | Calculation | Result |
|----------------------|-------------|--------|
| Average flow time | (4 + 9 + 16 + 24 + 34 + 47)/6 | 22.33 hours |
| Average number of jobs in system | [4 (6) + 5 (5) + 7 (4) + 8 (3) + 10 (2) + 13 (1)] /47 | 2.85 jobs |
| Average lateness | (0 + 0 + 0 + 12 + 0 + 0)/6 | 2.0 hours |
| Maximum lateness | — | 12 hours |

## Earliest Due Date (EDD)

| Job | Processing Time | Due Date |
|-----|-----------------|----------|
| A | 8 hours | 12 hours |
| B | 4 | 5 |
| C | 7 | 20 |
| D | 10 | 35 |
| E | 13 | 47 |
| F | 5 | 25 |

| Job Sequence | Flow Time | Lateness |
|--------------|-----------|----------|
| B | 0 + 4 = 4 | 0 |
| A | 4 + 8 = 12 | 0 |
| C | 12 + 7 = 19 | 0 |
| F | 19 + 5 = 24 | 0 |
| D | 24 + 10 = 34 | 0 |
| E | 34 + 13 = 47 | 0 |

| Performance Measure | Calculation | Result |
|---------------------|-------------|--------|
| Average flow time | (4 + 12 + 19 + 24 + 34 + 47)/6 | 23.33 hours |
| Average number of jobs in system | [4 (6) + 8 (5) + 7 (4) + 5 (3) + 10 (2) + 13 (1)]/47 | 2.98 jobs |
| Average lateness | (0 + 0 + 0 + 0 + 0 + 0)/6 | 0 hours |
| Maximum lateness | — | 0 hours |

## Job Slack

| Job | Processing Time | Due Date |
|-----|-----------------|----------|
| A | 8 hours | 12 hours |
| B | 4 | 5 |
| C | 7 | 20 |
| D | 10 | 35 |
| E | 13 | 47 |
| F | 5 | 25 |

| Job Sequence | Slack | Flow Time | Lateness |
|---|---|---|---|
| B | 5 − 4 = 1 | 0 + 4 = 4 | 0 |
| A | 12 − 8 = 4 | 4 + 8 = 12 | 0 |
| C | 20 − 7 = 13 | 12 + 7 = 19 | 0 |
| F | 25 − 5 = 20 | 19 + 5 = 24 | 0 |
| D | 35 − 10 = 25 | 24 + 10 = 34 | 0 |
| E | 47 − 13 = 34 | 34 + 13 = 47 | 0 |

| Performance Measure | Calculation | Result |
|---|---|---|
| Average flow time | (4 + 12 + 19 + 24 + 34 + 47)/6 | 23.33 hours |
| Average number of jobs in system | [4 (6) + 12 (5) + 19 (4) + 24 (3) + 34 (2) + 47 (1)]/47 | 2.98 jobs |
| Average lateness | (0 + 0 + 0 + 0 + 0 + 0)/6 | 0 hours |
| Maximum lateness | — | 0 hours |

## Critical Ratio (CR)

| Job | Processing Time | Due Date |
|---|---|---|
| A | 8 hours | 12 hours |
| B | 4 | 5 |
| C | 7 | 20 |
| D | 10 | 35 |
| E | 13 | 47 |
| F | 5 | 25 |

| Job Sequence | CR | Flow Time | Lateness |
|---|---|---|---|
| B | 5/4 = 1.25 | 0 + 4 = 4 | 0 |
| A | 12/8 = 1.5 | 4 + 8 = 12 | 0 |
| C | 20/7 = 2.86 | 12 + 7 = 19 | 0 |
| D | 35/10 = 3.5 | 19 + 10 = 29 | 0 |
| E | 47/13 = 3.62 | 29 + 13 = 42 | 0 |
| F | 25/5 = 5.0 | 42 + 5 = 47 | 22 |

| Performance Measure | Calculation | Result |
|---|---|---|
| Average flow time | (4 + 12 + 19 + 29 + 42 + 47)/6 | 25.5 hours |
| Average number of jobs in system | [4 (6) + 8 (5) + 7 (4) + 10 (3) + 13 (2) + 5 (1)]/47 | 3.26 jobs |
| Average lateness | (0 + 0 + 0 + 0 + 0 + 22)/6 | 3.67 hours |
| Maximum lateness | — | 22 hours |

## Summary

| Method | Average Flowtime | Average Number of Jobs in System | Average Lateness | Maximum Lateness |
|---|---|---|---|---|
| FCFS | 26.17 | 3.34 | 4.83 | 22 |
| SPT | 22.33 | 2.85 | 2.00 | 12 |
| EDD | 23.33 | 2.98 | 0 | 0 |
| SLACK | 23.33 | 2.98 | 0 | 0 |
| CR | 25.50 | 3.26 | 3.67 | 22 |

As the example shows, the sequencing technique chosen will affect various performance measures in different ways. Which technique is best? It depends upon the environment in which the manager is making the decision. No one sequencing rule is best for all performance measures or for all sets of jobs. For this particular set of jobs EDD or SLACK rules will provide excellent on-time completion of jobs. The SPT rule will provide the shortest average flow time and minimize the congestion of jobs in the shop, but some jobs will not be completed on time. Management must determine the most important performance measure and the sequencing rule that usually performs best on that measure. That particular sequencing rule would generally be the one to use for future applications.

The problem of developing schedules can be compounded in two ways. First, we have thus far considered a static set of jobs to be sequenced without any new arrivals. What happens if we consider dynamic arrivals to the single-machine system? Unless the shop is using the first-come, first-served rule, new arrivals always have the potential to resequence the jobs in the queue, resulting in a new schedule of start and finish times. Maintaining accurate schedules in a dynamic environment requires significant computing resources, even for fairly simple dispatching rules. Another way to complicate sequencing and scheduling is to have more than one operation. When we listed the dispatching rules, we discussed the "best" rules for several performance criteria. Actually, those rules are only guaranteed to be best in single-machine problems with no dynamic arrivals. These static problems are of mathematical interest and do provide insight into the factors that researchers should weigh when attempting to develop heuristics for complex scheduling systems.

## Johnson's Rule for Fixed Sequence, Two-Machine Problems

Exact solutions to scheduling problems that seek to improve shop performance are rare. In addition to the rules that apply to single-machine systems is **Johnson's rule,** a solution procedure for a very restricted two-machine problem.[3] It is an instructive topic but directly applicable in only a select number of cases. Consider an auto body repair shop that has six customers who want their cars fixed and are all available at the start of the week. Each car must have body work first, followed by painting. The reverse of this sequence never occurs. The manager develops the following estimates for the time required for each operation:

| Car | Body Work | Painting |
|-----|-----------|----------|
| A | 18 hours | 6 hours |
| B | 10 | 5 |
| C | 12 | 2 |
| D | 4 | 6 |
| E | 14 | 5 |
| F | 6 | 3 |

The problem is to complete work on all six cars in the minimum flow time. Because both operations can be performed simultaneously but not on the same

[3]S. M. Johnson, "Optimal Two- and Three-Stage Production Schedules with Setup Times Included," *Naval Research Logistics Quarterly* 1 (March 1954): 61–68.

car, the shop needs to begin with the car that requires very little body work so that the painting can begin. The reverse logic applies for the final job. The painting time on the last job should be short to avoid delays in completing all jobs. Using the rule requires the manager to take following steps:

1. Identify the minimum operation processing time, including set-up time, for the candidate (unsequenced) jobs.
2. If the first operation requires the least amount of time, place that job as early in the sequence as possible. If the second operation requires the least amount of time, assign it to the latest unassigned position in the sequence.
3. Break ties judiciously.
4. Repeat from step 1.

In this example the rule operates as follows: Two hours is the minimum processing time. It is the second operation for car C, so we assign that car to the last sequence position:

| _____ | _____ | _____ | _____ | _____ | C |

We remove car C from further consideration for its first operation processing time. Three hours is the shortest flow time remaining, also with the second operation, so we place car F follows:

| _____ | _____ | _____ | _____ | F | C |

Car D requires four hours on the first operation, so it assumes the earliest unassigned position:

| D | _____ | _____ | _____ | F | C |

Cars B and E are tied for an unassigned late position in the sequence. Choose this sequence:

| D | _____ | B | E | F | C |

because the first operation for car B brings it to the earlier position, consistent with the logic of this algorithm. We assign car A to the final position by default. We have established the sequence of D, A, B, E, F, C. Plotting the resulting schedule on a Gantt chart gives the following result:

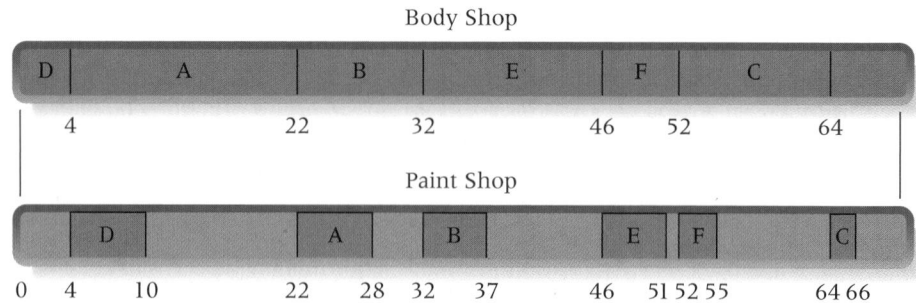

The minimum flow time for the completion of these six jobs is sixty-six hours. Although Johnson's rule has been extended to include a three-machine sequence, exact solutions to more complex scheduling problems have not yet been found.

# Data Collection and Order Disposition

Modern shop-floor control procedures include data that are proportional to the complexity of the operation. However, even in predictable operations we must know the location and status of an open order. The system should maintain records on actual use of material at each work center in order to maintain accurate material inventory records. Ideally, the system should include feedback on the status of machines and tooling. The Allen-Bradley plant described earlier in this chapter collected all this information electronically, using bar-coded information read from the product itself as it moved through production. By using bar codes the shop can match customer and order number with materials, track the order through machines, and always know the status of the order. If a quality problem requires rework, the system automatically reorders the defective part, and production of the replacement unit begins immediately. In transfer lot implementation the system can link the parent order to each transfer lot, avoiding a potential order-tracking and disposition problem. Finally, for accounting purposes the system can report the machine hours actually used.

All this information is not used for reports on the past performance of the shop alone. New orders arrive daily and require time and cost estimates before the shop can prepare bids and quotes for the customer. The data collected on recent shop performance provides a basis for more accurate estimation. Operations Management in Practice 15.1 discusses how Sun Microsystems used information to solve some of its critical shop-floor control problems.

# Innovative Control: Theory of Constraints[4]

Throughout this chapter we have commented on the general desire for high machine, people, and facility utilization. We proposed that a related issue, throughput, is a key performance measure. Managers can sometimes become so consumed by the desire for high utilization and throughput that products are produced whether they are needed or not. Producing products just for the sake of utilization and throughput can spell doom for organizations. An entire body of knowledge has been created recently to help managers understand how to best utilize resources to produce what is needed. The basic lesson is that focusing on utilization at every process is not good. Managers should identify the bottleneck operations that constrain output, and let them direct the flow of material through the facility. The information originally was known as **synchronous manufacturing**. The more recent term is **theory of constraints (TOC)**.

A *constraint* is anything that limits an organization's ability to improve. Constraints can be physical (machine capacity, resource availability, and so on) or nonphysical (policies, procedures, attitudes, and so on). For example, the electronics manufacturing industry often uses a process step called *bake* at the end of the production process. In this step manufactured electrical components go into an oven and are heated to eliminate all moisture before the component is sealed. Process steps ahead of the bake step often complete components much faster than the oven can complete its operation. The oven has a limited capacity

---

[4]Adapted from James T. Low, "Strategic Linkages Between Purchasing and Production Management," *American Production and Inventory Control Society—The Performance Advantage* 2 (December 1992): 33–34.

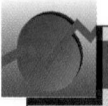

# Streamline Manufacturing: Sun Microsystems, Inc.

You can't improve productivity or quality without information on how your plant is currently operating. So how can you get that information and give it to the employees who can best make use of it? Here's how Sun Microsystems does it.

As a manufacturer of Unix workstations, Sun has shipped more than 150,000 systems since its founding in 1982. The company not only faces the challenge of high-volume production, but also must engage in custom manufacturing for its high-end systems. This shipment and product strategy has significantly affected Sun's manufacturing operations. One example of how Sun deals with this complex environment is its shop floor system (SFS) in use since 1987. This system is used in the manufacturing and testing of printed circuit boards (PCBs). SFS automates PCB routing, tracking, and quality data collection during work-in-process. By providing access to live, constantly changing plant and inventory data, SFS improves accuracy in inventory control and planning, and increases productivity.

Sun uses SFS in its Milpitas [California] facility where it builds desktop and server computers. At the heart of each system is a set of circuit boards made up of a central processing unit and several optional boards. Systems are configured in hundreds of ways by using combinations of up to 80 different boards. The boards are assembled by outside contractors. Once delivered to Sun, they undergo extensive testing. The test process involves five steps, with different steps for different board configurations. The 80 boards can move through any of 137 test and debug locations. Certain boards must be tested together and mated for the remainder of the process. Until 1987, routing, tracking, and recording of PCBs were done by hand. The board test space was an open floor space filled with workbenches grouped by test. Using hand carts, material handlers moved tote boxes of boards from station to station. Employees kept track of WIP and test results on pieces of paper, later typing data into an off-line system which generated reports. The need for an on-line system was apparent. Says program manager Michael Koclanes, "Doing all movement and inventory tracking manually resulted in some inventory control problems. Many of our board inventories weren't accurate. Printed circuit boards would go through the factory faster than we could track them. Our paper database made scheduling fairly difficult."

Now the PCBs are moved through Milpitas in totes on a conveyor in an interconnected system of carousels and testing sites. Boards to be tested are stored in a central area. The carousel operator pulls the tote of the requested boards from the carousel and puts it on the conveyor. Each board and tote have an embedded bar code. Once on the conveyor, the tote passes over laser readers and photo eyes to determine the next testing location. The impact of this SFS system on performance has been dramatic. "We've cut inventories by one-third, our output has doubled, and we're running between 98.5 and 99% accuracy now," asserts Koclanes.

and the process cannot be rushed. Managers would need to recognize this operation as a limiting operation in the process. It is the effective management of these constraint operations that makes the theory of constraints such a powerful concept. In operation the theory of constraints is a five-step process that can help managers get the most out of organizational resources:

**Step 1:** Identify the system's constraints, whether physical or nonphysical.

**Step 2:** Decide how to exploit the system's constraints. Get the most possible from the limit of the current constraints.

**Step 3:** Subordinate everything else to the decisions made in step 2. Avoid keeping nonconstraint resources busy doing unneeded work.

**Step 4:** Elevate the system's constraints. If possible, reduce the effects of the constraints. Offload some demand or expand capability. Make sure everyone in the company knows what the constraints are and what their effects are.

**Step 5:** If a constraint is relaxed in step 4, go back to step 1.
WARNING: Do not let inertia become a constraint.

Dr. Eliyahu Goldratt, a physicist, proposed the theory of constraints in the mid-1980s. TOC gained popularity after Goldratt and Jeff Cox wrote a book, *The Goal,* that highlighted the concepts.[5] The book provides a fictional account of the daily problems of a plant manager. It is well written and should be required reading for manufacturing managers worldwide. Goldratt and Cox cleverly teach the reader much about TOC within *The Goal* without doing so explicitly.

For example, the book uses a troop of Boy Scouts marching single file down a winding mountain trail to illustrate the effect of a bottleneck operation in a sequence of operations. One scout, Herbie, is much slower than the other boys. The scout leader (the plant manager) experiments by moving Herbie to different places in the line and observing the effects on the group. When Herbie is at the front of the line, the boys all bunch up behind him, and the entire group's progress is slow. When Herbie is at the back of the line, the other boys move at their pace and leave him behind. The leader observes that it does not matter that some boys may get to their destination early; the trip is not finished until they all arrive. While he was moving Herbie back and forth, he was thinking of the problems he was having with bottleneck processes in his manufacturing plant. Throughout the book the authors refer to the "goal" of any organization and how traditional techniques and attitudes are often not supportive of the goal.

According to TOC, the goal for most organizations is to make money today and in the future. Goldratt proposes three performance measures for evaluating progress toward the goal. The first measure is throughput. Goldratt's definition of *throughput* is somewhat different from our previous definition. He defines throughput as the rate at which the system generates money through sales. It is not simply output. The company must convert output to cash in order to count output as throughput. We can think of throughput as contribution margin, made up of selling price minus raw material costs. It does not include labor costs.

The second performance measure is inventory. Goldratt defines *inventory* as the money a company invests in things it could or plans to sell. Inventory includes raw material, finished goods, work in process, buildings, land, and machinery. Again, he does not include in inventory the labor component of work in process.

[5]Eliyahu M. Goldratt and Jeff Cox, *The Goal: A Process of Ongoing Improvement* (Croton-on-Hudson, N.Y.: North River Press, 1986).

His final measure is operating expense. He defines *operating expense* as any money spent in the transformation process that converts inventory to throughput. This includes wages, salaries, utilities, scrap, and the like. The challenge is to increase throughput while decreasing inventory and operating expense. Using these performance measures, we can relate the traditional terminology for measures of overall organizational results to Goldratt's terminology:

$$Net\ profit = \text{Throughput} - \text{Operating expense}$$
$$Return\ on\ investment = (\text{Throughput} - \text{Operating expense})/\text{Inventory}$$
$$Productivity = \text{Throughput}/\text{Operating expense}$$
$$Turnover = \text{Throughput}/\text{Inventory}$$

The TOC challenges many of the traditional practices and procedures that have guided businesses in the past. For example, some have criticized the way traditional cost accounting procedures allocate costs. Researchers have found that traditional cost accounting procedures sometimes lead managers to make incorrect decisions about which products to produce or not to produce. These criticisms have caused many companies to rethink traditional costing practices. TOC also challenges conventional approaches to determining product prices, production lot sizes, productivity measures, and performance incentives.

The control mechanism usually associated with synchronous manufacturing, or the theory of constraints, is referred to as **drum-buffer-rope (DBR)**. The *drum* provides a master production schedule, which directs production. Control points, or bottlenecks, set the "drum beat," or pace of production. The theory keys production at operations that are not bottlenecks to the production at the bottleneck operations. Because nonbottleneck operations do not produce faster than the bottleneck operation can absorb their output, needless work-in-process inventories do not build. The *buffer* is in the form of inventory, strategically placed ahead of bottleneck operations to help protect against the inevitable disruptions. Buffer inventories are not in place specifically to maximize utilization of the operation but to ensure that customer delivery dates are met. The *rope* is a communication device that ties the manufacturing process together and ensures the most efficient utilization of bottleneck and nonbottleneck operations. The rope ensures the synchronization of each production step to the master schedule. DBR creates an orderly flow of material that optimizes (not maximizes) throughput while minimizing inventory and operations expense. Operations Management in Practice 15.2 illustrates how North Carolina-based Quaker Furniture used synchronous manufacturing techniques to improve its operations.

The concepts of TOC have been incorporated into a software package called *Optimized Production Technology (OPT)*.[6] *OPT* is a complete production-planning and control system that focuses on identifying bottleneck operations and synchronizing the efficient flow of material through the facility. Many algorithms used by the software are proprietary, but the following general principles guide their application:

1. Do not balance capacity—balance the flow.
2. The level of utilization of a nonbottleneck resource is determined by some other constraint in the system, not by its own potential.

[6]*OPT* is a proprietary product of Dr. Eliyahu M. Goldratt and Creative Output, Inc., of Milford, Connecticut.

**OPERATIONS MANAGEMENT IN PRACTICE 15.2**

# Synchronous Manufacturing: Quaker Furniture

In October of 1990, sales began slowing at Quaker Furniture. Management at the Hickory, North Carolina-based office furniture manufacturer, which has annual sales in the $7 to $8 million range, almost welcomed the recession as an opportunity for the company to catch its breath.

Since its founding in 1966, Quaker had built a reputation for quality products and reliable delivery. But management knew that the company was struggling to meet customer demand for faster delivery and more options. Even with the recessionary slowdown, it took all of the company's perseverance to ship 15 percent of its annual output in the popular quick-ship time frame of three weeks. Regular orders took eight weeks or more to process, manufacture, and ship; that was far too long to provide satisfaction for Quaker's increasingly demanding customers. Something would have to change.

While other companies were throttling back to coast through the recession, Quaker management concluded that the company should adopt a different strategy. Why? Because if the company had trouble keeping up with demand during the recession, it could never accelerate when the market recovered.

Surveying the plant, management could not help but notice the large investment in work-in-process and finished goods inventory. Material was everywhere. A high percentage of that inventory was actually getting in the way of effective production. It was believed that there was inflexibility in the existing system, but it was not known exactly how to transform the operation into one that could manage material better and more flexibly.

The answer came in the form of a book titled *Synchronous Manufacturing* by Umble and Srikanth. The book suggested an approach to manufacturing that, in many respects, was the opposite of policies that Quaker had followed for years.

Synchronous manufacturing is an all encompassing manufacturing management philosophy. It employs a consistent set of principles, procedures and techniques to help managers evaluate every action in their operation in terms of its contribution to two vital goals: making money and maximizing existing resources. The whole purpose of synchronous manufacturing is to provide a process for developing methods which increase revenue generated by sales (throughput) while decreasing inventory and operating expenses.

Quaker's management had always believed that the way to boost productivity was to boost efficiencies. However, evidence was mounting that Quaker, which had admirable efficiencies at most of its individual operations, was not nearly as effective as it needed to be. It seemed to be locked in a vicious cycle. In pursuit of higher efficiency levels, the company kept releasing more and more material onto the shop floor. However, high efficiencies, even when achieved, often translated into unhappy customers—many of whom called frequently to complain about late deliveries.

"Bumping" orders was management's response. This satisfied complaining customers, but drove efficiencies back down. Major changes were needed in the traditional attitudes about how manufacturing should be done.

The company began by cutting inventory levels. Only the material which was needed to satisfy existing customer orders was released to the shop. The result was some very uncertain employees who had always equated large volumes of work-in-process inventory with job security. Through communication and training, the new way was finally accepted. While there is much more to synchronous manufacturing than simply cutting inventory, it was a valuable first step for Quaker.

With a little more than a year of experience with synchronous manufacturing, Quaker has cut work-in-process inventory by 39 percent while increasing inventory turns by 25 percent. Delivery performance of all regular orders has improved by 25 percent, cutting the eight-week lead time down to six. In addition, the operation has increased the percentage of orders shipped in the quick-ship time frame from 15 percent to 40 percent of total volume.

Not only has Quaker increased the volume of quick-ship orders, it also increased the number of model and fabric options available. These improvements were all made with a 16 percent smaller work force. Synchronous manufacturing has been an effective system for managing Quaker's materials to meet its goals.

3. *Utilization* of a resource means "making what is needed," whereas *activation* of a resource is "making parts to keep the resource busy." The terms are not synonymous.
4. Because bottleneck operations have no excess capacity, an hour lost on a bottleneck operation is an hour lost for the entire system.
5. Because nonbottleneck operations have extra capacity, an hour saved on a nonbottleneck operation is a mirage.
6. Bottlenecks govern both inventory and throughput in a system.
7. The transfer batch size may not, and in many cases should not, be the same as the process batch size.
8. The process batch may vary in size for various operations and over time. It should not be fixed.
9. All the system's constraints must be considered simultaneously in determining schedules. Lead times are a result of the schedule and are not fixed.

Many U.S. companies accepted and applied with success the concepts associated with TOC. The radical departure from traditional thought proposed by the philosophy has been a limiting factor in its acceptance. Although some companies may not accept the full philosophy of TOC, many have a greater understanding of the effects of bottleneck operations in their facilities as a result of TOC. They have modified procedures within their facilities to ensure better utilization of the bottlenecks.

## International Issues in Shop-Floor Control

Most studies of international operations management focus on strategic issues that tend to be long term and focused on executive decisions. Should a manufacturer enter an international market? Is this service acceptable in another culture? By comparison, the decisions that we have been describing relating to shop-floor control appear to be immediate and particular to the situation as it occurs in one facility. However, a study conducted by Boo-Ho Rho and D. Clay Whybark regarding manufacturing procedures in other countries provides some important insight for manufacturing managers who may be seeking to operate internationally.[7] Their study of manufacturing control practices compares Western European companies with those in South Korea in two industries: nonfashion textiles and small machine tools. Although these industries would seem to be very different, the study found greater differences in practice between Western European and Korean companies than it found between practices in the two industries. This study is just one of many that should be done in order to better understand the international environment of business.

The authors surveyed companies in each industry in South Korea and in a spectrum of Western European companies. Because Korea's is an emerging economy, European companies are showing considerable interest in engaging in joint ventures and combined operations, as well as traditional sourcing arrangements. The response to their mailed questionnaire was discouraging, so the researchers made follow-up visits and conducted telephone interviews. The final survey sample included 34 European and 33 Korean textile companies, and 24 European and 89 Korean machine tool makers. The researchers judged the participants to be representative of industry practice in each locale. Some of the nonfashion textile makers were vertically integrated, with spinning, weaving, and sewing operations. Others were involved in only one process. The small machine tool makers produced small drill presses, mills, and other metal-forming machines.

In several areas the differences in manufacturing practices were not dramatic. Korean companies had slightly fewer employees but substantially lower overall sales and investment in production equipment. This difference meant that the Korean companies in both industries had lower sales output per employee and lower investment in technology per employee. Korean companies were engaged in produce-to-order arrangements slightly more often than were the Western Europeans. Capacity utilization was almost the same in each region and between industries. Both regions exported approximately 25 percent of textile production, but machine tool exports were only 14 percent of the Korean production versus a more aggressive 32 percent for the Europeans. In the area of production planning the European companies appeared to consider available capacity more heavily in planning, whereas the order backlog and forecast of demand were more significant inputs for Korean managers. The production plans were produced by more senior managers using computer technology in Europe; Korean production plans were constructed by lower levels of management. This important distinction indicates that when negotiating a revision of production plans in multinational operations, individuals at very different levels of the organizations would probably be involved.

The individuals to whom they report and the criteria for shop-floor decision making are frequently different as well. In Korean companies production personnel decide when to release orders to the shop and establish the production sequences, but the criteria they use are definitely market and customer oriented. They typically communicate plans to the shop floor in writing. In the European sample, marketing or general management established the rules for order release

---

[7]Boo-Ho Rho and D. Clay Whybark, "Comparing Manufacturing and Control Practices in Europe and Korea," *International Journal of Production Research* 28 (December 1990): 2393–2404. Reproduced with permission of Taylor & Francis, Inc., Washington, D.C.

and sequencing, but used the criteria of processing time required and availability of material to establish the priorities.

In terms of performance Korean companies had higher mean lateness versus planned lead times and delivery promises, but the worst cases of lateness were more common in European companies. Typically, the reasons given for order lateness were also different. In Europe lateness was usually the result of labor unavailability or inflexibility; Korean companies usually cited a capacity limitation or quality concerns. European companies tend to use back orders to smooth production planning, whereas hiring and/or firing are more typical in South Korea.

In broad terms the production decision makers and the criteria they use are different and may be a confounding factor in joint operations. More important, the labor inflexibility in Europe seems to require greater investment in technology to meet production schedules. Labor flexibility provides a buffer to the less-capitalized Korean companies.

## ► Summary

Shop-floor control involves the process of executing production plans. This execution requires the manager to determine the best routing for jobs and to release orders to the shop when appropriate. SFC is also responsible for tracking the progress of jobs, reporting on status when it is needed, and providing measures to assess performance of the facility.

**Learning Objective 1: Discuss the key activities of shop-floor control in continuous, repetitive, and job shop operations.** In both continuous and repetitive operations the key activities of SFC include routine reporting of the status of the system and accurate prediction of the ability of the system to meet order requirements on time. The shop floor is organized to help ensure a steady flow of materials. In the much more complex, batch-oriented job shop operations, SFC is extremely complex. Key activities include determining lead times for order-promising purposes, determining the best route for a job to follow through the shop, and determining when to release jobs to the shop. The manager does all this while attempting to minimize congestion yet provide high utilization of people and machinery. Also important are the order-tracking and performance assessment activities of SFC.

**Learning Objective 2: Describe the difference between a job's planned lead time and its flow time.** The planned lead time is the estimated time that a job will spend in the shop. It is an estimate because it must be determined before the job is ever started. Managers often use planned lead time to quote promised dates to customers or determine whether they should accept the job, given the customer's specified due date. The job's flow time is the amount of time that it actually took to complete the job, including its processing times and all delays.

**Learning Objective 3: Describe the negative effects of high levels of work-in-process inventories.** WIP represents a commitment of raw material and processing time that have not yet generated cash flow. High levels of WIP also negatively affect flow times and lessen a company's flexibility in responding to changing customer needs. More WIP also increases congestion on the shop floor, which results in more confusion in an already complex environment.

**Learning Objective 4: Describe the measures of shop performance that are best served by SPT and EDD scheduling rules.** The rule for shortest processing time provides the minimum average flow time for the single-machine situation. It also works well for measuring shop congestion by keeping down the average number of jobs in the system. The rule for earliest due date works well for minimizing the maximum lateness of jobs in the system. It also minimizes the variance of lateness.

**Learning Objective 5: Construct Gantt charts to illustrate sequencing a set of jobs.** Once managers have determined which sequencing rule to apply, they perform the required calculations. Next, they sequence the jobs according to the chosen rule and determine the individual start and finish times for the job. Then they draw a horizontal bar chart with the time dimension across the bottom of the chart. They mark on the time line the start and finish times of the sequenced jobs. The finish time of the last job in the sequence will be the flow time for all jobs.

**Learning Objective 6: Describe the steps of Johnson's rule, and identify situations to which it is applicable.** Johnson's rule is applicable whenever a manager must sequence multiple jobs through two processing stations; the manager must determine the sequence for each job through each station, and the processes are always performed in the same order. For example, many processes include the sanding and painting of newly manufactured products. Never are they painted and then sanded. The manager would set up the steps in the procedure by first identifying the job with the shortest processing time, regardless of which process it is on. If the manager finds that one job will be in the first process for the least amount of time, it gets priority on the schedule. If the manager finds that one job will be in the last process for the least amount of time, it is scheduled to go through that process last. The manager sequences all other jobs for processing until all are sequenced.

**Learning Objective 7: Discuss the key performance measures promoted by the theory of constraints.** The first key performance measure is throughput, which is the rate at which the system generates money through sales. Throughput is not simply output. The second measure is inventory, which is the money invested in things the organization plans to or could sell. The third measure is operating expense, which is the money spent to transform inventory into throughput. The objective of TOC is to maximize throughput while minimizing inventory and operating expense.

## ► Key Terms

| | | |
|---|---|---|
| alternative routings | flow time | synchronous manufacturing |
| bottleneck operation | Johnson's rule | theory of constraints (TOC) |
| completion date | lead time | throughput |
| cycle time | operation processing time | transfer lots |
| delivery date | *Optimized Production Technology (OPT)* | utilization |
| drum-buffer-rope (DBR) | planned lead time | |

## ► Discussion Questions

1. What is shop-floor control, and what are its major subfunctions?
2. Under what conditions should a company refuse a customer's order?
3. Distinguish between planned and actual lead time. How would you use the difference between planned and actual lead times to adjust the delay multiplier?
4. What is the definition of a job? an order? a production lot? a transfer lot? flow time?
5. What are some typical performance measures for job shop floor control? Under what situations might each one be appropriate?
6. Why is it important to reduce work-in-process inventory? to reduce queue time?
7. Your local dry cleaner always specifies a three-day lead time, no matter the size of the order that you bring in. Other businesses also use this constant lead time policy. Suggest a reason that this is true.
8. How is the principal task of the shop-floor control manager in continuous, repetitive, and job shop operations linked to the skill and decision making expected of the workers?
9. Concurrent operations processing uses transfer lots. Explain what transfer lots are and why they are used.
10. Which sequencing rules are applicable to job shop operations? What are the advantages and disadvantages of each?
11. Under what conditions can managers apply Johnson's sequencing rule?
12. Describe a service application to which the principles of the theory of constraints could be applied.

# ► Problems

1. Apply Johnson's algorithm to the following jobs that require sanding and then staining in a woodworking job shop:

| Job | Sanding | Staining |
|-----|---------|----------|
| a | 35 minutes | 25 minutes |
| b | 32 | 58 |
| c | 20 | 20 |
| d | 12 | 7 |
| e | 0 | 25 |
| f | 80 | 65 |

Construct a Gantt chart for the sequence that you recommend. What is the total flow time for these jobs? What can you conclude about the sequence position of job f?

2. All incoming jobs require processing through two operations. Operation 1 must be done first, and there is no set-up time between jobs on either operation. Consider the estimated processing times (in hours) for following seven jobs:

| Job | Operation 1 | Operation 2 |
|-----|-------------|-------------|
| A | 4.5 | 1.5 |
| B | 2.0 | 5.0 |
| C | 6.0 | 3.5 |
| D | 1.5 | 6.5 |
| E | 0.8 | 1.0 |
| F | 3.0 | 0.5 |
| G | 5.5 | 6.0 |

a. What sequence gets the jobs out of the shop as quickly as possible?
b. How long will it take all 7 jobs to go through the first operation?
c. When will all the jobs be completely finished?

3. Ace Furniture Refinishers uses a 3 step process to refinish wooden furniture. Items are first dipped in chemicals for exactly 30 minutes to remove the old finish. They are then sanded and stained. The four orders that follow should be processed today. Remember, there is no easy way to schedule three operations. How should they be sequenced? Why?

| Job | Dip | Sand | Stain (in minutes) |
|-----|-----|------|--------------------|
| a | 30 | 15 | 20 |
| b | 30 | 5 | 10 |
| c | 30 | 40 | 80 |
| d | 30 | 90 | 50 |

4. The following data pertain to five jobs that are waiting to be processed:

| Job | Processing Time | Due Date (Days from Now) |
|-----|-----------------|--------------------------|
| A | 5 | 6 |
| B | 18 | 22 |
| C | 10 | 9 |
| D | 7 | 7 |
| E | 9 | 15 |

Use each of the following rules to develop a sequence for the jobs:
a. Earliest due date
b. Shortest processing time
c. Critical ratio
Which method would you say is best? Why?

5. The following data pertain to 6 jobs that are waiting to be processed:

| Job | Processing Time | Due Date (Days from Now) |
|-----|-----------------|--------------------------|
| A | 4 | 8 |
| B | 6 | 35 |
| C | 5 | 20 |
| D | 12 | 17 |
| E | 8 | 15 |
| F | 6 | 18 |

a. Evaluate the first-come, first-served (FCFS) sequence of jobs using the average lateness and maximum lateness criteria.
b. Evaluate the sequence using average flow time.
c. Would you expect FCFS to perform well on either of these performance measures? Why or why not?

6. Resequence the jobs from problem 5 by using shortest processing time (SPT).
a. Use average and maximum lateness criteria to evaluate this sequence.
b. Compare these results with those obtained using FCFS. Are these results surprising? Why or why not?

7. Use earliest due date (EDD) to resequence the jobs from problem 5.
a. Use average and maximum lateness criteria to evaluate this sequence.
b. Compare these results with those obtained from the SPT schedule and the FCFS schedule. Are these results what you expected? Why or why not?
c. Use average flow time to evaluate this sequence.
d. Compare this result with that obtained using SPT. Is this what you expected? Why or why not?

**8.** Use the following data to respond to problems 8a–c:

| Job | Processing Time | Due Date (Days from Now) |
|-----|------|------|
| A | 15 | 30 |
| B | 7 | 15 |
| C | 12 | 45 |
| D | 9 | 20 |
| E | 6 | 10 |

**a.** Calculate the slack time remaining for each job. Use the SLACK rule to determine a schedule for them.

**b.** Calculate the critical ratio for each job. Use the critical ratio rule to schedule these jobs.

**c.** How would you expect these sequences to compare with those that SPT and EDD, using the average and maximum lateness criteria, would yield? using the criterion of average flow time?

**9.** For the following five jobs, is there any schedule that will allow all the jobs to be finished on time? If so, write the schedule. If not, explain why scheduling these jobs for on-time completion is impossible.

| Job | Processing Time | Due Date (Days from Now) |
|-----|------|------|
| A | 15 | 40 |
| B | 10 | 30 |
| C | 20 | 60 |
| D | 12 | 55 |
| E | 9 | 25 |

**10.** Use the following data to respond to problems 10a–c:

| Job | Processing Time | Due Date (Days from Now) |
|-----|------|------|
| A | 10 | 16 |
| B | 6 | 12 |
| C | 20 | 48 |
| D | 16 | 40 |

**a.** Determine the job sequence using FCFS, SPT, and EDD. Draw a Gantt chart for each sequencing rule.

**b.** Rate each sequence on average flow time, average number of jobs in system, average lateness, and maximum lateness.

**c.** Which sequencing rule would you recommend? Why?

# ► Selected References

Gunn, Thomas. *Manufacturing for Competitive Advantage: Becoming a World-Class Manufacturer.* Cambridge, Mass.: Ballinger, 1987.

Kaplan, Robert S., ed. *Measures for Manufacturing Excellence.* Boston: Harvard Business School Press, 1990.

Melnyk, Steven, Philip Carter, David Dilts, and David Lyth. *Shop Floor Control.* Homewood, Ill.: Dow Jones-Irwin, 1985.

Schonberger, Richard. *World Class Manufacturing.* New York: Free Press, 1989.

Umble, M., and M. L. Srikanth. *Synchronous Manufacturing.* Cincinnati: South-Western Publishing, 1990.

Vollmann, Thomas, William Berry, and D. Clay Whybark. *Manufacturing Planning and Control Systems*, 2d ed. Homewood, Ill.: Richard D. Irwin, 1988.

# Hoops University

Basketball tickets are in short supply at Hoops University, a private institution in North Carolina. The university can never accommodate student demand for tickets, and the administration is concerned about the image of Hoops U on the nightly news: Thousands of undergraduates are camping out in front of the Hoop-Dome to be eligible for tickets on a first-come, first-served basis. Administrators also are concerned about the health and safety of the waiting students and are sensitive to students' complaints that student-rate tickets are being scalped.

The administrators have tried or discussed and dismissed a variety of plans for distributing tickets. Hoops wants to get the limited number of tickets to the students who want to attend the game. The administrators think that some rotation of tickets might eliminate the camping out, but they are having trouble figuring out how to make the rotation fair. Students continue to arrive throughout the night and early morning. Some break into the queue to join their friends. There have been a few nasty confrontations.

As students studying operations management at Hoops, you have been asked to devise a scheme for prioritizing the "orders" in this queue in a way that will be acceptable and fair to most students and will eliminate the need to spend the night out in cold winter weather. What sort of dispatching rule would you devise? What are the key criteria underlying your rule? What would be the principal criticism of your rule?

## CHAPTER 16

# Just-in-Time Production

*Our production cycle is about 81 hours from the mine to the finished machine in the freight car, or 3 days and 9 hours instead of the 14 days which we used to think was record breaking.*

HENRY FORD, *TODAY AND TOMORROW, 1926*

**Introduction**

**Just-in-Time Production**
*OPERATIONS MANAGEMENT IN PRACTICE 16.1: Back from the Future—Gearing Up for the Productivity Challenge*
*OPERATIONS MANAGEMENT IN PRACTICE 16.2: Just-in-Time at Acme Manufacturing*

**Total Business Cycle Management**

**Managing Material Flows**

**Just-in-Time System Requirements**
*OPERATIONS MANAGEMENT IN PRACTICE 16.3: Some Manufacturers Drop Efforts to Adopt Japanese Techniques*

**Implementation of Just-in-Time**

**Coordinating JIT and Material Requirements Planning**

# Introduction

Corporate strategies developed over the last several decades have reflected the importance of many measures of corporate performance. None has been as important or as comprehensive as the measure of time. The ability of an operation to respond quickly and effectively to changing markets or customers' wishes may mean the difference between long-term success and failure. Today's leading companies manage the time required to accomplish many diverse organizational tasks. These range from such complex tasks as new product and strategy development to simpler tasks such as processing expense vouchers and setting up a production machine. For the leading companies time has become the most powerful source of competitive advantage.

Many readers may find this discussion familiar. For example, our description of total quality management in Chapter 7 discussed the renewed focus on internal and external customer satisfaction through continuous process improvement. The improvement of a process often involves reducing the cycle time required to complete the process. But time is only one of the many measures of process improvement. In this chapter our concern is specifically the use of time for measuring the effectiveness of efforts to ensure excellent customer satisfaction and long-term competitiveness. We will talk about how to cut cycle times for all types of processes by identifying and eliminating waste. Some manufacturing organizations use the term **short-cycle manufacturing** to describe their philosophy of continuously improving cycle times by eliminating waste. Hypothetically, an organization that achieves the shortest cycle times possible would be doing things just in time.

A just-in-time (JIT) system is one manifestation of the operational task of eliminating waste and increasing the productive use of resources. At its extreme it portrays an organization that is totally devoid of inventories and able to respond immediately to changing market conditions. This ideal state will continue to be a target for American businesses but a reality for only a select few. JIT is essentially a system of beliefs and attitudes, combined with a collection of methods and procedures, all of which are shaped into a general management philosophy that describes how an operation should be managed. Whenever we refer to JIT as a *system* in this book, we are referring to this system of beliefs and attitudes. It is not a physical system such as computer hardware or software, which can be implemented and used.

Since the introduction of the JIT philosophy in this country in the 1970s, it has met with mixed reviews. Some believe it's the panacea that American industry has needed, whereas some believe that it's simply the next "strategy du jour." Many of those who have doubts about the potential of such a concept may not fully understand it. It is very important that the management philosophy known as JIT be better understood.

# Just-in-Time Production

Although most implementations of the JIT philosophy have been reported in manufacturing operations, the philosophy applies equally to any type of productive operation. Almost everyone produces something, be it computer hardware or software, hamburgers, financial reports, marketing plans, new strategic focuses, or whatever. Many people refer to the JIT philosophy as *JIT manufacturing*, but we call it *JIT production* to reflect the broad view of the concept. Companies that have earned the true benefits of JIT implementation have adopted it as the perspective of the entire organization rather than focusing only on improving manufacturing operations. After all, quality products manufactured in the most efficient and productive means possible, but not delivered on time because of transportation problems, do not contribute to excellent customer satisfaction. It is the overall buying experience, from the very first contact between supplier and customer to the very last contact, that determines the customer's perception of satisfaction. Just-in-time systems attempt to increase the flexibility and responsiveness between suppliers and customers (both internal and external) in order to eliminate waste and improve customer satisfaction and overall competitiveness. Operations Management in Practice 16.1 describes the experiences of one company that has used JIT to improve its competitive position.

# Origins of JIT Philosophy

More than any other single source the Japanese auto manufacturer Toyota is generally accepted as the originator of JIT concepts and methods. Toyota developed a manufacturing control system that is responsive and productive. In order to succeed Toyota had to secure the cooperation of its suppliers and distribution system. Because of this, many concepts that originated at Toyota spread through Japanese manufacturing practice, with each company making adjustments and improvements to the system. Today these JIT ideas are commonly referred to as *Japanese manufacturing techniques*.

But as the epigraph at the beginning of this chapter indicates, Henry Ford in the 1920s understood and practiced many concepts since designated as JIT concepts. Ford considered digging ore out of the ground the initial process of his automobile assembly operation. His complete material flow consisted of converting the ore into steel, stamping out parts for his cars, assembling the cars, and shipping the cars by rail to the ultimate customers. He constantly worked to improve this material flow, cutting the cycle time, and eliminating waste to improve productivity. His comment, "Our production cycle is about 81 hours from the mine to the finished machine in the freight car, or 3 days and 9 hours instead of the 14 days which we used to think was record breaking," describes his

# Back from the Future: Gearing Up for the Productivity Challenge

In 1987, managers at Tektronix, a diversified manufacturer of high technology equipment, realized that the product lines in their most profitable division were in danger of losing market share to competitors, both foreign and domestic. Knowing that it had to improve efficiency and reduce the cost of manufacturing, the company had already adopted JIT principles in its manufacturing operations. However, improvements in manufacturing alone were not going to be sufficient. The company also had to reduce the time it took a product to go from the concept stage to the marketplace. This meant applying the JIT philosophy to the firm's engineering division.

Tektronix's engineers were already committed to designing complex, high-quality products in the shortest time possible. But, as any engineer will attest, it is difficult to design according to a timetable. Also, there are many factors outside an engineer's control which make it harder to adhere to a schedule. To help overcome these difficulties, Tektronix selected a critical engineering project and assembled a cross-functional team of 30 people. These individuals then decided on their goal: to complete their design effort (normally a 24 month activity) in 12 months. To achieve this goal would require an entirely new design process. In formulating this new process, the team determined that the following five factors were the most critical in determining their success.

*Extraordinary Teamwork*: In order to achieve such a lofty goal, team members abandoned an "us vs. them" mentality and instead worked together towards the common goal. This spirit of teamwork extended beyond the team's border to include vendors—who were given desks in the teams project area—and management—which responded with a stated commitment to the team's efforts.

*Effective Communication*: The team discovered that talk is not cheap; what people say reveals what they think. Communication is the vehicle through which teamwork is accomplished. Improved communication dramatically improved the effectiveness of the team's meetings—they became shorter and more productive.

*Innovation*: To adhere to its ambitious schedule, the team developed new methods of dealing with prototypes. Designs were perfected as much as possible and then released. Needed changes were then applied to the next design. The constant updating created a new dynamism—and massive, month-long efforts to update prototypes were replaced by delivery of new designs every 2–3 weeks.

*View Obstacles as Occasions for Creativity*: When faced by an insurmountable obstacle, the team found new ways to proceed. For instance, the team discovered late in the project that the equipment used to measure key components was not capable of handling the new design, and there was no time to develop a new measurement device. However, a team member found a simple modification of the existing device did the trick. Not only was the team able to proceed, but a new marketing opportunity for the modified part was created.

*Coaching*: In athletics, the role of the coach is critical. But coaching is usually missing from the business environment. The Tektronix team members realized that coaching was essential to their support structure, which required that all team members succeed, and decided to coach each other. Team members found themselves surrounded not by critics, but by coaches. They learned to listen to each other and view coaching positively rather than defensively.

concern for total cycle time. Some believe that the Japanese learned their concept of JIT from the early experiences of Henry Ford.

## JIT Misunderstandings and Myths

Regardless of the origins of the JIT philosophy, it is a very important topic in today's manufacturing and service environments and one that is often misunderstood. Over the years industry has used such terms as *stockless production, kanban, zero inventories,* and many others to describe the activities associated with JIT. The plethora of terms has contributed little to understanding the philosophy and sometimes has contributed to the lack of understanding. Proponents of JIT point to several specific misunderstandings that tend to lessen the success of JIT usage. They include

- Thinking of JIT as a physical system to be implemented, rather than a management philosophy to be adopted
- Thinking of JIT as simply an inventory control system
- Thinking of JIT as strictly a management approach for manufacturers

Throughout this chapter we will address these misunderstandings and others. But first let's consider the improvements that a business can expect from a successful implementation of the JIT philosophy.

## Motivation for JIT Implementation

The number of JIT implementations in this country has been limited. Why? If it makes so much sense to reduce cycle times in order to become more responsive and provide better customer satisfaction, why is everyone not looking to JIT as the way of the future?

American companies have found meeting the competitive challenge presented by many international industries, including those in Japan, difficult. Understanding the economic development of Japan is an important factor in understanding the motivation that drives this approach to waste- and error-free operations. You have learned that the cost of carrying inventory is actually several categories of costs, including maintaining storage space and the opportunity that is lost when you trade a very liquid asset such as money for raw material, work-in-process, or finished goods inventory. Japan is a small country that lacks significant wealth in natural resources. The space that U.S. companies frequently devote to inventory storage is much more expensive in Japan. Similarly, the Japanese government was involved in directing the distribution of scarce capital in the developing postwar economy to companies that were producing products efficiently.

The companies could achieve high productivity by producing defect-free products and by minimizing the time required to produce a product from raw material and components to a finished product for sale. Doing this required coordination, training, and commitment from each member of the organization. The JIT philosophy included each of these elements: coordinating production schedules, producing defect-free products by using superior product and process designs, and gaining the involvement and commitment of people.

The specific practices used by Japanese companies reflect their culture and traditions. Because implementing the just-in-time philosophy is difficult, non-

# Just-in-Time at Acme Manufacturing

Acme manufacturing is a fictitious name for a company which was founded as an "oil tool" company in 1921. Acme's facilities include plants in Texas, Michigan, and Livingston, Scotland. Combined, they provide over 1.5 million square feet of administration, engineering, and manufacturing space.

During the last quarter of 1990, Acme management became aware that a change was needed in the way business was conducted. Inventories were climbing, cycle times were getting longer, and customers were showing signs of dismay. A major customer told Acme that by 1993, it was going to expect four-week deliveries of product after placement of a purchase order. If Acme was going to continue serving that customer, it was going to have to do something. At that time the average cycle time on products was 13 weeks which meant a 70 percent reduction would be required.

Around that same time, two of Acme's major customers, General Electric and Pratt & Whitney introduced it to the philosophy of JIT manufacturing. In January, 1991, a team of major managers from Acme participated in a five-day workshop on JIT education and implementation. Acme management hired the consulting firm which had put on the training workshop to help Acme implement JIT. By August 1991, the majority of Acme employees had been involved in some form of JIT training.

In order to achieve the 70 percent reduction in cycle times, an aggressive approach was initiated. Calculations were made to determine the minimum lead time (excluding queue time) for each manufactured part. These times became the beginning point for the improvement efforts. Aggressive target cycle times were established and periodic checks were performed on lead times to assess progress. Whenever it appeared that the shops were coming close to meeting the target cycle time, management established new target goals. Through these incremental improvements, Acme had realized a 39 percent reduction in cycle times by early 1993.

During the same period that cycle times were dropping, inventory levels at Acme steadily decreased. Inventory dropped from $54 million in January 1991 to $37 million in December 1991. The reduction in inventory was attributed to smaller batch sizes, better control of raw-material inventory, and frequent shipments of product to the customer. Inventory levels were expected to drop to $29 million by December 1992.

Continuous process improvement teams at Acme were activated to continue looking for areas to improve. Employee morale has improved and the amount of rework is continuing to decline due to increased quality.

Japanese companies that were frustrated in their attempts occasionally cited the homogeneity of Japanese society and American pride in individual versus group achievement as reasons that JIT would not work for them. Once American companies had greater experience in implementing JIT, they recognized the cultural differences were unique opportunities for implementing JIT in different societies. The underlying principles are not culturally dependent.

A summary of the motivations for JIT production would include

- Reducing raw material, purchased parts, work-in-process, and finished goods inventories
- Increasing the productivity of direct labor employees
- Improving the utilization of equipment on products that will be deployed quickly
- Producing defect-free and well-designed products
- Improving the company's responsiveness to changing markets and customers' requirements

Operations Management in Practice 16.2 relates the experiences of an organization through the early stages of JIT implementation.

How can JIT offer such dramatic improvements to organizations? To answer this question we must consider the more fundamental issue of time and how it affects the competitiveness of a company. This will provide a better foundation for understanding the JIT philosophy.

## Total Business Cycle Management

A company's **total business cycle** is the time that elapses between the identification and satisfaction of a customer's need and receipt of payment. It is sometimes referred to as the *cash flow cycle*, because the company spends money on a customer's order from order entry through procurement of raw material and component parts, production, and distribution of the final product. The company does not complete the cash flow cycle until it receives payment for the product or service. Figure 16.1 illustrates the cash flow cycle for a simplified supplier-customer experience.

The figure illustrates several key subcycles of a company's total business cycle. When a customer's order arrives, two important things happen. First, the cycle clock begins to tick, reflecting the time elapsed since the order came in.

FIGURE 16.1
Overall Cash Flow Cycle

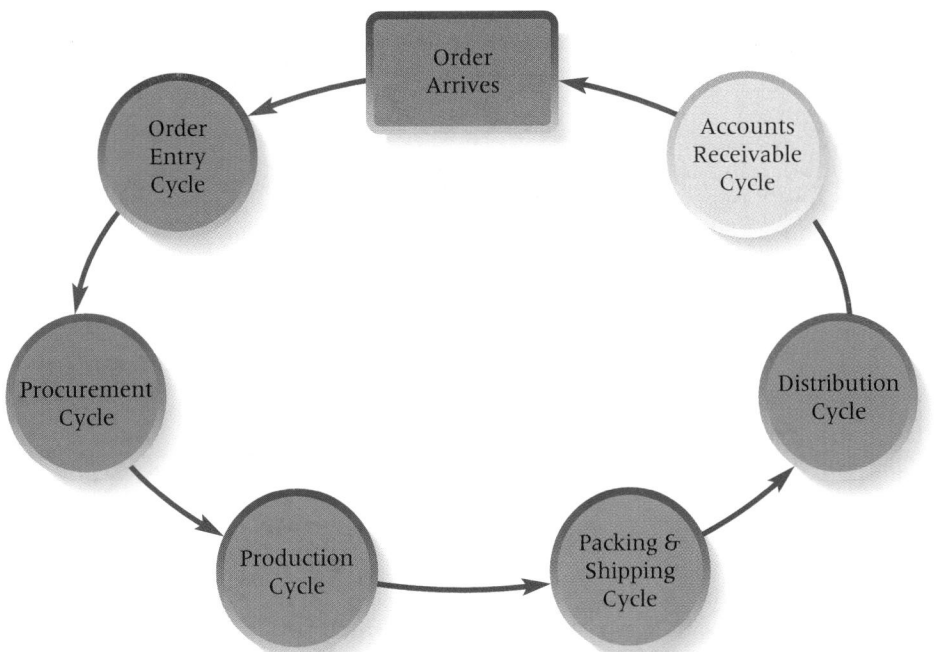

*Land's End is able to provide excellent customer satisfaction partly because of its well trained customer service staff. Customers' perception of quality is affected by every contact with company personnel from order entry staff to delivery and service personnel.*

Second, the company spends money on labor, material, and overhead to complete the order.

During the order entry cycle those involved in the process can track the average amount of time required to process an order. The tracking may be nearly instantaneous, as in a computer-oriented process, or may take days, as in a paper-oriented process. Either way, it is the responsibility of the order entry function to manage and continue to improve its cycle in order to support overall cycle reduction.

Part of the order entry process is notifying the procurement function of the new order so the procurement cycle may begin. Personnel in the procurement area may now look at what raw material and component parts will be required, determine which vendors to call for parts, and complete the purchasing process. They should maintain data on vendors' performance. The procurement area is responsible for establishing long-term relationships with vendors in order to cut procurement lead time and variability.

In a manufacturing environment the production cycle is usually the longest element of the overall business cycle. It is often called the *work-in-process (WIP) cycle.* It is measured from the time material is drawn from raw material stores and brought to the manufacturing floor until the finished product is placed in finished goods inventory. Manufacturing and engineering personnel usually are responsible for continually reducing the production or WIP cycle. In some repetitive manufacturing processes 90 percent of the total production cycle has turned out to be wasted time. An order is actually being worked on the production floor only 10 percent of the time. This implies excellent opportunities for improvement.

Once the product is produced to customer specifications, the packing and shipping cycle begins. Here the finished product is checked against the customer's order for quantity and quality, packaged, and shipped through the appropriate distribution channel. The distribution cycle is essentially the time required to transport the product through the channels of distribution to the customer. The selection of transportation type is partially a function of how well the overall cycle has been managed to that point. If unanticipated delays jeopardize the on-time delivery status of the order, the company may have to use extra fast transportation methods that result in higher transportation costs than the company expected.

At this point in the cycle the customer's order has been delivered, it is hoped on-time. The cycle clock stops ticking now, but the overall cash flow cycle is not yet complete. The customer has the usual time period to pay the invoice. The customer and supplier usually negotiate the duration of this accounts receivable cycle.

A company's total business cycle includes other critical cycles. For example, a company's **new product development cycle** is the time required to identify a new need in the marketplace and satisfy that need. A **new strategy development cycle**, the time required to develop a new strategy and complete its implementation, also might be part of the total business cycle.

# Managing Material Flows

In the ideal operation material would flow almost uninterrupted throughout the process. The material would stop only for value-adding activities. Whether the material is paperwork, information, products, or whatever, the concept remains the same. Time-based companies consider anything that interrupts the flow of material as a problem to be addressed and eliminated if possible. This definition of a problem would include partially completed products that are waiting for a machine to be set up, paperwork awaiting a signature, and any item waiting for approval, inspection, or engineering direction. Many activities considered problems under this definition are traditionally thought of as standard operating procedure and simply accepted as "givens" for the organization. Time-based companies challenge these givens—they recognize that they do not have to be given.

*Storage areas stacked to the ceiling with all types of inventory are expensive and often not needed.*

# Set-up Reduction and the EOQ Lot Size

Consider, for example, machine set-up times. If a changeover usually requires eight workers per hour to complete at $10 per worker per hour, and the changeover requires no material, a rough estimate of the cost of a set-up would be $80. (Assuming that set-up personnel are hourly workers.) Many companies would accept this information as given and simply plug the information, along with demand, production, and carrying cost data, into the economic lot size model developed in Chapter 12. The result would be the optimal lot size to produce.

Let's consider the effect of a particular lot size on the effectiveness of a time-conscious manufacturing operation. Suppose your repetitive manufacturing operation includes six processing steps, and your lot size calculation indicates the optimal lot size is one thousand units. If the lot size is to remain intact and each processing step has similar capacity, you will have one thousand units of work in process between each processing step. What does all this mean?

- Storing all this WIP will take large amounts of valuable floor space and may create a safety hazard.
- Financial investment in WIP inventory will be high.
- Because the production cycle time is the average amount of time that it takes one unit to work its way through the entire system, cycle time will be relatively long.

- The long production cycle time will result in decreased ability to respond to changes in customers' requirements.
- Workers who have to work around all the clutter caused by the excessive inventory may damage the product while moving it from place to place.
- If a processing problem is detected, the company may have to rework or scrap many units, increasing the cost of the units.

Suppose you could make changes that which would allow the lot size to be one hundred units rather than one thousand. WIP and its financial investment would decrease, as would the cycle time and the requirement for valuable floor space. Quality would increase, and costs of rework and scrap would drop. Most important, your time-sensitive company would increase its ability to respond to an increasingly demanding customer base. What if your lot size were ten or, ideally, one? How could you do this?

Consider again the formula that we developed in Chapter 12 for determining the economic lot size:

$$Q^* = \sqrt{\frac{2DC_s}{C_H}} \sqrt{\frac{p}{p-u}}$$

If you want to reduce the economic lot size $Q^*$, your only viable alternative is to reduce $C_s$, the set-up cost. The nonviable alternatives include reducing demand ($D$), increasing carrying cost ($C_H$), and increasing the production rate ($p$). By

FIGURE 16.2
Rocks in the Materials River

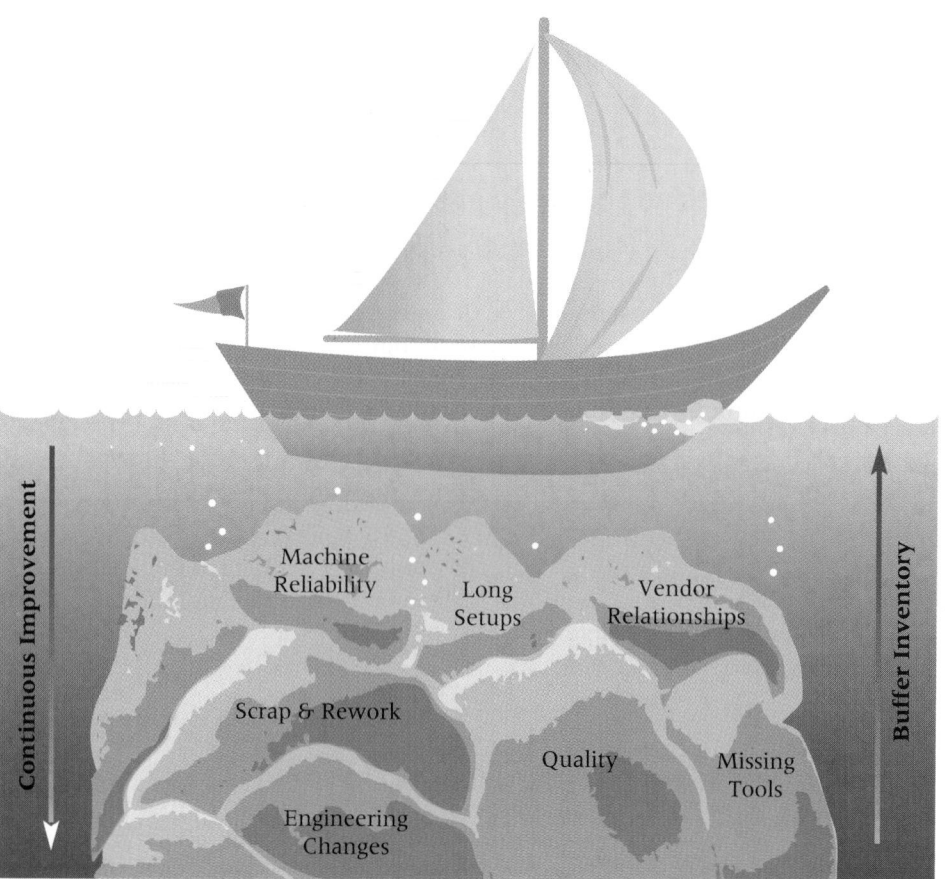

forming an improvement team and focusing on the current set-up process, you can reduce the time required to for set-up. These improvement efforts often quickly result in a 50 percent reduction in set-up time. The set-up time reduction procedures outlined in Chapter 15 have proved extremely useful. So the advantages of not accepting set-up times as given, and working toward continuous improvement of those times, are considerable.

## Inventory Reduction Caution

We need to sound one note of caution about reducing inventory. Most organizations hold inventory because of inherent uncertainties caused by operational problems. Companies hold raw material and component parts inventories because their suppliers may not perform as expected and because customers often change their minds. Companies hold finished goods because customer demand is uncertain or production yields are unexpectedly high. They hold work-in-process inventories because of problems with the production process. WIP builds because of low-quality products, long machine set-up times, large lot sizes, poor machine reliability, frequent engineering changes, frequent product rework, missing tools, and many other reasons. In each case companies are holding inventory as a buffer against the effects of the problem. So, as long as the problems exist, the company needs the inventory. The first step in reducing inventories is identifying the problems.

Many people use the term *rocks in the materials river* to refer to those problems that lead companies to hold inventory. As Figure 16.2 shows, the complete material flow is the river, and the operations area is the boat sailing on the river. The river bottom is not smooth; it is full of jagged rocks waiting to tear the bottom off the boat. To prevent this the captain sails the boat only in water deep enough to cover the dangerous rocks. In this metaphor the rocks are the operational problems and the water is the buffer inventory (raw material, WIP, and finished goods), which protects the organization from the problems. What the company needs is continuous amelioration of the problems so that it can reduce the "water level" systematically. To arbitrarily reduce inventory just for the sake of doing so may expose the organization to problems that will slow customer deliveries.

One useful way to illustrate WIP buildup specifically is by describing the productive operation as a funnel. As Figure 16.3 shows, work comes into a work area for processing at some particular rate. The input rate of work and the capacity of the work area essentially determine the rate at which finished work exits the work area. The small neck of the funnel represents the various problems that restrict the flow of product through the facility. It is easy to see that the company needs to balance the input rate and output rate. If inputs are too fast for the capacity of the operation, the funnel will fill up with WIP. Cycle time for the operation would be the average amount of time that an item needs for entering the work area, being processed, and exiting the work area.

Some managers believe that you can get a higher rate of output by increasing the rate of input. As the illustration shows, the only way to get sustainable increases in output rate is to expand the neck of the funnel—that is, continually identify those problems that are restricting the flow of work through the work area, and develop long-term solutions to those problems. Step by step, the flow of work would increase. As we noted earlier, the funnel for the ideal operation would have a top equal in size to its neck, implying a flow of material through

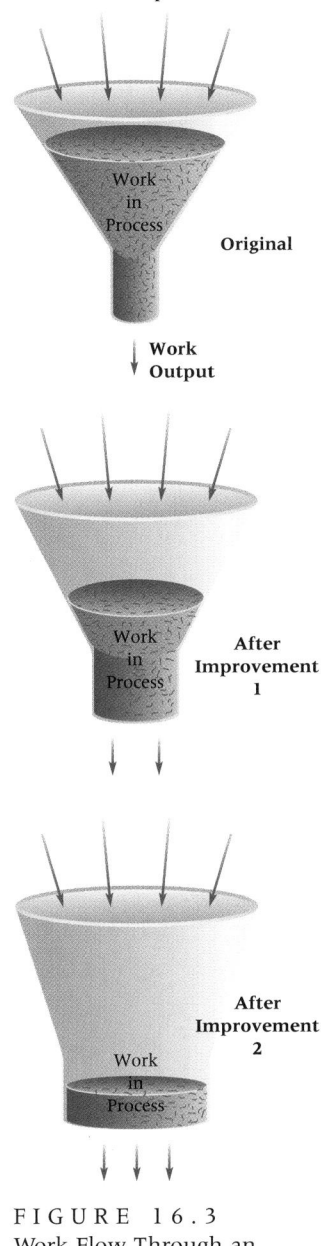

FIGURE 16.3
Work Flow Through an Operation

the work area. Very short cycle time, very low investment in WIP, and high levels of responsiveness would characterize the improved work area. It is this continued focus on identifying and eliminating the bottlenecks that characterizes the JIT approach and creates reference to JIT as *enforced problem solving*. Greater responsiveness and flexibility, not "just-in-case" inventory investment, address operational uncertainty.

## Just-in-Time System Requirements

The ideal JIT production system is able to respond to changing market demand for products by having the flexibility to produce exactly what is needed. Market-driven waste-free production is substantially different from the logic that drove much of manufacturing management for most of the twentieth century. The former "science of production" stated that a technology was set up to perform a certain operation and that it should produce large lots of identical parts. It saw frequent changes in production as a waste of potential production time. Once workers were making a repetitively produced item, mistakes were less likely and they were not wasting time in changing the tooling and fixtures on a machine to produce different items. An economically "efficient" lot of production was based in large part on the idea of spreading the cost and production time lost to changeovers over a large number of units. Upon completion, the company stacked in a warehouse in anticipation of future demand any units from the large lots that were not required for production. The "science of manufacturing" was probably appropriate for that particular time in history, when many industries faced only limited competition.

International competitive forces have caused organizations to challenge the old manufacturing logic. The new logic of JIT manufacturing attacks the assumption that changeover is necessarily a costly, time-consuming process. To respond to changing demand patterns companies need to develop methods of quickly changing production from one product to another. The requirements for JIT implementation include

- Production flexibility at every stage of supply
- Stability and flexibility in scheduling
- Comprehensive quality assurance
- Teams of competent, empowered employees who promote trust, commitment, and open communication
- A "signaling" system to pull production
- A logistics system to support JIT delivery

Each requirement is critical to the successful implementation of the JIT philosophy.

### Production Flexibility Along the Supply Chain

While implementing JIT, some large powerful companies have simply demanded that their suppliers make more frequent and smaller shipments of material. Their approach to inventory reduction is to push back to their suppliers the inventory that they normally would carry. These companies mistakenly think of JIT as a specific approach to reducing inventories, and they have irritated many important suppliers. A long-term JIT relationship is not likely to develop if the company buying parts or material simply requires its suppliers to maintain inventory and ship it when it needs it. To sustain JIT each channel member along the supply chain of buyers and sellers must develop the flexibility to produce quantities of intermediate products when they are needed. Sometimes members of the supply chain that are at more advanced stages of JIT implementation help the company do this.

## Schedule Stability and Discipline

A key element of JIT is replacing production of large batches with a continuous flow of smaller quantities. Proponents of JIT often suggest that companies can drive set-up-related costs so low that they can produce a lot size of one unit that would be economically feasible. Although companies seldom attain this lot size of one, making it a goal does focus manufacturing managers on the task of making fundamental changes in the design of the production process instead of attempting to patch a basically flawed system. Commitment to an ideal lot size of one forces managers to reexamine production practices and exposes waste—which is anything that does not add value to the product, such as unnecessary storage time, movement from place to place, or inspection.

What do these reductions in lot size imply for schedule stability? Instead of producing five distinct items at a workstation each week, setting up for each only once, a company could produce each of the five items every day or perhaps even several times a day as the economic lot size becomes smaller. A system that produces the correct amount of each product as it is needed is inherently stable. When demand changes, the company should not have to incur costly interruptions in manufacturing in order to expedite a special order. Normal production schedules include that item in production today, perhaps even this morning, and the company handles adjustments to demand at that time. There is virtually no rescheduling or no incidents that require unanticipated set-ups. The system is designed to respond quickly to changes in the pattern of demand without creating an inefficient production process.

A sales force that manages customers' demand in a manner that is positive for the company also can make its schedule more stable. Consider, for example, the practice of quantity discounts. Instead of inducing customers to purchase more frequently in smaller lots to help smooth out production, some companies offer incentives for them to order less frequently in larger quantities. But the less frequent orders of larger quantities often arrive at the most inopportune time, which means the company may incur extra costs. This is especially true if satisfying the customer's order means working overtime, adding an extra shift, or subcontracting the work out. The company usually does not pass this extra cost on to the customer, so it is producing more expensive products at a discount price. Customers order in economic lots for themselves by making the best use of the quantity discount. They store for future use those units their operations do not need immediately. But customers usually prefer to get the discount and have delivery quantities that more closely match their needs. Long-term supplier-customer relationships often make this arrangement possible, and both customer and supplier win.

## Comprehensive Quality Assurance

Failing to do things right the first time is the cause of much disruption of material flow through an operation. Jobs that must be done over again generate additional costs through scrap and rework that are usually not recoverable.

Consider the case of the multimillion dollar Hubble Space Telescope, which was delivered into orbit by a U.S. space shuttle late in 1992. Months later astronomers found that the telescope's lenses and other components were defective. The dilemma was how to deal with the problem. The telescope was nearly useless as it was, but the cost of attempting to repair the telescope would be phenomenal. In mid-1993 the National Aeronautics and Space Administration (NASA) decided to devote another shuttle mission to attempting to repair the flawed device. Late in 1993 the shuttle's crew nearly worked miracles to repair the telescope at another multimillion dollar cost. Not all product defects generate such an enormous cost to rework. But the cost of rework is a waste to be eliminated.

Most people who have office assistants have horror stories about how long an assistant took to accomplish what was supposed to be a simple task. One manager tells the story of giving a secretary a one-page memo to type. The manager put the draft in the secretary's in-basket and waited about three hours for the memo. After picking up the completed document and returning to the office, the manager found seven typographical errors and confronted the secretary, who smiled and promised to correct the errors as soon as possible. Two hours later the manager once again retrieved the completed document, only to find three typographical errors—two new ones and a mistake left over from the first memo. The apologetic secretary tried again, and the manager had the memo by the end of the day. The manager contemplated the day's dealings with the secretary. Could it be that the secretary didn't even have time for a coffee break today and came back from lunch early, just complete all the work that needed to be done? Might the secretary go home this afternoon talking about how much work had been accomplished?

The secretary probably did believe that a lot of work had been accomplished that day. But that thinking is based on the secretary's definition of the job. If the job is perceived to be that of typist and the person typed all day long with few interruptions, the person did a lot of work. If the job is perceived to be that of providing excellent customer satisfaction, the secretary did not accomplish much. The secretary's attitude may have been that there is no difference in typing five different things or typing one thing five times. Under the first definition of the job the secretary is correct. Under the second definition the secretary wasted almost the entire day, because the secretary probably had satisfied no customers that day. While the secretary was retyping the memo, other work was waiting for attention.

This attitude is prevalent in manufacturing areas. Some machine operators define their jobs as strictly machine operators. Therefore, they do not think that spending 50 percent of each day reworking product is a problem, because they are operating the machine almost continually. But the time they spend reworking product is in fact wasted time, for which the business will probably not be repaid. An organizational culture truly imbued in quality understands what happens when people fail to do things right the first time. Companies must design performance appraisal and reward systems that reflect and encourage the proper attitude about quality throughout the organization.

Under the JIT philosophy companies eliminate all waste—whether it is the waste of time, material, product, energy, money, or information. Internal and external customer satisfaction must drive the work effort. Rework is one penalty for failing to do things right the first time. Companies must design quality into products and processes, because it cannot be inspected in after the fact. Organizations need quality-oriented individuals who use quality processes in a quality-oriented culture. Everyone in the organization must understand that she or he is in the "quality business." If you walk into the accounting or marketing department of a manufacturing organization and ask, "Who is responsible for quality around here?" you should not be sent to the quality control area. The answer should be, "I am responsible for the quality of the work that I do." This is one clear sign that an organization is beginning to establish a quality culture.

## Creating Teams of Competent, Empowered Employees

The effective implementation of JIT requires a tremendous amount of dedication to creative problem solving. In each of the examples of JIT implementation we have described so far, resistance by senior managers, first-line supervisors, and workers could be an insurmountable block to effective change. Some individuals leave in frustration, usually because the new manufacturing environment is so unfamiliar and the "rules" of production have changed so dramatically that they lack the confidence to do their job.

Forming teams to solve problems requires fundamental changes in the roles of worker and supervisor; the supervisor must become a teacher, facilitator, and leader rather than an enforcer. Some workers and supervisors alike find the changes empowering. If production employees are responsible for production, routine maintenance, and quality, they must have the power to take appropriate action.

For supervisors the transition from enforcer to coach can be difficult. In many manufacturing environments first-line supervisors are not nearly as familiar with the details of the production technology as the workers are. Formally structured lines of communication, which sometimes inhibit communication, are a serious impediment to success. This fundamental change in working relations is most difficult if the traditional worker-supervisor context was adversarial or even one of quiet tolerance.

First-line managers must either change or leave the company when senior management makes the strategic choice to embrace JIT concepts. Senior managers must be prepared to exert incredible effort through a difficult transition period. For that reason the early implementers of JIT usually were companies under attack competitively—they had no choice but to take action. Success stories are more common today; strong leaders in successful companies seek to maintain or improve competitive position and market share, so the JIT philosophy continues to spread.

## JIT Systems and Signals

Every manufacturing and service delivery system has some sort of signal that triggers production at each work center. In a job shop the trigger is usually the arrival of a job in the queue at a work center. There, the relative priority of that job is compared with the priorities of other jobs in the queue. When no orders are waiting to be processed, work ceases. In a continuous process production continues at essentially the same rate on a continuous basis, so the trigger that initiates production occurs rarely; it may have been a single event when the facility was first brought on line. JIT systems are most frequently found in batch and repetitive environments.

**Push Versus Pull Production Systems** Some systems schedule production beginning with the first activities that have to be performed. Material requirements planning (MRP) systems are designed to initiate production at the lowest level of the bill of materials. Such a system is a called a **push production system**, because arrival of work in process at intermediate stages and the appearance of work orders on computer-generated schedules attempt to push the product through the system, completing it as needed and on schedule, it is hoped. In an attempt to maintain high measures of people and machine utilization, an MRP system often releases material down stream before an operation has the capacity to process it. The general philosophy is that if a station has material that it can process, it should process it immediately, and move it on to the next step in the process. The results are often high levels of work-in-process inventories, longer cycle times and more confusion, and less flexibility and lower quality.

Compare the push-type of production system with that used at McDonald's restaurants. If McDonald's used a push system, workers would prepare food according to some predetermined schedule. A key concern would be the utilization of kitchen personnel and equipment. Workers often would prepare food whether customers were in the restaurant or not. This application has no "schedule" that initiates the production of hamburgers. Rather, workers prepare limited numbers of hamburgers and store them as finished goods in a warm area for sale in the near future. Sales of finished goods pull more sandwiches from earlier stages of preparation. The number of hamburgers on hand, or some other signal from management, triggers production at each subsequent work center. If customer demand is zero, production of a particular item ceases. This type system would be more of a **pull production system**, in which work is authorized rather than scheduled in advance. The primary advantages of this type of system are in reducing costly work-in-process inventories and the ability to quickly respond to special customer needs. The primary disadvantage would be the potential underutilization of people and equipment in the kitchen. Pull production systems are characteristic of JIT production systems, because they focus on satisfying customers' needs just in time.

**JIT Signals and Kanban** JIT systems use a signal or sign to authorize the production or movement of material. In Japanese the term *kanban*, which literally translated means card, refers to this signaling device. The cards govern the flow of materials throughout the facility. The kanbans contain important information about the product, where it is produced, and where it is used. At Toyota the kanban system has two cards, a **production** *kanban*, which authorizes a work center to produce a part, and a **conveyance** *kanban*, which signals the need to move more parts to that department or work center. The absence of a production kanban at a work center is the signal that work should stop, because there is obviously no demand for that particular part. Variations on the operation of pull production systems and kanbans have emerged in response to special manufacturing situations.

**Modifications of the Signaling System** Individual companies that implement JIT signaling for production have customized the procedures to meet their needs. When the spatial distance between work centers is not great, companies use a single-card kanban system to authorize production when parts are needed. Some modified systems have no card at all. The signal to produce more parts may simply be a verbal command or an empty square taped on a table between workstations. Formal kanban systems such as the one-card or two-card systems are not necessary for every application.

**When to Use Kanban**  The JIT pull production systems are appropriate for many discrete unit production systems. Kanban signals are just one element of a JIT production system. Pull systems assume that lot sizes are small and workers can do set-ups quickly. They also assume that many of the rocks in the materials river have been removed. Finally, the material-handling and information systems must support truly fast pulls of parts from producing centers. Parts included in a JIT signaling system should be used daily. At least one container should always be on hand. The full containers are the work in process of a JIT system. By placing restrictions on the number of containers in the system, the system controls and reduces WIP. The validity of these assumptions directly affects the success of the pull production system.

Many novice manufacturing managers have learned about pull production systems and have been impressed enough to go back to work and give them a try. They are often amazed that WIP clears out the work area, quality seems to improve, workers' stress seems to be reduced, and everything goes well. Their attitude changes when something unexpected, such as a machine breakdown, unfavorable product yields, a long machine set-up, or an engineering problem arises. In a short period of time everything stops and no product is going out the door. The pull production system often gets the blame, when in fact conditions were not right for the pull system to be effective. Remember that inventory exists to protect the organization from various problems, and pull systems reduce much of that protective inventory. The company must first address the problems that create the need for inventory and eliminate the problems.

## Logistics Systems to Support JIT Delivery

As we noted in Chapter 10, using JIT production for strategic advantage often requires fast and regular supply from other companies. At one time Sony Corp. announced that it would build a color television manufacturing facility in a former Volkswagen plant near Pittsburgh. Several years earlier Sony had built a television picture tube manufacturing facility in the same area, so where to locate the television assembly plant to support JIT was obvious.

The Toyota–General Motors joint venture, called New United Motor Manufacturing, Inc. (NUMMI), in Fremont, California, has quick delivery arrangements in place with suppliers in Indiana, Ohio, and Michigan. NUMMI receives daily deliveries of parts required for exactly one day's production of nine hundred cars. Leaseway Transportation Corp. runs the system using Union Pacific railways and "piggyback" truck trailers that can be removed from trucks and attached to flat-top railcars. The network of trucks follows fifteen routes, bringing the parts to a central location in Chicago, where the trailers are mounted on the railcars on a train bound directly to Fremont. NUMMI began by holding three days' inventory of parts just in case it saw delays but planned to reduce that emergency inventory to a one-day supply more consistent with the just-in-time philosophy. After General Motors announced that its new Saturn division would locate in Spring Hill, Tennessee, many of Saturn's suppliers made similar announcements. Proximity between supplier and manufacturer was necessary in order to supply the frequent and small quantity deliveries that Saturn operations anticipated.

# Some Manufacturers Drop Efforts to Adopt Japanese Techniques

Some American manufacturers are discarding billions of dollars of investment they made in the 1980s to adopt Japanese manufacturing ideas. They haven't decided that the Japanese systems don't work. Rather, they realize that some of those systems, however useful in lifting productivity in Japan, haven't achieved much in their own plants.

The urgency of responding to customer needs is raising doubts about rigid pursuit of the concept of Just-in-Time delivery of parts. This system works well in Japan where suppliers tend to be clustered around their major customers. In the U.S., despite the greater distances, many companies have been relying on frequent, prompt deliveries from suppliers.

But GE Appliances found that low inventories of some parts—it gets 475 parts from 75 suppliers—prevented it from responding to customer demands quickly. So it recently increased by 24 percent its inventory of parts with long delivery times. The change helps it respond now to customer orders in 3.6 weeks, down from 18 weeks in 1990. "We are getting the factory closer to the customer," says Richard Burke, the unit's vice president of manufacturing.

The benefits of a faster order-to-delivery cycle more than offset the cost of stocking parts. John Cassidy, director of research at United Technologies Corporation, says many companies are learning that "the primary motive in just-in-time isn't reducing inventory." The Japanese devised it, he says, "to expose the weak points on the manufacturing line." Without the inventory buffer, workers have to keep production defect free.

"We misplaced the goal," says Mr. Cassidy, who spent a year studying manufacturing in Japan. "In order to eliminate inventory, we focused our efforts on materials handling. We forced the supplier to take extraordinary measures to solve our inventory problem, rather than looking at our own manufacturing processes."

James Harbour, a manufacturing specialist at a consulting firm bearing his name, says American companies have to think of manufacturing in broader terms. They must, for instance, design and engineer products and manufacturing processes with quality in mind. "The Americans adopted quality circles without upfront engineering and thought it would generate massive improvement in quality and productivity. They were living in a dream land," he says.

The cost of a logistics breakdown is obvious in JIT systems. An entire facility must literally shut down when parts or material do not arrive. Some U.S. companies have recently begun to abandon some concepts borrowed from the Japanese because of the difficulty of making them work. Operations Management in Practice 16.3 highlights some of these companies and concepts.

## Implementation of Just-in-Time

Many companies are overwhelmed when they consider the scope of changes required to fully implement the JIT philosophy. What activities should initiate the journey toward a time-conscious organization? It is impossible to provide a set of implementation steps that would work for any organization. As was the case in earlier discussions about TQM, each organization is unique, and failure to recognize and capitalize on those unique aspects can doom dramatic organizational changes. The general suggestions that follow are based upon the experiences of many JIT adopters in the United States:

1. Run a pilot project with one final assembly operation and a few select work centers that feed it. Choose the pilot project carefully, because it is important that early experiences with JIT have a good chance of success. Furthermore, a final assembly stage will not upset the entire facility while the company is learning to manufacture using JIT concepts.

2. Identify key supervisors for reorientation to the JIT philosophy. They need a do-or-die attitude, because JIT is counterintuitive to traditional shop-floor practice. It is useful to note that most early JIT adopters were under the gun competitively and that companies often need a moderate level of urgency in introducing fundamental changes.

3. Organize production areas well and design them to improve material flow and communication between work centers. Before attempting to implement defect-free production and abbreviated set-up plans, train workers in the proper use of equipment and procedures.

4. Invite suppliers to observe your JIT system so that they can understand the interface required to secure long-term sourcing arrangements.

Even with the best plans and intentions some forces always work against change. This is especially true when changes are as dramatic as those suggested by JIT.

In 1986 researchers studied companies in the process of implementing JIT.[1] They used respondents' comments to devise a list of barriers to successful implementation. The most frequently reported barrier was cultural resistance to change. The companies listed such specific problems as lack of union acceptance, lack of acceptance by management, general resistance to change, and skepticism about the success of the project. One respondent noted that difficulty in accepting failure was a barrier. Because implementation will involve many different projects, some projects probably will not be successful. Dealing with failure is not something that organizations usually train their employees to do. The second most frequently cited barrier was lack of resources; most respondents specified lack of training or education. One company noted that it had had problems with predicting the financial benefits of JIT in order to justify expenditures for training and education. The third barrier reported by most companies was lack of understanding or commitment on the part of top management. Respondents noted that many managers underestimate the magnitude of changes involved with JIT. Initial commitment may deteriorate over time as more and more changes occur. The last major barrier listed was performance measurement; companies found it difficult to refine performance measures to encourage desired behavior. They also said that the existence of individual incentives precluded implementation of JIT in some areas of their plants. As companies create teams to develop solutions to operational problems, they need to institute team incentives as well as individual incentives. Team activities cannot conflict with existing individual incentive programs.

---

[1]Karlene M. Crawford, J. H. Blackstone, Jr., and J. F. Cox, "A Study of JIT Implementation and Operating Problems," *International Journal of Production Research* 26 (September 1988): 1565–1566. Reproduced with permission from Taylor & Francis, Inc., Washington, DC.

# Coordinating JIT and Material Requirements Planning

The principles we have described for implementing JIT may seem different from those we described for achieving production control through material requirements planning. In fact, when JIT was being introduced in the United States in the 1980s, production trade magazines published many articles that compared JIT and MRP, indicating that they were fundamentally different. One problem with this thinking was that it sometimes led excellent companies—that had successfully developed and implemented MRP systems—to believe that inaugurating JIT would require dismantling all that they had worked hard to develop in their plants.

Certainly MRP and JIT have some differences. In this chapter we have described JIT as a pull production system, because demand at the end of the supply chain initiates production—reversing the production sequence—through departments. In contrast, MRP systems push production through departments according to a schedule of estimated times required for production at each work center. Demand for a product initiates production activity at the earliest stages.

In discussing the appropriate use of kanban systems, we said that they are most appropriate in operations that have a daily demand for parts. MRP systems are applicable to a much wider array of manufacturing situations. Companies sometimes develop hybrid systems that use JIT pull systems where they are useful and MRP push systems elsewhere.

Yamaha Motor Co., manufacturer of motorcycles, mopeds, and all-terrain vehicles, and Deere and Co., the U.S. farm equipment company, have coordinated MRP and JIT. Although the details of their implementations are different, both companies recognized that the benefits of MRP continued to be applicable to parts of their manufacturing planning and control system. Yamaha was never a major user of MRP but has retained the master production scheduling component of its MRP system. Forecasting and planning are two of the major benefits of MRP, and the only intrinsic response to those issues in JIT is to be flexible and responsive. Yamaha finds that it is easier to achieve this responsiveness with a formal planning system.

At the Deere and Co. tractor works in Waterloo, Iowa, a new facility produces two types of farm tractors with 25 percent less inventory than did the older facility that it replaced. The facility uses a carefully planned JIT system for all parts that are used daily for manufacturing John Deere tractors. Deere and Co. uses an MRP system for master planning and production of special parts or continuously produced products that require casting. Computers track inventories and schedule maintenance at the Deere facility, in contrast to what JIT purists might suggest. Deere has developed a system that focuses on a smooth flow of materials from start to finish. Its objective, coordinated flow, led Deere to select certain JIT principles rather than adopt the entire system.

As the examples illustrate, JIT and MRP are complementary, not contradictory. Shorter production cycle times result in shorter planned lead times, which decrease the cumulative lead time for end items. This in turn decreases the length of the frozen planning horizon, increasing the company's ability to respond to changing customer demand. The greater schedule stability of JIT produces more even work loads on the shop floor. The organization should then become more consistent in meeting order due dates. With less variability in order completion times the company can shorten planned lead times as the need for safety lead times decreases.

# ▶ Summary

In twenty years students will look back on the operations practices of the late twentieth century and probably will find the term *just-in-time* somewhat amusing. The objective is obvious. It is hardly a technical term that requires special educational background to appreciate its meaning. However, the effective implementation of these concepts is a challenge to managers and workers alike. Each principle described in this chapter requires a change from traditional ideas that made some managers successful in the past. Competing through time is the most significant recent development in the quest for superior customer satisfaction in ever-demanding markets.

**Learning Objective 1: Describe the origins of the just-in-time approach to production.** Toyota of Japan is generally accepted as the originator of the JIT philosophy. Some people refer to the concept as the *Toyota manufacturing system.* Toyota secured the cooperation of all members of its supply channel as well as the Japanese government to make the concept a reality. Many elements of the Toyota system, such as the minimization of all forms of inventory, were developed out of necessity. The physical lack of space in Japan forced Toyota to think of inventory as something that it could not afford.

**Learning Objective 2: Describe the complete cash flow cycle for a typical customer-ordered product.** The cash flow cycle is the time that elapses from the moment a customer places an order until the customer pays for the order. It is typically made up of the order entry cycle, procurement cycle, production cycle, packing and shipping cycle, distribution cycle, and accounts receivable cycle. The cash flow cycle is important because its length determines how rapidly operations costs are converted into revenue and reinvested.

**Learning Objective 3: Describe the relationship of material flows, work-in-process inventory, and cycle times in a manufacturing environment.** The ideal production environment is one in which incoming work is processed immediately and delivered to the customer exactly when needed. Material would flow uninterrupted throughout the series of necessary process steps. Unfortunately, operational problems that exist in any organization cause unexpected delays in the processing and movement of material. To ensure the movement of finished product in the face of the unexpected delays companies hold work-in-process inventory as a buffer. Because production cycle time is measured as the average amount of time required to start and finish a job, the more WIP inventory that exists on the operations floor, the longer the production cycle time is. Increased cycle time adversely affects the organization's ability to respond to customer and market demands. Time-conscious organizations seek to reduce total business cycle time by identifying problems that stop material from flowing. Once problems are resolved, the inventory held as a buffer against those problems becomes unnecessary. The result is shorter cycle times and greater responsiveness.

**Learning Objective 4: Explain the role of set-up time reduction in achieving production flexibility and responsiveness.** One key problem in achieving flexibility in operations is the number of units being produced in each lot or batch. Large lot sizes increase WIP, which increases cycle times and decreases flexibility and responsiveness. The high cost of completing a set-up for an operation is usually the reason for those large lot sizes. If the cost of a set-up is high, no one would want to set up often; large lots become the most efficient use of resources. Reducing the time required to set up an operation should decrease lot sizes, thereby increasing flexibility and responsiveness. Improved quality, lower costs, and smaller floor space are often additional benefits of cutting set-up time.

**Learning Objective 5: Describe the organizational requirements for JIT implementation.** The requirements for implementing JIT include production flexibility at every stage of supply; schedule stability and discipline; comprehensive quality assurance; teams of competent, empowered employees promoting trust, commitment, and open communications; a signaling system to pull production; and a logistics system to support JIT deliveries.

**Learning Objective 6: Compare traditional push production systems with the pull systems associated JIT production.** Push systems are traditional production systems; work is scheduled in advance in order to ensure high utilization of people and equipment. Manufacturing systems that use traditional MRP to initiate production at the lowest levels of the bill of materials are pull-type systems. In push systems line imbalances or operations problems result in increased WIP inventory. Pull systems are demand-driven production systems that sacrifice utilization for flexibility and reductions in WIP inventories. Work is not scheduled in advance; it is authorized when needed. Work begins only when information from a downstream operation signals the need for material. Line imbalances and operations problems result in idle time but no WIP buildup.

**Learning Objective 7: Describe the use of kanbans as signaling devices in organizations.** Pull produc-

tion systems require some form of signal to indicate when material should be produced. The term *kanban* is the Japanese word for card, the signaling device used by many Japanese and U.S. companies. The Toyota production system uses a two-card kanban signaling system that has production and conveyance kanbans to initiate production and movement, respectively. When downstream operations are located close to one another, the conveyance kanban may be unnecessary. Those situations may call for a one-card kanban system. Kanban is not a complex concept. It is simply some form of signaling system that controls the flow of material through a facility. Each organization designs its own kanban system to suit its individual needs. Kanban signaling devices can be cards, lights, squares taped atop a work table, colored golf balls, or whatever.

## ▶ Key Terms

conveyance *kanban*
*kanban*
new product development cycle

new strategy development cycle
production *kanban*
pull production system

push production system
short-cycle manufacturing
total business cycle

## ▶ Discussion Questions

1. Compare the triggers for production in just-in-time systems and for traditional production systems.
2. What is the motivation for implementing JIT systems?
3. To what extent are JIT systems culturally dependent—unlikely to be adaptable to American companies?
4. Discuss vendor relationships in JIT systems. How are they different from the buyer-seller relationships found in traditional manufacturing systems? Why might some vendors be hesitant to enter a JIT agreement?
5. Why is JIT implementation difficult for some managers? for some workers?
6. How relevant is the JIT philosophy in the service sector? Provide examples to support your views.
7. What difficulties did U.S. manufacturers have in attempting to implement JIT?

8. Why are shortened set-up times crucial to the development of JIT?
9. Outline a sequence of activities that a company should undertake to implement JIT. Give reasons for the sequence of activities that you provide.
10. Why does excess work-in-process inventory hide problems within a JIT manufacturing system?
11. Describe the typical way that JIT and MRP systems are integrated.
12. The idle time aspect of pull production systems is a source of concern for many managers. When a workstation has no authorization to produce material, what can workers do to help address the manager's concerns?
13. What is the role of quality assurance in a successful JIT system?

## ▶ Selected References

Dear, Anthony. *Working Towards Just-in-Time.* New York: Van Nostrand Reinhold, 1988.

Goddard, Walter E. *Just-in-Time: Surviving by Breaking Tradition.* Essex Junction, Vt.: Oliver Wight Publications, 1986.

Hall, Robert W. *Attaining Manufacturing Excellence.* Homewood, Ill: Dow Jones-Irwin, 1987.

Inman, R. Anthony, and Satish Mehra. "The Transferability of Just-in-Time Concepts to American Small Businesses." *Interfaces* 20 (March–April 1990): 30–37.

Japan Management Association. *The Canon Production System*. Cambridge, Mass.: Productivity Press, 1987.

Monden, Yasuhiro. *Toyota Production System*. Norcross, Ga.: Industrial Engineering and Management Press, 1983.

Monden, Yasuhiro, ed. *Applying Just-in-Time: The American/Japanese Experience*. Norcross, Ga.: Industrial Engineering and Management Press, 1986.

Schonberger, Richard J. *Japanese Manufacturing Techniques: Nine Hidden Lessons in Simplicity*. New York: Free Press, 1982.

Stalk, George, and Thomas M. Hout. *Competing Against Time: How Time-Based Competition Is Reshaping Global Markets*. New York: Free Press, 1990.

## CHAPTER 17

# Design and Scheduling of Service Systems

*The service system is all of the apparatus, physical and procedural, that the service people have at their disposal to meet the customer's needs.*

KARL ALBRECHT AND RON ZEMKE

**Introduction**

**The Evolution of the Service System**
*OPERATIONS MANAGEMENT IN PRACTICE 17.1: Pampering the American Motorist*

**Strategic Approaches to Service System Design**
*GLOBAL OPERATIONS MANAGEMENT 17.2: Innovative Retail Service Systems—ATMs in Japan*

**Strategies for Managing Service Demand**
*OPERATIONS MANAGEMENT IN PRACTICE 17.3: SABRE—The Evolution of an Airline Demand Management System*

**Strategies for Controlling Service Supply**

**Vehicle Routing**

**Case Study: National Technological University**

# Introduction

The operations manager in a service business contends with many of the same kinds of problems as the operations manager in a manufacturing business. Initially, both make a strategic decision about the market niche they will serve. Next they develop a product or service to provide to the consumer. Then they design and put in place some sort of a system that will provide the goods or service. They design and implement the system in a way that makes the system controllable with respect to its cost and the quality and timeliness of its product or service.

Figure 17.1 presents an overview of the design process. (Chapter 5 presented a more extensive discussion of product and services planning and design.) The design process begins with focusing on the customer and deciding upon an idea for the product or service that can be produced and sold for a profit. The marketing department is typically responsible for determining customers' needs

**FIGURE 17.1**
An Overview of the Design Process

Source: Adapted from Robert G. Murdick, Barry Render, and Roberta S. Russell, *Service Operations Management* (Boston: Allyn & Bacon, 1990), p. 91.

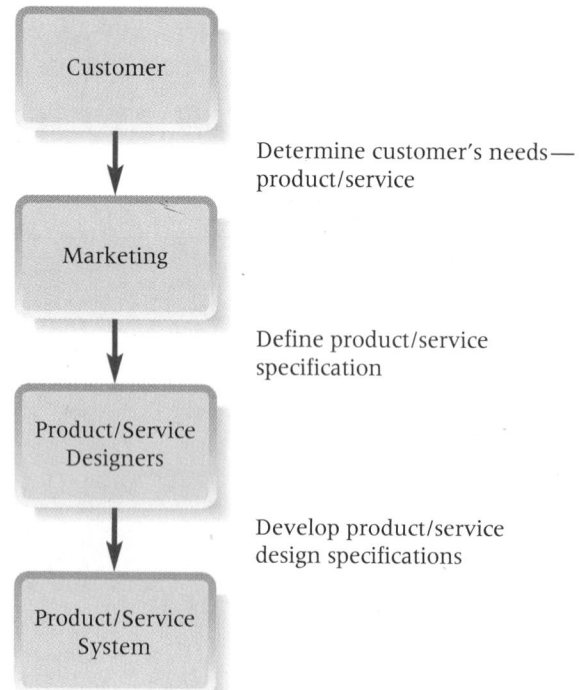

Customer → Determine customer's needs — product/service

Marketing → Define product/service specification

Product/Service Designers → Develop product/service design specifications

Product/Service System

and wants. The description of the product or service is called the **performance specification**, and it describes exactly what the product or service does for the customer. For example, an automatic car wash might have a performance specification of washing a car in less than two minutes. The next step is for the product/service designers or engineers to translate the performance specification into the **design specifications**. The design specifications state the type of service system that will satisfy the performance specification. For example, a mass transportation system for a large city might use subways, buses, or light rail as design specifications. The final step in the design process is putting the service system into place.

We must emphasize that several aspects of service organizations are critical. First, designing and managing a successful service delivery system requires the skillful organization and integration of marketing, human resources, and operations management. Marketing is a particularly critical factor, because the delivery process for services is based to a great extent on marketing. Similarly, people skills are important, because most service systems involve one-on-one interactions with customers. Second, service operations deliver a service product that is consumed as the service occurs. This has a number of significant implications for the design of the service delivery system, its supporting information system, and the management and motivation of the people providing the service. Third, many services are provided by geographically dispersed networks connected by a communications system and an overall marketing program.

In this chapter we examine some ways in which service companies deal with the issues involved in service system design and scheduling. We begin by showing how a service strategy is developed and used to define the service package, and then we discuss service system design, emphasizing the strategic nature of the process. The chapter also examines specific strategies for managing service demand and controlling service supply.

## The Evolution of the Service System

As Figure 17.2 shows, we can think of the evolution of a successful service system as a three-stage process. The evolution begins with defining the **service strategy**, which is what defines the service business—what it is and what it will do. The next stage is specifying a **service package**, which defines exactly what the customer will get. The final stage is determining the **service system**, which defines how the service is to be created and delivered to the customer.

### Service Strategy

Wickham Skinner has asserted that strategy involves matching what the organization is good at, its "distinctive competence," with its "primary task," the

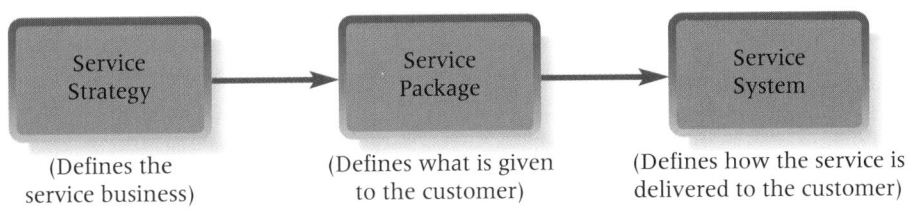

FIGURE 17.2
Evolution of a Service System

reasons for its existence and the markets it serves.[1] Michael Porter has argued persuasively that there are three generic competitive strategies: overall cost leadership, differentiation, and focus.[2] Overall cost leadership can yield high profits through low prices, high sales volume, and high market share. Differentiation involves making the product or service clearly different and more desirable than that of a competitor. Focus involves using a combination of cost and differentiation to achieve a market niche.

What is a service strategy? Karl Albrecht and Ron Zemke have a simple definition: "A service strategy is a distinctive formula for delivering service; such a strategy is keyed to a well-chosen benefit premise that is valuable to the customer and that establishes a competitive position."[3]

The service strategy positions the service product in the marketplace just as a product strategy positions a physical product in the marketplace.

An effective service strategy meets the following conditions:

1.  It is concrete and action oriented.
2.  It conveys a concept or mission that people in the organization can understand, relate to, and somehow put into action.
3.  Its premise offers a critical benefit that is important to the customer. It must focus on something the customer is willing to pay for.
4.  It differentiates the organization in some meaningful way from its competitors in the eyes of the customer.
5.  It is simple, easy to put into words, and easy to explain to the customer.[4]

The service strategy answers this question: Why should the customer choose us?

Developing an effective service strategy is a challenging and difficult task. No service is ever perfect, and it is unlikely that all customers are going to be completely satisfied with the service they receive. Service strategy involves the trade-offs between what the service organization can and will do, given the available resources and any external constraints imposed upon it by a corporate body or by government, and what the customer expects or requires.

Certain differences in formulating strategy for manufacturing companies and for service companies are important:

- Services find fewer barriers to entering their markets, because services usually require less capital than manufacturing and because the service that is offered often cannot be patented.
- Service businesses, particularly those that are people based, find acquiring technology that cannot be copied is more difficult than it is for manufacturing.
- Achieving uniqueness is more difficult for services than for manufacturers.
- Determining the costs associated with services is more difficult, so price competition is more difficult than it is for manufacturers.
- Using research and development to devise new services is not easy, because services lack a tangible product.

---

[1]Wickham Skinner, "Manufacturing—Missing Link in Corporate Strategy," *Harvard Business Review* 47 (May–June 1969): 136–145.
[2]Michael Porter, *Competitive Strategy* (New York: Free Press, 1985), pp. 11–26.
[3]Karl Albrecht and Ron Zemke, *Service America! Doing Business in the New Economy* (Homewood, Ill: Dow Jones-Irwin, 1985), p. 64.
[4]Albrecht and Zemke, *Service America!* p. 174.

■ Using acquisition as a growth strategy is risky for services, because key personnel, the major asset of any service company, can simply leave. As companies are acquired, their employees may be more inclined to leave than stay and face an uncertain future under the direction of the acquiring company.[5]

Service organizations have three major operations strategies:

1. Strategically locating the service unit (or units)
2. Establishing economies of scale
3. Developing service differentiation

Because a service is an abstract and perishable entity, it needs to be easily accessible to its customers. This makes either single-site or multisite location decisions very important. Multiple sites allow the service company to protect itself from competition by preventing other service companies without comparable financial, purchasing, or advertising resources from moving into the same geographical area. For example, a few large car rental companies have secured many airport locations and have effectively prevented other companies from entering this business. Strategically placed multisite facilities have also been the means by which many service companies have achieved spectacular growth.

Operations managers in service companies have many opportunities to establish economies of scale. Centralized purchasing and centralized advertising by food services are two examples. Many other examples of scale economies exist in equipment-based service businesses. One good example of this is the multiplex movie theater that is prevalent in suburban locations throughout the United States. A multiplex uses a single set of ticket sellers/takers, a single concession stand, and provides one set of restrooms.

**Service differentiation** refers to the service quality identification and customer loyalty achieved by established service companies. Past advertising, word-of-mouth recommendations, previous good service, or being the first entrant in a market can differentiate a service. Other services invest in technology to create differentiation. For example, Wal-Mart has made a tremendous investment in computers and information technology to track customers' purchases and inventory levels. This has enabled Wal-Mart to provide consistently high product service levels for its customers. It has loyal customers who perceive that they will be able to secure the products they want at a Wal-Mart store. By differentiating their services, businesses can create a barrier to competition by forcing competitors to spend heavily to overcome customers' loyalties.

A final question might well be "What does a good service strategy look like?" Albrecht and Zemke have chronicled some effective strategies developed and implemented by service organizations.[6] Table 17.1 summarizes five successful service organizations and the service strategies they use; these companies often have common themes, such as speed and convenience of service.

## The Service Package

A service company must decide what service it will provide, where and how it will provide it, and to whom. This requires the company to define the service

---

[5]Dan R.E. Thomas, "Strategy Is Different in Service Businesses," *Harvard Business Review* 56 (July–August 1978): 158–165.
[6]Albrecht and Zemke, *Service America!* pp. 70–73.

TABLE 17.1
Examples of Successful
Service Strategies

| Service Organization | Service Strategy |
|---|---|
| McDonald's | Speed, efficiency, low price, convenience |
| Deluxe Check Printers | Extremely fast response, maximum convenience |
| British Airways | Care and concern, solving customer problems quickly and effectively, flexibility in dealing with customer needs, fixing things that go wrong |
| Santa Monica Medical Center | Professional credibility, individualized attention, responsiveness |
| Holiday Inn | Convenience, moderate price |

Source: Karl Albrecht and Ron Zemke, *Service America! Doing Business in the New Economy* (Homewood: Ill.: Dow Jones-Irwin, 1985), pp. 70–73.

package that the customer is to receive. We can define the service package as a bundle of goods consisting of four features:

■ Supporting facilities—the physical resources that must be available in order to provide the service
■ Facilitating goods—the materials the customer purchases or consumes
■ Explicit services—the intrinsic benefits that are readily observable by the senses
■ Implicit services—the extrinsic, or psychological, benefits of the service[7]

These are the features the consumer encounters, and they form the basis for the consumer's perception of that service. Table 17.2 lists criteria for evaluating the four features of the service package and provides examples.

Also useful is distinguishing between a core service and the peripheral services that are part of the service package. The **core service** is the major or primary service that is offered as part of the service package; the **peripheral services** are the associated or secondary services offered as part of the service package. For an airline the core service is the actual transport of a person from, say, New York to Los Angeles. The peripheral services may include the cleanliness of the plane's interior, the attitude of the flight attendants, the food and drinks provided, and the general comfort of the flight.

Richard Normann states that the service package usually is a mixture of four ingredients:

■ Specialized capacity to deliver services. Because a service business competes with other service businesses and its own customers, it has to be able to do something better or less expensively than the customer (or the competition) can. For example, a building cleaning service does the same thing that a company's own maintenance staff can do.
■ Linkages and social relationships. A service business links customers and resources in new ways or in new contexts and promotes certain social relationships. A travel agency is a good example of a service business that provides linkages.

[7]Richard Normann, *Service Management: Strategy and Leadership in Service Businesses* (Chichester, England: Wiley, 1984), pp. 23–25.

T A B L E   1 7 . 2
Service Package Evaluation
Criteria

**Feature One: Supporting Facilities**
*Evaluation Criteria:*                                    *Examples:*

1. Exterior appearance                                    Ski resort
2. Interior decor                                         Restaurant
3. Facility layout                                        Hospital
4. Supporting equipment

**Feature Two: Facilitating Goods**
*Evaluation Criteria:*                                    *Examples:*

1. Consistency                                            Ski lifts
2. Quantity                                               Food items
3. Selection                                              Diagnostic equipment

**Feature Three: Explicit Services**
*Evaluation Criteria:*                                    *Examples:*

1. Service personnel training                             Location of ski resort
2. Comprehensiveness                                      Taste of food
3. Consistency                                            Intensive care
4. Availability

**Feature Four: Implicit Services**
*Evaluation Criteria:*                                    *Examples:*

1. Service personnel attitude                             Prestige of ski resort
2. Privacy and security                                   Waiter courtesy
3. Convenience                                            Doctor's credentials
4. Atmosphere
5. Waiting experience
6. Status
7. Sense of well being

Source: James A. Fitzsimmons and Robert S. Sullivan, *Service Operations Management* (New York: McGraw-Hill, 1982), pp. 17–19.

■  Transfer of know-how. A service business often exists because it has some special skill, knowledge, or know-how that it can transfer. A university is a classic example of a service business that specializes in transfer of knowledge.

■  Management and organization as a service product. Many service businesses sell "service management systems" as their major service. For example, service companies now provide systems for managing hotels.[8]

The service package also consists of both physical items and intangibles. The physical items in the service package include

1. Items that are purchased by the customer directly (such as meals in a restaurant or parts in an auto supply store) or items that are supplied free as samples.

[8]Normann, *Service Management*, pp. 23–29.

# Pampering the American Motorist

Innovative service companies are finding many new ways to make money by exploiting the American motorist's yearning to be pampered.

Using a blend of technology and time-saving concepts, automotive convenience services are proliferating. Among the many new services for motorists are Oilco, of Braintree, Massachusetts, which sends equipped vans to parking lots to do lubrications, change oil and filters, inspect motor fluids, replace worn filters, wipers, and lights, and adjust the tire pressure. "There's no waiting in line, no taking time off from work," exults John Cozzi, a marketing consultant who is helping to set up the company.

Turner's of Califon, in Califon, New Jersey, got started by changing oil in people's driveways. Now it restores and repairs luxury and antique cars, and its workers wear gloves to prevent smudging as they transport vehicles to its shop in a special van. A-Action Mobile Window Tinting, Inc., of Orlando will tint car windows with plastic film in the customer's driveway.

For automobile purchasers who find the negotiation process distasteful, Auto Consumers, Inc., of New York, will take over. They do the haggling and also advise their clients, who number more than one thousand annually, against certain models and options (notably rust-proofing contracts). Another consultant for car buyers, Stan Madeloff, founder of Jenlor Co. of Canton, Massachusetts, used to train and recruit personnel for car dealerships but "switched sides" in the mid-1980s. He says his mission now is to fend off "surprises and exorbitant overcharges" for consumers. Car/Puter helps people buy cars but does not do any negotiating. It furnishes computerized printouts with pricing information on the latest rebates and financial incentives for all makes of cars.

Service companies have also found pampering opportunities in rental cars. Instant Rent A Car, of Millburn, New Jersey, delivers its cars to customers' homes at a moment's notice. "About half of the people can't get here (to the car rental office) because their car is broken down, and about half don't want to," says owner Dennis Pryor.

One service company, Auto Tech Center, of New York City, tries to do it all. Employees at its six-floor garage on Manhattan's Upper East Side will pick up, park, and deliver your car, lease you a car and get special insurance discounts for it, "detail" your car for $185, repair your car, tint your car's windows, and sell and install items in your car, ranging from $4,500 leather seats to cellular phones. "We don't have any competition," boasts Michael Gluckman, the president and a principal shareholder. "We're a one-stop shop."

2.  Physical items that are altered during the service process. This covers repair of physical items owned by the customer or physical changes to the customers themselves. Examples of the latter include medical services or grooming services.

3.  Other physical items that are operationally a part of the service package but that may not be a part of the main service package, including admission tickets, programs, and souvenirs.

4.  Physical items that form part of the overall environment of the service operation. In a restaurant this includes the physical decor, the type of china and silverware used, and the dress of the servers.

The intangible elements of service in a service package include

1.  The nature of the service contact, which may be personal ("soft" contact) or impersonal ("hard" contact)
2.  The atmosphere of the service environment, which is created by the sights, sound, and comfort of the service
3.  The feelings created in the customer, which consist of the sense of security, status, and well being[9]

Obviously, the mixture of physical items and intangibles will vary greatly between service organizations. At one end of the spectrum is a self-service video store; almost 100 percent of its service package will consist of the physical items that customers rent or purchase. At an athletic event or musical performance almost 100 percent of the service package will consist of intangibles. In the middle of the spectrum might be an up-scale restaurant, where the consumer receives a blend of good food (physical items) and gracious service in comfortable surroundings, which produce a sense of well being (intangibles).

As the company is designing its service package in terms of its physical and intangible elements, it must identify the characteristics of potential customers. These characteristics are important both for the design of the service system and for setting standards of performance for the service package. For example, the design of a medical services facility for elderly people would be quite different from the design of a medical facility for children.

Setting standards for the service package is an important part of the overall service design process. These standards become the foundation for the design and operation of the service unit. They also become important in advertising and promoting the service to the customer. Matching what the service facility can deliver with what the service package promises is critical. Because most services are intangible, setting service package standards is much more difficult than setting standards of performance and quality for manufactured goods.

The effective management of a service operation requires the integration of four major elements:

- The service package
- The service package standards
- The service-producing unit
- The customers' expectations (to the degree they can be determined)[10]

As Figure 17.3 shows, these elements then must fit together to form a successful service operation.

Operations Management in Practice 17.1 presents several examples of service systems that offer convenience to motorists.

# Strategic Approaches to Service System Design

Figure 17.4 shows the options available in approaching service system design strategically. First, we can design a highly personalized service that is provided on

[9]Christopher Voss, Colin Armistead, Bob Johnson, and Barbara Morris, *Operations Management in Service Industries and the Public Sector* (Chichester, England: Wiley, 1985), pp. 51–53.
[10]Voss et al., *Operations Management*, p. 55.

FIGURE 17.3
Framework for a Successful
Service Operation

Source: Adapted from Christopher
Voss, Colin Armistead, Bob Johnston,
and Barbara Morris, *Operations
Management in Service Industries and
the Public Sector* (Chichester, England:
Wiley, 1985), p. 56.

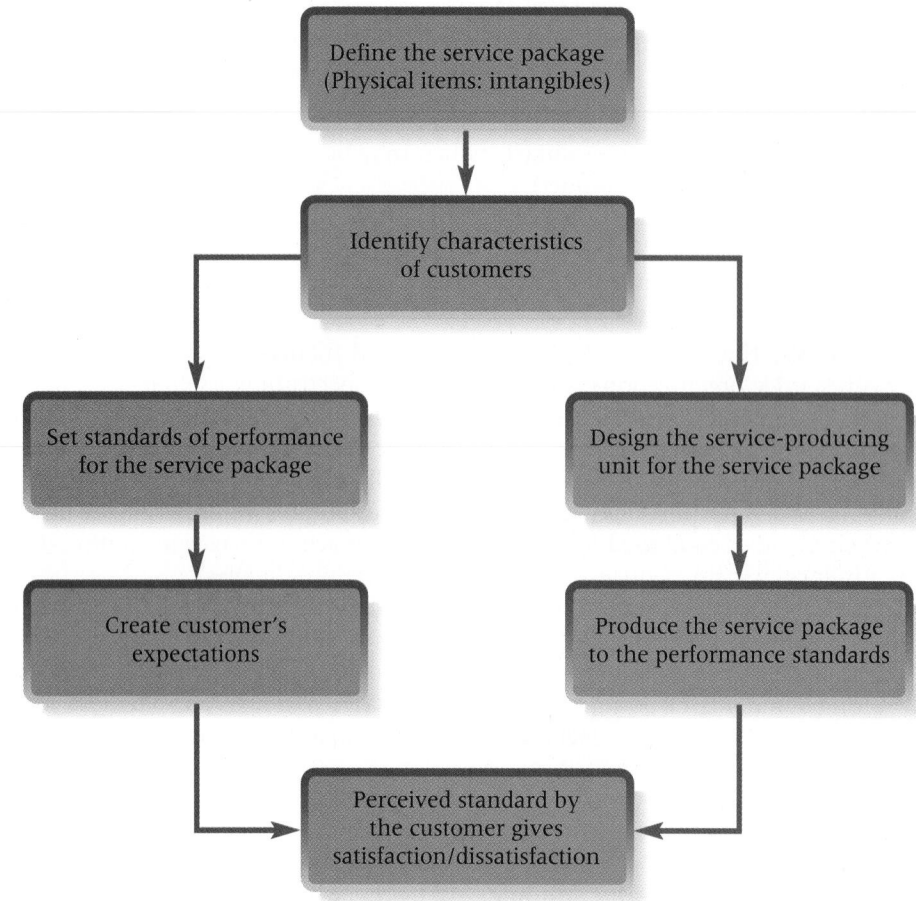

a one-to-one basis. Or we can deliver services by using a production-line approach—using technology and systems to achieve consistent quality and an efficient operation. An intermediate approach divides the service into high consumer-contact operations and low consumer-contact operations. Low consumer-contact operations have a technical core that isolates them from the consumer. Another approach to service system design emphasizes consumer participation. Self-service represents the ultimate in consumer participation.

## Production-Line Approach

Most of us think about service in personal and humanistic terms. Because the typical service involves the consumer in interacting with the service provider, we tend to think of services as custom designed to some degree. Theodore Levitt argues that this consumer orientation to designing a service system has created inefficiencies. He proposes that service companies adopt a technocratic approach to service system design, one that substitutes "technology and systems for people and serendipity."[11]

[11]Theodore Levitt, "Production-Line Approach to Service," *Harvard Business Review* 50 (September–October 1972): 41–52.

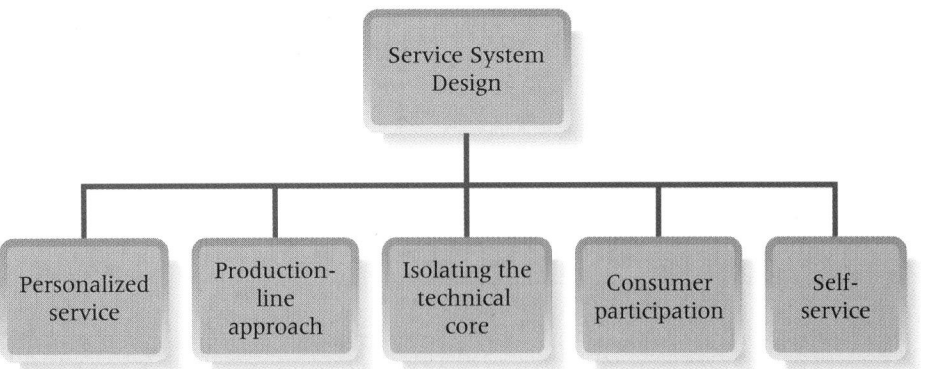

F I G U R E   1 7 . 4
Strategic Approaches to
Service System Design

Source: Adapted from James A.
Fitzsimmons and Robert S. Sullivan,
*Service Operations Management* (New
York: McGraw-Hill, 1982), p. 149.

*A hospital is a classic example of
the delivery of personalized
service on a one-to-one basis.*

McDonald's is a classic example of the production-line approach to service systems design. At McDonald's a central commissary carefully premeasures and prepackages raw hamburger patties. Individual store employees have no discretion as to size, quality, or consistency of raw material. McDonald's gives the same kind of attention to all its products, because it has designed storage and preparation space for and limited it to the company's predetermined mix of products. No space is available for any goods, beverages, or services that are not part of the original system's design.

Producing french fries depends heavily on technology and automation at McDonald's. McDonald's provides its outlets with precut, partially cooked, frozen potato slices. The fryer is designed to cook a certain quantity of fries, an amount that will not be so large as to create an inventory of soggy, greasy fries or so small as to require frequent frying. Employees empty the fries onto a wide, flat tray adjacent to the service counter and use a special wide-mouthed scoop with a funnel at one end to fill the french fry bags with generous, uniform portions. The tray's location prevents spilling, and the overall design prevents employees from touching the fries. The result is an ample portion of fries delivered in a speedy and efficient manner.

Other aspects of McDonald's production-line approach to service abound. The tissue paper that wraps each hamburger is color coded to denote the type of product (Big Mac, regular burger). Heated reserves hold preprepared hamburgers for rush orders. Frying surfaces have spatter guards to protect the cook's uniform. Large and highly visible trash cans dot the parking lot to promote the idea of customers' cleaning up after themselves.

McDonald's has achieved its remarkable success by applying a manufacturing style of thinking to a people-intensive service situation. We can look at its entire service system as a piece of equipment that can produce a standard, customer-satisfying output while requiring little operating discretion from its employees.[12]

The important features of the production-line approach to service system design can include

1. Using hard technologies—substituting machinery or tools for people-intensive performance of service work. Examples of hard technology include automatic teller machines instead of bank tellers, automatic coin receptacles at bridges, subway entrances, and toll roads instead of human collectors, and the machines that automatically check the credit of a credit card holder instead of manual credit checking.
2. Using soft technologies—substituting organized, preplanned systems for individual service operations. Examples of soft technology include the array of prepackaged vacation tours offered by American Express (that eliminates the need for time-consuming personal selling), supermarkets and open-stock libraries (that allow people to serve themselves quickly and efficiently), and mutual funds "families" (that allow the consumer a wide variety of investment options).
3. Standardizing service—limiting service options in order to achieve uniformity and predictability. Various franchise operations are examples of standardized service. Allstate Insurance, with its off-the-shelf insurance programs, and H&R Block, with its systematic approach to income tax preparation, are other advocates of the service standardization approach.
4. Dividing labor—breaking the job into a group of tasks to allow specialization. A modern medical center is an excellent example of a service facility that involves a high degree of division of labor. Clerks perform certain information-gathering and recordkeeping functions, nurses and technicians perform certain tests and procedures, and doctors diagnose, prescribe, and operate.
5. Limiting discretion of personnel—providing a well-defined set of tasks to the service employee in order to achieve standardization, uniformity, and quality. We find examples of this in various fast-food restaurants, such as McDonald's, Burger King, KFC, and Pizza Hut, and in limited-service, fast, low-priced repair facilities such as Midas Muffler and AAMCO transmission repair shops.

Global Operations Management 17.2 describes how the introduction of automatic teller machines in Japan has increased banking productivity.

[12]Levitt, "Production-Line Approach to Service," pp. 44–46.

# Innovative Retail Service Systems— ATMs in Japan

Automatic teller machines (ATMs) have made great contributions to Japanese banking by reducing labor costs and introducing a new source of bank income.

For several reasons ATMs have achieved widespread acceptance in Japan very rapidly. First, Japanese rarely use personal checks; they prefer to pay in cash or by direct transfer of funds. Second, most Japanese companies use a direct deposit system to transfer the salaries of workers directly to their personal accounts.

But the most important reason for the success of ATMs in Japan has been the concept of ATM sharing. By 1975 individual Japanese banks had completed ATM networks that included their own branches and were seeking ways to expand. Because of competition for prime ATM locations—in department stores and subway stations, for example—they decided to cooperate. So they formed the Nippon Cash Service (NCS), an individual company that allows banks to share ATMs. NCS established communications protocols and message formats that became the basis for all Japanese ATM-sharing systems.

In 1989 Japanese bankers formed Banks Cash Services (BANCS) to share ATMs actually installed by banks. BANCS, which is owned by the thirteen participating city banks, is quite different from the systems of shared ATM networks in the United States, such as Cirrus and Master Teller. The Japanese network allows the holder of an ATM card from any major bank access at any one of the network's machines. U.S. networks are not as all inclusive.

In Japan settlements and ATM crediting are done on a real-time basis. ATMs automatically count the number of bills in a customer's cash deposit and confirm that they are genuine. The system then updates the account ledger in real time, completing the credit processing. Japanese ATMs also have recycle functions—they can pay out and accept cash in real time. If the cash deposited by a customer is acceptable, other customers can withdraw it.

At Dai-Ichi Kangyo Bank, Ltd., ATMs have eliminated the need for five thousand workers, producing annual savings of $210 million. Transactions at DKB's ATMs have increased dramatically since 1975, when 12,600 bank employees handled about 25 million transactions each month. By 1988 the number of transactions had reached 51 million per month, whereas the number of employees was down to 5,900. The productivity of the employees has been boosted by a factor of four.

## Isolating the Technical Core Approach

Traditionally, we think of services as involving a great deal of personal contact with customers in order to assess their specific needs. So the extent of customer contact can have a big influence on service system design. **Customer contact** refers to the physical presence of the customer in the system.

Not all service businesses have the same degree of customer contact. Table 17.3 classifies some examples of service businesses according to whether the customer has a low, intermediate, or high degree of contact with the service system.

TABLE 17.3
Service Businesses Classified
According to Extent of
Customer Contact

| Low Contact | Intermediate Contact | High Contact |
|---|---|---|
| Mail order company | Motel | Medical center |
| Parcel service company | Bank | School |
| Discount broker | Post office | Gourmet restaurant |

**Extent of contact** refers to the percentage of time the customer is in the service system compared with the total time it takes to perform the service. Richard B. Chase argues that the degree to which a service operation can achieve efficiency is directly related to the extent of customer contact. He contends that the less direct contact the customer has with the service system, the greater the potential of the service system to operate at peak efficiency and vice versa. The low-contact system has the capability of decoupling operations and sealing off the **technical core** (the production processes) from the environment, whereas the high-contact system does not.[13]

It is important for the service operations manager to determine how much customer contact is required to provide the service, because it has a major bearing on every decision. Table 17.4 lists some key decisions in service system design, contrasting high-contact and low-contact systems applicable to each decision. From Table 17.4 we can make several generalizations about the two classes of service systems:

- High-contact operations require people with good public relations skills. The quality associated with the service is directly related to the consumer's interaction with the service employee.
- Low-contact systems have a greater ability to match supply and demand. A high-contact system's supply capacity will only match customer demand a certain percentage of the time. Also, high-contact systems have to devote some portion of their capacity to performing public relations duties as part of the service.
- High-contact systems generally suffer from lack of standardization and uncertainty with respect to day-to-day operations. This occurs because the customer is in the production schedule and must be accommodated.
- Because orders cannot be stored to smooth production flows in high-contact systems, time pressures are much more prevalent. High-contact systems often mean that customers must wait for service, so any delay of consequence has an immediate effect on the customer.

What can the service operations manager do to design an efficient service delivery system when consumers are part of the service process? Chase's research shows companies should divide the service delivery system into high-contact and low-contact operations. One group of people handles all high-contact activities, and another group handles all low-contact activities. The high-contact group should have particularly good public relations skills, whereas the low-

[13]Richard B. Chase, "Where Does the Customer Fit in a Service Operation?" *Harvard Business Review* 56 (November–December 1978): 137–142.

| Design Consideration | High-Contact Operation | Low-Contact Operation |
|---|---|---|
| Facility location | Operations must be near the customer. | Operations may be placed near supply, transportation, or labor. |
| Facility layout | Facility should accommodate the customer's physical and psychological needs and expectations. | Facility should enhance production. |
| Product design | Environment as well as the physical product define the nature of the service. | Customer is not in the service environment, so the product can be defined by fewer attributes. |
| Process design | Stages of production process have a direct, immediate effect on the customer. | Customer is not involved in the majority of processing steps. |
| Scheduling | Customer is in the production schedule and must be accommodated. | Customer is concerned mainly with completion dates. |
| Production planning | Orders cannot be stored, so smoothing production flow will result in loss of business. | Both backlogging and production smoothing are possible. |
| Worker skills | Direct work force makes up a major part of the service product and so must be able to interact well with the public. | Direct work force need only have technical skills. |
| Quality control | Quality standards are often in the eye of the beholder and hence variable. | Quality standards are generally measurable and hence fixed. |
| Time standards | Service time depends on customer needs, and therefore time standards are inherently loose. | Work is performed on customer surrogates (e.g., forms), and time standards can be tight. |
| Wage payment | Variable output requires time-based wage systems. | Fixable output permits output-based wage systems. |
| Capacity planning | To avoid lost sales, capacity must be set to match peak demand. | Storable output permits setting capacity at some average demand level. |
| Forecasting | Forecasts are short term, time oriented. | Forecasts are long term, output oriented. |

Source: Richard B. Chase, "Where Does the Customer Fit in a Service Operation?" *Harvard Business Review* 56 (November–December 1978): 139.

TABLE 17.4
Major Design Decisions in High-Contact and Low-Contact Service Systems

contact group should have strong technical and analytical skills. Essentially, the service system is divided into front office operations and back office operations.

A typical hotel is a good example of a service business that separates high-contact and low-contact operations. Its high-contact employees include registration clerks, the bell captain, concierge, cashiers, and bellhops. These individuals interact with the guests and maintain a friendly, personal, one-on-one relationship with them. They form the front office operation. The hotel's low-contact employees include housekeepers, maintenance personnel, food and beverage workers, laundry attendants, telephone operators, and bookkeepers.

*The modern gas station/convenience store is a good example of a low customer contact operation.*

They do not have much direct interaction with customers, although they do contribute to the overall service. They form the back office operation. The front office operations stress customer interaction. The back office operations stress efficiency, productivity, and high use of capacity.

## Consumer Participation Approach

Consumer participation in services can take many forms. One example is the formal relationship with your bank, which is continuous after you open an account or become a "subscriber" to the services it offers. Another example is your continuous but informal relationship with the police department or fire department in your city. Still another example, involving services that are available only at discrete times, is the mail service we receive six days a week. Table 17.5 presents several examples of continuous service delivery versus discrete service transactions and formal versus informal relationships between customers and the service organization.

In many service systems the consumer is present while the service is occurring. This presents opportunities for involving the consumer in the service process in a way that increases productivity.

The wide spectrum of service delivery systems in turn provides many possibilities for consumer participation in the service process. Self-service involves almost the total commitment of the consumer to the service process. A typical video store is a good example of self-service—the consumer makes the rental decision unassisted and is responsible for transporting and using the product and returning it intact and on time. At the other end of the spectrum is personalized service in which the customer is almost completely dependent on the service provider. Even so, opportunities for consumer involvement exist. A

| Nature of Service Delivery | Type of Relationship Between the Service Organization and Its Customers | |
|---|---|---|
| | *"Membership" Relationship* | *No Formal Relationship* |
| Continuous delivery of service | Insurance | Radio station |
| | Telephone subscription | Police protection |
| | College enrollment | Lighthouse |
| | Banking | Public highway |
| | American Automobile Association | |
| Discrete transactions | Long-distance calls from subscriber phone | Car rental |
| | Theater-series subscription | Mail service |
| | Travel on commuter ticket | Toll highway |
| | | Pay phone |
| | | Movie theater |
| | | Public transportation |
| | | Restaurant |

Source: Christopher B. Lovelock, *Services Marketing: Text, Cases & Readings* (Englewood Cliffs, N.J.: Prentice-Hall, 1984), p. 54.

T A B L E   1 7 . 5
Consumer Participation in Services

doctor, lawyer, and architect all provide very personalized services yet rely on their patients or clients for information and direction.

Service systems that involve increased consumer participation are becoming more prevalent because of rising wage levels, which require the service provider to substitute consumers' labor for employees' labor. At fast-food restaurants we are encouraged to clean up after ourselves. Airlines provide storage so that passengers can carry luggage aboard. Banks and other financial institutions promote the use of automatic teller machines. Restaurants feature salad bars and buffets. The list is endless and simply reinforces the fact that the modern consumer has become a producer in the service process.

Service system design built around smoothing service demand is another trend. The inherent nature of demand for service exhibits a great deal of variability by time period. At a restaurant or gas station the variation is by hour of the day, at a theater or dry-cleaning store the variation is by day of the week, at a golf course or ski resort the variation is by season. Certain service businesses attempt to smooth service demand to achieve more uniform use of capacity and to improve productivity. A restaurant may offer price incentives for certain hours of the day, and a golf course typically uses a reservation system.

When attempts to smooth demand fail, services achieve high use of capacity by forcing consumers to wait for service. This is another form of involving the consumer in the service process. In order for the wait to be acceptable to the consumer, the service must offer good service and reasonable prices.

## Strategies for Managing Service Demand

The major factor in the success of many service businesses is the extent to which they are able to use their available capacity when demand is erratic. Figure 17.5 shows the effects of cyclical variations in demand on service capacity. Figure 17.5

F I G U R E   1 7 . 5
Effects of Cyclical Variations
in Service Demand on
Service Capacity

Source: Christopher H. Lovelock,
*Services Marketing: Text, Cases &
Readings* (Englewood Cliffs, N.J.:
Prentice-Hall, 1984), p. 281.

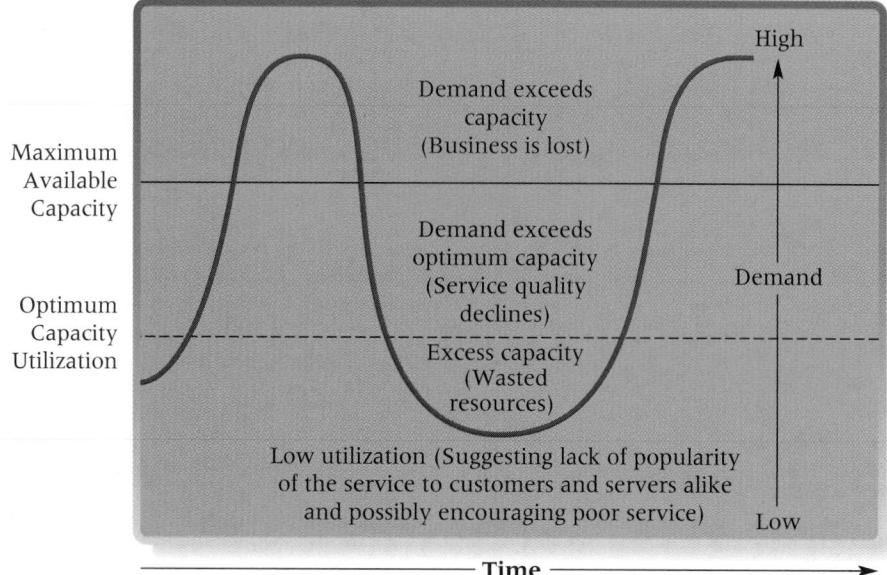

assumes that the maximum available capacity (solid line) is fixed over time. The optimum capacity utilization (broken line) is the level above which the consumer begins to perceive a deterioration in the quality of the service because of overcrowding. For example, when an airplane becomes more than about 75 percent full, service to its passengers typically deteriorates. The maximum available capacity reflects the upper limit on the capacity of the service facility. For some service facilities, particularly those involving amusement services, such as sports arenas and theaters, optimum and maximum capacity converge. These facilities are often built to a size that is smaller than that which would satisfy peak demand in order to encourage a sell out.

Figure 17.5 shows that a fixed-capacity service business may face one of four demand conditions:

■ Demand exceeds maximum available capacity—the business may lose customers.
■ Demand exceeds the optimum capacity level—no one is turned away, but all customers are likely to perceive a deterioration in the quality of service.
■ Demand and supply are well balanced at the level of optimum capacity.
■ Demand is below optimum capacity and productive resources are underused—the business is risking (in some instances) that customers may find the experience disappointing or have doubts about the viability of the service.

Christopher Lovelock suggests five common approaches to managing demand.[14] The first involves taking no action and simply letting demand seek its own level. This approach, while simple, reflects the absence of any strategy. The second and third approaches involve managing demand by reducing demand in

---

[14]Christopher H. Lovelock, "Strategies for Managing Capacity-Constrained Service Organizations," *Services Industry Journal* 4 (November 1984): 18–30.

peak periods and increasing demand in low periods, respectively. The fourth and fifth approaches involve inventorying demand, by using either a reservation system or a formalized queueing system. Table 17.6 links these five approaches to three demand/capacity scenarios, with commentary on the resulting interactions.

TABLE 17.6
Demand Management Approaches for Varying Capacity Situations

| | **Capacity Situation Relative to Demand** | | |
|---|---|---|---|
| *Approach Used to Manage Demand* | *Insufficient Capacity (Excess Demand)* | *Sufficient Capacity\* (Satisfactory Demand)* | *Excess Capacity (Insufficient Demand)* |
| Take no action | Unorganized queueing results. (May irritate customers and discourage future use.) | Capacity is fully utilized. (But is this the most profitable mix of business?) | Capacity is wasted. (Customers may have a disappointing experience for services like theater.) |
| Reduce demand | Pricing higher will increase profits. Communication can be employed to encourage usage in other time slots. (Can this effort be focused on less profitable desirable segments?) | Take no action (but see above). | Take no action (but see above). |
| Increase demand | Take no action unless opportunities exist to stimulate (and give priority to) more profitable segments. | Take no action unless opportunities exist to stimulate (and give priority to) more profitable segments. | Price lower selectively (try to avoid cannibalizing existing business; ensure all relevant costs are covered). Use communications and variation in products/distribution (but recognize extra costs, if any, and make sure appropriate trade-offs are made between profitability and usage levels). |
| Inventory demand by reservation system | Consider priority system for most desirable segments. Make other customers shift (a) outside peak period or (b) to future peak. | Try to ensure most profitable mix of business. | Clarify that space is available and that no reservations are needed. |
| Inventory demand by formalized queueing | Consider override for most desirable segments. Seek to keep waiting customers occupied and comfortable. Try to predict wait period accurately. | Try to avoid bottleneck delays. | Not applicable. |

\**Sufficient capacity* may be defined as maximum available capacity or optimum capacity, depending on the situation.
Source: Christopher H. Lovelock, "Strategies for Managing Capacity-Constrained Service Organizations," *Service Industries Journal* 4 (November 1984): 21.

## Price Incentives

Perhaps the simplest strategy for managing service demand is price incentives. Examples of price incentives are numerous, including

- The "Reach Out America" telephone call plan offered by AT&T that provides for less expensive long-distance rates on weekends and at night.
- Season-specific rates offered by resorts. For example, Table 17.7 lists some prices associated with the Deer Valley Ski Resort located near Park City, Utah.
- Pricing of airline tickets by virtually all domestic airlines to encourage travel on certain days of the week and over weekends.
- Movie theaters that offer lower prices for "rush hour" (before 6 P.M.) or matinee tickets.
- Golf courses or tennis courts that charge more for prime time or weekend use of facilities.

For price incentives to be effective as a demand management tool, the service operations manager must be able to determine whether the aggregate demand curve for a specific service varies sharply from one time period to another. Also, the operations manager needs to determine the shape and slope of the service's demand curve at various points in time. Further complications may arise because of demand curves for various aspects of the service that vary within time periods. For example, an automobile repair shop offers a wide range of services; the demand for tune-ups is quite different from the demand for transmission repairs. The service operations manager faces a difficult task in determining the nature of all these different demand curves. Field research, trial and error, and analyzing comparable service businesses are all ways to measure the effect of price incentives.

## Promoting Off-peak Demand

Promoting off-peak demand refers to the demand strategy of seeking different sources of demand in order to fill unused capacity. For example, many ski resorts have added "alpine" water slides and conference facilities to promote summertime use. Automobile repair facilities are often open at night and on weekends. Universities regularly use their athletic facilities to host a variety of youth sports camps during the summer. Public schools rent their facilities to church and civic organizations. Promoting off-peak demand also is a way to keep from overtaxing

**TABLE 17.7**
Nightly Room Rates
Deer Valley Ski Resort
(1993–1994)

| Property | Unit Type | Special Season | Regular Season | Holiday Season |
|---|---|---|---|---|
| Lakeside | 1 bedroom | $265 | $315 | $ 500 |
| Stag Lodge | 2 bedroom with spa | $715 | $815 | $1,365 |
| Mont Cervin | 2 bedroom | $680 | $765 | $1,120 |

NOTE: SPECIAL SEASON: Opening—December 19, 1993; January 2—21, 1994; March 27—Closing 1994
REGULAR SEASON: January 22–March 6, 1994
HOLIDAY SEASON: December 20, 1993–January 1, 1994

available capacity. Retail stores often conduct sales on certain slack days of the week (Tuesday or Wednesday) as a means of promoting off-peak demand.

## Partitioning Demand

Closely related to promoting off-peak demand is the strategy of partitioning demand. Because service demand usually does not originate from a homogeneous source, the operations manager can partition it into planned and random arrivals. An appointment system can control the planned arrivals, leaving the random arrivals to fill out the remaining capacity. Many repair service facilities operate in exactly this manner. So do restaurants and hotels.

## Inventorying Demand—Reservation Systems

Many services, particularly those of a personal nature, are provided by reservation or appointment. Doctors and dentists make appointments for routine patient care and allow some additional time for emergency situations.

Taking reservations presells the service capacity. It also allows customers to avoid waiting and to secure service at a specific time. The service business can assign demand to available capacity for a particular time period or at alternative locations. It is one way to inventory demand.

Problems arise when customers fail to keep appointments or when service businesses overbook. Strategies for dealing with these problems include requiring an advance fee for the reservation, which may not be refundable if the reservation is not kept, a practice of many hotels and even some doctors and dentists. Overbooking problems may mean that the service has to compensate the victims, as is typically done by airlines.

Operations Management in Practice 17.3 describes the evolution of American Airline's SABRE computerized reservation system.

## Inventorying Demand—Queueing Systems

Queueing systems, or waiting lines, are another way in which service companies can inventory demand. They can ask customers to wait in line for service on a first-come, first-served basis. Successful queueing systems require that the operations manager determine the maximum amount of time a person will wait and provide ways to make this interval pass quickly and pleasantly. Service companies try to do this by providing pleasant surroundings (nice furniture, music, entertainment), reading material, food and drink, and beginning the service process by both supplying and collecting preliminary information.

In some queueing systems certain users may receive a higher priority in the queue. Service companies can base this priority on the importance of the customer, on how long it will take to provide the service, or on the customer's willingness to pay a premium price for fast service. For example, most supermarkets and discount stores have an express lane to serve customers who want to purchase only a limited number of items. Hotels charge a premium price for valet parking or for quick laundry service. Preferred customers get the choice appointments at automobile repair shops. So operations managers have many ways to customize queueing systems to fit certain situations.

Waiting lines are discussed in detail in Tutorial 5 at the end of the textbook.

**OPERATIONS MANAGEMENT IN PRACTICE 17.3**

# SABRE— The Evolution of an Airline Demand Management System

SABRE, American Airline's computerized reservation system (CRS), and United Airline's APOLLO, the other leading CRS, have transformed service in the airline industry. SABRE has evolved through four distinct stages, over thirty years, and in each stage it has played a different role in the service offered by American Airlines.

American began working on a computerized reservation system in the late 1950s when its ability to handle its volume of reservations began to outrun its capacity. Initially, it was designed as a relatively simple inventory-management tool that could monitor available seats and attach passengers' names to the seats as they were booked. In 1963, the year SABRE debuted, it processed data related to 85,000 phone calls, 40,000 confirmed reservations, and 20,000 ticket sales. So, even at its inception it was a major technical breakthrough.

As the years went by the functionality of SABRE expanded greatly. By the mid-1970s SABRE was providing the basis for generating flight plans for aircraft, tracking spare parts, scheduling crews, and developing a range of decision support systems for management. SABRE became the control center through which American Airlines functioned.

In 1976, in response to United's single-channel sales channel called APOLLO, American developed and installed its own system in travel agencies. It soon included not only its own flights but also flights from other airlines. Through the mid-1980s American added new services to the data base (hotels, rail, rental cars), new features that helped travel agents offer better service, greatly increased the installed base of SABRE terminals, and created a training and support infrastructure. By the dawn of the 1990s the enhanced SABRE system was operating in more than 14,500 subscriber locations in forty-five countries.

continued

## Developing Complementary Services

Many service businesses have figured out that developing complementary services can expand their capacity. Restaurants routinely route waiting customers to the bar, producing revenue as well as providing a pleasant waiting experience for customers. Convenience stores have expanded their services by adding self-service gas pumps. Similarly, service stations have added convenience food operations. Video stores now sell food (popcorn, candy, soft drinks) as well as rent movies. By developing complementary services, services can make overall demand more uniform.

## Strategies for Controlling Service Supply

We have reviewed some strategies for managing service demand. Even so, operations managers often find that they cannot easily smooth demand for many services. So they must also have strategies for controlling service supply.

Earl W. Sasser suggests two basic strategies for controlling supply, whether patterns of demand can be predicted accurately in advance or not. They are the

Today SABRE can best be described as an "electronic travel supermarket" that links suppliers of travel and related services (including packaged tours, currency rates, Broadway shows) to retailers such as travel agents and directly to customers such as corporate travel departments. It has more than 45 million fares in its data base, with as many as 40 million changes entered each month. During peak periods SABRE handles almost 2,000 messages per second and creates more than 500,000 passenger name records per day. SABRE includes the schedules and fares of about 650 airlines, and American pays SABRE the same booking fees as other airlines do. SABRE's capacity to write tickets and issue boarding passes for American and other large carriers is similar. SABRE also sells SABRE's revenue-management expertise to other companies. Known as "yield management," it establishes different prices for seats on a flight and allocates seats to maximize revenues by calculating the optimal revenue yield per seat, flight by flight. SABRE's industry-leading U.S. market share is 40 percent of airline bookings.

Max D. Hopper, senior vice president for information systems at American Airlines, has been one of the major contributors to the evolution and success of the SABRE computerized reservation system. Looking to the future, he makes three observations about the emergence of an "information utility" in service systems:

- Powerful workstations will be common in offices and factories, and organizations will use them far more intensively and creatively than they do today.
- Companies will be technology developers rather than system builders, even for their most critical applications.
- Economies of scale will be more important than ever in information processing.

**chase-demand strategy** and the **level-capacity strategy**. Using the chase-demand strategy in a service business involves adjusting work force levels so that service output matches service demand throughout the planning period. It is appropriate when demand is volatile and unpredictable and the supply of relatively low-skilled labor for jobs requiring limited training is adequate. It requires more employees, and those employees exhibit a higher rate of turnover because the low-skill environment in which they operate is not very attractive. Using the level-capacity strategy in a service business involves maintaining a constant work force level throughout the planning period. Service operations managers use the level capacity strategy when more highly skilled people perform jobs for high pay, have some discretion, and work in a relatively pleasant environment. Recall that we discussed these strategies in detail in Chapter 11.

Table 17.8 reviews the chase-demand and level-capacity strategies. The top of the table contrasts the conditions that encourage the use of these alternative strategies. The bottom of the table summarizes the operating responses for the two strategies. Because the pure chase-demand strategy has a number of negative connotations, such as the sweatshop working conditions described in the table, service managers have sought ways to modify it to overcome volatile,

**(a) Conditions Encouraging:**

| Condition Encouraging: | Chase-Demand | Level-Capacity |
|---|---|---|
| Size of fluctuation in demand | Large | Small |
| Speed of fluctuation in demand | Fast | Slow |
| Predictability of fluctuation in demand | Unpredictable | Predictable |
| Cost structure | Highly variable | Highly fixed |
| Cost of poor service | Low | High |
| Cost of lost business | High | Low |

**(b) Operating Responses:**

| Operating Responses: | Chase-Demand | "Modified" Chase-Demand | Level-Capacity |
|---|---|---|---|
| Percentage of peak business covered with "base" capacity | Low | Moderate | High |
| Division of jobs | High | Low | Low |
| Labor skill level required | Low | Moderate | High |
| Job discretion | Low | Moderate | High |
| Compensation rate | Low | Improved | High |
| Working conditions | Sweat shop | Improved | Pleasant |
| Training required per employee | Low | (Greater cross-job training) | High |
| Labor turnover | High | Lower | Low |
| Hire-fire costs | High | Lower | Low |
| Error rate | High | Lower | Low |
| Amount of supervision required | High | Lower | Low |
| Type of budgeting and forecasting required | Short-run | Long-run | Long-run |

Source: James L. Heskett, W. Earl Sasser, Jr., and Christopher W.L. Hart, *Service Breakthroughs: Changing the Rules of the Game* (New York: Free Press, 1990), p. 151.

unpredictable demand. The modified chase-demand column in the middle of the lower half of the table reflects this effort.[15]

## Daily Work Shift Scheduling

Despite all they do to promote uniform demand, many service operations still experience erratic demand patterns. Daily work shift scheduling, or **shift scheduling**, is an important problem for such service organizations as telephone companies, banks, hospitals, police departments, and bus lines.

The general approach to daily work shift scheduling involves the following steps:

1. Forecast daily demand. Make a daily demand forecast that takes into account seasonality, weekday/weekend variations, and holidays.

[15]Earl W. Sasser, "Match Supply and Demand in Service Industries," *Harvard Business Review* 54 (November–December 1976): 133–140.

| Employee | M | T | W | Th | F | S | Su |
|---|---|---|---|---|---|---|---|
| Kim | X | Off | X | X | Off | X | X |
| Garcia | X | Off | X | X | Off | X | X |
| Eubank | X | X | X | X | X | Off | Off |
| Jones | X | X | X | X | X | Off | Off |
| Poldolsky | X | X | X | X | X | Off | Off |
| Stein | X | Off | X | X | X | X | Off |
| Greenbaum | X | X | Off | X | X | X | Off |
| Jefferson | X | X | X | Off | X | X | Off |
| Singhal | Off | X | X | X | X | X | Off |
| Stone | Off | X | X | X | X | X | Off |

|  | M | T | W | Th | F | S | Su | Total |
|---|---|---|---|---|---|---|---|---|
| **Capacity (C)** | 8 | 7 | 9 | 9 | 8 | 7 | 2 | 50 |
| **Requirements (R)** | 7 | 5 | 8 | 8 | 7 | 5 | 2 | 42 |
| **Excess (C − R)** | 1 | 2 | 1 | 1 | 1 | 2 | 0 | 8 |

2. Convert the forecast to hourly staffing requirements. Use the daily demand forecast to develop a profile of the number of workers required by hour.
3. Schedule work shifts. Use the hourly staffing requirements to devise work shifts that consist of a certain number of hours an employee is to work, including rest and meal periods.
4. Assign specific employees to specific shifts. Do this fairly, taking into consideration overtime work and scheduling of consecutive days off.

## Weekly Work Shift Scheduling

Daily work shift scheduling is only a part of the bigger problem of weekly work shift scheduling. Many services operate seven days a week. But most service employees want to be scheduled for five consecutive workdays with two consecutive days off. Weekly work shift scheduling tries to assign employees to a specific combination of workdays during a week or another standard period. Work force schedules translate the staffing plan into specific schedules of work for each employee (see Chapter 11 for a discussion of staffing plans).

**TABLE 17.9**
Initial Seven Oaks Health Care Center Work Force Schedule

**EXAMPLE 17.1**

Table 17.9 shows the weekly work force schedule for the Seven Oaks Health Care Center. The center is open seven days a week and is staffed by 10 employees.

The table shows the days of the week that each employee is to work; the Xs indicate the workdays for the employees. For example, Kim has Tuesday and Friday off each week, whereas Eubank has Saturday and Sunday off each week.

Determining the workdays for each employee determines the overall capacity for the staffing plan. For the work force schedule to be operational, it must also satisfy the daily work force requirements stated in the aggregate in the staffing plan. As Table 17.9 shows, the current work force schedule has a capacity of 50 people per week, a requirement of 42 people per week, and an excess of 8 people per week. If the work force schedule does not meet or exceed daily work force requirements, the scheduler has to rearrange days off until the requirements are satisfied. If this cannot be done, the center will need to hire more employees or schedule overtime hours.

A number of other constraints may be imposed on the work force schedule. Legal considerations may require that a certain number of doctors and nurses be on duty at all times. Behavioral considerations are also important. For example, the center may need to give personnel a certain number of consecutive days off each week or limit the consecutive workdays of employees to a certain maximum. Other considerations are vacations, holidays, or simply the preferences of the employees themselves.

Note that in Table 17.9 five employees did not receive two consecutive days off. Let us now consider an approach to work force scheduling that recognizes this constraint.[16] The goal of this method is to identify the two consecutive days off for each employee that minimize the total slack capacity while meeting the overall weekly requirement. The method has the following steps:

1. Choose the set of smallest requirements that includes at least two consecutive days. That is, choose the days with the lowest demand, next-lowest demand, and so forth, until there are at least two consecutive days.
2. Assign the employee the selected pair of days off. Subtract the requirement satisfied by the employee for each day worked from the total staffing requirement for that day.
3. If a tie occurs, ask the employee being scheduled to make the choice. If this is not possible, break the tie arbitrarily. For example, you could choose to give the employee Saturday and Sunday off instead of Sunday and Monday off.
4. Repeat steps 1 to 3 until all requirements are satisfied or a certain number of employees have been scheduled.

The initial set of requirements (see Table 17.9) is

| M | T | W | Th | F | S | Su | Assigned Employee |
|---|---|---|----|---|---|----|----|
| 7 | 5 | 8 | 8 | 7 | ⑤ | ② | Kim |

The unique pair of minimum requirements (circled) is S–Su. Consequently, the first employee, Kim, is scheduled to work Monday–Friday (Kim is scheduled to have Saturday and Sunday off).

We now reduce the requirements for M–F to reflect the scheduling of Kim. Observe that the requirements for S–Su are not reduced, because they were employee days off in the previous step. The second set of requirements is

| M | T | W | Th | F | S | Su | Assigned Employee |
|---|---|---|----|---|---|----|----|
| 6 | 4 | 7 | 7 | 6 | ⑤ | ② | Garcia |

[16]This approach is suggested by R. Riberwala, D. Phillipe, and J. Browne, "Optimal Scheduling of Two Consecutive Idle Periods," *Management Science* 19 (September 1972): 71–75.

The unique pair of minimum requirements (circled) is again S–Su. The second employee, Garcia, is scheduled to work Monday–Friday.

We now reduce the requirements for M–F to reflect the scheduling of Garcia. The third set of requirements is

| M | T | W | Th | F | S | Su | Assigned Employee |
|---|---|---|----|---|---|----|-------------------|
| 5 | 3 | 6 | 6 | 5 | ⑤ | ② | Eubank |

The pairs of minimum requirements are S–Su or Su–M. The third employee, Eubank, is (arbitrarily) scheduled to work Monday–Friday.

We now reduce the requirements for M–F to reflect the scheduling of Eubank. The fourth set of requirements is

| M | T | W | Th | F | S | Su | Assigned Employee |
|---|---|---|----|---|---|----|-------------------|
| ④ | ② | 5 | 5 | 4 | 5 | 2 | Jones |

The pairs of minimum requirements are Su–M or M–T. The fourth employee, Jones, is (arbitrarily) scheduled to work Wednesday–Sunday.

We now reduce the requirements for W–Su to reflect the scheduling of Jones. The fifth set of requirements is

| M | T | W | Th | F | S | Su | Assigned Employee |
|---|---|---|----|---|---|----|-------------------|
| 4 | 2 | 4 | 4 | 3 | ④ | ① | Poldolsky |

The pairs of minimum requirements are S–Su or Su–M. The fifth employee, Poldolsky, is (arbitrarily) scheduled to work Monday–Friday.

We now reduce the requirements for M–F to reflect the scheduling of Poldolsky. The sixth set of requirements is

| M | T | W | Th | F | S | Su | Assigned Employee |
|---|---|---|----|---|---|----|-------------------|
| ③ | ① | 3 | 3 | 2 | 4 | 1 | Stein |

The pairs of minimum requirements are Su–M, M–T, or T–W. The sixth employee, Stein, is (arbitrarily) scheduled to work Wednesday–Sunday.

We now reduce the requirements for W–Su to reflect the scheduling of Stein. The seventh set of requirements is

| M | T | W | Th | F | S | Su | Assigned Employee |
|---|---|---|----|---|---|----|-------------------|
| 3 | 1 | 2 | 2 | 1 | ③ | ⓪ | Greenbaum |

The pairs of minimum requirements are S–Su, Su–M, T–W, or Th–F. We break the tie by giving S–Su a preference. The seventh employee, Greenbaum, is scheduled to work Monday–Friday.

We now reduce the requirements for M–F to reflect the scheduling of Greenbaum. The eighth set of requirements is

| M | T | W | Th | F | S | Su | Assigned Employee |
|---|---|---|----|---|---|----|-------------------|
| 2 | 0 | 1 | ① | ⓪ | 3 | 0 | Jefferson |

The pairs of minimum requirements are T–W or Th–F. The eighth employee, Jefferson, is (arbitrarily) scheduled to work Saturday–Wednesday.

We now reduce the requirements for S–W to reflect the scheduling of Jefferson. The ninth set of requirements is

| M | T | W | Th | F | S | Su | Assigned Employee |
|---|---|---|---|---|---|----|-------------------|
| 1 | (0) | (0) | 1 | 0 | 2 | 0 | Singhal |

The unique pair of minimum requirements (circled) is T–W. The ninth employee, Singhal, is scheduled to work Thursday–Monday.

We now reduce the requirements of Th–M to reflect the scheduling of Singhal. The tenth set of requirements is

| M | T | W | Th | F | S | Su | Assigned Employee |
|---|---|---|---|----|---|----|-------------------|
| 0 | 0 | 0 | (0) | (0) | 1 | 0 | Stone |

We can make several pairs of assignments, so we chose one, Th–F, arbitrarily. The tenth and last employee, Stone, is assigned to work Saturday–Wednesday.

The final Seven Oaks Health Care Center work force schedule appears in Table 17.10. Because the amount of excess capacity is substantial, the work force schedule is not unique. Stone, for example, could have W–Th off without causing a capacity shortage. In fact, the Seven Oaks Health Care Center might be able to operate with one less employee, because of the total of eight days of excess capacity and because no day requires the presence of all ten employees.

## Part-time Staffing

In many service operations the demand pattern exhibits pronounced peaks at certain times of the day or days of the week. For example, restaurants exhibit demand peaks at meal times, and banks exhibit demand peaks on Fridays. When

**TABLE 17.10**
Final Seven Oaks Health Care Center Work Force Schedule

| Employee | M | T | W | Th | F | S | Su | Total |
|----------|---|---|---|----|---|---|----|-------|
| Kim | X | X | X | X | X | Off | Off | |
| Garcia | X | X | X | X | X | Off | Off | |
| Eubank | X | X | X | X | X | Off | Off | |
| Jones | Off | Off | X | X | X | X | X | |
| Poldolsky | X | X | X | X | X | Off | Off | |
| Stein | Off | Off | X | X | X | X | X | |
| Greenbaum | X | X | X | X | X | Off | Off | |
| Jefferson | X | X | X | Off | Off | X | X | |
| Singhal | X | Off | Off | X | X | X | X | |
| Stone | X | X | X | Off | Off | X | X | |
| **Capacity (C)** | 8 | 7 | 9 | 8 | 8 | 5 | 5 | 50 |
| **Requirements (R)** | 7 | 5 | 8 | 8 | 7 | 5 | 2 | 42 |
| **Excess (C − R)** | 1 | 2 | 1 | 0 | 1 | 0 | 3 | 8 |

this occurs, the businesses can use part-time employees to supplement regular employees. Using part-time employees helps trade off the risks associated with overstaffing and understaffing.

## Cross-training Employees

Cross-training employees so that they are multiskilled is perhaps one of the best strategies for controlling service supply. Many service systems involve several operations, not all of which may be busy at any one time. By cross-training employees to perform several or all operations, companies create flexibility and additional service supply. Cross-training also can help to build the morale of employees, because it can relieve them of the monotony of being idle.

A typical supermarket or discount store is a good example of the use of cross-training to increase supply. When business peaks occur and long waiting lines develop at checkout stands, these businesses use all their employees in the checkout process. When slow periods occur, employees stock shelves or clean up the store.

## Customer Self-service

We are all familiar with customer self service, because we are so routinely involved in the process. Fast-food restaurants have pretty much eliminated servers and table-cleaning personnel. Most gasoline stations are now all or mainly self-service.

In self-service operations consumers provide the demand exactly when they want it. Also, the consumer may smooth demand by choosing a time for service when the facility is not busy. Self-service businesses have fewer employees to manage and compensate. The customer expects faster and less expensive service as compensation for being a part of the service process.

## Adjusting or Sharing Capacity

Many service organizations attempt to physically design their facilities to allow for adjusting capacity. Restaurants have special rooms they open only to accommodate large groups or to alleviate heavy demand. Supermarkets and discount stores are regularly designed to have a large number of checkout stands. The actual number of checkout stands in use is constantly adjusted to prevailing demand conditions.

Service companies also share capacity. Airlines share gates, ramps, baggage-handling equipment, and ground personnel at airports. Schools and churches make their facilities available for use by other community groups.

By adjusting or sharing service capacity service companies are able to use their capacity effectively during slack periods. This enables them to avoid a large investment in equipment and facilities.

## Vehicle Routing

Scheduling customer service and routing service vehicles are key considerations in many service operations. Appliance repairs, installation of equipment, school busing, home repairs, and public health nursing are services in which the delivery of the service is essential to its overall performance. For trucking

*Routing bread delivery trucks is a key operations problem for a bakery.*

concerns, taxi companies, mail and package delivery companies, and mass transit services, the timely delivery of the product or the customer is the service.

In many service companies the routing of vehicles is a major operational problem that has a profound influence on the quality of service. We can describe the general vehicle-routing problem as follows. We have a certain number of customers with known delivery requirements and locations. We also have a fleet of vehicles with limited capacity. We seek to assign the trucks to specific routes in order to service all the customers while minimizing the total time or distance traveled. This general problem may be subject to various constraints. For example, union rules may restrict the time a driver can work, or customers may require that deliveries be made at certain times during the day. The general problem also has many variations. For example, school buses have to be routed to stop at various locations to pick up children, and mail delivery generally follows a certain street assignment.

## The Clarke-Wright Savings Heuristic

One procedure often used in vehicle-routing situations is the **Clarke-Wright savings heuristic**.[17] It is used to determine routes from a central depot or warehouse to $N$ delivery points or customers. The central depot is labeled zero (0). The initial assumption is that enough vehicles are available so that a unique (one) vehicle can be assigned to visit each of the $N$ customers. This means that $N$ vehicles are assigned to visit $N$ customers. Also, it is assumed that the time, cost, or distance associated with traveling between locations is symmetric.

[17]G. Clarke and J. W. Wright, "Scheduling of Vehicles from a Central Depot to a Number of Delivery Points," *Operations Research* 12 (July–August 1964): 568–581.

Customers

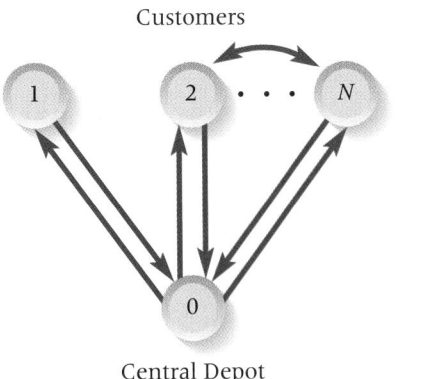

Central Depot

FIGURE 17.6
Initial Assignment of Routes

FIGURE 17.7
Illustration of Savings

Current Route                    Combined Route

The cost associated with going from location i to location j is $C_{ij}$. By symmetric costs we mean that $C_{ij} = C_{ji}$.

The initial assignment of $N$ vehicles to $N$ customers, which appears in Figure 17.6, is quite inefficient, because each vehicle must return to the depot after servicing each customer. The total cost of the initial assignment that uses $N$ vehicles is

$$\text{Total cost} = 2\,C_{01} + 2\,C_{02} + \ldots + 2\,C_{0N-1} + 2\,C_{0N} \qquad (17\text{-}1)$$

$$= \sum_{j=1}^{N} 2\,C_{0j}$$

An alternative is to combine routes in order to eliminate unnecessary return trips. For example, suppose that the routes to customers i and j are combined into one route. Does this new route achieve any cost savings when compared with the initial assignment? We now save one trip between i and 0 and one trip between 0 and j, but we add a new trip between i and j. Figure 17.7 illustrates this situation. The net savings, $S_{ij}$, achieved by linking locations i and j into the same route, is

$$S_{ij} = C_{i0} + C_{0j} - C_{ij} \qquad (17\text{-}2)$$

If this net savings is positive, linking the customers is beneficial.

The steps of the Clarke-Wright savings heuristic for a given set of route costs and customer requirements are as follows:

1.  Compute the net savings for all pairs of customers, using equation 17-2.
2.  Rank the net savings from biggest to smallest.

FIGURE 17.8
Banking Network

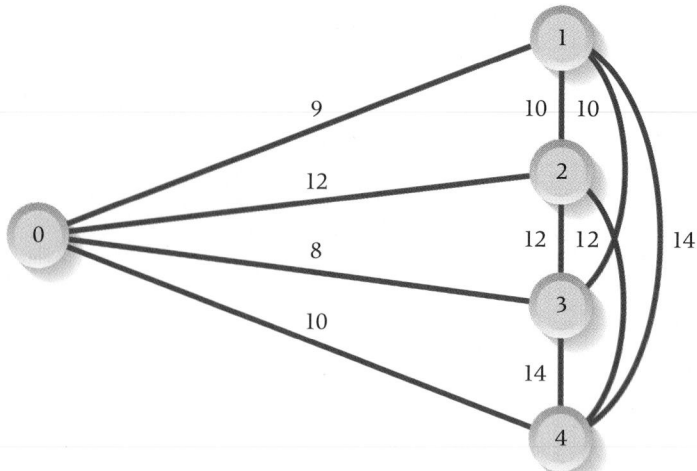

3. Choose the pair of customers with the biggest net savings, and determine whether it is feasible to link them. If this is possible, construct a new route by linking them. If not, discard the pair and choose the pair with the next biggest savings.
4. Continue with step 3 so long as the net savings is positive. The problem is solved when all positive savings have been used.

An urban bank has four branch offices in addition to its head office. The home office processes checks, so someone must pick the checks up from each branch office once a day and bring them to the home office. Figure 17.8 shows the network of the bank's home office and four branches, with distances shown in miles.

Table 17.11 presents the distances associated with the various routes, and only the top of the matrix is filled in, because the assumption is that all branch distances are symmetrical.

We use equation 17-2 to compute the net savings for each pair of locations. Consider linking locations 1 and 2. The net savings is

$$S_{12} = C_{01} + C_{02} - C_{12} \qquad (17\text{-}3)$$
$$= 9 + 12 - 10 = 11$$

Table 17.12 presents the net savings for all pairs of locations.

We start with an initial solution that services each branch office directly from the home office. The initial set of routes and their associated distances are

| Routes | Distances |
|--------|-----------|
| 0–1–0 | 9 + 9 = 18 |
| 0–2–0 | 12 + 12 = 24 |
| 0–3–0 | 8 + 8 = 16 |
| 0–4–0 | 10 + 10 = 20 |
| | Total 78 |

The next step is to choose the pair of branches (customers) with the greatest net savings and join them together. As we see in Table 17.12, the greatest net savings is 11 miles. If we connect branch offices 1 and 2, the routes and their associated distances are

| Routes | Distances |
|--------|-----------|
| 0–1–2–0 | 9 + 10 + 12 = 31 |
| 0–3–0 | 8 +  8 = 16 |
| 0–4–0 | 10 + 10 = 20 |
| | Total 67 |

Next we try to join branches 2 and 4, because this represents the next-greatest net savings (10 miles). If we connect branches 2 and 4, the routes and their associated distances are

| Routes | Distances |
|--------|-----------|
| 0–1–2–4–0 | 9 + 10 + 12 + 10 = 41 |
| 0–3–0 | 8 +  8 = 16 |
| | Total = 57 |

Next we try to join branches 2 and 3, because this represents the next-greatest net savings (8 miles). This is not feasible because we have already connected branch 2 with branches 1 and 4.

We next try to join branches 1 and 3, because this represents the next-greatest net savings (7 miles). If we connect branches 1 and 3, the route and its associated distance are

| Route | Distance |
|-------|----------|
| 0–3–1–2–4–0 | 8 + 10 + 10 + 12 + 10 = 50 |

Because we have connected all the branch offices with each other and the home office, we have solved the problem. We see that the overall distance traveled is 28 miles shorter than our original set of routes. Figure 17.9 shows the final network.

TABLE 17.11
Shortest Distance Matrix (Miles)

| From Branch | To Branch | 0 | 1 | 2 | 3 | 4 |
|-------------|-----------|---|---|---|---|---|
| 0 | | – | 9 | 12 | 8 | 10 |
| 1 | | | – | 10 | 10 | 14 |
| 2 | | | | – | 12 | 12 |
| 3 | | | | | – | 14 |
| 4 | | | | | | – |

TABLE 17.12
Net Savings Matrix (Miles)

| From Branch | To Branch | 0 | 1 | 2 | 3 | 4 |
|-------------|-----------|---|---|---|---|---|
| 0 | | – | – | – | – | – |
| 1 | | | – | 11 | 7 | 5 |
| 2 | | | | – | 8 | 10 |
| 3 | | | | | – | 4 |
| 4 | | | | | | – |

FIGURE 17.9
Final Network

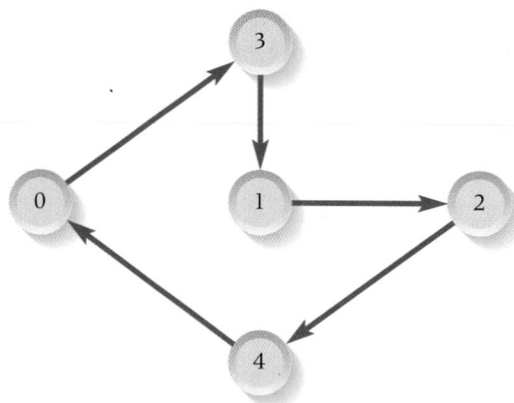

# ▶ Summary

Service system design and scheduling are formidable problems because of the unique nature of services. The service operations manager faces major challenges in scheduling and controlling services. Because of the cyclical and erratic nature of service demand, balancing this demand against service supply is a particularly difficult task.

**Learning Objective 1: Discuss the evolution of a service system.** A service system evolves in three stages. It begins with the definition of a service strategy, which defines the service business—what it is and what it will do. Then the business specifies the service package, which defines exactly what the customer will get. The final step is to determine the service delivery system.

**Learning Objective 2: Describe what is involved in developing a service strategy.** Developing a service strategy requires the matching of the distinctive competence of the organization with its primary task and the markets it serves. Several service strategies may be possible, including overall cost leadership, service differentiation, and service focus. The service strategy that is chosen should be clearly stated, focus on providing something a customer is willing to pay for, and convey a sense of mission for the organization.

**Learning Objective 3: List and describe the components of the service package.** The service package typically has four features: the supporting facilities or physical resources that must be available in order to provide the service; the facilitating goods or materials the buyer will consume; the explicit services, or

intrinsic benefits, that the service provides; and the extrinsic, or psychological, benefits of the service.

**Learning Objective 4: Discuss major approaches to service system design.** Major approaches to service system design include (1) the production-line approach, which uses technology and systems instead of people; (2) the technical core isolation approach, in which design of the service system is rooted in the extent of customer contact; and (3) the consumer participation approach, in which the consumer is an integral part of the service system.

**Learning Objective 5: Summarize strategies for altering service demand.** Typical ways to manage service demand are by offering price incentives, promoting demand in off-peak times or seasons, partitioning demand into planned and random arrivals, inventorying demand through reservation systems, inventorying demand through queueing systems, and developing complementary services.

**Learning Objective 6: Summarize strategies for controlling service supply.** Typical ways to control service supply are by adjusting work force levels so that service output matches service demand during the planning period (chase-demand strategy) or maintaining a constant work force level throughout the planning (level-capacity strategy). Other strategies for controlling service supply include daily and weekly shift scheduling, using part-time employees, cross-training employees, customer self-service, and adjusting or sharing capacity.

# ► Key Terms

| | | |
|---|---|---|
| chase-demand strategy | extent of contact | service package |
| Clarke-Wright savings heuristic | level-capacity strategy | service strategy |
| core service | performance specification | service system |
| customer contact | peripheral services | shift scheduling |
| design specifications | service differentiation | technical core |

# ► Discussion Questions

1. What are the major elements of the service package, and why are they important to the service operations manager?
2. What are the major ways in which service operations try to manage service demand?
3. What are the major ways in which service operations attempt to control service supply?
4. Why is a waiting line sometimes a desirable approach to balancing supply and demand for a service system?
5. What are the major ways in which service and manufacturing operations differ, and how are these differences important in scheduling services?
6. What are the important elements of a successful service strategy?
7. What are the major differences in developing a service strategy as opposed to a manufacturing strategy?

8. Provide some examples of your own of service organizations that have an effective service strategy, and describe what this service strategy involves.
9. Describe and discuss the major approaches to service system design.
10. Why is it important for the service operations manager to separate high-contact from low-contact customer services?
11. What are the savings in the Clarke-Wright savings heuristic?
12. What are some practical objectives that might be considered in evaluating routes for
    a. School buses?
    b. Emergency medical service vehicles?
    c. Bread delivery trucks?

# ► Problems

1. The Big Pig Grocery has determined its minimal personnel (checkout clerks) requirements for various days of the week. They are as follows:

| Day | Mon. | Tues. | Wed. | Thurs. | Fri. | Sat. | Sun. |
|---|---|---|---|---|---|---|---|
| Minimum Personnel | 3 | 4 | 5 | 6 | 6 | 7 | 5 |

   a. Develop a work force schedule that covers all requirements and gives each clerk 2 consecutive days off. (Assume that the clerks have no preference regarding which days they have off.)
   b. Specify the work schedule for each clerk.
   c. Determine how many clerks Big Pig needs.
2. The manager of the Universal Parcel Service forecasts the following minimal requirements for package handlers on a daily basis:

| Day | Mon. | Tues. | Wed. | Thurs. | Fri. | Sat. | Sun. |
|---|---|---|---|---|---|---|---|
| Minimum Personnel | 10 | 9 | 10 | 13 | 15 | 11 | 9 |

   a. Develop a work force schedule that covers all requirements and gives each package handler 2 consecutive days off. (Assume that the handlers have no preference regarding which days they have off.)
   b. Specify the work schedule for each handler.
   c. Determine how many handlers Universal needs.

**3.** Apply the Clarke-Wright savings heuristic to the data shown in the table that follows in order to compute the savings obtained by connecting
   **a.**  Location 2 with location 3
   **b.**  Location 2 with location 4
   **c.**  Location 2 with location 5
   **d.**  Location 3 with location 4
   **e.**  Location 3 with location 5
   **f.**  Location 4 with location 5

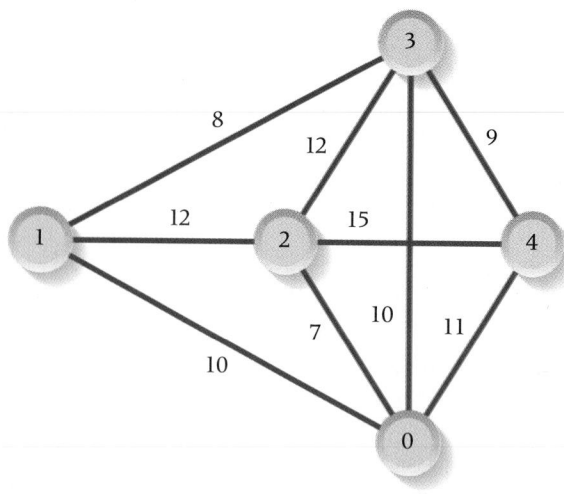

|  | To Location | | | | |
|---|---|---|---|---|---|
| From Location | *1* | *2* | *3* | *4* | *5* |
| 1 | – | 11 | 17 | 12 | 15 |
| 2 |  | – | 13 | 10 | 17 |
| 3 |  |  | – | 11 | 19 |
| 4 |  |  |  | – | 12 |
| 5 |  |  |  |  | – |

NOTE: Assume that location 1 is the central location.

**4.** Apply the Clarke-Wright savings heuristic to the data shown in the table that follows in order to compute the savings obtained by connecting
   **a.**  Node 1 and node 2
   **b.**  Node 1 and node 3
   **c.**  Node 1 and node 4
   **d.**  Node 2 and node 3
   **e.**  Node 2 and node 4
   **f.**  Node 3 and node 4

|  | To Node | | | | |
|---|---|---|---|---|---|
| From Node | *0* | *1* | *2* | *3* | *4* |
| 0 | – | 5 | 7 | 2 | 6 |
| 1 |  | – | 3 | 5 | 8 |
| 2 |  |  | – | 2 | 9 |
| 3 |  |  |  | – | 4 |
| 4 |  |  |  |  | – |

NOTE: Assume that node 0 is the central node.

**5.** Martinez Office Supply makes deliveries to 4 retail stores from a central warehouse, as shown in the following figure (distances are in miles):

Martinez Office Supply Network
   Use the Clarke-Wright savings heuristic to determine the best route in this situation.

**6.** The Clean-It-Up Refuse Collection Co. collects trash around Gotham City. It delivers the trash to 4 landfills, as shown in the following figure (distances are in miles):

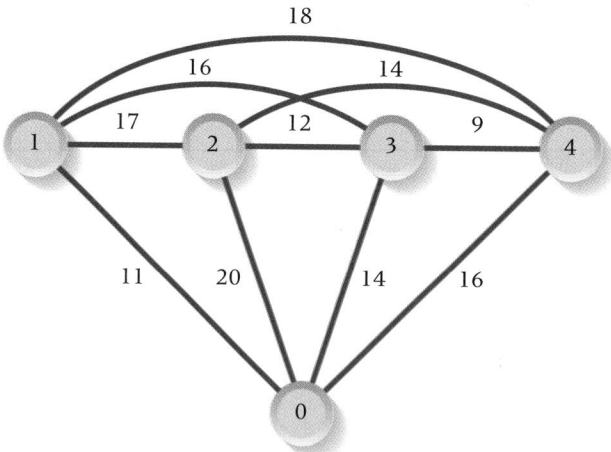

Clean-It-Up Refuse Collection Co. Network
   Use the Clarke-Wright savings heuristic to determine the best route in this situation.

7. Ace Auto Parts Co. has 4 retail outlets and 1 central warehouse. The table that follows shows the distances between all locations. Use this information with the Clarke-Wright savings heuristic to determine the best route for the company.

| | | | | | |
|---|---|---|---|---|---|
| 0–1 | 14 miles | 1–2 | 9 miles | 2–4 | 20 miles |
| 0–2 | 12 miles | 1–3 | 20 miles | 2–5 | 21 miles |
| 0–3 | 19 miles | 1–4 | 14 miles | 3–4 | 11 miles |
| 0–4 | 16 miles | 1–5 | 13 miles | 3–5 | 19 miles |
| 0–5 | 13 miles | 2–3 | 9 miles | 4–5 | 13 miles |

## ► Selected References

Albrecht, Karl. *At America's Service: How Corporations Can Revolutionize the Way They Treat Their Customers.* Homewood, Ill.: Dow Jones-Irwin, 1988.

Albrecht, Karl, and Ron Zemke. *Service America! Doing Business in the New Economy.* Homewood, Ill.: Dow Jones-Irwin, 1985.

Bowen, David E., Richard B. Chase, Thomas G. Cummings, and Associates. *Service Management Effectiveness: Balancing Strategy, Organization, Human Resources, Operations, and Marketing.* San Francisco: Jossey-Bass, 1990.

Collier, David A. *Service Management: The Automation of Services.* Reston, Va.: Reston, 1985.

————. *Service Management: Operating Decisions.* Englewood Cliffs, N.J.: Prentice-Hall, 1987.

Czepiel, John A., Michael R. Solomon, and Carol Suprenant. *The Service Encounter.* Lexington, Mass.: D.C. Heath, 1985.

Fitzsimmons, James A., and Mona J. Fitzsimmons. *Service Management for Competitive Advantage,* New York: McGraw-Hill, 1994.

Heskett, James L. *Managing in the Service Economy.* Boston: Harvard Business School Press, 1986.

Heskett, James L., W. Earl Sasser, Jr., and Christopher W.L. Hart, *Service Breakthroughs: Changing the Rules of the Game.* New York: Free Press, 1990.

Lovelock, Christopher H. *Services Marketing: Text, Cases & Readings.* Englewood Cliffs, N.J.: Prentice-Hall, 1984.

————. *Managing Services: Marketing, Operations, and Human Resources.* Englewood Cliffs, N.J.: Prentice-Hall, 1988.

Murdick, Robert G., Barry Render, and Roberta S. Russell. *Service Operations Management.* Boston: Allyn & Bacon, 1990.

Normann, Richard. *Service Management: Strategy and Leadership in Service Businesses.* Chichester, England: Wiley, 1984.

Sasser, W. Earl, R. Paul Olsen, and D. Daryl Wyckoff. *Management of Service Organizations: Text, Cases, and Readings.* Boston: Allyn & Bacon, 1978.

Shelp, Ronald K., John C. Stephenson, Nancy S. Truitt, and Bernard Wasow. *Service Industries and Economic Development.* New York: Praeger, 1985.

Voss, Christopher, Colin Armistead, Bob Johnston, and Barbara Morris. *Operations Management in Service Industries and the Public Sector.* Chichester, England: Wiley, 1985.

Zeithaml, Valerie A., A. Parasuraman, and Leonard L. Berry. *Delivering Service Quality.* New York: Free Press, 1990.

# National Technological University

## Introduction

The National Technological University (NTU) is a very unusual university:

- Its mission focuses exclusively on advanced technical education.
- It has no central campus but instead uses a satellite and other telecommunications technologies to deliver instruction.
- Its "campus" consists of forty-five member universities that provide an excellent faculty, hundreds of courses, and outstanding teaching facilities.
- Its students are working adults with challenging jobs in high-technology organizations.
- Its subscribing organizations include many of the best companies in the world—they are selective, enlightened, creative, and successful.

With a critical mission, sweeping curriculum, exceptionally strong faculty, and a nationwide delivery system, NTU truly symbolizes a higher order of education.

For the U.S. economy to remain vital, particularly with respect to manufacturing, a large percentage of working engineers and technical managers will have to continue their education beyond the undergraduate level. This will likely be especially true for older engineers and technical managers who were not exposed to technological changes during their formal education.

However, many companies cannot afford the time or cost to send their engineers and technical managers to full-time graduate programs at universities. But they recognize that what these employees need to enhance their productivity is career-long education that does not disrupt full-time work.

The National Technological University was established as a separate nonprofit, private educational corporation in January 1984. As an institution of higher education, it has the unique mission of serving the advanced educational needs of graduate engineers, technical professionals, and managers. It awards master's degrees to qualified individuals and provides research seminars in selected disciplines. It operates a modern telecommunications delivery system for convenient, flexible, and on-site service and offers noncredit short courses, tutorials, seminars, and research symposia to introduce advanced technology concepts to a broad range of technical professionals.

Three major building blocks comprise NTU: the service suppliers (the member universities), the service customers (the reception sites at the various facilities of the associated organizations), and the administration of the service delivery system (the coordination and other services provided by NTU headquarters).

## NTU's Service Suppliers

NTU offers graduate programs of study leading to master of science degrees in eleven disciplines:

- Computer engineering
- Computer science
- Electrical engineering
- Engineering management
- Hazardous waste management
- Health physics
- Management of technology
- Manufacturing systems engineering
- Materials science and engineering
- Software engineering
- Special majors

NTU's participating universities are chosen on the basis of their academic standing and reputation, experience with long-distance learning, and the interest of their faculty in the program. Table 1 lists the leading U.S. universities that participated during the 1992–1993 school year. Some universities participate in all eleven disciplines, whereas others provide courses only in selected subject areas. The *NTU Bulletin* lists more than 890 courses from these participating universities. Many of the universities produce the majority of the noncredit courses, tutorials, and research teleconferences offered by NTU; private companies, independent consultants, and private individuals produce the rest. Additional universities continue to join the NTU network.

## NTU's Service Customers

NTU's service customers are its subscribing corporations or government agencies. NTU today delivers instruction to 649 sites, each located at a facility operated by one of 131 sponsoring organizations. Six

**TABLE 1.** NTU Participating Universities

| | |
|---|---|
| Arizona State University | University of Alaska at Fairbanks |
| Boston University* | University of Arizona |
| Colorado State University | University of California—Berkeley |
| Columbia University | University of California—Davis |
| Cornell University | University of Colorado—Boulder |
| George Washington University | University of Delaware |
| Georgia Institute of Technology | University of Florida |
| GMI Engineering & Management Institute* | University of Idaho |
| Illinois Institute of Technology | University of Illinois at Urbana-Champaign |
| Iowa State University | University of Kentucky |
| Kansas State University | University of Maryland |
| Lehigh University | University of Massachusetts |
| Michigan State University | University of Michigan |
| Michigan Technological University | University of Minnesota |
| New Jersey Institute of Technology | University of Missouri—Rolla |
| | University of New Mexico |
| New Mexico State University | University of Notre Dame* |
| North Carolina State University | University of South Carolina |
| Northeastern University | University of Southern California* |
| Oklahoma State University | University of Tennessee—Knoxville |
| Old Dominion University | |
| Purdue University | University of Washington |
| Rensselaer Polytechnic Institute* | University of Wisconsin—Madison |
| Southern Methodist University | |

*Contributes only to noncredit Advanced Technology and Management Program

Canadian and Mexican sites are in NTU's satellite network, and NTU member corporations have 46 sites outside of North America. Additionally, 59 government sites are on the NTU network, and the NTU has community sites and is interconnected with other networks. NTU aired 528 graduate credit courses and 321 noncredit courses during the 1992–1993 academic year.

All NTU students are employees of a subscribing organization. Eighty-four percent of the students are men and 16 percent are women; their average ages are thirty-four and thirty-two, respectively. The predominant entry degree is the bachelor of science (60 percent); 30 percent hold master of science degrees, 5 percent hold doctorates, and the remainder bachelor of arts, master of business administration, or other degrees.

## NTU's Administration

The administrative headquarters for NTU, located in Fort Collins, Colorado, consists of two divisions, the credit and noncredit programs. The credit program consists of the eleven master's degree programs, each of which is offered on the basis of individual courses supplied by NTU member universities. Academic committees formed by professors from participating universities establish minimum requirements and standards for individual students, courses, credits, and all other academic matters. Students can earn and accumulate credits from any NTU member university, and transferring a limited amount of credits from nonmember universities is possible. NTU has established its own set of graduate requirements, which is independent of those at its member institutions.

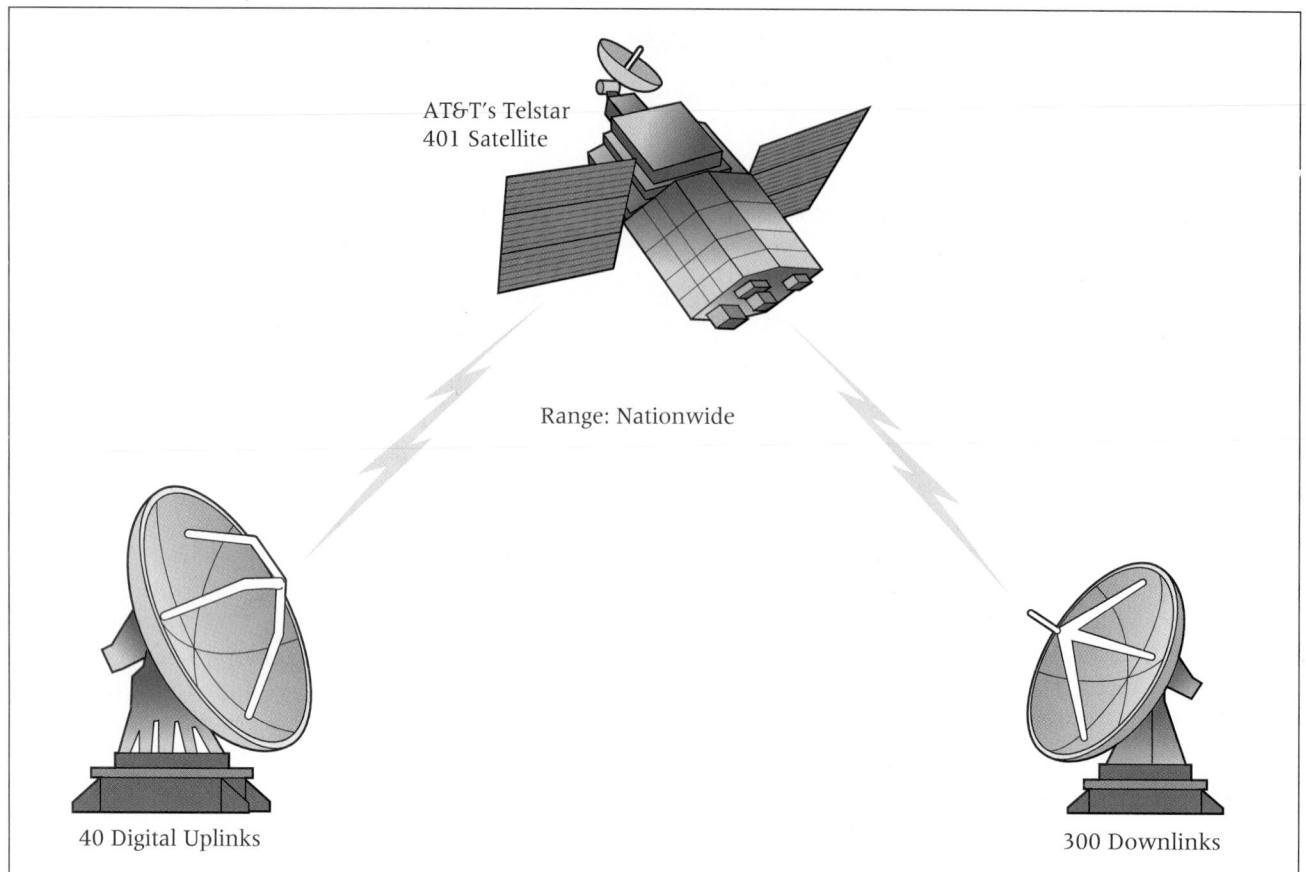

AT&T's Telstar
401 Satellite

Range: Nationwide

40 Digital Uplinks

300 Downlinks

**FIGURE 1.** Major Components of the NTU Satellite
Network

The main function of the administrative headquarters is coordinating the supply and demand for
courses, registering students, organizing broadcasts,
and training and providing support for the local site
coordinators. For the noncredit program NTU headquarters has main responsibility for marketing and
producing the individual short courses or seminars.
NTU headquarters also has the strategic objective of
expanding the bases of supply and demand for all
types of courses.

## The NTU Service Delivery System

NTU is a truly unique institution of higher education,
not only in the United States but throughout the
world. It built and operates a sophisticated satellite
telecommunications network. More important, it put
together and operates a unique academic network
that meets the advanced educational needs of thousands of technical professionals and managers at hundreds of geographically dispersed work sites.

Figure 1 shows the major components of the NTU
satellite network. The NTU network uses Telstar 401,
a new Ku-band domestic communications satellite, to
provide fourteen compressed digital video channels
throughout the day and night. The satellite operates
in the 12/14/GHz band. NTU has installed a series of
satellite uplink stations, and a network of television
receive-only terminals is at each organizational site of
participating graduate students. The technical operations of the network are controlled at the NTU Network Control Center, which prepares schedules and
monitors satellite channels for technical quality.

To make optimum financial use of satellite transponder time and to deal with the realities of the
working students' class time, courses are transmitted
around the clock, seven days a week. Videotape machines record most courses at the students' sites for

use at the convenience of the students. Electronic mail, fax, telephone, U.S. mail, and overnight mail service are the primary means that students and instructors use to communicate, although computer conferencing is also available. All students can participate and interact with students at other sites as well as with the instructors. Normal workday hours on the network are used for seminars, conferences, and classes that require real-time interaction.

NTU students use instructional services provided by the sponsoring organizations, including the instructional areas, computer access, selected equipment, laboratories, telecommunications equipment, and educational offices. Finally, the institutional and organizational libraries, combined with the public and academic libraries where the students are located, provide the learning materials the students need for their studies. Because of the satellite delivery facilities students have access to a range of materials beyond the normal capacity of any single institution.

## A Perspective on NTU

NTU has awarded degrees to 373 individuals since 1986; 118 were conferred in 1993. In the 1992–1993 academic year saw 5,213 course enrollments, up more than 11 percent from the previous year. By 1995 NTU is expected to become a top-ten provider of master's degrees in engineering. Virtually all graduates report that they would not have been able to get graduate degrees by any other means.

How do the employers evaluate NTU? Eastman-Kodak recently made an in-depth study of NTU, summarizing its findings as follows:

- Undergraduate level education is not enough to prepare our technical employees for many of the challenges they face in performing the required tasks.
- Master's level education significantly improves job performance.
- Courses are applicable to work assignment; students are able to apply many of the new tools immediately.
- National Technological University's faculty provide state-of-the-art information.
- The variety of courses offered by National Technological University is extremely important; it gives students/employees the pertinent information, when needed.[1]

[1]Lionel Baldwin, "The National Technological University in Early 1989," unpublished paper, p. 8.

In the Eastman-Kodak study technical professionals estimated that their effectiveness on the job had increased by 25 to 35 percent as a result of completing the NTU graduate program of study. They also cited specific examples of significant project savings in dollars and time that resulted from advanced study.

NTU has been guided by a clear set of goals from its inception—enhancing personal and corporate productivity by providing America's engineers and technical managers with a set of excellent classes, taught by excellent professors, at their work sites. It has been remarkably successful at providing a long-distance education service, and it has shown great flexibility in producing, transmitting, and distributing its educational services in a cost-effective manner. Its future seems secure and promising, and its mandate is likely to expand and diversify, both in the United States and abroad.

## ► Acknowledgements

The preparation of this case was greatly assisted by Dr. Lionel V. Baldwin, president, National Technological University. Material for the case was drawn from the following sources:

Baldwin, Lionel V. "The National Technological University in Early 1989," unpublished paper.

Fwu, Bih-jen et al. "National Technological University (NTU): A Case Study on Growth and Expansion in Distance Education" (paper presented at the XVth World Conference of the International Council of Distance Education, Caracas, November 1990).

Graham, Ellen. "Distance Education Uses Electronic Links to Recast the Campus," *Wall Street Journal*, September 13, 1991, pp. A1, A5.

National Technological University. *Long Range Plan, 1990–1995*. Fort Collins, Colo., October 1990.

_____. *National Technological University Bulletin*. Fort Collins, Colo., May 1991.

_____. *National Technological University Annual Report, 1992–1993*, Fort Collins, Colo., August 1993.

## ► Discussion Questions

1. What are some of the factors that make the National Technological University such an unusual university?
2. What are the major building blocks of NTU's service delivery system?
3. What types of technology does NTU use in its service delivery system?
4. Evaluate the unique mission of NTU.
5. What sorts of competitive pressures is NTU likely to confront in the future?

## CHAPTER 18

# Project Management

*The only things that evolve by themselves in an organization are disorder, friction, and malperformance.*

PETER DRUCKER

**Introduction**

**PERT and CPM**
*OPERATIONS MANAGEMENT IN PRACTICE 18.1: Project Management for Product Launch at Oldsmobile*

**Managing Project Resources**
*OPERATIONS MANAGEMENT IN PRACTICE 18.2: Using Project Management Tools in Building Construction at Michigan State University*

**PERT Networks and Uncertain Time Estimates**

**Guidelines for Managing Projects**
*OPERATIONS MANAGEMENT IN PRACTICE 18.3: Platform Teams in the U.S. Auto Industry*

*After completing this chapter you should be able to*

1. Describe how to use a work breakdown structure to manage projects
2. Describe how a project network differs from a Gantt chart
3. Discuss how project managers use the concepts of earliest and latest start times and the critical path
4. Describe how to use a project network to help manage project budgets
5. Discuss the assumptions used in PERT (program evaluation and review technique) to view project completion time in a probabilistic fashion
6. Discuss the importance of behavioral factors in project management

# Introduction

**Project management techniques** are fundamental tools for successfully planning, scheduling, and controlling complex projects. Manufacturers routinely use project management techniques to manage the production of certain low-volume products such as ships and aircraft. Other types of production and service systems also use these techniques. The most significant aspect of project management is that it provides powerful tools for managing the development and implementation of the new products, systems, and facilities that will increasingly determine a company's competitive advantage in the twenty-first century.

The recent trend toward fewer middle managers, flatter organizational structures, and empowered employees means that managers find themselves managing cross-functional projects and processes more frequently and managing narrowly defined functions less frequently. The ability to effectively lead a diverse team in the successful achievement of a goal is becoming increasingly important.

In general, projects have the following eight characteristics:

1. A one-time focus
2. A specific purpose and desired results
3. A start and a finish
4. A time frame for completion
5. The involvement of a cross-functional group of people
6. A limited set of resources
7. A logical sequence of interdependent activities
8. A clear user (client, customer) of the results[1]

Projects are successful if they are completed on time, within budget, and to performance requirements. As Figure 18.1 shows, time, cost, and performance usually are conflicting goals. Achieving performance goals requires time and money. However, reducing performance requirements and/or spending additional money (overtime, overnight mail, subcontracting, and so on) can often save time. Balancing these competing objectives is one of the most difficult and challenging tasks of the project manager.

A number of tools are available for managing projects. We illustrate these tools throughout this chapter by using the example of a new product development project.

[1]W. Alan Randolph and Barry Z. Posner, *Getting the Job Done! Managing Project Teams and Task Forces for Success* (Englewood Cliffs, New Jersey: Prentice Hall, 1992), p. 3.

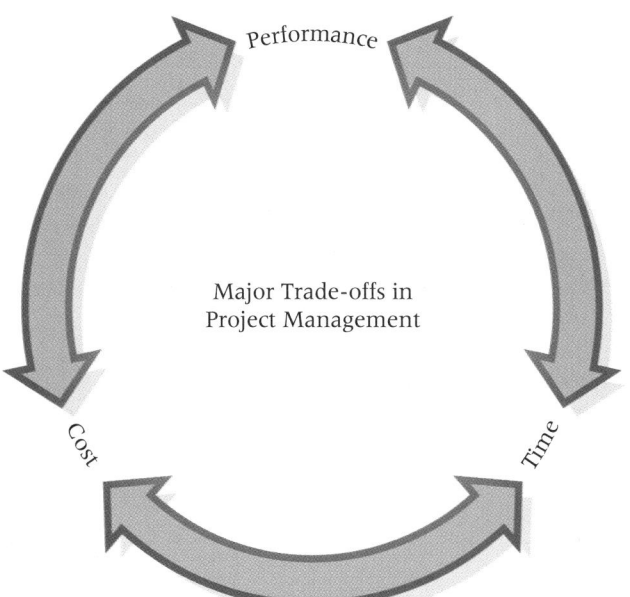

Performance

Major Trade-offs in
Project Management

Cost

Time

FIGURE  18.1
Trade-offs in Project
Management

**EXAMPLE 18.1**

A major manufacturer of bicycles is planning to enter the high-end market for mountain bikes by designing a new, state-of-the-art mountain bike. The bicycle is to be a completely new design, and management has directed the design team to incorporate the latest technology in every facet of the product—frame, gears, wheels, brakes, and so on—yet keep the price of the bike within $100 of leading competitors' prices.

The first step is a preliminary market analysis to determine which features are most important to buyers of the competing bikes. Once this is done, the engineering department will develop preliminary product design alternatives, while the manufacturing department will work in parallel on a preliminary manufacturing study. After the preliminary product design alternatives and manufacturing study are finished, the company will evaluate the product design alternatives in terms of their ability to meet the market demands and their manufacturability. The evaluation will result in the selection of the best product design. After making the selection the company will develop detailed marketing plans and detailed designs for the product and the manufacturing process. After the detailed product design is completed, it will build a prototype of the product. The company will finalize the product design after completing and testing the prototype and after finishing the design of the manufacturing process. Then the company will order component parts and production equipment. After the production equipment is received, it will be installed. When the new product development project is finished, new product introduction (which the company should also manage with project management tools) can begin. Table 18.1 provides time estimates for each of the new product development activities.

TABLE 18.1
Duration Times for Mountain
Bike Development Project

| Activity | Expected Duration (months) |
|---|---|
| A—Do preliminary market analysis | 1.0 |
| B—Develop preliminary product designs | 3.0 |
| C—Do preliminary manufacturing study | 1.0 |
| D—Evaluate and select best product design | 1.0 |
| E—Develop detailed marketing plans | 1.0 |
| F—Design manufacturing process | 3.0 |
| G—Develop detailed product design | 3.0 |
| H—Build and test prototype | 1.0 |
| I—Finalize product design | 1.5 |
| J—Order components | 1.0 |
| K—Order production equipment | 3.0 |
| L—Install production equipment | 2.0 |

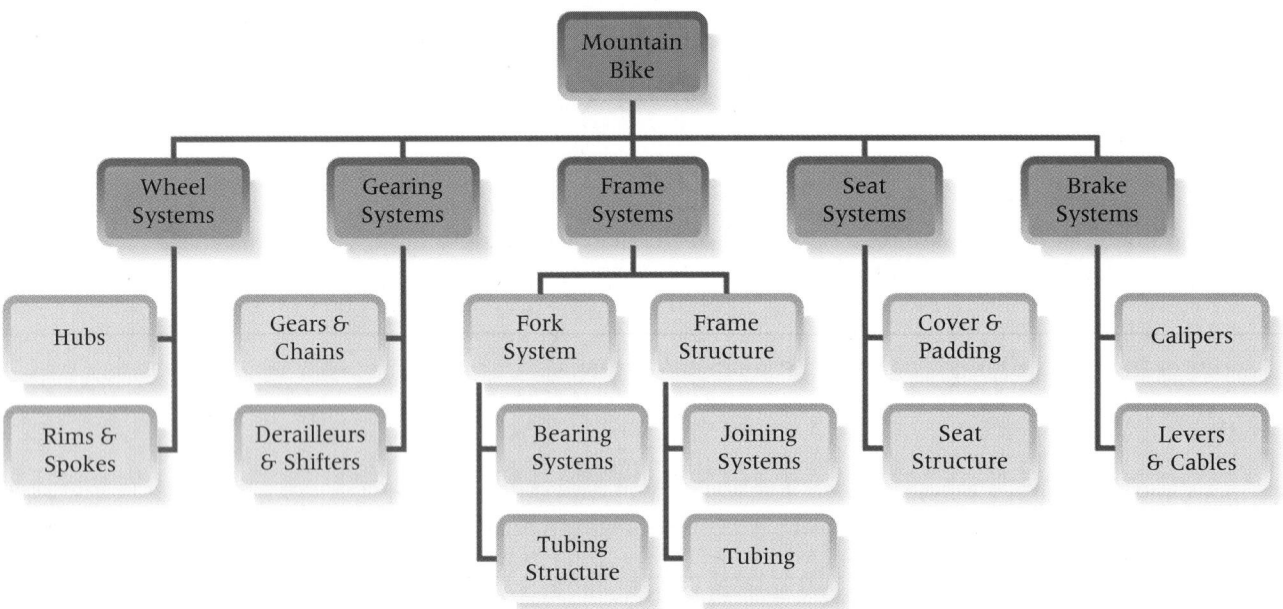

FIGURE 18.2
Work Breakdown Structure
for Mountain Bike
Development Project

# Work Breakdown Structures (WBS)

One tool available to a company for managing a project is a work breakdown structure. The National Aeronautics and Space Administration's *Handbook for Preparation of Work Breakdown Structures* provides a good definition for **work breakdown structure (WBS):**

> Generically, a WBS is a family tree subdivision of effort required to achieve an objective (e.g., program, project, contract, etc.). The WBS is developed by starting with the end objective required and successively subdividing it into manageable components in terms of size and complexity, such as program, project, system, subsystems, components, tasks, subtasks, and work elements. It should be product or

task oriented and should include all the necessary effort which must be undertaken to achieve the end objective.[2]

Figure 18.2 shows a WBS for the mountain bike project. Because it defines the work required to complete the project and helps to show the required interfaces, a WBS is useful for complex projects. The organizational structure of the project will in many cases parallel the WBS, because the company may assign responsibility for individual elements in the WBS to contractors, project teams, or individuals.

## Gantt Charts

Although the WBS is useful in project management, it does not address the timing of individual work elements. One way to show the timing of activities is with a **Gantt chart** (developed by Harry Gantt in 1916). This chart gives a time line for each activity of a project. Figure 18.3 is a Gantt chart for the new product development project.

Gantt charts have proved useful in a number of areas, including production scheduling. However, for project management purposes they have one weakness: They do not explicitly specify the precedence relationships of activities. Note that the detailed marketing, manufacturing, and product design activities in Figure 18.3 (activities E, F, and G) do not start until the company has evaluated and selected the best product design alternative (activity D), which is consistent with the order of activities given in the project description. Development of the Gantt chart in Figure 18.3 considered such precedence relationships, but the figure does not show these relationships explicitly.

FIGURE 18.3
Gantt Chart for Mountain
Bike Development Project

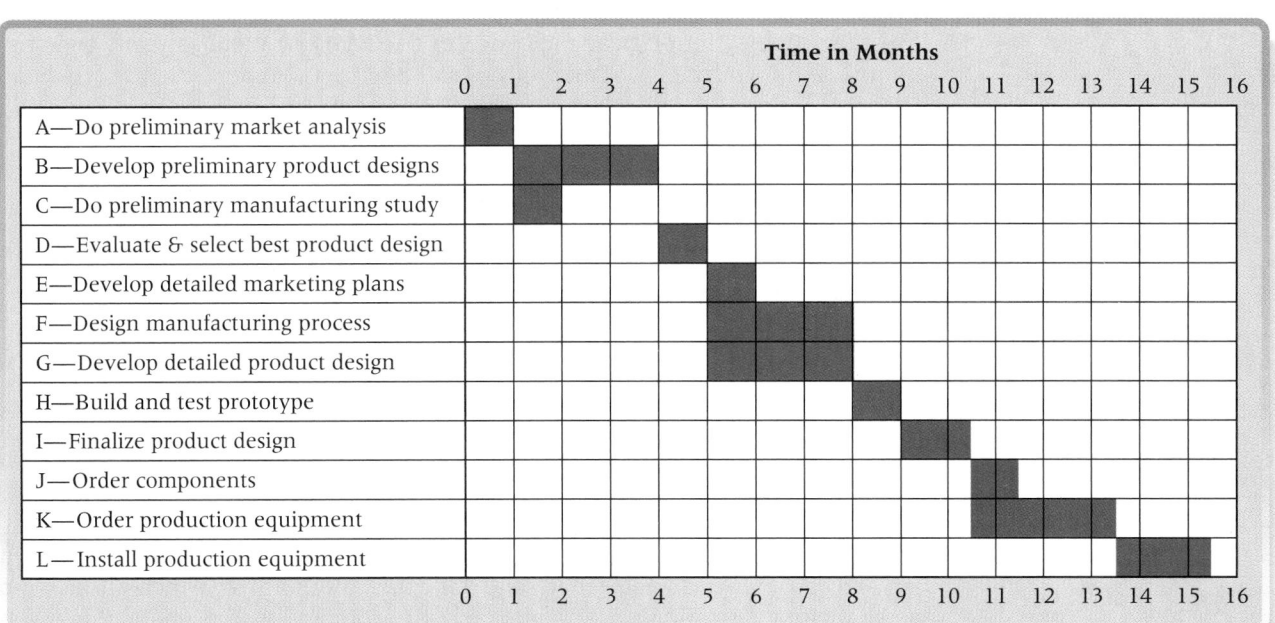

[2]National Aeronautics and Space Administration, *Handbook for Preparation of Work Breakdown Structures* (Washington, D.C.: U.S. Government Printing Office, 1975), p. 1.

*Mountain bikes, specifically designed for rough terrain, are both agile and durable.*

# PERT and CPM

PERT and CPM networks show precedence relationships explicitly. The **program evaluation and review technique (PERT)** is one of two project management techniques developed during the late 1950s. The Special Projects Office of the U.S. Navy developed PERT in the late 1950s during the development of the Polaris Submarine-Launched Ballistic Missile System. At the same time DuPont was developing the **critical path method (CPM)** to manage plant construction.[3] Although the two methods were developed independently, they are surprisingly similar. Still, they have two major differences:

- ■ PERT was developed to acknowledge uncertainty in the times required to complete activities. Thus, PERT treats activity time as a random variable, whereas CPM requires a single deterministic time value for each activity.
- ■ PERT focuses exclusively on the time variable, whereas CPM includes the analysis of time/cost trade-offs.

Today, project management software is based on both PERT and CPM concepts and usually includes features of both systems. A **project network** is used to portray graphically the interrelationships of the elements of a project and to show the order in which the activities must be performed.

One of two methods—activity on arc and activity on node—is used to construct project networks. The **activity-on-node** method uses circles, or *nodes*, to represent activities required by the project and arrows, or *arcs*, to indicate precedence relationships. The **activity-on-arc** method uses an arc to represent an activity, and each node represents an *event*, the point at which all activities leading into that node are completed. By convention an originating event

---

[3]Harvey M. Sapolsky, *The Polaris System Development: Bureaucratic and Programmatic Success in Government* (Cambridge, Mass.: Harvard University Press, 1972), pp. 118–119.

denotes the "start" of the project, and a terminal event marks the "end" of the project. The direction of the arrows or arcs shows the sequence of events. This chapter uses the activity-on-arc method, which is consistent with a PERT-type system. Figure 18.4 shows both methods.

## Construction of a Project Network

Two simple rules govern the construction of an activity-on-arc project network:

- Each activity must be represented by only one directed arc.
- No two activities may begin and end on the same two nodes (all activities are uniquely represented by their beginning and ending nodes).

For example, if activities A and B occur in parallel, the temptation is to represent this relationship as shown in Figure 18.5. But because we identify all activities by their beginning and ending node numbers, we must introduce a **dummy activity**, shown as *d* in Figure 18.6, to avoid identical representations for the two activities.

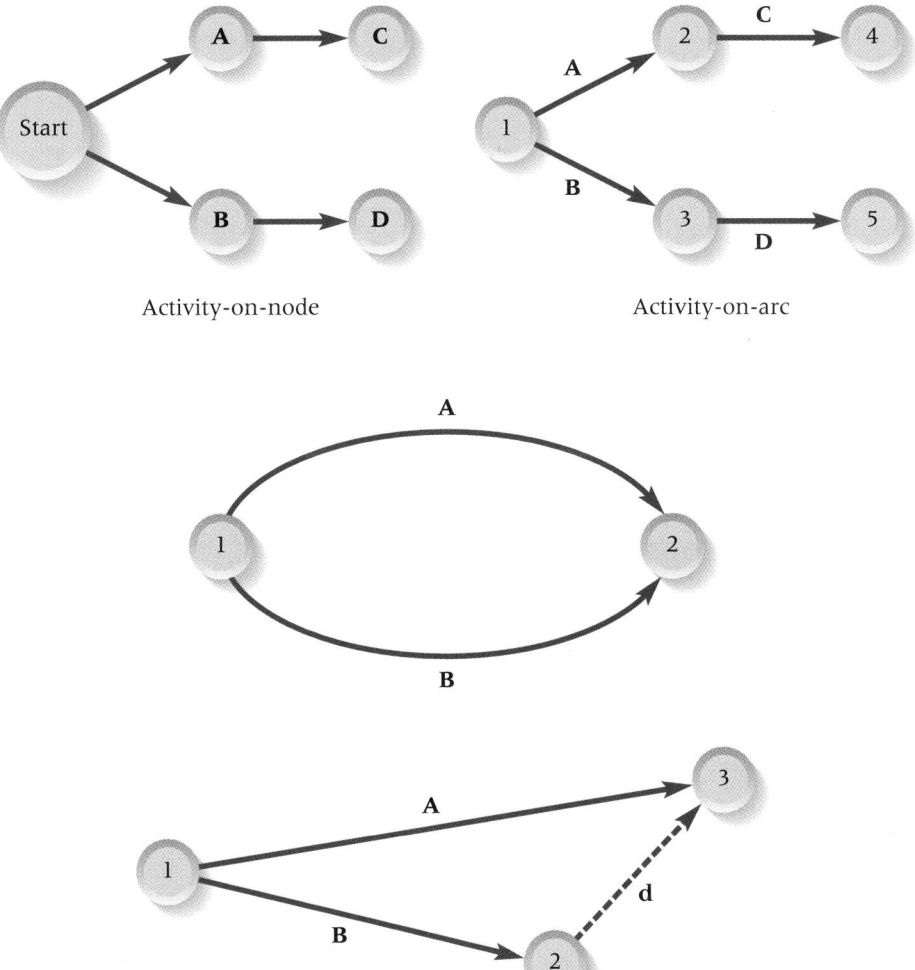

Activity-on-node                    Activity-on-arc

FIGURE 18.4
The Activity-on-Node and
Avtivity-on-Arc Methods

FIGURE 18.5
Incorrect Representation of
Parallel Activities

FIGURE 18.6
Correct Representation of
Parallel Activities Using a
Dummy Activity Arc

We also may need dummy activities to correctly represent precedence relationships. For example, suppose we need to represent the following activities in a project network:

| Activity | Immediate Predecessor |
|----------|-----------------------|
| A | – |
| B | – |
| C | A, B |
| D | B |

To show that activities A and B precede activity C, whereas only activity B precedes activity D, we use a dummy activity, as shown in Figure 18.7.

Whenever two or more activities share predecessor activities but do not share an identical set of predecessor activities, we will need at least one dummy activity to show the precedence relationships correctly.

Project managers find that simply constructing a project network is useful, because the process forces them to explicitly determine the activities that must be accomplished and the precedence relationships that exist. This process can lead to better communication in projects that involve more than one organization or functional area.

Constructing a project network is a trial-and-error process. Even with well-defined activities and precedence relationships, it usually takes two or three attempts to produce a neatly constructed network. Table 18.2 provides the

**FIGURE 18.7**
Using a Dummy Activity to Represent Precedence Relationships

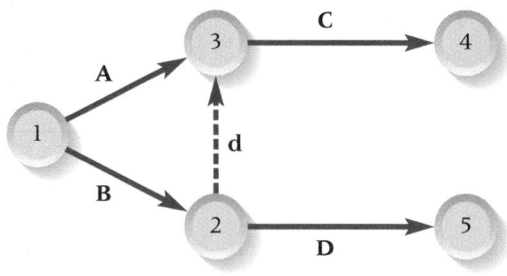

**TABLE 18.2**
Precedence Relationships in the Mountain Bike Development Project

| Activity | Immediate Predecessor |
|----------|-----------------------|
| A—Do preliminary market analysis | – |
| B—Develop preliminary product designs | A |
| C—Do preliminary manufacturing study | A |
| D—Evaluate and select best product design | B,C |
| E—Develop detailed marketing plans | D |
| F—Design manufacturing process | D |
| G—Develop detailed product design | D |
| H—Build and test prototype | G |
| I—Finalize product design | F,H |
| J—Order components | I |
| K—Order production equipment | I |
| L—Install production equipment | K |

precedence relationships for the mountain bike product development project described in Example 18.1. The first activity in the project is activity A. Two activities—activities B and C—follow activity A directly, whereas activity D immediately follows both B and C. Figure 18.8 shows how you may be tempted to draw the network for the first four activities. However, because each activity must have a unique pair of starting and ending nodes, we must use a dummy activity to draw the first four activities, as shown in Figure 18.9. Activities E, F, and G can start after activity D is completed, so we add them to the network, as Figure 18.10 shows. Figure 18.11 shows how to add activities H and I to the network (activity H follows activity G, and activity I follows both activities F and H).

No activities have activity E as a predecessor, so it ends at the terminal event. However, we still must add the last three activities—J, K, and L—to the network. Activity I precedes activities J and K, so we add them to the network after activity I. No activities have activity J as a predecessor, so it too ends at the

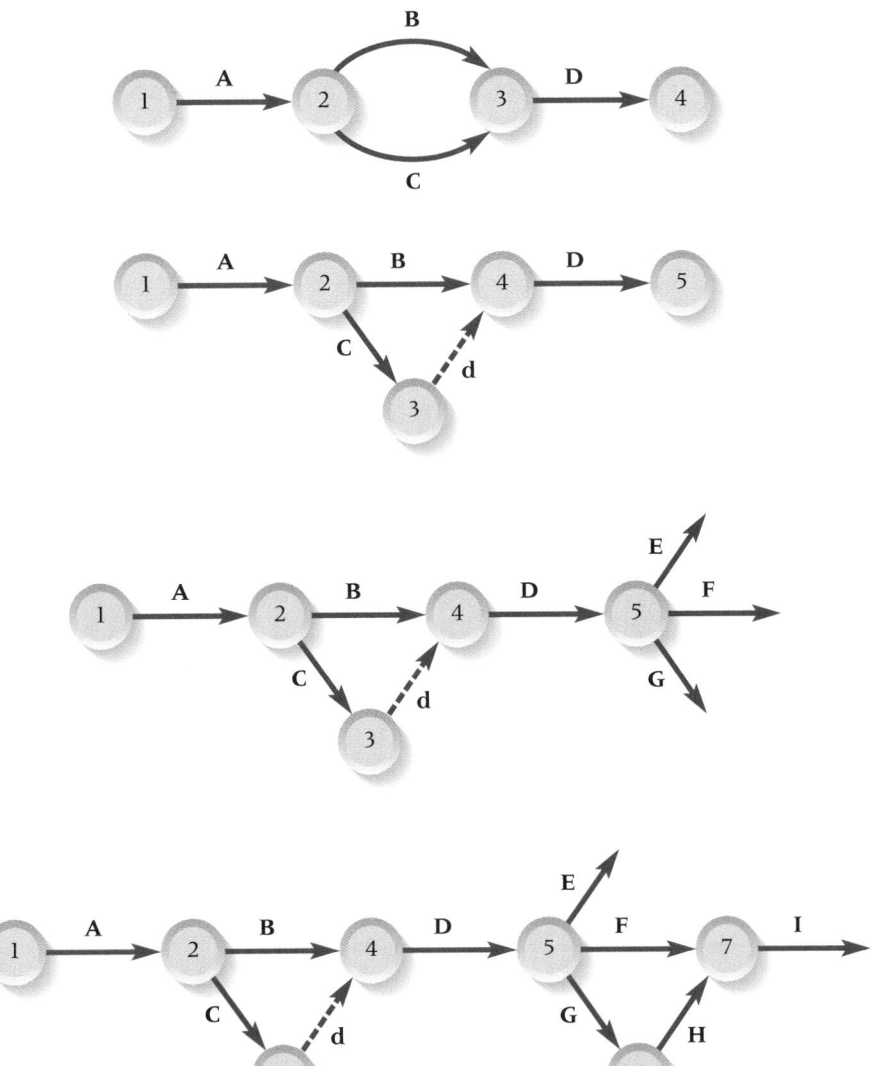

FIGURE 18.8
Incorrect Network for Four Activities

FIGURE 18.9
Correct Network for Four Activities

FIGURE 18.10
Adding Activities to a Network

FIGURE 18.11
Adding More Activities to a Network

terminal event. Activity L follows activity K, and no activities have activity L as a predecessor, so we draw activity L to start after activity K has ended and to end at the terminal event. Adding activities J, K, and L to the diagram results in the completed project network shown in Figure 18.12.

## Calculating the Completion Time for a Project

Given the activity durations in Table 18.1 and the project network of Figure 18.12, we can determine the minimum completion time for the project. We do this by starting at the originating event of the network (node 1) and determining the earliest time we can start an activity, given the activities that precede it—*assuming that all activities start as soon as possible and are completed as soon as possible.* If the mountain bike development project starts at time $T = 0$, the **earliest start (ES) time** for activity A is time $T = 0$ and the **earliest finish (EF) time** for activity A is time $T = 1.0$ (because the duration of this activity is one month). Activities B and C can start as soon as activity A is completed. Thus, the ES time for both activities is $T = 1.0$. The EF time for activity B is $T = 4.0$ (the ES time for the activity plus its duration), and the EF time for activity C is $T = 2.0$. Activity D can only start after *both* activities B and C are completed, so its earliest start (ES) time is $T = 4.0$. Because the duration for activity D is one month, its earliest finish (EF) time is $T = 5.0$. Continuing this process results in the network shown in Figure 18.13. This network shows the ES and EF times for each activity above its arc. Note that the activity timing in Figure 18.13 is consistent with the Gantt chart in Figure 18.3.

Figure 18.13 shows that, if everything goes as planned, the project will take 15.5 months to complete (the largest EF time for activities E, J and L). However, every activity need not start as early as possible for the project to be completed in 15.5 months. We can use a process similar to that used to develop Figure 18.13 to determine which activities we can delay, and by how much, without increasing the completion time of the project.

By starting at the terminal event (node 10), we can see that activities E, J, and L must all be completed within 15.5 months or the entire project will be delayed. Thus, the **latest finish (LF) time** for E, J, and L is time $T = 15.5$. This means that the **latest start (LS) time** for activities E and J is time $T = 14.5$, because they both have a duration of one month. Activity L has a LS time of 13.5, because it has a duration of two months. If the latest time activity L can start is 13.5 months into the project, then the latest finish (LF) time for activity K (its immediate predecessor) is time $T = 13.5$. Because its duration is 3.0,

**FIGURE 18.12**
Project Network for
Mountain Bike Development
Project

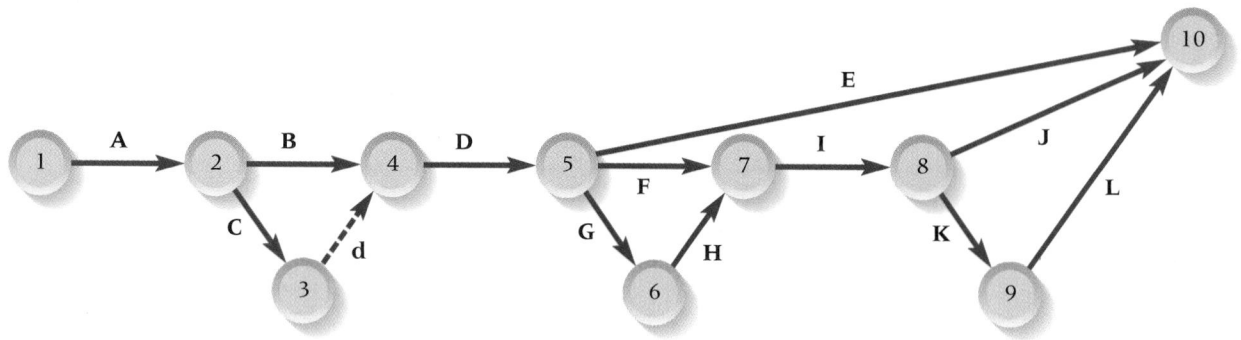

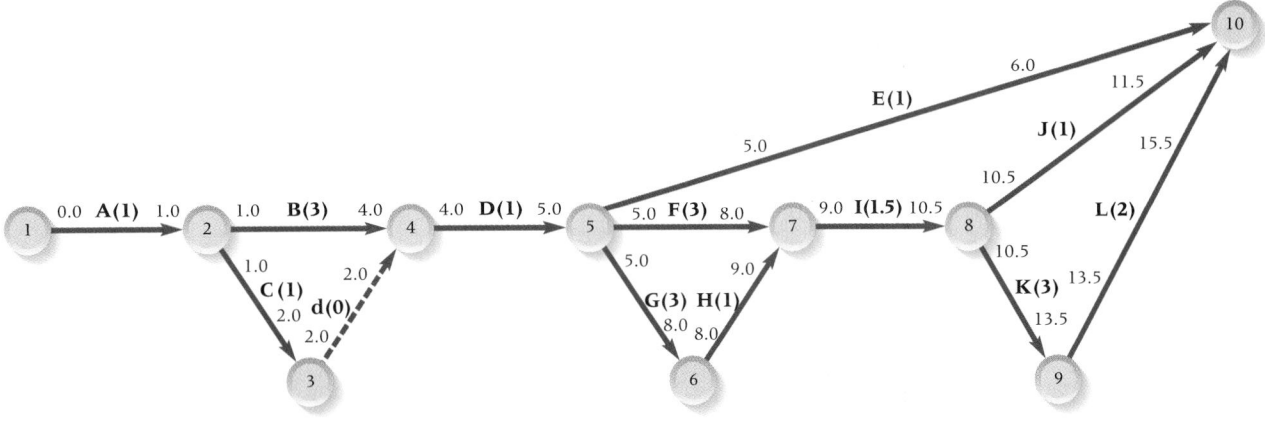

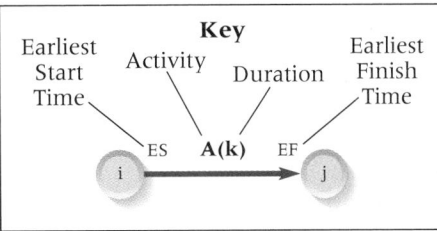

FIGURE 18.13
Project Network with Earliest
Start and Finish Times

activity K's latest start (LS) time is $T = 10.5$. Activity I must be completed before activities J and K can start. Because activity K has the *earliest* latest starting time of these two activities, activity I's latest finish (LF) time is 10.5. The latest start (LS) time for activity I is $T = 9.0$. We continue this process until we have determined the latest starting and latest finish times for all activities. Figure 18.14 shows the results of this process, which also are summarized in Table 18.3, which contains the early and late start and finish times for all activities.

Table 18.3 also shows the **slack time** for each activity. We can use either of two equations to determine the slack:

$$\text{Slack} = \text{LS} - \text{ES}$$

$$\text{Slack} = \text{LF} - \text{EF}$$

ES and EF are the earliest start and earliest finish times, respectively, and LS and LF are the latest start and latest finish times. The slack represents how long we can delay the activity without delaying the entire project, assuming its preceding activities are completed as early as possible. Note that the activities that have zero slack lie on a path through the network; this path is called the *critical path*. Every project has at least one critical path. Figure 18.14 shows the activities on the critical path of the mountain bike development project. The **critical path** is the set of activities that controls the duration of the project—any delay in these activities will result in a delay for the entire project. In managing a large scale and complex project, a project manager finds it extremely useful to know which activities are on the critical path and which activities have slack. Activities that lie on the critical path are called **critical activities.**

We could use another procedure to determine the critical path. The critical path is the *longest* path through the network, and the length of a path through the network is simply the sum of the activity times on the path. Thus, we can

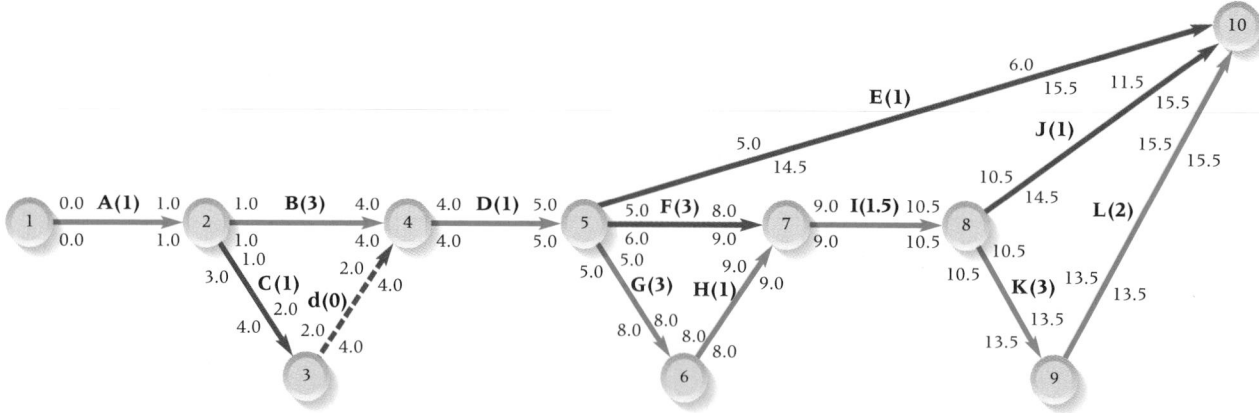

**FIGURE 18.14**
Project Network with Earliest
and Latest Start and Finish
Times

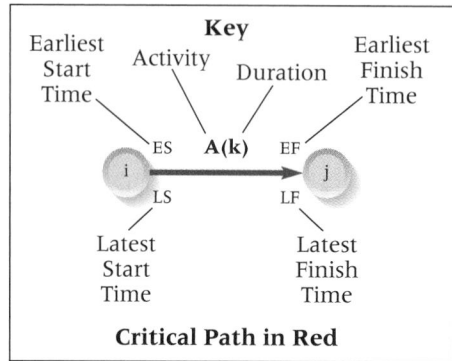

**TABLE 18.3**
Earliest and Latest Start and
Finish Times for Activities in
the Mountain Bike Project

| Activity | Duration | ES | EF | LS | LF | Slack |
|----------|----------|------|------|------|------|-------|
| **A** | **1.0** | **0.0** | **1.0** | **0.0** | **1.0** | **0.0** |
| **B** | **3.0** | **1.0** | **4.0** | **1.0** | **4.0** | **0.0** |
| C | 1.0 | 1.0 | 2.0 | 3.0 | 4.0 | 2.0 |
| **D** | **1.0** | **4.0** | **5.0** | **4.0** | **5.0** | **0.0** |
| E | 1.0 | 5.0 | 6.0 | 14.5 | 15.5 | 9.5 |
| F | 3.0 | 5.0 | 8.0 | 6.0 | 9.0 | 1.0 |
| **G** | **3.0** | **5.0** | **8.0** | **5.0** | **8.0** | **0.0** |
| **H** | **1.0** | **8.0** | **9.0** | **8.0** | **9.0** | **0.0** |
| **I** | **1.5** | **9.0** | **10.5** | **9.0** | **10.5** | **0.0** |
| J | 1.0 | 10.5 | 11.5 | 14.5 | 15.5 | 4.0 |
| **K** | **3.0** | **10.5** | **13.5** | **10.5** | **13.5** | **0.0** |
| **L** | **2.0** | **13.5** | **15.5** | **13.5** | **15.5** | **0.0** |

determine the critical path by identifying all paths through the network and
calculating the length of each path. The longest path through the network is the
critical path (there may be more than one critical path). The mountain bike
project has ten paths. These paths and their corresponding lengths are

| Path | Length (Months) |
|------|-----------------|
| A-B-D-E | 6 |
| A-B-D-F-I-J | 10.5 |

## OPERATIONS MANAGEMENT IN PRACTICE 18.1◀

# Project Management for Product Launch at Oldsmobile

Oldsmobile used a project management system, *Time Line* by Symantec, to manage the launch of six new Oldsmobile products in 1990: a new Toronado, Cutlass Supreme four-door, Silhouette minivan, Cutlass convertible, Calais Quad 442, and a restyled 88 Royale. The manager responsible for coordinating their introduction faced the problem of planning and implementing the launch. The project required coordinating eighteen departments at the Oldsmobile home office, including production, engineering, distribution, sales, and public relations. It also included 18 zone offices, 18 field marketing managers, Oldsmobile's advertising agency (Leo Burnett), and 3,200 Oldsmobile dealers. The resources involved in the project included hundreds of millions of dollars in launch advertising and promotion and hundreds of thousands of new vehicles that had to be sold to meet sales and production goals.

Project management techniques allowed the manager to decompose the project into manageable modules or subprojects. The project management system handled activity charting, resource assignment, cost budgeting and monitoring, and project-related timetables. It also automatically determined the critical paths for subprojects and the critical path for the overall project and generated timely status reports. The project management system highlighted subprojects and/or activities that were in danger of missing due dates. This allowed Oldsmobile management to allocate more resources to them to meet the schedule. On a weekly basis the manager responsible for the overall products launch presented launch status reports at the general sales managers' staff meetings and made recommendations based on information provided by the project management system.

Using project management for new product introduction at Oldsmobile in 1990 resulted in the smoothest and best-managed product launch possible. The only major glitch occurred when production was not able to meet its projected schedule because of the commitment to high quality. Because the project management system was tracking all elements of the launch simultaneously, Oldsmobile management was able to pull back its advertising buys in light of this delay and reschedule them accordingly.

| Path | Length (Months) |
|---|---|
| A-B-D-F-I-K-L | 14.5 |
| A-B-D-G-H-I-J | 11.5 |
| **A-B-D-G-H-I-K-L** | **15.5** |
| A-C-D-E | 4 |
| A-C-D-F-I-J | 8.5 |
| A-C-D-F-I-K-L | 12.5 |
| A-C-D-G-H-I-J | 9.5 |
| A-C-D-G-H-I-K-L | 13.5 |

This table shows that path A-B-D-G-H-I-K-L is the critical path, which is what Figure 18.14 and Table 18.3 show. This procedure for path analysis will be useful when considering time/cost trade-offs (project crashing).

Operations Management in Practice 18.1 discusses how Oldsmobile used a project management system to launch six new cars.

# Managing Project Resources

Like project networks, project management tools are not static documents but dynamic tools that evolve as the project proceeds. During the planning phase of a project, numerous iterations are usually required to develop the project network as the project becomes better defined. Once the project is underway, actual activities will diverge from the plan, and continuous monitoring is required to detect deviations from the plan so that corrective action can be taken. In the sections that follow we discuss how to use project networks to manage projects.

# Developing Project Budgets

A manager can use earliest and latest time estimates to develop a project budget. In developing a budget the manager assumes that the costs for an activity occur at a uniform rate throughout the duration of the activity. Given this assumption, the cash flows for the critical activities are fixed. However, this is not true for the noncritical activities, because these have slack associated with their starting and ending times. Although a manager could prepare an infinite number of budgets based on various assumed starting and ending times for noncritical activities, the most practical approach is to set boundaries by calculating two budgets: one based on all activities starting as *early* as possible, and one for which all activities start as *late* as possible. The steps for determining these budgets are as follows:

1. Determine the ES, EF, LS, and LF associated with each activity.
2. Determine the total cost for each activity, and calculate the budgeted cost per time period for each activity by dividing the total activity cost by the expected activity time.
3. Determine the expense per time period for each activity, first by using the earliest time estimates (ES and EF) and then by using the latest time estimates (LS and LF).
4. Add up the costs for each period (for each budget) to get a cumulative project cost per time period.

**TABLE 18.4**
Activity Durations and Cost Estimates

| Activity | Activity Duration (months) | Estimated Cost (Thousands) | Budgeted Cost per Month (Thousands) |
|:---:|:---:|:---:|:---:|
| A | 1.0 | $ 100 | $100 |
| B | 3.0 | 150 | 50 |
| C | 1.0 | 120 | 120 |
| D | 1.0 | 10 | 10 |
| E | 1.0 | 225 | 225 |
| F | 3.0 | 500 | 166.7 |
| G | 3.0 | 400 | 133.3 |
| H | 1.0 | 150 | 150 |
| I | 1.5 | 75 | 50 |
| J | 1.0 | 350 | 350 |
| K | 3.0 | 450 | 150 |
| L | 2.0 | 90 | 45 |
| | | $2,620 | |

We already have completed step 1 for the mountain bike development project (Table 18.3). Table 18.4 gives the activity cost estimates and a budgeted cost per time period (step 2). We can complete steps 3 and 4 for the earliest start times by using the budgeted cost per month information from Table 18.4 and the earliest start and finish (ES and EF) from Table 18.3 to prepare a monthly budgeted cost summary for the project, which is shown in Table 18.5. Note that activity A's ES time of $T = 0.0$ and EF time of $T = 1.0$ mean that activity A begins and ends in month 1.

Table 18.6 presents the budgeted cost schedule that results when we use the latest time estimates for all activities. If the project proceeds according to its time estimates, each activity will start somewhere between its earliest and latest start times. This means that the cumulative total cost per month should fall between the costs indicated on the earliest time cost schedule and the costs indicated on the latest time cost schedule. The best way to illustrate this is by plotting the estimated cumulative cost-to-date values for the two budgets, which are shown in Figure 18.15. For example, the cumulative total project cost to date by month 10 should be somewhere between $1,480,000 (latest time schedule) and $1,705,000 (earliest time schedule). This analysis is beneficial for cash flow planning in a project.

## Monitoring and Controlling Project Costs

So far the topics we have discussed have concerned planning and scheduling project activities and developing project budgets. However, the ultimate objective of project management is to monitor and control costs while keeping the project on schedule. Reviewing the actual project costs for all completed and partially completed activities at a given point and then comparing these costs with the

TABLE 18.5
Monthly Expenditures Based on ES and EF Times

| Activity | 1 | 2 | 3 | 4 | 5 | 6 | 7 | 8 | 9 | 10 | 11 | 12 | 13 | 14 | 15 | 16 |
|---|---|---|---|---|---|---|---|---|---|---|---|---|---|---|---|---|
| A | $100 | | | | | | | | | | | | | | | |
| B | | 50 | 50 | 50 | | | | | | | | | | | | |
| C | | 120 | | | | | | | | | | | | | | |
| D | | | | | 10 | | | | | | | | | | | |
| E | | | | | | 225 | | | | | | | | | | |
| F | | | | | | 166.7 | 166.7 | 166.6 | | | | | | | | |
| G | | | | | | 133.4 | 133.3 | 133.3 | | | | | | | | |
| H | | | | | | | | | 150 | | | | | | | |
| I | | | | | | | | | | 50 | 25* | | | | | |
| J | | | | | | | | | | | 175* | 175* | | | | |
| K | | | | | | | | | | | 75* | 150 | 150 | 75* | | |
| L | | | | | | | | | | | | | | 22.5* | 45 | 22.5* |
| Total Cost per Month | $100 | 170 | 50 | 50 | 10 | 525.1 | 300 | 299.9 | 150 | 50 | 275 | 325 | 150 | 97.5 | 45 | 22.5 |
| Cumulative Total Cost | $100 | 270 | 320 | 370 | 380 | 905.1 | 1,205 | 1,505 | 1,655 | 1,705 | 1,980 | 2,305 | 2,455 | 2,553 | 2,598 | $2,620 |

*These activities start or end in the middle of the month. The cost used for these months is half the monthly rate.

| Activity | Month | | | | | | | | | | | | | | | |
| --- | --- | --- | --- | --- | --- | --- | --- | --- | --- | --- | --- | --- | --- | --- | --- | --- |
| | 1 | 2 | 3 | 4 | 5 | 6 | 7 | 8 | 9 | 10 | 11 | 12 | 13 | 14 | 15 | 16 |
| A | $100 | | | | | | | | | | | | | | | |
| B | | 50 | 50 | 50 | | | | | | | | | | | | |
| C | | | | 120 | | | | | | | | | | | | |
| D | | | | | 10 | | | | | | | | | | | |
| E | | | | | | | | | | | | | | | 112.5* | 112.5* |
| F | | | | | | | 166.7 | 166.7 | 166.6 | | | | | | | |
| G | | | | | | 133.4 | 133.3 | 133.3 | | | | | | | | |
| H | | | | | | | | | 150 | | | | | | | |
| I | | | | | | | | | | 50 | 25* | | | | | |
| J | | | | | | | | | | | | | | | 175* | 175* |
| K | | | | | | | | | | | 75* | 150 | 150 | 75* | | |
| L | | | | | | | | | | | | | | 22.5* | 45 | 22.5* |
| Total Cost per Month | $100 | 50 | 50 | 170 | 10 | 133.4 | 300 | 300 | 316.6 | 50 | 100 | 150 | 150 | 97.5 | 332.5 | 310 |
| Cumulative Total Cost | $100 | 150 | 200 | 370 | 380 | 513.4 | 813.4 | 1,113 | 1,430 | 1,480 | 1,580 | 1,730 | 1,880 | 1,978 | 2,310 | $2,620 |

*These activities start or end in the middle of the month. The cost used for these months is half the monthly rate.

TABLE 18.6
Monthly Expenditures Based
on LS and LF Times

FIGURE 18.15
Graph of Early and Late
Time Budgets

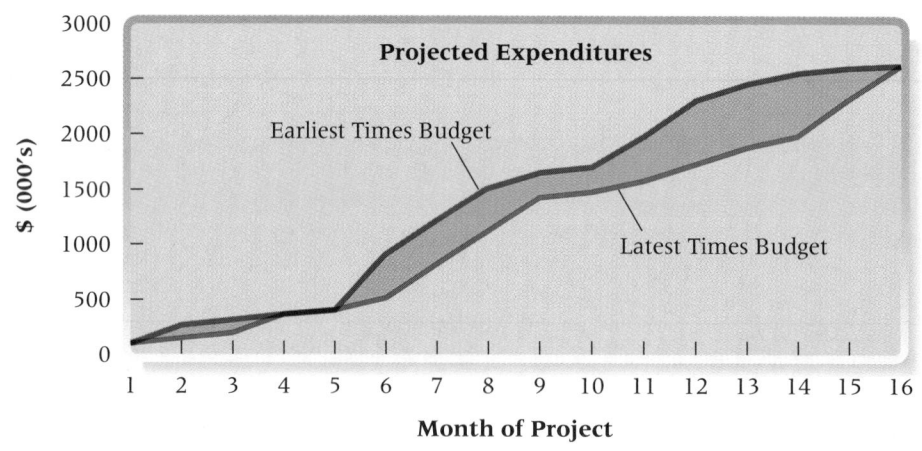

planned or budgeted costs for the project can identify cost overruns for which the manager may be able to initiate corrective action.

Suppose that management approved the mountain bike development project six months ago, and the preliminary marketing, product design, and manufacturing studies are complete, the new product design has been selected, and the detailed marketing, manufacturing, and design work has begun. At this point a manager is interested in not only how well the new product development project is going and whether it will be completed on time but also whether the project can be brought in within the projected cost. Determining whether the project is over or under budget requires both the expenditures to date and an estimate of the status of activities. Table 18.7 provides this data, as well as the evaluation of the budget performance of the project.

We can determine the value of the work completed for a given activity by multiplying the proportion of work completed with respect to the activity by the total budgeted cost for the activity. We calculate the activity cost difference by subtracting the value of the work completed from the actual cost of the work completed. After six months the mountain bike project had incurred cost overruns on completed activities A, B, and D and a cost underrun on completed activity C (see Figure 18.7). Activities E, F, and G are in progress, with cost overruns on activities E and G. This results in a current cost overrun of $62,000, or 8 percent ($62,000/$775,000 × 100 = 8%), which is significant. Because activities E, F, and G are still in progress, we should review them immediately to determine whether corrective action is required. The method we use to calculate the value of work completed assumes that expenditures are directly proportional to the percentage of work completed; that may not be the case and may explain cost overruns or underruns for work in progress. In this example the preliminary marketing and product design efforts (activities A and B) exceed the budgeted amounts, and the current efforts in marketing and product design (activities E and G) continue that trend. Thus, further examination of these activities, including the validity of the original budget estimates, is warranted.

One major difficulty in this type of analysis is the 95 percent barrier. It is a common human tendency to underestimate the amount of work remaining in a task, and it is not uncommon for a task to be reported to the project manager as 95 percent complete and remain at that level for an extended period of time. Project managers often find it difficult to obtain timely cost expenditure data and accurate estimates of completion, so their ability to take timely and effective corrective action can be limited.

TABLE 18.7
Comparison of Budgeted and Actual Costs for the Mountain Bike

| Activity | Total Budgeted Cost | Percentage of Task Completed | Value of Work Completed (Thousands) | Actual Cost (Thousands) | Difference (Actual – Budgeted Value) (Thousands) |
|---|---|---|---|---|---|
| A | $ 100 | 100 | $100 | $120 | $ 20 |
| B | 150 | 100 | 150 | 170 | 20 |
| C | 120 | 100 | 120 | 110 | −10 |
| D | 10 | 100 | 10 | 12 | 2 |
| E | 225 | 20 | 45 | 65 | 20 |
| F | 500 | 30 | 150 | 140 | −10 |
| G | 400 | 50 | 200 | 220 | 20 |
| H | 150 | 0 | 0 | 0 | 0 |
| I | 75 | 0 | 0 | 0 | 0 |
| J | 350 | 0 | 0 | 0 | 0 |
| K | 450 | 0 | 0 | 0 | 0 |
| L | $  90 | 0 | 0 | 0 | 0 |
|  | $2,620 | | $775 | $837 | $ 62 |

## Resource Limitations

The task of managing a project involves deploying resources to achieve a specific result. Resources usually are limited, and they can have a significant effect on the ability to complete a project on time and within budget. In the examples we have used thus far, we have assumed the activity durations or times to be known and constant. In reality activity times are generally related to the resources available. Providing more resources usually decreases the duration of an activity—but not always. For example, ship and aircraft construction are limited by space. Only so many workers can fit in the fuselage of an airplane or the hull of a ship. Adding too many workers can slow the production process, because workers are competing for access to the same work space.

When resources are limited, the task of developing and managing a project network becomes much more complicated. Several approaches have been developed to deal with resource limitations, but in practice it is usually a trial-and-error process. Most project-planning software packages allow the user to assign resources to activities and then calculate a time-based profile of resource usage for the project. If the time-based profile indicates the project needs more resources than are available, the manager can modify the project network or management can make additional resources available.

## Time/Cost Trade-offs in Project Management

The manager of a project often can shorten the duration of an activity by assigning more resources to it. Of course, such an action increases the cost of the activity. Project managers frequently find it is useful to have ways to consider such time/cost trade-offs. The time/cost trade-off problem usually occurs in well-defined projects, such as building construction, where time and cost estimates are accurate.

Shortening the project by assigning more resources to one or more of the critical activities is called **project crashing.** To perform a time/cost analysis we need two time estimates and two cost estimates for each activity:

| Time Estimates | Cost Estimates |
|---|---|
| Normal activity duration | Normal time cost |
| Crash activity duration | Crash time cost |

We will assume that we can add resources in any amount so that the activity duration can be anything between the normal duration and the crash duration and the costs will vary linearly with completion time. For example, if a task would normally take three months at a cost of $3,000 but can be completed in as little as two months at a cost of $4,000, the project can be completed in two and a half months at a cost of $3,500 or in two and a quarter months at a cost of $3,750.

When we assume that costs are linear, it is useful to calculate the crash cost per unit of time, which we can do by using the following formula:

$$\text{Crash cost/Unit time} = \frac{\text{Crash cost} - \text{Normal cost}}{\text{Normal time} - \text{Crash time}}$$

Table 18.8 lists the normal and crash times and the associated cost estimates for the mountain bike development project. It also shows the maximum number of

| Activity | Normal Time | Normal Cost (Thousands) | Crash Time | Crash Cost (Thousands) | Maximum Months Available | Cost/Month (Thousands) |
|---|---|---|---|---|---|---|
| A | 1.0 | $ 100 | 0.5 | $140 | 0.5 | $ 80 |
| B | 3.0 | 150 | 1.0 | 270 | 2.0 | 60 |
| C | 1.0 | 120 | 0.5 | 160 | 0.5 | 80 |
| D | 1.0 | 10 | 1.0 | 10 | – | – |
| E | 1.0 | 225 | 0.5 | 300 | 0.5 | 150 |
| F | 3.0 | 500 | 2.0 | 700 | 1.0 | 200 |
| G | 3.0 | 400 | 1.0 | 500 | 2.0 | 50 |
| H | 1.0 | 150 | 0.5 | 170 | 0.5 | 40 |
| I | 1.5 | 75 | 0.5 | 135 | 1.0 | 60 |
| J | 1.0 | 350 | 0.5 | 385 | 0.5 | 70 |
| K | 3.0 | 450 | 2.0 | 540 | 1.0 | 90 |
| L | 2.0 | 90 | 1.5 | 160 | 0.5 | $140 |
|   |   | $2,620 |   |   |   |   |

TABLE 18.8
Normal and Crash Times and Cost Estimates

months each activity can be crashed and the crash cost per month. Note that the normal times and normal costs in this table match the activity durations and estimated costs given in Table 18.4.

The critical path controls the length of the project. If one of the activities on the critical path is shortened, a different path may become the critical path and control the length of the project. Therefore, project-crashing procedures must consider the effect on all paths in the network of crashing one activity. As we noted earlier, the mountain bike development project has ten paths through its network:

| Path | Length (Months) |
|---|---|
| A-B-D-E | 6 |
| A-B-D-F-I-J | 10.5 |
| A-B-D-F-I-K-L | 14.5 |
| A-B-D-G-H-I-J | 11.5 |
| **A-B-D-G-H-I-K-L** | **15.5** |
| A-C-D-E | 4 |
| A-C-D-F-I-J | 8.5 |
| A-C-D-F-I-K-L | 12.5 |
| A-C-D-G-H-I-J | 9.5 |
| A-C-D-G-H-I-K-L | 13.5 |

We can use a *heuristic procedure*[4] for crashing project activity times while attempting to minimize the additional costs:

1. Compute the crash cost per time period for all activities in the network, using the formula provided.
2. Determine the critical path. (The process begins with the normal time estimates.) If there is more than one critical path, choose one arbitrarily. If

[4]A heuristic procedure is a rule-of-thumb technique that provides a good (and perhaps optimal) solution.

the critical path length is equal to or shorter than the target completion time, stop—the project can be completed within the target time. If the critical path is longer than the target completion time, select the activity on the critical path with the lowest crash cost per unit of time (one that has not already been crashed to the maximum extent possible). If there is a tie for lowest cost per unit of time, choose one of the activities arbitrarily. Crash this activity to the greatest extent possible or until you have achieved the deadline you are after, whichever is shorter.

3. Update the lengths of all project paths by adjusting for the time reduction of the crashed activity and update the cost of the project accordingly. Return to step 2.

**EXAMPLE 18.2**

Assume that to beat the competition to market with the new mountain bike, the company has to shorten the project duration to twelve months.

The critical path for the project network is A-B-D-G-H-I-K-L with a length of 15.5 months. In accordance with step 2 of the heuristic we should crash activity H to the maximum, half a month. After crashing this activity, the path lengths of the network become

| Path | Length (Months) |
|---|---|
| A-B-D-E | 6 |
| A-B-D-F-I-J | 10.5 |
| A-B-D-F-I-K-L | 14.5 |
| A-B-D-G-H-I-J | 11 |
| **A-B-D-G-H-I-K-L** | **15** |
| A-C-D-E | 4 |
| A-C-D-F-I-J | 8.5 |
| A-C-D-F-I-K-L | 12.5 |
| A-C-D-G-H-I-J | 9 |
| A-C-D-G-H-I-K-L | 13 |

The project length is now fifteen months, and the cost of the project has increased to $2,640,000. The critical path is still A-B-D-G-H-I-K-L. The activity with the next lowest crash cost per month on this path is activity G, with a crash cost per month of $50,000. When we crash this activity for two months, the following path lengths result:

| Path | Length (Months) |
|---|---|
| A-B-D-E | 6 |
| A-B-D-F-I-J | 10.5 |
| **A-B-D-F-I-K-L** | **14.5** |
| A-B-D-G-H-I-J | 9 |
| A-B-D-G-H-I-K-L | 13 |
| A-C-D-E | 4 |
| A-C-D-F-I-J | 8.5 |
| A-C-D-F-I-K-L | 12.5 |
| A-C-D-G-H-I-J | 7 |
| A-C-D-G-H-I-K-L | 11 |

Path A-B-D-F-I-K-L is now critical, with a length of 14.5 months and the project cost is now $2,740,000. Two (uncrashed) activities—activities B and I—are tied for the lowest crash cost per month. The heuristic procedure states that ties are to be broken arbitrarily, so we can crash either one. By choosing activity B arbitrarily and crashing it for the two months available, we obtain new path lengths of

| Path | Length (Months) |
|------|-----------------|
| A-B-D-E | 4 |
| A-B-D-F-I-J | 8.5 |
| **A-B-D-F-I-K-L** | **12.5** |
| A-B-D-G-H-I-J | 7 |
| A-B-D-G-H-I-K-L | 11 |
| A-C-D-E | 4 |
| A-C-D-F-I-J | 8.5 |
| **A-C-D-F-I-K-L** | **12.5** |
| A-C-D-G-H-I-J | 7 |
| A-C-D-G-H-I-K-L | 11 |

The project length is now 12.5 months at a cost of $2,860,000. Note that two paths are tied for the critical path; because the heuristic states that ties are broken arbitrarily, we can still use path A-B-D-F-I-K-L. Now activity I has the lowest crash cost per month. Note that we only need to crash I for half a month. The result is the following path lengths:

| Path | Length (Months) |
|------|-----------------|
| A-B-D-E | 4 |
| A-B-D-F-I-J | 8 |
| **A-B-D-F-I-K-L** | **12** |
| A-B-D-G-H-I-J | 6.5 |
| A-B-D-G-H-I-K-L | 10.5 |
| A-C-D-E | 4 |
| A-C-D-F-I-J | 8 |
| **A-C-D-F-I-K-L** | **12** |
| A-C-D-G-H-I-J | 6.5 |
| A-C-D-G-H-I-K-L | 10.5 |

Now we can complete the project in twelve months at a cost of $2,890,000. Table 18.9 summarizes the results of the project-crashing analysis.

The heuristic procedure for crashing a project demonstrates the trade-offs that characterize a project. Nevertheless, the procedure is unwieldy for analyzing large-scale networks. A project manager can use linear programming to crash a

TABLE 18.9
Summary of Project Crashing

| Step | Activity | Mean Project Completion Time (Months) | Completion Cost (Thousands) |
|------|----------|----------------------------------------|------------------------------|
| 0 | No crashing | 15.5 | $2,620 |
| 1 | H crashed by 0.5 month | 15.0 | 2,640 |
| 2 | G crashed by 2.0 months | 14.5 | 2,740 |
| 3 | B crashed by 2.0 months | 12.5 | 2,860 |
| 4 | I crashed by 0.5 month | 12.0 | 2,890 |

# Using Project Management Tools in Building Construction at Michigan State University

Project management techniques were important to the successful completion of the $20 million addition to Michigan State University's business school in 1993. According to Dan Bollman, project representative for Michigan State University, "Michigan State is a fairly sophisticated customer. We are constantly involved in building construction and renovation. In the last few years we have completed a new intramural sports facility, an indoor tennis facility, an addition to the engineering building, and the 18,000-seat Jack Breslin Student Events Center. We know the importance of project planning in complex construction projects, so the bid package for the business school addition included a $40,000 schedule management allowance."

Glenn Granger, vice president of corporate services for Granger Construction, says, "We were pleased that Michigan State included funds specifically for project management. Originally, Michigan State planned for an outside consulting firm to conduct all project scheduling, but after some discussion we convinced them that it would be better to hire a consultant to construct the original project network and schedule but let Granger handle management of the schedule during construction."

The primary benefit of having a project schedule is that it provides a common means of communication. According to Granger,

> The project schedule is an important communication tool which helps build trust between the general contractor and the building's owner, and trust is an important ingredient in a construction project. With good communication and trust we are better able to handle problems, which always occur in large projects. We have a good relationship with Michigan State, and whenever a problem arose, we were able to concentrate our efforts on fixing the problem correctly, because we had faith that Michigan State would compensate us fairly for any additional work, and they had faith that we would submit only fair and reasonable charges.

By using the project management network the contractor was able to find ways to reduce the length of the project. One example was the construction of two large lecture rooms. According to Granger,

> The lecture rooms required a significant amount of work in the ceilings—fire sprinklers, lighting, acoustic treatments, et cetera, and the only way to do this work effectively is to erect scaffolding so that the entire ceiling can be reached at one time. We originally planned to work on the lecture rooms in series because we only had enough scaffolding to do one room at a time. It turns out that this placed the lecture rooms on the critical path, and so it was possible to reduce the length of the project by working on the rooms in parallel. With the project network we were able to effectively communicate this to Michigan State. The university agreed that it would be beneficial to reduce the project length and agreed to spend ten thousand dollars to rent additional scaffolding. Without a good, realistic schedule, the university might not have felt that the promised reduction in project length would be realized.

project and optimally determine its associated time/cost trade-offs. Operations Management in Practice 18.2 describes how Michigan State University's contractor used project management methods to complete a $20 million addition to its business school on time.

## PERT Networks and Uncertain Time Estimates

The team responsible for the development of PERT during the Polaris program originally envisioned a system that would help managers make trade-offs in time, cost, and performance in project management. The team quickly recognized that this goal was too ambitious and decided to concentrate on the time aspect of project management. The enormous technical challenges of the Polaris program meant a high degree of uncertainty in regard to the completion time of many activities. Therefore, the team developed techniques, grounded in statistical theory, to treat time as a *random variable* and allow managers to look at project completion time in a probabilistic fashion. These probabilistic methods require three time estimates for each activity:

- **Optimistic time estimate** *(a)*—an estimate of the minimum time an activity will require
- **Most likely time estimate** *(m)*—an estimate of the normal time an activity will require
- **Pessimistic time estimate** *(b)*—an estimate of the maximum time an activity will require

These three estimates are considered to be related in the form of a unimodal probability distribution; *m*, the most likely time, is the modal value. Because the optimistic time and the pessimistic time may vary in their relationship to *m*, the unimodal probability distribution may be skewed to the right or to the left, as illustrated in Figure 18.16.

Converting *a*, *m*, and *b* to estimates of the *expected value* and *variance* of the time required by the activity requires two assumptions:

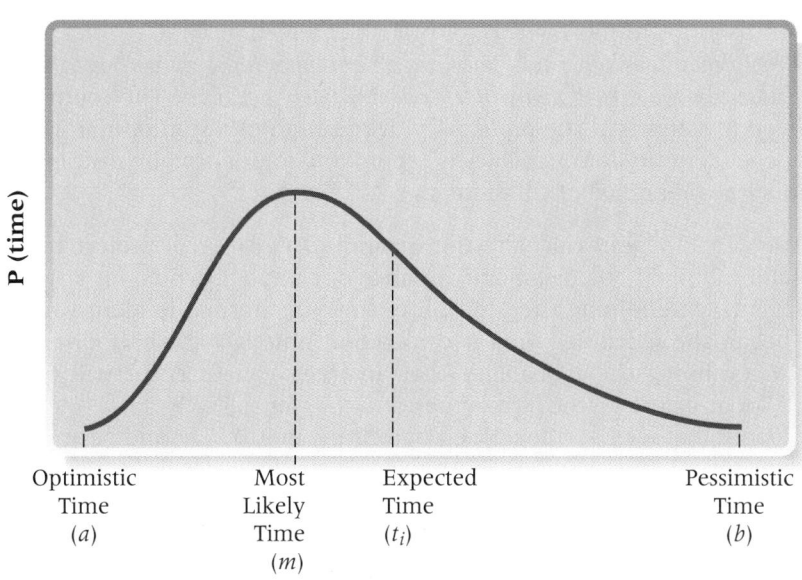

FIGURE 18.16
Unimodal Probability
Distribution

P (time)

| Optimistic Time (*a*) | Most Likely Time (*m*) | Expected Time (*t_i*) | | Pessimistic Time (*b*) |

■ The activity times are assumed to be beta distributed, so that the expected or **mean activity time** for an activity $i$, $t_i$, can be estimated as

$$t_i = \frac{a_i + 4m_i + b_i}{6}$$

■ The standard deviation of the time required by an activity is equal to one-sixth of the range of the reasonably possible time requirements. Thus we can estimate the standard deviation of the activity time for an activity $i$ as

$$\sigma_i = \frac{b_i - a_i}{6}$$

and the **variance of activity time** as

$$\sigma_i^2 = \left[\frac{b_i - a_i}{6}\right]^2$$

The rationale for the standard deviation and variance estimates is that the tails of many probability distributions are three standard deviations from the mean (the normal distribution, for example); therefore, there would be a spread of six standard deviations between tails.

To determine the probability of completing the project on schedule, we need three additional assumptions:

*Activity times are statistically independent.* Statistical independence means that the time that it takes to complete a given project activity does not affect the time it takes to complete any other project activity or task. If the activity times are statistically independent, we can total the mean activity times and variances of the activity times along a particular path in the project network to determine the mean completion time and the variance of completion time, respectively, for the path.

*The critical path always requires a significantly longer total duration time than any other path (in terms of mean time).* Under this assumption we can use the mean completion time for the critical path to estimate mean project completion time and the variance of the completion time for the critical path to estimate the variance of project completion time.

*Project completion time (or critical path completion time) has a normal distribution, because it is the sum of many independent random variables.* The central limit theorem states that the probability distribution of a sum of many independent random variables is (approximately) normally distributed under a wide range of conditions.

Given that we can calculate the mean and variance of project completion time (and, similarly, the mean and variance of completion time for any intermediate event), determining the probability that this normal random variable will be less than the scheduled project completion time is a straightforward process (as is determining the probability that an intermediate event will be accomplished on or before a scheduled time).

Suppose that we have developed optimistic, most likely, and pessimistic time estimates for all the activities in the mountain bike development project, as presented in Table 18.10, and that we have calculated the means or expected times and variances as we have described. Note that the expected times in this table are

TABLE 18.10
Duration Times for Mountain
Bike Development Project

| Activity | Optimistic Time Estimates (a) | Most Likely Time Estimates (m) | Pessimistic Time Estimates (b) | Expected Time ($t_i$) | Standard Deviation ($\sigma_i$) |
|---|---|---|---|---|---|
| A | 0.5 | 1.0 | 1.5 | 1.0 | 0.1667 |
| B | 2.5 | 3.0 | 3.5 | 3.0 | 0.1667 |
| C | 0.5 | 0.75 | 1.0 | 0.75 | 0.0833 |
| D | 0.5 | 1.0 | 1.5 | 1.0 | 0.1667 |
| E | 0.5 | 0.75 | 1.0 | 0.75 | 0.0833 |
| F | 2.0 | 2.5 | 3.0 | 2.5 | 0.1667 |
| G | 2.0 | 4.0 | 6.0 | 4.0 | 0.6667 |
| H | 1.0 | 2.0 | 3.0 | 2.0 | 0.3333 |
| I | 0.5 | 1.5 | 2.5 | 1.5 | 0.3333 |
| J | 0.5 | 1.0 | 1.5 | 1.0 | 0.1667 |
| K | 1.0 | 2.0 | 3.0 | 2.0 | 0.3333 |
| L | 1.0 | 1.5 | 2.0 | 1.5 | 0.1667 |

different than the duration times given in Table 18.3. One advantage of using multiple time estimates is that the manager of an activity may be able to be more honest about the estimates. Frequently, managers may either give the time estimates they think (or have been told) management expects or may hedge their time estimates because of uncertainties.

With the expected times in Table 18.10 the critical path is still A-B-D-G-H-I-K-L, but the length is now sixteen months. The paths through the project network, and their corresponding lengths, are as follows:

| Path | Length (Months) |
|---|---|
| A-B-D-E | 5.75 |
| A-B-D-F-I-J | 10 |
| A-B-D-F-I-K-L | 12.5 |
| A-B-D-G-H-I-J | 13.5 |
| **A-B-D-G-H-I-K-L** | **16** |
| A-C-D-E | 3.5 |
| A-C-D-F-I-J | 7.75 |
| A-C-D-F-I-K-L | 10.25 |
| A-C-D-G-H-I-J | 11.25 |
| A-C-D-G-H-I-K-L | 13.75 |

We can see that this project meets reasonably well the assumption that the critical path dominates the project. Although a path other than the critical path might delay the project, it is not likely to, so we will ignore the possibility.

Suppose that the mountain bike must be ready for introduction in eighteen months. Using the assumptions listed earlier, the mean completion time for the project is the sum of the expected completion times for the activities on the critical path, which is simply the length of the critical path—sixteen months. The variance of the completion time of the project is the sum of the variances of the activities on the critical path:

$$\sigma_p^2 = \sum_{\text{Critical Path}} \sigma_i^2 = \sigma_A^2 + \sigma_B^2 + \sigma_D^2 + \sigma_G^2 + \sigma_H^2 + \sigma_I^2 + \sigma_K^2 + \sigma_L^2$$

$$= 0.1667^2 + 0.1667^2 + 0.1667^2 + 0.6667^2 + 0.3333^2$$
$$+ 0.3333^2 + 0.3333^2 + 0.1667^2 = 0.8889$$

Because we assume the completion time for the project to be a normally distributed random variable, we can convert it to a standard normal random variable by subtracting the mean project completion time from it and then dividing the result by the standard deviation of project completion time, as shown in the formula that follows. Table 18.11 (a standard normal probability table) gives the probability that the project will be completed in eighteen months.

$$P \text{ (Completion time} \leq 18 \text{ months)} =$$
$$P\left(Z \leq \frac{18 - 16}{\sqrt{0.8889}}\right) = P(Z \leq 2.12) = 0.5 + 0.4830 = 0.9830, \text{ or } 98.3\%$$

# Guidelines for Managing Projects[5]

Project management experts W. Alan Randolph and Barry Posner have developed two acronyms based on guidelines for successful project management: GO-CARTS and DRIVER. GO-CARTS are rules for project planning—the means for successfully reaching the finish line of a project. GO-CARTS stands for

Set a clear **g**oal.
Determine the **o**bjectives.
Establish **c**heckpoints, **a**ctivities, **r**elationships, and **t**ime estimates.
Create a **s**chedule.

The goals of a project often are not clear, or there may be many different views of what the goals are. Clearly defined goals are necessary to make the proper trade-offs in time, schedule, and performance during the project. Goals tend to be general and somewhat abstract. The manager then must develop a set of clear concrete objectives, the completion of which will achieve the project's goals. Managers can satisfy the remaining rules by developing and analyzing a project network using the tools discussed earlier in this chapter.

DRIVER is Randolph and Posner's second acronym and represents rules for successfully leading a project team. DRIVER stands for

**D**evelop people individually and as a team.
**R**einforce the commitment and excitement of people.
**I**nform everyone connected with the project.
**V**italize people by building agreements.
**E**mpower yourself and others.
**R**isk approaching problems creatively.

Developing people is essential to a successful project. The project manager cannot do it alone—in fact, the project manager seldom if ever works directly on the project. Reinforcing the excitement and commitment of people is important as well. Project work can be extremely rewarding. Unlike many jobs, project work

[5]Adapted from W. Alan Randolph and Barry Z. Posner, *Getting the Job Done! Managing Project Teams and Task Forces for Success* (Englewood Cliffs, N.J.: Prentice-Hall, 1992).

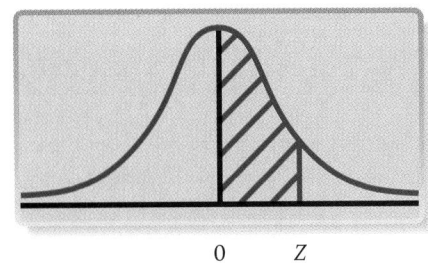

0        Z

| Z | .00 | .01 | .02 | .03 | .04 | .05 | .06 | .07 | .08 | .09 |
|-----|-------|-------|-------|-------|-------|-------|-------|-------|-------|-------|
| 0.0 | .0000 | .0040 | .0080 | .0120 | .0160 | .0199 | .0239 | .0279 | .0319 | .0359 |
| 0.1 | .0398 | .0438 | .0478 | .0517 | .0557 | .0596 | .0636 | .0675 | .0714 | .0753 |
| 0.2 | .0793 | .0832 | .0871 | .0910 | .0984 | .0987 | .1026 | .1064 | .1103 | .1141 |
| 0.3 | .1179 | .1217 | .1255 | .1293 | .1331 | .1368 | .1406 | .1443 | .1480 | .1517 |
| 0.4 | .1554 | .1591 | .1628 | .1664 | .1700 | .1736 | .1772 | .1808 | .1884 | .1879 |
| 0.5 | .1915 | .1950 | .1985 | .2019 | .2054 | .2088 | .2123 | .2157 | .2190 | .2224 |
| 0.6 | .2257 | .2291 | .2324 | .2357 | .2389 | .2422 | .2454 | .2486 | .2518 | .2549 |
| 0.7 | .2580 | .2612 | .2642 | .2673 | .2704 | .2734 | .2764 | .2794 | .2823 | .2852 |
| 0.8 | .2881 | .2910 | .2939 | .2967 | .2995 | .3023 | .3051 | .3078 | .3106 | .3133 |
| 0.9 | .3159 | .3186 | .3212 | .3238 | .3264 | .3289 | .3315 | .3340 | .3365 | .3389 |
| 1.0 | .3413 | .3438 | .3461 | .3485 | .3508 | .3531 | .3554 | .3577 | .3599 | .3621 |
| 1.1 | .3643 | .3665 | .3686 | .3708 | .3729 | .3749 | .3770 | .3790 | .3810 | .3830 |
| 1.2 | .3849 | .3869 | .3888 | .3907 | .3925 | .3944 | .3962 | .3980 | .3997 | .4015 |
| 1.3 | .4032 | .4049 | .4066 | .4082 | .4099 | .4115 | .4131 | .4147 | .4162 | .4177 |
| 1.4 | .4129 | .4207 | .4222 | .4236 | .4251 | .4265 | .4279 | .4279 | .4292 | .4306 |
| 1.5 | .4332 | .4345 | .4357 | .4370 | .4382 | .4394 | .4406 | .4418 | .4429 | .4441 |
| 1.6 | .4452 | .4463 | .4474 | .4484 | .4495 | .4505 | .4515 | .4525 | .4535 | .4545 |
| 1.7 | .4554 | .4564 | .4573 | .4582 | .4591 | .4599 | .4608 | .4616 | .4625 | .4633 |
| 1.8 | .4641 | .4649 | .4656 | .4664 | .4671 | .4678 | .4686 | .4693 | .4699 | .4706 |
| 1.9 | .4713 | .4719 | .4726 | .4732 | .4738 | .4744 | .4750 | .4756 | .4761 | .4767 |
| 2.0 | .4772 | .4778 | .4783 | .4788 | .4793 | .4798 | .4803 | .4808 | .4812 | .4817 |
| 2.1 | .4821 | .4826 | .4830 | .4834 | .4838 | .4842 | .4846 | .4850 | .4854 | .4857 |
| 2.2 | .4861 | .4864 | .4868 | .4871 | .4875 | .4878 | .4881 | .4884 | .4887 | .4890 |
| 2.3 | .4893 | .4896 | .4898 | .4901 | .4904 | .4906 | .4909 | .4911 | .4913 | .4816 |
| 2.4 | .4918 | .4920 | .4922 | .4925 | .4927 | .4929 | .4931 | .4932 | .4934 | .4936 |
| 2.5 | .4938 | .4940 | .4941 | .4943 | .4945 | .4946 | .4948 | .4949 | .4951 | .4952 |
| 2.6 | .4953 | .4955 | .4956 | .4957 | .4959 | .4960 | .4961 | .4962 | .4963 | .4964 |
| 2.7 | .4965 | .4966 | .4967 | .4968 | .4969 | .4970 | .4971 | .4972 | .4973 | .4974 |
| 2.8 | .4974 | .4975 | .4976 | .4977 | .4977 | .4978 | .4979 | .4979 | .4980 | .4981 |
| 2.9 | .4981 | .4982 | .4982 | .4983 | .4984 | .4984 | .4985 | .4985 | .4986 | .4986 |
| 3.0 | .49865 | .4987 | .4987 | .4988 | .4988 | .4989 | .4989 | .4989 | .4990 | .4990 |
| 4.0 | .49997 | | | | | | | | | |

TABLE 18.11
Area Under the Normal Curve

# Platform Teams in the U.S. Auto Industry

American auto makers are recognizing that product teams are the way to organize the task of designing cars. Chrysler credits "platform teams" with much of the success of its LH sedans, Dodge Ram pickups, and Dodge Neon compact cars. Tom Stallkamp, vice president of procurement and supply and general manager of large-car operations at Chrysler, describes the platform team concept:

In the past, vehicles were developed sequentially through the organization. First, a design would be approved and researched, then it would be passed off to engineering, then that was passed off to purchasing, which found suppliers, and then it would be turned over to manufacturing to be put together. That whole process took four and a half or five years, and there was not a lot of contact among groups along the way.

What the LH has shown us, and it was the first really big program we tried this on, was that we could shorten that process by having the designers work with the engineers while they were coming up with the concept of the car to see if it was feasible, by having the people in manufacturing work with the engineers to see if they could actually build the car. That's the concept of the platform groups—getting people to work together *simultaneously* rather than sequentially.

The first advantage is that it shortens the time frame. The LH took three and a quarter years. And I can't stress strongly enough that when people work together as a team, the job can be done with fewer people. They have broader jobs, but everyone plays a role in the entire vehicle rather than a tiny segmented role. We did the LH with a group of about 700 people, which is a lot fewer than before.

A lot of companies, particularly domestic, have tried this but have done it with part-time people. In the morning they might work on brakes for one car,

*Platform teams for new product development contributed immensely to the success of Chrysler's Dodge Ram pickups and Dodge Neon compact cars.*

and in the afternoon they'd work on brakes for another program. In our platform group, we have full-time people, dedicated to engineering, purchasing, finance, and all that, exclusively related to the platform, and who report to the platform chief. This concept is similar to what is being done by some of the Japanese companies. Frankly, we took an in-depth look at Honda and adapted what the Japanese do for the uniqueness of Chrysler.*

Ford is also embracing the platform team concept as a result of the Mustang "skunk works" team that redesigned the car in three years at $700 million dollars—25 percent less time and 30 percent less expensive than any comparable new car program at Ford in recent years. Ford gave the Mustang team unprecedented authority, and it set up what it called the Mustang Car Co. in a converted furniture warehouse in Allen Park, Michigan. The team grouped people into "chunk teams" responsible for a particular aspect, or "chunk," of the car. With a short development schedule the teams did away with the time-consuming process of selecting suppliers through competitive bidding. Instead, the Mustang team leaders agreed to just ask the best suppliers available to join the design process from the start.

The Mustang exceeded Ford's objectives for variable cost, investment, and time to market. The "skunk works" approach is likely to be a model for product development at Ford in the future. According to Kenneth K. Kohrs, Ford's vice president of car product development,

"It sets the guidelines for how production teams should be formed."**

*Richard Ceppos, "Q&A with Tom Stallkamp," *Automobile Magazine* 7 (June 1992): 62.
**Joseph B. White and Oscar Suris, "How a 'Skunk Works' Kept Mustang Alive—On a Tight Budget," *The Wall Street Journal*, Sept. 21, 1993, pp. 41–42.

results in a single concrete outcome to which team members can point and say, "I accomplished that." But project work can be demanding, with long hours required to meet deadlines and occasional frustrations and setbacks. Project managers must be just as concerned with team members' emotions and attitudes as they are with budgets and deadlines.

Things happen quickly in a project, and the manager must communicate new developments and changes to all affected members of the team. Frequently, the difficulty is determining who is affected. One effective way to encourage communication is with the co-located team approach, in which team members from all disciplines or functional areas are located in one facility to encourage cooperation. The automotive industry has embraced this approach in recent years. Operations Management in Practice 18.3 shows how Chrysler and Ford have used teams in new product development.

Conflicts are bound to occur in a project, and the way they are handled can have a significant effect on how successful the project is. According to Randolph and Posner,

By effectively managing and negotiating conflicts, you will achieve positive outcomes from the inevitable differences that arise in moving your GO-CARTS forward. You can get the job done most effectively when you build agreements which vitalize partici-

*Ford redesigned the Mustang in 25 percent less time and 30 percent less cost than any of its recent comparable car programs by using a platform team approach.*

pants. Conflict creates energy that is essential to managing projects and task forces from inception to implementation. Anticipating the sources of conflict and understanding the ebb and flow of conflicts in a project environment will increase your ability to harness this energy. Paradoxically, finding—or, if necessary creating—areas of agreement is an important place for negotiating differences.[6]

Empowerment is a popular concept in management today. Many successful projects are characterized by small dedicated project teams (the aircraft programs of Lockheed's skunk works, for example). One result of small project teams is that complex, limiting bureaucracies do not develop—there aren't enough people. The only option is to give people authority and responsibility—to empower them. Successful managers can best use their power by giving it away. We discuss the topic of employee empowerment in Chapter 9.

Finally, Randolph and Posner urge project managers to risk approaching problems creatively. Frequently, the safe approach is the riskiest, because it is unlikely to lead to innovation. Creating an environment in which employees feel they are free to pursue unique solutions can pay off handsomely. To encourage innovation the 3M Company expects its engineers and scientists to spend 15 percent of their time on nonprogrammed activities. It is important to remember that good ideas do not always appear to be good ideas when they are first introduced. Many excellent ideas, such as 3M Post-it™ notes and xerography (photocopying) were not received positively at first.

[6]Randolph and Posner, *Getting the Job Done!* p. 99.

# ► Summary

Project management is an important part of management today. Project management skills are likely to become a requirement for entering the ranks of management in the future. Successful project managers must have both organizational and behavioral skills. One of the many project management software programs available today can greatly aid project organization. These tools can help the manager communicate effectively with others in the project and can aid in making decisions. Successful project management requires an ability to manage conflicts in time, cost, and performance.

Project managers must also be able to lead, motivate, and communicate with people and organizations involved with the project. Project management tools such as work breakdown structures, Gantt charts and project networks can greatly increase communication, but they are not a substitute. The project manager also must realize that it is the project team and not the manager that does the work. The project manager's main function is to optimize the efforts of the project team.

**Learning Objective 1: Describe how to use a work breakdown structure to manage projects.** A work breakdown structure (WBS) breaks a large technical project into component parts. This technique is especially useful in the development of such complex systems as spacecraft and satellites. A WBS differs from Gantt charts and project networks in that it details the structure of the end product instead of defining the activities that must be accomplished to achieve the end product. In this respect it is similar to a product structure diagram or bill of material in MRP.

**Learning Objective 2: Describe how a project network differs from a Gantt chart.** A Gantt chart is a visual device that shows the duration of tasks in a project. It must reflect the precedence relationships of the project activities but does not show them explicitly. A project network is a diagram that explicitly shows precedence relationships among project activities. With a project network and activity duration times constructing a Gantt chart is a simple matter.

**Learning Objective 3: Discuss how project managers use the concepts of earliest and latest start times and the critical path.** The critical path (or paths) is the set of activities in a project network that controls the duration of the entire project. Any delays in the critical path activities will delay the entire project. The earliest and latest activity times reveal the degree of flexibility in starting and finishing an activity. If an activity has the same earliest and latest start times, it must have the same earliest and latest finish times and the slack for the activity must be zero, meaning the activity is critical. This information is useful to a manager trying to allocate resources to different activities.

**Learning Objective 4: Describe how to use a project network to help manage project budgets.** A project network allows a manager to determine the timing of project activities. Given cost estimates for the project's activities, the manager can develop boundaries for the project's cash flow. This will allow the project manager to determine the cash flows necessary over time to support the project and provide a way to determine whether expenditures are within reason. The manager also can use project crashing techniques to make time/cost trade-offs that allow the manager to determine cost-effective ways to reduce the time required to complete a project.

**Learning Objective 5: Discuss the assumptions used in PERT to view project completion time in a probabilistic fashion.** The manager needs to make assumptions about the distribution of activity times and the nature of the project activities. The manager assumes that activity times are beta distributed to estimate mean activity times and assumes that the standard deviation of activity time is equal to one-sixth of the range of reasonably possible time requirements to estimate standard deviations (and variances) of activity times. In the project the manager uses the critical path to make probabilistic statements about the completion time of the project. This requires statistically independent activity times and one critical path that is sufficiently greater than any other path in the network. Also, the manager recognizes that the distribution of critical path completion time is normal since it is the sum of a number of activities with independent completion times.

**Learning Objective 6: Discuss the importance of behavioral factors in project management.** Quantitative techniques are only one tool in the toolbox needed to manage a project. Project management is the job of getting a group of people to work together to achieve a goal. Planning and structuring the project is important, but leading and motivating team members is perhaps more important. A small dedicated project team has consistently proved to be a key factor in successful projects. One explanation is that with limited personnel resources, small project teams must by necessity empower team members.

# ▶ Key Terms

| | | |
|---|---|---|
| activity-on-arc | Gantt chart | project management techniques |
| activity-on-node | latest finish time (LF) | project crashing |
| critical activities | latest start time (LS) | project network |
| critical path | mean activity time | slack time |
| critical path method (CPM) | most likely time estimate ($m$) | variance of activity time |
| dummy activity | optimistic time estimate ($a$) | work breakdown structure (WBS) |
| earliest finish time (EF) | pessimistic time estimate ($b$) | |
| earliest start time (ES) | program evaluation and review technique (PERT) | |

# ▶ Discussion Questions

1. Why is project management likely to become more important to managers in the future?
2. What role do quantitative tools play in project management?
3. How does the function of a work breakdown structure differ from that of a project network?
4. Does the choice of activity on arc versus activity on node for a project network affect numerical calculations?
5. How do resource limitations affect the development and management of a project network?
6. How can a manager improve project cost management by using project networks?
7. What behavioral factors are important in project management?
8. How can a project network facilitate communication in a project?

# ▶ Problems

For problems 1 through 3 construct the project network, given the activity precedence information provided.

**1.**

| Activity | Immediate Predecessors |
|---|---|
| A | – |
| B | – |
| C | B |
| D | A |
| E | B |
| F | B |
| G | D,E |
| H | F |

**2.**

| Activity | Immediate Predecessors |
|---|---|
| A | – |
| B | – |
| C | A,B |
| D | B |
| E | B |
| F | C,D,E |
| G | E |

**3.**

| Activity | Immediate Predecessors |
|---|---|
| A | – |
| B | – |
| C | – |
| D | A |
| E | B |
| F | B |
| G | B,C |
| H | F,G |
| I | D,E,H |
| J | D,E,H |
| K | F,G |
| L | G |

For problems 4 through 6 construct the project network, given the precedence information provided, and calculate the ES, EF, LS, and LF times and the slack associated with each activity, and determine the critical path.

**4.**

| Activity | Immediate Predecessors | Duration |
|----------|------------------------|----------|
| A | – | 3 |
| B | – | 4 |
| C | A | 5 |
| D | A | 3 |
| E | B | 2 |
| F | B | 3 |
| G | C | 7 |
| H | D,E | 5 |

**5.**

| Activity | Immediate Predecessors | Duration |
|----------|------------------------|----------|
| A | – | 4 |
| B | – | 3 |
| C | – | 3 |
| D | A | 5 |
| E | B | 4 |
| F | C | 7 |
| G | C | 6 |
| H | D,E | 3 |
| I | H,F | 4 |
| J | G | 6 |

**6.**

| Activity | Immediate Predecessors | Duration |
|----------|------------------------|----------|
| A | – | 3 |
| B | A | 7 |
| C | A | 6 |
| D | B | 6 |
| E | C | 2 |
| F | C | 5 |
| G | D,E | 5 |
| H | F | 3 |
| I | F | 8 |
| J | G,H | 7 |
| K | G,H | 7 |
| L | I,K | 5 |

**7.** Fix-Em-Up Industries restores classic cars. The chairman, Hi Price, wants to develop a project network to plan future restoration jobs. The following activities are required to restore a car. First, workers must disassemble the entire car and tag and catalog the parts. Next, they must strip the paint from the body panels, rebuild the engine, rechrome the bumpers and trim, and reupholster the seats. Each activity begins once the car has been stripped. After the paint has been stripped from the body

panels, workers can paint the panels and the car frame. After painting, they can reassemble the body. After the car has been reassembled, they can install the interior panels and new carpet. They can install the reupholstered seats once they have installed the carpet and interior panels. After the engine is rebuilt and the body has been reassembled, the engine can be installed. With the car body reassembled, workers can install the rechromed bumpers and trim.

Given the following information,

**a.** Determine the precedence relationships of the activities and construct the project network

**b.** Calculate the ES, EF, LS, and LF times and slack for each activity, and determine the critical path

| Activity | Duration (Days) |
|----------|-----------------|
| A—Disassemble car & catalog parts | 4 |
| B—Strip paint | 2 |
| C—Paint | 3 |
| D—Rebuild engine | 3 |
| E—Rechrome bumper | 2 |
| F—Reuphoster seats | 2 |
| G—Reassemble body | 1.5 |
| H—Install carpet & interior panels | 1 |
| I—Install seats & interior trim | 1.5 |
| J—Install engine | 2 |
| K—Install bumpers & trim | 3 |

**8.** Holly White, chief operating officer of EEO Industries, wants to convert her manufacturing facility to an MRP system. She wishes to use a project network to plan this conversion and has identified the following activities that must be completed. First, the available MRP computer systems and software must be evaluated. Bills of material (BOM) must be developed for all products, and lead times for each part must be determined from company production records. Lot sizes or lot sizing methods must be determined for each part, but this should not be done until the BOMs are developed. After the MRP systems and software have been evaluated, the best system for EEO can then be purchased and installed. Once the system has been installed, data (BOM, lead times, lot sizes and so on) can be input and checked, and a detailed material inventory can be performed simultaneously. With all data entered and verified and a complete material inventory, the new MRP system can be tested by operating it in parallel with the current production-planning system. When all problems with the new MRP system have been corrected, the company can complete the changeover to the MRP system.

Given the following information,

| Activity | Duration (Weeks) |
|---|---|
| A—Evaluate MRP systems & software | 8 |
| B—Develop BOMs for all parts | 10 |
| C—Calculate lead times | 7 |
| D—Determine lot sizes | 4 |
| E—Purchase & install new MRP system | 6 |
| F—Input data | 10 |
| G—Inventory parts | 2 |
| H—Operate MRP system in parallel | 5 |
| I—Complete changeover | 2 |

a.  Determine the precedence relationships of the activitites and construct the project network
b.  Calculate the ES, EF, LS, and LF times and slack for each activity, and determine the critical path

9.  Given the following information (time is in weeks);

| Activity | Immediate Predecessor | Normal Time | Normal Cost | Crash Time | Crash Cost |
|---|---|---|---|---|---|
| A | – | 3 | $200 | 2 | $ 300 |
| B | A | 5 | 300 | 3 | 500 |
| C | A | 4 | 500 | 2 | 800 |
| D | A | 7 | 400 | 4 | 850 |
| E | C | 6 | 700 | 4 | 1,100 |
| F | B,E | 2 | 600 | 1 | 1,000 |
| G | C | 5 | 300 | 4 | 400 |
| H | D | 4 | 500 | 3 | 700 |
| I | H | 3 | 400 | 1 | 800 |
| J | F,G | 3 | $200 | 2 | $ 375 |

a.  Construct the project network
b.  Determine the critical path
c.  Crash the project to fifteen weeks

10.  Given the following information (time is in weeks);

| Activity | Immediate Predecessor | Normal Time | Normal Cost | Crash Time | Crash Cost |
|---|---|---|---|---|---|
| A | – | 3 | $ 700 | 2 | $ 900 |
| B | – | 4 | 900 | 2 | 1,250 |
| C | A | 2 | 1,100 | 1 | 1,400 |
| D | B | 6 | 600 | 3 | 900 |
| E | C,D | 8 | 800 | 7 | 950 |
| F | D | 7 | 1,300 | 4 | 2,200 |
| G | E | 4 | 500 | 3 | 800 |
| H | E,F | 9 | $ 800 | 6 | $1,250 |

a.  Construct the project network
b.  Determine the critical path
c.  Crash the project to twenty weeks

11.  Use the project network from problem 1 with the following cost and activity durations to determine the ES and LS weekly budgets for the project:

| Activity | Cost | Expected Time (Weeks) |
|---|---|---|
| A | $ 400 | 2 |
| B | 750 | 3 |
| C | 700 | 2 |
| D | 600 | 6 |
| E | 560 | 7 |
| F | 450 | 3 |
| G | 600 | 1 |
| H | 500 | 2 |

a.  If the project had incurred expenditures as given here, would you say the project was within budget (assuming activities were reasonably on schedule)?

| Week | Expenditures |
|---|---|
| 1 | $ 300 |
| 2 | 800 |
| 3 | 1100 |
| 4 | 1800 |
| 5 | 2500 |
| 6 | 2800 |
| 7 | 3300 |

b.  If you were given the following status for the project, would you say the project was within budget?

| Activity | Percent Complete | Current Expenditures |
|---|---|---|
| A | 100 | $400 |
| B | 100 | 750 |
| C | 100 | 650 |
| D | 90 | 500 |
| E | 80 | 350 |
| F | 100 | 450 |
| G | 0 | 0 |
| H | 100 | $500 |

12.  Use the project network from problem 2 with the following cost and expected times to determine the EST and LST weekly budget summaries for the project:

| Activity | Cost | Expected Time (Weeks) |
|---|---|---|
| A | $600 | 3 |
| B | 700 | 2 |
| C | 450 | 6 |
| D | 600 | 4 |
| E | 600 | 5 |
| F | 450 | 1 |
| G | 500 | 2 |

a.  If the project had incurred expenditures as given here, would you say the project was within budget (assuming activities were reasonably on schedule)?

| Week | Expenditures |
|------|--------------|
| 1 | $ 300 |
| 2 | 800 |
| 3 | 1100 |
| 4 | 1800 |
| 5 | 2100 |

**b.** If you were given the following status for the project, would you say the project was with budget?

| Activity | Percent Complete | Current Expenditures |
|----------|-----------------|---------------------|
| A | 100 | $420 |
| B | 100 | 700 |
| C | 40 | 270 |
| D | 80 | 500 |
| E | 50 | 300 |
| F | 0 | 0 |
| G | 0 | 0 |

**13.** Nail and Hammer, building contractors, have decided to build a model home on Lake Fairview. They have identified the major activities required to complete construction of the home and three time estimates (in weeks) for each task. This information and the logical order in which the activities must be accomplished are provided in the table that follows.

| Activity | Immed. Pred. | Times Opt. | Times Likely | Times Pess. |
|----------|------|------|--------|-------|
| A—Excavation | – | 1.0 | 2.0 | 3.0 |
| B—Foundation | A | 1.0 | 2.0 | 4.0 |
| C—Framing | B | 2.0 | 4.0 | 5.0 |
| D—Roof | C | 1.0 | 2.0 | 3.0 |
| E—Rough plumbing | C | 0.5 | 1.0 | 2.0 |
| F—Rough electrical | C | 0.5 | 1.0 | 1.5 |
| G—Heating & electrical | D | 1.0 | 2.0 | 3.0 |
| H—Drywall | E,F,G | 1.0 | 1.5 | 2.0 |
| I—Siding | D | 2.0 | 2.5 | 3.0 |
| J—Interior paint | H | 0.5 | 1.0 | 1.5 |
| K—Finish electrical | J | 0.5 | 1.0 | 2.0 |
| L—Finish plumbing | J | 0.5 | 1.0 | 1.5 |
| M—Flooring | K,L | 0.5 | 1.0 | 2.0 |
| N—Install fixtures | M | 1.0 | 1.5 | 2.0 |
| O—Exterior paint | I | 0.5 | 1.0 | 1.5 |

Given this information,

**a.** Construct the project network using the precedence information provided

**b.** Determine the critical path for the project network based on the expected time

**c.** Determine the probability that the project will be completed within eighteen weeks, nineteen weeks, and twenty weeks.

**14.** Forever, Inc., provides a wedding planning service. Bucks McBride wants to determine the minimum time required to plan the ideal wedding using project management. Bucks McBride has given the following information about the wedding planning process. A guest list must be developed before the caterers can be hired. Because of the close working relationship between the reception halls and caterers, a reception hall cannot be selected until the caterers have been specified. The photographer can be hired any time after the reception hall has been selected. Because the musicians will play at both the wedding and reception, they cannot be hired until both the church and reception hall have been selected. The wedding date must be set and the guest list must be completed before the church can be selected. The selection of the florist can be done at any time, but most couples wait until the last minute. Because the wedding couple's budget is usually limited, the wedding rings must be purchased before the caterers can be specified. The wedding rings can be purchased at any time.

Given this information,

| Activity | Opt. | Times Likely | Pess. |
|----------|------|--------------|-------|
| A—Choose church | 1 | 2 | 3 |
| B—Hire musicians | 2 | 3 | 4 |
| C—Hire photographer | 1 | 1.5 | 2 |
| D—Purchase rings | 2 | 3 | 5 |
| E—Rent reception hall | 1 | 2 | 4 |
| F—Set wedding date | 1 | 2 | 3 |
| G—Select florist | 0.5 | 1 | 1.5 |
| H—Select caterers | 1 | 2 | 3 |
| I—Develop guest list | 2 | 3 | 5 |

**a.** Construct the project network using the precedence information provided

**b.** Determine the critical path for the project network based on the expected time

**c.** Determine the probability that the project can be completed in ten weeks and 11 weeks.

► **Selected References**

Badiru, Adedeji Bodunde. *Quantitative Models for Project Planning, Scheduling, and Control.* Westport, Conn.: Quorum Books, 1993.

Kerzner, Harold. *Project Management: A Systems Approach to Planning, Scheduling and Controlling,* 4th ed. New York: Van Nostrand Reinhold, 1992.

National Aeronautics and Space Administration. *Handbook for Preparation of Work Breakdown Structures.* Washington, D.C.: U.S. Government Printing Office, 1975.

Randolph, W. Alan, and Barry Z. Posner. *Getting the Job Done! Managing Project Teams and Task Forces for Success.* Englewood Cliffs, N.J.: Prentice-Hall, 1992.

Sapolsky, Harvey M. *The Polaris System Development: Bureaucratic and Programmatic Success in Government.* Cambridge, Mass.: Harvard University Press, 1972.

# Quality Analysis, Measurement, and Improvement

*I am convinced that if the rate of change inside an institution is less than the rate of change outside, the end is in sight.*

JOHN F. WELCH, CHAIRMAN AND CHIEF
EXECUTIVE OFFICER, GENERAL ELECTRIC

Introduction

Total Quality Management
    Implementation Process

Process Analysis for Continuous
    Improvement
*OPERATIONS MANAGEMENT IN
    PRACTICE 19.1—19.5: Five Teams Win
    '93 Quality Cup*

Statistical Tools for Process
    Improvement

Case Study: Process Improvement
    Activities

## Introduction

This chapter focuses on analysis, measurement, and improvement of quality. In Chapter 7, Managing Quality, we discussed the strategic implications of quality management activities. We proposed that total quality management (TQM) was the philosophy most often implemented by successful companies. As we have noted previously, the most important element of TQM is the drive for continuous process improvement. In this chapter we will discuss the tools and improvement process that have proved most useful. Companies also can use these tools and the improvement process to support the cycle time reductions discussed in Chapter 16, Just-in-Time Production.

## Total Quality Management Implementation Process

To reemphasize the importance of continuous process improvement and the need for effective analytical tools, we will review the TQM implementation process, illustrated in Figure 19.1, which we introduced in Chapter 7. Of primary concern in this chapter is the critical element of continuous improvement of key processes. We will discuss and use examples to illustrate the tools that facilitate data collection, problem identification, and problem determination and will help formulate recommendations for improvement. Because quality-oriented organizations base their decisions on fact and analysis, these tools are extremely important to the problem solver.

## Process Analysis for Continuous Improvement

Companies today have recognized the need to become prevention oriented, rather than detection oriented, as is traditional, in their quality efforts. To support these prevention activities companies are developing a culture based on continuous improvement of key processes within the organization. From product or service design and delivery to support processes performed in personnel, marketing, financial, engineering, logistics, and customer service areas, companies are using teamwork to accomplish continuous process improvement. A systematic approach to process improvement is useful, whether the objective is to reduce cycle times, improve product or service quality, or improve productivity and efficiency. Operations Management in Practice 19.1, 19.2, 19.3, 19.4, and 19.5 illustrate the successful use of the team approach to continuous improve-

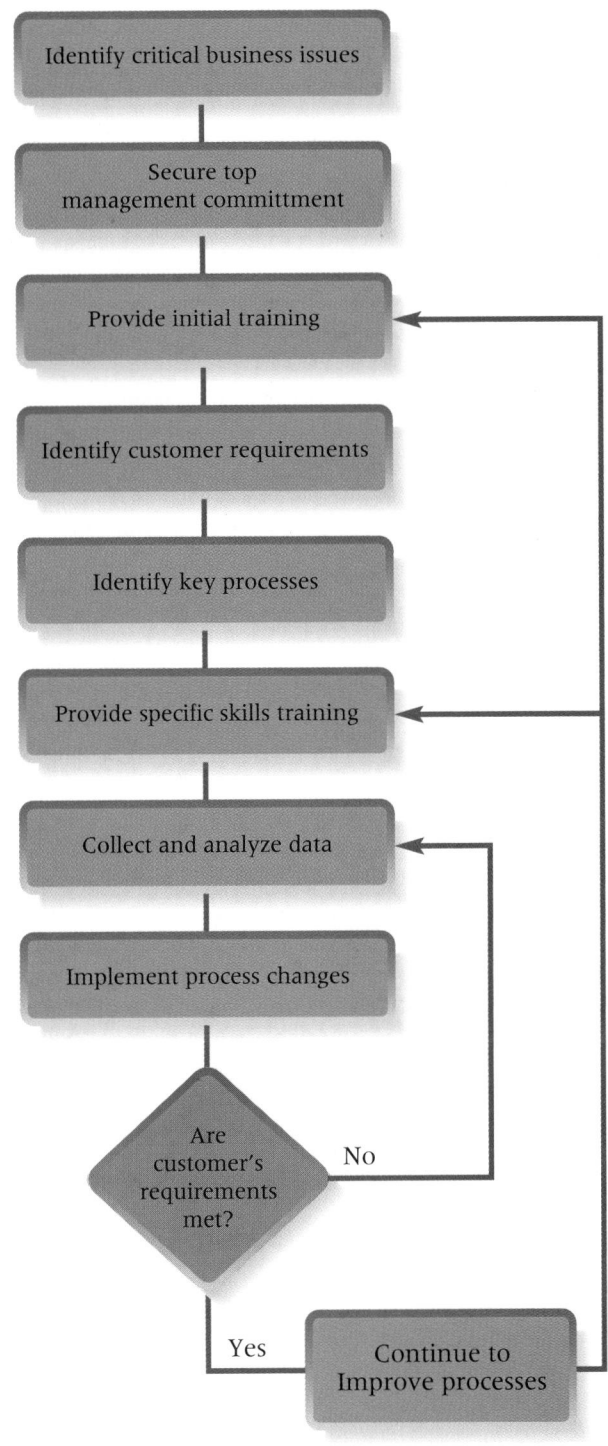

FIGURE  19.1
TQM Implementation Process

ment. These companies, operating in a wide variety of industries, won the 1993 Rochester Institute of Technology/USA TODAY Quality Cup in recognition of their success. The RIT/USA TODAY Quality Cup recognizes small teams or individuals, not entire companies or divisions, as is traditional for industry awards.

# Government Division: North Island Navy Depot

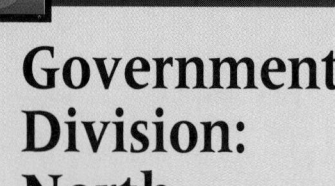

The workers in the North Island Navy Depot—250 craftsmen, machinists and managers—make replacement parts for the 1,262 mph, F/A-18 Hornet fighter planes. Building 472, where most of the work was accomplished, was dirty, dark, and lifeless. Around the Navy yard, people joked that it was an earthbound black hole where airplane parts, money and morale disappeared, never to be seen again. The commanding officer said that there were "all sorts of surly people were stalking around." "You almost needed armed bodyguards when you walked in the place."

He knew what was wrong. For years, the Navy has been preaching the virtues of what it calls total quality leadership (TQL), a management approach based on the teachings of consultant W. Edwards Deming. But Navy officers and middle managers often don't practice TQL. They use buzzwords like teamwork, trust and worker empowerment, but they cling to power and ignore front-line workers' ideas. In scores of U.S. companies, as well as the Navy, getting middle managers to buy into a total-quality approach is the biggest stumbling block to improvement.

The solution: Create a team of 10 middle managers drawn from various departments—planning, engineering, materials and others—and give it the power and money to rescue the money-losing operation. If it didn't work, the operation would be closed and 250 people would lose their jobs.

Mission accomplished. That tiny team revamped the manufacturing process by listening to workers and giving them the tools to do their jobs. Over the past 1.5 years, the team's improvements have saved the Navy at least $1.7 million. The time it takes to manufacture and deliver an F/A-18 part has dropped from 172 days to 100 days, a 42% decline. Perhaps the most impressive point, government workers are stealing work from private contractors.

These improvement activities netted the depot a RIT/USA TODAY Quality Cup and helped to avoid the ax in Pentagon cutbacks that will close three of six depots nationwide. Almost 90% of the Marine Corps' generals and 70% of the Navy's admirals have learned TQL. This year the Navy will train 11,000 at two Navy schools dedicated to TQL. Over the past five years, the navy's TQL effort has saved taxpayers at least $6 billion.

**T A B L E   1 9 . 1**
Eight-Step Process
Improvement Model

1. Define the problem in the context of the process.
2. Identify, analyze, and document the process.
3. Measure current performance.
4. Understand why the process is performing as it is.
5. Develop alternative solutions and select the best one.
6. Develop a strategy and implement the alternative chosen.
7. Evaluate the results of the new process.
8. Commit to continuous improvement of the process.

Source: Abstracted from Arthur R. Tenner and Irving J. DeToro, *Total Quality Management: Three Steps to Continuous Improvement* (Reading, Mass.: Addison-Wesley, 1992), p. 109.

This section of the text is devoted to describing a model for process improvement and to providing a set of tools that will be useful in implementing the model. Table 19.1 lists the steps of the overall process improvement model.

## Process Improvement Model

We are proposing an eight-step process improvement model that provides the structure needed to facilitate process improvement activities. This model can be effectively applied in all organizations, regardless of the type of organization or the type of process to be improved. It is important to follow the steps of the model to help ensure success of the improvement effort. In their haste to make things better newly commissioned improvement teams actually have made things worse by not mapping out an effective strategy for improvement. Hastily implemented solutions to poorly analyzed problems often result in performance worse than before the "improvement." Team leaders or team facilitators must restrain the excitement of a newly formed team and channel that enthusiasm within the guidelines of a proven process improvement model, such as that which follows.

## OPERATIONS MANAGEMENT IN PRACTICE 19.2

# Service Division: New York Telephone

Thieves cost New York Telephone millions of dollars a year. Some make long-distance international calls in a home without the owner's knowledge. Others are computer hackers who tap into corporate phone systems and place unauthorized calls. Until recently, some of the biggest losses stemmed from "call-sell" operations. Call-sell thieves set up a phone system in an apartment or storefront and subscribe to telephone service. Then they charge U.S. customers about $10 to make long-distance calls, often overseas. Many of their customers are illegal aliens who want to call family or friends back home. The more sophisticated thieves use three-way calling features offered by the phone company to link callers in two overseas countries. For instance, a call from France to Brazil would travel through New York and be billed to the New York phone number.

Call-sell thieves typically close shop and move on in less than a month, but not before taking in tens of thousands of dollars. How could the phone company detect unauthorized calls in time to catch the thieves? New York Telephone asked a team of 25 managers and hourly workers from several departments to attack the problem. The team developed a state-of-the-art fraud detection system. It now takes employees just three days to detect fraud, versus two to three weeks a couple of years ago. The system is saving the company an estimated $5 million to $8 million a year. That is money that New York Telephone loses when thieves walk away from their phone bills.

In 1991, a call-sell operation named the Amigo Scam charged customers in the Middle East $10 per minute for calls to Israeli-occupied territories. Israel had blocked calls from Arab countries. Amigo's operators in New York set up conference calls—and left New York Telephone with $750,000 in unpaid bills.

# Manufacturing Division: Boise Cascade's DeRidder Mill

At Boise Cascade, a ten member team was established to improve the way the mill makes newsprint, the paper used by newspapers. The team was made up of managers and hourly workers from three different departments. By spending the night in the wood yard counting and sorting fresh-cut pine that went into the mill, team members who usually work days learned some shocking things about the operation.

They found that the mill was using far more wood than anyone realized. They also found that mill workers had needlessly been diverting wood suitable for newsprint into cheap liner board. The team collected and analyzed data to dispel a company assumption that the better the wood that went into the mill, the better the pulp and, ultimately, the newsprint that came out. To improve the quality of the newsprint, the mill kept buying better and better wood. The team found through experimentation that there was no connection between the quality of the wood going into the mill and the quality of the pulp coming out. Therefore, high-quality paper could be made out of poor-quality wood. This finding alone saves the company at least $1.5 million a year.

Another surprise came when the team watched a woodyard crane pick up a load of wood for the mill. The company had always assumed that the crane picked up 12 cords (2.7 tons per cord) with each bite. So they simply counted the number of crane bites to determine how much wood was processed. To their surprise, they watched the crane pick up 17 cords per bite rather than 12. This helped to explain why they were using more wood than expected.

Why hadn't the plant always accurately measured how much wood it was using? Why did it go for years without running tests on the connection between the quality of wood and the quality of paper? While there is no answer to those two questions, team members now joke about a new motto for the plant: "In God we trust; all others must have data."

**Step 1: Define the Problem in the Context of the Process**   This is one of the most important steps. Although both process and results are important, the focus must be on the process, not specific results. For example, a results-oriented objective might be to "reduce the amount of time required for a student to wait to see an academic adviser." A process-oriented objective would be to "improve the process of academic advising in the college." Results of an improvement activity might be reported as, "The average amount of time required for a student to see an academic adviser has been reduced by 50 percent." To define the problem in the context of the process, we must answer several questions. For example, what are the outputs of the process? Who are the customers, both internal and external? What are the customers' requirements?

In many organizations the people responsible for the process tend to think they know exactly what the problem is and exactly how to fix it. This is possible, but a better approach to problem solving may be to first form an improvement team. Individuals with a vested interest in the process that needs improvement should be on the team. For example, a team might be made up of suppliers of information or material to the process, those responsible for actually accomplishing the process, and even customers of the product or service provided by the process. Do not forget to consider both internal customers and external customers. The team can determine the needs and expectations of various customers by talking with them. These needs and expectations should drive the improvement effort.

Improvements developed by a team of individuals are often better than improvements developed by one individual for at least two reasons. First, the old adage that "two heads are better than one" is usually true. By using group techniques (which we will discuss later), a team gathers a multitude of inputs from people with different views of the problem. This helps to ensure that any solution proposed will improve the total process and focus on the needs and

# OPERATIONS MANAGEMENT IN PRACTICE 19.4 ◀

## Small Organization Division: Fitchburg Coated Products

Fitchburg Coated Products had been doing business pretty much the same way for 30 years. And it was making money. Yet one corner of its business—the medical products group—was in trouble. The company makes adhesive products. Its medical group makes products like the patches used in EKG heart tests to attach sensors to a patient.

Customers were returning 4.5% of its products. And employees were demoralized by having to work long hours to redo work they had already done. Then the new CEO began preaching the gospel of change. Teamwork and total quality management—a system of bringing workers, managers and customers together to solve problems—had come to Fitchburg. It is thought that Fitchburg wouldn't be in the medical products business today if it was not for the teams working on the problems. It was a matter of survival.

The CEO set up 27 teams of employees from through the company—salesmen, the marketing vice president, production workers and customer service people. Team members met weekly in brainstorming sessions to identify problems and come up with solutions. The medical products team set up a system to track what customers wanted. Each one wanted its medical tape cut in different widths and lengths. Each wanted the products packed a different way. No one on the production floor knew the details.

Members of the team visited customers to see how the medical products were being used—and find out first hand what the problems were. Some changes were small, and common sense—but savings were big. For instance, materials were being damaged in storage, first by forklifts that ripped the bottom off 1,200 foot bandage rolls. At $10 per foot, they would lose around $100 worth. The company had simply assumed that it was a cost of doing business. The team designed a soft felt cradle to fit over the forklift. Now the material is treated more gently.

The big change was in attitude—among Fitchburg employees and between the company and its customers. Employees from production talked to sales people, managers talked to customer service reps.

Results for the medical group were dramatic. During the first six months of 1992, product returns were less than 1% as compared to 4.5% in the first half of 1991. Revenue jumped to $5 million last year from $4 million in 1991 and waste has decreased by 39%.

# Not-for-Profit Division: Swedish American Hospital

Doctors at Swedish American Hospital were griping to nurses. Nurses were shouting at lab technicians, who were trying to analyze dozens of blood samples. In the Intensive and Critical Care Units, critically ill patients were stuck on respirators and life-support systems longer than necessary because blood-test results were slow. The people trying to care for patients were furious.

A team of 10 doctors, nurses, therapists, laboratory technicians, medical technologists and staff members serving the ICCU cut the time needed to get the crucial blood tests from an average of 51 minutes to less than 20 minutes. Team members found that a test took 75 steps and filled a three page diagram before improvement. The team was surprised that there were so many opportunities for delays at every step. For example, it was found that vials sat for an average of 15 minutes before a runner from the lab picked them up. The team discovered that the process was much more complex than originally thought.

The team considered 40 solutions and made a number of changes. For example, doctors now stagger the times at which they need test results so lab technicians won't be deluged with samples. Also, most ICCU nurses were trained to collect the sample which was usually done by a specialist.

expectations of the customer. Second, a particular solution must be acceptable to those responsible for its implementation if it is to be implemented successfully. Assuming that the team developed the proposed solution, each team member will have an interest in seeing that the proposed solution provides desired results. Industry is full of good solutions that did not achieve the results expected, because those responsible for their implementation did not "buy in" to the solution.

Several tools are available to assist teams in defining the problem in terms of the process, including brainstorming, Pareto analysis, and process mapping.

**Step 2: Identify, Analyze, and Document the Process** Developing good solutions to problems is quite difficult unless everyone has a full understanding of the current process. People who report to work every day and do essentially the same piece of the overall process every day often do not understand the entire process. They have a good view of the trees but a limited view of the forest.

These improvement activities require a view of the entire forest and how each individual and activity fits into the overall process. Teams must identify and document every activity, however minor. They must analyze each activity to assess exactly what is done, who does it, why it is done, where it is done, how long it takes, and what its overall contribution to the process is. Check sheets and process maps are effective tools in this step of the overall improvement model.

**Step 3: Measure Current Performance** After identifying and analyzing the individual activities, the team must assess the strengths and weaknesses of the current overall process. Strengths and weaknesses are generally identified in terms of contributions to efficiency and customer satisfaction. How well are we doing now? What are some concrete measures of performance? The measures used will depend upon the process being analyzed. Measures of product or service quality, on-time delivery, waiting time, total cost, total processing time, and the number of processing steps all may be useful, depending upon the situation.

To determine which factors are most important, the team must talk to the customers. Teams often use customer surveys to do this. The surveys can help identify not only which factors are important to the customers but also customers' perception of how satisfied they are with the current process. Teams can also develop check sheets to collect actual performance data on important factors. Information collected in this step will be extremely valuable as a benchmark of current performance against which to compare the effectiveness of a chosen alternative solution. Without this basic measure of performance assessing the effect of improvements made to the process will be difficult. As we noted earlier, overzealous teams tend to overlook this step and go on to formulate and implement changes to the system. They often regret the oversight when they find they cannot assess improvement.

**Step 4: Understand Why the Process Is Performing as It Is**  Once the team has identified and measured critical performance factors, it must shift its attention to figuring out why the process is performing as it is. The objective of this exploratory analysis is to find the causes of the problems that the performance measures brought to light. Useful tools in this stage include brainstorming and cause-and-effect diagrams. Using these tools identifies areas for potential improvement. Inefficiencies, waste, redundancy, poor skills, attitudes and training, and convoluted information or material flows are just some of the typical causes of poor performance found during this stage.

**Step 5: Develop Alternative Solutions and Select the Best One**  At this point in the improvement process the team has identified customers' needs and expectations; identified, analyzed, and documented the current process; measured the current performance for critical factors; and understands why the process is performing as it is. Next, the team begins to develop alternative solutions to the problems it noted. It will evaluate various alternatives on how well they might contribute to the performance measures established earlier as critical measures. The team then chooses the best alternative for implementation.

Sometimes solutions that would be acceptable to management must involve no increase in budgets, no new hiring or layoffs, no expensive equipment, and so on. In this step management should make the team aware of any critical constraints that might affect its solutions.

**Step 6: Develop Strategy and Implement the Alternative Chosen**  Any alternative that is poorly implemented will stand little chance of providing the results expected. The strategy should include when, where, and how to implement the alternative. Generally, implementation on a small scale is better. If possible, the company should implement the solution in a small area until it can assess the performance of the improved process. At that time the company may modify the implementation strategy to include procedures for extending the new process to the entire work area. Sometimes implementing on a small scale first is not feasible. In those cases the strategy should include contingencies to deal with unexpected problems that the new process may create.

*Process improvement requires
careful monitoring and analysis
of the subject process.*

**Step 7: Evaluate the Results of the New Process**  The performance measures used to evaluate the new process should be the same measures identified in step 3. Only then can the team make an accurate comparison of the pre-improvement and postimprovement processes. The team will be able to assess some performance measures, such as waiting time and processing time, rather rapidly, but others may take a while longer. For example, customers' perceptions of the improvements may take longer to assess. Do not rush this step. Don't be quick to see the outcomes that you desperately want to see. Be objective. Be scientific.

**Step 8: Commit to Continuous Improvement of the Process**  Assuming that the assessment of the improved process is favorable, the company must take care to ensure that the improvement activity continues. At this point the team will probably disband, because it formed to study, recommend, implement, and measure. The term *continuous process improvement* means just that. Never be satisfied with current performance—continue to assess process performance and maintain customer contact. Many companies find that statistical process control is useful in the ongoing assessment of process performance. The commitment to continuous improvement of all processes is a reflection of management discipline. Properly trained and motivated managers who work in total quality cultures should possess the discipline to support and encourage continuous process improvement activities.

   We devote the remainder of this chapter to a description of the various tools and activities we mentioned in the steps of the process improvement model.

## Benchmarking

Whereas process improvement techniques encourage the identification of incremental improvements that the company can and should make to a process, sometimes a process is so critical to the business and so far behind the competition in performance that the company must set more aggressive improvement goals. This is the approach taken by benchmarking.

**Benchmarking** is the search for industry "best practices" that lead to superior business performance. This technique is based on the idea that companies with superior business processes will manufacture, deliver, and service products better than the competition will. In benchmarking, a company identifies processes that are important to its competitive position and then attempts to identify other companies or areas within the same company that are known for superior performance in this process. The benchmark partner may not even be in the same industry.

Imagine that you run a commercial airline. One activity crucial to customer service is baggage handling. A large percentage of passengers who check luggage rather than carrying it with them are changing planes en route to their final destination. Your company sorts thousands of bags daily, and the cost of an error is the cost of hand delivering the bag to the traveler and, even worse, the likelihood that the passenger will avoid booking flights with your airline in the future. Your company has determined that baggage handling is a critical process that it must improve.

The search now begins for a company that sorts and forwards items better than the others. One company that your airline might emulate is Federal Express. It operates in the same airport environment as you do, and its order-tracking system is renowned. Another company with superior performance is the catalog sales organization Lands' End. Although Lands' End's business is very different, it faces many of the same problems. Each day Lands' End receives shipments of items from manufacturers worldwide. These items must be sorted and stocked in a warehouse. The outflow of goods from the warehouse is similarly aggressive. Orders arrive by mail, fax, and telephone twenty-four hours a day. Many telephone customers want to know if an item is in stock and ready for shipment immediately. Lands' End has developed a item-tracking and -handling process that has characteristics similar to those needed in the airline industry.

After one of these organizations confirms that it might be a willing partner for benchmarking, both it and your airline must try to identify some reciprocal arrangement, because typically both partners must benefit if they are going to have sufficient incentive to benchmark. Federal Express wants to improve its employee training programs, and it notes that training is a process for which you have an excellent reputation. On this basis you agree to meet with a previously established agenda of questions to explore. You predetermine that neither company will disclose confidential information and that you will not publicly reveal the partner with whom you benchmarked. The first condition is especially important in those few cases in which you are benchmarking with competitors. The second condition helps to ensure that you and your benchmarking partner won't be deluged with requests for information from nonbenchmarking partners.

This exchange of information is the external portion of benchmarking, described as the planning stage in Table 19.2. Suppose that in this exercise, you determine that Federal Express's processes depend on significant use of bar coding technology and hand-held bar code label makers and readers. You might also determine how it organizes the department that routes packages and the vendors from which it purchased the technology. You disclose similar kinds of information regarding your employee training programs.

TABLE 19.2
Benchmarking Process Steps

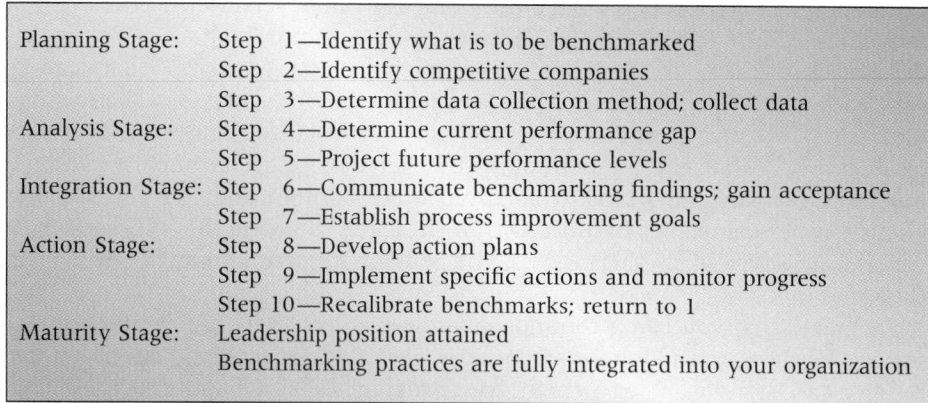

| | | |
|---|---|---|
| Planning Stage: | Step 1 | Identify what is to be benchmarked |
| | Step 2 | Identify competitive companies |
| | Step 3 | Determine data collection method; collect data |
| Analysis Stage: | Step 4 | Determine current performance gap |
| | Step 5 | Project future performance levels |
| Integration Stage: | Step 6 | Communicate benchmarking findings; gain acceptance |
| | Step 7 | Establish process improvement goals |
| Action Stage: | Step 8 | Develop action plans |
| | Step 9 | Implement specific actions and monitor progress |
| | Step 10 | Recalibrate benchmarks; return to 1 |
| Maturity Stage: | Leadership position attained |
| | Benchmarking practices are fully integrated into your organization |

Source: Robert C. Camp, "Benchmarking: The Search for Best Practices That Lead to Superior Performance," *Quality Progress* 22 (February 1989): 71.

Now that your airline has an idea of how the "best of the best" companies handles packages, its current rate of routing mistakes, and the technical solutions it uses to improve performance, the internal stages of the benchmarking process begin. Table 19.2 identifies these stages as analysis, integration, and action. Once the airline reaches the action stage, it repeats the process continually. At that point the process is in the maturity stage, signifying that your airline has become the "best." But achieving that status simply means that others will be benchmarking against you to reach and surpass the level of your process. To maintain the "best" status your airline must achieve continuous improvements in a never-ending quest for superiority of performance.

Companies considering benchmarking should exercise caution. According to research by Ernst & Young and the American Quality Foundation, benchmarking can actually hurt companies that are just beginning their quality quest.[1] The American Productivity and Quality Center in Houston operates the International Benchmarking Clearinghouse to help companies interested in identifying benchmarking partners. Table 19.3 lists the generally recognized U.S. leaders in a variety of disciplines.

## Data Collection, Analysis, and Presentation

Accurate collection, analysis, and presentation of data are the bases for benchmarking or other process improvement activities. As we mentioned earlier, many tools and procedures are available that contribute to the overall efficiency of data management. It is extremely important to include a legend whenever a chart, diagram, check sheet, or similar tool is used to collect or display data. A legend is simply a notation on the document that provides important information about the data presented. The legend might include the source of the data, exactly when they were collected, who collected them, why they were collected, and who to contact for additional information about the document. The legend is invaluable when conducting follow-up studies of some particular process. To accurately assess changes in a process teams need to use similar sampling techniques; an accurate and complete legend supplies that information.

---

[1] Otis Port and Geoffrey Smith, "Beg, Borrow—and Benchmark," *Business Week,* November 30, 1992, p. 75.

*Movement is underway in many educational institutions to incorporate quality concepts learned from business into the classroom.*

| America's World-Class Champs | |
|---|---|
| *General Area* | *Best Companies* |
| Benchmarking methods | AT&T, Digital Equipment, Ford, IBM, Motorola |
| Billing and collection | American Express, MCI, Fidelity Investments |
| Customer satisfaction | L.L. Bean, Federal Express, GE Plastics, Xerox |
| Distribution & logistics | L.L. Bean, Wal-Mart |
| Employee empowerment | Corning, Dow, Milliken, Toledo Scale |
| Equipment maintenance | Disney |
| Flexible manufacturing | Allen-Bradley, Baldor, Motorola |
| Health care programs | Allied-Signal, Coors |
| Marketing | Procter & Gamble |
| Product development | Beckman Instruments, Calcomp, Cincinnati Milacron, DEC, Hewlett Packard, 3M, Motorola, NCR |
| Quality methods | AT&T, IBM, Motorola, Westinghouse, Xerox |
| Quick shop-floor Changes | Dana, GM Lansing, Johnson Controls |
| Supplier management | Bose, Ford, Levi Strauss, 3M, Motorola, Xerox |
| Worker training | Disney, General Electric, Federal Express, Ford, Square D |

Source: Otis Port and Geoffrey Smith, "Beg, Borrow—and Benchmark," *Business Week,* November 30, 1992, pp. 74–75.

**Brainstorming** Brainstorming is a group technique for generating ideas in an environment free of criticism and intimidation. The group focuses on some specific problem or concern. Walt Disney has been credited with the concept of brainstorming (which he called *storyboarding*). During the development of the animated film *Steamboat Willie* in 1928 Disney used the technique to solicit ideas for the project.[2] Four basic principles should govern brainstorming meetings:[3]

1.  No criticism: Accept all ideas without judgment.
2.  No constraints: Do not be limited to how things are today or the constraints on the organization. Be creative. Often, several seemingly wild ideas combine to trigger an innovative one.
3.  Build on other people's ideas: Accept and encourage the modification, extension, or expansion of other people's ideas.
4.  Encourage participation: Encourage people to actively participate. The more ideas that are generated, the higher their quality will be. Some facilitators go around the room and ask each person for an idea. The process continues until each person says, "'I pass."

Brainstorming is especially useful for identifying problems, concerns, causes of problems, and potential solutions. Companies generally do not use brainstorming to determine a specific solution to a particular problem. Other techniques would be more appropriate for deciding upon a particular solution.

[2]Bruce Brocca and M. Suzanne Brocca, *Quality Management: Implementing the Best Ideas of the Masters* (Homewood, Ill.: Richard D. Irwin, 1992), p. 251.
[3]Kazuo Ozeki and Tetsuichi Asaka, *Handbook of Quality Tools* (Cambridge, Mass.: Productivity Press, 1990), p. 39.

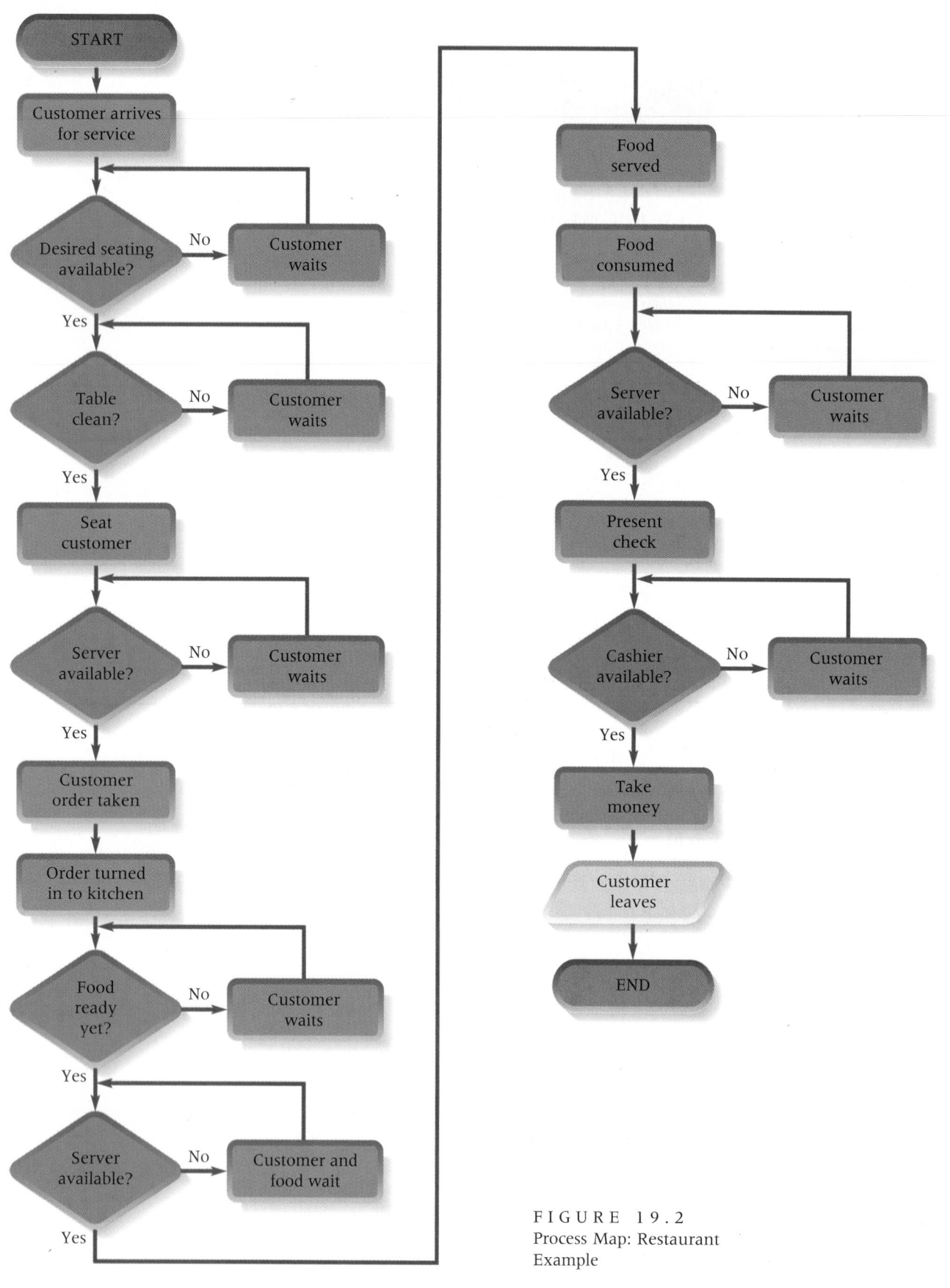

FIGURE 19.2
Process Map: Restaurant
Example

**Process Mapping** Process mapping is a technique that is useful for gaining an understanding of a process. Sometimes referred to as a *process flow chart*, process mapping is a graphic representation of the interrelationships of several activities that comprise a total process. Completing a process map requires a complete understanding of the entire process. The entire improvement team often develops the process map, because the team consists of individuals who at least understand their specific areas of the total process. Using generally accepted symbols to represent different stages of a process allows the mapping of the complete details of a process. Typical symbols include

to denote the start and end of a process

to denote an activity

to denote a decision point

to denote the delivered product or service

to denote the direction of flow

Consider the sample process map shown in Figure 19.2. This map represents the flow of customers through the process of being served in a restaurant. The restaurant manager could use this map to identify causes of delays in customer service and opportunities for improvement.

**Run Diagrams** Run diagrams show trends in some performance measure of a process. For example, if a director of university admissions wanted to track the number of freshman applications that come in each semester, the director could create a run diagram, as shown in Figure 19.3. The run diagram makes it easy to see long-term trends in the process being measured.

**Check Sheets** One of the most widely used tools of process improvement is the check sheet. Many of us use check sheets every day but do not think about it. Simple grocery lists and invitation lists are examples of check sheets. Most often, people use check sheets for collecting data about a process. After brainstorming and process mapping to understand the process, the team decides what data it needs to collect. Then it can design a check sheet to facilitate the data collection. Another example of the effective use of check sheets involves an office in which the phone rings constantly. Many of the calls are for another office and must be transferred to the appropriate party. The telephone process becomes a candidate for improvement. The office can develop a check sheet that allows the telephone answerer to mark down for whom the call was intended. The answerer might

FIGURE 19.3
Example of Run Diagram

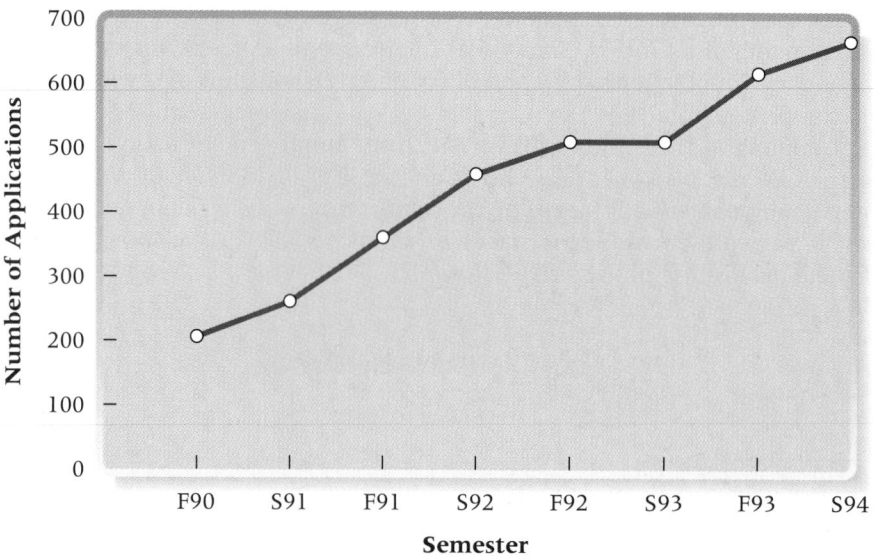

TABLE 19.4
Example of Check Sheet

| Error Type | Fridays in March 1993 | | | | Total |
| | *1st* | *2nd* | *3rd* | *4th* | |
|---|---|---|---|---|---|
| Addition | //// | /////// | /// | //// | 17 |
| Multiplication | ///// | /////// | /////// | //////// | 24 |
| Omission | // | / | | // | 5 |
| Routing | / | | // | | 3 |
| Typing | /// | //// | // | ///// | 14 |
| *TOTAL* | 15 | 17 | 13 | 18 | 63 |

Legend: Data gathered by Ronald Johnson (443-3344).
Purpose: Analyze types of processing errors created in billing department on Fridays.
Sampling plan: random samples of 100 jobs were sampled each Friday afternoon.

also be instructed to tell the caller, "I will be happy to transfer your call, but first, we are working to improve our operations, and we would like your help. Could you tell me where you got our telephone number?" The check sheet is designed for easy recording of the caller's response. The information will be important when the team gets to the heart of the telephone process problem.

The admissions office at Samford University in Birmingham, Alabama, successfully implemented a similar check sheet in 1993. The team used information collected on the check sheet to design a bookmark containing most of the phone numbers that entering freshmen and their parents needed. When the office mailed school catalogs to prospective students, each catalog contained a bookmark. This partial solution helped to decrease the number of calls that the admission office was transferring to financial aid or other departments on campus, thus improving the efficiency of the admissions office staff. Table 19.4 is another sample check sheet. A team designed this check sheet to identify the types and frequency of errors in the billing process. Preliminary analysis had indicated that most errors were occurring on Friday afternoons, so the check sheet was designed to collect data during that time period.

**Pareto Charts**  Another useful approach to strategic analysis of quality problems is developing Pareto charts. The Pareto analysis uses a bar chart to indicate the frequency of different sources of nonconformities in a product or service and indicates the potential improvement that will have the greatest effect on the overall quality of the item. The Pareto concept seeks to separate the vital few from the trivial many. Figure 19.4 provides the general format for a Pareto chart.

Suppose a manufacturer of hard contact lenses is experiencing too many defects after grinding the product. One approach to Pareto analysis of the problem would begin by classifying the defective lenses according to the type of defect present. For example, is the grinding problem frequently on the edges of the lenses or the center? Does the defect arise from inconsistent lens thickness? What is the frequency of nonconformities in each of the major contact lens product lines? Does the frequency of defects vary in relation to material from different suppliers of lens blanks? Do all operators and machines have the same frequency of defects? Figure 19.5 shows multiple applications of Pareto analysis to this problem.

Second, the analyst must decide which of the questions asked best separates one dominant source of nonconforming units, or the significant few, from the many other, less frequent sources of problems. In a group of 1,000 lenses, 85 have grinding problems. Those 85 include 60 lenses with edge-grinding defects and 25 with other nonconformities. Among the 60 with edge defects the suppliers of the lens blanks may vary according to the type of eyesight correction needed. Perhaps 50 of the 60 lenses originated from a single supplier. Pareto analysis has enabled us to identify one strategy for correcting 50 of 85 defective lenses. Working closely with the supplier of the nonconforming units and sharing information with that company about the problem may enable the two to jointly determine the source of this problem.

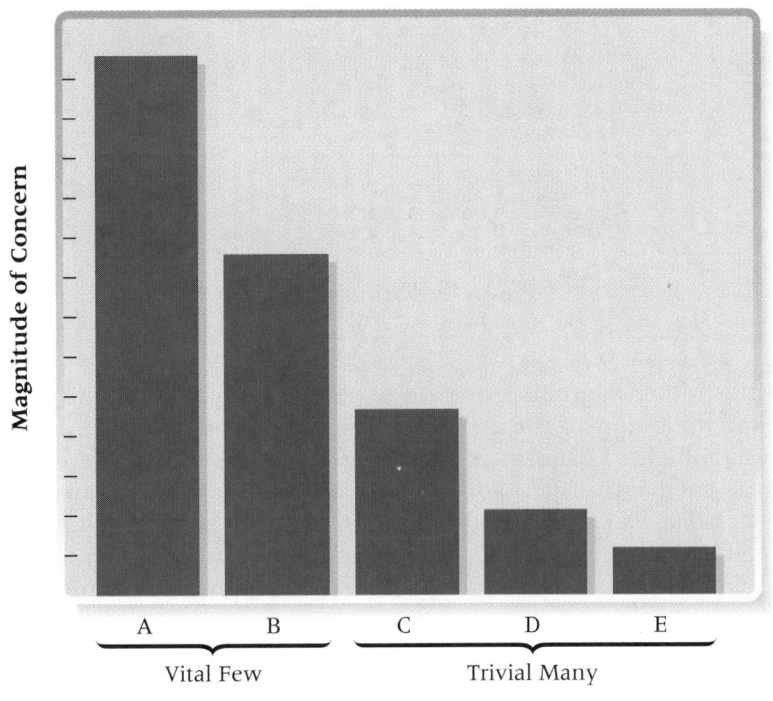

FIGURE 19.4
General Format for a Pareto Chart

FIGURE 19.5
Pareto Chart Examples

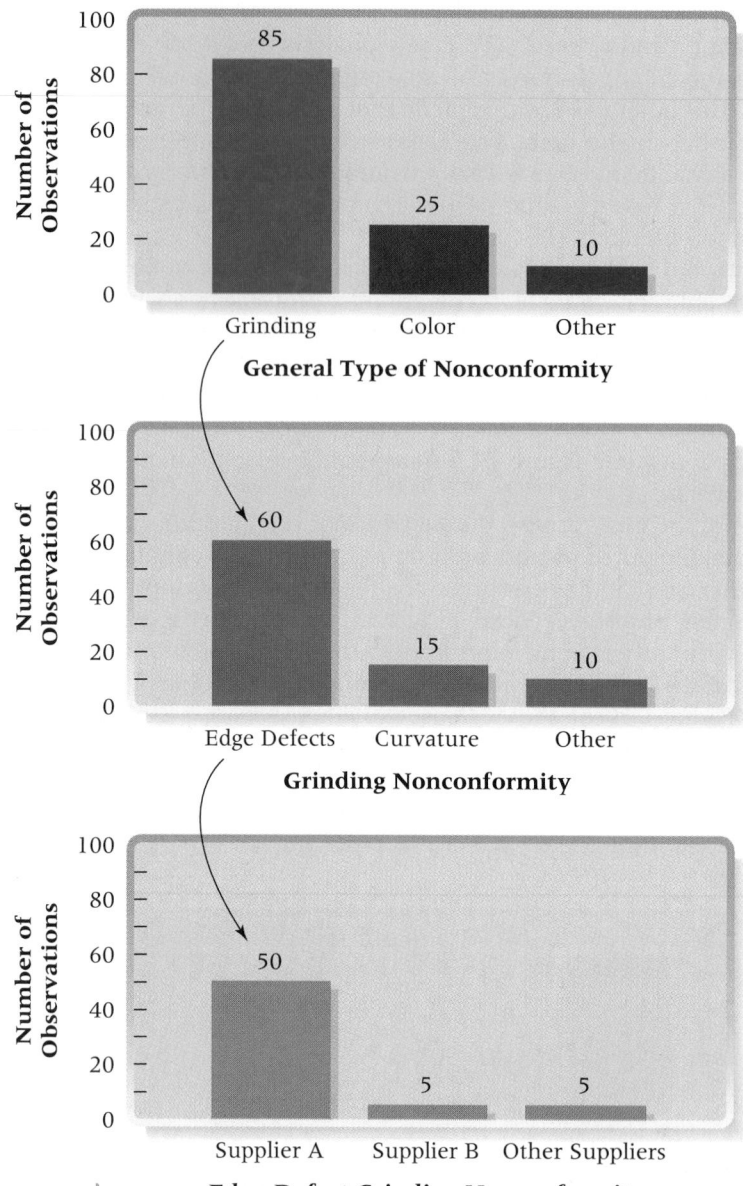

**General Type of Nonconformity**

**Grinding Nonconformity**

**Edge-Defect Grinding Nonconformity**

**Cause-and-Effect Diagrams** The path to restoring a system to statistical control requires identification of the assignable cause of the out-of-control condition. The cause-and-effect diagram is a tool for clarifying the causes of a quality problem. Sometimes called a *fishbone diagram* or an *Ishikawa diagram* (after the late Kaoru Ishikawa who fostered its use), the cause-and-effect diagram is useful for communicating the potential causes of an out-of-control quality characteristic and coordinating the choice of an approach to correcting the problem. Figure 19.6 illustrates the general structure of a cause-and-effect diagram. The team lists the concern or problem it is addressing (called the *effect*) on the right of the diagram. The factors that influence this concern are generally classified as labor, equipment, material, and methods. Users of cause-and-effect diagrams are

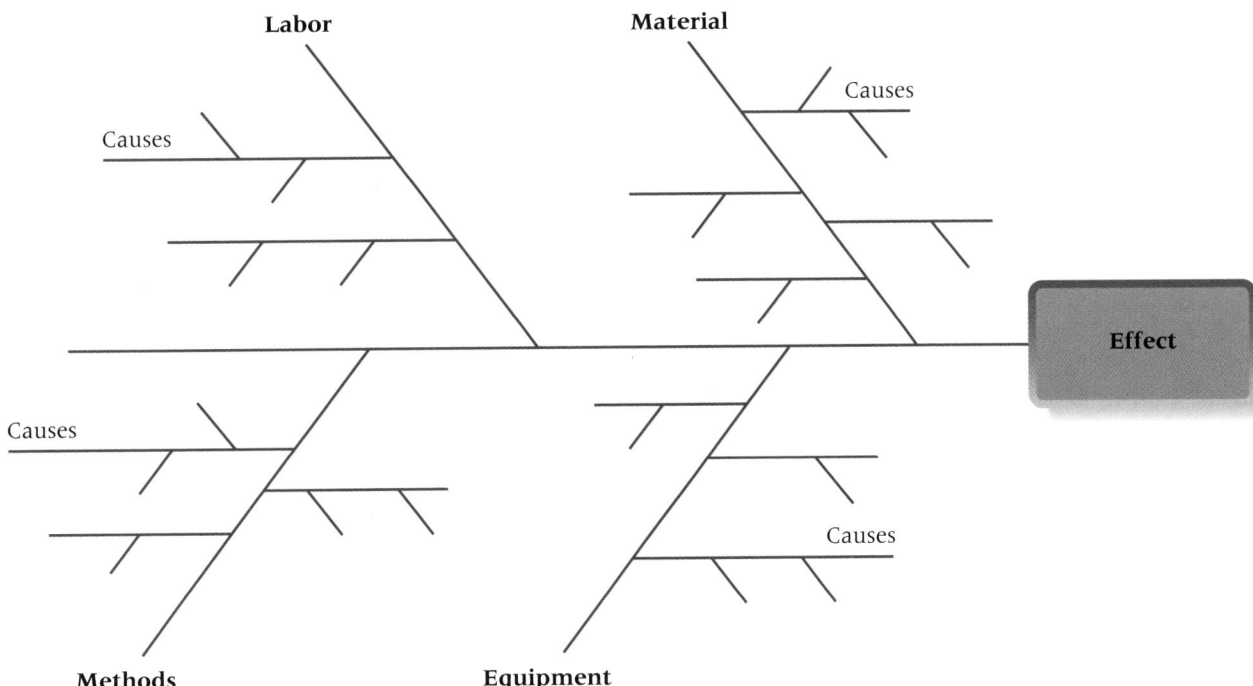

**Labor**

Causes

**Material**

Causes

Causes

Effect

Causes

Causes

**Methods**

**Equipment**

FIGURE  19.6
Cause-and-Effect Diagram
(Fishbone)

certainly not limited to those major factors. For each major branch or fishbone the process improvement team asks why a particular branch might not be contributing positively to the outcome desired. The team lists successive ideas as smaller branches on the four principal branches. Teams often use brainstorming to do this, listing ideas that they classify and place on the cause-and-effect diagram. They can then use the diagram to develop a set of strategies for corrective action.

Many professors across the country are using the continuous improvement process and tools to improve the learning experience for their students. Figure 19.7 is a cause-and-effect diagram generated by students of one such professor. The students brainstormed and decided that four major issues affected their "total course satisfaction": the instructor, the textbook, the instructor's methods, and the general classroom environment. The students used the cause-and-effect diagram along with additional input from students to develop recommendations for improvement.

The tools and procedures we have discussed thus far are basically nonstatistical by nature. That does not mean that they are not useful. Teams can successfully conduct many process improvement projects without using statistical tools, but statistical process control is very useful for some processes.

## Statistical Tools for Process Improvement

Most of the principles we describe in this section are well-known applications of standard statistical principles. These ideas are important, but they are certainly not new. In fact, if we could isolate one reason for the slip in competitiveness by North American companies in the seventies and eighties, we might well find it was the failure to adopt these principles.

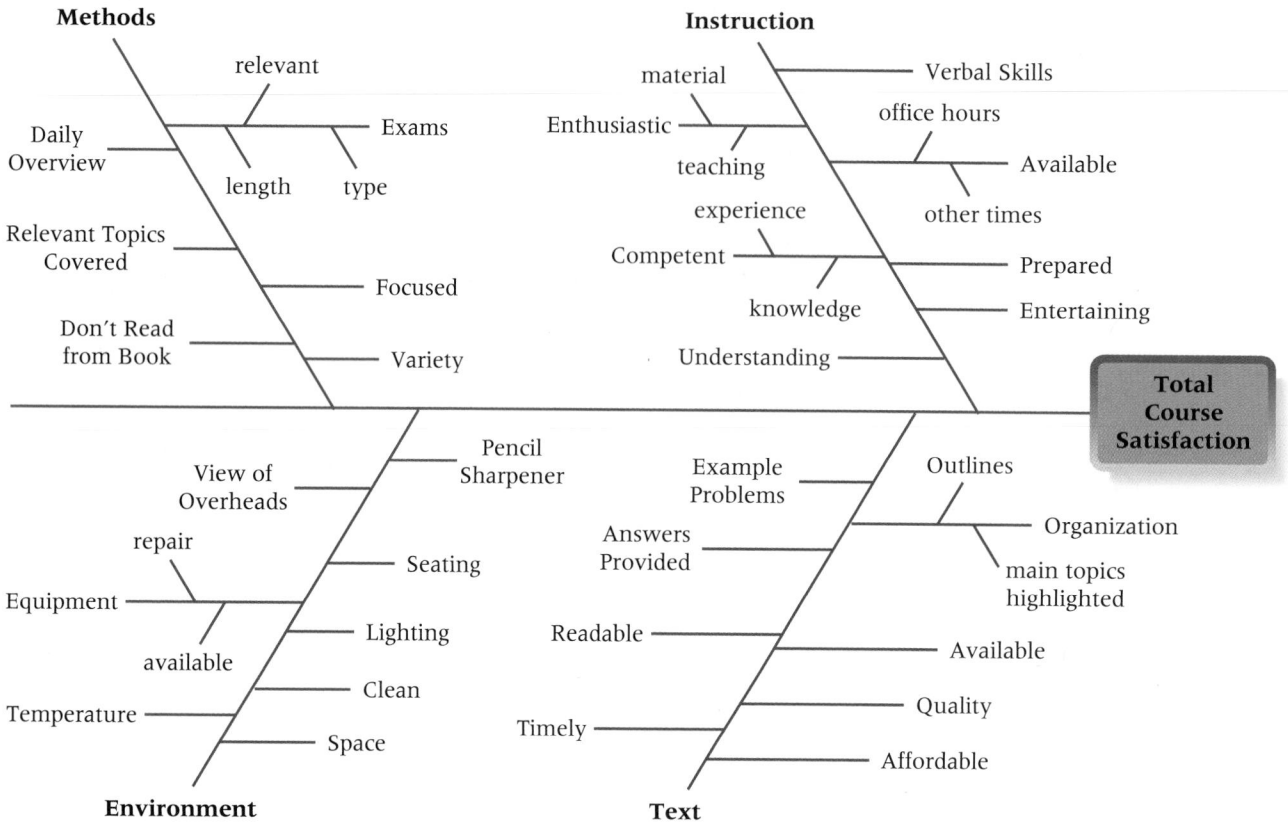

F I G U R E   1 9 . 7
Cause-and-Effect Diagram
from Class Activity

## Statistical Sampling and Control

Because manufacturing and service processes involve people, machines, and material operating together in some work environment, many factors can affect quality-related characteristics of the final product or service. Before statistical methods were available manufacturers compared each unit they produced with some master item and attempted to identify and correct any serious nonconformities. This approach could work if the manufacturer was meticulous, but it was expensive. Several scientists and engineers working at Bell Labs in the 1940s were convinced that they could use the then-new science of statistics to determine the natural variation to be expected in the measurement of some quality characteristic.

These quality characteristics might be a measurable variable, such as the number of ounces of milk in a carton, or the presence or absence of an attribute, such as rough or smooth surfaces on a table. When a process is stable, there will be a statistical distribution of natural variation from some assigned value. This means that when the milk carton filler is set to fill each carton with a mean of thirty-two ounces, actual measurements of filled cartons will form a distribution around that mean. Only redesigning the process, using different material, retraining the work force, or changing the environmental conditions under which the operation takes place can reduce the natural variation.

## Sampling and the Central Limit Theorem

No matter what the underlying distribution for the process variation might be, the central limit theorem of statistics states that the distribution of sample means from a population with any underlying distribution will be normally distributed. This assumes a sample size big enough to be statistically significant. Thus, for measurable variables such as ounces of milk, it doesn't matter what the distribution of individual observations of milk per carton might be; if someone took repeated samples of some number of cartons per sample and determined the average volume of milk in each sample, the distribution of those sampling means would be normally distributed. Because the normal distribution is well known, someone could collect statistics to determine the natural distribution of samples from a process. Presumably, someone could use the same information to determine whether the process has "drifted" out of control or whether some factor associated with material, technology, or workers is responsible for a change in the natural distribution. Figure 19.8 illustrates this concept.

## Using Statistics to Test Inferences About Quality Control

Using statistics to measure and control quality implies that no one measures every item produced or constantly monitors the process that produces them. Instead, someone takes samples of some predetermined size $n$ from a total population of size $N$. The goal is to correctly infer something about the state of the population based upon the observation of the sample; this process involves some risk. Elementary statistics suggests that two types of risk are associated with making an error in statistical inference, $\alpha$ and $\beta$.

Within the context of quality control $\alpha$ is the probability of a Type I error, sometimes called the **producer's risk,** which is the risk that a buyer would incorrectly reject a lot that is actually good. A lot is thought to be good if its measure falls within three standard deviations of the mean value for that measure. Such an error occurs when the mean of the sample of $n$ observations is unusually high or low but still belongs to a population that is in statistical control. Figure 19.9 illustrates the region(s) in the tail(s) of a normally distributed sampling distribution where such an error would occur.

If an analyst takes a random sample of ten televisions from an international shipment of two thousand units, the probability that some measurable quality characteristic of the sample units would have an unusually high or low value is quite small. Based on this test sample, the analyst might incorrectly reject the lot. Figure 19.9 also illustrates the probability that a lot or population that is actually out of statistical control is accepted as good. The probability that this occurs is called the **consumer's risk,** or $\beta$. The figure illustrates that the mean of the quality characteristic has actually shifted from $\mu$ to $\mu_1$, but the sample that was taken still falls within three standard deviations ($\pm 3\sigma$) of the value of $\mu$. No one detected this shift in the mean in the sample, and a Type II error occurs.

## Process Control Charts

By applying the concepts of sampling and risk analysis, we can measure some quality characteristic of products in order to make an inference about the state of the process. This process control approach attempts to identify and correct

FIGURE 19.8
The Concept of Statistical
Control

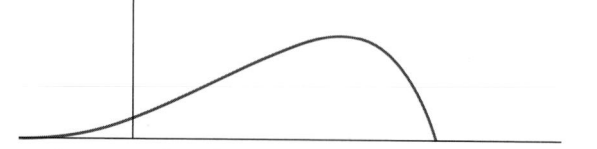

Observations of some quality characteristics from a natural distribution.

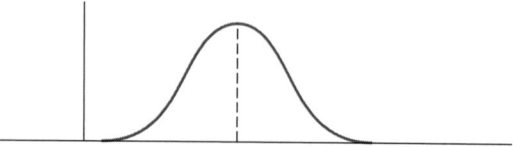

Samples of size $n$ of that same quality characteristics are normally distributed, as is predicted by the central limit theorem.

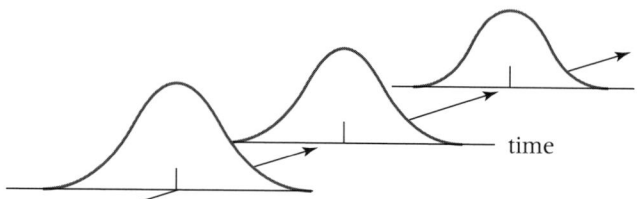

A process that is in statistical control has a stable mean and variance and is predictable.

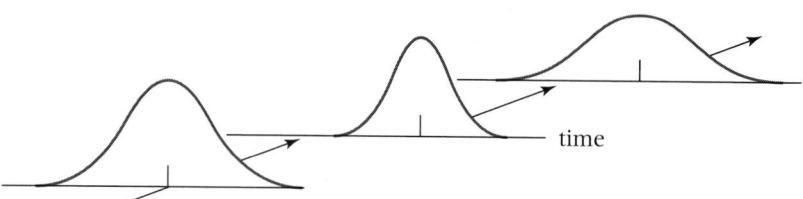

If assignable causes of variation are present, the process output is no longer stable or predictable. These assignable causes may effect the mean and/or the variance of the sampling distribution.

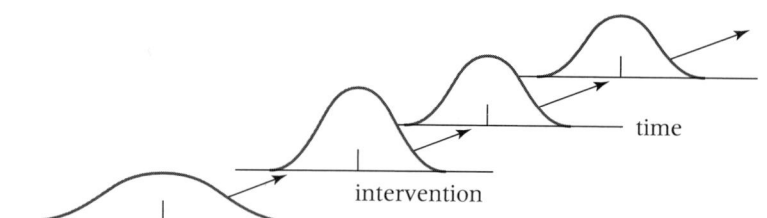

If these assignable causes of variation can be identified and eliminated, the process can be brought back into statistical control.

process changes before they produce a large number of nonconforming items. **Process control charts** are designed to detect shifts in the mean value of a process so that an analyst can find assignable causes and the company can take corrective action. Process control data also are useful in determining the capability of a process, which we will discuss in a later section. North American companies that develop process control charts commonly use the statistical decision rule—so long as samples stay within three standard deviations of the mean, the process is presumed to be in control. Assuming normality, the total risk

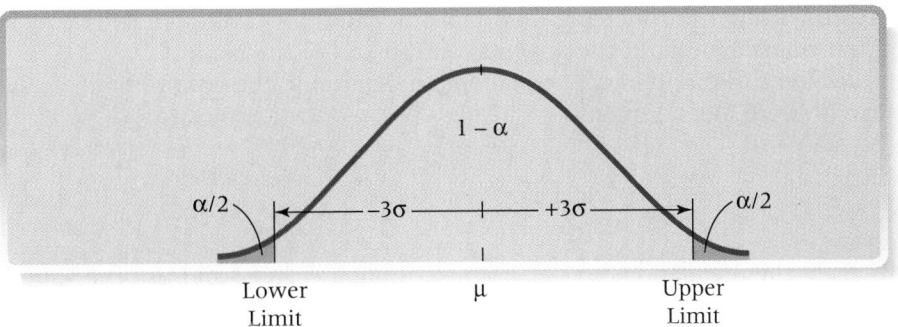

FIGURE 19.9
Control Chart for Quality
Characteristic Q

α: Probability of Type I error—incorrectly concluding that the process is out of statistical control.

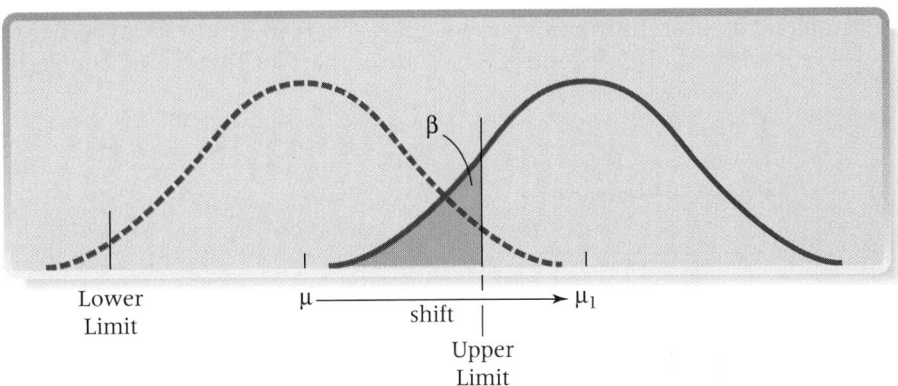

β: Probability of Type II error—incorrectly concluding that the process is in statistical control when a shift has occurred.

of exceeding these ±3σ limits is $P(\alpha) = 0.0026$. Figure 19.9 shows that the distribution of sample measurements can be collected periodically during manufacturing. If the sample observations stay within the ±3σ control limits and show no pattern, we conclude that the system is in statistical control. We interpret evidence of a nonrandom pattern in the control chart as a shift in the process, implying a Type II error. For any statistical sampling plan the selection of appropriate levels of alpha and beta risk and the sample size are crucial decisions for managers. It is beyond the scope of this discussion, but selecting the sample size *n* and one of either alpha or beta is sufficient to specify the risk of a sampling plan.

**Control Charts for Variable Data**  When the quality characteristic being monitored is measurable on a continuous scale, such as inches, miles per hour, ounces, or liters, that characteristic is called a *quality variable*. The data illustrated in Table 19.5 represent twenty samples of five measurements ($n = 5$) in each. For each of the samples we have calculated the mean ($\overline{X}$) and the difference between the biggest and smallest measurement [range ($R$)]. We can use the grand mean of these twenty samples ($\overline{\overline{X}}$) as an approximation of the mean value of the quality characteristic that we are measuring. We can use the mean of the twenty sample ranges ($\overline{R}$) as a way to estimate the standard deviation of the process. Because the variability of the sample mean depends on the sample size *n*, tables have been developed to assist in converting $\overline{R}$ into an estimate of three standard deviations for constructing control charts. This table of values for three standard deviation control charts appears in the appendix at the end of the book.

We can use the following equations to determine the control limits for the mean of these measurements:

Lower control limit: $\bar{\bar{X}} - A_2 \times \bar{R}$
Center line: $\bar{\bar{X}}$
Upper control limit: $\bar{\bar{X}} + A_2 \times \bar{R}$

We apply these equations to the example in Figure 19.12 and use the value of $A_2 = 0.58$ when sample size $n = 5$ (from the appendix) to determine that the

Lower control limit is $4.36 - (0.58 \times 0.37) = 4.145$
Center line is $4.36$
Upper control limit is $4.36 + (0.58 \times 0.37) = 4.575$

We can plot data from future samples on this $\bar{X}$-chart to determine whether the process remains in statistical control. The control chart for this example looks like this:

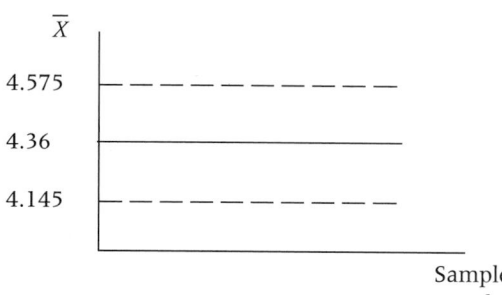

Suppose that the data in Table 19.5 represent the ounces of potato chips in an individual serving-size bag. Because potato chips come in a variety of sizes and shapes, it is not unusual to have some variation in the weight of a typical bag of this type. However, just monitoring the mean value of ounces per sample does not provide sufficient information to determine whether the process is in control. Within one sample of $n = 5$ the individual observations could be either very consistent or highly variable. If one bag is almost empty and the next is loaded with chips, the mean value of a sample of five successive measurements may be in control with regard to the mean, but the process is performing poorly. Therefore, the range of the measurements must be in control as well. Using the same three-sigma limits that we used with the $\bar{X}$-chart, we can construct an $R$-chart. Once again, we will use the mean value of some test sample ranges in conjunction with the sample size to determine the value of three standard deviations of the range $\sigma_R$, using table values provided in the appendix.

Lower control limit: $\bar{R} \times D_3$
Center line: $\bar{R}$
Upper control limit: $\bar{R} \times D_4$

For this example, where $n = 5$, $D_3 = 0.0$ and $D_4 = 2.11$. We then calculate the control limits for the $R$-chart as follows:

Lower control limit: $0.37 \times 0.0 = 0.0$
Center line: $0.37$
Upper control limit: $0.37 \times 2.11 = 0.781$

| **Data for Control Chart Construction** | | | | | | | |
|---|---|---|---|---|---|---|---|
| $(n = 5)$ Sample Batch | Measurements | | | | | $\overline{X}$ | $R$ |
| 1 | 4.5 | 4.6 | 4.5 | 4.4 | 4.4 | 4.48 | .20 |
| 2 | 4.6 | 4.5 | 4.4 | 4.3 | 4.1 | 4.38 | .50 |
| 3 | 4.6 | 4.1 | 4.4 | 4.4 | 4.1 | 4.32 | .50 |
| 4 | 4.4 | 4.3 | 4.4 | 4.2 | 4.3 | 4.32 | .20 |
| 5 | 4.3 | 4.3 | 4.4 | 4.2 | 4.3 | 4.30 | .20 |
| 6 | 4.6 | 4.6 | 4.2 | 4.5 | 4.4 | 4.46 | .40 |
| 7 | 4.1 | 4.3 | 4.6 | 4.5 | 4.2 | 4.34 | .50 |
| 8 | 4.5 | 4.5 | 4.4 | 4.6 | 4.4 | 4.48 | .20 |
| 9 | 4.4 | 4.2 | 4.6 | 4.6 | 4.2 | 4.40 | .40 |
| 10 | 4.2 | 4.2 | 4.2 | 4.5 | 4.2 | 4.26 | .30 |
| 11 | 4.3 | 4.2 | 4.3 | 4.4 | 4.2 | 4.28 | .20 |
| 12 | 4.4 | 4.4 | 4.4 | 4.4 | 4.1 | 4.34 | .30 |
| 13 | 4.3 | 4.2 | 4.4 | 4.6 | 4.6 | 4.42 | .40 |
| 14 | 4.2 | 4.4 | 4.4 | 4.1 | 4.4 | 4.30 | .30 |
| 15 | 4.2 | 4.3 | 4.1 | 4.5 | 4.6 | 4.34 | .50 |
| 16 | 4.6 | 4.4 | 4.3 | 4.5 | 4.1 | 4.38 | .50 |
| 17 | 4.6 | 4.6 | 4.6 | 4.2 | 4.5 | 4.50 | .40 |
| 18 | 4.4 | 4.6 | 4.3 | 4.1 | 4.3 | 4.34 | .50 |
| 19 | 4.3 | 4.6 | 4.2 | 4.2 | 4.1 | 4.28 | .50 |
| 20 | 4.2 | 4.5 | 4.1 | 4.4 | 4.4 | 4.32 | .40 |
| | | | | | | $\overline{\overline{X}} = 4.36$ | $\overline{R} = 0.370$ |

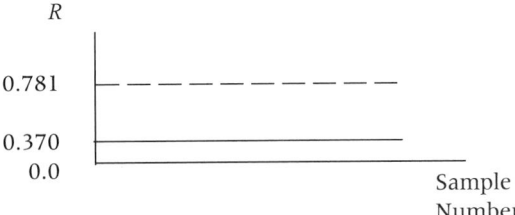

To conclude that the process is in statistical control using a quality characteristic measured by a variable, future samples must be within the control limits of *both* the $R$-chart and the $\overline{X}$-chart, and no nonrandom pattern should be apparent in a series of either chart. Exactly what constitutes a nonrandom pattern is up to the individual user. Some consider seven or more consecutive observations moving in the same direction and seven or more consecutive observations above or below the center line as nonrandom patterns significant enough to warrant investigation.

Thus far, we have used statistical techniques to characterize a process when the process is known to be in control. This characterization relates to the amount of natural variation exhibited in the process. We have measured both between-sample variability ($\overline{X}$-chart) and within-sample variability ($R$-chart) and have designed control charts that reflect that natural variability. We then monitor the process for a degree of variability not expected to occur naturally.

If a sample is below the center line of the $\overline{X}$-chart or below the center line of the $R$-chart, does it mean the same thing? Consider the potato chip bag-filling process. If an observation is below the center line of the $\overline{X}$-chart, the average weight of the sample is low. That could occur if the amount of potato chips in all bags were about right, except for one very light one, or if all bags were light. The $R$-chart would help complete the picture. If the range of that sample was high, the implication would be that the sample had a mixture of both heavy and light bags. Understand that observations going lower on the $R$-chart is a good event. After all, that is what process improvement is all about. Activities are directed at reducing variability, and the $R$-chart is designed to measure that variability.

How should you respond if the sample means are near the center line and the sample ranges continue to decrease toward zero? If the range values exceed the lower control limit, we would say that the process is no longer in statistical control, but that is not necessarily bad. Obviously, something about the environment has changed, causing more consistency in the process output. The appropriate response would be to treat this out-of-control situation just like any other. Investigate the cause of the improvement (in this case), and determine whether it is possible to make that improvement part of the natural process. For example, a new vendor may produce a particular component to closer tolerances than the usual vendors. That better-quality component may perform better within the process under consideration. Once the advantages of the particular vendor are properly documented, that vendor might become a sole supplier for the component. If that is the case, we would conclude that the environment now is different from the environment in which the control charts were originally constructed. We would need to establish new lower and upper control limits for the control charts.

Figure 19.10 illustrates the use of a control chart for tracking the performance of a machining process that shears a metal part. The quality measure for this process is the dimension of the part. An operator takes five readings at regular intervals throughout the day and computes the mean and range on the data record at the bottom of the chart. The operator then plots these data points on the charts and uses a straight line to connect new data points to previous ones. This line assists the operator in detecting nonrandom patterns. This illustration also includes the values for $A_2$, $D_3$, and $D_4$ that the operator used to construct the charts in the lower right corner.

**Control Charts for Attribute Data**  Many of the measurable quality characteristics of products are not continuous variables but the presence or absence of a quality attribute. As we would expect from statistics, the underlying distribution of this type of quality characteristic is binomial, because it describes characteristics that can have only one of two values, such as "success" or "failure." The control chart most associated with this type of attribute is the $P$-chart, which tracks the proportion of samples that is nonconforming.

The $P$-chart control limits are relatively easy to compute. For each of $M$ samples of size $n$, we add up the proportion of defectives from each sample. Then we divide the total by the number of samples, $M$. The result denotes the overall proportion of defectives. Because the $P$ statistic is binomial, the standard deviation of that statistic has a form familiar to students of statistics:

$$s_P = \sqrt{(\overline{P}(1 - \overline{P}))/n}$$

We determine three sigma-control limits by using the following equations:

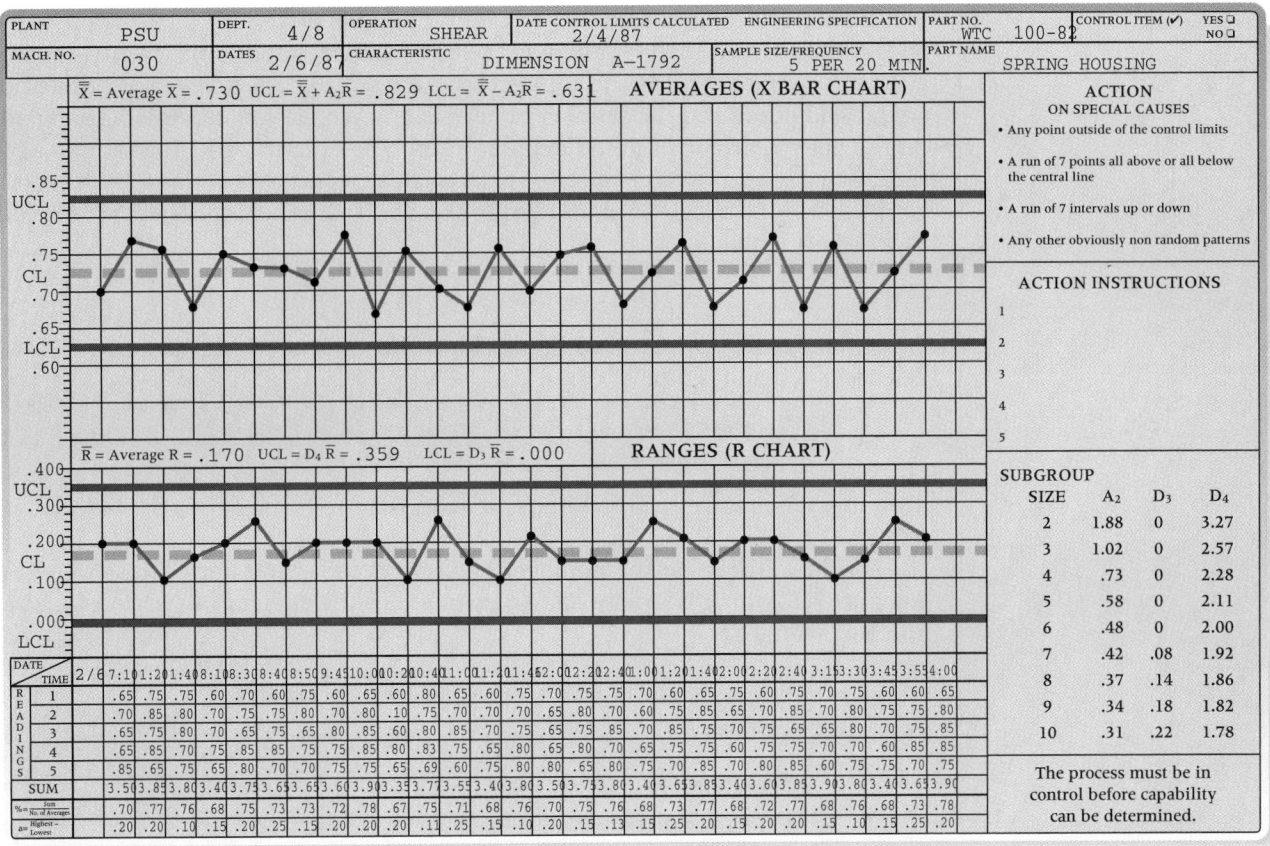

\* For sample sizes of less than seven, there is no lower control limit for ranges.

FIGURE 19.10
Sample Control Chart

Lower control limit: $\bar{P} - 3s_P$
Center line: $\bar{P}$
Upper control limit: $\bar{P} + 3s_P$

A second form of attribute control chart involves tracking the average number of defectives in a sample rather than the proportion of defectives in a sample. Such a control chart is referred to as an *nP-chart*. To use the *nP*-chart the size of each sample must be the same. This type of chart is a useful alternative to the *P*-chart, because it is easier to understand and the calculations are easier. The center line of the *nP*-chart is simply the sum of the defectives across all *M* samples, divided by *M*. Because the sample sizes are the same, another way to simply calculate the center line value is to multiply the sample size (*n*) by the overall proportion of defectives ($\bar{P}$). The resulting centerline is denoted $n\bar{P}$. An estimate of the standard deviation for the *nP*-chart is

$$s_{n\bar{P}} = \sqrt{n\bar{P}(1 - \bar{P})}$$

We then would determine three standard deviation control limits for the *nP*-chart as

Lower control limit: $n\bar{P} - 3s_{n\bar{P}}$
Center line: $n\bar{P}$
Upper control limit: $n\bar{P} + 3s_{n\bar{P}}$

Table 19.6 provides data that can be used to illustrate the construction of $P$- and $nP$-charts. An analyst randomly selected fifteen samples of twenty square glass plates and recorded the number and fraction of defectives. Note that the analyst did not record the number of defects on each glass plate. Any defect at all on the glass plate constitutes a defective unit. For example, the first sample had three defective plates out of twenty. Let's calculate control limits for a $P$-chart and an $nP$-chart for this data. Because $\bar{P} = 0.11$ and $n = 20$, the standard deviation for this $P$-chart would be

$$s_P = \sqrt{(\bar{P}(1 - \bar{P}))/n} = \sqrt{(0.11(1 - 0.11))/20} = 0.07$$

Three standard deviation control limits for this control chart for the proportion of defectives would then be

Lower control limit: $\bar{P} - 3s_P = 0.11 - 3(0.07) = -0.10 = 0$
Upper control limit: $\bar{P} + 3s_P = 0.11 + 3(0.07) = 0.32$

Note that when lower control limits are calculated to be negative, they are set at zero.

For the $nP$-chart for the number of defectives the center line of the chart was given as 2.2, which is simply $n\bar{p}$. An estimate of the standard deviation for the $nP$-chart would be

$$s_{n\bar{p}} = \sqrt{n\bar{p}(1 - \bar{P})} = \sqrt{2.2(1 - 0.11)} = 1.4$$

Three standard deviation control limits for the $nP$-chart would be

Lower control limit: $n\bar{p} - 3s_{n\bar{p}} = 2.2 - 3(1.4) = 0$ (truncated)
Upper control limit: $n\bar{p} + 3s_{n\bar{p}} = 2.2 + 3(1.4) = 6.4$

Other variations of the $P$-chart for attributes have been developed for special applications. For example, in the previous problem a glass plate was considered

T A B L E 1 9 . 6
Data for an Attribute Quality Characteristic

| Sample | # Defective | Fraction Defective |
|--------|-------------|--------------------|
| 1 | 3 | 0.15 |
| 2 | 2 | 0.10 |
| 3 | 4 | 0.20 |
| 4 | 0 | 0.00 |
| 5 | 1 | 0.05 |
| 6 | 2 | 0.10 |
| 7 | 4 | 0.20 |
| 8 | 1 | 0.05 |
| 9 | 2 | 0.10 |
| 10 | 3 | 0.15 |
| 11 | 3 | 0.15 |
| 12 | 0 | 0.00 |
| 13 | 2 | 0.10 |
| 14 | 4 | 0.20 |
| 15 | 2 | 0.10 |
| Total | 33 | 1.65 |
| Average | $n\bar{P} = 2.2$ | $\bar{P} = .11$ |

defective if it had any defect. What if some plates had more than one defect? That information would be totally lost when using the *P*-chart or *nP*-chart. In quality improvement efforts it is sometimes useful to look at the number of defects in each item. Examples of these quality characteristics would include the number of defects found among electrical components on a circuit board, the number of typographical errors per printed page, the number of surface defects on a 2.5-square-foot metal sheet, or the number of defects in a 10-meter length of wire.

We use the *C*-chart to track the countable number of defects in an item when the sample size is the same. For this situation the underlying statistical distribution is Poisson. The Poisson distribution has the property that the standard deviation is the square root of the mean. The center line of the chart would be $\bar{C}$, calculated as the total number of defects found divided by the number of items in the sample. The general form for the center line and three standard deviation control limits for a *C*-chart would be

$$\text{Lower control limit: } \bar{C} - 3\sqrt{\bar{C}}$$
$$\text{Center line: } \bar{C}$$
$$\text{Upper control limit: } \bar{C} + 3\sqrt{\bar{C}}$$

Here's how to construct the C-chart. Suppose you have collected a sample of twenty-five microwave oven cabinets. Defects on a cabinet might be scratches, dents, burrs, or any other surface problem. From the sample of twenty-five cabinets you found a total of forty defects, giving a $\bar{C}$ of 1.6 defects per cabinet. Computing the control limits for this example yields the following:

$$\text{Lower control limit: } 1.6 - 3\sqrt{1.6} = 0 \text{ (truncation)}$$
$$\text{Center line: } 1.6$$
$$\text{Upper control limits: } 1.6 + 3\sqrt{1.6} = 5.395$$

Table 19.7 summarizes the formulas to be used for constructing three standard deviation control limits for these control charts.

## Control Limits Versus Specification Limits

Measurements of product quality characteristics can indicate that a process is in statistical control. That does not guarantee that the products produced meet the requirements of the customer, however. When the control limits of quality characteristics are computed, they represent the natural variation produced by a

TABLE 19.7
3$\sigma$ Control Chart Formulas

| Control Chart Type | Center Line | Lower Control Limit | Upper Control Limit |
|---|---|---|---|
| $\bar{X}$ | $\bar{\bar{X}}$ | $\bar{\bar{X}} - A_2\bar{R}$ | $\bar{\bar{X}} + A_2\bar{R}$ |
| $R$ | $\bar{R}$ | $D_3\bar{R}$ | $D_4\bar{R}$ |
| $P$ | $\bar{P}$ | $\bar{P} - 3\sqrt{(\bar{P}(1-\bar{P}))/n}$ | $\bar{P} + 3\sqrt{(\bar{P}(1-\bar{P}))/n}$ |
| $nP$ | $n\bar{P}$ | $n\bar{P} - 3\sqrt{n\bar{P}(1-\bar{P})}$ | $n\bar{P} + 3\sqrt{n\bar{P}(1-\bar{P})}$ |
| $C$ | $\bar{C}$ | $\bar{C} - 3\sqrt{\bar{C}}$ | $\bar{C} + 3\sqrt{\bar{C}}$ |

process. Some processes are not precise enough for some applications. The natural variation of the wood cut produced by a chain saw makes it an unacceptable technology for cabinet making. These **specification limits** indicating acceptable variation are set by the designer or the customer. Operations managers must then select a capable process so that the natural control limits of the process are within the specifications of the customer. Figure 19.11 illustrates the idea of process capability.

In the first diagram the natural limits of the process fit easily within the specifications. Even if the process drifts from the midpoint of the specifications, operators would have an opportunity to correct the process and would be unlikely to produce unacceptable units while corrective action is taken. The second diagram indicates a process that is not capable. Even when the process is centered precisely between the specifications, units are produced that are either above or below the specified measurement.

The relationship between control limits of a process and the specification limits of design are useful in comparing process capabilities. One such **process capability** index ($C_p$) is defined as follows:

$$C_p = \frac{USL - LSL}{6\sigma}$$

where

FIGURE 19.11
Process Capability

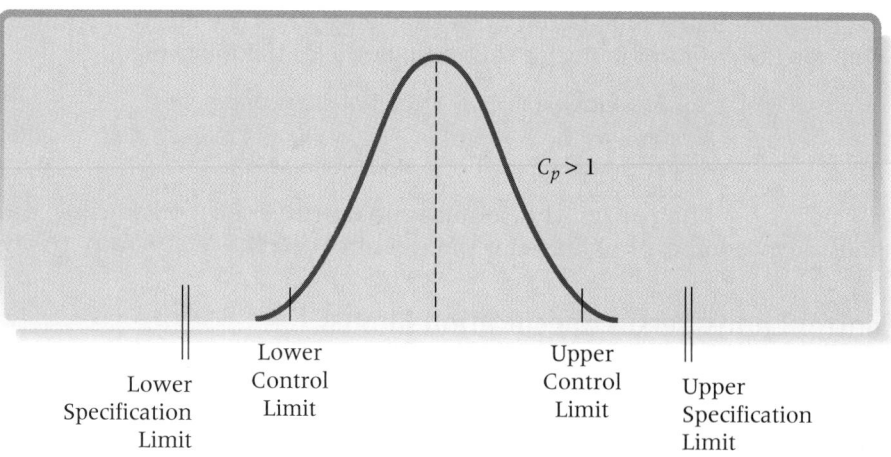

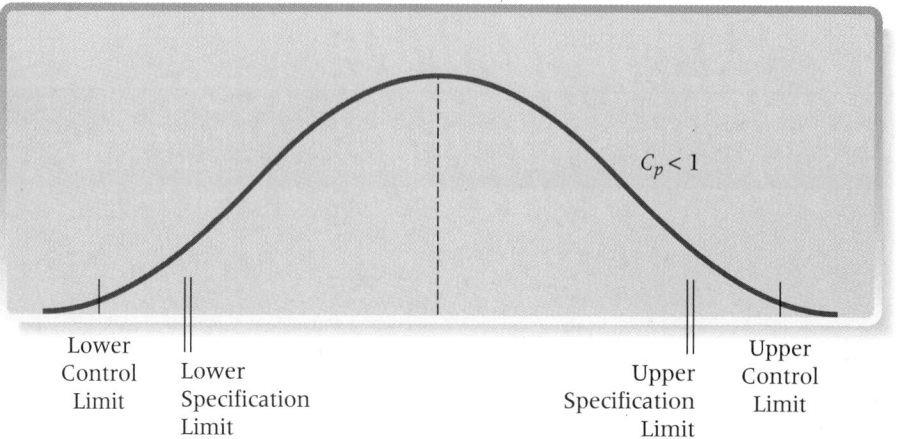

$USL$ = Upper specification limit

$LSL$ = Lower specification limit

$\sigma$ = Standard deviation of the process

We can estimate the standard deviation of the process by dividing the process $\bar{R}$ by the factor $d_2$. This factor is determined from the table of values based on sample size (see appendix), similar to the factors $A_2$, $D_3$, and $D_4$ that we used previously.

A process with a $C_p$ equal to one is just barely capable. If it is a very stable process with little tendency to drift out of statistical control, it may be tolerable. However, a very small shift in the mean increases the number of out-of-specification units produced. A $C_p$ greater than one indicates that the process is capable of producing items with values of the quality characteristic within specifications. Values of $C_p$ that are less than one are not feasible for manufacturing purposes.

While the $C_p$ relates the process spread to the specification spread, it does not consider how well the process is centered within the limits. Although a $C_p$ may be equal to or greater than one, if the process mean is not centered between the specification limits, some units may be produced outside the limits. In order to factor in the location of the process mean, $C_p$ must be modified. One adjusted capability index is $C_{pk}$. This new index is defined as

$$C_{pk} = C_p(1 - k)$$

where

$$k = 2|\text{design target} - \text{process average}| / \text{specification range}$$

Note that if the process average is equal to the design target value, $C_{pk}$ will be equal to $C_p$, indicating that the process is perfectly centered within the limits.

Suppose for a stable process $\bar{\bar{X}} = 200$, $\bar{R} = 2$, and $n = 5$. Suppose further that design specifications are $198 \pm 4$. From the table of factors for $n = 5$ we find that $d_2 = 2.326$. Thus, for this process

$$\sigma = 2/2.326 = 0.86 \quad \text{and} \quad C_p = (202 - 194) / 6(0.86) = 1.55.$$

This index of 1.55 indicates that the process is capable, but does that mean that it will not produce units outside the limits? By calculating $C_{pk}$, we gain more insight to the true characteristics of this process:

$$k = 2|198 - 200| / (202 - 194) = 0.5$$
$$C_{pk} = 1.55(1 - 0.5) = 0.775$$

After using this technique to factor in how the process is centered, we find that the process is *not* as capable of consistently delivering units within the specification limits as first thought. The primary problem with this process is not its natural variation. The process needs to be improved to better center the mean within the specification limits.

# Acceptance Sampling[4]

Inspecting incoming material and finished production lots in order to certify that they are acceptable is still a widespread practice in U.S. industry. The preference

[4]James R. Evans and William M. Lindsay, *The Management and Control of Quality,* 2d ed. (Minneapolis/ St. Paul: West, 1993), pp. 627–638.

of course would be that inspections would be unnecessary, but the realities indicate that some form of testing is necessary. If testing is necessary, companies would eliminate risk by inspecting 100 percent of the items. Technological breakthroughs in the areas of measurement and instrumentation are allowing a limited number of companies to automatically inspect 100 percent of the items produced. But for most organizations inspecting 100 percent would be too costly and time consuming. In addition, the testing process actually destroys such products as munitions, flash bulbs, camera film, military missile systems, and many others.

Given these concerns about 100 percent testing, the general procedure that companies use is to draw a random sample from the population of items, test the sample, and draw conclusions about the quality of the entire population based on the quality of the sample. This process is called **acceptance sampling.** The risk of drawing an incorrect conclusion is defined in the same way that it is for control charts. However, here we do not use the measurement of the quality characteristic to assess the statistical control of the process but to determine the acceptability of the items themselves. For finished goods the only corrective action that is possible is to sort through rejected lots and separate good items from bad and then rework or scrap the bad ones. Such sorting can do nothing to improve the quality of future production.

On both the outgoing and incoming material sides inspection increases cycle time and wastes resources. Because of the time required to return defective material to a supplier and get replacement units, many manufacturers do everything they can do to use the defective material. Inspecting items is a procedure that fails to improve manufacturing, and many feel that it is at odds with modern, prevention-oriented quality philosophies. But for the sake of completeness, we will address some of the basics of acceptance sampling.

Acceptance sampling is accomplished for both attribute and variable measures. Here we will discuss only acceptance sampling for attribute measures. One

*Xerox technicians perform final inspection on a piece of equipment before sending it to the customer.*

key issue in any acceptance sampling is the sampling plan. The **sampling plan** contains information about the sample size to be drawn and the accept/reject numbers for that sample size. The acceptance number describes the maximum number of defective items found in the sample that will be acceptable. Finding any less than that number of defective items in the sample will result in acceptance of the entire lot. The rejection number describes the minimum number of defective items in the sample that will result in rejection of the entire lot.

The simplest type of sampling plan is the single sampling plan—the accept/ reject decision is based on a single sample. The plan would consist of the sample size ($n$) to be drawn from the population of size ($N$). Also provided would be the acceptance number $c$, so that if the number of defective items is found to be less or equal to $c$, the lot would be accepted. Otherwise the lot would be rejected. An alternative is to specify the rejection number $r$, so that if the number of defective items is found to be $r$ or more, the lot would be rejected.

As we noted earlier, some risks are associated with statistical sampling. These risks are the producer's risk, or the probability of rejecting a lot of good quality, and the consumer's risk, or the probability of accepting a lot of poor quality. You must evaluate the trade-offs in these risks when determining the details of a specific sampling plan. You must ask yourself, "If the lot has a given percentage of nonconforming items, what is the probability that it will be accepted or rejected by a particular sampling plan?" We can estimate these probabilities for a particular sampling plan from the **operating characteristics curve,** which provides the probability of accepting a lot drawn from a population of various levels of quality. Figure 19.12 illustrates an operating characteristics curve. On the curve the horizontal axis shows the actual percentage of defectives in the lot, which is generally unknown. The vertical axis shows the probability that a lot will be accepted.

Suppose the lot was actually 3 percent defective. Using the curve, we would estimate the probability of accepting the lot at about 80 percent. If 3 percent

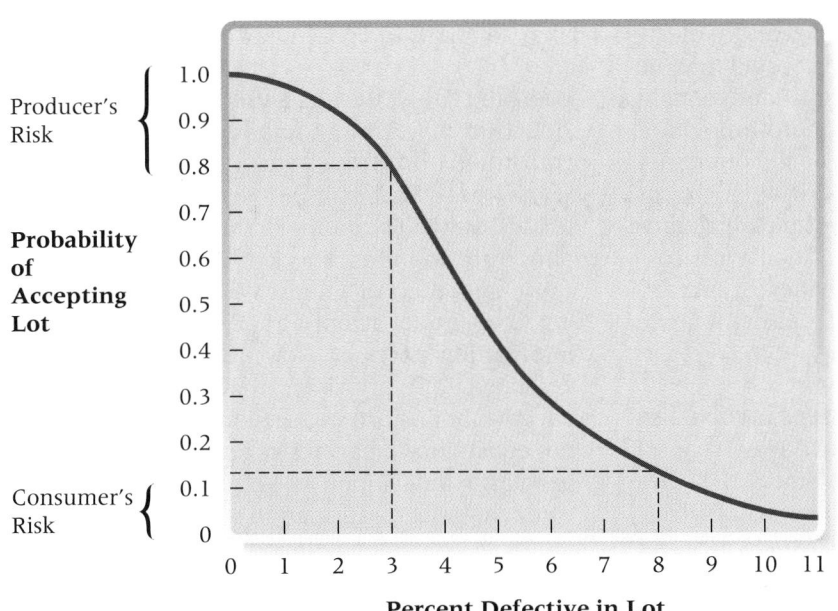

FIGURE 19.12
Operating Characteristics
Curve

defective was considered good quality, the probability of rejecting the lot (producer's risk) would be about 20 percent. If the percentage of defectives was 8 percent, the probability of accepting would be about 12 percent. If that was considered poor quality, the 12 percent would represent the consumer's risk. If these risk factors were unacceptable to management, a different sampling plan would be created. For different sampling plans the operating characteristics curve would change shape, yielding different probabilities.

## ► Summary

In an effort to reestablish themselves as competitive forces in their industries many companies are focusing on continuous process improvement. This focus is often part of an overall total quality management implementation throughout the organization. This chapter provided some tools and procedures that have proved effective in assisting companies in their improvement activities.

**Learning Objective 1: Describe the role of continuous process improvement in today's business environment.** Continuous process improvement is a useful activity, regardless of the type of organization involved. Manufacturing companies, service companies, government agencies, educational institutions, and other nonprofit organizations can benefit from the tools and procedures involved in continuous process improvement. Ideally, the concept of continuous improvement becomes ingrained in the culture of the organization—improvement activities would not be special efforts but a way of life. Process improvement activities foster improved communication throughout the organization. Traditional functional boundaries become more transparent as cross-functional teams form to analyze and improve cross-functional processes. They also enhance communication with customers and suppliers. Team activities, normally inherent to process improvement, also improve worker relations within the company.

**Learning Objective 2: Outline the steps involved in continuous process improvement.** The chapter outlined an eight-step improvement process: (1) Define the problem in context of the process; (2) identify, analyze, and document the process; (3) measure current performance; (4) understand why the process

is performing as it is; (5) develop alternative solutions and select the best one; (6) develop a strategy and implement the alternative chosen; (7) evaluate the results of the new process; (8) commit to continuous improvement of the process.

**Learning Objective 3: Define *benchmarking*, and outline the process of benchmarking for process improvement.** Benchmarking is the search for industry "best practices" that lead to superior business performance. Companies identify processes that are most important to their competitive position, then attempt to identify other companies or areas within the same company that are known for superior performance in those processes. The two parties negotiate to develop a mutually beneficial relationship in which each party shares performance information. The five stages of the benchmarking process are planning, analysis, integration, action, and maturity.

**Learning Objective 4: Describe the use and construction of various tools for process analysis and continuous improvement.** The chapter discussed several tools that have proved effective in improvement activities, including brainstorming, process mapping, run diagrams, check sheets, Pareto charts, and cause-and-effect diagrams. We noted that brainstorming is a group activity that is useful for soliciting information necessary for process improvement. We described four principles that are necessary for an effective brainstorming session: no criticism of ideas, no constraints that restrict creativity, encouraging people to build upon other people's ideas, and encouraging the participation of all members of the group. Process mapping is useful for helping a group understand how a process works. The process map is essentially a flow chart that uses special symbols to denote the flow of material and information throughout a process. Analyzing the map involves looking for nonvalue-adding activities and other inefficiencies. Run diagrams are useful for tracking the value of some quality measure over time, because they identify for further analysis long-term trends in some measure. Check sheets enhance the efficiency of data collection from a process. Those who know the process the best and those who will be involved in collecting the data should design the check sheet. Pareto charts are bar charts that are used to separate the vital few concerns from the trivial many. Pareto analysis identifies the most significant problems for further analysis. Cause-and-effect diagrams, sometimes called *fishbone diagrams* or *Ishikawa diagrams,* are used to further refine a problem or area of concern. Group activities help direct the process improvement effort and lead to the identification, discussion, and prioritizing of potential causes of the concern.

## Learning Objective 5: Develop lower and upper control limits for a process involving variable data.

The term *variable data* means that we can measure quality on some continuous scale such as inches, feet, centimeters, tons, pounds, or the like. To monitor the performance of a process involving variable data we must use both an $\bar{X}$-chart to track between-sample variability and an $R$-chart to track within-sample variability. Construction of both types of control charts involves the use of the appendix at the end of the text. The appendix provides the constant values necessary to construct three standard deviation $\bar{X}$ and $R$ control charts. After looking up the $A_2$, $D_3$, and $D_4$ values for a particular sample size, we would construct the $\bar{X}$-chart limits as $\bar{\bar{X}} \pm A_2\bar{R}$. For the $R$-chart we would construct the lower limit as $D_3\bar{R}$ and the upper control limit as $D_4\bar{R}$ with a center line of $\bar{R}$.

## Learning Objective 6: Develop lower and upper control limits for a process involving attribute data.

The term *attribute data* means that the quality measure is binary in nature. That is, it is either defective or it is not. The best way to monitor that particular type of performance measure is by using $nP$-charts or $P$-charts. If the actual number of defectives is the measure of concern, we can determine the upper and lower limits of the $nP$-chart by $n\bar{P} \pm 3\sqrt{n\bar{P}(1-\bar{P})}$. If the proportion of defectives is the measure of interest, we can determine the upper and lower control limits by $\bar{P} \pm 3\sqrt{(\bar{P}(1-\bar{P}))/n}$. If we wish to track the countable number of defects in each item we use $\bar{C} \pm 3\sqrt{\bar{C}}$.

## Learning Objective 7: Describe the concept of process capability, and calculate the capability index for a given process.

That a process is in statistical control does not guarantee that the process is within specifications as defined by the customer. Each process has a certain degree of variability inherent to the process. Control charts are designed to monitor the variability in a process to ensure that it does not exceed the level normally expected. The process capability index is a measure that relates the overall specification limits, dictated by process design or by customer desires, and the statistical control limits of the process. The process capability index $C_p$ can be determined by the following calculation:

$$C_p = \frac{USL - LSL}{6\sigma}$$

The process capability index, which assumes that the process is centered between the specification limits, should be at least one but should be much greater. One way to consider how the process is centered is to calculate a modified capability index:

$$C_{pk} = C_p(1 - k)$$

where

$k = 2|\text{design target-process average}|/\text{specification range}$

If the process is perfectly centered, $k$ will equal 0 and $C_{pk}$ will equal $C_p$.

## ► Key Terms

| | | |
|---|---|---|
| acceptance sampling | operating characteristics curve | producer's risk |
| benchmarking | process capability | sampling plan |
| consumer's risk | process control charts | specification limits |

# ▶ Discussion Questions

1. What role does continuous process improvement play in today's business environment?
2. What are the eight steps in the process improvement model?
3. Why should improvements developed by a team be better than those developed by individuals?
4. What is benchmarking and how is it used? If you were managing the food service operation at your university, against whom might you benchmark your operation?
5. What are the four basic principles of brainstorming, and why is each important?
6. What is a process map, and how are process maps used in the continuous improvement process?

7. Define *producer's risk* and *consumer's risk.*
8. What is the difference between attribute data and variable data? What types of control charts are appropriate for each kind of data?
9. How many standard deviations are normally used in setting process control limits? Why? What would be the effect of choosing larger or smaller limits?
10. What types of variability are monitored in $\bar{X}$- and $R$-charts?
11. What does the process capability index measure? Why is it useful?

# ▶ Problems

1. Consider the process you go through every morning when the alarm sounds. Construct a process map of the process.
2. Using the following data, which represent the number of ounces of cereal in boxes, plot the data. The horizontal axis should contain incremental box weights from the lightest box to the heaviest box. The vertical axis should show the frequency of occurrence of each weight. Suppose the control limits for this process are 16 ± 1 ounce. Does this data suggest that a problem exists?

| | | | |
|---|---|---|---|
| 15.1 | 16.5 | 16.3 | 15.8 |
| 16.2 | 16.5 | 15.8 | 16.6 |
| 16.4 | 15.9 | 16.2 | 16.4 |
| 15.2 | 16.1 | 16.3 | 16.0 |
| 15.4 | 15.7 | 16.6 | 16.4 |
| 16.5 | 15.9 | 16.2 | 16.4 |
| 15.2 | 16.1 | 15.7 | 16.1 |
| 16.2 | 16.8 | 15.2 | 16.1 |
| 15.7 | 15.1 | 16.1 | 16.3 |
| 16.2 | 16.3 | 16.7 | 16.5 |

3. Consider the following data, which have been collected from a manufacturing process in which 7 different product types are manufactured. Five types of defects have been found to be most frequent in this manufacturing area. Analyze the data, and construct Pareto charts to describe what is going on in the area.

| | | *Problem* | | | |
|---|---|---|---|---|---|
| *Product* | *Labels* | *Liner* | *Glue* | *Wrong Size* | *Warped* |
| A | 2 | | 8 | | |
| B | 1 | | 4 | | |
| C | | 4 | | 7 | 19 |
| D | | 2 | | | 5 |
| E | 3 | | 11 | | |
| F | 1 | | | | 3 |
| G | 1 | | | 2 | |

4. Construct a cause-and-effect diagram in which the effect is the desire to perform better on exams.
5. From a process known to be in control, 25 samples were taken at random, each containing 10 items. The mean and range of each sample were taken, yielding $\Sigma\bar{X}$ = 121.48 ounces and $\Sigma R$ = 8.25 ounces. Compute the center line and $3\sigma$ control limits for $\bar{X}$ and $R$.
6. Random samples of 5 items each were taken from a process while it was being operated under controlled conditions. The following measurements were recorded: The mean of the sample means was 6.5 inches, and the mean of the sample ranges was 0.15 inches. Establish center line and $3\sigma$ control limits for the mean and range of this process.
7. The following data were collected from a machine that cuts pieces of metal to a particular length (in meters). Ten random samples were collected, with each sample containing 5 cut pieces. The table contains the mean and range of each sample.

| Sample | Mean | Range | Sample | Mean | Range |
|--------|------|-------|--------|------|-------|
| 1 | 15.4 | 2.1 | 6 | 16.1 | 2.6 |
| 2 | 15.1 | 3.2 | 7 | 15.5 | 0.9 |
| 3 | 14.6 | 1.5 | 8 | 14.9 | 1.2 |
| 4 | 14.9 | 2.5 | 9 | 15.2 | 2.1 |
| 5 | 15.0 | 1.9 | 10 | 15.3 | 3.0 |

Draw and completely label the $3\sigma$ control charts for means and ranges.

8. From a process known to be in control, 6 random samples of 4 electrical transformers each were drawn and measured for output voltage. The data are as follows:

|  |  | Item # |  |  |
|---|---|---|---|---|
| Sample # | 1 | 2 | 3 | 4 |
| 1 | 12.5 | 12.6 | 13.2 | 12.1 |
| 2 | 13.2 | 12.9 | 13.2 | 13.0 |
| 3 | 12.5 | 12.5 | 12.8 | 12.0 |
| 4 | 11.8 | 12.5 | 13.0 | 12.4 |
| 5 | 12.1 | 12.5 | 12.2 | 12.2 |
| 6 | 12.3 | 11.9 | 12.2 | 12.7 |

What would be the center lines and $3\sigma$ control limits for the means and ranges for this process?

9. Quality control charts for manufacturing station 2 are shown in the figures that follow. The last 10 sample values have been posted. How would you describe to management the current situation at station 2?

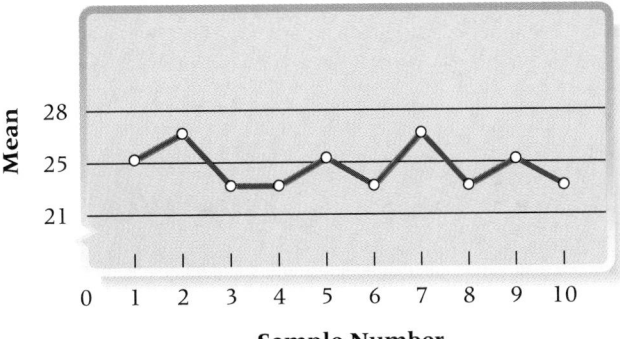

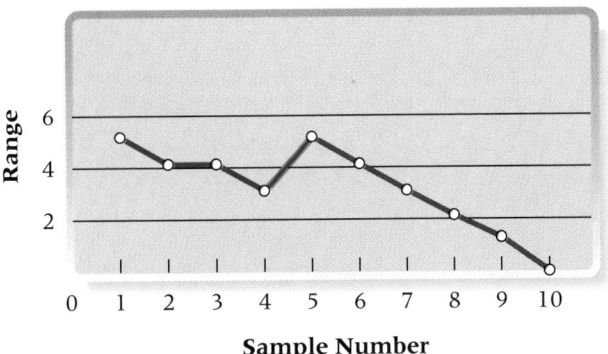

10. A mail order facility routinely conducts customer satisfaction surveys by randomly calling 50 customers each week. It usually expects to receive 1 customer complaint on the average each week. This week it received 3 complaints from the survey. Is there cause for concern? Why?

11. A law enforcement department has identified a particular section of town that seems to have a consistent crime rate. It has collected data over the past year and determined that there normally are 4.5 major crimes committed in this section of town each week. Establish $3\sigma$ control limits for a C chart to help the department monitor the section of town and determine whether the department needs to increase patrols.

12. An assembler of cordless telephones has collected data on the number of defectives found. In 15 samples of 10 telephones each, he found 1, 3, 2, 0, 1, 2, 1, 3, 1, 0, 1, 3, 1, 2, and 1 defective units. Assuming that the process is currently under control, determine the center line and $3\sigma$ control limits for the average number of defective units.

13. A manufacturer of VCRs would like to develop a control chart for the proportion of defective housings. Five samples of 100 VCRs each have been taken and the number of defective housings found are as follows:

| Sample # | 1 | 2 | 3 | 4 | 5 |
|----------|---|----|---|---|---|
| # defective | 3 | 14 | 8 | 2 | 6 |

What would be the center line and $3\sigma$ control limits for this process?

14. From a process known to be under control, several samples of 5 units each have been collected. The mean of the sample means was found to be 160 with an average range of 15. Customer specifications for the units are $155 \pm 20$ units. Is this process currently capable? What would be the process capability index for the process? Are there any sources of concern for the process?

## ► Selected References

Banks, Jerry. *Principles of Quality Control.* New York: Wiley, 1989.

Evans, James R., and William M. Lindsay. *The Management and Control of Quality,* 2d ed. Minneapolis: West, 1993.

Hradesky, John L. *Productivity and Quality Improvement.* New York: McGraw-Hill, 1988.

Imai, Masaaki. *KAIZEN: The Key to Japan's Competitive Success.* New York: McGraw-Hill, 1986.

Juran, Joseph M., and Frank M. Gryna, Jr. *Quality Planning and Analysis,* 2d ed. New York: McGraw-Hill, 1980.

Oakland, John S. *Statistical Process Control.* London: Heinemann, 1986.

Ozeki, Kazuo, and Tetsuichi Asaka. *Handbook of Quality Tools: The Japanese Approach.* Cambridge, Mass.: Productivity Press, 1990.

# Process Improvement Activities

You have been hired as a consultant by the Jonesville city council to help improve law enforcement and crime prevention in that city. You have been asked to study data previously collected by the police department and make recommendations for improvement.

You are given a check sheet (Table 1) that records various types of criminal activity reported in Jonesville during a period of several months. All data were gathered during the week and recorded on the check sheet Sunday night. The five most frequent crimes

**TABLE 1** Check Sheet for Reported Crime in Jonesville

**Crimes Reported**

| Month | Week | Homicide | Sexual Assault | Armed Robbery | Auto Theft | Narcotics Violation |
|---|---|---|---|---|---|---|
| July | 1 | / | // | / | /// | / |
| | 2 | | / | | // | /// |
| | 3 | | | / | | |
| | 4 | // | / | // | / | / |
| August | 1 | / | /// | | | / |
| | 2 | / | | | | // |
| | 3 | | / | / | // | |
| | 4 | // | | // | / | /// |
| September | 1 | / | | | | |
| | 2 | | | / | | // |
| | 3 | / | | // | | / |
| | 4 | | / | /// | | // |
| October | 1 | | / | | / | |
| | 2 | / | | | // | // |
| | 3 | | | / | | / |
| | 4 | /// | | / | / | |
| November | 1 | | / | / | | /// |
| | 2 | | | | | / |
| | 3 | | | | / | |
| | 4 | / | | /// | / | /// |
| December | 1 | | | | | // |
| | 2 | | | | / | /// |
| | 3 | / | / | / | | /// |
| | 4 | //// | | // | | |
| January | 1 | // | | / | / | //// |
| | 2 | | | / | | |
| | 3 | | | | | / |
| | 4 | // | | / | / | // |
| *Total Reported Crimes* | | 23 | 12 | 25 | 18 | 41 |

were homicide, sexual assault, armed robbery, auto theft, and narcotics violations.

Your job is to analyze the data and prepare a presentation for the police department and city council. Using the tools discussed in this chapter, conduct a detailed analysis of the data. Be prepared to answer the council's questions about the types and causes of problems in the city and what should be done to address the problems.

## ▶ Discussion Questions

1. What are the most significant crime problems in Jonesville?
2. What are the limitations of the data as provided?
3. If you were to repeat the data collection effort, how would you change the check sheet to make your job more effective? What additional information would be useful?
4. Based on your analysis of the data provided, what recommendations would you make to the city council for improvements in crime prevention in Jonesville?

## CHAPTER 20

# Building Competitive Advantage: Allen-Bradley's World Contactor Facility[1]

*You get it [wealth] out of mother earth. You mine it, farm it or fish it. Then you take that basic raw material and add value to it. That's what we call manufacturing. If we don't create wealth, we are going to become a third-class country.*

C. R. "BUD" WHITNEY, CHAIRMAN OF ALLEN-BRADLEY CO.

**Introduction**

**Allen-Bradley's World Contactors**

**Identifying Strategic Threats and Opportunities**

**The Competitive Challenge**

**Building Competitive Advantage: Toward World-Class Manufacturing**

**Technologies and Methods**

**World-Class Manufacturing: Outcomes and Benefits**

[1]This case study was adapted from several primary sources: Gregory T. Farnum, "Automating for Survival," *Manufacturing Engineering* 94 (April 1985): 45–48; John M. Martin, "How Allen-Bradley Managed CIM," *Managing Automation* (May 1986): 73–75; Gene Bylinsky, "Technology: A Breakthrough in Automating the Assembly Line," *Fortune*, May 26, 1986, pp. 64–66; Harvard Business School, "Allen-Bradley (A)," Harvard Business School Case Study 0-687-073 (Boston: HBS Case Services, Harvard Business School, 1987): 1–20; and Harvard Business School, "Allen-Bradley (B)," Harvard Business School Case Study 0-687-074 (Boston: HBS Case Services, Harvard Business School, 1987): 1–6. The author updated and expanded the information contained in these sources, based on recent conversations with John C. Rothwell, manager, World Contactor Facility, Allen-Bradley, and company material provided by him. Christine A. Zwicke, manager, public relations and employee communications, Allen-Bradley, also made substantial contributions to this case study.

*After completing this chapter you should be able to*

1. Explain what *competitive advantage* means, and identify the sources and outcomes of competitive advantage for Allen-Bradley
2. Describe the role of operations in enabling Allen-Bradley to become a world-class manufacturer
3. Explain how operations strategic planning contributed to the success of the World Contactor Facility

4. Explain what benchmarking competitors is
5. Describe the attributes of a world-class manufacturing facility
6. Identify the key human resources-related factors that contributed to the success of the World Contactor Facility
7. Describe the benefits achieved for Allen-Bradley by the World Contactor Facility

## Introduction

What is *competitive advantage*? Sometimes the term is used interchangeably with *distinctive competence* to mean relative superiority in skills and resources. Another widespread meaning is positional advantage and the resulting market share and profitability performance associated with it.[2] Although the term *competitive advantage* can be defined in several ways, these two definitions capture the essence of its meaning. Taken together they describe both the state of advantage and how it was gained.

This final chapter focuses on the competitive advantage that Allen-Bradley has achieved in the global marketplace for its World Contactor products (on-off switches). We will examine the market conditions that led to the development of these products, the competitive hurdles that Allen-Bradley had to overcome to become a global player, and the methods and technologies that enabled Allen-Bradley to attain world market share. Specifically, we will consider the vital role of operations in this success story and showcase the manufacturing technologies, systems, and methods that have made Allen-Bradley a world-class manufacturer.

## Allen-Bradley's World Contactors

Since 1985 Allen-Bradley's World Contactor assembly facility has been manufacturing Bulletin 100 contactors and Bulletin 700F control relays for the global market. Contactors and control relays are electromechanical devices that open and close electrical circuits. Contactors are switches for heavy-duty, high-amperage power circuits, whereas relays are used for lower current applications. A simplistic description of both products is boxlike switches that turn electric motors on and off. The primary difference between the contactor and the relay is in the composition of the contact points in the switch—the points in a contactor are rugged 90 percent silver and 10 percent tin, whereas the relay points are fine 99 percent silver and 1 percent tin.

The contactors and relays produced by Allen-Bradley's World Contactor Facility, which is part of Allen-Bradley's Operations Group (see the case study for Chapter 3, Operations Strategic Planning at Allen-Bradley), were designed to

[2]George S. Day and Robin Wensley, "Assessing Advantage: A Framework for Diagnosing Competitive Superiority, *Journal of Marketing* 52 (April 1988): 1–20.

meet International Electrotechnical Commission (IEC) standards. Markets for the products include the machine tool, petrochemical, automotive, mining, forestry, and heavy equipment industries.

Until the mid-1980s Allen-Bradley designed its products primarily for the North American market in accordance with National Electrical Manufacturers Association (NEMA) standards. NEMA products are durable and can be repaired with relative ease, simply by replacing worn-out parts. In contrast, IEC products are designed to be replaced rather than repaired, are generally smaller than NEMA products, and tend to be more application specific. Although contactors and relays built to meet international standards do not provide everything that NEMA-based contactors and relays can offer, Allen-Bradley has designed its contactors and relays with features that are important to U.S. users and original equipment manufacturers.

## The World Contactor Facility

The World Contactor automated assembly facility is a 45,000-square-foot operation located on the eighth floor of Allen-Bradley's Milwaukee headquarters. It is best described as a computer-integrated manufacturing (CIM) "factory within a factory." The operation can produce four varieties of contactors and three styles of relays, with more than one thousand different customer specifications, in lot sizes as small as one, with world-class quality, zero direct labor, and a lead time of twenty-four hours.

The World Contactor Facility has four key areas: a control room, a plastic molding cell, a contact fabrication cell, and the automated assembly line.

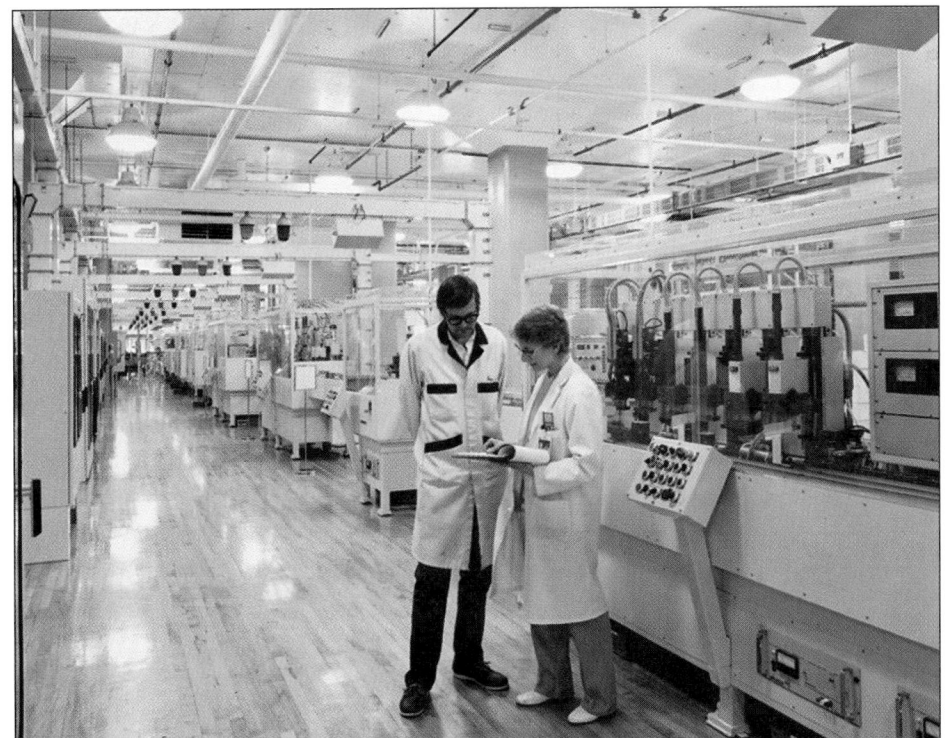

*Only a few attendants oversee operations at Allen-Bradley's $15 million World Contactor Facility in Milwaukee. The automated assembly line can produce hundreds of motor starters per hour with many variations and consistent quality. Courtesy of Allen-Bradley, a Rockwell International company.*

Purchased components such as brass, steel, silver, molding powder, coils, and springs enter the facility through an elevator door to the left of the control room, and finished products exit through an elevator door to the right of the control room. Figure 20.1 provides a simplified overview of the physical layout of the World Contactor Facility. The operation is controlled primarily by Allen-Bradley products and serves as a showcase for a number of the company's control and communication products. During its first eight years of operation nearly 35,000 customers toured the facility. As a CIM showcase it not only demonstrates the capabilities of the company's control and communication products but also proves that quality products can be produced at competitive prices by using advanced manufacturing technologies (see the section on the service factory in Chapter 1). Figure 20.2 provides a more detailed diagram of the physical layout of the facility.

## Identifying Strategic Threats and Opportunities

Until the mid-1980s Allen-Bradley built its contactors and relays primarily for the North American market in accordance with NEMA standards. However, not only was the global market for IEC standard products rapidly expanding but overseas manufacturers were bringing their IEC-type products into the United States, demonstrating the benefits of their IEC products to U.S. companies. The importation of the IEC-type product by overseas manufacturers was a serious threat to Allen-Bradley, because making contactors is one of its important businesses. Furthermore, Allen-Bradley's own market research indicated that IEC and NEMA would coordinate their standards in the United States by 1990. In

FIGURE 20.1
Simplified Overview of the
World Contactor Facility

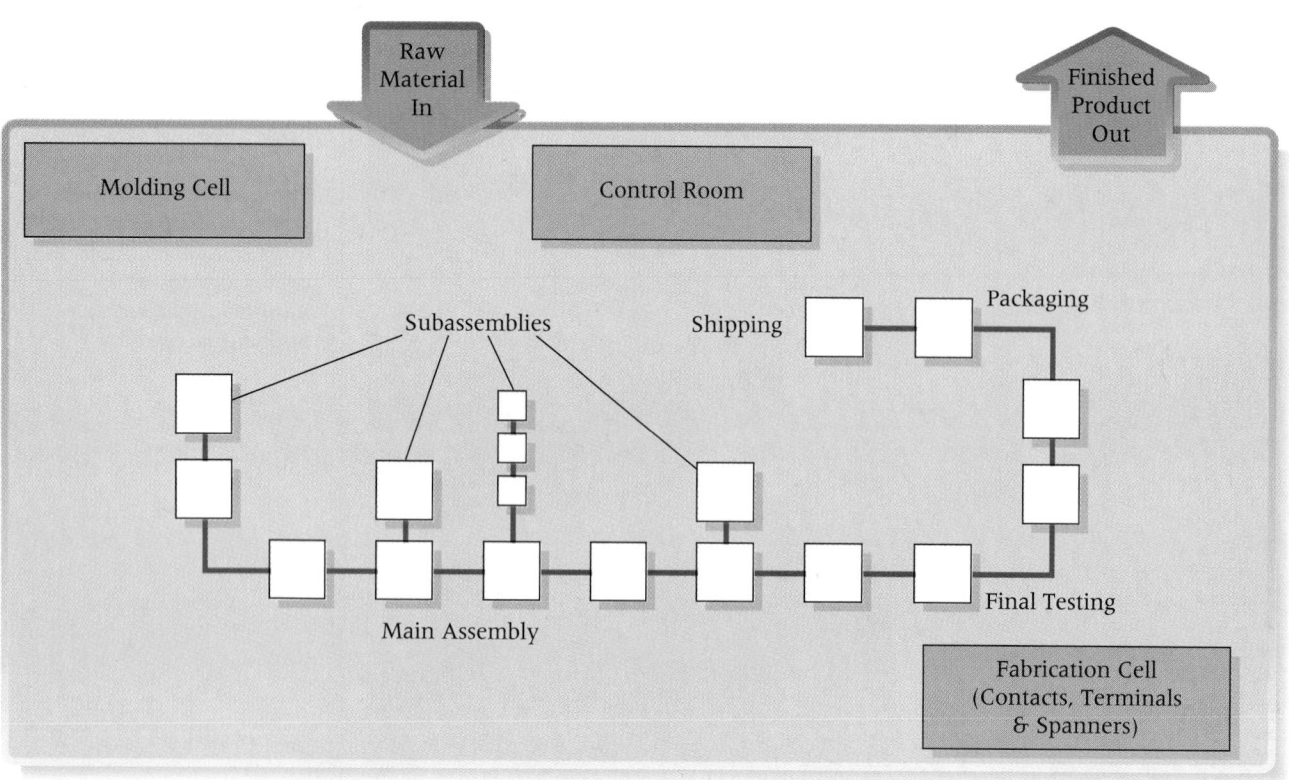

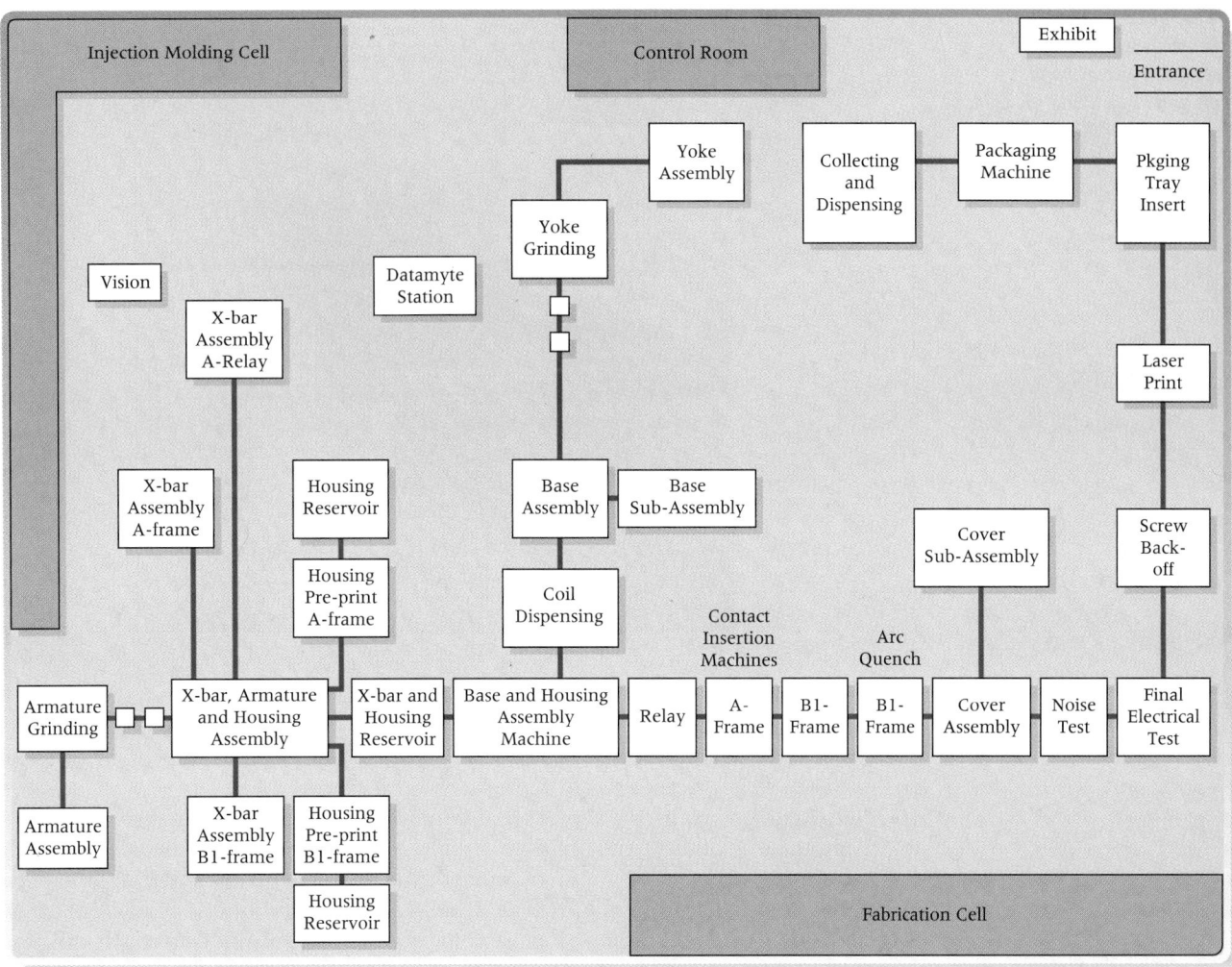

FIGURE 20.2
Physical Layout of the World
Contactor Facility

other words, the products of the future for most specific purpose applications would increasingly be IEC, although NEMA products would probably remain the industry standard for more general or demanding applications (such as hazardous, difficult, and high-reliability applications).

At the same time the rapidly expanding global market for IEC products posed an attractive opportunity for Allen-Bradley. The company at that time had a limited line of international products and wanted to become a global manufacturer. Allen-Bradley viewed the contactor product as an opportunity to penetrate the global marketplace and as a way to expand its distribution and sales networks worldwide.

## The Competitive Challenge

The challenge facing Allen-Bradley was to position its new IEC-type contactors and relays to have clear advantages over the competitions'. Allen-Bradley saw two ways to do this:

*A nine-alley reservoir holds different sizes of molded housings for relays and contactors, dispersing the correct casing for assembly to a base. Courtesy of Allen-Bradley, a Rockwell International company.*

- Differentiate the product from competitors' products
- Provide a product that cost less to make than competitors' in order to beat competitors' prices in the marketplace

Allen-Bradley's plans for achieving differentiation focused on unsurpassed quality, product flexibility (the ability to build a wide variety of products for different customers' needs), and rapid manufacturing in lot sizes as small as one. The objective was to build to order a wide variety of products characterized by one-day delivery lead times (inclusive of production lead time) in a cost-efficient way.

## Defining Competitive Advantage

In addition to identifying its strategic goals for the new products, Allen-Bradley needed to introduce its new line of contactors and relays within a two-year time frame or lose its window of opportunity. This was a monumental challenge—in the past the introduction of a new line of contactors had taken as long as seven years.

As we will see, Allen-Bradley's strategic objectives encompassed several of the *manufacturing competitive priorities* introduced in Chapter 3—design quality, quality of conformance, product reliability, product flexibility, production lead time, delivery speed, low manufacturing cost, and new product introduction. Because operations has the lion's share of responsibility for most of these priorities, the manufacturing functional area at Allen-Bradley would have to be an important player in building competitive advantage for the World Contactor facility.

**Cost**   Cost was a key priority. Allen-Bradley recognized that its product had to be cost competitive in all markets and that the international competition was stiff.

*A contact insertion machine automatically places lower contact and pressure plates in the correct configuration on relays and contactors made in the World Contactor Facility. Courtesy of Allen-Bradley, a Rockwell International company.*

For example, the company had to compete against overseas manufacturers that benefited from government subsidies—one French company was selling contactors for $4.50, although its material costs were more than $5.

Allen-Bradley's marketing people easily estimated target costs, because they knew the prices that contactors were bringing around the world, and the company's cost and financial experts knew what an acceptable gross margin would be. The bottom line was that Allen-Bradley would have to reduce its manufacturing costs by approximately 25 to 30 percent to be competitive on a global basis.

**Quality** Allen-Bradley managers knew that the quality of its contactors and relays would have to be better than the competitions' in order to gain world market share. Thus, achieving unsurpassed quality was a key competitive requirement for the World Contactors and acted as a key driver in the definition of both the product and the manufacturing process.

**Flexibility and Lead Times** The ability to build to order a wide variety of products in lot sizes as small as one with minimal lead times was also critical. Not even the Japanese had managed to do it. Although other companies can manufacture customized products, they cannot do it automatically—without stopping and starting the line—and at speeds approaching those of mass production.

## The Foundation for Success

Fortunately for Allen-Bradley, the manufacturing functional area already had initiated two parallel activities that contributed greatly to the success of the World Contactor project: the development of a strategic plan for manufacturing operations and a global examination of alternative manufacturing systems and methods. Essentially, Allen-Bradley had been expending a good bit of time and effort in benchmarking the competition.

**Operations Strategic Planning**    Allen-Bradley was one of the first companies to recognize the critical role of manufacturing in achieving competitive advantage. As Larry Yost, vice president of operations for Allen-Bradley's Operations Group, said, "When we decided to develop such a [strategic manufacturing] plan . . . we could find no one doing strategic planning for manufacturing. All we found were some consultants talking about it and a few books on the subject."[3] Aware of the important contributions that manufacturing can make to the competitiveness of a company, the executives at Allen-Bradley incorporated manufacturing strategic planning in their well-established business strategic planning process in the early 1980s.

The case study for Chapter 3 examined and discussed the process by which Allen-Bradley's Operations Group developed the strategic manufacturing plan (see Case Study Figure 2). Allen-Bradley evaluates the effectiveness of all manufacturing strategic planning in the Allen-Bradley's Operations Group in terms of seven key success factors: cost, quality, new product introduction, competitive delivery, asset utilization, business systems, and human resources (see Case Study Figure 3). For the World Contactor project the first four success factors were especially critical.

**Benchmarking the Competition**    As Allen-Bradley started operations strategic planning, it also began to comprehensively study and evaluate alternative manufacturing methods. Top Allen-Bradley managers attended trade shows and toured manufacturing facilities throughout the world to gain an in-depth understanding of different operations and systems. They visited many competitors' operations, examining what was different from Allen-Bradley's and why.

As a result of this benchmarking expedition Allen-Bradley managers developed various manufacturing theories and strategies and, in particular, a series of programs associated with "stockless production." The managers also began to disseminate to everyone in the Allen-Bradley organization the knowledge they had gained. They informed not only manufacturing people but also personnel in development engineering, cost and finance, marketing, and data processing. Thus, managers in various functional areas throughout the organization came to understand how various manufacturing strategies and methods would meet their specific objectives as well as the overall business objectives. Because many of the strategies and programs the managers studied during the benchmarking expedition were relevant to the World Contactor project, all functional areas within the organization had a solid grasp early on of the manufacturing concepts and systems that were critical to the success of the project.

## Building Competitive Advantage: Toward World-Class Manufacturing

Once they had clearly defined the competitive challenge, Allen-Bradley managers examined various ways to meet it. The company investigated the advantages and disadvantages of offshore manufacturing, joint ventures, making the contactors and relays under license, and manufacturing the products in house in the

[3]Martin, "How Allen-Bradley Managed CIM," p. 73.

United States. They ruled out low-cost offshore labor because the anticipated savings were substantially offset by the costs of materials handling, warehousing operations, and so on in a nonautomated operation. Finally, Allen-Bradley decided to manufacture its World Contactors in the United States. Two major advantages associated with this strategic choice were the availability of skilled labor and lower overall shipping costs, because production would take place within the world's biggest market for the products. Nevertheless, Allen-Bradley's decision introduced a new competitive hurdle: how to make the IEC products cost competitive with foreign-made contactors.

## Cost

To be competitive on a global basis Allen-Bradley had to reduce its costs by 25 to 30 percent. In the early 1980s Allen-Bradley's manufacturing costs broke down this way: material, 50 percent; overhead, 40 percent; and direct labor, 10 percent. To achieve cost savings of the magnitude it required Allen-Bradley recognized that it needed an automated manufacturing system.

The company's initial concept for its automated system eliminated direct labor. However, the 10 percent direct labor cost saving was too low to achieve the cost target. The company had to substantially reduce material and overhead costs as well. It could achieve some reductions in material costs by working with the company's own design engineers as well as its outside suppliers. However, the only way to achieve substantial reductions in overhead (reductions in materials handling, warehousing, manufacturing engineering support, and set-ups) was by installing and using a computer-integrated manufacturing system. A CIM system would eliminate the need for material handlers, inspectors, group leaders, supervisors, and a warehouse. The cost decrease in overhead, as well as the elimination of direct labor associated with such a system, would make Allen-Bradley's cost target reachable—the cost of a typical contactor could be reduced from $13.25 to $8.35. Still, it would cost Allen-Bradley $15 million to build such a system.

In evaluating the CIM investment Allen-Bradley dispensed with traditional, short-term return on investment methods, because they would preclude approval of the project. The World Contactor project was high in cost and risk—yet, if successful, it would allow the company to reap rich rewards in the world marketplace. As Yost said, "If you're not going to be among the survivors, ROI [return on investment] doesn't mean a damn."[4]

## Quality

To win a share of the world market, Allen-Bradley's World Contactors had to be better than the competitions'. Several factors contributed to this critical objective. Because the IEC contactors and relays were new products for the company, it could develop the products and their manufacturing process simultaneously. Allen-Bradley developed the product specifications in a cross-functional effort that involved manufacturing, marketing, development, quality control, management, and finance, and designed the product specifically for the automated process that would manufacture it.

[4]Bylinsky, "Technology," p. 66.

Also, Allen-Bradley integrated its total quality management system, which encompassed such quality methods as statistical process control (SPC) and process capability studies, into the new manufacturing system. The concern for quality extended to the company's suppliers as well—consistency of component parts is critical in an automated system. Allen-Bradley developed a set of quality standards for parts to be used in the automated system and required its suppliers to use SPC.

Finally, the company designed the manufacturing system itself to encompass 3,500 automated data collection points and 350 automated assembly test points to check each component and the final product; this ensured that work would meet quality standards as it moved from station to station. The system would automatically reject components and/or products that failed to satisfy standards.

## Flexibility and Lead Times

The original concept for the automated system called for assembly in batch mode. However, the company revised this to accommodate production to customer demand in lot sizes as small as one. It did this because Yost wanted a just-in-time manufacturing system, with its associated low inventories and high flexibility—he saw such a capability as an integral part of a truly global manufacturing strategy. At the same time the company needed to attain a delivery lead time of one day (inclusive of manufacturing time) to differentiate itself from its major competitors.

The ability to manufacture contactors and relays in lot sizes of one according to customer demand and at mass production speeds posed a monumental challenge to Allen-Bradley's engineers. The key was to identify each product being assembled so the line would not have to stop to assemble a different end item. Although the Japanese method of kanban uses serial numbers and special dummy objects to identify the start of a new batch, it is a manual approach that does not accommodate the production of lots of one at mass production speeds.

Allen-Bradley's engineers solved the problem when they realized that they could use bar codes to automatically identify different contactors and relays coming down the line. In the World Contactor facility a bar code not only identifies the catalog number of the product to be made but also specifies the exact operations required in its manufacture. However, using bar code technology required formulating and printing bar codes instantaneously as the contactor and relay bases moved by. An engineer found that a specially adapted high-speed printer could do this. Thus, using bar code technology in the World Contactor CIM system allowed Allen-Bradley to manufacture more than one thousand different styles of IEC products at an average production rate of six hundred units per hour.

## Technologies and Methods

Several manufacturing technologies and methods contributed greatly to the success of the World Contactor facility. Various chapters of this book introduced all of them. Their implementation and use in the World Contactor facility should enable you to understand the contribution that each can make to a company's competitive advantage.

## Concurrent Engineering and the Team Approach

Because Allen-Bradley's executives had concluded that the product and manufacturing process should be designed simultaneously (in other words, concurrent engineering), they established several task forces, or teams, and gave them responsibility for jointly designing the product and manufacturing process.

One task force was the Project Management Team. Its mission was to develop a contactor and relay that would be competitive on a global basis. The team consisted of a production engineering manager, a marketing manager, and a product development manager. The second team was the Automation Equipment Engineering Task Force. This task force was responsible for designing most of the equipment for the project. The team included a project manager charged with special equipment design, a project engineer responsible for designing the electrical system for the machinery, a supervisor of machine builders who managed the equipment construction process, a project supervisor for equipment planning, a project engineer for facility layout, and a maintenance superintendent for facilities. (As it happened, Allen-Bradley designed more than 90 percent of the equipment and built approximately 60 percent of it.)

In January 1983 the president of Allen-Bradley authorized the $15 million investment in the World Contactor Facility. Then the company formed another task force to determine the products' exact specifications and ideal features for the automated line. This task force was a multidisciplinary team; it included almost thirty people, representing all the departments that would be affected by the project: manufacturing, marketing, development engineering, management, quality, information systems, special equipment and finance. Headed by Yost, the team brought together all the functional areas that eventually would be involved in the World Contactor Facility, and it specifically designed the products in light of the automated process that would manufacture them.

After the products were designed and developed, Allen-Bradley's attention shifted to the automated line that would manufacture them. In the spring of 1984 the Implementation Task Force met for the first time. This team replaced the multidisciplinary task force headed by Yost and was charged with carrying on its work. John C. Rothwell, who had been appointed the department manager for the World Contactor Facility, headed the Implementation Task Force. Members included the project manager from Yost's team, who was familiar with the software that wrote the functional specification for the automated line, and representatives from the departments responsible for testing, planning and inventory control, manufacturing, and facilities and equipment. This team condensed and prioritized the features of the ideal system developed by Yost's multidisciplinary task force and also was responsible for facility layout, incoming equipment, and equipment design. Its goal was to have the manufacturing area ready by December 1, 1984.

By December 1984 most of the equipment was on the floor of the World Contactor Facility, and debugging of the automated line commenced in January 1985. On April 15, 1985, the World Contactor Facility began operation. Thus, within about two years Allen-Bradley had a world-class product ready for market and a fully operational CIM facility. Allen-Bradley management made the key factor clear: "[W]e wouldn't have been successful without a multidiscipline team approach."[5]

---

[5] Allen-Bradley Co., "With Computer-Integrated Manufacturing, We're Reshaping the Way We Think And Work," in *CIM Computer Integrated Manufacturing at Allen-Bradley*, publication no. 5052C (pamphlet), June 1990, p. 10.

## Computer-Integrated Manufacturing and the Productivity Pyramid

Chapter 8, Technological Developments in Operations Management, described various aspects of computer-integrated manufacturing. Allen-Bradley has its own definition of computer-integrated manufacturing:

> Computer-integrated manufacturing (CIM) integrates the "factors of production" to organize every event that occurs in a manufacturing business from receipt of a customer's order to delivery of the product. The ultimate goal is to integrate the production processes, the material, sales, marketing, purchasing, administration and engineering information flows into a single, closed-loop controlled system.[6]

Note the similarity of Allen-Bradley's definition of CIM and the definition of CIM provided in Chapter 8.

A complete control system includes the coordination of the control activities of an entire processing or production application. Allen-Bradley's approach to CIM is embodied in its *productivity pyramid*. The productivity pyramid is a step-by-step approach to automation. It divides the complete control system into five levels according to the tasks performed at those levels. It represents a systems approach to automated manufacturing in which each control level builds on the technology provided by the level beneath it. Because each level is linked to other levels, information and instructions must be communicated within and between them. Control systems within each level and communications between levels enable information and instructions to be communicated within and between levels. This unifies all levels within the productivity pyramid in a single automation network.[7]

The productivity pyramid is a schematic depiction of the activities required at each of five functional control levels in a typical manufacturing facility to link the machine level to order entry. It illustrates how Allen-Bradley products are configured in relationship to each other, which makes possible plantwide communications and control. Figure 20.3 shows Allen-Bradley's productivity pyramid.

The plant level receives orders from Allen-Bradley locations around the world. Sales personnel enter orders directly into computer terminals that are linked to Allen-Bradley's IBM mainframe. The company's MRP II system, which resides in its mainframe computer, integrates these orders with manufacturing, sales, and accounting data. Within twenty-four hours the system downloads the orders to the World Contactor Facility's DEC VAX 4000 area controller (center level). The area controller translates the orders into specific production requirements and downloads the information to the cell level, which is governed by an Allen-Bradley PLC 5-250™ master controller. In addition to downloading sales orders the DEC VAX 4000 area controller handles all production and maintenance reporting for the facility.

The PLC 5-250™ master controller (cell level) tells the automated line's twenty-six PLC 2/30® programmable controllers (station level) what actions the individual machines must take. Communication between the programmable controllers and the master controller flows along two local area networks (LANs), and a third LAN connects the master controller with the DEC VAX 4000 area

[6]Allen-Bradley Co., *CIM Computer Integrated Manufacturing at Allen-Bradley*, p. 2.
[7]Allen-Bradley Co., *The Allen-Bradley Company*, publication no. 5075, April 1990, p. 2.

At the plant level, orders are received from a vast world-wide network of sales personnel directly into the corporate mainframe. These orders are processed and downloaded to the next level each day.

The center level area controller receives orders and translates product catalog codes to UPC barcodes. In addition to downloading these orders, this computer is responsible for all production and maintenance reporting for the facility.

The PLC 5-250™ Master Controller is responsible for dispatching orders to the assembly line and consolidating them upon completion. Other features include facility security, order modification, and general line status.

At this level each machine is electrically controlled by a PLC-2/30®.

The 26 Assembly line stations.

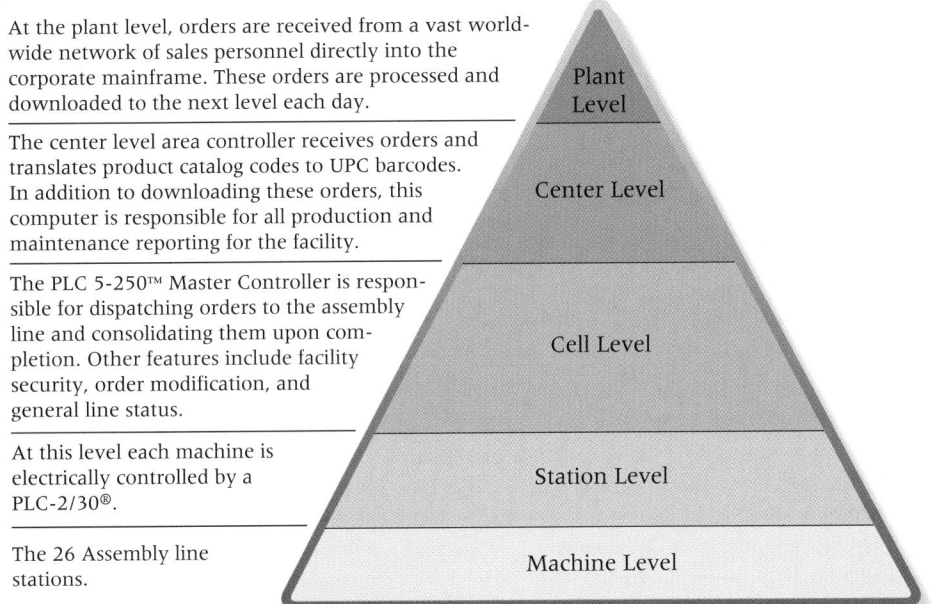

FIGURE 20.3
Allen-Bradley's Productivity Pyramid*

*Adapted from Harvard Business School, "Allen-Bradley (A)," Harvard Business School Case Study 0-687-073 (Boston: HBS Case Services, Harvard Business School, 1987): 18.

*As an Allen-Bradley proximity sensor notes the presence of a contactor cover (yellow), it sends a signal to a PLC-2/30® programmable controller. The controller instructs a robotic pick-and-place mechanism, which is driven by a DC drive, to place the cover on the contactor housing (black). Courtesy of Allen-Bradley, a Rockwell International company.*

controller. The master controller stores two orders—one held in memory and the one actually being assembled. Once an order is completely assembled, the system begins processing the order held in memory. At this point the DEC VAX 4000 automatically downloads a new order into the master computer's memory.

A multitude of sensors located at various points along the automated line generates the feedback needed to confirm that the instructions have been implemented and the line is running smoothly. Testing occurs progressively as a contactor or relay moves from one station to the next. If a component fails an inspection, it is immediately identified, and that station's PLC-2/30® signals for a replacement to be made. If three successive defects occur at any workstation, it is automatically shut down.

Each workstation has three lights that signal machine conditions or problems. A blue light comes on when a parts feeder is running low, a yellow light indicates a part is jammed, and a red light signals a machine malfunction (loss of power, loss of hydraulic fluid, loss of air pressure). When such a malfunction occurs, the machine is automatically shut down to prevent self-destruction. When an assembly station malfunctions, the system activates an automatic shutdown of all preceding processes. An Allen-Bradley Dataliner™ display panel mounted near the bank of lights provides an English-language description of the situation or problem requiring attention.

Six operators run the computer-integrated manufacturing system at the World Contactor Facility. The ultimate objective is for the manufacturing process to run itself with only one person—in the control room—to monitor it. To this end the company has experimented with such advanced technologies as voice simulation: a personal computer linked to a laser bar code reader linked to a voice simulation machine that reads the bar code as the product moves past it. When this technology is fully implemented, a computerized voice will alert the operator to important events on the shop floor, including problems.

## Bar Coding

As we noted earlier, bar coding was essential in enabling the automated line to produce lot sizes of one according to customer demand at mass production speeds. At the start of the manufacturing process the system labels individual parts with a bar code so the programmable logic controllers (PLCs) can identify which product variation is being made and direct the machines to perform the necessary operations. At the end of the process a laser-marking machine inscribes catalog numbers and other electrical information on the fully assembled product, which is then packaged and bar coded again. The final bar code allows the system to route the finished product to an appropriate sorting tray in an accumulator at the end of the line. An employee sends the order and an invoice printed automatically by the system down an elevator to the company's shipping department.

## Total Quality Management

Since Allen-Bradley's founding in 1903 product quality has been a cornerstone of its business philosophy. Before it started the World Contactor project, Allen-Bradley had succeeded in implementing a comprehensive total quality management system (TQMS). As we noted earlier, this system encompassed the use of such proven quality techniques as statistical process control and process capability studies. The TQMS and its associated techniques were the foundation for the unsurpassed quality that the World Contactor Facility achieved. Allen-Bradley also required its World Contactor suppliers to adhere to the TQMS doctrine—the company gave suppliers a rigid set of quality standards for component items and instructed them to apply SPC.

Allen-Bradley specifically designed the automated manufacturing process with quality management in mind. The automated line has 3,500 automated data collection points and 350 automated assembly test points to ensure that each component and the final product meet quality standards. For example, a Zygo Model 121 LTS laser gauge measures the surfaces of magnets to ensure adherence to tolerances during the grinding process. The system feeds information from the gauge back to the grinder. If the grinding wheel is breaking down and the magnets are not meeting the required tolerances, the system automatically adjusts the grinding wheel until the problem is corrected. A traditional manufacturing operation would first grind the magnets and then send them to an inspection machine that identifies defects.

The system includes equipment to automatically tests every contactor and relay immediately after assembly. It tests for coil continuity, sealed coil current, insulation voltage, low voltage pickup, crossbar stroke, return spring force, and pole continuity. This final set of automatic tests ensures that the products that Allen-Bradley customers receive are of the quality the customers expect from Allen-Bradley.[8]

## Just-in-Time Manufacturing

As we noted earlier, the original concept for the automated system called for assembly in batch mode. Later, this was revised to accommodate production to customer demand in lot sizes as small as one—in other words, flexible automation. The change derived from Yost's desire for a just-in-time manufacturing system with its associated low inventories and high flexibility—such a capability was viewed as an integral part of a global manufacturing strategy. The World Contactor's flexible, automated line has allowed Allen-Bradley to eliminate most of its inventories—parts, work in process, and finished goods. The company manufactures everything it requires for the contactors and relays, except springs, electrical coils, and screws. A local supplier delivers springs on a just-in-time basis, and Allen-Bradley orders screws and coils in economically large quantities and stores them until they are needed. Work-in-process inventories are practically nonexistent, because the system's six technicians load assembly machines overnight with just enough raw materials and parts to handle the next day's production. Allen-Bradley ships finished products immediately, so it has no end-item inventories.

Allen-Bradley has achieved nearly zero-inventory status in its World Contactor Facility. The inventory value of contactors and relays before the World Contactor project was approximately equal to the $15 million that the company invested in the project. Yost summarized the results this way: "Shifting assets from inventory to capital is a much better utilization of those assets."[9]

## Human Resource Management

Several months after start-up of the World Contactor facility, Rothwell was appointed its department manager. Rothwell had worked at Allen-Bradley since 1972, primarily in the Special Equipment Design Group, where he had been working on a project that used a data base to schedule long-term projects—including the World Contactor project. Rothwell quickly became involved in the

[8]Allen-Bradley Co., *IEC Contactors and Relays*, publication no. 100-1.0. October 1984, p. 6.
[9]Martin, "How Allen-Bradley Managed CIM," p. 74.

*John Rothwell, manager of the World Contactor Facility. Courtesy of Allen-Bradley, a Rockwell International company.*

World Contactor project, heading the first meeting of the Implementation Task Force in March 1984.

According to Yost, Allen-Bradley had several reasons for choosing Rothwell to head the World Contactor Facility:

> Automation requires a manager to understand high technology, for instance, computers. You need a new type of manager, a type of person who is technically competent and who has people skills. My feeling is you can take a person with a technical bent and teach them people skills, but you can't teach everybody technical skills.
>
> John had a broad background which was necessary. He had a smattering of all the technologies and worked well with it. He had formal training, and he had moved around the company and therefore had developed people skills. He was the only guy for the job. We made it known that he was the first of a new breed of manager.[10]

Rothwell was responsible for selecting the people to staff the World Contactor Facility. He interviewed 130 in-house applicants, looking for individuals who were self-starters and had a positive attitude toward automation; he eventually selected seven finalists. Rothwell viewed people as key to the success of a manufacturing facility:

> People will make or break the line; the quality of the people and the morale of the group are essential. I spend a lot of time thinking about my people and how I can make their job easier, and I work hard at taking care of them and making sure they get what they need to make the job satisfying.[11]

One method Rothwell used to increase employee satisfaction was to give employees a lot of freedom. For example, he permitted one employee to start and finish work a half-hour earlier on days he was scheduled to golf with the Allen-Bradley Golf League. And Rothwell gave workers considerable responsibility. He asked operators to set their own objectives, telling them they would be measured on performance—just as Rothwell was evaluated.

Job rotation has also contributed to the human resources success of the World Contactor Facility. The company cross-trained all attendants in the molding and fabrication cells and on the automated line for all job assignments and gave them a single union classification, that of manufacturing cell specialist. Assignments rotate on a three-month basis. Also noteworthy is that the company's major union, the United Electrical Workers, did not object to the World Contactor project, because Allen-Bradley did not make IEC contactors and relays before it built the World Contactor facility.

## World-Class Manufacturing: Outcomes and Benefits

The World Contactor Facility has enabled Allen-Bradley to achieve a distinct cost advantage over its competitors and a substantial profit margin for itself without resorting to offshore manufacturing. Depending on the competitiveness of the world market, the price for one of the Allen-Bradley contactors ranges from $8 in Australia to $20 in the United States. Allen-Bradley's cost is well under $8. Thus, the company's use of advanced manufacturing technologies and state-of-the-art manufacturing methods has led to profitable cost relationships. Furthermore, Allen-Bradley's innovative approach to manufacturing enabled the company to create many new jobs for U.S. workers.

[10]Harvard Business School, "Allen-Bradley (B)," p. 3.
[11]Harvard Business School, "Allen-Bradley (B)," pp. 1–2.

*The World Contactor team. Courtesy of Allen-Bradley, a Rockwell International company.*

Even more important, the World Contactor Facility has enabled Allen-Bradley to achieve its strategic goals of becoming a world-class manufacturer by the mid-1980s and gaining world market share for its products. The former president of Allen-Bradley, Tracy O'Rourke, claimed that no competitor could beat him on price or quality for IEC contactors and relays. Allen-Bradley's rapid delivery has also made a substantial contribution to its competitive advantage. For example, one big user of IEC contactors and relays switched his business from a European supplier to Allen-Bradley, because of the company's ability to deliver a finished product on a next-day delivery basis.

## ► Summary

Allen-Bradley's world-class World Contactor Facility has enabled the company to attain world market share for its IEC contactors and relays. This is a remarkable achievement, especially because Allen-Bradley did not even manufacture IEC products before it began the World Contactor project. The facility has also provided Allen-Bradley with a system/process showcase that demonstrates to potential customers the strategic benefits of computer-integrated manufacturing and of flexible automation. The World Contactor project and facility have also provided tangible illustrations of many of the concepts, technologies, and methods introduced in this textbook. It is a dynamic example of the vital role that operations management can play in building the competitive strength of a company.

**Learning Objective 1: Explain what *competitive advantage* means, and identify the sources and outcomes of competitive advantage for Allen-Bradley.** Competitive advantage is the positional advantage a company achieves over its competitors, with the resulting market share and profitability performance. The primary sources of competitive advantage for Allen-Bradley were low cost, superior product quality (encompassing design quality, conformance quality, and product reliability), product flexibility, minimum production lead time, and delivery speed. The major outcomes associated with Allen-Bradley's competitive advantage were the attainment of global market share along with appropriate profitability.

**Learning Objective 2: Describe the role of operations in enabling Allen-Bradley to become a world-class manufacturer.** Operations played a critical role in the success of the World Contactor Facility. Most competitive priorities set for the World Contactor project were the responsibility of operations and required manufacturing solutions (low cost, unsurpassed quality, minimum production lead time, delivery speed). Indeed, the use of advanced manufacturing technologies (computer-integrated manufacturing, flexible automation, bar coding, and so on) and methods (MRP II, just-in-time production, statistical process control) enabled the company to attain and sustain its competitive advantage.

**Learning Objective 3: Explain how operations strategic planning contributed to the success of the World Contactor Facility.** Allen-Bradley's incorporation of operations strategic planning in its business strategic planning process before starting the World Contactor project provided a solid foundation for the project. At Allen-Bradley operations is proactive, not reactive, and hence contributes immensely to the competitive advantage of the company.

**Learning Objective 4: Explain what benchmarking competitors is.** Benchmarking competitors is a first-hand comprehensive study and critical examination of a company's top competitors with respect to strategies, tactics, products, technologies, operations, systems, and methods and their associated outcomes.

**Learning Objective 5: Describe the attributes of a world-class manufacturing facility.** A world-class manufacturing facility produces products that are as good as or better than competing products in the world market; world-class products are the best in the world, based on the competitive dimensions of their global markets. For Allen-Bradley's World Contactor Facility world-class manufacturing offers competitive prices for its contactors and relays via low-cost manufacturing, the highest possible quality, and next-day delivery for made-to-order products. In general the attributes most often associated with world-class manufacturing are superior quality, competitive or lowest price, excellent service (presale and postsale), flexibility, and dependable and rapid delivery.

**Learning Objective 6: Identify the key human resources-related factors that contributed to the success of the World Contactor Facility.** One key factor was the appointment of John Rothwell as department manager of the World Contactor Facility. Rothwell possessed the two most important attributes for an operations manager, as discussed in Chapter 1 of this textbook: technical competence and people skills. The careful selection procedure Rothwell used for choosing the individuals who would serve as operators in the facility was also critical—he made sure they were self-starters with good attitudes about computers and automation. Also important were the independence and responsibility that Rothwell gave his employees (allowing them to determine the criteria that would be used to evaluate their performance). Finally, the use of cross-training and job rotation were also significant and positive factors.

**Learning Objective 7: Describe the benefits achieved for Allen-Bradley by the World Contactor Facility.** The most important benefits were achieving its strategic goal of becoming a world-class manufacturer by the mid-1980s, its attainment of world market share, and its appropriate profitability.

## ► Discussion Questions

1. What manufacturing competitive priorities were important to the World Contactor Facility?
2. What strategic threat faced Allen-Bradley in the 1980s with respect to contactors and relays? What strategic opportunity was available?
3. How did Allen-Bradley managers benchmark the competition?
4. What were the major advantages of a computer-integrated manufacturing system for Allen-Bradley? Should all companies implement computer-integrated manufacturing to achieve the same advantages? Why or why not?
5. What method(s) enabled Allen-Bradley to achieve its target two-year time frame for introducing its World contactors and relays?
6. What quality methods does the World Contactor Facility use?

7.  How did Allen-Bradley solve the problem of manufacturing in lot sizes of one at mass production speeds?
8.  Describe the five levels of the productivity pyramid.
9.  Do you agree with Larry Yost's statement: "My feeling is you can take a person with a technical bent and teach them people skills, but you can't teach everybody technical skills"? Why or why not?
10. Describe two examples of how advanced manufacturing technologies or methods contributed to the success of the World Contactor Facility.

# ► Selected References

Allen-Bradley Co. *IEC Contactors and Relays*. Publication no. 100-1.0. October 1984.

_____. *The Allen-Bradley Company*. Publication no. 5075. April 1990.

_____. "With Computer-Integrated Manufacturing, We're Reshaping the Way We Think And Work." In *CIM Computer Integrated Manufacturing at Allen-Bradley*. Publication no. 5052C. June 1990, pp. 8–13.

_____. "CIM Goes to Harvard." In *CIM Computer Integrated Manufacturing at Allen-Bradley*. Publication no. 5052C. June 1990, pp. 14–15.

Bylinsky, Gene. "Technology: A Breakthrough in Automating the Assembly Line." *Fortune,* May 26, 1986, pp. 64–66.

Day, George S., and Robin Wensley. "Assessing Advantage: A Framework for Diagnosing Competitive Superiority. *Journal of Marketing* 52 (April 1988): 1–20.

Farnum, Gregory T. "Automating for Survival." *Manufacturing Engineering* 94 (April 1985): 45–48

Harvard Business School. "Allen-Bradley (A)." Harvard Business School Case Study 0-687-073, Boston: HBS Case Services, Harvard Business School, 1987.

_____. "Allen-Bradley (B)." Harvard Business School Case Study 0-687-074, Boston: HBS Case Services, Harvard Business School, 1987.

Martin, John M. "How Allen-Bradley Managed CIM," *Managing Automation* (May 1986): 73–75.

# The Transportation Problem

## Introduction

The **transportation problem** involves the transportation or physical distribution of goods and services from several supply origins to several demand destinations. In general, a fixed amount or limited quantity of goods or services will be available at each **supply origin,** or location, and a fixed amount or desired quantity of goods or services will be required at each customer **demand destination,** or location. The structure of the transportation problem involves a variety of shipping routes and associated costs for the origin-to-destination movements possible. Solving the transportation problem requires the determination of how many units should be shipped from each origin to each destination, in order to satisfy all the destination demands while minimizing the total cost associated with transportation. Transportation problems typically arise in situations that involve the physical movement of goods from plants to warehouses, warehouses to customers, wholesalers to retailers, or retailers to consumers. The optimal solution to a transportation problem can provide useful information for making facility location or aggregate planning decisions.

In this tutorial we describe how to construct a transportation problem and find an optimal solution. The transportation problem has a special structure, and because of this special structure we will develop and use a special algorithm to solve it.

## Mathematical Structure of the Transportation Problem

The transportation problem is structured to describe a particular situation. A given product is available in known quantities at each of $m$ origins. Each of $n$ destinations requires known quantities of the same product. Also known is the per unit cost for shipping one unit of the given product from any origin to any destination. We need to determine a shipping schedule that will satisfy the requirements at each destination while minimizing the total cost of the shipments.

To develop the mathematical structure of the transportation problem, let

$a_i$ = the quantity of the product available at origin i

$b_j$ = the quantity of the product required at destination j

$c_{ij}$ = the unit cost associated with shipping one unit of product from origin i to destination j

$x_{ij}$ = the unknown quantity to be shipped from origin i to destination j

The transportation problem involves solving for the $x_{ij}$, which

$$\text{Minimize } Z = \sum_{i=1}^{m} \sum_{j=1}^{n} c_{ij} x_{ij} \text{ (Objective function)} \quad \text{(T1-1)}$$

subject to

$$\sum_{j=1}^{n} x_{ij} = a_i \qquad a_i > 0, i = 1, 2, \ldots, m$$

(Constraint set)

$$\sum_{i=1}^{m} x_{ij} = b_j \qquad b_j > 0, j = 1, 2, \ldots, n \quad \text{(T1-2)}$$

with $x_{ij} \geq 0$ (Nonnegativity conditions) \quad (T1-3)

Additionally, in the **balanced transportation problem** it is assumed that

$$\sum_{i=1}^{m} a_i = \sum_{j=1}^{n} b_j \quad \text{(T1-4)}$$

or that the total amount available at the $m$ origins will exactly satisfy the quantity required at the $n$ destinations. As we shall see later, the latter assumption (equation T1-4) is really no more restrictive than one in which the constraints have ≤ signs. For now we will concentrate on the balanced transportation problem.

It is convenient to use a matrix tableau, such as that shown in Table T1.1, to represent the transportation problem.

Each row in the tableau corresponds to an origin, and each column corresponds to a destination. The entries in the final column are the supply availabilities at the origins, and the entries in the bottom row are the demand requirements at the destinations. The $x_{ij}$ entry in cell $(i,j)$ denotes the allocation from origin $i$ to destination $j$, and the corresponding cost per unit allocated is $c_{ij}$. The sum of the $x_{ij}$ values across row $i$ must equal $a_i$ in any feasible solution, and the sum of the $x_{ij}$ values down column j must equal $b_j$ in any feasible solution. The lower right-hand box indicates that the total amount available at the $m$ supply origins exactly satisfies the total quantity required at the $n$ demand destinations.

## Solving the Transportation Problem

We can show how to structure and solve transportation problems by considering the situation faced by the Sea Treasures Seafood Co. This company has two seafood canneries, one in San Diego and one in New Orleans. It ships its main product, canned tuna fish, to four major distribution warehouses in Los Angeles, Kansas City, Atlanta, and Philadelphia. Recently, the demand for canned tuna fish has increased sharply. As a result, Sea Treasures is considering constructing and operating a third seafood cannery at Jacksonville, Florida. Assuming that the plant is located in Jacksonville, management would like to determine the minimum shipping cost from the three cannery locations (San Diego, New Orleans, and Jacksonville) to the four distribution warehouses (Los Angeles, Kansas City, Atlanta, and Philadelphia).

The shipping costs represent a major portion of the free-on-board (FOB) prices that Sea Treasures quotes to food wholesalers at the four major distribution warehouses. Sea Treasures estimates the demand at each of the four warehouses(in number of cases) for the forthcoming year as follows:

| Warehouses | *Estimated Yearly Demand (no. of cases)* |
|---|---|
| Los Angeles | 35,000 |
| Kansas City | 20,000 |
| Atlanta | 25,000 |
| Philadelphia | 45,000 |

Sea Treasures estimates the yearly production output (number of cases) from each of the three canneries as follows:

| Canneries | *Estimated Yearly Output (no. of cases)* |
|---|---|
| San Diego | 40,000 |
| New Orleans | 50,000 |
| Jacksonville, Fl. | 35,000 |

The company also has determined the per case shipping cost for each origin-destination pair, shown in Table T1.2.

**TABLE T1.1**
The Transportation Problem Tableau

| Origin | Destination | | | | | | Origin Availability, $a_i$ |
|---|---|---|---|---|---|---|---|
| | $D_1$ | $D_2$ | ... | $D_j$ | ... | $D_n$ | |
| $O_1$ | $c_{11}$ $x_{11}$ | $c_{12}$ $x_{12}$ | ... | $c_{1j}$ $x_{1j}$ | ... | $c_{1n}$ $x_{1n}$ | $a_1$ |
| $O_2$ | $c_{21}$ $x_{21}$ | $c_{22}$ $x_{22}$ | ... | $c_{2j}$ $x_{2j}$ | ... | $c_{2n}$ $x_{2n}$ | $a_2$ |
| ⋮ | ⋮ | ⋮ | ⋮ | ⋮ | ⋮ | ⋮ | ⋮ |
| $O_i$ | $c_{i1}$ $x_{i1}$ | $c_{i2}$ $x_{i2}$ | ... | $c_{ij}$ $x_{ij}$ | ... | $c_{in}$ $x_{in}$ | $a_i$ |
| ⋮ | ⋮ | ⋮ | ⋮ | ⋮ | ⋮ | ⋮ | ⋮ |
| $O_m$ | $c_{m1}$ $x_{m1}$ | $c_{m2}$ $x_{m2}$ | ... | $c_{mj}$ $x_{mj}$ | ... | $c_{mn}$ $x_{mn}$ | $a_m$ |
| Destination Requirement, $b_j$ | $b_1$ | $b_2$ | ... | $b_j$ | ... | $b_n$ | $\sum_{i=1}^{m} a_i = \sum_{j=1}^{n} b_j$ |

TABLE T1.2
Tuna Fish Shipping Costs
(per Case)

| From Cannery | To Warehouse | | | |
|---|---|---|---|---|
| | Los Angeles | Kansas City | Atlanta | Philadelphia |
| San Diego | $ 1.00 | $7.50 | $8.50 | $11.00 |
| New Orleans | 7.50 | 4.50 | 3.00 | 7.50 |
| Jacksonville | 10.00 | 6.50 | 1.00 | 6.00 |

## Finding an Initial Basic Feasible Solution

The transportation problem tableau shows a basic feasible solution to a transportation problem has exactly $(m + n - 1)$ positive $x_{ij}$ values (allocations), and that the sum of the allocations for each row is equal to $a_i$ for that row and the sum of the allocations for each column is equal to $b_j$ for that column.

The general procedure for constructing an initial basic feasible solution involves selecting the $(m + n - 1)$ basic variables one at a time and assigning a value to the variable that will satisfy either an origin availability or a destination requirement (but not both). We could, of course, satisfy both at a single point in time. Such a condition produces a degenerate basic feasible solution. For simplicity we will consider this possibility later. Selecting and assigning a value to a basic variable satisfies one additional constraint. By making such assignments to $(m + n - 1)$ variables, we will have constructed the entire basic feasible solution in a manner that satisfies all the constraints. Next we will develop two procedures for determining an initial basic feasible solution.

**Northwest Corner Rule** The first procedure used to determine an initial basic feasible solution is called the **northwest corner rule.** Using the northwest corner rule, and referring to Table T1.1, we begin with cell (1,1), which is the cell in the northwest corner of the tableau, and we set $x_{11} = $ min $(a_1, b_1)$. With this first step we satisfy either an origin availability or a destination requirement. If $a_1 > b_1$, we move to cell (1,2) and set $x_{12} = $ min $(a_1 - b_1, b_2)$. Conversely, if $b_1 > a_1$, we move to cell (2,1) and set $x_{21} = $ min $(b_1 - a_1, a_2)$. (Remember that if $a_1 = b_1$, degeneracy will occur.) With this second step we satisfy either the second origin availability or the second destination requirement. We continue in this way, satisfying either an origin availability or a destination requirement, at each step in the process. Eventually, we must obtain a basic feasible solution with $(m + n - 1)$ positive values, because after we have made $(m + n - 2)$ such allocations, we are forced to make a single final allocation that satisfies the last row and last column simultaneously. The initial basic feasible solution obtained by applying the northwest corner rule may be far from the

optimal basic feasible solution, because we completely ignored the costs associated with the various origin-destination routes.

## Example T1.1

To illustrate use of the northwest corner rule we now apply the procedure to our tuna fish shipping problem. Table T1.3 presents the initial basic feasible solution for this problem, using the northwest corner rule.

Observe first that the format for Table T1.3 is exactly that which we introduced earlier, in Table T1.1. Applying the northwest corner rule, the first allocation is $x_{11} = 35,000$, the min $(a_1 = 40,000; b_1 = 35,000)$. This exactly satisfies the destination requirement for column one (Los Angeles). Because $a_1 > b_1$, we move to cell (1,2) and set $x_{12} = 5,000$, the min $(a_1 - b_1 = 40,000 - 35,000 = 5,000; b_1 = 20,000)$. This completely uses the origin availability for row one (San Diego). We then proceed downward and to the right until we have used all row (origin) availabilities and have met all column (destination) requirements. The arrows in Table T1.3 show the order in which we determine the basic variables (allocations). The initial basic feasible solution obtained by using the northwest corner rule has $(m + n - 1) = (3 + 4 - 1) = 6$ positive allocations. The total shipping cost associated with this initial basic feasible solution is as follows:

| Shipping Route | Shipping Cost |
|---|---|
| San Diego-Los Angeles | 35,000 cases × $1.00 per case = $ 35,000 |
| San Diego-Kansas City | 5,000 cases × $7.50 per case = $ 37,500 |
| New Orleans-Kansas City | 15,000 cases × $4.50 per case = $ 67,500 |
| New Orleans-Atlanta | 25,000 cases × $3.00 per case = $ 75,000 |
| New Orleans-Philadelphia | 10,000 cases × $7.50 per case = $ 75,000 |
| Jacksonville-Philadelphia | 35,000 cases × $6.00 per case = $210,000 |
| | Total $500,000 |

**Matrix Minima Rule** A second procedure for determining an initial basic feasible solution involves the successive determination of matrix minima. Using the **matrix minima rule**, we begin by determining the lowest cost in the entire tableau. If a tie occurs, we may break it arbitrarily. Assuming that this occurs for cell (i,j), we then set $x_{ij} = $ min

Destination

| Origin | $D_1$ Los Angeles | $D_2$ Kansas City | $D_3$ Atlanta | $D_4$ Philadelphia | Origin Availability |
|---|---|---|---|---|---|
| $O_1$ San Diego | 1.00 (35,000) | 7.50 (5,000) | 8.50 | 11.00 | 40,000 |
| $O_2$ New Orleans | 7.50 | 4.50 (15,000) | 3.00 (25,000) | 7.50 (10,000) | 50,000 |
| $O_3$ Jacksonville | 10.00 | 6.50 | 1.00 | 6.00 (35,000) | 35,000 |
| Destination Requirement | 35,000 | 20,000 | 25,000 | 45,000 | 125,000 |

TABLE T1.3
Initial Basic Feasible Solution—Northwest Corner Rule

Destination

| Origin | $D_1$ Los Angeles | $D_2$ Kansas City | $D_3$ Atlanta | $D_4$ Philadelphia | Origin Availability |
|---|---|---|---|---|---|
| $O_1$ San Diego | 1.00 (35,000) | 7.50 | 8.50 | 11.00 (5,000) | 40,000 |
| $O_2$ New Orleans | 7.50 | 4.50 (20,000) | 3.00 | 7.50 (30,000) | 50,000 |
| $O_3$ Jacksonville | 10.00 | 6.50 | 1.00 (25,000) | 6.00 (10,000) | 35,000 |
| Destination Requirement | 35,000 | 20,000 | 25,000 | 45,000 | 125,000 |

TABLE T1.4
Initial Basic Feasible Solution—Matrix Minima Rule

($a_i$, $b_j$) and eliminate from further consideration either row i or column j, depending on which requirement is satisfied. If $x_{ij} = a_i$, we decrease $b_j$ by $a_i$, and if $x_{ij} = b_j$, we decrease $a_i$ by $b_j$. We then repeat this process throughout the remainder of the tableau. Whenever the search process reaches a point at which the minimum cost is not unique, choose among the minima arbitrarily. Degeneracy can again occur, a possibility that we will discuss more fully later. Using the matrix minima rule usually produces a better initial feasible solution than the northwest corner rule.

Applying the matrix minima rule to our tuna fish shipping problem, we obtain the initial basic feasible solution shown in Table T1.4.

## Example T1.2

Applying the matrix minima rule, the first allocation is $x_{11} = 35,000$, the min ($a_1 = 40,000$; $b_1 = 35,000$), because $c_1 = \$1$ is the minimum cost in the tableau. This allocation exactly satisfies the destination requirement for column one (Los Angeles), and we decrease $a_1$ by 35,000 too. The next-lowest cost in the tableau is $c_{33} = \$1$. We make the second allocation as $x_{33} = 25,000$, the min ($a_3 = 35,000$; $b_3 = 25,000$). We then decrease $a_3$ by $b_3 = 25,000$ and continue. We repeat this process throughout the remainder of the tableau, as indicated by the arrows in Table T1.4, until we have determined all the basic variables. Observe that we have again made $(m + n - 1) = (3 + 4 - 1) = 6$ positive allocations. The total shipping cost associated with this initial basic feasible solution is as follows:

| Shipping Route | Shipping Cost |
|---|---|
| San Diego-Los Angeles | 35,000 cases × $ 1.00 per case = $ 35,000 |
| San Diego-Philadelphia | 5,000 cases × $11.00 per case = $ 55,000 |
| New Orleans-Kansas City | 20,000 cases × $ 4.50 per case = $ 90,000 |
| New Orleans-Philadelphia | 30,000 cases × $ 7.50 per case = $225,000 |
| Jacksonville-Atlanta | 25,000 cases × $ 1.00 per case = $ 25,000 |
| Jacksonville-Philadelphia | 10,000 cases × $ 6.00 per case = $ 60,000 |
| | Total            $490,000 |

## Moving to an Optimal Solution: The Stepping-stone Method

In the previous section of this chapter we determined a basic feasible solution to the transportation problem having $(m + n - 1)$ of the basic variables, the $x_{ij}$, positive. We entered the values for the basic $x_{ij}$ in the appropriate cells, and we circled the values to indicate that they were basic. Now we must evaluate each of the unoccupied cells (unused shipping routes) to determine the effect upon the objective function of transferring one unit from an occupied cell to the unoccupied cell. The **stepping-stone method** involves two steps:

■ We evaluate all unoccupied cells for the net cost effect of transferring one unit from an occupied cell to the unoccupied cell. We make this transfer in a manner that maintains the row and column balance of the transportation problem (each row availability is exactly allocated, and each column requirement is exactly satisfied).

■ After we have evaluated all the unoccupied cells, we make a reallocation to the unoccupied cell that the tableau indicates would have the greatest net cost per unit savings.

We use the steps of the stepping-stone method repeatedly until there are no unoccupied cells for which an improvement in the objective function would occur.

To measure the effect on the objective function of transferring one unit to an unoccupied cell, we must find a closed loop or path between the unoccupied cell and selected occupied cells. This path consists of a series of steps leading from the unoccupied cell to the occupied cells (the stones) and back to the unoccupied cell. Because we are evaluating the effect of making a one-unit allocation to an unoccupied cell, we can do this by using the $c_{ij}$ values associated with the cells along the path.

The procedure for tracing out the closed loop is as follows:

1. Begin with the unoccupied cell to be evaluated and place a +1 in the unoccupied cell. This indicates that we are evaluating the effect of moving one unit into

this unoccupied cell (moving one unit into unoccupied cell (i,j) will incur a cost of + $c_{ij}$).

2. Draw an arrow from the unoccupied cell being evaluated to an occupied cell in the same row or to an occupied cell in the same column. Place a −1 in the cell to which the arrow was drawn. This signifies that we are compensating for the +1 unit moved into the unoccupied cell by subtracting (shifting) one unit from either an occupied cell in its same row or an occupied cell in its same column [moving one unit from occupied cell (k,j) will save a cost equal to $c_{kj}$]. This shifting is necessary in order to maintain the row or column balance.

3. Move horizontally or vertically (but never diagonally) from the occupied cell just selected to another occupied cell. Draw an arrow to this occupied cell, and place a +1 in the cell to which the arrow was drawn, again to maintain the row or column balance.

4. Repeat the process of moving from occupied cell to occupied cell until we loop back to the original unoccupied cell. Alternate the +1 and −1 allocations at each step of the looping process in order to maintain the row or column balance.

5. Throughout the looping process we maintain the important restriction that there is exactly one positive allocation (+1) and exactly one negative allocation (−1) in any row or column through which the loop happens to pass. Again, this restriction is necessary to maintain the row or column balance. Physically, this means that as we trace the closed loop, we will make orthogonal (90°, or right-angle) turns only at the occupied cells. It is also important to note that the number of cells involved in the closed loop process will always be an even integer equal to or greater than 4 (4, 6, 8, and so on).

6. After we have constructed the entire closed loop, we determine the net cost associated with the unoccupied cell by adding the $c_{ij}$ values in all the cells marked with a +1 and subtracting the $c_{ij}$ values in all the cells marked with a −1.

We evaluate all the unoccupied cells in this manner. Then we select the unoccupied cell in which the greatest per unit net cost savings occurs as the cell into which we will make a reallocation. If two or more cells tie in the evaluation process, we may break the tie arbitrarily. The steps just outlined are the variable entry criterion for the transportation problem.

The variable removal criterion for the transportation problem involves the cells on the closed loop that we marked as −1 during the evaluation process. Because the variable entry criterion involves a reallocation to a previously unoccupied cell, the variable removal criterion requires that we decrease the cells on the closed loop with an entry of −1 to maintain the row and column balance. We must examine each cell marked as −1; the cell marked as −1 and that has the minimum value will indicate the amount by which we can increase the current nonbasic variable. The cell selected in this manner will decrease to zero (in other words, it will become nonbasic), and the unoccupied cell we selected by using the variable entry criterion will increase to the amount that was originally in the cell marked as −1 (it will become basic). In this manner we will maintain the row and column balance. This process is the variable removal criterion for the transportation problem.

We should emphasize that in using the procedure for tracing the closed loop in order to evaluate an unoccupied cell, we begin by placing a +1 in the unoccupied cell we are evaluating and then proceed alternatively, placing −1 and +1 in the occupied cells along the closed loop. Additionally, we must assign the −1 and +1 values in a manner that maintains the row and column balance. To illustrate, consider Example T1.3.

## Example T1.3

In this example we are automatically assigning a +1 to the unoccupied cell we are evaluating. Assigning the −1 is uniquely determined to be the cell occupied by the amount of ten, because we can offset the assignment of −1 to this cell by assigning +1 to the cell occupied by the amount five (so we can maintain the row-column balance). We cannot assign the −1 to the cell occupied by the amount of twenty because doing so would throw the row out of balance—no other cell is occupied in the corresponding row. The number of cells in the closed loop process is the even value of four, that is, two occupied cells assigned as −1 and two cells—the unoccupied cell we are evaluating and the other occupied cell—assigned as +1.

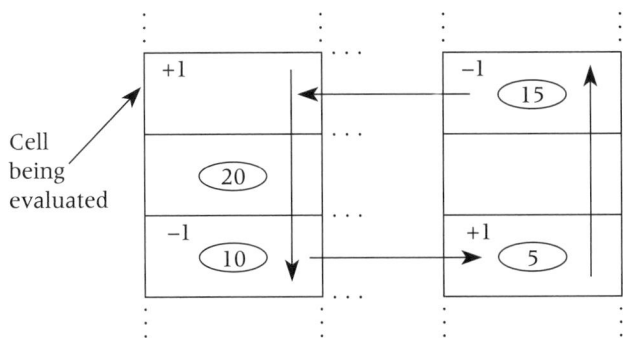

## Example T1.4

To illustrate the stepping-stone algorithm we will solve the tuna fish shipping problem by using the initial basic feasible solution determined by the northwest corner rule. Table T1.5 reproduces this tableau.

We will begin our analysis by considering cell (1,3), which is unoccupied and represents the San Diego → Atlanta shipping route. In the case of cell (1,3) a closed path consists of steps from this cell (1,3) to cell (2,3), from cell (2,3) to cell (2,2), from cell (2,2) to cell (1,2), and from cell (1,2) back to cell (1,3). We are evaluating the effect of adding one unit to cell (1,3), for which we then must compensate by subtracting one unit from cell (2,3). Then we must compensate for the reduction in cell (2,3) by adding one unit to cell (2,2). And we must compensate for the addition to cell (2,2) by subtracting one unit from cell (1,2). This completes the reallocation along the closed path from cell (1,3) and back to cell (1,3).

|  | Destination | | | | |
|---|---|---|---|---|---|
| Origin | $D_1$ Los Angeles | $D_2$ Kansas City | $D_3$ Atlanta | $D_4$ Philadelphia | Origin Availability |
| $O_1$ San Diego | 1.00 (35,000) | 7.50 (5,000) | 8.50 +2.50 | 11.00 +0.50 | 40,000 |
| $O_2$ New Orleans | 7.50 +9.50 | 4.50 (15,000) | 3.00 (25,000) | 7.50 (10,000) | 50,000 |
| $O_3$ Jacksonville | 10.00 +13.50 | 6.50 +3.50 | 1.00 −0.50 | 6.00 (35,000) | 35,000 |
| Destination Requirement | 35,000 | 20,000 | 25,000 | 45,000 | 125,000 |

NOTE: Total shipping cost (initial basic feasible solution) = $500,000.

TABLE T1.5
Tuna Fish Shipping Problem—Initial Basic Feasible Solution

We can determine the net change in the objective function that corresponds to this reallocation by adding and subtracting the appropriate transportation costs. By following our closed path, we obtain the following results:

Cell (1,3)

| | |
|---|---|
| Add one unit to cell (1,3): | +$8.50 |
| Subtract one unit from one cell (2,3): | – 3.00 |
| Add one unit to cell (2,2): | + 4.50 |
| Subtract one unit from cell (1,2): | – 7.50 |
| Net change | +$2.50 |

Cell (1,3)

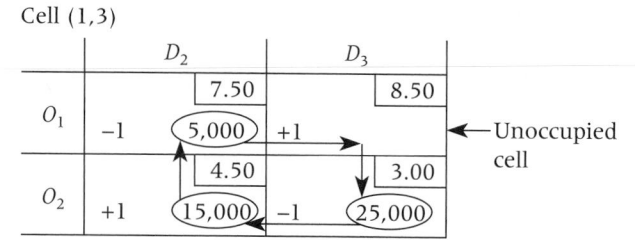

Allocating one unit to cell (1,3) will result in a +$2.50 net cost change in the objective function. We enter this net cost increase in cell (1,3) in the tableau.

We evaluate in the same manner the effect of allocating one unit to each of the other unoccupied cells. The computations for the other cells are

Cell (1,4)

| | |
|---|---|
| Add one unit to cell (1,4): | +$11.00 |
| Subtract one unit from cell (2,4): | – 7.50 |
| Add one unit to cell (2,2): | + 4.50 |
| Subtract one unit from cell (1,2): | – 7.50 |
| Net change | +$ 0.50 |

Cell (1,4)

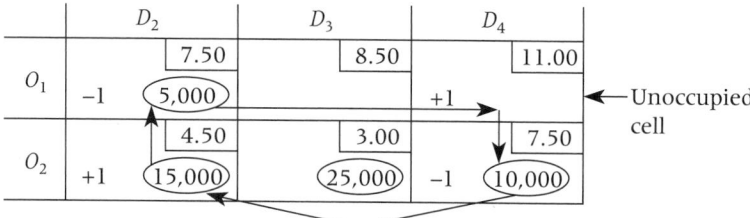

Cell (2,1)

| | |
|---|---|
| Add one unit to cell (2,1): | +$ 7.50 |
| Subtract one unit from cell (2,2): | – 4.50 |
| Add one unit to cell (1,2): | + 7.50 |
| Subtract one unit from cell (1,1): | – 1.00 |
| Net change | +$ 9.50 |

Cell (2,1)

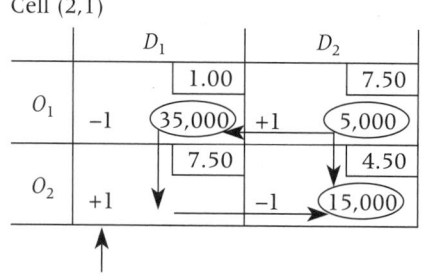

Cell (3,1)

| | |
|---|---|
| Add one unit to cell (3,1): | +$ 10.00 |
| Subtract one unit from one cell (3,4): | – 6.00 |
| Add one unit to cell (2,4): | + 7.50 |
| Subtract one unit from one cell (2,2): | – 4.50 |
| Add one unit to cell (1,2): | + 7.50 |
| Subtract one unit from cell (1,1): | – 1.00 |
| Net change | +$ 13.50 |

Cell (3,1)

Cell (3,2)

Cell (3,2)
Add one unit to cell (3,2):            +\$ 6.50
Subtract one unit from cell (3,4):      −  6.00
Add one unit to cell (2,4):            +  7.50
Subtract one unit from cell (2,2):     −  4.50
                    Net change  +\$ 3.50

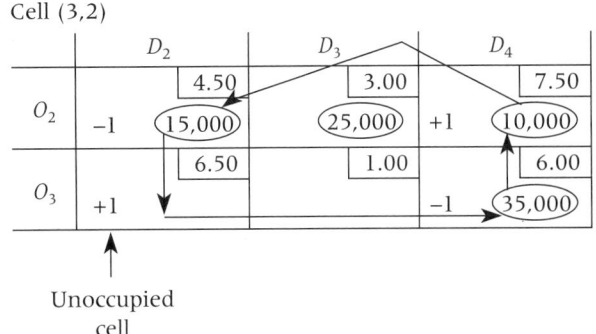

Unoccupied
cell

Cell (3,3)

Cell (3,3)
Add one unit to cell (3,3):            +\$ 1.00
Subtract one unit from cell (3,4):      −  6.00
Add one unit to cell (2,4):            +  7.50
Subtract one unit from cell (2,3):     −  3.00
                    Net change  −\$ 0.50

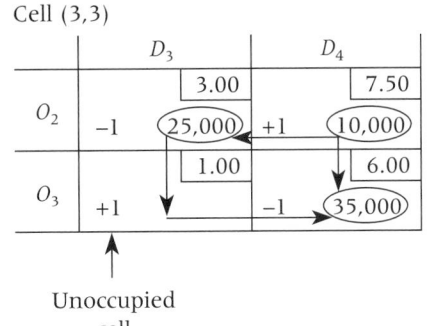

Unoccupied
cell

Table T1.5 shows the net cost changes for all the unoccupied cells. If all net cost changes are ≥ 0, the basic feasible solution is optimal. If one or more of the net cost changes is < 0, we can reduce the value of the objective function (shipping cost).

In Table T1.5 we observe that the net cost change for cell (3,3) is −0.50. We can decrease the objective function by making an allocation to the unoccupied cell (3,3). The question now is how much we can allocate to cell (3,3). We can answer by recalling that a basic feasible solution must have $(m + n − 1)$ occupied cells, and we must maintain our row and column balance (we must exactly satisfy the column requirements using the row availabilities exactly). The amount of the allocation we place in an unoccupied cell is always the *minimum* amount in the cells on the closed loop that we marked as −1 during the unoccupied cell evaluation process. The number of units that we can allocate to cell (3,3) is limited to an amount equal to the *minimum* of the number of units already allocated to cell (2,3) and cell (3,4), because one of these two cells will provide the units that will move into cell (3,3). Diagrammatically,

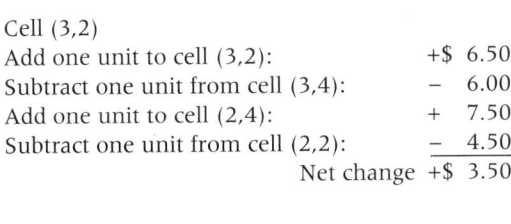

or

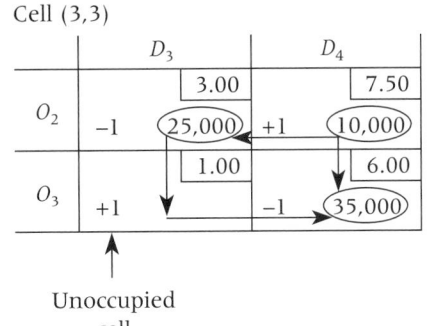

Note that in these diagrams we have marked each cell along the closed loop with a +1 or a −1. We compute the number of units to allocate to cell (3,3) as

$$\text{Allocation to cell (3,3)} = \text{minimum} \frac{\text{cell (2,3)} \quad \text{cell (3,4)}}{25,000 \quad 35,000}$$

$$= 25,000 \qquad \text{(T1-5)}$$

To maintain a basic feasible solution and the row-column balance, we must select the minimum value in these two cells. We move 25,000 units from cell (2,3) to cell (3,3). We compensate for this move by reducing the amount in cell (3,4) by 35,000 − 25,000 = 10,000. Then we increase the amount in cell (2,4) by 10,000 + 25,000 = 35,000. Finally, we reduce the amount in cell (2,3) by 25,000 − 25,000 = 0. We have, of course, simply moved 25,000 units around the closed path that we used to originally evaluate cell (3,3). Table T1.6 is the new tableau, which shows that we have made this change.

We must now evaluate the unoccupied cells in Table T1.6, the second tableau, to determine whether we can

Destination

| Origin | $D_1$ Los Angeles | $D_2$ Kansas City | $D_3$ Atlanta | $D_4$ Philadelphia | Origin Availability |
|---|---|---|---|---|---|
| $O_1$ San Diego | 1.00 (35,000) | 7.50 (5,000) | 8.50 +3.00 | 11.00 +0.50 | 40,000 |
| $O_2$ New Orleans | 7.50 +9.50 | 4.50 (15,000) | 3.00 +0.50 | 7.50 (35,000) | 50,000 |
| $O_3$ Jacksonville | 10.00 +13.50 | 6.50 +3.50 | 1.00 (25,000) | 6.00 (10,000) | 35,000 |
| Destination Requirement | 35,000 | 20,000 | 25,000 | 45,000 | 125,000 |

NOTE: Total shipping cost (second basic feasible solution) = $487,500.

T A B L E   T 1 . 6
Tuna Fish Shipping Problem—Second Basic Feasible Solution
(Optimal Solution)

make any further allocations that reduce the objective function. The computations for these cells are made in the same manner as they were for the previous tableau; the details will not be repeated here.

Because the net changes are for all unoccupied cells ≥ 0, in Table T1.6, we are optimal. The minimum-cost shipping plan is as follows:

| Shipping Route | Shipping Cost |
|---|---|
| San Diego-Los Angeles | 35,000 cases × $1.00 per case = $ 35,000 |
| San Diego-Kansas City | 5,000 cases × $7.50 per case = $ 37,500 |
| New Orleans-Kansas City | 15,000 cases × $4.50 per case = $ 67,500 |
| New Orleans-Philadelphia | 35,000 cases × $7.50 per case = $262,500 |
| Jacksonville-Atlanta | 25,000 cases × $1.00 per case = $ 25,000 |
| Jacksonville-Philadelphia | 10,000 cases × $6.00 per case = $ 60,000 |
| | Total    $487,500 |

## Special Situations

A number of special situations can arise in formulating and solving transportation problems.

## Alternative Optimal Solutions

A transportation problem can have more than one optimal solution (several alternative optimal solutions). We can recognize this situation because one or more of the unoccupied cells will have a net cost savings equal to zero. A reallocation to the cell (route) that has a net cost savings equal to zero will have no effect on the total transportation cost. This reallocation will provide another solution with the same total transportation cost, but the routes will be different than those for the original optimal solution.

## Unacceptable Transportation Routes

Practical transportation problems frequently make it desirable to discourage or even prevent shipment of a product from a certain origin to a certain destination. This can be accomplished very simply, by assigning an arbitrarily large cost, such as $c_{ij} = +M$, as the cost coefficient associated with this allocation. Using a cost of $+M$ will prevent the associated cell from entering the basis, so such an allocation will not be a part of the final solution.

## Degeneracy

**Degeneracy** occurs in transportation problems when less than $(m + n - 1)$ of the $x_{ij}$ values are strictly positive. Degeneracy can occur as we are determining an initial basic feasible solution, or it can occur as we are making an iteration.

Consider the transportation problem tableau shown in Table T1.7 in which the transportation planner used the northwest corner rule to determine the initial basic feasible solution. Using the rule results in an initial feasible solution that has positive allocations to only five cells, instead of the $(m + n - 1) = 6$ strictly positive allocations required for an initial basic feasible solution. This happened because the planner's assignment of the value $x_{23} = 15$ simultaneously satisfied the row two availability of 30 and the column three requirement of 15.

## Example T1.5

To resolve this problem we use the transportation tableau that appears in Table T1.8. In it the planner has added one

| Origin | Destination | | | | Origin Availability |
|---|---|---|---|---|---|
| | $D_1$ | $D_2$ | $D_3$ | $D_4$ | |
| $O_1$ | 2 / (15) | 6 | 3 | 4 | 15 |
| $O_2$ | 3 / (5) | 1 / (10) | 4 / (15) | 2 | 30 |
| $O_3$ | 3 | 6 | 3 | 2 / (20) | 20 |
| Destination Requirement | 20 | 10 | 15 | 20 | 65 |

TABLE T1.7
Degenerate Initial Feasible Solution (Using Northwest Corner Rule)

$Z = 115$

| Origin | Destination | | | | Origin Availability |
|---|---|---|---|---|---|
| | $D_1$ | $D_2$ | $D_3$ | $D_4$ | |
| $O_1$ | 2 / (15) | 6 / +6 | 3 / 0 | 4 / +3 | 15 |
| $O_2$ | 3 / (5) | 1 / (10) | 4 / (15) | 2 / (0) | 30 |
| $O_3$ | 3 / 0 | 6 / +5 | 3 / -1 | 2 / (20) | 20 |
| Destination Requirement | 20 | 10 | 15 | 20 | 65 |

TABLE T1.8
Modified Tableau—Initial Basic Feasible Solution

$Z = 155$

| Origin | Destination | | | | Origin Availability |
|---|---|---|---|---|---|
| | $D_1$ | $D_2$ | $D_3$ | $D_4$ | |
| $O_1$ | 2 / (15) | 6 / +6 | 3 / +1 | 4 / +3 | 15 |
| $O_2$ | 3 / (5) | 1 / (10) | 4 / +1 | 2 / (15) | 30 |
| $O_3$ | 3 / 0 | 6 / +5 | 3 / (15) | 2 / (5) | 20 |
| Destination Requirement | 20 | 10 | 15 | 20 | 65 |

TABLE T1.9
Optimal Solution (Nondegenerate)

Min $Z = 140$
(Optimal)

cell, (2,4), at a zero level and identified it with a broken circle. Because the planner has constructed an initial basic feasible solution with $(m + n - 1) = 6$ occupied cells, we can proceed to iterate, using the stepping-stone method. We obtain the second basic feasible solution, which is the optimal solution to this problem and appears in Table T1.9.

Note that this optimal solution is no longer degenerate.

## The Unbalanced Transportation Problem

It is very common in practical applications to encounter an **unbalanced transportation problem** in which the total supply is not equal to the total demand. If total supply is greater than total demand, we introduce one **slack**, or **dummy destination**; its demand is exactly equal to the excess of supply over demand. Conversely, if total demand is greater than total supply, we introduce one **slack**, or **dummy origin**—its supply is exactly equal to the excess of demand over supply. In both situations we assign a cost of zero for every route to a dummy destination and for every route from a dummy origin. We do this because we do not actually use the dummy destination or origin in the solution that we ultimately implement.

## Example T1.6

Table T1.10 presents an example of an unbalanced transportation problem. The origin availabilities total 245 units; the destination requirements total 180 units. We have added one slack destination with demand of $245 - 180 = 65$ units. The costs associated with this slack destination column are all zero. The matrix minima method was used to determine an initial basic feasible solution for this problem, using two cells in the dummy destination column. The stepping-stone method has been used to evaluate the costs associated with moving into the unoccupied cells for this tableau, and we observe that we can achieve a per unit cost savings of $2 by making an allocation to cell (1,6). We next determine that we can move 40 units into cell (1,6). By making this reallocation, we obtain the second basic feasible solution, shown in Table T1.11.

We continue to use the stepping-stone method and observe that we can achieve a per unit cost savings of $1 by making an allocation to cell (3, slack). We next determine that we can move 5 units into cell (3, slack). By making this reallocation, we obtain the third basic feasible solution, shown in Table T1.12.

In this third basic feasible solution the net changes are $\geq 0$ for all the unoccupied cells. The minimum-cost shipping plan that we have determined is as follows:

| Shipping Route | Shipping Cost |
|---|---|
| $O_1 \rightarrow D_1$ | 0 units × $ 5 per unit = $ 0 |
| $O_1 \rightarrow D_6$ | 45 units × $ 7 per unit = 315 |
| $O_2 \rightarrow D_3$ | 10 units × $10 per unit = 100 |
| $O_2 \rightarrow$ Slack destination | 60 units × $ 0 per unit = 0 |
| $O_3 \rightarrow D_2$ | 20 units × $11 per unit = 220 |
| $O_3 \rightarrow D_6$ | 5 units × $12 per unit = 60 |
| $O_3 \rightarrow$ Slack destination | 5 units × $ 0 per unit = 0 |
| $O_4 \rightarrow D_1$ | 50 units × $ 9 per unit = 450 |
| $O_4 \rightarrow D_4$ | 35 units × $ 8 per unit = 280 |
| $O_4 \rightarrow D_5$ | 15 units × $ 6 per unit = 90 |
| | Total            $1,515 |

This optimal basic feasible solution is degenerate [the number of occupied cells is less than $(m + n - 1) = 10$], because $x_{11} = 0$. Because supply exceeds demand by 65 units, our optimal solution is to ship the excess 65 units to the slack destination. Because we have no slack destination, solving the problem in this way means that we would have excesses of 60 units at origin $O_2$ and 5 units at origin $O_3$.

## Changes in Transportation Costs

Also note that once we have couched any transportation problem in the form given by equations T1-1, T1-2, T1-3, and T1-4, we can replace each $c_{ij}$ by $c_{ij} + \delta$, for any constant $\delta$, without changing the values of the $x_{ij}$, which yield an optimal solution. We can do this because the substitution of

| Origin | $D_1$ | $D_2$ | $D_3$ | $D_4$ | $D_5$ | $D_6$ | Slack Destination | Origin Availability |
|---|---|---|---|---|---|---|---|---|
| $O_1$ | 5 | 10 | 15 | 8 | 9 | 7 | 0 | |
| | (45) | +2 | +9 | +4 | +7 | -2 | +4 | 45 |
| $O_2$ | 14 | 13 | 10 | 9 | 20 | 21 | 0 | |
| | +5 | +1 | (10) | +1 | +14 | +8 | (60) | 70 |
| $O_3$ | 15 | 11 | 13 | 25 | 8 | 12 | 0 | |
| | +7 | (20) | +4 | +18 | +3 | (10) | +1 | 30 |
| $O_4$ | 9 | 19 | 12 | 8 | 6 | 13 | 0 | |
| | (5) | +7 | +2 | (35) | (15) | (40) | (5) | 100 |
| Destination Requirement | 50 | 20 | 10 | 35 | 15 | 50 | 65 | 245 |

Destination (header spanning the table)

TABLE T1.10
Initial Basic Feasible Solution—Unbalanced Transportation Problem

Destination

| Origin | $D_1$ | $D_2$ | $D_3$ | $D_4$ | $D_5$ | $D_6$ | Slack Destination | Origin Availability |
|--------|-------|-------|-------|-------|-------|-------|-------------------|---------------------|
| $O_1$ | 5 / (5) | 10 / +4 | 15 / +9 | 8 / +4 | 9 / +7 | 7 / (40) | 0 / +4 | 45 |
| $O_2$ | 14 / +5 | 13 / +3 | 10 / (10) | 9 / +1 | 20 / +14 | 21 / +10 | 0 / (60) | 70 |
| $O_3$ | 15 / +5 | 11 / (20) | 13 / +2 | 25 / +16 | 8 / +1 | 12 / (10) | 0 / −1 | 30 |
| $O_4$ | 9 / (45) | 19 / +9 | 12 / +2 | 8 / (35) | 6 / (15) | 13 / +2 | 0 / (5) | 100 |
| Destination Requirement | 50 | 20 | 10 | 35 | 15 | 50 | 65 | 245 |

TABLE T1.11
Second Basic Feasible Solution—Unbalanced Transportation Problem

Destination

| Origin | $D_1$ | $D_2$ | $D_3$ | $D_4$ | $D_5$ | $D_6$ | Slack Destination | Origin Availability |
|--------|-------|-------|-------|-------|-------|-------|-------------------|---------------------|
| $O_1$ | 5 / (0) | 10 / +4 | 15 / +10 | 8 / +4 | 9 / +7 | 7 / (45) | 0 / +5 | 45 |
| $O_2$ | 14 / +4 | 13 / +2 | 10 / (10) | 9 / 0 | 20 / +13 | 21 / +9 | 0 / (60) | 70 |
| $O_3$ | 15 / +5 | 11 / (20) | 13 / +3 | 25 / +16 | 8 / +1 | 12 / (5) | 0 / (5) | 30 |
| $O_4$ | 9 / (50) | 19 / +9 | 12 / +3 | 8 / (35) | 6 / (15) | 13 / +2 | 0 / +1 | 100 |
| Destination Requirement | 50 | 20 | 10 | 35 | 15 | 50 | 65 | 245 |

TABLE T1.12
Third Basic Feasible Solution—Unbalanced Transportation Problem (Optimal Solution)

the $c_{ij} + \delta$ for each $c_i$ will change only the value of the objective function by a constant amount, say, $K$:

$$K = \delta \sum_{i=1}^{m} a_i \text{ or } K = \delta \sum_{j=1}^{n} b_j \qquad \text{(T1-6)}$$

## Example T1.7

Assume that we have solved a transportation problem involving truck shipments from 10 plants to 25 warehouses and have determined that the minimum cost associated with shipping some 5,000 units of our product is $10,000.

We then learn that a gasoline price increase will increase the unit cost associated with each origin → destination route by 5 cents. We do not need to resolve the transportation problem to determine the values of the $x_{ij}$, which yield the optimal solution. They will remain as they are in the current solution, and the value of the objective function will simply increase by

$$K = \delta \sum_{j=1}^{n} b_j$$
$$= (0.05)(5,000) \qquad \text{(T1-7)}$$
$$= \$250$$

Also, note that the values of the $x_{ij}$ for the optimal solution to a transportation problem do not change if we add a constant $\lambda$ either to each cost in row i of the transportation tableau or to each cost in column j of the transportation tableau. Why this is true becomes apparent when we consider the nature of the stepping-stone algorithm used to solve the transportation problem. In evaluating the effect of moving one unit into an unoccupied cell, we move along a closed path from that unoccupied cell to various occupied cells and back to the unoccupied cell, always using an even number of steps. Within any row or any column, we will always make exactly two steps from the unoccupied cell to an occupied cell, from an occupied cell to another occupied cell, or from an occupied cell back to the unoccupied cell.

In making this evaluation we will always be using exactly two $c_{ij}$ values from any row or any column, and we will add one $c_{ij}$ value and subtract the other $c_{ij}$ value in the computation. If we now add a constant $\lambda$ to each of the $c_{ij}$ values in row i or to each of the $c_{ij}$ values in column j, the optimal solution will not change, because in evaluating each occupied cell involving row i or column j, we must both add and subtract the constant amount $\lambda$ one time. Once again, we do not need to resolve the transportation problem to determine the values of the $x_{ij}$, which yield the optimal solution. They will remain as they are in the current solution, and the value of the objective function will increase by

$$K = \lambda \cdot a_i, \text{ if } \lambda \text{ is added to each } c_{ij} \text{ value in row i} \quad \text{(T1-8)}$$
$$K = \lambda \cdot b_j, \text{ if } \lambda \text{ is added to each } c_{ij} \text{ value in column j} \quad \text{(T1-9)}$$

## Example T1.8

Assume that we have a plant → warehouse transportation problem in which we want to include the variable produc-

tion cost of 25 cents per unit for the 100 units produced at plant 2. We know that when we add this variable production cost to row two of the tableau, the values of the $x_{ij}$, which yield the optimal solution, will not change. They will remain as they are in the current solution, and the value of the objective function will increase by

$$K = \lambda \cdot a_i \quad \text{(T1-10)}$$
$$= (\$0.25) \cdot (100) = \$25$$

## Profit Maximization Transportation Problems

In certain transportation problems the structure of the problem may require that we maximize profits rather minimize costs. We can still use the stepping-stone algorithm to solve such a problem. However, we must make one of the two modifications that follow:

1. We solve the profit maximization transportation problem in exactly the same manner as the cost minimization transportation problem, except that the costs $c_{ij}$ are replaced by the profits $p_{ij}$ and the test of optimality is reversed. If all net changes are $\leq 0$, the basic feasible solution is optimal (all cell evaluations must be zero or negative).
2. We transform the profit maximization problem by subtracting all $p_{ij}$ values from the biggest $p_{ij}$. This transformation scales the original problem into a new problem that involves relative costs. We can solve this new relative cost problem in the usual cost minimization manner. We calculate the total maximum profit by multiplying the optimal values of the basic variables, the $x_{ij}$, by the original profits, the $p_{ij}$.

---

## ► Summary

This tutorial presented an overview of the stepping-stone method of solving the transportation problem. We also showed how to formulate transportation problems and reviewed the mathematical structure of such problems.

Transportation problems arise in many production and logistics situations involving the physical movement of products and also in situations involving

facility location decisions. We can also use the structure of the transportation problem to solve some aggregate planning problems.

A number of special situations can arise for transportation problems. A thorough understanding of how to deal with these special situations is important in effectively using the transportation problem methodology in practice.

# ► Key Terms

balanced transportation problem
degeneracy
demand destination
matrix minima rule

northwest corner rule
slack (dummy) destination
slack (dummy) origin
stepping-stone method

supply origin
transportation problem
unbalanced transportation problem

# ► Discussion Questions

1. Why will the matrix minima rule generally produce a better initial basic feasible solution than the northwest corner rule?
2. What indicates that degeneracy has occurred in a transportation problem? How is degeneracy resolved?
3. Briefly describe how to balance a transportation problem involving more units at the origins than are required at the destinations.

4. What are the basic steps in the stepping-stone method?
5. How do we know when we have obtained the optimal solution to a transportation problem?

# ► Problems

1. A paint manufacturer has 3 plants and 4 distribution warehouses. The shipping costs from each plant to the 4 distribution warehouses and the plant availabilities and destination requirements appear in the tableau that follows. The manufacturer seeks to develop a shipping schedule that minimizes her total shipping cost.

| Plant | Warehouse | | | | Plant Availability |
|---|---|---|---|---|---|
| | 1 | 2 | 3 | 4 | |
| 1 | 6.50 | 4.00 | 3.00 | 5.00 | 235 |
| 2 | 6.00 | 8.50 | 7.00 | 4.00 | 280 |
| 3 | 5.00 | 6.00 | 9.00 | 10.00 | 110 |
| Warehouse Requirement | 125 | 160 | 110 | 230 | 625 |

   a. Use the northwest corner rule to determine an initial basic feasible solution.
   b. Use the stepping-stone method to determine the optimal solution.
2. Solve the transportation problem that has the following costs, origin availabilities, and destination requirements. Use the northwest corner rule to obtain an initial basic feasible solution, and use the stepping-stone method to obtain the optimal solution.

Destination

| Origin | $D_1$ | $D_2$ | $D_3$ | $D_4$ | $D_5$ | $D_6$ | Origin Availability |
|---|---|---|---|---|---|---|---|
| $O_1$ | 2 | 3 | 2 | 5 | 6 | 4 | 40 |
| $O_2$ | 4 | 4 | 3 | 2 | 5 | 2 | 60 |
| $O_3$ | 4 | 3 | 5 | 9 | 6 | 2 | 85 |
| $O_4$ | 4 | 2 | 8 | 4 | 5 | 7 | 30 |
| Destination Requirement | 25 | 50 | 35 | 15 | 60 | 30 | 215 |

3. Solve problem 2 by using the matrix minima method to obtain an initial basic feasible solution. Use the stepping-stone method to determine the optimal solution.

4. Solve the transportation problem that has the following costs, origin availabilities, and destination requirements. Use the northwest corner rule to obtain an initial basic feasible solution, and use the stepping-stone method to obtain the optimal solution.

Destination

| Origin | $D_1$ | $D_2$ | $D_3$ | $D_4$ | $D_5$ | Origin Availability |
|---|---|---|---|---|---|---|
| $O_1$ | 2 | 1 | 3 | 3 | 2 | 40 |
| $O_2$ | 2 | 3 | 4 | 3 | 1 | 50 |
| $O_3$ | 2 | 3 | 5 | 4 | 3 | 60 |
| $O_4$ | 4 | 2 | 2 | 4 | 6 | 30 |
| Destination Requirement | 30 | 50 | 40 | 25 | 35 | 180 |

5. Solve problem 4 by using the matrix minima method to obtain an initial basic feasible solution. Use the stepping-stone method to determine the optimal solution.

6. Solve the following transportation problem by using the stepping-stone method and the northwest corner rule to obtain an initial basic feasible solution. HINT: Use cells marked with a zero to resolve degeneracy.

Destination

| Origin | $D_1$ | $D_2$ | $D_3$ | $D_4$ | $D_5$ | $D_6$ | Origin Availability |
|---|---|---|---|---|---|---|---|
| $O_1$ | 11 | 9 | 7 | 5 | 3 | 5 | 30 |
| $O_2$ | 8 | 13 | 11 | 9 | 6 | 8 | 40 |
| $O_3$ | 7 | 9 | 12 | 14 | 9 | 7 | 10 |
| $O_4$ | 5 | 4 | 9 | 11 | 15 | 14 | 80 |
| Destination Requirement | 50 | 20 | 10 | 30 | 20 | 30 | 160 |

**7.** Solve the following transportation problem, which involves shipments of iron ore from a series of ports to a series of steel mills and has this initial basic feasible solution: HINT: Use cells marked with a zero to resolve degeneracy.

Steel Mill

| Port | $SM_1$ | $SM_2$ | $SM_3$ | $SM_4$ | $SM_5$ | $SM_6$ | Port Availability |
|---|---|---|---|---|---|---|---|
| $P_1$ | 3 (30) | 1 (20) | 2 | 5 | 2 | 6 | 50 |
| $P_2$ | 4 | 2 (20) | 1 (25) | 6 | 3 | 4 | 45 |
| $P_3$ | 4 | 5 | 3 (10) | 4 (50) | 7 (20) | 1 | 80 |
| $P_4$ | 5 | 2 | 1 | 3 | 2 (40) | 1 (20) | 60 |
| Steel Mill Requirement | 30 | 40 | 35 | 50 | 60 | 20 | 235 |

**8.** A company has 3 warehouses containing 10,000, 7,500, and 12,000 units of its product. In the next month it must ship 3,500, 2,500, 7,000, 5,000, 500, and 3,500 units to 6 retail outlets. The unit cost of shipment from any warehouse to any retail outlet is contained in the matrix that follows. Determine the minimum-cost shipping plan.

Destination

| Origin | $D_1$ | $D_2$ | $D_3$ | $D_4$ | $D_5$ | $D_6$ |
|---|---|---|---|---|---|---|
| $O_1$ | 10 | 9 | 16 | 3 | 10 | 26 |
| $O_2$ | 17 | 23 | 18 | 9 | 11 | 19 |
| $O_3$ | 20 | 15 | 20 | 6 | 13 | 15 |

**9.** The Dixie Southern Railroad Co. has a problem that involves the distribution of its empty railroad cars. It has a shortage of railroad cars in certain cities and an oversupply of railroad cars in other cities. The imbalances are as follows:

| City | Shortage | Overage |
|---|---|---|
| New York | – | 50 |
| Boston | – | 75 |
| Philadelphia | – | 30 |
| Atlanta | 20 | – |
| Miami | – | 40 |
| Washington, D.C. | 30 | – |
| Pittsburgh | 40 | – |
| Cleveland | 25 | – |
| Detroit | 35 | – |

The costs associated with distributing the railroad cars are presented in the table that follows. Determine the minimum-cost shipping plan.

| | | | To | | |
|---|---|---|---|---|---|
| From | Atlanta | Washington | Pittsburgh | Cleveland | Detroit |
| New York | 40 | 30 | 50 | 60 | 90 |
| Boston | M | 50 | 70 | 90 | 100 |
| Philadelphia | 30 | 10 | 20 | 40 | 60 |
| Miami | 30 | 50 | 60 | 70 | M |

**10.** A producer of microcomputers manufactures its product in Los Angeles, Dallas, San Francisco, and Denver and maintains regional distribution centers in New York, Cleveland, Reno, and Tampa. The cost matrix that follows provides the shipping cost per microcomputer for every manufacturer-to-distribution-center combination. The matrix also provides information on origin availabilities and destination requirements. Determine a minimum-cost shipping plan for this company.

Regional Distribution Center

| Manufacturing Location | New York | | Cleveland | | Reno | | Tampa | | Availability |
|---|---|---|---|---|---|---|---|---|---|
| Los Angeles | | 45 | | 20 | | 20 | | 30 | 200 |
| Dallas | | 40 | | 25 | | 30 | | 35 | 75 |
| San Francisco | | 50 | | 25 | | 35 | | 40 | 105 |
| Denver | | 50 | | 30 | | 35 | | 35 | 150 |
| Requirement | 90 | | 75 | | 100 | | 195 | | |

# ▶ Selected References

Bradley, Stephen P., Arnoldo C. Hax, and Thomas L. Magnanti. *Applied Mathematical Programming*. Reading, Mass.: Addison-Wesley, 1977.

Dantzig, George B. *Linear Programming and Extensions*. Princeton, N.J.: Princeton University Press, 1963.

Hadley, George. *Linear Programming*. Reading, Mass.: Addison-Wesley, 1962.

Luenberger, D. G. *Linear and Nonlinear Programming*. Reading, Mass.: Addison-Wesley, 1985.

Markland, Robert E. *Topics in Management Science*, New York: Wiley, 1989.

Murty, K. G. *Linear Programming*. New York: Wiley, 1983.

Shapiro, Roy D. *Optimization Models for Planning and Allocation: Text and Cases in Mathematical Programming*. New York: Wiley, 1984.

# Decision Analysis

## Introduction

The managers of a company can significantly affect its success by the caliber of the decisions they make. Decision making is not the only function of a manager, but it is an important one. Two major factors influence the quality of a manager's decisions:

- Availability of information and opinions: Accurate and timely information is critical to making a good decision, but opinions are critical as well. Opinions are an analysis of the facts, hypotheses yet to be tested. According to author Peter Drucker, "The effective decision maker also knows that he starts out with opinions anyhow. The only choice he has is between using opinions as a productive factor in the decision making process and deceiving himself into false objectivity."[1]
- Mechanics of the decision process: With as much information and understanding as possible the manager must arrive at a decision by some evaluative process. The decision-making process used can significantly affect the quality of the decision made.

This tutorial will focus on the mechanics of the decision-making process. Management science techniques have been developed to help managers approach decision making in a rational fashion. The techniques are useful not only for arriving at a decision but also for helping managers understand the decision they are facing. We will use the following example to illustrate decision-making methods in this tutorial.

## Example T2.1

A first-tier automotive components supplier is trying to win a contract from a Big Three auto manufacturer to supply the

window-cranking mechanism for a new luxury sedan. The company must decide between two alternative manufacturing processes before submitting its proposal. Both processes can produce high-quality components and are acceptable to the auto manufacturer. The first alternative is a batch production process based on general purpose machines. The advantage of this approach is low fixed costs (equipment, training, and so on); however, variable costs are high because of high labor requirements. The second approach is to use special purpose, computer-controlled equipment in an assembly line. This approach requires a much greater investment in equipment and training but has lower variable production costs.

The auto manufacturer is offering a five-year contract for the window-cranking mechanism. The profitability of the contract depends on both the manufacturing technology chosen and the sales volume of the new luxury sedan. The supplier's accounting department has estimated the net present value (NPV) of the contract for both technologies under three sales-level assumptions—high, moderate, and low. These estimates appear in the payoff table in Figure T2.1.

A **payoff table** presents the potential economic outcomes of the alternatives available to the decision maker. The column headings of the table are **states of nature**—the potential future conditions facing the decision maker. Because the future is characterized by uncertainty, a payoff table typically presents a range of potential future events. In example T2.1, both the auto manufacturer and the supplier are uncertain about future sales of the new luxury automobile. The row headings of the table are the **decision alternatives,** the choices available to the decision maker. The outcomes are the table entries. In this problem the outcome of selecting the general purpose machinery *if* future demand turns out to be moderate is $1.5 million; that is, during the five years of the contract the time-discounted value of the difference between revenues and costs is equivalent to a profit today of $1.5 million.

Figure T2.1 is a payoff table because the outcomes are profits. However, decision problems frequently are stated in

[1]Peter F. Drucker, *Management: Tasks, Responsibilities, Practices* (New York: Harper & Row, 1974) p. 471.

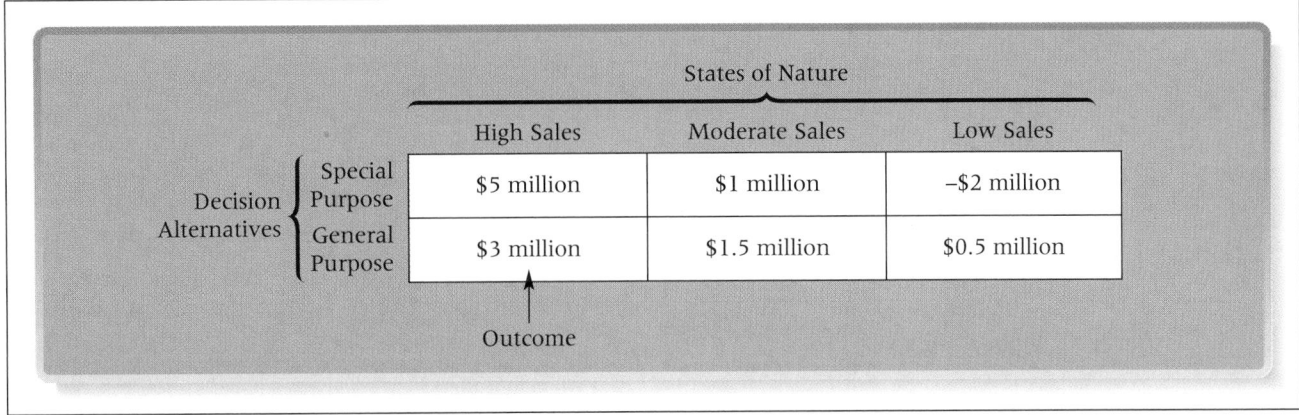

F I G U R E  T 2 . 1
Payoff Table for Example T2.1

terms of costs, and it is common to refer to a table such as Figure T2.1 in which the outcomes are costs as a **cost table.** Frequently, students are confused about how to modify decision-making methods when looking at costs instead of profits. In this tutorial we state the decision rules in terms of *best* and *worst* outcomes (rather than higher and lower outcomes). Stated in this fashion, the rules are easy to apply to both profits and costs. Another approach to a cost problem is to multiply all outcomes by $-1$ and treat the table as a payoff table.

The payoff table in Figure T2.1 shows the outcome of the decision depends on which state of nature actually occurs. In this tutorial we present various methods for making decisions. Such methods increase the likelihood that relevant information and opinions will be incorporated in the decision-making process and evaluated logically. Nevertheless, the result of any given method is not guaranteed to be optimal. If in this problem the decision maker selects the special purpose equipment, he will be making the wrong choice if the sales level is low, no matter what method was used to arrive at this decision.

## Dominated Alternatives

The first step in decision analysis is to determine whether there are any dominated alternatives. A **dominated alternative** is a decision alternative that has outcomes that are equivalent to or worse than the outcomes of another decision alternative for every state of nature. Stated mathematically, decision alternative $p$ dominates decision alternative $q$ if,

when outcomes are profits,

$$O_{pj} \geq O_{qj} \text{ for all states of nature } j$$

when outcomes are costs,

$$O_{pj} \leq O_{qj} \text{ for all states of nature } j$$
where $O_{pj}$ is the outcome for alternative $p$ under state of nature $j$

In Figure T2.1 neither alternative is dominated. The special purpose approach is better under the high-demand state of nature, and the general purpose approach is better under the moderate- and low-demand states of nature.

For purposes of illustration Figure T2.2 presents a payoff table with a dominated decision alternative. Note that alternative 1 is better than alternative 4 under states of nature A and C and equivalent under states of nature B and D. Thus, it would not make sense to consider decision alternative 4, because alternative 1 has outcomes that are always as good or better. Consequently, we should eliminate alternative 4 from further consideration.

## Decision Making Under Uncertainty

If a manager has the information presented in Figure T2.1 but is unable (or unwilling) to estimate the probability of occurrence of the various states of nature, the manager is facing a problem categorized as **decision making under uncertainty.** In this case a number of approaches are available for reaching a decision. Five possibilities are

- Optimistic criterion
- Pessimistic criterion
- Coefficient of optimism
- Equally likely
- Minimum regret

### Optimistic (Maximax) Criterion

The **optimistic criterion** is appropriate when (as the term says) the manager or decision maker is optimistic about the future. The idea behind this criterion is that the decision should be made to allow the decision maker the opportu-

F I G U R E   T 2 . 2
Payoff Table with a Dominated Alternative

F I G U R E   T 2 . 3
Optimistic Criterion

nity to get the best outcome possible. The decision approach is to

1.  Determine the best outcome for each alternative
2.  Choose the alternative with the best of the best outcomes

Figure T2.3 shows the optimistic criterion solution. Under this approach a manager would choose the special purpose equipment because the firm might make $5 million with this decision. If the general purpose equipment is chosen, the most the company can make is $3 million. The term *maximax* is sometimes applied to this decision criterion when the decision problem is described by a payoff table because the optimistic criterion will choose the alternative with the *maximum* of the *maximum* outcomes.

## Pessimistic (Maximin) Criterion

The **pessimistic criterion** is appropriate for a conservative decision maker. The decision approach is to

1.  Determine the worst outcome for each alternative
2.  Pick the alternative with the best of the worst outcomes

Figure T2.4 shows the decision alternative that the manager should choose using the pessimistic criterion. This criterion leads to the selection of the general purpose approach, because the worst that can happen under this alternative is a profit of $500,000. If the manager chooses the special purpose approach, the company could experience a loss of $2 million. The term *maximin* is sometimes used for this criterion, because for a payoff table the approach says to pick the alternative with the *maximum* of the *minimum* outcomes.

## Coefficient of Optimism (Hurwicz) Criterion

A decision maker is unlikely to be either totally optimistic or totally pessimistic. The **coefficient of optimism criterion,** suggested by Leonid Hurwicz, combines the best and the

| | High Sales | Moderate Sales | Low Sales | Worst Outcome |
|---|---|---|---|---|
| Special Purpose | $5 million | $1 million | –$2 million | –$2 million |
| General Purpose | $3 million | $1.5 million | $0.5 million | $0.5 million ✓ |

FIGURE  T2.4
Pessimistic Criterion

| | Best Outcome | Worst Outcome | Weighted Outcome |
|---|---|---|---|
| Special Purpose | $5 million | –$2 million | (0.7)*(5) + (0.3)*(–2) ✓ = $2.9 million |
| General Purpose | $3 million | $0.5 million | (0.7)*(3) + (0.3)*(0.5) = $2.25 million |

FIGURE  T2.5
Coefficient of Optimism (Hurwicz) Criterion

worst possible outcomes for a given alternative in a weighted average that reflects the level of optimism of the decision maker. We calculate the weighted average outcome by using the equation

$$\begin{array}{c} weighted \\ average \\ outcome \end{array} = (\alpha)\left(\begin{array}{c} optimistic \\ outcome \end{array}\right) + (1 - \alpha)\left(\begin{array}{c} pessimistic \\ outcome \end{array}\right)$$

where the coefficient $\alpha$ ($0 \leq \alpha \leq 1$) represents the decision maker's degree of optimism. When $\alpha = 1$, the decision maker is totally optimistic, and the weighted average outcome for a given alternative is the best outcome possible. When $\alpha = 0$, the decision maker is totally pessimistic, and the weighted average outcome for a given alternative is the worst outcome possible. Figure T2.5 shows the decision alternative that should be chosen using the coefficient of optimism criterion with $\alpha = 0.7$.

## Equally Likely Criterion

The coefficient of optimism approach has an advantage over the optimistic and pessimistic approaches because it considers more information by combining two outcomes for each decision alternative. The **equally likely criterion** uses all the information available by taking a weighted average of

*all* outcomes for each decision alternative. Because the manager does not have probability estimates for the states of nature, the manager assumes they are equally likely to occur. Thus, under the equally likely criterion the manager calculates a simple average of the outcomes for each decision alternative, as shown in Figure T2.6. Because this example has three states of nature, we assume the probability of each one to be one-third, i.e., 33.33 percent. The equally likely outcome is the average outcome we would expect if we had the same decision to make a great number of times and the probability that each state of nature would occur were indeed one-third.

## Minimax Regret Criterion

Rather than looking at the actual outcomes, a manager can consider the relative differences between outcomes under each decision alternative for a given state of nature. To facilitate such an analysis the manager constructs a **regret matrix.** To construct the regret matrix, each state of nature is analyzed in turn by assuming it has occurred. The manager compares the outcome for each decision alternative with the best outcome under that state of nature and enters the monetary difference in the regret matrix. Figure T2.7 shows the regret matrix for example T2.1. The entry for the

| | High Sales (1/3) | Moderate Sales (1/3) | Low Sales (1/3) | Equally Likely Outcome |
|---|---|---|---|---|
| Special Purpose | $5 million | $1 million | –$2 million | $(5 + 1 − 2) ÷ 3$ = $1.33 million |
| General Purpose | $3 million | $1.5 million | $0.5 million | $(3 + 1.5 + 0.5) ÷ 3$ ✓ = $1.67 million |

FIGURE T2.6
Equally Likely Criterion

| | High Sales | Moderate Sales | Low Sales | Maximum Regret |
|---|---|---|---|---|
| Special Purpose | 0 | $0.5 million | $2.5 million | $2.5 million |
| General Purpose | $2 million | 0 | 0 | $2 million ✓ |

FIGURE T2.7
Minimum Regret Criterion

special purpose alternative under the high-demand state of nature is zero, because if high demand occurs, the special purpose alternative provides the best outcome and the company would have no regrets about choosing it. If demand is high and the company chooses the general purpose alternative, the result is a regret of $2 million, because the company will earn $3 million with general purpose equipment but could have earned $5 million with the special purpose equipment. Similarly, if the demand is moderate and the company chooses the special purpose equipment, the regret will be $500,000, because it could have earned that much more under moderate demand by selecting special purpose equipment.

The regret matrix has three axioms:

- Regrets are always positive or zero: The decision maker either does or does not have regrets about a decision.
- There is always at least one zero under each state of nature in the regret matrix: Either one alternative is best (with a regret of zero), or there is a tie for the best alternative.
- Regrets are always bad: Whether the manager uses a payoff table (profits) or a cost table, the regret matrix

shows what the company would regret if it selected that alternative under a particular state of nature.

Once the regret matrix is constructed, the manager compares the maximum regret for each decision alternative and selects the alternative with the *minimum* of the *maximum* regrets, hence the term **minimax regret criterion.**

## Decision Making Under Risk

In **decision making under risk** the manager or decision maker has estimates of the probabilities of the various states of nature or is willing to make them. A popular decision criterion that uses these probability estimates is the expected value criterion. This technique is illustrated for example T2.1, and Figure T2.8 shows probabilities for the states of nature. This figure shows that the decision maker thinks there is a 30 percent chance that demand for the new luxury car will be high, a 50 percent chance that demand will be moderate, and a 20 percent chance that demand will be low. The manager should remember two rules of probability in assigning probability estimates to states of nature:

F I G U R E   T 2 . 8
Payoff Table with State of Nature Probabilities

- The probability of each state of nature must be between zero and one.
- The sum of the probabilities of all states of nature must be exactly one.

## Expected Value Criterion

The **expected value criterion** is useful when decision makers view the decision as being fairly routine—one of many similar decisions that they make regularly. Under the expected value criterion the manager calculates the expected value for each alternative by using the probability estimates specified for the states of nature. The expected value is the long-run average outcome that would result if we faced exactly the same decision many, many times and always chose the same alternative.

If in example T2.1 the manager repeated the decision many times and always chose the special purpose approach, sometimes demand for the car would be high and the

company would make $5 million, sometimes demand would be moderate and it would make $1 million, and sometimes demand would be low and the company would lose $2 million. In the long run, it is assumed high demand would occur 30 percent of the time, moderate demand would occur 50 percent of the time, and low demand would occur 20 percent of the time. Therefore, the long-run average outcome from facing this decision problem an infinite number of times and always selecting the special purpose alternative would be

$$(0.3)(\$5 \text{ million}) + (0.5)(\$1 \text{ million}) + (0.2)(-\$2 \text{ million}) = \$1.6 \text{ million}$$

Figure T2.9 shows that based on the expected value criterion the best alternative is to use general purpose equipment. We should note that in actuality the company would never earn a profit of $1.75 million: It will earn $3 million or $1.5 million or $0.5 million. The expected value is the long-run average outcome if the same decision situation were repeated many times.

## Decision Trees

The expected value solution shown in Figure T2.9 can be represented as a **decision tree**, as shown in Figure T2.10. A square node represents a decision, in this case special purpose versus general purpose equipment. A circular node represents chance events—in this case the future states of nature. In a decision tree we label each state of nature branch with the probability of that state of nature and its associated outcome. We calculate the expected value by multiplying the outcome of each branch coming out of the circular node by its associated probability and adding them up. Note that we place the resulting expected value near the circular node. We indicate the optimal choice by putting hash marks on the best decision branch.

The decision tree format of Figure T2.10 contains the same information as the payoff table in Figure T2.9. How-

F I G U R E   T 2 . 9
Expected Value Criterion

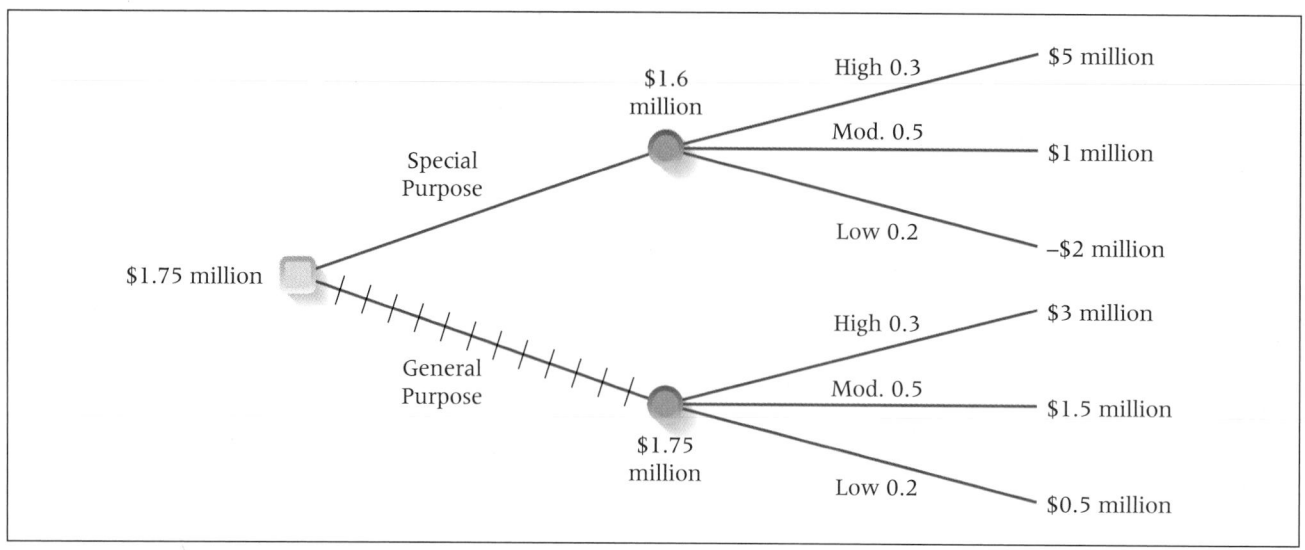

FIGURE  T2.10
Decision Tree Format for the Expected Value Problem

ever, the decision tree format is useful when considering the effect of additional information on the decision process.

## Decision Making with Additional Information

Managers often can obtain additional information about the probabilities of the states of nature to facilitate the decision process. Additional research, either internally or through consultants, is one source of additional information as to which state of nature is likely to occur. Two important questions about additional information are "What is the information worth?" and "How should I make my decision in light of the additional information?" We can use decision trees and Bayes' theorem to answer these questions. A critical factor in the value of additional information is the accuracy of the information source. As a first step in understanding how to evaluate additional information, we can determine the value of *perfect* information.

## Expected Value of Perfect Information

A meaningful measure of the value of perfect information is the long-run average improvement that would result from having the information available. This is known as the *expected value of perfect information*. To calculate this we must first calculate the long-run average outcome with the perfect information, or the expected value with perfect information. With perfect information decision makers cannot control which state of nature will occur, but they can

identify the best alternative for a given state of nature. Thus, we calculate the expected value with perfect information by using the *best* outcome under each state of nature, as shown in Figure T2.11. If we know the expected value *with* perfect information and the optimal expected value from the previous analysis, it is easy to determine the expected value *of* the perfect information. The **expected value of perfect information** is the difference between the expected value with perfect information and the optimal expected value. For example T2.1 it is

$$\$2.35 \text{ million} - \$1.75 \text{ million} = \$600,000$$

| | High Sales (0.3) | Moderate Sales (0.5) | Low Sales (0.2) |
|---|---|---|---|
| Special Purpose | $5 million | $1 million | −$2 million |
| General Purpose | $3 million | $1.5 million | $0.5 million |

Expected Value with Perfect Information
= (0.3)(5) + (0.5)(1.5) + (0.2)(0.5)
= $2.35 million

FIGURE  T2.11
Calculation of the Expected Value with Perfect Information

Thus, if perfect information were available to the company in example T2.1, it would be worth $600,000. The more difficult and practical question is "What is imperfect information worth?"

## Accuracy of Additional Information

Suppose the company in example T2.1 can obtain additional information regarding the sales potential of the new luxury sedan in the form of the opinion of Arlene Jean (A. J.) Zipp, noted auto industry analyst. Zipp has predicted the success of a number of new car introductions and has had a good deal of success in doing so. When evaluating a new car, Zipp predicts that a car will either be a hit or a miss. Although she has only two categories for her prediction and there are three sales outcome categories in this example, this will not be a problem.

Suppose the auto supplier has Zipp's hit or miss predictions for fourteen previous new car introductions and has classified the actual successes of these introductions according to the classification scheme of high, moderate, and low sales, as shown in Figure T2.12. The first table in this figure shows that the five times that actual demand for a new car was high, A. J. Zipp predicted a hit four times and predicted a miss once. In the five new car introductions that saw moderate actual demand, Zipp predicted a hit three times

and a miss two times. New car demand was low four times, and Zipp predicted a miss three of four times.

The second table shows the same information expressed as **conditional probabilities**. For example, five of the nineteen new cars introduced had high demand, and four of those five times Zipp predicted a hit, while one of the five times she predicted a miss. These conditional probabilities are expressed in statistical notation as

$$P(\text{hit}|\text{high}) = \frac{4}{5} = 0.8$$

$$P(\text{miss}|\text{high}) = \frac{1}{5} = 0.2$$

These conditional probabilities are representative of Zipp's accuracy in predicting new car demand. When the resulting demand is high, Zipp predicts a hit 80 percent of the time and incorrectly predicts a miss 20 percent of the time. To make use of this accuracy information, we use Bayes' theorem to calculate some new probabilities.

## Bayes' Theorem

Figure T2.13 shows how to use Bayes' theorem in this problem. The state of nature probabilities we introduced earlier are called **prior probabilities** in Bayes' theorem. The conditional probabilities in Figure 2.13 show how accurate the information source (A. J. Zipp) has been in the past. With prior and conditional probabilities we can use Bayes' theorem to calculate **marginal probabilities**, which indicate how likely it is that Zipp will predict a hit or miss in

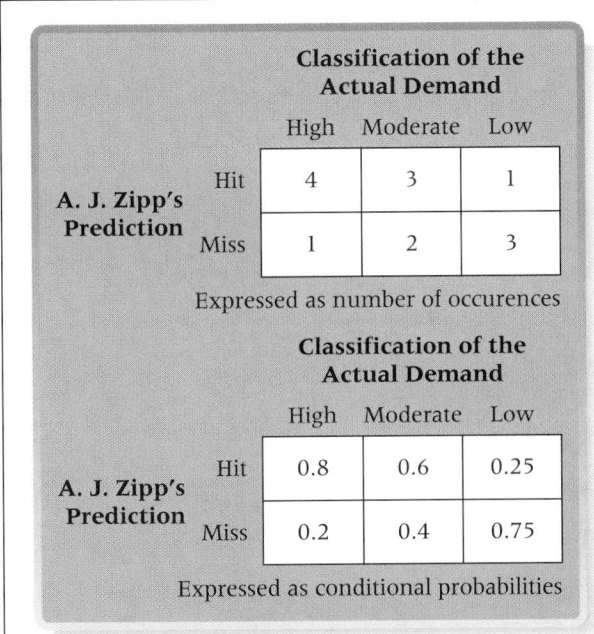

FIGURE T2.12
Accuracy of A. J. Zipp's Predictions Based on Fourteen Previous New Car Introductions

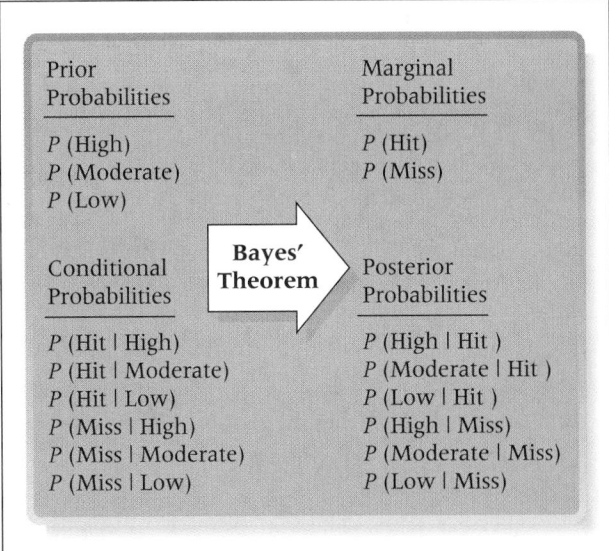

FIGURE T2.13
Use of Bayes' Theorem in Assessing Additional Information

the current situation, and **posterior probabilities,** which indicate how likely it is that the actual demand will be high, moderate, or low, given Zipp's prediction of hit or miss.

Frequently, students have trouble distinguishing between $P(\text{hit}|\text{high})$ and $P(\text{high}|\text{hit})$. $P(\text{hit}|\text{high})$ is the conditional probability that indicates how likely it is that Zipp will predict a hit, given that demand will turn out to be high. This is a measurement of Zipp's accuracy, based on previous experience. If Zipp predicts a hit, $P(\text{high}|\text{hit})$ tells us how likely it is that demand will actually turn out to be high. In other words, this is the probability that demand will be high when Zipp predicts a hit. This probability, the posterior probability, depends on two factors:

1.  Zipp's demonstrated accuracy [represented by conditional probabilities such as $P(\text{hit}|\text{high})$]
2.  The likelihood of high demand in our situation (represented by the prior probabilities)

Figure T2.14 gives the equations of **Bayes' theorem** that we use to calculate the marginal and posterior probabilities. The student new to decision analysis typically finds these equations difficult to use. Fortunately, there is a calculation device, the Bayes' tree, that makes the process much easier and allows the student to develop an intuitive understanding of Bayes' theorem. A word of warning is in order: Do not confuse the Bayes' *tree* with *decision* trees. A Bayes' tree is a device that simplifies the calculation of probabilities using Bayes' theorem. A decision tree is a device for evaluating decisions.

Figure T2.15 shows a Bayes' tree for this problem. Note that the tree is drawn vertically to help distinguish it from the decision tree, which is drawn horizontally (see Figure T2.10) The first set of branches in the Bayes' tree is for the

**Given:**

States of nature $S_1$, $S_2$, ..., $S_n$ with related probabilities $P(S_1)$, $P(S_2)$, ..., $P(S_n)$. Additional information predictions $I_1$, $I_2$, ..., $I_m$ and related conditional probabilities

$$\begin{matrix} P(I_1|S_1) & \cdots & P(I_m|S_1) \\ \vdots & \ddots & \vdots \\ P(I_1|S_n) & \cdots & P(I_m|S_n) \end{matrix}$$

**Calculate:**

Marginal Probabilities

$$P(I_t) = \sum_j P(I_t|S_j)P(S_j)$$

Posterior Probabilities

$$P(S_j|I_t) = \frac{P(I_t|S_j)P(S_j)}{P(I_t)}$$

prior probabilities, which are the initial probability estimates of the states of nature. The second set of branches is for the conditional probabilities, which depict the accuracy of the information source (in this case A. J. Zipp). Note that we place the conditional probabilities under the appropriate prior probability branches. The next step in the Bayes' tree method is to multiply down the tree—we multiply each conditional probability by the prior probability of the branch from which it is drawn. Under the branch at far left 0.24 is the result of multiplying the prior probability of high demand (0.3) by the probability that Zipp will predict a hit

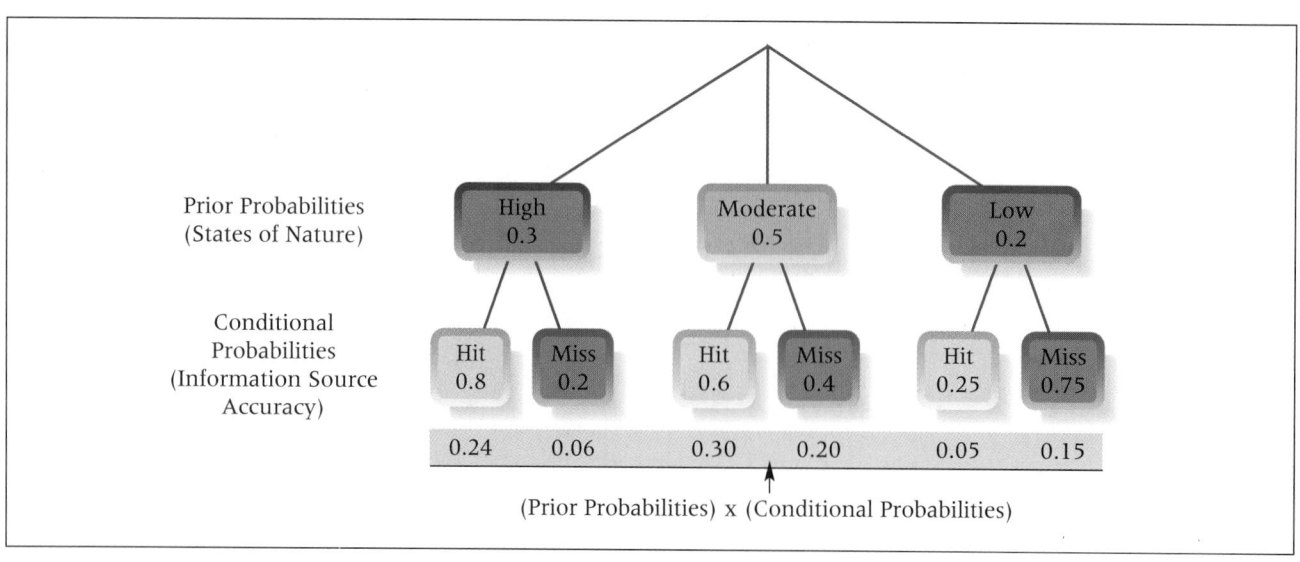

Bayes' Theorem Calculation Using a Bayes' Tree

given high demand (0.8). Similarly, we obtain the next value (0.06) by multiplying 0.3 by 0.2.

The results of the multiplication process provide a lot of information about what A. J. Zipp is likely to do if she makes a prediction in this case. There are three circumstances under which she can predict the new car to be a hit, and we know how likely each is. There is a 24 percent chance she will predict a hit and that actual demand will turn out to be high. There is a 30 percent chance she will predict a hit and the demand will be moderate and a 5 percent chance she will predict a hit and demand will be low. Similarly, there is 6 percent chance she will predict a miss and the demand will turn out to be high, a 20 percent chance she will predict a miss and demand will turn out to be moderate, and a 15 percent chance she will say miss and demand will turn out to be low. These six potential outcomes, which result from the combination of two predictions and three results, are the only outcomes possible, so these probabilities must add up to 1 (students should check this themselves). Note again that these probabilities result from multiplying the prior probabilities and the conditional probabilities, so these results depend both on the current situation, represented by the prior (state of nature) probabilities and A. J. Zipp's historical accuracy, represented by the conditional probabilities.

Calculating the marginal probabilities now is a simple matter. The marginal probabilities indicate how likely Zipp is to predict a hit or a miss in the current situation. Note that the Bayes' tree shows the likelihood Zipp will predict a hit in association with each of the three states of nature (high, moderate, and low demand). The probability Zipp will predict a hit is the sum of these probabilities, or

$$P(hit) = 0.24 + 0.3 + 0.05 = 0.59$$

Similarly, the probability that Zipp will predict a miss is the sum of the probabilities from the multiplication process in the Bayes' tree in which the prediction is miss, or

$$P(miss) = 0.06 + 0.2 + 0.15 = 0.41$$

Once we have the marginal probabilities it is easy to calculate the posterior probabilities. The posterior probability $P(high|hit)$ is the probability that demand will be high, given that Zipp predicts a hit. In the current situation the probability Zipp will predict a hit and demand will be high is 24 percent, and the probability Zipp will predict a hit is 59 percent, so

$$P(high|hit) = \frac{0.24}{0.59} = 0.41$$

Consider the implications of Bayes' theorem. Without Zipp's prediction the (prior) probability of high demand is 30 percent. However, if Zipp predicts a hit, Bayes' theorem revises the estimate of the probability of high demand to 41 percent.

Similarly, the probability that demand will be moderate when Zipp predicts a hit is

$$P(mod.|hit) = \frac{0.30}{0.59} = 0.51$$

FIGURE T2.16
Results from Bayes' Theorem Calculations

**Marginal Probabilities**

$$P(hit) = 0.59$$
$$P(miss) = \frac{0.41}{1.00}$$

**Posterior Probabilities**

$$P(high|hit) = 0.24/0.59 = 0.41$$
$$P(mod.|hit) = 0.30/0.59 = 0.51$$
$$P(low|hit) = 0.05/0.59 = \frac{0.08}{1.00}$$

$$P(high|miss) = 0.06/0.41 = 0.15$$
$$P(mod.|miss) = 0.20/0.41 = 0.49$$
$$P(low.vbmiss) = 0.15/0.41 = \frac{0.37}{1.01}$$

Figure T2.16 summarizes the Bayes' theorem calculations for example T2.1. Note that the sum of the marginal probabilities is 1: Either Zipp will predict a hit, or she will predict a miss; there is no other option. Also, when we add up the posterior probabilities for the same prediction condition, they add up to 1. In Figure T2.16 the posterior probabilities for the *predict hit* condition add up to 1.01 because of rounding error. If the probabilities are rounded to three decimal places, they add up to 1 exactly (0.146 + 0.488 + 0.366).

## Evaluating and Using Additional Information

With the probabilities we calculated using Bayes' theorem, we can construct a modified decision tree to determine the value of additional information and how the decision should be made in light of the additional information. In this example suppose A. J. Zipp is willing to make a prediction about the success of the new luxury sedan for the auto supplier for the modest sum of $50,000. Is this a good deal, and if so, how should her prediction be used?

We can use the expected value of perfect information we calculated earlier to check whether the deal has potential. The expected value of perfect information is $600,000, and Zipp wants only $50,000, so although Zipp's information is imperfect, it may be worth $50,000. If Zipp had asked $600,000 for her information, it would clearly not be worth the money. The expected value of perfect information should always be calculated first. If the expected value of perfect information is less than the asking price of the imperfect information, the manager can dismiss the information source out of hand, because imperfect information cannot be worth more than perfect information. Calculating the expected value of perfect information also provides a check on the calculation of the **expected value of sample information.** The expected value of sample information is

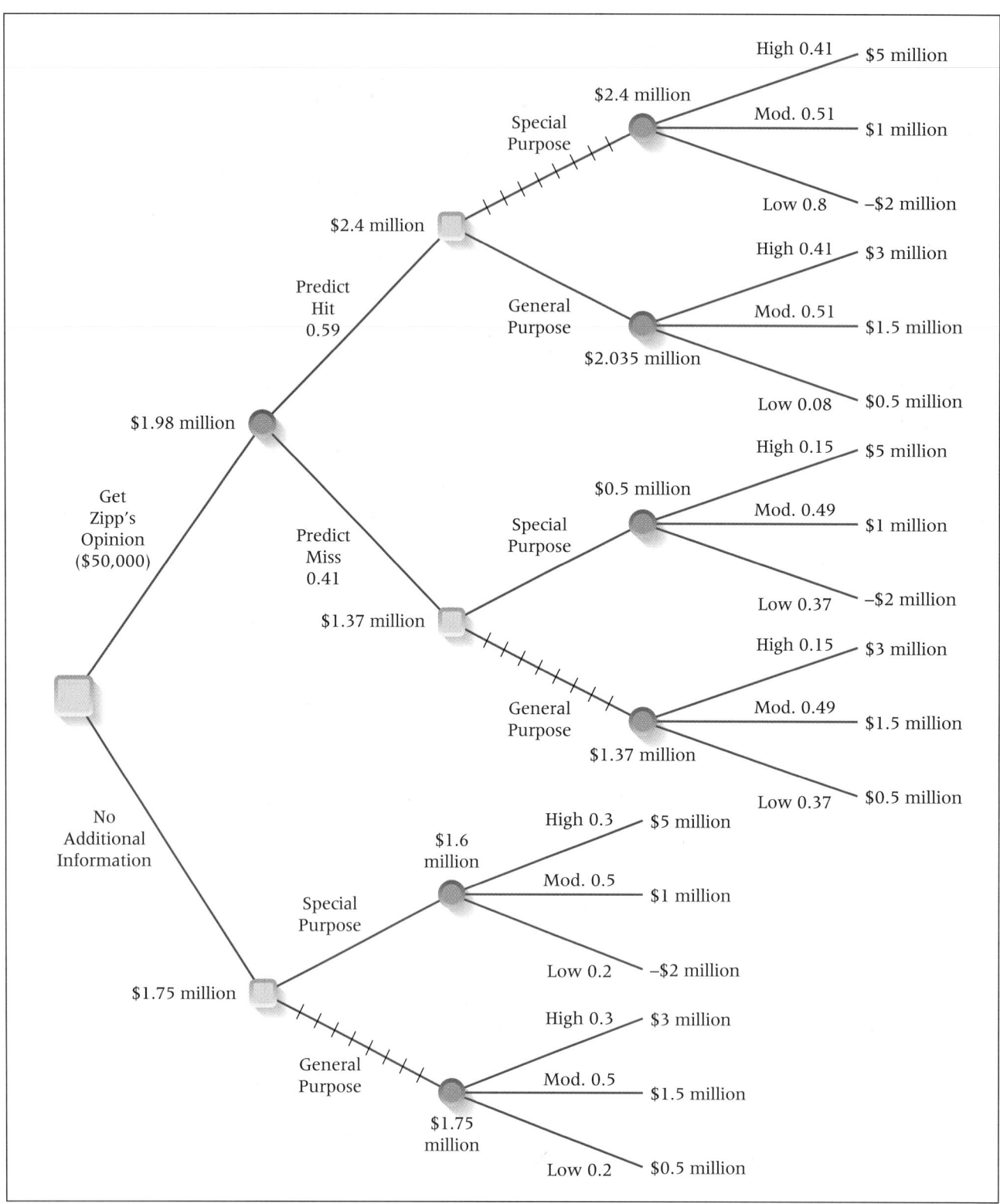

High 0.41 — $5 million
Mod. 0.51 — $1 million
Low 0.8 — –$2 million

$2.4 million

Special
Purpose

$2.4 million

High 0.41 — $3 million
Mod. 0.51 — $1.5 million
Low 0.08 — $0.5 million

General
Purpose

$2.035 million

Predict
Hit
0.59

$1.98 million

Get
Zipp's
Opinion
($50,000)

High 0.15 — $5 million
Mod. 0.49 — $1 million
Low 0.37 — –$2 million

$0.5 million

Special
Purpose

Predict
Miss
0.41

$1.37 million

High 0.15 — $3 million
Mod. 0.49 — $1.5 million
Low 0.37 — $0.5 million

General
Purpose

$1.37 million

No
Additional
Information

High 0.3 — $5 million
Mod. 0.5 — $1 million
Low 0.2 — –$2 million

$1.6
million

Special
Purpose

$1.75 million

High 0.3 — $3 million
Mod. 0.5 — $1.5 million
Low 0.2 — $0.5 million

General
Purpose

$1.75
million

FIGURE T2.17
Decision Tree for Evaluating Additional Information

the difference between the expected value of the decision process *with* additional information and the value of the decision process *without* it. The expected value of sample information must always be less than or equal to the expected value of perfect information.

Figure T2.17 shows a decision tree constructed to evaluate A. J. Zipp's predictions. Although the tree looks complicated, it is actually fairly simple to construct. The layout of the tree (from left to right) corresponds directly to the chronology of the decision process in real life.

In real life the first decision is whether to get the additional information before making the decision, and the decision tree shows this as the first decision. If the decision maker decides not to obtain additional information, the decision maker faces the same decision problem as before. Note that the portion of the decision tree after the branch labeled *no additional information* is identical to the decision tree presented in Figure T2.10. If the company obtains additional information, the cost is $50,000, which is clearly shown on the *get Zipp's opinion* branch.

If the managers of the auto supply company decide to pay Zipp for her opinion, they must wait for her opinion before deciding whether to go with general purpose or special purpose equipment. They cannot tell Zipp which opinion to give them, but the marginal probabilities calculated from Bayes' theorem indicate a 59 percent chance she will predict a hit and a 41 percent chance she will predict a miss. Next, management has to evaluate the special purpose versus general purpose decision under two conditions—a hit prediction and a miss prediction.

Suppose A. J. Zipp predicts a hit for the new luxury sedan. Note that the part of the decision tree after the *predict hit* branch is identical to the original decision tree, except that the probability estimates have changed. Rather than using the prior probabilities [in other words, $P(\text{high})$], we use the posterior probabilities [in other words, $P(\text{high} \mid \text{hit})$], because the equipment decision is being evaluated under the assumption that Zipp predicts a hit. Before her prediction we estimated the probability of high demand at 30 percent. But with the hit prediction this estimate has increased to 41 percent. The probability of moderate demand has increased slightly (1 percent), and the probability of low demand has decreased by 12 percent. With the revised probabilities the expected value of the special pur-

pose alternative is greater than the general purpose alternative because it is more likely that demand will be high. Note that the expected value of both alternatives is greater with a hit prediction than it was initially. Again, this indicates that Zipp has some degree of accuracy in her predictions, and higher demand is more likely with a hit prediction.

The portion of the decision tree after the *predict miss* branch is again identical to the original decision tree, with the exception of the modified probabilities for the states of nature. The expected values of both alternatives are much lower than they were originally, because the miss prediction means there is only a 15 percent chance of high volume and a 37 percent chance of low volume. With a miss prediction the general purpose equipment is the best choice.

Now we have two expected values, depending on Zipp's prediction. If Zipp predicts a hit the expected value of special purpose equipment is best at $2.4 million. If Zipp predicts a miss the expected value of general purpose equipment is best at $1.37 million. Because probability estimates for Zipp's predictions are available, we can calculate the expected value of the whole decision process with additional information:

$$(0.59) \times (\$2.4 \text{ million}) + (0.41) \times (\$1.37 \text{ million}) = \$1.98 \text{ million}$$

With Zipp's opinion the expected value increases by $230,000 ($1.98 million − $1.75 million). Note that this is less than the $600,000 that perfect information is worth. However, because the expected value of Zipp's opinion is $230,000 and she is asking only $50,000 for it, it is rational to pay for her information. With Bayes' theorem and a decision tree, we have answered the two questions posed initially:

■ Yes, the auto supplier should pay for the additional information.

■ If Zipp predicts a hit, the supplier should select special purpose equipment. If Zipp predicts a miss, the supplier should select general purpose equipment.

Note that the type of equipment selected depends on Zipp's prediction (additional information). If the expected value calculations had shown that general purpose equipment should be selected under both predictions, Zipp's information would not have had an effect on the decision, and the value of her information would have been zero.

## ► Summary

Decision making is a critical function for a manager, and operations managers frequently make important decisions. Although external events play a part in the success of a decision, careful information gathering and a rational decision process are important compo-

nents, and they are the only components over which the decision maker has control.

This tutorial presented five techniques for making decisions when no probability estimates are available and the expected value approach when probability estimates exist. In addition, we presented Bayes' theorem as a tool that can be used with decision trees to determine whether a source of additional information is sufficiently accurate to justify its cost and how the additional information can effectively be used.

## ► Key Terms

| | | |
|---|---|---|
| Bayes' theorem | dominated alternative | optimistic criterion |
| coefficient of optimism criterion | equally likely criterion | payoff table |
| conditional probabilities | expected value criterion | pessimistic criterion |
| cost table | expected value of perfect information | posterior probabilities |
| decision alternatives | expected value of sample information | prior probabilities |
| decision making under risk | marginal probabilities | regret matrix |
| decision making under uncertainty | minimax regret criterion | states of nature |
| decision tree | | |

## ► Discussion Questions

1. Discuss the relative importance of the two factors (availability of information and opinions and mechanics of the decision process) that affect the quality of a decision.

2. Why should a manager eliminate a dominated decision alternative in the decision process? Would it ever be selected?

3. How do the decision criteria differ when evaluating costs and profits?

4. Is there a best criterion for decision making under uncertainty? Are there conditions that favor one method over another?

5. Why is Bayes' theorem necessary for evaluating additional information?

6. What is the difference between a conditional probabilities and posterior probabilities?

## ► Problems

1. Given the following payoff table,

**States of Nature**

| Alternatives | $S_1$ | $S_2$ | $S_3$ | $S_4$ |
|---|---|---|---|---|
| $A_1$ | 25 | 15 | 35 | 5 |
| $A_2$ | 22 | 18 | 25 | 12 |
| $A_3$ | 35 | 10 | 20 | 20 |
| $A_4$ | 20 | 18 | 20 | 7 |

a. Are any decision alternatives dominated? If so, which one(s)?

b. Pick the best alternative(s) based on the following criteria:
   Optimistic
   Pessimistic
   Coefficient of optimism ($\alpha = 0.6$)
   Equally likely
   Minimum regret

2. Given the following cost table,

**States of Nature**

| Alternatives | $S_1$ | $S_2$ | $S_3$ |
|---|---|---|---|
| $A_1$ | 20 | 15 | 10 |
| $A_2$ | 15 | 18 | 10 |
| $A_3$ | 25 | 10 | 7 |
| $A_4$ | 20 | 12 | 15 |

a. Are any decision alternatives dominated? If so, which one(s)?

b. Pick the best alternative(s) based on the following criteria:
   Optimistic
   Pessimistic
   Coefficient of optimism ($\alpha = 0.8$)
   Equally likely
   Minimum regret

3. Given the following payoff table,

**States of Nature**

| Alternatives | $S_1$ | $S_2$ | $S_3$ |
|---|---|---|---|
| $A_1$ | 200 | 145 | 90 |
| $A_2$ | 150 | 180 | 110 |
| $A_3$ | 245 | 120 | 75 |

Pick the best alternative using,

a. Coefficient of optimism ($\alpha = 0.7$)

b. Equally likely

c. Minimum regret

4. A sportswear company is planning to market a commemorative football sweatshirt at Enormous State University (ESU) this fall. Sales of commemorative sweatshirts in the past have been highly correlated with the team's record. Estimated

market demand based on the team's performance is as follows:

| Season | Sales (Units) |
|---|---|
| 10–11 wins, top rate bowl game | 20,000 |
| 8–9 wins, warm weather bowl game | 18,000 |
| 6–7 wins, some kind of bowl game | 12,000 |
| 4–5 wins, no bowl game | 7,000 |
| < 3 wins, new coach | 3,000 |

The sweatshirts can be sold during the regular season for $25 each. Sweatshirts not sold during the season can be sold to the bookstore for $7 each. Shirts can be ordered before the beginning of the season for $10 each. If demand exceeds the amount ordered before the season, additional shirts can be procured for $15 each.
Construct the payoff table for this problem. Determine the best alternative based on the minimum regret criterion.

5. In problem 4 suppose that by aggregating a number of predictions by prominent sportswriters, we have arrived at the following probabilities:

| Season | Probability |
|---|---|
| 10–11 wins | 0.05 |
| 8–9 wins | 0.25 |
| 6–7 wins | 0.40 |
| 4–5 wins | 0.20 |
| < 3 wins | 0.10 |

Determine the best alternative using the expected value criterion.

6. A purchasing manager for an electric motor manufacturer is facing a make-or-buy decision for a relay in a new electric motor. His decision hinges on whether demand for the new motor will be sufficient to cover the fixed costs to start production of the relay. The marketing department has made the following market share estimates:

| Market Share | Probability |
|---|---|
| 10% | 0.2 |
| 30% | 0.3 |
| 40% | 0.4 |
| 50% | 0.1 |

The manufacturing engineering department has prepared cost estimates for manufacturing the relay, and the purchasing department has received competitive price quotes. Both the in-house manufacturing estimates and the price quotes were made for quantities that correspond to the four

market share estimates. These cost estimates are summarized as follows:

| Market Share | NPV of In-house Manufacturing Costs (in hundred thousand dollars) | NPV of Purchase Costs (in hundred thousand dollars) |
|---|---|---|
| 10% | 28 | 12 |
| 30% | 36 | 34 |
| 40% | 40 | 44 |
| 50% | 44 | 54 |

Construct a decision tree for this problem that shows whether to make or buy the part based on the expected value criterion. Calculate the expected value of perfect information.

7. An enterprising business student is planning to sell drinks outside the ESU football stadium on football Saturdays. The student has one insulated beverage container and has to decide whether to bring iced tea or coffee. Drink sales depend on the weather at game time, with profits as shown in the table:

| | Weather | |
|---|---|---|
| | *Hot* | *Cold* |
| Iced Tea | $400 | $ 0 |
| Coffee | $100 | $300 |

The student has to prepare the beverage the night before the game, so he has to guess what the weather will be and prepare the appropriate beverage.

a. If the probability of hot weather during a game at this time of year is 60 percent, what beverage should he bring based on the expected value criterion?

b. The local weather forecaster has demonstrated the following accuracy in predicting the weather for the previous twenty days:

| | Actual Weather | |
|---|---|---|
| Forecaster's Prediction | *Hot* | *Cold* |
| Hot | 8 | 3 |
| Cold | 2 | 7 |

Using Bayes' theorem and a decision tree, determine the value of the forecaster's information. If the information has value, determine how the student should use the information in making the beverage decision.

8. A major oil exploration company is trying to determine whether to drill for oil on a particular piece of land. Based on the location and history of similar drilling attempts, the company has determined the following probabilities for the results of drilling:

| Result | Probability |
|--------|-------------|
| Gusher | 0.05 |
| Moderate find | 0.35 |
| Dry hole | 0.6 |

   If the drilling results in a gusher, the company estimates the NPV of the find at $15 million. If the result is a moderate find, the NPV is $6 million. If the drilling results in a dry hole, the company will lose $2 million in drilling expenses. As an alternative, the company can sell the property to another exploration company for $1 million. Construct the payoff table for this problem, and determine the best course of action, using the expected value criterion.

9.   In problem 8 the company can obtain additional information from a seismic survey. If a seismic survey finds a dome structure, the probability of an oil deposit is greater (see figure).

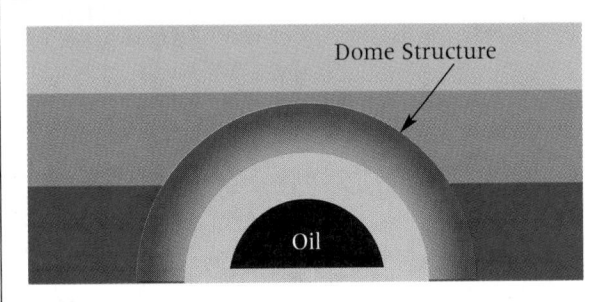

The accuracy of a dome structure in predicting the existence of oil is as follows:

| | **Results from Drilling** | | |
|---|---|---|---|
| | *Gusher* | *Moderate Find* | *Dry Hole* |
| **Dome** | 0.6 | 0.5 | 0.4 |
| **No Dome** | 0.4 | 0.5 | 0.6 |

   A seismic survey costs $500,000. Using Bayes' theorem and a decision tree, determine whether the survey should be conducted and, if so, how the results should be used.

10.   Slurry Chemical Co. produces Slime-away, a degreasing solution used in the metal-stamping industry. The active ingredient in Slime-away, trisodium phosphate, has recently been linked to a decrease in the southeastern slimey salamander population. The evidence is circumstantial, and the EPA has begun a study of the problem. The results of the study are due in two years. If the study proves that trisodium phosphate is responsible for the decreasing salamander population, the EPA will ban it. Slurry Chemical is trying to decide whether to stop using trisodium phosphate and switch to triglycerol sulfate, which is viewed as a safer chemical. The management of Slurry chemical has been presented with the following options:

■   Switch to triglycerol sulfate. During the next two years this option will increase raw material costs by $1.5 million. If the EPA concludes trisodium phosphate is the cause of the salamander problem, the company will be spared adverse publicity and high changeover costs. If trisodium phosphate is not the cause of the salamander problem, Slurry can switch back to trisodium phosphate at no additional cost.

■   Wait for the results of the EPA study. If the EPA bans trisodium phosphate, the company will have to change quickly to triglycerol sulfate. The switching costs will be higher, and sales will suffer because of the negative publicity. Total costs, if the company waits and the EPA bans trisodium phosphate, are estimated at $4 million. However, if the company waits for the EPA report and trisodium phosphate is not the cause of declining salamander populations, it will have saved $1.5 million in increased raw material costs.

Chemists for Slurry Chemical have estimated there is a 40 percent chance the EPA will ban trisodium phosphate.

a.   Construct the cost table for this problem. Determine the best decision alternative based on the expected value approach. Calculate the expected value of perfect information.

b.   Slurry's chemists can do short-term exposure tests on trisodium phosphate to get a better estimate of the likelihood that the EPA will ban it. They have done some research to compare the results of the short-term exposure test with the EPA's more exhaustive testing and have come up with the following probability estimates:

| | | **EPA Action** | |
|---|---|---|---|
| | | *Ban* | *No Ban* |
| **Short-term Exposure** | *Safe* | 0.1 | 0.8 |
| **Test Results** | *Unsafe* | 0.9 | 0.2 |

Slurry's chemists estimate the cost of running the short-term exposure test at $400,000. Using Bayes' theorem and a decision tree, determine whether Slurry should run the tests and, if so, how it should use the results.

## ► Selected References

Dannenbring, David G., and Martin K. Starr. *Management Science: An Introduction.* New York: McGraw-Hill, 1981.

Drucker, Peter F. *Management: Tasks, Responsibilities, Practices.* New York: Harper & Row, 1974.

Markland, Robert E. and James R. Sweigart. *Quantitative Methods: Applications to Managerial Decision Making.* New York: Wiley, 1987.

# Linear Programming

## Introduction

**Linear programming** involves the general problem of finding the best way to allocate scarce resources among competing activities. This allocation problem arises naturally in a number of situations, such as scheduling production to maximize profits, mixing ingredients for a product to minimize costs, selecting an optimum portfolio of investments, allocating sales personnel to sales territory, and defining a least cost shipping network. In each of these situations the common requirement is to allocate some type of scarce or limited resource to some specific activity. Because the resources generally produce profits or incur costs, the linear programming problem involves allocating the scarce resources so as to maximize profits or minimize costs.

Since George Dantzig introduced the simplex method for solving linear programming problems in 1947, it has been used in numerous applications. It is now a standard tool that has saved millions of dollars for companies all over the world. Many articles and textbooks about its applications are available. In fact, a 1970 IBM study estimated that 25 percent of all computer usage was devoted to some form of linear programming.

This tutorial presents a review of the basics of linear programming, but it neither delves into the theory of linear programming nor presents a comprehensive treatment of this vast subject. The material presented here is sufficient for understanding the applications presented in this book and for solving the end-of-chapter problems. The selected references at the end of the tutorial provide several opportunities for further study.

## Formulating a Linear Programming Model

We will begin our discussion of linear programming by illustrating the formulation of a typical production-scheduling problem. We will limit the scope of this example so that we can analyze and solve graphically the model that results.

### Example T3.1

The Braxton Machine Works produces machined metal parts to customers' specifications and operates in job shop fashion. Management is concerned with allocating excess production capacity to either or both of two new products:

Product 1: camshaft
Product 2: gear

The excess capacity that is available is as follows:

| Machine Type | Available Excess Capacity (machine hours per week) |
|---|---|
| Milling machine | 60 |
| Metal lathe | 40 |

The number of machine hours required to produce each unit of the two products is as follows:

| Machine Type | Required Machine Hours (machine hours per unit) | |
|---|---|---|
| | Product 1 | Product 2 |
| Milling machine | 5 | 10 |
| Metal lathe | 4 | 4 |

The marketing department has determined that the camshaft can be priced to produce a unit profit of $6 whereas the gear can be priced to produce a unit profit of $8.

We can formulate this problem situation as a linear programming model. Let $x_j$ ($j = 1, 2$) be the number of units (unknown) of product j to be produced in a week, where $x_1$ = number of camshafts produced per week and $x_2$ = number of gears produced per week. The $x_j$ are the **decision variables,** the values of which we seek to determine as we solve the problem. We are interested in maximizing profitability, so we can write the profit function for the model this way:

$$\text{Maximize } Z = \$6x_1 + \$8x_2 \qquad (\text{T3-1})$$

This is the **objective function** for our problem formulation. The values $6 and $8 are the profit parameters, or coefficients, of the objective function.

The resource availabilities in this situation are the excess capacities available on the two machines. A constraint must be developed for each of the two resource availabilities, which are referred to as **right-hand-side values,** or coefficients, and are the resource availability parameters.

The mathematical statement of the two resource availability constraints is

$$5x_1 + 10x_2 \le 60 \text{ hours (milling machine constraint)}$$
$$4x_1 + \ 4x_2 \le 40 \text{ hours (metal lathe constraint)} \qquad (\text{T3-2})$$

This is the **constraint set** for our problem formulation. The first constraint states that five hours per unit multiplied by the number of camshafts that are produced plus ten hours per unit multiplied by the number of gears that are produced must be less than or equal to the sixty hours of available excess capacity for the milling machine. The second constraint states that four hours per unit multiplied by the number of camshafts that are produced plus four hours per unit multiplied by the number of gears that are produced must be less than or equal to the forty hours of available excess capacity for the metal lathe. In each of these constraints the coefficients of the decision variables $x_1$ and $x_2$ are the **physical rates of usage,** or **physical rates of substitution.** The physical rates of usage are the parameters of the constraint set. They tell us the rate at which the resources (milling machine hours or metal lathe hours) are used in the production of the desired end products ($x_1$ = camshafts, $x_2$ = gears).

Finally, we must define the **nonnegativity restrictions** for our problem formulation:

$$x_1 \ge 0, x_2 \ge 0 \qquad (\text{T3-3})$$

The nonnegativity restrictions simply state that the factory must make nonnegative amounts of each of the two products.

## Assumptions Used in Linear Programming

Five basic assumptions are used in formulating and solving linear programming models. First, there must be limited resources (workers, equipment, money, or raw material). Without resource restrictions there is simply no problem to be solved. Second, some explicit objective must need to be achieved. Typical objectives are to produce goods or services in a manner that maximizes profits or minimizes costs. Third, the objective function and constraints must be ex-

pressed as linear functions. For example, if it takes one hour to make a part and this part produces a $5 profit, two parts will take two hours to make and will produce a $10 profit. Fourth, all products and resources must be homogeneous. For example, all hours available on a particular machine are equally productive, and all parts produced on a particular machine are identical. Fifth, the decision variables in linear programming are restricted to nonnegative values, and they can take on fractional as well as integer values. For example, a linear programming solution may indicate to produce 9.33 gallons of a product.

## Mathematical Structure of the Linear Programming Model

Now we can state the general mathematical structure of linear programming models. We seek to determine the values of $x_j$, $j = 1, 2, \ldots, n$, that maximize the linear function

$$\text{Maximize } Z = c_1x_1 + c_2x_2 + \ldots + c_nx_n \qquad (\text{T3-4})$$

subject to the linear restrictions of

$$a_{11}x_1 + a_{12}x_2 + \ldots + a_{1n}x_n \le b_1$$
$$a_{21}x_1 + a_{22}x_2 + \ldots + a_{2n}x_n \le b_2$$
$$\vdots \qquad \vdots \qquad \vdots \qquad \vdots \qquad (\text{T3-5})$$
$$a_{m1}x_1 + a_{m2}x_2 + \ldots + a_{mn}x_n \le b_m$$

with $\qquad x_1 \ge 0, x_2 \ge 0, \ldots, x_n \ge 0 \qquad (\text{T3-6})$

where $a_{ij}$, $b_i$, and $c_j$ are known (given) parameters of the model. The $c_j$ are the parameters of the objective function, the $a_{ij}$ are the parameters of the constraint set, and the $b_i$ are the right-hand-side parameters. The linear function being maximized is the objective function. The linear restrictions are the constraint set. The nonnegativity restrictions are for the decision variables, the $x_j$.

This general linear programming model can have other forms. First, we may seek to minimize, rather than maximize, the objective function. Second, the constraints need not be of the form "less than or equal to" ($\le$) but instead can be of the form "greater than or equal to" ($\ge$), or they can be strict "equalities" (=).

## Graphical Solutions to Linear Programming Problems

For simple two-variable linear programming problems,[1] we can use a graphical approach to obtain a solution. The

[1]Strictly speaking, three-variable linear programming problems can also be solved graphically. However, it is very difficult to obtain such a solution graphically because of the complexity associated with drawing in three dimensions.

graphical solution also provides a comprehensive illustration of the basic concepts of linear programming. The graphical procedure is limited to two-variable problems, and the simplex procedure is used for problems that have more than two variables.

## Example T3.2

We will now illustrate the graphical solution procedure using the profit maximization production-scheduling model. This small problem has only two decision variables, so we can use a two-dimensional graphical procedure. The procedure involves constructing a two-dimensional graph with $x_1$ as the horizontal axis and $x_2$ as the vertical axis. The nonnegativity restrictions, $x_1 \geq 0$, $x_2 \geq 0$, require $(x_1, x_2)$ to lie on the positive sides of the two axes (if not actually on either axis); they are shown in Figure T3.1.

Now, let us superimpose the constraint set on these nonnegativity conditions. The constraint set is composed of two linear inequalities, which we represent with straight lines that form boundaries for permissible values of the decision variables, the $x_j$. We can plot each of the two constraints (inequalities) from two intercept points. We use the intercept points $(x_1 = 0, x_2 = 6)$ and $(x_1 = 12, x_2 = 0)$ to plot the straight line representing the milling machine constraint, $5x_1 + 10x_2 \leq 60$. This first constraint states that no $(x_1, x_2)$ value can lie above the line $5x_1 + 10x_2 \leq 60$. Similarly, we use the intercept points $(x_1 = 0, x_2 = 10)$ and $(x_1 = 10, x_2 = 0)$ to plot the straight line representing the metal lathe constraint, $4x_1 + 4x_2 \leq 40$. This second constraint signi-

fies that no $(x_1, x_2)$ value can lie above the line $4x_1 + 4x_2 \leq 40$. Figure T3.2 is the graphical representation of the constraint set superimposed on the nonnegativity conditions.

Figure T3.2 shows the region of permissible values of $x_1, x_2$. The final step in solving the problem is to pick out the point that maximizes the value of the objective function $Z = 6x_1 + 8x_2$. After a little practice this step becomes easy. To see how it is done we proceed by trial and error. We graph the objective function as a series of straight lines (often referred to as **isoprofit,** or "equal profit," lines in a profit maximization problem) beginning at the origin ($x_1 = 0, x_2 = 0$), where the objective function has a value of $Z = 6x_1 + 8x_2 = 6(0) + 8(0) = 0$, and continuing upward, and to the right as a series of parallel lines to the point ($x_1 = 8, x_2 = 2$), where the objective function has its maximum value of $Z = 6x_1 + 8x_2 = 6(8) + 8(2) = 64$. The desired optimal solution to this problem is $x_1 = 8$, $x_2 = 2$, which indicates that the Braxton Machine Works should produce eight camshafts and two gears with its excess capacity, maximizing profit at $64. Figure T3.3 is the graphical representation of the complete profit maximization production-scheduling model.

From Figure T3.3 we can state several important definitions:

1. Any set of $x_j$ that satisfies the constraint set is termed a solution to the linear programming model.
2. Any set of $x_j$ that satisfies the constraint set and the nonnegativity restrictions is termed a feasible solution to the linear programming model.

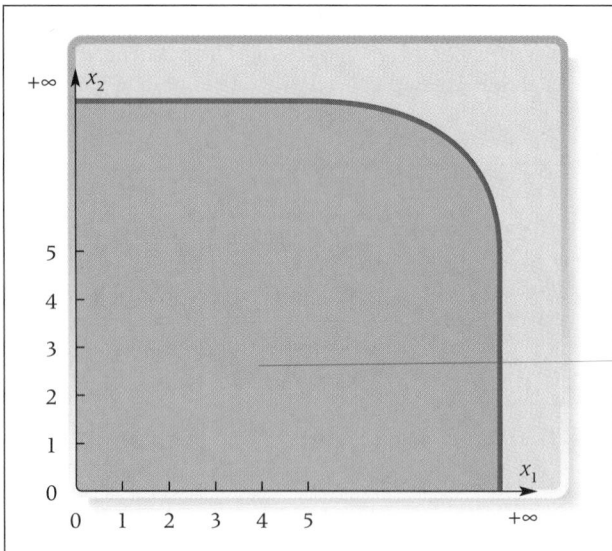

**FIGURE T3.1**
Graphical Representation—Nonnegativity Conditions

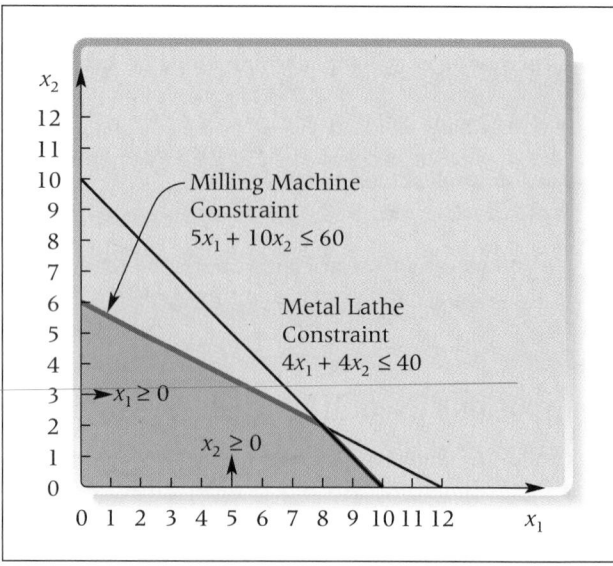

**FIGURE T3.2**
Graphical Representation—Nonnegativity Conditions and Constraint Set

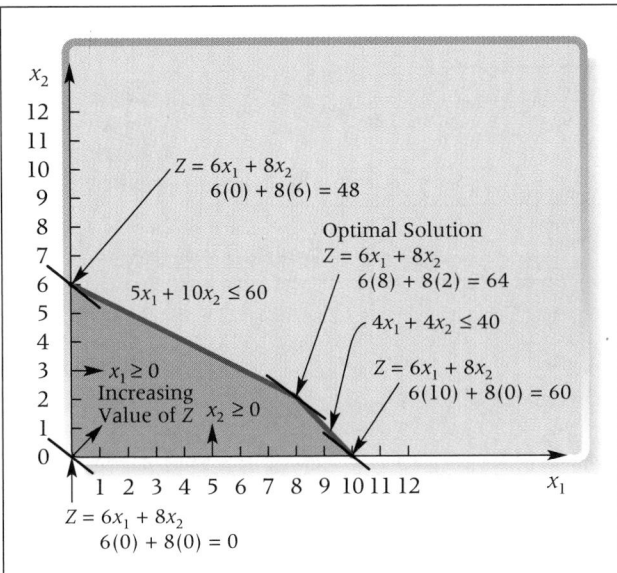

F I G U R E   T 3 . 3
Graphical Representation—Profit Maximization Production
Scheduling Model

3.   Any set of $x_j$ that satisfies the constraint set and the
      nonnegativity restrictions and optimizes (maximizes or
      minimizes) the objective function is termed an optimal
      feasible solution.

      Figure T3.3 illustrates these definitions. First, the **solu-
tion space** is defined by the constraint set that is bounded
by the two straight lines, $5x_1 + 10x_2 = 60$ and $4x_1 + 4x_2 = 40$.
Next, the **feasible solutions** are points within the **feasible
solution space** defined by the two constraints and the two
nonnegativity restrictions, $x_1 \geq 0$ and $x_2 \geq 0$. The feasible
solution space is shaded. Finally, the **optimal feasible
solution** is the point ($x_1 = 8$, $x_2 = 2$) within the feasible
solution space at which the value of the objective function
is the biggest [in other words, $Z = 6x_1 + 8x_2 = 6(8) + 8
(2) = 64$]. The values of the objective function, $Z$, are traced
over the feasible solution space, beginning at the origin
($x_1 = 0$, $x_2 = 0$), with a straight line that has the slope of the
objective function (Slope $= -c_1/c_2 = -6/8 = -3/4$). At
the origin the value of the objective function is obviously
$Z = 0$. As the isoprofit line with slope $= -3/4$ moves up and
to the right, the point ($x_1 = 0$, $x_2 = 6$) is reached, and at this
point $Z = 48$. Moving farther right and up we obtain the
point ($x_1 = 10$, $x_2 = 0$), at which the value of $Z = 60$. Finally,
we move to the point ($x_1 = 8$, $x_2 = 2$), which produces the
optimal feasible solution, $Z = 64$. To maximize profit we
have moved the isoprofit line (objective function) as far as
possible from the origin, increasing the values of $x_1$ and $x_2$,
but have remained within the feasible solution space.

# Solving Linear Programming Problems Using the Simplex Method

The **simplex method,** or **simplex algorithm,**[2] is an
algebraic procedure that uses a set of repetitive operations
to move to an optimal solution. It can be used to solve
problems consisting of many variables and constraints. In
practice, linear programming problems are solved by using
any of a number of linear programming computer software
packages. (The software package accompanying this book
allows you to solve linear programming problems.)

## Example T3.3

We will illustrate the steps in the simplex method by using
the Braxton Machine Works problem we formulated earlier
and solved graphically. This illustration will enhance your
understanding of linear programming in general and will
enable you to construct the input for computer programs
and to interpret the output from computer programs.

## Technical Steps in the Simplex Method

The technical steps in the simplex method are as follows for
the Braxton Machine Works problem.

**Step 1: Formulate the Problem**   Recall that our problem
formulation was

$$\text{Maximize (Profit) } Z = \$6x_1 + \$8x_2 \qquad \text{(T3-7)}$$

subject to
$$5x_1 + 10x_2 \leq 60$$
$$4x_1 + 4x_2 \leq 40 \qquad \text{(T3-8)}$$

with
$$x_1 \geq 0, \quad x_2 \geq 0 \qquad \text{(T3-9)}$$

**Step 2: Reformulate the Problem in Standard Linear
Programming Form**   To use the simplex method we must
adjust the original problem formulation. Each constraint
inequality is expanded by including a slack variable. The
**slack variable** represents the amount required to convert
the original constraint inequality to an equality. Think of
the slack variable as the amount of idle resources present.

For our problem we require two slack variables, $s_1$ for
the first constraint and $s_2$ for the second constraint. The
constraint equations are first rewritten as

$$5x_1 + 10x_2 + 1s_1 = 60 \qquad \text{(T3-10)}$$
$$4x_1 + 4x_2 + 1s_2 = 40$$

Then we adjust the constraint equations so that all variables
are represented in all equations. Any slack variable not

_____

[2] *Simplex* is a term used in n-dimensional geometry—it does not mean that
the method is simple!

| | Decision Variables | | | | Slack Variables | | | | | |
|---|---|---|---|---|---|---|---|---|---|---|
| $c_j$ | $c_1$ | $c_2$ | ... | $c_n$ | 0 | 0 | ... | 0 | | (Objective function coefficients) |
| $c_B$   **Basic Variables** | $x_1$ | $x_2$ | ... | $x_n$ | $s_1$ | $s_2$ | ... | $s_m$ | **Solution** | (Headings) |
| 0    $s_1$ | $a_{11}$ | $a_{12}$ | ... | $a_{1n}$ | 1 | 0 | ... | 0 | $b_1$ | |
| 0    $s_2$ | $a_{21}$ | $a_{22}$ | ... | $a_{2n}$ | 0 | 1 | ... | 0 | $b_2$ | (Constraint coefficients |
| ⋮    ⋮ | ⋮ | ⋮ | ⋱ | ⋮ | ⋮ | ⋮ | ⋱ | ⋮ | ⋮ | |
| 0    $s_m$ | $a_{m1}$ | $a_{m2}$ | ... | $a_{mn}$ | 0 | 0 | ... | 1 | $b_m$ | |
| $Z_j$ | $Z_1$ | $Z_2$ | ... | $Z_n$ | $Z_{s_1}$ | $Z_{s_2}$ | ... | $Z_{s_m}$ | Current value of objective function | (Contribution loss/unit) |
| $c_j - Z_j$ | $c_1 - Z_1$ | $c_2 - Z_2$ | ... | $c_n - Z_n$ | $c_{s_1} - Z_{s_1}$ | $c_{s_2} - Z_{s_2}$ | ... | $c_{s_m} - Z_{s_m}$ | | (Net contribution/unit) |

TABLE T3.1
General Form—Initial Simplex Tableau

associated with a constraint is given a coefficient of zero. The adjusted system of constraint equations is

$$5x_1 + 10x_2 + 1s_1 + 0s_2 = 60 \qquad \text{(T3-11)}$$
$$4x_1 + 4x_2 + 0s_1 + 1s_2 = 40$$

We also rewrite the objective function to reflect the addition of the two slack variables. Because they do not produce any profit, their coefficients are zero, and the reformulated objective function is

$$\text{Maximize } Z = 6x_1 + 8x_2 + 0s_1 + 0s_2 \qquad \text{(T3-12)}$$

Finally, the reformulated problem must have nonnegativity conditions for all variables, namely,

$$x_1 \geq 0, x_2 \geq 0, s_1 \geq 0, s_2 \geq 0 \qquad \text{(T3-13)}$$

**Step 3: Construct the Initial Simplex Tableau**  Table T3.1 presents the general form of the initial simplex tableau.

The initial simplex tableau is a representation of the standard linear programming form, with some supplemental rows and columns. The top row of the table presents the $c_j$, the objective function coefficients. The next row presents the headings for the various columns. The $m$ rows represent the constraint coefficients. Following is the $Z_j$ row, which represents the contribution loss per unit of the $j$th variable. The final row is the $c_j - Z_j$ row, which is the net contribution per unit of the $j$th variable. (We will have more to say about the $Z_j$ and $c_j - Z_j$ rows shortly.)

The far left column in the tableau gives the values of the objective function coefficients associated with the basic variables. With a set of ≤ constraints, the initial **basis** (set of basic variables) will consist of $m$ slack variables with $c_B$ values equal to zero. The next column is headed **Basic Variables** and lists those $m$ variables that are currently basic, or in the solution. The next $m + n$ columns contain the constraint coefficients. The final (far right) column displays the solution values of the basic variables.

Table T3.2 presents the initial simplex tableau for the Braxton Machine Works problem.

Pivot column
↓

| | $c_j$ | 6 | 8 | 0 | 0 | |
|---|---|---|---|---|---|---|
| $c_B$ | **Basic Variable** | $x_1$ | $x_2$ | $s_1$ | $s_2$ | Solution |
| Pivot row → 0 | $s_1$ | 5 | (10) | 1 | 0 | 60 |
| 0 | $s_2$ | 4 | 4 | 0 | 1 | 40 |
| | $Z_j$ | 0 | 0 | 0 | 0 | 0 |
| | $c_j - Z_j$ | 6 | 8 | 0 | 0 | |

Pivot element

TABLE T3.2
The Initial Simplex Tableau—Braxton Machine Works

The top row of Table T3.2 lists the $c_j$ values, or the contribution to profit associated with the production of one unit of each product. This row is a restatement of the reformulated objective function coefficients, and it remains the same for all subsequent tableaus. The first column, headed by $c_B$, lists the objective function coefficients, or profit per unit, for the variables in the solution at that stage of the problem solution. These "basic" variables in the initial solution are the two slack variables, $s_1$ and $s_2$, as shown in the second column. Their objective function coefficients are zero, because they contribute nothing to profit.

The coefficients of the constraint equations are listed in the rows of the tableau, directly under the headings for the respective variables. We can determine the substitution rates from the numbers in the various columns. For example, under the $x_1$ column are the numbers 5 and 4. This means that every unit of $x_1$ that is produced will require five units of the first resource and four units of the second resource.

The numbers shown in the Solution column refer to the number of units of each resource available. In the initial tableau this is a restatement of the right-hand side of each constraint equation.

The values in the $Z_j$ row, with the exception of the value under the Solution column, refer to the amount of gross profit that is given up by introducing one unit of that variable into the solution. The $Z_j$ value for the Solution column is the total profit for the solution. In the initial solution of a simplex problem, all values of $Z_j$ will be zero, because no real products are being produced.

The values in the $Z_j$ row are calculated by multiplying the elements in the $c_B$ column by the corresponding elements in the columns of the tableau and adding them. Performing these multiplications and additions, we obtain

$$Z_1 = 0(5) \quad + 0(4) = 0 \qquad \text{(T3-14)}$$
$$Z_2 = 0(10) + 0(4) = 0$$
$$Z_3 = 0(1) \quad + 0(0) = 0$$
$$Z_4 = 0(0) \quad + 0(1) = 0$$

A value in the $Z_j$ row represents the decrease in the value of the objective function that will result if one unit of the $j$th variable is brought into the solution.

In this initial simplex tableau we also observe that there is a zero in the $Z_j$ row in the last column (in other words $Z_0 = 0$ in the Solution column). This value is the objective function value, or profit, associated with the current basic solution. We obtained it by multiplying the current values of the basic variables, which are given in this last column, by their corresponding contributions to profit, as given in the $c_B$ column.

The final row, the $c_j - Z_j$ row, is determined by subtracting the appropriate $Z_j$ value from the corresponding objective function coefficient, $c_j$, for that column. This value is the difference between the contribution ($c_j$) and the loss

($Z_j$) that results from producing one unit of $x_j$. Each unit of $x_j$ brought into the solution will improve the value of the objective function by the amount $c_j$. For example, every unit of $x_1$ (camshaft) that Braxton produces will improve the objective function by the amount $c_1$, which is the $6 profit associated with each camshaft produced. The value of the objective function will also decrease by an amount $Z_1$ for each unit of $x_1$ that is produced. The net change in the objective function that results from producing one unit of $x_1$ is $c_1 - Z_1 = \$6 - 0 = \$6$. Each value in the $c_j - Z_j$ row represents the net profit, or net contribution, that is added by producing one unit of product j (if $c_j - Z_j$ is positive) or the net profit (or net contribution) that is subtracted by producing one unit of product j (if $c_j - Z_j$ is negative). Because there is no $c_0$ value, we do not compute $c_0 - Z_0$. Furthermore, because all the $Z_j$ values $j = 1, 2, \ldots, 4$ are equal to zero in the initial tableau, the $c_j - Z_j$ values in this example are identical to the coefficients in the $c_j$ row. Next we will show how to use the $c_j - Z_j$ row in performing an iteration.

**Step 4: Select the Variable to Bring into the Solution** We use the $c_j - Z_j$ row to determine which variable we should insert in the basis. Because we are maximizing profit in this example, a number in the $c_j - Z_j$ row represents the net profit that Braxton adds to its bottom line by producing one unit of j. Referring to the initial tableau, the $c_j - Z_j$ row shows that the objective function will increase by $6 for each unit of $x_1$ that Braxton produces and by $8 for each unit of $x_2$ that it produces. Because we are seeking to maximize profit, we naturally select $x_2$ to enter in the basis, because this choice will cause the greatest increase in net profit. This is the **variable entry criterion.**

**Variable Entry Criterion** The variable entry criterion is based upon the values in the $c_j - Z_j$ row of the simplex tableau. For a maximization problem the variable selected for entry is the one that has the largest (most positive) value of $c_j - Z_j$. When all values of $c_j - Z_j$ are zero or negative, we have the optimal solution. For a minimization problem the variable selected for entry is the one that has the smallest (most negative) value of $c_j - Z_j$. When all values of $c_j - Z_j$ are zero or positive, we have the optimal solution. For either maximization or minimization problems, if there are ties for the entering $c_j - Z_j$ value, we can break the tie arbitrarily (simply choose one of the corresponding variables for entry).

Applying the variable entry criterion to our present maximization example, the biggest $c_j - Z_j$ value is $c_2 - Z_2 = 8$. Thus, we choose $x_2$ as the variable to enter the basis.

**Step 5: Select the Variable to Leave the Solution** The Solution column and the column that contains the constraint equation coefficients for the entering variable $x_2$ are used to determine the variable to be removed from the basis as $x_2$ enters. We must determine which current basic variable is first driven to zero as we allow the current nonbasic variable $x_2$ to become basic. We do this by using the variable removal criterion.

## Variable Removal Criterion  The **variable removal criterion** is based upon the ratios formed as the values in the Solution column are divided by the corresponding values ($a_{ij}$ coefficients) in the column for the variable selected to enter the basis. Ignore any $a_{ij}$ values in the column that are zero or negative (do not compute the ratio). We choose as the variable to be removed from the basis the one that has the smallest ratio. In the case of ties between two or more variables for the smallest ratio, break the tie arbitrarily (simply choose one of the variables for removal). This variable removal criterion remains the same for both maximization and minimization problems.

In the variable removal criterion just stated, do not compute the ratios for any $a_{ij}$ values in the column (the denominators of the ratios) that are zero or negative. (Ratios involving either a zero or a negative number in the denominator are ignored, because they introduce a variable into the basis at either an infinite, or negative, level.)

Applying the variable removal criterion to our present problem, the following ratios are formed:

| Current Basic Variables | Solution ÷ $a_{i2}$ | Ratios |
|---|---|---|
| $s_1$ | 60 ÷ 10 | 60/10 = 6 (smallest) |
| $s_2$ | 40 ÷ 4 | 40/4 = 10 |

The current basic variable $s_1$ is replaced by the current nonbasic variable $x_2$. This occurs because the ratios we have formed indicate that $s_1$ is driven to zero first as $x_2$ is increased. The meaning of this ratio of "6" is that six units of entering product $x_2$ can be produced before the first constraint (corresponding to the current basic variable $s_1$) becomes binding. When $x_2 = 6$ and $s_1 = 0$, the first constraint is exactly satisfied, that is

$$5x_1 + 10x_2 + 1s_1 = 60 \qquad \text{(T3-15)}$$
$$5(0) + 10(6) + 1(0) = 60$$

If $x_2 > 6$, this constraint will be violated.

What we have accomplished so far is to identify the current nonbasic variable $x_2$, which will cause the greatest increase in profitability and determine the current basic variable $s_1$, to be removed from the basis (driven to zero) as $x_2$ is increased to the maximum possible value of six. These two steps have been done in a manner that maintains the feasibility of our solution.

## Step 6: Change the Solution—Perform the Pivoting Process, and Check the New Solution for Optimality  The next step in our basis-changing process requires the deter-

mination of our new solution by "pivoting" $x_2$ into the basis and pivoting $s_1$ out of the basis.

The **pivoting** process involves performing linear algebra row operations on the rows of the simplex tableau to solve the system of constraint equations in terms of the new set of basic variables. We initiate the pivoting process by identifying the variable $x_2$, to be entered in the basis by designating the **pivot column** (refer to Table T3.2). Similarly, we identify the variable $s_1$ to be removed from the basis by specifying the **pivot row** (refer to Table T3.2). We circle the element at the intersection of the pivot column and the pivot row to identify it as the **pivot element.** The pivot element is the number "10" in the simplex tableau, which is at the intersection of the row corresponding to leaving variable $s_1$ and the column corresponding to entering variable $x_2$ (refer to Table T3.2).

The actual pivoting operation involves two steps that are performed to obtain an identity matrix as the coefficient matrix of the new set of basic variables $x_2$ and $s_2$. The current basic variables must always form an identity matrix within the simplex tableau. Because $s_2$ was a basic variable in our previous solution, nothing needs to be done to its corresponding column. However, in the pivot column corresponding to the variable $x_2$ we need to obtain a 1 as the pivot element and zeros in all other positions. The two-step pivoting process proceeds as follows.

**Step 6a**  Converting the pivot element to 1 simply requires that we divide all values in the pivot row by 10. We immediately enter this new row in the second tableau, Table T3.3.

For our problem, the calculations for determining the new pivot row are

Pivot row (variable $s_1$): Divide the values in old row one by 10 to obtain new row one.

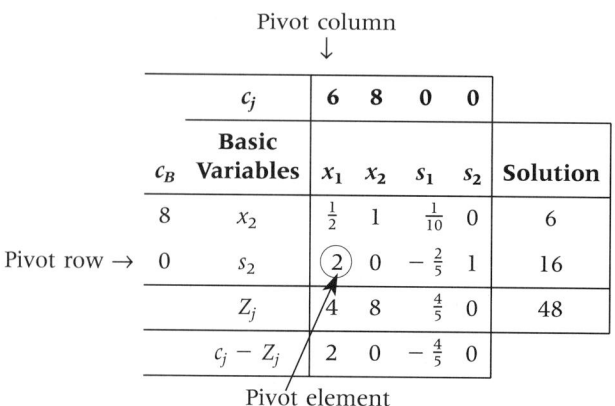

| | | $c_j$ | 6 | 8 | 0 | 0 | |
|---|---|---|---|---|---|---|---|
| $c_B$ | **Basic Variables** | | $x_1$ | $x_2$ | $s_1$ | $s_2$ | **Solution** |
| 8 | $x_2$ | | $\frac{1}{2}$ | 1 | $\frac{1}{10}$ | 0 | 6 |
| 0 | $s_2$ | | ②  | 0 | $-\frac{2}{5}$ | 1 | 16 |
| | $Z_j$ | | 4 | 8 | $\frac{4}{5}$ | 0 | 48 |
| | $c_j - Z_j$ | | 2 | 0 | $-\frac{4}{5}$ | 0 | |

Pivot column ↓

Pivot row →

Pivot element

TABLE 3.3
Second Simplex Tableau—Braxton Machine Works

| Column Heading | Pivot Row Calculation | New Pivot Row (Row One) | |
|---|---|---|---|
| $x_1$ | 5/10 | = 1/2 | |
| $x_2$ | 10/10 | = 1 (pivot element) | |
| $s_1$ | 1/10 | = 1/10 | |
| $s_2$ | 0/10 | = 0 | |
| Solution | 60/10 | = 6 | (T3-16) |

**Step 6b** The objective of the second step is to obtain zeros in all the elements of the pivot column, expect for the pivot element itself, of course. To do this we use elementary row operations that involve adding or subtracting the appropriate multiple of the new pivot row to or from the other original rows. Again, we use linear algebra to obtain a zero in the appropriate position in the pivot column. For our problem, the detailed calculations are as follows:

Row two (variable $s_2$): Multiply the new pivot row by $-4$ and add to old row two to obtain new row two.

Old Row Two + $(-4 \cdot$ New Pivot Row$)$ = New Row Two
| 4 | + | $(-4 \cdot 1/2)$ | = | 2 | |
|---|---|---|---|---|---|
| 4 | + | $(-4 \cdot 1)$ | = | 0 | |
| 0 | + | $(-4 \cdot 1/10)$ | = | $-2/5$ | |
| 1 | + | $(-4 \cdot 0)$ | = | 1 | |
| 40 | + | $(-4 \cdot 6)$ | = | 16 | (T3-17) |

The pivoting process is equivalent to solving the system of constraint equations for the new basic variables $x_2$ and $s_2$, with $x_1 = 0$ and $s_1 = 0$. We can write the system of equations that represents this second solution as

$$1x_2 + 0s_2 = 6 \qquad x_1 = 0$$
$$\text{with} \qquad \text{(T3-18)}$$
$$0x_2 + 1s_2 = 16 \qquad s_1 = 0$$

We can immediately identify the values of the basic variables as $x_2 = 6$, $s_2 = 16$.

Table T3.3 shows the complete second simplex tableau. Comparing the solution with Figure T3.3, in graphical terms we have moved vertically from the extreme point $x_1 = 0$, $x_2 = 0$ to the adjacent extreme point $x_1 = 0$, $x_2 = 6$.

Once again, we compute the $Z_j$ values in the second tableau in exactly the same manner as in the initial simplex tableau. To illustrate

| | | | |
|---|---|---|---|
| $Z_1 = 8(1/2)$ | + 0(2) | = 4 | |
| $Z_2 = 8(1)$ | + 0(0) | = 8 | |
| $Z_3 = 8(1/10)$ | + 0(-2/5) | = 4/5 | (T3-19) |
| $Z_4 = 8(0)$ | + 0(1) | = 0 | |
| $Z_0 = 8(6)$ | + 0(16) | = 48 | (current value of the objective function) |

We compute the $c_j - Z_j$ values by subtracting the corresponding $Z_j$ values we have just computed from the $c_j$ values shown in the top row of the tableau. We immediately

observe that $c_1 - Z_1 = 2$ (positive), so we know that we do not yet have the optimal solution and must make at least one more iteration.

**Step 7: Make Additional Iterations (As Necessary)** We select the next variable to enter the basis by again using the variable entry criterion. The choice is very simple in this instance, because we can improve profit only by entering the variable $x_1$ into the solution (the only positive $c_j - Z_j$ value is $c_1 - Z_1 = 2$). We select the variable $x_1$ to enter the basis.

We choose the variable to leave the basis by again using the variable removal criterion. Applying this criterion forms the following ratios:

| Current Basic Variables | Solution ÷ $a_{i1}$ | Ratios |
|---|---|---|
| $x_2$ | $6 \div 1/2$ | 12 |
| $s_2$ | $16 \div 2$ | 8 (smallest) |

The current basic variable $s_2$ is replaced by the current nonbasic variable $x_1$. The element located at the intersection of the row corresponding to $s_2$ and the column corresponding to $x_1$, the value 2, becomes the pivot element.

Pivoting is accomplished in exactly the same manner as before. First, we convert the pivot element 2 to the value 1, as follows:

Pivot row (variable $s_2$): Divide the values in old row two by 2 to obtain new row two.

| Column Heading | Pivot Row Calculation | New Pivot Row (Row Two) | |
|---|---|---|---|
| $x_1$ | 2/2 | = 1 (pivot element) | |
| $x_2$ | 0/2 | = 0 | |
| $s_1$ | $(-2/5)/2$ | = $-1/5$ | (T3-20) |
| $s_2$ | 1/2 | = 1/2 | |
| Solution | 16/2 | = 8 | |

Next, we proceed to obtain zeros for the remaining elements of the pivot column, except of course for the pivot element itself. Using row operations on the first row, we obtain

Row one (variable $x_2$): Multiply the new pivot row by $-1/2$ and add to old row one to obtain new row one.

Old Row One + $(-1/2 \cdot$ New Pivot Row$)$ = New Row One
| 1/2 | + | $(-1/2 \cdot 1$ | = $-1/2)$ | = 0 | |
|---|---|---|---|---|---|
| 1 | + | $(-1/2 \cdot 0$ | = 0) | = 1 | |
| 1/10 | + | $(-1/2 \cdot -1/5 = 1/10)$ | | = 1/5 | (T3-21) |
| 0 | + | $(-1/2 \cdot 1/2$ | = $-1/4)$ | = $-1/4$ | |
| 6 | + | $(-1/2 \cdot 8$ | = $-4)$ | = 2 | |

We can now construct the third simplex tableau, as shown in Table T3.4. Comparing this solution with Figure T3.3, in graphical terms we have moved from the extreme

| $c_j$ | | 6 | 8 | 0 | 0 | |
|---|---|---|---|---|---|---|
| $c_B$ | Basic Variables | $x_1$ | $x_2$ | $s_1$ | $s_2$ | Solution |
| 8 | $x_2$ | 0 | 1 | $\frac{1}{5}$ | $-\frac{1}{4}$ | 2 |
| 6 | $x_1$ | 1 | 0 | $-\frac{1}{5}$ | $\frac{1}{2}$ | 8 |
| | $Z_j$ | 6 | 8 | $\frac{2}{5}$ | 1 | 64 |
| | $c_j - Z_j$ | 0 | 0 | $-\frac{2}{5}$ | $-1$ | |

TABLE T3.4
Third Simplex Tableau (Optimal Solution)—Braxton Machine Works

point $x_1 = 0$, $x_2 = 6$ to the adjacent extreme point $x_1 = 8$, $x_2 = 2$. The $Z_j$ values and the $c_j - Z_j$ values for this tableau are computed in exactly the same manner as they were for the previous two tableaus. We will not repeat the details of these computations here.

In this third simplex tableau all $c_j - Z_j$ values are either zero or negative. We have obtained the optimal solution with $x_1 = 8$, $x_2 = 2$, $s_1 = 0$, $s_2 = 0$, and the optimal value of $Z = 64$. The optimal solution indicates that we will maximize profit if Braxton produces eight camshafts (product 1) and two gears (product 2).

## Summary of the Steps in the Simplex Method: Maximization Problems

We can summarize the steps used in the simplex method for a maximization problem as follows:

1. Formulate the problem in terms of an objective function, a set of constraints, and a set of nonnegativity conditions.
2. Reformulate the problem in standard linear programming format, adding slack variables where necessary, to convert the original constraint inequalities to equalities.
3. Construct the initial simplex tableau.
4. Select the variable to bring into the solution (largest $c_j - Z_j$ value).
5. Select the variable to leave the solution (smallest positive ratio of the Solution column values to the comparable values in the column selected in step 4).
6. Perform the pivoting process, and check the resulting new solution for optimality.
7. Repeat the process, steps 4 though 6, until optimality is achieved.

## Shadow Prices

The final simplex tableau (Table T3.4) gives the solution values for the basic variables and the optimal value of the objective function ($x_1 = 8$, $x_2 = 2$, and $Z = 64$). We can gain additional valuable information from this tableau.

The $c_j - Z_j$ values for the decision variables, $x_1$ and $x_2$, indicate how much additional profit Braxton can make by producing additional units of these products. Because $x_1$ and $x_2$ are both basic variables, the optimal solution already indicates the maximum amounts of these products that Braxton can produce. Consequently, their $c_j - Z_j$ values are zero.

The $c_j - Z_j$ values for the slack variables, $s_1$ and $s_2$, are called **shadow prices,** *marginal values,* or *opportunity costs.* They represent the marginal change in the objective function that will occur by making an additional unit of a resource available. The shadow price for $s_1 = \frac{2}{5} = 0.40$. This means that one additional hour of milling machine time is worth 40 cents. To see why this is the case, look at the column coefficients of the nonbasic variable, $s_1$, in the optimal simplex tableau. It is

$$s_1 \text{ (milling machine resource)}$$

$$[x_2] \quad \tfrac{1}{5}$$
$$[x_1] \quad -\tfrac{1}{5}$$

These column coefficients indicate the rate of substitution between the variable $s_1$ (milling machine resource) and the basic variables, $x_1$ and $x_2$. If one more unit of $s_1$ is available, we will produce one-fifth fewer units of $x_1$ and one-fifth more units of $x_2$. Because each unit of $x_1$ produces $6 profit, ($6 \times -\tfrac{1}{5} = -\tfrac{6}{5}$), we lose $6/5 from decreased production of $x_1$. But because each unit of $x_2$ produces $8 profit, ($8 \times \tfrac{1}{5} = \tfrac{8}{5}$), we gain $8/5 from increased production of $x_2$. The result is a net gain of $2/5 for each unit of resource 1 (milling machine resource) that we add. The rates of substitution also work in the other direction; reducing resource 1 by one unit results in a loss of $2/5 per unit.

The shadow price for resource 2 (metal lathe resource), $s_2 = 1$, can be interpreted similarly. Shadow prices can be very useful to operations managers as they make capacity decisions. They can compare the cost of additional units of capacity with the shadow price for the capacity to see whether working overtime, subcontracting, or developing other ways of expanding capacity is worthwhile.

Two points are important to remember in connection with shadow prices. First, the shadow prices apply only within a certain range of values. Once that range is exceeded in either direction, the shadow prices change. This occurs because the constraints have shadow prices associated with them because they are binding. If the amount of a resource is made large enough, at a certain point the constraint is no longer binding. For example, if constraint 1 were increased by 60 units, to 100, that constraint would no longer be binding, and there would be slack, or unused units, of the milling machine resource. Second, the constraints form a set in which they are interrelated. It may not be possible to increase both resources at the same time and improve the value of the objective function.

# Other Issues in Linear Programming

We encounter several other issues in formulating and solving linear programming problems.

## Other Types of Constraints ($\geq$ and =)

In our profit maximization example we dealt with a problem formulation composed entirely of less-than or equal-to ($\leq$) constraints. Other problem formulations can contain greater-than or equal-to ($\geq$) constraints or equality (=) constraints.

Recall that for $\leq$ constraints we added a slack variable to convert the inequality to an equality. For example, in the Braxton Machine Works example we converted the first inequality $5x_1 + 8x_2 \leq 60$ to an equality, using the slack variable $s_1$, as in $5x_1 + 8x_1 + 1s_1 = 60$. Suppose that in another situation we had a constraint of the form $3x_1 + 2x_2 \geq 30$. To convert this to an inequality we would subtract a **surplus variable,** $s_1$, as in $3x_1 + 2x_2 - 1s_1 = 30$. But now we cannot use the simplex method, because its initial solution has to be feasible. This means that each row has to have one variable with a +1 as its coefficient and that this same variable must have all zeros in the other rows. To overcome this problem, when we have to use surplus variables to create equalities for $\geq$ constraint, we also use **artificial variables,** which have +1 as their coefficients. Think of an artificial variable as a fictitious product that has a very high cost. It is permitted in the initial solution to the simplex problem but cannot appear in the final solution. Using $A_1$ as the corresponding artificial variable, we would write the constraint as

$$3x_1 + 2x_2 - 1s_1 + 1A_1 = 30 \qquad \text{(T3-22)}$$

Assuming that we were still maximizing profit, the objective function would appear as

$$\$6x_1 + \$8x_2 + 0s_1 - \$MA_1 \qquad \text{(T3-23)}$$

where $\$M$ is assumed to be a large amount, say a million or a billion dollars.[3]

We also use an artificial variable in equality constraints. For example, if we had another constraint for our problem given by $5x_1 + 7x_2 = 30$, we would have to change it to $5x_1 + 7x_2 + 1A_2 = 30$ to satisfy the starting simplex requirement of having a unique nonnegative variable in each constraint equation. It would also be reflected in the objective function, which we would now write as

$$\$6x_1 + \$8x_2 + 0s_1 - \$MA_1 - \$MA_2 \qquad \text{(T3-24)}$$

When artificial variables must be used, the simplex method begins with these artificial variables in solution. They are then removed from the basis during the pivoting process.

## Minimization Problems

For minimization problems the variable selected for entry is the one that has the smallest (most negative) value of $c_j - Z_j$. The procedure is identical to that described and illustrated earlier for a maximization problem. When all values of $c_j - Z_j$ are zero, or positive, we have the optimal solution.

## Sensitivity Analysis

The operations manager usually is interested in much more than the optimal solution. This optimal solution provides the user with the value of the objective function, the decision variable values, and the shadow prices. But these solution values are based on the assumption that the input parameters are constant. What happens when these parameter values change? Do we have to completely resolve the problem? How sensitive is the solution to parameter changes? **Sensitivity analysis,** or postoptimality analysis, addresses these types of questions.

Sensitivity analysis typically concerns the following two types of situations:

- Changes in the coefficients of the objective function
- Changes in the right-hand-side values of the constraint set

A detailed discussion of sensitivity analysis is beyond the scope of this tutorial. However, the linear programming module included in the software package accompanying this textbook will enable you to perform sensitivity analyses for the situations we have described.

---

[3]When we encounter a $\geq$ or = constraint in a minimization problem, we give the artificial variable a large positive coefficient in the objective function to prevent it from being in the final solution.

## ▶ Summary

This tutorial has presented an overview of the solution procedure (the simplex method) for linear programming problems. An understanding of the simplex method is necessary in order for a manager to be able to interpret and use the output from a linear programming software package.

In this tutorial we have also demonstrated how to formulate linear programming problems. Linear programming problem formulation requires a lot of practice and is something of an art. We also discussed the output from a linear programming solution, another important consideration. Finally, the manager should be aware of how sensitive the solution of the problem is to changes in the problem's input parameters.

## ▶ Key Terms

| | | |
|---|---|---|
| artificial variable | objective function | sensitivity analysis |
| basic variables | optimal feasible solution | shadow prices |
| basis | physical rates of substitution | simplex algorithm |
| constraint set | physical rates of usage | simplex method |
| decision variables | pivot column | slack variable |
| feasible solution space | pivot element | solution space |
| feasible solutions | pivot row | surplus variable |
| isoprofit | pivoting | variable entry criterion |
| linear programming | right-hand-side values | variable removal criterion |
| nonnegativity restrictions | | |

## ▶ Discussion Questions

1. What conditions must be present for linear programming to be used?
2. Why are slack variables used in the simplex method? Why are they necessary?
3. How do a solution, a feasible solution, a basic feasible solution, and the optimal feasible solution for a linear programming problem differ?
4. What type of information does the solution to a linear programming problem yield?
5. How do you know when you have obtained the optimal solution to a linear programming problem?
6. What happens to the entry and removal criteria if you have to solve a minimization instead of a maximization problem?
7. What type of information do the shadow prices provide?
8. Why are artificial variables used in some linear programming problems?
9. Why is a big value, $\pm M$, assigned to artificial variables?
10. Explain how you can obtain the values of the shadow prices directly from the optimal simplex tableau.

## ▶ Problems

1. Solve the following problem graphically:

$$\text{Maximize } Z = 3x_1 - 1x_2$$
$$\text{subject to } \quad 4x_1 + 2x_2 \le 8$$
$$3x_1 + 1x_2 \le 10$$
$$\text{with } x_1 \ge 0, x_2 \ge 0$$

2. Solve the following problem graphically:

$$\text{Minimize } Z = x_1 + 2x_2$$
$$\text{subject to } \quad 2x_1 - 3x_2 \le 7$$
$$1x_1 + 2x_2 \le 10$$
$$\text{with } x_1 \ge 0, x_2 \ge 0$$

**3.** Solve the following problem graphically:

$$\text{Maximize } Z = 1x_1 + 6x_2$$
$$\text{subject to} \quad 4x_1 + 8x_2 \leq 32$$
$$5x_1 + 7x_2 \leq 35$$
$$-3x_1 + 3x_2 \leq 9$$
$$\text{with } x_1 \geq 0, x_2 \geq 0$$

**4.** Solve the following problem graphically:

$$\text{Minimize } Z = 4x_1 + 8x_2$$
$$\text{subject to} \quad 7x_1 + 1x_2 \geq 7$$
$$2x_1 + 3x_2 \leq 6$$
$$3x_1 + 2x_2 \geq 6$$
$$1x_1 + 4x_2 \geq 4$$
$$\text{with } x_1 \geq 0, x_2 \geq 0$$

**5.** Janet Hudson has a basement macramé shop in which she weaves two types of macramé products; hanging flowerpot holders and wall hangings. To make each item she must use a combination of four ropes, but each rope type is available in a limited quantity. The rope availability is as follows:

| Rope Type | Rope Availability (ft) |
|-----------|------------------------|
| A | 150 |
| B | 210 |
| C | 130 |
| D | 190 |

The rope requirement to manufacture the two items is as follows:

| | Rope Requirement (ft) | |
|-----------|-----------------|--------------|
| Rope Type | Flowerpot Holder | Wall Hanging |
| A | 17 | 5 |
| B | 109 | 13 |
| C | 3 | 18 |
| D | 6 | 8 |

Hudson believes that she can sell her hanging flowerpot holders for $3 each and her wall hangings for $4 each. She can sell all that she produces. Formulate as a linear programming model.

**6.** Ye Olde Smokehouse, Ltd., prepares and packages three Christmas gift packages containing sausages and cheeses. The "Taster's Delight" gift package contains 3 sausages and 6 cheeses, the "Succulent Delight" contains 5 sausages and 4 cheeses, and the "Gourmet Delight" contains 6 sausages and 5 cheeses. The company has 2,500 sausages and 3,000 cheeses available for packaging, and it believes that all gift packages can be sold (based on previous demand). Profits are estimated at $2.50 for the "Taster's Delight" gift package, $3.50 for the "Succulent Delight" gift package, and $4.00 for the

"Gourmet Delight" gift package. Formulate as a linear programming model.

**7.** The Leather Boot Sporting Goods Co. manufactures two types of leather soccer balls, Competition Ball and Professional Ball. Each ball requires work by both semiskilled and skilled employees. Basically, the semiskilled employees use machines in the manufacture of the soccer balls, whereas the skilled employees hand sew the soccer balls. The available time (per week) for each type of employee and the time requirement for each type of soccer ball are:

| | Manufacturing Time Requirement (hr) | | |
|---------|---------|---------|---------|
| Type of Employee | Competition Ball | Professional Ball | Time Availability (hours per week) |
| Semiskilled | 2 | 3 | 80 |
| Skilled | 4 | 6 | 150 |

The cost of an hour of semiskilled labor is $5.50, and the cost of an hour of skilled labor is $8.50. To meet weekly demand requirements at least 15 Competition Balls and at least 10 Professional soccer balls must be manufactured. Formulate as a linear programming model.

**8.** La Vonda Wilson, R.N., is trying to develop a diet plan for her patients. The required nutritional elements and the total daily requirements of each nutritional elements are as follows:

| Required Nutritional Element | Total Daily Requirement |
|------------------------------|-------------------------|
| Calories | Not more than 2,700 calories |
| Carbohydrates | Not less than 300 grams |
| Protein | Not less than 250 grams |
| Vitamins | Not less than 60 grams |

Wilson has four basic food types to use in planning her menus. The units of nutritional elements per unit of food type are shown in the table that follows. Note that the cost associated with a unit of ingredient also appears at the bottom of this table.

| Required Nutritional Element | Units of Nutritional Elements per unit of Food Type | | | |
|------------------------------|---------|---------|---------|-----------|
| | Milk | Meat | Bread | Vegetable |
| Calories | 160 | 210 | 120 | 150 |
| Carbohydrates | 110 | 130 | 110 | 120 |
| Protein | 90 | 190 | 90 | 130 |
| Vitamins | 50 | 50 | 75 | 70 |
| Cost per Unit | $ 0.42 | $ 0.68 | $ 0.32 | $ 0.17 |

Formulate as a linear programming model.

9. Solve the following linear programming problem, using the simplex algorithm:

$$\text{Maximize } Z = 2x_1 - 1x_2 + 5x_3$$
$$\text{subject to:} \quad 3x_1 \qquad\quad - 2x_3 \leq 16$$
$$2x_1 + 5x_2 + 1x_3 \leq 10$$
$$3x_2 + 1x_3 \leq 12$$
$$\text{with } x_1, x_2, x_3, \geq 0.$$

10. Solve the following problem, using the simplex algorithm:

$$\text{Minimize } Z = 4x_1 + 3x_2 + 2x_3$$
$$\text{subject to} \quad 4x_1 + 1x_2 + 1x_3 \geq 10$$
$$3x_1 \qquad\quad - 1x_3 \leq 4$$
$$2x_1 + 2x_2 - 8x_3 \leq 3$$
$$\text{with } x_1 \geq 0, x_2 \geq 0, x_3 \geq 0.$$

11. Solve the following linear programming problem, using the simplex algorithm:

$$\text{Maximize } Z = \quad 4x_1 + 2x_2$$
$$\text{subject to} \quad 3x_1 + 2x_2 \leq 8$$
$$-4x_1 + 3x_2 \geq -7$$
$$7x_1 + 2x_2 = 14$$
$$\text{with } x_1 \geq 0, x_2 \geq 0.$$

12. Solve the following linear programming problem, using the simplex algorithm:

$$\text{Minimize } Z = \quad 2x_1 + 5x_2 + 3x_3$$
$$\text{subject to} \quad 9x_1 - 3x_2 + 2x_3 = 4$$
$$-3x_1 + 4x_2 + 3x_3 \geq 10$$
$$5x_1 \qquad\quad + 3x_3 \leq 9$$
$$\text{with } x_1, x_2, x_3, \geq 0.$$

13. A plastics company uses three extruding and curing machines in the manufacture of three types of children's toys. Toy 1 requires 4 hours on machine A, 1 hour on machine B, and 3 hours on machine C. Toy 2 requires 6 hours on machine A, 1½ hours on machine B, and 1 hour on machine C. Toy 3 requires 3 hours on machine A and 3 hours on machine B. There is an excess of 24 hours of machine A time, 12 hours of machine B time, and 12 hours of machine C time. Toy 1 produces $0.50 profit per unit, toy 2 produces $6 profit per unit, and toy 3 produces $5 profit per unit.
The linear programming formulation of this problem is

$$\text{Maximize } Z = 1/2 x_1 + 6x_2 + 5x_3$$
$$\text{subject to} \quad 4x_1 + 6x_2 + 3x_3 \leq 24$$
$$1x_1 + 3/2 x_2 + 3x_3 \leq 12$$
$$3x_1 + 1x_2 \qquad\quad \leq 12$$
$$\text{with } x_1 \geq 0, x_2 \geq 0, x_3 \geq 0.$$

The optimal tableau (solution) for this problem is

| | $c_j$ | $\frac{1}{2}$ | 6 | 5 | 0 | 0 | 0 | |
|---|---|---|---|---|---|---|---|---|
| $c_B$ | Basic Variables | $x_1$ | $x_2$ | $x_3$ | $s_1$ | $s_2$ | $s_3$ | Solution |
| 6 | $x_2$ | $\frac{2}{3}$ | 1 | 0 | $\frac{2}{9}$ | $-\frac{2}{9}$ | 0 | $\frac{8}{3}$ |
| 5 | $x_3$ | 0 | 0 | 1 | $-\frac{1}{9}$ | $\frac{4}{9}$ | 0 | $\frac{8}{3}$ |
| 0 | $s_3$ | $\frac{7}{3}$ | 0 | 0 | $-\frac{2}{9}$ | $\frac{2}{9}$ | 1 | $\frac{28}{3}$ |
| | $Z_j$ | 4 | 6 | 5 | $\frac{7}{9}$ | $\frac{8}{9}$ | 0 | $\frac{88}{3}$ |
| | $c_j - Z_j$ | $-\frac{7}{2}$ | 0 | 0 | $-\frac{7}{9}$ | $-\frac{8}{9}$ | 0 | |

a. What is the optimal production schedule for this firm?

b. What is the shadow price for an additional hour of time on machine A? machine B? machine C?

c. What is the opportunity cost assciated with toy 1? How can this opportunity cost be interpreted?

14. A company uses three machines in the manufacture of three products. Each unit of product 1 requires 3 hours on machine 1, 2 hours on machine 2, and 1 hour on machine 3. Each unit of product 2 requires 4 hours on machine 1, 1 hour on machine 2, and 3 hours on machine 3. Each unit of product 3 requires 2 hours on machine 1, 2 hours on machine 2, and 2 hours on machine 3. The contribution margin of the three products is $30, $40, and $35 per unit, respectively. Available for scheduling are 90 hours of machine 1 time, 54 hours of machine 2 time, and 93 hours of machine 3 time.
The linear programming formation of this problem is

$$\text{Maximize } Z = 30x_1 + 40x_2 + 35x_3$$
$$\text{subject to} \quad 3x_1 + 4x_2 + 2x_3 \leq 90$$
$$2x_1 + 1x_2 + 2x_3 \leq 54$$
$$1x_1 + 3x_2 + 2x_3 \leq 93$$
$$\text{with } x_1, x_2, x_3 \geq 0.$$

and the optimal tableau for this problem is:

| | $c_j$ | 30 | 40 | 35 | 0 | 0 | 0 | |
|---|---|---|---|---|---|---|---|---|
| $c_B$ | Basic Variables | $x_1$ | $x_2$ | $x_3$ | $s_1$ | $s_2$ | $s_3$ | Solution |
| 40 | $x_2$ | $\frac{1}{3}$ | 1 | 0 | $\frac{1}{3}$ | $-\frac{1}{3}$ | 0 | 12 |
| 35 | $x_3$ | $\frac{5}{6}$ | 0 | 1 | $-\frac{1}{6}$ | $\frac{2}{3}$ | 0 | 21 |
| 0 | $s_3$ | $-\frac{5}{3}$ | 0 | 0 | $-\frac{2}{3}$ | $-\frac{1}{3}$ | 1 | 15 |
| | $Z_j$ | 42.5 | 40 | 35 | 7.5 | 10 | 0 | 1215 |
| | $c_j - Z_j$ | $-12.5$ | 0 | 0 | $-7.5$ | $-10$ | 0 | |

**a.** What is the optimal production schedule for this company?

**b.** What is the marginal value of an additional hour of time on machine 1?

**c.** What is the opportunity cost associated with product 1? What interpretation should be given to this opportunity cost?

**d.** Management is considering the introduction of a new product that will require 4 hours on machine 1, 2 hours on machine 2, and 3 hours on machine 3. This new product will have a contribution margin of $55. Should it be produced? If it should, what will be the marginal value of producing one unit of this new product?

## ► Selected References

Bradley, Stephen P., Arnoldo C. Hax, and Thomas L. Magnanti. *Applied Mathematical Programming.* Reading, Mass.: Addison-Wesley, 1977.

Dantzig, George B. *Linear Programming and Extensions.* Princeton, N.J.: Princeton University Press, 1963.

Hadley, George. *Linear Programming.* Reading, Mass.: Addison-Wesley, 1962.

Luenberger, D. G. *Linear and Nonlinear Programming.* Reading, Mass.: Addison-Wesley, 1985.

Markland, Robert E. *Topics in Management Science,* 3d ed. New York: Wiley, 1989.

Murty, K. G. *Linear Programming.* New York: Wiley, 1983.

Shapiro, Roy D. *Optimization Models for Planning and Allocation: Text and Cases in Mathematical Programming.* New York: Wiley, 1984.

# Simulation

## Introduction

The rapid development of computer technology has led to an increased use of computer simulation to solve problems in science, engineering, and business. Simulation is developing a computer model that represents a real world system and then using the model to evaluate the performance of the system under varying conditions. Computer simulation has been used to model many **continuous systems,** systems having quantities of interest that are not countable. For example, computational fluid dynamics (CFD) allows aircraft designers to model the airflow around aircraft by using computer models, eliminating much of the time-consuming and expensive process of testing models in a wind tunnel.

In operations we typically use computer simulation to model **discrete systems,** systems in which the quantities of interest are countable. Computer simulation of discrete events is frequently referred to as **discrete event simulation.** For example, a fast-food restaurant might use discrete event simulation to model various arrangements of its carryout operation. The model might address the number of windows, the spacing between windows, the number of personnel used, and so on. A manufacturing company might use discrete event simulation to evaluate different factory layouts, worker assignment rules, job dispatching rules, and so on.

A major advantage of computer simulation is that it permits the evaluation of different system configurations without actually constructing the different arrangements. It is usually too expensive to conduct experiments involving the actual physical arrangement of a system. Even if the evaluation does not involve physical arrangement, the expense of experimentation may be prohibitive. For example, a factory manager may not be willing to experiment with different production-scheduling procedures in an operating factory, because trying procedures that prove inefficient causes a real loss of money.

A second advantage of computer simulation is animation capability. Computer animation of an operating simu-

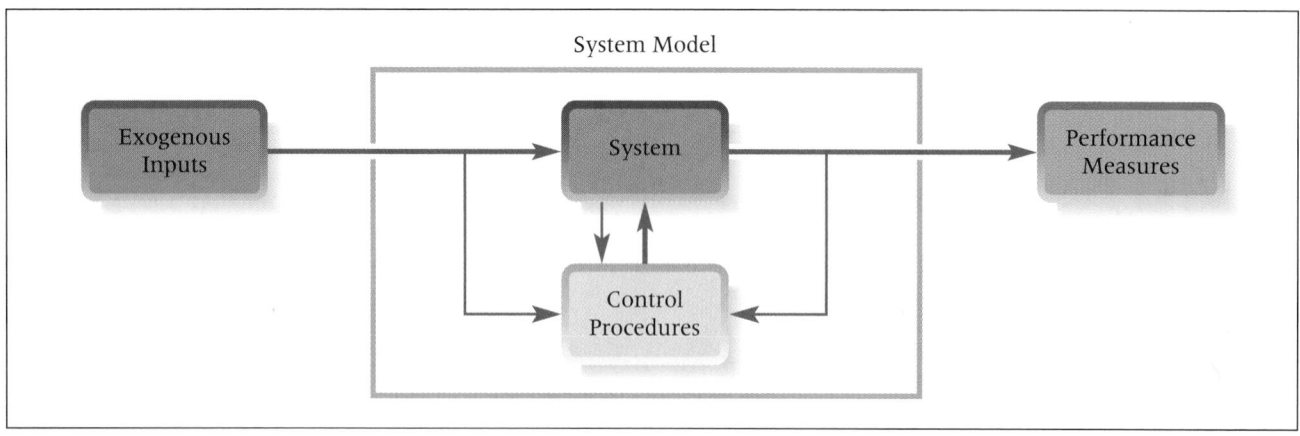

FIGURE T4.1
Overview of Simulation

lation model is one tool that the simulation programmer can use to test the simulation model's accuracy. Animation frequently provides the analyst with insights that cannot be gained from looking at paper output. Animation is also a useful tool in convincing management of the accuracy of the model and its results. If production managers can see animations that behave as their factories do, their confidence in the models will increase.

## An Overview of Simulation

The purpose of simulation is to develop a model that includes all important features of a system so that it behaves, for the most part, as the real system does. We then can evaluate the performance of the model under various external conditions, system arrangements, and control procedures. Figure T4.1 illustrates the simulation concept.

A simulation analysis has three basic components: the exogenous inputs, the system model, and the performance measures. The **system model** is the model of the system *and* its control procedures. The **exogenous** (external) **inputs** are those factors that are not under the control of the system's designers and operators. The number of customers and their arrival pattern, job orders, and equipment failures are all items that may be considered exogenous inputs. The **performance measures** are used to evaluate the success of the system's design or control procedures. Performance measures include such things as customer waiting time, facility utilization, factory throughput, and due date performance. As Figure T4.1 shows, the control procedure may use the system status, exogenous inputs, and the performance measures to determine system control inputs.

### Steps in a Simulation Study

The steps of a simulation study are

1. Construct a model of the system and its control procedures
2. Determine what items comprise the exogenous inputs
3. Subject the system to simulated exogenous inputs
4. Measure the system's performance
5. Evaluate the system and its controls
6. Make changes to the system or its controls, if the system does not perform satisfactorily, and return to step 3

### Simulating Exogenous Inputs

Simulation modelers must evaluate the system's performance in light of the exogenous inputs. The simulation modeler needs to identify the inputs, quantify them, and then develop a way to generate random exogenous inputs.

Three methods are available for generating inputs:

1. The simulation modeler may assume a theoretical distribution. Academic researchers typically use this method when they want generality in order to provide maximum applicability of the results. With this method the simulation modeler makes an assumption such as "processing times for a component are normally distributed with a mean of fifteen minutes and a standard deviation of three minutes."
2. The simulation modeler may fit a theoretical distribution to measured data. If the model is of an actual system, the simulation modeler can measure the exogenous inputs and, if they appear to match a theoretical distribution (normal, exponential, and so on), can determine the parameters of the distribution so that the theoretical distribution fits the empirical data.
3. The simulation modeler may use measured data to construct frequency ranges that can be used with uniform 0–1 random numbers to generate discrete input values. This method is the easiest to understand and use; however, it generates discrete values when the input may be continuous in nature.

Methods 1 and 2 are beyond the scope of this discussion. We will explain how to use method 3 next.

The first step is to collect data on the input of interest. This may be accomplished by making a special effort to measure the input or, what is more convenient, to obtain the data from company records. With the data collected the simulation modeler can construct a histogram. The number of observations and the width of the histogram's ranges will affect the accuracy of the inputs generated.

As an example, suppose we measured the serving time for two hundred customers in a fast-food restaurant and developed the frequency distribution histogram shown in Figure T4.2. We can easily convert the frequency distribution to a relative frequency distribution by dividing the number of observations in each service time range by the total number of observations. A relative frequency distribution shows the proportion of observations that fall into a particular category relative to the total. Figure T4.3 displays the data from Figure T4.2 as a relative frequency histogram.

Given the relative frequency distribution of Figure T4.3 and a series of uniformly distributed 0–1 random numbers, we can generate discrete inputs that approximate the service times that we used to generate Figures T4.2 and T4.3. Table T4.1 gives a series of five-digit uniformly distributed random numbers. Each digit in a uniformly distributed random number is itself uniformly distributed—that is, the probability that a digit will be a zero is 0.10, the probability that it will be a 1 is 0.10, the probability that it will be a 2 is 0.10, and so on.

The random numbers in Table T4.1 are actually **pseudo-random numbers.** A computer generated the numbers using a random number algorithm. All random number algorithms generate numbers that appear to be

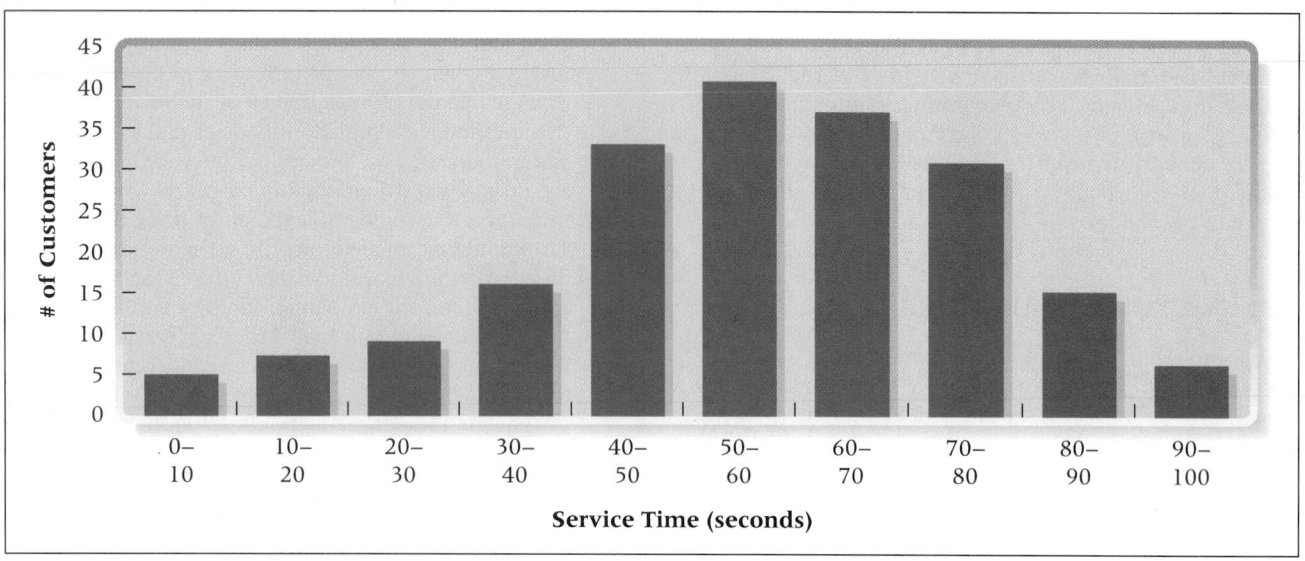

FIGURE T4.2
Service Time Frequency Histogram

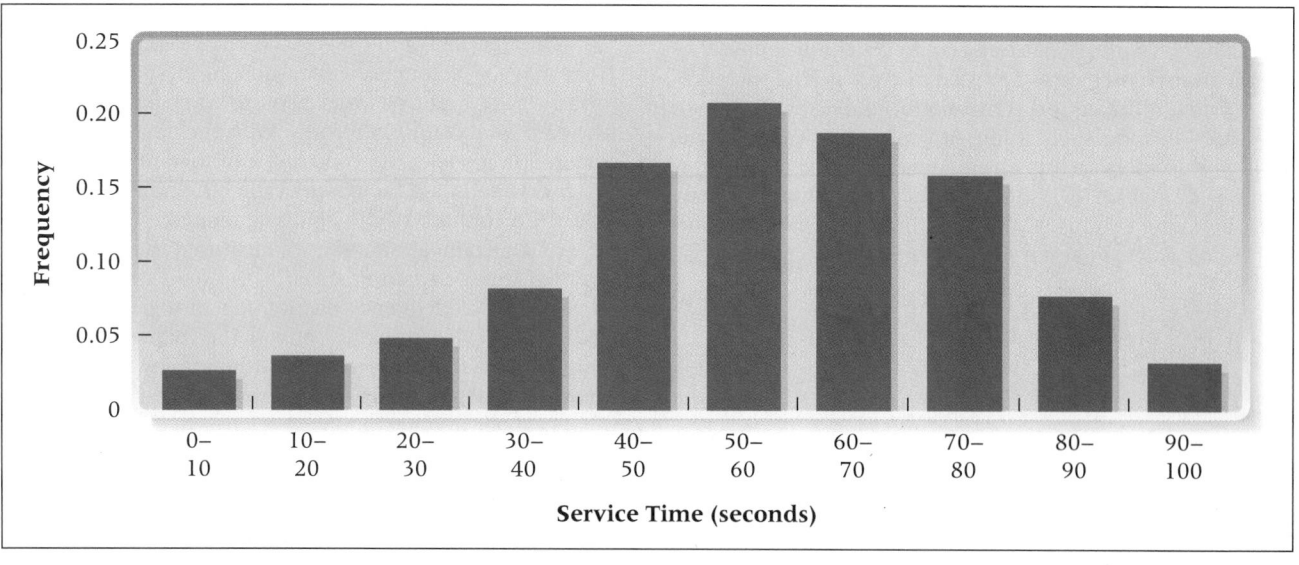

FIGURE T4.3
Service Time Relative Frequency Histogram

independent and uniformly distributed but eventually repeat themselves. Depending on the algorithm used, the numbers will repeat after about fifty thousand numbers, so for most practical purposes this is not a problem, and we can treat pseudo-random numbers as true random numbers.

We use the discrete probability distribution of service times in Figure T4.3 to generate cumulative probability ranges, as shown in Table T4.2. First, we add up the probabilities for each interval to obtain a cumulative prob-

ability distribution. The cumulative probability distribution shows that the probability of having a service time between 0 and 10 is 0.025, the probability of having a service time between 0 and 20 is 0.060, and so on. Next, we use the cumulative probabilities to develop cumulative probability ranges. The first cumulative probability range, for service times between 0 and 10 seconds, starts at 0.000 and goes to 0.001 less than the cumulative probability for the interval (0.025 − 0.001 = 0.024). The next cumulative probability

| | 1 | 2 | 3 | 4 | 5 | 6 | 7 | 8 | 9 | 10 |
|---|---|---|---|---|---|---|---|---|---|---|
| 1 | 07884 | 47156 | 38316 | 78046 | 07123 | 58618 | 57880 | 68001 | 34828 | 23858 |
| 2 | 78547 | 28206 | 28219 | 17473 | 22614 | 73669 | 78724 | 85374 | 65654 | 48299 |
| 3 | 50833 | 49635 | 88693 | 45874 | 66116 | 80220 | 57017 | 30550 | 65585 | 78550 |
| 4 | 74362 | 27523 | 21818 | 38495 | 10286 | 44699 | 88904 | 30422 | 50984 | 32668 |
| 5 | 68203 | 47661 | 04064 | 32289 | 05520 | 24527 | 31209 | 56451 | 07976 | 59107 |
| 6 | 96486 | 10017 | 96348 | 18648 | 40729 | 30671 | 97853 | 75825 | 77543 | 07276 |
| 7 | 69214 | 75562 | 11061 | 77455 | 41234 | 34510 | 12556 | 65430 | 73734 | 99965 |
| 8 | 44210 | 06111 | 35941 | 68504 | 89395 | 13213 | 58506 | 20521 | 18756 | 86233 |
| 9 | 85435 | 74685 | 04238 | 27427 | 72285 | 43852 | 47482 | 25774 | 40047 | 51412 |
| 10 | 12732 | 65567 | 53333 | 56759 | 88335 | 65896 | 72533 | 34706 | 24296 | 39538 |
| 11 | 11866 | 56050 | 91629 | 33755 | 36657 | 48266 | 93272 | 21095 | 27726 | 95622 |
| 12 | 74104 | 00854 | 03587 | 03235 | 72985 | 85801 | 17510 | 12453 | 37012 | 46535 |
| 13 | 47340 | 52175 | 36106 | 79658 | 31907 | 71470 | 02978 | 61927 | 17894 | 91406 |
| 14 | 98951 | 17105 | 08275 | 56488 | 41812 | 90777 | 42345 | 39906 | 24572 | 81408 |
| 15 | 18317 | 09124 | 30901 | 70855 | 93947 | 71517 | 07744 | 35280 | 70503 | 52658 |
| 16 | 35411 | 88491 | 90139 | 04697 | 36471 | 46901 | 48949 | 39826 | 79709 | 23782 |
| 17 | 91001 | 37856 | 01173 | 42306 | 11293 | 50960 | 96402 | 67894 | 04724 | 19852 |
| 18 | 86843 | 05003 | 52699 | 74463 | 24590 | 18978 | 82647 | 01497 | 22951 | 22510 |
| 19 | 99532 | 27585 | 31828 | 08528 | 71080 | 96599 | 92585 | 99106 | 41626 | 26025 |
| 20 | 17715 | 01197 | 81098 | 82718 | 91563 | 56510 | 09081 | 07129 | 39447 | 27244 |
| 21 | 10401 | 71913 | 75983 | 48514 | 78590 | 56571 | 84156 | 18936 | 88864 | 50376 |
| 22 | 84018 | 60439 | 94931 | 40408 | 66046 | 62855 | 15632 | 42386 | 93597 | 35838 |
| 23 | 87390 | 75781 | 70491 | 08500 | 96022 | 49388 | 56777 | 29379 | 55842 | 41780 |
| 24 | 40658 | 19873 | 92589 | 35681 | 40456 | 43117 | 73154 | 63755 | 60232 | 59719 |
| 25 | 24486 | 01121 | 32623 | 13058 | 60140 | 54401 | 97130 | 30019 | 40024 | 92607 |
| 26 | 10526 | 01037 | 07036 | 25350 | 81863 | 02542 | 85748 | 56140 | 72328 | 54781 |
| 27 | 51072 | 97729 | 13454 | 51428 | 98976 | 65865 | 79424 | 48966 | 20822 | 17849 |
| 28 | 11282 | 22393 | 46947 | 87111 | 40921 | 04568 | 85241 | 73261 | 17846 | 62152 |
| 29 | 11496 | 19426 | 04624 | 31458 | 69198 | 14279 | 52489 | 20251 | 04312 | 72766 |
| 30 | 55460 | 93635 | 08114 | 11275 | 57354 | 99109 | 67783 | 20867 | 57633 | 36530 |
| 31 | 79895 | 67443 | 78750 | 24739 | 81623 | 44340 | 62378 | 31994 | 33636 | 24128 |
| 32 | 13838 | 25085 | 77113 | 46462 | 19608 | 88120 | 48999 | 39298 | 68962 | 94980 |
| 33 | 21666 | 99684 | 13728 | 46551 | 95970 | 42861 | 62646 | 64706 | 98971 | 15591 |
| 34 | 39086 | 88577 | 30968 | 62474 | 79067 | 35948 | 62262 | 91817 | 52374 | 85428 |
| 35 | 06401 | 87947 | 50768 | 13083 | 08536 | 50008 | 47252 | 79628 | 47161 | 90389 |
| 36 | 29648 | 97363 | 25453 | 91936 | 29043 | 54051 | 57840 | 66415 | 79440 | 04299 |
| 37 | 37470 | 98176 | 06614 | 75092 | 98873 | 48501 | 49962 | 95042 | 31395 | 52399 |
| 38 | 29428 | 28754 | 16682 | 51951 | 27962 | 40230 | 19272 | 92997 | 49048 | 17325 |
| 39 | 65520 | 92394 | 25938 | 62612 | 28708 | 58306 | 41236 | 98395 | 57274 | 11889 |
| 40 | 86231 | 95334 | 95372 | 64746 | 92053 | 6767 | 04008 | 81467 | 69269 | 63788 |

TABLE T4.1
Random Five-Digit Numbers

range, for the service time interval 10–20, starts at the cumulative probability for the previous interval and goes to 0.001 less than the cumulative probability for the current interval. Note that the cumulative probability intervals start at 0.000 and end at 0.999. Why we construct the intervals in this fashion will become clear in a moment.

Now we can use the random numbers in Table T4.1 with the cumulative probability ranges in Table T4.2 to generate inputs that approximate the service time distribution for the fast-food restaurant. To generate ten random service times we can use the first ten random numbers in column 1 of Table T4.1. To use these numbers with the cumulative probability ranges in Table T4.2 we convert

them to three-digit 0–1 random numbers by taking the first three digits of the number and placing a decimal point in front of the first digit. This gives us the following three-digit 0–1 uniform random numbers: 0.078, 0.785, 0.508, 0.743, 0.682, 0.964, 0.692, 0.442, 0.854, and 0.127. Now *both* the cumulative probability ranges and the 0–1 uniform random numbers range in value from 0.000 to 0.999. We convert these 0–1 uniform random numbers to simulated service times by finding the cumulative probability range that contains the 0–1 uniform random number and using the mean service time as the simulated service time. Thus, the ten 0–1 uniform random numbers generate the following service times: 25, 75, 55, 75, 65, 85, 65, 55, 75, and 35. The

| Service Time Interval | Mean Service Time | Probability | Cumulative Probability | Cumulative Probability Range |
|---|---|---|---|---|
| 0–10 | 5 | 0.025 | 0.025 | 0.000–0.024 |
| 10–20 | 15 | 0.035 | 0.060 | 0.025–0.059 |
| 20–30 | 25 | 0.045 | 0.105 | 0.060–0.104 |
| 30–40 | 35 | 0.080 | 0.185 | 0.105–0.184 |
| 40–50 | 45 | 0.165 | 0.350 | 0.185–0.349 |
| 50–60 | 55 | 0.205 | 0.555 | 0.350–0.554 |
| 60–70 | 65 | 0.185 | 0.740 | 0.555–0.739 |
| 70–80 | 75 | 0.155 | 0.895 | 0.740–0.894 |
| 80–90 | 85 | 0.075 | 0.970 | 0.895–0.969 |
| 90–100 | 95 | 0.030 | 1.000 | 0.970–0.999 |

T A B L E   T 4 . 2
Development of Cumulative Probability
Ranges

service times generated by this method are random, and the long-run frequency distribution closely approximates the one shown in Figure T4.3. To demonstrate this, Figure T4.4 compares the original observations of Figure T4.2 with two hundred simulated service times generated from the first five columns of Table T4.1. This figure shows that the

distribution of the simulated service times agrees quite well with the original distribution.

It should now be clear why we set up the cumulative probability ranges as we did. The cumulative probability ranges extend from 0.000 to 0.999. Because of the way we generated the random numbers, their values must also range from 0.000 to 0.999. If we had constructed the ranges differently, the generation process would be biased.

This method generates service times that do not exactly represent the service times of the fast-food restaurant. One source of inaccuracy lies in the use of discrete values to simulate service times that can take continuous values between 0 and 100 (and perhaps above 100, because the upper limit of 100 in Figures T4.2 and T4.3 derives from the fact that we did not observe a service time above 100 in the sample of two hundred service time observations, not because a service time above 100 is not possible). With this method we can only generate service times of 5 seconds, 10 seconds, 15 seconds, and so on and not service times of 4.6 seconds, 8.4 seconds, and so on. Also, we developed the frequency ranges in Figure T4.4 from a *sample* of the distribution of interest and not the true distribution.

We can reduce the inaccuracy of this method to some extent by taking more observations and using narrower frequency ranges.

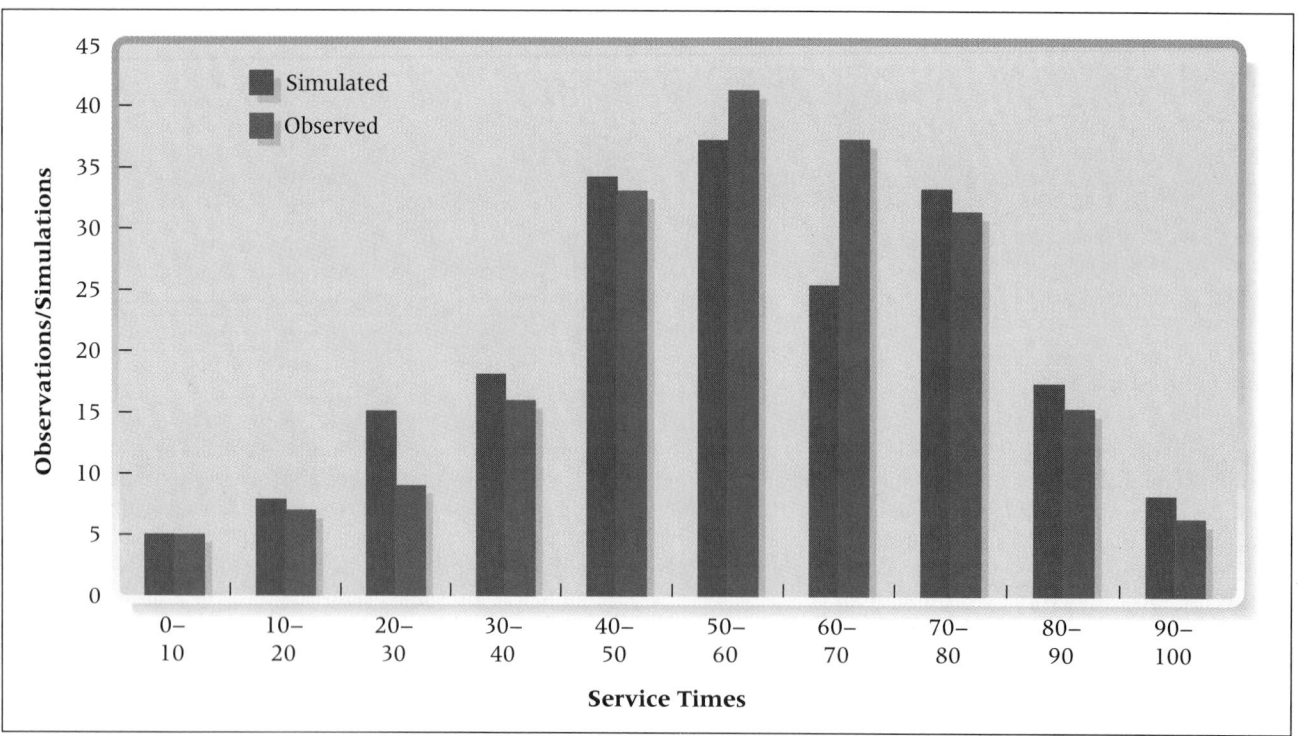

F I G U R E   T 4 . 4
Comparison of Simulated Services Time Distribution with Observed Distribution

Now that we have developed a method of generating exogenous inputs, we will present a simple manual simulation study.

## Example T4.1

A manufacturing company is developing a production process for a new product. The process engineering department is planning to perform two operations at one work center by using two workers who will work independently. Each worker will perform both operations in sequence. The first operation requires an expensive special tool. The process planning department is trying to decide whether providing only one tool in the work center is reasonable. Figure T4.5 illustrates the process. The company has developed the following information concerning component interarrival times and processing times for both operations of the work center:

*Component Interarrival Time*
*(Minutes)*

| Interarrival Time | Probability |
|---|---|
| 1–2 | 0.2 |
| 2–3 | 0.1 |
| 3–4 | 0.3 |
| 4–5 | 0.4 |

*Processing Time—Operation 1*
*(Minutes)*

| Processing Time | Probability |
|---|---|
| 2–3 | 0.2 |
| 3–4 | 0.3 |
| 4–5 | 0.4 |
| 5–6 | 0.1 |

*Processing Time—Operation 2*
*(Minutes)*

| Processing Time | Probability |
|---|---|
| 0–1 | 0.1 |
| 1–2 | 0.2 |
| 2–3 | 0.5 |
| 3–4 | 0.2 |

## Simulating the System

We use interarrival time data to generate arrival times for incoming component parts. Figure T4.6 illustrates how interarrival times relate to arrival times. Interarrival times are easy to generate, and we generate the arrival times by adding a component's interarrival time to the previous component's arrival time. As a side note, many simulation

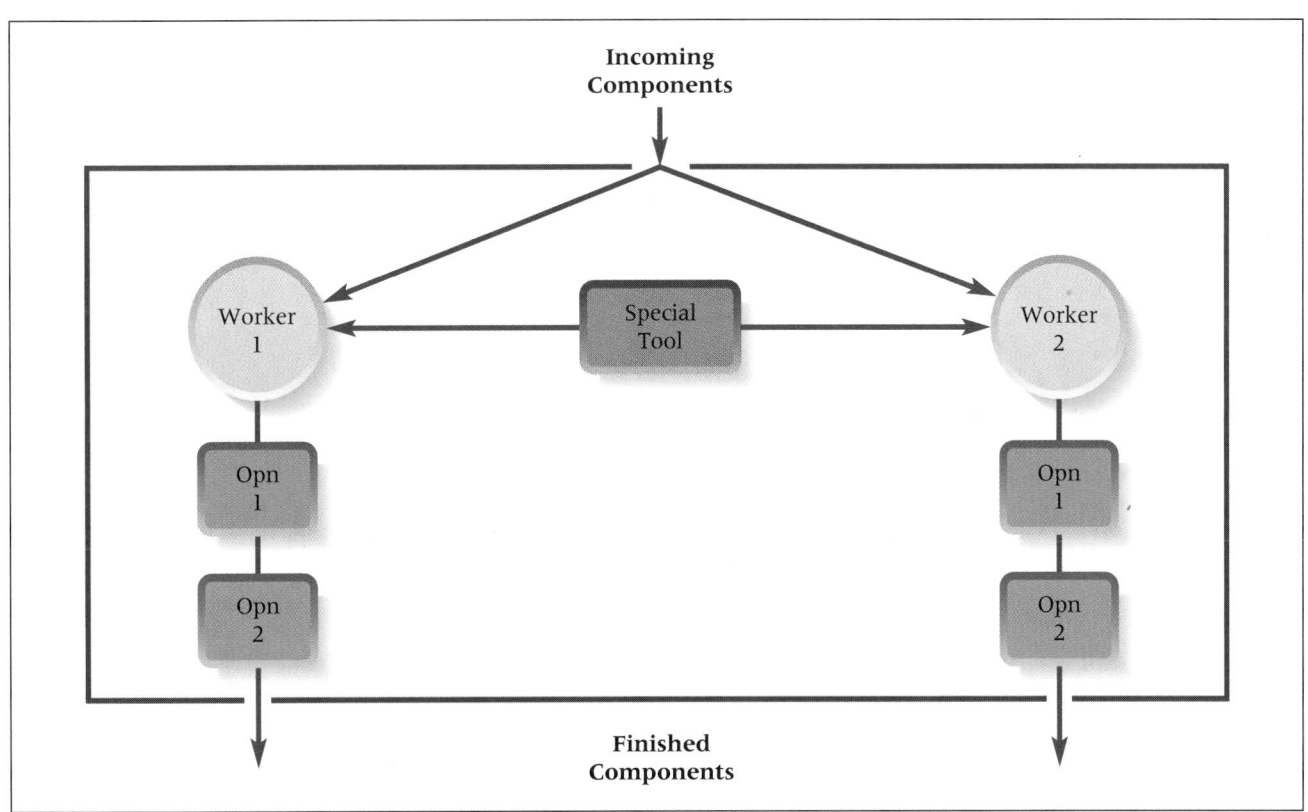

FIGURE T4.5
Production Process for Example T4.1

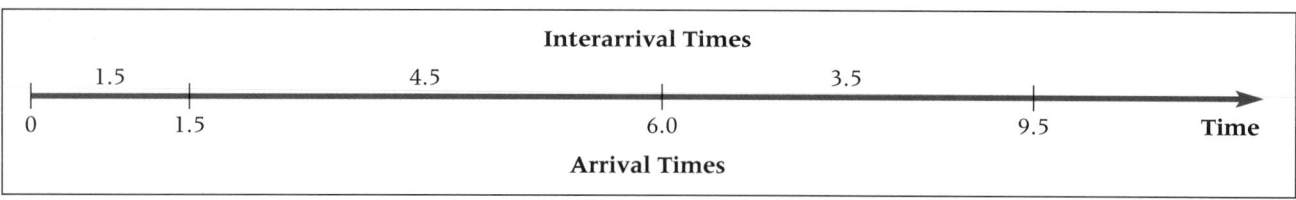

FIGURE  T4.6
Relationship Between Arrival Times and Interarrival Times

studies use the exponential distribution to generate interarrival times. The exponential distribution has a number of properties that make it good choice to represent arrival processes.

First, we must convert the relative frequency or probability data for the exogenous inputs to cumulative probability ranges. The cumulative probability ranges for this problem are

*Component Interarrival Time*
*Frequency Ranges*

| Mean Interarrival Time | Cumulative Probability Range |
|---|---|
| 1.5 | 0.00–0.19 |
| 2.5 | 0.20–0.29 |
| 3.5 | 0.30–0.59 |
| 4.5 | 0.60–0.99 |

*Processing Time—Operation 1*
*Frequency Ranges*

| Mean Processing Time | Cumulative Probability Range |
|---|---|
| 2.5 | 0.00–0.19 |
| 3.5 | 0.20–0.49 |
| 4.5 | 0.50–0.89 |
| 5.5 | 0.90–0.99 |

*Processing Time—Operation 2*
*Frequency Ranges*

| Mean Processing Time | Cumulative Probability Range |
|---|---|
| 0.5 | 0.00–0.09 |
| 1.5 | 0.10–0.29 |
| 2.5 | 0.30–0.79 |
| 3.5 | 0.80–0.99 |

| Component No. | RN1 | Interarrival Time | RN2 | Process 1 Time | RN3 | Process 2 Time |
|---|---|---|---|---|---|---|
| 1 | 0.07 | 1.5 | 0.47 | 3.5 | 0.38 | 2.5 |
| 2 | 0.78 | 4.5 | 0.28 | 3.5 | 0.28 | 1.5 |
| 3 | 0.50 | 3.5 | 0.49 | 3.5 | 0.88 | 3.5 |
| 4 | 0.74 | 4.5 | 0.27 | 3.5 | 0.21 | 1.5 |
| 5 | 0.68 | 4.5 | 0.47 | 3.5 | 0.04 | 0.5 |
| 6 | 0.96 | 4.5 | 0.10 | 2.5 | 0.96 | 3.5 |
| 7 | 0.69 | 4.5 | 0.75 | 4.5 | 0.11 | 1.5 |
| 8 | 0.44 | 3.5 | 0.06 | 2.5 | 0.35 | 2.5 |
| 9 | 0.85 | 4.5 | 0.74 | 4.5 | 0.04 | 0.5 |
| 10 | 0.12 | 1.5 | 0.65 | 4.5 | 0.53 | 2.5 |
| 11 | 0.11 | 1.5 | 0.56 | 4.5 | 0.91 | 3.5 |
| 12 | 0.74 | 4.5 | 0.00 | 2.5 | 0.03 | 0.5 |
| 13 | 0.47 | 3.5 | 0.52 | 4.5 | 0.36 | 2.5 |
| 14 | 0.98 | 4.5 | 0.17 | 2.5 | 0.08 | 0.5 |
| 15 | 0.18 | 1.5 | 0.09 | 2.5 | 0.30 | 2.5 |
| 16 | 0.35 | 3.5 | 0.88 | 4.5 | 0.90 | 3.5 |
| 17 | 0.91 | 4.5 | 0.37 | 3.5 | 0.01 | 0.5 |
| 18 | 0.86 | 4.5 | 0.05 | 2.5 | 0.52 | 2.5 |
| 19 | 0.99 | 4.5 | 0.27 | 3.5 | 0.31 | 2.5 |
| 20 | 0.17 | 1.5 | 0.01 | 2.5 | 0.81 | 3.5 |

TABLE  T4.3
Exogenous Inputs for Example T4.1

| | | Worker 1 | | | Worker 2 | | | Performance Measures | |
| | | | | | | | | Component Wait for Worker | Total Worker Idle (waiting for component or tool) |
| Comp. | Arrival Time | Operation 1 Start | Operation 2 Start | Operation 2 End | Operation 1 Start | Operation 2 Start | Operation 2 End | | |
|---|---|---|---|---|---|---|---|---|---|
| 1 | 1.5 | 1.5 | 5.0 | 7.5 | | | | — | 1.5 |
| 2 | 6.0 | | | | 6.0 | 9.5 | 11.0 | — | 6.0 |
| 3 | 9.5 | 9.5 | 13.0 | 16.5 | | | | — | 2.0 |
| 4 | 14.0 | | | | 14.0 | 17.5 | 19.0 | — | 3.0 |
| 5 | 18.5 | 18.5 | 22.0 | 22.5 | | | | — | 2.0 |
| 6 | 23.0 | | | | 23.0 | 25.5 | 29.0 | — | 4.0 |
| 7 | 27.5 | 27.5 | 32.0 | 33.5 | | | | — | 5.0 |
| 8 | 31.0 | | | | 32.0 | 34.5 | 37.0 | 1.0 | 3.0 |
| 9 | 35.5 | 35.5 | 40.0 | 40.5 | | | | — | 2.0 |
| 10 | 37.0 | | | | 40.0 | 44.5 | 47.0 | 3.0 | 3.0 |
| 11 | 38.5 | 44.5 | 49.0 | 52.5 | | | | 6.0 | 4.0 |
| 12 | 43.0 | | | | 49.0 | 51.5 | 52.0 | 6.0 | 2.0 |
| 13 | 46.5 | | | | 52.0 | 56.5 | 59.0 | 5.5 | — |
| 14 | 51.0 | 56.5 | 59.0 | 59.5 | | | | 5.5 | 4.0 |
| 15 | 52.5 | | | | 59.0 | 61.5 | 64.0 | 6.5 | — |
| 16 | 56.0 | 61.5 | 66.0 | 69.5 | | | | 5.5 | 2.0 |
| 17 | 60.5 | | | | 66.0 | 69.5 | 70.0 | 5.5 | 2.0 |
| 18 | 65.0 | 69.5 | 72.0 | 74.5 | | | | 4.5 | — |
| 19 | 69.5 | | | | 72.0 | 75.5 | 78.0 | 2.5 | 2.0 |
| 20 | 71.0 | 75.5 | 78.0 | 81.5 | | | | 4.5 | 1.0 |
| | | | | | | | Averages | 2.8 | 2.43 |

TABLE T4.4
Simulation of Single Tool Problem

We can use these ranges with the random numbers in Table T4.1 to generate random inputs. Table T4.3 shows the exogenous inputs we generated for twenty components. We took the random numbers from the first three columns in Table T4.1. Each exogenous input requires a different set of random numbers because the inputs are assumed to be independent.

Now that we have the exogenous inputs we can simulate operation of the system with one tool, as shown in Table T4.4. The first column in Table T4.4 identifies the component, and the second column shows when the component enters the system. We obtain the arrival time from the interarrival times in Table T4.3. The first interarrival time in Table T4.3 is 1.5. We start the simulation at time zero, so the first component arrives at time 1.5. The interarrival time for the second component is 4.5, so it arrives 4.5 minutes later than the first component, or at time 6.0. We calculate the remaining interarrival times similarly (by adding the component's interarrival time to the arrival time of the previous component).

Table T4.4 has columns for each of the two workers assigned to the work center that keep track of

1. When the worker starts operation 1 (which is when the worker is free to start working on the component *and* the special tool is available)

2. When operation 2 starts (and operation 1 ends)
3. When operation 2 ends

The information in these eight columns is sufficient for keeping track of the system and calculating the following performance measures:

1. The time a *component* spends waiting for processing—component wait time
2. The *total* time a *worker* spends idle (waiting for a part and/or the special tool)

In Table T4.4 we assume the first component goes to the first worker. The first worker is ready to begin processing the first component at its arrival time (1.5 minutes) and begins operation 1 immediately, because the special tool is available. The first operation is completed in 3.5 minutes (from Table T4.3), so operation 2 begins at time 1.5 + 3.5 = 5.0. Operation 2 takes 2.5 minutes (Table T4.3 again), so the first component is completed at time 7.5. The first worker was idle for 1.5 minutes until the first component arrived, so the worker's idle time for the first component is 1.5 minutes.

The second component arrives at time 6. When it arrives, worker 1 is performing operation 2 on the first component, so worker 2 takes the second component and begins operation 1 immediately, because the special tool is available. Worker 2 completes operation 1 at time 9.5 and operation 2 at time 11.0. The worker's idle time is 6.0 minutes, the difference between the time the simulation started and the time worker 2 took began processing component 2.

Component 3 is handled similarly. When component 3 arrives, worker 2 is starting operation 2 on component 2. Worker 1 is available, having finished with component 1 at time 7.5. Worker 2 was done with the special tool at time 9.5, so the first operation can begin immediately at time 9.5. Worker 1 is finished with component 3 at time 16.5 and was idle for 2 minutes between completing component 1 and starting component 3.

The simulation continues in this fashion until component 6 arrives. Both workers 1 and 2 are available. Because worker 2 has been idle longer, we will assume worker 2 takes the part. When component 8 arrives, the second worker is available but cannot begin processing the part at time 31.0, because worker 1 does not finish with the special tool until time 32.0. Thus, operation 1 on component 8 begins at time 32.0. Note that component 1 had to wait one minute for the special tool. The worker's idle time for this component is three minutes. As already defined, the worker's idle time includes time waiting for a part and/or waiting for the special tool, so the idle time for the worker for component 8 is the time between the completion of component 6 and the start of operation 1 on component 8 (32.0 − 29.0 = 3.0).

Component 11 arrives while both workers 1 and 2 are busy. Worker 1 is the first worker available, but worker 2 is not finished with the special tool until 44.5, so worker 1 remains idle for 4 minutes until 44.5. Note that the component had to wait 6 minutes for processing to begin.

The simulation of Table T4.4 shows an average worker idle time (waiting for a component and/or special tool) of 2.43 minutes and an average component waiting time of 2.8 minutes.

Table T4.5 is a simulation of the same system with a special tool for each worker. We used the exogenous inputs from Table T4.3 in Table T4.5. The technique of using the same random numbers has a number of names, including **pairing, blocking** and using **common random numbers.** This technique provides for stronger statistical tests. When comparing two system designs under the same conditions (exogenous inputs), any differences in the performance

| | | Worker 1 | | | Worker 2 | | | Performance Measures | |
|---|---|---|---|---|---|---|---|---|---|
| Comp. | Arrival Time | Operation 1 Start | Operation 2 Start | Operation 2 End | Operation 1 Start | Operation 2 Start | Operation 2 End | Component Wait for Worker | Total Worker Idle (waiting for component) |
| 1 | 1.5 | 1.5 | 5.0 | 7.5 | | | | — | 1.5 |
| 2 | 6.0 | | | | 6.0 | 9.5 | 11.0 | — | 6.0 |
| 3 | 9.5 | 9.5 | 13.0 | 16.5 | | | | — | 2.0 |
| 4 | 14.0 | | | | 14.0 | 17.5 | 19.0 | — | 3.0 |
| 5 | 18.5 | 18.5 | 22.0 | 22.5 | | | | — | 2.0 |
| 6 | 23.0 | | | | 23.0 | 25.5 | 29.0 | — | 4.0 |
| 7 | 27.5 | 27.5 | 32.0 | 33.5 | | | | — | 5.0 |
| 8 | 31.0 | | | | 31.0 | 33.5 | 36.0 | — | 2.0 |
| 9 | 35.5 | 35.5 | 40.0 | 40.5 | | | | — | 2.0 |
| 10 | 37.0 | | | | 37.0 | 41.5 | 44.0 | — | 1.0 |
| 11 | 38.5 | 40.5 | 45.0 | 48.5 | | | | 2.0 | — |
| 12 | 43.0 | | | | 44.0 | 46.5 | 47.0 | 1.0 | — |
| 13 | 46.5 | | | | 47.0 | 51.5 | 54.0 | 0.5 | — |
| 14 | 51.0 | 51.0 | 53.5 | 54.0 | | | | — | 2.5 |
| 15 | 52.5 | 54.0 | 56.5 | 59.0 | | | | 1.5 | — |
| 16 | 56.0 | | | | 56.0 | 60.5 | 64.0 | — | 2.0 |
| 17 | 60.5 | 60.5 | 64.0 | 64.5 | | | | — | 1.5 |
| 18 | 65.0 | | | | 65.0 | 67.5 | 70.0 | — | 1.0 |
| 19 | 69.5 | 69.5 | 73.0 | 75.5 | | | | — | 5.0 |
| 20 | 71.0 | | | | 71.0 | 73.5 | 77.0 | — | 1.0 |
| | | | | | | | Averages | 0.25 | 2.075 |

TABLE T4.5
Simulation of Dual Tool Problem

measures are the result of system differences rather than the particular exogenous inputs used in the study.

The simulation in Table T4.5 is simpler than that in Table T4.4, because the workers never have to wait for the special tool. The simulation in Table T4.5 shows that the addition of the special tool significantly reduces the waiting time for the components. The average component waiting time with one special tool was 2.8 minutes, whereas with two special tools this is reduced by 91 percent to 0.25 minutes. The worker's idle time was reduced by 15 percent to 2.075 minutes. The results of the simulation suggest that the second tool will improve the system's performance by increasing throughput, but we cannot know definitively without performing statistical tests. But before we can perform a statistical test, we must determine whether the simulated system is in **steady state,** or equilibrium, operation when we measure its performance.

The simulations in Tables T4.4 and 4.5 started with two idle workers and no components, but this is not the usual status for the system and is not representative of normal operating conditions. Because the system started empty and idle, it will go through a **transient phase** before it reaches steady state operation, if in fact it does reach a steady state. In many situations it is the steady state behavior that is of interest; however, in some situations the transient behavior is of interest. For example, a bank may be interested in how to schedule tellers to minimize labor costs while maintaining an acceptable level of performance. A bank starts empty and should end empty, and it is the transient behavior that is of interest. This is an example of a **regenerative simulation**—the system starts and ends empty over a specific period. In this case we can average the performance

measures for each regeneration period and use them as independent observations for statistical tests. In the case of a steady state simulation, obtaining independent observations is much more complicated.

There are no sure techniques for determining when a simulation reaches steady state behavior; however, one useful approach is to plot a performance measure as a function of time. For Example T4.1 we developed simulation models in the MOR/DS (Microcomputer Support for Operations Research/Discrete Simulation) simulation language. Figure T4.7 plots the waiting times (defined in this case as total time in the system) for the first five hundred components for the single tool case. It is obvious from this figure that the waiting times grow with each new component. Thus, the single tool problem does not reach a steady state; speaking of an average waiting time is not meaningful. Clearly, with only one tool this work center cannot keep pace with the rest of the production process. Figure T4.8 shows the waiting time for the first five hundred components with two special tools. The pattern of results indicates a steady state has been attained. This figure shows that with two special tools, the workers can keep up with the work load. Thus, these simulation results clearly show that this production process requires two special tools.

Because the waiting times in Figure T4.8 go through a number of cycles within the first five hundred components, it seems reasonable to assume that the system is in steady state behavior and thus represents normal operating conditions. Under this assumption we ran the simulation for an additional one thousand components to determine the steady state behavior of the system. With two tools the average worker utilization is 87.9 percent, meaning that the workers

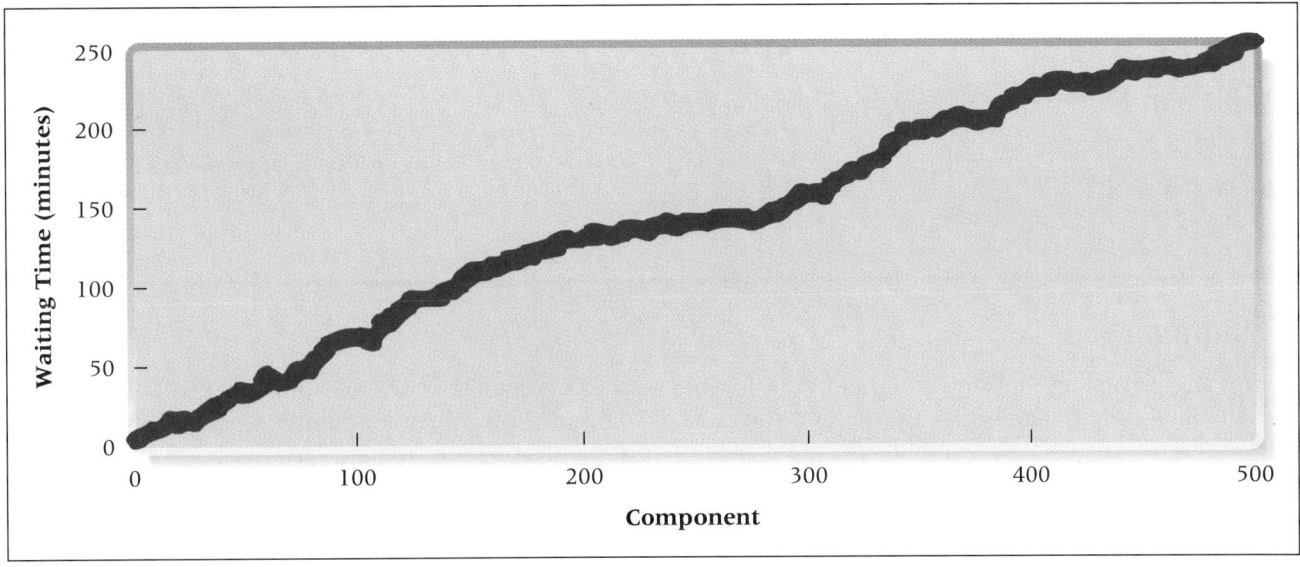

FIGURE T4.7
Waiting Time for Components with a Single Tool

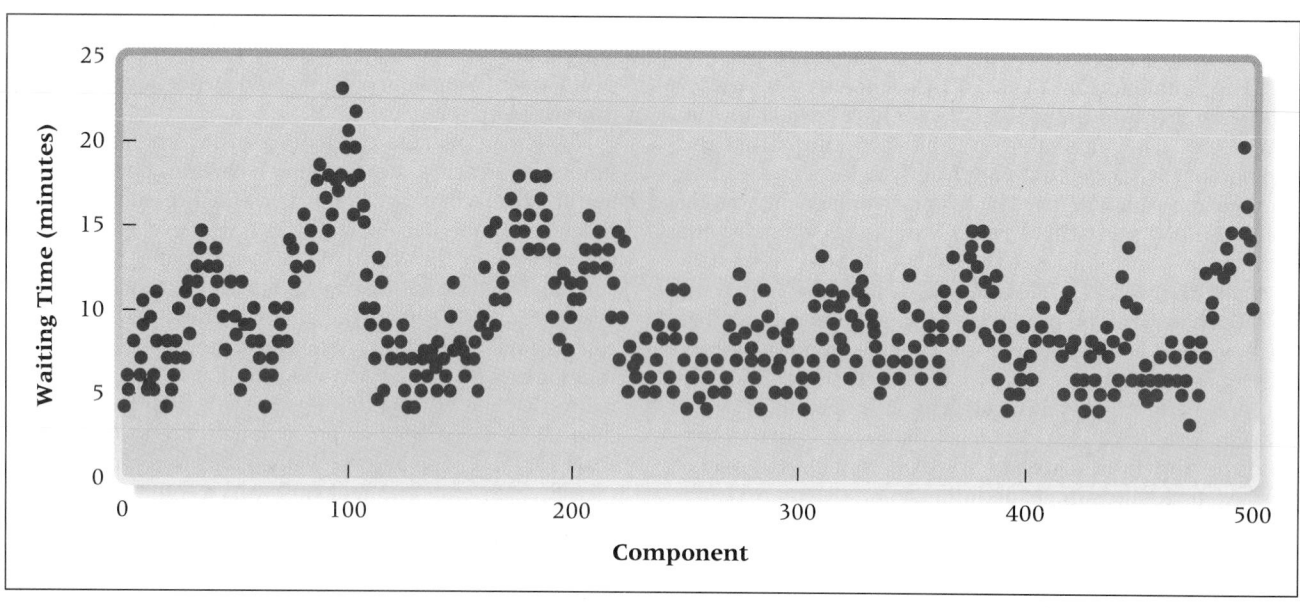

FIGURE T4.8
Waiting Times for Dual Tool Simulation

are idle 12.1 percent of the time. The average utilization of each special tool is 55.2 percent. This shows that there is more work than one tool can handle, even if we ignore the timing problems associated with sharing one tool. The average time a component spends waiting for a worker is 2.341 minutes, not the 0.25 minutes we calculated in Table T4.5, with a maximum observed time of 15 minutes. The average number of components waiting for a worker is 0.39, with a maximum of 5 observed.

## Simulation Languages

Although we can write simulations in a programming language such as FORTRAN, it is more common to use a special purpose simulation language. More than forty simulation languages have been developed, which gives an indication of the popularity of simulation. Some, such as the very capable MOR/DS language, are available for less than $100. Some languages with sophisticated animation capabilities cost more than $10,000. Some of the more popular simulation languages are GPSS, SIMAN, SLAM, and SIMSCRIPT.[1]

_____

[1]For a comparison of simulation languages, see James Swain, "Simulation Survey," *OR/MS Today* (October 1991): 81–102.

## ► Summary

Computer technology improved dramatically during the 1980s. At the beginning of the decade the personal computer was primarily a hobbyist's toy. Today, personal computers have the power of mainframe computers, and the increases in software capabilities and user friendliness are truly astounding. Students of business should learn about the growth in computer capabilities during the 1980s in order to have some idea of the magnitude of change that will occur by the end of the century. Computer simulation software is growing in performance, and with the increases in multimedia capabilities and virtual reality, the potential for computer simulation is unlimited. Simulation will increasingly become a required tool of the modern operations manager.

# ► Key Terms

| | | |
|---|---|---|
| blocking | exogenous inputs | regenerative simulation |
| common random numbers | pairing | steady state |
| continuous systems | performance measures | system model |
| discrete event simulation | pseudo-random numbers | transient phase |
| discrete systems | | |

# ► Discussion Questions

1. What are some circumstances that make computer simulation an important tool in problem solving?
2. How can simulation contribute to the study of such operations management problems as facility layout, staffing, or shop-floor control?
3. How does animation improve the usefulness of a simulation model?
4. What is an exogenous input? How can you identify exogenous inputs?
5. What is a performance measure? How can you determine appropriate performance measures?
6. Describe the steps in the simulation process for a study of a production control system.

7. Why do we use interarrival times to generate arrival times rather than generating arrival times directly?
8. How can the use of common random numbers improve a simulation study?
9. What is the difference between the transient phase of a simulation and its steady state performance?
10. What is a regenerative simulation? What are some cases in which a regenerative simulation can be used?
11. How can future developments in computer technology, such as virtual reality, be used to improve simulation methods?

# ► Problems

1. Given the following operation time data for a production process, construct frequency ranges to generate inputs that simulate the process:

| Processing Time (Minutes) | Probability |
|---|---|
| 0–4 | 0.15 |
| 4–8 | 0.20 |
| 8–12 | 0.35 |
| 12–16 | 0.30 |

2. The table that follows gives the transit times for shipping components from a factory to its main warehouse. Construct frequency ranges from this table, and generate ten outputs using the first ten random numbers from the second column of Table T4.1.

| Shipping Time (Hours) | Probability |
|---|---|
| 3.00–3.10 | 0.05 |
| 3.10–3.20 | 0.15 |
| 3.20–3.30 | 0.25 |
| 3.30–3.40 | 0.30 |
| 3.40–3.50 | 0.25 |

3. The interarrival times at a hospital emergency room were measured for 150 patients. Use this data to construct frequency ranges, and generate the arrival times for ten patients using the first ten random numbers from the fifth column of Table T4.1.

| Interarrival Time (Minutes) | Number of Patients |
|---|---|
| 0.0–2.0 | 30 |
| 2.0–4.0 | 30 |
| 4.0–6.0 | 35 |
| 6.0–8.0 | 45 |
| 8.0–10.0 | 10 |

4. John Blarney, a recent business school grad, plans to set up a financial planning business at a local mall. He plans to run the business by himself at first and wants to see whether he will be able to handle customer demand by himself. He has surveyed mall patrons and has determined that he can expect customers to arrive with the following frequency:

| Interarrival Time (Minutes) | Probability |
|---|---|
| 0.00–10.0 | 0.10 |
| 10.0–15.0 | 0.20 |
| 15.0–20.0 | 0.20 |
| 20.0–25.0 | 0.30 |
| 25.0–30.0 | 0.20 |

From his survey work, Blarney has evaluated customer needs and determined that three levels of consulting will be required. He has developed the following distribution for customer consulting time:

| Consulting Time (Minutes) | Probability |
|---|---|
| 10 | 0.2 |
| 20 | 0.6 |
| 30 | 0.2 |

Simulate the arrival of twenty customers, and calculate the average customer waiting time. Use column 3 of Table T4.1 to generate the arrival times and column 7 to generate the consulting times.

5. Repeat the simulation study in problem 4, but assume that customers are not willing to wait for more than ten minutes before being served. Instead of average customer waiting time, calculate the percentage of customers leaving because of an excessive waiting time.

6. A bank has a computer system with a disk drive unit that breaks frequently. The bank has purchased a spare disk drive unit so that it may immediately replace the original disk drive unit when it breaks. The bank then will immediately send the broken disk drive unit to the manufacturer to be repaired, even if the other disk drive is still being repaired. After the broken unit is repaired and returned to the bank, it will be used as the spare unit. The probability of time between breakdowns (in days) for the disk drive is as follows:

| Time Between Breakdowns (days) | Probability |
|---|---|
| 20 | 0.1 |
| 30 | 0.3 |
| 40 | 0.3 |
| 50 | 0.2 |
| 60 | 0.1 |

| Time for Disk Drive Repair (days) | Probability |
|---|---|
| 30 | 0.2 |
| 40 | 0.2 |
| 50 | 0.3 |
| 60 | 0.3 |

Simulate the operation of the computer system with the disk drive for ten breakdowns, using column 8

from Table T4.1 for the breakdown times and column 9 for the repair times. Calculate the percentage of time that the computer is unavailable because of disk drive failure.

7. A bank has a two tellers and a single waiting line. Customers wait in a single line and then are served by one and only one teller. The time between arrivals of customers follows these probabilities:

| Interarrival Time (Minutes) | Probability |
|---|---|
| 1.0 | 0.1 |
| 1.5 | 0.1 |
| 2.0 | 0.2 |
| 2.5 | 0.3 |
| 3.0 | 0.3 |

The teller service times are as follows:

| Teller Service Time (Minutes) | Probability |
|---|---|
| 3.0 | 0.2 |
| 4.0 | 0.3 |
| 5.0 | 0.3 |
| 6.0 | 0.2 |

Simulate the bank for ten customers, using column 4 from Table T4.1 for the arrival times and column 6 for the service times. Calculate the average waiting time per customer.

8. Althea Jones is the maintenance supervisor at Vroom Auto Products. She is interested in developing a preventative maintenance program for a group of machines and wants to simulate the current performance of the equipment. From past experience she knows there is a 30 percent chance that a machine will break down on any given day. If a breakdown does occur, the repair time is distributed as follows:

| Repair Time | Probability |
|---|---|
| 1 day | 0.2 |
| 2 days | 0.6 |
| 3 days | 0.2 |

Simulate the operation of one of the machines for a ten-day period. Use column 2 from Table T4.1 to generate the breakdowns and column 3 to determine the length of the breakdowns.

## ► Selected References

Curry, G. L., B. L. Deuermeyer, and R. M. Feldman. *Discrete Simulation: Fundamentals and Microcomputer Support.* Oakland, Calif.: Holden-Day, 1989.

Kleijnen, J.P.C. *Statistical Tools for Simulation Practitioners.* New York: Marcel Dekker, 1987.

Law, A. M., and W. D. Kelton. *Simulation Modeling and Analysis.* New York: McGraw-Hill, 1982.

Shannon, R. E. *Systems Simulation: The Art and Science.* Englewood Cliffs, N.J.: Prentice-Hall, 1975.

# Waiting Line Models

## Introduction

**Waiting lines,** or **queues,** are a common occurrence in our everyday lives. All of us have waited in line to purchase a ticket at a sporting event or waited to pay for groceries at a supermarket. Waiting lines are also common in a variety of operations management situations. Waiting lines form whenever the arrivals, or demand, for service from a facility exceeds the capacity of that facility. Waiting lines can consist of people, machines, customers' orders, computer jobs to be processed, or parts awaiting assembly. Examples of common waiting line situations are presented in Table T5.1.

In this tutorial we consider how to analyze waiting lines and how to evaluate the cost and effectiveness of service systems. If the demands to be placed on a service facility were known in advance and could be accurately predicted, scheduling the service facility in an efficient manner would be a relatively simple chore. However, it is often difficult to predict when units will arrive for service and/or how much time will be required to provide the needed service. Consequently, waiting line analysis is characterized by the following:

1. Customers, or arrivals, that require service
2. Uncertainty in regard to the magnitude of the demand for service and the timing of the arrivals for service
3. Service facilities, or servers, that perform the service operation
4. Uncertainty concerning the time duration of the service operation
5. Uncertainty concerning the behavior of the customers as they arrive for service and/or wait in the queue

Based on these five characteristics the objective of queueing analysis becomes the provision of adequate but not excessive service. Providing too much service to the extent that the service facility is often idle, or empty, represents an incurrence of unnecessary costs, namely, the direct cost of idle employees or the loss associated with low morale from being idle. Conversely, excessive waiting has a cost in terms of customers' frustration and loss of goodwill. The goal of waiting line analysis is to achieve an economic balance between the cost of the service and the cost associated with the wait required for that service. Figure

| Situation | Arrivals (Demand) | Servers | Service Mechanism |
|---|---|---|---|
| Doctor's office | Patients | Doctor and nurse | Providing medical care |
| Movie theater box office | Movie patrons | Ticket seller | Selling tickets |
| Traffic intersection | Automobiles | Traffic signal | Moving through intersection |
| Port | Ships | Dock workers | Unloading and loading ships |
| Garage | Automobiles | Repairers | Repairing automobiles |
| Registrar's office | Prospective students | Registration clerks | Registering students |
| Pizza restaurant | Hungry people | Pizza makers | Making and serving pizzas |
| Airport | Airplanes | Runways, gates, and terminals | Arriving and departing airplanes |
| Mail-order store | Mail orders | Clerks | Filling orders |
| Telephone exchange | Calls | Switching equipment | Completing call connections |

TABLE T5.1
Examples of Common Waiting Line Situations

T5.1 shows the relationship between the level of service provided, the cost of the service, the cost associated with the wait required for that service, and the total cost (the sum of the service cost and the waiting cost).

Queueing theory originated in the research of a Danish engineer, A. K. Erlang, who studied the fluctuating demands on telephone service. In 1913 he published some of his findings in a report entitled, *Solution of Some Problems in the Theory of Probabilities of Significance in Automatic Telephone Exchanges.* After World War I Erlang's work was expanded to encompass numerous applications of waiting lines to busi-

ness situations. Queueing theory is a standard tool of operations management in such areas as scheduling, assembly line balancing, service system design, and machine loading.

## Structure of Waiting Line Problems

We begin our analysis of waiting line problems with a description of their structure. Figure T5.2 presents the major elements common to all waiting line problems.

These major elements have properties and characteristics that we must examine before we can develop and apply mathematical models of waiting lines.

### The Input Process

The input process for a queueing problem, described in terms of three characteristics, is concerned with the manner in which items or customers enter into or arrive at the service system.

**Size of the Input Source**  The source of arrivals is referred to as the **input source,** or **calling population.** The size of the input source is either infinite or finite and represents the total number of potential customers requiring service for a given period of time. The assumption of an infinite-size input source is applicable to situations in which the number of arrivals at any particular moment is only a small portion of the potential arrivals. Examples of unlimited calling populations include cars arriving at a stop light, customers arriving at a convenience store, or voters arriving at a poll to vote. We assume a finite-size calling population if the

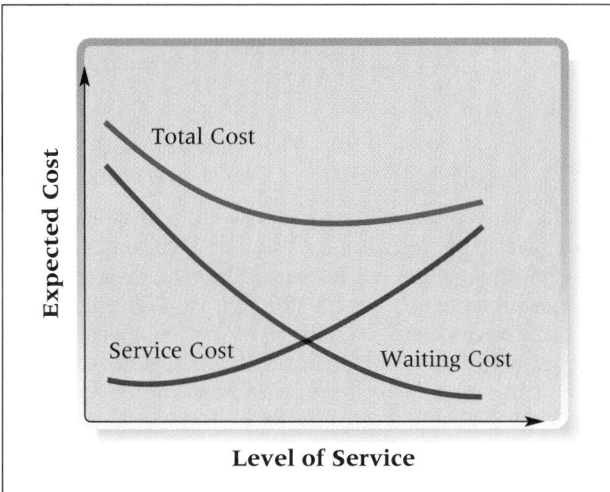

**FIGURE T5.1**
Service Level–Cost Relationships—Waiting Line Model

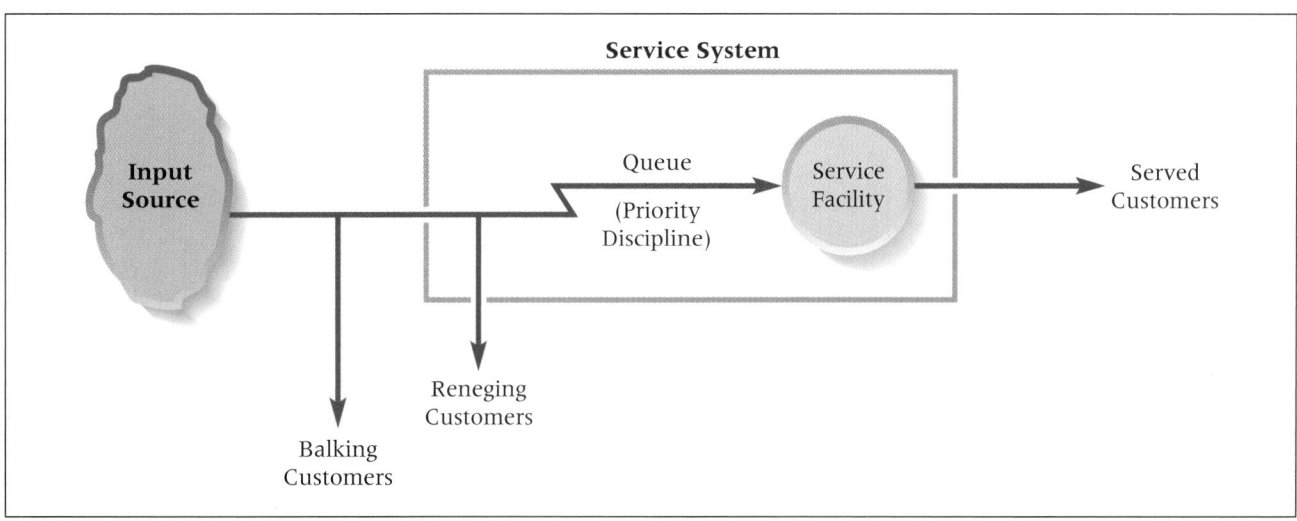

**FIGURE T5.2**
Major Elements of Waiting Line Problems

number of customers in the queueing system significantly affects the rate at which the input source generates new customers. An example of a finite-size input source is an airplane—it has a fixed capacity (number of passenger seats).

**Arrival Pattern for the System**  Customers, or objects, can arrive at a service facility according to some known, or deterministic, pattern. For example, arrivals at a particular theater might follow a known pattern that corresponds to the times at which the movie is being shown.

However, arrivals often occur in a random pattern. For example, calls coming to an 800 telephone number typically arrive randomly, as do the arrivals at emergency medical facilities. A random arrival pattern has two important char-

acteristics. First, a random arrival pattern is one in which each arrival is independent of all other arrivals. Second, the probability of a particular arrival happening during a specific time period does not depend on what happened up to the beginning of the period but only on the length of the time period. Such a random arrival pattern is said to be *memoryless* (it has no memory of past events).

The **Poisson distribution** is commonly used to describe the random pattern of number of customers arrivals to a waiting line system during some time period. Using the Poisson distribution, if there is an average of λ arrivals in a time period $T$, the probability of $x$ arrivals in the same time period is expressed as

$$P[x \text{ arrivals during the period } T] = \frac{e^{-\lambda T}(\lambda T)^x}{x!} \quad \text{(T5-1)}$$

where

$e = 2.71828$ (the base of natural logarithms)
$x! = (x)(x-1)(x-2)\ldots(3)(2)(1)$ ($x$ factorial)

The Poisson distribution is a discrete probability distribution, because it describes the number of customer arrivals for a specific time period. In Figure T5.3 the Poisson distribution is presented for several different values of the mean, λ. As the mean becomes larger, the Poisson distribution becomes flatter and more symmetrical. Referring to Figure T5.3b, if the mean arrival rate is three customers per time period, the probabilities associated with the different number of arrivals are as shown in Table T5.2.[1]

With respect to the calling population, if the number of arrivals per time period is Poisson distributed with a mean arrival rate of λ, the time between arrivals (interarrival time) is distributed as the negative exponential probability distribution with mean of $1/\lambda$. For example, if the mean

[1]The Appendix presents a table of Poisson probability values for various values of $x$ and λ.

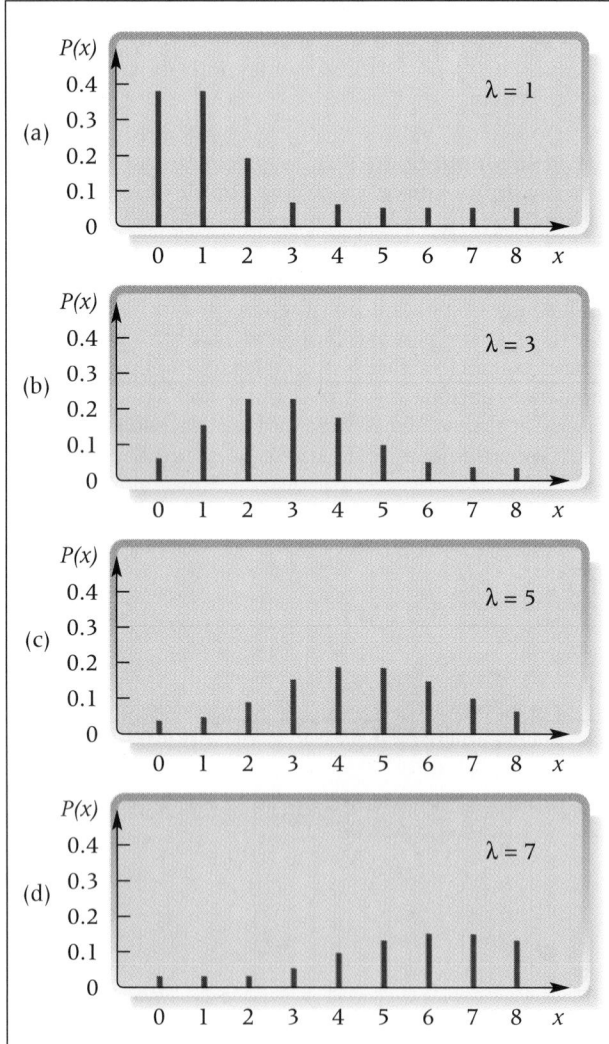

FIGURE  T5.3
Poisson Distribution—Varying Values of Mean, λ

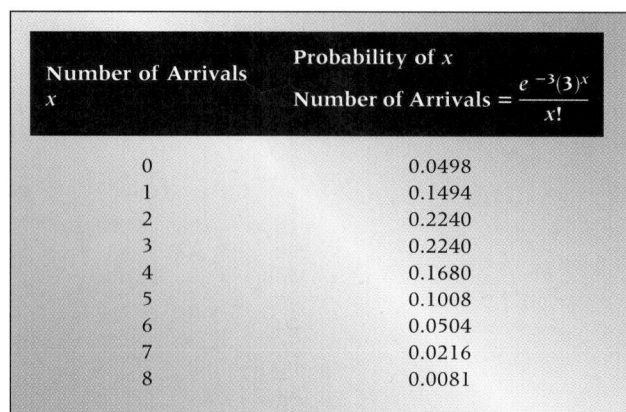

| Number of Arrivals $x$ | Probability of $x$ Number of Arrivals $= \dfrac{e^{-3}(3)^x}{x!}$ |
|---|---|
| 0 | 0.0498 |
| 1 | 0.1494 |
| 2 | 0.2240 |
| 3 | 0.2240 |
| 4 | 0.1680 |
| 5 | 0.1008 |
| 6 | 0.0504 |
| 7 | 0.0216 |
| 8 | 0.0081 |

TABLE  T5.2
Probability of $x$ Arrivals (Poisson Arrivals, λ = 3 Customers per Time Period)

| Arrival Rate | Interarrival Time |
|---|---|
| Poisson distributed | Negative exponentially distributed |
| Mean = | Mean = $1/\lambda$ |
| $\lambda$ = 5 customers per 10-minute time period | $1/\lambda = 1/\left(\dfrac{5\ customers}{10\text{-minute time period}}\right)$ |
| | = 2 minutes/arrival |

TABLE T5.3
Relationship Between Arrival Rate and Interarrival Time

arrival rate per ten-minute time period is five customers, the mean time between arrivals is two minutes (10 minutes/5 minutes = 2 minutes/arrival). Table T5.3 summarizes the relationship between the arrival rate and the interarrival time.

**Behavior of Arrivals** Considering the behavior of arrivals to the waiting line is also part of the analysis. Waiting line analysis proceeds on the basis that the arrivals are patient and form into queues awaiting service. However, some waiting line models allow for arrivals who balk or renege. **Balking** refers to the phenomenon of arrivals who refuse to join the waiting line because it is simply too long. **Reneging** refers to the situation in which the arrivals initially join the queue but then leave without completing the service. Virtually all of us have practiced balking or reneging with respect to some type of waiting line. When this happens, the service facility loses a customer and a source of revenue.

## The Waiting Line (Queue)

The focal point of waiting line analysis and the second major component of a waiting line problem is the waiting line itself. We describe a waiting line by three characteristics.

**Length of the Waiting Line** The length of a waiting line can be either limited or unlimited. An example of a limited queue situation would be a small theater that can seat a limited number of people for any performance. An example of an unlimited queue situation would be the toll booth at a bridge. In general, we treat waiting line models in this tutorial under the assumption of unlimited queue length.

**Number of Waiting Lines** Queues can be designed to have a single line or multiple lines. Figure T5.4 presents an example of each.

**Queue Discipline** A third characteristic of waiting lines is the queue discipline. The **queue discipline** specifies the

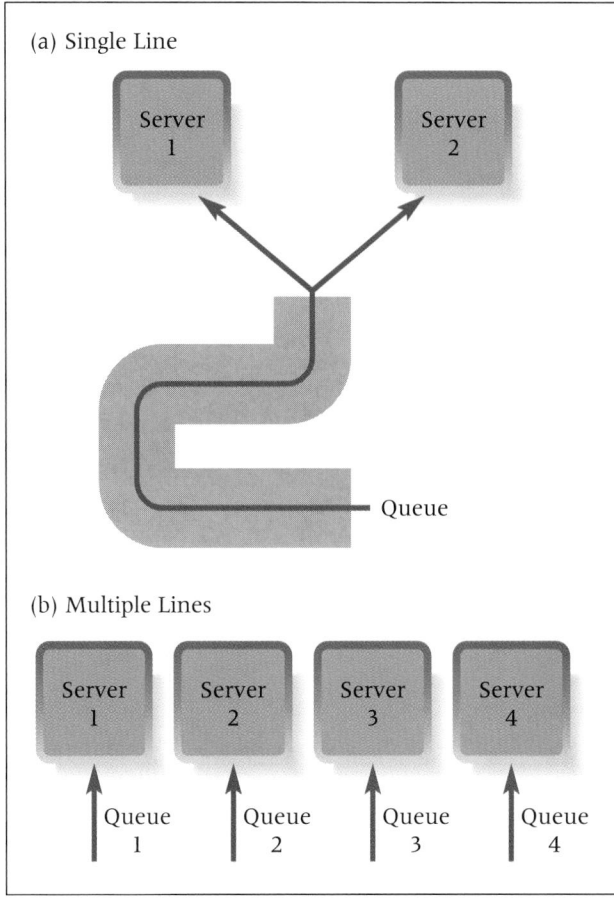

(a) Single Line

Server 1

Server 2

Queue

(b) Multiple Lines

Server 1

Server 2

Server 3

Server 4

Queue 1

Queue 2

Queue 3

Queue 4

FIGURE T5.4
Waiting Line Configurations

order in which customers entering the queueing system are served. Common types of queue disciplines are

1. First come, first served. Customers are served in the order in which they enter the queue. Standing in line to purchase tickets at a movie theater is an example of a first-come, first-served queue discipline.
2. Last come, first served. Customers are served in the reverse order in which they enter the queue. An elevator in which people move to the rear as they enter is an example of a last-come, first-served queue discipline.
3. Random. This queue discipline has no order of service. Question-and-answer sessions in televised news conferences often appear to be a random queue discipline.
4. Priority. This queue discipline has a predefined rule that determines the order of service. For example, people with chronic respiratory problems may be selected first in the general population of a city for a flu inoculation.

## The Service Facility

The service facility for the queueing system is concerned with the manner in which items or customers are served and leave the queueing system. We describe the service facility in terms of two characteristics.

### Number and Configurations of Service Facilities
The service mechanism may consist of a single-service facility or multiple-service facilities. A queueing system with multiple-service facilities arranged in parallel is called a *multiple-channel queueing system.* A queueing system with multiple-service facilities arranged in series is called a *multiple-phase queueing system.* The number of **channels** in a queueing system refers to the number of parallel service facilities

available for service arrivals. The number of **phases** in a queueing system refers to the number of sequential service steps through which each individual arrival must pass. Service facility configurations fall into five basic structure categories, according to customer volume and the type of services provided. Figure T5.5 shows each category.

An example of a single-channel, single-phase queueing system would be a small grocery store with only one checkout station. An example of a multiple-channel, single-phase queueing system would be a large grocery store with several checkout stations. An example of a single-channel, multiple-phase queueing system would be a dentist's office in which a patient is first treated by a dental hygienist and then by the dentist. If the office has several dentists, it would be an example of a multiple-channel, multiple-phase

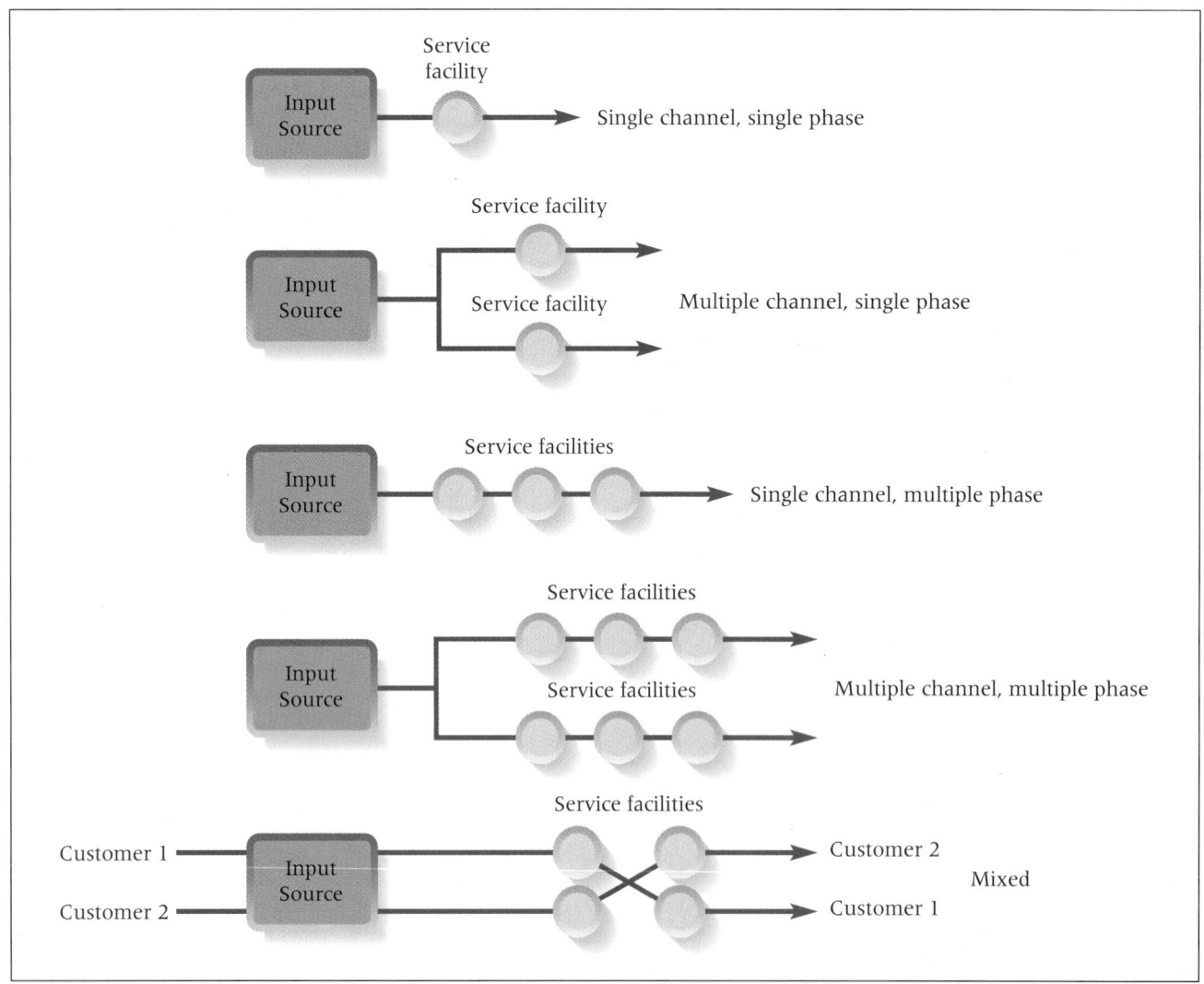

FIGURE T5.5
Basic Configurations of Service Facilities

queueing system. In the mixed arrangement each customer has a specific routing between service facilities, and service cannot be neatly described in phases.

**Service Pattern for the System**  The time needed for completing the service is referred to as the **service time,** or **holding time.** The service time is generally dependent upon the customer's service requirement, but it may also be partially dependent on the state of the service mechanism. For example, the servers may tend to speed up their service if they perceive that many customers are waiting.

In typical waiting line situations the times required for serving customers also follow a random pattern. As was the case for the random arrival pattern for customers to a waiting line system, we can use a probability distribution to describe the random service time pattern. In the case of random arrivals we were interested in the number of arrivals during a time period. Consequently, we used the discrete Poisson distribution. Service times are continuous, and we use a continuous probability distribution, the negative exponential distribution (or, as it is often called, simply the **exponential distribution),** to describe the random pattern of customer service times in a waiting line system. Using the negative exponential distribution, if $\mu$ is the average service rate ($\mu$ is the inverse of the average service time), the (exponential) probability density function for the service time, $t$, is expressed as

$$f(t) = \mu e^{-\mu t} \text{ for } t \geq 0 \qquad \text{(T5-2)}$$

where

$$e = 2.71828 \text{ (base of natural logarithms)}$$

The negative exponential distribution is a continuous probability distribution, which is used to describe the time required to perform a service. Figure T5.6 presents the negative exponential probability distribution for the service time, $t$.

We can see from Figure T5.6 that short service times have the highest probability of occurrence. As the service time increases, the probability distribution decreases exponentially toward a zero probability.

Using this (exponential) probability density function,[2] we can determine the probability that the service time, $t$, will exceed some specified length of time, $T$. This probability is expressed as

$$P(\text{service time, } t, \text{ exceeds } T) = P(t > T) = e^{-\mu T} \qquad \text{(T5-3)}$$

Conversely, the probability that the service time, $t$, will be less than or equal to some specified length of time, $T$, is expressed as

$$P(\text{service time, } t, \text{ is less than or equal to } T) = P(t \leq T) = 1 - e^{-\mu T}$$
$$\text{(T5-4)}$$

[2]The Appendix presents a table of the exponential functions, $e^x$ and $e^{-x}$ for various values of $x$.

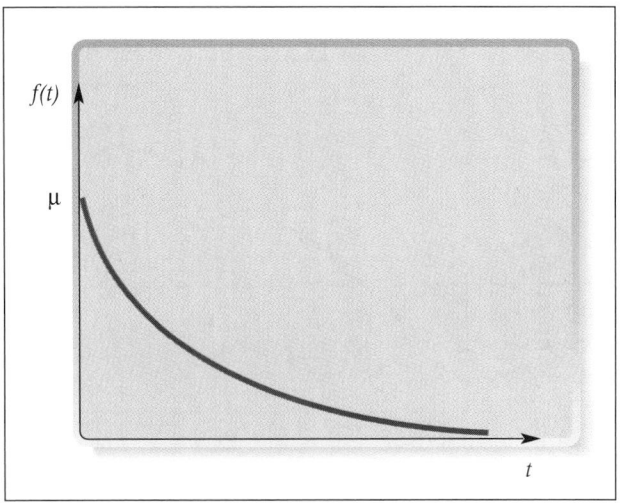

FIGURE T5.6
Negative Exponential Probability Distribution for Service Time, $t$

To illustrate the use of these formulas let us assume that we operate a muffler shop that can service an average of three automobiles per hour. Using equation T5-4 we can compute the probability that an automobile will have a new muffler installed within a specified service time, $T$. For example,

$$P[\text{service time} \leq 0.1 \text{ hours}] = 1 - e^{-3(0.1)} = 0.2592$$
$$P[\text{service time} \leq 0.2 \text{ hours}] = 1 - e^{-3(0.2)} = 0.4512 \quad \text{(T5-5)}$$
$$P[\text{service time} \leq 0.4 \text{ hours}] = 1 - e^{-3(0.4)} = 0.6988$$
$$P[\text{service time} \leq 0.6 \text{ hours}] = 1 - e^{-3(0.6)} = 0.8347$$

Consequently, using the exponential distribution with $\mu = 3$, we would expect 25.92 percent of the automobiles to have a new muffler installed within 6 minutes or less ($T \leq 0.1$ hours), 45.12 percent in 12 minutes or less, 69.88 percent in 24 minutes or less, and 83.47 percent in 36 minutes or less. Figure T5.7a shows graphically the probability that an automobile will have a new muffler installed within a specified time, $T$, given $\mu = 3$.

Using equation T5-3, we can compute the probability that an automobile will take more than a specified service time $T$ to have a muffler installed. For example,

$$P[\text{service time} > 0.1 \text{ hours}] = e^{-3(0.1)} = 0.7408$$
$$P[\text{service time} > 0.2 \text{ hours}] = e^{-3(0.2)} = 0.5488$$
$$P[\text{service time} > 0.4 \text{ hours}] = e^{-3(0.4)} = 0.3012$$
$$P[\text{service time} > 0.6 \text{ hours}] = e^{-3(0.6)} = 0.1653 \quad \text{(T5-6)}$$

Consequently, using the exponential distribution with $\mu = 3$, we would expect 74.08 percent of the automobiles to require more than 6 minutes ($T > 0.1$ hours) to have a muffler installed, 54.88 percent to require more than 12 minutes, 30.12 percent to require more than 24 minutes, and 16.53 percent to require more than 36 minutes. Figure

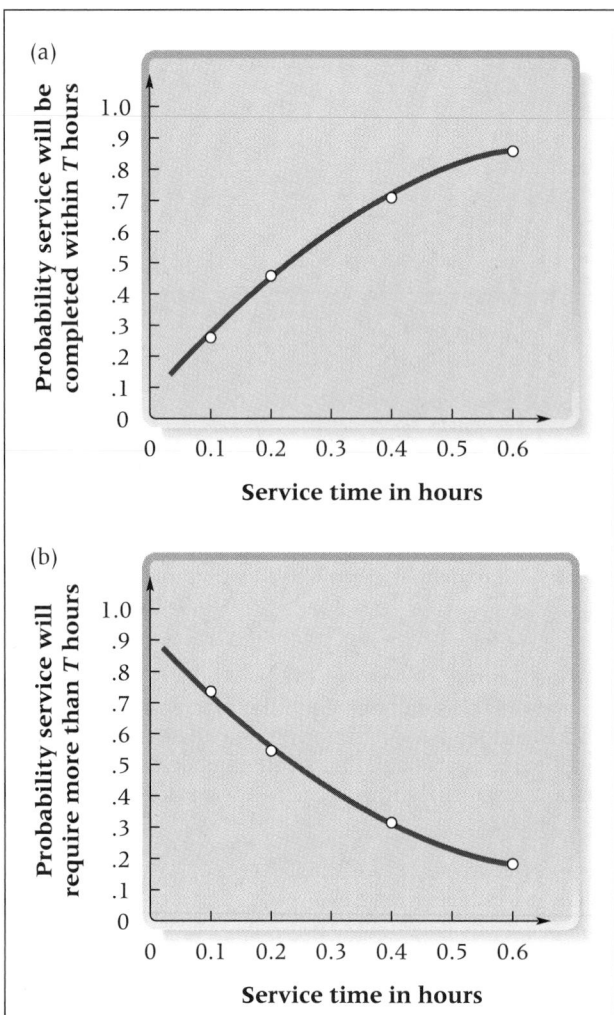

(a)

(b)

FIGURE T5.7
Service Time—Exponential Distribution

T5.7b shows graphically the probability that an automobile will require more than a specified time $T$ to have a muffler installed, given $\mu = 3$.

With respect to the service facility, when the expected service completion time, $1/\mu$, follows the negative exponential distribution, the mean service rate, $\mu$, follows a Poisson distribution. For example, if the mean service completion time is twelve minutes per customer, the mean service rate is five customers per hour. Table T5.4 summarizes the relationship between the service time and the service rate.

## Operating Characteristics of Waiting Line Models

The basic objective of waiting line analysis is to balance the level of service provided with the cost associated with

| Service Time | Service Rate |
|---|---|
| Negative exponentially distributed | Poisson distributed |
| Mean = $1/\mu$ | Mean = $\mu$ |
| $1/\mu = 1/\left(\dfrac{5 \text{ customers}}{1 \text{ hour time period}}\right)$ | $\mu = 5$ customers/hour |
| $= 12$ minutes/customer | |

TABLE T5.4
Relationship Between Service Time and Service Rate

providing that level of service. However, unlike linear programming models, there is no procedure for the optimization of waiting line models. For a given waiting line model, we typically try to identify its operating characteristics. Important **operating characteristics** include

1. The average number of units in the waiting line
2. The average number of units in the system
3. The average time each unit spends in the waiting line
4. The average time each unit spends in the system
5. The service facility utilization
6. The probability of a specific number of units (customers) in the system (in the waiting line or being served)

Given this information about operating characteristics and estimates of service cost and customer waiting time cost, the operations manager seeks to make decisions that will balance service levels and service costs.

## Notation Used for Waiting Line Models

In later sections of this tutorial we will consider some examples of the application of waiting line models in operations management. We will use the following notation in presenting these examples:

$\lambda$ = **mean arrival rate** (arrivals per unit of time)
$\mu$ = **mean service rate** per server (services per unit of time)
$1/\lambda$ = mean time between arrivals
$1/\mu$ = mean time per unit served (service time per unit)
$s$ = number of servers
$L$ = average number of units in the service system
$L_q$ = average number of units in the waiting line
$W$ = average time spent in the system (including service)
$W_q$ = average time spent in the waiting line
$n$ = number of units in the service system
$P_n$ = probability that there are $n$ units in the system
$\rho$ = average use of the service facility (defined as $\lambda/\mu$ or $\lambda/s\mu$)

In the next section of this tutorial we analyze problems involving the single-channel, single-phase; and multiple-channel, single-phase models. Many more advanced waiting line models are available, and examples of their application can be found in the references at the end of this tutorial.

## Data Collection and Model Validation

To use a particular queueing model we often must collect data on the average arrival rate, $\lambda$, and the average service time, $1/\mu$. To determine the average arrival rate we tally the number of arrivals per unit of time: minute, hour, day, week, and so forth. Then we compute an average arrival rate over all time periods which for we collected data. To determine the average service rate we tally the time required to perform several individual services. Then we use these individual service times to compute an average service time, $1/\mu$, and the average service rate, $\mu$.

After collecting data and determining the average arrival rate, $\lambda$, and the average service time, $1/\mu$, we try to validate the queueing model we are attempting to apply to the problem situation. For example, if we propose to use a single-channel waiting line model with a Poisson arrival rate and an exponential service time, we need to verify that our actual queueing problem fits that particular queueing model. We must confirm that the system has only one service facility, that the (actual) average arrival rate data fit the Poisson distribution, and that the (actual) average service time data fit the negative exponential distribution. The chi-square ($\chi^2$) goodness of fit test is typically used to determine whether the actual arrival rate data fit the Poisson distribution and the actual service time data fit the negative exponential distribution.

## Decision Variables in the Analysis of Waiting Lines

When operations managers analyze waiting line problems, a number of variables may affect the decisions they make. These variables include

1. Arrival rates. Price incentives, reservation systems, or advertising can affect the rate of demand for servers ($\lambda$).
2. Service rates. Server training programs, wage incentives, development of improved work methods, and using labor saving equipment can affect the service rate of the service facility ($\mu$).
3. Number of service facilities. This key variable in the analysis of waiting line problems determines the overall capacity of the service system.
4. Number of servers per facility. The service rate ($\mu$) of the facility reflects the number of servers per facility.
5. Number of phases. Efficiently completing the service may require sequential phases.
6. Queue configuration. The basic decision here is between a single-line queue or multiple-line queues for multiple-phase service facilities.

7. Queue discipline. The operations manager has to specify the queue discipline that the service system will follow.

The effect of these decision variables on the operating characteristics of queueing models will become more apparent in the applications that follow.

## The Single-Channel, Single-Phase Waiting Line Model

The single-channel, single-phase waiting line model is one of the simplest yet most widely applicable queueing models. Its derivation and use are predicated on the following assumptions:

- Arrivals come from an infinite population.
- The Poisson distribution describes the arrivals.
- The average arrival rate is constant over time = $\lambda$.
- Arrivals are served on a first-come, first-served basis.
- There is no balking or reneging in the service line (every arrival waits in a single line to be served, regardless of the length of the queue that forms).
- The negative exponential distribution describes service times.
- The average service time is constant over time = $1/\mu$.
- The average service time is greater than the average arrival rate.
- There is a single server.
- There is one service phase.

The operating characteristic equations for the single-channel, single-phase waiting line model are as follows:[3]
The expected number of units in the queue

$$= L_q = \lambda^2/\mu(\mu - \lambda) = L - \lambda/\mu \qquad (T5\text{-}7)$$

The expected number of units in the queueing system

$$= L = \lambda/(\mu - \lambda) \qquad (T5\text{-}8)$$

The expected waiting time in the queue

$$= W_q = \lambda/\mu(\mu - \lambda) = L_q/\lambda = W - 1/\mu \qquad (T5\text{-}9)$$

The expected waiting time in the queueing system

$$= W = 1/(\mu - \lambda) = L/\lambda \qquad (T5\text{-}10)$$

The utilization factor for the queueing system

$$= \rho = \lambda/\mu \qquad (T5\text{-}11)$$

The probability that there are $n$ units in the queueing system

$$= P_n = (\lambda/\mu)^n (1 - \lambda/\mu) \qquad (T5\text{-}12)$$

[3]The mathematics used to derive the operating characteristics equations presented in this tutorial is complicated and beyond the scope of this text. We will simply present these equations and illustrate their use. The reader interested in the derivations should consult Harvey M. Wagner, *Principles of Operations Research* (Englewood Cliffs, N.J.: Prentice-Hall, 1975), pp. 867–880.

## Application of the Single-Channel, Single-Phase Waiting Model

Susan Gonzalez is the owner and manager of Sue's Frame-It Shop, which provides picture-framing services for its customers. Her existing facility can serve an average of twelve customers per hour, and it has an average of ten customers per hour needing service. Gonzalez has studied waiting line models as part of her operations management course at a local university. She feels that her picture-framing shop satisfies all the assumptions necessary for application of a single-channel, single-phase waiting line model. She would like to use this model to answer a number of questions about her business.

**Question 1** What are the operating characteristics of Sue's Frame-It Shop for an arrival rate of ten customers per hour and a service rate of twelve customers per hour?

The operating characteristics can be calculated as follows:

$$\lambda = 10 \text{ customers/hour arriving}$$
$$\mu = 12 \text{ customers/hour being served}$$
$$s = \text{one service channel}$$

The expected number of customers in the queueing system:

$$L = \lambda/(\mu - \lambda) = 10/(12 - 10) = 10/2 = 5 \text{ customers} \quad (T5\text{-}13)$$

The expected number of customers in the queue:

$$L_q = \lambda^2/\mu(\mu - \lambda) = 10^2/12 (12 - 10) = 100/24 = 4.17 \text{ customers} \quad (T5\text{-}14)$$

The expected waiting time in the queueing system:

$$W = 1/(\mu - \lambda) = 1/(12 - 10) = 1/2 \text{ hour (30 minutes)} \quad (T5\text{-}15)$$

The expected waiting time in the queue:

$$W_q = \lambda/\mu (\mu - \lambda) = 10/12(12 - 10) = 5/12 \text{ hour (25 minutes)} \quad (T5\text{-}16)$$

The utilization factor for the queueing system:

$$\rho = \lambda/\mu = 10/12 = 0.833 \quad (T5\text{-}17)$$

**Question 2** Because of limited space in her shop, Gonzalez would like for there to be a 60 percent probability, or more, that not more than five customers will be in her store at any one time (waiting or being served). What is the present level of service for the five-customer limit?

Table T5.5 presents computational results for $n = 0, 1, 2, \ldots, 5$.

The probability that there are five or fewer customers in Gonzalez's shop is 0.665, which exceeds her desired 60 percent probability level.

**Question 3** Gonzalez worries that her customers may be having to wait too long in the queueing system. She would

| $n$ | $P_n = (\lambda/\mu)^n (1 - \lambda/\mu)$ $= (10/12)^n (1 - 10/12)$ |
|---|---|
| 0 | 0.167 |
| 1 | 0.139 |
| 2 | 0.116 |
| 3 | 0.096 |
| 4 | 0.080 |
| 5 | 0.067 |
| Total | 0.665 |

TABLE T5.5
Probability of $n$ Customers in Sue's Frame-It Shop ($\lambda = 10$, $\mu = 12$)

like to determine what service rate would be needed to cut the average wait to only 20 minutes (0.333 hour).

To answer this question we use the equation for the average time in the system and solve for $\mu$.

$$W = 1/(\mu - \lambda)$$
$$20 \text{ min} = 0.333 \text{ hr} = 1/(\mu - 10)$$
$$0.333\mu - 3.333 = 1 \quad (T5\text{-}18)$$
$$\mu = 13 \text{ customers/hour}$$

**Question 4** Gonzalez would like to determine the service rate required to have only a 5 percent chance of more than five customers in the system.

Answering this question requires using the same logic and relationships as in question 2, except that $\mu$ is now the decision variable. It is easier to first determine the average utilization rate by trial and error and then solve for the service rate.

Having only a 5 percent chance of more than five customers in the system is equivalent to having a 95 percent chance of five or fewer customers in the system, namely,

$$0.95 = P_0 + P_1 + P_2 + P_3 + P_4 + P_5$$
$$0.95 = (1 - \lambda/\mu)(\lambda/\mu)^0 + (1 - \lambda/\mu)(\lambda/\mu)^1 + (1 - \lambda/\mu)(\lambda/\mu)^2 + (1 - \lambda/\mu)(\lambda/\mu)^3 + (1 - \lambda/\mu)(\lambda/\mu)^4 + (1 - \lambda/\mu)(\lambda/\mu)^5$$
$$0.95 = (1 - \lambda/\mu)[1 + (\lambda/\mu)^1 + (\lambda/\mu)^2 + (\lambda/\mu)^3 + (\lambda/\mu)^4 + (\lambda/\mu)^5]$$
$$0.95 = (1 - \lambda/\mu)(1 + \rho + \rho^2 + \rho^3 + \rho^4 + \rho^5) \quad (T5\text{-}19)$$

If $\rho = 0.55$

$$0.95 \ ? \ (1 - 0.55) (1 + 0.55 + 0.303 + 0.166 + 0.092 + 0.05)$$
$$0.95 \ ? \ (0.45) (2.161)$$
$$0.95 \neq 0.972 \quad (T5\text{-}20)$$

If $\rho = 0.60$

$$0.95 \ ? (1 - 0.60) (1 + 0.60 + 0.36 + 0.216 + 0.130 + 0.078)$$
$$0.95 \ ? (0.40) (2.384)$$
$$0.95 \sim 0.9536 \quad (T5\text{-}21)$$

Therefore, for a utilization rate of 60 percent, the probability of having more than five customers in the system is 95 percent. For $\lambda = 10$ customers/hour, the service rate must be

$$\rho = \lambda/\mu$$
$$0.60 = 10/\mu$$
$$\mu = 16.67 \text{ customers/hour} \quad \text{(T5-22)}$$

# The Multiple-Channel, Single-Phase Waiting Line Model

The multiple-channel, single-phase waiting line model's derivation and use are predicated on the same assumptions as for the single-channel, single-phase waiting line model, except the number of servers is now $s$ (where $s > 1$). The operating characteristics equations for the multiple-channel, single-phase waiting line model are as follows:

The probability that the queueing system is empty
= probability that there are 0 units in the queueing system
$= P_0$

$$= \frac{1}{\left[ \displaystyle\sum_{n=0}^{n=s-1} \frac{(\lambda/\mu)^n}{n!} + \frac{(\lambda/\mu)^s}{s!} \frac{1}{1 - (\lambda/s\mu)} \right]} \quad \text{for } s\mu > \lambda \quad \text{(T5-23)}$$

The probability that there are $n$ units in the queueing system
$= P_n$

$$= \frac{(\lambda/\mu)^n}{n!} P_0 \quad \text{for } n \leq s$$

$$\frac{(\lambda/\mu)^n}{s!s^{n-s}} P_0 \quad \text{for } n > s \quad \text{(T5-24)}$$

The expected number of units in the queue

$$= L_q = \frac{(\lambda/\mu)_s (\lambda/\mu s) P_0}{s! (1 - \lambda/\mu s)^2} \quad \text{(T5-25)}$$

The expected number of units in the queueing system

$$= L = L_q + \lambda/\mu \quad \text{(T5-26)}$$

The expected waiting time in the queue

$$= W_q = L_q/\lambda \quad \text{(T5-27)}$$

The expected waiting time in the queueing system

$$= W = W_q + 1/\mu = L/\lambda \quad \text{(T5-28)}$$

The utilization factor for the queueing system

$$= \rho = \lambda/\mu s \quad \text{(T5-29)}$$

## Application of the Multiple-Channel, Single-Phase Waiting Line Model

Susan Gonzalez, the owner and operator of Sue's Frame-It Shop, has the opportunity to rent the store next door to her shop. If she does this, she can effectively expand her current facility to provide space to serve two customers simultaneously. Gonzalez could then assign workers to each of the two service facilities and operate a two-channel waiting line system. She would now like to use a multiple-channel, single-phase waiting line model to answer various questions about her proposed business expansion.

**Question 1** What are the operating characteristics of Sue's Frame-It Shop, expanded to two service facilities, with an arrival rate of ten customers per hour and a service rate of twelve customers per hour (for each service facility)?

The operating characteristics can be calculated as follows:

$$\lambda = 10 \text{ customers/hour arriving}$$
$$\mu = 12 \text{ customers/hour being served}$$
$$s = \text{two service channels}$$

The probability that the queueing system is empty[4]

$= P_0$

$$= \frac{1}{\left[ \displaystyle\sum_{n=0}^{n=s-1} \frac{(\lambda/\mu)^n}{n!} + \frac{(\lambda/\mu)^s}{s!} \frac{1}{1 - (\lambda/s\mu)} \right]}$$

$$= \frac{1}{\left[ \displaystyle\sum_{n=0}^{n=1} \frac{(10/12)^n}{n!} + \frac{(10/12)^2}{2!} \frac{1}{1 - (10/2\cdot12)} \right]}$$

$$= \frac{1}{\left[ \frac{(10/12)^0}{0!} + \frac{(10/12)^1}{1!} + \frac{(10/12)^2}{2!} \frac{1}{1 - (10/24)} \right]}$$

$$= \frac{1}{[1 + 0.833 + (0.347)(1.714)]}$$

$$= \frac{1}{[1 + 0.833 + 0.595]} = \frac{1}{2.428} = 0.412 \quad \text{(T5-30)}$$

The expected number of units in the queue:

$$= L_q = \frac{(\lambda/\mu)^s (\lambda/\mu s) P_0}{s! (1 - \lambda/\mu s)^2} = \frac{(10/12)^2 (10/12 \cdot 2) (0.412)}{(2 \cdot 1)(1 - 10/24)^2}$$

$$= \frac{(25/36)(5/12)(0.412)}{(2)(49/144)} = \frac{(125/332)(0.412)}{(98/144)}$$

$$= (125/98)(0.412/3) = 0.175 \text{ customer} \quad \text{(T5-31)}$$

The expected number of units in the queueing system

$$= L = L_q + \lambda/\mu = 0.175 + 10/12 = 1.01 \text{ customers} \quad \text{(T5-32)}$$

The expected waiting time in the queue

$$= W_q = L_q/\lambda = 0.175/10 = 0.018 \text{ hour (1.08 minutes)} \quad \text{(T5-33)}$$

The expected waiting time in the queueing system

$$= W = W_q + 1/\mu = 0.018 + 1/12 = 0.101 \text{ hour (6.06 minutes)} \quad \text{(T5-34)}$$

The utilization factor for the queueing system

$$\rho = \lambda/\mu s = 10/12.2 = 10/24 = 0.417 \quad \text{(T5-35)}$$

**Question 2** With the expanded space Gonzalez would like an 80 percent probability or more that not more than five customers will be in her store at any one time (waiting or being served). What is the present level of service in the expanded facility for the five-customer level?

[4]Observe that considerable computational effort is required for computing the value of $P_0$. To assist you, a table of values of $P_0$, for various combinations of $\lambda/\mu s$ (utilization factor) and $s$ (number of channels) has been provided in the Appendix.

| $n$ | $P_n$ |
|-----|-------|
| 0 | 0.412 |
| 1 | 0.343 |
| 2 | 0.143 |
| 3 | 0.060 |
| 4 | 0.025 |
| 5 | 0.010 |
| *Total* | 0.850 |

**TABLE T5.6**
Probability of $n$ Customers in Sue's Frame-It Shop
(Expanded) ($\lambda = 10$, $\mu = 12$, $s = 2$)

Computational results for $n = 0, 1, 2, \ldots, 5$ are presented in Table T5.6.

The probability that there are five or fewer customers in Sue's Frame-It Shop (expanded) is 0.850, which exceeds her desired 80 percent probability level.

**Question 3** Gonzalez would like to compare the daily operating costs of her present facility with the daily operating costs of the expanded facility. She knows that her total labor costs (wages and benefits) are $7.50 per hour per employee. She estimates that customer dissatisfaction and loss of goodwill cost her $5 per hour of the time the customer spends in the waiting line system. Her overhead costs (rent, lights, heating/cooling, and so on) are $50 per day per service facility. Her shop is open ten hours each day.

Computations of the relevant daily operating cost for the two configurations are as follows:

**Configuration 1 (Existing Facility)**

| | |
|---|---|
| Daily labor cost (1 worker × 10 hours/day × $7.50/hour) | $ 75.00 |
| Daily overhead cost (single service facility) | 50.00 |
| Daily customer waiting cost (10 customers/hour × 10 hours/day × 0.5 hour average wait × $5/hour—waiting cost) | 250.00 |
| Total | $375.00 |

**Configuration 2 (Expanded Facility)**

| | |
|---|---|
| Daily labor cost (2 workers × 10 hours/day × $7.50/hour) | $150.00 |
| Daily overhead costs (double service facility) | 100.00 |
| Daily customer waiting cost (10 customers/hour × 10 hours/day × 0.101 hour average wait × $5/hour—waiting cost) | 50.50 |
| Total | $300.50 |

Gonzalez could conclude that expanding her shop to double its service capacity is desirable. By so doing, she would reduce her total daily operating cost by $74.50, or about 20 percent.

## Other Waiting Line Models

Operating characteristics have been derived for more complex waiting line models describing the following situations:

1. Limited, or finite, input sources
2. Arrivals that follow various probability distributions other than the Poisson
3. Service times that follow various probability distributions other than the exponential
4. Arrivals that occur in groups rather than one at a time
5. Mean arrival rates that vary according to the number of units waiting for service
6. Queue disciplines that are not first come, first served
7. Mean service rates that vary according to the number of units waiting for service

The operating characteristics for these waiting line models are generally more complex than those presented in this tutorial, which is meant to be an introduction to the basic ideas and applications of queueing theory. If you want to consider more complex queueing models, consult the list of references at the end of this tutorial.

## ► Summary

Waiting line problems occur in many everyday situations as well as in many operations management environments. In this tutorial we discussed the general structure of queueing models and presented the operating characteristics for two of the more common queueing models. We also presented applications of these models, emphasizing the economic analysis that should accompany the use of a particular queueing model in a decision-making framework.

# ► Key Terms

| | | |
|---|---|---|
| balking | mean arrival rate | queue |
| calling population | mean service rate | queue discipline |
| channels | operating characteristics | reneging |
| exponential distribution | phases | service time (holding time) |
| input source | Poisson distribution | waiting line |

# ► Discussion Questions

1. What is the difference between a channel and a phase?
2. Discuss the cost of trade-offs that must be made in managing waiting line situations.
3. What is the difference between balking and reneging in a waiting line situation?
4. Briefly describe the structure and major components of a waiting line model.
5. Provide an example of an infinite queue.
6. Provide an example of a finite queue.
7. Suppose somebody said to you, "Queueing models are too difficult for the operations manager to use."

How would you reply to this statement? (Note: "Yes, you are right," is not an appropriate reply.)

8. What does the utilization factor measure? If the utilization factor is greater than 100 percent, what happens to the queue length?
9. Describe some queue disciplines you have encountered. What kind of a queue discipline do you think is most common? Why?
10. Does the result, "the expected number of customers in the queue = 1/2," make sense? Why or why not?

# ► Problems

1. Speedy's fast-food restaurant has a single drive-through order window. Its owner has surveyed activities at the restaurant and has observed that customers arrive at the restaurant according to a Poisson input process at a mean arrival rate of 60 per hour. Customer orders follow an exponential distribution and can be prepared at an average rate of 80 orders per hour. Compute the operating characteristics for this queueing system.

2. An automatic bank teller machine at the Chapin Bank will provide service to customers at the rate of 20 customers per hour. Customers typically arrive at a rate of 15 customers per hour. Compute the operating characteristics for this queueing system. What assumptions did you use in computing these operating characteristics?

3. Police Car 89 is assigned to an area of the Manassas Precinct. The precinct lieutenant, Lee, complains that the car has been arriving late to the scene of its calls and suggests that the car's officers, Jefferson and Davis, are spending too much time at a local restaurant. The officers defend their position by arguing that they are overworked, and they suggest that an additional car be assigned to their patrol area.

   Using your knowledge of queueing theory, analyze this situation. A 6-month record of police calls indicates that the rate of police calls has been 4

per hour and follows a Poisson distribution. The mean service rate for Jefferson and Davis is 6 calls per hour, with the service time following the exponential distribution.

   Compute the operating characteristics for this queueing system. As a part of your analysis determine the probabilities associated with $n$ units in the queueing system for $n = 1, 2, 3, 4,$ and 5.

4. On the Mississippi River at Alton, Illinois, barges arrive according to a Poisson distribution at the rate of 3 barges per hour. On the average it takes 15 minutes to move a barge through the lock. Determine
   a. The probability that the lock is empty
   b. The expected number in the queue
   c. The expected number in the queueing system
   d. The expected waiting time in the queue
   e. The expected waiting time in the queueing system
   f. The utilization rate for the lock
   g. The probability of there being no more than 3 boats in the lock

5. Assume that we are given a single-channel waiting line situation in which arrivals occur at an average rate of 6 per hour ($\lambda = 6$) and the mean service rate is 8 per hour ($\mu = 8$). Construct a probability distribution for the probability that there are $n$ units in the queueing system, for values of $n = 0, 1, 2, 3,$

4, 5, and 6. Suppose that we want to avoid having a waiting line of 3 or more customers. What is the probability of this happening?

6. Consider a single-channel queueing model, with a mean service rate of $\mu = 6$. Plot the probability that the system is empty for $\lambda = 0, 1, \ldots, 6$.

7. Assume that we have a single-channel waiting line facility in which arrivals occur at an average rate of 4 per hour. By altering the assignment of personnel within our service facility we can alter the service rate. However, an increase in the service rate will be accompanied by an increase in the service cost per hour. The service rate and the service cost per hour vary as follows:

| Service Rate ($\mu$) | Service Cost/Hour |
|---|---|
| 6 customers/hour | $ 5.00 |
| 6.5 " | 7.00 |
| 7 " | 9.00 |
| 7.5 " | 11.00 |
| 8 " | 13.00 |

The cost associated with customers' having to wait is $15 per hour. For this situation perform an economic analysis for an 8-hour time period.

a. Illustrate the economic analysis graphically, showing service cost, customer waiting cost, and total cost for the various possible service rates.

b. What is the optimal service level (service rate), and what is the expected total cost?

8. The Pickens & Laurens Railroad finds that it must steam clean its cars once a year. It is considering two alternatives for its steam-cleaning operation. Under alternative 1, the railroad would operate two steam-cleaning booths in parallel, at a total annual cost of $100,000. The service time distribution under this alternative is exponential with a mean of 5 hours. Under alternative 2, the railroad would operate one large steam-cleaning booth at a total annual cost of $150,000. However, the service time distribution under this alternative would be exponential with a mean of 3 hours. Under both alternatives the railroad cars arrive according to a Poisson input process with a arrival rate of 1 car every 8 hours. The cost of an idle hour is thought to be $15 per hour. Assume that the steam-cleaning booths operate (8 hours per day × 250 days per year) = 2,000 hours per year. Which alternative should the railroad choose?

9. Chemical trucks arrive at the Irmo plant of Allied Fibers according to a Poisson distribution at a rate of 4 trucks per hour. A worker unloads them at a rate of 6 trucks per hour, following approximately the exponential distribution. The plant manager, Tim Fry, is considering the hiring of a second worker to unload trucks, believing that this will result in a total of 12 trucks per hour (6 per worker) being unloaded. The hourly labor cost associated with each worker unloading trucks is $10. The cost associated with having a truck waiting to be unloaded is $20 per hour (once the truck is actually being unloaded, the waiting cost is not incurred). Perform a queueing analysis and an economic analysis for this situation.

10. The manager of the St. Andrews Video Store is trying to decide how many cash registers to have open each Saturday (its busiest day). The decision criteria include the customer waiting time (and the associated waiting cost) and the service costs associated with employing additional checkout clerks. Jane Mahaffey, the manager of the St. Andrews Video Store, has conducted a survey of customers and has concluded that the store suffers about $7 in lost sales and goodwill for every hour of customer time spent waiting in the checkout line. Checkout clerks are paid an average of $5 per hour. The customers typically arrive at the checkout stand at a rate of 60 customers per hour. A single clerk can service 70 customers per hour. If two clerks are used, each of the two clerks can service 40 customers per hour. What service configuration should be employed, and why?

11. At Shem Creek in Mt. Pleasant, South Carolina, shrimp boats arrive to be unloaded. The manager of the Low Country Seafood Co., Jerry Granou, estimates that during the shrimping season, shrimp boats arrive at an average rate of 3 boats per hour, following the Poisson distribution, and each worker can unload 1/2 boats per hour. She also knows that the workers who unload the shrimp boats earn $10 per hour in wages and benefits whether they are busy or idle. She estimates that the cost of a shrimp boat's being idle (having to wait to be unloaded) is $100 per hour. How many workers should be employed to unload the shrimp boats?

12. A. A. Berry offers clothes shopping by telephone. Its current operation has one clerk to answer telephone inquiries. If this clerk is busy, the caller is put on hold and asked to wait. Calls are arriving at an average rate of 30 calls per hour, and the clerk can answer calls at an average rate of 35 calls per hour. Calls follow the Poisson distribution, whereas the service times follow the exponential distribution. The clerk servicing the telephone calls is paid $8 per hour, but the management of A. A. Berry estimates that there is a loss of about $15 per hour of customers' time spent waiting for the clerk to take an order.

a. What is the average time that customers must wait before their order is taken?

**b.** What is the average number of customers waiting to place an order?

**c.** The management of A. A. Berry is considering the addition of a second clerk to take calls. If this second clerk has the same service rate and receives the same $8 per hour, should the company hire a second clerk? Explain.

## ▶ Selected References

Bartfai, P., and J. Tomko, *Point Processes Queueing Problems.* New York: Elsevier-North Holland Publishing, 1981.

Cooper, Robert E., *Introduction to Queueing Theory.* New York: Elsevier-North Holland Publishing, 1980.

Gorney, Leonard, *Queueing Theory: A Problem-Solving Approach.* Princeton, N.J.: Petrocelli, 1981.

Hillier, Frederick S. et al., *Queueing Tables and Graphs.* New York: Wiley, 1981.

Markland, Robert E., *Topics in Management Science.* New York: Wiley, 1989.

Newell, Gordon F., *Approximate Behavior of Tandem Queues.* New York: Springer-Verlag, 1980.

————., *Applications of Queueing Theory.* New York: Chapman and Hall, 1982.

Saaty, Thomas L. *Elements of Queueing Theory.* New York: McGraw-Hill, 1961.

Srivastava, H. M., and B. R. Kashyap, *Special Functions in Queueing Theory and Related Stochastic Processes.* New York: Academic Press, 1982.

Wagner, Harvey M., *Principles of Operations Research.* Englewood Cliffs, N.J.: Prentice-Hall, 1975.

# Tables

**1.** Standard Normal Distribution
**2.** Poisson Distribution—Individual Terms
**3.** Exponential Functions
**4.** Probability of Zero Units in the Queueing System ($P_0$) for Multiple Server Models
**5.** 36 Control Chart Factors

TABLE A1
Standard Normal Distribution

This table gives the area under the standardized normal curve from 0 to Z, as shown by the shaded portion of the following figure.

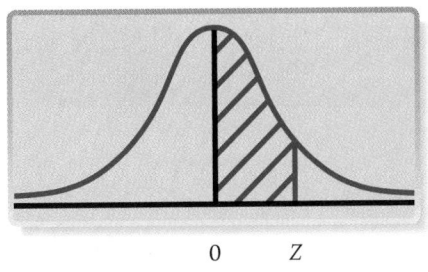

0     Z

Examples: if Z is the standardized normal random variable, then

$P(0 \leq Z \leq 1.25) = 0.3944$
$P(Z \geq 1.25) = 0.5000 - 0.3944 = 0.1056$
$P(Z \leq 1.25) = 0.5000 + 0.3944 = 0.8944$
$P(Z \leq -1.25) = 0.1056$ (by symmetry)

| Z | 0.00 | 0.01 | 0.02 | 0.03 | 0.04 | 0.05 | 0.06 | 0.07 | 0.08 | 0.09 |
|---|------|------|------|------|------|------|------|------|------|------|
| 0.0 | 0.0000 | 0.0040 | 0.0080 | 0.0120 | 0.0160 | 0.0199 | 0.0239 | 0.0279 | 0.0319 | 0.0359 |
| 0.1 | 0.0398 | 0.0438 | 0.0478 | 0.0517 | 0.0557 | 0.0596 | 0.0636 | 0.0675 | 0.0714 | 0.0753 |
| 0.2 | 0.0793 | 0.0832 | 0.0871 | 0.0910 | 0.0948 | 0.0987 | 0.1026 | 0.1064 | 0.1103 | 0.1141 |
| 0.3 | 0.1179 | 0.1217 | 0.1255 | 0.1293 | 0.1331 | 0.1368 | 0.1406 | 0.1443 | 0.1480 | 0.1517 |
| 0.4 | 0.1554 | 0.1591 | 0.1628 | 0.1664 | 0.1700 | 0.1736 | 0.1772 | 0.1808 | 0.1844 | 0.1879 |
| 0.5 | 0.1915 | 0.1950 | 0.1985 | 0.2019 | 0.2054 | 0.2088 | 0.2123 | 0.2157 | 0.2190 | 0.2224 |
| 0.6 | 0.2257 | 0.2291 | 0.2324 | 0.2357 | 0.2389 | 0.2422 | 0.2454 | 0.2486 | 0.2518 | 0.2549 |
| 0.7 | 0.2580 | 0.2612 | 0.2642 | 0.2673 | 0.2704 | 0.2734 | 0.2764 | 0.2794 | 0.2823 | 0.2852 |
| 0.8 | 0.2881 | 0.2910 | 0.2939 | 0.2967 | 0.2995 | 0.3023 | 0.3051 | 0.3078 | 0.3106 | 0.3133 |
| 0.9 | 0.3159 | 0.3186 | 0.3212 | 0.3238 | 0.3264 | 0.3289 | 0.3315 | 0.3340 | 0.3365 | 0.3389 |
| 1.0 | 0.3413 | 0.3438 | 0.3461 | 0.3485 | 0.3508 | 0.3531 | 0.3554 | 0.3577 | 0.3599 | 0.3621 |
| 1.1 | 0.3643 | 0.3665 | 0.3686 | 0.3708 | 0.3729 | 0.3749 | 0.3770 | 0.3790 | 0.3810 | 0.3830 |
| 1.2 | 0.3849 | 0.3869 | 0.3888 | 0.3907 | 0.3925 | 0.3944 | 0.3962 | 0.3980 | 0.3997 | 0.4015 |
| 1.3 | 0.4032 | 0.4049 | 0.4066 | 0.4082 | 0.4099 | 0.4115 | 0.4131 | 0.4147 | 0.4162 | 0.4177 |
| 1.4 | 0.4192 | 0.4207 | 0.4222 | 0.4236 | 0.4251 | 0.4265 | 0.4279 | 0.4292 | 0.4306 | 0.4319 |
| 1.5 | 0.4332 | 0.4345 | 0.4357 | 0.4370 | 0.4382 | 0.4394 | 0.4406 | 0.4418 | 0.4429 | 0.4441 |
| 1.6 | 0.4452 | 0.4463 | 0.4474 | 0.4484 | 0.4495 | 0.4505 | 0.4515 | 0.4525 | 0.4535 | 0.4545 |
| 1.7 | 0.4554 | 0.4564 | 0.4573 | 0.4582 | 0.4591 | 0.4599 | 0.4608 | 0.4616 | 0.4625 | 0.4633 |
| 1.8 | 0.4641 | 0.4649 | 0.4656 | 0.4664 | 0.4671 | 0.4678 | 0.4686 | 0.4693 | 0.4699 | 0.4706 |
| 1.9 | 0.4713 | 0.4719 | 0.4726 | 0.4732 | 0.4738 | 0.4744 | 0.4750 | 0.4756 | 0.4761 | 0.4767 |
| 2.0 | 0.4772 | 0.4778 | 0.4783 | 0.4788 | 0.4793 | 0.4798 | 0.4803 | 0.4808 | 0.4812 | 0.4817 |
| 2.1 | 0.4821 | 0.4826 | 0.4830 | 0.4834 | 0.4838 | 0.4842 | 0.4846 | 0.4850 | 0.4854 | 0.4857 |
| 2.2 | 0.4861 | 0.4864 | 0.4868 | 0.4871 | 0.4875 | 0.4878 | 0.4881 | 0.4884 | 0.4887 | 0.4890 |
| 2.3 | 0.4893 | 0.4896 | 0.4898 | 0.4901 | 0.4904 | 0.4906 | 0.4909 | 0.4911 | 0.4913 | 0.4916 |
| 2.4 | 0.4918 | 0.4920 | 0.4922 | 0.4925 | 0.4927 | 0.4929 | 0.4931 | 0.4932 | 0.4934 | 0.4936 |
| 2.5 | 0.4938 | 0.4940 | 0.4941 | 0.4943 | 0.4945 | 0.4946 | 0.4948 | 0.4949 | 0.4951 | 0.4952 |
| 2.6 | 0.4953 | 0.4955 | 0.4956 | 0.4957 | 0.4959 | 0.4960 | 0.4961 | 0.4962 | 0.4963 | 0.4964 |
| 2.7 | 0.4965 | 0.4966 | 0.4967 | 0.4968 | 0.4969 | 0.4970 | 0.4971 | 0.4972 | 0.4973 | 0.4974 |
| 2.8 | 0.4974 | 0.4975 | 0.4976 | 0.4977 | 0.4977 | 0.4978 | 0.4979 | 0.4979 | 0.4980 | 0.4981 |
| 2.9 | 0.4981 | 0.4982 | 0.4982 | 0.4983 | 0.4984 | 0.4984 | 0.4985 | 0.4985 | 0.4986 | 0.4986 |
| 3.0 | 0.49865 | 0.4987 | 0.4987 | 0.4988 | 0.4988 | 0.4989 | 0.4989 | 0.4989 | 0.4990 | 0.4990 |
| 4.0 | 0.4999683 | | | | | | | | | |

TABLE A2
Poisson Distribution—
Individual Terms

The Poisson probability function is given by

$$f(x;\lambda) = \frac{\lambda^x e^{-\lambda}}{x!} \quad \text{for } \lambda > 0,\, x = 0, 1, 2, \ldots$$

The following table contains the individual terms of $f(x; \lambda)$ for specified values of $x$ and $\lambda$.

| x | 0.01 | 0.02 | 0.03 | 0.04 | 0.05 | 0.06 | 0.07 | 0.08 | 0.09 | 0.10 | 0.15 | x |
|---|------|------|------|------|------|------|------|------|------|------|------|---|
| 0 | 0.990 | 0.980 | 0.970 | 0.961 | 0.951 | 0.942 | 0.932 | 0.923 | 0.914 | 0.905 | 0.861 | 0 |
| 1 | 0.010 | 0.020 | 0.030 | 0.038 | 0.048 | 0.057 | 0.065 | 0.074 | 0.082 | 0.090 | 0.129 | 1 |
| 2 | | | | 0.001 | 0.001 | 0.002 | 0.002 | 0.003 | 0.004 | 0.005 | 0.010 | 2 |

λ

| x | 0.20 | 0.25 | 0.30 | 0.40 | 0.50 | 0.60 | 0.70 | 0.80 | 0.90 | 1.0 | 1.1 | 1.2 | 1.3 | 1.4 | 1.5 | 1.6 | 1.7 | 1.8 | 1.9 | 2.0 | x |
|---|------|------|------|------|------|------|------|------|------|-----|-----|-----|-----|-----|-----|-----|-----|-----|-----|-----|---|
| 0 | 0.819 | 0.779 | 0.741 | 0.670 | 0.607 | 0.549 | 0.497 | 0.449 | 0.407 | 0.368 | 0.333 | 0.301 | 0.273 | 0.247 | 0.223 | 0.202 | 0.183 | 0.165 | 0.150 | 0.135 | 0 |
| 1 | 0.164 | 0.195 | 0.222 | 0.268 | 0.303 | 0.329 | 0.348 | 0.359 | 0.366 | 0.368 | 0.366 | 0.361 | 0.354 | 0.345 | 0.335 | 0.323 | 0.311 | 0.298 | 0.284 | 0.271 | 1 |
| 2 | 0.016 | 0.024 | 0.033 | 0.054 | 0.076 | 0.099 | 0.122 | 0.144 | 0.165 | 0.184 | 0.201 | 0.217 | 0.230 | 0.242 | 0.251 | 0.258 | 0.264 | 0.268 | 0.270 | 0.271 | 2 |
| 3 | 0.001 | 0.002 | 0.003 | 0.007 | 0.013 | 0.020 | 0.028 | 0.038 | 0.049 | 0.061 | 0.074 | 0.087 | 0.100 | 0.113 | 0.126 | 0.138 | 0.150 | 0.161 | 0.171 | 0.180 | 3 |
| 4 | | | | 0.001 | 0.002 | 0.003 | 0.005 | 0.008 | 0.011 | 0.015 | 0.020 | 0.026 | 0.032 | 0.039 | 0.047 | 0.055 | 0.063 | 0.072 | 0.081 | 0.090 | 4 |
| 5 | | | | | | | 0.001 | 0.001 | 0.002 | 0.003 | 0.004 | 0.006 | 0.008 | 0.011 | 0.014 | 0.018 | 0.022 | 0.026 | 0.031 | 0.036 | 5 |

λ

| x | 2.1 | 2.2 | 2.3 | 2.4 | 2.5 | 2.6 | 2.7 | 2.8 | 2.9 | 3.0 | 3.1 | 3.2 | 3.3 | 3.4 | 3.5 | 3.6 | 3.7 | 3.8 | 3.9 | 4.0 | x |
|---|-----|-----|-----|-----|-----|-----|-----|-----|-----|-----|-----|-----|-----|-----|-----|-----|-----|-----|-----|-----|---|
| 0 | 0.122 | 0.111 | 0.100 | 0.091 | 0.082 | 0.074 | 0.067 | 0.061 | 0.055 | 0.050 | 0.045 | 0.041 | 0.037 | 0.033 | 0.030 | 0.027 | 0.025 | 0.022 | 0.020 | 0.018 | 0 |
| 1 | 0.257 | 0.244 | 0.231 | 0.218 | 0.205 | 0.193 | 0.181 | 0.170 | 0.160 | 0.149 | 0.140 | 0.130 | 0.122 | 0.113 | 0.106 | 0.098 | 0.091 | 0.085 | 0.079 | 0.073 | 1 |
| 2 | 0.270 | 0.268 | 0.265 | 0.261 | 0.257 | 0.251 | 0.245 | 0.238 | 0.231 | 0.224 | 0.216 | 0.209 | 0.201 | 0.193 | 0.185 | 0.177 | 0.169 | 0.162 | 0.154 | 0.147 | 2 |
| 3 | 0.189 | 0.197 | 0.203 | 0.209 | 0.214 | 0.218 | 0.220 | 0.222 | 0.224 | 0.224 | 0.224 | 0.223 | 0.221 | 0.219 | 0.216 | 0.212 | 0.209 | 0.205 | 0.200 | 0.195 | 3 |
| 4 | 0.099 | 0.108 | 0.117 | 0.125 | 0.134 | 0.141 | 0.149 | 0.156 | 0.162 | 0.168 | 0.173 | 0.178 | 0.182 | 0.186 | 0.189 | 0.191 | 0.193 | 0.194 | 0.195 | 0.195 | 4 |
| 5 | 0.042 | 0.048 | 0.054 | 0.060 | 0.067 | 0.074 | 0.080 | 0.087 | 0.094 | 0.101 | 0.107 | 0.114 | 0.120 | 0.126 | 0.132 | 0.138 | 0.143 | 0.148 | 0.152 | 0.156 | 5 |
| 6 | 0.015 | 0.017 | 0.021 | 0.024 | 0.028 | 0.032 | 0.036 | 0.041 | 0.045 | 0.050 | 0.056 | 0.061 | 0.066 | 0.072 | 0.077 | 0.083 | 0.088 | 0.094 | 0.099 | 0.104 | 6 |
| 7 | 0.004 | 0.005 | 0.007 | 0.008 | 0.010 | 0.012 | 0.014 | 0.016 | 0.019 | 0.022 | 0.025 | 0.028 | 0.031 | 0.035 | 0.039 | 0.042 | 0.047 | 0.051 | 0.055 | 0.060 | 7 |
| 8 | 0.001 | 0.002 | 0.002 | 0.002 | 0.003 | 0.004 | 0.005 | 0.006 | 0.007 | 0.008 | 0.010 | 0.011 | 0.013 | 0.015 | 0.017 | 0.109 | 0.022 | 0.024 | 0.027 | 0.030 | 8 |
| 9 | | | | 0.001 | 0.001 | 0.001 | 0.001 | 0.002 | 0.002 | 0.003 | 0.003 | 0.004 | 0.005 | 0.006 | 0.007 | 0.008 | 0.009 | 0.010 | 0.012 | 0.013 | 9 |
| 10 | | | | | | | | | 0.001 | 0.001 | 0.001 | 0.001 | 0.002 | 0.002 | 0.002 | 0.003 | 0.003 | 0.004 | 0.005 | 0.005 | 10 |

λ

| x | 4.1 | 4.2 | 4.3 | 4.4 | 4.5 | 4.6 | 4.7 | 4.8 | 4.9 | 5.0 | 5.1 | 5.2 | 5.3 | 5.4 | 5.5 | 5.6 | 5.7 | 5.8 | 5.9 | 6.0 | x |
|---|-----|-----|-----|-----|-----|-----|-----|-----|-----|-----|-----|-----|-----|-----|-----|-----|-----|-----|-----|-----|---|
| 0 | 0.017 | 0.015 | 0.014 | 0.012 | 0.011 | 0.010 | 0.009 | 0.008 | 0.007 | 0.007 | 0.006 | 0.006 | 0.005 | 0.005 | 0.004 | 0.004 | 0.003 | 0.003 | 0.003 | 0.002 | 0 |
| 1 | 0.068 | 0.063 | 0.058 | 0.054 | 0.050 | 0.046 | 0.043 | 0.040 | 0.036 | 0.034 | 0.031 | 0.029 | 0.026 | 0.024 | 0.022 | 0.021 | 0.019 | 0.018 | 0.016 | 0.015 | 1 |
| 2 | 0.139 | 0.132 | 0.125 | 0.119 | 0.112 | 0.106 | 0.100 | 0.095 | 0.089 | 0.084 | 0.079 | 0.075 | 0.070 | 0.066 | 0.062 | 0.058 | 0.054 | 0.051 | 0.048 | 0.045 | 2 |
| 3 | 0.190 | 0.185 | 0.180 | 0.174 | 0.169 | 0.163 | 0.157 | 0.152 | 0.146 | 0.140 | 0.135 | 0.129 | 0.124 | 0.119 | 0.113 | 0.108 | 0.103 | 0.098 | 0.094 | 0.089 | 3 |
| 4 | 0.195 | 0.194 | 0.193 | 0.192 | 0.190 | 0.188 | 0.185 | 0.182 | 0.179 | 0.175 | 0.172 | 0.168 | 0.164 | 0.160 | 0.156 | 0.152 | 0.147 | 0.143 | 0.138 | 0.134 | 4 |
| 5 | 0.160 | 0.163 | 0.166 | 0.169 | 0.171 | 0.173 | 0.174 | 0.175 | 0.175 | 0.175 | 0.175 | 0.175 | 0.174 | 0.073 | 0.171 | 0.170 | 0.168 | 0.166 | 0.163 | 0.161 | 5 |
| 6 | 0.109 | 0.114 | 0.119 | 0.124 | 0.128 | 0.132 | 0.136 | 0.140 | 0.143 | 0.146 | 0.149 | 0.151 | 0.154 | 0.156 | 0.157 | 0.158 | 0.159 | 0.160 | 0.160 | 0.161 | 6 |
| 7 | 0.064 | 0.069 | 0.073 | 0.078 | 0.082 | 0.087 | 0.091 | 0.096 | 0.100 | 0.104 | 0.109 | 0.113 | 0.116 | 0.120 | 0.123 | 0.127 | 0.130 | 0.133 | 0.135 | 0.138 | 7 |
| 8 | 0.033 | 0.036 | 0.039 | 0.043 | 0.046 | 0.050 | 0.054 | 0.058 | 0.061 | 0.065 | 0.069 | 0.073 | 0.077 | 0.081 | 0.085 | 0.089 | 0.092 | 0.096 | 0.100 | 0.103 | 8 |
| 9 | 0.015 | 0.017 | 0.019 | 0.021 | 0.023 | 0.026 | 0.028 | 0.031 | 0.033 | 0.036 | 0.039 | 0.042 | 0.045 | 0.049 | 0.052 | 0.055 | 0.059 | 0.062 | 0.065 | 0.069 | 9 |
| 10 | 0.006 | 0.007 | 0.008 | 0.009 | 0.010 | 0.012 | 0.013 | 0.015 | 0.016 | 0.018 | 0.020 | 0.022 | 0.024 | 0.026 | 0.029 | 0.031 | 0.033 | 0.036 | 0.039 | 0.041 | 10 |
| 11 | 0.002 | 0.003 | 0.003 | 0.004 | 0.004 | 0.005 | 0.006 | 0.006 | 0.007 | 0.008 | 0.009 | 0.010 | 0.012 | 0.013 | 0.014 | 0.016 | 0.017 | 0.019 | 0.021 | 0.023 | 11 |
| 12 | 0.001 | 0.001 | 0.001 | 0.001 | 0.002 | 0.002 | 0.002 | 0.003 | 0.003 | 0.003 | 0.004 | 0.005 | 0.005 | 0.006 | 0.007 | 0.007 | 0.008 | 0.009 | 0.010 | 0.011 | 12 |
| 13 | | | | | 0.001 | 0.001 | 0.001 | 0.001 | 0.001 | 0.001 | 0.002 | 0.002 | 0.002 | 0.002 | 0.003 | 0.003 | 0.004 | 0.004 | 0.005 | 0.005 | 13 |
| 14 | | | | | | | | | | 0.001 | 0.001 | 0.001 | 0.001 | 0.001 | 0.001 | 0.001 | 0.001 | 0.002 | 0.002 | 0.002 | 14 |
| 15 | | | | | | | | | | | | | | | | | 0.001 | 0.001 | 0.001 | 0.001 | 15 |

T A B L E   A 2
Poisson Distribution—
Individual Terms (Continued)

| x | 6.1 | 6.2 | 6.3 | 6.4 | 6.5 | 6.6 | 6.7 | 6.8 | 6.9 | 7.0 | 7.1 | 7.2 | 7.3 | 7.4 | 7.5 | 8.0 | 8.5 | 9.0 | 9.5 | 10.0 | x |
|---|---|---|---|---|---|---|---|---|---|---|---|---|---|---|---|---|---|---|---|---|---|
| 0 | 0.002 | 0.002 | 0.002 | 0.002 | 0.002 | 0.001 | 0.001 | 0.001 | 0.001 | 0.001 | 0.001 | 0.001 | 0.001 | 0.001 | 0.001 | | | | | | 0 |
| 1 | 0.014 | 0.013 | 0.012 | 0.011 | 0.010 | 0.009 | 0.008 | 0.008 | 0.007 | 0.006 | 0.006 | 0.005 | 0.005 | 0.005 | 0.004 | 0.003 | 0.002 | 0.001 | 0.001 | | 1 |
| 2 | 0.042 | 0.039 | 0.036 | 0.034 | 0.032 | 0.030 | 0.028 | 0.026 | 0.024 | 0.022 | 0.021 | 0.019 | 0.018 | 0.017 | 0.016 | 0.011 | 0.007 | 0.005 | 0.003 | 0.002 | 2 |
| 3 | 0.085 | 0.081 | 0.077 | 0.073 | 0.069 | 0.065 | 0.062 | 0.058 | 0.055 | 0.052 | 0.049 | 0.046 | 0.044 | 0.041 | 0.039 | 0.029 | 0.021 | 0.015 | 0.011 | 0.008 | 3 |
| 4 | 0.129 | 0.125 | 0.121 | 0.116 | 0.112 | 0.108 | 0.103 | 0.099 | 0.095 | 0.091 | 0.087 | 0.084 | 0.080 | 0.076 | 0.073 | 0.057 | 0.044 | 0.034 | 0.025 | 0.019 | 4 |
| 5 | 0.158 | 0.155 | 0.152 | 0.149 | 0.145 | 0.142 | 0.138 | 0.135 | 0.131 | 0.128 | 0.124 | 0.120 | 0.117 | 0.113 | 0.109 | 0.092 | 0.075 | 0.061 | 0.048 | 0.038 | 5 |
| 6 | 0.160 | 0.160 | 0.159 | 0.159 | 0.157 | 0.156 | 0.155 | 0.153 | 0.151 | 0.149 | 0.147 | 0.144 | 0.142 | 0.139 | 0.137 | 0.122 | 0.107 | 0.091 | 0.076 | 0.063 | 6 |
| 7 | 0.140 | 0.142 | 0.144 | 0.145 | 0.146 | 0.147 | 0.148 | 0.149 | 0.149 | 0.149 | 0.149 | 0.149 | 0.148 | 0.147 | 0.146 | 0.140 | 0.129 | 0.117 | 0.104 | 0.090 | 7 |
| 8 | 0.107 | 0.110 | 0.113 | 0.116 | 0.119 | 0.121 | 0.124 | 0.126 | 0.128 | 0.130 | 0.132 | 0.134 | 0.135 | 0.136 | 0.137 | 0.140 | 0.138 | 0.132 | 0.123 | 0.113 | 8 |
| 9 | 0.072 | 0.076 | 0.079 | 0.082 | 0.086 | 0.089 | 0.092 | 0.095 | 0.098 | 0.101 | 0.104 | 0.107 | 0.110 | 0.112 | 0.114 | 0.124 | 0.130 | 0.132 | 0.130 | 0.125 | 9 |
| 10 | 0.044 | 0.047 | 0.050 | 0.053 | 0.056 | 0.059 | 0.062 | 0.065 | 0.068 | 0.071 | 0.074 | 0.077 | 0.080 | 0.083 | 0.086 | 0.099 | 0.110 | 0.119 | 0.124 | 0.125 | 10 |
| 11 | 0.024 | 0.026 | 0.029 | 0.031 | 0.033 | 0.035 | 0.038 | 0.040 | 0.043 | 0.045 | 0.048 | 0.050 | 0.053 | 0.056 | 0.059 | 0.072 | 0.085 | 0.097 | 0.107 | 0.114 | 11 |
| 12 | 0.012 | 0.014 | 0.015 | 0.016 | 0.018 | 0.019 | 0.021 | 0.023 | 0.025 | 0.026 | 0.028 | 0.030 | 0.032 | 0.034 | 0.037 | 0.048 | 0.060 | 0.073 | 0.084 | 0.095 | 12 |
| 13 | 0.006 | 0.007 | 0.007 | 0.008 | 0.009 | 0.010 | 0.011 | 0.012 | 0.013 | 0.014 | 0.015 | 0.017 | 0.018 | 0.020 | 0.021 | 0.030 | 0.040 | 0.050 | 0.062 | 0.073 | 13 |
| 14 | 0.003 | 0.003 | 0.003 | 0.004 | 0.004 | 0.005 | 0.005 | 0.006 | 0.006 | 0.007 | 0.008 | 0.009 | 0.009 | 0.010 | 0.011 | 0.017 | 0.024 | 0.032 | 0.042 | 0.052 | 14 |
| 15 | 0.001 | 0.001 | 0.001 | 0.002 | 0.002 | 0.002 | 0.002 | 0.003 | 0.003 | 0.003 | 0.004 | 0.004 | 0.005 | 0.005 | 0.006 | 0.009 | 0.014 | 0.019 | 0.027 | 0.035 | 15 |
| 16 | | 0.001 | 0.001 | 0.001 | 0.001 | 0.001 | 0.001 | 0.001 | 0.001 | 0.001 | 0.002 | 0.002 | 0.002 | 0.002 | 0.003 | 0.005 | 0.007 | 0.011 | 0.016 | 0.022 | 16 |
| 17 | | | | | | | | | | 0.001 | 0.001 | 0.001 | 0.001 | 0.001 | 0.001 | 0.002 | 0.004 | 0.006 | 0.009 | 0.013 | 17 |
| 18 | | | | | | | | | | | | | | | | 0.001 | 0.002 | 0.003 | 0.005 | 0.007 | 18 |
| 19 | | | | | | | | | | | | | | | | | 0.001 | 0.001 | 0.002 | 0.004 | 19 |
| 20 | | | | | | | | | | | | | | | | | | 0.001 | 0.001 | 0.002 | 20 |

T A B L E   A 3
Exponential Functions

| x | $e^x$ | $e^{-x}$ | x | $e^x$ | $e^{-x}$ |
|---|---|---|---|---|---|
| 0.00 | 1.0000 | 1.0000 | 0.25 | 1.2840 | 0.7788 |
| 0.01 | 1.0101 | 0.9900 | 0.26 | 1.2969 | 0.7710 |
| 0.02 | 1.0202 | 0.9802 | 0.27 | 1.3100 | 0.7633 |
| 0.03 | 1.0305 | 0.9704 | 0.28 | 1.3231 | 0.7558 |
| 0.04 | 1.0408 | 0.9608 | 0.29 | 1.3364 | 0.7482 |
| 0.05 | 1.0513 | 0.9512 | 0.30 | 1.3499 | 0.7408 |
| 0.06 | 1.0618 | 0.9418 | 0.31 | 1.3634 | 0.7334 |
| 0.07 | 1.0725 | 0.9329 | 0.32 | 1.3771 | 0.7261 |
| 0.08 | 1.0833 | 0.9231 | 0.33 | 1.3910 | 0.7189 |
| 0.09 | 1.0942 | 0.9139 | 0.34 | 1.4049 | 0.7118 |
| 0.10 | 1.1052 | 0.9048 | 0.35 | 1.4191 | 0.7046 |
| 0.11 | 1.1163 | 0.8958 | 0.36 | 1.4333 | 0.6977 |
| 0.12 | 1.1275 | 0.8869 | 0.37 | 1.4477 | 0.6907 |
| 0.13 | 1.1388 | 0.8780 | 0.38 | 1.4623 | 0.6839 |
| 0.14 | 1.1503 | 0.8693 | 0.39 | 1.4770 | 0.6770 |
| 0.15 | 1.1618 | 0.8607 | 0.40 | 1.4918 | 0.6703 |
| 0.16 | 1.1735 | 0.8521 | 0.41 | 1.5068 | 0.6636 |
| 0.17 | 1.1853 | 0.8436 | 0.42 | 1.5220 | 0.6570 |
| 0.18 | 1.1972 | 0.8353 | 0.43 | 1.5373 | 0.6505 |
| 0.19 | 1.2092 | 0.8269 | 0.44 | 1.5527 | 0.6440 |
| 0.20 | 1.2214 | 0.8187 | 0.45 | 1.5683 | 0.6376 |
| 0.21 | 1.2337 | 0.8106 | 0.46 | 1.5841 | 0.6313 |
| 0.22 | 1.2461 | 0.8025 | 0.47 | 1.6000 | 0.6250 |
| 0.23 | 1.2586 | 0.7945 | 0.48 | 1.6161 | 0.6188 |
| 0.24 | 1.2712 | 0.7866 | 0.49 | 1.6323 | 0.6126 |

TABLE A3
Exponential Functions
(Continued)

| x | $e^x$ | $e^{-x}$ | x | $e^x$ | $e^{-x}$ |
|---|---|---|---|---|---|
| 0.50 | 1.6487 | 0.6065 | 1.00 | 2.7183 | 0.3678 |
| 0.51 | 1.6653 | 0.6005 | 1.05 | 2.8577 | 0.3499 |
| 0.52 | 1.6820 | 0.5945 | 1.10 | 3.0042 | 0.3329 |
| 0.53 | 1.6989 | 0.5886 | 1.15 | 3.1582 | 0.3166 |
| 0.54 | 1.7160 | 0.5827 | 1.20 | 3.3201 | 0.3012 |
| 0.55 | 1.7333 | 0.5769 | 1.25 | 3.4903 | 0.2865 |
| 0.56 | 1.7507 | 0.5712 | 1.30 | 3.6693 | 0.2625 |
| 0.57 | 1.7683 | 0.5655 | 1.35 | 3.8574 | 0.2592 |
| 0.58 | 1.7860 | 0.5599 | 1.40 | 4.0552 | 0.2466 |
| 0.59 | 1.8040 | 0.5543 | 1.45 | 4.2631 | 0.2346 |
| 0.60 | 1.8221 | 0.5488 | 1.50 | 4.4817 | 0.2231 |
| 0.61 | 1.8404 | 0.5433 | 1.55 | 4.7115 | 0.2122 |
| 0.62 | 1.8589 | 0.5379 | 1.60 | 4.9530 | 0.2019 |
| 0.63 | 1.8776 | 0.5326 | 1.65 | 5.2070 | 0.1921 |
| 0.64 | 1.8965 | 0.5273 | 1.70 | 5.4739 | 0.1821 |
| 0.65 | 1.9155 | 0.5220 | 1.75 | 5.7546 | 0.1738 |
| 0.66 | 1.9348 | 0.5168 | 1.80 | 6.0496 | 0.1653 |
| 0.67 | 1.9542 | 0.5117 | 1.85 | 6.3593 | 0.1572 |
| 0.68 | 1.9739 | 0.5066 | 1.90 | 6.6850 | 0.1496 |
| 0.69 | 1.9937 | 0.5016 | 1.95 | 7.0287 | 0.1423 |
| 0.70 | 2.0138 | 0.4965 | 2.00 | 7.3891 | 0.1353 |
| 0.71 | 2.0340 | 0.4916 | 2.05 | 7.7679 | 0.1287 |
| 0.72 | 2.0544 | 0.4867 | 2.10 | 8.1662 | 0.1224 |
| 0.73 | 2.0751 | 0.4819 | 2.15 | 8.5849 | 0.1165 |
| 0.74 | 2.0959 | 0.4771 | 2.20 | 9.0250 | 0.1108 |
| 0.75 | 2.1170 | 0.4723 | 2.25 | 9.4877 | 0.1054 |
| 0.76 | 2.1383 | 0.4677 | 2.30 | 9.9742 | 0.1003 |
| 0.77 | 2.1598 | 0.4630 | 2.35 | 10.486 | 0.0954 |
| 0.78 | 2.1815 | 0.4584 | 2.40 | 11.023 | 0.0907 |
| 0.79 | 2.2034 | 0.4538 | 2.45 | 11.588 | 0.0863 |
| 0.80 | 2.2255 | 0.4493 | 2.50 | 12.182 | 0.0821 |
| 0.81 | 2.2479 | 0.4448 | 2.55 | 12.807 | 0.0781 |
| 0.82 | 2.2705 | 0.4404 | 2.60 | 13.464 | 0.0743 |
| 0.83 | 2.2933 | 0.4360 | 2.65 | 14.154 | 0.0707 |
| 0.84 | 2.3164 | 0.4317 | 2.70 | 14.880 | 0.0672 |
| 0.85 | 2.3396 | 0.4274 | 2.75 | 15.643 | 0.0639 |
| 0.86 | 2.3632 | 0.4231 | 2.80 | 16.445 | 0.0608 |
| 0.87 | 2.3869 | 0.4189 | 2.85 | 16.288 | 0.0578 |
| 0.88 | 2.4109 | 0.4148 | 2.90 | 18.174 | 0.0550 |
| 0.89 | 2.4351 | 0.4106 | 2.95 | 19.106 | 0.0523 |
| 0.90 | 2.4596 | 0.4066 | 3.00 | 20.086 | 0.0498 |
| 0.91 | 2.4843 | 0.4025 | 3.05 | 21.115 | 0.0474 |
| 0.92 | 2.5093 | 0.3985 | 3.10 | 22.198 | 0.0450 |
| 0.93 | 2.5345 | 0.3945 | 3.15 | 23.336 | 0.0429 |
| 0.94 | 2.5600 | 0.3906 | 3.20 | 24.533 | 0.0408 |
| 0.95 | 2.5857 | 0.3867 | 3.25 | 25.790 | 0.0389 |
| 0.96 | 2.6117 | 0.3829 | 3.30 | 27.113 | 0.0369 |
| 0.97 | 2.6379 | 0.3790 | 3.35 | 28.503 | 0.0351 |
| 0.98 | 2.6645 | 0.3753 | 3.40 | 29.964 | 0.0333 |
| 0.99 | 2.6912 | 0.3716 | 3.45 | 31.500 | 0.0317 |

Tables **Appendix**

TABLE A3
Exponential Functions
(Continued)

| $x$ | $e^x$ | $e^{-x}$ | $x$ | $e^x$ | $e^{-x}$ |
|---|---|---|---|---|---|
| 3.50 | 33.115 | 0.0302 | 6.10 | 445.86 | 0.0022 |
| 3.55 | 34.813 | 0.0287 | 6.20 | 492.75 | 0.0020 |
| 3.60 | 36.598 | 0.0273 | 6.30 | 544.57 | 0.0018 |
| 3.65 | 38.475 | 0.0260 | 6.40 | 601.85 | 0.0017 |
| 3.70 | 40.447 | 0.0247 | 6.50 | 665.14 | 0.0015 |
| 3.75 | 42.521 | 0.0235 | 6.60 | 735.10 | 0.0014 |
| 3.80 | 44.701 | 0.0224 | 6.70 | 812.41 | 0.0012 |
| 3.85 | 46.993 | 0.0213 | 6.80 | 897.85 | 0.0011 |
| 3.90 | 49.402 | 0.0202 | 6.90 | 992.27 | 0.0010 |
| 3.95 | 51.935 | 0.0193 | 7.00 | 1096.6 | 0.0009 |
| 4.00 | 54.598 | 0.0183 | 7.10 | 1212.0 | 0.0008 |
| 4.05 | 57.397 | 0.0174 | 7.20 | 1339.4 | 0.0007 |
| 4.10 | 60.340 | 0.0166 | 7.30 | 1480.3 | 0.0007 |
| 4.15 | 63.434 | 0.0158 | 7.40 | 1636.0 | 0.0006 |
| 4.20 | 66.686 | 0.0150 | 7.50 | 1808.0 | 0.0006 |
| 4.25 | 70.105 | 0.0143 | 7.60 | 1998.2 | 0.0005 |
| 4.30 | 73.700 | 0.0136 | 7.70 | 2208.3 | 0.0005 |
| 4.35 | 77.478 | 0.0129 | 7.80 | 2440.6 | 0.0004 |
| 4.40 | 81.451 | 0.0123 | 7.90 | 2697.3 | 0.0004 |
| 4.45 | 85.627 | 0.0117 | 8.00 | 2981.0 | 0.0003 |
| 4.50 | 90.017 | 0.0111 | 8.10 | 3294.5 | 0.0003 |
| 4.55 | 94.632 | 0.0107 | 8.20 | 3641.0 | 0.0003 |
| 4.60 | 98.844 | 0.0101 | 8.30 | 4023.9 | 0.0002 |
| 4.65 | 104.58 | 0.0096 | 8.40 | 4447.1 | 0.0002 |
| 4.70 | 109.95 | 0.0091 | 8.50 | 4914.8 | 0.0002 |
| 4.75 | 115.58 | 0.0087 | 8.60 | 5431.7 | 0.0002 |
| 4.80 | 121.51 | 0.0082 | 8.70 | 6002.9 | 0.0002 |
| 4.85 | 127.74 | 0.0078 | 8.80 | 6634.2 | 0.0002 |
| 4.90 | 134.29 | 0.0074 | 8.90 | 7332.0 | 0.0001 |
| 4.95 | 141.17 | 0.0070 | 9.00 | 8103.1 | 0.0001 |
| 5.00 | 148.41 | 0.0067 | 9.10 | 8955.3 | 0.0001 |
| 5.10 | 164.02 | 0.0061 | 9.20 | 9897.1 | 0.0001 |
| 5.20 | 181.27 | 0.0055 | 9.30 | 10938 | 0.0001 |
| 5.30 | 200.34 | 0.0050 | 9.40 | 12088 | 0.0001 |
| 5.40 | 221.41 | 0.0045 | 9.50 | 13360 | 0.0001 |
| 5.50 | 244.69 | 0.0041 | 9.60 | 14765 | 0.0001 |
| 5.60 | 270.43 | 0.0037 | 9.70 | 16318 | 0.0001 |
| 5.70 | 298.87 | 0.0033 | 9.80 | 18034 | 0.0001 |
| 5.80 | 330.30 | 0.0030 | 9.90 | 19930 | 0.0001 |
| 5.90 | 365.04 | 0.0027 | 10.00 | 22026 | 0.0000 |
| 6.00 | 403.43 | 0.0025 | | | |

823

TABLE A4
Probability of Zero Units in
the Queueing System ($P_0$)
for Multiple Server Models

| System Utilization Ratio $\rho = \lambda/s\mu$ | Number of Servers (s) | | | | | | | | |
|---|---|---|---|---|---|---|---|---|---|
| | 2 | 3 | 4 | 5 | 6 | 7 | 8 | 9 | 10 |
| 0.05 | 0.9048 | 0.8607 | 0.8187 | 0.7788 | 0.7408 | 0.7047 | 0.6703 | 0.6376 | 0.6065 |
| 0.10 | 0.8182 | 0.7407 | 0.6703 | 0.6065 | 0.5488 | 0.4966 | 0.4493 | 0.4066 | 0.3679 |
| 0.15 | 0.7391 | 0.6373 | 0.5487 | 0.4724 | 0.4066 | 0.3499 | 0.3012 | 0.2592 | 0.2231 |
| 0.20 | 0.6667 | 0.5479 | 0.4491 | 0.3678 | 0.3012 | 0.2466 | 0.2019 | 0.1653 | 0.1353 |
| 0.25 | 0.6000 | 0.4706 | 0.3673 | 0.2863 | 0.2231 | 0.1738 | 0.1353 | 0.1054 | 0.0821 |
| 0.30 | 0.5385 | 0.4035 | 0.3002 | 0.2228 | 0.1652 | 0.1224 | 0.0907 | 0.0672 | 0.0498 |
| 0.35 | 0.4815 | 0.3451 | 0.2449 | 0.1731 | 0.1222 | 0.0862 | 0.0608 | 0.0428 | 0.0302 |
| 0.40 | 0.4286 | 0.2941 | 0.1993 | 0.1343 | 0.0903 | 0.0606 | 0.0407 | 0.0273 | 0.0183 |
| 0.45 | 0.3793 | 0.2496 | 0.1616 | 0.1039 | 0.0666 | 0.0426 | 0.0272 | 0.0174 | 0.0111 |
| 0.50 | 0.3333 | 0.2105 | 0.1304 | 0.0801 | 0.0490 | 0.0298 | 0.0182 | 0.0110 | 0.0067 |
| 0.55 | 0.2903 | 0.1762 | 0.1046 | 0.0614 | 0.0358 | 0.0208 | 0.0121 | 0.0070 | 0.0040 |
| 0.60 | 0.2500 | 0.1460 | 0.0831 | 0.0466 | 0.0260 | 0.0144 | 0.0080 | 0.0044 | 0.0024 |
| 0.65 | 0.2121 | 0.1193 | 0.0651 | 0.0350 | 0.0187 | 0.0099 | 0.0052 | 0.0028 | 0.0015 |
| 0.70 | 0.1765 | 0.0957 | 0.0502 | 0.0259 | 0.0132 | 0.0067 | 0.0034 | 0.0017 | 0.0009 |
| 0.75 | 0.1429 | 0.0748 | 0.0377 | 0.0187 | 0.0091 | 0.0044 | 0.0021 | 0.0010 | 0.0005 |
| 0.80 | 0.1111 | 0.0562 | 0.0273 | 0.0130 | 0.0061 | 0.0028 | 0.0013 | 0.0006 | 0.0003 |
| 0.85 | 0.0811 | 0.0396 | 0.0186 | 0.0085 | 0.0038 | 0.0017 | 0.0008 | 0.0003 | 0.0001 |
| 0.90 | 0.0526 | 0.0249 | 0.0113 | 0.0050 | 0.0021 | 0.0009 | 0.0004 | 0.0002 | 0.0001 |
| 0.95 | 0.0256 | 0.0118 | 0.0051 | 0.0022 | 0.0009 | 0.0004 | 0.0002 | 0.0001 | 0.0000 |

NOTE: $\lambda$ = arrival rate (Poisson); $s$ = number of servers; $\mu$ = service rate (per individual server and exponential service time).

| Sample Size (n) | Factor for $\overline{X}$-Chart ($A_2$) | Factors for R-Chart | | Sample Size (n) | Factor for Estimating s from $\overline{R}$ ($d_2$) |
|---|---|---|---|---|---|
| | | Lower Limit ($D_3$) | Upper Limit ($D_4$) | | |
| 2 | 1.880 | 0 | 3.267 | 2 | 1.128 |
| 3 | 1.023 | 0 | 2.574 | 3 | 1.693 |
| 4 | 0.729 | 0 | 2.282 | 4 | 2.059 |
| 5 | 0.577 | 0 | 2.114 | 5 | 2.326 |
| 6 | 0.483 | 0 | 2.004 | 6 | 2.534 |
| 7 | 0.419 | 0.076 | 1.924 | 7 | 2.704 |
| 8 | 0.373 | 0.136 | 1.864 | 8 | 2.847 |
| 9 | 0.337 | 0.184 | 1.816 | 9 | 2.970 |
| 10 | 0.308 | 0.223 | 1.777 | 10 | 3.078 |
| 11 | 0.285 | 0.256 | 1.744 | 11 | 3.173 |
| 12 | 0.266 | 0.283 | 1.717 | 12 | 3.258 |
| 13 | 0.249 | 0.307 | 1.693 | 13 | 3.336 |
| 14 | 0.235 | 0.328 | 1.672 | 14 | 3.407 |
| 15 | 0.223 | 0.347 | 1.653 | 15 | 3.472 |
| 16 | 0.212 | 0.363 | 1.637 | 16 | 3.532 |
| 17 | 0.203 | 0.378 | 1.622 | 17 | 3.588 |
| 18 | 0.194 | 0.391 | 1.608 | 18 | 3.640 |
| 19 | 0.187 | 0.403 | 1.597 | 19 | 3.689 |
| 20 | 0.180 | 0.415 | 1.585 | 20 | 3.735 |
| 21 | 0.173 | 0.425 | 1.575 | 21 | 3.778 |
| 22 | 0.167 | 0.434 | 1.566 | 22 | 3.819 |
| 23 | 0.162 | 0.443 | 1.557 | 23 | 3.858 |
| 24 | 0.157 | 0.451 | 1.548 | 24 | 3.895 |
| 25 | 0.153 | 0.459 | 1.541 | 25 | 3.931 |

## A

AAMCO Transmission, 616
ABC analysis, 437
ABC classification, 435–36
Abernathy, William J., 183*n*
Absolute measures, of forecasting
 error, 144–45
Acceptance sampling, 255, 713–16
Ace Office Supply Co., 451
Acme manufacturing, 586
Activity-on-arc project network, 652
 construction of, 653–56
Activity-on-node, 652
Actual capacity, 195–96
Actual output rate, 195–96
Adaptive organizations, characteristics
 of, 327
Advertising promotions, 389
Aerogels, 159
Age Discrimination in Employment
 Act (ADEA), 330
Aggregate production planning,
 382–84, 477
 bridging approach to, 387
 framework for, 386–93
 managerial issues in implementing,
  415–16
 in manufacturing companies, 409
 methods in, 406–8
 in service companies, 408, 411
 strategies for, 391–93
 techniques for, 393
  mathematical techniques, 400
  trial-and-error method, 393–400
Aggregation, 382–83
 by labor, 383
 by products, 383
 by time, 384
Airlines
 capacity measuring by, 195
 demand management system for, 626
Air shipments, 367–68
Albrecht, Karl, 605, 608
Alfa-Laval Thermal Co., 214
Algorithm, simplex, 779
Allen-Bradley's World Contactors, 28,
 29–30, 724–25
 building competitive advantage of,
  730–38
 competitive challenge of, 727–30
 identifying strategic threats and
  opportunities, 726–27
 world-class manufacturing, 738–39
 world contactor facility, 725–26

Allison Transmission, 197, 198
Allocation problem, 210
Allstate Insurance, 616
Alternative optimal solutions, 750
Alternative routings, 560
American Airlines, 313, 367
 SABRE system of, 625, 626
American Express, 68, 333, 334,
 616
American National Standards Institute
 (ANSI), 257
American Production and Inventory
 Control Society, 550
American Society for Quality Control
 (ASQC), 272
American Society for Training and
 Development, 341
American Society of Mechanical
 Engineers (ASME), 20
American Society of Quality Control
 (ASQC), 261
American Steinway and Sons, 268
Americans with Disabilities Act
 (ADA), 330
Ames Rubber Corp., 263, 264
Anheuser-Busch, 195
Animated computer simulation
 techniques, 181
Answer Computer, Inc., 62
Anticipation stock, 432
Apple Computer, 327
Appraisal costs, 273
ARA Services, 50
Arco, 313
Ark, Bart van, 7*n*
Armistead, Colin, 613*n*
Arnold, Danny R., 74*n*
Artificial intelligence (AI), 310–12
Artificial variables, 485
Asaka, Tetsuichi, 695*n*
Ashland Chemical, 359
Assembler-supplier relationship, in
 Japan, 95–97
Assemble-to-order company (ATO),
 11–12
Assembly lines, 179–80
Associative forecasting methods, 119,
 136–37
Assurance, 271
Atlas Door, 27
AT&T
 global operations at, 230
 green manufacturing at, 12
 network systems group at, 263
 Universal Card Services, 263

Attribute data, control charts for,
 708–11
Audit, in capacity planning, 203, 205
Austin, M. Jill, 537*n*
Automated guided vehicles (AGV),
 307
Automated storage and retrieval
 system (AS/RS), 307
Automatic identification of parts,
 307–9
Automatic teller machines (ATMs),
 45, 617
Automation
 definition of, 300
 fixed, 301
 flexible, 301
 programmable, 301
 in services, 63
 wariness of United States
  manufacturers on, 307
Automobile industry
 advanced options in, 302
 operations in, 16–17
 platform teams in, 674
Auto Tech Center, 612
Available seat miles (ASMs), 195–96
Average, 113
 simple, 126
 simple moving, 126–29
 weighted moving, 129
Average-aggregate inventory value,
 430–31
Average flow time, 563
Average lateness, 563
Average outgoing quality limit
 (AOQL), 255
Avoidance of Refuse Ordinance, 375

## B

Backlog, 387, 389
Back order, 434–35
 costs of, 391
Balanced transportation problem,
 742–43
Baldridge, Malcolm, National Quality
 Award, 68, 256–63, 268
 winners of, 263, 264–65
Balking, 807
Ballou, Ronald H., 356*n*, 372, 373*n*
Banks Cash Services (BANCS), 617
Bar coding, 65, 89, 307–8, 736
Base planned lead time
 on the number of operations, 557
 on total processing time, 556

Basic variables, 780
Basis, 780
Batch production, 14, 15, 179
Bay Area Rapid Transit (BART) system, 308–9
Bayes' theorem, 767–69
Bayes' tree, 768
Bean, L. L., 68, 263, 433
Bell, Daniel, 56*n*
Bell Labs, 255
Benchmarking, 692–94, 730
Benders decomposition approach, 227
Benefits, 342–44
Benetton, 374
Benton, W. C., 538*n*
Berger, Joan, 66*n*
Bernstein, Aaron, 335*n*
Berry, Leonard L., 51*n*, 271
Best operating level, 201
Bill of material (BOM), 476, 478–80
   modular, 498
Bill of material file, 476
Biomedical Computer Programs (BMDP), 150
Bizzell, Bobby G., 74*n*
Blackburn, Joseph D., 27*n*
Black & Decker Co., 171, 382
Blackston, J., Jr., 550*n*
Blanc fountain pen, 269
Blocking, 798
BMW, 233
Boeing Co., 230, 314, 364
Boesendorfer, 268
Boise Cascade, continuous improvement at, 688
Boisseau, Charles, 338*n*
Borsig Valve Co., capacity planning in, 537
Bottleneck operation, 196, 558
Bowersox, Donald J., 367*n*
Bowman, Edward H., 402, 403
Bradley, Peter, 68*n*
Brainstorming, 695–96
Braun, 170
Bridging approach, to aggregate planning, 387
British Airways, 60
Brocca, Bruce, 695*n*
Brocca, M. Suzanne, 695*n*
Brown, Paul B., 272*n*
Brown, Ronald, 264
Browne, J., 630*n*
Bryan, William Jennings, 73
Budget, developing project, 660–61
Buffer, 572
Bumping, 573
Burger King (BK), 202, 616
Burlington Northern, 367
Burroughs Wellcome Co., 2, 3
Business cycle, in service sector, 60

Business environment, role of technology in, 293–98
Business-level strategic planning, 74, 75–77
   functional area involvement in, 77
Business logistics
   best value for money in, 364
   component integration in, 358–60
   components of, 357–58
   customer service in, 372–73
   definition of, 356–57
   elements of, 360–61
   international sourcing in, 164
   make-or-buy decision in, 362–63
   purchasing in, 361–67
   scope of, 357–61
   sources of goods and services in, 363–64
   supplier evaluation, 365–66
   transportation in, 367–71
   value analysis in, 365
   warehousing in, 372
Business managers, tasks of, 75–76
Business mission statement, 76
Business parks
   proliferation of, 228–29
   types of, 228
Business process reengineering, 280, 282–85
Business strategies, generic, 77
Bylinsky, Gene, 723*n*, 731

C

Cadillac Motor Car Co., 263, 334
Calgon Consumer Products, 362
Calling population, 805–6
Cannondale, 553–54
Capacity
   adjusting or sharing, 633
   defining and measuring, 195–96
Capacity bills, capacity planning using, 518, 525–27
Capacity changes
   sizing, 201–2
   strategic timing of, 199–201
Capacity cushion, 90, 199
Capacity decisions, 90
Capacity efficiency, 196
Capacity planning, 194, 202–3
   capacity bills in, 518, 525–27
   decision trees in, 205–206
   defining and measuring capacity in, 195–96
   detailed, 531, 532–36
   focused facilities in, 197
   importance of, 194–95
   long-range, 90
   measuring system effectiveness in, 196–97
   need for, 516–17

   overall factors in, 518, 521–25
   production planning and scheduling framework, 517–21
   resource profiles in, 518, 527–31
   rough-cut, 385, 517, 521–23
   in service operations, 536–38
   steps in, 203–5
   strategic implications of, 517
   as trial-and-error process, 519, 521
Capacity requirements planning (CRP), 386, 518–19, 532–36
Capacity strategies, 90, 197–99
   capacity cushions in, 199
   location options in, 208
   sizing capacity changes in, 201–2
   strategic timing of capacity changes in, 199–201
Capacity utilization, 196
Carey, John, 297*n*
Carrier Corp., 186
Carrying cost, 434
Cash flow cycle, 587
Cassidy, Jack, 598
Caterpillar, 80–81
Causal methods, 119
Cause-and-effect diagrams, 700–701
*C*-chart, 711
Cellular manufacturing, 181
Cellular telephones, 314
Census, 119
Center of gravity method, in single-facility location decision, 218–20
Central limit theorem, and sampling, 703
Ceppos, Richard, 675*n*
Champy, James, 28*n*, 282*n*
Change, inevitability of, as human resources issues, 345
Charlotte Panthers, 216
Chase, Richard B., 28*n*, 618*n*
Chase-demand strategy, 627
Chase strategy, 392
Check sheets, 697–98
Chemical production, 13
Child components, 478
Chillers, 185
Chi-square goodness of fit test, 811
Chrysler Corp., 173, 260–61, 553
   and defect control, 260–61
Chung, Chen, 405, 406*n*
CIM. *See* Computer integrated manufacturing
Cipau, Gabriel R., 10
Citicorp, 68
Clark, G., 634*n*
Clark, Kim, 8*n*, 81*n*
Clark-Wright savings heuristic, 634–38
Clausing, Don, 164*n*
Clevenger, Charlie, 198

Cliburn, Van, 268

Closed loop materials requirements planning (MRP), 24, 474–75, 478, 498

Closs, D. J., 367*n*

Coaching, 584

Coca-Cola, 276

Coefficient of determination, 142

Coefficient of optimism (Hurwicz) criterion, 762–63

Coincident indicators, 111

Colgate-Palmolive, 375

Commonality, 479

Common carriers, 367

Common random numbers, 798

Communications, technological improvements in, 314–15

Community considerations, in location decisions, 211

Company activities, and strategic advantage, 15–18

Compensation, as human resources issue, 344–45

Competition, time-based, 27–28

Competitive advantage, 724

Competitive analysis, performing, 165–66

Competitiveness, improving, in services, 59–63

Competitive priorities, at Meiji Seika Kaisha, Ltd., 86

Competitors, performing technical comparison with, 167

Complementary services, 389 developing, 626

Completion data, 557

Compliance, 296

Component, 474

Comprehensive quality assurance, 593–95

Computer-aided design (CAD), 26, 65, 303, 304

Computer-aided manufacturing (CAM), 26, 303, 304–5

Computer-integrated manufacturing (CIM), 89, 302–4 and the productivity pyramid, 734–36

Computer numerically controlled (CNC) machines, 305

Computer-related operations technologies, 26

Computers in forecasting, 150 in improving service, 62

Computer simulation, advantages of, 790–91

Computer technology, 314–15

Computer time, calculation of, for project, 656–59

Concurrent engineering, 27–28, 172–74 team approach in, 733

Conditional probabilities, 767

Conformance to specifications, 84

Connors, H. M., 226*n*

Constant demand rate, 455, 457–58

Constant lead time, 455, 456–57

Constraint set, 777

Consumer contact with, in service operations, 45–46 problem of intangibility for, 48

Consumerism, 112–13

Consumer participation approach, 620–21 in service process, 46

Consumer services, mass, 43

Consumer's risk, 703

Containerization, 368

Container on rail-flat car (COFC), 368–69

Continuous flow production, 13, 45, 180–81

Continuous improvement, 25–26 of key processes, 277–78 process analysis for, 684–87 acceptance sampling in, 713–16 benchmarking in, 692–94 control limits versus specification limits in, 711–13 data collection, analysis, and presentation in, 694–701 process improvement model in, 687–92 sampling and the central limit theorem in, 703 statistical sampling and control in, 702

Continuous process improvement (CPI), 275

Continuous process shop-floor control, 552

Continuous quality improvement (CQI), 275

Continuous review system, 453–54, 465 comparison of, with periodic review system, 465–67 determining reorder point in, 454–59 service levels, safety stock, and shortages in, 459–63

Continuous systems, 790–91

Contract carriers, 367

Control chart, 149 for attribute data, 708–11 for variable data, 705–8

Control Data learning center, 48

Control limit, 147 versus specification limits, 711–13

Controlling service supply, strategies for, 626–33

Conveyance kanban, 596

Cooke, James Aaron, 375*n*

Cooper, Randolph B., 501*n*

Cooperative arrangements, costs, 390

Coors, 195

Copacino, W. C., 368, 370*n*

Copyright, 48

Core service, 610

Corporate downsizing, 337–38

Corporate-level strategic planning, 74

Correlation coefficient, 141

Correlations, 167

Cost analysis, in making single-facility location decision, 215

Cost leadership, 78

Costs in building competitive advantage, 731 monitoring and controlling project, 661–63 of quality, 272–74

Cost table, 761

Council of Logistics Management, 356

Counting methods, 119

Cox, James F., III, 550*n*, 599*n*

Cox, Jeff, 571*n*

Cozzi, John, 612

Crabapple Microcomputer Co., 205

Crawford, Karlene M., 599*n*

Critical activities, 657

Critical path, 657–59

Critical path method (CPM), 652–53

Critical ratio, 563

Critical resources, 14

Crook, C. W., 404–5

Crosby, Philip, 255, 267–68, 269, 274

Cross-border ownership, 230

Cross-cultural training, 341

Cross-functional team, 18, 172 implementing, in DFM, 174

Cross-training employees, 633

Customer attributes, 164–65

Customer contact, 617–18

Customer-driven new product ideas, 162–64

Customers assessing needs and wants to, 158–60 voice of, 159–60, 164–65

Customer satisfaction, 161–71 focusing on, 276–77

Customer satisfaction teams, 278

Customer self-service, 633

Customer service, 17, 372–73

Customer waiting time, 791

Customization, 84

Cycle counting, 438, 501

Cycle-service level, 456–57

Cycles of mistrust, 336
Cycle stock, 432
Cycle time, 172, 555
Cyclical, 114

# D

Dai-Ichi Kangyo Bank, Ltd., 617
Daily work shift scheduling, 628–29
Dantzig, George, 776
Dartnell Co., 223–25
Data collection
  analysis, and presentation, 694–701
  and order disposition, 569
  and validation of waiting line
    model, 811
Davidow, William, 62
Day, George S., 724n
Decision alternatives, 760
Decision analysis, 760–71
  decision making under risk, 764–65
  decision making under uncertainty,
    761
    coefficient of optimism (Hurwicz)
      criterion, 762–63
    equally likely criterion, 763
    minimax regret criterion, 763–64
    optimistic (maximax) criterion,
      761–62
    pessimistic (maximin) criterion,
      762
  decision making with additional
    information, 766
    accuracy of additional
      information, 767
    Bayes' theorem, 767–69
    evaluating and using additional
      information, 769–71
    expected value of perfect
      information, 766–67
  decision trees, 765–76
  dominated alternatives, 761
  expected value criterion, 765
Decision Support Systems for
  Production/Operations
  Management, 150
Decision trees, 765–76
  in capacity planning, 205–6
Decision variables, 776–77
  in analysis of waiting lines, 811
Deckro, Richard, 405n
Deere and Co., 600
Defect, 161
Degeneracy, 750
Delivery date, 554
Delivery dependability, 84
Delivery speed, 84
Delphi method, 123–24
  of waste in India, 123–24
Delta Airlines, 3, 68

Demand
  characteristics of, 110–14
  components of, 113–14
  factors influencing, 111–13
  inventorying, 625
  partitioning, 625
Demand destination, 742
Demand forecast, 47
Demand management, 385
  top-down approach to, 100
De Meyer, Arnoud, 85n
Deming, W. Edwards, 25, 265–66,
  323, 335, 686
Deming Prize, 265–66
Dependent demand, 429
Dependent demand inventory
  management, material
  requirements planning (MRP)
  development of, 474–75
  closed loop, 498–99
  examples of, 482–83
  fixed order quantity, 493–94
  freezing master production
    schedule, 490
  gross-to-net requirements
    explosion, 483–86
  implementation of, 499–504
  information requirements, 500
  inventory control, 500–1
  loss of visibility for low-level
    components, 486–87
  lot-for-lot procedure, 493
  lot sizing, 492–93, 495–96
  low-level coding, 483
  lumpiness of demand, 490–92
  manufacturing resource planning,
    499
  material, 498
  minimum length for planning
    horizon, 487
  modular bills of material, 498
  period order quantity, 494
  prerequisites, 475–80
  record calculations, 481–82
  records in, 480
  system nervousness, 487–89, 495
  timing conventions, 480–81
  uncertainty in, 497–98
  use of, 496–97
Dependent variable, 136
Dertouzos, Michael, 8n
Design capacity, 195
Design for manufacturability,
  172–74
Design for the Environment (DFE),
  185–87
Design innovation, 84
Design quality, 84
Design specifications, 607
Design trade-offs, evaluating, 167–68

Detailed capacity planning, 531,
  532–36
DeToro, Irving J., 686n
DFM, implementing cross-functional
  teams in, 174
Differentiation, 78
Digital Equipment Corp. (DEC), 12,
  100, 187
Digital Matchprint, 298
Discrete event simulation, 790
Discrete systems, 790
Diseconomies of scale, 201
Disney World, 163, 170, 276
Dispatching rules, 262
Distinctive competence, 75–76, 724
Distribution System Stimulator, 226
Dodge, Harold, 255
Dominated alternatives, 761
Donno, Luca, 203n
Double Eagle Double Stack, 371
Double exponential smoothing,
  133–35
Dougherty, John R., 300n, 304n, 306n
Dow Chemical, 359
  Waste Reduction Always Pays
    program, 11
Droge, Cornelia, 78n
Drucker, Peter, 647, 760n
Drum-buffer-rope (DBR), 572
Dubashi, Jagannath, 298n
DuBois, Frank L., 408
Due date performance, 791
Dumaine, Brian, 327n
Dummy activity, 653
Dummy destination, 751–52
Dummy origin, 752
DuPont, 187
Durability, 270

# E

Ealey, Lance A., 279n
Earliest due date (EDD) rule, 262
Earliest finish (EF) time, 656
Earth Summit, 297
Eastman Chemical Co., 263, 264–65
Eastman Kodak, 343
Ecologically sound manufacturing,
  9, 11
Econometric models, 143–44
Economic lot size, 432, 589–91
Economic order quantity (EOQ), 432,
  493–94
Economic order quantity (EOQ)
  models, 438
  constant demand, no shortages,
    439–43
  constant demand, shortages
    allowed, 443–46
  quantity discounts, 450–52

Economic order quantity (EOQ) models, (*continued*)
  sensitivity analysis for, 452–53
  uniform replenishment rate, constant demand, no shortages, 447–48
Economies of scale, 201
Ed, William T., 433
Effective capacity, 195
Effective leadership, 279
Eisman, Regina, 330*n*
Electromation, Inc., 335
Electronic data interchange (EDI), 27, 65, 89, 314, 552
Electronic Data Systems, General Motors purchase of, 364
Electronic mail, 314
Electronic pagers, 314
Elemental standard times, 347, 350
Ellett Brothers, inventory management at, 437
Elmore, David, 50
Embassy Suites, 163
Empathy, 271
Employees
  cross-training of, 633
  morale of, in service operations, 48
Empowered employees, creating teams of competent, 595
Empowerment, 676
Emshwiller, John R., 159*n*
End item, 474, 525
Enforced problem solving, 592
Engineer, voice of, 166–67
Engleman, Robert, 295*n*
Enterprise integration, 302
Environment
  designing for, 185–87
  technology and, 294–96
Environmental sensitivity, 375–76
Equally likely criterion, 763
Erland, A. K., 804
Ernst, Scott, 334
Ethics
  influence of operations manager in, 9
  in purchasing, 366–67
European Community, 98
Evans, Dale, 65
Evans, James R., 713*n*
Evans, Phillip, 93*n*
EXCEL, 393
Excellence, quality as, 268
Exception reports, 496–97
Executive Furniture, Inc. (EFI), 2, 3
Executive opinion, jury of, 12
Exogenous (external) inputs, 791
  simulating, 791–95
Expected value
  of perfect information, 766–67
  of sample information, 769, 771

Expected value criterion, 765
Expert system, 310
Exponential distribution, 809
Exponential smoothing
  double, 133–35
  single, 129–33
Extent of contact, 618
External environment, analysis of, 75
External factors, influencing demand, 111
External failure costs, 272–73
External information, 6

**F**

Facility layout problem, 210
Facility utilization, 791
Factor rating systems, in single-facility location decision, 216–18
Factory focus, 91
Factory throughput, 791
Family location, 209
Farber, Barry, 68*n*
Farnum, Gregory T., 723*n*
Feasible solutions, 779
Feasible solution space, 779
Federal Express, 27, 68, 263, 293, 328, 367, 375
  and use of benchmarking, 693
Federal Quality Institute (FQI), 275
Feigenbaum, Armand, 255, 269
Ferdows, Kasra, 85*n*
Figuiolo, Lee, 62
Fill rate, 459
Final assembly schedule, 498
Finished goods, 429
Firm infrastructure, 17
Firm planned orders (FPOs), 487–88
First come, first served (FCFS), 262
First-tier suppliers, 96
Fishbone diagram, 700
Fitchburg Coated Products, continuous improvement at, 689
Fitness concept, 269
Fitness for use, quality as, 269
Fixed automation, 301
Fixed automation programmable automation, 89
Fixed order interval system, 463
Fixed order quantity, 454, 493–94
Fixed time period system, 463
Flexibility, 12, 306
  in building competitive advantage, 729, 732
Flexible automation, 301
Flexible manufacturing system (FMS), 26, 89, 184, 306–7
Florida Power & Light, 68
Flow shop, 178
Flow time, 555
Fly-in parks, 228

Focus, 78*n*
Focused facilities, 197
Focused stores, 198
Food processing, 13
Ford, Henry, 21–23, 581, 583, 585
Ford Motor Co.
  advanced options at, 302
  capacity at, 195
  concurrent engineering at, 173–74
  global operations of, 230
  inventory measurement at, 431
  negative cushion at, 90
  reengineering at, 28, 29
  sociotechnical system concept at, 326
  worker productivity at, 328
Forecasting, 114–15
  accuracy of, 115
  approaches to, 119
  computers in, 150
  definition of, 110
  determining what in, 115
  establishing objectives for, 115
  gathering and analyzing data in, 117
  making, 118
  monitoring and controlling, 118–19
  presenting results, 118
  qualitative forecasting methods, 119, 121
    associative methods, 119, 136–37
    Delphi method, 121–22, 123–24
    econometric models, 143–44
    jury of executive opinion, 121
    market research surveys, 122
    naïve extrapolation, 121
    quantitative forecasting methods, 136–37
    regression models, 137–43
    sales force composite, 121
    time series analysis models, 125
    time series decomposition, 135–36
    time series smoothing, 125–35
  selecting method for, 117–18
  specifying time period for, 116–17
  subjective, 115
Forecasting error, 118, 144
  absolute measures of, 144–45
  relative measures of, 146
Forest Hills Tennis Racket Co., 393–400, 415–16
FORTRAN, 800
Franklin, Benjamin, 427
Freezing the master production system, 489, 490
Freight consolidation, 369–71
Functional-level strategic planning, 74, 77
Furniture industry, operations in, 16
Fuzzy logic, 311–12

# G

Game plan, 385
Gantt, Harry, 651
Gantt charts, 651
   construction, 563–67
Garvin, David, 28n, 254n, 278n
Gendex, MRP and the real cost of
   inventory losses at, 503
General Electric Co.
   environmental concerns of, 189
   and freight consolidation, 370
   and inventory control, 428
   and just-in-time, 586, 598
   robots at, 306
   sociotechnical system concept at, 326
   *Time Series Forecasting System,* 118
General Foods, 326
General Motors Corp., 195, 260, 301,
   326, 341, 364, 370n, 428
   and capacity measurement, 195
   and cross-cultural and training, 341
   and defect control, 260
   purchase of Electronic Data Systems
      by, 364
   Quad 4 Engine Plant, 2
   sociotechnical system concept at,
      326
   and use of new technology, 301
General purpose plant, 223
Generic business strategies, 77
GeneSysData Technologies, Inc., 62
Geoffrion, Arthur M., 227n
Georgia-Pacific Corp., 209, 239–48
Giffi, Craig, 92n
Gilbreth, Frank, 350
Glaskowsky, Nicholas A., Jr., 367n
Global integration, of operations,
   97–100
Globally integrated purchasing
   operations, 98
Globe Metallurgical, Inc., 263
Goal programming, 405
Goldratt, Eliyahu, 571
Goodman, D. A., 405n
Goods, 41
Goodwill, 435
Gorman, Leon, 68
Government regulations, as human
   resources issue, 330
GPSS, 800
Granite Rock Co., 263
Greene, James H., 305n
Green manufacturing, 9, 12
Greenpeace, 186
Groover, Mikell P., 301n, 306n
Gross requirements, 481
Gross-to-net requirements explosion,
   483–86
Growth rate of productivity, 8
Gryna, F. M., 266n

# H

Hakanson, William P., 309n
Hales, H. Lee, 303
Hamburger, Michael J., 225n
Hammer, Michael, 28n, 282n
Hampton, William J., 187
Hansmann, Fred, 402
Harbour, James, 598
Harker, Patrick T., 63n
Harrington, T. C., 355
Hart, Christopher W. L., 55n
Haskell, strategic positioning at, 80
Hauser, John, 164n
Hax, Arnoldo C., 3n
Hayes, Robert, 8n, 77n, 81n, 199n,
   205n, 299
Hebert, John, 405n
Heinz, 339
Helferich, O. K., 367n
Henkoff, Ronald, 340n
Herman, Stanley, 331–32
Heskett, James L., 55n, 357
Hess, Sydney W., 402
Heuristics, 665–66
   in making multiple-facility location
      decisions, 225–26
Hewlett-Packard, 326
   environmental concerns at, 12
   global operation at, 28
   and innovation, 80
   quality concerns at, 30, 230
   sociotechnical system concept at,
      326
   and worker productivity, 328, 342,
      343
Heye, Christopher, 8n
Hickory Furniture Co., 220–21
Hierarchical framework, aggregate
   planning in, 382
Hierarchical production planning
   (HPP), 416–21
   at Owens-Corning fiberglass, 420
High-technology business services,
   43
Hill, Terry, 258
Hiring/firing workers, costs of, 390
Hitachi, 163
Hodde, James A., 205n
Hoerr, John, 333n
Holcomb, Mary C., 361
Holding cost, 434
Holding time, 809
Holiday Inn University, 48
Holt, Charles, 400–1
Honda Motor Co., 230, 260
Hoole, Richard W., 97n
Hopper, Max D., 627
House of Quality, 164–68
H&R Block, 3, 616
Hudson, D. R., 367n

Human resource management, 17
   in building competitive advantage,
      737–38
Human resources
   issues of the 1990s, 330
      government regulations in, 330
      work force diversity in, 330–31
   manager as leader in, 331
   participative management in,
      331–32
   strategic planning in, 91–92,
      324–25
   team activities, 332–35
      benefits in, 342–44
      compensation in, 344–45
      fear in the workplace in, 335–38
      inevitability of change in, 345
      recognition and rewards in, 345
      training and development in,
         338–41
   work measurement, 346
Humphreys, Richard W., 350n
Hunt-Wesson Foods, Inc., 227
Hurwicz, Leonid, 762–63
Hybrids, 15
Hyrnick, Michael S., 205n

# I

IBM
   and concurrent engineering, 173
   *Consumer Goods System (COGS),* 118
   environmental concerns at, 12
   and global concerns at, 230
   marketing of Distribution System
      Stimulator by, 226
   multiechelon inventory
      management at, 466
   and quality function deployment,
      170
   Rochester site, 263
   sociotechnical system concept at,
      326
   and strategic alliances, 296
   and worker productivity, 328, 343
Inbound logistics, 17, 357
Incentive programs, 342
Indented bills of material, 481
Independent demand, 429
Independent demand inventory
   management, 427, 428–29
   basic concepts in, 429–38
   comparing continuous review and
      periodic review systems in, 465–67
   continuous review system in,
      453–63
   dependent demand in, 429
   economic order quantity models in,
      438–53
   independent demand in, 429
   periodic review system in, 463–64

Independent variable, 136
Indicators
    coincident, 111
    lagging, 111
    leading, 111
Industrial parks, 228
Industrial robots, 89
Industrial services, 43
Industrial society, 56
Inevitability of change, as human
    resources issue, 345
Information
    decision making with additional,
        766–71
    effective collection and analysis of,
        278
    expected value of sample, 769, 771
    external, 6
    internal, 6
Infrastructure, 87
Innovative control, 569, 571–72, 574
Input-output control, 560–61
Input source, 805–6
Inspection, 255
Instant Rent A Car, 612
Integrated capacity and facilities
    strategy, considerations in
    developing, 90–91
Intelligence, artificial, 310–12
Interchangeability parts, 20
Intermittent, job shop operations
    scheduling, 560–69
    shop-floor control in, 554–60
Intermittent flow configurations,
    176–78
Intermittent production, 13, 176
Internal capabilities, analysis of, 75
Internal decisions, that influence
    demand, 111
Internal failure costs, 272
Internal information, 6
Internal operations, 358
Internal Revenue Service (IRS), 313
International competition in services,
    57–59
International issues, in shop-floor
    control, 574–76
International service transactions, 57
International Sourcing, 364
In-transit inventory, 432
Inventories, 389
    comparing continuous review and
        periodic review systems, 465–67
    continuous review system, 453–54
        determining reorder point,
            454–59
        service levels, safety stock, and
            shortages in, 459–63
    costs in, 433–35
    definition of, 429

economic order quantity models in,
    438
    constant demand, no shortages,
        439–43
    constant demand, shortages
        allowed, 443–46
    quantity discounts, 450–52
    sensitivity analysis for, 452–53
    uniform replenishment rate,
        constant demand, no shortages,
        447–48
    methods of measuring, 430–31
    periodic review system, 463–65
    reasons for holding, 432
    records in, 436–38
    types of, 429–30
    zero, 428
Inventory carrying costs, 391
Inventory control, objectives of, 438
Inventorying demand, 625
Inventory items, classifying, 435–36
Inventory level, 386
*Inventory Management Program and
    Control Technique (IMPACT)*, 118
Inventory records, 476, 480
Inventory reduction caution, 591–92
Inventory turnover, 428, 431
IRT/USA TODAY Quality Cup, 685
Ishikawa, Kaoru, 278, 700
Ishikawa diagram, 700
ISO9000 international standards,
    257
Isoprofit, 778
Item cost, 435
Item master file, 500
Ivie, R. M., 367n

**J**

Jacob, Rahul, 275n
Jaikumar, Ramchandran, 299
Japan
    assembler-supplier relationships in,
        95–97
    manufacturing techniques in, 583,
        598
Japan Telephone & Telegraph Corp.,
    278
Jencks, Herb, 295
Jenlor Co., 612
Jiffy-Lube oil change shop, 42
Job, 555
Jobbers, 176
Job rotation, 738
Job shop, 13, 44, 176, 178
Job shop floor control, performance
    measures in, 557–60
John, Elton, 268
Johnson, Bob, 613n
Johnson, S. M., 567n

Johnson's rule for fixed sequence,
    two-machine problems, 567–68
Johnston, William B., 231n
Jones, C. W., Hauling Services, 401n,
    408–11
Jones, Daniel T., 95n
Judgment methods, 119, 120
Juran, Joseph, 255, 266–67, 269, 274
Jury of executive opinion, 121
Just-in-time (JIT)
    coordinating materials requirements
        planning and, 600
    implementation, 598–99
    misunderstandings and myths, 585
    motivation for implementation,
        585–87
    systems requirements, 592–99
Just-in-time (JIT) delivery, logistics
    systems to support, 597–98
Just-in-time (JIT) philosophy, origins
    of, 583, 585
Just-in-time (JIT) production, 24–25,
    582–83, 737
Just-in-time total quality
    management (JIT/TQM) production
    system, 95

**K**

*Kaizen*, 25–26, 91, 277
Kanban, 585, 596, 597
    conveyance, 596
    production, 596
Kellogg, mission statement of, 76
Kenmore, 197
KFC, 616
Khumawala, B. M., 408
Kimball International, Inc., 303
Kitchen Aid, 197
Kleiner, Art, 11n
Kmart, 42, 293
Koepp, Stephen, 67n
Koselka, Rita, 375n
Kotler, Phillip, 74n, 75n
Krajewski, Lee, 405, 406n
Kuehn, Alfred A., 225n

**L**

Labor, aggregation by, 383
Labor intensiveness, in service
    operation, 47–48
Lag demand, 201
Lagging indicators, 111
Lakernick, Philip, 62
Lambert, D. M., 355
Land's End
    benchmarking at, 693
    inventory at, 433
Langley, C. John, Jr., 361

Lao-Tze, 549
Latest finish (LF) time, 656
Latest start (LS) time, 656
Leadership
  effective, 279
  quality management, 263, 265–69
Leading indicators, 111
Lead time, 439, 554
  in building competitive advantage, 729, 732
  planned, 555
Least square, 138–39
Lee, Sang M., 406$n$
Lee, W. B., 408
Lehman, Shearson, 313
Lele, Miland M., 160$n$
Leong, G. Keong, 87$n$
Less than full truck load (LTL), 367
Lester, Richard K., 8–9
Level-capacity strategy, 627
Level strategy, 392
Levi, Daniel, 300$n$
Levinson, Marc, 7$n$
Levi Strauss, 327, 343
Levitt, Theodore, 614$n$
Licensing agreements, 48
Lindsay, William M., 713$n$
Linear decision rule, 400–401
Linear programming, 402, 776–85
  assumptions used in, 777
  constraints in, 785
  formulating linear programming model in, 776–77
  graphical solutions to problems in, 777–79
  mathematical structure of model for, 777
  minimization problems in, 785
  in project crashing, 667, 669
  sensitivity analysis, 785
  shadow prices in, 784–85
  simplex method in, 779–84
  transportation method in, 223–25, 403–4
Line-flow production, 13, 15, 45
Linkages
  definition of, 17
  vertical, 92–97
Livy, 381
Local decisions, factors affecting, 209–13, 215
Locational cost-volume-profit analysis, in single-facility location decision, 220–22
Location-allocation problem, 210
Location decision, 90, 194, 207
  dominant facility location factors in manufacturing in, 212–13
  dominant facility location factors in services in, 213, 215

factors affecting, 209–13, 215
general approach to making, 208–9
importance of, 207–8
making multiple-facility, 222
  business park proliferation, 228–29
  factories: research and development linkages, 229
  globalization of production, 229–31
  heuristics, 225–26
  optimization methods, 226
  plant charters approach to, 222–23
  simulation, 226
  sun belt phenomenon, 232
  transportation method, 223–25
making single-facility, 215
  center of gravity method, 218–20
  detailed cost analysis in, 215
  factor rating systems, 216–18
  locational cost-volume-profit analysis, 220–22
  regional, community, and site considerations in, 210–12
  strategic trends in, 227–28
Location problem, 210
Logistics
  just-in-time, 376, 597–98
  reverse, 375
Logistics management, 357
  strategic trends in, 373–74
Long-range capacity planning, 90
Long-range planning, 385
Loss function, 158
Loss minimization, designing for, 158
Lot-for-lot (LFL) procedure, 493
Lot sizing, 492–93
  fixed order quantity, 493–94
  importance of lot sizing, 495–96
  lot-for-lot (LFL) procedure, 493
  and MRP system nervousness, 495
  period order quantity, 494
Lot-to-lot, 483
Lotus 1-2-3, 393
Love, Robert, 386$n$, 402$n$
Lovelock, Christopher H., 47$n$, 622
Low, James T., 569$n$
Low-level coding, 483
Low production cost, 84
Lublin, Joann S., 341$n$
Luciano, Lani, 342$n$, 343$n$
Lyne, Jack, 229$n$

## M

Mabert, Vincent A., 538$n$
MacArthur, Douglas, 25
Macroanalysis, 210

Madden, Thomas J., 205$n$
Madeloff, Stan, 612
Maffei, Richard B., 226$n$
Magee, John, 368, 370$n$, 372$n$
Magnet, Myron, 63$n$
Main, Jeremy, 342$n$
Make-or-buy decision in, 362–63
Make-to-order (MTO) company, 11
Make-to-stock (MTS) company, 11
Man, Charles C., 65$n$
Management coefficient model, 402
Management science, 23
Manager as leader, as human resources issue, 331
Managerial issues, in aggregate production plans, 415
Manor Care, Inc., 50
Manufacturability, design for, 172–74
Manufacturing companies, aggregate planning in, 409
Manufacturing Futures Survey, 84–85
Manufacturing operation, 2, 6
  classifying, 43
  distinctions between service operations, 3, 43
  dominant facility location factors in, 212–13
  ecologically sound, 11
  increased productivity in, 41
  organization in, 91
  productivity in, 7–9
  resource planning in, 499
Manufacturing operations
  process design and layout for, 174–82
  role of quality in, 258–59
Manufacturing planning-and-control (MPC) system, 385
Manufacturing resource planning (MRP II), 24, 475
Maquiladora plants, 231
Marcus, Stanley, 259
Margin, 16
Marginal probabilities, 767
Market-area plant, 222–23
Marketing, 17
Market research, new product ideas in, 1599
Market research surveys, 122
Markland, Robert, 78$n$, 216, 226$n$
Markoff, John, 296$n$
Marlow Industries, 263
Marriott, J. Willard, Sr., 68
Marriott's Learning Center, 48
Marshall, Colin, 60
Martin, John E., 284
Martin, John M., 723$n$, 730$n$, 737$n$
Martin Co., 255

Massachusetts Institute of Technology (MIT)
Commission on Industrial Productivity, 8
Council on Industrial Productivity, 8–9
Mass consumer services, 43
Master production schedule (MPS), 385, 476, 477–78, 516
constraints on, 419
freezing, 489, 490
Material flow, managing, 589–92
Material handling, reduction of, 560
Material requirements planning (MRP), 24, 386, 420, 474, 497, 516, 595–96
closed loop, 498
information requirements, 500
inventory control, 500–501
coordinating just-in-time and, 600
development of, 474–75
example of, 482–83
freezing master production schedule, 489, 490
gross-to-net requirements explosion, 483–86
and hierarchial production planning, 419
implementation of, 499
existing systems and informal systems, 499–500
keys to successful implementation, 499
planning in, 501–4
loss of visibility for low-level components, 486–87
lot sizing, 492–93
fixed order quantity, 493–94
importance of, 495–96
lot-for-lot procedure, 493
period order quantity, 494
and system nervousness, 495
low-level coding, 483
lumpiness of demand, 490–92
manufacturing resource planning (MRP II), 499
minimum length for planning horizon, 487
modular bills of material, 498
prerequisites, 475–80
bills of material, 478–80
master production schedule, 475–80
records in, 480, 481–82
system nervousness, 487–89
timing conventions, 480–81
uncertainty in, 497–98
use of, 496–97
Materials management, 357

Mathematical techniques, 400
goal programming, 405
linear decision rule, 400–401
linear programming, 402, 403
management coefficient model, 401
mixed integer programming, 405–6
parametric production planning, 401
production-switching heuristic, 402
search decision rule, 401
simulation models, 406
Matrix minima rule, 744–46
Matsushita, 163
Maximum lateness, 563
Maxwell, John C., 276n
Mayazawa, Kiichi, 297
Mazda, 230
McCormick Harvester Co., 254
McDonald's
and employee productivity, 50
Hamburger University, 48
production line approach of, 181–82, 615, 616
push production system of, 596
and service product matrix at, 52
McGrath, Michael E., 97n
Mean activity time, 670
Mean arrival rate, 810
Mean service rate, 810
Mean time between failures (MTBF), 270
Mean time to failure (MTTF), 270
Medium-range planning, 385
Meiji Seika Kaisha, Ltd, competitive priorities at, 86
Mellichamp, Joseph, 386n, 402n
Merced County, California, 313
Methods-time measurement (MTM), 350–51
Michigan State University, 3
project management tools at, 668
Microanalysis, 211
Microcomputer Support for Operations Research/Discrete Simulation (MOR/DS), 799, 800
Midas Muffler, 616
Millard, Richard, 50
Miller, Herman, 186
Miller, Jeffrey G., 85n
Miller, Phineas, 19
Milliken and Co., 263, 333, 340
MIL-STD (military standard) tables, 255
Minimax regret criterion, 763–64
Minimization problems, 785
Minnesota Mining & Manufacturing (3M) Co., 298
Pollution Prevention Pays programs at, 11
Minnesota Wire & Cable Co., at capacity planning, 520

Mirsky, Jeanette, 18–19n
Mixed integer programming, 405–6
Mixed-model assembly, in repetitive manufacturing, 553–54
Mixed strategy, 393
Mixed-use parks, 228
Modigliani, Franco, 400–401
Modular bills of material, 498
Moody, Patricia E., 27n
Moore, Laurence J., 406n
Morison, Elting E., 515
Morris, Barbara, 613n
Most likely time estimate, 669
Motorola, Inc.
environmental concerns at, 296
as MBNQ winner, 263
participative management program at, 333
sociotechnical system concept at, 326
time-based competition at, 27
training and education center, 339
and worker productivity, 328, 343
Movement inventories, 432
Moving average
simple, 126–29
weighted, 129
MRP Systems Directory and Buyers Guide, 503
Multimedia technology, 315
Multinational company, and global integration, 99
Multiple-channel, single-phase waiting line model, 813–14
Multiple channel queueing system, 808
Multiple linear regression, 143
Multiple-phase queueing system, 808
Murdick, Robert G., 46n, 215n

## N

Naïve extrapolation, 121
associative forecasting methods in, 136–37
Delphi method in, 121–22, 123–24
econometric models in, 143–44
jury of executive opinion on, 121
market research surveys in, 122
quantitative forecasting methods in, 136–37
regression models in, 137–43
sales force composite in, 121
time series analysis models in, 125
time series decomposition in, 135–36
time series smoothing in, 125–35
Nakane, Jinichiro, 85n
Nasar, Sylvia, 328n
National Bureau of Standards, 261
National Labor Relations Act (1935), 334

National Labor Relations Board (NLRB), 334–35, 335
National Technological University (NTU), 47, 642–45
Navy, U.S., use of total quality leadership by, 686
Negative correlation, 141
Negative cushion, 90
Neiman Marcus, 259
Neural networks, 310–11
Neurocomputers, 312
New operations technologies, 89
New product
  application of quality function deployment (QFD) to, 170
  customer-driven, 162–64
  developing, 88
  development cycle for, 589
  introduction of, 84
  from market research, 159
  technology-driven, 159
News Life Health Clubs, Inc., 218
New strategy development cycle, 589
New United Motor Manufacturing, Inc. (NUMMI), 597
New York telephone, continuous improvement at, 687
Nonnegativity restrictions, 777
Nordstrom, Inc., 68
Normal time, 349
Normann, Richard, 48n, 610n, 611n
North American Free Trade Agreement (NAFTA), 98, 231
Northern Telecom, 12, 35, 299
Northwest Airlines, 308
Northwest corner rule, 744
nP-chart, 709–10
NQI, Inc., 186
Nucor Corp., 179
Numerically controlled machines, 305
NYNEX, 313

**O**

Objective function, 777
O'Brien Corp., 461–63
Oestreich, Daniel, 335–36
Office parks, 228
Off-peak demand, promoting, 624–25
Oldsmobile, project management for product launch at, 659
Oliff, Michael D., 408
On-time delivery, 17
Opening door, 163
Open order, 481
Operating characteristics, 810
Operating characteristics curve, 715
Operating expense, 572
Operating strategy, 55
Operation competitive priorities, 82
Operation processing time, 555

Operations, 17
  as competitive weapon, 83–84
  global integration of, 97–100
Operations competitive priorities, 84–85
Operation setback chart, 528
Operations management
  definition of, 2
  field of, 23
  history of, 18–23
  recent trends in, 24–26
  technological developments in, 292–315
Operations manager, role of, in managing transformation process, 9–10
Operations planning and control, 92
Operations requirements, 168
Operations strategic planning, 75, 77, 81–83, 730
Operations strategy, 81–82
  choices in, 85, 87–88
Opportunity cost, 434
Optimal feasible solution, 779
Optimistic (maximax) criterion, 761–62
Optimistic time estimate, 669
Optimization methods, in making multiple-facility location decision, 226
Optimized Production Technology (OPT), 572
Option modules, 498
Order cycle time, 12
Ordering cost, 433
Order review and release, 561–62
Order winner, 259
Orlicky, Joseph, 496n
O'Rourke, Tracy, 739
Otis Elevator Co., 62
Ottinger, Lisa, 315
Outbound logistics, 17, 358
Output
  in service operations, 48
  variable, nonstandard, 48
Outsourcing, 93, 374
Overall factors, capacity planning using, 518, 521–25
Overtime, effect of, on capacity, 196
Overtime/slack time, 389
  costs of, 390
Owens-Corning Fiberglas, improved hierarchical production planning at, 420
Ozeki, Kazuo, 695n

**P**

Pairing, 798
Paper production, 13
Paradice, David, 315

Parallel service, 808
Parametric production planning, 401
Parasuraman, A., 51n, 271
Parent component, 478
Pareto charts, 699–700
Participative management, 331–32
Partitioning demand, 625
Parts families, 181
Parts Inventory Management System (PIMS), 466
Part-time staffing, 389, 632–33
  costs of, 390
Pasmore, William, 326
Patents, 48
Pavilion Technologies, 311, 318–21
Pay-for-performance, 344
Payoff table, 760–61
P-chart, 708
Pegging, 496
Penney, J. C., 65, 293, 328
People skills, operations manager need for, 9
Performance measures, 791
  in job shop floor control, 557–60
Performance specification, 607
Periodic counts, 501
Periodic review system, 463–65, 465
  comparison of, with continuous review system, 465–67
Period order quantity, 494
Peripheral services, 610
Perishability, of services, 46
Personal services
  skilled, 43
  unskilled, 42–43
Pessimistic (maximin) criterion, 762
Pessimistic time estimate, 669
Peters, Thomas, 67
Petroleum refining, 13
Philip, N. V., 230
Physical distribution, 358
Physical rates
  of substitution, 777
  of usage, 777
Physical supply, 357–58
Pilat, Dirk, 7n
Pipeline inventory, 432
Pipelines, 368
Pisano, Gary P., 77n
Pitney Bowes, 293, 294
Pivot column, 782
Pivot element, 782
Pivoting process, 782
Pivot row, 782
Pizza Hut, 50, 616
Planned lead time, 555
Planned order receipts, 481
Planned order releases, 481
Planning horizon, 477
  minimum length of, 487

Plant charters approach, in making multiple-facility locations decisions, 222–23
Plants within plants (PWPs), 197
Pohang Iron and Steel Co., Ltd. (POSCO), 249–52
Poisson distribution, 806–7
Poka-yoke, 277
Pollard, William, 54
Pollini, Maurizio, 268
Port, Otis, 267n, 694n, 695n
Porter, Michael, 15n, 17n, 75n, 78n, 92n, 608
Positioning, 55
Positive correlation, 141
Posner, Barry, 648n, 672, 675–77
Posterior probabilities, 768
Postindustrial society, 56, 69
Postoptimality analysis, 785
Postsale customer service, 84
Pratt & Whitney, 586
Predetermined standard times, 350–51
Preindustrial society, 55–56, 69
Prevention costs, 273
Price, quality as value for, 269–70
Price incentives, 389, 624
Primary activities, 16
Prior probabilities, 767
Private carriers, 367
Problem-solving teams, 278, 332
Process analysis, for continuous improvement, 684–87
    acceptance sampling in, 713–16
    benchmarking in, 692–94
    control limits versus specification limits in, 711–13
    data collection, analysis, and presentation, 694–701
    process improvement model in, 687–92
    sampling and the central limit theorem in, 703
    statistical sampling and control in, 702
Process capability index ($C_p$), 712–13
Process capability studies, 732
Process Characteristics Matrix, 168
Process control charts, 703–11
Process design
    for manufacturing and service systems, 174–82
    strategic issues in, 182–87
    and technology management, 88–89
Processes, 277
    continuous improvement of key, 277–78
Process flow chart, 697
Process improvement, statistical tools for, 701

Process improvement model, 687–92
Process improvement teams, 278
Process industries, 13
Process innovation, 183–84
Process mapping, 697
Process-oriented layout, 176
Process plant, 223
Process technology, 88–89
Proctor & Gamble, 163, 326, 343
Procurement, 17, 357
Producer's risk, 703
Product
    aggregation by, 383
    durability of, 84
    effective design of, 279–80
    flexibility of, 84
    selecting features for, 161–62
Product innovation, 183–84
Production
    batch, 15
    continuous flow, 13
    intermittent, 13
    just-in-time, 24–25
    line-flow, 13
Production flexibility, along the supply chain, 592–93
Production kanban, 596
Production lead time, 84
Production-line approach, 614–16
    to service, 181–82
Production lot, 555
Production planning, 383, 384–86.
    See also Aggregate production planning
    long-range, 385
    medium-range, 385
    short-range, 386
Production planning and scheduling framework, and capacity planning, 51
Production-planning environment, 387–91
Production rate, 386
Production-switching rule, 421
Productivity
    definition of, 7
    improving, in services, 59–63
    in sociotechnical organization, 327–30
    and the transformation process, 7–9
Productivity pyramid
    computer-integrated manufacturing in, 734–36
Productivity studies, focus of, 7
Product-level strategic planning, 74
Product life cycle, 111–13, 182
    compression of, 184
Product mix flexibility, 84
Product-oriented layout, 178
Product planning, 88

Product planning and process design, 158
    assessing customers' needs and wants, 158–60
    customer satisfaction, 161–71
    design for manufacturability, 172–74
    process design and layout for manufacturing and service systems, 174–82
    strategic issues in process design, 182–87
Product plant, 222
Product process matrix, 88, 184–85
Product reliability, 84, 270
Product structure diagram, 478
Product-switching heuristic, 402
Profit maximization transportation problems, 754
Program evaluation and review technique (PERT), 652–53
Programmable automation, 301
Programmable logic controllers (PLCs), 736
Progressive Casualty Insurance Co., 62
Project, 44, 175
Project crashing, 664–67
Project management
    calculating completion time for project in, 656–59
    critical path method in, 652–53
    Gantt charts in, 651
    managing project resources in, 660
    budgets, 660–61
    monitoring and controlling project costs, 661–63
    resource limitations, 664
    time/cost trade-offs in, 664–67, 669
    program evaluation and review technique in, 652–53
    program evaluation and review technique networks and uncertain time estimates in, 669–76
    techniques in, 648
    work breakdown structures in, 650–51
Project manufacturing, 12–13
Project network, 652
Prototype, 162
Pseudo-random numbers, 791–94
Public/private partnership, 187
Pull production systems, 595–96
Purchasing
    definition of, 361–62
    ethics in, 366–67
    globally integrated operations in, 98
Purchasing planning and control, 386
Push production systems, 595–96

# Q

QFD. *See* Quality function deployment
Quaker furniture, 573–74
Quaker Oats, 359
Qualifiers, 259
Qualitative forecasting methods, 117, 119, 121
Quality, 84. *See also* Continuous improvement; Total quality management
in building competitive advantage, 729, 731–32
and business process reengineering, 282–85
costs of, 272–74
definitions of, 268–70
difficulty of measuring, in services, 51
greater emphasis on, in services, 67–68
historical perspective of, 254–55
role of, in manufacturing strategy, 258–59
and total quality management, 275–82
Quality assurance, 14, 255
comprehensive, 593–95
Quality circles, 278, 332
Quality control, using statistics to test inferences about, 703
Quality function deployment, 164
application to new product design, 170
Quality management, 91
as strategic issue, 256–63
Quality management leadership, 263, 265–69
Quality-related product characteristics, 270
Quality-related service characteristics, 271–72
Quality variable, 705
Quantitative forecasting methods, 117, 136–37
Quantity discount, 435, 450–52
Queue discipline, 807
Queueing systems, 625. *See* Waiting line models
Queueing theory, 805
Queues, 804. *See* Waiting line models
Queue times, reduction of, 560

# R

Radio frequency (RF) identification systems, 308–9
Rail, 367
Ralston Purina Co., 226
Ramsay, Martin, 257*n*

Randolph, W. Alan, 648*n*, 672, 675–77, 676
Random error, 114
Raw materials, 429
RCA, global operations at, 230
*R*-chart, 706–7
Recognition and rewards, 345
Recycling old automobiles, 186–87
Reebok, 160
Reengineering, business process, 28, 282–85
Regenerative simulation, 799
Regional considerations, in location decisions, 211
Regression equation, 137
Regression models, 137–43
Regret matrix, 763
Reich, Robert B., 229
Reichheld, Frederick F., 159*n*
Relative measures, of forecasting error, 146
Reliability, 259, 271
Render, Barry, 46*n*
Render, Murdick, 63*n*
Rendez, Barry, 215*n*
Reneging, 807
Reorder point, 439
determining, 454–59
Reorder point system (ROP), 454
Repetitive manufacturing, mixed-model assembly in, 553–54
Repetitive operation, shop-floor control in, 552–53
Repetitive process, 179
Reservations, 389
Reservation systems, 625
Resource allocation, 77
Resource planning, 385
Resource profiles, capacity planning using, 527–31
Responsiveness, 128, 271
Reverse logistics, 375
Rework, 594
Reynolds, Larry, 275*n*
Rho, Boo-Ho, 575*n*
Riberwala, R., 630*n*
Richardson Sports, 216
Right-hand-side values, 777
Rightsizing, 337–38
Risk, decision making under, 764–65
Ritz-Carlton Hotel Co., 256–63
Ritzman, Larry P., 538*n*
RJR Nabisco, 342–43
Roach, Stephen S., 59
Roadway Express, 367
Roberts, W. Jack, 67
Robotics, 305–6
Rohan, Thomas M., 345*n*
Rolex watch, 269
Romig, Harry, 255

Roos, Daniel, 95*n*
Roper, 197
Rose, Jack, 520
Rosenfield, D. B., 368, 370*n*
Roth, Aleda V., 92*n*
Rothwell, John, 723*n*, 733, 738
Rough-cut capacity planning, 385, 517, 521–23
Routing and standard time data, 525
Run diagrams, 697
Russell, Roberta S., 46*n*, 215*n*
Ryan, Kathleen, 335–36

# S

Saatchi and Saatchi's, 230
Safety lead time, 497–98
Safety stock, 432, 459, 497–98
Sales, 17
Sales force composite, 121
Sample, 119
Sampling and the central limit theorem, 703
Sampling plan, 715
Sapolsky, Harvey M., 652*n*
Sasser, Earl W., 626–27, 628*n*
Sasser, W. E., Jr., 159*n*
Sasser, W. Earl, 55*n*
Saturn, 207
Scatter diagram, 136–37
Scheduled receipts, 481
Schedule stability and discipline, 593
Scheduling and sequencing, 562–63
Scheuing, Eberhard E., 362
Schmenner, Roger W., 52*n*, 90*n*, 213*n*, 223*n*
Schneider, Benjamin, 48*n*
Scholtes, Peter R., 277*n*
Science parks, 228
Scientific management approach, 20
Scrap allowance, 497–98
Seal, Gregory M., 92*n*
Search decision rule, 401
Sears, Roebuck, and Co., 431
Seasonal, 114
Second-tier suppliers, 96
Self-managing work team, 333
Sematech, 296
Sensitivity analysis, 785
for the EOQ model, 452–53
Sentara Norfolk General Hospital, 329
Serviceability, 270
Service companies
aggregate planning in, 408, 411
efforts in raising productivity, 50
Service concept, 55
Service delivery system, 55
Service demand, strategies for managing, 621–23
Service differentiation, 609
Service facility, 808–10

Service factories, 28–31, 52
Service jobs, adequacy of, 63–67
Service levels, 459
Service master, 54
ServiceMasters, 55
Service operation, 3
    and capacity planning, 536–38
    characteristics of, 45–51
    distinctions between manufacturing
        operations, 3
    labor intensiveness in, 47–48
    outputs of, 6–7
    strategic approaches to, 51
Service organization, 91
Service output, intangibility of, 48
Service package, 607, 609–13
Service planning, 88
Service process, consumer
    participation in, 46
Service process matrix, 51–54
Service productivity, difficulty of
    measuring, 49–51
Services, 40
    business cycles in, 60
    classifying, 43
    comparing manufacturing
        operations, 43
    defining, 41–43
    difficulty of measuring quality in,
        51
    dominant facility location factors in,
        213, 215
    effective design of, 279–80
    greater quality emphasis in, 67–68
    improving productivity and
        competitiveness in, 59–63
    increased international competition
        in, 57–59
    perishability of, 46
    production line approach to,
        181–82
    selecting features for, 161–62
    technology and automation in, 63
    using computers to improve, 62
Service sector trends, 55
Service shops, 52
Service strategy, 607–9
Service system
    evolution of, 607–13
    integration in, 55
    process design and layout for,
        174–82
    strategic approaches to design of,
        613
Service time, 809
Set-up reduction, 589–91
Set-up times, reduction of, 558–59
Sewell, Carl, 271–72
Shadow prices, 784–85
Shapiro, Roy D., 357
Sharp, 230

Shelp, Ronald K., 43n
Sheridan, John H., 303n
Sherman, Stratford, 296n
Sherwin-Williams, 326
Shewhart, W. A., 255
Shift scheduling, 628–29
    daily work in, 628–29
    weekly work in, 629–32
Shingo, Shigeo, 25n
Shop-floor control manager, task of,
    551–52
Shop-floor control (SFC), 550
    continuous process, 552
    in intermittent, job shop
        operations, 554–60
    international issues in, 574–76
    repetitive operation, 552–53
Shortages, 434, 459
    cost of, 434
Short-cycle manufacturing, 582
Shortest processing time (SPT), 262
Short-range planning, 386
Shouldice Hospital (Toronto), 55
Showalter, Michael J., 538n
Shulman, Lawrence E., 93n
Shycon, Harvey N., 226n
Sierra Club, 186
Siferd, Sue Perrott, 538n
Signaling system, modifications of,
    596–97
SIMAN, 800
Simon, Herbert, 400–1
Simon, Ruth, 306n
Simple average, 126
Simple exponential smoothing, 130
Simple linear regression, 137
Simple moving average, 126–29
Simplex algorithm, 779
Simplex method, 402, 776
    technical steps in, 779–84
Simplification, improving designs
    through, 170
SIMSCRIPT, 800
Simulation, 790–91
    making multiple-facility location
        decision, 226
Simulation languages, 800
Simulation models, 406
Simulation study, 791
    simulating system, 795–800
    stimulating exogenous inputs in,
        791–95
Sinai, Allen, 61n
Sinatra, Frank, 268
Singer Sewing Machine Co., 254
Single-channel, single-phase waiting
    line model, 811–13
Single exponential smoothing,
    129–33
Site considerations, in location
    decisions, 211–12

Site selection, dictation of, by
    consumer location, 47
Site selection survey, 229
Skilled personal services, 43
Skinner, Wickham, 77n, 91n, 197n,
    608n
Slack destination, 751–52
Slack origin, 752
Slack time, 657
Slack time remaining, 563
Slack variable, 779–82
SLAM, 800
Sleep Inn, 50
Slem, Charles, 300n
Sloan, Alfred P., Jr., 22–23
Smith, Frederick W., 27
Smith, Garry D., 74n
Smith, Geoffrey, 694n, 695n
Smith, Roger, 301
SmithKline Beecham Consumer
    Brands, 362
Snyder, David L., 87n
Sociotechnical organizations, 324,
    325–27
    adaptive organizational structures
        in, 327
    keys to worker productivity in,
        327–30
Sociotechnical system (STS), 326
Sofianou, Zaharo, 61n
Solectron Corp., 263
Solution space, 779
Sony, 230, 269
Sourcing decisions, 363–64
Southeastern Steel Co., 218
Special purpose teams, 333
Specification limits, versus control
    limits, 711–13
Specifications, quality as conformance
    to, 268–69
Spencer, M., 550n
Spiegel, 313
Spitzer, Kirk, 214
Sports, role of technological advances
    in, 293–94, 295
Spreadsheet program, 393
Stability, 128
Staffing plan, 383
    developing, 414–15
Stalk, George, 93n
Stallkamp, Tom, 675n
Standard error of the estimate, 140
Standard linear programming form,
    reformulation of problem in,
    779–82
Standard time, 346
States of nature, 760
Statistical Analysis System (SAS), 150
Statistical Package for Social Scientists
    (SPSS), 150
Statistical process control (SPC), 732

Statistical quality control, 255
Statistical sampling and control, 702
Statistical tools, for process improvement, 701
Statistics, testing inferences about quality control, 703
Steady state, 799
Steelcase, MRP at, 475
Steele, Daniel C., 495n
Stephenson, John C., 43n
Stepping-stone method, 746–50
Step-up cost, 434
Stevens, Graham, 93n
Stocker, Gregg, 164n, 168n
Stock keeping units (SKUs), 372
Stockless production, 585
Stock out, 434
    costs of, 391, 434
Stopwatch studies, 346–50
Storage cost, 434
Storyboarding, 695
Strategic advantage, and company activities, 15–18
Strategic alliances, 174
    technology-focused, 296–97
Strategic approaches, to service operations management, 51
Strategic business units (SBU), 74
Strategic human resources planning, 324–25
Strategic issue
    in process design, 182–87
    quality management, 256–63
Strategic operations choices, 85, 87–88
    categories of, 87, 88–92
Strategic operations management, 3–4
Strategic planning
    business-level, 74, 75–77
        functional area involvement in, 77
    corporate-level, 74
    functional-level, 74
    hierarchy in, 74
    operations, 75, 77, 81–83
    product-level, 74
    purpose of, 74
Strategic positioning, 78
    ultimate purpose of, 79
Strategic quality planning, 275–76
Strategic service vision, 55
Strategic threats and opportunities, identifying, 726–27
Strategic trends
    in location decisions, 227–28
    in logistics management, 373–74
Subcontracting, 389
    costs of, 390
    effect of, on capacity, 196
Subjective forecast, 115
Sun belt, growth in, 232

Sun Microsystems, Inc., 374–75, 570
Supplier evaluation, 365–66
Supply chain
    management of, 93–95
    production flexibility along the, 592–93
Supply origin, 742
Support activities, 16–17
    technological improvements for, 309–15
Suris, Oscar, 675n
Surplus variables, 485
Swain, James, 800n
Swart, William, 203n
Swedish American Hospital, continuous improvement at, 690
Synchronous manufacturing, 569
System model, 791

T

Taco Bell, 28
    reengineering at, 284–85
Taguchi, Genichi, 158, 279
Tanelian, Katherine, 343
Tangibles, 271
Tanzer, Andrew, 306n
Target market segments, 55
Taubert, William H., 401–2
Tavistock Institute, 325, 326
Taylor, Frederick Winslow, 20–21, 346
Team activities, in sociotechnical operations, 332–35
Team approach, and concurrent engineering, 733
Teamwork, effective use of, 278–79
Technical comparison, performing, 167
Technical core, 618
    isolating the, 617–20
Technical knowledge base, operations manager need for, 9
Technical requirements, 166–67
Technological developments
    automation in, 300–2
    in business environment, 293–98
    in communications, 314–15
    computer-aided design in, 304
    computer-aided manufacturing in, 304–9
    computer-integrated manufacturing in, 302–4
    implementation of new technology, 299–300
    in operations management, 292–315
    in sports, 293–94, 295
    support improvements in, 309–15
Technology
    definition of, 293
    and environment, 294–96

implementing new, 299–300
    in services, 63
    in today's business environment, 293–98
    transferring new product from concept to reality, 298
Technology component groups (TCGs), 466
Technology-driven new product ideas, 159
Technology-focused strategic alliances, 296–97
Technology transfer, 298
Tektronic, 28, 30
Tektronix, 584
Temporary labor, 389
    costs of, 390
Tenner, Arthur R., 686n
Texaco, 313
Texas Instruments Inc., global operations at, 230, 263, 328
Theory of constraints (TOC), 569, 571–72, 574
Therbligs, 350
Thermalux, 159
Third-party logistics services, 374–75
Thomas, Dan R. E., 609n
Thomas, Rich, 7n
Thornburg, Linda, 341n, 344n
Through-put, 558, 571
Thurow, Lester, 65
Time, aggregation by, 384
Time-based competition, 27–28
Time buckets, 480–81
Time/cost trade-offs, in project management, 664–67, 669
Time fences, 490–92
Time horizon, 382
Time-phasing, 479–80
Time series, 110
    analysis methods, 119, 120
    analysis models, 125
    decomposition of, 135–36
    smoothing, 125–35
Time studies, 346–50
Timex, 269
Timing conventions, in MRP, 480–81
Top-down approach, to demand management, 100
Top quality management, 582
Toshiba America, 230
Total business cycle, 587
    management of, 587–89
Total quality control (TQC), 275
Total quality leadership (TQL), 686
Total quality management (TQM), 25–26, 187, 275, 436–437
    barriers to implementing, 282
    implementation process, 280–82, 684
    requirements, 275–80

# Index

Total revenue, 15
Toyota Motor Corp., 27, 80, 97, 260, 428, 553, 583
Tracking signal, 147
Trademarks, 48
Training
  effective use of, 278–79
  in sociotechnical organizations, 338–41
Trans-Alaska Pipeline, 368
Transfer lots, 555
Transformation process, 6–7
  operations manager in, 9
  and productivity, 7–9
Transient phase, 799
Transocean movements, 369
Transportation, 367
  freight consolidation, 369–71
    environmental sensitivity, 375–76
    just-in-time logistics, 376
    third-party logistics services, 374–75
  legal forms of carriers, 367
  transportation mode selection, 367
Transportation method of linear programming, 223–25, 403–4
Transportation problem, 742–55
  balanced, 742–43
  changes in transportation costs, 752–75
  finding initial basic feasible solution, 744
    alternative optimal solutions, 750
    degeneracy in, 750
    matrix minima rule in, 744–46
    Northwest corner rule in, 744
    stepping-stone method in, 746–50
    unacceptable transportation routes in, 750
  mathematical structure of, 742–43
  profit maximization, 754
  solving, 743
  unbalanced, 751
Trend, 113–14
Triage, 554
Trial-and-error method, 393–400
Trist, Eric, 325, 326
Truck, 367
Truck trailers on rail flat cars (TOFC), 368
Truitt, Nancy S., 43n
Turner's of Califon, 612
Two-bin system, 453–54

## U

Ulvila, Jacob W., 205n
Unbalanced transportation problem, 751

Uncertainty, decision making under, 761–64
Union Pacific (UP), 367, 371
United Parcel Service (UPS), 293, 367
United States research facilities, 229
United Steel Works, 7
United Technologies Corporation, 598
Universal product code (UPC), 308
Unskilled personal services, 42–43
Utilization, 558
  measures of, 196
Uttal, Bro, 68n
Utterback, James M., 183n

## V

Value, definition of, 15
Value activities, 16
Value analysis, 96–97, 365
  improving designs through, 170–71
Value chain, 15–18
Value-cost leveraging, 55
Van Winkle, Kenneth, 303
Variable
  artificial, 485
  basic, 780
  dependent, 136
  independent, 136
  slack, 779–82
  surplus, 485
Variable data, control charts for, 705–8
Variable demand rate, 456–59
Variable entry criterion, 781
Variable lead time, 457–59
Variable removal criterion, 782
Variance of activity time, 670
Vehicle routing, 633–34
Venable, Tim, 229n
Vergin, Roger C., 408n
Vertical integration, 93, 364
Vertical linkages, 92–97
Vickery, Shawnee K., 78n
Virtual reality, 312–13, 314
Volume flexibility, 84
Voss, Christopher, 613n

## W

Waiting line models, 804–14
  data collection and model validation, 811
  decision variables in the analysis of waiting lines, 811
  multiple-channel, single-phase waiting line model, 813–14
  notation used for, 810–11
  operating characteristics, 810
  other models, 814
  single-channel, single-phase waiting line model, 811–13

  waiting line problems, 805
    service facility, 808–10
    structure of, 805
    waiting line (queue), 807
Waiting lines, 804
Wallace, Thomas, 24n, 300n, 304n, 306n, 345, 475n, 501, 503n
Wallace Co., 263
Wallace Manufacturing, 345
Wal-Mart, 42, 293, 328, 367, 376
Ward, Peter T., 87n
Warehousing, 372
Wasow, Bernard, 43n
Water transportation, 368
Weekly work shift scheduling, 629–32
Weeks of supply, 431
Weighted moving average, 129
Welch, John F., 683
Weldcrack Expert, 311
Wellcome, Burroughs Co., 10
  batch production systems at, 15
  tablet production at, 14
Wemmerlöv, Urban, 496n
Wensley, Robin, 724n
Westinghouse Electric Corp., 263, 328, 333
  Achievements in Clean Technology project, 11
"What-if" analysis, 393
Wheelwright, Steven, 8n, 81n, 199n, 205n
Whirlpool Corp., 197, 230
White, Joseph B., 675n
Whitehead, Alfred North, 473
Whitney, C. R. "Bud," 723
Whitney, Daniel E., 291
Whitney, Eli, 18–20
Whitney Arms Co., 20
Wiggenhorn, William, 339n, 340
Wilhoit, Joan, 137
Winters' triple exponential smoothing model, 135, 136
Wolcott, Oliver, 20
Womack, James P., 95n
Wonder, Stevie, 268
Wood, Robert Chapman, 21n
Woodruff, Robert, 276
Work breakdown structures (WBS), 650–51
Work force diversity, as human resources issue, 330–31
Work force level, 386
Work in process (WIP), 429
Work-in-process (WIP) cycle, 588
Work-in-process (WIP) inventory, 432, 517, 557
Work measurement, 346
  elemental standard times, 350
  time studies of, 346–50
Workplace, fear in, as human resource issue, 335–38

Wright, J. W., 634*n*
Wright Line, Inc., 387
Wycoff, Joyce, 68*n*

## X

*X*-chart, 706–7
Xerox Corp., 359
   as adaptive organization, 327
   development cycle at, 172
   and employee potential, 328
   global manufacturing integration at, 99
   and logistics integration, 359
   as MBNQ award winner, 263
   sociotechnical system concept at, 326
   and team projects, 333–34

## Y

Yamaha Motor Co., 268, 600
Yellow Freight, 367
Yost, Larry, 730, 738
Young, Andrew, 300*n*

## Z

Zeithaml, Valarie A., 51*n*
Zemke, Ron, 325*n*, 605, 608, 609*n*
Zero defections, 159
Zero defects, 26
Zero inventories, 428, 585
Zipp, Arlene Jean, 767, 769, 771
Zmud, Robert W., 501*n*
Zwicke, Christine A., 723*n*
Zytec Corp., 263

## OPERATIONS MANAGEMENT IN PRACTICE/GLOBAL OPERATIONS MANAGEMENT BOX SOURCES

**10 Box 1.1** Interview with Dr. Gabriel R. Cipau, Senior Vice President of Production and Engineering, Burroughs Wellcome (USA) April, 1992. **12 Box 1.2** Adaptation from Barbara N. Berkman, "AT&T's Big Push to Stay Ahead of Environmental Woes" (September 18, 1989), pp. 33–36. Reproduction with permission from *Electronic Business Buyer,* c. 1989 Reed Elsevier, Inc. **14 Box 1.3** Shawnee K. Vickery, Multi-state Lot Sizing for Serial Production, Ph.D. Dissertation, University of South Carolina, 1983. **29 Box 1.4** Selected Adaptation from *Reengineering the Corporation* by Michael Hammer and James Champy. Copyright (c) 1993 by Michael Hammer and James Champy. Reprinted by permission of Harper Collins Publishers. **50 Box 2.1** David Wessel, "With Labor Scarce, Service Firms Strive to Raise Productivity" (June 1, 1989), pp. A1 & A16. Reprinted with permission of *The Wall Street Journal* (c) Dow Jones and Company, Inc. All rights reserved worldwide. **54 Box 2.2** Tim Ferguson, "Inspired from Above Service Master Dignifies Those Below" (May 8, 1990), p. A25. Reprinted with permission of *The Wall Street Journal,* (c) 1990 Dow Jones and Company, Inc. All rights reserved worldwide. **60 Box 2.3** Lynn McCloud, "Sir Colin Marshall of British Airways: To Fly, To Serve," *USAir Magazine* (March 1993), pp. 52–55, 96. **62 Box 2.4** Paul B. Carroll, "Computers Cut Through the Service Maze" (May 1, 1990), p.1. Reprinted by permission of *The Wall Street Journal,* (c) Dow Jones and Company, Inc. All rights reserved worldwide. **80 Box 3.1** Interview with Joseph F. Wojdak, Chief Executive Officer, Haskell of Pittsburgh, Verona, Pennsylvania, Spring, 1991. **86 Box 3.2** Interviews with Japanese managers of Meiji Seika Kasha, Ltd. (Odawara Plant) conducted by Yoshito Higuchi, August, 1990. **99 Box 3.3** Reprinted by permission of *Harvard Business Review* from "Manufacturing's New Economies of Scale," Vol. 70, No.3, (May–June 1992) by Michael McGrath and Richard Hoole. Copyright (c) 1992 by the President and Fellows of Harvard College; all rights reserved. **123 Box 4.1** Robin T. Petersen, "Sales Force Composite Forecasting–An Exploratory Analysis." *The Journal of Business Forecasting* (Summer 1990), pp. 16–21. **124 Box 4.2** H. D. Sharma, Sushil, and A. D. Gupta, "Present and Future Status of System Waste: A National-Level Delphi in India," *Technological Forecasting and Social Change* 44 (1993): 199–218. **160 Box 5.1** Brian Dumaine, "Design that Sells and Sells and ...", *Fortune* (March 11, 1991), p. 86. Copyright (c) 1991 Time Inc. All rights reserved. **185 Box 5.2** Scott McMurray, "Air-Conditioner Firms Put Chill on Plans to Phase Out Use of Chlorofluorocarbons" (May 10, 1993), pp. B1–B2. Reprinted by permission of *The Wall Street Journal,* (c) 1993 Dow Jones and Company, Inc. All rights reserved worldwide. **187 Box 5.3** Kimberly Alanis, Project Coordinator, VEDCO Energy Corporation, 1994. **198 Box 6.1** Clyde E. Witt, "Partnerships Drive Alison's Focused Factory," *Material Handling Engineering* (January 1992), pp.37–40. **214 Box 6.2** "How Alfa-Laval Got Employees Moving," by Joyce E. Santora. Copyright (c) January 1991. Reprinted with permission of *Personnel Journal,* ACC Communications, Inc., Costa Mesa, California; all rights reserved. **216 Box 6.3** Patricia K. Guseman, "How to Pick the Best Location," copyright (c) August 1988, pp. 42–43. Reprinted with permission from American Demographics, Ithaca, New York. **231 Box 6.4** "Maquiladora Industry Generates $3 Billion a Year," April 20, 1991, Special Advertising Section, p. A19. Reprinted by permission of *The Wall Street Journal,* (c) 1991 Dow Jones and Company, Inc. All rights reserved worldwide. **233 Box 6.5** Robert Ady, "Why BMW Cruised into Spartanburg" (July 8, 1992), p. A10. Reprinted with permission of *The Wall Street Journal,* (c) 1992 Dow Jones and Company, Inc. All rights reserved worldwide. **258 Box 7.1** The Ritz Carlton Hotel Company promotional literature, 1992. **260 Box 7.2** Douglas Lavin, "Chrysler Mounts Campaign to Cut Defects" (January 27, 1994), pp. B1&B5. Reprinted by permission of *The Wall Street Journal,* (c) 1994 Dow Jones and Company, Inc. All rights reserved worldwide. **264 Box 7.3** Karen Bemowski, "A Pat On The Back Is Worth A Thousand Words" (March 1994), pp. 51–54. Copyright (c) 1994 American Society for Quality Control. Reprinted with permission. **284 Box 7.4** Michael Hammer and James Champy, *Reengineering the Corporation, A Manifesto for Business Revolution,* pp.171–181. **294 Box 8.1** Mark Alpert, "Jumping Ahead by Going High Tech," *Fortune* (October 19, 1992), pp. 113–114. Copyright (c) 1992 Time, Inc. All rights reserved. **295 Box 8.2** Gene Bylinsky, "High Technology Olympians," *Technology Review* (January 1993) pp. 22-30. **297 Box 8.3** Fred Pearce, "Can Toyota Save the World?" *Audubon* (November/December 1992), p. 132 and Frederick Myers, "Japan Bids for Global Leadership in Clean Industry," *Science* (May 22, 1992), Vol. 256, pp. 1144–1145. Copyright 1992 by the AAAS. **302 Box 8.4** John Teresko, "How Should Management Assess Today's Advanced Manufacturing Options?" Reprinted with permission from *Industry Week,* (May 26, 1986). Copyright (c) Penton Publishing, Inc., Cleveland, Ohio. **307 Box 8.5** William R. Neikirk, *Chicago Tribune,* "Factories Wrestling With Robots," *Bryan-College Eagle* (July 19, 1987), p. F1. **311 Box 8.6** "Future View: Tomorrow's Manufacturing Technologies," *Manufacturing Engineering* (January 1992), p. 78. Reprinted with permission of the Society of Manufacturing Engineering, January 1992. **314 Box 8.7** Gene Bylinsky, "The Marvels of 'Virtual Reality'," *Fortune* (June 3, 1991), p. 138. Copyright (c) 1991 Time Inc. All rights reserved. **329 Box 9.1** Martha T. Moore, "Dramatic Turnaround: X-Ray Processing Time Cut 81%," *USA Today* (April 10, 1992), p. 5B. Copyright (c) USA *Today.* Reprinted with permission. **334 Box 9.2** Lore Croghan, "American Express Office Takes Team Approach to Work," *The Hartford Courant* (October 4, 1993), p.11. **339 Box 9.3** Ronald Henkoff, "Reducing the Bile Factor at Heinz," *Fortune* (April 9, 1990), p.42. Copyright (c) 1989 Time, Inc. All rights reserved. **343 Box 9.4** Richard Louv, "Should Corporations Care About Child Care?" *Business and Safety Review* Vol. 81, 1993, p.60. From *Childhood's Future.* Copyright (c) 1990 by Richard Louv. As published in *Business and Safety Review.* Reprinted by permission of Houghton Mifflin Co. All rights reserved. **362 Box 10.1** Lisa H. Harrington, "Integrated Logistics Systems: Still More Talk Than Action," *Traffic World* (May 4, 1992), p. 35. **371 Box 10.2** Jeff Jordan, "Double Eagle - Last Year's Vision, This Year's Reality," *INFOMAGAZINE* (March/April 1991), pp. 11–13. **374 Box 10.3** "How Managers Can Succeed Through SPEED," *Fortune* (February 13, 1989), p.59. Copyright (c) 1989 Time, Inc. All rights reserved.

# Acknowledgments

387 **Box 11.1** Reprinted with the permission of APICS, Inc., "MRP and Aggregate Planning—A Problem Solution," by Marcia Migliorelli and Robert J. Swan, *Production and Inventory Management* (Second Quarter, 1988), pp. 42–45. 409 **Box 11.2** Vic Gilgeous, "Aggregate Planning in U.K. Manufacturing Companies," *International Journal of Operations and Production Management,* Vol. 7, No.1 (1987), pp. 50-61. 414 **Box 11.3** Reprinted by permission of Kenneth Chelst, "A Public Safety Merger in Gross Pointe Park, Michigan–A Short and Sweet Study," *Interfaces*, Vol. 18, No. 4, (July/August 1988) pp. 1-11. Copyright 1988 the Operations Research Society of America and The Institutes of Management Sciences, 290 Westminster Street, Providence, Rhode Island 02903. 420 **Box 11.4** Reprinted with permission from *Journal of Operations Management,* Vol. 8, No. 2, G. Keong Leong, Michael D. Oliff, and Robert E. Markland, "Improved Hierarchical Production Planning," (April 1989) p. 95, Elsevier Science Ltd., Oxford, England. 433 **Box 12.1** Tim W. Ferguson, "Shrink Inventory? Lands' End Likes It Loose," *The Wall Street Journal* (January, 18, 1994), p. A7. Reprinted by permission of *The Wall Street Journal,* (c) 1994 Dow Jones & Company, Inc. All rights reserved. 437 **Box 12.2** Ellert Brothers Inventory–no source. 466 **Box 12.3** Reprinted by permission of Morris Cohen, et al., "Optimizer: IBM's Multi-Echelon System for Managing Service Logistics," *Interfaces*, Vol. 20, No. 1 (January/February 1990), pp. 65–82. Copyright (c) 1990 the Operations Research Society of America and The Institutes of Management Sciences, 290 Westminster Street, Providence, Rhode Island 02903. 475 **Box 13.1** Interview with James Austof, Production and Inventory Control Manager, Steelcase, Inc., Spring 1992. 503 **Box 13.2** Interview with Jim Kettner of Gendex, February 25, 1993. 520 **Box 14.1** Interview with Jack Rose, Computer Operations Manager, Minnesota Wire and Cable, Co., July 3, 1993. 537 **Box 14.2** Interview with Bill Neufeld of Nichols-Radtke, July 15, 1993. 570 **Box 15.1** Leslie C. Jasany, "Streamline Manufacturing; Sun Microsystems Inc.," *Controls and Systems* (February 1992), p.38. 573 **Box 15.2** William Libby, "Quaker Furniture Manages Materials Using Synchronous Manufacturing," *APICS–The Performance Advantage,* (March 1992) pp. 24–26. 584 **Box 16.1** Richard D. Massimilian and Laura Pedro, "Back from the Future: Gearing Up for the Productivity Challenge." Reprinted by permission of the publisher from *Management Review,* (February 1990) pp. 41–43. Copyright 1990 American Management Association, New York. All rights reserved. 586 **Box 16.2** Reprinted with the permission of APICS, Inc., "Acme Manufacturing: A Case Study in JIT Implementation," *Production and Inventory Management Journal* (Second Quarter, 1993), pp. 82–86. 598 **Box 16.3** Amal Kumar Naj, "Some Manufacturers Drop Efforts to Adopt Japanese Techniques" (May 7, 1993), p. A1. Reprinted by permission of *The Wall Street Journal,* copyright (c) 1993 Dow Jones and Company, Inc. All rights reserved worldwide. 612 **Box 17.1** Brent Bowers, "Pampering Motorists Proves Profitable," *The Wall Street Journal* (September 13, 1990), pp. B1,B2. 617 **Box 17.2** Tadashi Katagiri, "ATMs in Japan," *Bank Administration* (February 1989), pp. 16–20. 626 **Box 17.3** Max D. Hopper, "Rattling SABRE–New Ways to Compete on Information," *Harvard Business Review* (May–June 1990), pp. 118–125. 668 **Box 18.2** Interview with Dan Bollman, Project Representative for Michigan State University and Glenn Granger, Vice President of Corporate Services for Granger Construction on August 12, 1993. 674 **Box 18.3** Richard Ceppos, "Q&A with Tom Stallkamp," *Automobile Magazine,* Vol.7, No.3 (June 1992), and Joseph B. White and Oscar Suris, "How a 'Skunk Work' Kept Mustang Alive—On A Tight Budget," *The Wall Street Journal,* Vol.LXXIV, No.238 (September 21,

1993). 686 **Box 19.1** Listening to Workers Pays Off," *USA TODAY* (April 2, 1993), pp. 1B–2B. Copyright (c) 1993, *USA TODAY.* Reprinted with permission. 687 **Box 19.2** "Fraud Crackdown Rings Up Savings," *USA TODAY* (April 2, 1993), p. 4B. Copyright (c) 1993, *USA TODAY.* Reprinted with permission. 688 **Box 19.3** "Night in the Wood Yard Opens Eyes, Saves Millions," *USA TODAY* (April 2, 1993), p. 4B. Copyright (c) 1993, *USA TODAY.* Reprinted with permission. 689 **Box 19.4** "Review Kept Firm from Falling Apart," *USA TODAY* (April 2, 1993), p. 5B. Copyright (c) 1993, *USA TODAY.* Reprinted with permission. 690 **Box 19.5** "New Ideas Without New Blood," *USA TODAY* (April 2, 1993), p. 5B. Copyright (c) 1993, *USA TODAY.* Reprinted with permission.

## TEXT ACKNOWLEDGMENTS

15 **Footnote 9** Adapted and reprinted with permission of The Free Press, an imprint of Simon & Schuster from "The Value Chain and Competitive Advantage," Chapter 2 in *Competitive Advantage: Creating and Sustaining Superior Performance* by Michael E. Porter, 1985. 16 **Figure 1.4** Adapted and reprinted with permission of The Free Press, an imprint of Simon & Schuster from "The Value Chain and Competitive Advantage," Chapter 2 in *Competitive Advantage: Creating and Sustaining Superior Performance* by Michael E. Porter, 1985. 17 **Table 1.1** Adapted and reprinted with permission of The Free Press, an imprint of Simon & Schuster from "The Value Chain and Competitive Advantage," Chapter 2 in *Competitive Advantage: Creating and Sustaining Superior Performance* by Michael E. Porter, 1985. 18 **Figure 1.5** Adapted and reprinted with permission of The Free Press, an imprint of Simon & Schuster from "The Value Chain and Competitive Advantage," Chapter 2 in *Competitive Advantage: Creating and Sustaining Superior Performance* by Michael E. Porter, 1985. 21 **Footnote 13** Excerpt from Robert Chapman Wood, "A Lesson Learned and a Lesson Forgotten," February 6, 1989, pp. 71-72. Reprinted with permission of FORBES magazine. Copyright (c) Forbes Inc., 1989. 28 **Footnote 27** Selected adaptation from RE-ENGINEERING THE CORPORATION by Michael Hammer and James Champy. Copyright (c) 1993 by Michael Hammer and James Champy. Reprinted by permission of Harper Collins Publishers, Inc. 28 **Footnote 28** Reprinted by permission of *Harvard Business Review.* An excerpt from "The Service Factory," July–August 1989, pp. 61–69 by Richard Chase and David Garvin. Copyright (c) 1989 by the President and Fellows of Harvard College; all rights reserved. 37 **Case Study, Chapter 1** Reprinted by permission of *Harvard Business Review.* An excerpt from "How Northern Telecom Competes on Time," July–August 1989, pp. 108–114 by Roy Merrils, 1989. Copyright (c) 1989 by the President and Fellows of Harvard College; all rights reserved. 42 **Figure 2.2** Earl W. Sasset, R. Paul Olsen and D. Daryl Wyckoff, *Management of Service Operations: Text, Cases, and Readings.* Copyright (c) 1978 Allyn and Bacon. Reprinted by permission. 46 **Footnote 2** Adapted from Robert G. Murdick, Barry Render, and Roberta S. Russell, *Service Operations Management.* Copyright (c) 1990 by Allyn and Bacon. Reprinted by permission. 49 **Figure 2.3** Reprinted by permission of *Harvard Business Review.* An excerpt from "Strategy Is Different in Service Businesses," by Dan R.E. Thomas, July–August 1978. Copyright (c) 1978 by the President and Fellows of Harvard College; all rights reserved. 52 **Footnote 7** Reprinted from "How Can Service Businesses Survive and Prosper?" by Roger Schmenner, Sloan Management Review 27, No. 3 (Spring 1986):29 by permission of publisher. Copyright (c) 1986 by the Sloan Management Review Association. All rights reserved. 53 **Figure 2.4** Reprinted from "How Can Service Busi-

# Acknowledgments

nesses Survive and Prosper?" by Roger Schmenner, Sloan Management Review 27, No. 3 (Spring 1986):29, by permission of publisher. Copyright (c) 1986 by the Sloan Management Review Association. All rights reserved. **55 Footnote 8** Reprinted with permission of Macmillan College Publishing Company from *Service Breakthroughs: Changing the Rules of the Game* by James L. Heskett, W. Earl Sasser, Jr., Christopher W.L. Hart. Copyright (c) 1990 by Macmillan College Publishing Company, Inc. **58–59 Table 2.4** Reprinted by permission of *Harvard Business Review.* An exhibit from "Services Under Siege–The Restructuring Imperative" by Stephen S. Roach, (September–October 1991):89. Copyright (c) 1991 by the President and Fellows of Harvard College; all rights reserved. **61 Figure 2.7** Reprinted by permission of *Harvard Business Review.* An exhibit from "Services Under Siege–The Restructuring Imperative" by Stephen S. Roach, (September–October 1991):89. Copyright (c) 1991 by the President and Fellows of Harvard College; all rights reserved. **64 Table 2.5** David A. Collier, *Service Management: The Automation of Services, 1985,* pp. 22–23, (Burr Ridge, Illinois: Business One-Irwin and Reston, Virginia: Reston Publishing Company, 1985). **71–72 Case Study Chapter 2** Bernie Ward, "Profile: H. Wayne Huizenga/Blockbuster Entertainment Corp.," December 1993. The article has been reprinted/republished through the courtesy of Halsey Publishing Co., publishers of Delta Airlines' *SKY Magazine.* **74 Footnote 1** Phillip Kotler, *Marketing Management: Analysis, Planning, Implementation and Control, 6th ed.* Copyright (c) 1988, pp. 36–49. Adapted by permission of Prentice-Hall, Englewood Cliffs, New Jersey. **75 Footnote 3** Adapted and reprinted with permission of The Free Press, an imprint of Simon & Schuster from *Competitive Advantage: Creating and Sustaining Superior Performance* by Michael E. Porter. Copyright (c) 1985 by Michael E. Porter. **78 Footnote 7** Adapted and reprinted with permission of The Free Press, an imprint of Simon & Schuster from *Competitive Advantage: Creating and Sustaining Superior Performance* by Michael E. Porter. Copyright (c) 1985 by Michael E. Porter. **92 Footnote 16** Adapted and reprinted with permission of The Free Press, an imprint of Simon & Schuster from *Competitive Advantage: Creating and Sustaining Superior Performance* by Michael E. Porter. Copyright (c) 1985 by Michael E. Porter. **95 Footnote 19** Adapted with the permission of Rawson Associates, an imprint of Simon & Schuster from *The Machine that Changed the World,* Harper Perennial 1991. Copyright (c) James P. Womack, Daniel T. Jones, Daniel Roos and Donna Sammons Carpenter. **97 Footnote 20** Reprinted with permission of *Harvard Business Review.* Adapted from "Manufacturing's New Economies of Scale," by Michael McGrath and Richard Hoole, May–June 1992. Copyright (c) 1992 by the President and Fellows of Harvard College; all rights reserved. **120 Table 4.4** Reprinted by permission of *Harvard Business Review.* An excerpt from "Manager's Guide to Forecasting," by David Georgoff and Robert Murdick, January–February 1986, pp. 110–120. Copyright (c) 1986 by the President and Fellows of Harvard College; all rights reserved. **202 Footnote 3** Reprinted with permission of William Swart and Luca Donno, "Simulation Modeling Improves Operations Planning and Productivity of Fast Food Restaurants," *Interfaces,* Volume 11 (December 1981), pp. 35–46. Copyright (c) 1981 the Operations Research Society of America and The Institute of Management Sciences, 290 Westminster Street, Providence, Rhode Island 02903. **215 Footnote 7** Adaptation from Robert Murdick, Barry Render and Roberta Russell, *Service Operations Management.* Copyright (c) 1990 by Allyn and Bacon. Reprinted by permission. **230 Footnote 16** Reprinted with permission of *Harvard Business Review.* An excerpt from "Who Is Us?" by Robert B. Reich (January/February 1990).

Copyright (c) 1990 by the President and Fellows of Harvard College; all rights reserved. **254 Footnote 1** Adapted and reprinted with the permission of *The Free Press,* an imprint of Simon & Schuster from *Managing Quality: The Strategic and Competitive Edge* by David A. Garvin. Copyright (c) 1988 by David A. Garvin. **256 Table 7.1** Adapted and reprinted with the permission of *The Free Press,* an imprint of Simon & Schuster from *Managing Quality: The Strategic and Competitive Edge* by David A. Garvin. Copyright (c) 1988 by David A. Garvin. **266 Figure 7.1** Reprinted from "The Deming Chain Reaction" from *Out of the Crisis* by W. Edwards Deming, reprinted in *The Deming Management Method* by Mary Walton, by permission of MIT and The W. Edwards Deming Institute. Published by MIT, Center for Advanced Engineering Study, Cambridge, MA 02139. Copyright 1986. **266 Figure 7.1** and **Table 7.4** Reprinted by permission of the Putnam Publishing Group from *The Deming Management Method* by Mary Walton. Copyright (c) 1986 by Mary Walton. **266 Footnote 4** J.M. Juran and F.M. Gryna, *Quality Planning and Analysis, Third Edition,* McGraw-Hill 1993. Reproduced with permission of McGraw-Hill. **267 Table 7.5** J.M. Juran and F.M. Gryna, *Quality Planning and Analysis, Third Edition,* McGraw-Hill 1993. Reproduced with permission of McGraw-Hill. **272 Footnote 10** From *Customers for Life* by Carl Sewell and Paul B. Brown. Copyright (c) 1990 by Carl Sewell. Used by permission of Doubleday, a division of Bantam Doubleday Dell Publishing Group, Inc. **277 Footnote 14** From *The Team Handbook* by Peter R. Scholtes. Copyright (c) 1988. Joiner Associates, Inc. All rights reserved. Reprinted and adapted with permission. **282 Footnote 17** Selected Adaptation from *Reengineering the Corporation: A Manifesto For Business* by Michael Hammer and James Champy. Copyright (c) 1992 by Michael Hammer and James Champy. Reprinted by permission of Harper Collins Publishers, Inc. **294** The Gallup Poll Monthly, April 1991. **297 Footnote 5** John Carey, "Hey You In the Ivory Tower," pp. 32–33. Reprinted from October 12, 1992 issue of *Business Week* by special permission, copyright (c) by McGraw-Hill, Inc. **298 Table 8.1** John Carey, "Hey You In the Ivory Tower," pp. 32–33. Reprinted from October 12, 1992 issue of *Business Week* by special permission, copyright (c) by McGraw-Hill, Inc. **300 Footnote 8** Andrew Young, Daniel Levi, and Charles Slem, "Dispelling Some Myths About People Tech," (November 1987) pp. 52–69. Reprinted from *Industrial Engineering Magazine,* November 1987. Copyright (c) 1987, Institute of Industrial Engineers, 25 Technology Park, Atlanta, Georgia 30092. **300 Table 8.2** William H. Miller, "CAD Comes Into Its Own," (May 18, 1992) p. 62. Reprinted with permission from *Industry Week,* May 18, 1992. Copyright Penton Publishing, Inc., Cleveland, Ohio. **308 Table 8.4** Joe LaFeir, "Everything You've Needed To Know About Bar Coding," *Fortune,* (May 1992) p. 26. Copyright (c) 1992 Time, Inc. All rights reserved. **309 Figure 8.1** Mark Alpert, "Building a Better Bar Code," *Fortune,* (June 15, 1992) p. 101. Copyright (c) 1992 Time, Inc. All rights reserved. Artwork credit belongs to Tony Mikolajozyk. **312 Footnote 25** Future View: Tomorrow's Manufacturing Technologies, *Manufacturing Engineering* (January 1992). Reprinted with permission of the Society of Manufacturing Engineers. **313 Table 8.5** Evan I. Schwartz and James B. Treece, "Smart Programs Go To Work." Reprinted from March 2, 1992 issue of *Business Week* by special permission, copyright (c) 1992 by McGraw-Hill, Inc. **325 Figure 9.1** Cynthia Fisher, Lyle Schoenfeldt, James Shaw, *Human Resource Management, First Edition,* p. 688. Copyright (c) 1990 by Houghton Mifflin Company. Reprinted with permission. **326 Footnote 2** William Pasmore, *Designing Effective Organizations,* 1988, p. 49. Copyright (c) 1988. Reprinted by permission of John Wiley & Sons, Inc.

**331 Footnote 7** Stanley Herman, "Participative Management is a Double-Edged Sword," (January 1989) p. 55. Reprinted with permission from the January 1989 issue of *Training* Magazine. Copyright (c) 1989, Lakewood Publications, Minneapolis, MN. All rights reserved. Not for resale. **332 Figure 9.2** John Hoerr, "The Payoff from Teamwork." Reprinted from July 10, 1989 issue of *Business Week* by special permission, copyright (c) 1989 by McGraw-Hill, Inc. **333 Footnote 8** John Hoerr, "The Payoff from Teamwork." Reprinted from July 10, 1989 issue of *Business Week* by special permission, copyright (c) 1989 by McGraw-Hill, Inc. **340 Footnote 15** Ronald Henkoff, "Companies That Train Best," *Fortune,* (March 22, 1993). Copyright (c) 1993 Time, Inc. All rights reserved. **341 Table 9.1** Ronald Henkoff, "Companies That Train Best," *Fortune,* (March 22, 1993). Copyright (c) 1993 Time, Inc. All rights reserved. **359 Figure 10.2** Ronald H. Ballou, *Business Logistics Management, 3e,* (c) 1992, p. 24. Reprinted by permission of Prentice Hall, Englewood Cliffs, New Jersey. **368 Footnote 7** *Modern Logistics Management*, by John F. Magee, W.C. Copacino and D.B. Rosenfield. Copyright (c) 1985. Reprinted by permission of John Wiley & Sons, Inc. **372 Table 10.3** *Modern Logistics Management*, by John F. Magee, W.C. Copacino and D.B. Rosenfield. Copyright (c) 1985. Reprinted by permission of John Wiley & Sons, Inc. **372 Footnote 8** *Modern Logistics Management*, by John F. Magee, W.C. Copacino and D.B. Rosenfield. Copyright (c) 1985. Reprinted by permission of John Wiley & Sons, Inc. **417 Figure 11.8** Reprinted with permission from *Operations Research* 30, Vol. 2, (March/April 1982). Copyright (c) 1982, Operations Research Society of America. No further reproduction permitted without consent of the copyright owner. **418 Figure 11.9** Reprinted by permission of *Harvard Business Review.* An exhibit from "Putting Production Decisions Where They Belong," by Harlan C. Meal (March/April 1984), pp. 101 & 106. Copyright (c) 1984 by the President and Fellows of Harvard College; all rights reserved. **418 Figure 11.10** Reprinted by permission of *Harvard Business Review.* An exhibit from "Putting Production Decisions Where They Belong," by Harlan C. Meal (March/April 1984), pp. 101 & 106. Copyright (c) 1984 by the President and Fellows of Harvard College; all rights reserved. **421 Table 11.14** Reprinted with permission from The Journal of Operations Management, Vol. 8, No. 2, G. Keong Leong, Michael D. Oliff, and Robert E. Markland, "Improved Hierarchical Production Planning" (April 1989), p. 95, Elsevier Science Ltd., Oxford, England. **575 Footnote 7** From *International Journal of Production Research* 1190, Vol. 28(12), pp. 2393–2404. "Comparing Manufacturing and Control Practices in Europe and Korea by Boo-Ho Rho and Clay Whybank. Taylor & Francis, Inc., Washington, D.C.. Reproduced with permission. **599 Footnote 1** From *International Journal of Production Research*, 1988, Vol. 26(9), pp. 1565–1566. "A Study of JIT Implementation and Operating Problems" by Karlene Crawford, J.H. Blackstone, Jr., and J.F. Cox. Taylor & Francis, Inc., Washington, D.C.. Reproduced with permission. **606 Figure 17.1** Adaptation from Robert Murdick, Barry Render and Roberta Russell, *Service Operations Management.* Copyright (c) 1990 by Allyn and Bacon. Reprinted by permission. **608 Footnote 2** Adapted and reprinted with the permission of The Free Press, an imprint of Simon and Schuster from *Competitive Advantage: Creating and Sustaining Superior Performance* by Michael E. Porter. Copyright (c) 1985 by Michael E. Porter. **610 Table 17.1** Karl Albrecht and Ron Zemke, *Service America Doing Business in the New Economy* (Homewood, IL: Dow Jones–Irwin, 1985), pp. 70–73. **611 Table 17.2** James A. Fitzsimmons and Robert S. Sullivan, *Service Operations Management* (McGraw-Hill, 1982) pp. 17–19. Reproduced with permission of

McGraw-Hill. **613 Footnotes 9 and 10** Christopher Voss, Colin Armistead, Box Johnston and Barbara Morris, *Operations Management in Service Industries and the Public Sector* (Chichester, England: Wiley, 1985), p. 56. **614 Figure 17.3** Adapted from Christopher Voss, Colin Armistead, Box Johnston and Barbara Morris, *Operations Management in Service Industries and the Public Sector* (Chichester, England: Wiley, 1985), p. 56. **618 Footnote 13** Richard B. Chase, "Where Does the Customer Fit In a Service Operation?" Reprinted with permission of *Harvard Business Review* 56 (November–December 1978) pp. 137–142. Copyright 1978 by the President and Fellows of Harvard College; all rights reserved. **619 Table 17.4** Richard B. Chase, "Where Does the Customer Fit In a Service Operation?" Reprinted with permission of *Harvard Business Review* 56 (November–December 1978) pp. 137–142. Copyright 1978 by the President and Fellows of Harvard College; all rights reserved. **621 Table 17.5** Christopher B. Lovelock, *Services Marketing, Text, Cases and Readings* (Englewood Cliffs, N.J.: Prentice-Hall, 1984), p. 54. Reprinted with permission of Prentice-Hall. **622 Figure 17.5** Christopher B. Lovelock, *Services Marketing, Text, Cases and Readings* (Englewood Cliffs, N.J.: Prentice-Hall, 1984), p. 54. Reprinted with permission of Prentice-Hall. **623 Table 17.6** Christopher Lovelock, "Strategies for Managing Capacity-Constrained Service Organizations," *Service Industries Journal* 4 (November 1984), p. 21. **628 Table 17.8** James Heskett, W. Earl Sasser, Jr., and Christopher W.L. Hart, *Service Breakthroughs: Changing the Rules of the Game* (New York: Free Press, 1990), p. 151. **628 Footnote 15** Adapted by permission of *Harvard Business Review* An exhibit from "Match Supply and Demand in Service Industries," by W. Earl Sasser (November–December 1976). Copyright (c) 1976 by the President and Fellows of Harvard College; all rights reserved. **686 Table 19.1** Arthur R. Tenner and Irving J. DeToro, *Total Quality Management: Three Steps to Continuous Improvement* (Reading, MA: Addison-Wesley Publishing Co., 1992), p. 109. **694 Table 19.2** Robert C. Camp, "Benchmarking: The Search for Best Practices That Lead to Superior Performance," *Quality Progress* (February 1989), p. 71. Copyright (c) 1989 American Society for Quality Control. Reprinted with permission. **694 Footnote 1** Otis Port and Geoffrey Smith, "Beg, Borrow–and Benchmark." Reprinted from the November 30, 1992 issue of *Business Week* by special permission, copyright (c) 1992 by McGraw-Hill, Inc. **695 Table 19.3** Otis Port and Geoffrey Smith, "Beg, Borrow–and Benchmark." Reprinted from the November 30, 1992 issue of *Business Week* by special permission, copyright (c) 1992 by McGraw-Hill, Inc.

## PHOTO CREDITS

**vii** Photo courtesy of Ford Motor Company. **viii** Terry Vine, Tony Stone Worldwide. **ix** Frank Herholdt, Tony Stone Worldwide. **xii** Photo courtesy of Hewlett Packard Company. **xvi** Photo courtesy of Allen-Bradley, a Rockwell International Company. **1** Joe Cornish, Tony Stone Worldwide. **2** Photo courtesy of General Motors Corporation. **5** Photo courtesy of Ford Motor Company. **22** Photo courtesy of Ford Motor Company. **39** Photo courtesy of Blockbuster Entertainment Corporation. **41** Photo courtesy of Deer Valley Ski Resort. **45** Photo courtesy of the University of South Carolina. **52** Photo courtesy of Delta Air Lines. **66** Photo courtesy of L.L. Bean. **73** Terry Vine, Tony Stone Worldwide. **81, top left** Photo courtesy of Haskell of Pittsburgh, Inc. **81, top right** Photo courtesy of Haskell of Pittsburgh, Inc. **81, bottom** Photo courtesy of Caterpillar Inc. **98** Photo courtesy of Xerox Corporation. **109** Bill Pogue, Tony Stone Worldwide. **117** Frank Herholdt, Tony Stone World-

# Acknowledgments

wide. **125** Photo courtesy of Hewlett-Packard Company. **124** Rhoda Sidney, Stock Boston. **157** Seth Resnick, Stock Boston. **162** Photo courtesy of MacDonald's Corporation. **175** Bob Daemmrich, Stock Boston. **180** Photo courtesy of Ford Motor Company. **193** Photo courtesy of Sony Electronics Inc. **207** Photo courtesy of Saturn Corporation. **230** Bob Daemmrich, Stock Boston. **212** Photo courtesy of Baylor University Medical Center. **253** Photo courtesy of The Ritz-Carlton Hotel Company. **261** Photo courtesy of Eastman Chemical Company. **265** AP/Wide World. **283** Photo courtesy of Taco Bell Corp. **291** Photo courtesy of United Parcel Service. **294** Ellis Herwig, Stock Boston. **305** Andy Sacks, Tony Stone Worldwide. **313** Peter Menzel, Stock Boston. **323** John Coletti, Stock Boston. **330** John Coletti, Stock Boston. **333** Paul Avis, Liason International. **340** Photo courtesy of The Boeing Company. **355** Photo courtesy of Burlington Northern Railroad. **368** Photo courtesy of Burlington Northern Railroad. **369** Bruce Hands, Tony Stone Worldwide. **372** David Joel, Stock Boston. **381** Photo courtesy of Norwest Corporation. **390** Photo courtesy of Black & Decker Corporation. **406** Photo courtesy of Cadbury-Schweppes. **417** Photo courtesy of United Parcel Services. **427** John Lund, Tony Stone Images.

**440** Photo courtesy of Hewlett Packard Company. **454** Herb Snitzer, Stock Boston. **463** Photos courtesy of Miller Brewing Company. **473** Photo courtesy of Steelcase, Inc. **476** Photo courtesy of Steelcase, Inc. **503** Photo courtesy of Hewlett-Packard Company. **515** Bob Daemmrich, Stock Boston. **520** Photo courtesy of Minnesota Wire and Cable Co. **536** George Hunter, Tony Stone Worldwide. **549** Billy Barnes, Stock Boston. **554** Andy Sacks, Tony Stone Worldwide. **557** IMS Photo by Steve Swope. **560** John Feingersch, Stock Boston. **581** Starr, Stock Boston. **588** Photo courtesy of Land's End, Inc. **589** Richard Pasley, Stock Boston. **605** Photo courtesy of Knott's Camp Snoopy, Mall of America. **615** Arles Gupton, Tony Stone Worldwide. **620** Photo courtesy of FINA Inc. **634** Lawrence Migdale, Stock Boston. **642** Photo courtesy of National Technological University. **647** David Sharrock, Tony Stone Worldwide. **652** David Hiser, Tony Stone Worldwide. **674, left** Photo courtesy of Chrysler Corporation. **674, right** Photo courtesy of Chrysler Corporation. **676** Photo courtesy of Ford Motor Company. **683** Bob Daemmrich, Stock Boston. **692** Martin Rogers, Stock Boston. **694** Photo courtesy of Loras College, Dubuque, Iowa. **714** Photo courtesy of Xerox Corporation.

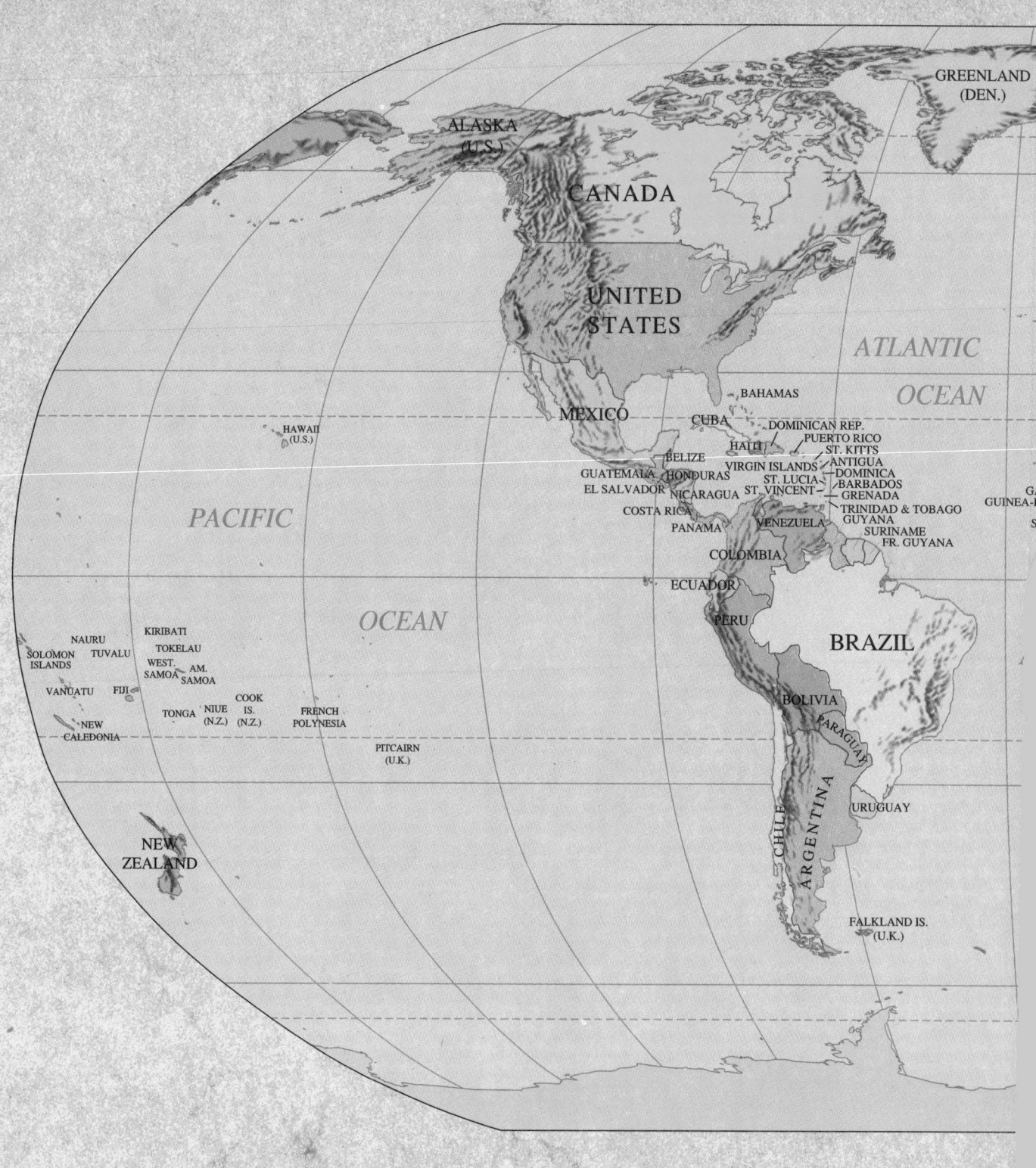

GREENLAND
(DEN.)

ALASKA
(U.S.)

CANADA

UNITED
STATES

ATLANTIC

OCEAN

MEXICO

BAHAMAS

CUBA

DOMINICAN REP.
PUERTO RICO
ST. KITTS
ANTIGUA
DOMINICA
BARBADOS
GRENADA
TRINIDAD & TOBAGO
GUYANA
SURINAME
FR. GUYANA

HAITI

BELIZE
VIRGIN ISLANDS
ST. LUCIA
ST. VINCENT

GA
GUINEA-B

SI

HAWAII
(U.S.)

PACIFIC

GUATEMALA
EL SALVADOR
COSTA RICA
PANAMA

HONDURAS
NICARAGUA

VENEZUELA

COLOMBIA

ECUADOR

PERU

OCEAN

BRAZIL

NAURU
SOLOMON
ISLANDS

TUVALU

KIRIBATI
TOKELAU
WEST.
SAMOA AM.
SAMOA

BOLIVIA

PARAGUAY

VANUATU FIJI

TONGA

NIUE
(N.Z.)

COOK
IS.
(N.Z.)

FRENCH
POLYNESIA

NEW
CALEDONIA

URUGUAY

PITCAIRN
(U.K.)

CHILE
ARGENTINA

NEW
ZEALAND

FALKLAND IS.
(U.K.)